Lecture Notes in Computer Science 2996

Edited by G. Goos, J. Hartmanis, and J. van Leeuwen

T0189864

Springer
Berlin
Heidelberg
New York
Hong Kong
London
Milan
Paris
Tokyo

Volker Diekert   Michel Habib (Eds.)

STACS 2004

21st Annual Symposium
on Theoretical Aspects of Computer Science
Montpellier, France, March 25-27, 2004
Proceedings

 Springer

Series Editors

Gerhard Goos, Karlsruhe University, Germany
Juris Hartmanis, Cornell University, NY, USA
Jan van Leeuwen, Utrecht University, The Netherlands

Volume Editors

Volker Diekert
Universität Stuttgart, FMI
Universitätsstr. 38, 70569 Stuttgart, Germany
E-mail: diekert@informatik.uni-stuttgart.de

Michel Habib
LIRMM, Université Montpellier II
161, rue Ada, 34392 Montpellier, Cedex 5, France
E-mail: habib@lirmm.fr

Cataloging-in-Publication Data applied for

A catalog record for this book is available from the Library of Congress.

Bibliographic information published by Die Deutsche Bibliothek
Die Deutsche Bibliothek lists this publication in the Deutsche Nationalbibliografie;
detailed bibliographic data is available in the Internet at <http://dnb.ddb.de>.

CR Subject Classification (1998): F, E.1, I.3.5, G.2

ISSN 0302-9743
ISBN 3-540-21236-1 Springer-Verlag Berlin Heidelberg New York

Springer-Verlag is a part of Springer Science+Business Media

springeronline.com

© Springer-Verlag Berlin Heidelberg 2004
Printed in Germany

Typesetting: Camera-ready by author, data conversion by PTP-Berlin, Protago-TeX-Production GmbH
Printed on acid-free paper   SPIN: 10991633   06/3142   5 4 3 2 1 0

Preface

The Symposium on Theoretical Aspects of Computer Science (STACS) is alternately held in France and in Germany. The conference of March 25–27, 2004 at the Corum, Montpellier was the twenty-first in this series. Previous meetings took place in Paris (1984), Saarbrücken (1985), Orsay (1986), Passau (1987), Bordeaux (1988), Paderborn (1989), Rouen (1990), Hamburg (1991), Cachan (1992), Würzburg (1993), Caen (1994), München (1995), Grenoble (1996), Lübeck (1997), Paris (1998), Trier (1999), Lille (2000), Dresden (2001), Antibes (2002), and Berlin (2003).

The symposium looks back at a remarkable tradition of over 20 years. The interest in STACS has been increasing continuously during recent years and has turned it into one of the most significant conferences in theoretical computer science. The STACS 2004 call for papers led to more than 200 submissions from all over the world.

The reviewing process was extremely hard: more than 800 reviews were done. We would like to thank the program committee and all external referees for the valuable work they put into the reviewing process of this conference.

We had a two-day meeting for the program committee in Montpellier during November 21–22, 2003. Just 54 papers (i.e., 27% of the submissions) could be accepted, as we wanted to keep the conference in its standard format with only two parallel sessions. This strict selection guaranteed the very high scientific quality of the conference.

We would like to thank the three invited speakers Claire Kenyon (École Polytechnique, Palaiseau), Erich Grädel (RWTH, Aachen), and Robin Thomas (Georgia Institute of Technology, Atlanta) for presenting their recent results at STACS 2004.

Special thanks for the local organization go to Christophe Paul and Celine Berger, who spent a lot of time and effort, and did most of the organizational work, and thanks also go to the Ph.D. students of the graph algorithms project for their support. We acknowledge the financial support STACS 2004 received from the CNRS, the Montpellier Agglomeration, the Languedoc Roussillon region, the University of Montpellier, and the LIRMM.

Montpellier, January 2004   Volker Diekert
                                                              Michel Habib

Organization

STACS 2004 was organized by the Computer Science Department of the LIRMM (Laboratoire d'Informatique, de Robotique et de Microélectronique de Montpellier), University of Montpellier (France).

Program Committee

O. Carton (Paris, France)
P. Darondeau (Rennes, France)
V. Diekert (Stuttgart, Germany), Co-chair
M. Droste (Dresden, Germany)
C. Gavoille (Bordeaux, France)
B. Gärtner (Zurich, Switzerland)
M. Habib (Montpellier, France), Chair
K. Jansen (Kiel, Germany)
P. Koiran (Lyon, France)
K. G. Larsen (Aalborg, Denmark)
S. Leonardi (Rome, Italy)
A. Pelc (Québec, Canada)
G. Pighizzini (Milan, Italy)
C. Schindelhauer (Paderborn, Germany)
U. Schöning (Ulm, Germany)

Organizing Committee

T. Bennouas
C. Berger, Co-chair
M. Bouklit
C. Crespelle
F. de Montgolfier
C. Paul, Chair

Referees[1]

K. Abdollah	A. Atserias	L. Bernardinello	B. Borchert
P. Abdulla	V. Auletta	J. Berstel	A. Borghese
L. Aceto	H. Austinat	P. Berthome	A. Bouajjani
U. Adamy	E. Badouel	E. Bertino	S. Boucheron
G. Agosta	E. Bampis	D. Besozzi	V. Bouchitté
S. Aguzzoli	P. Baptiste	M. Bienkowski	M. Bousquet-
D. Aharonov	A. Bar-Noy	M. Bläser	Mélou
E. Allender	E. Barcucci	J. Blömer	U. Brandes
N. Alon	O. Baudon	A. Blumensath	A. Brandstädt
L. Alonso	C. Bazgan	L. Boasson	G. Brassard
K. Ambos-Spies	O. Beaumont	O. Bodini	P. Bro Miltersen
C. Ambühl	D. Beauquier	H. Bodlaender	A. Brodsky
P. Arnaud	L. Becchetti	P. Boldi	H. Buhrman
J. Arpe	P. Berenbrink	N. Bonichon	

---

[1] This list was automatically compiled from the database of the conference. We apologize for any omissions or inaccuracies.

A. Bulatov
G. Buntrock
S. Buss
B. Caillaud
T. Calamoneri
G. Calinescu
A. Carpi
J. Castro
M. Charikar
V. Chepoi
J. Chlebikova
B. Chlebus
C. Choffrut
M. Chrobak
B. Codenotti
M. Cochand
O. Cogis
A. Cohen
R. Cole
H. Comon
C. Crépeau
P. Csorba
E. Csuhaj-Varju
A. Czumaj
J. Czyzowicz
F. D'Amore
G. Dabosville
V. Damerow
I. Damgaard
O. Dantona
M. De Berg
G. De Giacomo
G. De Marco
M. Dekhtyar
C. Delhomme
G. Della Vedova
O. Delmas
C. Demetrescu
A. Dessmark
M. Dietzfelbinger
K. Diks
T. Dimtirios
I. Dinur
S. Dobrev
R. Dowgird
F. Dragan
P. Duchon

J. Durand-Lose
A. Durand
M. Durand
C. Durr
L. Engebretsen
D. Eppstein
T. Erlebach
Z. Ésik
M. Farach-Colton
J. Feldman
R. Feldmann
P. Ferragina
M. Ferrari
A. Ferreira
G. Fertin
C. Fiorentini
K. Fischer
A. Fishkin
E. Fleury
F. Fomin
L. Fortnow
M. Fouquet
H. Fournier
P. Fraigniaud
P.G. Franciosa
H. Fuks
J. Gabarro
A. Gajardo
B. Ganter
L. Gargano
L. Gasieniec
S. Gaubert
R. Gavalda
O. Gerber
H. Gimbert
R. Giroudeau
R. Glantz
A. Goerdt
M. Goldwurm
J. Goubault-
    Larrecq
E. Graedel
S. Grigorieff
M. Grohe
G. Grossi
J. Gruska
D.J. Guan

D. Gunopulos
J. Guo
D. Gusfield
J. Gustedt
S. Haar
T. Hagerup
H. Handschuh
C. Hanen
N. Hanusse
F. Henne
F. Hennecke
M. Hermann
P. Hertling
U. Hertrampf
J. Hitchcock
M. Hoffmann
T. Holenstein
B. Hollas
S. Homer
H.J. Hoogeboom
P. Hoyer
J. Hromkovic
M. Hutter
J.I. Alvarez-
    Hamelin
J. Illum
A. Ingolfsdottir
A. Itai
K. Iwama
H.V. Jagadish
A. Jakoby
P. Janssen
E. Jeandel
O. Jensen
J. Johannsen
D. Jost
B. Jouvencel
V. Kabanets
C. Kaklamanis
B. Kaliski
L. Kari
A. Karlin
C. Kenyon
R. Kenyon
A. Kesselman
T. Kimbrel
L. Kirousis

D. Kirsten
H. Klauck
J. Klein
P. Klein
O. Klima
A. Klivans
T. Knapik
D. Kobler
J. Koebler
J. Koenemann
B. König
J.-C. König
S. Kontogiannis
K. Korovin
G. Kortsarz
M. Korzeniowski
L. Kowalik
D. Kowalski
R. Kralovic
D. Kratsch
M. Kraus
W. Krieger
M. Krivelevich
D. Krizanc
J. Krokowski
P. Krysta
A. Kucera
M. Kufleitner
M. Kurowski
E. Laber
C. Lagoze
K.-J. Lange
S. Laplante
R. Lavi
E. Lebhar
V.B. Le
A. Lemay
S. Lewandowski
P. Liberatore
V. Liberatore
W. Lindner
A. Lingas
Z. Lipták
M. Liskiewicz
M. Lohrey
S. Lokam
S. Lombardy

L. Longpre
Z. Lotker
F. Luccio
A. Maciel
F. Magniez
A. Malinowski
G. Malod
B. Mans
B. Manthey
M. Margenstern
E. Markou
P. Massazza
D. Matijevic
J.M. Maubach
G. Mauri
M. Mavronicolas
A. May
E. Mayordomo
F. Mazoit
J. Mazoyer
B. McKay
R. McConnell
P. McKenzie
C. Meinel
C. Mereghetti
W. Merkle
J. Messner
U. Meyer
D. Micciancio
P. Michiardi
F. Mignosi
P. Milman
A. Miquel
A. Mitchell
D. Mix
  Barrington
F. Montgolfier
C. Moore
M. Morvan
D. Mount
J.-M. Muller
A. Muscholl
P. Mutzel
J. Neraud
P. Nesi
F. Neven
P. Nguyen

R. Niedermeier
B. Nielsen
L. Nourine
D. Nowotka
Y. Okamoto
P. Oliva
A. Orlitsky
I. Pak
B. Palano
A. Panconesi
M. Parente
D. Parkes
C. Paul
C. Pech
A. Pecher
A. Pelc
D. Peleg
M. Pellegrini
G. Persiano
H. Petersen
P. Phillips
C. Picouleau
J.-E. Pin
A. Piperno
N. Pisanti
W. Plandowski
M. Pocchiola
D. Pointcheval
N. Portier
M. Prabhakaran
D. Pretolani
T. Przytycka
P. Pudlak
U. Rabinovitch
H. Räcke
M. Raffinot
A. Raspaud
R. Ravi
A. Razborov
O. Regev
D. Reidenbach
J. Reimann
R. Reischuk
E. Remila
R. Renner
E. Rivals
H. Rivano

Y. Robert
M. Robson
G. Rote
T. Roughgarden
A. Roumy
S. Rührup
A. Russell
N. Sabadini
V. Sagar
  Malhotra
J. Sakarovitch
L. Salvail
K. Salzwedel
P. Sanders
M. Santha
J. Sawada
N. Schabanel
C. Scheideler
I. Schiermeyer
R. Schuler
I. Schurr
M. Schwartzbach
S. Schwoon
M. Sciortino
D. Seese
L. Segoufin
P. Sen
A. Sengupta
H. Shachnai
S. Shenker
C. Silvano
R. Silvestri
I. Simon
M. Skutella
S. Skyum
J. Snoeyink
C. Sohler
R. Solis-Oba
S. Spallinger
E. Speckenmeyer
J. Srba
G.S. Brodal
L. Staiger
G. Steiner
M. Sviridenko
U. Szabó
A. Ta-Shma

H. Tamaki
E. Tardos
P. Tesson
T. Teobald
J. Thorsten
T. Thierauf
E. Thierry
D. Thilikos
W. Thomas
H. Thuillier
S. Tiga
I. Todinca
J. Toran
M. Torelli
R. Treinen
R. Tripathi
M. Trubian
D. Trystram
P. Urzyczyn
U. Vaccaro
S. Vadhan
M. Valiev
D. Van Melkebeek
Y. Vaxes
F. Verner Jensen
M.-C. Vilarem
B. Vöcking
H. Vogler
W. Vogler
K. Volbert
H. Vollmer
L. Vuillon
K. Wagner
I. Walukiewicz
R. Wanka
O. Watanabe
J. Watrous
B. Weber
I. Wegener
P. Weil
E. Welzl
M. Westermann
K. Wich
T. Wilke
C. Witt
G.J. Woeginger
H. Wu

T. Yamakami   T. Zeugmann   M. Ziegler   U. Zwick
Y. Yurirabinovich G.-Q. Zhang   M. Zito
A. Zeliko   H. Zhang

Sponsoring Institutions

Table of Contents

Pattern Inference and Statistics

Satisfiability – Constraint Satisfaction Problem

Scheduling (I)

Algorithms

Networks (I)

Automata Theory and Words

Structural Complexity (II)

Path Algorithms

Cryptography

Networks (II)

Logic and Formal Languages

Graphs Algorithms (II)

Game Theory and Complexity

Networks (III)

Structural Complexity (III)

Scheduling (II)

Algorithmic Information

Errata to STACS 2003

Approximation Schemes for Metric Clustering Problems

Claire Kenyon

LIX, Ecole Polytechnique, France.

Problem statement and motivation.   The problem of partitioning a data set into a small number of *clusters* of related items has a crucial role in many information retrieval and data analysis applications, such as web search and classification [5,6,22,11], or interpretation of experimental data in molecular biology [21].

We consider a set V of n points endowed with a distance function δ. These points have to be partitioned into a fixed number k of subsets $C_1, C_2, \ldots, C_k$ so as to minimize the cost of the partition, which is defined to be the sum over all clusters of the sum of pairwise distances in a cluster. We call this problem k-Clustering. In the settings that we consider, this optimization problem is NP-hard to solve exactly even for $k = 2$ (using arguments similar to those in [8, 7]).

The k-Clustering problem was proposed by Sahni and Gonzalez [19] in the setting of arbitrary weighted graphs. Unfortunately, only poor approximation guarantees are possible [16,12]. Guttman-Beck and Hassin [14] initiated the study of the problem in metrics. Schulman [20] gave probabilistic algorithms for ℓ_2^2 k-Clustering.

The results which we present.   The results presented deal with the case that δ is an arbitrary metric. We first present polynomial time algorithms which for every fixed $\epsilon > 0$ compute partitions into two parts which maximize the sum of intercluster distances: this objective function that is the complement of Metric 2-Clustering (polynomial time approximation scheme for metric Max Cut [8]). We next present a polynomial time algorithm for 2-clustering [15] which uses the Metric Max Cut approximation scheme. Finally, we present an extension to algorithms for every fixed integer k and for every fixed $\epsilon > 0$ that compute a partition into k clusters of cost at most $1 + \epsilon$ times the cost of an optimum partition [9]. The running time is $O(f(k,\epsilon)n^{3k})$. Note that Bartal, Charikar, and Raz [4] gave a polynomial time approximation algorithm with polylogarithmic performance guarantees for Metric k-Clustering where k is arbitrary (i.e., part of the input).

It is interesting to note that both Schulman's algorithm for k-Clustering and the algorithm of Fernandez de la Vega and Kenyon for Mertic Max Cut use a similar idea of sampling data points at random from a biased distribution that depends on the pairwise distances. In recent research on clustering problems,

V. Diekert and M. Habib (Eds.): STACS 2004, LNCS 2996, pp. 1–3, 2004.

sampling has been the core idea in the design of provably good algorithms for various objective functions. Examples include [2,1,17].

The Metric k-Clustering algorithm

1. By exhaustive search, guess the optimal cluster sizes $n_1 \geq n_2 \geq \cdots \geq n_k$.
2. By exhaustive search, for each pair of large cluster indices i and j, guess whether C_i^* and C_j^* are close or far.
3. Taking the equivalence relation which is the transitive closure of the relation "C_i^* and C_j^* are close", define a partition of large cluster indices into groups.
4. For each large cluster C_i^*, let c_i be a random uniform element of V. Assign each point $x \in V$ to the group G which minimizes $\min_{i \in G}[n_i \delta(x, c_i)]$.
5. By exhaustive search, for each group G thus constructed, guess $|G \cap S|$, where $S = \cup_{i \text{ small}} C_i^*$ is the union of small clusters. For each x assigned to group G, let $f(x) = \min_{i \in G} \delta(x, c_i)$. Remove from G's assignment the $|G \cap S|$ elements with largest value $f(x)$.
6. Partition each group of large clusters into the appropriate number h of clusters using the PTAS for Max-h-Cut with error parameter $\epsilon' = \epsilon^2 \epsilon^{3j_0}/(3k^3)$.
7. Recursively partition the removed elements into the appropriate number of clusters.

References

1. N. Alon, S. Dar, M. Parnas, and D. Ron. Testing of clustering. In *Proc. of the 41th Ann. IEEE Symp. on Foundations of Computer Science(FOCS)* 2000, 240-250.
2. N. Alon and B. Sudakov. On two segmentation problems. *Journal of Algorithms*, 33:173–184, 1999.
3. S. Arora, D. Karger, and M. Karpinski. Polynomial time approximation schemes for dense instances of NP-hard problems. *J. Comp. System. Sci.*, 58:193–210, 1999.
4. Y. Bartal, M. Charikar, and D. Raz. Approximating min-sum k-clustering in metric spaces. In *Proc. of the 33rd Ann. ACM Symp. on Theory of Computing*, July 2001, pages 11–20.
5. A. Broder, S. Glassman, M. Manasse, and G. Zweig. Syntactic clustering of the Web. In *Proc. of the 6th Int'l World Wide Web Conf.*(WWW), 1997, pages 391–404.
6. S. Deerwester, S.T. Dumais, T.K. Landauer, G.W. Furnas, and R.A. Harshman. Indexing by latent semantic analysis. *Journal of the Society for Information Science*, 41(6):391–407, 1990.
7. W. Fernandez de la Vega, M. Karpinski, and C. Kenyon. A polynomial time approximation scheme for metric MIN-BISECTION. *ECCC TR02-041*, 2002.
8. W. Fernandez de la Vega and C. Kenyon. A randomized approximation scheme for metric MAX CUT. In *Proc. of the 39th Ann. IEEE Symp. on Foundations of Computer Science (FOCS)*, 1998, pages 468-471, also in JCSS 63 (2001). pages 531-541.

9. W. Fernandez de la Vega, Marek Karpinski, Claire Kenyon and Yuval Rabani, Approximation Schemes for Clustering Problems, STOC'03.
10. P. Drineas, A. Frieze, R. Kannan, S. Vempala, and V. Vinay. Clustering in large graphs and matrices. In *Proc. of the 10th Ann. ACM-SIAM Symp. on Discrete Algorithms (SODA)*, 1999, pages 291–299.
11. C. Faloutsos, R. Barber, M. Flickner, J. Hafner, W. Niblack, D. Petkovic, and W. Equitz. Efficient and effective querying by image content. *Journal of Intelligent Information Systems*, 3(3):231–262, 1994.
12. N. Garg, V. Vazirani, and M. Yannakakis. Approximate max-flow min-(multi)cut theorems and their applications. *SIAM Journal on Computing*, 25(2):235–251, 1996.
13. O. Goldreich, S. Goldwasser, and D. Ron. Property testing and its connection to learning and approximation. *J. of the ACM*, 45:653–750, 1998.
14. N. Guttmann-Beck and R. Hassin. Approximation algorithms for min-sum p-clustering. *Disc. Applied Math.*, 89:125–142, 1998.
15. P. Indyk. A sublinear time approximation scheme for clustering in metric spaces. In *Proc. of the 40th Ann. IEEE Symp. on Foundations of Computer Science (FOCS)*, 1999, 154-159.
16. V. Kann, S. Khanna, J. Lagergren, and A. Panconesi. On the hardness of approximating Max k-Cut and its dual. In *Proc. of the 4th Israeli Symp. on Theory of Computing and Systems (ISTCS)*, 1996. Also in *Chicago Journal of Theoretical Computer Science*, 1997.
17. N. Mishra, D. Oblinger, and L. Pitt. Sublinear time approximate clustering. In *Proc. of the 12th Ann. ACM-SIAM Symp. on Discrete Algorithms (SODA)*, January 2001, pages 439–447.
18. R. Ostrovsky and Y. Rabani. Polynomial time approximation schemes for geometric clustering problems. *J. of the ACM*, 49(2):139–156, March 2002.
19. S. Sahni and T. Gonzalez. P-complete approximation problems. *Journal of the ACM*, 23(3):555–565, 1976.
20. L.J. Schulman. Clustering for edge-cost minimization. In *Proc. of the 32nd Ann. ACM Symp. on Theory of Computing (STOC)*, 2000, pages 547–555.
21. R. Shamir and R. Sharan. Algorithmic approaches to clustering gene expression data. In T. Jiang, T. Smith, Y. Xu, M.Q. Zhang eds., *Current Topics in Computational Biology*, MIT Press, to appear.
22. M.J. Swain and D.H. Ballard. Color indexing. *International Journal of Computer Vision*, 7:11–32, 1991.

Positional Determinacy of Infinite Games*

Erich Grädel

Aachen University

Abstract. We survey results on determinacy of games and on the existence of positional winning strategies for parity games and Rabin games.
We will then discuss some new developments concerning positional determinacy for path games and for Muller games with infinitely many
priorities.

1   Introduction

1.1   Games and Strategies

We study infinite two-player games with complete information, specified by an
arena (or game graph) and a *winning condition*. An arena $\mathcal{G} = (V, V_0, V_1, E, \Omega)$,
consists of a directed graph (V, E), equipped with a partitioning $V = V_0 \cup V_1$ of
the nodes into positions of Player 0 and positions of Player 1, and a function
$\Omega : V \to C$ that assigns to each position a *priority* (or colour) from a set C.
Although the set V of positions may be infinite, it is usually assumed that C is
finite. (We will drop this assumption in Section 4 where we discuss games with
infinitely many priorities.)

In case $(v, w) \in E$ we call w a successor of v and we denote the set of
all successors of v by vE. To avoid tedious case distinctions, we assume that
every position has at least one successor. A *play* of $\mathcal{G}$ is an infinite path $v_0 v_1 \ldots$
formed by the two players starting from a given initial position v_0. Whenever the
current position v_i belongs to V_0, then Player 0 chooses a successor $v_{i+1} \in v_i E$, if
$v_i \in V_1$, then $v_{i+1} \in v_i E$ is selected by Player 1. The *winning condition* describes
which of the infinite plays $v_0 v_1 \ldots$ are won by Player 0, in terms of the sequence
$\Omega(v_0)\Omega(v_1) \ldots$ of priorities appearing in the play. Thus, a winning condition is
given by a set $W \subseteq C^\omega$ of infinite sequences of priorities.

Winning conditions can be specified in several ways. In the theory of Gale-
Stewart games as developed in descriptive set theory, the winning condition is
just an abstract set $W \subseteq \{0, 1\}^\omega$. In computer science applications winning
conditions are often specified by formulae from a logic on infinite paths, such
as LTL (linear time temporal logic), FO (first-order logic), or MSO (monadic
second-order logic) over a vocabulary that uses the linear order $<$ and monadic
predicates P_c for each priority $c \in C$. Of special importance are also *Muller
conditions*, where the winner of a play depends on the set of priorities that have
been seen infinitely often.

---

* This research has been partially supported by the European Community Research
Training Network "Games and Automata for Synthesis and Validation" (GAMES)

V. Diekert and M. Habib (Eds.): STACS 2004, LNCS 2996, pp. 4–18, 2004.

A *(deterministic) strategy* for Player σ is a partial function $f : V^*V_\sigma \to V$ that maps initial segments $v_0v_1 \ldots v_m$ of plays ending in a position $v_m \in V_\sigma$ to a successor $f(v_0 \ldots v_m) \in v_mE$. A play $v_0v_1 \cdots \in V^\omega$ is *consistent with* f, if Player σ always moves according to f, i.e., if $v_{m+1} = f(v_0 \ldots v_m)$ for every m with $v_m \in V_\sigma$. We say that such a strategy f is winning from position v_0, if every play that starts at v_0 and that is consistent with f, is won by Player σ. The *winning region* of Player σ, denoted W_σ, is the set of positions from which Player σ has a winning strategy.

1.2 Determinacy

A game $\mathcal{G}$ is *determined* if $W_0 \cup W_1 = V$, i.e., if from each position one of the two players has a winning strategy. On the basis of the axiom of choice it is not difficult to prove that there exist nondetermined games. The classical theory of infinite games in descriptive set theory links determinacy of games with topological properties of the winning conditions. Usually the format of Gale-Stewart games is used where the two players strictly alternate, and in each move a player selects an element of $\{0, 1\}$; thus the outcome of a play is an infinite string $\pi \in \{0, 1\}^\omega$. Gale-Stewart games can be viewed as graph game, for instance on the infinite binary tree, or on a bipartite graph with four nodes. Zermelo [21] proved already in 1913 that if in each play of a game, the winner is determined already after a finite number of moves, then one of the two players has a winning strategy. In topological terms the winning sets in such a game are clopen (open and closed). Before we mention further results, let us briefly recall some basic topological notions.

Topology. We consider the space B^ω of infinite sequences over a set B, endowed with the topology whose basic open sets are $O(x) := x \cdot B^\omega$, for $x \in B^*$. A set $L \subseteq B^\omega$ is *open* if it is a union of sets $O(x)$, i.e., if $L = W \cdot B^\omega$ for some $W \subseteq B^*$. A tree $T \subseteq B^*$ is a set of finite words that is closed under prefixes. It is easily seen that $L \subseteq B^\omega$ is *closed* (i.e., the complement of an open set) if L is the set of infinite branches of some tree $T \subseteq B^*$, denoted $L = [T]$. This topological space is called *Cantor space* in case $B = \{0, 1\}$, and *Baire space* in case $B = \omega$.

The class of *Borel sets* is the closure of the open sets under countable union and complementation. Borel sets form a natural hierarchy of classes Σ_η^0 for $1 \le \eta < \omega_1$, whose first levels are

$$\Sigma_1^0 \; (\text{or } G) : \quad \text{the open sets}$$
$$\Pi_1^0 \; (\text{or } F) : \quad \text{the closed sets}$$
$$\Sigma_2^0 \; (\text{or } F_\sigma) : \quad \text{countable unions of closed sets}$$
$$\Pi_2^0 \; (\text{or } G_\delta) : \quad \text{countable intersections of open sets}$$

In general, Π_η^0 contains the complements of the Σ_η^0-sets, $\Sigma_{\eta+1}^0$ is the class of countable unions of Π_η^0-sets, and $\Sigma_\lambda^0 = \bigcup_{\eta < \lambda} \Sigma_\eta^0$ for limit ordinals λ.

In the 1950s, Gale and Stewart showed that all open games and all closed games are determined. This was then extended in several papers to higher levels of the Borel hierarchy, until Martin [14] proved in 1975 that in fact all games with Borel winning conditions are determined. The theory of infinite games from there branched in several directions. In descriptive set theory one aims to prove determinacy result for stronger, non-Borel games. For game theory that relates to computer science, determinacy is just a first step in the analysis of a game. Rather than in the mere existence of winning strategies, one is interested in reasonably simple winning strategies that can be effectively constructed, are computationally efficient and do not require too much memory. We will focus on this last aspect here.

1.3 Positional Determinacy

In general, winning strategies can be very complicated. It is of interest to determine which games admit simple strategies, in particular *finite memory strategies* and *positional strategies*. While positional strategies only depend on the current position, not on the history of the play, finite memory strategies have access to bounded amount of information on the past. Finite memory strategies can be defined as strategies that are realisable by finite automata.

More formally, a strategy with memory M for Player σ is given by a triple (m_0, U, F) with initial memory state $m_0 \in M$, a memory update function $U : M \times V \to M$ and a next-move function $F : V_\sigma \times M \to V$. Initially, the memory is in state m_0 and after the play has gone through the sequence $v_0 v_1 \ldots v_m$ the memory state is $u(v_0 \ldots v_m)$, defined inductively by $u(v_0 \ldots v_m v_{m+1}) = U(u(v_0 \ldots v_m), v_{m+1})$. In case $v_m \in V_\sigma$, the next move from $v_1 \ldots v_m$, according to the strategy, leads to $F(v_m, u(v_0 \ldots v_m))$. In case $M = \{m_0\}$, the strategy is positional; it can be described by a function $F : V_\sigma \to V$.

We will say that a game is *positionally determined* if it is determined and both players have positional winning strategies on their winning regions.

2   Muller Games, Streett-Rabin Games, and Parity Games

Parity games are graph games with priority labeling $\Omega : V \to \{0, \ldots, d\}$ for some $d \in \mathbb{N}$ and parity winning condition: Player 0 wins a play π if the least priority occurring infinitely often in π is even. Parity games are of importance for several reasons [19,20].

- Parity games are positionally determined. This has been first established by Mostowski [16] and by Emerson and Jutla [5]. An immediate consequence of positional determinacy is that winning regions of parity games can be decided in NP ∩ Co-NP.
- Many complicated games can be reduced to parity games (over larger game graphs).

– Parity games arise as the model checking games for fixed point logics. In particular the model checking problem for the modal μ-calculus can be solved in polynomial time if, and only if, winning regions for parity games can be decided in polynomial time.

Parity games are a special case of Muller games.

Definition 1 A *Muller condition* over a finite set C of priorities is written in the form $(\mathcal{F}_0, \mathcal{F}_1)$ where $\mathcal{F}_0 \subseteq \mathcal{P}(C)$ and $\mathcal{F}_1 = \mathcal{P}(C) - \mathcal{F}_0$. A play π in a game with Muller winning condition $(\mathcal{F}_0, \mathcal{F}_1)$ is won by Player σ if, and only if, $\text{Inf}(\pi)$, the set of priorities occurring infinitely in π, belongs to $\mathcal{F}_\sigma$.

The *Zielonka tree* for a Muller condition $(\mathcal{F}_0, \mathcal{F}_1)$ over C is a tree $Z(\mathcal{F}_0, \mathcal{F}_1)$ whose nodes are labelled with pairs (X, σ) such that $X \in \mathcal{F}_\sigma$. We define $Z(\mathcal{F}_0, \mathcal{F}_1)$ inductively as follows. Let $C \in \mathcal{F}_\sigma$ and $C_0, \ldots, C_{k-1}$ be the maximal sets in $\{X \subseteq C : X \in \mathcal{F}_{1-\sigma}\}$. Then $Z(\mathcal{F}_0, \mathcal{F}_1)$ consists of a root, labeled by (C, σ), to which we attach as subtrees the Zielonka trees $Z(\mathcal{F}_0 \cap \mathcal{P}(C_i), \mathcal{F}_1 \cap \mathcal{P}(C_i))$, for $i = 0, \ldots, k - 1$.

It has been proved by Gurevich and Harrington [8] that Muller games are determined via finite memory strategies. However, Muller games need not be positionally determined, not even for solitaire games (where only one player moves). Consider, for instance, the game with three positions $1, 2, 3$, all belonging to Player 0, with possible moves $(1, 2), (2, 1), (1, 3), (3, 1)$, and winning condition $\mathcal{F}_0 = \{\{1, 2, 3\}\}$ (i.e., all three positions must be seen infinitely often). Clearly Player 0 can win this game, but not with a positional strategy.

Besides parity games there are other important special cases of Muller games. Of special relevance for us are games with Rabin and Street conditions because these are positionally determined for one player [11].

Definition 2 A *Streett-Rabin condition* is a Muller condition $(\mathcal{F}_0, \mathcal{F}_1)$ such that $\mathcal{F}_0$ is closed under union.

In the Zielonka tree for a Streett-Rabin condition, the nodes labeled $(X, 1)$ have only one successor. We remark that in the literature, Streett and Rabin conditions are often defined in a different manner, based on a collection $\{(E_i, F_i) : i = 1, \ldots k\}$ of pairs of sets. However, it is not difficult to see that the definitions are equivalent [22]. Further, it is also easy to show that if both $\mathcal{F}_0$ and $\mathcal{F}_1$ are closed under union, then $(\mathcal{F}_0, \mathcal{F}_1)$ is equivalent to a parity condition. The Zielonka tree for a parity condition is just a finite path.

In a Streett-Rabin game, Player 1 has a positional wining strategy on his winning region. On the other hand, Player 0 can win, on his winning region, via a finite memory strategy, and the size of the memory can be directly read of from the Zielonka tree. We present an elementary proof of this result. The exposition is inspired by [4]. In the proof we use the notion of an attractor.

Definition 3 Let $\mathcal{G} = (V, V_0, V_1, E, \Omega)$ be an arena and let $X, Y \subseteq V$, such that X induces a subarena of $\mathcal{G}$ (i.e., every position in X has a successor in X). The *attractor* of Player σ of Y in X is the set $\text{Attr}_\sigma^X(Y)$ of those positions $v \in X$ from which Player σ has a strategy to force the play into Y. More formally $\text{Attr}_\sigma^X(Y) = \bigcup_\alpha Z^\alpha$ where

$$Z^0 = X \cap Y,$$
$$Z^{\alpha+1} = Z^\alpha \cup \{v \in V_\sigma \cap X : vE \cap Z^\alpha \neq \emptyset\} \cup \{v \in V_{1-\sigma} \cap X : vE \subseteq Z^\alpha\}$$
$$Z^\lambda = \bigcup_{\alpha < \lambda} Z^\alpha \quad \text{for limit ordinals } \lambda$$

On $\text{Attr}_\sigma^X(Y)$, Player σ has a *positional attractor strategy* to bring the play into Y. Moreover $X \setminus \text{Attr}_\sigma^X(Y)$ is again a subarena.

Theorem 4 *Let $\mathcal{G} = (V, V_0, V_1, E, \Omega)$ be game with Streett-Rabin winning condition $(\mathcal{F}_0, \mathcal{F}_1)$. Then $\mathcal{G}$ is determined, i.e. $V = W_0 \cup W_1$, with a finite memory winning strategy of Player 0 on W_0, and a positional winning strategy of Player 1 on W_1. The size of the memory required by the winning strategy for Player 0 is bounded by the number of leaves of the Zielonka tree for $(\mathcal{F}_0, \mathcal{F}_1)$.*

Proof. We proceed by induction on the number of priorities in C or, equivalently, the depth of the Zielonka tree $Z(\mathcal{F}_0, \mathcal{F}_1)$. Let ℓ be number of leaves of $Z(\mathcal{F}_0, \mathcal{F}_1)$. We distinguish two cases.

We first assume that $C \in \mathcal{F}_1$.

$$X_0 := \{v : \text{Player 0 has a winning strategy with memory of size} \leq \ell \text{ from } v\},$$

and $X_1 = V \setminus X_0$. It suffices to prove that Player 1 has a positional winning strategy on X_1. To construct this strategy, we combine three positional strategies of Player 1, a trap strategy, an attractor strategy, and a winning strategy on a subgame with fewer priorities.

First, we observe that X_1 is a trap for Player 0; this means that Player 1 has a positional trap-strategy t on X_1 to enforce that the play stays within X_1.

Since $\mathcal{F}_0$ is closed under union, there is a unique maximal subset $C' \subseteq C$ with $C' \in \mathcal{F}_0$. Let $Y := X_1 \cap \Omega^{-1}(C \setminus C')$ and let $Z = \text{Attr}_1^{X_1}(Y) \setminus Y$. Observe that Player 1 has a positional attractor strategy a, by which he forces from any position $z \in Z$ that the play reaches Y.

Finally, let $V' = X_1 \setminus (Y \cup Z)$ and let $\mathcal{G}'$ be the subgame of $\mathcal{G}$ induced by V', with winning condition $(\mathcal{F}_0 \cap \mathcal{P}(C'), \mathcal{F}_1 \cap \mathcal{P}(C'))$. Since this game has fewer priorities, the induction hypothesis applies, i.e. $V' = W_0' \cup W_1'$, Player 0 has a winning strategy with memory $\leq \ell$ on W_0' and Player 1 has a positional winning strategy g' on W_1'. However, $W_0' = \emptyset$; otherwise we could combine the strategies of Player 0 to obtain a winning strategy with memory $\leq \ell$ on $X_0 \cup W_0' \supsetneq X_0$ contradicting the definition of X_0. Hence $W_1' = V'$.

We can now define a positional strategy g for Player 1 on X_1 by

$$g(x) = \begin{cases} g'(x) & \text{if } x \in V' \\ a(x) & \text{if } x \in Z \\ t(x) & \text{if } x \in Y \end{cases}$$

Consider any play π that starts at a position $v \in X_1$ and is consistent with g. Obviously π stays within X_1. If it hits $Y \cup Z$ only finitely often, then from some point onward, it stays within V_1 and coincides with a play consistent with g'. It is therefore won by Player 1. Otherwise π hits $Y \cup Z$, and hence also Y, infinitely often. Thus, $\mathrm{Inf}(\pi) \cap (C \setminus C') \neq \emptyset$ and therefore $\mathrm{Inf}(\pi) \in \mathcal{F}_1$.

We now consider the second case, $C \in \mathcal{F}_0$. There exist maximal subsets $C_0, \ldots, C_{k-1} \subseteq C$ with $C_i \in \mathcal{F}_1$. Observe that for every set $D \subseteq C$, we have that if $D \cap (C \setminus C_i) \neq \emptyset$ for all $i < k$, then $D \in \mathcal{F}_0$. Let

$$X_1 := \{v : \text{Player 1 has a positional winning strategy from } v\},$$

and $X_0 = V \setminus X_1$. We claim that Player 0 has a finite memory winning strategy of size $\leq \ell$ on X_0. To construct this strategy, we proceed in a similar way as above, for each of the sets $C \setminus C_i$. We will obtain strategies $f_0, \ldots, f_{k-1}$ for Player 0, such that f_i has finite memory M_i, and we will use these strategies to build a winning strategy f on X_0 with memory $M_0 \cup \cdots \cup M_{k-1}$.

For $i = 0, \ldots, k-1$, let $Y_i = X_0 \cap \Omega^{-1}(C \setminus C_i)$ let $Z_i = \mathrm{Attr}_0^{X_0}(Y_i) \setminus Y_i$, and let a_i be a positional attractor strategy, by which Player 0 can force a play from any position in Z_i to Y_i. Further, let $U_i = X_0 \setminus (Y_i \cup Z_i)$ and let $\mathcal{G}_i$ be the subgame of $\mathcal{G}$ induced by U_i, with winning condition $(\mathcal{F}_0 \cap \mathcal{P}(C_i), \mathcal{F}_1 \cap \mathcal{P}(C_i))$. The winning region of Player 1 in $\mathcal{G}_i$ is empty; indeed, if Player 1 could win $\mathcal{G}_i$ from v, then, by induction hypothesis, he could win with a positional winning strategy. By combining this strategy with the positional winning strategy of Player 1 on X_1, this would imply that $v \in X_1$; but $v \in U_i \subseteq V \setminus X_1$.

Hence, by induction hypothesis, Player 0 has a winning strategy f_i with finite memory M_i on U_i. Let $(f_i + a_i)$ be the combination of f_i with the attractor strategy a_i. From any position $v \in U_i \cup Z_i$ this strategy ensures that the play either remains inside U_i and is winning for Player 1, or it eventually reaches a position in Y_i.

We now combine the finite-memory strategies $(f_0 + a_0), \ldots, (f_{k-1} + a_{k-1})$ to a winning strategy f on X_0, which ensures that either the play ultimately remains within one of the regions U_i and coincides with a play according to f_i, or that it cycles infinitely often through all the regions $Y_0, \ldots, Y_{k-1}$.

At positions in $\bigcap_{i<k} Y_i$, Player 0 just plays with a (positional) trap strategy ensuring that the play remains in X_0. At the first position $v \notin \bigcap_{i<k} Y_i$, Player 0 takes the minimal i such that $v \notin Y_i$, i.e. $v \in U_i \cup Z_i$, and uses the strategy $(f_i + a_i)$ until a position in $w \in Y_i$ is reached. At this point, Player 0 switches from i to $j = i + \ell \pmod{k}$ for the minimal ℓ such that $w \notin Y_j$. Hence $w \in U_j \cup Z_j$; Player 0 now plays with strategy $(f_j + a_j)$ until a position in Y_j is reached. There Player 0 again switches to the appropriate next strategy, and so on.

Assuming that $M_i \cap M_j = \emptyset$ for $i \neq j$ it is not difficult to see that f can be implemented with memory $M = M_0 \cup \cdots \cup M_{k-1}$. We leave a formal definition of f to the reader.

It remains to prove that f is winning on X_0. Let π be a play that starts in X_0 and is consistent with f. If π eventually remains inside some U_i then it coincides, from some point onwards, with a play that is consistent with f_i, and therefore won by Player 0. Otherwise it hits each of the sets $Y_0, \ldots, Y_{k-1}$ infinitely often. But this means that $\text{Inf}(\pi) \cap (C \setminus C_i) \neq \emptyset$ for all $i \leq k$; as observed above this implies that $\text{Inf}(\pi) \in \mathcal{F}_0$.

Note that, by induction hypothesis, the size of the memory M_i is bounded by the number of leaves of the Zielonka subtrees $Z(\mathcal{F}_0 \cap \mathcal{P}(C_i), \mathcal{F}_1 \cap \mathcal{P}(C_i)$. Consequently the size of M is bounded by the number of leaves of $Z(\mathcal{F}_0, \mathcal{F}_1)$.

$\square$

Of course it also follows from this Theorem that parity games are positionally determined.

3   Path Games

Another interesting variant of two-player games on graphs are *path games* where in each move a player can select a path of arbitrary finite length rather than just an edge. Such games arise in several contexts.

3.1   Banach-Mazur Games

In descriptive set theory, path games have been studied in the form of *Banach-Mazur games* (see [9, Chapter 6] or [10, Chapter 8.H]). In their original variant (see [15, pp. 113–117], the winning condition is a set W of real numbers; in the first move, one of the players selects an interval d_1 on the real line, then his opponent chooses an interval $d_2 \subset d_1$, then the first player selects a further refinement $d_3 \subset d_2$ and so on. The first player wins if the intersection $\bigcap_{n \in \omega} d_n$ of all intervals contains a point of W, otherwise his opponent wins.

By identifying real numbers with infinite sequences of natural numbers, this game is essentially equivalent to a path game on the ω-branching tree T^ω with winning condition $W \subseteq \omega^\omega$. Player 0 starts by selecting a finite path $a_0 a_1 \ldots a_m$ from the root, and in each further move, the player extend the path by another finite sequence of numbers. The outcome of the play is an infinite path π through $\mathcal{T}^\omega$; Player 0 has won if $\pi \in W$, otherwise Player 1 has won. This game is usually denoted $G^{**}(W)$.

A classical result due to Banach and Mazur characterises, in terms of topological properties, the winning conditions W such that one of the two players has a winning strategy for the game $G^{**}(W)$. We recall that a set X in a topological space is *nowhere dense* if its closure does not contain a non-empty open set. A set is *meager* if it is a union of countably many nowhere dense sets and it has the *Baire property* if its symmetric difference with some open set is meager. In particular, every Borel set has the Baire property.

Theorem 5 (Banach-Mazur)   (1) *Player 1 has a winning strategy for the game $G^{**}(W)$ if, and only if, W is meager.*

(2) *Player 0 has a winning strategy for $G^{**}(W)$ if, and only if, there exists a finite word $x \in \omega^*$ such that $x \cdot \omega^\omega \setminus W$ is meager (i.e., W is co-meager in some basic open set).*

As a consequence, it can be shown that for any class $\Gamma \subseteq \mathcal{P}(\omega^\omega)$ that is closed under complement and under union with open sets, all games $G^{**}(W)$ with $W \in \Gamma$ are determined if, and only if, all sets in Γ have the Baire property. Since Borel sets have the Baire property, it follows that Banach-Mazur games are determined for Borel winning conditions. (Via a coding argument, this can also been easily derived form Martin's Theorem.)

3.2   Path Games in Computer Science

Pistore and Vardi [17] use path games as a tool for task planning in nondeterministic domains. In their scenario, the desired infinite behaviour of a system is specified by formulae in LTL, and it is assumed that the outcome of actions may be nondeterministic; hence a plan has not only one possible execution path, but an execution tree. Between weak planning (some possible execution path satisfies the specification) which is of course not very useful, and strong planning (all possible outcomes are consistent with the specification) which is often unrealistic, there is a spectrum of intermediate cases such as for instance strong cyclic planning: every possible partial execution of the plan can be extended to an execution reaching the desired goal. In this context, planning can be modelled by a game between a friendly player E and a hostile player A selecting the outcomes of nondeterministic actions. This game is a path game on the execution tree of the plan, and the question is whether the friendly player E has a strategy to ensure that the outcome (an infinite path through the execution tree) satisfies the given LTL-specification.

In [1] we have studied path games in a quite different scenario: once upon a time in the west, two players set out on an infinite ride. More often than not, they had quite different ideas on where to go, but for reasons that have by now been forgotten they were forced to stay together – as long as they were both alive. They agreed on the rule that each player can determine on every second day, where the ride should go. Hence, one of the players began by choosing the first day's ride: he indicated a finite, non-empty path p_1 from the starting point v; on the second day his opponent selected the next stretch of way, extending p_1 to a finite path p_1q_1; then it was again the turn of the first player to extend the path to $p_1q_1p_2$ and so on. After ω days, an infinite ride is completed and it is time for payoff. The scenario is quite useful to capture the interest of the audience at at conference, and provides good motivation to study general issues like positional determinacy, algorithmic complexity and logical definability of path games.

In the Banach-Mazur games $G^{**}(W)$, the players strictly alternate. But it is also interesting to study cases, where after a few alternations, one of the players is eliminated, and the games then becomes a solitaire game. In the planning application studied in [17] these are in fact the most relevant cases. For instance, strong cyclic planning corresponds to what we call an AE^ω-game: a single move by A is followed by actions of E. In the scenario of the wild west as investigated in [1] it is of also quite realistic that one of players may not make to the end (see e.g. [12,13]). To describe the alternation pattern between the players we call the players Ego and Alter, and denote a move where Ego selects a finite path by E and an ω-sequence of such moves by E^ω; for Alter we use corresponding notation A and A^ω. For any fixed triple $\mathcal{G} = (G, W, v)$ consisting of an arena G, a winning condition W and an initial position v, we then have the following games.

- $(EA)^\omega(\mathcal{G})$ and $(AE)^\omega(\mathcal{G})$ are the path games with infinite alternation of finite path moves.
- $(EA)^k E^\omega(\mathcal{G})$ and $A(EA)^k E^\omega(\mathcal{G})$, for arbitrary $k \in \mathbb{N}$, are the games ending with an infinite path extension by Ego.
- $(AE)^k A^\omega(\mathcal{G})$ and $E(AE)^k A^\omega(\mathcal{G})$ are the games where Alter chooses the final infinite lonesome ride.

This infinite collection of games collapses to a finite lattice of just eight different games, a result that has been proved independently in [17] and [1].

Theorem 6 *For every triple $\mathcal{G} = (G, W, v)$*

$$E^\omega(\mathcal{G}) \succeq EAE^\omega(\mathcal{G}) \succeq AE^\omega(\mathcal{G})$$

$$\curlyvee| \qquad\qquad \curlyvee|$$

$$(EA)^\omega(\mathcal{G}) \succeq (AE)^\omega(\mathcal{G})$$

$$\curlyvee| \qquad\qquad \curlyvee|$$

$$EA^\omega(\mathcal{G}) \succeq AEA^\omega(\mathcal{G}) \succeq A^\omega(\mathcal{G})$$

Further, every path game on $\mathcal{G}$ is equivalent to one of these eight games.

For each comparison $\succeq$ in the diagram there are simple games for which it is strict.

3.3 Positional Determinacy of Path Games

Path games with only finitely many alternations between the two players are trivially determined, for whatever winning condition, and for path games with infinite alternations, the Banach-Mazur Theorem establishes determinacy for a very large class of winning conditions, covering almost all path games that are likely to appear in computer science applications.

As for the usual graph games, the question arises, which path games admit positional winning stratgies. Observe that a positional strategy for a path game on the graph $G = (V, F)$ has the form $f : V \to V^*$ assigning to every node v a finite path from v through G.

We first look at path games with infinite alternations.

Proposition 7 *If Ego has a winning strategy for a path game $(EA)^\omega(G, W, v)$ with $W \in \Sigma_2^0$, then he also has a positional winning strategy.*

Proof. Let $G = (V, F)$ be the game graph. Since W is a countable union of closed sets, we have $W = \bigcup_{n<\omega} [T_n]$ where each $T_n \subseteq V^*$ is a tree. Further, let f be any (non-positional) winning strategy for Ego. We claim that, in fact, Ego can win with one move.

We construct this move by induction. Let x_1 be the initial path chosen by Ego according to f. Let $i \geq 1$ and suppose that we have already constructed a finite path $x_i \notin \bigcup_{n<i} T_n$. If $x_i y \in T_i$ for all finite y, then all infinite plays extending x_i remain in W, hence Ego wins with the initial move $w = x_i$. Otherwise choose some y_i such that $x_i y_i \notin T_i$, and suppose that Alter prolongs the play from x_i to $x_i y_i$. Let $x_{i+1} := f(x_i y_i)$ the result of the next move of Ego, according to his winning strategy f.

If this process did not terminate, then it would produce an infinite play that is consistent with f and won by Alter. Since f is a winning strategy for Ego, this is impossible. Hence there exists some $m < \omega$ such that $x_m y \in T_m$ for all y. Thus, if Ego moves to x_m in his opening move, then he wins, no matter how the play proceeds afterwards. In particular, Ego wins with a positional strategy. □

We cannot extend this observation beyond the Σ_2-level of the Borel hierarchy. Consider the path game on the completely connected directed graph with nodes 0 and 1, with a Π_2-winning condition for Ego, consisting of those infinite plays that have infinitely many initial segments containing more ones than zeros. Clearly, Ego has a winning strategy for $(EA)^\omega(G, W, v)$, but not a positional one.

Muller and S1S winning conditions. We recall that there are very simple examples of Muller games that do not admit positional winning strategies. For path games the situation is different.

Proposition 8 *All path games $(EA)^\omega(\mathcal{G})$ with a Muller winning condition admit positional winning strategies.*

Proof. We will write $v \leq w$ to denote that position w is reachable from v in the arena G. For every position v, let $C(v)$ be the set of priorities reachable from v, that is, $C(v) := \{\Omega(w) : v \leq w\}$. Obviously, $C(w) \subseteq C(v)$ whenever $v \leq w$. We call v a *stable* position if $C(w) = C(v)$ for all w that are reachable from v. Note that from every u some stable position is reachable. Further, if v is stable, then every reachable position $w \geq v$ is stable as well.

Let the set of winning plays in $\mathcal{G}$ be defines by a Muller condition $(\mathcal{F}_0, \mathcal{F}_1)$. We claim that Ego has a winning strategy in $(EA)^\omega(\mathcal{G})$ iff there is a stable position v that is reachable from the initial position v_0, so that $C(v) \in \mathcal{F}_0$. To see this, let us assume that there is such a stable position v with $C(v) \in \mathcal{F}_0$. Then, for every $u \geq v$, we choose a path p from u so that, when moving along p, each colour of $C(u) = C(v)$ is visited at least once, and set $f(u) := p$. In case v_0 is not reachable from v, we assign $f(v_0)$ to some path that leads from v_0 to v. Now f is a positional winning strategy for Ego in $(EA)^\omega(\mathcal{G})$, because, after the first move, no colours other then those in $C(v)$ are seen. Moreover, every colour in $C(v)$ is visited at each move of Ego, hence, infinitely often.

Conversely, if for every stable position v reachable from v_0 we have $C(v) \in \mathcal{F}_1$, then we can construct a winning strategy for Alter in a similar way.   □

Note that in a finite arena all positions of a strongly connected component that is terminal, i.e., with no outgoing edges, are stable. Thus, the above characterisation translates as follows: Ego wins the game iff there is a terminal component whose set of colours belongs to $\mathcal{F}_0$. Obviously this can be established in linear time w.r.t. the size of the arena and the description of the winning condition.

Corollary 9 *On a finite arena G, path games with a Muller winning condition $(\mathcal{F}_0, \mathcal{F}_1)$ can be solved in time $O(|G| \cdot |\mathcal{F}_\sigma|)$.*

In fact, this result can be extended to a very large class of path games, with general winning conditions definable in S1S. For path games with finite alternations there are, however, also some cases where memory is required. The situation is summarized by the following result.

Theorem 10 *Let $\gamma(G, \varphi)$ denote the path game on the arena G with alternation pattern γ and winning condition defined by the S1S-formula φ.*

(1) *All S1S path games $\gamma(G, \varphi)$ are determined via finite memory strategies.*

(2) *All S1S path games $(EA)^\omega(G, \varphi)$ and $(AE)^\omega(G, \varphi)$ are positionally determined.*

(3) *For future conditions $\varphi \in$ S1S, all path games $\gamma(G, \varphi)$ are positionally determined.*

(4) *For any game prefix γ with finite alternations there exist games $\gamma(G, \varphi)$ with $\varphi \in$ S1S that do not admit positional winning strategies.*

Here, a future condition is a formula that does not depend on initial segments: for any ω-word π and any pair of finite words x and y, we have $x\pi \models \psi$ if, and only if, $y\pi \models \psi$. We just sketch the proof. First of all, it is not difficult to prove that path games with parity winning condition are positionally determined for any game prefix. (By Theorem 6 it suffices to consider the eight prefixes $E^\omega, A^\omega, AE^\omega, EA^\omega, EAE^\omega, AEA^\omega, (EA)^\omega$, and $(AE)^\omega$.)

One can then use parity games as an instrument to investigate path games with winning conditions specified in by arbitrary S1S-formulae. It is well known that every S1S-formula φ is equivalent to a deterministic parity automaton $\mathcal{A}$ (see e.g. [6]). To prove (1), we analyse a path game on G with winning condition φ by considering two games on the product arena $G \times \mathcal{A}$, one, denoted $\mathcal{H}[G]$ with the priority labelling inherited from G and winning condition φ, the other one, denoted $\mathcal{H}[\mathcal{A}]$ with priorities inherited from $\mathcal{A}$ and the parity winning condition.

– A play through $G \times \mathcal{A}$ is winning for Ego in $\mathcal{H}[G]$ if and only if it winning for Ego in $\mathcal{H}[\mathcal{A}]$.

– The two arenas G and $\mathcal{H}[G]$ are bisimilar.

The positional determinacy of parity path games then implies positional determinacy of $\mathcal{H}[G]$ which in turn implies obtains finite memory determinacy for the original game; the value $f(v, q)$ of a winning strategy depends on the current position v in G and a state q of the automaton $\mathcal{A}$.

To prove (2) we have to unify, for each position $v \in G$, the values $f(v, q)$ for those pairs (v, q) that are reachable in a play of according to f. Let us assume that Ego wins the game $(EA)^\omega(G, \varphi)$ starting from position v_0. We will base our argumentation on the assiciated game $\mathcal{H}[G]$ for which Ego has a positional winning strategy f.

For any v, we denote by $Q_f(v)$ the set of states q so that the position (v, q) can be reached from position (v_0, q_0) in a play according to f. Let $\{q_1, q_2, \ldots, q_n\}$ be an enumeration of $Q_f(v)$, in which the initial state q_0 is taken first, in case it belongs to $Q_f(v)$. We construct a path associated to v along the following steps. First, set $p_1 := f(v, q_1)$; for $1 < i \le n$, let (v', q') be the node reached after playing the path $p_1 \cdot p_2 \cdots p_{i-1}$ from position (v, q_i) and set $p_i := f(v', q')$. Finally, let $f'(v)$ be the concatenation of $p_1, p_2, \ldots, p_n$.

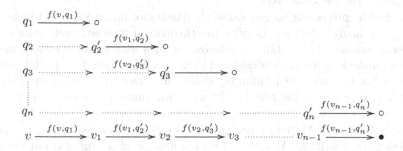

Fig. 1. Merging strategies at node v

Now, consider a play in $\mathcal{H}[G]$ in which Ego chooses the path $f'(v)$ at any node $(v, q) \in V \times Q$. This way, the play will start with $f(q_0, v_0)$. Further, at any position (v, q) at which Ego moves, $f'(v)$ contains some segment of the form $(v', q') \cdot f(v', q')$. In other words, every move of Ego has some "good part" which would also have been produced by f at the position (v', q'). But this means that the play coincides with a play where Ego always moves according to the strategy f while all the "bad parts" were produced by Alter. This proves that f' is a positional strategy for Ego in the game $\mathcal{H}[G]$. Since the values do not depend on the second component, f' induces a positional strategy for Ego in $(EA)^\omega(G, \psi)$. The same construction works for the case $(AE)^\omega(G, \psi)$, if we take instead of $Q_f(v)$ the set $Q(v) := \{\delta(q_0, s) : s \text{ is a path from } v_0 \text{ to } v\}$.

The argument for (2) relies on players always taking turns. If we consider games where the players alternate only finitely many times, the situation changes. Consider, for instance, the winning condition $\psi \in \text{S1S}$ that requires the number of zeroes occurring in a play to be odd on the completely connected arenea with two positions $0, 1$. When starting from position 1, Ego obviously has winning strategies for each of the games $E^\omega(G, \psi)$, $AE^\omega(G, \psi)$, and $EAE^\omega(G, \psi)$, but no positional ones. Nevertheless, such games are always positionally determined for one of the players. Indeed, if a player wins a game $\gamma(G, \psi)$ finally controlled by his opponent, he always has a positional winning strategy. This is trivial when $\gamma \in \{E^\omega, A^\omega, AE^\omega, EA^\omega\}$; for the remaining cases EAE^ω and AEA^ω a positional strategy can be constructed as above. For a proof of (3) the reader is refered to [1].

4   Games with Infinitely Many Priorities

Muller games and parity games have been studied extensively both for the cases of finite and for infinite game graphs. However, even in the case of infinite game graphs, it has always been assumed that the positions are labelled with a finite set of priorities, and this is essential for the proofs of positional determinacy exhibitted above, that proceed by induction on the number of priorities or on the depth of the Zielonka tree.

We find it interesting to generalise the theory of infinite games to the case of infinitely many priorities. Besides the theoretical interest, such games arise in several contexts. For instance, pushdown games with winning conditions depending on stack contents as considered in [2,3] can be viewed as special cases of Muller or parity games with infinitely many priorities. We have started to and report here on some of the results. For more information the reader is referred to [7].

The definition of Muller games (Definition 1) directly generalises to countable sets C of priorities[1]. However, a representation of a Muller condition by a Zielonka tree is not always possible, since we may have sets $D \in \mathcal{F}_\sigma$ that have subsets in $\mathcal{F}_{1-\sigma}$ but no maximal ones. Further, it turns out that the condition that $\mathcal{F}_0$ and $\mathcal{F}_1$ are both closed under finite unions is no longer sufficient for positional determinacy. To see this let us discuss the possible generalisations of parity games to the case of priority assigments $\Omega : V \to \omega$. For parity games with finitely many priorities it is of course purely a matter of taste whether we let the winner be determined by the least priority seen infinitely often or by the greatest one. Here this is no longer the case.

Parity games are games where Player 0 wins the plays in which the least priority seen infinitely often is even, or where no priority appears infinitely often. Thus,

$$\mathcal{F}_0 = \{X \subseteq \omega : \min(X) \text{ is even}\} \cup \{\emptyset\}$$
$$\mathcal{F}_1 = \{X \subseteq \omega : \min(X) \text{ is odd}\}$$

---

[1] With minor modifications, it can also be generalised to uncountable sets C. See [7] for a discussion of this.

Max-parity games are games where Player 0 wins if the maximal priority occurring infinitely often is even, or does not exist, i.e.

$$\mathcal{F}_0 = \{X \subseteq \omega : \text{ if } X \text{ is finite and non-empty, then } \max(X) \text{ is even}\}$$
$$\mathcal{F}_1 = \{X \subseteq \omega : X \text{ is finite, non-empty, and } \max(X) \text{ is odd}\}$$

Note that for both definitions, $\mathcal{F}_0$ and $\mathcal{F}_1$ are closed under finite unions. Nevertheless the two conditions behave quite differently. The parity condition has a very simple Zielonka tree, namely just a Zielonka path

$$\omega \longrightarrow \omega \setminus \{0\} \longrightarrow \omega \setminus \{0, 1\} \longrightarrow \omega \setminus \{0, 1, 2\} \longrightarrow \cdots$$

whereas there is no Zielonka tree for the max-parity condition since $\omega \in \mathcal{F}_0$ has no maximal subset in $\mathcal{F}_1$ (and $\mathcal{F}_1$ is not closed under unions of chains). This is in fact related to a much more important difference concerning the memory needed for winning strategies. Indeed, consider the max-parity game with positions $V_0 = \{0\}$ and $V_1 = \{2n+1 : n \in \mathbb{N}\}$ (where the name of a position is also its priority), such that Player 0 can move from 0 to any position $2n + 1$ and Player 1 can move back from $2n + 1$ to 0. Clearly Player 0 has a winning strategy from each position but no winning strategy with finite memory.

Hence positional determinacy, and even finite-memory determinacy fails for max-parity games with infinitely many priorities. On the other hand we prove in [7] that parity games with priorities in ω do admit positional winning strategies for both players. In fact, parity games over ω turn out to be the only Muller games with this property.

Theorem 11 *A Muller condition $(\mathcal{F}_0, \mathcal{F}_1)$ over a countable set C of priorities admits positional winning strategies if, and only if, it is isomorphic to a parity condition over $n \leq \omega$ priorities.*

This discrepancy between (min-)parity games and max-parity games has an interesting application to a classical problem posed in [18]. The curious reader is refered to [7].

References

1. D. BERWANGER, E. GRÄDEL, AND S. KREUTZER, *Once upon a time in the west. Determinacy, complexity and definability of path games*, in Proceedings of the 10th International Conference on Logic for Programming and Automated Reasoning, LPAR 2003, Almaty, Lecture Notes in Computer Science Nr. 2850, Springer-Verlag, 2003, pp. 226–240.
2. A. BOUQUET, O. SERRE, AND I. WALUKIEWICZ, *Pushdown games with unboundedness and regular conditions*. Submitted for publication.
3. T. CACHAT, J. DUPARC, AND W. THOMAS, *Solving pushdown games with a σ_3 winning cndition*, in Computer Science Logic, CSL 2002, Lecture Notes in Computer Science Nr. 2471, Springer-Verlag, 2002, pp. 322–336.

4. S. DZIEMBOWSKI, M. JURDZIŃSKI, AND I. WALUKIEWICZ, *How much memory is needed to win infinite games?*, in Proceedings of 12th Annual IEEE Symposium on Logic in Computer Science (LICS 97), 1997, pp. 99–110.
5. A. EMERSON AND C. JUTLA, *Tree automata, mu-calculus and determinacy*, in Proc. 32nd IEEE Symp. on Foundations of Computer Science, 1991, pp. 368–377.
6. E. GRÄDEL, W. THOMAS, AND T. WILKE, eds., *Automata, Logics, and Infinite Games*, Lecture Notes in Computer Science Nr. 2500, Springer, 2002.
7. E. GRÄDEL AND I. WALUKIEWICZ, *Positional determinacy of games with infinitely many priorities*. Submitted for publication.
8. Y. GUREVICH AND L. HARRINGTON, *Trees, automata and games*, in Proceedings of the 14th Annual ACM Symposium on Theory of Computing, STOC '82, 1982, pp. 60–65.
9. A. KANAMORI, *The Higher Infinite*, Springer, 1991.
10. A. KECHRIS, *Classical Descriptive Set Theory*, Springer, 1995.
11. N. KLARLUND, *Progress measures, immediate determinacy, and a subset construction for tree au tomata*, Annals of Pure and Applied Logic, 69 (1994), pp. 243–268.
12. S. LEONE, *The Good, the Bad and the Ugly*, with Clint Eastwood, Eli Wallach, Lee Van Cleef et al., 1966.
13. S. LEONE, *Once Upon a Time in the West*, with Charles Bronson, Claudia Cardinale, Henry Fonda et al., 1969.
14. D. MARTIN, *Borel determinacy*, Annals of Mathematics, 102 (1975), pp. 336–371.
15. R. MAULDIN, ed., *The Scottish Book. Mathematics from the Scottish Café*, Birkhäuser, 1981.
16. A. MOSTOWSKI, *Games with forbidden positions*, Tech. Rep. Tech. Report 78, University of Gdansk, 1991.
17. M. PISTORE AND M. VARDI, *The planning spectrum — one, two, three, infinity*, in Proc. 18th IEEE Symp. on Logic in Computer Science, 2003.
18. J. SWIFT, *Gulliver's Travels*, George Routledge & Sons, London, 1906. First published in 1726.
19. W. THOMAS, *On the synthesis of strategies in infinite games*, in Proceedings of STACS 95, Lecture Notes in Computer Science Nr. 900, Springer-Verlag, 1995, pp. 1–13.
20. W. THOMAS, *Languages, automata, and logic*, in Handbook of Formal Languages Vol. 3, G. Rozenberg and A. Salomaa, eds., Springer, 1997, pp. 389–455.
21. E. ZERMELO, *Über eine Anwendung der Mengenlehre auf die Theorie des Schachpiels*, in Proc. 5th Internat. Congr. Mathematics, vol. 2, Cambridge, 1913, pp. 501–504.
22. W. ZIELONKA, *Infinite games on finitely coloured graphs with applications to automata on infinite trees*, Theoretical Computer Science, 200 (1998), pp. 135–183.

Individual Communication Complexity*

Extended Abstract

Harry Buhrman[1], Hartmut Klauck[2], Nikolai Vereshchagin[3], and Paul Vitányi[1]

[1] CWI, Kruislaan 413, 1098 SJ Amsterdam, The Netherlands,
{buhrman,paulv}@cwi.nl;
[2] IAS, Einstein Drive, Princeton, NJ 08540-0631, USA, klauck@ias.edu;
[3] Dept. Math. Logic and Theory of Algorithms, Faculty of Mechanics and
Mathematics, Moscow State University, Leninskie gory, Moscow, 119992 Russia.
ver@mccme.ru.

Abstract. We initiate the theory of communication complexity of individual inputs held by the agents, rather than worst-case or average-case. We consider total, partial, and partially correct protocols, one-way versus two-way, with (not in this version) and without help bits.

1 Introduction

Suppose Alice has input x, Bob has input y, and they want to compute a function $f(x, y)$ by communicating information and local computation according to a fixed protocol $P = (P_A, P_B)$. Here P_A is the protocol executed by Alice, and P_B is the protocol executed by Bob. To be more precise, let us assume that Alice outputs $f(x, y)$. We are only interested in minimizing the number of bits communicated between Alice and Bob as is customary in the communication complexity setting [8,3]. Usually, one considers the worst-case or average-case over all inputs x, y of given length n. However, in current situations like replicated file systems, and cache coherence algorithms, in multiprocessor systems and computer networks, the worst-case or average-case are not necessarily significant. The files or updates can be very large; but in real life they may typically be non-random and have considerable regularities or correlations that allow the communicated information to be greatly compressible. Neither the worst-case nor the average-case may be relevant; one wants to analyze the individual case. This gives also much more information: from the individual case-analysis one can easily derive the worst-case and the average-case, but not the other way around. Indeed, certain phenomena have no counterpart in more traditional settings: For example, there are inputs for Bob such that irrespective of Alice's input, every "simple" total protocol requires arbitrarily higher communication complexity than some more "complex" total protocol. Our results are expressed

* The authors are partially supported by EU project QAIP, IST–1999–11234, EU project RESQ, IST-2001-37559, the NoE QUIPROCONE IST–1999–29064, the ESF QiT Programmme, the EU NeuroCOLT II Working Group EP 27150, the EU NoE PASCAL, and by the Netherlands Organization for Scientific Research (NWO).

V. Diekert and M. Habib (Eds.): STACS 2004, LNCS 2996, pp. 19–30, 2004.

in terms of Kolmogorov complexity [5], the minimal number of bits from which the data can be decompressed by effective computation. We use the "plain" Kolmogorov complexity denoted as $C(x), C(x|y), C(x,y)$ for the absolute complexity of x, the conditional complexity of x given y, and the joint complexity of x, y. Increased compression of the data approximates the Kolmogorov complexity more and more, but the actual value is uncomputable in general. Given x, y, and assuming that Alice and Bob have a protocol P that works correctly on x, y, we study the *individual communication complexity* $CC^P(x,y)$ defined as the number of bits Alice with input x and Bob with input y exchange using protocol P. We refer to a standard definition of communication protocol [3]. We assume that the protocol identifies the length n of the strings on which it works. By the complexity of a protocol P we mean its plain Kolmogorov complexity conditional to n, denoted as $C(P|n)$.

Results and Related Work: We use the framework of communication complexity as in [8,3]. As far as we are aware there is no previous work on individual communication complexity. We formulate a theory of individual communication complexity, and first analyze the "mother" problem, the indentity function, where Alice outputs the input of Bob. We look at special functions such as the inner product, random functions, and the equality function. We then turn to the question of analyzing the communication complexity, with respect to the best protocol of given complexity, for the mother problem (identity function). For total protocols that are always correct, the power of one-way protocols equals that of two-way protocols, but for partially correct protocols or partial protocols, two-way protocols are remarkably more powerful. We establish a relation with Kolmogorov's Structure function, and the existence of strange "non-communicable" inputs of possibly low Kolmogorov complexity for total protocols—for which the communication complexity of every total protocol is necessarily very large (almost the literal uncompressed input needs to be communicated) unless all of the input is hard-wired in the protocol. It is shown that for partial protocols two-way is more powerful than one-way when we use help bits (omitted in this extended abstract for space reasons).

2   The Mother Function: Identity

We start with listing some easy facts that establish lower and upper bounds on individual communication complexity with respect to individual protocols P expressed in terms of $C(y|n)$, $C(y|P)$ and compared to $C(y|x)$. We assume that the protocols do not depend on x, y, they are uniform, and they compute the function concerned on strings of length n. Let C be a constant such that $C(y|n) \leq n + C$ for all y.

Let $I(x,y) = y$ be the identity function: Alice with input x and Bob with input y compute output y by Alice. This is the "mother" function: for if Alice can compute I then she can compute every computable function f.

(1) For all n there is a protocol P of complexity $n + O(1)$ to compute the identity function such that for all x, y of length n we have $CC_I^P(x,y) \leq C(y|n)$.

Indeed, assume Bob knows $L_n = |\{p \mid |p| \leq n + C, \ U(p) \text{ halts}\}|$. ($U$ is the reference universal Turing machine.) Then Bob can find all halting programs of length at most $n+C$ by enumerating them until he obtains L_n halting programs. This allows him to find a shortest program y^* for y. He transmits that program to Alice and Alice computes y. The complexity of this protocol is $C(L_n)+O(1) = n + O(1)$.

(2) The complexity bound $n + O(1)$ on $C(P|n)$ in item (1) is tight. For every protocol of complexity less than n the assertion of item (1) is false: for all P there are x, y such that $CC_I^P(x, y) \geq n$ but $C(y|P) = O(1)$ (and hence $C(y|n) \leq C(P|n) + O(1)$, that is $C(y|n)$ is much smaller than $CC_I^P(x, y)$ if $C(P|n)$ is much smaller than n).

Indeed, let ϵ be the empty string and let y be the first string such that $CC_I^P(\epsilon, y) \geq n$ (by counting arguments there is such y).

(3) For every protocol P to compute identity function and for every x, y we have $CC_I^P(x, y) \geq C(y|P) - O(1)$.

Let c be the conversation between Alice and Bob on inputs x, y. It suffices to prove that given P, c we can find y. It is known [3] that the set of all pairs (x', y') such that the conversation between Alice and Bob on input (x', y') is equal to c is a rectangle, that is, has the form $X \times Y$, for some $X, Y \subset \{0, 1\}^n$. The set Y is a one-element set, as for every $y' \in Y$ Alice outputs y also on the input (x, y') (the output of Alice depends on c, P, x only). We can find Y given P, c and since $Y = \{y\}$ we are done.

By item (2), for every protocol there are x, y such that the right hand side of the inequality $CC_I^P(x, y) \geq C(y|P) - O(1)$ is much less than its left hand side, more specifically, $C(y|P) = O(1)$ and $CC_I^P(x, y) \geq n$.

(4) How is $CC_I^P(x, y)$ related to $C(y|x)$? By item (3) we have $CC_I^P(x, y) \geq C(y|x) - C(P) - O(\log C(P))$ for all x, y. For all P this inequality is not tight for some x, y: there are x, y such that $C(y|x) = O(1)$ but $CC_I^P(x, y) \geq n$.

Indeed, let $x = y$. We need to prove that for some x it holds $CC_I^P(x, x) \geq n$. For every x let $c(x)$ denote the conversation on the pair (x, x). For every x the set of input pairs (x', y') producing the conversation $c(x)$ is a rectangle of height 1, as we have seen in item (3). Therefore $c(x)$ are pairwise different for different x hence for some x we have $|c(x)| \geq n$.

(5) However, for some P, x, y the inequality $CC_I^P(x, y) \geq C(y|x) - C(P|n) - O(\log C(P|n))$ is close to an equality: for all α there are P, x, y such that $CC_I^P(x, y) = C(y|x) - \alpha + O(1)$ and $C(P|n) \leq \alpha + O(1)$.

Indeed, let x be some string. Let y be a random string of length n, independent of x, that is, $C(y|x) = n + O(1)$. Let P be the following protocol: Bob first looks whether his string y' has the same prefix of length α than y. If this is the case he sends to Alice 0 and then $n - \alpha$ remaining bits of y' and Alice prefixes the $n - \alpha$ received bits by α first bits of y and outputs the resulting string. Otherwise Bob sends to Alice 1 and then y'. The complexity of this protocol is at most $\alpha + O(1)$, as both Alice and Bob need to know only the first α bits of y. And we have $CC_I^P(x, y) = n - \alpha = C(y|x) - \alpha + O(1)$.

3   Other Functions

Because Alice can compute every computable function once she knows Bob's input, for all f, P there is P' with $CC_f^{P'}(x,y) \leq CC_f^P(x,y)$ and $C(P') \leq C(P,f) + O(1)$.

The trivial lower bound on the individual communication complexity of a function f is $CC^P(x,y) \geq C(f(x,y) \mid x, P) - O(1)$ (and hence $TCC_f^\alpha(x,y) \geq C(f(x,y) \mid x) - \alpha - O(\log \alpha)$ anticipating on a later defined notion). In this section we establish some nontrivial lower bounds on $CC^P(x,y)$ for P computing f on all arguments for the inner product function, the equality function and for random Boolean functions. We omit the proofs for space reasons.

Initially, Alice has a string $x = x_1, \ldots, x_n$ and Bob has a string $y = y_1, \ldots, y_n$ with $x, y \in \{0,1\}^n$. Alice and Bob compute the inner product of x and y modulo 2

$$f(x,y) = \sum_{i=1}^n x_i \cdot y_i \bmod 2$$

with Alice ending up with the result. The following result is proven by extending an argument introduced in [2].

Theorem 1. *Every deterministic protocol P computing the inner product function f requires at least $CC^P(x,y) \geq C(x, y \mid P) - n - O(1)$ bits of communication on all x, y.*

Remark 1. The result of the theorem is only significant for $C(x,y) > n$, but for some x, y it cannot be improved. Namely, if $x = 00 \ldots 0$ then $f(x,y) = 0$ for all y's and there is a protocol P computing the Identity function such that $CC^P(x,y) = 0$ for all such x, y. If y is any random string (relative to P) then the right hand side of the inequality $CC^P(x,y) \geq C(x,y \mid P) - n - O(1)$ becomes $O(1)$ while the left hand side is equal to 0, thus both sides are almost the same.

Assume Alice has $x = x_1 \ldots x_n$ and Bob has $y_1 \ldots y_n$, and $f : \{0,1\}^{2n} \to \{0,1\}$ satisfies

$$C(f \mid n) \geq 2^{2n} - n. \tag{1}$$

The latter condition means that the truth table describing the outcomes of f for the 2^n possible inputs x (the rows) and the 2^n possible inputs for y (the columns) has high Kolmogorov complexity. If we flip the truth table for a prospective f using a fair coin, then with probability at least $1 - 2^{-n}$ it will satisfy (1).

Theorem 2. *Every deterministic protocol P computing a function f satisfying (1) (without help bits) requires at least $CC_f^P(x,y) \geq \min\{C(x \mid P), C(y \mid P)\} - \log n - O(1)$.*

Theorem 3. *Let f be the equality function, with $f(x,y) = 1$ if $x = y$ and 0 otherwise. For every deterministic protocol P computing f we have $CC^P(x,x) \geq C(x \mid P) - O(1)$ for all x,y. On the other hand there is P of complexity $O(1)$ such that there are x,y ($x \neq y$) with $C(x \mid P), C(y \mid P) \geq n - 1$ for which $CC_f^P(x,y) = 2$.*

Generalizing this idea, every function that contains large monochromatic rectangles, of size say $2^{2n}/n^{O(1)}$, has many pairs x,y of complexity close to n for which the individual communication complexity drops to $O(\log n)$: In round 1 Bob tells Alice in which large rectangle (if any) his input is situated, by sending the index of the rectangle to Alice, and 0 otherwise. If Bob did send an index, and Alice's input is in that rectangle as well, then Alice outputs the color ("0" or "1") of the rectangle. Otherwise, Alice starts a default protocol.

4   Total Protocols

Let f be a function defined on pairs of strings of the same length. Assume that Alice has x, Bob has y and Alice wants to compute $f(x,y)$. As the complexity measure we consider the number of bits communicated between Alice and Bob. The naive definition of the individual communication complexity of the value of the function f on the argument (x,y) is the number of communicated bits in the "best" communication protocol. Then, for every x,y there is a protocol with no communication at all on (x,y): the string y is hard wired into the protocol. To meaningfully capture the individual communication complexity of computing a function $f(x,y)$ we define now the following notion.

Definition 1. *Let α be a natural number parameter. Let $TCC_f^\alpha(x,y)$ stand for the minimum $CC^P(x,y)$ over all total protocols P of complexity at most α that always compute f correctly (being total such a protocol terminates for all inputs, and not only for (x,y)).*

For $\alpha = n + O(1)$ we have $TCC_f^\alpha(x,y) = 0$ for all computable f and all x,y, since we can hard wire y into the protocol. Therefore it is natural to consider only α that are much smaller than n, say $\alpha = O(\log n)$. Since computation of the Identity function suffices to compute all other (recursive) functions we have $TCC_f^{\alpha+O(1)}(x,y) \leq TCC_I^\alpha(x,y)$. The trivial lower bound is $TCC_f^\alpha(x,y) \geq C(f(x,y) \mid x) - \alpha - O(\log \alpha)$. For $f = I$ this gives $TCC_I^\alpha(x,y) \geq C(y \mid x) - \alpha - O(\log \alpha)$.

4.1   One-Way Equals Two-Way for Identity

Let $TCC_{f,1\text{-way}}^\alpha(x,y)$ stand for the minimum $TCC^P(x,y)$ over all one-way (Bob sends a message to Alice) total protocols P of complexity at most α computing f (over all inputs, and not only on (x,y)). It is clear that $TCC_{f,1\text{-way}}^\alpha(x,y)$ does not depend on x: indeed, consider for given (x,y) the best protocol P; that protocol sends the same message on every other pair (x', y) hence $TCC^\alpha_{f,1\text{-way}}(x', y) \leq TCC^\alpha_{f,1\text{-way}}(x, y)$. Obviously,

$$TCC^\alpha_f(x, y) \leq TCC^\alpha_{f,1\text{-way}}(x, y)$$

for all α, x, y, f.

Surprisingly, for $f = I$, the Identity function, this inequality is an equality. That is, for total protocols "1-way" is as powerful as "2-way." More specifically, the following holds.

Theorem 4. *There is a constant C such that for all α, x, y we have*

$$TCC^{\alpha+C}_{I,1\text{-way}}(x, y) \leq TCC^\alpha_I(x, y).$$

Proof. Pick a two-way protocol P witnessing $TCC^\alpha_I(x, y) = l$. Let $c = c(x, y)$ be the conversation according to P between Alice and Bob on inputs x, y. It is known that the set of all pairs (x', y') such that the conversation between Alice and Bob on input (x', y') is equal to c is a rectangle, that is, has the form $X \times Y$, for some $X, Y \subset \{0, 1\}^n$. The set Y is a one-element set, as for every $y' \in Y$ Alice outputs y also on the input (x, y') (the output of Alice depends on c, P, x only).

Consider the following 1-way protocol P': find an x' with minimum $c(x', y)$ and send $c(x', y)$ to Alice. Alice then finds the set of all pairs (x'', y') such that the conversation between Alice and Bob on input (x'', y') is equal to $c(x', y)$. As we have seen that set has the form $X \times \{y\}$ for some X. Thus Alice knows y. As $|c(x', y)| \leq |c(x, y)| = TCC^\alpha_I(x, y)$ and $C(P'|P) = O(1)$ we are done.

4.2   Non-communicable Objects

The function $TCC^\alpha_{I,1\text{-way}}(x, y)$, as a function of y, α, essentially coincides with *Kolmogorov structure function* $h_y(\alpha)$ studied in [7]. The latter is defined by

$$h_y(\alpha) = \min_S \{\log |S| : S \ni y, \ C(S) \leq \alpha\},$$

where S is a finite set and $C(S)$ is the length (number of bits) in the shortest binary program from which the reference universal machine U computes a listing of the elements of S and then halts. More specifically we have

$$TCC^{\alpha+O(1)}_{I,1\text{-way}}(x, y) \leq h_y(\alpha), \tag{2}$$

$$h_y(\alpha + O(\log n)) \leq TCC^\alpha_{I,1\text{-way}}(x, y).$$

To prove the first inequality we have to transform a finite set $S \ni y$ into a one-way protocol P of complexity at most $\alpha = C(S) + O(1)$ witnessing $TCC^\alpha_{I,1\text{-way}}(x, y) \leq \log |S|$. The protocol just sends the index of y in S, or y literally if $y \notin S$.

To prove the second inequality we have to transform a one-way total protocol P into a finite set $S \ni y$ of complexity at most $C(P) + O(\log n)$ with $\log |S| \leq$

$CC^P(y)$. The set consists of all y' on which P sends the message of the same length l as the length of the message on y. Obviously, $|S| \le 2^l = 2^{CC^P(y)}$ and to specify S we need a program describing P and l. Thus $C(S) \le C(P) + O(\log TCC^\alpha_{I,1\text{-way}}(x,y)) \le C(P) + O(\log n)$.

For the properties of $h_y(\alpha)$, which by Theorem 4 are also properties of $TCC^\alpha_{I,1\text{-way}}(x,y)$, its relation with Kolmogorov complexity $C(y)$ of y and possible shapes of the function $\alpha \mapsto h_y(\alpha)$ we refer to [7].

We will present here only a few properties. First, two easy inequalities: For all $\alpha \ge O(1)$ and all x, y we have

$$C(y|n) - \alpha - O(\log \alpha) \le TCC^\alpha_{I,1\text{-way}}(x,y) \le n - \alpha + O(1). \qquad (3)$$

The first inequality is the direct consequence of the inequality $C(y|n) \le CC^P(x,y) + C(P|n) + O(\log C(P|n))$, which is trivial. To prove the second one consider the protocol that sends $n - \alpha + C$ bits of y (for appropriate constant C) and the remaining α bits are hardwired into the protocol. Its complexity is at most $\alpha - C + O(1) \le \alpha$ for appropriate choice of C.

The second property is not so easy. Given y, consider values of α such that

$$TCC^\alpha_{I,1\text{-way}}(x,y) + \alpha = C(y) + O(1). \qquad (4)$$

That is, the protocol P witnessing (4) together with the one-way communication record Bob sends to Alice form a two-part code for y that is—up to an independent additive constant—as concise as the shortest one-part code for y (that has length $C(y)$ by definition). Following the usage in [7] we call P a "sufficient" protocol for y. The description of the protocol plus the communication precisely describe y, and in fact, it can be shown that the converse holds as well (up to a constant additive term). There always exists such a protocol, since the protocol that contains y hard wired in the form of a shortest program of length $C(y)$ satisfies the equality with $\alpha = C(y) + O(1)$ and $TCC^\alpha_I(y) = 0$. By definition we cannot have $TCC^\alpha_{I,1\text{-way}}(x,y) + \alpha < C(y) - O(1)$, but for α sufficiently small we have $TCC^\alpha_I(y) + \alpha > C(y) + O(1)$. In fact, for every form of function satisfying the obvious constraints on TCC^α_I there is a y such that $TCC^\alpha_{I,1\text{-way}}(x,y)$ realizes that function up to logarithmic precision. This shows that there are essentially non-communicable strings. More precisely:

Theorem 5. *For every $k \le n$ and for every function $h(\alpha)$ on integer domain $[0,k]$ with $h(0) = n$, $h(k) = 0$, $C(h) = O(\log n)$ such that $h(\alpha) + \alpha$ does not increase there is a string y of length n and $C(y) = k + O(\log n)$ such that*

$$TCC^{\alpha+O(\log n)}_{I,1\text{-way}}(x,y) \le h(\alpha),$$
$$h(\alpha + O(\log n)) \le TCC^\alpha_{I,1\text{-way}}(x,y).$$

The proof is by combining Theorem 1 of [7] with (2). In particular, for every $k < n - O(\log n)$ there are strings y of length n and complexity k such that $TCC^\alpha_{I,1\text{-way}}(x,y) > n - \alpha - O(\log n)$ for all $\alpha < k - O(\log n)$ while

$TCC^\alpha_{I,1\text{-way}}(x,y) = O(1)$ for $\alpha \geq k + O(1)$. We call such strings y *non-communicable*. For example, with $k = (\log n)^2$ this shows that there are y of complexity $C(y) \approx (\log n)^2$ with $TCC^\alpha_{I,1\text{-way}}(x,y) \approx n - (\log n)^2$ for all $\alpha < C(y) - O(\log n)$ and $O(1)$ otherwise. That is, Bob can hold a highly compressible string y, but cannot use that fact to reduce the communication complexity significantly below $|y|$! Unless *all* information about y is hard wired in the (total) protocol the communication between Bob and Alice requires sending y almost completely literally. For such y, irrespective of x, the communication complexity is *exponential* in the complexity of y for all protocols of complexity less than that of y; when the complexity of the protocol is allowed to pass the complexity of y then the communication complexity suddenly drops to 0.

Corollary 1. *For every n, k with $k \leq n$ there are y of length n and $C(y) = k + O(\log n)$ such that for every x $TCC^\alpha_{I,1\text{-way}}(x,y) \geq n - \alpha - O(\log n)$ for $\alpha < C(y) - O(\log n)$; while for every x, y we have $TCC^\alpha_{I,1\text{-way}}(x,y) = O(1)$ for $\alpha \geq C(y) + O(1)$.*

This follows by combining Theorems 4, 5. If we relax the requirement of total and correct protocols to partial and partially correct protocols then we obtain the significantly weaker statements of Theorem 6 and Corollary 2.

5   Partially Correct and Partial Protocols

The individual communication complexity can decrease if we do not require the communication protocol to be correct on all the input pairs. Let $CC^\alpha_f(x,y)$ stand for the minimum $CC^P(x,y)$ over all P of complexity at most α computing f correctly on input (x,y) (on other inputs P may output incorrect result). The minimum of the empty set is defined as ∞. Let $CC^\alpha_{f,1\text{-way}}(x,y)$ stand for the minimum $CC^P(x,y)$ over all one-way (Bob sends a message to Alice) P of complexity at most α computing $f(x,y)$ (again, on other inputs P may work incorrectly). For instance, if f is a Boolean function then $CC^{O(1)}_{f,1\text{-way}}(x,y) = 0$ for all x, y (either the protocol outputting always 0 or the protocol outputting always 1 is computes $f(x,y)$ for specific pair (x,y)).

5.1   Partially Correct and Partial Protocols versus Total Ones

It is easy to see that in computing the Identity function for some (x,y) total, partially correct, protocols are more powerful than totally correct ones. A total partially correct protocol P computes $f(x,y)$ correctly for some (x,y), but may err on some inputs (u,v), in which case we set $CC^P(x,y) = \infty$. Being total such a protocol terminates for all inputs.

Definition 2. Let α be a natural number parameter. Let $CC^\alpha_f(x,y)$ stand for the minimum $CC^P(x,y)$ over all total partially correct protocols P of complexity at most α.

For instance, for every n there is a total protocol $P = P_n$ computable from n such that $CC^P_{I,1\text{-way}}(x,x) = 0$ (Alice outputs her string), thus $CC^{O(1)}_I(x,x) = 0$. On the other hand, for random x of length n we have $TCC^\alpha_I(x,x) \geq TCC^{\alpha - O(1)}_{I,1\text{-way}}(x,x) \geq C(x|n) - \alpha - O(\log \alpha) \geq n - \alpha - O(\log \alpha)$.

We also consider partial protocols that on some x, y are allowed to get stuck, that is, give no instructions at all about how to proceed. Formally, such a protocol is a pair of programs (P_A, P_B). The program P_A tells Alice what to do for each c (the current part of the conversation) and x: either wait the next bit from Bob, or to send a specific bit to Bob, or to output a certain string and halt. Similarly, the program P_B tells Bob what to do for each c and y: either to wait the next bit from Alice or to send a bit to Alice, or to halt. This pair must satisfy the following requirements for all $(x,y) \in \{0,1\}^n$ and all c: if a party gets the instruction to send a bit then another party gets the instruction to wait for a bit. However we do not require that for all $(x,y) \in \{0,1\}^n$ and all c both parties get some instruction, it is allowed that P_A, P_B start some endless computation. In particular, Alice may wait for a bit and at the same time Bob has no instruction at all.

Definition 3. The complexity of a partial protocol $P = (P_A, P_B)$ is defined as $C(P|n)$. We say that P computes f on the input (x,y) if Alice outputs $f(x,y)$ when P_A, P_B are run on (x,y). On other pairs Alice is allowed to output a wrong answer or not output anything at all. If protocol P does not terminate, or gives an incorrect answer, for input (x,y), then $CC^P(x,y) = \infty$. Two-way and one-way individual communication complexities with complexity of the partial protocol upper bounded by α are denoted as $PCC^\alpha_f(x,y)$ and $PCC^\alpha_{f,1\text{-way}}(x,y)$ respectively.

Since the total, partially correct, protocols are a subset of the partial protocols, we always have $PCC^\alpha_f(x,y) \leq CC^\alpha_f(x,y) \leq TCC^\alpha_f(x,y)$. Consider again the Identity function. We have the following obvious lower bound

$$C(y|x) - \alpha - O(\log \alpha) \leq PCC^\alpha_I(x,y) \tag{5}$$

for all α, x, y. On the other hand we have the following upper bound if α is at least $\log C(y) + O(1)$:

$$PCC^\alpha_{I,1\text{-way}}(x,y) \leq C(y). \tag{6}$$

Indeed, we hardwire the value $C(y)$ in the protocol using $\log C(y)$ bits. This enables P_B to find a shortest description y^* of y and to send it to Alice; subsequently P_A decompresses the message received from Bob. Note that the program P_B gives no instruction to Bob if the complexity of Bob's input is greater than $C(y)$. Therefore, this protocol is not total. Comparing Equation (6) to Equation (3) we see that for PCC we have a better upper bound than for TCC. It turns out that for some pairs (x,y) the communication complexity for totally correct (and even for partially correct) protocols is close to the upper bound $n - \alpha$ while the communication complexity for partial protocols is close to the lower bound $C(y|x) - \alpha \ll n$.

Theorem 6. *For all* α, n, x *there are* y *of length* n *such that* $CC_I^\alpha(x, y) \geq n - \alpha$ *and* $C(y|x) \leq \alpha + O(1)$.

Proof. Fix a string x. By counting arguments, there is a string y with $CC_I^\alpha(x, y) \geq n - \alpha$. Indeed, there are less than $2^{\alpha+1}$ total protocols of complexity at most α. For each total protocol P there are at most $2^{n-\alpha-1}$ different y's with $CC^P(x, y) < n - \alpha$. Therefore the total number of y's with $CC_I^\alpha(x, y) < n - \alpha$ is less than $2^{\alpha+1}2^{n-\alpha-1} = 2^n$.

Let y be the first string with $CC_I^\alpha(x, y) \geq n - \alpha$. To identify y conditional to x we only need to know the number of total protocols of complexity at most α: given that number we enumerate all such protocols until we find all them. Given all those protocols and x we run all of them on all pairs (x, y) to find $CC_I^\alpha(x, y)$ (here we use that the protocols are total) for every y, and determine the first y for which it is at least $n - \alpha$. Hence $C(y|x) \leq \alpha + O(1)$.

Corollary 2. *Fix constants* C_1, C_2 *such that* $PCC_{I,1\text{-way}}^{\log C(y)+C_1}(x, y) \leq C(y) \leq n + C_2$. *Applying the theorem to the empty string* ϵ *and to (say)* $\alpha = 2\log n$ *we obtain a* y *of length* n *with exponential gap between* $CC_I^{2\log n}(\epsilon, y) \geq n - 2\log n - O(1)$ *and* $PCC_{I,1\text{-way}}^{\log(n+C_2)+C_1}(\epsilon, y) \leq C(y) \leq 2\log n + O(1)$.

Using a deep result of An. Muchnik [6] we can prove that $PCC_{I,1\text{-way}}^\alpha$ is close to $C(y|x)$ for $\alpha \geq O(\log n)$.

Theorem 7 (An. Muchnik). *For all* x, y *of length* n *there is* p *such that* $|p| \leq C(y|x) + O(\log n)$, $C(p|y) = O(\log n)$ *and* $C(y|p, x) = O(\log n)$, *where the constants in* $O(\log n)$ *do not depend on* n, x, y.

Corollary 3. *For all* x, y *of length* n *we have* $PCC_{I,1\text{-way}}^{O(\log n)}(x, y) \leq C(y|x) + O(\log n)$.

Proof. Let p be the program of Muchnik's theorem, let q be the program of length $O(\log n)$ for the reference computer to reconstruct p from y and let r the program of length $O(\log n)$ for the reference computer to reconstruct y from the pair (x, p). The protocol is as follows: Bob finds p from y, q and sends p to Alice; Alice reconstructs y from x, r. Both q and r are hardwired into the protocol, so its complexity is $O(\log n)$. This protocol is partial, as both Bob and Alice may be stuck when reconstructing p from y', q and y from x', r.

For very small values of $C(y|x)$, $C(y)$ we can do even better using the coloring lemma 3.9 and theorem 3.11 from [1].

Lemma 1. *Let* k_1, k_2 *be such that* $C(x) \leq k_1$ *and* $C(y \mid x) \leq k_2$, *and let* $m = |\{(x, y) : C(x) \leq k_1, C(y \mid x) \leq k_2\}|$. *For* $M = 2^{k_1}$, $N = 2^{k_2}$ *and every* $1 \leq B \leq N$ *Bob can compute the recursive function* $R(k_1, k_2, m, y) = r_y \leq (N/B)e(MN)^{1/B}$ *such that Alice can reconstruct* y *from* x, r_y, m *and at most* $b \leq \log B$ *extra bits.*

Using k_1, k_2, m, y, Bob can compute r_y and send it in $\log r_y$ bits to Alice. The latter computes y from x, m, r_y using additionally $b \leq \log B$ special bits provided by the protocol. Then, the number of bits that need to be communicated, 1 round, from Bob to Alice, is

$$\log r_y \leq k_2 - \log B + \frac{k_2 + k_1}{B}.$$

The protocol $P = (P_A, P_B)$ uses $\leq 2(k_1 + k_2) + b + O(1)$ bits.

Corollary 4. *If $C(x), C(y|x) = O(\log\log n)$ and $b = \Theta(\log\log n)$ then $PCC_{I,1-way}^{\Theta(\log\log n)}(x, y) \leq C(y|x) - \Theta(\log\log n)$.*

5.2 Two-Way Is Better than One-Way for Partially Correct Protocols

Note that for the Identity function all our upper bounds hold for one-way protocols and all our lower bounds hold for two-way protocols. The following question arises: are two-way protocols more powerful than one-way ones (to compute the Identity function)? Theorem 4 implies that for total protocol it does not matter whether the communication is one-way or two-way. For partially correct total protocols and partial protocol the situation is different. It turns out that partially correct total two-way protocols are stronger than even partial one-way protocols.

Theorem 8. *For every k, l, s such that $k \geq s + l 2^s$ there are strings x, y of length $(2^s + 1)k$ such that $CC_I^{O(1)}(x, y) \leq 2^s \log(2k)$ but $PCC_{I,1-way}^s(x, y) \geq l$.*

Proof. We let $x = z_0 z_1 \ldots z_{2^s}$ where $z_0, \ldots, z_{2^s}$ have length k and $y = z_j 00 \ldots 0$ for some j.

To prove the upper bound consider the following two-way protocol: Alice finds a set of indexes $I = \{i_1, \ldots, i_{2^s}\}$ such that for every distinct j, m there is $i \in I$ such that ith bit of z_j is different from ith bit of z_m (such set does exist, which may be shown by induction). Then she sends to Bob the string $i_1 \ldots i_{2^s}$ and Bob sends to Alice ith bit of y for all $i \in I$. Alice knows now y.

We need to find now particular $z_0, z_1, \ldots, z_{2^s}$ such that no one-way protocol is effective on the pair (x, y) obtained from them in the specified way. To this end let $P_1, \ldots, P_N$ be all the one-way partial protocols of complexity less than s computing the identity function. For every z and $i \leq N$ let $c(z, i)$ denote the message sent by Bob in protocol P_i when his input is $z00 \ldots 0$ provided the length of the message is less than l. Otherwise let $c(z, i) = \infty$. Let $c(z)$ stand for the concatenation of $c(z, i)$ over all i. The range of $c(z)$ has $(2^l)^N < 2^{l 2^s}$ elements. Hence there is c such that for more than $2^{k - 2^s l} \geq 2^s$ different z's we have $c(z) = c$. Pick such c and pick different $z_0, z_1, \ldots, z_{2^s}$ among those z's. Let y_j stand for the string obtained from z_j by appending 0s. We claim that $CC_I^{P_i}(x, y_j) \geq l$ for some j for all $i \leq N$. Assume that this is not the case. That is, for every j there are i such that $CC_I^{P_i}(x, y_j) < l$. There are $j_1 \neq j_2$ for which i is the same. As $c(z_{j_1}, i) = c(z_{j_2}, i) \neq \infty$ Alice receives the same message in P_i on inputs $(x, y_{j_1}), (x, y_{j_2})$ and should output both answers y_{j_1}, y_{j_2}, which is a contradiction.

Corollary 5. *Let in the above theorem $s = (\log k)/3$ and $l = k^{2/3}/\log k$. These values satisfy the condition $k \geq s + l2^s$ and hence there are x, y of length about $k^{4/3}$ with almost quadratic gap between $CC_I^{O(1)}(x,y) \leq k^{1/3}\log 2k$ and $PCC_{I,1\text{-way}}^{(\log k)/3}(x,y) \geq k^{2/3}/\log k$. Letting $s = \log\log k$ and $l = k/(2\log k)$ we obtain x, y of length about $k\log k$ with an exponential gap between $CC_I^{O(1)}(x,y) \leq \log k \log(2k)$ and $PCC_{I,1\text{-way}}^{\log\log k}(x,y) \geq k/(2\log k)$.*

6   Summary of Some Selected Results for Comparison

- $\forall_{x,y,\alpha}[TCC_I^\alpha(x,y) \geq CC_I^\alpha(x,y) \geq PCC_I^\alpha(x,y)]$ by definition.
- $\forall_{\alpha,x,y}[TCC_{I,1\text{-way}}^{\alpha+O(1)}(x,y) = TCC_I^\alpha(x,y) + O(1)]$ Theorem 4 and discussion.
- $\forall_{n,k,\alpha}\exists_{y,|y|=n,C(y)=k}\forall_x[\alpha < C(y) - O(\log n) \Rightarrow TCC_I^\alpha(x,y) \geq n - \alpha]$ Corollary 1.
- $\forall_{x,y,\alpha}[\alpha \geq C(y) - O(1) \Rightarrow TCC_I^\alpha(x,y) = O(1)]$ Corollary 1.
- $\forall_{n,x,\alpha}\exists_{y,|y|=n}[C(y|x) \leq \alpha + O(1)\&CC_I^\alpha(x,y) \geq n - \alpha]$ Theorem 6.
- $\forall_{x,y,\alpha}[PCC_I^\alpha(x,y) \geq C(y|x) - \alpha - O(\log\alpha)]$ (5).
- $\forall_{n,x,y}[PCC_{I,1-way}^{\log C(y)+O(1)}(x,y) \leq C(y)]$ (6).
- $\forall_n\forall_{x,y,|x|=|y|=n}[PCC_{I,1-way}^{O(\log n)}(x,y) \leq C(y|x) + O(\log n)]$ Corollary 3.
- $\forall_{k,l,s:k \geq s+l2^s}\exists_{x,y,|x|=|y|=(2^s+1)k}[CC_I^{O(1)}(x,y) \leq 2^s \log(2k)\&PCC_{I,1-way}^s(x,y) \geq l]$ Theorem 8.

The situation gets different when we allow help bits. For space reasons we defer our results to the full version of this paper.

References

1. C.H. Bennett, P. Gács, M. Li, P.M.B. Vitányi, and W. Zurek, Information Distance, *IEEE Trans. Information Theory*, IT-44:4(1998) 1407–1423.
2. H. Buhrman, T. Jiang, M. Li, P. Vitanyi, New applications of the incompressibility method: Part II, *Theoretical Computer Science*, 235:1(2000), 59–70.
3. E. Kushilevitz, N. Nisan, *Communication Complexity*, Cambridge University Press, 1997.
4. L. A. Levin, Average Case Complete Problems, *SIAM J.Comput.*, 15:1(1986), 285–286.
5. M. Li and P.M.B. Vitányi, *An Introduction to Kolmogorov Complexity and its Applications*, Springer-Verlag, New York, 2nd Edition, 1997.
6. An.A. Muchnik, Conditional complexity and codes, *Theoret. Comput. Sci.*, 271:1/2(2002), 97–111.
7. N.K. Vereshchagin and P.M.B. Vitányi, Kolmogorov's structure functions and an application to the foundations of model selection, *Proc. 47th IEEE Symp. Found. Comput. Sci.*, 2002, 751–760.
8. A.C. Yao. Some complexity questions related to distributive computing. In: *Proc. 11th ACM Symposium on Theory of Computing*, 1979, 209–213.

The Complexity of Satisfiability Problems over Finite Lattices

Bernhard Schwarz

Department of Computer Science, University of Würzburg
schwarzb@informatik.uni-wuerzburg.de

Abstract. We study the computational complexity of problems defined by formulas over fixed finite lattices. We consider evaluation, satisfiability, tautology, counting, and quantified formulas. It turns out that evaluation and tautology always can be decided in alternating logarithmic time. For satisfiability we obtain the following dichotomy result: If the lattice is distributive, satisfiability is in alternating logarithmic time. Otherwise, it is NP-complete. Counting is #P-complete for every lattice with at least two elements. For quantified formulas over non-distributive lattices we obtain PSPACE-completeness, while the problem is in alternating logarithmic time, if the lattice is distributive.

1 Introduction

Goldmann and Russell [6] investigated the computational complexity of determining if an equation over some fixed finite group has a solution. Formally, an equation over a group $\mathcal{G} = (G, \circ)$ or more generally over an algebra $\mathcal{A} = (A, f_1, \ldots, f_m)$, is given as

$$H(x_1, \ldots, x_n) = a$$

where H is a formula over the variables $x_1, \ldots, x_n$, the constants $c \in A$, and the functions $f_1, \ldots, f_m$, and $a \in A$ is the target. The satisfiability problem over $\mathcal{A}$ is to determine if there is an assignment to the variables such that the equation is satisfied. Goldmann and Russell [6] showed, that this problem lies in P for nilpotent groups, but is NP-complete for any non-solvable group. Barrington et al. [2] extended these results by considering the computational complexity of satisfiability over a fixed finite monoid.

Satisfiability over the boolean algebra $\mathcal{B} = (\{0, 1\}, \{\wedge, \vee, \neg\})$ is the classical NP-complete problem [4], while satisfiability over the monotone boolean algebra $\mathcal{M} = (\{0, 1\}, \{\wedge, \vee\})$, considering only monotone boolean formulas, can be decided in alternating logarithmic time.

Formulas over lattices generalize monotone formulas. A lattice is a partially ordered set with the functions $\wedge$ (greatest lower bound) and $\vee$ (smallest upper bound). While the monotone boolean algebra $\mathcal{M}$ is a distributive lattice, lattices can be non-distributive as well. We study the computational complexity of

V. Diekert and M. Habib (Eds.): STACS 2004, LNCS 2996, pp. 31–43, 2004.

problems defined by formulas over both, distributive and non-distributive finite
lattices. We observe the following dichotomy for a finite lattice V:

$$V \text{ is distributive} \quad \Rightarrow \quad \text{Satisfiability over } V \text{ is in ALOGTIME.}$$
$$V \text{ is non-distributive} \quad \Rightarrow \quad \text{Satisfiability over } V \text{ is NP-complete.}$$

The paper is organized as follows. In Section 2 we define the problems to study
over arbitrary algebras. We recall results that lead to monotone formulas and
finally to finite lattices. Section 3 introduces lattices and classifies the tautology
and counting problems for lattices. Section 4 deals with distributive lattices.
We show that most problems are easy in this case. In Section 5 we complete
the dichotomy, proving several completeness results for non-distributive lattices.
The last section gives an overview of all results, and mentions open problems.

We use standard notations [3,7,5]. Most proofs are given in sketch. For more
detail we refer to the Technical Report [9].

2   Algebras

We study problems that are defined by formulas over algebras. An *algebra* is a
pair of sets (A, M) where A is a set of elements and $M \subseteq \{f : A^{n_f} \to A\}$ is a
set of total functions. The algebra is called *finite*, if A and M are finite.

Definition 1. *For an algebra $\mathcal{A} = (A, M)$ the set of all $\mathcal{A}$-formulas $\mathrm{F}(\mathcal{A})$ is
given by*

(1) *For each $c \in A : c$ is an $\mathcal{A}$-formula (constant).*
(2) *For each $i \geq 1 : x_i$ is an $\mathcal{A}$-formula (variable).*
(3) *If $F_1, \ldots, F_n$ are $\mathcal{A}$-formulas, and $f \in M$ is a function $f : A^n \to A$,
    then $f(F_1, \ldots, F_n)$ is an $\mathcal{A}$-formula.*

For an $\mathcal{A}$-formula $F \in \mathrm{F}(\mathcal{A})$, n_F denotes the number of different indices of
variables occuring in F. Let $i_1 < \ldots < i_{n_F}$ be all indices of variables in F.
For arbitrary $w = (a_1, \ldots, a_{n_F}) \in A^{n_F}$, $F(w)$ denotes the *value* of F, when
replacing each x_{i_j} by a_j and applying the functions occuring in F. We also write
$F(x_1, \ldots, x_n)$ to make clear that F is an $\mathcal{A}$-formula that contains at most the
variables $x_1, \ldots, x_n$.

Definition 2. *For a fixed algebra $\mathcal{A} = (A, M)$ and $a \in A$ we define the following
evaluation, tautology, satisfiability and counting problems:*

$$\mathrm{VAL}_{\mathcal{A}}^{a} =_{\mathrm{df}} \{(F, w) \mid F \in \mathrm{F}(\mathcal{A}), w \in A^{n_F}, F(w) = a\}.$$
$$\mathrm{VAL}_{\mathcal{A}} =_{\mathrm{df}} \{(F, w, b) \mid (F, w) \in \mathrm{VAL}_{\mathcal{A}}^{b}\}.$$
$$\mathrm{TAUT}_{\mathcal{A}}^{a} =_{\mathrm{df}} \{F \in \mathrm{F}(\mathcal{A}) \mid \forall w \in A^{n_F} : F(w) = a\}.$$
$$\mathrm{TAUT}_{\mathcal{A}} =_{\mathrm{df}} \{(F, b) \mid F \in \mathrm{TAUT}_{\mathcal{A}}^{b}\}.$$
$$\mathrm{SAT}_{\mathcal{A}}^{a} =_{\mathrm{df}} \{F \in \mathrm{F}(\mathcal{A}) \mid \exists w \in A^{n_F} : F(w) = a\}.$$
$$\mathrm{SAT}_{\mathcal{A}} =_{\mathrm{df}} \{(F, b) \mid F \in \mathrm{SAT}_{\mathcal{A}}^{b}\}.$$
$$\#_{\mathcal{A}}^{a} : \mathrm{F}(\mathcal{A}) \to \mathrm{N} \ : \ F \mapsto \#\{w \in A^{n_F} \mid F(w) = a\}.$$
$$\#_{\mathcal{A}} : \mathrm{F}(\mathcal{A}) \times \mathcal{A} \to \mathrm{N} \ : \ (F, b) \mapsto \#_{\mathcal{A}}^{b}(F).$$

If we have a sequence of quantifiers $Q_1, \dots, Q_n \in \{\forall, \exists\}$, *then we define the number of alternations* $\kappa(Q_1 \cdots Q_n) =_{df} \#\{i \in \mathbb{N} \mid 1 \leq i \leq n-1, Q_i \neq Q_{i+1}\}$. *Now define for* $k \geq 1$ *the following problems of quantified formulas:*

$$\text{QAF}^a_{\mathcal{A}} =_{df} \{Q_1 \dots Q_n F \mid F \in \text{F}(\mathcal{A}), n = n_F, Q_1, \dots, Q_n \in \{\forall, \exists\},$$
$$Q_1 a_1 \in A \cdots Q_n a_n \in A : F(a_1, \dots, a_n) = a\}.$$

$$\text{QAF}_{\mathcal{A}} =_{df} \{(qF, b) \mid qF \in \text{QAF}^b_{\mathcal{A}}\}.$$

$$\Sigma^a_{k,\mathcal{A}} =_{df} \{Q_1 \dots Q_n F \in \text{QAF}^a_{\mathcal{A}} \mid Q_1 = \exists, \kappa(Q_1 \cdots Q_n) = k-1\}.$$

$$\Sigma_{k,\mathcal{A}} =_{df} \{(qF, b) \mid qF \in \Sigma^b_{k,\mathcal{A}}\}.$$

$$\Pi^a_{k,\mathcal{A}} =_{df} \{Q_1 \dots Q_n F \in \text{QAF}^a_{\mathcal{A}} \mid Q_1 = \forall, \kappa(Q_1 \cdots Q_n) = k-1\}.$$

$$\Pi_{k,\mathcal{A}} =_{df} \{(qF, b) \mid qF \in \Pi^b_{k,\mathcal{A}}\}.$$

These definitions are a generalization of the well known problems. If the algebra is finite, we can determine upper bounds for the problems:

Theorem 1. *Let* $\mathcal{A} = (A, M)$ *be a finite algebra,* $a \in A$ *and* $k \geq 1$.

1. $\text{VAL}_{\mathcal{A}}, \text{VAL}^a_{\mathcal{A}} \in \text{ALOGTIME}$.
2. $\text{TAUT}_{\mathcal{A}}, \text{TAUT}^a_{\mathcal{A}} \in \text{coNP}$.
3. $\text{SAT}_{\mathcal{A}}, \text{SAT}^a_{\mathcal{A}} \in \text{NP}$.
4. $\#_{\mathcal{A}}, \#^a_{\mathcal{A}} \in \#\text{P}$.
5. $\Sigma_{k,\mathcal{A}}, \Sigma^a_{k,\mathcal{A}} \in \Sigma^P_k$, $\Pi_{k,\mathcal{A}}, \Pi^a_{k,\mathcal{A}} \in \Pi^P_k$ *and* $\text{QAF}_{\mathcal{A}}, \text{QAF}^a_{\mathcal{A}} \in \text{PSPACE}$.

Proof. The first statement follows from a result by Buss [3]: Every parenthesis context-free language is in ALOGTIME. The other statements are trivial, since $\mathcal{A}$ is finite.

Theorem 1 cannot be improved in general, since the upper bounds are strict in the case of the boolean algebra:

Theorem 2 (Bu87,RW99). *Let be* $\mathcal{B} =_{df} (\{0,1\}, \{\wedge, \vee, \neg\})$ *and* $k \geq 1$.

1. $\text{VAL}^1_{\mathcal{B}}$ *is* $\leq^{logtime}_m$*-complete for* ALOGTIME.
2. $\text{TAUT}^1_{\mathcal{B}}$ *is* $\leq^{log}_m$*-complete for* coNP.
3. $\text{SAT}^1_{\mathcal{B}}$ *is* $\leq^{log}_m$*-complete for* NP.
4. $\#^1_{\mathcal{B}}$ *is* $\leq^{log}_m$*-complete for* $\#$P.
5. $\Sigma^1_{k,\mathcal{B}}, \Pi^1_{k,\mathcal{B}}$, *and* $\text{QAF}^1_{\mathcal{B}}$, *resp. are* $\leq^{log}_m$*-complete for* Σ^P_k, Π^P_k, *and* PSPACE, *resp.*

On the other hand, if we drop the negation, most problems turn to be easy:

Theorem 3 (Bu87,RW99). *Let be* $\mathcal{M} =_{df} (\{0,1\}, \{\wedge, \vee\})$ *and* $k \geq 1$.

1. $\text{VAL}^1_{\mathcal{M}} \in \text{ALOGTIME}$.
2. $\text{TAUT}^1_{\mathcal{M}} \in \text{ALOGTIME}$.
3. $\text{SAT}^1_{\mathcal{M}} \in \text{ALOGTIME}$.
4. $\#^1_{\mathcal{M}}$ *is* $\leq^{log}_{1-T}$*-complete for* $\#$P. *If* $\#^1_{\mathcal{M}}$ *is* $\leq^p_m$*-complete for* $\#$P *then* $\text{P} = \text{NP}$.
5. $\Sigma^1_{k,\mathcal{M}}, \Pi^1_{k,\mathcal{M}}, \text{QAF}^1_{\mathcal{M}} \in \text{ALOGTIME}$.

Turning to finite lattices, we show that non-distributivity nearly replaces the negation in the different results of Theorem 2 and Theorem 3.

3   Lattices

Now we want to study lattices. For binary functions it is usual to use infix notation. The previous results hold unchanged in this case. An algebra $V = (V, \{\wedge, \vee\})$ is called *lattice*, if both binary functions $\wedge$ and $\vee$ are commutative and associative, and if they satisfy

$$\forall a, b \in V : (a \wedge b) \vee b = b \text{ and } (a \vee b) \wedge b = b.$$

In a lattice V we can define a *partial order* $\leq$ by $a \leq b \Leftrightarrow_{\mathrm{df}} a \wedge b = a$. So we have usual relations like $<, >$ and $\geq$.

Definition 3. *An element $a \in V$ is called* a direct predecessor *of $b \in V$, if*

$$a < b \text{ and } \{v \in V \mid a \leq v \leq b\} = \{a, b\}.$$

We denote this as $a <_1 b$, and we call a and b neighbours.

Now we determine a lower bound for the counting problems in finite lattices:

Theorem 4. *If V is a finite lattice with at least two elements, then the counting problem $\#_V^v$ for any $v \in V$ is $\leq_{1-T}^{log}$-complete for $\#P$.*

Proof. Let $a \in V$ be a direct predecessor of $b \in V$. We reduce $\#3SAT$ to $\#_V^a$ and $\#_V^b$. Define $f(x) =_{\mathrm{df}} ((x \vee a) \wedge b)$ and divide V into the sets $V_0 =_{\mathrm{df}} \{v \in V \mid f(v) = a\}$ and $V_1 =_{\mathrm{df}} \{v \in V \mid f(v) = b\}$. Let F be an instance of 3SAT with variables $x_1, \ldots, x_n$. Replace every literal x_k ($\neg x_k$, resp.) by $f(x_k)$ ($f(x_{k+n})$, resp.). We obtain a V-formula $H_0(x_1, \ldots, x_{2n})$. Let $H_1 =_{\mathrm{df}} \bigwedge_{i=1}^n (f(x_i) \vee f(x_{n+i}))$, $H_2 =_{\mathrm{df}} \bigvee_{i=1}^n (f(x_i) \wedge f(x_{n+i}))$, and $H_3 =_{\mathrm{df}} ((H_0 \wedge H_1) \vee H_2)$. We obtain:

$$\#3SAT(F) \cdot |V_0 \times V_1|^n = \#_V^b(H_3) - \#_V^b(H_2)$$
$$= \#_V^b(H_3) - (|V|^{2n} - (|V|^2 - |V_1|^2)^n)$$
$$= (|V|^2 - |V_1|^2)^n - \#_V^a(H_3)$$

Corollary 1. *If V is a finite lattice with at least two elements, then the counting problem $\#_V$ is $\leq_{1-T}^{log}$-complete for $\#P$.*

In a finite lattice V we always have a *bottom element* $0 =_{\mathrm{df}} \bigwedge_{v \in V} v$ and a *top element* $1 =_{\mathrm{df}} \bigvee_{v \in V} v$. These elements satisfy $(\forall v \in V : 0 \leq v \leq 1)$.
Then the monotonity of the functions $\wedge$ and $\vee$ gives us the following Proposition:

Proposition 1. *Let V be a finite lattice, $H(x_1, \ldots, x_n) \in F(V)$ and $a \in V$. Then the following equivalence holds:*

$$(\forall w \in V^n : H(w) = a) \Leftrightarrow H(0, \ldots, 0) = H(1, \ldots, 1) = a.$$

Theorem 5. *Let V be a finite lattice and let be a $\in V$. Then the problems* TAUT_V *and* TAUT_V^a *belong to* ALOGTIME.

Proof. Using Proposition 1 it is easy to reduce a tautology problem to an evaluation problem. So the tautology problems belong to ALOGTIME.

Theorem 6. *Let V be a finite lattice, $k \geq 1$, and $a \in V$. It holds:*

$$\Sigma_{2k,V}^a, \Sigma_{2k,V} \in \Sigma_{2k-1}^{\mathrm{P}}, \quad \text{and} \quad \Pi_{2k+1,V}^a, \Pi_{2k+1,V} \in \Pi_{2k}^{\mathrm{P}}.$$

Proof. The last quantifier in a quantified formula of the given problems is $\forall$. So let $Q_1, \ldots, Q_n \in \{\forall, \exists\}$ and $i \in \mathbb{N}$ with $\exists = Q_i \neq Q_{i+1} = \ldots = Q_n = \forall$. It holds:

$$Q_1 \cdots Q_n F(x_1, \ldots, x_n) \in \mathrm{QAF}_V^a$$

if and only if

$$Q_1 a_1 \in V \cdots Q_i a_i \in V : F(a_1, \ldots, a_i, x_{i+1}, \ldots, x_n) \in \mathrm{TAUT}_V^a.$$

After Theorem 5 we know $\mathrm{TAUT}_V^a \in \mathrm{ALOGTIME} \subseteq \mathrm{P}$. Furthermore there is one alternation less in $Q_1 \cdots Q_i$ than in $Q_1 \cdots Q_n$.

4   Distributive Lattices

Distributivity is usually a property of a whole lattice, but we introduce distributive elements, too. An element a of a lattice V is called *distributive*, if

$$\forall b, c \in V : a \wedge (b \vee c) = (a \wedge b) \vee (a \wedge c) \quad \text{and}$$
$$\forall b, c \in V : a \vee (b \wedge c) = (a \vee b) \wedge (a \vee c).$$

A lattice is called *distributive*, if each element is distributive.

Proposition 2. *Let V be a lattice, $H(x_1, \ldots, x_n) \in F(V)$ and $w \in V^n$. Each distributive element $a \in V$ satisfies:*

$$a \wedge H(w) \leq H(a, \ldots, a) \leq a \vee H(w).$$

Proof. We prove both via the structure of H:

(1) $H(x_1, \ldots, x_n) = v \in V$:
     $a \wedge H(w) \leq H(w) = H(a, \ldots, a) = H(w) \leq a \vee H(w)$.
(2) $H(x_1, \ldots, x_n) = x_i$:
     $a \wedge H(w) \leq a = H(a, \ldots, a) = a \leq a \vee H(w)$.
(3) $H(x_1, \ldots, x_n) = F(x_1, \ldots, x_n) \wedge G(x_1, \ldots, x_n)$:

$$a \wedge H(w) = a \wedge (F(w) \wedge G(w)) = (a \wedge F(w)) \wedge (a \wedge G(w))$$
$$\leq F(a, \ldots, a) \wedge G(a, \ldots, a) = H(a, \ldots, a)$$
$$\leq (a \vee F(w)) \wedge (a \vee G(w))$$
$$= a \vee (F(w) \wedge G(w)) = a \vee H(w).$$

(4) $H(x_1, \ldots, x_n) = F(x_1, \ldots, x_n) \vee G(x_1, \ldots, x_n)$: Dual to (3).

Proposition 3. *Let V be a lattice, $H(x_1, \ldots, x_n) \in F(V)$, and let $a \in V$ be a distributive element. Then the following equivalence holds:*

$$(\exists w \in V^n : H(w) = a) \Leftrightarrow H(a, \ldots, a) = a.$$

Proof. Let $H(x_1, \ldots, x_n) \in F(V)$ and $w \in V^n$ such that $H(w) = a$. From Proposition 2 we obtain $a = a \wedge H(w) \leq H(a, \ldots, a) \leq a \vee H(w) = a$. So this yields $H(a, \ldots, a) = a$. The converse is easy, since $(a, \ldots, a) \in V^n$.

Theorem 7. *Let V be a finite lattice and let $a \in V$ be a distributive element. Then the satisfiability problem SAT_V^a belongs to ALOGTIME.*

Proof. Using Proposition 3 it is easy to reduce the satisfiability problem SAT_V^a to the evaluating problem VAL_V^a. So SAT_V^a belongs to ALOGTIME.

Corollary 2. *Let V be a finite, distributive lattice. Then the satisfiability problem SAT_V belongs to ALOGTIME.*

Corollary 3. *Let V be a finite lattice and let $a \in V$ be a distributive element. If $\#_V^a$ is $\leq_m^p$-complete for $\#P$ then $P = NP$.*

Theorem 8. *Let V be a finite lattice, $k \geq 1$, and let $a \in V$ be a distributive element. The problems $\Sigma_{k,V}^a$, $\Pi_{k,V}^a$, and QAF_V^a belong to ALOGTIME.*

Proof. It is sufficient to show $\mathrm{QAF}_V^a \in$ ALOGTIME. For $v \in \{0, 1\}$ (bottom and top element in V) define $\beta_v^a(\forall) =_{\mathrm{df}} v$ and $\beta_v^a(\exists) =_{\mathrm{df}} a$. We show the following.

$$Q_1 \cdots Q_n F(x_1, \ldots, x_n) \in \mathrm{QAF}_V^a$$

$$\text{if and only if}$$

$$F(\beta_0^a(Q_1), \ldots, \beta_0^a(Q_n)) = F(\beta_1^a(Q_1), \ldots, \beta_1^a(Q_n)) = a.$$

For $n = 0$ this statement is obvious.

For $n \geq 0$: Let $F(x_1, \ldots, x_{n+1}) \in F(V)$ be a V-formula and let $Q_1, \ldots, Q_{n+1} \in \{\forall, \exists\}$. We define $G(x, y) =_{\mathrm{df}} F(x, \beta_y^a(Q_2), \ldots, \beta_y^a(Q_{n+1}))$. By induction hypothesis, it remains to prove the following equivalence for $Q \in \{\forall, \exists\}$:

$$(Qv \in V : G(v, 0) = G(v, 1) = a) \Leftrightarrow G(\beta_0^a(Q), 0) = G(\beta_1^a(Q), 1) = a.$$

$Q = \exists$: Proposition 3 shows the equivalence, since a is distributive.
$Q = \forall$: We use Propostion 1 and obtain:

$$(\forall v \in V : G(v, 0) = G(v, 1) = a) \Leftrightarrow G(0, 0) = G(1, 0) = G(0, 1) = G(1, 1) = a.$$

The monotonity of $\wedge$ and $\vee$ yields anyway $G(0, 0) \leq G(0, 1) \leq G(1, 1)$ and $G(0, 0) \leq G(1, 0) \leq G(1, 1)$, and we obtain the equivalence.

So it is sufficient to evaluate F at the following two positions: Replace every $\exists$-quantified variable by a, and replace every $\forall$-quantified variable by 0 (1, resp.) for the first (second, resp.) evaluation. The quantified formula is in QAF_V^a if and only if both evaluations of F return the value a.

Now it is easy to reduce the problems $\Sigma_{k,V}^a$, $\Pi_{k,V}^a$, and QAF_V^a to an evaluation problem. So these problems belong to ALOGTIME.

Corollary 4. *Let V be a finite, distributive lattice and $k \geq 1$. Then the problems $\Sigma_{k,V}$, $\Pi_{k,V}$, and QAF_V belong to* ALOGTIME.

So most of the problems are easy in finite, distributive lattices. But what happens, if the finite lattice is non-distributive?

5   Non-distributive Lattices

According to Birkhoff [1], each non-distributive lattice has at least one of the following two lattices as a sublattice:

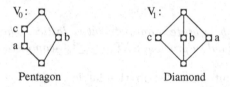

Pentagon   Diamond

Definition 4. *Let V be a non-distributive lattice. A triple $(a,b,c) \in V^3$ such that $a \wedge b = c \wedge b$, $a \vee b = c \vee b$, and either $a < c$ or $(a \neq c, a \wedge c = a \wedge b$ and $a \vee c = a \vee b)$, is called* non-distributive.

Definition 5. *A non-distributive triple $(a,b,c) \in V^3$ is called* maximal non-distributive, *if each non-distributive triple $(a',b',c') \in V^3$ satisfies:*

(M1) $a' \wedge b' \not> a \wedge b$,
(M2) $a' \wedge b' = a \wedge b \Rightarrow a' \vee b' \not< a \vee b$,
(M3) $(a' \wedge b' = a \wedge b, a' \vee b' = a \vee b, a \not< c) \Rightarrow a' \not< c'$.

Obviously each finite non-distributive lattice has at least one such triple.

Lemma 1. *Let V be a lattice and let $(a,b,c) \in V^3$ be a maximal non-distributive triple. Then each $c^+ \in V$ satisfies: $(c^+ \geq c$ and $c^+ \quad c \vee b) \Rightarrow c^+ \wedge b = c \wedge b$.*

Proof. At first let us define $b' =_{\text{df}} c^+ \wedge b$, $c' =_{\text{df}} b' \vee c$, and $a' =_{\text{df}} b' \vee a$. Supposing $b' \neq c \wedge b$ we get one of the following four cases, all of them leading to a contradiction:

| Case 1a | Case 1b | Case 2a | Case 2b |

Case 1: $a < c$. (Pentagon-case)

Case 1a: $a' < c'$. Here we obtain the situation shown in the first picture. (a', b, c') is a non-distributive triple, contradicting (M1).

Case 1b: $a' = c'$. Here we obtain the situation shown in the second picture. (a, b', c) is a non-distributive triple, contradicting (M2).

Case 2: $a \not< c$. (Diamond-case)

Case 2a: $b \le a'$, therefore $a' = a \vee b$. Here we obtain the situation shown in the third picture. (b', a, b) is a non-distributive triple, contradicting (M3).

Case 2b: $b \quad a'$, therefore $a' < a \vee b$. Here we obtain the situation shown in the last picture. Let $V' =_{\mathrm{df}} \{v \in V \mid v \ge b'\}$. We get $a', b, c' \in V'$ and $(a' \vee c') \wedge b \quad (a' \wedge b) \vee (c' \wedge b)$. This implies, that V' is a non-distributive sublattice. Hence V' contains at least one non-distributive triple, contradicting (M1).

Theorem 9. *Let V be a finite, non-distributive lattice. Then there exists a $c' \in V$, so that the satisfiability problem $\mathrm{SAT}_V^{c'}$ is $\le_m^{log}$-complete for NP.*

Proof. Let V be a finite, non-distributive lattice, $(a, b, c) \in V^3$ a maximal non-distributive triple, and $c' \in V$ such that $c \le c' <_1 c \vee b$.

We reduce 3SAT to $\mathrm{SAT}_V^{c'}$. Let F be an instance of 3SAT with variables $x_1, \ldots, x_n$, i. e. $F = \bigwedge_{i=1}^m \bigvee_{j=1}^3 x_{ij}$ with $x_{ij} \in \{x_1, \ldots, x_n, \neg x_1, \ldots, \neg x_n\}$.

First we define $f(x) =_{\mathrm{df}} ((x \vee c') \wedge (c \vee b))$ and $n_{ij} =_{\mathrm{df}} \begin{cases} k & \text{if } x_{ij} = x_k, \\ n + k & \text{if } x_{ij} = \neg x_k. \end{cases}$

So we can define the following V-formulas:

$$H_0(x_1, \ldots, x_{2n}) =_{\mathrm{df}} \bigwedge_{i=1}^m \bigvee_{j=1}^3 f(x_{n_{ij}}),$$

$$H_1(x_1, \ldots, x_{2n}) =_{\mathrm{df}} \bigwedge_{i=1}^n (f(x_i) \vee f(x_{n+i})),$$

$$H_2(x_1, \ldots, x_{2n}) =_{\mathrm{df}} \bigvee_{i=1}^n (f(x_i) \wedge f(x_{n+i})),$$

$$H_0'(x_1, \ldots, x_{2n}) =_{\mathrm{df}} (H_0 \wedge b) \vee a,$$

$$H_1'(x_1, \ldots, x_{2n}) =_{\mathrm{df}} (H_1 \wedge b) \vee a,$$

$$H_2'(x_1, \ldots, x_{2n}) =_{\mathrm{df}} (H_2 \wedge b) \vee c', \quad \text{and}$$

$$H(x_1, \ldots, x_{2n}) =_{\mathrm{df}} H_0' \wedge H_1' \wedge H_2'.$$

With $c' <_1 c \vee b$ each $v \in V$ holds: $f(v) \in \{c', c \vee b\}$. So we get for each $w \in V^{2n}$: $H_0(w), H_1(w), H_2(w) \in \{c', c \vee b\}$. With $V_0 =_{\mathrm{df}} \{v \in V \mid f(v) = c'\}$ and $V_1 =_{\mathrm{df}} \{v \in V \mid f(v) = c \wedge b\}$ we can define Ω_y for each $y = (y_1, \ldots, y_n) \in \{0, 1\}^n$

by $\Omega_y =_{df} \{(w_1,\dots,w_{2n}) \in V^{2n} \mid \forall i (1 \le i \le n) : (w_i, w_{n+i}) \in V_{y_i} \times V_{\overline{y_i}}\}$.
We show:

$$w \in \bigcup_{F(y)=1} \Omega_y \Leftrightarrow H(w) = c'.$$

First, let be $y \in \{0,1\}^n$ such that $F(y) = 1$, and let $w \in \Omega_y$. We can calculate $H_0(w) = c \vee b$, $H_1(w) = c \vee b$ and $H_2(w) = c'$. So we obtain $H_0'(w) = c \vee b$, $H_1'(w) = c \vee b$ and $H_2'(w) = c'$, and it holds $H(w) = c'$.

Now let $w = (w_1,\dots,w_{2n}) \notin \bigcup_{F(y)=1} \Omega_I$. We obtain at least one of the following three cases:

(1) $w \in \bigcup_{F(y)=0} \Omega_y$.
(2) $\exists i (1 \le i \le n) : f(w_i) = f(w_{n+i}) = c'$.
(3) $\exists i (1 \le i \le n) : f(w_i) = f(w_{n+i}) = c \vee b$.

As consequences we obtain from the three cases:

(1') $H_0(w) = c'$, therefore by Lemma 1: $H_0'(w) = a$.
(2') $H_1(w) = c'$, therefore by Lemma 1: $H_1'(w) = a$.
(3') $H_2(w) = c \vee b$, therefore we obtain: $H_2'(w) = c \vee b$.

If $H_0'(w) = a$ or $H_1'(w) = a$, then $H(w) \le a$, so $H(w) \ne c'$, because $c' \quad a$. Otherwise $H_0'(w) = H_1'(w) = c \vee b$ and with (3') this yields $H(w) = c \vee b \ne c'$. So each $w \notin \bigcup_{F(y)=1} \Omega_I$ satisfies $H(w) \ne c'$. Now we have:

$$F \in 3\text{SAT} \Leftrightarrow H \in \text{SAT}_V^{c'}.$$

The V-formula H is computable with input F by a log-space algorithm, so the satisfiability problem $\text{SAT}_V^{c'}$ is $\le_m^{log}$-complete for NP.

This completes the dichotomy to Corollary 2:

Theorem 10. *Let V be a finite lattice.*

$$V \text{ is distributive} \quad \Rightarrow \quad \text{SAT}_V \in \text{ALOGTIME}.$$

$$V \text{ is non-distributive} \quad \Rightarrow \quad \text{SAT}_V \text{ is } \le_m^{log}\text{-complete for NP}.$$

This is the main dichotomy result, and we will extend it by similar results for quantified formulas over finite lattices.

Let $\mathcal{B} =_{df} (\{0,1\}, \{\wedge, \vee, \neg\})$. A $\mathcal{B}$-formula $F \in F(\mathcal{B})$ is called *simple*, if $\neg$ only occurs at variables. Now we define a simple version of QBF, which is still $\le_m^{log}$-complete for PSPACE:

$$\text{SQBF} =_{df} \{Q_1 \cdots Q_n F(x_1,\dots,x_n) \in \text{QAF}_\mathcal{B}^1 \mid F \text{ is simple}\}.$$

Theorem 11. *Let V be a finite, non-distributive lattice and $k \ge 1$. Then there is a $c' \in V$ such that:*

$\Sigma^{c'}_{2k-1,V}$ is $\leq^{log}_m$-complete for Σ^P_{2k-1},
$\Pi^{c'}_{2k,V}$ is $\leq^{log}_m$-complete for Π^P_{2k}, and
$\mathrm{QAF}^{c'}_V$ is $\leq^{log}_m$-complete for PSPACE.

Proof. The proof of Theorem 9 does not need the formula F to be in 3CNF. It is sufficient, that F is simple. We obtain the V-formula H_0 from a simple instance F by replacing every literal x_i by $f(x_i)$ and replacing every literal $\neg x_i$ by $f(x_{n+i})$.

So let $Q_1 \cdots Q_n F(x_1, \ldots, x_n)$ be an instance of SQBF. We are now using the notations of the proof of Theorem 9, in particular the elements $c', c \vee b \in V$, the function f, and the V-formula $H(x_1, \ldots, x_{2n})$. Furthermore we define additional quantifiers $Q_{n+i} =_{df} \exists$ for $i = 1, \ldots, n$ and a mapping $\alpha : V \to \{0,1\}$ by

$$\forall v \in V : \alpha(v) =_{df} \begin{cases} 0 & \text{if } f(v) = c', \\ 1 & \text{if } f(v) = c \vee b. \end{cases}$$

Finally we define $\alpha_k(v_1, \ldots, v_k) =_{df} (\alpha(v_1), \ldots, \alpha(v_k))$ as a shortcut. We prove by induction on $i (0 \leq i \leq n)$:

$$y \in \{0,1\}^i, Q_{i+1} \cdots Q_n F(y, x_{i+1}, \ldots, x_n) \in \text{SQBF}$$
$$\Rightarrow \forall v \in \alpha_i^{-1}(y) : Q_{i+1} \cdots Q_{2n} H(v, x_{i+1}, \ldots, x_{2n}) \in \mathrm{QAF}^{c'}_V$$

and

$$v \in V^i, Q_{i+1} \cdots Q_{2n} H(v, x_{i+1}, \ldots, x_{2n}) \in \mathrm{QAF}^{c'}_V$$
$$\Rightarrow Q_{i+1} \cdots Q_n F(\alpha_i(v), x_{i+1}, \ldots, x_n) \in \text{SQBF}.$$

Case $i = n$: Already shown in the proof of Theorem 9.
Case $i \leq n$: Let $Q_i = \forall$ ($Q_i = \exists$, resp.).
First let $y \in \{0,1\}^{i-1}$ and $Q_i \cdots Q_n F(y, x_i, \ldots, x_n) \in \text{SQBF}$. Then we have:

$$Q_i y_i \in \{0,1\} : Q_{i+1} \cdots Q_n F(y, y_i, x_{i+1}, \ldots, x_n) \in \text{SQBF},$$

which results in:

$$Q_{i+1} \cdots Q_n F(y, 0, x_{i+1}, \ldots, x_n) \in \text{SQBF}$$
$$\text{and (or, resp.)}$$
$$Q_{i+1} \cdots Q_n F(y, 1, x_{i+1}, \ldots, x_n) \in \text{SQBF}.$$

By induction hypothesis, we obtain for all $v \in \alpha_{i-1}^{-1}(y)$:

$$\forall v_i \in \alpha^{-1}(0) : Q_{i+1} \cdots Q_{2n} H(v, v_i, x_{i+1}, \ldots, x_{2n}) \in \mathrm{QAF}^{c'}_V$$
$$\text{and (or, resp.)}$$
$$\forall v_i \in \alpha^{-1}(1) : Q_{i+1} \cdots Q_{2n} H(v, v_i, x_{i+1}, \ldots, x_{2n}) \in \mathrm{QAF}^{c'}_V.$$

Furthermore $V = \alpha^{-1}(0) \cup \alpha^{-1}(1)$. (In particular: $c' \in \alpha^{-1}(0) \neq \emptyset$ and $c \vee b \in \alpha^{-1}(1) \neq \emptyset$.) Hence it holds:

$$\forall v \in \alpha_{i-1}^{-1}(y) : Q_i v_i \in V : Q_{i+1} \cdots Q_{2n} H(v, v_i, x_{i+1}, \ldots, x_{2n}) \in \mathrm{QAF}_V^{c'}.$$

So we have: $\forall v \in \alpha_{i-1}^{-1}(y) : Q_i \cdots Q_{2n} H(v, x_i, \ldots, x_{2n}) \in \mathrm{QAF}_V^{c'}$. Hence the first statement is proved. To prove the second statement, let $v \in V^{i-1}$ and $Q_i \cdots Q_{2n} H(v, x_i, \ldots, x_{2n}) \in \mathrm{QAF}_V^{c'}$. Then we have:

$$Q_i v_i \in V : Q_{i+1} \cdots Q_{2n} H(v, v_i, x_{i+1}, \ldots, x_{2n}) \in \mathrm{QAF}_V^{c'}.$$

By induction hypothesis we get:

$$Q_i v_i \in V : Q_{i+1} \cdots Q_n F(\alpha_i(v, v_i), x_{i+1}, \ldots, x_n) \in \mathrm{SQBF}.$$

Together with $\alpha(V) = \{0, 1\}$ this yields: $Q_i \cdots Q_n F(\alpha_{i-1}(v), x_i, \ldots, x_n) \in \mathrm{SQBF}$. This completes the proof of the second statement.
In particular, the two statements for $i = 0$ result in:

$$Q_1 \cdots Q_n F(x_1, \ldots, x_n) \in \mathrm{SQBF} \Leftrightarrow Q_1 \cdots Q_{2n} H(x_1, \ldots, x_{2n}) \in \mathrm{QAF}_V^{c'}.$$

The reduction does not change the number of alternations between $\forall$ and $\exists$, if the last quantifier is an $\exists$-quantifier.

Together with Theorem 6 this completes the dichotomy to Corollary 4:

Theorem 12. *Let V be a finite lattice, and $k \geq 1$.*

$$V \text{ is distributive} \quad \Rightarrow \quad \Sigma_{k,V}, \Pi_{k,V}, \mathrm{QAF}_V \in \mathrm{ALOGTIME}.$$

$$V \text{ is non-distributive} \quad \Rightarrow \quad \begin{cases} \Sigma_{2k-1,V}, \Sigma_{2k,V} \text{ are } \leq_m^{log}\text{-complete for } \Sigma_{2k-1}^{\mathrm{P}}. \\ \Pi_{2k,V}, \Pi_{2k+1,V} \text{ are } \leq_m^{log}\text{-complete for } \Pi_{2k}^{\mathrm{P}}. \\ \mathrm{QAF}_V \text{ is } \leq_m^{log}\text{-complete for PSPACE.} \end{cases}$$

At last we show that a counting problem of a finite lattice can be $\leq_m^{log}$-complete for #P. In Corollary 1 we have only shown $\leq_{1-T}^{log}$-completeness.

Theorem 13. *Let V_1 be the "diamond"-lattice. The counting problem $\#_{V_1}^c$ is $\leq_m^{log}$-complete for #P.*

Proof. We reduce #3SAT to $\#_{V_1}^c$:
Let F be an instance of 3SAT with variables $x_1, \ldots, x_n$. Replace every literal x_k by $(x_k \vee b)$ and replace every literal $\neg x_k$ by $(x_{n+k} \vee b)$. We obtain a V_1-formula $H_3(x_1, \ldots, x_{2n})$. Furthermore let $H_1 =_{\mathrm{df}} \bigvee_{i=1}^n (((x_i \wedge x_{n+i}) \vee c) \wedge a)$, $H_2 =_{\mathrm{df}} \bigvee_{i=1}^n (((x_i \wedge x_{n+i}) \vee b) \wedge a)$, $H_4 =_{\mathrm{df}} \bigwedge_{i=1}^n (((x_i \vee c) \wedge a) \vee b)$, $H_5 =_{\mathrm{df}} \bigwedge_{i=1}^n (((x_{n+i} \vee c) \wedge a) \vee b)$, and $H =_{\mathrm{df}} H_1 \vee H_2 \vee (H_3 \wedge H_4 \wedge H_5 \wedge c)$. We obtain:

$$\#_{V_1}^c(H) = \#3\mathrm{SAT}(F)$$

6   Results and Open Questions

Let V be a finite lattice with at least two elements, and $k \geq 1$.

Problem	Complexity of the problem, if V is	
	distributive	non-distributive
VAL_V	ALOGTIME	ALOGTIME
TAUT_V	ALOGTIME	ALOGTIME
SAT_V	ALOGTIME	$\leq_m^{log}$-complete for NP
$\Sigma_{2k-1,V}$	ALOGTIME	$\leq_m^{log}$-complete for $\Sigma_{2k-1}^{\mathrm{P}}$
$\Sigma_{2k,V}$	ALOGTIME	$\leq_m^{log}$-complete for $\Sigma_{2k-1}^{\mathrm{P}}$
$\Pi_{2k,V}$	ALOGTIME	$\leq_m^{log}$-complete for Π_{2k}^{P}
$\Pi_{2k+1,V}$	ALOGTIME	$\leq_m^{log}$-complete for Π_{2k}^{P}
QAF_V	ALOGTIME	$\leq_m^{log}$-complete for PSPACE
$\#_V$	$\leq_{1-T}^{log}$-complete for #P if $\mathrm{P} \neq \mathrm{NP}$: not $\leq_m^{p}$-complete for #P	$\leq_{1-T}^{log}$-complete for #P

For the "diamond"-lattice V_1 the counting problem $\#_{\mathrm{V}_1}$ is $\leq_m^{log}$-complete for #P. So the question arises, which finite lattices have counting problems that are $\leq_m^{p}$-complete for #P?

It was shown that $\mathrm{P} \neq \mathrm{NP}$ implies that distributive lattices do not have counting problems, being $\leq_m^{p}$-complete for #P. But maybe this claim can be shown independently.

We showed that for a distributive element $a \in V$ the element-specific problem SAT_V^a is in ALOGTIME. On the other hand we showed, that in every non-distributive lattice V there is at least one element $c' \in V$, so that $\mathrm{SAT}_V^{c'}$ is $\leq_m^{log}$-complete for NP. Of course this element is not distributive. But which computational complexity has the problem SAT_V^a for an arbitrary element a?

Acknowledgments. I have benefited greatly from discussions with Klaus Wagner, and I want to thank Christian Glasser for helpful discussions.

References

[1] G. Birkhoff, *Lattice Theory*, Colloquium Publications Vol. XXV, American Mathematical Society, Providence, RI, 1967.

[2] D. M. Barrington, P. McKenzie, C. Moore, P. Tesson, and D. Therien, *Equation Satisfiability and Program Satisfiability for Finite Monoids*, Proceedings of the 25th International Symposium on Mathematical Foundations of Computer Science, pages 172-181, 2000.

[3] S. R. Buss, *The Boolean formula value problem is in* ALOGTIME, Proceedings of the 19th Symposium on Theory of Computing, pages 123-131, 1987.

[4] S. A. Cook, *The complexity of theorem-proving procedures*, Proceedings of the Third ACM Symposium on Theory of Computing, pages 151-158, 1971.

[5] M. R. Garey, D. S. Johnson, *Computers and Intractability*, W. H. Freeman and Company, 1979.

[6] M. Goldmann, A. Russell, *The complexity of solving equations over finite groups*, Proceedings of the 14th Annual IEEE Conference on Computational Complexity, pages 80-86, 1999.

[7] C. H. Papadimitriou, *Computational Complexity*, Addison-Wesley, Reading, MA, 1994.

[Ru81] W. L. Ruzzo, *On uniform circuit complexity*, Journal of Computer System Sciences, 22:265-383, 1981

[8] Steffen Reith, Klaus W. Wagner, *The Complexity of Problems Defined by Subclasses of Boolean Functions*, Technical Report 218, Inst. für Informatik, Univ. Würzburg, 1999. Available via ftp from *http://www.informatik.uni-wuerzburg.de/reports/tr.html*

[9] Bernhard Schwarz, *The Complexity of Satisfiability Problems over Finite Lattices*, Technical Report 314, Institut für Informatik, Universität Würzburg, 2004. Available via ftp from *http://www.informatik.uni-wuerzburg.de/reports/tr.html*

Constant Width Planar Computation Characterizes ACC^0

Kristoffer Arnsfelt Hansen

Department of Computer Science, University of Aarhus, Denmark
arnsfelt@daimi.au.dk

Abstract. We obtain a characterization of $\mathbf{ACC^0}$ in terms of a natural class of constant width circuits, namely in terms of constant width polynomial size planar circuits. This is shown via a characterization of the class of acyclic digraphs which can be embedded on a cylinder surface in such a way that all arcs flow along the same direction of the axis of the cylinder.

1   Introduction

This paper deals with the relationship between the computational power of *width* restricted circuits and *depth* restricted circuits. We relate constant width polynomial size *planar* circuits and also nondeterministic branching programs to constant depth polynomial size circuits.

Constant width polynomial size circuits (and branching programs) were shown to have surprising computational power by Barrington [1]. The class of functions computed by constant width polynomial size circuits is exactly $\mathbf{NC^1}$, and is thus considerably more than the functions computed by constant depth polynomial size circuits, being $\mathbf{AC^0}$.

Such connections are very interesting to explore, since they might provide the means for a better understanding of the classes involved, thus approaching lower bounds. Currently however, obtaining lower bounds for $\mathbf{NC^1}$ seems out of reach.

The smallest natural circuit class lacking lower bounds is $\mathbf{ACC^0}$, the subclass of $\mathbf{NC^1}$ computed by constant depth polynomial size circuits allowing MOD gates. By restricting the digraph representation of circuits geometrically, we obtain a characterization of $\mathbf{ACC^0}$ in terms of constant width circuits.

Theorem 1. *Constant width, polynomial size planar circuits compute exactly* $\mathbf{ACC^0}$.

Although Barrington and Thérien gave a characterization of $\mathbf{ACC^0}$ in terms of finite monoids [4] and Yao proved a nontrivial upper bound for $\mathbf{ACC^0}$ in terms of a class of threshold circuits [16], our result is the first alternative characterization of $\mathbf{ACC^0}$ by a circuit model.

Planarity has been previously employed in circuit lower bounds. While for general circuits, the best lower bounds for explicit functions are linear, superlinear lower bounds are known for general planar circuits. This was first obtained

V. Diekert and M. Habib (Eds.): STACS 2004, LNCS 2996, pp. 44–55, 2004.

by Lipton and Tarjan based on their planar separator theorem [10], although their lower bound did not allow inputs to appear more than once, as we require in the above characterization. For general planar circuits allowing inputs to occur several times, superlinear lower bounds were proved by Turán, [13] and improved to the current best lower bound of $\Omega(n \log^2 n)$ by Gröger [7].

The circuits of Theorem 1 are restricted in two more aspects than planarity, namely that of constant width and of monotonicity in gate operations. Thus there is hope of obtaining much better lower bounds than just slightly superlinear. Furthermore one could hope that the geometric perspective on computation can lead to new ways of understanding the internal structure of NC^1, thus obtaining progress towards separating ACC^0 and NC^1.

Much of the naturalness of ACC^0 comes from the algebraic characterizations by Barrington and Thérien of the classes AC^0, ACC^0 and NC^1 in terms of restrictions of finite monoids [4]. The class AC^0 has also been characterized in terms of geometric restrictions by Vinay [14] and Barrington et al [2,3]. It was shown that the class of functions computed by constant width polynomial size *upwards planar* circuits (and nondeterministic branching programs) is exactly AC^0.

An intermediate geometric restriction between upwards planarity and planarity was studied in [8]. There progress towards characterizing ACC^0 was obtained by relaxing the geometrical restriction of upwards planarity to that of cylindricality. While the exact relation to constant depth circuits is unknown under this restriction, it was shown that constant width polynomial size cylindrical circuits (and nondeterministic branching programs) can compute a strict superclass of AC^0, while still only computing functions in ACC^0. It is by building upon this result that we obtain Theorem 1.

The restrictions of upwards planarity and cylindricality are similar in the sense that each layer of the circuit is drawn "together", in such a way that all arcs flow in a common direction. Under the restriction of planarity, nodes are in contrast allowed to be placed in an arbitrary way in the plane.

The results on the computational power of cylindrical circuits, as well as the characterization of AC^0 in terms of upwards planar circuits are actually based upon the algebraic characterizations by Barrington and Thérien[4]. Thus with the present characterization of ACC^0 and the previous characterizations of AC^0 in terms of geometric restrictions, the link between algebra and geometry in a computational setting seems very strong.

The key to applying the results on the computational power of cylindrical circuits for proving Theorem 1, is in identifying exactly which planar digraphs are cylindrical.

Theorem 2. *A layered digraph D is layered cylindrical if and only if it is a subgraph of an acyclic planar layered digraph with a unique source and sink.*

This theorem is implicit in the works of Tamassia and Tollis [12] on *tessellation representations* of graphs in the plane and on a sphere. By "cutting" a digraph along a path from the source to the sink, they effectively reduce the spherical case (or equivalently the cylindrical case) to the planar case.

We give another proof of the theorem, working directly on the given planar embedding, taking advantage of the digraph being layered. This allows us to directly extract the combinatorial characterization of cylindricality used in [8] and also makes later uniformity considerations easier. With appropriate definitions of uniformity we can obtain the following uniform version of Theorem 1.

Theorem 3. *Logspace-uniform constant width, polynomial size planar circuits compute exactly logspace-uniform* **ACC⁰**.

Organisation of Paper. In Sect. 2 we introduce the notions of embeddings and circuits we will consider. We also state some basic properties about planar embeddings of certain digraphs. In Sect. 3 we prove Theorem 2, and in Sect. 4 we prove Theorem 1, as well as characterizing the computational power of planar branching programs. We introduce combinatorial embeddings in Sect. 5 as a means for dealing with uniformity issues. We conclude with some discussions and open problems in Sect. 6.

2   Preliminaries

Bounded Depth Circuits. $\mathbf{AC^0}$ is the class of functions computed by polynomial size bounded depth circuits consisting of NOT gates and unbounded fanin AND and OR gates. $\mathbf{ACC^0}$ is the class of functions computed when we also allow unbounded fanin MOD gates computing MOD_m for constants m.

Planar and Cylindrical Embeddings of Digraphs. A digraph $D = (V, A)$ is called *layered* if there is a partition $V = V_0 \cup V_1 \cup \cdots \cup V_h$ such that each arc of A goes from *layer* V_i to the *next layer* V_{i+1} for some i. Given such a partition, we call h the *depth* of D, $|V_i|$ the width of layer i and $k = \max |V_i|$ the width of D.

A digraph is *planar* if it can be embedded in the plane. It is called *upward planar* if it can be embedded in the plane, in a way such that all arcs are monotonically increasing in the vertical direction. It is called *cylindrical* if it can be embedded on a cylinder surface, in a way such that all arcs are monotonically increasing in the direction of the axis of the cylinder.

We call a layered digraph *layered cylindrical* if it can be embedded on a cylinder surface, such that all arcs are monotonically increasing in the direction of the axis of the cylinder and that layers correspond to disjoint circles of the cylinder, which contain all the nodes of the layer.

In [11] the following properties of planar embeddings are proved. They are stated under the assumption of the digraph being 2-connected, but the proof does not use this assumption.

Lemma 4. *Let D be a planar acyclic digraph with a unique source and sink, and let $\widehat{D}$ be any planar embedding of D. Then*

1. *Each face of $\widehat{D}$ consists of two directed paths.*
2. *For any vertex v of $\widehat{D}$ all ingoing (outgoing) arcs of v appear consecutively around v.*

Bounded Width Branching Programs and Circuits. A *nondeterministic branching program* is an acyclic digraph where all arcs are labelled by either a literal, i.e. a variable or a negated variable, or a boolean constant, and an initial and a terminal node. An input is accepted if and only if there is a path from the initial node to the terminal node in the graph that results from substituting constants for the literals according to the input and then deleting arcs labelled by 0.

When referring to constant width branching programs we will mean a nondeterministic branching program, which when viewed as a digraph, is layered and of constant bounded width.

By a *constant width circuit* we mean a circuit consisting of fanin 2 AND and OR gates and fanin 1 COPY gates, which when viewed as a digraph, like for branching programs, is layered and of constant bounded width. Input nodes can be literals or boolean constants, and can occur anywhere in the circuit.

Viewing nondeterministic branching programs and circuits as digraphs, it makes sense to restrict them geometrically. Since all cylindrical embeddings considered are layered cylindrical, we will usually just write cylindrical instead of layered cylindrical.

3   Embedding Digraphs on a Cylinder

In this section we will prove Theorem 2. The "only if" part is easily obtained: Consider a layered cylindrical embedding of a layered digraph D. By adding new arcs one can eliminate sources and sinks appearing in all layers except the first and the last. Now add a new first layer with a single node with arcs to all nodes in the previous first layer. Similarly add a new last layer with a single node with arcs from all nodes in the previous last layer. We have thus obtained an acyclic layered cylindrical superdigraph of D with a unique source and sink. The proof is completed by observing that every cylindrical embedding can be transformed into a planar embedding.

The "if" part is proved in several steps. First we will obtain a suitable partition of the planar embedding, and then later use this to obtain a new embedding on a cylinder surface.

Consider a planar embedding $\widehat{D}$ of a layered digraph D. Let $V(D) = V_0 \cup \cdots \cup V_h$ be the layers of D. Let C be a closed curve in the plane, partitioning the plane into two regions R_1 and R_2. We say that C is a *separating curve* for layer i if the following two properties hold.

1. The intersection of C and $\widehat{D}$ consists exactly of the nodes in V_i.
2. One of the regions R_j contain the embedding of subdigraph induced by $V_0 \cup \cdots \cup V_{i-1}$ as well as the arcs from V_{i-1} to V_i, and the other region contains the embedding of the subdigraph induced by $V_{i+1} \cup \cdots \cup V_h$ as well as the arcs from V_i to V_{i+1}

The following proposition shows that we can find separating curves for all layers in an acyclic planar layered digraph with a unique source and sink. This is illustrated in Fig. 1.

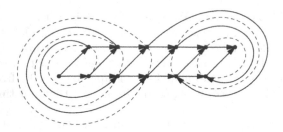

Fig. 1. Curves separating an acyclic planar layered digraph.

Proposition 5. *Let D be an acyclic planar layered digraph with a unique source and sink, with layers $V(D) = V_0 \cup \cdots \cup V_h$, and let $\widehat{D}$ be a planar embedding of D. Then there exists disjoint curves $C_1, \ldots, C_{h-1}$ such that C_i is a separating curve for layer i with respect to $\widehat{D}$ for all i.*

Proof. We will construct the separating curves by an iterative process. Assume that we have found separating curves $C_1, \ldots, C_{i-1}$.

Let v be a node in D which is neither the source nor the sink. That is, v has at least one ingoing arc and one outgoing arc, and by Lemma 4 all the ingoing arcs and outgoing arcs appear consecutively around v in $\widehat{D}$. It is then meaningful to talk about the rightmost ingoing (outgoing) arc, and the leftmost ingoing (outgoing) arc.

Since the ingoing arcs to V_{i-1} and outgoing arcs from V_{i-1} are separated by C_{i-1} it follows, that when traversing C_{i-1} from a node between the leftmost ingoing and outgoing arcs the next node is approached between the rightmost ingoing and outgoing arcs.

We now find a separating curve C_i for layer i by the following process: Start in an arbitrary node v in layer i. Follow along the left of the leftmost ingoing arc a to a node w in layer $i - 1$. If a is the leftmost outgoing arc of w we follow the curve C_{i-1} to the next node w' and follow the rightmost arc to a node v' in layer i. Otherwise we follow the next outgoing arc (in the counterclockwise order) to a node v' in layer i. Since both v and v' belong to the boundary of the face of $\widehat{D}$ we are within and because they belong to the same layer of D, it follows from Lemma 4 that v' is approached along the rightmost ingoing arc.

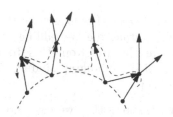

Fig. 2. Finding separating curves.

We now continue the same process, as illustrated in Fig. 2, until a closed curve C_i is found. It is clear that C_i has the following properties:

1. C_i only intersects $\widehat{D}$ in nodes from V_i.
2. C_i is disjoint from $C_1, \ldots, C_{i-1}$.
3. The region R partitioned by C_i containing C_{i-1} does not contain nodes from layers $i, \ldots, h$.

of which the last holds because D has a unique sink.

Now, since all nodes in V_i have an ingoing arc, and since they are not in the region R containing C_{i-1} by (3), it follows from (1) that C_i intersects *exactly* the nodes in V_i. From this and (3) it follows that C_i is a separating curve for layer i.

The next step is to associate an orientation (clockwise or counterclockwise) to each of the separating curves. These will give the order in which the nodes of each layer is to be drawn around a circle of the cylinder.

We give the first curve C_1 the counterclockwise orientation. Now assume we have assigned orientations to $C_1, \ldots, C_{i-1}$. We assign an orientation to C_i based on whether it contains C_{i-1} or vice versa. There will be three cases as illustrated in Fig. 3:

(a) C_{i-1} is inside the region bounded by C_i.
(b) The regions bounded by C_{i-1} and C_i are disjoint.
(c) C_i is inside the region bounded by C_{i-1}.

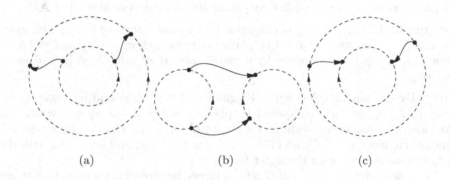

(a)   (b)   (c)

Fig. 3. Orienting the separating curves.

In cases (a) and (c) we assign the same orientation to C_i as C_{i-1}. In case (b) we assign the opposite orientation to C_i as C_{i-1}.

From the properties of separating curves it follows that case (b) can only occur once. In fact there is a k such that if $i < k$, C_i is oriented counterclockwise and if $i > k$, C_i is oriented clockwise.

For nodes a and b on a curve C, define the *segment from a to b*, to be the segment of C traversed by following C from a to b (inclusive) along the orientation associated to C.

The crucial property is now the following: Let a and b be nodes of layer $i-1$ with arcs to c and d in layer i respectively. Then nodes (except a and b) on the segment from a to b have only arcs to the segment from c to d (see Fig. 3). This is in fact, basically the characterization of cylindricality that was used in [8].

In fact, by this property, it follows that in Proposition 5, the separating curves found are actually traversed according to the orientations assigned above.

Furthermore, assign an ordering of the outgoing (ingoing) arcs from (to) a layer by traversing the separating curve according to the associated orientation, and including the outgoing arcs (ingoing arcs) of each node in counterclockwise (clockwise) order. Then it follows from the above property that the ordering of the outgoing arcs from a layer coincide with the ordering of the next layer, where the arcs are ingoing.

We are now in position to create a layered cylindrical embedding of D. The nodes in layer i are placed in a circle around the cylinder in the order they are met, when traversing the curve C_i according to the associated orientation, and the arcs between layers are simply drawn in the order described above.

This completes the embedding and the proof of Theorem 2.

4   Planar Branching Programs and Circuits

In this section we characterize the computational power of planar circuits (and nondeterministic branching programs). First we show how to compute any **ACC⁰** function by a constant width polynomial size planar circuit.

The core of the simulation is the following substitution lemma for planar circuits. Using this we only need to show how to compute AND, OR and MOD_m by planar circuits, to establish that planar circuits can compute all of **ACC⁰**.

Lemma 6. *If $f(x_1, \ldots, x_n)$ is computed by a planar circuit of size s_1 and width w_1 and $g_1, \ldots, g_n$ are computed by planar circuits each of size s_2 and width w_2 then $f(g_1, \ldots, g_n)$ is computed by a planar circuit of size $O(s_1 s_2^2)$ and width $O(w_1 w_2)$.*

Proof. By exchanging AND with OR gates and vice versa and by negating inputs, $\bar{g}_1, \ldots, \bar{g}_n$ are also computed by planar circuits of size s_2 and width w_2. Consider any planar embedding of a circuit C for f and choose planar embeddings of circuits $C_1, \ldots, C_n$ and $\bar{C}_1, \ldots, \bar{C}_n$ for $g_1, \ldots, g_n$ and $\bar{g}_1, \ldots, \bar{g}_n$ with the output gate appearing on the outer face.

We now stretch each layer of C into s_2 layers, by replacing each arc by a string of $s_2 - 1$ COPY gates, preserving planarity of the embedding. This ensures that input nodes in different layers are at least s_2 layers apart, and only increases the size by a factor $O(s_2)$ and the width by a factor 2.

This now allows us to simply substitute the embedding of C_i for x_i and the embedding of $\bar{C}_i$ for $\bar{x}_i$ in the embedding of C preserving the planarity, without increasing the width by more than a factor $O(w_2)$.

In [8] the construction for AND, OR and MOD_m is given in terms of cylindrical branching programs, and hence also in terms of planar circuits. For completeness we provide the details of the constructions directly in terms of planar circuits here.

The AND (and OR) of n inputs is easily computed by a planar circuit of width 2 and size $O(n)$ as shown in Fig. 4.

Fig. 4. A planar circuit computing AND.

The construction for MOD$_m$ is more complicated, an example of it is shown in Fig. 5.

It can be computed by a planar circuit of width $O(m)$ and size $O(mn)$ constructed as follows: We will have $2n+1$ layers. The first layer consists of a single input gate with the constant 1. In the last $2n$ layers the main part consists of m sufficiently long strings, which we number $0, \ldots, m-1$, of alternating AND and OR gates taking each other as input, the AND gates in odd layers and the OR gates in even layers.

String 0 starts with an AND gate and all other strings start with an OR gate. The constant input 1 in layer 0 will take the place of an OR gate in string 0. The construction will ensure that the OR gate in layer $2i$ of string j evaluates to 1 if and only if $\sum_{k=1}^{i} \equiv j \pmod{m}$.

The first AND gate in string 0 takes the constant input 1 as input. The first OR gate in the other strings takes a constant input 0 as input. The AND gate in layer $2i+1$ of every string takes $\bar{x}_i$ as the other input. The first $m-1$ OR gates in string 0 take a constant input 0 as the other input. The other OR gates in string 0, say in layer $2i$, take an AND gate as the other input, which is fed by x_i and the OR gate in layer $2(i-1)$ of string $m-1$. In general the OR gate in layer $2i$ of string j takes an AND gate as the other input, which is fed by x_i and the OR gate in layer $2(i-1)$ of string $j-1$. The output gate is the last OR gate of string 0.

Note, that while the above constructions are cylindrical, once we use Lemma 6 to substitute a circuit computing MOD$_m$ on more than m inputs, we leave the class of cylindrical circuits.

To conclude, we can from an **ACC^0** circuit construct a constant width, polynomial size planar circuit computing the same function as follows: Expand the **ACC^0** circuit into an **ACC^0** formula, and move the NOT gates to the layer just above the inputs by the usual constructions. Now proceeding layer by layer, we build appropriate components for the AND, OR and MOD$_m$ gates, and compose these using the substitution lemma.

We now prove the last part of Theorem 1, that constant width, polynomial size planar circuits only compute functions in **ACC^0**.

We need the following theorem from [8].

Theorem 7. *Every boolean function computed by a constant width, polynomial size cylindrical circuit is in* **ACC^0**.

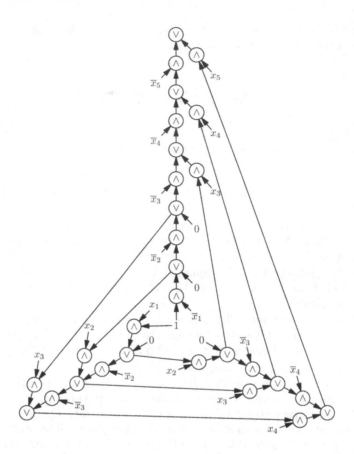

Fig. 5. A planar circuit of width 9 computing MOD$_3$ on 5 inputs.

Corollary 8. *Let p be a polynomial and w any constant. Then there is a polynomial q and a constant h such that every boolean function on n inputs computed by a cylindrical circuit of size $3p(n)$ and width $2w$ is computed by an* **ACC^0** *circuit of size $q(n)$ and depth h.*

Now consider a planar circuit C on n inputs of size at most $p(n)$ and width at most w. Let q and h be the polynomial and the constant from Corollary 8. We show that C is computed by an **ACC^0** circuit of size $q(p(n))^w$ and depth wh, assuming without loss of generality that $1 + p(n) \leq q(p(n))$.

If the width of C is in fact 1, then the function computed by C is certainly also computed by an **ACC^0** circuit of size $q(p(n))$ and depth h.

Otherwise, pick a node v in the first layer of C and let D be the subdigraph of the digraph representation of C, which is induced by the nodes which are on a path from v to the output node of C.

Removing the nodes in D, note that the remaining components are digraph representations of planar circuits. There are at most $p(n)$ of these each of size $p(n)$, but with width $w - 1$, since at least one node is removed from each layer.

By induction, all these are computed by $\mathbf{ACC^0}$ circuits of size $q(p(n))^{w-1}$ and depth $(w-1)h$.

Now by Theorem 2, D is cylindrical, and we construct a cylindrical embedding of it. For all AND and OR gates that have indegree 1 in D we will add a new input variable in the previous layer. In order to preserve layered cylindricality, we first stretch each layer into two layers using COPY gates. Together this will yield a cylindrical circuit of size at most $3p(n)$ and width at most $2w$ on at most $p(n)$ inputs, which by Corollary 8 is computed by an $\mathbf{ACC^0}$ circuit of size $q(p(n))$ and depth h. Now substitute the functions constructed inductively in this circuit to obtain an $\mathbf{ACC^0}$ circuit of size $q(p(n)) + p(n)q(p(n))^{w-1} \le q(p(n))^w$ and depth wh computing the function computed by C. This completes the proof of Theorem 1.

Turning to the computational power of planar nondeterministic branching programs, we can easily characterize this by Theorem 2. Indeed we can assume, without loss of generality that every node is on a path from the initial node to the terminal node, and hence Theorem 2 applies to give the following theorem.

Theorem 9. *Constant width, polynomial size planar branching programs compute the same boolean functions as constant width, polynomial size cylindrical branching programs.*

As noted in [8] this class of functions does not seem to capture all of $\mathbf{ACC^0}$. The compositional approach that worked so well for planar circuits using Lemma 6 fails for planar branching programs: in order to substitute a branching program for an arc, preserving planarity, one would need an embedding of it with both the initial and the terminal node on the external face. By a theorem by Kelly [9] and Battista and Tamassia [5] they would then need to be upwards planar and thus by the results by Barrington et al [2], substituted branching programs can only contribute with $\mathbf{AC^0}$ functions.

5   Uniformity Considerations

When considering uniformity, we need to be more precise when we talk about embeddings. We will employ the concept of combinatorial planar embeddings based on Edmonds' permutation technique [6] (see also [15] pages 70–73).

Combinatorial embeddings are most conveniently introduced for undirected graphs. Let $G = (V, E)$ be an undirected graph. For a vertex u define the set of neighbours $N(u) = \{v \| \{u, v\} \in E\}$ and let $A = \{uv \,|\, \{u, v\} \in E\}$ be the set of all oriented arcs obtained from E. Now let $p_u : N(u) \to N(u)$ be a cyclic permutation of the neighbours of u. Define $P : A \to A$ by $P(uv) = vp_v(u)$. Observe that P is a permutation of A.

As Edmonds now observed, there is a one-to-one correspondence between choices of $\{p_u\}$ and *2-cell embeddings* of G into closed orientable surfaces, where faces of the embedding correspond to the orbits of P.

We can thus say that $\{p_u\}$ is a combinatorial planar embedding of G if and only if Euler's formula $v - e + f = c + 1$ is satisfied, where $v = |V|$, $e = |E|$, f is the number of orbits in P and c is the number of connected components of G.

A description of a combinatorial planar embedding of a digraph D then simply consists of having for each vertex a list of the neighbours, in clockwise order around the vertex, say, according to an embedding. A description of a layered cylindrical embedding consists of an ordering of the nodes in each layer, corresponding to their order around the cylinder in an embedding.

We thus say that a family of planar circuits or cylindrical circuits are log-space-uniform, if there is a $O(\log n)$ space bounded Turing machine which on input 1^n outputs the description of the circuit on n inputs as well as the above defined description of the embedding.

With these definitions it is not difficult to realize Proposition 5 in logspace and using this also obtain Theorem 3. More details on this will be given in the final version of this paper.

6   Conclusion

We have obtained a characterization of $\mathbf{ACC^0}$ in terms of a geometrical restriction of the digraph representation of circuits. Together with the previous characterizations of $\mathbf{AC^0}$ this shows a striking similarity to the algebraic characterizations by Barrington and Thérien, as summarized in the following table.

Circuit Class	$\mathbf{AC^0}$	$\mathbf{ACC^0}$	$\mathbf{NC^1}$
Nonuniform Automata on Monoids	Aperiodic	Solvable	Unrestricted
Constant Width Branching Programs	Upwards planar	?	Unrestricted
Constant Width Circuits	Upwards planar	Planar	Unrestricted

It would be very interesting to further investigate the link between algebra and geometry in this setting. Intuitively, a cylindrical circuit correspond in some sense to an $\mathbf{ACC^0}$ circuit with just one layer of MOD gates. One could hope to explain this by tightening this link. In [8] a $\mathbf{\Pi_2} \circ \mathbf{MOD} \circ \mathbf{AC^0}$ lower bound and an $\mathbf{ACC^0}$ upper bound was proved. Perhaps one could give a seemingly better upper bound than $\mathbf{ACC^0}$, for example $\mathbf{AC^0} \circ \mathbf{MOD} \circ \mathbf{AC^0}$.

We don't have a characterization of $\mathbf{ACC^0}$ in terms of geometric restrictions of branching programs, yet they remain attractive for their simplicity. It might very well be within reach to obtain lower bounds for constant width planar branching programs, providing a first step for employing planarity in lower bounds for $\mathbf{ACC^0}$.

Acknowledgement. I am grateful to my advisor Peter Bro Miltersen for introducing me to constant width computation and for helpful comments and suggestions.

The author is supported by BRICS, Basic Research in Computer Science, a Centre of the Danish National Research Foundation.

References

1. David A. Barrington. Bounded-width polynomial-size branching programs recognize exactly those languages in NC^1. *J. Comput. System Sci.*, 38(1):150–164, 1989.
2. David A. Mix Barrington, Chi-Jen Lu, Peter Bro Miltersen, and Sven Skyum. Searching constant width mazes captures the AC^0 hierarchy. In *Proceedings of the 15th Annual Symposium on Theoretical Aspects of Computer Science*, pages 73–83, 1998.
3. David A. Mix Barrington, Chi-Jen Lu, Peter Bro Miltersen, and Sven Skyum. On monotone planar circuits. In *14th Annual IEEE Conference on Computational Complexity*, pages 24–31. IEEE Computer Society Press, 1999.
4. David A. Mix Barrington and Denis Thérien. Finite monoids and the fine structure of NC^1. *Journal of the ACM (JACM)*, 35(4):941–952, 1988.
5. Giuseppe Di Battista and Roberto Tamassia. Algorithms for plane representations of acyclic digraphs. *Theoretical Computer Science*, 61(2-3):175–198, 1988.
6. D. Edmonds. A combinatorial representation for polyhedral surfaces. *Notices Amer. Math. Soc.*, 7:646, 1960.
7. Hans Dietmar Gröger. A new partition lemma for planar graphs and its application to circuit complexity. In *8th International Symposium on Fundamentals of Computation Theory*, volume 529 of *Lecture Notes in Computer Science*, pages 220–229. Springer, 1991.
8. Kristoffer Arnsfelt Hansen, Peter Bro Miltersen, and V Vinay. Circuits on cylinders. In *14th International Symposium on Fundamentals of Computation Theory*, volume 2751 of *Lecture Notes in Computer Science*, pages 171–182. Springer, 2003.
9. David Kelly. Fundamentals of planar ordered sets. *Discrete Mathematics*, 63(2,3):197–216, 1987.
10. Richard J. Lipton and Robert Endre Tarjan. Applications of a planar separator theorem. *SIAM Journal on Computing*, 9(3):615–627, August 1980.
11. Roberto Tamassia and Ioannis G. Tollis. A unified approach to visibility representations of planar graphs. *Discrete & Computational Geometry*, 1(1):312–341, 1986.
12. Roberto Tamassia and Ioannis G. Tollis. Tessellation representations of planar graphs. In *Proceedings 27th Annual Allerton Conference on Communications, Control and Computing*, pages 48–57. University of Illinois at Urbana-Champaign, September 1989.
13. György Turán. On restricted boolean circuits. In *7th International Symposium on Fundamentals of Computation Theory*, volume 380 of *Lecture Notes in Computer Science*, pages 460–469. Springer, 1989.
14. V Vinay. Hierarchies of circuit classes that are closed under complement. In *11th Annual IEEE Conference on Computational Complexity*, pages 108–117. IEEE Computer Society, 1996.
15. Arthur T. White. *Graphs, Groups and Surfaces*. Elsevier Science Publishers B.V, 1984.
16. A. C.-C. Yao. On ACC^0 and threshold circuits. In *Proceedings 31st Annual Symposium on Foundations of Computer Science*, pages 619–627. IEEE Computer Society Press, 1990.

A Simple and Fast Approach for Solving Problems on Planar Graphs[*]

Fedor V. Fomin[1] and Dimtirios M. Thilikos[2]

[1] Department of Informatics, University of Bergen, N-5020 Bergen, Norway,
fomin@ii.uib.no
[2] Departament de Llenguatges i Sistemes Informàtics, Universitat Politècnica de
Catalunya, Campus Nord – Mòdul C5, c/Jordi Girona Salgado 1-3, E-08034,
Barcelona, Spain, sedthilk@lsi.upc.es

Abstract. It is well known that the celebrated Lipton-Tarjan planar separation theorem, in a combination with a divide-and-conquer strategy leads to many complexity results for planar graph problems. For example, by using this approach, many planar graph problems can be solved in time $2^{O(\sqrt{n})}$, where n is the number of vertices. However, the constants hidden in big-Oh, usually are too large to claim the algorithms to be practical even on graphs of moderate size. Here we introduce a new algorithm design paradigm for solving problems on planar graphs. The paradigm is so simple that it can be explained in any textbook on graph algorithms: Compute tree or branch decomposition of a planar graph and do dynamic programming. Surprisingly such a simple approach provides faster algorithms for many problems. For example, INDEPENDENT SET on planar graphs can be solved in time $O(2^{3.182\sqrt{n}}n + n^4)$ and DOMINATING SET in time $O(2^{5.043\sqrt{n}}n + n^4)$. In addition, significantly broader class of problems can be attacked by this method. Thus with our approach, LONGEST CYCLE on planar graphs is solved in time $O(2^{2.29\sqrt{n}(\ln n + 0.94)}n^{5/4} + n^4)$ and BISECTION is solved in time $O(2^{3.182\sqrt{n}}n + n^4)$. The proof of these results is based on complicated combinatorial arguments that make strong use of results derived by the Graph Minors Theory. In particular we prove that branch-width of a planar graph is at most $2.122\sqrt{n}$. In addition we observe how a similar approach can be used for solving different fixed parameter problems on planar graphs. We prove that our method provides the best so far exponential speed-up for fundamental problems on planar graphs like VERTEX COVER, (WEIGHTED) DOMINATING SET, and many others.

1 Introduction

The design of (exponential) algorithms that are significantly faster than exhaustive search is one of the basic approaches of coping with NP-hardness [17]. Nice

[*] This work was partially supported by the IST Program of the EU under contract number IST-1999-14186 (ALCOM-FT). The last author was supported by EC contract IST-1999-14186: Project ALCOM-FT (Algorithms and Complexity) - Future Technologies and by the Spanish CICYT project TIC-2002-04498-C05-03 (TRACER).

V. Diekert and M. Habib (Eds.): STACS 2004, LNCS 2996, pp. 56–67, 2004.
© Springer-Verlag Berlin Heidelberg 2004

examples of fast exponential algorithms are Eppstein's graph coloring algorithm [16] and the algorithm for 3-SAT [10]. For a good overview of the field see the recent survey written by Gerhard Woeginger [31].

It is well known that by making use of the well-known approach of Lipton & Tarjan [25] based on the celebrated planar separator theorem [24] one can obtain algorithms with time complexity $c^{O(\sqrt{n})}$ for many problems on planar graphs. However, the constants "hidden" in $O(\sqrt{n})$ can be crucial for practical implementations. During the last few years a lot of work has been done to compute and to improve the "hidden" constants [3,4]. In this paper we observe a general approach for obtaining sub-exponential time *exact* algorithms for many problems on planar graphs. Our approach is based on dynamic programming for graphs of bounded branch-width (tree-width). Combining our upper bound for branch-width of planar graphs with this simple approach one can obtain exponential speed-up for many known algorithms for many different planar graph problems. INDEPENDENT SET, DOMINATING SET, SAT, MIN-BISECTION, LONGEST CYCLE (PATH) on planar graphs are just a few examples of such problems.

Another field for implementation of our graph theoretical bounds is in the designing of parameterized algorithms. The last ten years were the evidence of rapid development of a new branch of computational complexity: Parameterized Complexity. (See the book of Downey & Fellows [15].) Roughly speaking, a parameterized problem with parameter k is *fixed parameter tractable* if it admits a solving algorithm with running time $f(k)|I|^{\beta}$. (Here f is a function depending only on k, $|I|$ is the length of the non parameterized part of the input and β is a constant.) Typically, $f(k) = c^k$ is an exponential function for some constant k. However, it appears, that for a large variety of planar graph problems algorithms with growth of the form $f(k) = c^{\sqrt{k}}$ are possible. During the last two years much attention was paid to the construction of algorithms with running time $c^{\sqrt{k}}$ for different problems on planar graphs. The first paper on the subject was the paper by Alber et al. [1] describing an algorithm with running time $O(4^{6\sqrt{34k}}n)$ (which is approximately $O(2^{70\sqrt{k}}n)$) for the PLANAR DOMINATING SET problem. Different fixed parameter algorithms for solving problems on planar and related graphs are discussed in [4,23]. We observe that our technique can serve also as a simple unified approach for solving many parameterized problems on planar graphs in subexponential time. Again, our approach is based on combinatorial bounds on planar branch-width and tree-width and provides a better running time for such basic parameterized problem like VERTEX COVER, DOMINATING SET and many others.

The crucial part of our paper is devoted to the proof that such a simple approach *guarantees* better time bounds and here we use complicated combinatorial arguments coming from Robertson-Seymour's Graph Minor Theory. More precisely, our proof is based on a new upper bound to the branch-width and the tree-width of planar graphs. Both these parameters where introduced (and served) as basic tools by Robertson and Seymour in their Graph Minors series of papers. Tree-width and branch-width are related parameters (See Theorem 1) and can be considered as measures of the "global connectivity" of a graph. Moreover, they appear to be of a major importance in algorithmic design as many NP-hard problems admit polynomial or even linear time solutions when their inputs are restricted to graphs of bounded tree-width or branch-width. This motivated the search for graphs where these parameters are relatively small. In this direction, Alon, Seymour & Thomas proved in [5] that given a minor closed graph class $\mathcal{G}$, any n-vertex graph G in $\mathcal{G}$ has tree-width/branch-width $O(\sqrt{n})$. As a consequence of this, any n-vertex planar graph G has tree-width/branch-width $\leq 14.697\sqrt{n}$.

We show that every n-vertex planar graph G has branch-width $\leq 2.122\sqrt{n}$ and tree-width $\leq 3.182\sqrt{n}$. To our knowledge, this is the best known upper bound for the value of these parameters on planar graphs. To obtain the new upper bounds we use deep "dual" and "min-max" theorems from Graph Minors series papers of Robertson & Seymour.

1.1   Previous Results and Our Contribution

Computation of constants α_t and α_b such that for every planar graph on n vertices $\mathbf{tw}(G) \leq \alpha_t\sqrt{n}+O(1)$ and $\mathbf{bw}(G) \leq \alpha_b\sqrt{n}+O(1)$ is of a great theoretical importance. In [5] Alon, Seymour & Thomas proved that any K_r-minor free graph on n vertices has tree-width$\leq r^{1.5}\sqrt{n}$. (Here K_r is complete graph on r vertices.) Since no planar graph contains K_5 as a minor, we have that $\alpha_t(G) \leq 6^{1.5} \leq 14.697$.

The first objective of this paper is to reduce the constant α_b to 2.122 (for the case of branch-width) and α_t to 3.182 (for the case of tree-width).

Lipton & Tarjan [25] were first to observe the existence of time $2^{O(\sqrt{n})}n^{O(1)}$ algorithms for several problems on planar graphs. However the constants hidden in big-Oh of the exponent make these algorithms unpractical. Later, a lot of work was done on computing and reducing these constants. The best known so far results can be found in [4], where generalizations and complicated improvement of Lipton-Tarjan (together with kernel reduction techniques) are used to obtain subexponential parameterized algorithms.

Thus, for example, the approach suggested in [4] provides an $O(2^{9.07\sqrt{n}}n\ln n)$ algorithm for INDEPENDENT SET and an $O(2^{18.61\sqrt{n}}n\ln n)$ algorithm for DOMINATING SET.

Here we suggest a unified approach based on branch decompositions (see Section 2 for the definitions). Our algorithm is simple and is performed in two steps: First we compute the branch decomposition of a planar graph and then do dynamic programming on graphs of bounded branch-width. Optimal branch decomposition of a planar graph can be constructed in polynomial time by using the algorithm due to Seymour & Thomas (Sections 7 and 9 in [29]). (See also the results of Hicks [21] on implementations of Seymour & Thomas algorithm.) For graphs with n vertices this algorithm can be implemented in $O(n^4)$ steps. And what is important for practical applications, there is no *large hidden constants* in the running time of this algorithm. As for the second stage, well known dynamic programming algorithms on tree decompositions can be easily translated to branch decompositions. Using upper bounds for branch-width we prove that our approach provides *more efficient* solutions for many well known problems on planar graphs.

The following table summarize some known and new results on some problems on planar graphs (for more problems see Section 3).

	Known results	New results
PLANAR INDEPENDENT SET	$O(2^{9.07\sqrt{n}}n\ln n)$ [4]	$O(2^{3.182\sqrt{n}}n + n^4)$
PLANAR DOMINATING SET	$O(2^{18.61\sqrt{n}}n\ln n)$ [4]	$O(2^{5.043\sqrt{n}}n + n^4)$
PLANAR (k,r)-CENTER		$O((2r+1)^{3.182\sqrt{n}}n + n^4)$
PLANAR LONGEST CYCLE		$O(2^{2.29\sqrt{n}(\ln n+0.94)}n^{5/4} + n^4)$
PLANAR LONGEST PATH		$O(2^{2.29\sqrt{n}(\ln n+0.94)}n^{5/4} + n^4)$
PLANAR BISECTION		$O(2^{3.182\sqrt{n}}n + n^4)$
PLANAR WEIGHTED DOMINATING SET		$O(2^{6.37\sqrt{n}}n + n^4)$
PLANAR PERFECT CODE		$O(2^{6.37\sqrt{n}}n + n^4)$
PLANAR TOTAL DOMINATING SET		$O(2^{7.4\sqrt{n}}n + n^4)$
PLANAR H-COLORING		$O(2^{\log h \cdot 2.12\sqrt{n}}hn^{3/2} + n^4)$
PLANAR KERNEL		$O(2^{3.37\sqrt{n}}n^2 + n^4)$
PLANAR H-COVERING		$O(2^{9.55\sqrt{nh}}n + n^4)$

Similar approach works well also for parameterized problems. The next table summarize results on the most fundamental fixed parameter problems on planar graphs. (See [3] for an overview of the results on this subject.) We include the result from [18] because it is based on the main combinatorial result of this paper and is obtained by similar approach.

	Known results	New results
PLANAR k-VERTEX COVER	$O(2^{4\sqrt{3k}}n)$ [3]	$O(2^{4.5\sqrt{k}}k + k^4 + kn)$
PLANAR k-DOMINATING SET	$O(2^{27\sqrt{k}}n)$ [23]	$O(2^{15.13\sqrt{k}}k + k^4 + n^3)$[18]
PLANAR k-INDEPENDENT SET	$O(2^{4\sqrt{6k}}n)$ [3]	$O(k^4 + 2^{4\sqrt{4.5k}}k + n)$

Thus our approach provides exponential speedup for the main basic parameterized problems. Our method is quite universal and can be implemented to obtain an exponential speed-up for many known algorithms for different problems with fixed parameters. Mention just a few parameterized versions of the following problems: INDEPENDENT DOMINATING SET, PERFECT DOMINATING SET, PERFECT CODE, WEIGHTED DOMINATING SET, TOTAL DOMINATING SET, EDGE DOMINATING SET, FACE COVER, VERTEX FEEDBACK SET, MINIMUM MAXIMAL MATCHING, CLIQUE TRANSVERSAL SET, DISJOINT CYCLES, and DIGRAPH KERNEL. Another advantage of our results is that they apply not only on planar graphs but on different generalizations of planar graphs, e.g. $K_{3,3}$-minor-free or K_5-minor-free graphs.

2   Definitions

All graphs in this paper are undirected, loop-less and, unless otherwise mentioned, they may have multiple edges.

Tree-width and branch-width. A *tree decomposition* of a graph G is a pair $(\{X_i \mid i \in V(T)\}, T)$, where $\{X_i \mid i \in V(T)\}$ is a collection of subsets of

$V(G)$ and T is a tree, such that (1) $\bigcup_{i \in V(T)} X_i = V(G)$, (2) for each edge $\{v, w\} \in E(G)$, there is an $i \in V(T)$ such that $v, w \in X_i$, and (3) for each $v \in V(G)$ the set of nodes $\{i \mid v \in X_i\}$ forms a subtree of T.

The *width* of a tree decomposition $(\{X_i \mid i \in V(T)\}, T)$ equals $\max_{i \in V(T)}(|X_i| - 1)$. The *tree-width* of a graph G, $\mathbf{tw}(G)$, is the minimum width over all tree decompositions of G.

A *branch decomposition* of a graph (or a hyper-graph) G is a pair (T, τ), where T is a tree with vertices of degree 1 or 3 and τ is a bijection from the set of leaves of T to $E(G)$. The *order* of an edge e in T is the number of vertices $v \in V(G)$ such that there are leaves t_1, t_2 in T in different components of $T(V(T), E(T) - e)$ with $\tau(t_1)$ and $\tau(t_2)$ both containing v as an endpoint.

The *width* of (T, τ) is the maximum order over all edges of T, and the *branch-width* of G, $\mathbf{bw}(G)$, is the minimum width over all branch decompositions of G.

It is easy to see that if H is a subgraph of G then $\mathbf{bw}(H) \le \mathbf{bw}(G)$. The following result is due to Robertson & Seymour [(5.1) in [26]].

Theorem 1 ([26]). *For any connected graph G where $|E(G)| \ge 3$, $\mathbf{bw}(G) \le \mathbf{tw}(G) + 1 \le \frac{3}{2}\mathbf{bw}(G)$.*

From Theorem 1, any upper bound on tree-width implies an upper bound on branch-width and vice versa.

Planar graphs: slopes and majorities. In this paper we use the expression Σ-*plane graph* for any planar graph drawn in the sphere Σ. To simplify notations we do not distinguish between a vertex of a Σ-plane graph and the point of Σ used in the drawing to represent the vertex or between an edge and the *open* line segment representing it. We also consider G as the union of the points corresponding to its vertices and edges. That way, a subgraph H of G can be seen as a graph H where $H \subseteq G$. We call by *region* of G any connected component of $\Sigma - E(G) - V(G)$. (Every region is an open set.) We use the notation $V(G), E(G)$, and $R(G)$ for the set of the vertices, edges and regions of G. A *path* of G is any connected subgraph P of G with two vertices of degree 1 (we call them *extremes*) and all other vertices (we call them *internal*) of degree 2. A *sub-path* of a path P is any path $P' \subseteq P$. A *cycle* of G is any connected subgraph C of G with all the vertices of degree 2. The length $|C|$ ($|P|$) of a cycle C (path $|P|$) is the number of its edges.

If $\Delta \subseteq \Sigma$, then $\overline{\Delta}$ denotes the *closure* of Δ, and the boundary of Δ is $\mathbf{bd}(\Delta) = \overline{\Delta} \cap \overline{\Sigma - \Delta}$. An edge e (a vertex v) is incident with a region r if $e \subseteq \mathbf{bd}(r)$ ($v \subseteq \mathbf{bd}(r)$).

We call a Σ-plane graph G *triangulated* if all of its regions are triangles, i.e. for every region r, $\mathbf{bd}(r)$ is a cycle of three edges and three vertices. Given a region r of a triangulated graph G we call the cycle $\mathbf{bd}(r)$ *triangle* of G. A *triangulation* H of a Σ-plane graph G is any triangulated Σ-plane graph H where $G \subseteq H$. Notice that any Σ-plane graph with all regions of size ≥ 3 has a triangulation. A triangle of a triangulated Σ-plane graph G is a *regional triangle* if it bounds a region of G.

Let G be a Σ-plane graph. A subset of Σ meeting the drawing only in vertices of G is called G-*normal*. A subset of Σ homeomorphic to the closed interval $[0, 1]$

is called I-*arc*. If the extreme points of a G-normal I-arc L are both vertices of G then we call it *line* of G. If a simple closed curve $F \subseteq \Sigma$ is G-normal then we call it *noose*.

The length of a line is the number of its vertices minus 1 and the length of a noose is the number of its vertices. We denote by $|N|$ ($|L|$) the length of a noose N (line L). $\Delta \subseteq \Sigma$ is an open disc if it is homeomorphic to $\{(x, y) : x^2 + y^2 < 1\}$. We say that a disc D is *bounded* by a noose N if $N = \mathbf{bd}(D)$. From the theorem of Jordan, any noose N bounds exactly two closed discs Δ_1, Δ_2 in Σ where $\Delta_1 \cap \Delta_2 = N$. We call Θ-*structure* $S = (L_1, L_2, L_3)$ of G the union of three mutually touching lines. If for $i, j, 1 \leq i < j \leq 3$ the noose $L_i \cup L_j$ has size $\leq k$ then we say that S is a Θ-structure of length $\leq k$. We call a Θ-structure *non-trivial* if at least two of its lines have length ≥ 2. We call the 6 closed discs bounded by the nooses $L_i \cup L_j, 1 \leq i < j \leq 3$ *closed discs bounded* by S.

The *radial graph of* a Σ-plane graph G is the bipartite Σ-plane graph R_G obtained by selecting a point in every region r of G and connecting it to every vertex of G incident to that region. We call the vertices of R_G that are not vertices of G *radial* vertices.

Slopes and majorities are important tools for improving upper bounds.

Slopes (*Robertson & Seymour [27]*). Let G be a Σ-plane graph and let $k \geq 1$ be an integer. A *slope* in G of order $k/2$ is a function $\mathbf{ins}$ which assigns to every cycle C of G of length $< k$ one of the two closed discs $\mathbf{ins}(C) \subseteq \Sigma$ bounded by C such that

[S1] If C, C' are cycles of length $< k$ and $C \subseteq \mathbf{ins}(C')$ then $\mathbf{ins}(C) \subseteq \mathbf{ins}(C')$.

[S2] If P_1, P_2, P_3 are three paths of G joining the same pair u, v of distinct vertices but otherwise disjoint, and the three cycles $P_1 \cup P_2, P_1 \cup P_3, P_2 \cup P_3$ all have length $< k$ then $\mathbf{ins}(P_1 \cup P_2) \cup \mathbf{ins}(P_1 \cup P_3) \cup \mathbf{ins}(P_2 \cup P_3) \neq \Sigma$.

A slope is *uniform* if for every region $r \in R(G)$ there is a cycle C of G of length $< k$ such that $r \subseteq \mathbf{ins}(C)$.

We need the following deep result proved in the Graph Minors papers by Robertson & Seymour. This result follows from Theorems (6.1) and (6.5) in [27] and Theorem (4.3) in [26]. (See also Theorems (6.2) and (7.1) in [29].)

Theorem 2 ([27]). *Let G be a connected Σ-plane graph where $|E(G)| \geq 2$ and let $k \geq 1$ be an integer. The radial drawing R_G has a uniform slope of order $\geq k$ if and only if G has branch-width $\geq k$.*

Majorities (*Alon, Seymour & Thomas [6]*). Let G be a Σ-plane graph and let $k \geq 0$ be an integer. A *majority of order k* is a function $\mathbf{big}$ that assigns to every noose N of length $\leq k$ a closed disc $\mathbf{big}(N) \subseteq \Sigma$ bounded by N such that

[M1] If P_1, P_2, P_3 is a Θ-structure of G with length $\leq k$ and $P_3 \subseteq \mathbf{big}(P_1 \cup P_2)$, then $\mathbf{big}(P_1 \cup P_3) \subseteq \mathbf{big}(P_1 \cup P_2)$ or $\mathbf{big}(P_2 \cup P_3) \subseteq \mathbf{big}(P_1 \cup P_2)$.

[M2] If N is a noose of length $\leq \min(2, k)$ then either $\mathbf{big}(N) - N$ contains a vertex or $\mathbf{big}(N)$ includes at least two edges of G.

The following result gives an upper bound on the order of a majority (statement (3.7) of [6]). This is a basic ingredient of our bound for the branch-width of planar graphs.

Theorem 3 ([6]). *Any majority of a Σ-plane graph G has order $\leq$ $\sqrt{4.5 \cdot |V(G)|} - 1$.*

Our bounds on branch-width and tree-width follows from the following theorem that is the main combinatorial result of the paper.

Theorem 4. *Let G, $|V(G)| \geq 5$, be a triangulated Σ-plane graph without multiple edges, drawn in Σ along with its radial graph and let $k \geq 2$ be an integer. If there exists a uniform slope of order $k + 1$ in R_G then G contains a majority of order k.*

The proof of Theorem 4 is rather long and technical. Due to space restrictions we sketch here the main ideas of the proof.

Sketch of the proof of Theorem 4. We want to correspond nooses of G to cycles of R_G and try to translate the slope axioms to majority axioms. Corresponding nooses to cycles is not direct as not every noose is a cycle of the radial graph. To overcome this problem we need to work with "classes" of similar structures.

Let G be a Σ-plane graph without loops or multiple edges and let $S \subseteq \Sigma$ be an I-arc (simple closed curve) in Σ. We use the notation $\kappa_G(S) = (v_1, \ldots, v_{|S \cap V(G)|})$ for the ordering (cyclic ordering) of the vertex set $S \cap V(G)$ that represents the way the vertices of G are met by S. Notice that κ can be applied to both cycles and nooses but also to paths and lines. Especially for cycles and paths of graphs without multiple edges, we can directly represent them with the output of the function κ (we will use the same notation for a cycle/path and the (cyclic) ordering of the vertices that it meets).

Let S be one of the following structures in G: a noose, a line, or a Θ-structure. A *variation* of S is the operation that transforms S to a structure S' of the same type in a way that $\mathbf{dif}(S, S') := \overline{(S \cup S') - (S \cap S')}$ is a noose of size 2 where one of the closed discs D it bounds has the following two properties: (1) $D - \mathbf{bd}(D)$ contains no vertices of G, (2) D contains at most one edge of G.

If two structures S_1 and S_2 are variations each of the other, we denote it as $S_1 \sim S_2$. If a structure S' is the result of a finite number of consecutive variations with S as starting point, we call S' *vibration* of S and we denote this fact as $S \sim^* S'$. Notice that if $S \sim^* S'$ then $V(G) \cap S = V(G) \cap S'$ and S, S' have the same length.

The importance of vibrations is that in a triangulated Σ-plane graph without multiple edges every noose is a vibration of a cycle of the radial graph. This fact is intuitively clear but needs a technical proof.

Let $\mathbf{ins}$ be a uniform slope of order $k + 1$ in R_G. To construct a majority we need to define the function $\mathbf{big}$. Every noose N in Σ of size $\leq k$ is a vibration of a cycle C in R_G and the length of C is $\leq 2k$. Cycle C is also a noose in Σ and because C and N are vibrations of each other, they "separate" the same vertex sets in G. In other words, if $\mathbf{ins}(C), \overline{\Sigma - \mathbf{ins}(C)}$ are closed discs bounded by C then for one of the closed discs D bounded by N, we have that $D \cap V(G) = \overline{\Sigma - \mathbf{ins}(C)} \cap V(G)$. We define $\mathbf{big}(N) = D$.

The proof of the fact that the function $\mathbf{big}$ defined via $\mathbf{ins}$ satisfies majority axioms is quite technical. It uses some results about vibrations of Θ-structures and requires a series of auxiliary results assuring that the basic topological properties involved in the majority axioms are invariants under vibrations.

Theorem 4 implies our main combinatorial result.

Theorem 5. *For any planar graph* G, $\mathbf{bw}(G) \le \sqrt{4.5|V(G)|} \le 2.122\sqrt{|V(G)|}$.

Proof. We assume that G has no multiple edges (notice that the duplication of an edge does not increase the branch-width of a graph with branch-width ≥ 2). It is easy to see that G has a triangulation H without multiple edges. It is enough to prove the bound of the theorem for H. By Theorem 3, H does not have any majority of order $\ge (3/\sqrt{2})\sqrt{|V(G)|}$. By Theorem 4, R_H has no slope of order $\ge (3/\sqrt{2})\sqrt{|V(G)|} + 1$. The result now follows from Theorem 2.   □

Since $9/(2\sqrt{2}) < 3.182$, Theorems 1 and 5 imply that for any planar graph G, $\mathbf{tw}(G) \le 3.182\sqrt{|V(G)|}$. In the next section examine the algorithmic consequences of our combinatorial bounds.

3   Algorithmic Consequences

In this section we discuss some applications of our results for different problems on planar graphs. The following simple theorem is the source for obtaining subexponential algorithms for many graph problems.

Theorem 6. *Let* Π *be an optimization problem that is solvable on graphs of branch-width* $\le \ell$ *in time* $f(\ell)g(n)$. *Then on planar graphs problem* Π *is solvable in time* $O(f(2.122\sqrt{n})g(n) + n^4)$

Proof. First we compute an optimal branch decomposition of planar graph. To compute an optimal branch decomposition of a planar graph one can use the algorithm due to Seymour & Thomas (Sections 7 and 9 in [29]). This algorithm can be implemented in $O(n^4)$ steps. Then Theorem 5 implies the proof.   □

Corollary 1. *Let* Π *be an optimization problem that is solvable on graphs of branch-width/tree-width* $\le \ell$ *in time* $2^{o(\ell^2)}\mathrm{poly}(n, \ell)$. *Then on planar graphs problem* Π *is solvable in subexponential time (in* $2^{o(n)}$ *steps).*

In spite of its simplicity, Theorem 6 provides a general framework for obtaining subexponential algorithms for a broad range of problems. And the only thing one needs to know to estimate the running time of the algorithm is how fast a problem can be solved on graphs of bounded branch-width/tree-width[1]. But really surprising is that such a trivial approach provides better time estimation than many, complicated to analyze, algorithms based on separator theorems.

---

[1] Any algorithm solving a problem on graphs of tree-width $\le \ell$ in time $f(\ell)g(n)$ can be translated to an algorithm for graphs of branch-width $\le \ell$ with running time $O(f(3/2\ell)g(n) + m)$ where m is the number of edges of the input graph.

Let us give just few examples. It is well known that on graphs of tree-width ℓ INDEPENDENT SET can be solved in time $O(2^{\ell}n)$ and hence on graphs of branch-width $\leq \ell$ it can be solved in time $O(2^{(3/2)\ell}n)$. Thus by Theorem 6 we obtain that INDEPENDENT SET on planar graphs is solvable in $O(2^{3.182\sqrt{n}}n+n^4)$. DOMINATING SET on graphs of branch-width $\leq \ell$ is solvable is time $O(2^{3\log_4 3 \cdot \ell}m)$ [11]. Thus on planar graphs, DOMINATING SET is solvable in $O(2^{5.043\sqrt{n}}n+n^4)$. Similar arguments, based on the algorithms in [1], work for the planar versions of different variations of the DOMINATING SET problem like INDEPENDENT DOMINATING SET, PERFECT DOMINATING SET, PERFECT CODE, WEIGHTED DOMINATING SET, RED BLUE DOMINATING SET where the time is $O(2^{6.37\sqrt{n}}n+n^4)$, and for TOTAL DOMINATING SET and TOTAL PERFECT DOMINATING SET where the time is $O(2^{7.4\sqrt{n}}n + n^4)$.

LONGEST CYCLE and LONGEST PATH problems on graphs of tree-width ℓ are solved in $O(\ell!2^{\ell}n)$ time [7] implying an $O(2^{2.29\sqrt{n}(\ln n+0.94)}n^{5/4} + n^4)$ algorithm on planar graphs. MIN-BISECTION is solvable in $O(2^{\ell}n)$ [22] on graphs of tree-width ℓ and the planar version of the problem is solvable in $O(2^{3.182\sqrt{n}}n + n^4)$. In [19], Gutin et al. gave a time $O(3^{\ell}kn)$ algorithm for finding a kernel of size k in a digraph whose underlying graph has treewidth at most ℓ. This implies that KERNEL is solvable in $O(2^{3.37\sqrt{n}}n^2+n^4)$. The H-COLORING problem is solvable in $O(h^{\ell+1}\ell n)$ on graphs of tree-width ℓ [13], therefore its planar version is solvable in time $O(2^{\log h \cdot 2.12\sqrt{n}}hn^{3/2} + n^4)$. H-COVER is solvable in time $O(n2^{3\ell h})$ [30] on graphs of tree-width $\leq \ell$ and thus for planar graphs in time $O(2^{9.546\sqrt{n}h}n+n^4)$. Finally, (k,r)-CENTER is solvable in time $O((2r+1)^{\frac{3}{2}\cdot\ell}m)$ on graphs of branch-width $\leq \ell$ [11] providing an $O((2r+1)^{3.182\sqrt{n}}n+n^4)$ algorithm for the planar version of the problem.

More generally, almost every natural problem expressible in MSOL is solvable in time $O(c^{\ell}n^{O(1)})$, $O(\ell^{\ell}n^{O(1)})$ or $O(\ell!c^{\ell}n^{O(1)})$, and by Corollary 1 is solvable in subexponential time on planar graphs. Examples of such problems where c is a small constant are VERTEX FEEDBACK SET, DISJOINT CYCLES, FACE COVER. EDGE DOMINATING SET, CLIQUE TRANSVERSAL, and MAXIMAL MATCHING (see [8,12]). For all these problems Corollary 1 provides subexponential algorithms with small hidden constants.

Actually, one can further strengthen the conditions of Corollary 1 towards extending the framework where subexponential algorithms are possible. Indeed, it is enough to have a time $(\mathsf{poly}(\ell,n))^{o(\ell^2)}$ algorithm for the problem Π for graphs of treewidth/branchwidth at most ℓ. Notice that such problems are not necessarily expressible in MSOL. As an example we mention the problems of finding a non-preemptive multicoloring with minimum sum/makespan. These problems can be solved in time $O(n\cdot(\ell p\log n)^{\ell+1})$ for graphs with tree-width $\leq \ell$ (see [20]). Therefore, they can be solved in time $O(pn^{3/2}\log n\cdot 2^{1.15\cdot\log p\log n\log\log n\sqrt{n}}+n^4)$ on planar graphs.

Similar ideas work for parameterized problems. Let $\mathcal{L}$ be a parameterized problem, i.e. $\mathcal{L}$ consists of pairs (I,k) where k is the *parameter* of the problem. *Reduction to linear problem kernel* is the replacement of problem inputs (I,k) by a reduced problem with inputs (I',k') (linear kernel) with constants c_1,c_2 such that $k' \leq c_1 k$, $|I'| \leq c_2 k'$ and $(I, k) \in \mathcal{L} \Leftrightarrow (I', k') \in \mathcal{L}$. (We refer to Downey & Fellows [15] for discussions on fixed parameter tractability and the ways of constructing kernels.)

Theorem 7. *Let $\mathcal{L}$ be a parameterized problem (I, k) (here I can be a graph, hypergraph or matroid) such that*
— There is a linear problem kernel computable in time $T_{kernel}(|I|, k)$ with constants c_1, c_2 and such that an optimal branch decomposition of the kernel is computable in time $T_{bw}(|I'|)$.
— On graphs (hypergraphs, matroids) of branch-width $\leq \ell$ and ground set of size n the problem $\mathcal{L}$ can be solved in $O(2^{c_3 \ell} n)$, where c_3 is a constant.
— $\mathbf{bw}(I') \leq c_4 \sqrt{k}$, where c_4 is a constant. Then $\mathcal{L}$ can be solved in time $O(2^{c_3 c_4 \sqrt{k}} k + T_{bw}(|I'|) + T_{kernel}(|I|, k))$.

Proof. The algorithm works as follows. First we compute a linear kernel in time $T_{kernel}(|I|, k)$. Then we construct a branch decomposition of the kernel in $T_{bw}(|I'|)$ steps. The size of the kernel is at most $c_1 c_2 k = O(k)$. The branch-width of the kernel is at most $c_4 \sqrt{k}$ and it takes $O(2^{c_3 c_4 \sqrt{k}} k + T_{bw}(|I'|) + T_{kernel}(|I|, k))$ to solve the problem. $\square$

Let us give some examples, where Theorem 7 provides *proven* better bounds for different parameterized problems.

The PLANAR k-VERTEX COVER problem is the task to compute, given a planar graph G and a positive integer k, a vertex cover of size k or to report that no such a set exists. A linear problem kernel of size $2k$ (with constants $c_1 = 1$ and $c_2 = 2$) for the k-VERTEX COVER problem (not necessary planar) was obtained by Chen et al. [9]. The running time of the algorithm constructing a kernel of a graph on n vertices is $O(kn + k^3)$. So in this case $T_{kernel}(|I|, k) = O(kn + k^3)$. It is well known that the VERTEX COVER problem on graphs on n vertices and with bounded tree-width $\leq \ell$ can be solved in $O(2^\ell n)$ time. The dynamic programming algorithm for the VERTEX COVER on graphs with bounded tree-width can be easy translated to the dynamic programming algorithm for graphs with bounded branch-width with running time $O(2^{3/2\ell} m)$, where m is the number of edges in a graph, and we omit it here. For planar graphs $2^{3/2\ell} m = O(2^{3/2\ell} n)$, thus $c_3 \leq 3/2$.

From the constructions used in the reduction algorithm of Chen et al. [9] it follows that if G is a planar graph then the kernel graph is also planar. To compute an optimal branch decomposition of a planar graph one can use the algorithm due to Seymour & Thomas [29]. This algorithm (applied to the kernel graph) can be implemented in $O(k^4)$ steps. The kernel graph I' has at most $2k$ vertices. Then by Theorem 5, $c_4 \leq \sqrt{4.5\sqrt{2}} = 3$. Thus by making use of Theorem 7, we conclude that PLANAR k-VERTEX COVER can be solved in $O(k^4 + 2^{4.5\sqrt{k}} k + kn)$.

A k-*dominating* set D of a graph G is a set of k vertices such that every vertex outside D is adjacent to a vertex of D. The PLANAR k-DOMINATING SET problem is the task to compute, given a planar graph G and a positive integer k, a k-dominating set or to report that no such a set exists.

Alber, Fellows & Niedermeier [2] show that the PLANAR DOMINATING SET problem admits a linear problem kernel. (The size of the kernel is $335k$.) This reduction can be performed in $O(n^3)$ time. DOMINATING SET problem on graphs of branch-width $\leq \ell$ can be solved in $O(2^{3\log_4 3 \cdot \ell} m)$ steps [18]. Thus $c_3 \leq 3\log_4 3$. It is proved in [18] that for every planar graph G with dominating set k, the branch-width of G is at most $3\sqrt{4.5}\sqrt{k}$, i.e. $c_4 \leq 3\sqrt{4.5}$. Then by Theorem 7, PLANAR DOMINATING SET can be solved in $O(2^{15.13\sqrt{k}}k + n^3 + k^4)$.

Other problems and generalizations. Our ideas can be adapted to different problems by using the bounds and tree-width (branch-width) based algorithms in the same fashion as it is done in [1,3,8,12]. That way, our upper bound implies the construction of faster algorithms for a series of problems when their inputs are restricted to planar graphs. As a sample we mention parameterized versions of the following problems: INDEPENDENT DOMINATING SET, PERFECT DOMINATING SET, PERFECT CODE, WEIGHTED DOMINATING SET, TOTAL DOMINATING SET, EDGE DOMINATING SET, FACE COVER, VERTEX FEEDBACK SET, MINIMUM MAXIMAL MATCHING, CLIQUE TRANSVERSAL SET, DISJOINT CYCLES, and DIGRAPH KERNEL (see [1,3,8,12] for the exact definitions).

Finally let us note that our upper bound for treewidth holds not only on planar graphs but on different generalizations of planar graphs. This follows directly from the results of [12] and implies an exponential speed-up of all the aforementioned problems on certain classes of non-planar graphs such as $K_{3,3}$-minor-free or K_5-minor-free graphs.

References

1. J. ALBER, H. L. BODLAENDER, H. FERNAU, T. KLOKS, AND R. NIEDERMEIER, *Fixed parameter algorithms for dominating set and related problems on planar graphs*, Algorithmica, 33 (2002), pp. 461–493.
2. J. ALBER, M. R. FELLOWS, AND R. NIEDERMEIER, *Efficient data reduction for dominating set: A linear problem kernel for the planar case*, in SWAT 2002, Springer, vol. 2368, Berlin, 2002, pp. 150–159.
3. J. ALBER, H. FERNAU, AND R. NIEDERMEIER, *Parameterized complexity: Exponential speed-up for planar graph problems*, in Electronic Colloquium on Computational Complexity (ECCC), Germany, 2001.
4. J. ALBER, H. FERNAU, AND R. NIEDERMEIER, *Graph separators: a parameterized view*, J. of Computer and System Sciences, (2003), to appear.
5. N. ALON, P. SEYMOUR, AND R. THOMAS, *A separator theorem for nonplanar graphs*, J. Amer. Math. Soc., 3 (1990), pp. 801–808.
6. ———, *Planar separators*, SIAM J. Discrete Math., 7 (1994), pp. 184–193.
7. H. L. BODLAENDER, *On linear time minor tests with depth-first search*, J. Algorithms, 14 (1993), pp. 1–23.
8. M.-S. CHANG, T. KLOKS, AND C.-M. LEE, *Maximum clique transversals*, in WG 2001, vol. 2204 of Lecture Notes in Comput. Sci., Springer, Berlin, 2001, pp. 32–43.
9. J. CHEN, I. A. KANJ, AND W. JIA, *Vertex cover: further observations and further improvements*, J. Algorithms, 41 (2001), pp. 280–301.
10. E. DANTSIN, A. GOERDT, E. A. HIRSCH, R. KANNAN, J. KLEINBERG, C. PAPADIMITRIOU, P. RAGHAVAN, AND U. SCHÖNING, *A deterministic $(2 - 2/(k+1))^n$ algorithm for k-SAT based on local search*, Theoret. Comput. Sci., 289 (2002), pp. 69–83.

11. E. D. DEMAINE, F. V. FOMIN, M. HAJIAGHAYI, AND D. M. THILIKOS, *Fixed-parameter algorithms for the (k, r)-center in planar graphs and map graphs*, in ICALP 2003, vol. 2719 of Lecture Notes in Comput. Sci., Springer, Berlin, 2003, pp. 829–844.

12. E. D. DEMAINE, M. HAJIAGHAYI, AND D. M. THILIKOS, *Exponential speedup of fixed parameter algorithms on $K_{3,3}$-minor-free or K_5-minor-free graphs*, in ISAAC 2002, Springer, Lecture Notes in Computer Science, Berlin, vol. 2518, 2002, pp. 262–273.

13. J. DIAZ, M. SERNA, AND D. M. THILIKOS, *Counting H-colorings of partial k-trees*, Theoretical Computer Science, 281 (2002), pp. 291–309.

14. H. N. DJIDJEV AND S. M. VENKATESAN, *Reduced constants for simple cycle graph separation*, Acta Informatica, 34 (1997), pp. 231–243.

15. R. G. DOWNEY AND M. R. FELLOWS, *Parameterized complexity*, Springer-Verlag, New York, 1999.

16. D. EPPSTEIN, *Small maximal independent sets and faster exact graph coloring*, in WADS 2001, vol. 2125 of Lecture Notes in Comput. Sci., Springer, Berlin, 2001, pp. 462–470.

17. U. FEIGE, *Coping with the NP-hardness of the graph bandwidth problem*, in SWAT 2000, vol. 1851 of Lecture Notes in Comput. Sci., Springer, Berlin, 2000, pp. 10–19.

18. F. V. FOMIN AND D. M. THILIKOS, *Dominating sets in planar graphs: Branch-width and exponential speed-up*, in SODA 2003, pp. 168–177.

19. G. GUTIN, T. KLOKS, AND C. M. LEE, *Kernels in planar digraphs*, in Optimization Online, Mathematical Programming Society, Philadelphia, 2001.

20. M. M. HALLDÓRSSON AND G. KORTSARZ, *Tools for multicoloring with applications to planar graphs and partial k-trees*, Journal of Algorithms, 42 (2002), pp. 334–366.

21. I. V. HICKS, *Branch Decompositions and their applications*, PhD thesis, Rice University, 2000.

22. K. JANSEN, M. KARPINSKI, A. LINGAS, AND E. SEIDEL, *Polynomial time approximation schemes for Max-Bisection on planar and geometric graphs*, in STACS 2001, vol. 2010 of Lecture Notes in Comput. Sci., Springer, Berlin, 2001, pp. 365–375.

23. I. KANJ AND L. PERKOVIĆ, *Improved parameterized algorithms for planar dominating set*, in MFCS 2002, Springer, Lecture Notes in Computer Science, Berlin, vol. 2420, 2002, pp. 399–410.

24. R. J. LIPTON AND R. E. TARJAN, *A separator theorem for planar graphs*, SIAM J. Appl. Math., 36 (1979), pp. 177–189.

25. ———, *Applications of a planar separator theorem*, SIAM J. Comput., 9 (1980), pp. 615–627.

26. N. ROBERTSON AND P. D. SEYMOUR, *Graph minors. X. Obstructions to tree-decomposition*, J. Combin. Theory Ser. B, 52 (1991), pp. 153–190.

27. ———, *Graph minors. XI. Circuits on a surface*, J. Combin. Theory Ser. B, 60 (1994), pp. 72–106.

28. N. ROBERTSON, P. D. SEYMOUR, AND R. THOMAS, *Quickly excluding a planar graph*, J. Combin. Theory Ser. B, 62 (1994), pp. 323–348.

29. P. D. SEYMOUR AND R. THOMAS, *Call routing and the ratcatcher*, Combinatorica, 14 (1994), pp. 217–241.

30. J. A. TELLE AND A. PROSKUROWSKI, *Algorithms for vertex partitioning problems on partial k-trees*, SIAM J. Discrete Math., 10 (1997), pp. 529–550.

31. G. J. WOEGINGER, *Exact algorithms for NP-hard problems: a survey*, in Combinatorial Optimization—Eureka, You Shrink!, M. Junger, G. Reinelt, and G. Rinaldi, eds., Springer, LNCS 2570, Berlin, 2003, pp. 185–207.

Sum-Multicoloring on Paths

Annamária Kovács*

Max-Planck Institut für Informatik,
Stuhlsatzenhausweg 85,
66123 Saarbrücken, Germany
panni@mpi-sb.mpg.de

Abstract. The question whether the *preemptive Sum Multicoloring* (pSMC) problem is hard on paths was raised by Halldórsson et al. in [8]. The pSMC problem is a scheduling problem where the pairwise conflicting jobs are represented by a conflict graph, and the time lengths of jobs by integer weights on the nodes. The goal is to schedule the jobs so that the *sum* of their finishing times is minimized. In the paper we give an $\mathcal{O}(n^3 p)$ time algorithm for the pSMC problem on paths, where n is the number of nodes and p is the largest time length. The result easily carries over to cycles.

1 Introduction

In scheduling problems there is a set of jobs, each with a given time length. There might be conflicts between jobs, then they cannot be worked on at the same time, due to e.g. some non-sharable resource they use. Real-life situations of this kind can be found in operating systems, in areas like traffic intersection control, frequency assignment for mobile phones, VLSI routing etc. (see [7]).

In the mathematical model the jobs are represented as nodes of a simple undirected graph $G = (V, E)$, where two nodes representing conflicting jobs are connected by an edge. The *demand* of $v \in V$ is a positive integer $x(v)$ modeling the number of time units needed to finish the job of v. A proper schedule $\Psi : V \to 2^{\mathbb{N}}$ of the jobs assigns a set $\Psi(v)$ of positive integers to each $v \in V$ s.t. $|\Psi(v)| = x(v)$ and the sets assigned to adjacent vertices do not intersect (i.e., they are never scheduled at the same time). In this way the scheduling problem becomes a graph *coloring* problem if $x(v) = 1$ for each $v \in V$, and graph *multicoloring* problem in the general case. (The name stems from regarding the $\Psi(v)$ as sets of colors. In the paper, however, we continue to view the problem as a *scheduling* problem since we will use colors for something else.)

A traditional optimization goal is to minimize the overall finishing time, respectively the number of colors used to color all the vertices. Another reasonable

---

* Partially supported by the Future and Emerging Technologies programme of the EU under contract number IST-1999-14186 (ALCOM-FT) and the Marie-Curie Training Site programme of the EU.

goal is to minimize the average finishing time of the jobs. That is, if $f(v)$ denotes the largest integer assigned to v, we search for a schedule (multicoloring), such that $\sum_{v \in V} f(v)$ is minimum over all proper schedules. The latter is called the *sum multicoloring* (SMC) problem.

In the paper we consider *preemptive* scheduling, where the $\Psi(v)$ are arbitrary sets of positive integers (pSMC problem). There has been much related work done concerning the *non-preemptive* SMC (npSMC) problem, where the assigned $\Psi(v)$ sets must be contiguous, see e.g. [7,8].

Our result. The question, if the pSMC problem is hard on paths, was raised as an open problem by Halldórsson et al. in [8]. In this paper we provide a pseudo-polynomial algorithm for the problem. Let $G = (V, E)$ be a path, $|V| = n$, and $p = \max_{v \in V} x(v)$. Our algorithm takes $\mathcal{O}(n^3 p)$ time. It is based on a technique that is interesting in its own right. With minor modifications the approach can be applied to the pSMC problem on cycles.

Related work. Here we just mention the most relevant results. For a more comprehensive history of the SMC and related problems see, e.g. [2,8].

The *sum coloring* problem, the special case of SMC with unit time requirements, was first raised by Kubicka in [4], where a polynomial algorithm was given for the case of trees. The sum coloring problem is NP-hard even on bipartite graphs [1], interval graphs [9], planar graphs [2], and line graphs [6]. These results imply the hardness of the corresponding SMC problems.

The general SMC problem was introduced by Bar-Noy et al. [7] within a comprehensive study on the approximability of both the pSMC and npSMC on different graph classes.

In [8] two efficient algorithms are provided for the *non-preemptive* (npSMC) problem on trees. They run in $\mathcal{O}(n^2)$ and in $\mathcal{O}(np)$ time, respectively. On paths the first one runs in $\mathcal{O}(n \log p / \log \log p)$ time. For the *preemptive* (pSMC) problem on trees, a polynomial time approximation scheme is given.

Marx proved the hardness of the pSMC problem on trees in [5]. He has shown that pSMC is NP-hard even on binary trees, even when p is polynomially bounded. Thus, the SMC problem on trees turned out to be one of the few scheduling-type of problems in which the preemptive version is essentially harder than the non-preemptive version. It is natural to go on asking, on which graph-classes pSMC is efficiently solvable. In [8] the question is raised, whether pSMC is hard on paths. For this problem, an algorithm polynomial in n and p is given in this paper. It can serve as a first step towards characterizing these graph-classes.

Overview. Section 2 describes the basic notation we use and establishes a few elementary facts. In Section 3 we give the ingredients of a pseudo-polynomial algorithm. Section 4 contains the details of an improved algorithm of $\mathcal{O}(n^4 p)$ steps. Unfortunately we could not get rid of the factor p, but we conclude by sketching a further improvement in the exponent of n and the modifications for the case when the graph is not a path but a cycle.

2   Notation, Definitions, and Basic Facts

The nodes in the path are numbered from left to right by $1, \ldots, n$. If $i < j$, we denote the subpath of starting node i and ending node j by $[i, j]$. If i is a node, then $x(i) \in \mathbb{N}^+$, is the *demand* of i. Let $p = \max_{1 \leq i \leq n} x(i)$ be the largest demand. $\Psi(i) \subset \mathbb{N}$ is the set of numbers or time units assigned to i in schedule Ψ. $f_\Psi(i)$ denotes the finishing time (the largest number assigned to i). We simply write $f(i)$ when Ψ is clear from the context. We also use $f(i, j) \overset{\text{def}}{=} \max(f(i), f(j))$. We add nodes 0 and $n + 1$ to the path with demands $x(0) = x(n + 1) = 0$.

Definition 1. *We call Ψ a (proper) schedule, if $|\Psi(i)| = x(i)$ and $\Psi(i) \cap \Psi(i + 1) = \emptyset$ $(1 \leq i \leq n - 1)$. Ψ is an* optimal *schedule, if $\sum_{i=1}^n f_\Psi(i)$ is minimum over all schedules. Ψ is a* square-optimal *schedule, if it is optimal, and the sum $\sum_{i=1}^n f(i)^2$ is maximum over all optimal schedules.*

Intuitively, in a square-optimal schedule small $f(i)$ values are as small as possible and large $f(i)$ are as large as possible.

We will give a pseudo-polynomial algorithm (polynomial in n and p) that computes an optimal schedule, for given demands on nodes of a path.

Definition 2. *Given a schedule Ψ, we say that node i is*

a local minimum, *if $i = 0$, or $i = n + 1$, or $f(i - 1) > f(i) < f(i + 1)$;*

a local maximum, *if $f(i - 1) < f(i) > f(i + 1)$;*

a stair *otherwise, in particular a* stair-up, *if $f(i - 1) < f(i) < f(i + 1)$, and a* stair-down, *if $f(i - 1) > f(i) > f(i + 1)$;*

compact, if $f(i) = x(i)$.

Let us use the following visualizing expressions. We say that i is *black* on level a, if $a \in \Psi(i)$, and i is *white* on level a if $a \notin \Psi(i)$ (see Fig. 1). For example, if i is compact then it is not white on any level under $f(i)$.

For $i < j$ we will also say, that the ordered pair (i, j) is *black-white, black-black,...* etc. on level a. Note that $(i, i + 1)$ cannot be black-black on any level.

The following is easy to see:

Proposition 1. *In an optimal schedule the number of levels where (i, j) is black-black is at most p. The same holds for white-black and for black-white levels. The number of levels under $f(i, j)$ where (i, j) is white-white, is at most $2p$.*

Definition 3. *An (i, j) pair is* conflicting *on level a, if either*

$i \equiv j \pmod 2$ and (i, j) is black-white, or white-black, or

$i \not\equiv j \pmod 2$ and (i, j) is black-black, or white-white.

Proposition 2. *If (i, j) is conflicting on level a, then $\exists k \in [i, j - 1]$ such that $(k, k + 1)$ is white-white on level a.*

Definition 4. *Suppose that $\forall k \in [i, j]$, $f(k) \geq \max(a, b)$ in a schedule Ψ. We say that we change the levels a and b on $[i, j]$, if $\forall k \in [i, j]$ we make k white (black) on level a if and only if according to Ψ it was white (black) on level b, and we make k white (black) on level b, if and only if it was white (black) on level a.*

After carrying out this operation, we may have to make corrections to get a proper schedule again. Note that we will have to check the pairs $(i - 1, i)$ and $(j, j + 1)$ on the levels a and b.

Proposition 3. *If i is a stair-up in a square-optimal schedule Ψ, then $(i - 1, i)$ is either white-black or black-white on any level $a \leq f(i)$. A symmetric statement holds if i is a stair-down.*

Proof. We need to show that $(i - 1, i)$ is not white-white on any level below $f(i)$. Suppose $(i - 1, i)$ is white-white on level $a < f(i)$. Let M be the first local maximum to the right of i, and let's change the levels a and $f(i)$ on $[i, M]$. Now we decreased $f(i)$ by at least one, and got a proper schedule on $[i - 1, i]$, since $i - 1$ is white on the level a. If it is a proper schedule on $[M, M + 1]$, then we decreased the optimum sum, contradiction; if it is not a proper schedule on $[M, M + 1]$, then we make M white either on the level a or on the level $f(i)$, and make it black on the level $f(M) + 1$ (increase $f(M)$ by one). Now we created another optimal schedule, but increased the sum of squares of finishing times, again a contradiction since Ψ was square-optimal. $\square$

Corollary 1. *In a square-optimal schedule let i be a local minimum and M the first local maximum to the right of i, and let $i < k < M$. Then $f(k) = x(k - 1) + x(k)$ holds, and $\Psi(k)$ is determined above the level $f(i)$. Moreover, $\Psi(i)$ determines the whole $\Psi(k)$. A symmetric statement holds for stair-downs.*

Proposition 4 is also based on a simple level-changing argument (see [3]):

Proposition 4. *For any local minimum k in an optimal schedule, $f(k) \leq 3x(k)$.*

3   An Outline of the Algorithm and Further Definitions

Definition 5. *With respect to a given schedule Ψ, let $i < j$ be both local minima with the property that if $i < k < j$ is a local minimum between them, then $f(k) \geq \max(f(i), f(j))$. We will say that such an (i, j) pair is a convex pair.*

Definition 6. *For a convex pair (i, j), in a schedule Ψ, let $pit(i, j) = k$ if*
 $i < k < j$ and k is a local minimum, and
 if $i < k' < j$ and k' is a local minimum, then $f(k) < f(k')$ or $(f(k) = f(k')$ and $k \leq k')$.
 If there is no local minimum between i and j, then let $pit(i, j) = \emptyset$ and let $top(i, j)$ denote the unique local maximum between i and j.

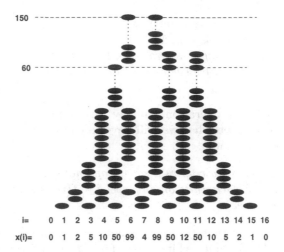

Fig. 1. A square-optimal solution for the given pSMC problem on a path of length 15. The convex pairs are $(0, 16)$, $(0, 7)$, $(7, 16)$, $(7, 10)$, and $(10, 16)$. Other examples: $pit(7, 16) = 10$; $top(7, 10) = 8$; $\ell(10) = 7$, and $r(10) = 13$.

Note that $pit(i, j)$ is the (leftmost) local minimum of smallest finishing time between i and j, and both $(i, pit(i, j))$ and $(pit(i, j), j)$ are convex pairs.

The algorithm tests for every pair (i, j), whether it can be a convex pair in a square-optimal schedule. It proceeds from short distances to long ones – i.e., first it tests for each pair of the form $(i, i + 2)$, and at last $(0, n + 1)$. It proceeds dynamically by testing for each k between i and j, if it can be $pit(i, j)$, or $top(i, j)$. We will add up the computed optimum on $[i + 1, k - 1]$, and on $[k + 1, j - 1]$, and $f(k)$, to obtain a possible sum of finishing times on $[i + 1, j - 1]$.

Of course, an optimum that we calculated this way is only realizable if we can indeed 'glue' two optimal schedules by the schedule of k. Thus, we will also have to one by one fix and test some characteristic of the schedule on i, j and k.

For the time being, let us suppose that if $k = pit(i, j)$ then $f(k) < f(i+1)$ and $f(k) < f(j-1)$. That is, we disregard the fact that there might be several stairs on the two sides of $[i, j]$, having finishing time smaller than $f(k)$, or stair-downs finishing under $f(i)$ if, e.g., $f(i) > f(j)$ (see $(i, k, j) = (7, 10, 16)$ on Fig. 1).

We will fix the number of black-black, white-black, black-white, and white-white levels concerning the (i, j) pair. Since we just fix the number, and not the location of these levels, even testing for all $\mathcal{O}(p^4)$ possibilities would result in a pseudo-polynomial algorithm.

Definition 7. *For a convex pair (i, j) in a fixed schedule Ψ, let $C(i, j) \in [0, 2p]^4$ be the 4-tuple denoting the number of levels under $f(i, j)$, where (i, j) is black-black, white-black, black-white, and white-white, respectively. We will call $C(i, j)$ the scheme of (i, j). For the triple $i < k = pit(i, j) < j$, we will talk about the scheme $C(i, k, j) \in [0, 2p]^8$ under the level $f(k)$, in the same sense.*

We denote by $C(i, k, j) \Rightarrow C(i, j)$, when they are consistent with each other, i.e., the number of black-white-black and the number of black-black-black levels of (i, k, j) sum up to the number of black-black levels of (i, j), and so on. Similarly, we use the notations $C(i, k, j) \Rightarrow C(i, k)$ and $C(i, k, j) \Rightarrow C(k, j)$.

Remark 1. Note that the four numbers in $C(i, j)$ sum up to $f(i, j)$ and the eight numbers in $C(i, k, j)$ sum up to $f(k)$. Note also, that $C(i, k, j) \Rightarrow C(i, j)$ implies that the number of white-white-white plus the number of white-black-white levels in $C(i, k, j)$ equals the number of white-white levels in $C(i, j)$ plus $f(k) - f(i, j)$. Here is where we implicitly exploit that (i, j) is supposed to be a convex pair, and therefore $f(k) \geq f(i, j)$: for a fixed $C(i, j)$ we will want to test for all possible $C(i, k, j)$, for which $C(i, k, j) \Rightarrow C(i, j)$ holds. Suppose, we wanted to calculate the optimum by taking also $f(k) < f(i, j)$ values into consideration. For this calculation we would need in advance the scheme of (i, j) under each possible $f(k)$ level. On the other hand, knowing $C(i, j)$ under all of the levels, boils down to having $\Psi(i)$ and $\Psi(j)$, and that is exactly what we tried to avoid, as testing all that, would lead beyond polynomial time.

For each pair $i < j$ and each possible scheme $C(i, j)$ of the pair, the algorithm computes an optimum sum of finishing times $F(i, j, C(i, j)) = \sum_{l=i+1}^{j-1} f(l)$ supposing that (i, j) is a convex pair. In particular, we test for each $k \in [i+1, j-1]$ to be $pit(i, j)$ and for each scheme $C(i, k, j) \Rightarrow C(i, j)$.

For $C(i, k, j) \Rightarrow C(i, k)$ and $C(i, k, j) \Rightarrow C(k, j)$ we have a previously computed $F(i, k, C(i, k))$ and a $F(k, j, C(k, j))$ value. We obtain the sum of finishing times for this k and $C(i, k, j)$ by $F(i, k, C(i, k)) + F(k, j, C(k, j)) + f(k)$. We also test if k can be $top(i, j)$. In that case the sum of finishing times is computed easily based on Corollary 1 and on $C(i, j)$. Finally we choose the smallest sum of finishing times to be $F(i, j, C(i, j))$ and remember one $k = pit(i, j)$ and one $C(i, k, j)$, or a $k = top(i, j)$ that yielded this value. In the end of this process we will have all the local minima and maxima in an optimal schedule and the schemes of convex pairs of minima. This is sufficient information to create such a schedule, starting with a minimum of smallest finishing time.

The algorithm is still a bit more complicated than this, because we may have stairs on the two sides of $[i, j]$ that we did not yet consider. Before we elaborate on this we shall need one more definition:

Definition 8. *Let i be a local minimum in a schedule Ψ. Let $i < r(i) \leq n+1$ be the node with the property $f(r(i)) < f(i)$ and $\forall k, i < k < r(i)$ $f(k) \geq f(i)$. We define $0 \leq \ell(i) < i$ symmetrically.*

Now, with these terms in hand, suppose we are testing the pair (i, j) and e.g. $f(i) > f(j)$ holds. Then we will need $C(i, r(i))$ instead of $C(i, j)$ and if $f(k) \geq f(i)$, then we will need $C(\ell(k), k, r(k))$ instead of $C(i, k, j)$ (see Fig. 1). This won't make so much difference, because $[i + 1, \ell(k)]$ consists of stair-ups as well as $[r(k), j - 1]$ consists of stair-downs only, and there the schedule and finishing times have a simple one-to-one correspondance to those of i and j. Let's say that all of $i \leq \ell(k) < k < r(k) \leq r(i) \leq j$ are fixed. The *schemes* $C(i, r(i))$ and $C(\ell(k), k, r(k))$, and the *consistency* $C(\ell(k), k, r(k)) \Rightarrow C(i, r(i))$ can be defined like before. In the latter, now we have to correct all the four values in $C(i, r(i))$ with the appropriate values that sum up to $f(k) - f(i)$ (not only the white-white value, see Remark 1).

The values $f(i, j)$, $C(i, j)$, $pit(i, j)$, etc. may carry an appended subscript $_\Psi$ in order to stress that they are relative to a schedule Ψ, or a subscript $_A$ when a value was yielded by the algorithm and is not necessarily realized by a schedule.

4   An $\mathcal{O}(n^4 p)$ Algorithm

In Section 3 the main idea of the algorithm was presented. Turning to the exact description we will make use of two technical theorems – Theorems 1 and 2 – that will help us simplify the algorithm and improve its performance. The detailed proofs omitted from this section can be found in [3].

Here we present an $\mathcal{O}(n^4 p)$ time algorithm. In the conclusions we will give a short argument on how to reduce its time bound to $\mathcal{O}(n^3 p)$.

Theorems 1 and 2 are based on the following lemmas:

Lemma 1. *Let i be a local minimum in a square-optimal schedule, such that it is not compact, and let $\ell(i) \leq k \leq r(i)$. Then the following hold:*
The (i, k) pair is not conflicting on the level $f(i)$;
The (i, k) pair is not conflicting on any level where i is white.

Proof. Suppose for example, that $i < k \leq r(i)$, and (i, k) is conflicting on the level $f(i)$. There must be an $i \leq s < k$ such that $(s, s+1)$ is white-white on level $f(i)$. Let M be the first local maximum to the left of i. Now all the finishing times on $[M, s]$ are not smaller than $f(i)$. Let i be white on the level $a < f(i)$. Let's change the levels a and $f(i)$ on $[M, s]$. Since $(s, s + 1)$ was white-white, this remains a proper schedule on $[s, s + 1]$ and it reduces $f(i)$ by at least 1. If it is not a proper schedule on $[M - 1, M]$, we can correct it by increasing $f(M)$ by 1 (like in the proof of Proposition 3). This remains an optimal schedule, but improves the former schedule concerning square-optimality, a contradiction.

If (i, k) is conflicting on the level a, the argument is essentially the same. $\square$

Corollary 2. *If $f(i) > x(i)$ then $i \not\equiv r(i) (\mathrm{mod} 2)$, and $i \not\equiv \ell(i) (\mathrm{mod} 2)$, otherwise $(\ell(i), i)$ or $(i, r(i))$ would be conflicting on the level $f(i)$.*

Lemma 2. *Let (i, j) be a convex pair in a square-optimal schedule Ψ. If $f(i) = f(j)$ then i and j are compact and $f(i) = x(i) = x(j) = f(j)$.*

In the proof we first point out that $\Psi(i)$ and $\Psi(j)$ must be the same. After that, a similar level-changing argument shows that they must be compact.

Lemma 3. *If i is a non-compact local minimum in a square-optimal schedule, then for any level $a \leq f(i)$ there is at most one $i \leq k < r(i)$ and at most one $\ell(i) \leq k < i$ such that $(k, k + 1)$ is white-white on the level a.*

Proof. Suppose we have $i \leq k < k' < r(i)$ such that $(k, k+1)$ and $(k', k'+1)$ are both white-white on level a. Note that by Lemma 1 i must be black on level a. Let i be white on level b. If $i \equiv k \pmod 2$ then k is white on level b (see Lemma 1). Then we change the levels a and b on $[k+1, k']$; if $i \not\equiv k \pmod 2$ then k is white on the level $f(i)$. Then we change the levels a and $f(i)$ on $[k+1, k']$. In both cases we obtain a proper square-optimal schedule that contradicts Lemma 1, because $(i, k+1)$ is conflicting on level $f(i)$ or on level b. $\square$

Now suppose (i, j) is a convex pair, $f(i) > f(j)$, and $k = pit(i, j)$. Theorem 1 implies that in most cases $C(i, r(i))$ determines $\ell(k)$, $r(k)$, and $C(\ell(k), k, r(k))$ if i, $r(i)$, and k are fixed. In turn, Theorem 2 shows that i, j, and $f(i)$ are sufficient to determine $r(i)$ and $C(i, r(i))$. In conclusion, the factor of p^7 in the running time of the rough algorithm can be reduced to p.

The proof of Theorem 1 is basically the same as that of Lemma 3:

Theorem 1. *Let (i, j) be a convex pair, $k = pit(i, j)$, and k be non-compact in a square-optimal schedule.*
(1) If $f(i, j) > \max(x(i), x(j))$ then $(\ell(k), k, r(k))$ can only be black-white-black, black-black-white, white-black-black or white-black-white.
(2) If $f(i, j) = \max(x(i), x(j))$ then in addition to the previous four, a black-black-black triple is also possible.

In Fig. 1, for example, (1) holds if $(i, k, j) = (7, 10, 16)$, and (2) holds, if $(i, k, j) = (0, 7, 16)$. Compare the levels 2 and 3 of $(\ell(k), k, r(k)) = (2, 7, 14)$.

Definition 9. *Let (i, j) be a convex pair. According to $f(i) > f(j)$, $f(i) < f(j)$, or $f(i) = f(j)$ we will use the name* relevant scheme *of (i, j) for the scheme $C(i, r(i))$, $C(\ell(j), j)$ or $C(i, j)$, respectively.*

Theorem 2. *Let (i, j) be a convex pair in a square-optimal schedule. If either $f(i, j) \neq \max(x(i), x(j))$ or $(f(i, j) = \max(x(i), x(j)))$, and $k = top(i, j))$ is known, then the relevant scheme of (i, j) can be computed in $\mathcal{O}(n)$ time.*

Sketch of proof. Note that interestingly, knowing if $f(i)$ or $f(j)$ is larger, is not a condition in the theorem. Namely, it is either obvious or irrelevant: If, e.g., $f(i, j) > x(j-1) + x(j)$ then $f(i, j) = f(i) > f(j)$ and we have to compute $r(i)$ and then $C(i, r(i))$. On the other hand, if $\max(x(i), x(j)) \leq f(i, j) \leq \min(x(i) + x(i+1), x(j) + x(j-1))$ then exactly one of $f(i) = f(j)$, $\ell(j) = i$ or $r(i) = j$ holds, and we have to compute $C(i, j)$. In any case, we need a $C(s, t)$ value, where (s, t) is not white-white on any level, because either one of them is compact, or one is a non-compact local minimum and they are of different parity. We get that the number of white-black levels is $f(s, t) - x(s)$, the number of black-white levels is $f(s, t) - x(t)$, and the number of black-black levels is $x(s) + x(t) - f(s, t)$.

Now we show how to obtain $r(i)$ if, e.g., $f(i, j) = f(i) > f(j)$. First let $f(i) > x(i)$. Note that $r(i) \ldots (j-1)$ is a (possibly empty) series of step-downs. Let s be a node, for which $x(s-1) + x(s) \geq f(i) > x(s) + x(s+1) > \ldots > x(j-1) + x(j)$ holds. If such an s exists, we can find it in $\mathcal{O}(n)$ steps. We claim that $r(i) = s$. If

$r(i)-1$ is also a step-down, then the claim is trivial, if it is a local maximum, then a short argument is needed to prove it. Second, if $f(i) = x(i)$ and $k = top(i,j)$ then $r(i) = \max(k+1, s)$, or $r(i) = k+1$ if s does not exist. $\square$

The following two simple lemmas describe two basic steps of the algorithm:

Lemma 4. *Let (i,j) be a convex pair of minima in a square-optimal solution Ψ, and let $k = top_\Psi(i,j)$. We can compute $f_\Psi(k)$ in $\mathcal{O}(n)$ steps if $f_\Psi(i,j)$ is known.*

Sketch of proof. If $k = top(i,j)$, then the schedule on the stairs $[i+1, k-1]$ and $[k+1, j-1]$ is determined by $\Psi(i)$ and $\Psi(j)$ in a greedy manner. Finally, the local maximum k is black on a level if and only if $(k-1, k+1)$ is white-white.

E.g., let $f(i) > f(j)$. We proceed along the levels from the bottom up, and sum up the number of levels, where k is black. Under level $f(i,j)$ we obtain this number from $C(i, r(i))$, where $C(i, r(i))$ can be computed in $\mathcal{O}(n)$ time. Since above the level $f(i,j)$ we know the schedule on $[i+1, j-1]$, here the summing up is straightforward by way of merging two increasing number series: the finishing times of stairs on the two sides. Merging and summing takes $\mathcal{O}(n)$ time. $\square$

Lemma 5. *Let (i,j) be a convex pair of minima in a square-optimal solution Ψ, and let $k = pit_\Psi(i,j)$. If $f_\Psi(i,j)$ is known and $f_\Psi(i,j) > \max(x(i), x(j))$, then it is possible to compute $f_\Psi(k)$ in $\mathcal{O}(n)$ steps.*

The proof of Lemma 5 is much the same as that of Lemma 4: we proceed from the bottom and sum up the levels where k is black (see Theorem 1), until the sum reaches $x(k)$. We also obtain $\ell(k)$ and $r(k)$. Under $f(i,j)$ we use $C(i, r(i))$, above that we know the schedule on $[i+1, \ell(k)]$ and on $[r(k), j-1]$.

We will run the algorithms of Lemma 4 and 5 on all possible $(i,j,f(i,j),k)$. The results, denoted by $fmax_A(i,j,f,k)$ and $fmin_A(i,j,f,k)$, respectively, provide the finishing time of k, if (i,j) is a convex pair and $k = top(i,j)$ resp. $pit(i,j)$ in a square-optimal schedule. If the setting (i,j,f,k) is not feasible, we may get no numeric result, which we denote by $fmax/fmin(i,j,f,k) = \infty$.

We continue with an exact description of the algorithm. It has two phases:
Phase 1. In this phase we compute an optimal structure: locations and finishing times of local minima, and locations of local maxima. We will not do the scheduling here, but we will get the optimum sum of finishing times as a result.

For all $0 \le i < j \le n+1$ where $i+2 \le j$ and all f where $\max(x(i), x(j)) \le f \le 3\max(x(i), x(j))$, we will compute $F_A(i,j,f)$ with the following meaning: if in a Ψ square-optimal solution (i,j) is a convex pair of minima, and $f_\Psi(i,j) = f$, then $\sum_{s=i+1}^{j-1} f_\Psi(s) = F_A(i,j,f)$. We proceed from short $[i,j]$ subpaths to longer ones, using a dynamic programming strategy. First we compute

$$Fmax = \min_{k \in [i+1, j-1]} \left(\sum_{s=i+1}^{k-1} (x(s-1) + x(s)) + fmax_A(i,j,f,k) + \right.$$

$$\left. + \sum_{s=k+1}^{j-1} (x(s+1) + x(s)) \right)$$

```
for d = 2 ... n + 1 do
  for 0 ≤ i < j ≤ n + 1, j − i = d do
    for f = max(x(i), x(j)) ... 3 max(x(i), x(j)) do
      for k = i + 1 ... j − 1 do
        compute fmax(i, j, f, k) in time O(n) (Lemma 4)
      end for
      Fmax := min_{i<k<j}(∑_{s=i+1}^{k−1}(x(s−1)+x(s)) + fmax(i,j,f,k) + ∑_{s=k+1}^{j−1}(x(s+1)+x(s)))
      top(i, j, f) := the k providing the minimum value
      for k = i + 2 ... j − 2 do
        if f = max(x(i), x(j)) then
          compute min_{x(k)≤f'≤3x(k)}(F(i,k,f') + f' + F(k,j,f'))
          fmin(i, j, f, k) := the f' providing the minimum
        else
          compute fmin(i, j, f, k) in time O(n) (Lemma 5)
        end if
      end for
      Fmin := min_{i<k<j}(F(i,k,fmin(i,j,f,k)) + fmin(i,j,f,k) + F(k,j,fmin(i,j,f,k)))
      pit(i, j, f) := the k providing the minimum value
      if Fmax ≤ Fmin then
        F(i, j, f) := Fmax and pit(i, j, f) := ∅
      else
        F(i, j, f) := Fmin and top(i, j, f) := ∅
      end if
    end for
  end for
end for
```

Fig. 2. Phase 1 of the $\mathcal{O}(n^4 p)$ algorithm.

in $\mathcal{O}(n^2)$ time (see Lemma 4). Second, if $f > \max(x(i), x(j))$ then we compute

$$Fmin = \min_{k \in [i+2, j-2]} (F_A(i, k, fmin_A(i, j, f, k)) + fmin_A(i, j, f, k) +$$

$$+ F_A(k, j, fmin_A(i, j, f, k)))$$

in $\mathcal{O}(n^2)$ time (see Lemma 5). If $f = \max(x(i), x(j))$, then we have to test for all the possible values of the finishing time of $k = pit(i, j)$. Thus, we compute

$$Fmin = \min_{k \in [i+2, j-2], f' \in [x(k), 3x(k)]} (F_A(i, k, f') + f' + F_A(k, j, f'))$$

in $\mathcal{O}(np)$ time. If k and f' provided the minimum sum, then we assign the f' value to $fmin_A(i, j, f, k)$.

We obtain $F_A(i, j, f) = \min(Fmax, Fmin)$.

Again, $F_A(i, j, f) = \infty$ means that (i, j) has lost the chance to be a convex pair of minima with $f(i, j) = f$ in any square-optimal schedule. If $F_A(i, j, f) \neq \infty$ then together with the value $F_A(i, j, f)$ we also store which $k \in [i + 1, j − 1]$ resulted the minimum. If it was a unique local maximum (that is if $Fmax \leq Fmin$) then we record it by $top_A(i, j, f) = k$. Otherwise we record $pit_A(i, j, f) = k$. The computation for one (i, j) pair takes $\mathcal{O}(n^2 p)$ time. Overall computation of Phase 1 takes $\mathcal{O}(n^4 p)$ time.

The proof of the following theorem is straightforward by induction on the lengths of subpaths:

Theorem 3. *If Φ is a valid schedule of the given demands on the path $[1, n]$, then $\sum_{s=1}^{n} f_\Phi(s) \geq F_A(0, n + 1, 0)$.*

```
procedure main()
schedule(0, n + 1, 0)


procedure schedule(i, j, f)
if top(i, j, f) ≠ ∅ then
    k := top(i, j, f)
    greedy(i, k − 1)
    greedy(j, k + 1)
    greedy(k)
else
    k := pit(i, j, f)
    fk := fmin(i, j, f, k)
    minschedule(i, j, f, fk)
    schedule(i, k, fk)
    schedule(k, j, fk)
end if


procedure greedy(k)
make k black on the smallest
x(k) levels where both
k − 1 and k + 1 are white
```

```
procedure minschedule(i, j, k, fk)
ℓ(k) := min{s ≥ i|x(s + 1) + x(s) ≥ fk}
r(k) := max{s ≤ j|x(s − 1) + x(s) ≥ fk}
greedy(i, ℓ(k))
greedy(j, r(k))
first make k black below fk, where it doesn't
conflict with both of Ψ(ℓ(k)) and Ψ(r(k))
if there are < x(k) black levels then
    fill up from the bottom the missing black levels
end if

procedure greedy(i, j)
if i < j then
    for k := i + 1 . . . j do
        if k is not scheduled then
            make k black on the smallest x(k)
            levels where k − 1 is white
        end if
    end for
end if
if j < i then
    proceed symmetrically
end if
```

Fig. 3. Phase 2.

Phase 2. In this phase we give an optimal schedule Φ. Now we proceed from long subpaths – starting with $[0, n + 1]$ – to shorter ones. Phase 1 provided the local minima in the form of $pit_A()$ values and their finishing times as $fmin_A()$, and the local maxima in the form of $top_A()$ values. While computing the schedule of these nodes we will basically follow the same algorithm as in Lemma 4 and 5 when we calculated their finishing times. Along the way, it is straightforward to show – we won't do this here – that Φ is a valid schedule and optimal, because $\sum_{s=1}^{n} f_\Phi(s) = F_A(0, n + 1, 0)$ (see Theorem 3).

First we take $pit_A(0, n + 1, 0)$ or $top_A(0, n + 1, 0)$. One of them must exist, because there exist valid schedules on the path.

If we have a $k = top_A(0, n + 1, 0)$ then there is just one local maximum in our optimal schedule. Then we do the scheduling in the greedy way on the stair-ups of $[1, k − 1]$ and on the stair-downs of $[k + 1, n]$. Finally we do the greedy scheduling on k, that is, we make k black where $(k − 1, k + 1)$ is white-white.

If on the other hand we have $k = pit_A(0, n+1, 0)$, then k will be the (leftmost) smallest local minimum in Φ. We have the finishing time $f_\Phi(k) := fmin_A(0, n + 1, 0, k)$ as well. Let $f_\Phi(k) \neq x(k)$ (otherwise $\Phi(k)$ is trivial). Now we obtain $\ell(k)$ and $r(k)$ again, while we are doing the greedy scheduling on the stairs $[1, \ell(k)]$ and $[r(k), n]$. In the meantime we schedule k : since k is not compact, $\ell(k) \not\equiv k \not\equiv r(k) \pmod 2$, and we make k black where $(\ell(k), r(k))$ is not black-black. If $x(k)$ is not used up till we reach $fmin_A(0, n + 1, 0, k)$, then we are free to assign the 'extra' black levels from bottom up (see node 7 on Fig. 1).

Now we proceed recursively, first make the schedule on $[0, k]$ then on $[k, n+1]$. Exactly one of $top_A(0, k, fmin_A(k))$ or $pit_A(0, k, fmin_A(k))$ exists, in the first case we make the schedule on the whole subpath $[0, k]$, in the latter case on $k' = pit(0, k)$, on $[\ell(k) + 1, \ell(k')]$, and on $[r(k'), k − 1]$. And so on...

Computing the pit_A, $fmin_A$ etc. values in Phase 1, corresponds to creating the schedule in Phase 2. This guarantees that we make ends meet: e.g., the $fmin_A$ values are not higher than the stairs on both sides, and all these details.

Analysis. Let a be a *preemption level*, if there is a node i s.t. i is black on a and white on $a + 1$, or vice versa. In our schedule, any preemption level is either the finishing time of a node, or the last of extra black levels in a local minimum (e.g. level 2 of node 7 on Fig. 1). Hence, there are $\mathcal{O}(n)$ preemption levels. We could record the preemption levels of any node, by way of merging or revisiting preemption levels of at most two other nodes. So, Phase 2 requires $\mathcal{O}(n^2)$ time.

5   Conclusions

The $\mathcal{O}(n^3p)$ Algorithm on Paths and Cycles. Let's regard a fixed triple (i, j, f) in Phase 1. We claim that we can compute $fmax_A(i, j, f, k)$ and $fmin_A(i, j, f, k)$ overall for all $k \in [i + 1, j - 1]$ in $\mathcal{O}(n)$ time. This reduces the time to $\mathcal{O}(n^3p)$ (compare Figure 2). First, in Theorem 2, the part of the computation taking $\mathcal{O}(n)$ time doesn't depend on k. Second, in Lemma 4 and 5, the merging and summing procedure is exactly the same for k's of the same parity. If the $x(k)$ demands of e.g. all even k's are sorted in non-decreasing order, during the merging of the two sides and summing the black levels, we can in parallel record the $fmax$ resp. $fmin$ finishing times of all the k's (sorted by demands). Let's sort the odd and even nodes by their demands at the beginning of Phase 1.

Finally, let's regard the case of cycles: First we compute $F_A(i, j, f)$ for <u>all</u> $[i, j]$ subpaths of the cycle and all possible f values. Since on a cycle a node of minimum finishing time is compact, the optimum sum will be $\min_{1 \le i \le n}(F_A(i, i, x(i)) + x(i))$, where $F_A(i, i, x(i))$ is the computed optimum on $i + 1, i + 2, \ldots, i + n - 1 = i - 1 (\bmod n)$. Finally, we start the scheduling with the compact local minimum.

Future work. It remains challenging to find an algorithm for this problem, polynomial in n (and $\log p$). We firmly believe that this is possible.

There is no obvious way to exploit our idea on conflict-graphs of maximum node degree ≥ 3. However, it may be interesting to examine graph-classes with just a small number of nodes of degree ≥ 3.

Acknowledgements. I would like to thank Dániel Marx for the idea of considering square-optimal schedules. Special thanks to Katalin Friedl, for directing me to the problem, and for her advice and lot of help during the writing of this paper.

References

1. A. Bar-Noy and G. Kortsarz. The minimum color-sum of bipartite graphs. *Journal of Algorithms*, 28:339–365, 1998.

2. M. M. Halldórsson and G. Kortsarz. Tools for multicoloring with applications to planar graphs and partial k-trees. *Journal of Algorithms*, 42(2):334–366, 2002.
3. A. Kovács. Sum-multicoloring on paths. Research Report MPI-I-2003-1-015, Max-Planck-Institut für Informatik, July 2003.
4. E. Kubicka. *The Chromatic Sum of a Graph*. PhD thesis, Western Michigan University, 1989.
5. D. Marx. The complexity of tree multicolorings. In *Proc. 27th Intl. Symp. Math. Found. Comput. Sci. (MFCS)*, LNCS. Springer, 2002.
6. A. Bar-Noy M. Bellare M. M. Halldórsson H. Shachnai and T. Tamir. On chromatic sums and distributed resource allocation. *Inf. and Comput.*, 140:183–202, 1998.
7. A. Bar-Noy M. M. Halldórsson G. Kortsarz H. Shachnai and R. Salman. Sum multicoloring of graphs. *Journal of Algorithms*, 37:422–450, 2000.
8. M. M. Halldórsson G. Kortsarz A. Proskurowski R. Salman H. Shachnai and J. A. Telle. Multi-coloring trees. *Information and Computation*, 180(2):113–129, 2002.
9. T. Szkaliczki. Routing with minimum wire length in the dogleg-free Manhattan model is NP-complete. *SIAM Journal on Computing*, 29(1):274–287, 1999.

Matching Algorithms Are Fast in Sparse Random Graphs*

Holger Bast[1], Kurt Mehlhorn[1], Guido Schäfer[1], and Hisao Tamaki[2]**

[1] Max-Planck-Institut für Informatik, Saarbrücken, Germany,
{bast,mehlhorn,schaefer}@mpi-sb.mpg.de
[2] Meiji University, Kawasaki, Japan, tamaki@cs.meiji.ac.jp

Abstract. We present an improved average case analysis of the maximum cardinality matching problem. We show that in a bipartite or general random graph on n vertices, with high probability every non-maximum matching has an augmenting path of length $O(\log n)$. This implies that augmenting path algorithms like the Hopcroft–Karp algorithm for bipartite graphs and the Micali–Vazirani algorithm for general graphs, which have a worst case running time of $O(m\sqrt{n})$, run in time $O(m \log n)$ with high probability, where m is the number of edges in the graph. Motwani proved these results for random graphs when the average degree is at least $\ln(n)$ [*Average Case Analysis of Algorithms for Matchings and Related Problems*, Journal of the ACM, **41**(6), 1994]. Our results hold, if only the average degree is a large enough constant. At the same time we simplify the analysis of Motwani.

1 Introduction

We consider the problem of computing a matching of maximum cardinality in an undirected graph $G = (V, E)$ with vertex set V and edge set E. A matching is a subset $M \subseteq E$ of the edges of G such that no two edges in M have a vertex in common. The edges in M are called *matching edges*, edges not in M are called *free edges*. A vertex is *matched* if it has an incident matching edge, otherwise it is *free*.

Augmenting Path Algorithms. Most matching algorithms are augmenting path algorithms. An *augmenting path* for a non-maximum matching M is a simple path between two free vertices, where the edges along the path are alternately free edges and matching edges. For every non-maximum matching, an augmenting path exists (e.g., obtained by taking the symmetric difference of the set of matching edges with the edge set of an arbitrary optimal matching). By making each free edge a matching edge and vice versa along such a path, a matching that is larger by one edge is obtained. Augmenting path algorithms search for

---

* Partially supported by the Future and Emerging Technologies programme of the EU under contract number IST-1999-14186 (ALCOM-FT).

** This work was done while the author was visiting the Max-Planck Institut für Informatik.

augmenting paths and augment, until the matching is maximum. The algorithms differ in the way they search for augmenting paths.

Complexity. Maximum matchings can be computed efficiently. Let n and m denote the number of vertices and edges of G, respectively. In bipartite graphs, the algorithm of Hopcroft and Karp [10] computes a maximum matching in time $O(m\sqrt{n})$. For dense graphs, i.e., with $m = \Theta(n^2)$, slightly better algorithms are known. Cheriyan and Mehlhorn [3] obtained $O(n^{2.5}/\log n)$ and Feder and Motwani [7] achieved, via graph compression, $O(m\sqrt{n}/\varphi(n,m))$, where $\varphi(n,m) = \log n/\log(n^2/m)$. In general graphs, Edmonds' blossom-shrinking algorithm [5,4,8] computes a maximum matching in time $O(nm\alpha(m,n))$, where $\alpha(m,n)$ denotes the inverse of Ackermann's function. Micali and Vazirani [13] gave an $O(m\sqrt{n})$ algorithm, which is similar to the algorithm of Hopcroft and Karp for bipartite graphs.

The algorithms of Hopcroft and Karp [10] and Micali and Vazirani [13] are of particular interest in this paper. The algorithms run in phases. In each phase we first construct a maximal set of vertex-disjoint shortest augmenting paths, and then augment the current matching along these paths. A phase requires time $O(m)$. In both algorithms the length of the shortest augmenting path strictly increases from one phase to the next and thus a bound on the maximal length of shortest augmenting paths implies a bound on running time: If every non-maximum matching in a bipartite (general) graph has an augmenting path of length at most $f(n)$, then the Hopcroft–Karp (Micali–Vazirani) algorithm runs in time $O(m \cdot f(n))$.

In practice, augmenting path algorithms perform significantly better than suggested by the worst case running times, see, e.g., [11,2]. The worst case running time seems to be an over-pessimistic estimation of the actual running time in practice. We are therefore interested in the average case behavior of augmenting path algorithms.

Random Graph Models. We define the probability distribution on graphs according to the model introduced by Erdös and Rényi [6]. We consider both bipartite and general graphs. We denote by $G(n;n)$ the set of all undirected bipartite graphs with n vertices on each side, and by $G(n;n;p)$ the probability distribution on $G(n;n)$, where each of the n^2 potential edges is present with probability p, independent of other edges. Similarly, we denote by $G(n)$ the set of all undirected graphs with n vertices and by $G(n;p)$ the probability distribution on $G(n)$, where each of the $n(n-1)/2$ potential edges is present with probability p, independent of other edges. The average degree of each vertex in a graph drawn from $G(n;n;p)$ or $G(n;p)$ is pn and $p(n-1)$, respectively. We will use c to denote the average degree of a random graph.

Our Results. We prove that in a random graph drawn from $G(n;n;c/n)$ or from $G(n;c/(n-1))$, with high probability every non-maximum matching has an augmenting path of length $O(\log n)$, if only c is above a certain constant. For bipartite graphs, our analysis requires that $c \geq 8.83$, for general graphs it requires that $c \geq 32.67$. It follows that under these conditions, the running time of the algorithms of Hopcroft and Karp on bipartite random graphs and Micali and Vazirani on general random graphs is $O(m\log n)$ with high probability.

We conjecture the existence of short augmenting paths for every value of c. Observe that for tiny values of c, for example $c < 1$, all paths are of length $O(\log n)$ and hence also all augmenting paths must be short. It is conceivable that our analysis can be strengthened so as to cover all values of c; we comment further on this in our conclusions.

Related Work. Motwani [12] presented the first average case analysis for matching algorithms. He showed that every non-maximum matching in a random graph from $G(n; n; c/n)$ or from $G(n; c/(n-1))$ with $c \geq \ln n$ has a logarithmic length augmenting path with high probability. The analysis rests on two key observations: (i) expander graphs[1] admit short augmenting paths with respect to any non-maximum matching, and (ii) random graphs with $c \geq \ln n$ are structurally so similar to expander graphs that the short augmenting path property carries over. Motwani's analysis breaks down when c is significantly below $\ln n$. When c is constant, for example, with high probability a constant fraction of the vertices is isolated and a constant fraction of the vertices has degree one, and such graphs are certainly not structurally similar to expanders.

Novelty. Nevertheless, on a high level our approach is similar to that of Motwani. We grow alternating trees as they are constructed in augmenting path algorithms at two free vertices connected by an augmenting path and show that the trees meet with high probability after $\Theta(\log n)$ layers. Our main technical lemma states that such trees exhibit exponential growth after $\Theta(\log n)$ layers; we remark that they may stay skinny for up to $\Theta(\log n)$ layers. In the proof, we exploit several structural properties of these trees, such as connectivity, degree-one descendence due to the matching edges, etc. In contrast to this, Motwani works with expansion for plain sets of vertices, which only holds for $c \geq \ln n$ and gives rise to several complications in the analysis, which we can avoid here. Our analysis is therefore at the same time stronger and simpler.

2 Main Result

In this section we state our main result, Theorem 1, explain the central ideas of its proof, and give an overview of the rest of the paper.

Theorem 1. *There is a constant c_0 such that a random graph from $G(n; n; c/n)$ or from $G(n; c/(n-1))$, where $c \geq c_0$, with high probability has the property that every non-maximum matching has an augmenting path of length $O(\log n)$. In a graph with this property, a maximum matching can be computed in $O(m \log n)$ time, where m is the number of edges.*

Remark 1. For a random graph from $G(n; n; c/n)$, the theorem holds for $c \geq 8.83$. For a random graph from $G(n; c/(n-1))$, it holds for $c \geq 32.67$.

---

[1] In an expander graph the cardinality of the set of neighbors of any vertex set S with $|S| \leq n/2$ is at least $(1 + \epsilon)|S|$ for some positive constant ϵ.

A central notion in our analysis will be that of an *augmenting path tree*. Augmenting path trees arise in the standard breadth-first search for augmenting paths for a given non-maximum matching: start from a free vertex, add all its neighbours, if none of them is free (otherwise an augmenting path is found) add all the incident matching edges and their other endpoints, and so on. We first give the formal definition, then Figure 1 provides an example.

Definition 1. *For a rooted tree T, let* $\mathrm{Even}(T)$ *denote the set of vertices at even non-zero levels (i.e., excluding the root), and let* $\mathrm{Odd}(T)$ *denote the set of vertices at odd levels, where the root has level 0, its children have level 1, and so on. The largest level of a vertex in T is denoted by* $\mathrm{depth}(T)$.

An augmenting path tree *is a rooted tree T of even depth, where each vertex of* $\mathrm{Odd}(T)$ *has exactly one child; in particular,* $|\mathrm{Odd}(T)| = |\mathrm{Even}(T)|$. *An augmenting path tree is* for *a particular matching, if its root is free with respect to that matching, and all edges between an odd level and the next larger even level are in the matching.*

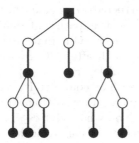
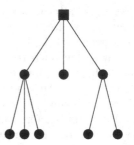

Fig. 1. Left: An augmenting path tree T with $|\mathrm{Even}(T)| = |\mathrm{Odd}(T)| = 8$. Right: The tree with vertices on odd levels "removed", as used in the proof of Lemma 2.

Our approach to proving Theorem 1 is as follows. Given a non-maximum matching, we pick the two free vertices of an augmenting path, and from each of these vertices we grow two augmenting path trees T_1 and T_2. The following lemma names a set of properties, which are sufficient for the existence of a short augmenting path.

Lemma 1. *Let T_1 and T_2 be two augmenting path trees for a given non-maximum matching in a given graph. Then the following properties imply that there is an augmenting path of length at most* $\mathrm{depth}(T_1) + \mathrm{depth}(T_2) + 1$

(a) T_1 and T_2 are (vertex and edge) disjoint;
(b) One of the following holds:
    (b1) either there is a free vertex adjacent to $\mathrm{Even}(T_1)$ or to $\mathrm{Even}(T_2)$,
    (b2) or there is an edge between $\mathrm{Even}(T_1)$ and $\mathrm{Even}(T_2)$.

Proof. If property (b1) holds, there is an augmenting path via just one of the trees, of length at most $\max\{\mathrm{depth}(T_1), \mathrm{depth}(T_2)\} + 1$. If property (b2) holds, then owing to (a) there is an augmenting path from the root of T_1 to the root of T_2 of length at most $\mathrm{depth}(T_1) + \mathrm{depth}(T_2) + 1$.

$\square$

Our construction of the trees T_1 and T_2 with these properties will be incremental, terminating as soon as property (b1) or (b2) is fulfilled. In Section 3, we will give the construction for bipartite random graphs. In Section 4, we deal with general random graphs.

The main difficulty will be to prove that the construction terminates with at most logarithmic depth for both trees. The key will be the following lemma, which establishes an expansion property for augmenting path trees, when the average degree is above a certain constant.

While the lemma is formulated and proven completely independently from its later use, some readers might prefer to first study the construction from Section 3 in more detail, see how the lemma is used there, and then come back to this section. In the lemma below, as well as in our constructions, we will use $\Gamma_G(X)$ to denote the *neighbourhood* of a vertex set X in G, i.e., the set of vertices adjacent to X in G.

Lemma 2. *For each $\varepsilon > 0$ and $\beta > 1 + \varepsilon$, there exist constants α and c_0 such that a random graph G from $G(n; n; c/n)$ or from $G(n; c/(n-1))$, where $c \geq c_0$, with high probability has the following property: for each augmenting path tree T with $\alpha \cdot \log n \leq |\mathrm{Even}(T)| \leq n/\beta$, it holds that $|\Gamma_G(\mathrm{Even}(T))| \geq (1+\varepsilon) \cdot |\mathrm{Even}(T)|$.*

Remark 2. For a random graph from $G(n; n; c/n)$, for $\varepsilon = 0.001$ and $\beta = 2.57$, the lemma holds with $c_0 = 8.83$. For a random graph from $G(n; c/(n-1))$, for $\varepsilon = 2.01$ and $\beta = 6.03$, the lemma holds with $c_0 = 32.67$. These will be the settings when we apply the lemma in Sections 3 and 4. The derivation of these constants is explained at the end of Section 3.

Proof. If a graph G does not have the property from the lemma, the following *bottleneck*[2] constellation occurs in G:

(i)   an augmenting path tree T with $\alpha \log n \leq |\mathrm{Even}(T)| \leq n/\beta$;
(ii) a set $\Gamma \supseteq \mathrm{Odd}(T)$ with $|\Gamma| \leq (1 + \varepsilon) \cdot |\mathrm{Even}(T)|$;
(iii) for each vertex from $\Gamma \backslash \mathrm{Odd}(T)$, an edge to a vertex from $\mathrm{Even}(T)$ (the edges from $\mathrm{Odd}(T)$ to $\mathrm{Even}(T)$ are already taken care of in (i));
(iv) no edge between $\mathrm{Even}(T)$ and $V \backslash \Gamma$, where V is the set of all vertices of G.

We will show that the probability that any such bottleneck constellation occurs is polynomially small in n. We first give the proof for a bipartite random graph, and then describe the (few) changes required for a general random graph.

If a fixed bottleneck constellation occurs in a graph from $G(n; n)$, the following events occur, where we write $l = |\mathrm{Even}(T)|$ and $r = |\Gamma|$: (i) the $2l$ edges from T are present, (ii) the $r - l$ edges from $\Gamma \backslash \mathrm{Odd}(T)$ to $\mathrm{Even}(T)$ are present, and (iii) none of the $l(n - r)$ edges between $\mathrm{Even}(T)$ and $V' \backslash \Gamma$ are present,

---

[2] In his work, Motwani uses this name in a related context.

where V' is the side of the bipartite graph containing Γ and we exploit that in a bipartite graph Even(T) and Γ lie on opposite sides of the graph. It follows that the probability that each of these, obviously independent, events occurs in a random graph from $G(n; n; c/n)$ is at most

$$(c/n)^{l+r} \cdot (1 - c/n)^{l(n-r)},$$

which, using that $l \leq n/\beta$, $l \leq r \leq (1 + \varepsilon) \cdot l$, and $1 - c/n \leq e^{-c/n}$, is bounded by

$$n^{-(l+r)} \cdot c^{(2+\varepsilon) \cdot l} \cdot e^{-c(1-(1+\varepsilon)/\beta) \cdot l} = n^{-(l+r)} \cdot \left(\frac{c^{2+\varepsilon}}{e^{c(1-(1+\varepsilon)/\beta)}}\right)^l.$$

The number of potential bottleneck constellations, i.e., the number of different bottleneck constellations in the complete bipartite graph on $2n$ vertices, with $|\text{Even}(T)| = l$ and $|\Gamma| = r$ is (i) the number of augmenting path trees T with $|\text{Even}(T)| = l$, times (ii) the number of ways to choose the $r - l$ vertices for $\Gamma\backslash\text{Odd}(T)$ from $V'\backslash\text{Odd}(T)$, where V' are the vertices on that side of the bipartite graph containing Odd(T) (vertices on the other side of the graph cannot be in the neighbourhood of Even(T)), times (iii) the number of ways to choose for each of these $r - l$ vertices an edge to one of the l vertices from Even(T).

Clearly, the number for (iii) is l^{r-l}, and the number for (ii) is $\binom{n-l}{r-l} \leq \binom{n}{r-l}$. To count the number of augmenting path trees T with $|\text{Even}(T)| = l$, observe that via "removing" the vertices in Odd(T), as illustrated by an example in Figure 1, each such tree corresponds to a unique combination of a tree on $l + 1$ vertices, and a sequence of l distinct vertices. By Cayley's theorem [1] the number of trees on $l + 1$ vertices is $(l + 1)^{l-1}$, and the number of sequences of l distinct vertices from one side of a graph from $G(n; n)$ is $n \cdot (n - 1) \cdots (n - l + 1) \leq n^l$.

The total number of potential bottleneck constellations in a $G(n; n)$ graph is hence at most

$$\binom{n}{l+1} \cdot (l+1)^{l-1} \cdot \binom{n}{r-l} \cdot l^{r-l} \cdot n^l \leq n^{r+l+1} \cdot e^{r+1} \cdot \left(\frac{l}{r-l}\right)^{r-l} \leq n^{r+l+1} \cdot e^{r+1} \cdot \left(\varepsilon^{-\varepsilon}\right)^l,$$

where the last inequality holds[3] for $r \leq (1 + \varepsilon) \cdot l$ and $\varepsilon \leq 1/e$.

Combining the bounds, we conclude that a random graph from $G(n; n; c/n)$ contains *any* bottleneck constellation with $|\text{Even}(T)| = l$ and $|\Gamma| = r$, with probability at most

$$en \cdot \left(\frac{\varepsilon^{-\varepsilon} e^{1+\varepsilon} c^{2+\varepsilon}}{e^{c(1-(1+\varepsilon)/\beta)}}\right)^l = en \cdot q^l,$$

where q is just an abbreviation for the fractional term. For sufficiently large c, we have $q < 1$; in particular, this holds for the values stated in the remark to the lemma: $\varepsilon = 0.001$, $\beta = 2.57$, and $c \geq 8.83$.

We finally sum over all r, l with $\alpha \cdot \log n \leq l \leq n/\beta$ and $l \leq r \leq (1 + \varepsilon) \cdot l$, and get a total probability of at most

$$en^3 \cdot q^{\alpha \log n} = en^{3-\alpha \log(1/q)},$$

---

[3] Let $r = (1 + \kappa) \cdot l$ with $0 \leq \kappa \leq \varepsilon$. If $\kappa = 0$, the claim is obvious (recall $0^0 = 1$). If $\kappa > 0$, we have $(l/(r - l))^{r-l} = (1/\kappa)^{\kappa \cdot l} \leq (1/\varepsilon)^{\varepsilon \cdot l}$, since $(1/\kappa)^\kappa$ is increasing for $\kappa \leq 1/e$.

which for sufficiently large α is polynomially small in n. This finishes the proof of Lemma 2 for bipartite random graphs.

In a random graph from $G(n; c/(n-1))$, the bound on the probability that a fixed constellation with $|\text{Even}(T)| = l$ and $|\Gamma| = r$ occurs, is

$$(c/(n-1))^{l+r} \cdot (1 - c/n)^{l(n-r)} \leq (n-1)^{-(l+r)} \cdot \left(\frac{c^{2+\varepsilon}}{e^{c(1-(1+\varepsilon)/\beta)}} \right)^l .$$

The number of bottleneck constellations can be bounded just like before by

$$\binom{n}{l+1} \cdot (l+1)^{l-1} \cdot \binom{n}{r-l} \cdot l^{r-l} \cdot n^l \leq n^{r+l+1} \cdot e^{r+1} \cdot \left(\frac{l}{r-l} \right)^{r-l} \leq n^{r+l+1} \cdot e^{r+1} \cdot 1.45^l,$$

where the last inequality now holds for $r \leq (1+\varepsilon) \cdot l$, but without restriction on ε (for arbitrary random graphs, we will apply the lemma with $\varepsilon > 2$). Altogether, a random graph from $G(n; c/(n-1))$ then contains *any* bottleneck constellation with probability at most

$$\sum_{\alpha \log n \leq l \leq n} \sum_{l \leq r \leq n} e^3 n \cdot \left(\frac{e^{1.38+\varepsilon} c^{2+\varepsilon}}{e^{c(1-(1+\varepsilon)/\beta)}} \right)^l \leq e n^3 \cdot q^{\alpha \log n} = e n^{3-\alpha \log(1/q)},$$

where the additional e^2 factor comes from $(n-1)^{-(l+r)} \cdot n^{r+l} \leq (1 + 1/(n-1))^{r+l} \leq e^2$, the 1.38 is just a number $\geq 1+\ln 1.45$, and q is again an abbreviation for the fractional term. For sufficiently large c, and in particular for $\varepsilon = 2.01$, $\beta = 6.03$ and $c \geq 32.67$, we have $q < 1$, and then for large enough α the probability is negligible. This proves Lemma 2 also for arbitrary random graphs. $\square$

The following simple property of random graphs was already stated and proven in [12, Lemma 3(d)], except that Motwani did not make the threshold on c explicit. We remark that this threshold is one of the major bottlenecks for reducing the threshold on c in our main result, Theorem 1.

Lemma 3. *For every $\beta > 1$, and for $c > 2 \cdot \beta^2 \cdot H(1/\beta) \cdot \ln 2$, where $H(x) = -x \log_2 x - (1-x) \log_2(1-x)$ is the binary entropy function, a random graph from $G(n; n; c/n)$ or from $G(n; c/(n-1))$ with high probability has the property that every two disjoint sets of vertices, both of size at least n/β, have an edge between them.*

Proof. The probability that no edge runs between two disjoint sets of sizes l and r is exactly $(1 - c/n)^{lr}$. If two disjoint subsets of size at least n/β and with no edge between them exist, then there exist also two subsets of size exactly $\lceil n/\beta \rceil$ with no edge between them (just remove the necessary number of vertices from each set), and this happens with probability at most

$$\binom{n}{\lceil n/\beta \rceil}^2 \cdot (1 - c/n)^{\lceil n/\beta \rceil^2} .$$

Now $\binom{n}{k} \leq 2^{n \cdot H(k/n)}$, where H is the binary entropy function as stated in the lemma. Since $H(x)/x$ is monotonically decreasing on $(0,1)$, we have

$$\binom{n}{\lceil n/\beta \rceil} \leq 2^{n \cdot H(\lceil n/\beta \rceil/n)} = 2^{H(\lceil n/\beta \rceil/n) \cdot n/\lceil n/\beta \rceil \cdot \lceil n/\beta \rceil} \leq 2^{\beta \cdot H(1/\beta) \cdot \lceil n/\beta \rceil}$$

The quantity $(1 - c/n)^{\lceil n/\beta \rceil^2}$ we bound by $e^{-c/\beta \cdot \lceil n/\beta \rceil}$. This give us the following bound on the above probability

$$\left(2^{\beta \cdot H(1/\beta)} \cdot e^{-c/(2\beta)} \right)^{2\lceil n/\beta \rceil}.$$

This is a negligible probability, provided that $c > 2 \cdot \beta^2 \cdot H(1/\beta) \cdot \ln 2$. We remark that, had we estimated the binomial coefficient via the standard $\binom{n}{k} \leq (en/k)^k$, we would have obtained the slightly more restrictive condition $c > 2\beta(1 + \ln \beta)$. □

3   Constructing the Trees for Bipartite Random Graphs

For a given non-maximum matching of a graph G from $G(n;n)$, consider an augmenting path and pick its two free endpoints, f_1 and f_2. Note that since every augmenting path has odd length, in a bipartite graph these two free vertices lie on opposite sides of G. The following procedure constructs T_1 and T_2.

0. Initially let T_1 and T_2 be the trees with f_1 and f_2 as the only vertex and root, respectively. Each of the following iterations will add two more levels to T_1 and to T_2.
1. Let $\Gamma(T) = \Gamma_G(\text{Even}(T)) \backslash \text{Odd}(T)$, for $T = T_1, T_2$.
2. If $\Gamma(T_1)$ or $\Gamma(T_2)$ contains a free vertex, STOP.
3. If $\Gamma(T_1)$ contains a vertex which is already in $\text{Even}(T_2)$, or vice versa, STOP.
4. If there is a matching edge between $\Gamma(T_1)$ and $\Gamma(T_2)$, add it, together with the endpoint and edge connecting it to (say) T_1, then STOP.
5. Otherwise add to T all the vertices from $\Gamma(T)$, together with the edges connecting them to $\text{Even}(T)$ (by construction all vertices from $\Gamma(T)$ are in fact adjacent to the largest level of T), for $T = T_1, T_2$.
6. Add the matching edges incident to $\Gamma(T)$ together with their other endpoints to T, for $T = T_1, T_2$.
7. Repeat 1.–6.

We first show that this construction fulfills the properties of Lemma 1. When the procedure stops in step 2, we have property (b1). When it stops in step 3 or 4, we have an edge between $\text{Even}(T_1)$ and $\text{Even}(T_2)$, which is property (b2). Since the roots of T_1 and T_2 lie on opposite sides of the bipartite graph G, we have $\text{Even}(T_1) \cap \text{Even}(T_2) = \text{Odd}(T_1) \cap \text{Odd}(T_2) = \emptyset$. Steps 3 and 4 ensure that $\text{Odd}(T_1) \cap \text{Even}(T_2) = \text{Odd}(T_2) \cap \text{Even}(T_1) = \emptyset$, hence we have complete disjointness of T_1 and T_2, which is property (a).

It remains to show that the procedure terminates within $O(\log n)$ iterations (note that by what we have shown so far, the procedure could run forever, namely when at some point $\Gamma(T) = \emptyset$ in step 1). Since each iteration adds two levels to each tree, the depth of the trees would then be $O(\log n)$, which by Lemma 1 would prove Theorem 1.

By construction, in step 6 of every iteration at least the matching edge of the augmenting path starting in f_1 is added to T_1, and the same holds for f_2 and T_2. After $\alpha \log n$ iterations therefore, $|\text{Even}(T)| \geq \alpha \cdot \log n$. Consider an iteration i, for $i > \alpha \cdot \log n$, which passes steps 2–4. Let T denote one of the trees (the following argument holds for T_1 as well as for T_2) at the beginning of the iteration, and let T' denote the tree at the end of the iteration, with two new levels added to it. We apply Lemma 2 with $\varepsilon = 0.001$ and $\beta = 2.57$; the value for ε is just a small one satisfying the requirement $\varepsilon > 0$ of Lemma 2, the choice for β will be explained in the next but one paragraph. When $|\text{Even}(T)| < n/\beta$, Lemma 2 gives that $|\Gamma_G(\text{Even}(T))| \geq (1 + \varepsilon) \cdot |\text{Even}(T)|$. Since $|\text{Even}(T')| = |\text{Even}(T)| + |\Gamma(T)| = |\text{Even}(T)| + |\Gamma_G(\text{Even}(T)) \backslash \text{Odd}(T)| = |\Gamma_G(\text{Even}(T))|$, we have $|\text{Even}(T')| \geq (1 + \varepsilon) \cdot |\text{Even}(T)|$. This proves that when the procedure runs for $\alpha \log n + \log_{1+\varepsilon}(n/\beta) = O(\log n)$ iterations, then certainly $|\text{Even}(T)| \geq n/\beta$, for $T = T_1, T_2$.

Consider the first iteration, where both $|\text{Even}(T_1)|$ and $|\text{Even}(T_2)|$ are at least n/β. By property (a), already established above, the two sets are disjoint, hence by Lemma 3, with high probability there is an edge between them. With such an edge, the procedure stops in step 3. This proves that with high probability the procedure terminates within $O(\log n)$ iterations, and hence with two trees of depth $O(\log n)$. This finishes the proof of Theorem 1 for random bipartite graphs.

We finally comment on our choice of $\beta = 2.57$ above, and how it leads to the requirement $c \geq 8.83$ in Theorem 1. Both Lemma 2 and Lemma 3 put a lower bound on c. For Lemma 2, this bound comes from the quantity q, defined in the proof of that lemma, which has to be strictly less than 1; this quantity depends on both β and c, hence let us write $q(\beta, c)$. Lemma 3 gives an explicit lower bound on c, depending only on β; let us write $c(\beta)$ for this bound. We are looking for the smallest β, where $q(\beta, c(\beta)) < 1$, which, in turn, will give us the smallest c for which our argument goes through. Using Gnuplot [9], we find that we can choose β as small as 2.57; then for $c \geq 8.83$, both lemmas (just) hold. For the analysis of the construction for arbitrary random graphs, given in the next section, the values are found in the same manner, though with a different q (see the proof of Lemma 2), and with $\varepsilon = 2.01$, because the construction there requires that $\varepsilon > 2$.

4   Constructing the Trees for Arbitrary Random Graphs

For a given non-maximum matching of a graph G from $G(n)$, consider an augmenting path and pick its two free endpoints, f_1 and f_2. The procedure for constructing T_1 and T_2 is similar as for bipartite graphs but with three complications: (i) two vertices from the neighborhood of $\text{Even}(T_1)$ or of $\text{Even}(T_2)$ may be incident to the same matching edge, so that we can add only one of them to the tree (step 5 below), (ii) the disjointness of the neighborhoods of $\text{Even}(T_1)$ and $\text{Even}(T_2)$ has to be taken care of explicitly now (step 6 below), and (iii) because only part of the neighborhood of $\text{Even}(T)$ is eventually added to T, for $T = T_1, T_2$, starting from the free vertices alone it could now indeed happen that $\Gamma(T_1) = \emptyset$ or $\Gamma(T_2) = \emptyset$ in one of the first $\alpha \log n$ iterations; therefore in step 0 we now start with a piece of size $2\lceil \alpha \log n \rceil$ of the augmenting path for each tree.

0. Let T_1 be the prefix of length $2\lceil \alpha \log n \rceil$ of the augmenting path starting at f_1, and let T_2 be the suffix of length $2\lceil \alpha \log n \rceil$. If the two are not disjoint, i.e., the length of the augmenting path is $4\alpha \log n$ or less, remove $T_1 \cap T_2$ from one of the trees and STOP (the properties of Lemma 1 are then fulfilled). Otherwise, $|\text{Even}(T_1)|, |\text{Even}(T_2)| \geq \alpha \log n$, and each of the following iterations will add two more levels to both T_1 and T_2.

1. Let $\Gamma(T_1) = \Gamma_G(\text{Even}(T_1)) \backslash (T_1 \cup \text{Odd}(T_2))$, and let $\Gamma(T_2) = \Gamma_G(\text{Even}(T_2)) \backslash (T_2 \cup \text{Odd}(T_1))$.

2. If $\Gamma(T_1)$ or $\Gamma(T_2)$ contains a free vertex, STOP.

3. If $\Gamma(T_1)$ contains a vertex which is already contained in $\text{Even}(T_2)$, or vice versa, STOP.

4. If there is a matching edge between $\Gamma(T_1)$ and $\Gamma(T_2)$, add it, together with the endpoint and edge connecting it to (say) T_1, then STOP.

5. Let $\Gamma'(T)$ be a maximal subset of $\Gamma(T)$ in which no two vertices match each other, for $T = T_1, T_2$; then $|\Gamma'(T)| \geq \lceil |\Gamma(T)|/2 \rceil$.

6. Let $\Gamma''(T_1) \subseteq \Gamma'(T_1)$ and $\Gamma''(T_2) \subseteq \Gamma'(T_2)$ such that $|\Gamma''(T_1)| = |\Gamma''(T_2)| \geq \lfloor \min\{|\Gamma'(T_1)|, |\Gamma'(T_2)|\}/2 \rfloor$ and $\Gamma''(T_1) \cap \Gamma''(T_2) = \emptyset$; this takes from $\Gamma'(T_1)$ and $\Gamma'(T_2)$ two maximally large subsets that are disjoint and of equal size (the worst case is when $\Gamma'(T_1)$ and $\Gamma'(T_2)$ are equal and of odd size).

7. Add to T the vertices from $\Gamma''(T)$, together with the edges connecting them to $\text{Even}(T)$ (not necessarily only to vertices at the largest level of T, as in the bipartite case), for $T = T_1, T_2$.

8. Add the matching edges incident to $\Gamma''(T)$ together with their other endpoints, to T, for $T = T_1, T_2$.

9. Repeat 1.–8.

Like in the bipartite case, it is easy to see that the properties of Lemma 1 are fulfilled. After step 0, T_1 and T_2 are disjoint, and by steps 3, 4, 5, and 6, disjoint sets of vertices are added to T_1 and T_2 in steps 7 and 8, which yields property (a). When the procedure stops in step 2, we have property (b1), if it stops in step 3 or 4, we have property (b2).

Let T denote one of the trees at the beginning of a fixed iteration, assuming that it has passed steps 2–4. Assume that $|\text{Even}(T)| < n/\beta$. Then by Lemma 2, applied with $\varepsilon = 2.01$ and $\beta = 6.19$, $|\Gamma_G(\text{Even}(T))| \geq (3 + 9\varepsilon')|\text{Even}(T)|$, where $\varepsilon' = 0.001$. Steps 0 and 6 ensure that at the beginning and end of every iteration, $|\text{Even}(T_1)| = |\text{Even}(T_2)|$, so that $|\text{Even}(T_1)|, |\text{Odd}(T_1)|, |\text{Even}(T_2), |\text{Odd}(T_2)|$ are all equal, and thus $|T_1 \cup \text{Odd}(T_2)| = |T_2 \cup \text{Odd}(T_1)| = 3|\text{Even}(T)| + 1$. Hence after step 1, $|\Gamma(T)| = |\Gamma_G(\text{Even}(T))| - (3|\text{Even}(T) + 1) \geq 9\varepsilon'|\text{Even}(T)| - 1 \geq 8\varepsilon'|\text{Even}(T)|$, where we assume without loss of generality that $\alpha \geq 1/\varepsilon'$ and hence $\varepsilon'|\text{Even}(T)| \geq \varepsilon'\alpha \log n \geq 1$. Then after step 5, $|\Gamma'(T)| \geq 4\varepsilon'|\text{Even}(T)|$, and since this holds for $T = T_1$ and for $T = T_2$, after step 6, $|\Gamma''(T)| \geq \lfloor 4\varepsilon'|\text{Even}(T)|/2 \rfloor \geq 2\varepsilon'|\text{Even}(T)| - 1 \geq \varepsilon'|\text{Even}(T)|$. In step 8, one vertex per vertex in $\Gamma''(T)$ is added, so that, if T' denotes the tree at the end of the iteration, we have

$$|\text{Even}(T')| = |\text{Even}(T)| + |\Gamma''(T)| \geq |\text{Even}(T)| + \varepsilon'|\text{Even}(T)| = (1+\varepsilon')|\text{Even}(T)|.$$

This proves that within $O(\log n)$ iterations, either the procedure terminates or at some point $|\text{Even}(T_1)| = |\text{Even}(T_2)| \geq n/\beta$.

As for the bipartite case, once $\text{Even}(T_1)$ and $\text{Even}(T_2)$ contain n/β or more vertices each, by Lemma 3 there will be an edge between the two sets, and the procedure will stop in step 3. This proves that with high probability the procedure terminates within $O(\log n)$ iterations, so that upon termination both trees have depth $O(\log n)$. This finishes the proof of Theorem 1 for arbitrary random graphs.

5   Conclusion

We proved that in a random graph on n vertices with high probability every non-maximum matching has an augmenting path of length $O(\log n)$. Motwani could prove this when the average degree is at least $\ln n$, whereas we only require that c is above a certain constant. Our expansion lemma is more powerful than Motwani's and at the same time makes the whole analysis simpler; in fact, the present writeup contains all proofs with all details.

While the expansion property on which the analysis in [12] is built does not hold when c is significantly smaller than $\ln n$, our condition on c does not appear to reflect a principal limit of our analysis. More refined versions of Lemma 2 (an idea would be to consider augmenting path trees which have expansion not in every level but only over a certain constant number of levels, we have not pursued this further yet), and of Lemma 3 (so far, we have not exploited the special structure of the two large sets between which we need an edge), might well be able to do without any condition on c.

References

1. M. Aigner and G. M. Ziegler. *Proofs from THE BOOK*. Springer, 2001.
2. B. V. Cherkassky, A. V. Goldberg, P. Martin, J. C. Setubal, and J. Stolfi. Augment or push: A computational study of bipartite matching and unit-capacity flow algorithms. *The ACM Journal of Experimental Algorithmics*, 3, 1998. http://www.jea.acm.org/1998/CherkasskyAugment.
3. J. Cheriyan and K. Mehlhorn. Algorithms for dense graphs and networks on the random access computer. *Algorithmica*, 15(6):521–549, 1996.
4. J. Edmonds. Maximum matching and a polyhedron with $(0, 1)$ vertices. *Journal of Research of the National Bureau of Standards*, 69(b):125–130, 1965.
5. J. Edmonds. Paths, trees and flowers. *Canadian Journal of Mathematics*, 17:449–467, 1965.
6. P. Erdös and A. Rènyi. On random graphs. *Publ. Math. Debrecen*, 6:290–297, 1959.

92   H. Bast et al.

7. T. Feder and R. Motwani. Clique partitions, graph compression and speeding-up algorithms. *Journal of Computer and System Sciences (JCSS)*, 51(2):261–272, 1995.
8. H. N. Gabow. An efficient implementation of Edmond's algorithm for maximum matching on graphs. *Journal of the ACM*, 23:221–234, 1976.
9. Gnuplot. http://www.gnuplot.info.
10. J. E. Hopcroft and R. M. Karp. An $n^{5/2}$ algorithm for maximum matchings in bipartite graphs. *SIAM Journal of Computing*, 2(4):225–231, 1973.
11. K. Mehlhorn and S. Näher. *LEDA: A Platform for Combinatorial and Geometric Computing*. Cambridge University Press, 1999.
12. R. Motwani. Average-case analysis of algorithms for matchings and related problems. *Journal of the ACM*, 41(6):1329–1356, 1994.
13. S. Micali and V. Vazirani. An $O(|V|^{0.5}|E|)$ algorithm for finding maximum matchings in general graphs. In *Foundations of Computer Science*, pages 17–27, 1980.

Algebraic Results on Quantum Automata

Andris Ambainis[1], Martin Beaudry[2], Marats Golovkins[1], Arnolds Ķikusts[1],
Mark Mercer[3], and Denis Thérien[3]

[1] Institute of Mathematics and Computer Science, University of Latvia,
Raiņa bulv. 29, Riga, Latvia[†]
{ambainis,marats}@lanet.lv, arnolds@usa.com
[2] Département de Mathématiques et d'Informatique 2500, Boul. Université,
Sherbrooke (PQ) J1K 2R1, Canada [‡]
beaudry@DMI.USherb.ca
[3] School of Computer Science, McGill University, 3480 rue University, Montréal
(PQ), H3A 2A7, Canada [‡]
{jmerce1,denis}@cs.mcgill.ca

Abstract. We use tools from the algebraic theory of automata to investigate the class of languages recognized by two models of Quantum Finite Automata (QFA): Brodsky and Pippenger's end-decisive model, and a new QFA model whose definition is motivated by implementations of quantum computers using nucleo-magnetic resonance (NMR). In particular, we are interested in the new model since nucleo-magnetic resonance was used to construct the most powerful physical quantum machine to date. We give a complete characterization of the languages recognized by the new model and by Boolean combinations of the Brodsky-Pippenger model. Our results show a striking similarity in the class of languages recognized by the end-decisive QFAs and the new model, even though these machines are very different on the surface.

1 Introduction

In the classical theory of finite automata, it is unanimously recognized that the algebraic point of view is an essential ingredient in understanding and classifying computations that can be realized by finite state machines, i.e. the regular languages. It is well known that to each regular language L can be associated a canonical finite monoid (its syntactic monoid, $M(L)$) and unsurprisingly the algebraic structure of $M(L)$ strongly characterizes the combinatorial properties of L. The theory of pseudo-varieties of Eilenberg (which in this paper will be called **M**-varieties for short) provides an elegant abstract framework in which these correspondences between monoids and languages can be uniformly discussed.

[†] Research supported by Grant No. 01.0354 from the Latvian Council of Science; European Commission, contract IST-1999-11234. Also for the fourth and fifth authors, the University of Latvia, Kristaps Morbergs fellowship.
[‡] Research supported by NSERC and FCAR.

V. Diekert and M. Habib (Eds.): STACS 2004, LNCS 2996, pp. 93–104, 2004.

Finite automata are a natural model for classical computing with finite memory, and likewise *quantum finite automata* (QFA) are a natural model for quantum computers that use a finite dimensional state space as memory. Quantum computing's more general model of *quantum circuits* [19] gives us an upper bound on the capability of quantum machines, but the fact that several years have passed without the construction of such circuits (despite the efforts of many scientists) suggests that the first quantum machines are not going to be this strong. Thus it is not only interesting but practical to study simpler models alongside of the more general quantum circuit model.

There are several models of QFA [17,15,8,5,9,7] which differ in what quantum measurements are allowed. The most general model (independently [9] and [7]) allows any sequence of unitary transformations and measurements. The class of languages recognized by this model is all regular languages. In contrast, the model of [17] allows unitary transformations but only one measurement at the end of computation. The power of QFAs is then equal to that of permutation automata [17,8] (i.e. they recognize exactly group languages). In intermediate models [15,8,5], more than one measurement is allowed but the form of those measurements is restricted. The power of those models is between [17] and [9,7] but has not been characterized exactly, despite considerable effort [4,2]. The most general model of QFAs describes what is achievable in principle according to laws of quantum mechanics while some of the more restricted models correspond to what is actually achieved by current implementations of quantum computers.

In view of the enduring success of the algebraic approach to analyze classical finite state devices, it is natural to ask if the framework can be used in the quantum context as well. The work that we present here answers the question in the affirmative. We will analyze two models of QFA: the model [8] and a new model whose definition is motivated by the properties of nucleo-magnetic resonance (NMR) quantum computing. Among various physical systems used to implement quantum computing, liquid state NMR has been the most successful so far, realizing quantum computers with up to 7 quantum bits [26]. Liquid state NMR imposes restrictions of what measurements can be performed, and the definition of the new model reflects this. In both cases we are able to provide an algebraic characterization for the languages that these models can recognize. It turns out that the class of languages recognized by these two models coincide almost exactly (that is, up to Boolean combinations), which is quite surprising considering the differences between the two models (for example, the NMR model allows mixed states while the [8] model does not). It is a pleasant fact that the M-variety that turns up in analyzing these QFA is a natural one that has been extensively studied by algebraists. Besides using algebra, our arguments are also based on providing new constructions to enlarge the class of languages previously known to be recognizable in these models, as well as proving new impossibility results using subspace techniques (as developed in [4]), information theory (as developed in [18]), and quantum Markov chains (as developed in [3]). In particular, we show that the Brodsky-Pippenger model cannot recognize the language $a\Sigma^*$ (it is already known [15] that Σ^*a is not recognizable), and that our new quantum model cannot recognize $a\Sigma^*$ or Σ^*a.

The paper is organized as follows. In Section 2 we give an introduction to the algebraic theory of automata and we define the models. In the next two sections we give our results on the two models we introduced, and in the last section we outline some open problems.

2   Preliminaries

2.1   Algebraic Theory of Automata

An **M**-variety is a class of finite monoids which is closed under taking submonoids, surjective homomorphisms, and direct products. Given an **M**-variety **V**, to each finite alphabet Σ we associate the class of regular languages $\mathcal{V}(\Sigma^*) = \{L \subseteq \Sigma^* : M(L) \in \mathbf{V}\}$. It can be shown that $\mathcal{V}(\Sigma^*)$ is a Boolean algebra closed under quotients (i.e. if $L \in \mathcal{V}(\Sigma^*)$ then for all $w \in \Sigma^*$ we have $w^{-1}L = \{x : wx \in L\} \in \mathcal{V}(\Sigma^*)$ and $Lw^{-1} = \{x : xw \in L\} \in \mathcal{V}(\Sigma^*)$) and inverse homomorphisms (i.e. if $\varphi : \Sigma^* \to \Sigma^*$ is a homomorphism and $L \in \mathcal{V}(\Sigma^*)$, then $\varphi^{-1}(L) \in \mathcal{V}(\Sigma^*)$). Any class of languages satisfying these closure properties is called a *-variety of languages. A theorem of Eilenberg [10] says that there is a 1-1 correspondence between **M**-varieties and *-varieties of languages: a driving theme of the research in automata theory has been to find explicit instantiations of this abstract correspondence.

The **M**-variety that plays the key role in our work is the so-called block groups [20], classically denoted **BG**. This variety is ubiquitous: it appears in topological analysis of languages [20], in questions arising in the study of non-associative algebras [6] and in constraint satisfaction problems [14]. It can be defined by the following algebraic condition: M is a block group iff for any $e = e^2$ and $f = f^2$ in M, $eM = fM$ or $Me = Mf$ implies $e = f$. For any language L, $M(L)$ is a block group iff L is a Boolean combination of languages of the form $L_0 a_1 L_1 \ldots a_k L_k$, where each $a_i \in \Sigma$ and each L_i is a language that can be recognized by a finite group: this class of languages is the largest *-variety that does not contain $a\Sigma^*$ or Σ^*a for arbitrary alphabet satisfying $|\Sigma| \geq 2$ [20].

2.2   Models

We adopt the following conventions. Unless otherwise stated, for any machine M where these symbols are defined, Q is the set of classical states, Σ is the input alphabet, q_0 is the initial state, and $Q_{acc} \subseteq Q$ ($Q_{rej} \subseteq Q$) are accepting (rejecting) states. If Q_{acc} and Q_{rej} are defined then we require $Q_{acc} \cap Q_{rej} = \emptyset$. Also, each model in this paper uses distinct start and endmarkers, ¢ and $ respectively. On input w, M processes the characters of ¢$w$$ from left to right.

Let $|Q| = n$. For all QFA in this paper, the state of the machine M is a *superposition* of the n classical states. Superpositions can be expressed mathematically as vectors in $\mathbb{C}^n$. For each $q \in Q$ we uniquely associate an element of the canonical basis of $\mathbb{C}^n$, and we denote this element $|q\rangle$. Now the superposition can be written as the vector $\sum_{q_i \in Q} \alpha_i |q_i\rangle$. We say α_i is the *amplitude* with which we are in state q_i. We now require each such vector to have an l_2 norm of 1, where the l_2 norm $\| \sum \alpha_i |q_i\rangle \|_2$ of $\sum \alpha_i |q_i\rangle$ is $\sqrt{\sum |\alpha_i|^2}$. Superpositions are also sometimes called *pure states*. There are also cases where the quantum state of the machine is a random variable; in other words, the state is a 'classical' probability distribution of superpositions $\{(p_i, \psi_i)\}$, each ψ_i with probability p_i. In this case we say the system is in a *mixed state*. Mixed states can be expressed in terms of *density matrices* [19], and these are usually denoted ρ.

A *transformation* of a superposition is a linear transformation with respect to a unitary matrix. $A \in \mathbb{C}^{n \times n}$ is called unitary if $A^* = A^{-1}$, where A^* is the Hermitian conjugate of A and is obtained by taking the conjugate of every element in A^T. Unitary transformations are length preserving, and they are closed under product. A set $\{A_\sigma\}$ of transformations is defined for each machine, with one transformation for each $\sigma \in \Sigma \cup \{\mathcal{c}, \$\}$.

An outside observer cannot gain a priori information about the state of a quantum mechanical system except through a *measurement* operation. A measurement of a superposition ψ probabilistically projects ψ onto exactly one of j prespecified disjoint subspaces $E_1 \oplus \cdots \oplus E_j$ spanning $\mathbb{C}^n$. The index of the selected subspace is communicated to the outside observer. For all i, let P_i be the projection operator for E_i. Then the probability of projecting into E_i while measuring $E_1 \oplus \cdots \oplus E_j$ is $\|P_i \psi\|_2^2$.

We will consider two modes of acceptance. For a probabilistic machine M, we say M recognizes L with *bounded (two-sided) error* if M accepts any $w \in L$ and rejects any $w \notin L$ with probability at least p, where $p > \frac{1}{2}$. We say M recognizes L with *bounded positive one-sided error* if any $w \in L$ is accepted with probability $p > 0$ and any $w \notin L$ is rejected with probability 1.

Liquid state NMR is the technique used to implement quantum computing on 7 quantum bits [26]. NMR uses nuclei of atoms as quantum bits, and the state of the machine is a molecule in which 7 different atoms can be individually adressed. One of features of NMR is that quantum transformations are simultaneously applied to a liquid containing 10^{21} molecules. Thus, we have the same quantum computation carried out by 10^{21} identical quantum computers. Applying a measurement is problematic, however. On different molecules, the measurement can have a different result. We can determine the fraction of molecules that produce each outcome, but we cannot separate the molecules by the measurement outcome. Because of that, the operations performed cannot be conditional on the outcome of a measurement. On the other hand, measurements which do not affect the next transformation are allowed. This situation is reflected in the definition of our new model, given below:

Latvian QFA (LQFA). A superset of this model has been studied in [18,5]. A LQFA is a tuple $M = (Q, \Sigma, \{A_\sigma\}, \{P_\sigma\}, q_0, Q_{acc})$ such that $\{A_\sigma\}$ are unitary matrices, and $\{P_\sigma\}$ are measurements (each P_σ is defined as a set $\{E_1, \ldots, E_j\}$ of orthogonal subspaces). We define $Q_{rej} = Q \backslash Q_{acc}$ and we require that $P_\$$

is a measurement w.r.t. $E_{acc} \oplus E_{rej}$, where $E_{acc} = span\{Q_{acc}\}$ and $E_{rej} = span\{Q_{rej}\}$. Let ψ be the current state. On input σ, $\psi' = A_\sigma\psi$ is computed and then measured w.r.t. P_σ. After processing the \$, the state of M will be in either E_{acc} or E_{rej} and M accepts or rejects accordingly. The acceptance mode for LQFA is bounded error. This model is introduced as QRA-M-C in the classification of QFAs introduced in [12].

Also in [12], a probabilistic automata model related to LQFA was introduced, which they called '1-way probabilistic reversible C-automata' (we abbreviate this to PRA). A PRA is a tuple $M = (Q, \Sigma, \{A_\sigma\}, q_0, Q_{acc})$, where each A_σ is a *doubly stochastic* matrix. A matrix is doubly stochastic if the sum of the elements in each row and column is 1. The acceptance mode for PRA is bounded error. The two models are related in the following way: If M is a LQFA such that each P_σ measures with respect to $\bigoplus_{q \in Q} span\{|q\rangle\}$ for every $\sigma \in \Sigma$, then M can be simulated by a PRA. Conversely, a PRA can be simulated by a LQFA if each A_σ of the PRA has a *unitary prototype* [12]. A matrix $U = [u_{ij}]$ is a unitary prototype for $S = [s_{ij}]$ if for all i,j: $|u_{i,j}|^2 = s_{i,j}$. When S has a unitary prototype it is called unitary stochastic [16]. This relationship between LQFA and PRA is helpful in proving that certain languages are recognized by LQFA.

Brodsky-Pippenger QFA (BPQFA). The BPQFA model is a variation on the model introduced by Kondacs and Watrous [15] (we will call this model KWQFA). A KWQFA is defined by a tuple $M = (Q, \Sigma, \{A_\sigma\}, q_0, Q_{acc}, Q_{rej})$ where each A_σ is unitary. The state sets Q_{acc} and Q_{rej} will be halt/accept and halt/reject states, respectively. We also define $Q_{non} = Q\backslash(Q_{acc} \cup Q_{rej})$ to be the the the set of nonhalting states. Lastly, for $\mu \in \{acc, rej, non\}$ we define $E_\mu = span\{Q_\mu\}$, and P_μ to be the projection onto E_μ. Let ψ be the current state of M. On input σ the state becomes $\psi' = A_\sigma\psi$ and then ψ' is measured w.r.t. $E_{acc} \oplus E_{rej} \oplus E_{non}$. If after the measurement the state is in E_{acc} or E_{rej}, M halts and accepts or rejects accordingly. Otherwise, ψ' was projected into E_{non} and M continues. We require that after reading \$ the state is in E_{non} with probability 0. The acceptance mode for KWQFA is bounded error.

The BPQFA model is one of several variations introduced by Brodsky and Pippenger in [8], which they called 'end-decisive with positive one-sided error'. A BPQFA M is a KWQFA where M is not permitted to halt in an accepting state until \$ is read, and the acceptance mode is changed to bounded positive one-sided error. Any BPQFA can be simulated by a KWQFA [8].

3 Latvian QFA

Our main result for this model is a complete characterization of the languages recognized by LQFA:

Theorem 1. *LQFA recognize exactly those languages whose syntactic monoid is in* **BG**.

Proof: We begin by showing that the languages recognized by LQFA forms a *-variety of languages. It is straightforward to show:

Theorem 2. *The class of languages recognized by LQFA is closed under union, complement, inverse homomorphisms, and word quotient.*

Next, to prove that LQFA cannot recognize any language whose syntactic monoid is not in **BG**, we need to show that LQFA cannot recognize Σ^*a or $a\Sigma^*$. We note that LQFA are a special case of Nayak's EQFA model [18], and EQFAs cannot recognize Σ^*a. We sketch the proof that $a\Sigma^*$ is not recognizable below.

Theorem 3. *LQFAs cannot recognize $a\Sigma^*$.*

Finally, we prove the following theorem below:

Theorem 4. *LQFAs recognize any language whose syntactic monoid is in **BG**.*

This will compete the characterization.   □

Proof of Theorem 3 (sketch) Suppose the LQFA M recognized $a\Sigma^*$. Let ρ_w be the state of M on reading w as a density matrix. Suppose σ and τ are of the form $\sigma = \sum_{w\in S\subseteq a\Sigma^*} p_w\rho_w$, $\tau = \sum_{w\in T\subseteq b\Sigma^*} p_w\rho_w$ with $\sum p_w = 1$. By linearity we can distinguish between σ and τ using $P_\$$ with some fixed probability $p > 1/2$. We show that a sequence $\sigma_1, \sigma_2, \ldots$ of σ matrices and a sequence $\tau_1, \tau_2, \ldots$ of τ matrices converge to the same limit, causing a contradiction.

We will need some notions from quantum information theory [19]. A *completely positive superoperator* is a linear operation that is a completely positive map on the space of $d \times d$ (particularly, density) matrices. For any density matrix ρ, the *Von Neumann entropy* $S(\rho)$ of ρ is $\sum -\lambda_i \log \lambda_i$, where the λ_is are the eigenvalues of ρ. It can be shown that any sequence of unitary transformations and measurements forms a CPSO E satisfying $S(E\rho) \geq S(\rho)$ for any ρ.

For all CPSOs E, we define E' to be the (CPSO) operation that performs the operation E with probability $1/2$, and the identity otherwise.

Lemma 1. *For any CPSO E such that $S(E\rho) \geq S(\rho)$ and any mixed state ρ, the sequence $E'\rho, (E')^2\rho \ldots$ converges. Let E_{lim} be the map $\rho \to lim_{i\to\infty}(E')^i\rho$. Then, E_{lim} is a CPSO and $S(E_{lim}\rho) \geq S(\rho)$ for any density matrix ρ.*

Lemma 2. *Let A, B be two sequences of unitary transformations and measurements. Let $C = A_{lim}B_{lim}$ and $D = B_{lim}A_{lim}$. Then, $C_{lim} = D_{lim}$.*

Let A, B, be the operations corresponding to reading a, b. We also consider A_{lim}, B_{lim}, $C = A_{lim}B_{lim}$, $D = B_{lim}A_{lim}$, C_{lim} and D_{lim}. Let Q_a (Q_b) be the set of density matrices corresponding to all probabilistic combinations of states ρ_{ax} (ρ_{bx}). Let $\overline{Q_a}$ and $\overline{Q_b}$ be the closures of Q_a and Q_b.

Lemma 3. *Let ρ be the state after reading the start marker ¢. Then, $C_{lim}\rho \in \overline{Q_a}$ and $D_{lim}\rho \in \overline{Q_b}$.*

By Lemmas 2 and 3, there exists sequences corresponding to $C_{lim}\rho$ and $D_{lim}\rho$, that are respectively probabilistic combinations of ρ_{ax} and ρ_{bx}, and they converge to the same limit.   □

The next theorem will assist in our proof of Theorem 4.

Theorem 5. *LQFA can recognize languages of the form* $\Sigma^* a_1 \Sigma^* \ldots a_k \Sigma^*$.

Proof: We start with construction of a PRA that recognizes $\Sigma^* a_1 \Sigma^* \ldots a_k \Sigma^*$ with probability $(\frac{n-1}{n})^k$, where n is any natural number. We construct our PRA inductively on the length of the subword. For $k = 1$ we construct $M^{(1)} = (Q^{(1)}, q_0, \Sigma, \{A_\sigma^{(1)}\}, Q_{acc}^{(1)})$ as follows. Let $Q^{(1)} = \{q_0, q_2, \ldots, q_n\}$, $A_{a_1}^{(1)} = \frac{1}{n}\mathbf{1}$ (where $\mathbf{1}$ is a $n \times n$ matrix of all ones), $A_\sigma^{(1)} = I$ for all $\sigma \neq a_1$, and $Q_{acc}^{(1)} = Q^{(1)} \backslash \{q_0\}$. It is easy to check that this machine accepts any $w \in \Sigma^* a_1 \Sigma^*$ with probability $(\frac{n-1}{n})$ and rejects any $w \notin \Sigma^* a \Sigma^*$ with probability 1.

Assume we have a machine $M^{(i-1)} = (Q^{(i-1)}, q_0, \Sigma, \{A_\sigma^{(i-1)}\}, Q_{acc}^{(i-1)})$ recognizing inputs containing the subword $a_1 \ldots a_{i-1}$ with probability $(\frac{n-1}{n})^{i-1}$, we construct $M^{(i)} = (Q^{(i)}, q_0, \Sigma, \{A_\sigma^{(i)}\}, Q_{acc}^{(i)})$ recognizing inputs containing the subword $a_1 \ldots a_i$ with probability $(\frac{n-1}{n})^i$. Our augmentation will proceed as follows. First let $Q_{acc}^{(i)}$ be a set of $(n-1)^i$ new states all distinct from $Q^{(i-1)}$, and let $Q^{(i)} = Q^{(i-1)} \cup Q_{acc}^{(i)}$. For each of the states $q \in Q_{acc}^{(i-1)}$ we uniquely associate n-1 states $q_2, \ldots, q_n \in Q_{acc}^{(i)}$. We leave q_0 unchanged.

Finally, we construct each $A_\sigma^{(i)}$ from $A_\sigma^{(i-1)}$. Define $\tilde{A}_\sigma^{(i-1)}$ to be the transformation that acts as $A_\sigma^{(i-1)}$ on $Q^{(i-1)} \subset Q^{(i)}$ and as the identity elsewhere. We let $A_\sigma^{(i)} = \tilde{A}_\sigma^{(i-1)} B_\sigma^{(i)}$, where $B_\sigma^{(i)}$ is an additional transformation that will process the a_i character (note that the matrices are applied from right to left). For all $\sigma \neq a_i$ we define $B_\sigma^{(i)} = I$. For $\sigma = a_i$ and we define $B_\sigma^{(i)}$ so that, independently for each $q \in Q_{acc}^{(i-1)}$, the transformation $\frac{1}{n}\mathbf{1}$ is applied to $\{q, q_2, q_3, \ldots, q_n\}$. At the end we have a machine $M = M^{(k)}$ that recognizes $\Sigma^* a_1 \Sigma^*, \ldots, a_k \Sigma^*$.

To simplify notation, we define $Q^{(0)} = Q_{acc}^{(0)} = \{q_0\}$ and $B_\sigma^{(1)} = A_\sigma^{(1)}$ for all σ. The correctness of the construction follows from this lemma:

Lemma 4. *Let w be any word. As we process w with M, for all $0 \leq i < k$ the total probability of M being in one of the states of $Q^{(i)}$ is nonincreasing.*

Proof of Lemma 4: Every nontrivial A_σ matrix can be decomposed into a product of $B_{a_i}^{(i)}$ matrices operating on different parts of the state space. All of these matrices operate on the machine state in such a way that for any $\{q, q'\} \subseteq Q_{acc}^{(j)}$, at any time there is an equal probability of being in state q or q'. Thus it is sufficient to keep track of the total probability of being in $Q_{acc}^{(j)}$. For any $S \subseteq Q$, denote by $P(S)$ the sum probability of being in one of the states of S.

For all $0 \leq i < k$ the machine can only move from $Q^{(i)}$ to $Q \backslash Q^{(i)}$ when $B_{a_{i+1}}^{(i+1)}$ is applied, and this matrix has the effect of averaging $Q_{acc}^{(i)} \cup Q_{acc}^{(i+1)}$. Since $|Q_{acc}^{(i+1)}| = (n\text{-}1)|Q_{acc}^{(i)}|$, it follows that a $B_{a_{i+1}}^{(i+1)}$ operation will not increase $P(Q^{(i)})$ unless $P(Q_{acc}^{(i+1)}) > (n\text{-}1)P(Q_{acc}^{(i)})$. It can easily be shown by induction on the sequence of $B_{a_j}^{(j)}$ matrices forming the transitions of M that this condition is never satisfied. Thus $P(Q^{(i)})$ is nonincreasing for all i. $\qquad \square$

First we show that any $w \notin L$ is rejected with certainty. The transitions are constructed in such a way that M can only move from $Q^{(i-1)}$ to $Q^{(i)}$ upon reading a_i, and M cannot move from $Q^{(i-1)}$ to $Q^{(i+1)}$ in one step (even if $a_i = a_{i+1}$). Next we show that any $w \in L$ is accepted with probability $\left(\frac{n-1}{n}\right)^k$. After reading the first a_1, $P(Q_{acc}^{(1)}) \geq \left(\frac{n-1}{n}\right)$ and by Lemma 4 this remains satisfied until a_2 is read, at which point M will satisfy $P(Q_{acc}^{(2)}) \geq \left(\frac{n-1}{n}\right)^2$. Inductively after reading subword a, M satisfies $P(Q_{acc}) \geq \left(\frac{n-1}{n}\right)^k$. Thus M indeed recognizes $\Sigma^* a_1 \Sigma^* \ldots a_k \Sigma^*$.

All that remains is to show that we can simulate each A_σ using LQFA transformations. Recall that each A_σ is a product of $B_{a_i}^{(i)}$ matrices operating on different parts of the state space. If each $B_{a_i}^{(i)}$ has a unitary prototype, then each A_σ could be simulated using the series of l transformations and measurements. We first show that we can collapse this operation into one transformation and one measurement. Assume we have a sequence of l unitaries U_i on a space E, each of them followed by a measurement $E_{i1} \oplus \cdots \oplus E_{ik_i}$. Define a new space E' of dimension $(\dim E) \cdot \prod_i k_i$. It is spanned by states $|\psi\rangle|j_1\rangle \ldots |j_l\rangle$, $|\psi\rangle \in E$, $j_i \in \{0, \ldots, (k_i-1)\}$. Each U_i can be viewed as a transformation on E' that acts only on the $|\psi\rangle$ part of the state. Replace the measurements by unitary transformations V_i defined by:

$$V_i|\psi\rangle|j_1\rangle \ldots |j_i\rangle \ldots |j_l\rangle = |\psi\rangle|j_1\rangle \ldots |(j_i + j) \bmod k_i\rangle \ldots |j_l\rangle$$

for $|\psi\rangle \in E_{ij}$. Consider a sequence of l unitaries and l measurements on E. Starting from $|\psi\rangle$, it produces a mixed state $\{(p_i, |\psi_i\rangle)\}$, where each $(p_i, |\psi_i\rangle)$ corresponds to a specific sequence of measurement outcomes. Then, if we start $|\psi\rangle|j_1\rangle \ldots |j_l\rangle$ and perform $U_1, V_1, \ldots, U_l, V_l$ and then measure all of $j_1, \ldots, j_l$, the final state is $|\psi_i\rangle|j_1'\rangle \ldots |j_l'\rangle$ for some $j_1', \ldots, j_l'$ with probability p_i. Thus, when we restrict to $|\psi\rangle$ part of the state, the two sequences of transformations are effectively equivalent. Finally, composing the U_i and V_i transformations gives one unitary U and we get one unitary followed by one measurement. It is now sufficient to prove that each $B_{a_i}^{(i)}$ has a unitary prototype.

Observe that any block diagonal matrix such that all of the blocks have unitary prototypes is itself a unitary prototype, and that unitary prototypes are trivially closed under permutations. Each $B_{a_i}^{(i)}$ can be written as a block diagonal matrix, where each block is the 1×1 identity matrix or the $\frac{1}{n}\mathbf{1}$ matrix, so it remains to show that there is a unitary prototype for $\frac{1}{n}\mathbf{1}$ matrices. Coincidentally the quantum Fourier transform matrix [19], which is the basis for most efficient quantum algorithms, is a unitary prototype for $\frac{1}{n}\mathbf{1}$. This completes the proof that A_σ can be simulated by an LQFA, and the proof of the theorem.   □

Proof of Theorem 4: We give a PRA construction recognizing the language L defined by $w \in L$ if and only if $w = w_0 a_1 w_1 \ldots a_k w_k$ where for each i, $w_0 a_1 w_1 \ldots w_i \in L_i$ for some prespecified group languages $L_0, \ldots, L_k$. By the cancellative law of groups, this is sufficient to show that PRA recognize any language of the form $L_0 a_1 L_1 \ldots a_k L_k$. We will see that each transition matrix has a unitary prototype, thus there is an LQFA recognizing this language as well.

This along with the closure properties of LQFA is sufficient to prove that any language whose syntactic monoid is in **BG** is recognized by an LQFA.

For all i let $G_i = M(L_i)$. Also let $\varphi_i : \Sigma^* \to G_i$ and F_i be such that $\varphi_i^{-1}(F_i) = L_i$. We compose these groups into a single group $G = G_0 \times \cdots \times G_k$ with identity $1 = (1, 1, \ldots, 1)$.

Let $M = (Q, q_0, \Sigma, \{A_\sigma\}, Q_{acc})$ be a PRA recognizing the subword $a_1 \ldots a_k$ constructed as in Theorem 5. From M we construct $M' = (Q', q_0', \Sigma, \{A_\sigma'\}, Q_{acc}')$ recognizing L. We set $Q' = Q \times G$, $q_0' = (q_0, 1)$, $Q_{acc}' = Q_{acc} \times F_k$, and $A_\varphi = A_\$ = I$. For each $\sigma \in \Sigma$ define A_σ' as follows. Let P_σ be the permutation matrix that maps (q, g) to $(q, g\sigma)$ for each $q \in Q$ and $g \in G$. For each $1 \leq i \leq k$ let $A_{i\sigma}'$ be the matrix that, for each $f \in F_{i-1}$, acts as the transformation $B_\sigma^{(i)}$ on $Q^{(i)} \times \{f\}$ and as the identity everywhere else. Finally, $A_\sigma' = P_\sigma A_{\sigma 1}' \ldots A_{\sigma k}'$.

The A_σ' are constructed so that M' keeps track of the current group element at every step. If M is in state (q, g), then after applying $A_1', \ldots, A_k'$ it remains in $Q \times \{g\}$ with probability 1. The P_σ matrix 'translates' all of the transition probabilities from $Q \times \{g\}$ to $Q \times \{g\sigma\}$. Initially M is in $Q \times \{1\}$, so after reading any partial input w, M will be in $Q \times \{1w\}$ with probability 1. In this way M will always keep track of the current group element.

Each A_σ' matrix refines A_σ from the $\Sigma^* a_1 \Sigma^* a_2 \ldots a_k \Sigma^*$ construction in such a way that, on input σ after reading w, we do not move from $Q^{(i-1)}$ to $Q^{(i)}$ (the action performed by $B_{a_i}^{(i)}$) unless $\sigma = a_i$ and $w \in F_{i-1}$. This is exactly what we need to recognize L. The transition matrices can be simulated by LQFA by the same argument as in Theorem 5.

Lemma 5. *Let w be any word. As we process the characters of w in M, for all $0 \leq i < k$ the total probability of being in one of the states of $Q^{(i)} \times G$ is nondecreasing.*

Proof: Same argument as in Lemma 4 holds.

Proof of correctness: It is easy to see that M will reject any word not in L. We do not move out of $Q^{(0)} \times G$ unless we read a_1 in the correct context. Inductively, we do not move into Q_{acc} unless we have read each subword letter on the correct context and the current state corresponds to a group element $f \in F_k$. Now suppose $w \in L$. Rewrite w as $w_0 a_1 \cdots a_k w_k$. Clearly M does not move out of $Q^{(0)} \times G$ while reading w_0. The character a_1 is now read, and M moves to $(Q^{(1)} \times G) \backslash (Q^{(0)} \times G)$ with probability $\frac{n-1}{n}$. By the previous lemma, this probability does not decrease while reading w_1. So now after reading $w_0 a_1 w_1$ we will be in $Q_{acc}^{(1)} \times G$ with probability $\frac{n-1}{n}$. If a_2 is read we move to $Q^{(2)}$ with probability $(\frac{n-1}{n})^2$. By induction after reading $w_0 a_1 \ldots w_{k-1} a_k$ we move to $(Q^{(k)} \times G) \backslash (Q^{(k-1)} \times G)$ with total probability at least $(\frac{n-1}{n})^k$. Finally, after reading w_k we move to Q_{acc}' with total probability at least $(\frac{n-1}{n})^k$, and so we accept any $w \in L$ with this probability. By choosing a suitable n we can recognize L with arbitrarily high probability. $\qquad\square$

4   Results for BPQFA

Our main result for BPQFA is given below:

Theorem 6. *The language L has its syntactic monoid in* **BG** *iff it is a Boolean combination of languages recognized by BPQFA.*

Proof: Similar to the LQFA case, we first show that this class of languages forms a *-variety. BPQFAs have been shown to be closed under inverse homomorphisms and word quotient [8], and we get Boolean combinations by definition. Next, we give the lower bounds. It is known that BPQFA cannot recognize $\Sigma^* a$, since KWQFA cannot recognize $\Sigma^* a$ [15] and any BPQFA can be simulated by a KWQFA. This proof can be easily extended to Boolean combinations of BPQFA. We prove the following theorem later in the section:

Theorem 7. *The language $a\Sigma^*$ is not a Boolean combination of languages recognized by BPQFA.*

Thus L is a Boolean combination of languages recognized by BPQFA only if $M(L)$ is in **BG**. Finally, we prove the following upper bound, by extending a construction of [8] in a manner similar to Theorem 4:

Theorem 8. *Any language whose syntactic monoid is in* **BG** *is a Boolean combination of languages recognized by BPQFA.*

This completes the proof of the main result. $\square$

Proof of Theorem 7: We use a technique introduced in [15] to analyze BPQ-FAs. Let ψ be an unnormalized state vector of M. Define $A'_\sigma = P_{non} A_\sigma$, and for any word $w = w_1 \ldots w_k$ let $A'_w = A'_{w_k} \cdots A'_{w_1}$. Then if ψ is the start vector, the vector $\psi_w = A'_w \psi$ completely describes the probabilistic behaviour of M, since M halts while reading w with probability $1 - \|\psi_w\|_2^2$, and continues in state $\frac{\psi_w}{\|\psi_w\|_2}$ with probability $\|\psi_w\|_2^2$. We also use the following lemma from [4]:

Lemma 6. *[4] Let $\{x, y\} \subseteq \Sigma^+$. Then there are subspaces E_1, E_2 s.t. $E_{non} = E_1 \oplus E_2$ and (1) if $\psi \in E_1$, then $A'_x(\psi) \in E_1$ and $A'_y(\psi) \in E_1$ and $\|A'_x(\psi)\| = \|\psi\|$ and $\|A'_y(\psi)\| = \|\psi\|$; (2) if $\psi \in E_2$, then for any $\epsilon > 0$, and for any word $t \in (x|y)^*$ there exists a word $t' \in (x|y)^*$ such that $\|A_{tt'}(\psi)\| < \varepsilon$.*

We first show that, for any BPQFA M, any $\varepsilon > 0$, and for any two prefixes $v, w \in \{a, b\}^+$, there exists $v', w' \in \{a, b\}^*$ such that $\|A'_{vv'}\psi - A'_{ww'}\psi\|_2^2 < \varepsilon$. In other words, any input with prefix vv' is indistinguishable from an input with prefix ww' by M. Let $\psi = A'_\ell(|q_0\rangle)$, and let b be some letter in $\Sigma \backslash \{a\}$. As in Lemma 6, separate E_{non} into two subspaces E_1 and E_2 with respect to the words $x = a$ and $y = b$. Then we can rewrite ψ as $\psi = \psi_1 + \psi_2$, where $\psi_i \in E_i$. By the lemma, and since A'_a and A'_b act unitarily on E_1, for any ε' there exists v' and w' such that $\|A'_{vv'}\psi - \psi_1\|_2^2 < \varepsilon'$ and $\|A'_{ww'}\psi - \psi_1\|_2^2 < \varepsilon'$. For sufficiently small ε' we have $\|A'_{vv'}\psi - A'_{ww'}\psi\|_2^2 < \varepsilon$.

Suppose we have a language L that is a Boolean combination of m languages $L_1, \ldots, L_m$ recognized by BPQFA. As above, we can construct inductively on the L_i languages two words $v = v_1 v_2 \cdots v_m \in \{a, b\}^*$ and $w = w_1 w_2 \ldots w_m \in \{a, b\}^*$ such that av and bw are indistinguishable for every L_i. Thus we must have either $\{av, bw\} \subseteq L$ or $L \cap \{av, bw\} = \emptyset$. Either way, the Boolean combination of BPQFAs does not recognize $a\Sigma^*$. $\qquad\square$

Note that in our characterization we have to take 'Boolean combinations' because BPQFA are not closed under complement. This follows from the theorem below, which we will prove in the full version:

Theorem 9. *Over any Σ s.t. $\{a, b\} \subseteq \Sigma$, BPQFA cannot recognize $\overline{\Sigma^* b \Sigma^* a \Sigma^*}$.*

5   Conclusion

In this paper we have produced algebraic characterizations for the languages that can be recognized by Brodsky-Pippenger Quantum Finite Automata and by a new model which we called Latvian Quantum Finite Automata. A somewhat surprising consequence of our results is that the two models are equivalent in power, up to Boolean combinations. It has been shown that a language L is recognizable by an LQFA iff its syntactic monoid is a block group; hence membership in the class is decidable. The situation is more complicated for BPQFA since the corresponding class of languages is not closed under complement. The good news is that we have shown that the class forms what is known as a *positive* $*$-variety and thus is amenable to algebraic description through the mechanism of *ordered monoids* [22]. We know that this positive $*$-variety strictly contains the regular languages that are open in the group topology and a precise characterization seems to be within reach.

Another open problem is to characterize algebraically the Kondacs-Watrous model. It is an easy consequence of our results on BPQFA that KWQFA can recognize any language whose syntactic monoid is in **BG**. However, outside of **BG** the question of language recognition is still unresolved.

The class of languages recognized by KWQFA is known not be closed under union [4], hence does not form a $*$-variety. It is nevertheless meaningful to ask for an algebraic description of the $*$-variety generated by those languages. We conjecture that the right answer involves replacing block groups by a 1-sided version $\mathbf{V}$ of this $\mathbf{M}$-variety defined by the following condition: for any $e = e^2$ and $f = f^2$ in M, $eM = fM$ imply $e = f$. The corresponding variety of languages can be described as largest variety that does not contain $\Sigma^* a$ for $|\Sigma| \geq 2$.

References

1. A. Ambainis and R. Freivalds. 1-way Quantum Finite Automata: Strengths, Weaknesses, and Generalizations. *Proceedings of the 39th IEEE Symposium on Foundations of Computer Science*, pp. 332–341. 1998.

2. A. Ambainis, A. Ķikusts: Exact Results for Accepting Probabilities of Quantum Automata. *Theoretical Computer Science*, 295, pp. 3–25, 2003.
3. D. Aharonov, A. Ambainis, Julia Kempe, Umesh Vazirani. Quantum walks on graphs. *Proceedings of STOC'01*, pp. 50–59.
4. A. Ambainis, A. Ķikusts, and M. Valdats. On the class of Languages Recognized by 1-way Quantum Finite Automata. *Proceedings of STACS 2001*, pp. 75–86. 2001.
5. A. Ambainis, A. Nayak, A. Ta-Shma and U. Vazirani. Quantum dense coding and quantum finite automata. *Journal of ACM*, 49, pp. 496–511, 2002.
6. M. Beaudry, F. Lemieux, and D. Thérien. Finite loops recognize exactly the regular open languages, *Proceedings of the 24th ICALP Colloquium on Automata, Languages and Programming*, LNCS 1256, Springer-Verlag. 1997.
7. A. Bertoni, C. Mereghetti, B. Palano. Quantum computing: 1- way quantum finite automata. *Proceedings of DLT'2003*, LNCS 2730, pp. 1–20. 2003.
8. A. Brodsky and N. Pippenger. Characterizations of 1-Way Quantum Finite Automata", *SIAM Journal on Computing*, 31(5), pp. 1456–1478, 2002.
9. M. P. Ciamarra. Quantum Reversibility and a New Model of Quantum Automaton. *FCT 2001*, pp. 376–379.
10. S. Eilenberg. Automata, Languages and Machines Vol B. *Academic Press*. 1976.
11. C. Fuchs, J. van de Graaf. Cryptographic distinguishability measures for quantum mechanical states. *IEEE Transactions on Information Theory*, 45(4), pp. 1216–1227, 1999.
12. M. Golovkins and M. Kravtsev. Probabilistic Reversible Automata and Quantum Automata. *COCOON 2002*. pp. 574–583. 2002.
13. J. Gruska. Quantum Computing. *McGraw-Hill*, p. 160. 1999.
14. P. Jeavons, D. Cohen and M. Gyssens. *Closure Properties of Constraint Satisfaction Problems*. JACM, 44, 4. pp. 527–548. 1997.
15. A. Kondacs and J. Watrous. On the power of Quantum Finite State Automata. *FOCS 1997*, pp. 66–75. 1997.
16. A. Marshall, I. Olkin. Inequalities: Theory of Majorization and Its Applications. *Academic Press*, 1979.
17. C Moore, J. Crutchfield. Quantum Automata and Quantum Grammars. *Theoretical Computer Science*, 237(1-2), pp. 275–306, 2000.
18. A. Nayak. Optimal Lower Bounds for Quantum Automata and Random Access Codes. *Proc. 40th FOCS*, pp 369–377. 1997.
19. M. Nielsen, I. Chuang. *Quantum Computation and Quantum Information*, Cambridge University Press, 2000.
20. J. E. Pin. BG=PG: A success story. *NATO Advanced Study Institute Semigroups, Formal Languages and Groups*, pp. 33-47. 1995.
21. J. E. Pin. On languages accepted by finite reversible automata. *Proceedings of the 14th International Colloquium on Automata, Languages, and Programming*. LNCS 267, pp. 237–249. 1987.
22. J. E. Pin, A variety theorem without complementation, *Russian Mathematics (Izvestija vuzov.Matematika)* 39, pp. 80–90. 1995.
23. J. E. Pin. Varieties of Formal Languages. *North Oxford Academic Publishers, Ltd, London*. 1986.
24. M. Rabin. Probabilistic Automata. *Information and Control*, 6(3), pp. 230–245. September 1963.
25. I. Simon. Piecewise Testable Events. *Proc. 2nd GI Conf.*, pp. 214–222, 1975.
26. L. Vandersypen, M. Steffen, G. Breyta, C. Yannoni, M. Sherwood, I Chuang. Experimental realization of Shor's quantum factoring algorithm using nuclear magnetic resonance. *Nature*, 414, 883–887, 2001.

Quantum Identification of Boolean Oracles

Andris Ambainis[1], Kazuo Iwama[2,3], Akinori Kawachi[2,3], Hiroyuki Masuda[2,3],
Raymond H. Putra[2,3], and Shigeru Yamashita[4]

[1] Institute of Mathematics and Computer Science, University of Latvia
ambainis@lanet.lv
[2] Quantum Computation and Information, ERATO,
Japan Science and Technology Corporation (JST)
[3] Graduate School of Informatics, Kyoto University
{iwama, kawachi, hiroyuki, raymond}@kuis.kyoto-u.ac.jp
[4] Graduate School of Information Science, Nara Institute of Science and Technology
ger@is.aist-nara.ac.jp

Abstract. The oracle identification problem (OIP) is, given a set S of
M Boolean oracles out of 2^N ones, to determine which oracle in S is the
current black-box oracle. We can exploit the information that candidates
of the current oracle is restricted to S. The OIP contains several concrete
problems such as the original Grover search and the Bernstein-Vazirani
problem. Our interest is in the quantum query complexity, for which
we present several upper bounds. They are quite general and mostly
optimal: (i) The query complexity of OIP is $O(\sqrt{N \log M \log N} \log \log M)$
for *any* S such that $M = |S| > N$, which is better than the obvious
bound N if $M < 2^{N/\log^3 N}$. (ii) It is $O(\sqrt{N})$ for *any* S if $|S| = N$,
which includes the upper bound for the Grover search as a special case.
(iii) For a wide range of oracles ($|S| = N$) such as random oracles and
balanced oracles, the query complexity is $O(\sqrt{N/K})$, where K is a simple
parameter determined by S.

1 Introduction

An *oracle* is given as a Boolean function of n variables, denoted by
$f(x_0, \ldots, x_{n-1})$, and so there are 2^{2^n} (or 2^N for $N = 2^n$) different oracles.
An *oracle computation* is, given a specific oracle f which we do not know, to determine, through queries to the oracle, whether or not f satisfies a certain property. Note that f has N black-box 0/1-values, $f(0, \ldots, 0)$ through $f(1, \ldots, 1)$.
($f(0, \ldots, 0)$ is also denoted as $f(0)$, $f(1, \ldots, 1)$ as $f(N-1)$, and similarly for an
intermediate $f(j)$.) So, in other words, we are asked whether or not these N bits
satisfy the property. There are many interesting such properties: For example,
it is called *OR* if the question is whether all the N bits are 0 and *Parity* if the
question is whether the N bits include an even number of 1's. The most general
question (or job in this case) is to obtain all the N bits. Our complexity measure
is the so-called *query complexity*, i.e., the number of oracle calls, to get a right
answer with bounded error. Note that the trivial upper bound is N since we can

V. Diekert and M. Habib (Eds.): STACS 2004, LNCS 2996, pp. 105–116, 2004.
© Springer-Verlag Berlin Heidelberg 2004

tell all the N bits by asking $f(0)$ through $f(N-1)$. If we use a classical computer, this N is also a lower bound in most cases. If we use a quantum computer, however, several interesting speedups are obtained. For example, the previous three problems have a (quantum) query complexity of $O(\sqrt{N})$, $\frac{N}{2}$ and $\frac{N}{2} + \sqrt{N}$, respectively [22,12,20,18].

In this paper, we discuss the following problem which we call the *oracle identification* problem: We are given a set S of M different oracles out of the 2^N ones for which we have the complete information (i.e., for each of the 2^N oracles, we know whether it is in S or not). Now we are asked to determine which oracle in S is currently in the black-box. A typical example is the Grover search [22] where $S = \{f_0, \ldots, f_{N-1}\}$ and $f_i(j) = 1$ iff $i = j$. (Namely, exactly one bit among the N bits is 1 in each oracle in S. Finding its position is equivalent to identifying the oracle itself.) It is well-known that its query complexity is $\Theta(\sqrt{N})$. Another example is the so-called Bernstein-Vazirani problem [14] where $S = \{f_0, \ldots, f_{N-1}\}$ and $f_i(j) = 1$ iff the inner product of i and j (mod 2) is 1. A little surprisingly, its query complexity is just one.

Thus the oracle identification problem is a promise version of the oracle computation problem. For both oracle computation and oracle identification problems, Ambainis developed a very general method for proving their lower bounds of the query complexity [4]. Also, many nontrivial upper bounds are known as mentioned above. However all those upper bounds are for specific problems such as the Grover search; no general upper bounds for a wide class of problems have been known so far.

Our Contribution. In this paper, we give general upper bounds for the oracle identification problem. More concretely we prove: (i) The query complexity of the oracle identification for *any* set S is $O(\sqrt{N \log M \log N} \log \log M)$ if $|S| = M > N$. (ii) It is $O(\sqrt{N})$ for *any* S if $|S| = N$. (iii) For a wide range of oracles ($M = N$) such as random oracles and balanced oracles, the query complexity is $O(\sqrt{\frac{N}{K}})$, where K is a parameter determined by S. The bound in (i) is better than the obvious bound N if $M < 2^{N/\log^3 N}$. Both algorithms for (i) and (ii) are quite tricky, and the result (ii) includes the upper bound for the Grover search as a special case. Result (i) is almost optimal, and results (ii) and (iii) are optimal; to prove their optimality we introduce a general lower bound theorem whose statement is simpler than that of Ambainis [4].

Related Results. Query complexity has constantly been one of the central topics in quantum computation; to cover everything is obviously impossible. For the upper bounds of the query complexity, the most significant result is due to Grover [22], known as the Grover search, which also derived many applications and extensions [10,12,16,23,24]. In particular, some results showed efficient quantum algorithms by combining the Grover search with other (quantum and classical) techniques. For example, quantum counting algorithm [15] gives an approximate counting method by combining the Grover search with the quantum Fourier transformation, and quantum algorithms for the claw-finding and the element distinctness problems [13] also exploit classical random sampling and sorting. Most recently, Ambainis developed an optimal quantum algorithm with

$O(N^{2/3})$ queries for element distinctness problem [6], which makes use of quantum walk and matches to the lower bounds shown by Shi [26]. Aaronson and Ambainis also showed an efficient quantum search algorithm for spacial regions [3] based on recursive Grover search, which is applicable to some geometrically structured problems such as search on a 2-D grid.

On the lower-bound side, there are two popular techniques to derive quantum lower bounds, i.e., the polynomial method and the quantum adversary method. The polynomials method was firstly introduced for quantum computation by [9] who borrowed the idea from the classical counterpart. For example, it was shown that for bounded error cases, evaluations of AND and OR functions need $\Theta(\sqrt{N})$ number of queries, while parity and majority functions at least $N/2$ and $\Theta(N)$, respectively. Recently, [1,26] used the polynomials method to show the lower bounds for the collisions and element distinctness problems.

The classical adversary method was used in [11,27], which is also called the hybrid argument. Their method can be used, for example, to show the lower bound of the Grover search. As mentioned above, Ambainis introduced a quite general method, which is known as the quantum adversary argument, for obtaining lower bounds of various problems, e.g., the Grover search, AND of ORs and inverting a permutation [4]. [7] recently established a lower bound of $\Omega(\sqrt{N})$ on the bounded-error quantum query complexity of read-once Boolean functions by extending [4], and [8] generalized the quantum adversary method from the aspect of semidefinite programming. Furthermore, [17,2] showed the lower bounds for graph connectivity and local search problem respectively using the quantum adversary method. Ambainis also gave a comparison between the quantum adversary method and the polynomial method [5].

2 Formalization

Our model is basically the same as standard ones (see e.g., [4]). An *oracle* is given as a Boolean function $f(x_0, \ldots, x_{n-1})$ of n variables, which transfers a quantum state from $|x_0, \ldots, x_{n-1}\rangle|b\rangle$ to $(-1)^{b \cdot f(x_0, \ldots, x_{n-1})}|x_0, \ldots, x_{n-1}\rangle|b\rangle$. A *quantum computation* is a sequence of unitary transformations $U_0 \to O \to U_1 \to O \to \cdots \to O \to U_t$, where O is a single oracle call against our *black-box oracle* (sometimes called an *input oracle*), and U_j may be any unitary transformation without oracle calls. The above computation sequence involves t oracle calls, which is our measure of the complexity (*the query complexity*). Let $N = 2^n$ and hence there are 2^N different oracles.

Our problem is called the *Oracle Identification Problem* (*OIP*). An OIP is given as an infinite sequence $S_1, S_2, S_4, \ldots, S_N, \ldots$. Each S_N ($N = 2^n, n = 0, 1, \ldots$) is a set of oracles (Boolean functions with n variables) whose size, $|S_N|$, is denoted by M ($\leq 2^N$). A (quantum) algorithm A which solves the OIP is a quantum computation as given above. A has to determine which oracle ($\in S_N$) is the current input oracle with bounded error. If A needs at most $g(N)$ oracle calls, we say that the query complexity of A is $g(N)$. It should be noted that A knows the set S_N completely; what is unknown for A is the current input oracle.

For example, the Grover search is an OIP whose S_N contains N (i.e., $M = N$) Boolean functions $f_1, \ldots, f_N$ such that

$$f_i(j) = 1 \quad \text{iff} \quad i = j.$$

Note that $f(j)$ means $f(a_0, a_1, \ldots, a_{n-1})$ ($a_i = 0$ or 1) such that $a_0, \ldots, a_{n-1}$ is the binary representation of the number j. Note that S_N is given as a $N \times M$ Boolean matrix. More formally, the entry at row i ($0 \le i \le M - 1$) and column j ($0 \le j \le N - 1$) shows $f_i(j)$. Fig. 1 shows such a matrix of the Grover search for $N = M = 16$. Each row corresponds to each oracle in S_N and each column to its Boolean value. Fig. 2 shows another famous example given by an $N \times N$ matrix, which is called the Bernstein-Vazirani problem [14]. It is well known that there is an algorithm whose query complexity is just one for this problem [14].

As described in the previous section, there are several similar (but different subtly) settings. For example, the problem in [25,4] is given as a matrix which includes all the rows (oracles) each of which contains $N/2$ 1's or $(1/2 + \varepsilon)N$ 1's for $\varepsilon > 0$. We do not have to identify the current input oracle itself but have only to answer whether the current oracle has $N/2$ 1's or not. (The famous Deutsch-Jozsa problem [19] is its special case.) The l-target Grover search is given as a matrix consisting of all (or a part of) the rows containing l 1's. Again we do not have to identify the current input oracle but have to answer with a column which has value 1 in the current input. Fig. 3 shows an example, where each row contains $N/2 + 1$ ones. One can see that the multi-target Grover search is easy ($O(1)$ queries are enough since we have roughly one half 1's), but identifying the input oracle itself is much harder.

In [4], Ambainis gave a very general lower bounds for oracle computation. When applying to the OIP (the original statement is more general), it claims the following:

Proposition 1. *Let S_N be a given set of oracles, and X, Y be two disjoint subsets of S_N. Let $R \subset X \times Y$ be such that*
1. For every $f_a \in X$, there exist at least m different $f_b \in Y$ such that $(f_a, f_b) \in R$.
2. For every $f_b \in Y$, there exist at least m' different $f_a \in X$ such that $(f_a, f_b) \in R$.
Let $l_{f_a, i}$ be the number of $f_b \in Y$ such that $(f_a, f_b) \in R$ and $f_a(i) \ne f_b(i)$ and $l_{f_b, i}$ be the number of $f_a \in X$ such that $(f_a, f_b) \in R$ and $f_a(i) \ne f_b(i)$. Let l_{max} be the maximum of $l_{f_a, i} l_{f_b, i}$ over all $(f_a, f_b) \in R$ and $i \in \{0, \ldots, N - 1\}$ such that $f_a(i) \ne f_b(i)$. Then, the query complexity for S_N is $\Omega\left(\sqrt{\frac{mm'}{l_{max}}}\right)$.

In this paper, we always assume that $M \ge N$. If $M \le N/2$, then we can select M columns out of the N ones while keeping the uniqueness property of each oracle. Then by changing the state space from n bits to at most $n - 1$ bits, we have a new $M \times M$ matrix, i.e., a smaller OIP problem.

3   General Upper Bounds

As mentioned in the previous section, we have a general lower bound for the OIP. But we do not know any nontrivial general upper bounds. In this section,

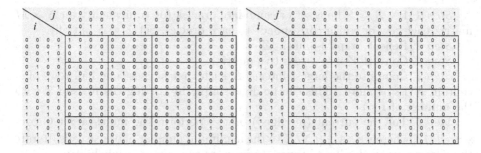

Fig. 1. $f_i(j) = 1$ iff $i = j$ **Fig. 2.** $f_i(j) = i \cdot j = \sum_x i_x \cdot j_x$ mod 2

we give two general upper bounds for the case that $M > N$ and for the case that $M = N$. The former is almost tight as described after the theorem, and the latter includes the upper bound for the Grover search as a special case. An $N \times M$ OIP denotes an OIP whose S_N (or simply S by omitting the subscript) is given as an $N \times M$ matrix as described in the previous section. Before proving the theorems, we introduce a convenient technique called a *Column Flip*.

Column Flip. Suppose that S is any $N \times M$ matrix (a set of M oracles). Then any quantum computation for S can be transformed into a quantum computation for an $N \times M$ matrix S' such that the number of 1's is less than or equal to the number of 0's in every column. (We say that such a matrix is 1-*sensitive*.) The reason is straightforward. If some column in S holds more 1's than 0's, then we "flip" all the values. Of course we have to change the current oracle into the new ones but this can be easily done by adding an extra circuit to the output of the oracle.

Theorem 1. *The query complexity of any $N \times M$ OIP is $O(\sqrt{N} \log M \log N \log \log M)$ if $M > N$.*

Proof. To see the idea, we first prove an easier bound, i.e., $O(\sqrt{N} \log M \log \log M)$. (Since M can be an exponential function in N, this bound is significantly worse than that of the theorem.) If necessary, we convert the given matrix S to be 1-sensitive by Column Flip. Then, just apply the Grover search against the input oracle. If we get a column j (the input oracle has 1 there), then we can eliminate all the rows having 0 in that column. The number of such removed rows is at least one half by the 1-sensitivity. Just repeat this (including the conversion to 1-sensitive matrices) until the number of rows becomes 1, which needs $O(\log M)$ rounds. Each Grover Search needs $O(\sqrt{N})$ oracle calls. Since we perform many Grover searches, the $\log \log M$ term is added to take care of the success probability.

In this algorithm we counted $O(\sqrt{N})$ oracle calls for the Grover search, which is the target of our improvement. More precisely, our algorithm is the following quantum procedure. Let $S = \{f_0, ..., f_{M-1}\}$ be the given $N \times M$ matrix:

Step 1. Let $Z \subseteq S$ be a set of candidate oracles (or equivalently an $N \times M$ matrix each row of which corresponds to each oracle). Set $Z = S$ initially.

Step 2. Repeat Steps 3-6 until $|Z| = 1$.

Step 3. Convert Z into 1-sensitive matrix.

Step 4. Compute the largest integer K such that at least one half rows of Z contain K 1's or more. (This can be done simply by sorting the rows of Z with the number of 1's.)

Step 5. For the current (modified) oracle, perform the multi-target Grover search [12] where we set $\frac{9}{2}\sqrt{N/K}$ to the maximum number of oracle calls. Iterate this Grover search $\log \log M$ times (to increase the success probability).

Step 6. If we succeeded in finding 1 by the Grover search in the previous step, i.e., a column j such that the current oracle actually has 1 in that column, then eliminate all the rows of Z having 0 in their column j. (Let Z be this reduced matrix.) Otherwise eliminate all the rows of Z having at least K 1's.

Now we estimate the number of oracle calls in this algorithm. Let M_r and K_r be the number of the rows of Z and the value of K in the r-th repetition respectively. Initially, $M_1 = M$. Note that the number of the rows of Z becomes $|Z|/2$ or less after Step 6, i.e., $M_{r+1} \leq M_r/2$ even if the Grover search is successful or not in Step 5 since the number of 1's in each column of the modified matrix is less than $|Z|/2$ and the number of the rows which have at least K 1's is $|Z|/2$ or more. Assuming that we need the T repetitions to identify the current input oracle, the total number of the oracle calls is

$$\frac{9}{2}\left(\sqrt{\frac{N}{K_1}} + \cdots + \sqrt{\frac{N}{K_T}}\right) \log \log M.$$

We estimate the lower bounds of K_r. Note that there are no identical rows in Z and the number of possible rows that contain at most K_r 1's is $\sum_{i=0}^{K_r}\binom{N}{i}$ in the r-th repetition. Thus, it must hold that $\frac{M_r}{2} \leq \sum_{i=0}^{K_r}\binom{N}{i}$. Since $\sum_{i=0}^{K_r}\binom{N}{i} \leq 2N^{K_r}$, $K_r = \Omega\left(\frac{\log M_r}{\log N}\right)$ if $M_r \geq N$, otherwise $K_r \geq 1$. Therefore the number of the oracle calls is at most

$$\frac{9}{2}\sqrt{N} \log \log M \sum_{i=1}^{T'}\sqrt{\frac{\log N}{\log M_i}} + \frac{9}{2}\sqrt{N} \log \log M \log N,$$

where the number of rows of Z becomes N or less after the T'-th repetition. For $\{M_1, ..., M_{T'}\}$, there exists a sequence of integers $\{k_1, ..., k_{T'}\}$ $(1 \leq k_1 < \cdots < k_{T'} \leq \log M)$ such that

$$1 \leq \frac{M}{2^{k_{T'}}} < M_{T'} \leq \frac{M}{2^{k_{T'}-1}} \leq \cdots \leq \frac{M}{2^{k_2}} < M_2 \leq \frac{M}{2^{k_1}} < M_1 = M$$

since $M_r/2 \geq M_{r+1}$ for $r = 1, ..., T'$. Thus, we have

$$\sum_{i=1}^{T'}\frac{1}{\sqrt{\log M_i}} \leq \sum_{i=1}^{T'}\frac{1}{\sqrt{\log(M/2^{k_i})}} \leq \sum_{i=0}^{\log M-1}\frac{1}{\sqrt{\log M - i}} \leq 2\sqrt{\log M}.$$

Then, the total number of the oracle calls is $O\left(\sqrt{N \log M \log N} \log \log M\right)$.

Next, we consider the success probability of our algorithm. By the analysis of the Grover search in [12], if the number of 1's of the current modified oracle is larger than K_r in the r-th repetition, then we can find 1 in the current modified oracle with probability at least $1 - (3/4)^{\log\log M}$. This success probability worsens after T rounds of repetition but still keeps a constant as follows: $(1 - (3/4)^{\log\log M})^T \geq (1 - 1/\log M)^{\log M} = \Omega(1)$. $\square$

Theorem 2. *There is an OIP whose query complexity is $\Omega(\sqrt{\frac{N}{\log N}}\log M)$.*

Proof. This can be shown in the same way as Theorem 5.1 in [4] as follows. Let X be the set of all the oracles whose values are 1 at exactly K positions and Y be the set of all the oracles that have 1's at exactly $K + 1$ positions. We consider the union of X and Y for our oracle identification problem. Thus, $M = |X| + |Y| = \binom{N}{K} + \binom{N}{K+1}$, and therefore, we have $\log M < K \log N$. Let also a relation R be the set of all (f, f') such that $f \in X$, $f' \in Y$ and they differ in exactly a single position. Then the parameters in Theorem 5.1 in [4] take values $m = \binom{N-K}{1} = N - K$, $m' = \binom{K+1}{1} = K + 1$ and $l = l' = 1$. Thus the lower bound is $\Omega(\sqrt{(N-K)(K+1)})$. Since $\log M = O(K \log N)$, K can be as large as $\Omega(\frac{\log M}{\log N})$, which implies our lower bound. $\square$

Thus the bound in Theorem 1 is almost tight but not exactly. When $M = N$, however, we have another algorithm which is tight within a factor of constant. Although we prove the theorem for $M = N$, it also holds for $M = poly(N)$.

Theorem 3. *The query complexity of any $N \times N$ OIP is $O(\sqrt{N})$.*

Proof. Let S be the given $N \times N$ matrix. Our algorithm is the following procedure:

Step 1. Let $Z = S$. If there is a column in Z which has at least $\sqrt{N}$ 0's and at least $\sqrt{N}$ 1's, then perform a *classical* oracle call with this column. Eliminate all the inconsistent rows and update Z.

Step 2. Modify Z to be 1-sensitive. Perform the multi-target Grover search [12] to obtain column j.

Step 3. Find a column k which has 0 and 1 in some row while the column j obtained in the Step 2 has 1 in that row (there must be such a column because any two rows are different). Perform a *classical* oracle call with column k and remove inconsistent rows. Update Z. Repeat this step until $|Z| = 1$.

Since the correctness of the algorithm is obvious, we only prove the complexity. A single iteration of Step 1 removes at least $\sqrt{N}$ rows, and hence we can perform at most $\sqrt{N}$ iterations (at most $\sqrt{N}$ oracle calls). Note that after this step each column of Z has at most $\sqrt{N}$ 0's or at most $\sqrt{N}$ 1's. Since we perform the Column Flip in Step 2, we can assume that each column has at most $\sqrt{N}$ 1's. The Grover search in Step 2 needs $O(\sqrt{N})$ oracle calls. Since column j has at most $\sqrt{N}$ 1's, the classical elimination in Step 3 needs at most $\sqrt{N}$ oracle calls. $\square$

4   Tight Upper Bounds for Small M

In this section, we investigate the case that $M = N$ in more detail. Note that Theorem 3 is tight for the whole $N \times N$ OIP but not for its subfamilies. (For example, the Bernstein-Vazirani needs only $O(1)$ queries.) To seek optimal bounds for subfamilies, we introduce the following parameter: Let S be an OIP given as an $N \times M$ matrix. Then $\#(S)$ be the maximum number of 1's in a single column of the matrix. We first give a lower bound theorem in terms of this parameter, which is a simplified version of Proposition 1.

Theorem 4. *Let S be an $N \times M$ matrix and $K = \#(S)$. Then S needs $\Omega(\sqrt{M/K})$ queries.*

Proof. Without loss of generality, we can assume that S is 1-sensitive, i.e., $K \leq M/2$. We select X (Y, resp.) as the upper (lower, resp.) half of S (i.e., $|X| = |Y| = M/2$) and set $R = X \times Y$ (i.e., $(x, y) \in R$ for every $x \in X$ and $y \in Y$). Let δ_j be the number of 1's in the j-th column of Y. Now it is not hard to see that we can set $m = m' = \frac{M}{2}$, $l_{x,j} l_{y,j} = \max\{\delta_j(\frac{M}{2} - K_j + \delta_j), (\frac{M}{2} - \delta_j)(K_j - \delta_j)\}$ where K_j is the number of 1's in column j. Since $K_j \leq K$, this value is bounded from above by $\frac{M}{2} K$. Hence, Proposition 1 implies $\Omega\left(\sqrt{\frac{mm'}{l_{max}}}\right) \geq \Omega\left(\sqrt{\frac{(\frac{M}{2})^2}{\frac{M}{2}K}}\right) = \Omega\left(\sqrt{\frac{M}{K}}\right)$. $\square$

Although this lower bound looks much simpler than Proposition 1, it is equally powerful for many cases. For example, we can obtain $\Omega(\sqrt{N})$ lower bound for the OIP given in Fig. 3 which we denote by X. Note in general that if we need t queries for an matrix S, then we also need at least t queries for any $S' \supseteq S$. Therefore it is enough to obtain a lower bound for the matrix X' which consists of the $N/2$ upper-half rows of X and all the 1's of the right half can be changed to 0's by the Column Flip. Since $\#(X') = 1$, Theorem 4 gives us an lower bound of $\Omega(\sqrt{N})$.

Now we give tight upper bounds for three subfamilies of $N \times N$ matrices. The first one is not a worst-case bound but an average-case bound: Let $AV(K)$ be an $N \times N$ matrix where each entry is 1 with the probability K/N.

Theorem 5. *The query complexity for $AV(K)$ is $\Theta(\sqrt{N/K})$ with high probability if $K = N^\alpha$ for $0 < \alpha < 1$.*

Proof. Suppose that X is an $AV(K)$. By using a standard Chernoff-bound argument, we can show that the following three statements hold for X with high probability (Proofs are omitted). (i) Let c_i be the number of 1's in column i. Then for any i, $1/2K \leq c_i \leq 2K$. (ii) Let r_j be the number of 1's in row j. Then for any j, $1/2K \leq r_j \leq 2K$. (iii) Suppose that D is a set of any d columns in X (d is a function in α which is constant since α is a constant). Then the number of rows which have 1's in all the columns in D is at most $2 \log N$.

Our lower bound is immediate from (i) by Theorem 4. For the upper bound, our algorithm is quite simple. Just perform the Grover search independently d

times. Each single round needs $O(\sqrt{N/K})$ oracle calls by (ii). After that the number of candidates is decreased to $2 \log N$ by (iii). Then we simply perform the classical elimination, just as step 3 of the algorithm in the proof of Theorem 3, which needs at most $2 \log N$ oracle calls. Since d is a constant, the overall complexity is $O(\sqrt{N/K}) + \log N = \sqrt{N/K}$ if $K = N^\alpha$. $\square$

The second subfamily is called a *balanced matrix*. Let $B(K)$ be a family of $N \times N$ matrices in which every row and every column has exactly K 1's. (Again the theorem holds if the number of 1's is $\Theta(K)$.)

Theorem 6. *The query complexity for $B(K)$ is $\Theta(\sqrt{N/K})$ if $K \leq N^{1/3}$.*

Proof. The lower-bound part is obvious by Theorem 4. The upper-bound part is to use a single Grover search $+$ K classical elimination. Thus the complexity is $O(\sqrt{N/K} + K)$, which is $O(\sqrt{N/K})$ if $K \leq N^{1/3}$. $\square$

The third one is somewhat artificial. Let $H(k)$, called an *hybrid matrix* because it is a combination of Grover and Bernstein-Vazirani, be an matrix defined as follows: Let $a = (a_1, a_2, \ldots, a_{n-k}, a_{n-k+1}, \ldots, a_n)$ and $x = (x_1, x_2, \ldots, x_{n-k}, x_{n-k+1}, \ldots, x_n)$. Then $f_a(x) = 1$ iff (i) $(a_1, ..., a_{n-k}) = (x_1, ..., x_{n-k})$ and (ii) $(a_{n-k+1}, ..., a_n) \cdot (x_{n-k+1}, ..., x_n) = 0 \pmod 2$. Fig. 4 shows the case that $k = 2$ and $n = 4$.

Theorem 7. *The query complexity for $H(k)$ is $\Theta(\sqrt{N/K})$, where $K = 2^k$.*

Proof. We combine the Grover search [22,12] with BV algorithm[14] to identify the oracle f_a by determining the hidden value a of f_a. We first can determine the first $n - k$ bits of a. Fixing the last k bits to $|0\rangle$, we apply the Grover search using oracle f_a for the first $n - k$ bits to determine $a_1, ..., a_{n-k}$. It should be noted that $f_a(a_1, \ldots, a_{n-k}, 0, \ldots, 0) = 1$ and $f_a(x_1, \ldots, x_{n-k}, 0, \ldots, 0) = 0$ for any $x_1, ..., x_k \neq a_1, ..., a_k$. Next, we apply BV algorithm to determine the remaining k bits of a. This algorithm requires $O(\sqrt{N/K})$ queries for the Grover search and $O(1)$ queries for BV algorithm to determine a. Therefore we can identify the oracle f_a using $O(\sqrt{N/K})$ queries. $\square$

5   Classical Lower and Upper Bounds

The lower bound for the general $N \times M$ OIP is obviously N if $M > N$. When $M = N$, we can obtain bounds being smaller than N for some cases.

Theorem 8. *The deterministic query complexity for $N \times N$ OIP S with $\#(S) = K$ is at least $\lfloor \frac{N}{K} \rfloor + \lfloor \log K \rfloor - 2$.*

Proof. Let f_a be the current input oracle. The following proof is due to the standard adversary argument. Let A be any deterministic algorithm using the oracle f_a. Suppose that we determine $a \in \{0,1\}^n$ to identify the oracle f_a. Then the execution of A is described as follows: (i) In the first round, A calls the oracle

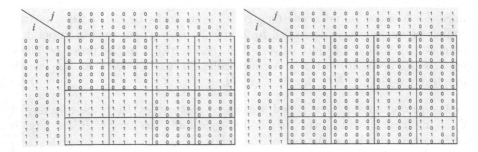

Fig. 3. Our problem is much harder   **Fig. 4.** $H(k)$ with $n = 4$ and $k = 2$

with the predetermined value x_0 and the oracle answers with $d_0 = f_a(x_0)$. (ii) In the second round, A calls the oracle with value x_1, which is determined by d_0 and the oracle answers with $d_1 = f_a(x_1)$. (iii) In the $(i+1)$-st round, A calls the oracle with x_i which is determined by $d_0, d_1, ..., d_{i-1}$ and the oracle answers with $d_i = f_a(x_i)$. (iv) In the m-th round A outputs a which is determined by $d_0, d_1, ..., d_{m-1}$ and stops. Thus, the execution of A is completely determined by the sequence $(d_0, d_1, ..., d_{m-1})$ which is denoted by $A(a)$. (Obviously, if we fix a specific a, then $A(a)$ is uniquely determined).

Let $m_0 = \lfloor N/K \rfloor + \lfloor \log K \rfloor - 3$ and suppose that A halts in the m_0-th round. We compute the sequence $(c_0, c_1, \dots, c_{m_0})$, $c_i \in \{0, 1\}$, and another sequence $(L_0, L_1, \dots, L_{m_0})$, $L_i \subseteq \{a | a \in \{0, 1\}^n\}$, as follows (note that $c_0, \dots, c_{m_0}$ are similar to $d_0, ..., d_{m-1}$ above and are chosen by the adversary): (i) $L_0 = \{0, 1\}^n$. (ii) Suppose that we have already computed $L_0, ..., L_i$, and $c_0, ..., c_{i-1}$. Let x_i be the value with which A calls the oracle in the $(i+1)$-st round. (Recall that x_i is determined by $c_0, ..., c_{i-1}$.) Let $L^0 = \{s \mid f_s(x_i) = 0\}$ and $L^1 = \{s \mid f_s(x_i) = 1\}$. Then if $|L_i \cap L^0| \geq |L_i \cap L^1|$ then we set $c_i = 0$ and $L_{i+1} = L_i \cap L^0$. Otherwise, i.e., if $|L_i \cap L^0| < |L_i \cap L^1|$, then we set $c_i = 1$ and $L_{i+1} = L_i \cap L^1$.

Now we can make the following two claims.

Claim 1. $|L_{m_0}| \geq 2$. (Reason: Note that $|L_0| = N$ and the size of L_i decreases as i increases. By the construction of L_i, one can see that until $|L_i|$ becomes $2K$, its size decreases additively by at most K in a single round and after that it decreases multiplically at most one half. The claim then follows by a simple calculation.)

Claim 2. If $a \in L_{m_0}$, then $(c_0, \dots, c_{m_0}) = A(a)$. (Reason: Obvious since $a \in L_0 \cap L_1 \cap \cdots \cap L_{m_0}$.)

Now it follows that there are two different a_1 and a_2 in L_{m_0} such that $A(a_1) = A(a_2)$ by Claims 1 and 2. Therefore A outputs the same answer for two different a_1 and a_2, a contradiction.   □

For the classical upper bounds, we only give the bound for the hybrid matrix. Similarly for $AV(K)$ and $B(K)$.

Theorem 9. *The deterministic query complexity for $H(k)$ is $O(\frac{N}{K} + \log K)$.*

Proof. Let f_a be the current input oracle. The algorithm consists of an exhaustive and a binary search to identify the oracle f_a by determining the hidden value a of f_a. First, we determine the first $n - k$ bits of a by fixing the last k bits to all 0's and using exhaustive search. Second, we determine the last k bits of a by using binary search. This algorithm needs $2^{n-k}(= \frac{N}{K})$ queries in the exhaustive search, and $O(k)(= O(\log K))$ queries in the binary search. Therefore, the total complexity of this algorithm is $O(2^{n-k} + k) = O(\frac{N}{K} + \log K)$. □

6   Concluding Remarks

Some future directions are as follows: The most interesting one is a possible improvement of Theorem 1, for which our target is $O(\sqrt{N \log M})$. Also, we wish to have a matching lower bound, which is probably possible by making the argument of Theorem 2 a bit more exact. As mentioned before, in a certain situation, we do not have to determine the current oracle completely but have only to do that "approximately", e.g., have to determine whether it belongs to some subset of oracles. It might be interesting to investigate how this approximation makes the problem easier (or basically not).

References

1. S. Aaronson. Quantum lower bound for the collision problem. In *Proceedings of the 34th Symposium on Theory of Computing*, pages 635–642, 2002.
2. S. Aaronson. Lower bounds for local search by quantum arguments. In *quant-ph/0307149*, 2003.
3. S. Aaronson and A. Ambainis. Quantum search of spatial regions. In *Proceedings of the 44th Symposium on Foundations of Computer Science*, pages 200–209, 2003.
4. A. Ambainis. Quantum lower bounds by quantum arguments. *Journal of Computer and System Sciences*, 64:750–767, 2002.
5. A. Ambainis. Polynomial degree vs. quantum query complexity. In *Proceedings of the 44th IEEE Symposium on Foundations of Computer Science*, pages 230–239, 2003.
6. A. Ambainis. Quantum walks and a new quantum algorithm for element distinctness. In *quant-ph/0311001*, Invited talk in EQIS 2003, 2003.
7. H. Barnum and M. Saks. A lower bound on the quantum complexity of read-once functions. In *Electronic Colloquium on Computational Complexity*, 2002.
8. H. Barnum, M. Saks, and M. Szegedy. Quantum query complexity and semi-definite programming. In *Proceedings of the 18th IEEE Conference on Computational Complexity*, pages 179–193, 2003.
9. R. Beals, H. Buhrman, R. Cleve, M. Mosca, and R. de Wolf. Quantum lower bounds by polynomials. In *Proceedings of 39th IEEE Symposium on Foundation of Computer Science*, pages 352–361, 1998.
10. D. Biron, O. Biham, E. Biham, M. Grassl, and D. A. Lidar. Generalized Grover Search Algorithm for Arbitrary Initial Amplitude Distribution. In *Proceedings of the 1st NASA International Conference on Quantum Computing and Quantum Communication, LNCS, Vol. 1509, Springer-Verlag*, pages 140–147, 1998.

11. C. Bennett, E. Bernstein, G. Brassard, and U. Vazirani. Strengths and weaknesses of quantum computing. *SIAM J. Comput.*, 26(5):1510–1523, 1997.
12. M. Boyer, G. Brassard, P. Høyer, and A. Tapp. Tight bounds on quantum searching. *Fortschritte der Physik*, vol. 46(4-5), 493-505, 1998.
13. H. Buhrman, C. Dürr, M. Heiligman, P. Høyer, F. Magniez, M. Santha and R. de Wolf. Quantum Algorithms for Element Distinctness. In *Proceedings of the 16th IEEE Annual Conference on Computational Complexity (CCC'01)*, pages 131–137, 2001.
14. E. Bernstein and U. Vazirani. Quantum complexity theory. *SIAM J. Comput.*, 26(5):1411–1473, October 1997.
15. G. Brassard, P. Høyer, M. Mosca, A. Tapp. Quantum Amplitude Amplification and Estimation. In *AMS Contemporary Mathematics Series Millennium Volume entitled "Quantum Computation & Information"*, to appear.
16. D. P. Chi and J. Kim. Quantum Database Searching by a Single Query. In *Proceedings of the 1st NASA International Conference on Quantum Computing and Quantum Communication, LNCS, Vol. 1509, Springer-Verlag*, pages 148–151, 1998.
17. C. Dürr, M. Mhalla, and Y. Lei. Quantum query complexity of graph connectivity. In *quant-ph/0303169*, 2003.
18. W. van Dam. Quantum oracle interrogation: getting all information for almost half the price. In *Proceedings of the 39th IEEE Symposium on the Foundation of Computer Science*, pages 362–367, 1998.
19. D. Deutsch, R. Jozsa. Rapid solutions of problems by quantum computation. In *Proceedings of the Royal Society, London, Series A*, 439, pages 553–558, 1992.
20. E. Farhi, J. Goldstone, S. Gutmann, and M. Sipser. A Limit on the Speed of Quantum Computation in Determining Parity. *Phys. Rev. Lett. 81*, 5442–5444, 1998.
21. E. Farhi, J. Goldstone, S. Gutmann, and M. Sipser. How many functions can be distinguished with k quantum queries? *Phys. Rev. A 60*, 6, 4331–4333, 1999.
22. L. K. Grover. A fast quantum mechanical algorithm for database search. In *Proceedings of the 28th ACM Symposium on Theory of Computing*, pages 212–219, 1996.
23. L. K. Grover. A framework for fast quantum mechanical algorithms. In *Proceedings of the 30th ACM Symposium on Theory of Computing*, pages 53–62, 1998.
24. L. K. Grover. Rapid sampling through quantum computing. In *Proceedings of the 32th ACM Symposium on Theory of Computing*, pages 618–626, 2000.
25. A. Nayak and F. Wu. The quantum query complexity of approximating the median and related statistics. In *Proceedings of the 31th ACM Symposium on Theory of Computing*, pages 384–393, 1999.
26. Y. Shi. Quantum lower bounds for the collision and the element distinctness problems. In *Proceedings of the 43rd IEEE Symposium on the Foundation of Computer Science*, pages 513–519, 2002.
27. U. Vazirani. On the power of quantum computation. *Philosophical Transaction of the Royal Society of London, Series A*, (356):1759–1768, 1998.

Local Limit Distributions in Pattern Statistics: Beyond the Markovian Models*

Alberto Bertoni[1], Christian Choffrut[2], Massimiliano Goldwurm[1], and Violetta Lonati[1]

[1] Dipartimento di Scienze dell'Informazione, Università degli Studi di Milano
Via Comelico 39/41, 20135 Milano – Italy
{bertoni,goldwurm,lonati}@dsi.unimi.it

[2] L.I.A.F.A. (Laboratoire d'Informatique Algorithmique, Fondements et Applications),
Université Paris VII, 2 Place Jussieu, 75221 Paris – France
Christian.Choffrut@liafa.jussieu.fr

Abstract. Motivated by problems of pattern statistics, we study the limit distribution of the random variable counting the number of occurrences of the symbol a in a word of length n chosen at random in $\{a, b\}^*$, according to a probability distribution defined via a finite automaton equipped with positive real weights. We determine the local limit distribution of such a quantity under the hypothesis that the transition matrix naturally associated with the finite automaton is primitive. Our probabilistic model extends the Markovian models traditionally used in the literature on pattern statistics.

This result is obtained by introducing a notion of symbol-periodicity for irreducible matrices whose entries are polynomials in one variable over an arbitrary positive semiring. This notion and the related results we prove are of interest in their own right, since they extend classical properties of the Perron–Frobenius Theory for non-negative real matrices.

Keywords: Automata and Formal Languages, Pattern statistics, Local Limit Theorems, Perron–Frobenius Theory.

1   Introduction

A typical problem in pattern statistics studies the frequency of occurrences of given strings in a random text, where the set of strings (patterns) is fixed in advance and the text is a word of length n randomly generated according to a probabilistic model (for instance, a Markovian model). In this context, relevant goals of research concern the asymptotic evaluations (as n grows) of the mean value and the variance of the number of occurrences of patterns in the text, as well as its limit distribution. This kind of problems are widely studied in the literature and they are of interest for the large variety of applications in different areas of computer science, probability theory and molecular biology (see for instance [8,12,11,14]). Many results show a normal limit distribution of the number of pattern occurrences in the sense of the central or local limit theorem [1]; here we recall

* This work has been supported by the Project M.I.U.R. COFIN 2003-2005 "Formal languages and automata: methods, models and applications".

V. Diekert and M. Habib (Eds.): STACS 2004, LNCS 2996, pp. 117–128, 2004.
© Springer-Verlag Berlin Heidelberg 2004

that the "local" result is usually stronger since it concerns the probability of single point values, while the "central" limit refers to the cumulative distribution function. In [10] limit distributions are obtained for the number of (positions of) occurrences of words from a regular language in a random string of length n generated in a Bernoulli or a Markovian model. These results are extended in [3] to the so-called *rational stochastic model*, where the pattern is reduced to a single symbol and the random text is a word over a two-letter alphabet, generated according to a probability distribution defined via a weighted finite automaton or, equivalently, via a rational formal series. The symbol frequency problem in the rational model includes, as a special case, the general frequency problem of regular patterns in the Markovian model studied in [10]. In the same paper [3], a normal local limit theorem is obtained for a proper subclass of primitive models. In this paper, we present a complete solution for primitive models, i.e. when the matrix associated with the rational formal series (counting the transitions between states) is primitive.

We now turn to a brief description of this paper. In Section 3, we introduce a notion of x-periodicity for irreducible matrices whose entries are polynomials in the variable x over an arbitrary positive semiring. Intuitively, considering the matrix as a labeled graph, its x-period is the GCD of the differences between the number of occurrences of x in (labels of) cycles of the same length. This notion and the related properties we prove are of interest in their own right, since they extend the classical notion of periodicity of non-negative matrices, studied in the Perron–Frobenius Theory for irreducible and primitive matrices [13]. In particular, these results are useful to study the eigenvalues of matrices of the form $Ax + B$, where A and B are matrices with coefficients in $\mathbb{R}_+$ and $x \in \mathbb{C}$ with $|x| = 1$ (see Theorem 2).

In Section 4 we prove our main result, concerning the local limit distribution of the random variable Y_n representing the number of occurrences of the symbol a in a word of length n chosen at random in $\{a, b\}^*$, according to any primitive rational model. Such a model can be described by means of a primitive matrix of the form $Ax + B$, where A and B are non-negative real matrices. If $Ax + B$ has x-period d, then we prove the existence of positive real constants α, β and non-negative real constants $C_0, C_1, \ldots, C_{d-1}$ with $\sum C_i = 1$ such that, as n tends to ∞, the relation

$$P\{Y_n = k\} = \frac{d\, C_{\langle k \rangle_d}}{\sqrt{2\pi\alpha n}} \cdot e^{-\frac{(k-\beta n)^2}{2\alpha n}} + o\left(\frac{1}{\sqrt{n}}\right)$$

holds uniformly for each $k = 0, 1, \ldots, n$ (here $\langle k \rangle_d = k - \lfloor k/d \rfloor$). If, in particular, $d = 1$ we get a normal local limit distribution, as already stated in [3].

2   Preliminaries

In this section we recall some basic notions and properties concerning rational formal series [2] and matrices over positive semirings [13].

2.1 Rational Formal Series and Weighted Automata

Let S be a positive semiring [9], that is a semiring such that $x+y = 0$ implies $x = y = 0$ and $x \cdot y = 0$ implies $x = 0$ or $y = 0$. Examples are given by $\mathbb{N}$, $\mathbb{R}_+$ or the Boolean algebra $\mathbb{B}$. Given a finite alphabet Σ, we denote by Σ^* the set of all finite strings over Σ and by 1 the empty word. Moreover, for each $w \in \Sigma^*$, we denote by $|w|$ its length and by $|w|_b$ the number of occurrences of the symbol $b \in \Sigma$ in w.

We recall that a *formal series* over Σ with coefficients in S is a function $r : \Sigma^* \longrightarrow S$. Usually, the value of r at w is denoted by (r, w) and we write $r = \sum_{w \in \Sigma^*} (r, w) \cdot w$. Moreover, r is called *rational* if there exists a *linear representation*, that is a triple (ξ, μ, η) where, for some integer $m > 0$, ξ and η are (column) vectors in S^m and $\mu : \Sigma^* \longrightarrow S^{m \times m}$ is a monoid morphism, such that $(r, w) = \xi^T \mu(w) \eta$ holds for each $w \in \Sigma^*$. We say that m is the *size* of the representation. Observe that considering such a triple (ξ, μ, η) is equivalent to defining a (weighted) non–deterministic automaton, where the state set is given by $\{1, 2, \ldots, m\}$ and the transitions, the initial and the final states are assigned weights in S by μ, ξ and η respectively.

It is convenient to represent the morphism μ by its *state diagram*, see Figure 1, which is a labeled directed graph where the vertices are given by the set $\{1, 2, \ldots, m\}$ and where there exists an edge with label $b \in \Sigma$ from vertex p to vertex q if $\mu(b)_{pq} \neq 0$. A *path* of *length* n is a sequence of labeled edges of the form

$$\ell = q_0 \xrightarrow{b_1} q_1 \xrightarrow{b_2} q_2 \ldots q_{n-1} \xrightarrow{b_n} q_n \; ;$$

in particular, if $q_n = q_0$ we say that ℓ is a q_0-cycle. Moreover we say that $w = b_1 b_2 \ldots b_n$ is the label of ℓ and we denote by $|\ell|_b = |w|_b$ the number of occurrences of b in ℓ.

Since we are interested in the occurrences of a particular symbol $a \in \Sigma$, we may set $A = \mu(a)$, $B = \sum_{b \neq a} \mu(b)$ and consider the *a-counting matrix* $M(x) = Ax + B$, which can be interpreted as a matrix whose entries are polynomials in $S[x]$ of degree lower than 2. Moreover, observe that for every $n \in \mathbb{N}$ we can write

$$\xi^T M(x)^n \eta = \sum_{|w|=n} (r, w) \cdot x^{|w|_a} . \tag{1}$$

Therefore $M(x)^n$ is related to the paths of length n of the associated state diagram, in the sense that the pq-entry of $M(x)^n$ is the sum of monomials of the form sx^k where $k = |\ell|_a$ for some path ℓ of length n from p to q in the state diagram.

2.2 Matrix Periodicity

We now recall the classical notion of periodicity of matrices over positive semirings. Given a finite set Q and a positive semiring S, consider a matrix $M : Q \times Q \to S$. We say that M is *positive* whenever $M_{pq} \neq 0$ holds for all $p, q \in Q$, in which case we write $M > 0$.

To avoid the use of brackets, from now on, we use the expression $M^n{}_{pq}$ to denote the pq-entry of the matrix M^n. For every index q, we call *period* of q the greatest common divisor (GCD) of the positive integers h such that $M^h{}_{qq} \neq 0$, with the convention that

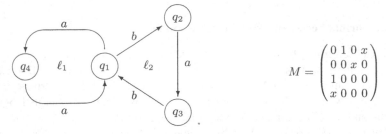

Fig. 1. Example of state diagram and a-counting matrix

$GCD(\varnothing) = +\infty$. Moreover, we recall that a matrix M is said to be *irreducible* if for every pair of indices p, q, there exists a positive integer $h = h(p, q)$ such that $M^h{}_{pq} \neq 0$; in this case, it turns out that all indices have the same period, which is finite and is called the *period* of M. Finally, the matrix is called *primitive* if there exists a positive integer h such that $M^h > 0$, which implies $M^n > 0$ for every $n \geq h$. It is well-known that M is primitive if and only if M is irreducible and has period 1.

When S is the semiring of positive real numbers an important result is given by the following theorem (see [13]).

Theorem 1 (Perron–Frobenius). *Let M be a primitive matrix with entries in $\mathbb{R}_+$. Then, M admits exactly one eigenvalue λ of maximum modulus (called the Perron–Frobenius eigenvalue of M), which is a simple root of the characteristic polynomial of M. Moreover, λ is real and positive and there exist strictly positive left and right eigenvectors u and v associated with λ such that $v^T u = 1$.*

A consequence of this theorem is that, for any primitive matrix M with entries in $\mathbb{R}_+$, the relation $M^n \sim \lambda^n \cdot uv^T$ holds as n tends to $+\infty$, where λ, u and v are defined as above. A further application is given by the following proposition [13, Exercise 1.9], to be used in the next sections.

Proposition 1. *Let C be a complex matrix, set $|C| = (|C_{pq}|)$ and let γ be one of the eigenvalues of C. If M is a primitive matrix over $\mathbb{R}_+$ such that $|C_{pq}| \leq M_{pq}$ for every p, q and if λ is its Perron–Frobenius eigenvalue, then $|\gamma| \leq \lambda$. Moreover, if $|\gamma| = \lambda$, then necessarily $|C| = M$.*

3   The Symbol-Periodicity of Matrices

In this section we introduce the notion of x-periodicity for matrices in the semiring $S[x]$ of polynomials in the variable x with coefficients in S and focus more specifically on the case of irreducible matrices.

3.1   The Notion of x-Periodicity

Given a polynomial $F = \sum_k f_k x^k \in S[x]$, we define the x-*period* of F as the integer $d(F) = GCD\{|h - k| \mid f_h \neq 0 \neq f_k\}$, where we assume $GCD(\{0\}) = GCD(\varnothing) = +\infty$. Observe that $d(F) = +\infty$ if and only if $F = 0$ or F is a monomial.

Now consider a finite set Q and a matrix $M : Q \times Q \to S[x]$. For any index $q \in Q$ and for each integer n we set $d(q,n) = d(M^n{}_{qq})$ and we define the x-period of q as the integer $d(q) = \mathrm{GCD}\ \{d(q,n) \mid n \geq 0\}$, assuming that any non-zero element in $\mathbb{N} \cup \{+\infty\}$ divides $+\infty$. Notice that if M is the a-counting matrix of some linear representation, this definition implies that for every index q and for every pair of q-cycles C_1 and C_2 of equal length, $|C_1|_a - |C_2|_a$ is a multiple of $d(q)$.

Proposition 2. *If M is an irreducible matrix over $S[x]$, then all indices have the same x-period.*

Proof. Consider an arbitrary pair of indices p, q. By symmetry, it suffices to prove that $d(p)$ divides $d(q)$, and this again can be proven by showing that $d(p)$ divides $d(q,n)$ for all $n \in \mathbb{N}$. As M is irreducible, there exist two integers s, t such that $M^s{}_{pq} \neq 0 \neq M^t{}_{qp}$. Then the polynomial $M^{s+t}{}_{pp} = \sum_r M^s{}_{pr} M^t{}_{rp} \neq 0$ and for some $k \in \mathbb{N}$ there exists a monomial in $M^{s+t}{}_{pp}$ with exponent k. Therefore, for every exponent h in $M^n{}_{qq}$, the integer $h + k$ appears as an exponent in $M^{n+s+t}{}_{pp}$. This proves that $d(p, n + s + t)$ divides $d(q, n)$ and since $d(p)$ divides $d(p, n + s + t)$, this establishes the result. $\square$

Definition 1. *The x-period of an irreducible matrix over $S[x]$ is the common x-period of its indices.*

Example 1. We compute the x-period of the matrix M over $\mathbb{B}[x]$ corresponding to the state diagram represented in Figure 1. Consider for instance state q_1 and let C_1 and C_2 be two arbitrary q_1-cycles having the same length. Clearly they can be decomposed by using the simple q_1-cycles of the automaton, namely $\ell_1 = q_1 \xrightarrow{a} q_4 \xrightarrow{a} q_1$, $\ell_2 = q_1 \xrightarrow{b} q_2 \xrightarrow{a} q_3 \xrightarrow{b} q_1$. Hence, except for their order, C_1 and C_2 only differ in the number of cycles ℓ_1 and ℓ_2 they contain: for $k = 1, 2$, let $s_k \in \mathbb{Z}$ be the difference between the number of ℓ_k contained in C_1 and the number of ℓ_k contained in C_2. Then, necessarily, $s_1|\ell_1| + s_2|\ell_2| = 0$, that is $2s_1 + 3s_2 = 0$. This implies that $s_1 = 3n$ and $s_2 = -2n$ for some $n \in \mathbb{Z}$. Hence

$$|C_1|_a - |C_2|_a = 3n|\ell_1|_a - 2n|\ell_2|_a = 6n - 2n = 4n$$

This proves that 4 is a divisor of the x-period of M. Moreover, both the q_1-cycles $\ell_1{}^3$ and $\ell_2{}^2$ have length equal to 6 and the numbers of occurrences of a differ exactly by 4. Hence, in this case, the x-period of M is exactly 4. $\square$

In the particular case where the entries of the matrix are all linear in x, the matrix decomposes $M = Ax + B$, where A and B are matrices over S; this clearly happens when M is the a-counting matrix of some linear representation. If further M is primitive, the following proposition holds.

Proposition 3. *Let A and B be matrices over S and set $M = Ax + B$. If M is primitive and $A \neq 0 \neq B$, then the x-period of M is finite.*

Proof. Let q be an arbitrary index and consider the finite family of pairs $\{(n_j, k_j)\}_{j \in J}$ such that $0 \le k_j \le n_j \le m$ where m is the size of M and k_j appears as an exponent in $M^{n_j}{}_{qq}$. Notice that since M is irreducible J is not empty. Since every cycle can be decomposed into elementary cycles all of which of length at most equal to m, the result is proved once we show that $d(q) = +\infty$ implies either $k_j = 0$ for all $j \in J$ or $k_j = n_j$ for all $j \in J$: in the first case we get $A = 0$ while in the second case we have $B = 0$.

Because of equality $M^{\prod_j n_j} = (M^{n_i})^{\prod_{j \ne i} n_j}$, the polynomial $M^{\prod_j n_j}{}_{qq}$ contains the exponent $k_i \prod_{j \ne i} n_j$ for each $i \in J$. Now, suppose by contradiction that $d(q)$ is not finite. This means that all exponents in $M^{\prod_j n_j}{}_{qq}$ are equal to a unique integer h such that $h = k_i \prod_{j \ne i} n_j$ for all $i \in J$. Hence, h must be a multiple of the least common multiple of all products $\prod_{j \ne i} n_j$. Now we have $\text{LCM}\{\prod_{j \ne i} n_j \mid i \in J\} \cdot \text{GCD}\{n_j \mid j \in J\} = \prod_j n_j$ and by the primitivity hypothesis $\text{GCD}\{n_j \mid j \in J\} = 1$ holds. Therefore h is a multiple of $\prod_j n_j$. Thus the conditions $k_j \le n_j$ leave the only possibilities $k_j = 0$ for all $j \in J$ or $k_j = n_j$ for all $j \in J$. $\qquad\square$

Observe that the previous theorem cannot be extended to the case when M is irreducible or when M is a matrix over $S[x]$ that cannot be written as $Ax + B$ for some matrices A and B over S.

Example 2. The matrix M with entries $M_{11} = M_{22} = 0$, $M_{12} = x$ and $M_{21} = 1$ is irreducible but it is not primitive since it has period 2. It is easy to see that the non-null entries of all its powers are monomials, thus M has infinite x-period. $\qquad\square$

Example 3. Consider again Figure 1 and set $M_{2,3} = x^3$. Then we obtain a primitive matrix over $\mathbb{B}[x]$ that cannot be written as $Ax + B$ and it does not have finite x-period. $\qquad\square$

3.2 Properties of x-Periodic Matrices

Given a positive integer d, consider the cyclic group $C_d = \{1, g, g^2, \dots, g^{d-1}\}$ of order d and the semiring $\mathcal{B}_d = \langle \mathcal{P}(C_d), +, \cdot \rangle$ (which is also called $\mathbb{B}$-algebra of the cyclic group) where $\mathcal{P}(C_d)$ denotes the family of all subsets of C_d and for every pair of subsets A, B of C_d we set $A + B = A \cup B$ and $A \cdot B = \{a \cdot b \mid a \in A, b \in B\}$; hence $\varnothing$ is the unit of the sum and $\{1\}$ is the unit of the product. Now, given a positive semiring S, consider the map $\varphi_d : S[x] \to \mathcal{B}_d$ which associates any polynomial $F = \sum_k f_k x^k \in S[x]$ with the set $\{g^k \mid f_k \ne 0\} \in \mathcal{B}_d$. Note that since the semiring S is positive φ_d is a semiring morphism. Intuitively, φ_d associates F with the set of its exponents modulo the integer d. Of course φ_d extends to the semiring of $Q \times Q$-matrices over $S[x]$ by setting $\varphi_d(T)_{pq} = \varphi_d(T_{pq})$, for every matrix $T : Q \times Q \to S[x]$ and all $p, q \in Q$. Observe that, since φ_d is a morphism, $\varphi_d(T)^n{}_{pq} = \varphi_d(T^n)_{pq} = \varphi_d(T^n{}_{pq})$.

Now, let $M : Q \times Q \to S[x]$ be an irreducible matrix with finite x-period d. Simply by the definition of d and φ_d, we have that for each $n \in \mathbb{N}$ all non-empty entries $\varphi_d(M^n)_{pp}$ have cardinality 1. The following results also concern the powers of $\varphi_d(M)$.

Proposition 4. *Let M be an irreducible matrix over $S[x]$ with finite x-period d. Then, for each integer n and each pair of indices p and q, the cardinality of the subset $\varphi_d(M)^n{}_{pq}$ of C_d is not greater than 1; moreover, if $\varphi_d(M)_{qq} \ne \varnothing$, then $\varphi_d(M)^n{}_{qq} = (\varphi_d(M)_{qq})^n$.*

Proof. Let n be an arbitrary integer and p, q an arbitrary pair of indices. By the remarks above we may assume $p \neq q$ and $M^n{}_{pq} \neq 0$. M being irreducible, there exists an integer t such that $M^t{}_{qp} \neq 0$. Note that if B is a non–empty subset of C_d then $|A \cdot B| \geq |A|$ holds for each $A \subseteq C_d$ and $\varphi_d(M)^{n+t}{}_{pp} \supseteq \varphi_d(M)^n{}_{pq} \cdot \varphi_d(M)^t{}_{qp}$. Therefore, since $|\varphi_d(M)^{n+t}{}_{pp}| \leq 1$, we have also $|\varphi_d(M)^n{}_{pq}| \leq 1$. The second statement is proved in a similar way reasoning by induction on n. $\square$

Proposition 5. *Let M be an irreducible matrix over $\mathcal{S}[x]$ with finite x-period d. Then, for each integer n, all non-empty diagonal elements of $\varphi(M)^n$ are equal.*

Proof. Let n be an arbitrary integer and let p, q be an arbitrary pair of indices such that $M^n{}_{pp} \neq 0 \neq M^n{}_{qq}$. By the previous proposition, there exist h, k such that $\varphi(M)^n{}_{pp} = \{g^h\}$ and $\varphi(M)^n{}_{qq} = \{g^k\}$. If t is defined as in the previous proof then the two elements $\varphi(M)^t{}_{qp} \cdot \{g^h\}$ and $\{g^k\} \cdot \varphi(M)^t{}_{qp}$ belong to $\varphi(M)^{t+n}{}_{qp}$; since this subset contains only one element they must be equal and this completes the proof. $\square$

Proposition 6. *Let M be a primitive matrix over $\mathcal{S}[x]$ with finite x-period d. There exists an integer $0 \leq \gamma < d$ such that for each integer n and each index q, if $M^n{}_{qq} \neq 0$, then $\varphi_d(M)^n{}_{qq} = \{g^{\gamma n}\}$.*

Proof. Since M is primitive, there exists an integer t such that $M^n{}_{pq} \neq \varnothing$ for every $n \geq t$ and for every pair of indices p and q. In particular, since $dt + 1 > t$, we have $|\varphi_d(M^{dt+1}{}_{qq})| = 1$ for each q and hence there exists $0 \leq \gamma < d$ such that $\varphi_d(M)^{dt+1}{}_{qq} = \{g^\gamma\}$. Observe that γ does not depend on q, by Proposition 5. Therefore, by Proposition 4, we have

$$\{g^{\gamma n}\} = \varphi_d(M)^{dtn+n}{}_{qq} \supseteq \varphi_d(M)^{dtn}{}_{qq} \cdot \varphi_d(M)^n{}_{qq} = \{1\} \cdot \varphi_d(M)^n{}_{qq}$$

which proves the result. $\square$

If M is the a-counting matrix of a linear representation, then the previous propositions can be interpreted by considering its state diagram. For any pair of states p, q, all paths of the same length starting in p and ending in q have the same number of occurrences of a modulo d. Moreover, if C_k is a q_k-cycle for $k = 1, 2$ and C_1 and C_2 have the same length, then they also have the same number of occurrences of a modulo d. Finally, if M is primitive, for each cycle ℓ we have $|\ell|_a = \gamma|\ell|$ modulo d for some integer γ.

We conclude this section with an example showing that Proposition 6 cannot be extended to the case when M is irreducible but not primitive.

Example 4. Consider the a-counting matrix M associated with the state diagram of Figure 2. Then M is irreducible with x-period 2, but it is not primitive since also its period equals 2. Consider the path $\ell = q_1 \xrightarrow{b} q_2 \xrightarrow{a} q_1$. We have $|\ell| = 2$ and $|\ell|_a = 1$, hence for any γ, $\gamma|\ell|$ cannot be equal to $|\ell|_a$ modulo 2. Thus, Proposition 6 does not hold in this case.

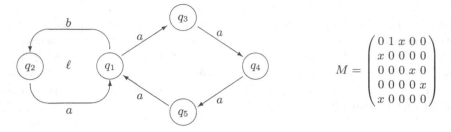

Fig. 2. State diagram and matrix of Example 4

3.3 Eigenvalues of x-Periodic Matrices

In this section we consider the semiring $\mathbb{R}_+$ of non–negative real numbers and we study the eigenvalues of primitive matrices $M(x)$ over $\mathbb{R}_+[x]$ when x assumes the complex values z such that $|z| = 1$. The next theorem shows how the eigenvalues of $M(z)$ are related to the x-period of the matrix.

Theorem 2. *Let $M(x)$ be a primitive matrix over $\mathbb{R}_+[x]$ with finite x-period d, set $M = M(1)$ and let λ be the Perron-Frobenius eigenvalue of M. Then, for all $z \in \mathbb{C}$ with $|z| = 1$, the following conditions are equivalent:*
1. $M(z)$ and M have the same set of moduli of eigenvalues;
2. If $\lambda(z)$ is an eigenvalue of maximum modulus of $M(z)$, then $|\lambda(z)| = \lambda$;
3. z is a d-th root of unity in $\mathbb{C}$.

Proof (outline). Clearly condition 1) implies condition 2). To prove that condition 2) implies condition 3) we reason by contradiction, that is we assume that z is not a d-th root of unity. It is possible to prove that in this case there exists an integer n such that $|M(z)^n| < M^n$. Therefore we can apply Proposition 1 and prove that λ^n is greater than the modulus of any eigenvalue of $M(z)^n$. In particular we have $\lambda^n > |\lambda(z)|^n$ which contradicts the hypothesis.

Finally we show that condition 3) implies condition 1). The case $d = 1$ is trivial; thus suppose $d > 1$ and assume that z is a $d-$th root of unity. It suffices to prove that if ν is an eigenvalue of M, then νz^γ is an eigenvalue of $M(z)$ with the same multiplicity, where γ is the constant introduced in Proposition 6. To this end, set $\hat{T} = I\nu z^\gamma - M(z)$ and $T = I\nu - M$. We now verify that $\mathrm{Det}\hat{T} = z^{\gamma m} \, \mathrm{Det}\, T$ holds, where m is the size of M. To prove this equality, recall that $\mathrm{Det}\, \hat{T} = \sum_\rho (-1)^{\sigma(\rho)} \hat{T}_{1\rho(1)} \cdots \hat{T}_{m\rho(m)}$. By Proposition 6, since z is a d-th root of 1 in $\mathbb{C}$, we have $\hat{T}_{qq} = (\nu - M_{qq})z^\gamma = z^\gamma T_{qq}$ for each state q and $\hat{T}_{q_0 q_1} \cdots \hat{T}_{q_{s-1} q_0} = z^{\gamma s} \, T_{q_0 q_1} \cdots T_{q_{s-1} q_0}$ for each simple cycle $(q_0, q_1, \ldots, q_{s-1}, q_0)$ of length $s > 1$. Therefore, for each permutation ρ, we get $\hat{T}_{1\rho(1)} \cdots \hat{T}_{m\rho(m)} = z^{\gamma m} \cdot T_{1\rho(1)} \cdots T_{m\rho(m)}$ which concludes the proof. $\square$

Example 5. Let us consider again the primitive matrix of Figure 1. We recall that here $d = 4$; moreover it is easy to see that $\gamma = 3$. Indeed, for each $k = 1, 2$, we have that $|\ell_k| - 3|\ell_k|_a$ is equal to 0 modulo 4. Now consider the characteristic polynomial of the matrix $M(x)$, given by $\chi_x(y) = y^4 - y^2 x^2 - yx$ and let ν be a root of χ_1. This implies that $\chi_1(\nu) = \nu^4 - \nu^2 - \nu = 0$ and hence $-i\nu$ is a root of the polynomial χ_i, $-\nu$ is a root of the polynomial χ_{-1} and $i\nu$ is a root of the polynomial χ_{-i}. This is consistent with Theorem 2, since $1, i, -1$ and $-i$ are the four roots of unity.   □

4   Local Limit Properties for Pattern Statistics

In this section we turn again our attention to pattern statistics and study the symbol frequency problem in the rational stochastic model under primitivity hypothesis; our goal is to determine the local limit distribution of the corresponding random variable.

Formally, given a rational formal series $r : \{a, b\}^* \to \mathbb{R}_+$, let (ξ, μ, η) be a linear representation of r of size m. Set $A = \mu(a)$, $B = \mu(b)$ and, to avoid trivial cases, assume $A \neq 0 \neq B$. We also set $M(x) = Ax + B$ and $M = M(1)$. Then, consider the probability space of all words of length n in $\{a, b\}^*$ equipped with the probability function given by

$$\mathrm{P}\{w\} = \frac{(r, w)}{\xi^T M^n \eta} = \frac{\xi^T \mu(w) \eta}{\xi^T M^n \eta}$$

for every $w \in \{a, b\}^n$. Now, consider the random variable $Y_n : \{a, b\}^n \to \{0, 1, \dots, n\}$ such that $Y_n(w) = |w|_a$ for every $w \in \{a, b\}^n$. For sake of brevity, we say that $\{Y_n\}_n$ *counts the occurrences of a in the model defined by r*. We study the asymptotic behaviour of Y_n under the hypothesis that the matrix $M(x)$ is primitive, obtaining a local limit distribution that strongly depends on the x-period of $M(x)$.

In the following analysis we consider triples (ξ, μ, η) where both ξ and η have just one non-null entry which is equal to 1: indeed, it turns out that the general case can be reduced to this kind of representation. To show this fact first observe that, for n large enough, all entries of the matrix M^n are strictly positive and thus for every integer $0 \leq k \leq n$ we have

$$\mathrm{P}\{Y_n = k\} = \sum_{|w|=n,\ |w|_a=k} \frac{\xi^T \mu(w) \eta}{\xi^T M^n \eta} = \sum_{p,q=1}^m \left(\frac{\xi_p M^n_{\ pq} \eta_q}{\xi^T M^n \eta} \sum_{|w|=n,\ |w|_a=k} \frac{\mu(w)_{pq}}{M^n_{\ pq}} \right). \quad (2)$$

Since $M(x)$ is primitive, by the Perron–Frobenius Theorem, M admits exactly one eigenvalue λ of maximum modulus, which is real and positive. Furthermore, we can associate to λ strictly positive left and right eigenvectors u and v such that $v^T u = 1$ and we know that, as n tends to infinity we have $M^n \sim \lambda^n \cdot uv^T$. Hence

$$\frac{\xi_p M^n_{\ pq} \eta_q}{\xi^T M^n \eta} \sim \frac{\xi_p u_p v_q \eta_q}{(\xi^T u)(v^T \eta)}.$$

Now, let Y_n^{pq} be the random variable associated with the linear representation (e_p, μ, e_q), where e_i denotes the characteristic vector of entry i. Thus, equation (2) can be reformulated as

$$\mathrm{P}\{Y_n = k\} = \sum_{p,q=1}^m C_{pq} \cdot \mathrm{P}\{Y_n^{pq} = k\} \quad (3)$$

where C_{pq} are non-negative constants such that $\sum C_{pq} = 1$.

Theorem 3. *Let $r : \{a, b\}^* \to \mathbb{R}_+$ be a rational formal series with a linear representation of the form (e_p, μ, e_q) such that $\mu(a) \neq 0 \neq \mu(b)$. Assume that its a-counting matrix $M(x)$ is primitive and let d be its x-period. Also let $\{Y_n^{pq}\}_n$ count the occurrences of a in the model defined by r. Then, there exist two real constants $0 < \alpha, \beta \leq 1$ and an integer $0 \leq \rho \leq d - 1$, all of them depending on $M = M(1)$, such that as n tends to $+\infty$ the relation*

$$
P\{Y_n^{pq} = k\} =
\begin{cases}
\dfrac{d}{\sqrt{2\pi\alpha n}} \cdot e^{-\frac{(k-\beta n)^2}{2\alpha n}} + o\left(\dfrac{1}{\sqrt{n}}\right) & if \ \ k \equiv \rho \ mod \ d \\[3mm]
0 & otherwise
\end{cases}
$$

holds uniformly for all integers $0 \leq k \leq n$.

Proof. For the sake of simplicity, for any integer $0 \leq k \leq n$ set

$$
p_n(k) = P\{Y_n^{pq} = k\} = \sum_{|w|=n, \ |w|_a=k} \frac{\mu(w)_{pq}}{M^n_{pq}} .
$$

Observe that by Proposition 4 there exists an integer $0 \leq \rho < d$ such that the number of occurrences of a in paths of the same length starting in p and ending in q are equal to ρ modulo d. Hence, $p_n(k) = 0$ for each $k \not\equiv \rho \bmod d$. Now, consider the smallest integer N such that $Nd \geq n + 1$ and apply the N-Discrete Fourier Transform to the array

$$
(p_n(\rho), \ p_n(\rho + d), \dots, \ p_n(\rho + (N - 1)d)) \in \mathbb{C}^N
$$

where the last coefficient is null if $n < \rho + (N - 1)d$. We get the following values $f_n(s)$, for integers s such that $-\lceil N/2 \rceil < s \leq \lfloor N/2 \rfloor$:

$$
f_n(s) = \sum_{j=0}^{N-1} p_n(\rho + jd) \cdot e^{\frac{2\pi i}{N} sj}
$$

Observe that these coefficients are related to the characteristic function $F_n(\theta)$ of the random variable Y_n^{pq}, i.e.

$$
F_n(\theta) = \sum_k p_n(k)e^{i\theta k} = \sum_{|w|=n} \frac{\mu(w)_{pq}}{M^n_{pq}} e^{i\theta|w|_a} \tag{4}
$$

Indeed, for any $-\lceil N/2 \rceil < s \leq \lfloor N/2 \rfloor$, we have

$$
f_n(s) = e^{-\frac{2\pi i}{Nd} s\rho} \cdot F_n\left(\frac{2\pi s}{Nd}\right)
$$

Hence to obtain the values $p_n(\rho + jd), j \in \{0, 1, \dots, N - 1\}$, it is sufficient to compute the N-th Inverse Transform of the $f_n(s)$'s. So, we have

$$
p_n(\rho + jd) = \frac{1}{N} \sum_{s=-\lceil \frac{N}{2} \rceil+1}^{\lfloor \frac{N}{2} \rfloor} f_n(s) \cdot e^{-\frac{2\pi i}{N} sj} = \frac{1}{N} \sum_{s=-\lceil \frac{N}{2} \rceil+1}^{\lfloor \frac{N}{2} \rfloor} F_n\left(\frac{2\pi s}{Nd}\right) e^{-\frac{2\pi i}{Nd} s(\rho+jd)}
$$

$$
\tag{5}
$$

To evaluate $p_n(k)$ we now need asymptotic expressions of the function $F_n(\theta)$ in the interval $\theta \in \left(-\frac{\pi}{d}, \frac{\pi}{d}\right]$. To this aim observe that relations (4) and (1) imply

$$F_n(\theta) = \frac{M(e^{i\theta})^n{}_{pq}}{M^n{}_{pq}}$$

Now, by Theorem 2, we know that the eigenvalues of $M(e^{i\theta})$ are in modulus smaller than λ, for each $\theta \in \left[\frac{-\pi}{d}, \frac{\pi}{d}\right]$ different from 0. This property allows us to argue as in [3, Theorem 5]. As a consequence, for each $\theta \in \left[\frac{-\pi}{d}, \frac{\pi}{d}\right]$ we can approximate the function $F_n(\theta)$ with the function $\hat{F}_n(\theta) = \exp\left(-\frac{\alpha}{2}n\theta^2 + i\beta n\theta\right)$, where α and β are positive constants depending on M. Thus, we get

$$\left| F_n(\theta) - \exp\left(-\frac{\alpha}{2}n\theta^2 + i\beta n\theta\right) \right| = \Delta_n(\theta)$$

where, as n tends to $+\infty$,

$$\Delta_n(\theta) = \begin{cases} O\left(\frac{1}{n^\varepsilon}\right) & \text{if } |\theta| \in [0, \frac{2\pi}{(n+1)^\varepsilon}] \\ O\left(e^{-\alpha\pi^2 n^{1-2\varepsilon}}\right) & \text{if } |\theta| \in [\frac{2\pi}{(n+1)^\varepsilon}, \theta_0] \\ O\left(\tau^n\right) & \text{if } |\theta| \in [\theta_0, \frac{\pi}{d}] \end{cases}$$

for some $0 < \theta_0 < \frac{\pi}{d}$, $0 < \tau < 1$, and for every $\frac{1}{3} < \varepsilon < \frac{1}{2}$.

Therefore, to find the approximation for $p_n(k)$ it is sufficient to replace into (5) the values $F_n\left(\frac{2\pi s}{Nd}\right)$ by their approximations $\hat{F}_n\left(\frac{2\pi s}{Nd}\right)$, so getting the following values for each $k \equiv \rho \bmod d$.

$$\hat{p}_n(k) = \frac{1}{N} \sum_{s=-\lceil\frac{N}{2}\rceil+1}^{\lfloor\frac{N}{2}\rfloor} \hat{F}_n\left(\frac{2\pi s}{Nd}\right) \cdot e^{-\frac{2\pi i}{Nd}ks} \tag{6}$$

Indeed, one can verify that $\left| p_n(k) - \hat{p}_n(k) \right| = O\left(\frac{1}{n^{2\varepsilon}}\right)$ for any $1/3 < \varepsilon < 1/2$ and every $k \equiv \rho \bmod d$. Finally, the sum in (6) can be computed by using the definition of Riemann integral and by means of standard mathematical tools: we find the following approximation which holds as n tends to $+\infty$, uniformly for all $k \equiv \rho \bmod d$:

$$\hat{p}_n(k) \approx \int_{-\frac{1}{2}}^{\frac{1}{2}} \hat{F}_n\left(\frac{2\pi}{d}t\right) \cdot e^{-i\frac{2k\pi}{d}t}\,dt = \int_{\frac{1}{2}}^{\frac{1}{2}} e^{-\frac{\alpha}{2}n(\frac{2\pi}{d}t)^2} \cdot e^{i\beta n\frac{2\pi}{d}t} \cdot e^{-i\frac{2k\pi}{d}t}\,dt$$

$$\approx \int_{-\infty}^{+\infty} e^{-\frac{2\alpha\pi^2 n}{d^2}t^2} \cdot e^{-i2\pi\frac{k-\beta n}{d}t}\,dt = \frac{d}{\sqrt{2\pi\alpha n}} \cdot e^{-\frac{(k-\beta n)^2}{2\alpha n}}$$

$\square$

Applying the theorem above to equation (3), we obtain the following result.

Theorem 4. *Let $r : \{a,b\}^* \to \mathbb{R}_+$ be a rational formal series with a linear representation (ξ, μ, η) such that $\mu(a) \neq 0 \neq \mu(b)$. Assume that its a-counting matrix $M(x)$ is primitive and let d be its x-period. Also let $\{Y_n\}_n$ count the occurrences of a in the model defined by r. Then, there exist two constants $0 < \alpha, \beta \leq 1$ depending on $M = M(1)$ and d constants $C_0, C_1, \ldots, C_{d-1}$ depending on M, ξ and η such that $C_i \geq 0$ for every $i = 0, \ldots, d-1$, $\sum_i C_i = 1$, and as n tends to $+\infty$ the relation*

$$P\{Y_n = k\} = \frac{d\, C_{\langle k\rangle_d}}{\sqrt{2\pi\alpha n}} \cdot e^{-\frac{(k-\beta n)^2}{2\alpha n}} + o\left(\frac{1}{\sqrt{n}}\right)$$

holds uniformly for all integers $0 \leq k \leq n$ (here $\langle k\rangle_d = k - \lfloor k/d\rfloor$).

Summarizing the previous results, Theorem 3 states that if the weighted automaton associated with the linear representation has just one initial and one final state, then the local limit distribution has a sort of periodic behaviour: it reduces to 0 everywhere in the domain of possible values except for an integer linear progression of period d, where it approaches a normal density function expanded by a factor d. We also observe that the main terms of mean value and variance of Y_n^{pq} are given by βn and αn, respectively, which do not depend on the initial and final states.

In the general case, when the automaton has more than one initial or final state, by Theorem 4 the required limit distribution is given by a superposition of behaviours of the previous type, all of which have the same main terms of mean value and variance. In the case $d = 1$ the limit probability function of Y_n reduces exactly to a Gaussian density function as already proved in [3]. Such a limit density is the same obtained in the classical DeMoivre–Laplace Local Limit Theorem (see for instance [7, Sec. 12]).

References

1. E. A. Bender. Central and local limit theorems applied to asymptotic enumeration. *Journal of Combinatorial Theory*, 15:91–111, 1973.
2. J. Berstel and C. Reutenauer. *Rational series and their languages*, Springer-Verlag, New York - Heidelberg - Berlin, 1988.
3. A. Bertoni, C. Choffrut, M. Goldwurm, and V. Lonati. On the number of occurrences of a symbol in words of regular languages. *Theoretical Computer Science*, 302(1-3):431–456, 2003.
4. D. de Falco, M. Goldwurm, and V. Lonati. Frequency of symbol occurrences in simple non-primitive stochastic models. *Proceedings 7th D.L.T. Conference*, Z. Esig and Z. Fülop editors, Lecture Notes in Computer Science, vol. n. 2710, Springer, 2003, 242–253.
5. P. Flajolet and R. Sedgewick. The average case analysis of algorithms: multivariate asymptotics and limit distributions. *Rapport de recherche* n. 3162, INRIA Rocquencourt, May 1997.
6. P. Flajolet and R. Sedgewick. Analytic combinatorics: functional equations, rational and algebraic functions. *Rapport de recherche* n. 4103, INRIA Rocquencourt, January 2001.
7. B.V. Gnedenko. *The theory of probability* (translated by G. Yankovsky). Mir Publishers - Moscow, 1976.
8. L. J. Guibas and A. M. Odlyzko. String overlaps, pattern matching, and nontransitive games. *Journal of Combinatorial Theory. Series A*, 30(2):183–208, 1981.
9. W. Kuich and A. Salomaa. *Semirings, automata, languages*. Springer–Verlag, New York Heidelberg Berlin Tokyo, 1986.
10. P. Nicodème, B. Salvy, and P. Flajolet. Motif statistics. *Theoretical Computer Science*, 287(2):593–617, 2002.
11. B. Prum, F. Rudolphe and E. Turckheim. Finding words with unexpected frequencies in deoxyribonucleic acid sequence. *J. Roy. Statist. Soc. Ser. B*, 57:205–220, 1995.
12. M. Régnier and W. Szpankowski. On pattern frequency occurrences in a Markovian sequence. *Algorithmica*, 22(4):621–649, 1998.
13. E. Seneta. *Non-negative matrices and Markov chains*, Springer–Verlag, New York Heidelberg Berlin, 1981.
14. M. Waterman. *Introduction to computational biology*, Chapman & Hall, New York, 1995.

A Discontinuity in Pattern Inference

Daniel Reidenbach*

Fachbereich Informatik, Technische Universität Kaiserslautern,
Postfach 3049, 67653 Kaiserslautern, Germany
reidenba@informatik.uni-kl.de

Abstract. This paper examines the learnability of a major subclass
of E-pattern languages – also known as erasing or extended pattern languages – in Gold's learning model: We show that the class of terminal-free
E-pattern languages is inferrable from positive data if the corresponding
terminal alphabet consists of three or more letters. Consequently, the
recently presented negative result for binary alphabets is unique.

1 Introduction

Pattern languages have been introduced by Angluin (cf. [1]), though some publications by Thue can already be interpreted as investigations of pattern structures (cf. e.g. [18]). Following Angluin, a pattern is a finite string that consists
of *variables* and of *terminal* symbols. A word of its language is generated by
a uniform *substitution* of all variables with arbitrary strings of terminals. For
instance, the language generated by the pattern $x_1 \, \mathsf{a} \, x_2 \, \mathsf{b} \, x_1$ (with x_1, x_2 as variables and a, b as terminals) contains, among others, the words $w_1 = \mathsf{a\,a\,a\,b\,a}$,
$w_2 = \mathsf{a\,a\,b\,b\,b\,a}$, $w_3 = \mathsf{a\,b\,b}$, whereas the following examples are not covered by
α: $v_1 = \mathsf{a}$, $v_2 = \mathsf{b\,a\,b\,b\,a}$, $v_3 = \mathsf{b\,b\,b\,b\,b}$. Thus, numerous regular and nonregular
languages can be described by patterns in a compact and "natural" way.

Pattern languages have been the subject of several analyses within the scope
of formal language theory, e.g. in [5] and [6] (for a survey see [16]). These examinations reveal that a definition disallowing the substitution of variables with the
empty word – as given by Angluin – leads to a language with particular features
being quite different from the one allowing the empty substitution (that has
been applied when generating w_3 in our example). Languages of the latter type
have been introduced by Shinohara (cf. [17]); they are referred to as *extended*,
erasing, or *E-pattern languages*.

When dealing with pattern languages, manifold questions arise from the man-
ifest problem of computing a pattern that is common to a given set of words.
Therefore pattern languages have been a focus of interest of algorithmic learning
theory from the very beginning. In the most elementary learning model of inductive inference – introduced by Gold (cf. [4]) and known as *learning in the limit*
or *Gold style learning* – a class of languages is said to be *inferrable from positive*

---

* Supported by the Deutsche Forschungsgemeinschaft (DFG), Grant Wi 1638/1-2

V. Diekert and M. Habib (Eds.): STACS 2004, LNCS 2996, pp. 129–140, 2004.

data if and only if there exists a computable device (the so-called *learning strategy*) that, for every of these (potentially infinite) languages and for every full enumeration of the words of the particular language to be learned, converges to a distinct and complete description of the language in finite time. According to [4], this task is too challenging for many well-known classes of formal languages: All superfinite classes of languages – i.e. all classes that contain every finite and at least one infinite language – such as the regular, context-free and context-sensitive languages are not inferrable from positive data. Thus, the number of rich classes of languages that are known to be learnable is rather small.

The current state of knowledge concerning the learnability of pattern languages considerably differs when regarding standard or E-pattern languages, respectively: The learnability of the class of standard pattern languages was shown by Angluin when introducing its definition in 1979 (cf. [1]). In the sequel there has been a variety of profound studies (e.g. in [7], [19], [14], and many more) on the complexity of learning algorithms, consequences of different input data, efficient strategies for subclasses, and so on. Regarding E-pattern languages, however, appropriate approaches presumably need to be more sophisticated and therefore progress has been rather scarce. Apart from positive results for the full class of E-pattern languages over the trivial unary and infinite terminal alphabets in [11], the examinations in the past two decades restricted themselves to the learnability of subclasses (cf. [17], [11], [12], and – indirectly – [20]). In spite of all effort, it took more than twenty years until at least for binary terminal alphabets the non-learnability of the subclass of *terminal-free* E-pattern languages (generated by patterns that only consist of variables) and, thus, of the full class could be proven (cf. [13]).

In this paper we revert to the class of terminal-free E-pattern languages – that has been a subject of some language theoretical examinations (cf. [3] and [6]) as well – with a rather surprising outcome: We show that it is inferrable from positive data *if and only if* the terminal alphabet does not consist of two letters. Thus, we present the first class of pattern languages to be known for which different non-trivial alphabets imply different answers to the question of learnability. Using several theorems in [2] and [6], our respective reasoning is chiefly combinatorial; therefore it touches on some prominent topics within the research on word monoids and combinatorics of words.

2   Definitions and Preliminary Results

For standard mathematical notions and recursion-theoretic terms not defined explicitly in this paper we refer to [15]; for unexplained aspects of formal language theory, [16] may be consulted.

For an arbitrary set A of symbols, A^+ denotes the set of all non-empty words over A and A^* the set of all (empty and non-empty) words over A. We designate the *empty* word as e. For the word that results from the n-fold concatenation of a letter a we write a^n. $|\cdot|$ denotes the size of a set or the length of a word, respectively, and $|w|_a$ the frequency of a letter a in a word w.

Σ is an alphabet of *terminal* symbols and $X = \{x_1, x_2, x_3, \cdots\}$ an infinite set of *variable* symbols, $\Sigma \cap X = \emptyset$. We designate Σ as *trivial* if and only if $|\Sigma| = 1$ or $|\Sigma| = \infty$. Henceforth, we use lower case letters from the beginning of the Latin alphabet as terminal symbols; words of terminal symbols are named as u, v, or w. For every j, $j \geq 1$, $y_j \in X$ is an unspecified variable, i.e. there may exist $j, j' \in \mathbb{N}$ such that $j \neq j'$ and $y_j = y_{j'}$. A *pattern* is a word over $\Sigma \cup X$, a *terminal-free pattern* is a word over X; naming patterns we use lower case letters from the beginning of the Greek alphabet. $\mathrm{var}(\alpha)$ denotes the set of all variables of a pattern α. We write Pat for the set of all patterns and Pat_{tf} for the set of all terminal-free patterns.

A *substitution* is a morphism $\sigma : (\Sigma \cup X)^* \longrightarrow \Sigma^*$ such that $\sigma(\mathbf{a}) = \mathbf{a}$ for every $\mathbf{a} \in \Sigma$. The *E-pattern language* $L_\Sigma(\alpha)$ of a pattern α is defined as the set of all $w \in \Sigma^*$ such that $\sigma(\alpha) = w$ for any substitution σ. For any word $w = \sigma(\alpha)$ we say that σ *generates* w, and for any language $L = L_\Sigma(\alpha)$ we say that α *generates* L. If there is no need to give emphasis to the concrete shape of Σ we denote the E-pattern language of a pattern α simply as $L(\alpha)$. We use ePAT_{tf} as an abbreviation for the full class of terminal-free E-pattern languages. For any class ePAT^* of E-pattern languages we write ePAT^*_Σ if the corresponding alphabet is of interest.

According to [10] we call a word w *ambiguous* (in respect of a pattern α) if and only if there exist at least two substitutions σ and σ' such that $\sigma(\alpha) = w = \sigma'(\alpha)$, but $\sigma(x_j) \neq \sigma'(x_j)$ for an $x_j \in \mathrm{var}(\alpha)$. The word $w = \mathbf{a}\,\mathbf{a}$, for instance, is ambiguous in respect of the pattern $\alpha = x_1\,\mathbf{a}\,x_2$ since it can be generated by the substitutions σ, $\sigma(x_1) = \mathbf{a}$, $\sigma(x_2) = e$, and σ', $\sigma'(x_1) = e$, $\sigma(x_2) = \mathbf{a}$.

Following [11], we designate a pattern α as *succinct* if and only if $|\alpha| \leq |\beta|$ for all patterns β with $L(\beta) = L(\alpha)$, and we call a pattern *prolix* if and only if it is not succinct. The pattern $\alpha = x_1x_1$, for instance, is succinct because there does not exist any shorter pattern that exactly describes its language, whereas $\beta = x_1x_2x_1x_2$ is prolix since $L(\beta) = L(\alpha)$ and $|\alpha| < |\beta|$.

Let ePAT^* be any set of E-pattern languages. We say that the *inclusion problem* for ePAT^* is *decidable* if and only if there exists a computable function which, given two arbitrary patterns α, β with $L(\alpha), L(\beta) \in \mathrm{ePAT}^*$, decides whether or not $L(\alpha) \subseteq L(\beta)$. In [6] it is shown that the inclusion problem for the full class of E-pattern languages is not decidable. Fortunately, this fact does not hold for terminal-free E-pattern languages. As this is of great importance for the following studies, we now cite two respective theorems of [6]:

Fact 1. *Let Σ be an alphabet, $|\Sigma| \geq 2$, and $\alpha, \beta \in X^*$ two arbitrarily given terminal-free patterns. Then $L_\Sigma(\beta) \subseteq L_\Sigma(\alpha)$ iff there exists a morphism $\phi : X^* \longrightarrow X^*$ such that $\phi(\alpha) = \beta$.*

Fact 2. *The inclusion problem for ePAT_{tf} is decidable.*

We now introduce our notions on Gold's learning model (cf. [4]): Each function $t : \mathbb{N} \longrightarrow \Sigma^*$ satisfying $\{t(n) \mid n \geq 0\} = L(\alpha)$ is called a *text* for $L(\alpha)$. Let S be any total computable function reading initial segments of texts and returning patterns. Each such function is called a *strategy*. If α is a pattern and t a text for $L(\alpha)$ we say that S *identifies* $L(\alpha)$ *from* t, if and only if the sequence of patterns returned by S, when reading t, converges to a pattern β, such that $L(\beta) = L(\alpha)$. Any class ePAT* of E-pattern languages is *learnable (in the limit)* if and only if there is a strategy S identifying each language $L \in$ ePAT* from any corresponding text. In this case we write ePAT$^\star \in$ LIM-TEXT for short.

The analysis of the learnability of certain classes of languages is facilitated by some profound criteria given by Angluin (cf. [2]). Because of Fact 2 and since Pat$_{tf}$ is recursively enumerable, we can use the following:

Fact 3. *Let* Pat* *be an arbitrary, recursively enumerable set of patterns and* ePAT* *the corresponding class of E-pattern languages, such that the inclusion problem for* ePAT* *is decidable. Then* ePAT$^\star \in$ LIM-TEXT *iff for every pattern* $\alpha \in$ Pat* *there exists a set* T_α *such that*

- $T_\alpha \subseteq L(\alpha)$,
- T_α *is finite, and*
- *there does not exist a pattern* $\beta \in$ Pat* *with* $T_\alpha \subseteq L(\beta) \subset L(\alpha)$.

If T_α exists, then it is called a *telltale* (for $L(\alpha)$) (in respect of ePAT*).

Roughly speaking, ePAT* is, thus, inferrable from positive data if and only if every of its languages contains a finite subset that may be interpreted (by a strategy) as an exclusive signal to distinguish between that distinct language and all of its sub-languages in ePAT*.

We conclude this section with the seminal learnability result on ePAT$_{tf}$ that has been presented in [13]:

Fact 4. *Let* Σ *be an alphabet,* $|\Sigma| = 2$. *Then* ePAT$_{tf,\Sigma} \notin$ LIM-TEXT.

In [13] it is stated that the proof of this theorem cannot easily be extended on finite alphabets with more than two letters and it is conjectured that even the opposite of Fact 4 holds true for these alphabets. In the following section we discuss this fairly counter-intuitive assumption.

3   On the Learnability of ePAT$_{tf}$

Trivial alphabets, for which ePAT$_{tf}$ is learnable (cf. [11]), considerably ease the construction of telltales. Consequently, the recent negative result on binary alphabets (cf. Fact 4) – revealing that the assumed uniqueness of the approaches on trivial alphabets indeed might not be a matter of the methods, but of the subject – promotes the guess that ePAT$_{tf}$ should not be learnable for every non-trivial alphabet. This surmise is supported by the fundamental algebraic theorem that for the free semigroup with two generators and for every $n \in \mathbb{N}$ there exists a free sub-semigroup with n generators and, thus, that the expressive power of words over three or more letters does not exceed that of words over two letters. Furthermore, there also exists a pattern specific hint backing this expectation since there seems to be no significant difference between terminal-free E-pattern languages over two and those over three letters (derived directly from Fact 1):

Theorem 1. *Let Σ_1, Σ_2 be finite alphabets, $|\Sigma_1| = 2$ and $|\Sigma_2| \geq 3$. Let α, β be terminal-free patterns. Then $L_{\Sigma_1}(\alpha) \neq L_{\Sigma_1}(\beta)$ iff $L_{\Sigma_2}(\alpha) \neq L_{\Sigma_2}(\beta)$.*

Thus, there is some evidence to suggest that Fact 4 might be extendable on all non-trivial terminal alphabets. In fact, our main result finds the opposite to be true:

Theorem 2. *Let Σ be a finite alphabet, $|\Sigma| \geq 3$. Then $\text{ePAT}_{tf,\Sigma} \in \text{LIM-TEXT}$.*

The proof of this theorem requires a broad combinatorial reasoning; it is accomplished in Section 3.1.

With Theorem 2 we can give a complete characterisation of the learnability of ePAT_{tf}, subject to alphabet size (for those cases not covered by Theorem 2, refer to [11] or Fact 4, respectively):

Corollary 1. *Let Σ be an alphabet. Then $\text{ePAT}_{tf,\Sigma} \in \text{LIM-TEXT}$ iff $|\Sigma| \neq 2$.*

Consequently, we can state a discontinuity in the learnability of terminal-free E-pattern languages that – though it has been conjectured in [13] – seems to be rather unexpected and that might explain the lack of comprehensive results on this subject in the past decades. The following section is dedicated to the proof of Theorem 2, but a precise and language theoretical explanation of the demonstrated singularity of terminal-free E-pattern languages over two letters is still open.

3.1 Proof of the Main Result

The proof of Theorem 2 consists of several steps: a characterisation of prolix patterns, a particular type of substitution, a learnability criterion for classes of terminal-free E-pattern languages, and some lemmata combining these elements.

To begin with, we give the characterisation of prolix patterns, that – although not implying a new decidability result (cf. Fact 2) – is a crucial instrument for our proof of the main theorem (see explanation after Theorem 4) as it gives a compact description of prolixness. Actually, in our reasoning we only use the *if* part of the following theorem, but we consider the characterisation of some interest since prolix terminal-free patterns may be seen as solution candidates for Post's Correspondence Problem if the empty substitution is allowed (the other case has been analysed e.g. in [9] and [8]).

Theorem 3. *A terminal-free pattern α is prolix iff there exists a decomposition*

$$\alpha = \beta_0 \, \gamma_1 \, \beta_1 \, \gamma_2 \, \beta_2 \, \cdots \, \beta_{n-1} \, \gamma_n \, \beta_n$$

for an $n \geq 1$, arbitrary $\beta_i \in X^*$ and $\gamma_i \in X^+$, $i \leq n$, such that

1. *$\forall i : |\gamma_i| \geq 2$,*
2. *$\forall i, i' : \text{var}(\gamma_i) \cap \text{var}(\beta_{i'}) = \emptyset$,*
3. *$\forall i \, \exists \, y_i \in \text{var}(\gamma_i) : (|\gamma_i|_{y_i} = 1 \wedge \forall i' \leq n : (y_i \in \text{var}(\gamma_{i'}) \implies \gamma_i = \gamma_{i'}))$.*

Proof. We first prove the *if* part of the theorem. Hence, let $\alpha \in \text{Pat}_{\text{tf}}$ be a pattern such that there exists a decomposition satisfying conditions 1, 2, and 3. We show that then there exist a pattern $\delta \in \text{Pat}_{\text{tf}}$ and two morphisms ϕ and ψ with $|\delta| < |\alpha|$, $\phi(\alpha) = \delta$, and $\psi(\delta) = \alpha$. Thus, we use Fact 1 as a criterion for the equivalence of E-pattern languages.

We define $\delta := \beta_0 \, y_1 \, \beta_1 \, y_2 \, \beta_2 \, \cdots \, \beta_{n-1} \, y_n \, \beta_n$ with y_i derived from condition 3 for every $i \le n$. Then condition 1 implies $|\delta| < |\alpha|$; the existence of ϕ and ψ (ϕ mapping y_i on γ_i and ψ mapping γ_i on y_i for every $i \le n$, both of the morphisms leaving all other variables unchanged) results from conditions 2 and 3.

Due to space constraints and as it is not needed for our subsequent reasoning, the proof of the *only if* part is merely given as an extended sketch.

Assume that $\alpha \in \text{Pat}_{\text{tf}}$ is prolix. We show that then there exists at least one decomposition of α satisfying conditions 1, 2, and 3: Because of the assumption and Fact 1, there exist a succinct pattern $\delta \in \text{Pat}_{\text{tf}}$ and two morphisms ϕ and ψ with $|\delta| < |\alpha|$, $\phi(\alpha) = \delta$, and $\psi(\delta) = \alpha$. Since δ is succinct it is obvious that $|\psi(x_j)| \ge 1$ for every $x_j \in \text{var}(\delta)$. Moreover, we may conclude that for every $x_j \in \text{var}(\delta)$ there exists an $x_{j'} \in \text{var}(\psi(x_j))$ such that $|\delta|_{x_j} = |\alpha|_{x_{j'}}$, as otherwise δ would be prolix – according to the *if* part and because of $\phi(\alpha) = \delta$, leading to $x_j \in \text{var}(\phi(x_{j''}))$ for some $x_{j''} \in \text{var}(\alpha)$. Therefore the following fact (later referred to as $(\star)$) is evident: Without loss of generality, δ, ϕ, and ψ can be chosen such that $x_j \in \text{var}(\psi(x_j))$ for every $x_j \in \text{var}(\delta)$, $\phi(x_j) = x_j$ for every $x_j \in \text{var}(\alpha) \cap \text{var}(\delta)$, and $\phi(x_{j'}) = e$ for every $x_{j'} \in \text{var}(\alpha) \setminus \text{var}(\delta)$.

In order to provide a basic decomposition of α we now define some appropriate subsets of $\text{var}(\alpha)$: First, $Y_1 := \{x_{j_1} \in \text{var}(\alpha) \mid |\psi(\phi(x_{j_1}))| \ge 2\}$, second, $Y_2 := \{x_{j_2} \in \text{var}(\alpha) \mid \phi(x_{j_2}) = e\}$, and finally $Y_3 := \text{var}(\alpha) \setminus (Y_1 \cup Y_2)$. These definitions entail $Y_1 \cap Y_2 = \emptyset$, $Y_2 \ne \emptyset$ (because of $|\delta| < |\alpha|$), and $|\phi(x_{j_3})| = |\psi(\phi(x_{j_3}))| = 1$ for all $x_{j_3} \in Y_3$ (because of $(\star)$). Using these sets of variables we examine the following decomposition: $\alpha = \beta_0 \, \gamma_1 \, \beta_1 \, \gamma_2 \, \beta_2 \, \cdots \, \beta_{m-1} \, \gamma_m \, \beta_m$ with $\beta_0, \beta_m \in Y_3^*$, $\beta_i \in Y_3^+$ for $0 < i < m$, and $\gamma_i \in (Y_1 \cup Y_2)^+$ for all $i \le m$.

This decomposition is unique. Obviously, it satisfies condition 2, and because of $(\star)$ we may state fact $(\star\star)$: $\gamma_i = \psi(\phi(\gamma_i))$ for every i, $1 \le i \le m$.

This leads to $\text{var}(\gamma_i) \cap Y_1 \ne \emptyset$ for all $i \le m$, and therefore condition 1 is satisfied. Now we can identify the following two cases:

Case A: $\forall i, 1 \le i \le m : \sum_{x_{j_1} \in Y_1} |\gamma_i|_{x_{j_1}} = 1$
Consequently, if $\text{var}(\gamma_i) \cap \text{var}(\gamma_{i'}) \cap Y_1 \ne \emptyset$ for some i, i', $i \ne i'$, then $\phi(\gamma_i) = \phi(\gamma_{i'})$ and also $\psi(\phi(\gamma_i)) = \psi(\phi(\gamma_{i'}))$. Thus, with $(\star\star)$ we can state $\gamma_i = \gamma_{i'}$, and therefore condition 3 for the basic decomposition is satisfied.

Case B: $\exists \hat{\imath}, 1 \le \hat{\imath} \le m : \sum_{x_{j_1} \in Y_1} |\gamma_i|_{x_{j_1}} = p \ne 1$ for a $p \in \mathbb{N}$
Because of condition 1 being satisfied, we can assume in this case that $p \ge 2$. Hence, we examine all modified decompositions of α that match the following principle for every $\hat{\imath}$ meeting the requirement of Case B:

$$\alpha = \beta_0 \, \gamma_1 \, \beta_1 \, \gamma_2 \, \beta_2 \, \cdots \, \beta_{\hat{\imath}-1} \, \overbrace{\gamma_{\hat{\imath}_1} \, \beta_{\hat{\imath}_1} \, \gamma_{\hat{\imath}_2} \, \beta_{\hat{\imath}_2} \, \cdots \, \beta_{\hat{\imath}_{p}-1} \, \gamma_{\hat{\imath}_p}}^{\gamma_{\hat{\imath}}} \, \beta_{\hat{\imath}+1} \, \cdots \, \beta_{m-1} \, \gamma_m \, \beta_m$$

such that β_i for all i and γ_i for all $i \neq \hat{\imath}$ derive from the previous definition, and, furthermore, such that $\beta_{\hat{\imath}_k} = e$ for all k, $1 \leq k \leq p-1$, and $\gamma_{\hat{\imath}_k} = \gamma_{\hat{\imath}_k,l}\, x_{j_1,\hat{\imath}_k}\, \gamma_{\hat{\imath}_k,r}$ for all k, $1 \leq k \leq p$, with $|\gamma_{\hat{\imath}_k}| \geq 2$ and $\gamma_{\hat{\imath}_k,l}, \gamma_{\hat{\imath}_k,r} \in Y_2^*$ and $x_{j_1,\hat{\imath}_k} \in Y_1$. Then, for all of these newly created decompositions, conditions 1 and 2 still are satisfied. Because of $\psi(x_{j_1,\hat{\imath}_1}\, x_{j_1,\hat{\imath}_2} \ldots x_{j_1,\hat{\imath}_p}) = \gamma_{\hat{\imath}}$, one of these decompositions meets the requirement of Case A. $\square$

As an illustration of Theorem 3 we now analyse some terminal-free patterns:

Example 1. $x_1x_2x_2x_1x_2x_2$ is prolix since $\gamma_1 = \gamma_2 = x_1x_2x_2$ and $\beta_0 = \beta_1 = \beta_2 = e$. $x_1x_2x_2x_1x_2x_2x_2$ and $x_1x_2x_1x_3x_4x_2x_4x_3$ are succinct since no variable for every of its occurrences has the same "environment" (i.e. a suitable γ) of length greater or equal 2 such that this environment does not share any of its variables with any potential β. $x_1x_2x_1x_2x_3x_3x_2x_4x_4x_5x_3x_2x_4x_4x_5$ is prolix since $\gamma_1 = \gamma_2 = x_1x_2$, $\gamma_3 = \gamma_4 = x_2x_4x_4x_5$, $\beta_0 = \beta_1 = \beta_4 = e$, $\beta_2 = x_3x_3$, $\beta_3 = x_3$.

As pointed out in [13], certain words due to their ambiguity are unsuitable for being part of a telltale. In the following definition we introduce a particular type of substitution that – depending on the pattern it is applied to – may lead to ambiguous words as well; nevertheless, it can be used to generate telltale words as it imposes appropriate restrictions upon their ambiguity. This feature is relevant for the learnability criterion in Theorem 4.

Definition 1. *Let α be a terminal-free pattern, $|\alpha| =: n$, and σ a substitution. For any $m \leq n$ let $\alpha\backslash_m = y_1 y_2 \cdots y_m$ be the prefix of length m of α. Let r_1, r_2, $\ldots$, r_{n-1} and l_2, l_3, $\ldots$, l_n be the smallest natural numbers such that for every substitution σ' with $\sigma'(\alpha) = \sigma(\alpha)$ and for $m = 1, 2, \ldots, n-1$:*

$$|\sigma(\alpha\backslash_m)| - r_m \leq |\sigma'(\alpha\backslash_m)| \leq |\sigma(\alpha\backslash_m)| + l_{m+1}.$$

Furthermore, define $l_1 := 0 =: r_n$.

Then we call the substitution σ (λ, ρ)-significant (for α) iff there exist two mappings $\lambda, \rho : \mathbb{N} \longrightarrow \mathbb{N}$ such that, for every $x_j \in \mathrm{var}(\alpha)$, $\lambda(j) = \max\{l_m \mid y_m = x_j\}$, $\rho(j) = \max\{r_m \mid y_m = x_j\}$, and $|\sigma(x_j)| \geq \lambda(j) + \rho(j) + 1$. We designate a word w as significant (for α) iff for some λ, ρ there exists a (λ, ρ)-significant substitution σ such that $w = \sigma(\alpha)$.

The following example illustrates Definition 1:

Example 2. Let $\alpha := x_1x_2x_3x_4x_1x_4x_3x_2$. Obviously, α is terminal-free and prolix (cf. Theorem 3). Let the substitution σ be given by $\sigma(x_1) := \mathsf{a}$, $\sigma(x_2) := \mathsf{a\,b}$, $\sigma(x_3) := \mathsf{b}$, and $\sigma(x_4) := \mathsf{a\,a}$. With little effort it can be seen that there exists only one different substitution σ' such that $\sigma'(\alpha) = \sigma(\alpha)$, namely $\sigma'(x_1) = \mathsf{a\,a}$, $\sigma'(x_2) = \mathsf{b}$, $\sigma'(x_3) = \mathsf{b\,a}$, and $\sigma'(x_4) = \mathsf{a}$. In terms of Definition 1 this implies the following:

$$\sigma(\alpha\backslash_1) = \mathsf{a} \quad \sigma(\alpha\backslash_2) = \mathsf{a\,a\,b} \quad \sigma(\alpha\backslash_3) = \mathsf{a\,a\,b\,b} \quad \sigma(\alpha\backslash_4) = \mathsf{a\,a\,b\,b\,a\,a} \; \cdots$$
$$\sigma'(\alpha\backslash_1) = \mathsf{a\,a} \quad \sigma'(\alpha\backslash_2) = \mathsf{a\,a\,b} \quad \sigma'(\alpha\backslash_3) = \mathsf{a\,a\,b\,b\,a} \quad \sigma'(\alpha\backslash_4) = \mathsf{a\,a\,b\,b\,a\,a} \; \cdots$$

Thus, $l_2 = l_4 = l_6 = l_8 = 1$, $l_1 = l_3 = l_5 = l_7 = 0$, and $r_k = 0$ for $1 \leq k \leq 8$. Then, with $\lambda(1) = \lambda(3) = 0$, $\lambda(2) = \lambda(4) = 1$, and $\rho(j) = 0$ for $1 \leq j \leq 4$, the substitution σ is (λ, ρ)-significant for α, since $|\sigma(x_j)| \geq \lambda(j) + \rho(j) + 1$ for every j, $1 \leq j \leq 4$. Consequently, there are certain subwords in $w := \sigma(\alpha) = \sigma'(\alpha)$ that are generated for every possible substitution by the same variable; therefore we may regard the following variables and subwords – that, in a different example, of course can consist of more than one letter each – as "associated":

$$w = \underbrace{\text{a}}_{x_1} \text{ a } \underbrace{\text{b}}_{x_2} \underbrace{\text{b}}_{x_3} \text{ a } \underbrace{\text{a}}_{x_4} \underbrace{\text{a}}_{x_1} \text{ a } \underbrace{\text{a}}_{x_4} \underbrace{\text{b}}_{x_3} \text{ a } \underbrace{\text{b}}_{x_2}.$$

That is the particular property of significant words which serves our purposes.

A second (and "comprehensive") example for a substitution generating significant words is given in Lemma 1.

Now we present the learnability criterion to be used, that is a generalisation of two criteria in [13]. As mentioned in Example 2, this criterion utilizes the existence of certain subwords in significant words that may be mapped to a distinct variable. In these subwords we place a single letter as a *marker* for its variable such that the exact shape of the generating pattern can be extracted from a suitable set of these words. The need for this distinct marker is an oblique consequence of a method used in [13] – the so-called *inverse substitution*.

Theorem 4. *Let Σ be an alphabet. Let $\text{Pat}^\star_{\text{tf}}$ be a recursively enumerable set of terminal-free patterns and $\text{ePAT}^\star_{\text{tf},\Sigma}$ the corresponding class of E-pattern languages. Then $\text{ePAT}^\star_{\text{tf},\Sigma} \in \text{LIM-TEXT}$ if for every $\alpha \in \text{Pat}^\star_{\text{tf}}$ there exists a finite set $\text{SUB} := \{\sigma_i \mid 1 \leq i \leq n\}$ of substitutions and mappings λ_i and ρ_i such that*

1. *every $\sigma_i \in \text{SUB}$ is (λ_i, ρ_i)-significant for α and*
2. *for every $x_j \in \text{var}(\alpha)$ there exists a substitution $\sigma_{j'} \in \text{SUB}$ with $\sigma_{j'}(x_j) = u_{j',j} \, \text{a} \, v_{j',j}$ for a letter $\text{a} \in \Sigma$ and some $u_{j',j}, v_{j',j} \in \Sigma^*$, $|u_{j',j}| \geq \lambda_{j'}(j)$ and $|v_{j',j}| \geq \rho_{j'}(j)$, such that $|\sigma_{j'}(\alpha)|_\text{a} = |\alpha|_{x_j}$.*

Proof. Given $\alpha \in \text{Pat}^\star_{\text{tf}}$, we define a set T_α of words by $T_\alpha := \{w_i \mid \sigma_i(\alpha) = w_i \text{ for a } \sigma_i \in \text{SUB}\}$. We now show that T_α is a telltale for $L(\alpha)$ in respect of $\text{ePAT}^\star_{\text{tf},\Sigma}$. For that purpose assume $T_\alpha \subseteq L(\beta) \subseteq L(\alpha)$ for some $\beta \in \text{Pat}^\star_{\text{tf}}$. Then (due to Fact 1) there exists a morphism $\phi : X^* \longrightarrow X^*$ such that $\phi(\alpha) = \beta$.

Because every $\sigma_i \in \text{SUB}$ is (λ_i, ρ_i)-significant for α and because of condition 2 we may conclude that for every $x_j \in \text{var}(\alpha)$ and for every σ' with $\sigma'(\beta) = w_{j'} = \sigma_{j'}(\alpha)$ – that necessarily exists since $T_\alpha \subseteq L(\beta)$ – holds the following: $\sigma'(\phi(x_j)) = u'_{j',j} \, \text{a} \, v'_{j',j}$ for a letter $\text{a} \in \Sigma$, and two words $u'_{j',j}, v'_{j',j} \in \Sigma^*$; for these words, due to the significance of $w_{j'}$, it is evident that $u'_{j',j}$ is a suffix of $u_{j',j}$ (or vice versa) and $v'_{j',j}$ is a prefix of $v_{j',j}$ (or vice versa). In addition it is obvious that $|\sigma'(\beta)|_\text{a} = |\alpha|_{x_j}$ can be stated for the examined σ'. Therefore, in order to allow appropriate substitutions to generate the single letter a, ϕ for all $x_j \in \text{var}(\alpha)$ must have the shape $\phi(x_j) = \gamma_1 \, x_{j_\text{a}} \, \gamma_2$ with $\gamma_1, \gamma_2 \in X^*$ and a single variable $x_{j_\text{a}} \in \text{var}(\phi(x_j))$, i.e. $|\beta|_{x_{j_\text{a}}} = |\alpha|_{x_j}$. Hence, the morphism $\psi : X^* \longrightarrow X^*$, defined by $\psi(x_k) := x_j$ for $k = j_\text{a}$ and $\psi(x_k) := e$ for $k \neq j_\text{a}$, leads to $\psi(\beta) = \alpha$ and – with the assumption $L(\beta) \subseteq L(\alpha)$ – to $L(\beta) = L(\alpha)$. Consequently, $L(\beta) \not\subseteq L(\alpha)$ for every pattern β with $T_\alpha \subseteq L(\beta)$ and, thus, T_α is a telltale for $L(\alpha)$ in respect of $\mathrm{ePAT}_{\mathrm{tf}}^\star$ (because of Fact 3). $\qquad\square$

In prolix patterns, there exist variables that cannot be substituted in such a way that the resulting word is significant. For instance, in the pattern $\alpha = x_1\, x_2\, x_1\, x_2$ every subword generated by x_1 can be generated by x_2 as well, and vice versa. Therefore, when applying Theorem 4 to $\mathrm{ePAT}_{\mathrm{tf}}$, $\mathrm{Pat}_{\mathrm{tf}}^\star$ necessarily has to consist of succinct patterns only.

The following two lemmata prove that for every succinct terminal-free pattern (and, thereby, for every language in $\mathrm{ePAT}_{\mathrm{tf}}$) there exists a set of substitutions satisfying the conditions of Theorem 4.

Lemma 1. *Let α be a succinct pattern, $\alpha \in \mathrm{Pat}_{\mathrm{tf}}$, and Σ an alphabet such that $\{\mathrm{a}, \mathrm{b}, \mathrm{c}\} \subseteq \Sigma$. Let for every $x_j \in \mathrm{var}(\alpha)$ and for every $i \in \{j \mid x_j \in \mathrm{var}(\alpha)\}$ the substitution σ_i^{tf} be given by*

$$\sigma_i^{\mathrm{tf}}(x_j) := \begin{cases} \mathrm{a\,b}^{3j-2}\,\mathrm{a\,a\,b}^{3j-1}\,\mathrm{a\,a\,b}^{3j}\,\mathrm{a} & , \quad i \neq j, \\ \mathrm{a\,b}^{3j-2}\,\mathrm{a\,c\,b}^{3j-1}\,\mathrm{a\,a\,b}^{3j}\,\mathrm{a} & , \quad i = j, \end{cases}$$

Then for every σ_i' with $\sigma_i'(\alpha) = \sigma_i^{\mathrm{tf}}(\alpha)$, for every $x_j \in \mathrm{var}(\alpha)$, and for some $u_j, v_j \in \Sigma^*$:

$$\sigma_i'(x_j) = \begin{cases} u_j\,\mathrm{a\,a\,b}^{3j-1}\,\mathrm{a\,a}\,v_j & , \quad i \neq j, \\ u_j\,\mathrm{a\,c\,b}^{3j-1}\,\mathrm{a\,a}\,v_j & , \quad i = j, \end{cases}$$

Proof. To begin with we explain the following terms that are used frequently: A *segment of* $\sigma_i^{\mathrm{tf}}(x_j)$ is a subword $\mathrm{a\,b}^{3j-q}\,\mathrm{a}$, $0 \leq q \leq 2$. As the natural extension thereof, the term segment of $\sigma_i^{\mathrm{tf}}(\delta)$ for every $\delta \in X^*$ designates any segment of $\sigma_i^{\mathrm{tf}}(x_j)$ with $x_j \in \mathrm{var}(\delta)$. An *outer segment* of $\sigma_i^{\mathrm{tf}}(x_j)$ is the subword $\mathrm{a\,b}^{3j-2}\,\mathrm{a}$ or the subword $\mathrm{a\,b}^{3j}\,\mathrm{a}$. The *inner segment* of $\sigma_i^{\mathrm{tf}}(x_j)$ is the subword $\mathrm{a\,b}^{3j-1}\,\mathrm{a}$. $\sigma_i'(x_{j'})$ *contains segments of* $\sigma_i^{\mathrm{tf}}(x_j)$ means that the segments of $\sigma_i^{\mathrm{tf}}(x_j)$ occur in natural order (i.e. in that order specified by σ_i^{tf}), consecutively (apart from the potential necessity of inserting the letter c), and non-overlapping.

Let σ_i' be an arbitrary substitution with $\sigma_i'(\alpha) = \sigma_i^{\mathrm{tf}}(\alpha)$ and $\sigma_i'(x_j) \neq \sigma_i^{\mathrm{tf}}(x_j)$ for an $x_j \in \mathrm{var}(\alpha)$. Then we define the following subsets of $\mathrm{var}(\alpha)$: Let Y_1 be the set of all $x_{j_1} \in \mathrm{var}(\alpha)$ such that $\sigma_i'(x_{j_1})$ contains the inner segment of $\sigma_i^{\mathrm{tf}}(x_{j_1})$, of every outer segment at least one letter, and at least one segment of the substitution σ_i^{tf} of a neighbouring variable. Consequently, $\sigma_i'(x_{j_1})$ contains at least two segments of $\sigma_i^{\mathrm{tf}}(x_{j_1})$, and for all $x_{j_1} \in Y_1$: $\alpha \neq \delta_1\, x_{j_1} x_{j_1}\, \delta_2$ with $\delta_1, \delta_2 \in X^*$. Let Y_2 be the set of all $x_{j_2} \in \mathrm{var}(\alpha)$ such that $\sigma_i'(x_{j_2})$ contains of at least one segment of $\sigma_i^{\mathrm{tf}}(x_{j_2})$ no letter. Then $Y_1 \cap Y_2 = \emptyset$. Finally, let Y_3 be given by $Y_3 := \mathrm{var}(\alpha) \setminus (Y_1 \cup Y_2)$. Then $\sigma_i'(x_{j_3})$ for all $x_{j_3} \in Y_3$ contains the inner segment of $\sigma_i^{\mathrm{tf}}(x_{j_3})$ and of both outer segments at least one letter, but no complete segment of a neighbouring variable.

Now assume to the contrary $Y_2 \neq \emptyset$, that implies $Y_1 \neq \emptyset$ as for every variable there are three unique corresponding segments (for two segments, depending on

α and σ'_i, we might face the situation that $Y_2, Y_3 \neq \emptyset$, but $Y_1 = \emptyset$). We show that this assumption entails α being prolix. The subsequent argumentation on this utilizes Theorem 3 and an evident fact (referred to as $(\star)$): For every $\delta \in Y_2^+$, $\sigma'_i(\delta)$ contains of at least one segment of $\sigma_i^{\text{tf}}(\delta)$ no letter.

As the starting point of our reasoning we use the following decomposition: $\alpha = \beta_0 \, \gamma_1 \, \beta_1 \, \gamma_2 \, \beta_2 \, \cdots \, \beta_{n-1} \, \gamma_n \, \beta_n$ with $n \geq 1$, $\beta_0, \beta_n \in Y_3^*$, $\beta_k \in Y_3^+$ for $0 < k < n$, and $\gamma_k \in (Y_1 \cup Y_2)^+$ for $1 \leq k \leq n$. This decomposition is unique, and it obviously satisfies condition 2 and – due to $(\star)$ – condition 1 of Theorem 3. However, concerning condition 3 it possibly deserves some modifications. To this end, the following procedure reconstructs the above decomposition such that in every γ_k there is exactly one occurrence of a variable in Y_1 (using $(\star)$ again):

PROCEDURE:

Define $k := 1$.

STEP 1: Let y_1, y_2 be the leftmost variables in γ_k with $y_1, y_2 \in Y_1$ and $\gamma_k = \delta_1 \, y_1 \, y_2 \, \delta_2$ for $\delta_1, \delta_2 \in X^*$. IF these variables exist, THEN define $\gamma_{n+1} := \gamma_n, \, \ldots \, , \gamma_{k+2} := \gamma_{k+1}$, $\beta_{n+1} := \beta_n, \, \ldots \, , \beta_{k+1} := \beta_k$, $\gamma_k := \delta_1 \, y_1$, $\beta_k = e$, and $\gamma_{k+1} := y_2 \, \delta_2$; finally, define $n := n + 1$. END IF. IF $k < n$, THEN define $k := k + 1$ and go to STEP 1. ELSE rename all pattern fragments as follows: $\alpha =: \beta_{0_1} \, \gamma_{1_1} \, \beta_{1_1} \, \gamma_{2_1} \, \beta_{2_1} \, \cdots \, \beta_{(n-1)_1} \, \gamma_{n_1} \, \beta_{n_1}$. Finally, define $k_1 := 1_1$ and go to STEP 2. END IF.

STEP 2: Let $y_1 \in Y_2$ and $y_2 \in Y_1$ be the leftmost variables in γ_{k_1} with $\gamma_{k_1} = \delta_1 \, y_1 \, y_2 \, \delta_2$ for $\delta_1, \delta_2 \in X^*$, such that at least one segment of $\sigma_i^{\text{tf}}(y_1)$ is generated by variables in δ_1. IF these variables exist, THEN IF $\sigma'_i(y_2)$ contains a segment of $\sigma_i^{\text{tf}}(\delta_2)$ (thus, necessarily the leftmost segment), THEN extend the decomposition as described in STEP 1. Finally, define $k_1 := (k+1)_1$, $n_1 := (n+1)_1$, and go to STEP 2. ELSE define $Y_1 := Y_1 \setminus \{y_2\}$ and $Y_3 := Y_3 \cup \{y_2\}$, reconstruct all pattern fragments β_{k_1} and γ_{k_1} accordingly and go to STEP 2. END IF. ELSE IF $k_1 < n_1$, THEN define $k_1 := (k + 1)_1$ and go to STEP 2. ELSE rename all pattern fragments as follows: $\alpha =: \beta_{0_2} \, \gamma_{1_2} \, \beta_{1_2} \, \gamma_{2_2} \, \beta_{2_2} \, \cdots \, \beta_{(n-1)_2} \, \gamma_{n_2} \, \beta_{n_2}$. Finally, define $k_2 := 1_2$ and go to STEP 3. END IF. END IF.

STEP 3: Let $y_1 \in Y_1$ and $y_2 \in Y_2$ be the leftmost variables in γ_{k_2} with $\gamma_{k_2} = \delta_1 \, y_1 \, y_2 \, \delta_2$ for $\delta_1, \delta_2 \in X^*$, such that at least one segment of $\sigma_i^{\text{tf}}(y_2)$ is generated by variables in δ_2. Modify γ_{k_2} analogously to Step 2. When this has been done for every k_2, then rename all pattern fragments as follows: $\alpha =: \beta_{0_3} \, \gamma_{1_3} \, \beta_{1_3} \, \gamma_{2_3} \, \beta_{2_3} \, \cdots \, \beta_{(n-1)_3} \, \gamma_{n_3} \, \beta_{n_3}$. Define $k_3 := 1_3$ and go to STEP 4.

STEP 4: Let y_1, y_2 be the leftmost variables in γ_{k_3} with $y_1, y_2 \in Y_2$ and $\gamma_{k_3} = \delta_1 \, y_1 y_2 \, \delta_2$ for $\delta_1, \delta_2 \in X^*$, such that at least one segment of $\sigma_i^{\text{tf}}(y_1)$ is contained in $\sigma'_i(\delta_1)$ and at least one segment of $\sigma_i^{\text{tf}}(y_2)$ is contained in $\sigma'_i(\delta_2)$. IF these variables exist, THEN extend the decomposition as described in STEP 1. Finally, define $k_3 := (k + 1)_3$, $n_3 := (n + 1)_3$, and go to STEP 4. END IF. IF $k_3 < n_3$, THEN define $k_3 := (k + 1)_3$ and go to STEP 4. ELSE rename all pattern fragments as follows: $\alpha =: \beta_{0_4} \, \gamma_{1_4} \, \beta_{1_4} \, \gamma_{2_4} \, \beta_{2_4} \, \cdots \, \beta_{(n-1)_4} \, \gamma_{n_4} \, \beta_{n_4}$. END IF.

END OF PROCEDURE

Obviously, $\forall k_4, k'_4 : \text{var}(\gamma_{k_4}) \cap \text{var}(\beta_{k'_4}) = \emptyset$. So the following is left to be shown:

a) $\forall k_4 : |\gamma_{k_4}| \geq 2$

b) $\forall k_4 : \sum_{x_{j_1} \in Y_1} |\gamma_{k_4}|_{x_{j_1}} = 1$

c) $\forall k_4, k_4' : (\text{var}(\gamma_{k_4}) \cap \text{var}(\gamma_{k_4'}) \cap Y_1 \neq \emptyset \Longrightarrow \gamma_{k_4} = \gamma_{k_4'})$

ad a) As a consequence of $(\star)$, the first decomposition of α is modified by Steps 1 - 4 if and only if there exists a γ_k that contains at least two variables $y_1, y_2 \in Y_1$. The procedure splits this γ_k in such a way that all new $\gamma_{k_1}, \gamma_{k_2}, \gamma_{k_3}$, and γ_{k_4} contain at least one $x_{j_2} \in Y_2$ and a sequence of variables that generates a segment of $\sigma_i^{\text{tf}}(x_{j_2})$ by σ_i'. Thus, $|\gamma_{k_4}| \geq 2$ for all k_4.

ad b) As mentioned in a), every γ_k contains at least one variable $x_{j_2} \in Y_2$. Moreover, there must also be a variable $x_{j_1} \in Y_1$ in every γ_k (again due to $(\star)$). The procedure splits only those γ_k that contain at least two variables of Y_1, and obviously – if possible – in such a way that every γ_{k_4} contains exactly one $x_{j_1} \in Y_1$. If this due to a) is not possible (e.g. for $\gamma_k = y_1\, y_2\, y_3$ with $y_1, y_3 \in Y_1$, $y_2 \in Y_2$, and necessarily $y_1 \neq y_3$), then in Step 2 or Step 3 either y_1 or y_3 is removed from Y_1 and therefore it is removed from γ_{k_1} or γ_{k_2}, respectively.

ad c) Because of a) and b) it is obvious that every γ_{k_4} begins or ends with a variable from Y_2. We consider that case where γ_{k_4} begins with $x_{j_2,k_4} \in Y_2$; the second case is symmetrical and the argumentation for the case that both aspects hold true derives from the combination of both approaches.

Hence, without loss of generality $\gamma_{k_4} = x_{j_2,k_4} \delta_1$ for $\delta_1 \in X^*$. Due to $(\star)$ and the construction of γ_{k_4}, to the right of x_{j_2,k_4} there is a pattern fragment $\gamma_{k_4,1}, |\gamma_{k_4,1}| \geq 1$, such that $\sigma_i'(\gamma_{k_4,1})$ contains at least one segment of $\sigma_i^{\text{tf}}(x_{j_2,k_4})$. If $\gamma_{k_4,1} \in Y_2^+$, then to the right of this pattern fragment there is a second pattern fragment $\gamma_{k_4,2}, |\gamma_{k_4,2}| \geq 1$, that – with σ_i' – again generates the segments "missing" in $\sigma_i'(\gamma_{k_4,1})$ and so on. As every γ_{k_4} has finite length, there must exist a $x_{j_1,k_4} \in Y_1$ in γ_{k_4} concluding this argumentation.

Consequently, $\gamma_{k_4} = x_{j_2,k_4}\, \gamma_{k_4,1}\, \gamma_{k_4,2}\, \cdots\, \gamma_{k_4,p-1}\, \gamma_{k_4,p}\, x_{j_1,k_4}$ for a $p \in \mathbb{N}$. However, since all variables in $\gamma_{k_4,l}, 1 \leq l \leq p$ of at least one of their segments do not generate any letter, x_{j_1,k_4} by σ_i' exactly determines the shape of $\gamma_{k_4,p}$, $\gamma_{k_4,p}$ that of $\gamma_{k_4,p-1}$ etc. up to $\gamma_{k_4,1}$ determining x_{j_2,k_4}.

This holds true for every occurrence of x_{j_1,k_4} and therefore $\forall k_4, k_4' \forall x_{j_1} \in Y_1 : ((x_{j_1} \in \text{var}(\gamma_{k_4}) \wedge x_{j_1} \in \text{var}(\gamma_{k_4'})) \Longrightarrow \gamma_{k_4} = \gamma_{k_4'})$. This proves c).

Thus, with a), b), c), and Theorem 3, α is prolix. This is a contradiction. Consequently, we may conclude $Y_1 = Y_2 = \emptyset$; this proves the lemma. $\qquad \square$

With Lemma 1, the major part of our reasoning is accomplished. Now the following lemma can be concluded without effort:

Lemma 2. *Let α be a succinct pattern, $\alpha \in \text{Pat}_{\text{tf}}$. Then for every i, $i \in \{j \mid x_j \in \text{var}(\alpha)\}$, there exist mappings $\lambda_i, \rho_i : \mathbb{N} \longrightarrow \mathbb{N}$ such that σ_i^{tf} (cf. Lemma 1) is (λ_i, ρ_i)-significant for α.*

Proof. Directly from Lemma 1, since for every $x_j \in \text{var}(\alpha)$ we can state $\lambda_i(j) \leq 3j - 1$, $\rho_i(j) \leq 3j + 1$, and $|\sigma_i^{\text{tf}}(x_j)| \geq 9j + 3$. $\qquad \square$

Consequently, for every succinct terminal-free pattern there exists a set of significant words. However, no word generated by any σ_i^{tf} needs to consist of three different letters in order to be significant – a and b would be sufficient. Indeed, due to the marker c, the given set of all σ_i^{tf} satisfies the second condition of Theorem 4. Thus, Theorem 4 is applicable for ePAT$_{tf}$ and therefore the main result of this paper, given in Theorem 2, is proven.

References

1. D. Angluin. Finding patterns common to a set of strings. In *Proc. STOC 1979*, pages 130–141, 1979.
2. D. Angluin. Inductive inference of formal languages from positive data. *Inf. Control*, 45:117–135, 1980.
3. G. Filè. The relation of two patterns with comparable language. In *Proc. STACS 1988*, volume 294 of *LNCS*, pages 184–192, 1988.
4. E.M. Gold. Language identification in the limit. *Inf. Control*, 10:447–474, 1967.
5. T. Jiang, E. Kinber, A. Salomaa, K. Salomaa, and S. Yu. Pattern languages with and without erasing. *Int. J. Comput. Math.*, 50:147–163, 1994.
6. T. Jiang, A. Salomaa, K. Salomaa, and S. Yu. Decision problems for patterns. *J. Comput. Syst. Sci.*, 50:53–63, 1995.
7. S. Lange and R. Wiehagen. Polynomial-time inference of arbitrary pattern languages. *New Generat. Comput.*, 8:361–370, 1991.
8. M. Lipponen and G. Păun. Strongly prime PCP words. *Discrete Appl. Math.*, 63:193–197, 1995.
9. A. Mateescu and A. Salomaa. PCP-prime words and primality types. *RAIRO Inform. théor.*, 27(1):57–70, 1993.
10. A. Mateescu and A. Salomaa. Finite degrees of ambiguity in pattern languages. *RAIRO Inform. théor.*, 28(3–4):233–253, 1994.
11. A.R. Mitchell. Learnability of a subclass of extended pattern languages. In *Proc. COLT 1998*, pages 64–71, 1998.
12. D. Reidenbach. A non-learnable class of E-pattern languages. *Theor. Comp. Sci.*, to appear.
13. D. Reidenbach. A negative result on inductive inference of extended pattern languages. In *Proc. ALT 2002*, volume 2533 of *LNAI*, pages 308–320, 2002.
14. R. Reischuk and T. Zeugmann. Learning one-variable pattern languages in linear average time. In *Proc. COLT 1998*, pages 198–208, 1998.
15. H. Rogers. *Theory of Recursive Functions and Effective Computability*. MIT Press, Cambridge, Mass., 1992. 3rd print.
16. G. Rozenberg and A. Salomaa. *Handbook of Formal Languages*, volume 1. Springer, Berlin, 1997.
17. T. Shinohara. Polynomial time inference of extended regular pattern languages. In *Proc. RIMS Symposia on Software Science and Engineering, Kyoto*, volume 147 of *LNCS*, pages 115–127, 1982.
18. A. Thue. Über unendliche Zeichenreihen. *Kra. Vidensk. Selsk. Skrifter. I Mat. Nat. Kl.*, 7, 1906.
19. R. Wiehagen and T. Zeugmann. Ignoring data may be the only way to learn efficiently. *J. Exp. Theor. Artif. Intell.*, 6:131–144, 1994.
20. K. Wright. Identification of unions of languages drawn from an identifiable class. In *Proc. COLT 1989*, pages 328–333, 1989.

Algorithms for SAT Based on Search in Hamming Balls

Evgeny Dantsin[1], Edward A. Hirsch[2]*, and Alexander Wolpert[1]

[1] Roosevelt University, 430 S. Michigan Av., Chicago, IL 60605, USA
{edantsin,awolpert}@roosevelt.edu
[2] Steklov Institute of Mathematics, 27 Fontanka, St. Petersburg 191023, Russia
hirsch@pdmi.ras.ru.

Abstract. We present two simple algorithms for SAT and prove upper bounds on their running time. Given a Boolean formula F in conjunctive normal form, the first algorithm finds a satisfying assignment for F (if any) by repeating the following: Choose an assignment A at random and search for a satisfying assignment inside a Hamming ball around A (the radius of the ball depends on F). We show that this algorithm solves SAT with a small probability of error in at most $2^{n-0.712\sqrt{n}}$ steps, where n is the number of variables in F. To derandomize this algorithm, we use covering codes instead of random assignments. The deterministic algorithm solves SAT in at most $2^{n-2\sqrt{n/\log_2 n}}$ steps. To the best of our knowledge, this is the first non-trivial bound for a deterministic SAT algorithm with no restriction on clause length.

1 Introduction

The propositional satisfiability problem (SAT) can be solved by an obvious algorithm in 2^n steps where n is the number of variables in the input formula. During the past decade there was a significant progress in proving better upper bounds for the restricted version of SAT (known as k-SAT) that allows clauses of length at most k. Both deterministic and randomized algorithms were developed for k-SAT; the currently best known bounds are as follows:

- $poly(n)\,(2 - \frac{2}{k+1})^n$ for a deterministic k-SAT algorithm [4,3];
- $poly(n)\,2^{(1-\frac{\mu_k}{k-1})n+o(n)}$ for a randomized k-SAT algorithm, where $k > 4$ and $\mu_k \to \frac{\pi^2}{6}$ as $k \to \infty$ [8];
- $O(1.324^n)$ for a randomized 3-SAT algorithm and $O(1.474^n)$ for a randomized 4-SAT algorithm [7]; these bounds and other recent bounds for 3-SAT, e.g., [1,6,11], are based on Schöning's local search algorithm [12,13] or on the randomized DPLL approach of Paturi, Pudlák, Saks, and Zane [9,8].

* Supported in part by RAS program of fundamental research "Research in principal areas of contemporary mathematics", RFBR grant #02-01-00089, and by Award No. RM1-2409-ST-02 of the U.S. Civilian Research & Development Foundation for the Independent States of the Former Soviet Union (CRDF).

V. Diekert and M. Habib (Eds.): STACS 2004, LNCS 2996, pp. 141–151, 2004.
© Springer-Verlag Berlin Heidelberg 2004

However, the progress for SAT without the restriction on the clause length is much more modest. Pudlak gives a randomized algorithm (based on [8]) that solves SAT in expected time $poly(n) \, m \, 2^{n-\varepsilon\sqrt{n}}$ where n is the number of variables, m is the number of clauses, and ε is a positive constant [10]. The most recent bound for a randomized SAT algorithm is given by Schuler in [14]: his algorithm (using the algorithm of [8]) runs in expected time $poly(n) \, m \, 2^{n-\frac{n}{1+\log_2 m}}$. There are also bounds that are "more" dependent on the number of clauses or other input parameters, e.g., $poly(n) \, m \, 2^{0.30897m}$ [5] for a deterministic SAT algorithm.

In this paper, we give a randomized algorithm that solves SAT in expected time $poly(n) \, m^2 \, 2^{n-0.712\sqrt{n}}$ and a deterministic algorithm that solves SAT in time $poly(n) \, m^2 \, 2^{n-2\sqrt{n/\log_2 n}}$. To the best of our knowledge, the latter is the first non-trivial bound for a deterministic SAT algorithm with no restriction on clause length. The bound for the randomized algorithm is worse than Schuler's bound [14]. However, our randomized algorithm uses another idea (the approach of [3] based on covering the search space by Hamming balls) and has a derandomized version (our deterministic algorithm).

Both our algorithms are based on the *multistart local search* approach that proved to be successful in randomized and deterministic algorithms for k-SAT [13,3]. Similarly to other local search algorithms, our algorithms choose some assignment of truth values to variables and then modify it step by step; sometimes the algorithm is restarted. There are two versions of this approach: "randomized" search [13] where the algorithm performs a random walk and "deterministic" search [3] where the algorithm recursively examines several possibilities to change the current assignments. In both versions, the random walk or the recursion is terminated after a specified number of steps, and the algorithm is restarted. We use the "deterministic" approach [3] for both deterministic and randomized algorithms: they search for a satisfying assignment inside a Hamming ball of a certain radius R around the initial assignment. More exactly, the search implementation either uses a minor modification of the procedure in [3] or examines all assignments in the Hamming ball, whichever is faster.

The analysis of a randomized algorithm based on the multistart local search usually contains two parts: the estimation of the probability that the initial assignment is close enough to a satisfying assignment, and the estimation of the time needed to perform the search started from the initial assignment. In the analysis of a deterministic algorithm based on the same approach, the first part is replaced by the estimation of the number of initial assignments that are needed to guarantee that all 2^n assignments (the points of the Boolean cube $\{0,1\}^n$) are covered by Hamming balls of radius R around the initial assignments[1]. In both cases, R is chosen to tradeoff between the number of initial assignments

---

[1] For example, the paper [3] gives two constructions of such coverings; we use the one that finds the set of assignments for $n/6$ variables by a greedy algorithm for the Set Cover problem, and then takes the direct product of 6 instances of the constructed set. The construction is optimal both in time and the number of assignments; however, the algorithm uses exponential space.

and the running time inside each ball. Our analysis follows this general scheme and, in addition, takes into account the fact that the time needed to find a solution inside a ball varies from one initial assignment to another. Our key lemma (Lemma 5) estimates the probability that this time is small enough, i.e., the lengths of clauses used by the algorithm are bounded by a certain function of n.

Organization of the paper. Sect. 2 defines basic notions and notation used in the paper. The randomized algorithm and its analysis are given in Sect. 3. This algorithm is derandomized in Sect. 4.

2   Definitions and Notation

Formulas and assignments. We deal with Boolean formulas in conjunctive normal form (CNF). By a *variable* we mean a Boolean variable that takes truth values $\top$ (true) or $\bot$ (false). A *literal* is a variable x or its negation $\neg x$. If l is a literal then $\neg l$ denotes the opposite literal, i.e., if l is x then $\neg l$ denotes $\neg x$, and if l is $\neg x$ then $\neg l$ denotes x. Similarly, if v denotes one of the truth values $\top$ or $\bot$, we write $\neg v$ to denote the opposite truth value. A *clause* is a disjunction C of literals such that C contains no opposite literals. The *length* of C (denoted by $|C|$) is the number of literals in C. A *formula* is a conjunction of clauses.

An *assignment* to variables $x_1, \ldots, x_n$ is a mapping from $\{x_1, \ldots, x_n\}$ to $\{\top, \bot\}$. This mapping is extended to literals: each literal $\neg x_i$ is mapped to the truth value opposite to the value assigned to x_i. We say that a clause C is *satisfied* by an assignment A if A assigns $\top$ to at least one literal in C. Otherwise, we say that C is *falsified* by A. The formula F is *satisfied* by A if every clause in F is satisfied by A. In this case, A is called a *satisfying* assignment for F.

Let F be a formula and l be a literal such that its variable occurs in F. We write $F|_{l=\top}$ to denote the formula obtained from F by assigning the value $\top$ to l. This formula is obtained from F as follows: the clauses that contain l are deleted from F, and the literal $\neg l$ is deleted from the other clauses. Note that $F|_{l=\top}$ may contain the empty clause or may be the empty formula. Let A and A' be two assignments differ only in the values assigned to a literal l. Then we say that A' is obtained from A by *flipping* the value of l.

Covering by balls. We identify $\top$ and $\bot$ with 1 and 0 respectively. Then any assignment to variables $x_1, \ldots, x_n$ can be identified with a point in Boolean cube $\{0, 1\}^n$. Let A and A' be assignments to $x_1, \ldots, x_n$, i.e., $A, A' \in \{0, 1\}^n$. The *Hamming distance* between A and A' is the number of variables x_i such that A and A' assign different values to x_i, i.e., the number of coordinates where A and A' are different. The *Hamming ball* (or simply *ball*) of radius R around an assignment A is the set of all assignments whose Hamming distance to A is less than or equal to R. The assignment A is called the *center* of the ball. The *volume* of a ball is the number of assignments that belong to the ball. We write $V(n, R)$ to denote the volume of a ball of radius R in $\{0, 1\}^n$. It is well known that the volume of a Hamming ball can be estimated in terms of the *binary entropy function*:

$$H(x) = -x \log_2 x - (1 - x) \log_2(1 - x) \ .$$

Let $A_1, \ldots, A_t \in \{0, 1\}^n$. Consider the balls of radius R around $A_1, \ldots, A_t$. We say that these balls *cover* $\{0, 1\}^n$ if any point in $\{0, 1\}^n$ belongs to at least one of these balls. The centers of the balls that cover $\{0, 1\}^n$ are then called a *covering code* of length n and radius R, see e.g., [2]. The number t of the code words is called the *size* of the covering code.

Notation. Here is a summary of the notation used in the paper.

- F denotes a formula; n denotes the number of variables in F; m denotes the number of clauses in F; k denotes the maximum length of clauses in F;
- C denotes a clause; $|C|$ denotes its length;
- A denotes an assignment;
- $F|_{l=\top}$ denotes the formula obtained from A by assigning $\top$ to literal l;
- R denotes the radius of a ball; $V(n, R)$ denotes the volume of a ball of radius R in $\{0, 1\}^n$;
- $H(x)$ denotes the binary entropy function.

3   Randomized Algorithm

In this section we desribe our randomized algorithm for SAT and analyze its probability of error and running time. The algorithm is called *Random-Balls*, it invokes procedures called *Ball-Checking* and *Full-Ball-Checking*. We start with the definition of these procedures. Given a formula F, an assignment A, and a radius R, each of the procedures searches for a satisfying solution to F in the Hamming ball of radius R around A.

Procedure *Ball-Checking*(F, A, R)

Input: formula F, assignment A, number R.
Output: satisfying assignment or "no".

1. If all clauses in F are true under A then return A.
2. If $R \leq 0$ then return "no".
3. If F contains an empty clause then return "no".
4. Choose a shortest clause $l_1 \vee \ldots \vee l_k$ in F that is falsified by A.
5. For $i \leftarrow 1$ to k
   Invoke *Ball-Checking*$(F_i, A_i, R - 1)$ where F_i is $F|_{l_i=\top}$ and A_i is obtained from A by flipping the value of l_i. If this call returns an assignment S, return S.
6. Return "no".

This procedure differs from its counterpart in [3] only in the choice of an unsatisfied clause at step 4: the procedure above chooses a *shortest* unsatisfied clause, while [3] allows choosing *any* unsatisfied clause.

Lemma 1. *If Ball-Checking(F, A, R) returns an assignment then this assignment satisfies F and belongs to the Hamming ball of radius R around A. If Ball-Checking(F, A, R) returns "no" then F has no satisfying assignments in the ball of radius R around A.*

Proof. The same as the proof of Lemma 2 in [3].   □

The following lemma gives a natural upper bound on the worst-case running time of Procedure *Ball-Checking*.

Lemma 2. *The running time of Ball-Checking(F, A, R) is at most $poly(n) \, m k^R$, where k is the maximum length of clauses occurring at steps 4 in all recursive calls.*

Proof. The recursion tree has at most k^R leaves because the maximum degree of branching is k and the maximum depth is R.   □

The next procedure *Full-Ball-Checking* searches a satisfying solution in a ball using a "less intelligent" method: this procedure simply checks the input formula on all points of the ball.

Procedure *Full-Ball-Checking(F, A, R)*

Input: formula F over variables $x_1, \ldots, x_n$, assignment A, number R.
Output: satisfying assignment or "no".

1. For $j \leftarrow 0$ to R
   For all subsets $\{i_1, \ldots, i_j\} \subseteq \{1, \ldots, n\}$
   a) Flip the values of variables $x_{i_1}, \ldots, x_{i_j}$ in A. Let A' be the new assignment obtained from A by these flips.
   b) If A' satisfies F, return A'.
2. Return "no".

Clearly, *Full-Ball-Checking* runs in time at most $poly(n) \, m \, V(n, R)$.

Next we define Algorithm *Random-Balls*. Given a formula F, this algorithm either returns a satisfying assignment for F or replies that F is unsatisfiable. In addition to F, the algorithm takes two numbers as input: R (radius of balls) and l ("threshold length" of clauses). The algorithm generates a certain number of random assignments step by step. For each such assignment A, the algorithm searches for a satisfying solution in the ball of radius R around A. To do it, the algorithm invokes either Procedure *Ball-Checking* or Procedure *Full-Ball-Checking*. The first one is executed if all clauses that would occur at its steps 4 are shorter than the specified "threshold" l. Otherwise, the algorithm invokes Procedure *Full-Ball-Checking*.

Algorithm *Random-Balls(F, R, l)*

Input: formula F over n variables, numbers R and l such that $0 \le R \le l \le n$.
Output: satisfying assignment or "no".

1. $N = \lceil \sqrt{8R(1 - R/n)} \; 2^{n(1-H(R/n))} \rceil$.
2. Repeat N times the following:
   a) Choose an assignment A uniformly at random.
   b) If F contains a clause that has at least l literals falsified by A and at most R literals satisfied by A, invoke *Full-Ball-Checking(F, A, R)*. Otherwise invoke *Ball-Checking(F, A, R)*. If the invoked procedure finds a satisfying assignment, return it.
3. Return "no".

Obviously, if the algorithm *Random-Balls* returns an assignment S then S satisfies the input formula, but the answer "no" may be incorrect. Thus, the algorithm is a one-sided error Monte Carlo algorithm that makes no mistake on unsatisfiable formulas, but may err on satisfiable ones. The following theorem estimates its probability of error.

Lemma 3. *For any R and l, the following holds:*

1. *If an input formula F is unsatisfiable then Algorithm Random-Balls returns "no" with probability 1.*
2. *If F is satisfiable then Algorithm Random-Balls finds a satisfying assignment with probability at least $1/2$.*

Proof. The first part follows from Lemma 1. Consider the second part: F has a satisfying assignment S, but all N trials of the algorithm return "no". This is possible only if for each of the N random assignments (chosen at step 2a), its Hamming distance from S is greater than R. Therefore, the probability of error does not exceed $(1 - p)^N$ where p is the probability that a random assignment belongs to the Hamming ball of radius R around S. To estimate p, we observe that $p = V(n, R)/2^n$ where $V(n, R)$ is the volume of a Hamming ball of radius R in the Boolean cube $\{0,1\}^n$. For $R \le n/2$, the volume $V(n, R)$ can be estimated as follows, see e.g. [2, Lemma 2.4.4]:

$$\frac{1}{\sqrt{8R(1 - R/n)}} \cdot 2^{H(R/n)n} \; \le \; V(n, R) \; \le \; 2^{H(R/n)n} \; .$$

Therefore $p \ge 2^{n(H(R/n)-1)}/\sqrt{8R(1 - R/n)}$. Using this lower bound on p, we get the stated upper bound on the probability of error: $(1-p)^N \le e^{-pN} \le 1/2$. $\square$

The following lemma is needed to estimate the running time of the algorithm *Random-Balls*.

Lemma 4. *Consider the execution of Random-Balls(F, R, l) that invokes Procedure Ball-Checking. For any input R and l, the maximum length of clauses chosen at steps 4 of Procedure Ball-Checking is less than l.*

Proof. The proof follows from the condition of step 2(b) of *Random-Balls*. More formally, let C be a clause of length at least l occurring in step 4 in some recursive call of *Ball-Checking*(F, A, R). Then C is a "decendent" of some clause D in F, i.e., C is obtained from D by removing $|D| - |C|$ literals where $|D| - |C| < R$. The removed $|D| - |C|$ literals must be true under the initial assignment A; the remaining $|C|$ literals must be false under it.   □

Lemma 5. *For any input R and l, let p be the probability (taken over random assignment A) that Random-Balls invokes Procedure Ball-Checking at step 2(b). Then we have the following bound on p:*

$$p \leq m \, 2^{l\left(H\left(\frac{R}{l+R}\right)-1\right)} .$$

Proof. We estimate the probability that a clause D in formula F meets the condition of step 2(b). If this condition holds, at least $\max(l, |D| - R)$ literals must be false under A. There are

$$\sum_{i=\max(l,|D|-R)}^{|D|} \binom{|D|}{i} = V(|D|, \min(|D| - l, R))$$

such assignments to the variables of D. Since $\min(|D| - l, R) \leq \frac{|D|}{2}$, this volume is at most $2^{H(\min(|D|-l,R)/|D|)|D|}$. If $|D| - l < R$, the exponent transforms to

$$H(1 - l/|D|)|D| \leq H(1 - l/(l + R))|D| = H(R/(R + l))|D| .$$

Otherwise, the exponent transforms just to $H(R/|D|)|D| \leq H(R/(R + l))|D|$. Therefore, there are at most $2^{H(R/(R+l))|D|}$ such assignments to the variables of D and at most

$$2^{H\left(\frac{R}{R+l}\right)|D|+n-|D|} = 2^{\left(H\left(\frac{R}{R+l}\right)-1\right)|D|+n} \leq 2^{l\left(H\left(\frac{R}{R+l}\right)-1\right)+n}$$

assignments to the variables of F. Multiplying this bound by the number of clauses in F and dividing by the total number 2^n of assignments, we get the claim.   □

Theorem 1. *For $R = 0.339\sqrt{n}$ and $l = 1.87\sqrt{n}$, the expected running time of Random-Balls(F, R, l) is at most*

$$poly(n) \, m^2 \, 2^{n-0.712\sqrt{n}} .$$

Proof. We need to estimate $N \cdot T$, where N is the number of random balls used by the algorithm *Random-Balls* and T is the expected running time of search inside a ball (i.e., of either *Ball-Checking*(F, A, R) or *Full-Ball-Checking*(F, A, R)). Using Lemma 5 and the upper bound on $V(n, R)$, we get the following upper bound on T:

$$T \leq poly(n) \, m \, (p \, V(n, R) + (1 - p) \, l^R)$$
$$\leq poly(n) \, m \, (p \, V(n, R) + l^R)$$
$$\leq poly(n) \, m \left(m \, 2^{l\left(H\left(\frac{R}{R+l}\right)-1\right)+H\left(\frac{R}{n}\right)n} + l^R \right) .$$

Hence we have

$$N \cdot T \le m \cdot poly(n) \cdot 2^{n - H\left(\frac{R}{n}\right)n} \cdot \left(m\, 2^{l\left(H\left(\frac{R}{R+l}\right) - 1\right) + H\left(\frac{R}{n}\right)n} + l^R \right)$$

$$= m \cdot poly(n) \cdot \left(m\, 2^{n + l\left(H\left(\frac{R}{R+l}\right) - 1\right)} + 2^{n - H\left(\frac{R}{n}\right)n + R\log_2 l} \right)$$

$$\le m^2 \cdot poly(n) \cdot 2^n \cdot (2^{-\phi} + 2^{-\psi})$$

where

$$\phi = l\left(1 - H\left(\frac{R}{R+l} \right) \right) \quad \text{and} \quad \psi = H\left(\frac{R}{n} \right) n - R\log_2 l \ .$$

Thus, we need to minimize $2^{-\phi} + 2^{-\psi}$. Let us estimate ϕ and ψ taking $R = a\sqrt{n}$ and $l = b\sqrt{n}$ where $a \le b$. In the estimation we use the fact that $\ln(1 + x) = x + o(x)$ for small x:

$$\phi = b\sqrt{n}\left(1 - H\left(\frac{a}{a+b} \right) \right)$$

$$= b\sqrt{n}\left(1 - \frac{a}{a+b}\log_2\frac{a+b}{a} - \frac{b}{a+b}\log_2\frac{a+b}{b} \right)$$

$$= b\sqrt{n}\left(1 - \log_2(a+b) + \frac{a\log_2 a + b\log_2 b}{a+b} \right) \ ;$$

$$\psi = H\left(\frac{a}{\sqrt{n}} \right) n - a\sqrt{n}\log_2(b\sqrt{n})$$

$$= \left(\frac{a}{\sqrt{n}}\log_2\frac{\sqrt{n}}{a} + \frac{\sqrt{n} - a}{\sqrt{n}}\log_2\frac{\sqrt{n}}{\sqrt{n} - a} \right) n - a\sqrt{n}\log_2(b\sqrt{n})$$

$$= a\sqrt{n}\log_2\frac{\sqrt{n}}{a} + \sqrt{n}(\sqrt{n} - a)(\log_2 e)\ln\left(1 + \frac{a}{\sqrt{n} - a} \right) - a\sqrt{n}\log_2(b\sqrt{n})$$

$$= a\sqrt{n}\log_2\frac{\sqrt{n}}{a} + a\sqrt{n}\log_2 e - a\sqrt{n}\log_2(b\sqrt{n}) + o(\sqrt{n})$$

$$= a\sqrt{n}\log_2\frac{e}{ab} + o(\sqrt{n}) \ .$$

Taking $a = 0.339$ and $b = 1.87$, we get $\phi, \psi > 0.712\sqrt{n}$, which gives us the stated overall upper bound. $\square$

4   Derandomization

In this section we describe the derandomization of our algorithm. The only part of the randomized algorithm where random bits are used is the choice of initial assignments. Our deterministic algorithm (Algorithm *Deterministic-Balls* described below) chooses initial assignments from a *covering code* (see Sect. 2). Such code can be, for example, constructed by a greedy algorithm, as formulated in the following lemma.

Lemma 6 ([3]). *Let $d \geq 2$ be a divisor of $n \geq 1$, and $0 < R < n/2$. Then there is a polynomial $q_d(n)$ such that a covering code of length n, radius at most R, and size at most $q_d(n) \cdot 2^{(1-H(R/n))n}$ can be constructed in time $q_d(n) \left(2^{3n/d} + 2^{(1-H(R/n))n} \right)$.*

Algorithm *Deterministic-Balls(F, R, l)*

Input: formula F over n variables, numbers R and l such that $0 \leq R \leq l \leq n$.
Output: satisfying assignment or "no".

1. Let $\mathcal{C}$ be a covering code of length n and radius R constructed in Lemma 6. For each assignment $A \in \mathcal{C}$ do the following:
   If F contains a clause that has at least l literals falsified by A and at most R literals satisfied by A, invoke *Full-Ball-Checking(F, A, R)*. Otherwise invoke *Ball-Checking(F, A, R)*. If the invoked procedure finds a satisfying assignment, return it.
2. Return "no".

Theorem 2. *Taking $R = \frac{2}{\log_2 e} \sqrt{\frac{n}{\log_2 n}}$ and $l = \frac{\log_2 e}{2} \sqrt{n \log_2 n}$, Algorithm Deterministic-Balls runs on F, R, and l in time at most*

$$poly(n) \; m^2 \; 2^{n-2\sqrt{\frac{n}{\log_2 n}}} \; .$$

Proof. For each ball, the algorithm invokes one of the two procedures: either *Full-Ball-Checking* or *Ball-Checking*. Let b_1 be the number of balls for which *Full-Ball-Checking* is called and b_2 be the number of balls where *Ball-Checking* is called. Lemma 5 gives the upper bound on b_1:

$$b_1 \; \leq \; p \, 2^n \; = \; m \, 2^{l(H(\frac{R}{R+l})-1)+n} \; .$$

In each of these b_1 balls, the algorithm examines at most $V(n, R)$ assignments. The number b_2 is obviously not greater than the size of $\mathcal{C}$:

$$b_2 \leq poly(n) \, 2^n / V(n, R) \; .$$

In each of these b_2 balls, the algorithm examines at most l^R assignments. Therefore, the total number of examined assignments can be estimated as follows:

$$b_1 \cdot V(n, R) + b_2 \cdot l^R \leq m \, 2^{l(H(\frac{R}{R+l})-1)+n+H(\frac{R}{n})n} + poly(n) \, 2^{n+R\log_2 l - H(\frac{R}{n})n}$$
$$= m \, 2^{S_1} + poly(n) \, 2^{S_2} \; .$$

We now estimate the exponents S_1 and S_2 taking $R = \frac{1}{\Delta}\sqrt{n}$ and $l = \Delta\sqrt{n}$ where Δ is a function of n such that $\Delta > \sqrt{2}$ for sufficiently large n. Due to this condition on Δ, we have $l > 2R$ and therefore $H(R/(R+l)) < H(R/l)$. We get

$$S_1 = l \left(H \left(\frac{R}{R+l} \right) - 1 \right) + n + H \left(\frac{R}{n} \right) n$$

$$< l \left(H \left(\frac{R}{l} \right) - 1 \right) + n + H \left(\frac{R}{n} \right) n$$

$$= \Delta\sqrt{n} \cdot \left(H \left(\frac{1}{\Delta^2} \right) - 1 \right) + n + H \left(\frac{1}{\Delta\sqrt{n}} \right) n$$

$$= n - \sqrt{n} \cdot \left(-\frac{2}{\Delta} \log_2 \Delta + \Delta + \Delta \left(1 - \frac{1}{\Delta^2} \right) \log_2 \left(1 - \frac{1}{\Delta^2} \right) \right.$$

$$\left. -\frac{1}{\Delta} \log_2(\Delta\sqrt{n}) + \left(\sqrt{n} - \frac{1}{\Delta} \right) \log_2 \left(1 - \frac{1}{\Delta\sqrt{n}} \right) \right)$$

$$= n - \sqrt{n} \cdot \left(-\frac{3}{\Delta} \log_2 \Delta + \Delta - \Delta \left(1 - \frac{1}{\Delta^2} \right) \frac{1}{\Delta^2} \log_2 e \right.$$

$$\left. -\frac{1}{2\Delta} \log_2 n - \left(\sqrt{n} - \frac{1}{\Delta} \right) \frac{1}{\Delta\sqrt{n}} \log_2 e + o \left(\frac{1}{\Delta} \right) \right)$$

$$= n - \sqrt{n} \cdot \left(-\frac{3}{\Delta} \log_2 \Delta + \Delta - \frac{1}{2\Delta} \log n + O \left(\frac{1}{\Delta} \right) \right) .$$

Substituting $\Delta = \delta\sqrt{\log_2 n}$, we get

$$S_1 = n - \sqrt{n} \left(\delta\sqrt{\log_2 n} - \frac{\log_2 n}{2\delta\sqrt{\log_2 n}} + o(1) \right)$$

$$= n - \sqrt{n \log_2 n} \left(\delta - \frac{1}{2\delta} + o(1) \right) .$$

For $\delta > 1/\sqrt{2}$, we have $S_1 \leq n - c\sqrt{n \log_2 n}$, where c is a positive constant. We now estimate S_2 as follows:

$$S_2 = n + R \log_2 l - H \left(\frac{R}{n} \right) n$$

$$= n + \frac{\sqrt{n}}{\Delta} \log_2(\Delta\sqrt{n}) - \frac{\sqrt{n}}{\Delta} \log_2(\Delta\sqrt{n}) - \sqrt{n} \left(\frac{\Delta\sqrt{n} - 1}{\Delta} \right) \log_2 \left(\frac{\Delta\sqrt{n}}{\Delta\sqrt{n} - 1} \right)$$

$$= n - \sqrt{n} \left(\frac{\Delta\sqrt{n} - 1}{\Delta} \right) \log_2 e \ln \left(1 + \frac{1}{\Delta\sqrt{n} - 1} \right)$$

$$= n - \frac{\sqrt{n} \log_2 e}{\Delta} - \sqrt{n} \cdot o \left(\frac{1}{\Delta} \right) .$$

Taking $\Delta = \delta\sqrt{\log_2 n}$, we have $S_2 \leq n - ((\log_2 e)/\delta)\sqrt{n/\log_2 n}$. Since S_2 dominates S_1, the total number of examined assignments is at most

$$m \, 2^{S_1} + poly(n) \, 2^{S_2} \leq poly(n) \, m \, 2^{n - \frac{\log_2 e}{\delta}\sqrt{\frac{n}{\log_2 n}}}$$

where $\delta > 1/\sqrt{2}$. If we take $\delta = (1/2) \log_2 e > 1/\sqrt{2}$, we get the claim.   □

Remark 1. In the proof of Theorem 2 one could take δ arbitrarily close to $1/\sqrt{2}$ getting the bound $$poly(n) \; m^2 \; 2^{n-(\sqrt{2}\log_2 e-\varepsilon)\sqrt{\frac{n}{\log_2 n}}}$$ for any $\varepsilon > 0$. To improve the bound even more, one could construct a code with proportion $O(p)$ of balls where *Full-Ball-Checking* is invoked. Such a code *exists*; however, we leave *constructing* it as an open question.

References

1. S. Baumer and R. Schuler. Improving a probabilistic 3-SAT algorithm by dynamic search and independent clause pairs. Electronic Colloquium on Computational Complexity, Report No. 10, February 2003.
2. G. Cohen, I. Honkala, S. Litsyn, and A. Lobstein. *Covering Codes*, volume 54 of *Mathematical Library*. Elsevier, Amsterdam, 1997.
3. E. Dantsin, A. Goerdt, E. A. Hirsch, R. Kannan, J. Kleinberg, C. Papadimitriou, P. Raghavan, and U. Schöning. A deterministic $(2 - \frac{2}{k+1})^n$ algorithm for k-SAT based on local search. *Theoretical Computer Science*, 289(1):69–83, October 2002.
4. E. Dantsin, A. Goerdt, E. A. Hirsch, and U. Schöning. Deterministic algorithms for k-SAT based on covering codes and local search. In Montanari, Rolim,Welzl, eds, *Proc. of the 27th International Colloquium on Automata, Languages and Programming, ICALP'2000*, vol. 1853 of *Lecture Notes in Computer Science*, pages 236–247. 2000.
5. E. A. Hirsch. New worst-case upper bounds for SAT. *Journal of Automated Reasoning*, 24(4):397–420, 2000.
6. T. Hofmeister, U. Schöning, R. Schuler, and O. Watanabe. A probabilistic 3-SAT algorithm further improved. In Alt, Ferreira, eds, *Proc. of the 19th Annual Symposium on Theoretical Aspects of Computer Science, STACS'02*, vol. 2285 of *Lecture Notes in Computer Science*, pages 192–202. 2002.
7. K. Iwama and S. Tamaki. Improved upper bounds for 3-SAT. Electronic Colloquium on Computational Complexity, Report No. 53, July 2003.
8. R. Paturi, P. Pudlák, M. E. Saks, and F. Zane. An improved exponential-time algorithm for k-SAT. In *Proceedings of the 39th Annual IEEE Symposium on Foundations of Computer Science, FOCS'98*, pages 628–637, 1998.
9. R. Paturi, P. Pudlák, and F. Zane. Satisfiability coding lemma. In *Proceedings of the 38th Annual IEEE Symposium on Foundations of Computer Science, FOCS'97*, pages 566–574, 1997.
10. P. Pudlák. Satisfiability — algorithms and logic. In L. Brim, J. Gruska, and J. Zlatuska, editors, *Proceedings of the 23rd International Symposium on Mathematical Foundations of Computer Science (MFCS'98)*, volume 1450 of *Lecture Notes in Computer Science*, pages 129–141. Springer-Verlag, 1998.
11. D. Rolf. 3-SAT in $RTIME(O(1.32793^n))$ — improving randomized local search by initializing strings of 3-clauses. Electronic Colloquium on Computational Complexity, Report No. 54, July 2003.
12. U. Schöning. A probabilistic algorithm for k-SAT and constraint satisfaction problems. In *Proceedings of the 40th Annual IEEE Symposium on Foundations of Computer Science, FOCS'99*, pages 410–414, 1999.
13. U. Schöning. A probabilistic algorithm for k-SAT based on limited local search and restart. *Algorithmica*, 32(4):615–623, 2002.
14. R. Schuler. An algorithm for the satisfiability problem of formulas in conjunctive normal form. Manuscript, 2003.

Identifying Efficiently Solvable Cases of Max CSP

David Cohen[1], Martin Cooper[2], Peter Jeavons[3], and Andrei Krokhin[4]

[1] Department of Computer Science, Royal Holloway, University of London,
Egham, Surrey, TW20 0EX, UK
d.cohen@rhul.ac.uk
[2] IRIT, University of Toulouse III, 31062 Toulouse, France
cooper@irit.fr
[3] Computing Laboratory, University of Oxford, Oxford OX1 3QD, UK
peter.jeavons@comlab.ox.ac.uk
[4] Department of Computer Science, University of Warwick,
Coventry, CV4 7AL, UK
ak@dcs.warwick.ac.uk

Abstract. In this paper we study the complexity of the maximum constraint satisfaction problem (Max CSP) over an arbitrary finite domain. We describe a novel connection between this problem and the supermodular function maximization problem (which is dual to the submodular function minimization problem). Using this connection, we are able to identify large classes of efficiently solvable subproblems of Max CSP arising from certain restrictions on the constraint types. Until now, the only known polynomial-time solvable cases for this form of optimization problem were restricted to constraints over a 2-valued (Boolean) domain. Here we obtain the first examples of general families of efficiently solvable cases of Max CSP for arbitrary finite domains, by considering supermodular functions on finite lattices. Finally, we show that the equality constraint over a non-Boolean domain is non-supermodular, and, when combined with some simple unary constraints, gives rise to cases of Max CSP which are hard even to approximate.

1 Introduction

The main object of our study in this paper is the maximum constraint satisfaction problem (MAX CSP) where one is given a collection of constraints on overlapping sets of variables and the goal is to find an assignment of values to the variables that maximizes the number of satisfied constraints. A number of classic optimization problems including MAX k-SAT, MAX CUT and MAX DICUT can be represented in this framework, and it can also be used to model optimization problems arising in more applied settings, such as database design [9].

The Max-CSP framework has been well-studied in the Boolean case, that is, when the set of values for the variables is $\{0, 1\}$. Many fundamental results have been obtained, containing both complexity classifications and approximation

V. Diekert and M. Habib (Eds.): STACS 2004, LNCS 2996, pp. 152–163, 2004.
© Springer-Verlag Berlin Heidelberg 2004

properties (see, e.g., [7,17,20]). In the non-Boolean case, a number of results have been obtained that concern approximation properties (see, e.g., [9,11]). However, there has so far been very little study of efficient exact algorithms and complexity for subproblems of non-Boolean MAX CSP, and the present paper is aimed at filling this gap.

We study a standard parameterized version of the MAX CSP, in which restrictions may be imposed on the types of constraints allowed in the instances. In particular, we investigate which restrictions make such problems *tractable*, by allowing a polynomial time algorithm to find an optimal assignment. This setting has been extensively studied and completely classified in the Boolean case [7, 20]. In contrast, we consider here the case where the set of possible values is an *arbitrary finite* set.

Experience in the study of various forms of constraint satisfaction [2,3,4, 5,19] has shown that the more general form of such problems, in which the domain is an arbitrary finite set, is often considerably more difficult to analyze than the Boolean case. The techniques developed for the Boolean case typically involve the careful manipulation of logical formulas [7]; such techniques do not readily extend to larger domains. For example, Schaefer [25] obtained a complete classification of complexity for the standard constraint satisfaction problem in the Boolean case using such techniques in 1978; although he raised the question of generalizing this result to larger domains in the same paper, little progress was made for the next twenty years.

The key step in the analysis of the standard constraint satisfaction problem [3,4] was the discovery that the characterization of the tractable cases over the Boolean domain can be restated in an algebraic form [19]. This algebraic description of the characterization has also proved to be a key step in the analysis of the counting constraint satisfaction problem [5] and the quantified constraint satisfaction problem [2]. However, this form of algebraic description does not provide a suitable tool for analyzing the MAX CSP, which is our focus here.

The main contribution of this paper is the first general approach to and the first general results about the complexity of subproblems of *non Boolean* MAX CSP. We point out that the characterization of the tractable cases of MAX CSP over a Boolean domain can also be restated in an algebraic form, but using a rather different algebraic framework: we show that they can be characterized using the property of *supermodularity*. We also show how this property can be generalized to the non-Boolean case, and hence used to identify large families of tractable subproblems of the non-Boolean MAX CSP. Moreover, we give some results to demonstrate how non-supermodularity can cause hardness of the corresponding subproblem.

The properties of sub- and supermodularity have been extensively used to study combinatorial optimization problems in other contexts. In particular, the problem of minimizing a submodular set function has been thoroughly studied, due to its applications across a variety of research areas [13,16,18,21,22]. The dual problem of maximizing a supermodular function has found interesting applications in diverse economic models, such as supermodular games (see [28]).

Submodular functions defined on (products of) totally ordered sets correspond precisely to Monge matrices and arrays (see, for example, survey [6]) which play an important role in solving a number of optimization problems including travelling salesman, assignment and transportation problems [6]. Hence this paper also unifies, for the first time, the study of the MAX CSP with many other areas of combinatorial optimization.

The structure of the paper is as follows. In Section 2 we discuss the MAX CSP problem, its Boolean case, its complexity, and the relevance of sub- and supermodularity. In Sections 3 and 4, we give two different generalizations for the (unique) non-trivial tractable case of Boolean MAX CSP: one to general supermodular constraints on restricted types of ordered domains (distributive lattices), and the other to a restricted form of supermodular constraint on more general ordered domains (arbitrary lattices). For the second case, we are able to give a cubic time algorithm, based on a reduction to the MIN CUT problem. Section 5 describes an even more efficient algorithm for all *binary* supermodular constraints on a totally ordered domain and then shows that the only tractability-preserving way of extending this set of constraints is with further supermodular functions; all other extensions give rise to hard problems. As further evidence that non-supermodularity causes hardness of MAX CSP, Section 6 establishes the surprising result that, in the non-Boolean case, allowing just the (non-supermodular) equality constraint and unary constraints gives rise to versions of MAX CSP that are hard even to approximate. Finally, in Section 7 we discuss our ideas in light of the results obtained, and describe possible future work. Proofs of all results are omitted due to space constraints.

2   Preliminaries

Throughout the paper, let D denote a finite set, $|D| > 1$. Let $R_D^{(m)}$ denote the set of all m-ary predicates over D, that is, functions from D^m to $\{0,1\}$, and let $R_D = \bigcup_{m=1}^{\infty} R_D^{(m)}$.

Definition 1. *A constraint over a set of variables $V = \{x_1, x_2, \ldots, x_n\}$, is an expression of the form $f(\mathbf{x})$ where*

- *$f \in R_D^{(m)}$ is called the* constraint function*;*
- *$\mathbf{x} = (x_{i_1}, \ldots, x_{i_m})$ is called the* constraint scope*.*

The constraint f is said to be satisfied *on a tuple $\mathbf{a} = (a_{i_1}, \ldots, a_{i_m}) \in D^m$ if $f(\mathbf{a}) = 1$.*

Definition 2. *An instance of* MAX CSP *is a collection of constraints $\{f_1(\mathbf{x}_1), \ldots, f_q(\mathbf{x}_q)\}$, $q \geq 1$, over a set of variables $V = \{x_1, \ldots, x_n\}$, where $f_i \in R_D$ for all $1 \leq i \leq q$. The goal is to find an assignment $\phi : V \to D$ that maximizes the number of satisfied constraints.*

Arguably, it is more appropriate for our purposes to consider the $0, 1$ values taken by constraint functions as *integers* and not as Boolean values; the goal in a MAX CSP instance is then to maximize the function $f : D^n \to \mathbb{Z}^+$ (where $\mathbb{Z}^+$ is the set all non-negative integers), defined by

$$f(x_1, \dots, x_n) = \sum_{i=1}^{q} f_i(\mathbf{x}_i).$$

The *weighted* version of the MAX CSP problem, in which each constraint $f_i(\mathbf{x}_i)$ has associated weight $\rho_i \in \mathbb{Z}^+$, can be viewed as the problem of maximizing the function

$$f(x_1, \dots, x_n) = \sum_{i=1}^{q} \rho_i \cdot f_i(\mathbf{x}_i).$$

In fact, the two versions of MAX CSP can be shown to be equivalent (as in [7, Lemma 7.2]).

Throughout the paper, $\mathcal{F}$ will denote a *finite* subset of R_D, and MAX CSP($\mathcal{F}$) will denote the restriction of MAX CSP to instances where all constraint functions belong to $\mathcal{F}$. The central problem we consider in this paper is the following.

Problem 1. Identify efficiently solvable problems of the form MAX CSP($\mathcal{F}$).

Recall that **PO** and **NPO** are optimization analogs of **P** and **NP**; that is, they are classes of optimization problems that can be solved in deterministic polynomial time and non-deterministic polynomial time, respectively. We will call problems in **PO** tractable. An optimization problem is called **NP**-hard if it admits a polynomial time Turing reduction from some **NP**-complete problem. The approximation complexity class **APX** consists of all **NPO** problems for which there is a polynomial time approximation algorithm whose performance ratio is bounded by a constant. A problem in **APX** is called **APX**-complete if every problem in **APX** has a special approximation-preserving reduction, called an *AP*-reduction, to it. It is well-known that every **APX**-complete problem is **NP**-hard. For more detailed definitions of approximation and optimization complexity classes and reductions, the reader is referred to [1,7,23].

Proposition 1. MAX CSP($\mathcal{F}$) *belongs to* **APX** *for every* $\mathcal{F}$.

A complete classification of the complexity of MAX CSP($\mathcal{F}$) for a two-element set D can be found in [7]. Before stating that result we need to give some definitions.

Definition 3. *An* endomorphism *of* $\mathcal{F}$ *is a unary operation* π *on* D *such that* $f(a_1, \dots, a_m) = 1 \Rightarrow f(\pi(a_1), \dots, \pi(a_m)) = 1$ *for all* $(a_1, \dots, a_m) \in D^m$ *and all* $f \in \mathcal{F}$. *We will say that* $\mathcal{F}$ *is a* core *if every endomorphism of* $\mathcal{F}$ *is injective (i.e. a permutation).*

The intuition here is that if $\mathcal{F}$ is not a core then it has a non-injective endomorphism π, which implies that, for every assignment ϕ, there is another assignment $\pi\phi$ that satisfies all constraints satisfied by ϕ and uses only a restricted set of values, so the problem can be reduced to a problem over this smaller set. For example, if $D = \{0, 1\}$ then $\mathcal{F}$ is a not a core if and only if $f(a, \dots, a) = 1$ for some $a \in D$ and all $f \in \mathcal{F}$. Obviously, in this case the assignment that assigns the value a to all variables satisfies all constraints, so it is optimal, and hence MAX CSP($\mathcal{F}$) is trivial.

Definition 4 ([7]). *A function* $f \in R_{\{0,1\}}^{(n)}$ *is called* 2-monotone *if it can be expressed as follows:*

$$f(x_1, \dots, x_n) = 1 \Leftrightarrow (x_{i_1} \wedge \dots \wedge x_{i_s}) \vee (\bar{x}_{j_1} \wedge \dots \wedge \bar{x}_{j_t}),$$

where either of the two disjuncts may be empty (i.e., the values of s or t may be zero).

Theorem 1 ([7]). *Let* $\mathcal{F} \subseteq R_{\{0,1\}}$ *be a core. If every $f \in \mathcal{F}$ is 2-monotone, then (weighted)* MAX CSP($\mathcal{F}$) *is in* **PO***, otherwise it is* **APX***-complete.*

As we announced in the introduction, the main new tools which we introduce to generalize (the tractability part of) this result will be the conditions of sub- and supermodularity. We will consider the most general type of sub- and supermodular functions, that is, those defined on a (general) lattice, as in [28]. Recall that a partial order $\sqsubseteq$ on a set D is called a *lattice* order if, for every $x, y \in D$, there exist a greatest lower bound $x \sqcap y$ and a least upper bound $x \sqcup y$. The algebra $\mathcal{L} = (D, \sqcap, \sqcup)$ on D with two binary operations $\sqcap$ and $\sqcup$ is called a *lattice*, and we have $x \sqsubseteq y \Leftrightarrow x \sqcap y = x \Leftrightarrow x \sqcup y = y$. As is well known, every finite lattice has a least element and a greatest element, which we will denote by $0_\mathcal{L}$ and $1_\mathcal{L}$, respectively. (For more information about lattices, see, e.g., [10].)

For tuples $\mathbf{a} = (a_1, \dots, a_n)$, $\mathbf{b} = (b_1, \dots, b_n)$ in D^n, let $\mathbf{a} \sqcap \mathbf{b}$ and $\mathbf{a} \sqcup \mathbf{b}$ denote the tuples $(a_1 \sqcap b_1, \dots, a_n \sqcap b_n)$ and $(a_1 \sqcup b_1, \dots, a_n \sqcup b_n)$, respectively.

Definition 5. *Let* $\mathcal{L} = (D, \sqcap, \sqcup)$ *be a lattice. A function* $f : D^n \to \mathbb{Z}^+$ *is called* submodular *on* $\mathcal{L}$ *if*

$$f(\mathbf{a} \sqcap \mathbf{b}) + f(\mathbf{a} \sqcup \mathbf{b}) \leq f(\mathbf{a}) + f(\mathbf{b}) \quad \textit{for all } \mathbf{a}, \mathbf{b} \in D^n.$$

It is called supermodular *on* $\mathcal{L}$ *if*

$$f(\mathbf{a} \sqcap \mathbf{b}) + f(\mathbf{a} \sqcup \mathbf{b}) \geq f(\mathbf{a}) + f(\mathbf{b}) \quad \textit{for all } \mathbf{a}, \mathbf{b} \in D^n.$$

The sets of all submodular and supermodular functions on $\mathcal{L}$*, will be denoted* Sbmod$_\mathcal{L}$ *and* Spmod$_\mathcal{L}$*, respectively.*

Note that sub- and supermodular functions are usually defined to take values in $\mathbb{R}$, but, in the context of MAX CSP, it is appropriate to restrict the range to consist of non-negative integers.

The properties of sub- and supermodularity are most often considered for functions defined on subsets of a set, which corresponds to the special case of Definition 5 where $|D| = 2$. Recall that a function on subsets of a set is submodular if $f(X \cap Y) + f(X \cup Y) \leq f(X) + f(Y)$ for all subsets X, Y, and it is supermodular if the inverse inequality holds [13,22]. The problem of minimizing a submodular set function is tractable [16,18,26]. Some results have also been obtained that concern minimization of a submodular function defined on a family of subsets [14,16,18,26], or on a finite grid (or integer lattice) [27], or on general lattices [28].

Observation 2 *Let f_1 and f_2 be submodular functions on a lattice $\mathcal{L}$.*

- *For any constants, $\alpha_1, \alpha_2 \in \mathbb{Z}^+$, the function $\alpha_1 f_1 + \alpha_2 f_2$ is also submodular.*
- *If $K \in \mathbb{Z}^+$ is an upper bound for the values taken by f_1, then the function $f' = K - f_1$, is supermodular.*
- *The function f_1 is submodular on the dual lattice $\mathcal{L}^\partial$ obtained by reversing the order of $\mathcal{L}$.*

(Corresponding statements also hold when the terms submodular and supermodular are exchanged throughout.)

The next proposition shows that the non-trivial tractable case of Boolean Max CSP identified in Theorem 1 can be characterized using supermodularity.

Proposition 2. *A function $f \in R_{\{0,1\}}$ is 2-monotone if and only if it is supermodular.*

Proposition 2 is a key step in extending tractability results for Max CSP from the Boolean case to an arbitrary finite domain, as it allows us to re-state Theorem 1 in the following form.

Corollary 1. *Let $\mathcal{F} \subseteq R_{\{0,1\}}$ be a core. If $\mathcal{F} \subseteq \mathrm{Spmod}_{\{0,1\}}$, then (weighted) Max CSP$(\mathcal{F})$ is in **PO**, otherwise it is **APX**-complete.*

3   Supermodular Constraints on Distributive Lattices

In this section we consider constraints given by supermodular functions on a finite *distributive* lattice. Recall that a finite lattice $\mathcal{D} = (D, \sqcap, \sqcup)$ is distributive if and only if it can be represented by subsets of a set A, where the operations $\sqcup$ and $\sqcap$ are interpreted as set-theoretic union and intersection, respectively [10]. It is well-known [10] that A can be chosen so that $|A| \leq |D|$. Note that if $\mathcal{D}$ is a finite distributive lattice, then the product lattice $\mathcal{D}^n = (D^n, \sqcap, \sqcup)$ is also a finite distributive lattice, which can be represented by subsets of a set of size at most $|D| \cdot n$, since every element of $\mathcal{D}$ can represented using at most $|D|$ bits.

It was shown in [18,26] that a submodular function on a finite distributive lattice[1] representable by subsets of an n-element set can be minimized in polynomial time in n (assuming that computing the value of the function on a given argument is a primitive operation). The complexity of the best known algorithm is $O(n^5 \min\{\log nM, n^2 \log n\})$ where M is an upper bound for the values taken by the function [18].

Using this result, and the correspondence between sub- and supermodular functions, we obtain the following general result about tractable subproblems of Max CSP.

Theorem 3. *Weighted Max CSP$(\mathcal{F})$ is in **PO** whenever $\mathcal{F} \subseteq \mathrm{Spmod}_\mathcal{D}$ for some distributive lattice $\mathcal{D}$ on D.*

---

[1]   referred to in [26] as a *ring family*.

It is currently not known whether submodular functions on non-distributive lattices can be minimized in polynomial time, and this problem itself is of interest due to some applications (see [18]). Obviously, any progress in this direction would imply that MAX CSP for supermodular constraints on the corresponding lattices could also be solved efficiently.

4   Generalized 2-Monotone Constraints

In this section we give a cubic-time algorithm for solving MAX CSP($\mathcal{F}$) when $\mathcal{F}$ consists of supermodular functions of a special form which generalizes the class of 2-monotone Boolean constraints defined above.

Definition 6. *A function $f \in R_D^{(n)}$ will be called* generalized 2-monotone *on a lattice $\mathcal{L}$ on D if it can be expressed as follows*

$$f(\mathbf{x}) = 1 \Leftrightarrow ((x_{i_1} \sqsubseteq a_{i_1}) \wedge \ldots \wedge (x_{i_s} \sqsubseteq a_{i_s})) \vee ((x_{j_1} \sqsupseteq b_{j_i}) \wedge \ldots \wedge (x_{j_t} \sqsupseteq b_{j_t})) \tag{1}$$

where $\mathbf{x} = (x_1, \ldots, x_n)$, and $a_{i_1}, \ldots, a_{i_s}, b_{j_1}, \ldots, b_{j_t} \in D$, and either of the two disjuncts may be empty (i.e., the value of s or t may be zero).

It is easy to check that all generalized 2-monotone functions are supermodular (but the converse is not true in general). To obtain an efficient algorithm for MAX CSP($\mathcal{F}$) when $\mathcal{F}$ consists of generalized 2-monotone functions, we construct a reduction to the MIN CUT problem, which is known to be solvable in cubic time [15].

To outline the reduction, we need to give some more notation and definitions. Recall that a *principal ideal* in a lattice $\mathcal{L}$ is a set of the form $\{x \in \mathcal{L} \mid x \sqsubseteq a\}$, for some $a \in \mathcal{L}$, and a principal *filter* (or dual ideal) is a set of the form $\{x \in \mathcal{L} \mid x \sqsupseteq b\}$, for some $b \in \mathcal{L}$. For any generalized 2-monotone function f, we will call the first disjunct in Equation 1 of Definition 6 (containing conditions of the form $x \sqsubseteq a$), the *ideal part* of f, and the second disjunct in this equation (containing conditions of the form $x \sqsupseteq b$), the *filter part* of f.

For any lattice $\mathcal{L}$, and any $c, d \in \mathcal{L}$, we shall write $c \prec d$ if $c \sqsubset d$ and there is no $u \in \mathcal{L}$ with $c \sqsubset u \sqsubset d$. Finally, let B_b denote the set of all maximal elements in $\{x \in \mathcal{L} \mid x \not\sqsupseteq b\}$. Now we are ready to describe the digraph used in the reduction.

Definition 7. *Let $\mathcal{L}$ be a lattice on a finite set D, and let $\mathcal{F}$ be a set of generalized 2-monotone functions on $\mathcal{L}$.*

Let $\mathcal{I} = \{\rho_1 \cdot f_1(\mathbf{x}_1), \ldots, \rho_q \cdot f_q(\mathbf{x}_q)\}$, $q \geq 1$, be an instance of weighted MAX CSP($\mathcal{F}$), over a set of variables $V = \{x_1, \ldots, x_n\}$, and let ∞ denote an integer greater than $\sum \rho_i$.

We construct a digraph $G_{\mathcal{I}}$ as follows:

- *The vertices of $G_{\mathcal{I}}$ are as follows*
  - $\{T, F\} \cup \{x_d \mid x \in V, d \in D\} \cup \{e_i, \bar{e}_i \mid i = 1, 2, \ldots, q\}$.

For each f_i where the ideal part is empty, we identify the vertices e_i and F. Similarly, for each f_i where the filter part is empty, we identify the vertices $\bar{e}_i$ and T.

- *The arcs of $G_{\mathcal{I}}$ are defined as follows:*
  - *For each $c \prec d$ in $\mathcal{L}$ and for each $x \in V$, there is an arc from x_c to x_d with weight ∞;*
  - *For each f_i, there is an arc from $\bar{e}_i$ to e_i with weight ρ_i;*
  - *For each f_i, and each conjunct of the form $x \sqsubseteq a$ in f_i, there is an arc from e_i to x_a with weight ∞;*
  - *For each f_i, and each conjunct of the form $x \sqsupseteq b$ in f_i, there is an arc from every x_u, where $u \in B_b$, to $\bar{e}_i$ with weight ∞.*

Arcs with weight less than ∞ will be called constraint *arcs.*

It is easy to see that $G_{\mathcal{I}}$ is a digraph with source T and sink F.

Example 1. Let $\mathcal{L}_\diamond$ be the lattice on $\{0, a, b, 1\}$ such that $0 = 0_{\mathcal{L}_\diamond}$, $1 = 1_{\mathcal{L}_\diamond}$, and the "middle" elements a and b are incomparable. Consider the following instance $\mathcal{I}$ of Max CSP$(\mathcal{F})$

$$f(x, y) = \rho_1 \cdot f_1(x) + \rho_2 \cdot f_2(x) + \rho_3 \cdot f_3(x, y) + \rho_4 \cdot f_4(y)$$

where the constraint functions f_i are defined as follows:

$$f_1(x) = 1 \Leftrightarrow (x \sqsubseteq a)$$
$$f_2(x) = 1 \Leftrightarrow (x \sqsupseteq b)$$
$$f_3(x, y) = 1 \Leftrightarrow (y \sqsubseteq 0) \vee (x \sqsupseteq 1)$$
$$f_4(y) = 1 \Leftrightarrow (y \sqsupseteq 1)$$

Note that, in $\mathcal{L}_\diamond$, $B_1 = \{a, b\}$, and $B_b = \{a\}$. One can check that the digraph shown in Figure 1 is the graph $G_{\mathcal{I}}$ specified in Definition 7 above.

It can be shown that, for any instance $\mathcal{I}$ of weighted Max CSP$(\mathcal{F})$, the total weight of constraints that are *not* satisfied by an optimal solution is equal to the weight of a minimum cut in the graph $G_{\mathcal{I}}$. The proof essentially uses the fact that the order $\sqsubseteq$ is a lattice order. Hence, we get the following result.

Theorem 4. *Let $\mathcal{L}$ be a lattice on a finite set D. If $\mathcal{F}$ consists of generalized 2-monotone functions on $\mathcal{L}$, then (weighted)* Max CSP$(\mathcal{F})$ *is solvable in $O(q^3 + n^3|D|^3)$ time, where q is the number of constraints and n is the number of variables in an instance.*

Theorem 4 shows that when the constraints in a Max CSP instance are described by generalized 2-monotone functions, then an optimal solution can be found much more efficiently than by invoking the general algorithm for submodular function minimization.

This result suggests that it may be worthwhile to look for other forms of constraint for which there exist efficient optimization algorithms. In the next section, we show that when we consider *totally ordered* lattices then such efficient algorithms can be obtained for a wide range of supermodular constraints.

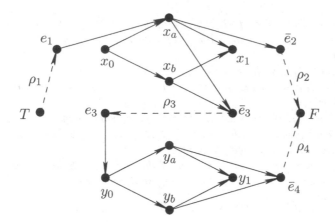

Fig. 1. The digraph $G_\mathcal{I}$ corresponding to the MAX CSP instance defined in Example 1. Dashed lines denote constraint arcs, and solid lines denote arcs of weight ∞.

5   Binary Supermodular Constraints on a Chain

In this section we consider supermodular functions on a finite *totally ordered* lattice, or *chain*. One reason why chains are especially interesting in our study is the following lemma.

Lemma 1. *Every unary function is supermodular on a lattice $\mathcal{L}$ if and only if $\mathcal{L}$ is a chain.*

It is easy to see that a chain is a distributive lattice, which implies that Theorem 3 can be applied, and hence that MAX CSP($\mathcal{F}$) is tractable for all sets $\mathcal{F}$ consisting of supermodular constraints on a chain. Furthermore, by Lemma 1, such sets of functions can include all unary functions.

We will now show that, for supermodular constraints which are at most *binary*, this result can be further strengthened, to obtain a more efficient special-purpose optimization algorithm. We obtain this result by using a reduction to the MIN CUT problem as in the preceding section, but in this case we can eliminate the dependence of the running time on the number of constraints. The proof uses the fact that binary submodular functions on a chain precisely correspond to square Monge matrices and hence can be decomposed into a sum of simpler functions [6].

Theorem 5. *Let $\mathcal{C}$ be a chain on a finite set D. If $\mathcal{F} \subseteq \mathrm{Spmod}_\mathcal{C}$, and each $f \in \mathcal{F}$ is at most binary, then MAX CSP($\mathcal{F}$) is solvable in $O(n^3|D|^3)$ time, where n is the number of variables in an instance.*

The next theorem is the main result of this section. It shows that the *only* tractability-preserving way of extending the set $\mathcal{F}$ from Theorem 5 is with further supermodular functions; all other extensions give rise to hard problems.

Theorem 6. *Let $\mathcal{C}$ be a chain on a finite set D, and let $\mathcal{F} \subseteq R_D$ contain all binary supermodular functions on $\mathcal{C}$.*

*If $\mathcal{F} \subseteq \mathrm{Spmod}_\mathcal{C}$, then (weighted) MAX CSP($\mathcal{F}$) is in **PO**, otherwise it is **NP**-hard.*

6   A Simple Non-supermodular Constraint

We have established in the previous section that for chains, in the presence of all binary supermodular functions, supermodularity is the only possible reason for tractability. It can be shown using results of [24] that the binary supermodular functions on a finite chain determine the chain (up to reverse order). However, by Lemma 1, all *unary* functions are supermodular on *every* chain. It is therefore an interesting question to determine whether supermodularity on a chain is the only possible reason for tractability of MAX CSP($\mathcal{F}$) when $\mathcal{F}$ contains all *unary* functions.

In this section we give some evidence in favour of a positive answer to this question, by considering a simple equality constraint. Interestingly, in all of the various versions of the constraint satisfaction problem for which complexity classifications have previously been obtained, an equality constraint can be combined with any tractable set of constraints without affecting tractability. However, we show here that such a constraint gives rise to hard subproblems of MAX CSP, in the presence of some simple unary constraints.

Definition 8. *Let D be a finite set. We define the function $f_{eq} \in R_D^{(2)}$, and the functions $c_d \in R_D^{(1)}$ for each $d \in D$, as follows*

$$f_{eq}(x,y) = 1 \Leftrightarrow (x = y) \quad and \quad c_d(x) = 1 \Leftrightarrow (x = d).$$

It is easy to check that f_{eq} on D is supermodular if $|D| = 2$. However, the next result shows that $|D| = 2$ is the only case for which this is true.

Lemma 2. *If $|D| > 2$ then $f_{eq}(x, y)$ is not supermodular on any lattice on D.*

Note that MAX CSP($\{f_{eq}\}$) is clearly tractable. However, this does not give us an interesting tractable subproblem of MAX CSP, since $\{f_{eq}\}$ is not a core. In fact, the core obtained from $\{f_{eq}\}$ is one-element.

The next theorem shows that the equality constraint f_{eq}, when considered together with the set of unary functions c_d (to make a core), gives rise to a hard problem.

Theorem 7. *For any finite set D with $|D| > 2$, if $\mathcal{F} \supseteq \{c_d \mid d \in D\} \cup \{f_{eq}\}$, then MAX CSP($\mathcal{F}$) is **APX**-complete.*

The proof is by reduction from the **APX**-complete MINIMUM 3-TERMINAL CUT problem [8]. In fact, in Theorem 7, it is enough to require that $\mathcal{F}$ contains at least three functions of the form c_d.

7   Conclusion

We believe that the most interesting feature of the research presented in this paper is that it brings together several different methods and directions in combinatorial optimization which have previously been studied separately: MAX CSP, submodular functions, and Monge properties. We hope that the ideas and results presented here will stimulate research in all of these areas, and perhaps also impact on other related areas of combinatorial optimization. In particular, the problem of minimizing submodular functions on non-distributive lattices becomes especially important in view of the links we have discovered.

The close connection we have established between tractable cases of MAX CSP and the property of supermodularity leads us to conjecture that supermodularity is the only possible reason for tractability in MAX CSP. Regardless of whether this conjecture holds, the results we have given above demonstrate that significant progress can now be made in developing efficient algorithms for all the known tractable cases of MAX CSP by exploiting the large body of existing results concerning sub- and supermodularity, and Monge properties (e.g., [6, 24,28]).

One possible direction to extend our results would be a further study of the approximability of constraint satisfaction problems over arbitrary finite domains. For example, the techniques presented here can be further fine-tuned to establish **APX**-completeness for at least some of the remaining **NP**-hard cases of MAX CSP. However, to complete the study of approximability properties, it is likely to be necessary to define appropriate notions of expressiveness for a given set of constraint functions, and this has previously only been developed for the Boolean case [7].

References

1. G. Ausiello, P. Creszenzi, G. Gambosi, V. Kann, A. Marchetti-Spaccamela, and M. Protasi. *Complexity and Approximation.* Springer, 1999.
2. F. Börner, A. Bulatov, P. Jeavons, and A. Krokhin. Quantified constraints: Algorithms and complexity. In *Proceedings of CSL'03*, volume 2803 of *LNCS*, pages 58–70, 2003.
3. A. Bulatov. A dichotomy theorem for constraints on a three-element set. In *Proceedings of FOCS'02*, pages 649–658, 2002.
4. A. Bulatov. Tractable conservative constraint satisfaction problems. In *Proceedings of LICS'03*, pages 321–330, 2003.
5. A. Bulatov and V. Dalmau. Towards a dichotomy theorem for the counting constraint satisfaction problem. In *Proceedings of FOCS'03*, pages 562-571, 2003.
6. R.E. Burkard, B. Klinz, and R. Rudolf. Perspectives of Monge properties in optimization. *Discrete Applied Mathematics*, 70:95–161, 1996.
7. N. Creignou, S. Khanna, and M. Sudan. *Complexity Classifications of Boolean Constraint Satisfaction Problems*, volume 7 of *SIAM Monographs on Discrete Mathematics and Applications*. 2001.
8. E. Dahlhaus, D.S. Johnson, C.H. Papadimitriou, P.D. Seymour, and M. Yannakakis. The complexity of multiterminal cuts. *SIAM Journal on Computing*, 23(4):864–894, 1994.
9. M. Datar, T. Feder, A. Gionis, R. Motwani, and R. Panigrahy. A combinatorial algorithm for MAX CSP. *Information Processing Letters*, 85(6):307–315, 2003.
10. B.A. Davey and H.A. Priestley. *Introduction to Lattices and Order*. Cambridge University Press, 1990.
11. L. Engebretsen and V. Guruswami. Is constraint satisfaction over two variables always easy? In *Proceedings of RANDOM'02*, volume 2483 of *LNCS*, pages 224–238, 2002.

12. T. Feder and M.Y. Vardi. The computational structure of monotone monadic SNP and constraint satisfaction: A study through Datalog and group theory. *SIAM Journal on Computing*, 28:57–104, 1998.

13. S. Fujishige. *Submodular Functions and Optimization*, volume 47 of *Annals of Discrete Mathematics*. North-Holland, Amsterdam, 1991.

14. M.X. Goemans and V.S. Ramakrishnan. Minimizing submodular functions over families of subsets. *Combinatorica*, 15:499–513, 1995.

15. A. Goldberg and R.E. Tarjan. A new approach to the maximum flow problem. *Journal of the ACM*, 35:921–940, 1988.

16. M. Grötschel, L. Lovász, and A. Schrijver. *Geometric Algorithms and Combinatorial Optimization*. Springer-Verlag, New York, 1988.

17. J. Håstad. Some optimal inapproximability results. *Journal of the ACM*, 48:798–859, 2001.

18. S. Iwata, L. Fleischer, and S. Fujishige. A combinatorial strongly polynomial algorithm for minimizing submodular functions. *Journal of the ACM*, 48(4):761–777, 2001.

19. P. Jeavons. On the algebraic structure of combinatorial problems. *Theoretical Computer Science*, 200:185–204, 1998.

20. P. Jonsson. Boolean constraint satisfaction: Complexity results for optimization problems with arbitrary weights. *Theoretical Computer Science*, 244(1-2):189–203, 2000.

21. H. Narayanan. *Submodular Functions and Electrical Networks*. North-Holland, 1997.

22. G.L. Nemhauser and L.A. Wolsey. *Integer and Combinatorial Optimization*. Wiley, 1988.

23. C.H. Papadimitriou and M. Yannakakis. Optimization, approximation, and complexity classes. *Journal of Computer and System Sciences*, 43(3):425–440, 1991.

24. R. Rudolf. Recognition of d-dimensional Monge arrays. *Discrete Applied Mathematics*, 52(1):71–82, 1994.

25. T.J. Schaefer. The complexity of satisfiability problems. In *Proceedings STOC'78*, pages 216–226, 1978.

26. A. Schrijver. A combinatorial algorithm minimizing submodular functions in polynomial time. *Journal of Combinatorial Theory, Ser.B*, 80:346–355, 2000.

27. A. Shioura. Minimization of an M-convex function. *Discrete Applied Mathematics*, 84:215–220, 1998.

28. D. Topkis. *Supermodularity and Complementarity*. Princeton University Press, 1998.

The Complexity of Boolean Constraint Isomorphism[*]

Elmar Böhler[1], Edith Hemaspaandra[2], Steffen Reith[3], and Heribert Vollmer[4]

[1] Theoretische Informatik, Universität Würzburg, Am Hubland, D-97074 Würzburg,
Germany, boehler@informatik.uni-wuerzburg.de
[2] Department of Computer Science, Rochester Institute of Technology, Rochester,
NY 14623, U.S.A., eh@cs.rit.edu
[3] LengfelderStr. 35b, D-97078 Würzburg, Germany, streit@streit.cc
[4] Theoretische Informatik, Universität Hannover, Appelstr. 4, D-30167 Hannover,
Germany, vollmer@thi.uni-hannover.de

Abstract. We consider the Boolean constraint isomorphism problem, that is, the problem of determining whether two sets of Boolean constraint applications can be made equivalent by renaming the variables. We show that depending on the set of allowed constraints, the problem is either coNP-hard and GI-hard, equivalent to graph isomorphism, or polynomial-time solvable. This establishes a complete classification of the complexity of the problem, and moreover, it identifies exactly all those cases in which Boolean constraint isomorphism is polynomial-time many-one equivalent to graph isomorphism, the best-known and best-examined isomorphism problem in theoretical computer science.

1 Introduction

Constraint satisfaction problems (or, constraint networks) were introduced in 1974 by U. Montanari to solve computational problems related to picture processing [26]. It turned out that they form a broad class of algorithmic problems that arise naturally in different areas [20]. Today, they are ubiquitous in computer science (database query processing, circuit design, network optimization, planning and scheduling, programming languages), artificial intelligence (belief maintenance and knowledge based systems, machine vision, natural language understanding), and computational linguistics (formal syntax and semantics of natural languages).

A constraint satisfaction instance is given by a set of variables, a set of values that the variables may take (the so-called *universe*), and a set of constraints. A constraint restricts the possible assignments of values to variables; formally a k-place constraint is a k-ary relation over the universe. The most basic question one is interested in is to determine if there is an assignment of values to the variables such that all constraints are satisfied.

---

[*] Research supported in part by grants NSF-INT-9815095/DAAD-315-PPP-gü-ab, NSF-CCR-0311021, DAAD D/0205776, DFG VO 630/5-1, and by an RIT FEAD grant.

V. Diekert and M. Habib (Eds.): STACS 2004, LNCS 2996, pp. 164–175, 2004.
© Springer-Verlag Berlin Heidelberg 2004

This problem has been studied intensively in the past decade from a computational complexity point of view. In a particular case, that of 2-element universes, a remarkable complete classification was obtained, in fact already much earlier, by Thomas Schaefer [28]. Note that in this case of a Boolean universe, the variables are propositional variables and the constraints are Boolean relations. A constraint satisfaction instance, thus, is a propositional formula in conjunctive normal form where, instead of the usual clauses, arbitrary Boolean relations may be used. In other words, the constraint satisfaction problem here is the satisfiability problem for generalized propositional formulas. Obviously the complexity of this problem depends on the set $\mathcal{C}$ of constraints allowed, and is therefore denoted by $CSP(\mathcal{C})$ ($\mathcal{C}$ will always be finite in this paper). In this way we obtain an infinite family of NP-problems, and Schaefer showed that each of them is either NP-complete or polynomial-time solvable. This result is surprising, since by Ladner's Theorem [25] there is an infinite number of complexity degrees between P and NP (assuming P $\neq$ NP), and consequently it is well conceivable that the members of an infinite family of problems may be located anywhere in this hierarchy. Schaefer showed that for the generalized satisfiability problem this is not the case: Each $CSP(\mathcal{C})$ is either NP-complete, that is in the highest degree, or in the lowest degree P. Therefore his result is called a *dichotomy theorem*.

For larger universes, much less is known. Satisfiability of constraint networks is always in NP, and for large families of allowed sets of constraints, NP-completeness was proven while for others, tractability (i.e., polynomial-time algorithms) was obtained. Research in this direction was strongly influenced by the seminal papers [15,13], and many deep and beautiful results have been proven since then, see, e. g., [14,24,16,4]. Only recently, a dichotomy theorem for the complexity of satisfiability of constraint networks over 3-element universes was published [6], but for larger domains such a complete classification still seems to be out of reach. For Boolean universes, however, a number of further computational problems have been addressed and in most cases, dichotomy theorems were obtained. These problems concern, among others, the problems to count how many satisfying solutions an instance has [7], to enumerate all satisfying solutions [8], to determine in certain ways optimal satisfying assignments [10, 18,27], to determine if there is a unique satisfying assignment [17], learnability questions related to propositional formulas [11], the inverse satisfiability problem [21], and the complexity of propositional circumscription [19,12]. Results about approximability of optimization problems related to Boolean CSPs appeared in [31,23]. We point the reader to the monograph [9] that discusses much of what is known about Boolean constraints.

In this paper, we address a problem that is not a variation of satisfiability, namely, the *isomorphism problem* for Boolean constraints. Perhaps the most prominent isomorphism problem in computational complexity theory is the *graph isomorphism problem*, GI, asking given two graphs if they are isomorphic. Graph isomorphism has been well studied because it is one of the very few problems in NP neither known to be NP-complete nor known to be in P (in fact, there is strong evidence that GI is not NP-complete, see [22]); thus GI may be in one of the "intermediate degrees" mentioned above.

Another isomorphism problem studied intensively in the past few years is the propositional formula isomorphism. This problem asks, given two propositional formulas, if there is a renaming of the variables that makes both equivalent. The history of this problem goes back to the 19th century, where Jevons and Clifford, two mathematicians, were concerned with the task to construct formulas or circuits for all n-ary Boolean functions, but since there are too many (2^{2^n}) of them they wanted to identify a small set of Boolean circuits from which all others could then be obtained by some simple transformation. This problem has been referred to since as the "Jevons-Clifford-Problem." One of the transformations they used was renaming of variables (producing an *isomorphic* circuit), another one was first renaming the variables and then negating some of them (producing what has been called a *congruent* circuit). Hence it is important to know how many equivalence classes for isomorphism and congruence there are, and how to determine if two circuits or formulas are isomorphic or congruent. (A more detailed discussion of these developments can be found in [29, pp. 6–8].) However, the exact complexity of the isomorphism problem for Boolean circuits and formulas (the congruence problem turns out to be of the same computational complexity; technically: both problems are polynomial-time many-one equivalent) is still unknown: It is trivially hard for the class coNP (of all complements of NP-problems) and in Σ_2^p (the second level of the polynomial hierarchy), and Agrawal and Thierauf showed that it is most likely not Σ_2^p-hard (that is, unless the polynomial hierarchy collapses, an event considered very unlikely by most complexity-theorists) [2].

In this paper we study the Boolean formula isomorphism problem restricted to formulas in the Schaefer sense, in other words: the *isomorphism problem for Boolean constraints*. In a precursor, the present authors showed that this problem is either coNP-hard (the hard case, the same as for general formula isomorphism) or reducible to the graph isomorphism problem (the easy case) [3]. This result is not satisfactory, since it leaves the most interesting questions open: Are there "really easy" cases for which the isomorphism problem is tractable (that is, in P)? What exactly are these? And are the remaining cases which reduce to graph isomorphism actually equivalent to GI?

The present paper answers these questions affirmatively. To state precisely our main result (Theorem 7) already here (formal definitions of the relevant classes of constraints will be given in the next section), constraint isomorphism is coNP-hard and GI-hard for classes $\mathcal{C}$ of constraints that are neither Horn nor anti-Horn nor affine nor bijunctive, it is in in P if $\mathcal{C}$ is both affine and bijunctive, and in all other cases, the isomorphism problem is *equivalent to graph isomorphism*. This classification holds for constraint applications with as well as without constants. As in the case of Schaefer's dichotomy, we thus obtain simple criteria to determine, given $\mathcal{C}$, which of the three cases holds. This theorem gives a complete classification of the computational complexity of Boolean constraint isomorphism. Moreover, it determines exactly all those cases of the Boolean constraint isomorphism problem that are equivalent to graph isomorphism, the most prominent and probably most studied isomorphism problem so far.

The next section formally introduces constraint satisfaction problems and the relevant properties of constraints. Section 3 then contains the proof of our main theorem: In Section 3.1 we identify those classes of constraints for which isomorphism is in P and Section 3.2 contains the main technical contribution of this paper proving GI-hardness for all other cases. Due to space restrictions, most proofs in this paper had to be omitted. We refer the reader to the ACM Computing Research Repository Report cs.CC/0306134.

2 Preliminaries

We start by formally introducing constraint problems. The following section is essentially from [3], following the standard notation developed in [9].

Definition 1.   1. A *constraint* C (of arity k) is a Boolean function from $\{0,1\}^k$ to $\{0,1\}$.
   2. If C is a constraint of arity k, and $x_1, x_2, \ldots, x_k$ are (not necessarily distinct) variables, then $C(x_1, x_2, \ldots, x_k)$ is a *constraint application of C*. In this paper, we view a constraint application as a Boolean function on a specific set of variables. Thus, for example, $x_1 \vee x_2 = x_2 \vee x_1$
   3. If C is a constraint of arity k, and for $1 \le i \le k$, x_i is a variable or a constant (0 or 1), then $C(x_1, x_2, \ldots, x_k)$ is a *constraint application of C with constants*.
   4. If A is a constraint application [with constants], and X a set of variables that includes all variables that occur in A, we say that A is a constraint application [with constants] *over variables X*. Note that we do not require that every element of X occurs in A.

The complexity of Boolean constraint problems depends on those properties of constraints that we define next.

Definition 2. Let C be a constraint.

   – C is *0-valid* if $C(\mathbf{0}) = 1$. Similarly, C is *1-valid* if $C(\mathbf{1}) = 1$.
   – C is *Horn* (or *weakly negative*) [*anti-Horn* (or *weakly positive*)] if C is equivalent to a CNF formula where each clause has at most one positive [negative] literal.
   – C is *bijunctive* if C is equivalent to a 2CNF formula.
   – C is *affine* if C is equivalent to an XOR-CNF formula.
   – C is *2-affine* (or, affine with width 2) if C is equivalent to a XOR-CNF formula such that every clause contains at most two literals.

Let $\mathcal{C}$ be a finite set of constraints. We say $\mathcal{C}$ is 0-valid, 1-valid, Horn, anti-Horn, bijunctive, or affine if *every* constraint $C \in \mathcal{C}$ is 0-valid, 1-valid, Horn, anti-Horn, bijunctive, or affine, respectively. Finally, we say that $\mathcal{C}$ is *Schaefer* if $\mathcal{C}$ is Horn or anti-Horn or affine or bijunctive.

The question studied in this paper is that of whether a set of constraint applications can be made equivalent to a second set of constraint applications using a suitable renaming of its variables. We need some definitions.

Definition 3. 1. Let S be a set of constraint applications with constants over variables X and let π be a permutation of X. By $\pi(S)$ we denote the set of constraint applications that results when we replace simultaneously all variables x in S by $\pi(x)$.

2. Let S be a set of constraint applications over variables X. The number of satisfying assignments of S, $\#_1(S)$, is defined as $||\{ I \mid I$ is an assignment to all variables in X that satisfies every constraint application in $S \}||$.

The isomorphism problem for Boolean constraints, first defined and examined in [3] is formally defined as follows.

Definition 4. 1. ISO($\mathcal{C}$) is the problem of, given two sets S and U of constraint applications of $\mathcal{C}$ over variables X, to decide whether S and U are isomorphic, i.e., whether there exists a permutation π of X such that $\pi(S)$ is equivalent to U.

2. ISO$_c(\mathcal{C})$ is the problem of, given two sets S and U of constraint applications of $\mathcal{C}$ with constants over variables X, to decide whether S and U are isomorphic.

Böhler et al. obtained results about the complexity of the just-defined problem that, interestingly, pointed out relations to another isomorphism problem: the graph isomorphism problem (GI).

Definition 5. GI is the problem of, given two graphs G and H, to determine whether G and H are isomorphic, i.e., whether there exists a bijection $\pi \colon V(G) \to V(H)$ such that for all $v, w \in V(G)$, $\{v, w\} \in E(G)$ iff $\{\pi(v), \pi(w)\} \subset E(H)$. Our graphs are undirected, and do not contain self-loops. We also assume a standard enumeration of the edges, and will write $E(G) = \{e_1, \ldots, e_m\}$.

GI is a problem that is in NP, not known to be in P, and not NP-complete unless the polynomial hierarchy collapses. For details, see, for example, [22]. Recently, Torán showed that GI is hard for NL, PL, Mod$_k$L, and DET under logspace many-one reductions [30]. Arvind and Kurur showed that GI is in the class SPP [1], and thus, for example in $\oplus P$.

The main result from [3] can now be stated as follows.

Theorem 6. *Let $\mathcal{C}$ be a set of constraints. If $\mathcal{C}$ is Schaefer, then ISO($\mathcal{C}$) and ISO$_c(\mathcal{C})$ are polynomial-time many-one reducible to GI, otherwise, ISO($\mathcal{C}$) and ISO$_c(\mathcal{C})$ are coNP-hard.*

Note that if $\mathcal{C}$ is Schaefer the isomorphism problems ISO($\mathcal{C}$) and ISO$_c(\mathcal{C})$ cannot be coNP-hard, unless NP = coNP. (This follows from Theorem 6 and the fact that GI is in NP.) Under the (reasonable) assumption that NP $\neq$ coNP, and that GI is neither in P, nor NP-complete, Theorem 6 thus distinguishes a hard case (coNP-hard) and an easier case (many-one reducible to GI).

Böhler et al. also pointed out that there are some bijunctive, Horn, or affine constraint sets $\mathcal{C}$ for which actually ISO($\mathcal{C}$) and ISO$_c(\mathcal{C})$ are equivalent to graph isomorphism. On the other hand, certainly there are $\mathcal{C}$ for which ISO($\mathcal{C}$) and ISO$_c$($\mathcal{C}$) are in P. In the upcoming section we will completely classify the complexity of ISO($\mathcal{C}$) and ISO$_c$($\mathcal{C}$), obtaining for which $\mathcal{C}$ exactly we are equivalent to GI and for which $\mathcal{C}$ we are in P.

3   A Classification of Boolean Constraint Isomorphism

The main result of the present paper is a complete complexity-theoretic classification of the isomorphism problem for Boolean constraints.

Theorem 7. *Let $\mathcal{C}$ be a finite set of constraints.*

1. *If $\mathcal{C}$ is not Schaefer, then ISO($\mathcal{C}$) and ISO$_c$($\mathcal{C}$) are coNP-hard and GI-hard.*
2. *If $\mathcal{C}$ is Schaefer and not 2-affine, then ISO($\mathcal{C}$) and ISO$_c$($\mathcal{C}$) are polynomial-time many-one equivalent to GI.*
3. *Otherwise, $\mathcal{C}$ is 2-affine and ISO($\mathcal{C}$) and ISO$_c$($\mathcal{C}$) are in P.*

The rest of this section is devoted to a proof of this theorem and organized as follows. The coNP lower-bound part from Theorem 7 follows from Theorem 6. In Section 3.1 we will prove the polynomial-time upper bound if $\mathcal{C}$ is 2-affine (Theorem 10). The GI upper bound if $\mathcal{C}$ is Schaefer again is part of Theorem 6. In Section 3.2 we will show that ISO$_c$($\mathcal{C}$) is GI-hard if $\mathcal{C}$ is not 2-affine (Theorems 15 and 17). Theorem 18 finally shows that ISO($\mathcal{C}$) is GI-hard if $\mathcal{C}$ is not 2-affine.

3.1   Upper Bounds

A central step in our way of obtaining upper bounds is to bring sets of constraint applications into a unique normal form. This approach is also followed in the proof of the coIP[2]^{NP} upper bound[1] for the isomorphism problem for Boolean formulas [2] and the GI upper bound from Theorem 6 [3].

Definition 8. *Let $\mathcal{C}$ be a set of constraints. nf is a normal form function for $\mathcal{C}$ if and only if for all sets S and U of constraint applications of $\mathcal{C}$ with constants over variables X, and for all permutations π of X,*

1. *$nf(S, X)$ is a set of Boolean functions over variables X,*
2. *$S \equiv nf(S, X)$ (here we view S as a set of Boolean functions, and define equivalence for such sets as logical equivalence of corresponding propositional formulas),*
3. *$nf(\pi(S), X) = \pi(nf(S, X))$, and*
4. *if $S \equiv U$, then $nf(S, X) = nf(U, X)$ (here, "=" is equality between sets of Boolean functions).*

It is important to note that $nf(S, X)$ is not necessarily a set of constraint applications of $\mathcal{C}$ with constants.

---

[1] Here IP[2] means an interactive proof system where there are two messages exchanged between the verifier and the prover.

An easy property of the definition is that $S \equiv U$ iff $nf(S, X) = nf(U, X)$. Also, it is not too hard to observe that using normal forms removes the need to check whether two sets of constraint applications with constants are equivalent, more precisely: S is isomorphic to U iff there exists a permutation π of X such that $\pi(nf(S)) = nf(U)$.

There are different possibilities for normal forms. The one used by [3] is the maximal equivalent set of constraint applications with constants, defined by $nf(S, X)$ to be the set of all constraint applications A of $\mathcal{C}$ with constants over variables X such that $S \rightarrow A$. For the P upper bound for 2-affine constraints, we use a normal form described in the following lemma. Note that this normal form is not necessarily a set of 2-affine constraint applications with constants.

Lemma 9. *Let $\mathcal{C}$ be a set of 2-affine constraints. There exists a polynomial-time computable normal form function nf for $\mathcal{C}$ such that for all sets S of constraint applications of $\mathcal{C}$ with constants over variables X, the following hold:*

1. *If $S \equiv 0$, then $nf(S, X) = \{0\}$.*
2. *If $S \not\equiv 0$, then $nf(S, X) = \{\overline{Z}, O\} \cup \bigcup_{i=1}^{\ell}\{(X_i \wedge \overline{Y_i}) \vee (\overline{X_i} \wedge Y_i)\}$, where $Z, O, X_1, Y_1, \ldots, X_\ell, Y_\ell$ are pairwise disjoint subsets of X such that $X_i \cup Y_i \neq \emptyset$ for all $1 \leq i \leq \ell$, and for W a set of variables, W in a formula denotes $\bigwedge W$, and $\overline{W}$ denotes $\neg \bigvee W$.*

Making use of the normal form, it is not too hard to prove our claimed upper bound.

Theorem 10. *Let $\mathcal{C}$ be a set of constraints. If $\mathcal{C}$ is 2-affine, then $\mathrm{ISO}(\mathcal{C})$ and $\mathrm{ISO}_c(\mathcal{C})$ are in P.*

Proof.   Let S and U be two sets of constraint applications of $\mathcal{C}$ and let X be the set of variables that occur in $S \cup U$. Use Lemma 9 to bring S and U into normal form. Using the first point in that lemma, it is easy to check whether S or U are equivalent to 0. For the remainder of the proof, we now suppose that neither S nor U is equivalent to 0. Let $Z, O, X_1, Y_1, \ldots, X_\ell, Y_\ell$ and $Z', O', X_1', Y_1', \ldots, X_k', Y_k'$ be subsets of X such that:

1. $Z, O, X_1, Y_1, \ldots, X_\ell, Y_\ell$ are pairwise disjoint and $Z', O', X_1', Y_1', \ldots, X_k', Y_k'$ are pairwise disjoint,
2. $X_i \cup Y_i \neq \emptyset$ for all $1 \leq i \leq \ell$ and $X_i' \cup Y_i' \neq \emptyset$ for all $1 \leq i \leq k$,
3. $nf(S, X) = \{\overline{Z}, O\} \cup \bigcup_{i=1}^{\ell}\{(X_i \wedge \overline{Y_i}) \vee (\overline{X_i} \wedge Y_i)\}$, and $nf(U, X) = \{\overline{Z'}, O'\} \cup \bigcup_{i=1}^{k}\{(X_i' \wedge \overline{Y_i'}) \vee (\overline{X_i'} \wedge Y_i')\}$.

We need to determine whether S is isomorphic to U. Since nf is a normal form function for $\mathcal{C}$, it suffices to check if there exists a permutation π on X such that $\pi(nf(S, X)) = nf(U, X)$. Note that

$$\pi(nf(S, X)) = \{\overline{\pi(Z)}, \pi(O)\} \cup \bigcup_{i=1}^{\ell}\{(\pi(X_i) \wedge \overline{\pi(Y_i)}) \vee (\overline{\pi(X_i)} \wedge \pi(Y_i))\}.$$

It is immediate that $\pi(nf(S, X)) = nf(U, X)$ if and only if

- $\ell = k$, $\pi(Z) = Z'$, $\pi(O) = O'$, and
- $\{\{\pi(X_1), \pi(Y_1)\}, \ldots, \{\pi(X_\ell), \pi(Y_\ell)\}\} = \{\{X'_1, Y'_1\}, \ldots, \{X'_\ell, Y'_\ell\}\}$.

Since $Z, O, X_1, Y_1, \ldots, X_\ell, Y_\ell$ are pairwise disjoint subsets of X, and since $Z', O', X'_1, Y'_1, \ldots, X'_k, Y'_k$ are pairwise disjoint subsets of X, it is easy to see that there exists a permutation π on X such that $nf(\pi(S), X) = nf(U, X)$ if and only if

- $\ell = k$, $||Z|| = ||Z'||$, $||O|| = ||O'||$, and
- $[\{||X_1||, ||Y_1||\}, \ldots, \{||X_k||, ||Y_k||\}] = [\{||X'_1||, ||Y'_1||\}, \ldots, \{||X'_k||, ||Y'_k||\}]$;
  here $[\cdots]$ denotes a multi-set.

It is easy to see that the above conditions can be verified in polynomial time. It follows that $\mathrm{ISO}(\mathcal{C})$ and $\mathrm{ISO}_c(\mathcal{C})$ are in P.   □

3.2 GI-Hardness

In this section, we will prove that if $\mathcal{C}$ is not 2-affine, then GI is polynomial-time many-one reducible to $\mathrm{ISO}_c(\mathcal{C})$ and $\mathrm{ISO}(\mathcal{C})$. As in the upper bound proofs of the previous section, we will often look at certain normal forms. In this section, it is often convenient to avoid constraint applications that allow duplicates.

Definition 11. Let $\mathcal{C}$ be a set of constraints.

1. A is a constraint application of $\mathcal{C}$ *without duplicates* if there exists a constraint $C \in \mathcal{C}$ of arity k such that $A = C(x_1, \ldots, x_k)$, where $x_i \neq x_j$ for all $i \neq j$.
2. Let S be a set of constraint applications of $\mathcal{C}$ [without duplicates] over variables X. We say that S is a maximal set of constraint applications of $\mathcal{C}$ [without duplicates] over variables X if for all constraint applications A of $\mathcal{C}$ [without duplicates] over variables X, if $S \to A$, then $A \in S$.
   If X is the set of variables occurring in S, we will say that S is a maximal set of constraint applications of $\mathcal{C}$ [without duplicates].

The following lemma is easy to see.

Lemma 12. *Let $\mathcal{C}$ be a set of constraints. Let S and U be maximal sets of constraint applications of $\mathcal{C}$ over variables X [without duplicates]. Then S is isomorphic to U iff there exists a permutation π of X such that $\pi(S) = U$.*

Note that if $\mathcal{C}$ is not 2-affine, then $\mathcal{C}$ is not affine, or $\mathcal{C}$ is affine and not bijunctive. We will first look at some very simple non-affine constraints.

Definition 13 ([9, p. 20]).

1. OR_0 is the constraint $\lambda xy. x \vee y$.
2. OR_1 is the constraint $\lambda xy. \overline{x} \vee y$.
3. OR_2 is the constraint $\lambda xy. \overline{x} \vee \overline{y}$.
4. OneInThree is the constraint $\lambda xyz. (x \wedge \overline{y} \wedge \overline{z}) \vee (\overline{x} \wedge y \wedge \overline{z}) \vee (\overline{x} \wedge \overline{y} \wedge z)$.

As a first step in the general GI-hardness proof, we show that GI reduces to some particular constraints. The reduction of GI to $\mathrm{ISO}(\{\mathrm{OR}_0\})$ already appeared in [5]. Reductions in the other cases follow similar patterns.

Lemma 14.   *1. GI is polynomial-time many-one reducible to* $\mathrm{ISO}(\{\mathrm{OR}_i\})$, $i \in \{0, 1, 2\}$.

2. *Let h be the 4-ary constraint* $h(x, y, x', y') = (x \vee y) \wedge (x \oplus x') \wedge (y \oplus y')$. *GI is polynomial-time many-one reducible to* $\mathrm{ISO}(\{h\})$.

3. *Let h be a 6-ary constraint* $h(x, y, z, x', y', z') = \mathrm{OneInThree}(x, y, z) \wedge (x \oplus x') \wedge (y \oplus y') \wedge (z \oplus z')$. *Then GI is polynomial-time many-one reducible to* $\mathrm{ISO}(\{h\})$.

The constraints OR_0, OR_1, and OR_2 are the simplest non-affine constraints. However, it is not enough to show that GI reduces to the isomorphism problem for these simple cases. In order to prove that GI reduces to the isomorphism problem for all sets of constraints that are not affine, we need to show that all such sets can "encode" a finite number of simple cases.

Different encodings are used in the lower bound proofs for different constraint problems. All encodings used in the literature however, allow the introduction of auxiliary variables. In [9], Lemma 5.30, it is shown that if C is not affine, then C plus constants can encode OR_0, OR_1, or OR_2. This implies that, for certain problems, lower bounds for OR_0, OR_1, or OR_2 transfer to C plus constants. However, their encoding uses auxiliary variables, which means that lower bounds for the isomorphism problem don't automatically transfer. For sets of constraints that are not affine, we will be able to use part of the proof of [9], Lemma 5.30, but we will have to handle auxiliary variables explicitly, which makes the constructions much more complicated.

Theorem 15. *If C is not affine, then GI is polynomial-time many-one reducible to* $\mathrm{ISO}_c(C)$.

Proof.   First suppose that C is weakly negative and weakly positive. Then C is bijunctive [7]. From the proof of [9, Lemma 5.30] it follows that there exists a constraint application $A(x, y, z)$ of C with constants such that $A(0, 0, 0) = A(0, 1, 1) = A(1, 0, 1) = 1$ and $A(1, 1, 0) = 0$. Since C is weakly positive, we also have that $A(1, 1, 1) = 1$. Since C is bijunctive, we have that $A(0, 0, 1) = 1$. The following truth-table summarizes all possibilities (this is a simplified version of [9], Claim 5.31).

xyz	000	001	010	011	100	101	110	111
$A(x, y, z)$	1	1	a	1	b	1	0	1

Thus we obtain $A(x, x, y) = (\overline{x} \vee y)$, and the result follows from Lemma 14.1.

So, suppose that C is not weakly negative or not weakly positive. We follow the proof of [9], Lemma 5.30. From the proof of [9], Lemma 5.26, it follows that there exists a constraint application A of C with constants such that $A(x, y) = \mathrm{OR}_0(x, y)$, $A(x, y) = \mathrm{OR}_2(x, y)$, or $A(x, y) = x \oplus y$. In the first two cases, the result follows from Lemma 14.1.

Consider the last case. From the proof of [9], Lemma 5.30, there exist a set $S(x, y, z, x', y', z')$ of C constraint applications with constants and a ternary function h such that $S(x, y, z, x', y', z') = h(x, y, z) \wedge (x \oplus x') \wedge (y \oplus y') \wedge (z \oplus z')$, $h(000) = h(011) = h(101) = 1$, and $h(110) = 0$.

The following truth-table summarizes all possibilities:

xyz	000	001	010	011	100	101	110	111
$h(x, y, z)$	1	a	b	1	c	1	0	d

We will first show that in most cases, there exists a set U of constraint applications of C with constants such that $U(x, y, x', y') = (x \vee y) \wedge (x \oplus x') \wedge (y \oplus y')$. In all these cases, the result follows from Lemma 14.2 above.

- $b = 0, d = 1$. In this case, $S(x, y, x, x', y', x') = (x \vee y') \wedge (x \oplus x') \wedge (y \oplus y') = (x \vee y') \wedge (x \oplus x') \wedge (y \oplus y')$.
- $b = 1, d = 0$. In this case, $S(x, y, x, x', y', x') = (x' \vee y') \wedge (x \oplus x') \wedge (y \oplus y')$.
- $c = 0, d = 1$. In this case, $S(x, y, y, x', y', y') = (x' \vee y) \wedge (x \oplus x') \wedge (y \oplus y')$.
- $c = 1, d = 0$. In this case, $S(x, y, y, x', y', y') = (x' \vee y') \wedge (x \oplus x') \wedge (y \oplus y')$.
- $b = c = 1$. In this case, $S(x, y, 0, x', y', 1) = (x' \vee y') \wedge (x \oplus x') \wedge (y \oplus y')$.
- $b = c = d = 0; a = 1$. In this case, $S(0, y, z, 1, y', z') = (y' \vee z) \wedge (y \oplus y') \wedge (z \oplus z')$.

The previous cases are analogous to the cases from the proof of [9], Claim 5.31. However, we have to explicitly add the $\oplus$ conjuncts to simulate the negated variables used there, which makes Lemma 14.2 necessary.

The last remaining case is the case where $a = b = c = d = 0$. In the proof of [9], Claim 5.31, it suffices to note that $(\overline{y} \vee z) = \exists! x h(x, y, z)$. But, since we are looking at isomorphism, we cannot ignore auxiliary variables. Our result uses a different argument and follows from Lemma 14.3 above and the observation that $S(x, y, z, x', y', z') = \text{OneInThree}(x, y, z') \wedge (x \oplus x') \wedge (y \oplus y') \wedge (z \oplus z')$. □

In the case where C is affine but not 2-affine, we first show GI-hardness of a particular constraint and then turn to the general result. (The proofs, using similar constructions as in the proofs of Lemma 14 and Theorem 15, are given in the full paper.)

Lemma 16. *Let h be the 6-ary constraint such that $h(x, y, z, x', y', z') = (x \oplus y \oplus z) \wedge (x \oplus x') \wedge (y \oplus y') \wedge (z \oplus z')$. GI is polynomial-time many-one reducible to $\text{ISO}(\{h\})$.*

Theorem 17. *If C is affine and not bijunctive, then GI is polynomial-time many-one reducible to $\text{ISO}_c(C)$.*

Finally, to finish the proof of statement 2 of Theorem 7, it remains to show GI-hardness of $\text{ISO}(C)$ for C not 2-affine. In the full paper we show that it is possible to remove the introduction of constants in the previous constructions of this section.

Theorem 18. *If C is not 2-affine, then $\text{GI} \leq^p_m \text{ISO}(C)$.*

Acknowledgements. We would like to thank Lane Hemaspaandra for helpful conversations and suggestions, and the anonymous referees for helpful comments.

References

1. V. Arvind and P. Kurur. Graph isomorphism is in SPP. In *Proceedings 43rd Symposium on Foundations of Computer Science*, pages 743–750. IEEE Computer Society Press, 2002.
2. M. Agrawal and T. Thierauf. The formula isomorphism problem. *SIAM Journal on Computing*, 30(3):990–1009, 2000.
3. E. Böhler, E. Hemaspaandra, S. Reith, and H. Vollmer. Equivalence and isomorphism for Boolean constraint satisfaction. In *Computer Science Logic*, volume 2471 of *Lecture Notes in Computer Science*, pages 412–426, Berlin Heidelberg, 2002. Springer Verlag.
4. A. Bulatov, A. Krokhin, and P. Jeavons. The complexity of maximal constraint languages. In *Proceedings 33rd Symposium on Theory of Computing*, pages 667–674. ACM Press, 2001.
5. B. Borchert, D. Ranjan, and F. Stephan. On the computational complexity of some classical equivalence relations on Boolean functions. *Theory of Computing Systems*, 31:679–693, 1998.
6. A. Bulatov. A dichotomy theorem for constraints on a three-element set. In *Proceedings 43rd Symposium on Foundations of Computer Science*, pages 649–658. IEEE Computer Society Press, 2002.
7. N. Creignou and M. Hermann. Complexity of generalized satisfiability counting problems. *Information and Computation*, 125:1–12, 1996.
8. N. Creignou and J.-J. Hébrard. On generating all solutions of generalized satisfiability problems. *Informatique Théorique et Applications/Theoretical Informatics and Applications*, 31(6):499–511, 1997.
9. N. Creignou, S. Khanna, and M. Sudan. *Complexity Classifications of Boolean Constraint Satisfaction Problems*. Monographs on Discrete Applied Mathematics. SIAM, 2001.
10. N. Creignou. A dichotomy theorem for maximum generalized satisfiability problems. *Journal of Computer and System Sciences*, 51:511–522, 1995.
11. V. Dalmau. *Computational complexity of problems over generalized formulas*. PhD thesis, Department de Llenguatges i Sistemes Informàtica, Universitat Politécnica de Catalunya, 2000.
12. A. Durand and M. Hermann. The inference problem for propositional circumscription of affine formulas is coNP-complete. In *Proceedings 20th Symposium on Theoretical Aspects of Computer Science*, volume 2607 of *Lecture Notes in Computer Science*, pages 451–462. Springer Verlag, 2003.
13. T. Feder and M. Vardi. The computational structure of monotone monadis SNP and constraint satisfaction: a study through Datalog and group theory. *SIAM Journal on Computing*, 28(1):57–104, 1998.
14. P. Jeavons, D. Cohen, and M. C. Cooper. Constraints, consistency and closure. *Artificial Intelligence*, 101:251–265, 1998.
15. P. Jeavons, D. Cohen, and M. Gyssens. Closure properties of constraints. *Journal of the ACM*, 44(4):527–548, 1997.
16. P. Jeavons, D. Cohen, and M. Gyssens. How to determine the expressive power of constraints. *Constraints*, 4:113–131, 1999.

17. L. Juban. Dichotomy theorem for generalized unique satisfiability problem. In *Proceedings 12th Fundamentals of Computation Theory*, volume 1684 of *Lecture Notes in Computer Science*, pages 327–337. Springer Verlag, 1999.

18. L. Kirousis and P. Kolaitis. The complexity of minimal satisfiability problems. In *Proceedings 18th Symposium on Theoretical Aspects of Computer Science*, volume 2010 of *Lecture Notes in Computer Science*, pages 407–418. Springer Verlag, 2001.

19. L. Kirousis and P. Kolaitis. A dichotomy in the complexity of propositional circumscription. In *Proceedings 16th Logic in Computer Science*, pages 71–80, 2001.

20. P. Kolaitis. Constraint satisfaction, databases, and logic. In *Proceedings 18th International Joint Conference on Artificial Intelligence*, pages 1587–1595, 2003.

21. D. Kavvadias and M. Sideri. The inverse satisfiability problem. *SIAM Journal of Computing*, 28(1):152–163, 1998.

22. J. Köbler, U. Schöning, and J. Torán. *The Graph Isomorphism Problem: its Structural Complexity*. Progress in Theoretical Computer Science. Birkhäuser, 1993.

23. S. Khanna, M. Sudan, L. Trevisan, and D. Williamson. The approximability of constraint satisfaction problems. *SIAM Journal on Computing*, 30(6):1863 – 1920, 2001.

24. P. Kolaitis and M. Vardi. Conjunctive-query containment and constraint satisfaction. In *Proceedings 17th ACM Symposium on Principles of Database Systems*, pages 205–213, 1998.

25. R. Ladner. On the structure of polynomial-time reducibility. *Journal of the ACM*, 22:155–171, 1975.

26. U. Montanari. Networks of constraints: fundamental properties and applications to picture processing. *Information Sciences*, 7:95–132, 1974.

27. S. Reith and H. Vollmer. Optimal satisfiability for propositional calculi and constraint satisfaction problems. *Information and Computation*, 186(1):1–19, 2003.

28. T. Schaefer. The complexity of satisfiability problems. In *Proccedings 10th Symposium on Theory of Computing*, pages 216–226. ACM Press, 1978.

29. T. Thierauf. *The Computational Complexity of Equivalence and Isomorphism Problems*, volume 1852 of *Lecture Notes in Computer Science*. Springer Verlag, Berlin Heidelberg, 2000.

30. J. Torán. On the hardness of graph isomorphism. In *Proceedings 41st Foundations of Computer Science*, pages 180–186, 2000.

31. U. Zwick. Finding almost-satisfying assignments. In *Proceedings 30th Symposium on Theory of Computing*, pages 551–560. ACM Press, 1998.

On Minimizing the Total Weighted Tardiness on a Single Machine

Stavros G. Kolliopoulos[1]* and George Steiner[2]**

[1] Department of Computing and Software, McMaster University
stavros@mcmaster.ca
[2] Management Science and Information Systems, McMaster University
steiner@mcmaster.ca

Abstract. Given a single machine and a set of jobs with due dates, the classical NP-hard problem of scheduling to minimize total tardiness is a well-understood one. Lawler gave an FPTAS for it some twenty years ago. If the jobs have positive weights the problem of minimizing total weighted tardiness seems to be considerably more intricate. To our knowledge there are no approximability results for it. In this paper, we initiate the study of approximation algorithms for the problem. We examine first the weighted problem with a fixed number of due dates and we design a pseudopolynomial algorithm for it. We show how to transform the pseudopolynomial algorithm to an FPTAS for the case where the weights are polynomially bounded. For the general case with an arbitrary number of due dates, we provide a quasipolynomial randomized algorithm which produces a schedule whose expected value has an additive error proportional to the weighted sum of the due dates.

1 Introduction

We study the problem of scheduling jobs on a single machine to minimize total weighted tardiness. We are given a set of n jobs. Job j, $1 \leq j \leq n$, becomes available at time 0, has to be processed without interruption for an integer time p_j, has a due date d_j, and has a positive weight w_j. For a given sequencing of the jobs the *tardiness* T_j of job j is defined as $\max\{0, C_j - d_j\}$, where C_j is the completion time of the job. The objective is to find a processing order of the jobs which minimizes $\sum_{j=1}^{n} w_j T_j$. In the 3-field notation used in scheduling the problem is denoted $1 | | \sum_j w_j T_j$.

According to Congram et al., $1| |\sum_j w_j T_j$ is an "NP-hard archetypal machine scheduling problem" whose exact solution appears very difficult even on very small inputs [1]. We proceed to review what is known on the complexity of the problem. In the case of one machine it has long been known that an optimal preemptive schedule has the same total weighted tardiness as an optimal nonpreemptive schedule [7]. Early on the problem was shown to be NP-hard in

---

* Research partially supported by NSERC Grant 227809-00;
** Research partially supported by NSERC Grant OG0001798;

the ordinary sense by Lenstra et al. [6] when the jobs have only two distinct due dates by a reduction from the knapsack problem. It was shown to be strongly NP-hard for an arbitrary number of due dates by Lawler [3]. Lawler and Moore [5] have presented a pseudopolynomial solution for the case when all jobs have a single common due date. From the algorithmic point of view we are not aware of any non-trivial approximation algorithm. The only case that seems to be better understood is the usually easier case of *agreeable weights:* in that case $p_j < p_i$ implies $w_j \geq w_i$. Lawler gave a pseudopolynomial algorithm for the agreeable-weighted case [3]. In 1982 he showed how to modify that algorithm to obtain an FPTAS for the case of unit weights [4]. Interestingly, the complexity of the unit weight problem, $1| |\sum_j T_j$ was an open problem for many years until Du and Leung showed it is NP-hard [2].

In this paper we make progress on the problem of minimizing total weighted tardiness by examining first the case where the number of distinct due dates is fixed. Our main contribution is a pseudopolynomial algorithm whose complexity depends on the total processing time. This implies that the problem is in $\mathcal{P}$ when the processing times are polynomially bounded. We then show how to modify the pseudopolynomial algorithm in two steps: first so that its complexity depends on the maximum tardiness and second so that it yields an FPTAS when the maximum job weight is bounded by a polynomial in n. Our main approach is based on viewing the problem as having to pack the jobs into a finite number of bins where the cost of each job depends on which bin it is assigned to and some jobs may be split between two bins. Hopefully some of the ideas we introduce could be of use for further study of approximating the long-open general case with an arbitrary number of due dates.

For the general case with an arbitrary number of distinct due dates we give a result that may be of interest when the due dates are concentrated around small values. Under the assumption that the maximum processing time is bounded by a polynomial in n, we provide a quasipolynomial randomized algorithm which produces a schedule whose expected value has an additive error equal to $\delta \sum_j w_j d_j$ for any fixed $\delta > 0$. We obtain this result by combining a partition of the time horizon into geometrically increasing intervals with a random shift of the due dates. To our knowledge this type of randomized input perturbation has not been used before in a scheduling context.

2   Pseudopolynomial Algorithm

Let us assume that the jobs have been numbered in *weighted shortest processing time* (WSPT) order, i.e., $p_1/w_1 \leq p_2/w_2 \leq ... \leq p_n/w_n$. We call a job *straddling a due date,* or *straddling* in short, if it is the last job to start before that due date. A job is *early* in a schedule if its processing is completed by its due date, and a job is *tardy* if it completes after its due date.

First we develop the pseudopolynomial solution for the problem with two fixed due dates $D_1 < D_2$. We say that job j *belongs to job class m* if $d_j = D_m$ for $m \in \{1,2\}$. We denote these job classes by $\mathcal{C}_m$ for $m \in \{1,2\}$. Our approach could be viewed as a generalization to multiple due dates of the classical approach of Lawler and Moore [5] which was known to work only for the single-due-date case before. As it is observed in [5], there appears to be no way to identify the straddling jobs in an optimal schedule before finding that schedule. Therefore we are going to enumerate all possible pairs. Let k_1, k_2 be the (fixed) straddling jobs and let S_{k_1} and S_{k_2} be their starting times in a schedule. Note that if $S_{k_1} + p_{k_1} \geq D_2$, then the second straddler does not exist and we denote this case by $k_2 = \Phi$. Define $P \doteq \sum_{j=1}^{n} p_j$ and $P_m^i \doteq \sum_{j \in C_m \setminus \{k_1, k_2\}, j \leq i} p_j$ for $m = 1, 2$, and $1 \leq i \leq n$. The fixed due dates partition the total processing interval $[0, P]$ into subintervals $I_1 = [0, D_1], I_2 = [D_1, D_2]$ and $I_3 = [D_2, P]$. These intervals can be viewed as bins where we have to pack the jobs. Let $e_{i,m}$ be the total processing time of early jobs from $C_m \setminus \{k_1, k_2\}$ scheduled in interval I_i for $m \in \{1, 2\}$ and $1 \leq i \leq m$. Similarly, let $t_{i,m}$ be the total processing time of tardy jobs from $C_m \setminus \{k_1, k_2\}$ scheduled in interval I_i for $m \in \{1, 2\}$ and $m + 1 \leq i \leq 3$. Let $E_m = \sum_{i=1}^{m} e_{i,m}$ represent the total amount of early processing for jobs from $C_m \setminus \{k_1, k_2\}$. A Gantt chart showing this partition of a partial schedule for the first j jobs is in Fig. 1. Since any early job scheduled from job class 2 in I_2 remains early anywhere in I_2, any job that is scheduled to be early in I_2 must follow all jobs which are scheduled tardy in I_2. In other words, the jobs in the part $t_{2,1}$ precede the jobs in the part $e_{2,2}$. Notice that in a partial schedule for the first j jobs $(j = 1, 2, ..., n)$, we always have

$$t_{3,1} = P_1^j - t_{2,1} - E_1 \text{ and } t_{3,2} = P_2^j - E_2. \tag{1}$$

Fig. 1. The Gantt chart for a typical partial schedule with two due dates.

Observe that when $k_2 = \Phi$, then $t_{2,1} = 0$ and $e_{2,2} = 0$ must hold. Finally let $F(S_{k_1}, S_{k_2}, E_1, E_2, t_{2,1}, j)$ denote the minimum total weighted tardiness of the job set $\{1, 2, ..., j\} \cup \{k_1, k_2\}$ in a schedule in which k_1, k_2 are the straddling jobs with start times S_{k_1} and S_{k_2}, respectively, the amount of early processing from $C_m \setminus \{k_1, k_2\}$ is E_m $(m \in \{1, 2\})$ and the total processing time of the tardy jobs from $C_1 \setminus \{k_1, k_2\}$ in interval I_2 is equal to $t_{2,1}$.

First we make a few observations which will be useful later.

Lemma 1. *In any optimal schedule the non-straddling tardy jobs scheduled in any interval $I_i (i > 1)$ must appear in WSPT order.*

Proof. Let J_i be the set of non-straddling tardy jobs scheduled in I_i in an optimal schedule. Assume that the jobs in J_i do not follow the WSPT order. Then there exist two adjacent jobs $j, l \in J_i$ such that $p_j/w_j < p_l/w_l$, but j is scheduled in the position immediately following l. A simple interchange argument shows that switching j in front of l would reduce the total weighted tardiness of the schedule, which contradicts its optimality.   □

The following result is due to McNaughton [7], we include its easy proof here for the sake of completeness.

Lemma 2. *The preemptive and non-preemptive versions of any instance of the total weighted tardiness problem have the same minimum total weighted tardiness.*

Proof. Consider any optimal preemptive schedule. Take all but the last piece of a job and insert these immediately before its last piece while shifting every other job as much to the left as possible. The total weighted tardiness of the resulting schedule is clearly not worse than that of the original schedule. Repeat this operation for every preempted job.   □

Let $l(j) \doteq \max\{\{0, 1, 2, ..., j\} \setminus \{k_1, k_2\}\}$ for $j = 0, 1, ..., n$. We can define the following recursive computation for $F(S_{k_1}, S_{k_2}, E_1, E_2, t_{2,1}, j), j \neq k_1, k_2$. For notational convenience we use f as an abbreviation of $F(S_{k_1}, S_{k_2}, E_1, E_2, t_{2,1}, j)$.

If $d_j = D_1$ then

$$f = \min \begin{cases} F(S_{k_1}, S_{k_2}, E_1 - p_j, E_2, t_{2,1}, l(j-1)) & \text{if } E_1 - p_j \geq 0 \\[2ex] F(S_{k_1}, S_{k_2}, E_1, E_2, t_{2,1} - p_j, l(j-1)) + & \text{if } p_j \leq t_{2,1} \\ w_j(S_{k_1} + p_{k_1} + t_{2,1} - D_1) & \\[2ex] F(S_{k_1}, S_{k_2}, E_1, E_2, t_{2,1}, l(j-1)) + & \text{if } p_j \leq t_{3,1}, \ t_{3,1} + t_{3,2} \leq \\ w_j(S_{k_2} + p_{k_2} + t_{3,1} + t_{3,2} - D_1) & P - (S_{k_2} + p_{k_2}) \\[2ex] \infty & \text{otherwise} \end{cases}$$

(2)

and if $d_j = D_2$ then

$$f = \min \begin{cases} F(S_{k_1}, S_{k_2}, E_1, E_2 - p_j, t_{2,1}, l(j-1)) & \text{if } E_2 - p_j \geq 0 \\[2ex] F(S_{k_1}, S_{k_2}, E_1, E_2, t_{2,1}, l(j-1)) + & \text{if } p_j \leq t_{32}, \ t_{3,1} + t_{3,2} \leq \\ w_j(S_{k_2} + p_{k_2} + t_{3,1} + t_{3,2} - D_2) & P - (S_{k_2} + p_{k_2}) \\[2ex] \infty & \text{otherwise} \end{cases}$$

(3)

The initial conditions are:

$$F(S_{k_1}, S_{k_2}, E_1, E_2, t_{2,1}, 0) = w_{k_1} max\{0, S_{k_1} + p_{k_1} - d_{k_1}\} + $$
$$+ w_{k_2} max\{0, S_{k_2} + p_{k_2} - d_{k_2}\}$$
$$\text{for all } k_1, k_2 \neq \Phi, S_{k_1}, S_{k_2}, E_1, E_2, t_{2,1} \text{ values} \qquad (4)$$

and

$$F(S_{k_1}, S_{k_2}, E_1, E_2, t_{2,1}, 0) = w_{k_1} max\{0, S_{k_1} + p_{k_1} - d_{k_1}\}$$
$$\text{for all } k_1, S_{k_1}, S_{k_2}, E_1, E_2, t_{2,1} \text{ values if } k_2 = \Phi$$
$$(5)$$

To explain the above computations, consider first the case when $d_j = D_1$: The first line of the computation calculates the resulting function value if we can insert job j into the interval I_1 to make it early, i.e, the time length E_1 is large enough for this. Since the relative order of early jobs from the same job class does not affect the tardiness of the schedule, we can assume that j gets inserted at the end of E_1. The next calculation applies when job j is tardy and scheduled in I_2. Any job that is scheduled to be early in I_2 will follow all jobs which are scheduled tardy in I_2. Note that since the jobs are indexed in WSPT order, by Lemma 1 job j should be at the end of $t_{2,1}$ and thus the second term correctly represents its tardiness. The third calculation corresponds to the case when j is tardy and is scheduled in I_3. By Lemma 1 again, job j should finish at the end of the combined tardy processing time $t_{3,1} + t_{3,2}$. Recall that although $t_{3,1}$ and $t_{3,2}$ are not state variables, they are uniquely determined by the state variables and can be easily derived by equation (1). Consider now the case $d_j = D_2$: The first calculation deals with the case when job j is made early. Since the relative order of early jobs from the same job class does not affect the tardiness of the schedule, we can assume that j gets inserted at the end of E_2. Note that although $E_2 = e_{1,2} + e_{2,2}$ is the union of these two parts, we don't need to keep track of $e_{1,2}$ and $e_{2,2}$ explicitly. We only need to ensure that E_2 is large enough to schedule job j at its end, possibly preemptively (part of it in $e_{2,2}$ and the remaining part in $e_{1,2}$.) Thus the insertion of j into E_2 may actually mean preemptively scheduling it in $I_1 \cup I_2$, but by Lemma 2 computing the total weighted tardiness of a possibly preemptive schedule here is acceptable. Finally, the last calculation deals with the case when j can be inserted at the end of the combined part $t_{3,1} + t_{3,2}$ to make it tardy.

The recursion can be implemented as a dynamic program. We have n choices for k_1, at most $n - 1$ choices for k_2, at most $n - 1$ choices for j, at most $p_{max} = max_{1 \leq j \leq n} p_j$ choices for S_{k_1} and S_{k_2}, and no more than P choices for each of E_1, E_2 and $t_{2,1}$. The optimal total weighted tardiness can be obtained by finding

$$\min\{F(S_{k_1}, S_{k_2}, E_1, E_2, t_{2,1}, l(n)) | k_1 \in \{1, 2, ..., n\}, k_2 \in \{1, 2, ..., n\} \backslash k_1,$$

$$S_{k_1} \in \{D_1 - p_{k_1}, ..., D_1 - 1\}, \max\{S_{k_1} + p_{k_1}, D_2 - p_{k_2}\} \leq S_{k_2} \leq \min\{S_{k_1} + p_{k_1}, D_2\},$$

$$E_1 \in \{1, 2, ..., S_{k_1}\}, 0 \le t_{2,1} \le S_{k_2} - (S_{k_1} + p_{k_1}), E_2 = S_{k_2} - t_{2,1} - p_{k_1} - E_1\}$$

and

$$\min\{F(S_{k_1}, S_{k_2}, E_1, E_2, t_{2,1}, l(n)) | k_1 \in \{1, 2, ..., n\}, S_{k_1} \in \{D_1 - p_{k_1}, ..., D_1 - 1\},$$

$$S_{k_1} + p_{k_1} \ge D_2, k_2 = \Phi, E_1 \in \{1, 2, ..., S_{k_1}\}, t_{2,1} = 0, E_2 = S_{k_1} - E_1\},$$

and accepting the best overall solution from the two sets. The inequalities in the last calculations ensure that we consider only feasible combinations of the state variables and we consider all of these. Thus we have proved the following theorem.

Theorem 1. *The recursion (2)-(5) gives a pseudopolynomial algorithm which computes the minimum total weighted tardiness for a problem with two distinct due dates in $O(n^3 p_{\max}^2 P^3)$ time.*

It can be easily seen that the above recursion can be extended to any fixed number of distinct due dates. The number of due dates matters only for the complexity of the resulting pseudopolynomial algorithm, as the running time of the algorithm depends exponentially on the number of distinct due dates, but it does not affect the logic of the argument. We state the result without including the details in this extended abstract.

Theorem 2. *There is a pseudopolynomial algorithm with complexity $O((nP)^{O(k)})$ which computes the minimum total weighted tardiness for a problem with a fixed number k of distinct due dates.*

We state next an immediate consequence of the previous two theorems, which sharpens the boundary between polynomially solvable and NP-hard versions of $1 || \sum w_j T_j$.

Corollary 1. *There is a polynomial algorithm which computes the minimum total weighted tardiness for a problem with a fixed number of distinct due dates if the job processing times are polynomially bounded.*

3 A Fully Polynomial Approximation Scheme

Let σ^* be an optimal sequence minimizing the total weighted tardiness. We use $T(\sigma^*)$ to denote the minimum total weighted tardiness of σ^* and $T_{\max}(\sigma^*)$ for the maximum tardiness of the jobs in σ^*. We show, as an intermediate step, that the complexity of the pseudopolynomial algorithm of the previous section can be bounded by a polynomial function of $T_{\max}(\sigma^*)$. First observe that we can limit the dynamic programming recursion to consider only (partial or full) schedules whose maximum tardiness does not exceed $T_{\max}(\sigma^*)$. Accordingly, none of the variables $t_{2,1}, t_{3,1}$ or $t_{3,2}$ can be larger than $T_{\max}(\sigma^*)$. By (1) this implies that we need to consider at most $T_{\max}(\sigma^*) + 1$ different values for E_1 and E_2 for any fixed combination of the other state variables. Finally, notice that the tardiness of a straddling job k_i will be $S_{k_i} + p_{k_i} - D_i$ for $i = 1, 2$, and thus $D_i - p_{k_i} \leq S_{k_i}$ and $S_{k_i} + p_{k_i} - D_i \leq T_{\max}(\sigma^*)$ imply that S_{k_i} can have at most $\min\{p_{k_i}, T_{\max}(\sigma^*) + 1\}$ different values. In summary, the complexity of the pseudopolynomial algorithm of Theorem 1 can be upperbounded by $O(n^3[T_{\max}(\sigma^*)]^5)$.

Similarly to [4], we are going to scale and round down the processing times and scale down the due dates by a constant K, which is to be determined later. Accordingly, let us define $\bar{d}_j \doteq d_j/K$ and $\bar{p}_j \doteq \lfloor p_j/K \rfloor$ for $j = 1, 2, ..., n$. Assume that we apply the pseudopolynomial algorithm of the preceding section to this scaled down problem and let σ_A be the optimal sequence found by the algorithm. Let $\overline{T}_{\sigma_A(j)}$ be the tardiness of the jth job in this sequence with the scaled down data and let $T_{\sigma_A(j)}$ be the tardiness of the same job in σ_A with the original data. Then we clearly have $\overline{T}_{\sigma_A(j)} \leq T_{\sigma_A(j)}/K$ for $j = 1, 2, ..., n$. Furthermore, $\overline{T}_{\sigma_A} \doteq \sum_{j=1}^{n} w_{\sigma_A(j)} \overline{T}_{\sigma_A(j)} \leq T(\sigma^*)/K$ since σ_A is optimal for the scaled down data. Let T'_{σ_A} denote the total weighted tardiness of the sequence σ_A when we use processing times $p'_j \doteq K\bar{p}_j$ for each job j and the original due dates d_j. Note that $p'_j = K\bar{p}_j \leq p_j \leq K(\bar{p}_j + 1)$. If we define $T_{\sigma_A} \doteq \sum_{j=1}^{n} w_{\sigma_A(j)} T_{\sigma_A(j)}$, then we can write

$$K\overline{T}_{\sigma_A} \leq T(\sigma^*) \leq T_{\sigma_A} \leq \sum_{j=1}^{n} w_{\sigma_A(j)} \max\{K \sum_{i=1}^{j} (\bar{p}_{\sigma_A(i)} + 1) - d_{\sigma_A(j)}, 0\}$$

$$\leq T'_{\sigma_A} + w_{\max} K n(n+1)/2, \quad (6)$$

where $w_{\max} \doteq \max_{1 \leq j \leq n} w_j$.

Furthermore,

$$K\overline{T}_{\sigma_A} = K \sum_{j=1}^{n} w_{\sigma_A(j)} \max\{\sum_{i=1}^{j} \bar{p}_{\sigma_A(i)} - \bar{d}_{\sigma_A(j)}, 0\}$$

$$= \sum_{j=1}^{n} w_{\sigma_A(j)} \max\{\sum_{i=1}^{j} K\bar{p}_{\sigma_A(i)} - d_{\sigma_A(j)}, 0\} = T'_{\sigma_A} \quad (7)$$

Combining (6) and (7), we obtain

$$T'_{\sigma_A} \leq T(\sigma^*) \leq T_{\sigma_A} \leq T'_{\sigma_A} + w_{\max} K n(n+1)/2,$$

which implies

$$T_{\sigma_A} - T(\sigma^*) \leq w_{\max} K n(n+1)/2. \quad (8)$$

Since we do not need to consider schedules for which $T_{\sigma_A(j)}$ would exceed $T_{\max}(\sigma^*)$ for any $j \in \{1, 2, ..., n\}$, the complexity of the dynamic program for the scaled problem will be bounded by $O(n^3[T_{\max}(\sigma^*)/K]^5)$.

It is well known that the earliest due date (EDD) order minimizes the maximum tardiness with any number of due dates. Let $T_{\max}$ be the maximum tardiness and T_{EDD} the total weighted tardiness of this schedule. We can assume without the loss of generality that $w_j \geq 1$ for all jobs j. Then we have

$$T_{\max} \leq T_{\max}(\sigma^*) \leq T(\sigma^*) \leq T_{EDD} \leq nw_{\max}T_{\max}. \tag{9}$$

Let us assume now that $w_{\max}$ does not grow too fast with n, i.e., there is a polynomial $g(n)$ such that we have $w_{\max} \leq g(n)$. If we choose $K = \varepsilon w_{\max}T_{\max}/(g^2(n) \cdot n(n+1)/2)$, then substituting into inequality (8) and using (9) yields

$$T_{\sigma_A} - T(\sigma^*) \leq g(n)Kn(n+1)/2 \leq \varepsilon T_{\max} \leq \varepsilon T_{\max}(\sigma^*) \leq \varepsilon T(\sigma^*).$$

Furthermore, the algorithm's complexity is upperbounded by $O(n^3[nw_{\max}T_{\max}/K]^5) \leq O(n^3[n^3g^2(n)/\varepsilon]^5)$. Thus we have proved the following.

Theorem 3. *If the job weights are bounded by a polynomial in n, then there is a fully polynomial time approximation scheme (FPTAS) for the minimum total weighted tardiness problem on a single machine with two different due dates.*

It is clear that the above scaling and rounding would also work for any fixed number of distinct due dates. Thus based on Theorem 2, we state the following result without proof.

Theorem 4. *If the job weights are bounded by a polynomial in n, then there is a fully polynomial time approximation scheme (FPTAS) for the minimum total weighted tardiness problem on a single machine with any fixed number of distinct due dates.*

4   Arbitrary Number of Due Dates

In this section we examine a general instance of the problem with an arbitrary number of due dates. Our goal is to transform the given instance into one with a reduced, although not necessarily constant, number of due dates. We then apply our previous algorithm whose complexity depends exponentially on the number of distinct due dates.

We are given an instance I with due dates d_j, $j = 1, \ldots, n$ and we will produce an instance I' with due dates d'_j, $j = 1, \ldots, n$. For a given schedule S let $cost(S)$ denote the total tardiness under the d_j and $cost'(S)$ the total tardiness under the d'_j. Similarly use T_j, T'_j to denote the tardiness of job j in each case with reference to the same schedule S. Let the *original optimum* OPT refer to the optimal tardiness of instance I under the d_j and the *modified optimum* OPT' to the optimal tardiness of I' under the d'_j.

What is a good way to generate d'_j? Assume for example that we adopt the following strategy: for every job j, enforce $d'_j < d_j$. Then for a fixed schedule S, we have $T'_j \geq T_j$, for all j, and hence $cost'(S) \geq cost(S)$. Computing S as a near-optimal schedule for the d'_j forces us to shoot for a modified optimum $OPT' \geq OPT$. When we calculate the cost of S under the original d_j it will potentially decrease. In order to analyze the performance guarantee we have to deal with two opposing effects: (i) upperbound the increase of OPT' with respect to OPT and (ii) lowerbound the difference $cost'(S) - cost(S)$. Symmetric considerations apply if we choose to set $d'_j > d_j$ for every j.

A mixed strategy where for some jobs the due dates increase and for others the due dates decrease seems to be more flexible. To counter the opposing effects inherent in the analysis, we choose to use randomization: for every job j we determine a_j, b_j such that $d_j \in [a_j, b_j]$, and we set d'_j to a_j with some probability λ_j and to b_j with probability $1 - \lambda_j$. We proceed with the analysis and will determine later suitable a_j, b_j, λ_j values for each job. We emphasize again that for time efficiency the resulting number of distinct due dates and hence the number of distinct a_j, b_j values must be small.

Lemma 3. *Under the instance transformation defined above,*

$$E[OPT'] \leq OPT + \sum_j w_j \lambda_j (d_j - a_j).$$

Proof. Consider the schedule S_o which achieves the original optimum OPT under the d_j. We establish the relation of $cost'(S_o)$ to OPT. If job j is tardy in S_o with respect to d_j, the expectation of $T'_j - T_j$ is at most $\lambda_j(d_j - a_j)$. If j is early with respect to d_j, $E[T'_j] \leq \lambda_j(d_j - a_j)$. The lemma follows.   □

We now examine the effect of calculating the expected cost of a schedule under the original due dates d_j.

Lemma 4. *Consider any schedule S. Define $B_j \doteq -\lambda_j(d_j - a_j) + (1 - \lambda_j)(b_j - d_j)$. If $B_j \geq 0$, $j = 1, \ldots, n$, then*

$$E[cost(S)] \leq E[cost'(S)] + \sum_j w_j B_j.$$

Proof. Let C_j be the completion time of job j in schedule S. If $C_j \leq d_j$, the tardiness T_j is zero. If $C_j > d_j$ we estimate $E[T_j - T'_j]$. Case 1: $d'_j = a_j$. This event happens with probability λ_j and the tardiness under d_j decreases with respect to T'_j by $(d_j - a_j)$. Case 2: $d'_j = b_j$. This event happens with probability $(1 - \lambda_j)$ and the tardiness increases with respect to T'_j by at most $(b_j - d_j)$. It follows that for a fixed schedule S, we have $E[T_j - T'_j] \leq B_j$. Because we assume that B_j is nonnegative for all j, including the jobs for which $T_j = 0$, the lemma follows.   □

Observe that in the upcoming theorem we consider for added generality the existence of a non-standard approximation scheme that finds a $(1 + \varepsilon)$-approximation for $\varepsilon \geq 0$, i.e., we also consider the existence of an exact algorithm.

Theorem 5. *Let I' be an instance derived from I based on the transformation defined above and let $\mathcal{A}$ be an approximation scheme for total weighted tardiness with running time $T(\mathcal{A}, I', \varepsilon)$ on instance I' for any $\varepsilon \geq 0$. If $B_j \geq 0$, $j = 1, \ldots, n$, we can compute in time $T(\mathcal{A}, I', \varepsilon)$ a schedule S such that*

$$E[cost(S)] \leq (1 + \varepsilon)OPT + \sum_j w_j \left(\varepsilon \lambda_j (d_j - a_j) + (1 - \lambda_j)(b_j - d_j) \right).$$

Proof. By Lemma 3, $E[OPT'] \leq OPT + \sum_j w_j \lambda_j (d_j - a_j)$. Invoking algorithm $\mathcal{A}$ on I' yields a schedule S with cost $cost'(S) \leq (1 + \varepsilon)OPT'$, which implies

$$E[cost'(S)] \leq E[(1 + \varepsilon)OPT'] \leq (1 + \varepsilon)OPT + (1 + \varepsilon)\sum_j w_j \lambda_j (d_j - a_j).$$

Mapping back the due dates to the original d_j values yields by Lemma 4

$$E[cost(S)] \leq E[(1 + \varepsilon)OPT'] + \sum_j w_j B_j.$$

Substituting the upper bound on the expectation of OPT' yields

$$E[cost(S)] \leq (1 + \varepsilon)(OPT + \sum_j w_j \lambda_j (d_j - a_j)) + \sum_j w_j B_j \Rightarrow$$

$$E[cost(S)] \leq (1 + \varepsilon)OPT + \sum_j w_j \left(\varepsilon \lambda_j (d_j - a_j) + (1 - \lambda_j)(b_j - d_j) \right).$$

$\square$

We demonstrate now a way to define the a_j's and the b_j's. We follow the method of partitioning the time horizon from 0 to $\sum_j p_j$ in geometrically increasing intervals whose endpoints are powers of $1 + \delta$ for fixed $\delta > 0$. Any due date that falls on a power of $1 + \delta$ or at the endpoints of the time horizon is left unchanged. Otherwise if $d_j \in ((1 + \delta)^l, (1 + \delta)^{l+1})$ define $a_j \doteq (1 + \delta)^l$, $b_j \doteq (1 + \delta)^{l+1}$ and denote l by l_j. Observe that for many different j, the l_j values may coincide. Let L denote the number of distinct due dates after this transformation. Under the assumption that the processing times are bounded by a polynomial in n, we can apply the algorithm described in Theorem 2 on the transformed instance I'. The running time of the algorithm will be $O(n^{O(L)})$. In our case $L = \lceil \log_{1+\delta} \sum_j p_j \rceil + 2$, therefore we obtain that $L = O(\log n / \log(1+\delta))$ under our assumption, i.e., the algorithm will be quasipolynomial. Hence we have the following theorem.

Theorem 6. *If the job processing times are bounded by a polynomial in n, then for any fixed $\delta > 0$, we can compute in quasipolynomial randomized time a schedule S such that*

$$E[cost(S)] \leq OPT + \delta \sum_j w_j d_j.$$

Proof. Consider the instance I' produced from the original instance by the above transformation. We will show at the end that for the chosen a_j, b_j values, we can choose λ_j's so that $B_j \geq 0$, $j = 1, \ldots, n$. Under this assumption and by using Theorem 2, Theorem 5 applies with $\varepsilon = 0$ and one can compute a schedule S such that

$$E[cost(S)] \leq OPT + \sum_j w_j(1 - \lambda_j)((1 + \delta)^{l_j+1} - d_j)$$

We now upperbound the additive error factor for job j.

$$\sum_j w_j(1 - \lambda_j)((1 + \delta)^{l_j+1} - d_j) \leq \sum_j w_j(1 - \lambda_j)((1 + \delta)^{l_j}(1 + \delta - 1)) \leq$$

$$\delta \sum_j w_j(1 + \delta)^{l_j} \leq \delta \sum_j w_j d_j.$$

The above derivation went through without imposing any constraint on λ_j. Ensuring that $B_j = -\lambda_j(d_j - a_j) + (1 - \lambda_j)(b_j - d_j) \geq 0$, is equivalent to $\lambda_j \leq (b_j - d_j)/(b_j - a_j)$. Since for all j, $0 < a_j < d_j < b_j$ it is always possible to choose λ_j to meet this constraint. $\square$

References

1. R. K. Congram, C. N. Potts, and S. L. van de Velde. An iterated dynasearch algorithm for the single-machine total weighted tardiness scheduling problem. *IN-FORMS Journal on Computing*, 14(1):52–67, 2002.
2. J. Du and J.Y.T. Leung. Minimizing total tardiness on one machine is NP-hard. *Mathematics of Operations Research*, 15:483–495, 1990.
3. E. L. Lawler. A "pseudopolynomial" algorithm for sequencing jobs to minimize total tardiness. *Annals of Discrete Mathematics*, 1:331–342, 1977.
4. E. L. Lawler. A fully polynomial approximation scheme for the total tardiness problem. *Operations Research Letters*, 1:207–208, 1982.
5. E. L. Lawler and J. M. Moore. A functional equation and its application to resource allocation and sequencing problems. *Management Science*, 16:77–84, 1969.
6. J.K. Lenstra, A.H.G. Rinnooy Kan, and P. Brucker. Complexity of machine scheduling problems. *Annals of Discrete Mathematics*, 1:343–362, 1977.
7. R. McNaughton. Scheduling with deadlines and loss functions. *Management Science*, 6:1–12, 1959.

Online Competitive Algorithms for Maximizing Weighted Throughput of Unit Jobs

Yair Bartal[1], Francis Y.L. Chin[2], Marek Chrobak[3], Stanley P.Y. Fung[2],
Wojciech Jawor[3], Ron Lavi[1], Jiří Sgall[4], and Tomáš Tichý[4]

[1] Institute of Computer Science, The Hebrew University of Jerusalem, Israel.
{yair,tron}@cs.huji.ac.il
[2] Department of Computer Science and Information Systems, The University of
Hong Kong, Hong Kong. {chin,pyfung}@csis.hku.hk
[3] Department of Computer Science, University of California, Riverside, CA 92521.
{marek,wojtek}@cs.ucr.edu
[4] Mathematical Institute, AS CR, Žitná 25, CZ-11567 Praha 1, Czech Republic.
{sgall,tichy}@math.cas.cz

Abstract. We study an online scheduling problem for unit-length jobs,
where each job is specified by its release time, deadline, and a nonnegative
weight. The goal is to maximize the *weighted throughput*, that is the
total weight of scheduled jobs. We first give a randomized algorithm
RMIX with competitive ratio of $e/(e-1) \approx 1.582$. Then we consider
s-bounded instances where the span of each job is at most s. We give
a 1.25-competitive randomized algorithm for 2-bounded instances, and
a deterministic algorithm EDF_α, whose competitive ratio on s-bounded
instances is at most $2 - 2/s + o(1/s)$. For 3-bounded instances its ratio
is $\phi \approx 1.618$, matching the lower bound.
We also consider 2-uniform instances, where the span of each job is 2.
We prove a lower bounds for randomized algorithms and deterministic
memoryless algorithms. Finally, we consider the multiprocessor case and
give an $1/(1 - (\frac{M}{M+1})^M)$-competitive algorithm for M processors. We
also show improved lower bounds for the general and 2-uniform cases.

1 Introduction

Network protocols today offer only the 'best-effort service', the term—misnomer,
in fact—that describes the most basic level of service that does not involve firm
guarantees for packet delivery. Next-generation networks, however, will provide
support for differentiated services, to meet various quality-of-service (QoS) demands from the users. In this paper we consider an online buffer management
problem that arises in such QoS applications.

In the *bounded delay buffer problem* [8,1], packets arrive and are buffered at
network switches. At each integer time step, one packet is sent along the link.
Each packet is characterized by its QoS value, which can be thought of as a
benefit gained by forwarding the packet. Network switches can use this value
to prioritize the packets. Each packet has a deadline that indicates the latest
time when a packet can be sent. In overload conditions, some packets will not be

V. Diekert and M. Habib (Eds.): STACS 2004, LNCS 2996, pp. 187–198, 2004.
© Springer-Verlag Berlin Heidelberg 2004

sent by their deadline, do not contribute to the benefit value, and can as well be dropped. The objective is to maximize the total value of the forwarded packets.

It is easy to see that this buffer management problem is equivalent to the following unit-job scheduling problem. We are given a set of n unit-length jobs, with each job j specified by a triple (r_j, d_j, w_j) where r_j and d_j are integral release times and deadlines, and w_j is a non-negative real weight. One job can be processed at each integer time. The goal is to compute a schedule for the given set of jobs that maximizes the *weighted throughput* or *gain*, that is, the total weight of the jobs completed by their deadline.

In this paper we focus on the online version of this problem, where each job arrives at its release time. At each time step, an online algorithm needs to schedule one of the pending jobs, without the knowledge of the jobs released later in the future. An online algorithm $\mathcal{A}$ is called R-competitive, if its gain on any instance is at least $1/R$ times the optimum (offline) gain on this instance. The smallest such value R is called the *competitive ratio* of $\mathcal{A}$. The competitive ratio is commonly used as a performance measure for online algorithms, and we adopt this measure in this paper.

For unit jobs, some restrictions on instances have been proposed in the literature [8,1,5]. In *s-bounded instances*, the span of the jobs (defined as the difference between the deadline and the release time) is at most s, and in *s-uniform instances* the span of each job is exactly s. In the context of QoS buffer management, these cases correspond to QoS situations in which the end-to-end delay is critical and only a small amount of delay is allowed at each node [8].

The unit-job scheduling problem is related to another scheduling problem which also arises from QoS applications. In *metered-task model* [2,6], each job is specified by four real numbers: release time, deadline, processing time (not necessarily unit), and weight. Preemptions are allowed. Unlike in classical scheduling, even non-completed jobs contribute to the overall gain. Specifically, the gain of a job is proportional to the amount of it that was processed.

Past work. A naive greedy algorithm that always schedules the heaviest job is known to be 2-competitive [8,7]. No better algorithm, deterministic or randomized, is known for the general case. For the deterministic case, a lower bound of $\phi \approx 1.618$ was shown in [1,5,7]. In the randomized case, [5] gives a lower bound of 1.25. (The proof in [5] was for metered tasks, but it carries over to unit jobs.) Both of those lower bounds apply even to 2-bounded instances.

For the 2-bounded case, a ϕ-competitive algorithm was presented in [8]. Deterministic algorithms for 2-uniform instances were studied by [1], who established a lower bound of $\frac{1}{2}(\sqrt{3}+1) \approx 1.366$ and an upper bound of $\sqrt{2} \approx 1.414$.

In [8], a version of the buffer management problem was studied in which the output port has *bandwidth* M (that is, M packets at a time can be sent). This corresponds to the problem of scheduling unit-time jobs on M processors. In [8] a lower bound of $4 - 2\sqrt{2} \approx 1.172$, for any M, was presented that applies even to the 2-bounded model. For the 2-uniform case, a lower bound of 10/9 was given.

Our results. First, we give a randomized algorithm with competitive ratio $e/(e-1) \approx 1.582$, which is the first algorithm for this problem with competitive ratio below 2. Our algorithm has been inspired by the techniques developed in [6].

For 2-bounded instances, we give a 1.25-competitive randomized algorithm, matching the known lower bound from [5].

We also give a deterministic algorithm EDF_α whose competitive ratio on 3-bounded instances is $\phi = 1.618$, matching the lower bound. This result extends previous results from the literature for 2-bounded instances [8], and it provides evidence that a ϕ-competitive deterministic algorithm might be possible for the general case. For 4-bounded instances, EDF_α is $\sqrt{3} \approx 1.732$ competitive, and for s-bounded instances it is $2 - 2/s + o(1/s)$ competitive. However, without the restriction on the span, it is only 2-competitive.

For 2-uniform instances, we prove a lower bound of $4 - 2\sqrt{2} \approx 1.172$ for randomized algorithms, improving the $10/9$ bound from [8]. In the deterministic case, we prove a lower bound of $\sqrt{2} \approx 1.414$ on algorithms that are memoryless (we say that an algorithm is memoryless if its decision at each step depends only on the pending jobs and is invariant under multiplying all weights of pending jobs by a constant). This matches the previously known upper bound in [1]. We remark that all competitive algorithms for unit-job scheduling in the literature are memoryless.

Finally, we study the M-processor case, that corresponds to the buffer management problem in which the output port has *bandwidth* M, meaning that it can send M packets at a time. We give a $1/(1 - (\frac{M}{M+1})^M)$-competitive algorithm for the case of M processors. For randomized algorithms, we also show improved lower bounds of 1.25 for the general and $4 - 2\sqrt{2} \approx 1.172$ for the 2-uniform cases.

In addition to those results, we introduce a new algorithm called BAL_β, where β is a parameter, and we analyze it in several cases. On 2-uniform instances, $\text{BAL}_{\sqrt{2}/2}$ is $\sqrt{2}$-competitive, matching the bound from [1]. On 2-bounded instances, BAL_β is ϕ-competitive (and thus optimal) for two values of $\beta \in \{2 - \phi, \phi - 1\}$. It is also ϕ-competitive for 3-bounded instances. Although we can show that BAL_β cannot be ϕ-competitive in general, we conjecture that for some values of β its ratio is better than 2.

Our results show the power of randomization for the problem of scheduling unit jobs. For the general version, our randomized algorithm outperforms all deterministic algorithms, even on the special case of span at most 2. For span at most 2, we give a tight analysis of the randomized case, showing a surprisingly low competitive ratio of 1.25, compared to 1.618 in the deterministic case.

2 Preliminaries

As we noted in the introduction, the QoS buffer management problem is equivalent to the unit-job scheduling problem. We will henceforth use scheduling terminology in this paper. We number the jobs $1, 2, \ldots, n$. Each job j is specified by a triple (r_j, d_j, w_j), where r_j and d_j are integral release times and deadlines, and w_j is a non-negative real weight. To simplify terminology and notation, we will often use the weights of jobs to identify jobs. Thus, we will say "job w" meaning "the job with weight w". A *schedule* S specifies which jobs are executed, and for each executed job j it specifies an integral time t when it is scheduled, where $r_j \le t < d_j$. Only one job can be scheduled at any given time step. The *throughput* or *gain* of a schedule S on instance I, denoted $gain_S(I)$, is the total weight of the jobs in I that are executed in S. Similarly, if $\mathcal{A}$ is a scheduling algorithm, $gain_{\mathcal{A}}(I)$ is the gain of the schedule computed by $\mathcal{A}$ on I. The optimal gain on I is denoted by $opt(I)$. We say that an instance is s-bounded if $d_j - r_j \leq s$ for all jobs j. Similarly, an instance is s-uniform if $d_j - r_j = s$ for all jobs j. The difference $d_j - r_j$ is called the span of a job j. A job i is pending in schedule S at t if $r_i \leq t < d_i$ and i has not been scheduled before t.

We often consider offline (canonical) earliest-deadline schedules. In such schedules, the job that is scheduled at any time t is chosen (from the ones that are executed in the schedule) as the pending job with the earliest deadline. Any schedule can easily be converted into an earliest-deadline schedule by rearranging its jobs. Jobs with the same deadline are ordered by decreasing weights. (Jobs with equal weights are ordered arbitrarily, but consistently by all algorithms.)

We often view the behavior of an online algorithm $\mathcal{A}$ as a game between $\mathcal{A}$ and an adversary. Both algorithms schedule jobs released by the adversary who tries to maximize the ratio $opt(I)/gain_{\mathcal{A}}(I)$. In most of the proofs we give a potential function argument by defining a potential function Φ that maps all possible configurations into real numbers. At each time step, an online algorithm and the adversary execute a job. The proofs are based on the following lemma.

Lemma 1. *Let $\mathcal{A}$ be an online algorithm. Let Φ be a potential function that is 0 on configurations with no pending jobs, and at each step satisfies $R \cdot \Delta gain_{\mathcal{A}} \geq \Delta adv + \Delta \Phi$, where $\Delta \Phi$ represents the change of the potential, and $\Delta gain_{\mathcal{A}}$, Δadv represent $\mathcal{A}$'s and the adversary gain in this step. Then $\mathcal{A}$ is R-competitive.*

The lemma above applies to randomized algorithms as well. In that case, however, $\Delta gain_{\mathcal{A}}$ and $\Delta \Phi$ are the expected values of the corresponding quantities, with respect to the algorithm's random choices at the given step.

In some proofs we use a different approach called charging. In a charging scheme, the weight of each of the jobs in the adversary schedule is charged to a job, or several jobs, in our schedule, in such a way that each job in our schedule is charged at most R times its weight. If such a charging scheme exists, it implies that our algorithm is R-competitive.

As discussed in the introduction, our problem is related to the metered-task model. Consider the discrete metered-task model, in which jobs have integral release times, deadlines and processing lengths, and the algorithm can only switch jobs at integral times. (In [5] this model is called non-timesharing.) Then:

Theorem 1. *The unit-job scheduling problem with a single processor is equivalent to the single processor discrete metered-task model. The unit-job scheduling problem with M processors is a special case of the M-processor discrete metered-task model (assuming jobs can migrate from one machine to another); they are equivalent when, in addition, all jobs in the metered-task model are of unit length.*

The continuous version of the metered-task model [2,6,5] bears some resemblance to the randomized case of unit-job scheduling, although it is not clear whether the results from the former model can be automatically translated into results for the latter model. One may attempt to convert a deterministic algorithm $\mathcal{D}$ for metered tasks into a randomized $\mathcal{R}$ algorithm for unit jobs, by setting the probability of $\mathcal{R}$ executing a given job j to be equal to $\mathcal{D}$'s fraction of the processor power devoted to j. It is, however, not clear how to extend this into a full specification of an algorithm that would match the performance of $\mathcal{D}$.

3 Randomized Algorithm RMIX

In this section we give the first randomized algorithm for scheduling unit jobs with competitive ratio smaller than 2.

Algorithm RMIX. At each step, let h_1 be the heaviest pending job. Select a real number $x \in (0,1)$ uniformly at random. Schedule the job j with earliest deadline among the pending jobs with $w_j \geq e^{-x} w_{h_1}$.

Notation. At each step we select inductively a sequence of pending jobs $h_2, \ldots, h_k$ so that h_{i+1} is the heaviest job j such that $w_j > w_{h_1}/e$ and $d_j < d_{h_i}$; if such j does not exist, we set $k = i$. In case of ties, prefer jobs with earlier deadlines. Denote $v_i = w_{h_i}$ for $i = 1, \ldots, k$ and $v_{k+1} = w_{h_1}/e$. Let $\delta_i = \ln(v_i) - \ln(v_{i+1})$. Note that RMIX schedules the job h_i with probability δ_i and $\sum_{i=1}^{k} \delta_i = 1$. At a given time step, the expected gain of RMIX is $\omega = \sum_{i=1}^{k} \delta_i v_i$.

Theorem 2. *Algorithm* RMIX *is* $\frac{e}{e-1} \approx 1.582$-*competitive.*

Proof. At a given time step, let X be the set of pending jobs in RMIX, and let Y be the set of pending jobs in the adversary schedule that he will schedule in the future. We assume that the adversary schedule is canonical earliest-deadline.

Define the potential $\Phi = \sum_{i \in Y-X} w_i$. Job arrivals and expirations cannot increase the potential as these jobs are not in $Y - X$: the arriving job is always in X and the expiring job is never in Y by the definition of Y. So we only need to analyze how the potential changes after job execution. By Lemma 1, denoting by j the job scheduled by the adversary, it sufficient to prove that $w_j + \Delta\Phi \leq \frac{e}{e-1}\omega$.

Assume that $j \in Y \cap X$. Inequality $\ln x \leq x - 1$ for $x = v_{i+1}/v_i$ implies that, for any $i \leq k$,

$$v_i - v_{i+1} \leq v_i(\ln v_i - \ln v_{i+1}) = \delta_i v_i . \tag{1}$$

We have $w_j \leq v_1$ as $j \in X$. Let $p \in \{1, \ldots, k+1\}$ be the largest index such that $w_j \leq v_p$. By the assumption that the adversary schedule is earliest-deadline, we know that he will not execute any h_i, $i = p, \ldots, k$, in the future, so these are not in Y. The expected increase of Φ is then at most $\sum_{i=1}^{p-1} \delta_i v_i$. So, using $v_{k+1} = v_1/e$ and (1), we have $w_j + \Delta\Phi \leq v_p + \sum_{i=1}^{p-1} \delta_i v_i = \frac{e}{e-1}(v_p - v_{k+1}) + \frac{1}{e-1}(v_1 - v_p) + \sum_{i=1}^{p-1} \delta_i v_i = \frac{e}{e-1}\sum_{i=p}^{k}(v_i - v_{i+1}) + \frac{1}{e-1}\sum_{i=1}^{p-1}(v_i - v_{i+1}) + \sum_{i=1}^{p-1} \delta_i v_i \leq \frac{e}{e-1}\sum_{i=p}^{k} \delta_i v_i + \frac{1}{e-1}\sum_{i=1}^{p-1} \delta_i v_i + \sum_{i=1}^{p-1} \delta_i v_i = \frac{e}{e-1}\omega$.

The easy case when $j \in Y - X$ is omitted.

4   An Optimal Randomized Algorithm for 2-Bounded Instances

In this section we give a 1.25-competitive randomized algorithm for 2-bounded instances. This matches the lower bound from [5], and thus completely resolves this case.

Algorithm R2B. Define $p_{ab} = 1$ if $a \geq b$ and $p_{ab} = \frac{4a}{5b}$ otherwise. Let $q_{ab} = 1 - p_{ab}$. Let a and b denote the heaviest jobs of span 1 and span 2, respectively, released at this time step. If the currently pending job is x, let $u = \max(x, a)$. Execute u with probability p_{ub} and b with probability q_{ub}.

Theorem 3. *Algorithm* R2B *is 1.25-competitive.*

Proof. Without loss of generality, we can assume that at each step exactly one job of span 1 is issued. All jobs of span 1 except the heaviest one can be simply ignored; if no job is issued, we treat it as a job of weight 0. Similarly, we can assume that at each step (except last) exactly one job of span 2 is issued. This can be justified as follows: If, at a given time t, the optimum schedule contains a job of span two released at t, we can assume that it is the heaviest such job. A similar statement holds for Algorithm R2B. Thus all the other jobs of span 2 can be ignored in this step, and treated as if they are issued with span 1 in the following time step.

First note that p_{ab} satisfies the following properties for any $a, b \geq 0$.

$$5p_{ab}a \geq 4a - b \quad (2) \qquad\qquad 5p_{ab}a + 2q_{ab}b \geq 4a \quad (4)$$

$$5(p_{ab}a + q_{ab}b) \geq 4b \quad (3) \qquad\qquad 5p_{ab}a + 2q_{ab}b \geq b . \quad (5)$$

Algorithm R2B is memoryless and randomized, so its state at each step is given by a pair $\langle x, s \rangle$, where x is the job of span 2 issued in the previous step, and s is the probability that x was executed in the previous step (i.e., no job is pending). Denote $t = 1 - s$ the probability that x is pending.

Denoting by $z \in \{0, x\}$ the pending job of the adversary, the complete configuration at this step is described by a triple $\langle x, s, z \rangle$. Let Φ_{xsz} denote the potential function in the configuration $\langle x, s, z \rangle$. We put $\Phi_{xs0} = 0$ and $\Phi_{xsx} = \frac{1}{4}x \cdot \max(5s - 1, 3s)$.

Consider one step, where the configuration is $\langle x, s, z \rangle$, two jobs a, b are issued, of span 1 and span 2, respectively. The new configuration is $\langle b, s', z' \rangle$, where $s' = sq_{ab} + tq_{x'b}$, $x' = \max(a, x)$, and $z' \in \{0, b\}$. Using Lemma 1, we need to show that for each adversary move:

$$R \cdot \Delta gain_{\text{R2B}} - \Phi_{bs'z'} + \Phi_{xsz} \geq \Delta adv \quad (6)$$

where $\Delta gain_{\text{R2B}}$ is the expected weight of a job scheduled by R2B and Δadv the weight of the job scheduled by the adversary.

<u>Case 1</u>: Adversary schedules b. Then $\Phi_{xsz} \geq 0$, $\Delta adv = b$, $z' = 0$, and $\Phi_{bs'z'} = 0$. For a fixed value of u in the algorithm, the expected gain of the algorithm is $p_{ub}u + q_{ub}b$ and (3) implies $\frac{5}{4}(p_{ub}u + q_{ub}b) \geq b$. By averaging over $u \in \{a, x'\}$ we get $R \cdot \Delta gain_{\text{R2B}} \geq b$, which implies (6).

Case 2: Adversary does not schedule b. Then $z' = b$, $\Phi_{bs'z'} = \frac{1}{4}b \cdot \max(5s'-1, 3s')$, $\Delta gain_{\text{R2B}} = s'b + sp_{ab}a + tp_{x'b}x'$. Substituting into (6), it is enough to prove that

$$\min(b, 2s'b) + 5sp_{ab}a + 5tp_{x'b}x' + 4 \cdot \Phi_{xsz} \geq 4 \cdot \Delta adv . \qquad (7)$$

Case 2.1: Adversary schedules a. Then $\Delta adv = a \leq x'$ and $\Phi_{xsz} \geq 0$. For the first term of the minimum, we use (2) twice and get $b + 5sp_{ab}a + 5tp_{x'b}x' = s(b + 5p_{ab}a) + t(b + 5p_{x'b}x') \geq 4sa + 4tx' \geq 4a$. For the second term of the minimum, we use (4) twice and get $2s'b + 5sp_{ab}a + 5tp_{x'b}x' = s(5p_{ab}a + 2q_{ab}b) + t(5p_{x'b}x' + 2q_{x'b}b) \geq 4sa + 4tx' \geq 4a$

Case 2.2: Adversary schedules $z = x$. It must be the case that $x' = x \geq a$, as otherwise the adversary would prefer to schedule a. We have $\Delta adv = x$.

If $x \geq b$, then $p_{xb} = 1$. We use $4\Phi_{xsz} = 4\Phi_{xsx} \geq (5s-1)x$ and obtain $5tp_{xb}x + 4\Phi_{xsz} \geq 5tx + 5sx - x = 4x$, which implies (7).

It remains to consider the case $x < b$. Using (2), (5) and (4) we obtain $b + 5tp_{xb}x \geq b + t(4x - b) = 4tx + sb$ and $2s'b + 5sp_{ab}a + 5tp_{xb}x = s(2q_{ab}b + 5p_{ab}a) + t(2q_{xb}b + 5p_{xb}x) \geq sb + 4tx$. Together with with $4\Phi_{xsz} = 4\Phi_{xsx} \geq 3sx$ and $x < b$ this implies $\min(b, 2s'b) + 5sp_{ab}a + 5tp_{xb}x + 4\Psi_{xsz} \geq 4tx + sb + 3sx \geq 4x$ and (7) follows.

5   Deterministic Algorithm for s-Bounded Instances

The 2-bounded (deterministic) case is now well understood. A ϕ-competitive algorithm was given in [1], matching the lower bound from [8,7]. In this section, we extend the upper bound of ϕ to 3-bounded instances. For the general case, the best known competitive ratio for deterministic algorithm is 2, [8,7].

We define two algorithms. They both use a real-valued parameter, α or β, and they are both ϕ-competitive for 3-bounded instances for an appropriate value of the parameter. In this section, h always denotes the heaviest pending job. The first algorithm schedules a relatively heavy job with the smallest deadline. The idea of the second algorithm is to balance the maximum gain in the next step against the discounted projected gain in the following steps, if no new jobs are issued. A *plan* (at time t) is an optimal schedule of jobs pending at time t. A plan can be computed by iteratively scheduling pending jobs, from heaviest to lightest, at their latest available slots.

Algorithm EDF_α: Execute the earliest-deadline job with weight $\geq \alpha w_h$.

Algorithm BAL_β: At each step, execute the job j that maximizes $w_j + \beta\pi_j$, where π_j is the total weight of the plan in the next time step, if j is executed in the current step. (In case of a tie, the algorithm chooses the earliest-deadline job, and if there are several, the heaviest one among those.)

We establish the following facts about BAL_β. The proofs are omitted. All positive results can be shown using Lemma 1. (a) Let $\beta \in \{\phi - 1, 2 - \phi\}$, where $\phi \approx 1.618$ is the golden ratio. Then BAL_β is ϕ-competitive for 2-bounded instances. (b) $\text{BAL}_{\sqrt{2}/2}$ is $\sqrt{2}$-competitive for 2-uniform instances (this is the best ratio for memoryless algorithms, as discussed in Section 6). (c) $\text{BAL}_{\phi-1}$ is

ϕ−competitive for 3-bounded instances and is not ϕ−competitive for 8-bounded instances.

Theorem 4. $\mathrm{EDF}_{\phi-1}$ *is ϕ-competitive for 3-bounded instances.*

Proof. We fix a canonical earliest-deadline adversary schedule A. Let E be the schedule computed by $\mathrm{EDF}_{\phi-1}$. We use the following charging scheme: Let j be the job scheduled by the adversary at time t. If j is executed in E before time t, charge j to its copy in E. Otherwise, charge j to the job in E scheduled at t.

Fix some time step t, and let f be the job scheduled in E at time t. Let also h be the heaviest pending job in E at time t. By the definition of $\mathrm{EDF}_{\phi-1}$, f is the earliest-deadline job with $w_f \geq (\phi - 1)w_h = w_h/\phi$. Denote also by j the job scheduled in A at time t.

Job f receives at most two charges: one from j and one from itself, if f is executed in A at some later time. Ideally, we would like to prove that the sum of the charges is at most ϕw_f. It turns out that in some cases this is not true, and, if so, we then show that for the job g scheduled by E in the next step, the total of all charges to f and g is at most $\phi(w_f + w_g)$. Summing over all such groups of one or two jobs, the ϕ-competitiveness of $\mathrm{EDF}_{\phi-1}$ follows.

If f receives only one charge, it is at most ϕw_f: If this charge is from f, it is trivially at most w_f. If the charge is from j (not scheduled before t in E), then j is pending at t in E and thus $w_j \leq w_h \leq \phi w_f$, by the definition of $\mathrm{EDF}_{\phi-1}$. In this case the group consist of a single job and we are done.

It remains to handle the case when f receives both charges. Since in A job j is before f, we have $d_j \leq d_f$ (and for $d_j = d_f$, the tie is broken in favor of j) But at time t, $\mathrm{EDF}_{\phi-1}$ chooses f, so j is not eligible for execution by $\mathrm{EDF}_{\phi-1}$, that is $w_j < (\phi-1)w_h$. If $w_f = w_h$, then f is charged at most $w_f + w_j \leq (1+\phi-1)w_h = \phi w_f$, and we have a group with a single job again.

Otherwise, $w_f < w_h$ and the adversary does not schedule f at time t, hence $d_f \geq t + 2$. By the rule of $\mathrm{EDF}_{\phi-1}$, $d_h > d_f$. As the span is bounded by 3, it has to be the case that $d_h = t + 3$ and $d_f = t + 2$. Thus the adversary schedules f at time $t + 1$. The weight of the job g scheduled at time $t + 1$ in E is $w_g \geq (\phi - 1)w_h$, as $h \neq f$ is still pending in E. Furthermore, g gets only the charge from itself, as the adversary at time $t + 1$ schedules f which is charged to itself. The total weight of the jobs charged to f and g is thus at most $w_j + w_f + w_g \leq (\phi - 1)w_h + w_f + w_g \leq \frac{3}{2}(w_f + w_g)$, since both w_h and w_f are at least $(\phi - 1)w_h$. In this case we have a group of two jobs.

A more careful analysis yields an upper bound of $2 - \Theta(1/s)$ on the competitive ratio of EDF_α on s-bounded instances.

Theorem 5. *For each $s \geq 4$, algorithm $\mathrm{EDF}_{1/\lambda_s}$ is λ_s-competitive for s-bounded instances, where λ_s is the unique non-negative solution of equation*

$$(2 - \lambda_s)(\lambda_s^2 + \lfloor \frac{s}{3} \rfloor \lambda_s + s - 2 - 2 \lfloor \frac{s}{3} \rfloor) = \lambda_s^2 - \lambda_s .$$

We get $\lambda_4 = \sqrt{3} \approx 1.732$. For larger s, the equation is cubic. It can be verified that $2 - \frac{2}{s} \leq \lambda_s \leq 2 - \frac{1}{s}$, and in the limit for $s \to \infty$, $\lambda_s = 2 - 2/s + o(1/s)$.

Recall that, by Theorem 1, results for discrete metered tasks can be applied to unit-job scheduling. Here we describe two such results. We say that a pending job i *dominates* another pending job j if $d_i \leq d_j$ and $w_i > w_j$. A pending job is *dominant* if no other pending job dominates it. In [4], the authors considered the case of the metered-task model when there are at most s dominant jobs at each time, and proposed an online algorithm GAP for this case. In s-bounded instances there can be at most s pending dominant jobs at any time. Thus, the results from [4] imply that:

Theorem 6. GAP *is r_s-competitive for s-bounded instances, where r_s is the unique positive real root of the equation $r_s = 1 + r_s^{-1/(s-1)}$.*

We can show that $r_s = 2 - \Theta(\frac{1}{s})$. EDF$_\alpha$ has a smaller competitive ratio for s-bounded instances, but GAP can also be applied to the more general set of instances that have at most s dominant jobs at any time. GAP can also be slightly modified to give the same performance without knowing the value of s in advance. In [3], an algorithm FIT was given for the discrete metered-task model. Its competitive ratio is better than 2 when the ratio of maximum to minimum job weights is at most ξ. By Theorem 1, we have:

Theorem 7. FIT *is $(2 - 1/(\lceil \lg \xi \rceil + 2))$-competitive for unit-job scheduling.*

6   2-Uniform Instances

We first prove a lower bound of $4 - 2\sqrt{2} \approx 1.172$ on the competitive ratio of randomized algorithms. This improves a lower bound of $10/9$ from [8].

Theorem 8. *No randomized algorithm can be better than $(4 - 2\sqrt{2})$-competitive for 2-uniform instances.*

Proof. We use Yao's minimax principle [9], by showing a distribution on instances that forces each online algorithm $\mathcal{A}$ to have ratio at least $4 - 2\sqrt{2}$.

We will generate an instance randomly. Fix a large integer n and let $a = \sqrt{2} + 1$ and $p = 1/a = \sqrt{2} - 1$. Each instance consists of stages $0, 1, \ldots$, where in stage j we have three jobs: two jobs j, j' of weight a^j issued at time $2j$ and one job j'' of weight a^{j+1} issued at time $2j + 1$. After each stage $j \leq n$, we continue with probability p or stop with probability $1 - p$. After stage n, at time $2n + 2$, we issue two jobs of weight a^{n+1}, and stop.

Fix a deterministic online algorithm $\mathcal{A}$. We compute the expected gain of $\mathcal{A}$ and the adversary in stage $j \leq n$, conditioned on stage j being reached. At time $2j$, $\mathcal{A}$ executes a job of weight a^j (it has no choice), say j. If it executes j'' at time $2j + 1$, its gain in stage j is $a^j + a^{j+1} = (1 + a)a^j = (2 + \sqrt{2})a^j$. If it executes j', its gain is either $2a^j + a^{j+1}$ or $2a^j$, depending on whether we stop, or continue generating more stages. Thus its expected gain is $(1 - p) \cdot (2a^j + a^{j+1}) + p \cdot 2a^j = (2 + \sqrt{2})a^j$, same as in the previous case. Since the probability of reaching this stage is p^j, the contribution of this stage to $\mathcal{A}$'s expected gain is $2 + \sqrt{2}$.

We now calculate the adversary gain in stage j. If we stop, the adversary gains $2a^j + a^{j+1}$, otherwise he gains $a^j + a^{j+1}$, so his expected gain is $(1 - p) \cdot$

$(2a^j + a^{j+1}) + p \cdot (a^j + a^{j+1}) = a^j(2 - p + a) = 4a^j$. Thus the contribution of this stage to the adversary's gain is 4.

Summarizing, for each step, except the last one, the contributions towards the expected value are $2 + \sqrt{2}$ for $\mathcal{A}$ and 4 for the adversary independent of j. The contributions of stage $n + 1$ are different, but also constant. So the overall ratio will be, in the limit for $n \to \infty$, the same as the ratio of the contributions of stages $0, \ldots, n$, which is $4/(2 + \sqrt{2}) = 4 - 2\sqrt{2}$, as claimed.

Deterministic algorithms for 2-uniform instances were studied in [1], where an upper bound of $\sqrt{2}$ was given. As we show below, it is not possible to beat ratio $\sqrt{2}$ with any deterministic memoryless algorithm. We define an online algorithm $\mathcal{A}$ to be *memoryless* if its decision at each step depends only on the pending jobs and is invariant under multiplying all weights of pending jobs by a constant. Due to space constraints the proof of the following theorem is omitted.

Theorem 9. *No deterministic memoryless algorithm can achieve competitive ratio better than $\sqrt{2}$ for 2-uniform instances.*

7   The Multiprocessor Case

The greedy 2-competitive algorithm [8,7] applies to both uniprocessor and multiprocessor cases. For M processors we give an algorithm with competitive ratio $(1 - (\frac{M}{M+1})^M)^{-1}$, showing that the competitive ratio improves with a larger number of processors. When $M \to \infty$ this ratio tends to $e/(e-1) \approx 1.58$, beating the $\phi \approx 1.618$ bound for $M = 1$ [5]. The basic idea of our algorithm is similar to algorithm MIXED [5] and our randomized algorithm RMIX. We divide the processing effort between M processors, such that each processor works on the earliest-deadline job with weight above a certain threshold. This threshold decreases geometrically for each processor. If no job is above the threshold, we select the heaviest remaining job, and reset the threshold to the weight of this job. Throughout this section let $\beta = M/(M + 1)$, $R = (1 - (\frac{M}{M+1})^M)^{-1}$.

Algorithm DMIX-M. Let X be the set of pending jobs at a time t. The algorithm chooses jobs $h_1, \ldots, h_M$ as shown below and schedules them for execution.

$i \leftarrow 1$;
repeat
    $g \leftarrow$ heaviest job in $X - \{h_1, \ldots, h_{i-1}\}$; $h_i \leftarrow g$; $j \leftarrow i$;
    repeat
        $i \leftarrow i + 1$;
        $f \leftarrow$ earliest-deadline job in $X - \{h_1, \ldots, h_{i-1}\}$ with $w_f \geq \beta^{i-j} w_g$;
        if f exists then $h_i \leftarrow f$;
    until f does not exist

Fix a time step t. Denote $v_i = w_{h_i}$ for all i. Normalize the weights so that $v_1 = 1$. We call those h_i selected in the outer repeat loop *g-jobs*. We only prove the case of two g-jobs, and leave the complete proof to the full paper. Suppose the g-jobs are h_1 and h_k, $1 < k \leq M$. By the choices of DMIX-M, we have $v_i \geq \beta^{i-1}$ for $i \in \{1, 2, \ldots, k-1\}$, $v_k < \beta^{k-1}$, and $v_i \geq v_k \beta^{i-k}$ for $i \in \{k+1, \ldots, M\}$.

Lemma 2. *(i)* $(k - 1) + (M - k + 1)v_k \leq R \cdot \left(\sum_{i=0}^{k-2} \beta^i + v_k \sum_{i=k}^{M} \beta^{i-k} \right)$.

(ii) $M\beta^{p-k}v_k + \sum_{i=1}^{p} v_i \leq R \cdot \sum_{i=1}^{M} v_i$ *for any positive integer* $p \in \{k, ..., M\}$.

Theorem 10. DMIX-*M* *is* $(1 - (\frac{M}{M+1})^M)^{-1}$-*competitive for* M *processors.*

Proof. (Sketch.) For a given input instance, let D be a schedule of DMIX-M and A the adversary schedule. As usual, we assume that A is canonical earliest-deadline. Fix a time step t. Let

$H = \{h_1, ..., h_M\}$, the jobs executed by DMIX-M, at time t,
$J =$ the set of M jobs executed by the adversary at time t,
$X =$ the pending jobs of DMIX-M at time t,
$Y =$ the pending jobs of the adversary at time t that will be executed at time t or later.

For a set of jobs I, let $w(I) = \sum_{i \in I} w_i$ denote the total weight of I. Define the potential function $\Phi = w(Y - X)$. By Lemma 1, it is thus sufficient to show that $w(J) + \Delta\Phi \leq R \cdot w(H)$.

Job arrivals and expirations cannot increase the potential. So we only need to analyze how the potential changes after job executions. The change in the potential due to the adversary executing the jobs in J is $-w(J - X)$, as the jobs in $J - X$ contribute to the current potential but will not contribute in the next step. A job h_i executed by DMIX-M does not contribute to the potential in the current step, but if $h_i \in Y - J$, then, in the next step, h_i will be pending in A but not in D, so it will contribute to the new potential. Thus the change due to DMIX-M executing the jobs in H is $w(H \cap Y - J)$. We conclude that $\Delta\Phi = -w(J - X) + w(H \cap Y - J)$. Therefore, in order to prove the theorem it is sufficient to show that $w(J \cap X) + w(H \cap Y - J) \leq R \cdot w(H)$.

Case 1: $H \cap Y - J = \emptyset$. Jobs $j \in J \cap X$ must have weight at most 1, at most $k - 1$ of them can have weights larger than v_k, since otherwise DMIX-M would choose the g-jobs differently. Thus, using Lemma 2, we get: $w(J \cap X) + w(H \cap Y - J) \leq (k - 1) + (M - k + 1)v_k + 0 \leq R \cdot \left(\sum_{i=0}^{k-2} \beta^i + v_k \sum_{i=k}^{M} \beta^{i-k} \right) \leq R \cdot \left(\sum_{i=1}^{k-1} v_i + \sum_{i=k}^{M} v_i \right) = R \cdot w(H)$.

Case 2: $H \cap Y - J \neq \emptyset$. Let p be the largest index for which $h_p \in Y - J$. In other words, h_p is the highest-indexed job in H that will be executed in A at a later time. Since A is earliest-deadline, we have $d_j \leq d_{h_p}$ for all $j \in J$. We distinguish two subcases.

Case 2.1: $p \geq k$. In this case, $w_j < \beta^{p-k}v_k$ for any $j \in J \cap X - H$, since otherwise they would be scheduled instead of h_k. Thus by Lemma 2, $w(J \cap X) + w(H \cap Y - J) = w(J \cap X - H) + w(H \cap Y) \leq M\beta^{p-k}v_k + \sum_{i=1}^{p} v_i \leq R \cdot w(H)$.

Case 2.2: $p \leq k$. We have $w_j \leq v_k$ for any $j \in J \cap X - \{h_1, ..., h_k\}$, since otherwise they would be scheduled instead of h_k. Thus by Lemma 2 with $p = k$, $w(J \cap X) + w(H \cap Y - J) = w(J \cap X - H) + w(H \cap Y) \leq \sum_{j \in X - \{h_1, ..., h_k\}} w_j + \sum_{i=1}^{p} v_i \leq Mv_k + \sum_{i=1}^{k} v_i \leq R \cdot w(H)$.

The lower bound proofs in [5] and Theorem 8 can easily be generalized to the multiprocessor case, improving the bounds in [8] $(4 - 2\sqrt{2}$ for the general case and $10/9$ for the 2-uniform case):

Theorem 11. *No deterministic or randomized algorithm can be better than $5/4$-competitive, for any number of processors M. No deterministic or randomized algorithm can be better than $4 - 2\sqrt{2}$-competitive, for 2-uniform instances on any number of processors M.*

Acknowledgements. M. Chrobak and W. Jawor were supported by NSF grants CCR-9988360 and CCR-0208856. J. Sgall and T. Tichý were partially supported by Institute for Theoretical Computer Science, Prague (project LN00A056 of MŠMT ČR), grant 201/01/1195 of GA ČR, and grant A1019401 of GA AV ČR. M. Chrobak, W. Jawor, J. Sgall and T. Tichý were partially supported by cooperative grant KONTAKT-ME476/CCR-9988360-001 from MŠMT ČR and NSF. F. Y. L. Chin and S. P. Y. Fung were supported by a RGC Grant HKU7142/03E.

References

1. N. Andelman, Y. Mansour, and A. Zhu. Competitive queueing policies for QoS switches. In *Proc. of the 14th ACM-SIAM SODA*, pages 761–770, 2003.
2. E.-C. Chang and C. Yap. Competitive online scheduling with level of service. In *Proc. 7th COCOON*, pages 453–462. Springer, 2001.
3. F. Y. L. Chin and S. P. Y. Fung. Online scheduling with partial job values and bounded importance ratio. In *Proc. of ICS*, pages 787–794, 2002.
4. F. Y. L. Chin and S. P. Y. Fung. Improved competitive algorithms for online scheduling with partial job values. *9th COCOON*, pages 425–434, 2003.
5. F. Y. L. Chin and S. P. Y. Fung. Online scheduling for partial job values: does timesharing or randomization help? *Algorithmica* 37(3):149–164, 2003.
6. M. Chrobak, L. Epstein, J. Noga, J. Sgall, R. van Stee, T. Tichy, and N. Vakhania. Preemptive scheduling in overloaded systems. In *Proc. of 29th ICALP*, pages 800–811, 2002.
7. B. Hajek. On the competitiveness of online scheduling of unit-length packets with hard deadlines in slotted time. In *CISS*, 2001.
8. A. Kesselman, Z. Lotker, Y. Mansour, B. Patt-Shamir, B. Schieber, and M. Sviridenko. Buffer overflow management in QoS switches. In *Proc. of the 33rd STOC*, pages 520–529, 2001.
9. A. Yao. Probabilistic computations: Towards a unified measure of complexity. In *Proc. of the 18th FOCS*, pages 222–227, 1977.

Optimal and Online Preemptive Scheduling on Uniformly Related Machines

Tomáš Ebenlendr[1] and Jiří Sgall[2]

[1] Faculty of Mathematics and Physics, Charles University, Praha. ebik@ucw.cz
[2] Mathematical Institute, AS CR, Žitná 25, CZ-11567 Praha 1, Czech Republic.
sgall@math.cas.cz

Abstract. We consider the problem of preemptive scheduling on uniformly related machines. We present a semi-online algorithm which, if the optimal makespan is given in advance, produces an optimal schedule. Using the standard doubling technique, this yields a 4 competitive deterministic and $e \approx 2.71$ competitive randomized online algorithms. In addition, it matches the performance of the previously known algorithms for the offline case, with a considerably simpler proof. Finally, we study the performance of greedy heuristics for the same problem.

1 Introduction

We consider the scheduling problem denoted $Q|pmtn|C_{\max}$ in the three-field notation. We are given m uniformly related machines, each characterized by its speed, and a sequence of jobs, each characterized by its processing time. If a job with processing time p is assigned to a machine of speed s it requires time p/s. Allowing preemption means that any job may be divided into several pieces that may be processed on several machines; however, the time slots assigned to different pieces need to be disjoint. The goal is to minimize the length of the schedule (makespan), i.e., the time when all jobs are finished.

In the online problem $Q|online\text{-}list, pmtn|C_{\max}$ the jobs arrive in a sequence and we have to assign each job without any knowledge of the future requests; the algorithm has to determine immediately all the machines and all the time slots in which the current job is scheduled. We also consider the semi-online variant in which an algorithm is given in advance the value of the optimal makespan. (Semi-)online algorithms are evaluated by the competitive ratio, which is the worst case ratio of the length of the produced schedule to the minimal length.

Finally, we also study the performance of two well-known greedy heuristics, LIST and LPT. LIST (LIST scheduling) is an online algorithm which schedules each coming job so that it finishes as soon as possible. For preemptive scheduling, it means that at each time the job is scheduled on the fastest available machine. LPT (Largest Processing Time first) uses the same strategy, but the jobs are sorted and processed from the largest one; i.e., it is no longer an online algorithm.

Preemptive scheduling on uniformly related machines is a classical scheduling problem, yet it did not receive much attention in the online version. One motivation for its study is the expectation that, similarly as for identical machines, the

V. Diekert and M. Habib (Eds.): STACS 2004, LNCS 2996, pp. 199–210, 2004.
© Springer-Verlag Berlin Heidelberg 2004

problem should be tractable, as the structure of the optimum is well understood, and at the same time it could provide a useful insight for constructing efficient randomized algorithms for the non-preemptive version.

We describe known results and our contribution in each area separately.

Optimal offline and semi-online algorithms

For offline preemptive scheduling the optimal solution was given already by Horvath et al. [14] and Gonzales and Sahni [13]. The algorithm of Gonzales and Sahni is more efficient: First, the total number of preemptions in the schedule is $2(m-1)$, which is the best possible bound for schedules with the optimal makespan. Second, its running time is $O(n + m \log m)$ and this is also best possible: the term $m \log m$ is caused by sorting the largest m jobs, which is necessary to obtain an optimal schedule. Another algorithm using $2(m-1)$ preemptions was given in [15]; it simplifies the algorithm of Gonzales and Sahni, but it also sorts the jobs, so it is not semi-online and needs time $O(n \log n)$.

An optimal (1-competitive) semi-online algorithm with the optimal makespan known in advance was previously known only for two machines, see Epstein [8].

Our results. We give an optimal (1-competitive) semi-online algorithm for the studied problem. It generates at most $2(m-1)$ preemptions and runs in time $O(n + m \log m)$, thus it is as efficient as the offline algorithm of Gonzales and Sahni. In addition it has the advantage of being semi-online, i.e., the jobs can be scheduled in an arbitrary order after computing the optimal makespan.

Since the value of the optimal makespan can be easily computed, our algorithm can be also used as an efficient offline algorithm instead of the algorithm of Gonzales and Sahni. The efficiency is the same and we believe that our algorithm is significantly simpler and easier to understand.

Online algorithms

For $Q|online\text{-}list|C_{\max}$, non-preemptive scheduling on uniformly related machines, the first constant competitive algorithm was given by Aspnes et al. [1]; it is deterministic and its competitive ratio is 8. This was improved by Berman et al. [3]; they present a 5.828 competitive deterministic and a 4.311 competitive randomized algorithms. For an alternative very nice presentation see [2].

These algorithms can also be used for preemptive scheduling. Woeginger [18] observed that the optimal non-preemptive makespan is at most twice the optimal preemptive makespan for uniformly related machines. Consequently, the previous algorithms that do not use preemption are also 11.657 competitive deterministic and 8.622 competitive randomized algorithms for $Q|online\text{-}list, pmtn|C_{\max}$. No better preemptive online algorithms were known before for the general case.

All these algorithms are based on a semi-online algorithm and a doubling strategy for guessing the optimal value. This common tool was first used for online scheduling in [16,1].

The lower bounds for $Q|online\text{-}list|C_{\max}$ are 2.438 for deterministic algorithms [3] and 2 for randomized algorithms; the same lower bound of 2 works for $Q|online\text{-}list, pmtn|C_{\max}$ both for deterministic and randomized algorithms [11].

Our results. Using our 1-competitive semi-online algorithm and the same doubling strategy as in the previous results, we obtain a 4 competitive deterministic and $e \approx 2.7183$ competitive randomized algorithms for $Q|online\text{-}list, pmtn|C_{\max}$.

Greedy algorithms

Both LIST and LPT were previously studied for the non-preemptive case, $Q|online\text{-}list|C_{\max}$. The competitive ratio of LIST is not constant, it is asymptotically $\Theta(\log m)$, see [5,1]. However, sorting the jobs improves the performance dramatically. The competitive ratio of LPT is between 1.52 and 1.66 [12]; a better upper bound of 1.58 is claimed in [6], but the proof appears to be incomplete.

Our results. We show that with preemption, $Q|online\text{-}list, pmtn|C_{\max}$, the situation is similar. The competitive ratio of LIST is $\Theta(\log m)$ and the competitive ratio of LPT is 2. More precisely, it is between $2 - 2/(m+1)$ and $2 - 1/m$.

Special cases

We conclude by a few cases in which we know the exact competitive ratio for preemptive scheduling from previous results.

The first case is that of identical machines (i.e., all the speeds are equal to 1), denoted by $P|online\text{-}list, pmtn|C_{\max}$. Chen et al. [4] gives an optimal deterministic algorithm and a matching lower bound which works even for randomized algorithms. The optimal competitive ratio is $4/3$ for $m = 2$ and increases to $e/(e-1) \approx 1.582$ as $m \to \infty$.

For the special case of two related machines the optimal competitive ratio for preemptive scheduling, $Q2|online\text{-}list, pmtn|C_{\max}$, was given independently by Wen and Du [17] and Epstein et al. [10] for any combination of speeds. If the ratio of the two speeds is $s \geq 1$, the optimal competitive ratio is $1 + s/(s^2+s+1)$ (this is equal to $4/3$ for $s = 1$ and decreases to 1 as $s \to \infty$); randomization does not help here either. The semi-online deterministic case of $Q2|online\text{-}list, pmtn|C_{\max}$ with jobs arriving sorted was completely analyzed in [9].

The special case of non-decreasing speed ratios was solved in [7]. Extending the technique for identical machines, the exact competitive ratio is given for all combinations of speeds satisfying the given restriction; all these values are smaller than or equal to 2.

2 Preliminaries

Let M_i, $i = 1, \ldots, m$, denote the m machines and let $s_i \geq 0$ be the speed of machine M_i. We assume, w.l.o.g., that the machines are sorted so that $s_1 \geq s_2 \geq \ldots$. The input sequence of jobs is denoted $J = (p_j)_{j=1}^n$, where n is the number of jobs and $p_j \geq 0$ is the processing time of jth job.

Let OPT be the makespan of the optimal schedule. There are two easy lower bounds on OPT. First, OPT is bounded by the total work that can be done on all machines. Thus

$$OPT \geq \frac{\sum_{j=1}^n p_j}{\sum_{i=1}^m s_i}. \tag{1}$$

Second, OPT is bounded by the optimal makespan of any k jobs. An optimal schedule of k jobs uses only k fastest machines: if it used a slower machine, some faster one would be idle at the same time. Thus, for all $k = 1, \ldots, m$,

$$OPT \geq \frac{\sum_{j=1}^k \bar{p}_j}{\sum_{i=1}^k s_i}, \tag{2}$$

where $\bar{p}_j$ is the jth largest processing time. It is known that the actual value of OPT is the minimal value satisfying the conditions (1) and (2) [14,13]. In particular, we can compute the value OPT in time $O(n + m \log m)$.

3   An Optimal Semi-online Algorithm

We present the semi-online algorithm, which, given T, generates a schedule with makespan at most T, if some such schedule exists.

The idea of the algorithm is to schedule each job on two adjacent machines using one preemption so that it spans over the whole interval $[0, T)$, i.e., it is always running on one of the machines. Thus at each time exactly one of these machines remains idle. Such a pair of machines can be thought as one *virtual machine* with possibly changing speed. For the subsequent jobs, such virtual machines are used in place of real ones. See Fig. 1 for an example. If a job is too small, we create a machine with zero speed, to fit this scheme. To prove that this outline works, it remains to check that if a job is too long to fit on a machine, T is smaller than OPT, as one of the conditions (1) and (2) is violated.

3.1   Preliminaries

We assume in this section, w.l.o.g., that $p_j > 0$ for all j; the algorithm can skip the jobs with zero processing times. We define machines $M_{m+1}, M_{m+2}, \ldots$ as machines with zero speed. These machines only serve to simplify the description of the algorithm as otherwise we would need to analyze separately a case when a job is too small to occupy the slowest machine for the whole time interval $[0, T)$.

We define a *virtual machine* as a set of adjacent machines, such that exactly one of them is idle at any time in $[0, T)$. Let V_i denote the ith virtual machine. Scheduling a job on V_i at time t means that we schedule it on the machine in V_i that is idle at time t. The speed of virtual machine V_i is denoted $v_i(t)$; it is defined to be the speed of the unique machine in V_i which is idle at time t. Let $W_i = \int_0^T v_i(t)dt$ be the total work which can be done on V_i. Note that a virtual machine is defined so that all this work can be used by a single job.

3.2   Algorithm InTime

The algorithm is defined to schedule in the interval $[offset, offset + time)$ instead of $[0, time)$. This is used later in the online variants of the algorithm.

Invariants: The algorithm works with sets V_i and numbers W_i. The following properties of the virtual machines are invariants of the algorithm:

1. Sets V_i are virtual machines. Every real machine belongs to exactly one virtual machine. $W_i = \int_0^T v_i(t)dt$.
2. For all i and t, $v_i(t) \geq v_{i+1}(t)$. This also implies $W_i \geq W_{i+1}$.
3. Each job that is already processed is scheduled on machines that belong to a single virtual machine. For every i, there are exactly $|V_i| - 1$ jobs that are scheduled on the machines that belong to V_i.

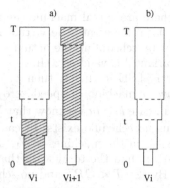

Fig. 1. One step of the algorithm InTime. The vertical axis is the time. The width of the columns is proportional to the speed of the machines and thus the area is proportional to the work done on a given job. (a) Two machines with one job that spans over $[0, T)$. (b) The new virtual machine obtained by merging the two idle parts. There is a new postponed preemption at time t.

Algorithm *InTime(T)*
  − Initialization:
  procedure *InitInTime(offset, time)*
    $T :=$ *time*; $o :=$ *offset*
    For all i **do** $V_i := \{M_i\}$; $W_i := s_i \cdot T$
  − Step: (schedule a job with processing time p)
  function *DoInTime(p)*
    1. **Find** i **such that** $W_i \geq p > W_{i+1}$ **or return FALSE**
    2. **Find** t **such that** $\int_0^t v_i(\tau)d\tau + \int_t^T v_{i+1}(\tau)d\tau = p$
    3. **Schedule job** p **on** V_i **in time interval** $[o, o+t)$ **and on** V_{i+1}
       in $[o+t, o+T)$.
    4. $V_i := V_i \cup V_{i+1}$; $W_i := W_i + W_{i+1} - p$;
       For all $j > i$ **do** $V_j := V_{j+1}$; $W_j := W_{j+1}$
    5. **return TRUE**
  − Main body:
  InitInTime(0, T); **for** $j := 0$ **to** n **do if not** *DoInTime(p_j)* **fail**

Theorem 3.1. *Algorithm InTime maintains all the invariants and generates a schedule with makespan at most T whenever such a schedule exists.*

Proof. All invariants are satisfied after the initialization. Now we show that the function *DoInTime()* maintains the invariants and that it can fail only in line 1.

In line 2, t exists because the left-hand side of condition is continuous in t, and p lies between values of the left-hand side for 0 and T (i.e., W_{i+1} and W_i). The value t can be computed since the function $v_i(t)$ changes its value at most m times. Line 3 is correct, because virtual machines are idle by definition. The real schedule can be generated because the algorithm knows the mappings to determine $v_i(t)$. Line 4 merges the two half-used virtual machines to one virtual machine that satisfy invariant 1. Invariant 2 is not broken because the two virtual machines are adjacent. If there are k real machines and $k - 1$ jobs in V_i and l machines and $l - 1$ jobs in V_{i+1}, we create one virtual machine with $k + l$ real machines and $k + l - 1$ jobs by scheduling the actual job and merging the two virtual machines. Thus invariant 3 is valid as well.

If $DoInTime()$ returns FALSE in line 1, then $p_j > W_1$ when processing some job j (we always have a machine of speed zero). We know that $V_1 = \{M_1, \ldots, M_k\}$, for some k. In case $k \geq m$ we know that $\sum_{j'=1}^{j} p_{j'} > T \cdot \sum_{i=1}^{m} s_i$. By (1), $T < OPT$ and thus no schedule exists. In case $k < m$ we know that there are $k - 1$ jobs scheduled on the machines of V_1. So, including j, we have k jobs that are together larger than the total work that can be done on the k fastest machines before T. By (2), $T < OPT$ and no schedule exists again.   □

Our algorithm can also be used as an optimal offline algorithm. As noted above, the exact preemptive optimum can be computed using conditions (1) and (2). Using the computed value as T in $InTime(T)$, the previous theorem guarantees that the produced schedule is optimal.

3.3   Efficiency of the Algorithm

The number of preemptions. There are two types of preemptions in the algorithm. *Immediate preemptions* are created by dividing a job between two virtual machines. *Postponed preemptions* are generated by scheduling on the virtual machine as its speed changes. It is clear that every immediate preemption generates at most one postponed preemption.

Define zero virtual machine as a set of real machines with zero speed. When scheduling on a non-zero virtual machine and a zero virtual machine, no immediate preemption occurs because the job is completed on the non-zero one. On the other hand, after scheduling on two non-zero machines, the number of non-zero machines decreases. Because we have m non-zero virtual machines after the initialization, the algorithm creates at most $m - 1$ immediate preemptions and thus no more than $2m - 2$ preemptions overall.

The time complexity and implementation. Even with a simple implementation using linked lists to store both the list of machines and the lists of preemptions on the machines, the algorithm is quite efficient. If a job is scheduled partially on a zero virtual machine, it is processed in time $O(1)$. The analysis of the number of preemptions implies that only $m - 1$ jobs are scheduled on two non-zero virtual machines; each such step takes $O(m)$ time, including searching for the time of the new preemption, actual scheduling and merging the lists of remaining preemptions. Thus the total time is $O(n + m^2)$. This bound can be further improved to $O(n + m \log m)$ by using search trees instead of linked lists; the details are omitted.

3.4   Generalizations

It is easy to generalize our algorithm so that the real machines change their speeds over time arbitrarily. It is necessary to preprocess the speed profiles so that at each time the machines are sorted according to their speeds; this is easy to do using additional preemptions to "glue" the initial virtual machines from pieces of different real machines. The same lower bounds (1) and (2) then hold for the optimum and the algorithm gives a matching schedule. Naturally, the time and the number of preemptions depend on the speed profiles of the machines.

4 Doubling Online Algorithms

When the optimal makespan is not known in advance, we guess it and if the guess turns out to be too small, we double it. It is well known that this technique can be improved by initial random guess with an exponential distribution; it is also not hard to optimize the multiplicative constants. The standard proof is omitted.

Algorithm *Double()*
Initialization: $G := p_1/s_1$; $B := 0$; $InitInTime(B, G)$
Step j: **while not** $DoInTime(p_j)$ **do** $B := B+G$; $G := 2 \cdot G$; $InitInTime(B, G)$

Theorem 4.1. *The algorithm Double is a 4 competitive deterministic online algorithm for preemptive scheduling on uniformly related machines.*

Algorithm *DoubleRand()*
Initialization:
    $r := rand([0, 1])$; (r is uniformly distributed in $[0, 1]$)
    $G := e^r \cdot p_1/s_1$; $B := 0$; $InitInTime(B, G)$
Step j: **while not** $DoInTime(p_j)$ **do** $B := B+G$; $G := e \cdot G$; $InitInTime(B, G)$

Theorem 4.2. *The algorithm DoubleRand is an e competitive randomized algorithm for preemptive scheduling on uniformly related machines.*

5 Greedy Algorithms

The greedy rule for scheduling on related machines instructs us to schedule each coming job so that it ends as soon as possible. With preemptions, this is achieved by scheduling the job from time 0 on the fastest idle machine (if there is any), for every time t, until it is completed. Thus the first job is scheduled on the fastest machine. The second job on the second fastest, with a preemption at the end of first job (if it is not completed earlier), and then on the fastest machine, etc. See Fig. 2 for an example. This algorithm is called LIST scheduling. If, in addition, the jobs arrive ordered so that their sizes are non-increasing, the algorithm is called LPT (Largest Processing Time first).

We prove that LIST and LPT have asymptotically the same competitive ratio as in the non-preemptive case. However, note that this is not a straightforward consequence of the non-preemptive case, as the preemptive and non-preemptive versions of LIST can generate different schedules on the same instance.

Notation. For a given instance, $NOPT$ denotes a non-preemptive optimal schedule and its makespan. It is known that $NOPT \leq 2 \cdot OPT$. this is proved as

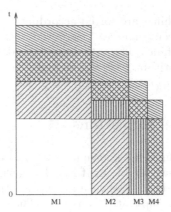

Fig. 2. An example of a schedule generated by the LIST algorithm. Similarly shaded regions correspond to the same job.

an upper bound on the non-preemptive LPT algorithm in [18]; we use the same proof in Theorem 5.7.

For input sequences J and J', $J' \subseteq J$ denotes that J' is a subsequence of J (not necessarily a contiguous segment). We say that J dominates J' if $p_j \geq p'_j$ for all j. In both cases trivially $OPT(J') \leq OPT(J)$.

5.1   Analysis of LIST

LIST is a simple online algorithm. However, we show that its competitive ratio is $\Theta(\log m)$ and thus it is not very good. Let $LIST(J)$ denote both the schedule generated by LIST on the input sequence of jobs J and its makespan.

We start by the upper bound. First we show that decreasing the size of jobs can only improve the schedule. This implies that removing short jobs decreases the makespan by a constant multiple of OPT; doing this in logarithmic number of phases we obtain the desired bound.

Lemma 5.1. *Suppose that J dominates J'. Then $LIST(J) \geq LIST(J')$.*

Proof. Consider the schedule after scheduling job p_j and let $t_{i,j}$, $i \leq j$, denote the ith smallest completion time of a job. Note that the sequence $T_j = (t_{i,j})_{i=1}^j$ is non-decreasing. Define $t_{0,j} = 0$. The job p_{j+1} is scheduled on machine M_{j+1-i} in the interval $[t_{i,j}, t_{i+1,j})$ and on M_1 after $t_{j,j}$; of course this holds only until it is completed (it may be too short to reach M_1 or even slower machines). The corresponding times for J' are denoted by $t'_{i,j}$ and the sequences T'_j.

We prove by induction on j that for all i, $t'_{i,j} \leq t_{i,j}$, i.e., T'_j is pointwise smaller than or equal to T_j. The induction assumption for zero jobs is trivial. The induction step says that $t'_{i,j} \leq t_{i,j}$ implies $t'_{i,j+1} \leq t_{i,j+1}$ assuming that $p'_{j+1} \leq p_{j+1}$.

By the induction assumption, the job p'_{j+1} in $LIST(J')$ is, at every time t, processed by a machine that is at least as fast as the machine that processes the job p_j in $LIST(J)$ at the same time. Moreover, $p'_{j+1} \leq p_{j+1}$. So the job p'_{j+1}

must be completed earlier than or at the same time when p_{j+1} is. The sequence T'_{j+1} is obtained from T'_j by inserting the completion time of p'_j, while T_{j+1} is obtained from T_j by inserting the completion time of p_j. Since a smaller or equal number is inserted into a pointwise smaller or equal sorted sequence T'_j, it necessarily remains pointwise smaller than or equal to T_j and the inductive claim follows. □

Lemma 5.2. *Let $J' \subseteq J$. Let t be a time such that all jobs $j \in J \setminus J'$ are completed at time t in $LIST(J)$. Then $LIST(J) \le t + LIST(J')$.*

Proof. Let J'' be obtained from J' by replacing each job p_j by p'_j which is equal to the part of p_j not processed in $LIST(J)$ by time t. Then the schedule $LIST(J'')$ is exactly the same as the interval $[t, LIST(J))$ of the schedule $LIST(J)$, except for the shift by t. By its definition, J'' is dominated by J'. Using Lemma 5.1 we get $LIST(J) = t + LIST(J'') \le t + LIST(J')$. □

Lemma 5.3. *All jobs j with $p_j \le p_{max}/m$ are completed by time $3 \cdot OPT$.*

Proof. First we claim that all jobs are started in $LIST$ by the time OPT. Otherwise all machines are busy until some time $t > OPT$, the total work processed is $\sum_{j=1}^n p_j \ge t \cdot \sum_{i=1}^m s_j > OPT \cdot \sum_{i=1}^m s_j$, a contradiction with (1).

Second, we claim that all machines with speed $s \le s_1/m$ are idle at and after time $2 \cdot OPT$. Let I be the indices of the slow machines, $I = \{i : s_i \le s_{max}/m\}$. The total capacity of them is small, namely $\sum_{i \in I} s_i \le (m-1)s_1/m < s_1 \le \sum_{i \notin I} s_i$ and thus $2\sum_{i \notin I} s_i > \sum_{i=1}^m s_i$. Suppose some machine from I is not idle at time $2 \cdot OPT$. Then all machines from $M \setminus I$ are busy for all the time from 0 till $2 \cdot OPT$ and the total size of jobs processed on them is at least $2 \cdot OPT \cdot \sum_{i \notin I} s_i > OPT \cdot \sum_{i=1}^m s_i$, which is a contradiction with (1) as well.

It follows that after time $2 \cdot OPT$, each job is scheduled and moreover it is scheduled only on machines faster than s_1/m. If $p_j \ge p_{max}/m$, then the job p_j is completed by time $2 \cdot OPT + p_j/(s_1/m) \le 2 \cdot OPT + p_{max}/s_1 \le 3 \cdot OPT$. □

Lemma 5.4. *All the jobs with $p_j \le 2p_{min}$ are completed by time $3 \cdot NOPT$.*

Proof. Let M_k denote the slowest machine used in a non-preemptive optimal schedule $NOPT$. Then $p_{min}/s_k \le NOPT$. We also know that is M_k idle in $LIST$ at time $NOPT$, as otherwise $LIST$ would schedule more total work of jobs than $NOPT$. Then the any job with $p_j \le 2p_{min}$ is completed by time $NOPT + p_j/s_k \le NOPT + 2p_{min}/s_k \le 3 \cdot NOPT$. □

Theorem 5.5. *$LIST$ is a $(9 + 6\log_2 m)$ competitive algorithm for preemptive scheduling on related machines.*

Proof. Let J be the input sequence, let $k = \lceil \log_2 m \rceil$. We define job sequences $J_k \subseteq \cdots \subseteq J_1 \subseteq J_0 \subseteq J$; $p_j^{(i)}$ and $p_{min}^{(i)}$ then refer to the processing times in the sequence J_i. Define J_0 as the sequence J without jobs with

$p_j \leq p_{max}/m$. Define J_{i+1} as the sequence J_i without jobs with $p_j^{(i)} \leq 2p_{min}^{(i)}$. It follows that J_k is an empty sequence and $LIST(J_k) = 0$. By Lemmas 5.3 and 5.2, $LIST(J) \leq 3 \cdot OPT + LIST(J_0)$. By Lemmas 5.4 and 5.2, $LIST(J_i) \leq 3 \cdot NOPT + LIST(J_{i+1}) \leq 6 \cdot OPT + LIST(J_{i+1})$. Putting this together, we have $LIST(J) \leq 3 \cdot OPT + LIST(J_0) \leq 3 \cdot OPT + 6k \cdot OPT + LIST(J_k) \leq (9 + 6\log_2 m) \cdot OPT$. $\square$

Now we turn to the lower bound. The instance uses groups of machines with geometrically decreasing speeds, but the number of machines increases even faster so that the total capacity of slow machines is larger than the capacity of the fast machines.

Theorem 5.6. *The competitive ratio of LIST is at least $\Omega(\log m)$.*

Proof. Let us construct the hard instance. Choose integers a, b, g such that $a \geq 2b > 4$ and g is arbitrary. The set of machines consists of groups $G_0, \ldots, G_g$, where the group G_i consists of a^i machines with speed b^{-i}. The jobs are in similar groups named J_i, each containing a^i jobs of length b^{-i}. The input sequence is a concatenation of these groups starting with the smallest job, that is, $J = J_g, \ldots, J_0$. We name the phases by the groups of jobs processed in each phase (i.e., we start by phase J_g, note that the indices of the groups are decreasing).

By scheduling each J_k to G_k we get $OPT = 1$, so it remains to prove that $LIST \geq \Omega(\log m)$.

For $k = 1, \ldots, g$, let $i_k = \sum_{l=0}^{k-1} a^l$ be the number of processors in groups $G_0, \ldots, G_{k-1}$. The choice of a guarantees that the number of jobs in I_k is $a^k \geq 2i_k$.

To prove a lower bound on $LIST(J)$, we construct a sequence J' dominated by J. Each group J_k, for $k = g, \ldots, 1$, is replaced by a corresponding group J'_k, defined inductively below. The last group J_0 with a single job is unchanged, so the sequence J' is defined as the concatenation of the groups $J'_g, \ldots, J'_1, J_0$.

To modify the group J_k, consider the schedule $LIST(J'_g, \ldots, J'_{k+1}, J_k)$. All the jobs in J_k have the same length, thus their completion times are non-decreasing. We construct a group J'_k by shortening the last i_k jobs in J_k so that their completion times are equal. Denote this common completion time τ_k. For $k = 0$, the sequence is not modified and τ_0 is the completion time of the single job in J_0. Define also $\tau_{g+1} = 0$.

We prove by induction that, for each $k = g, \ldots, 0$, (i) $1 \geq \tau_k - \tau_{k+1} \geq \Omega(1)$ and (ii) in the schedule $LIST(J'_g, \ldots, J'_{k+1}, J'_k)$, all the i_k processors in groups $G_0, \ldots, G_{k-1}$ are busy until time τ_k and all the machines are idle after time τ_k.

To start, note that (ii) for $k = g + 1$ holds trivially. Using (ii) for $k + 1$, it is feasible to schedule all jobs in J_k on machines G_k starting from time τ_{k+1} without preemptions and completing at time $1 + \tau_{k+1}$. The greedy schedule may schedule the jobs on faster processors which can only decrease their completion times and thus the first inequality of (i) holds. Using (ii) for $l > k$, it follows that the work done on any job in J_k before time τ_{k+1} is at most $\sum_{l=k+1}^{g} (\tau_l - \tau_{l+1}) b^{-l} \leq \sum_{l=k+1}^{\infty} b^{-l} = b^{-k}/(b-1)$. Consequently, all the completion times of jobs in J_k are larger than τ_{k+1}; thus $\tau_k > \tau_{k+1}$ and (ii) holds for k by the structure of

LIST schedule. Since the first i_k jobs from I_k are not shortened, the work done on the machines in $G_0, \ldots, G_{k-1}$ between τ_{k+1} and τ_k is at least

$$i_k \left(b^{-k} - \frac{1}{b-1} b^{-k} \right) \geq \frac{b-2}{b-1} b^{-k} a^{k-1}.$$

The total capacity of the machines in $G_0, \ldots, G_{k-1}$ is $\sum_{l=0}^{k-1} a^l b^{-l} < a^k b^{-k}$, using $a/b \geq 2$. Thus

$$\tau_k - \tau_{k+1} \geq \frac{\frac{b-2}{b-1} b^{-k} a^{k-1}}{a^k b^{-k}} = \frac{(b-2)}{a(b-1)} = \Omega(1);$$

this finishes the proof of (i) and the whole induction.

Using Lemma 5.1, $LIST(J) \geq LIST(J') = \tau_0 = \sum_{k=0}^{g} (\tau_k - \tau_{k+1}) \geq g \cdot \Omega(1) = \Omega(\log m)$. □

5.2   The Analysis of LPT

LPT is a simple approximation algorithm (no longer online), thus it is interesting to know its performance. We show that the approximation ratio of LPT for preemptive variant is between $2 - \frac{2}{m+1}$ and $2 - \frac{1}{m}$. The proof of the upper bound is the same as the proof for non-preemptive case from [18]. Non-preemptive LPT is there used as an upper bound on NOPT in comparison to OPT. We need to analyze the preemptive version of LPT, which possibly gives a different schedule than the non-preemptive LPT. Examining the proof shows that the properties of the non-preemptive LPT used in [18] are satisfied by the preemptive LPT as well. The proof is omitted.

Theorem 5.7. *Preemptive LPT produces schedules with makespan at most* $2 - \frac{1}{m}$ *times (preemptive) OPT.*

An almost matching lower bound is shown by an instance consisting of m identical machines and $m + 1$ identical jobs. Assuming unit jobs and machines, LPT produces a schedule of makespan 2 (no preemptions are used), while the optimal preemptive makespan is $\frac{m+1}{m}$. This yields a lower bound of $2 - \frac{2}{m+1}$ on the competitive ratio.

Conclusions

Our main result is an improvement of online algorithms for preemptive scheduling on uniformly related machines, $Q|online\text{-}list, pmtn|C_{max}$, by a factor of more than 2. Still, some gap remains. Our intuition is that, similarly to the case of identical machines, $P|online\text{-}list, pmtn|C_{max}$, randomization should not help for preemptive online scheduling and thus the deterministic 4 competitive algorithm can be improved.

Some proofs omitted in this version appear in the full version of the paper.

Acknowledgments. We are grateful to Yossi Azar for useful discussions and to anonymous referees for useful comments. This work was partially supported by the Institute for Theoretical Computer Science, Prague (project LN00A056 of MŠMT ČR), a cooperative grant KONTAKT-ME476/CCR-9988360-001 from MŠMT ČR and NSF, grant 201/01/1195 of GA ČR, and grant A1019401 of GA AV ČR.

References

1. J. Aspnes, Y. Azar, A. Fiat, S. Plotkin, and O. Waarts. On-line load balancing with applications to machine scheduling and virtual circuit routing. *Journal of the ACM*, 44:486–504, 1997.
2. A. Bar-Noy, A. Freund, and J. Naor. New algorithms for related machines with temporary jobs. *Journal of Scheduling*, 3:259–272, 2000.
3. P. Berman, M. Charikar, and M. Karpinski. On-line load balancing for related machines. *Journal of Algorithms*, 35:108–121, 2000.
4. B. Chen, A. van Vliet, and G. J. Woeginger. An optimal algorithm for preemptive on-line scheduling. *Operations Research Letters*, 18:127–131, 1995.
5. Y. Cho and S. Sahni. Bounds for list schedules on uniform processors. *SIAM Journal on Computing*, 9:91–103, 1980.
6. G. Dobson. Scheduling independent tasks on uniform processors. *SIAM Journal on Computing*, 13:705–716, 1984.
7. L. Epstein. Optimal preemptive scheduling on uniform processors with non-decreasing speed ratios. *Operations Research Letters*, 29:93-98, 2001.
8. L. Epstein. Bin stretching revisited. *Acta Informatica*, 39:97–117, 2003.
9. L. Epstein and L. M. Favrholdt. Optimal preemptive semi-online scheduling to minimize makespan on two related machines. *Operations Research Letters*, 30:269–275, 2002.
10. L. Epstein, J. Noga, S. S. Seiden, J. Sgall, and G. J. Woeginger. Randomized on-line scheduling for two related machines. *Journal of Scheduling*, 4:71–92, 2001.
11. L. Epstein and J. Sgall. A lower bound for on-line scheduling on uniformly related machines. *Operations Research Letters*, 26(1):17–22, 2000.
12. D. K. Friesen. Tighter bounds for LPT scheduling on uniform processors. *SIAM Journal on Computing*, 16:554–560, 1987.
13. T. F. Gonzales and S. Sahni. Preemptive scheduling of uniform processor systems. *Journal of the ACM*, 25:92–101, 1978.
14. E. Horwath, E. C. Lam, and R. Sethi. A level algorithm for preemptive scheduling. *Journal of the ACM*, 24:32–43, 1977.
15. H. Shachnai, T. Tamir, and G. J. Woeginger. Minimizing Makespan and Preemption Costs on a System of Uniform Machines In *Proc. 10th ESA*, LNCS 2416, pp. 859–871. Springer, 2002.
16. D. B. Shmoys, J. Wein, and D. P. Williamson. Scheduling parallel machines on-line. *SIAM Journal on Computing*, 24:1313–1331, 1995.
17. J. Wen and D. Du. Preemptive on-line scheduling for two uniform processors. *Operations Research Letters*, 23:113–116, 1998.
18. G. J. Woeginger. A comment on scheduling on uniform machines under chain-type precedence constraints. *Operations Research Letters*, 26:107–109, 2000.

Parallel Prefetching and Caching Is Hard

Christoph Ambühl[*1] and Birgitta Weber[**2]

[1] Instituto Dalle Molle di Studi sull' Intelligenza Artificiale
Galleria 2, 6928 Manno, SWITZERLAND
christoph@idsia.ch
[2] Institute of Theoretical Computer Science, ETH Zentrum,
8092 Zürich, SWITZERLAND
weberb@inf.ethz.ch

Abstract. In this paper we study integrated prefetching and caching in parallel disk systems. This topic has gained a lot of interest in the last years which manifests itself in numerous recent approximation algorithms. This paper provides the first negative result in this area by showing that optimizing the stall time is $\mathcal{APX}$-hard. This also implies that computing the optimal processing time is $\mathcal{NP}$-hard, which settles an open problem posed by Kimbrel and Karlin.

1 Introduction

In modern computer systems, the processor performance has increased at a much faster rate than memory access times. Especially disk accesses are very time consuming and represent a severe bottleneck in today's systems. Hence, it is of growing importance to find advanced techniques to facilitate efficient interaction between fast and slow memory.

In general, disks are partitioned into pages of a few KBytes in size. When some data on the page is needed, the whole page is copied into (fast) RAM memory and is accessed from there. Common tools to improve the performance of memory hierarchies are prefetching and caching. The cache of a computer system consists of a few memory blocks that can hold pages read from the disks. Keeping disk pages in cache, one can satisfy multiple requests to the same page. This results in an overall increase of the performance of the system. Because in general only a small fraction of the disk pages can be held in the cache, it is often necessary to evict a page from the cache in order to make room for the newly fetched one.

Caching strategies [4] load a page into the cache upon request. The processor then stalls until the page is in cache. Prefetching [5] means to load a page into

---

* Supported by the Swiss National Science Foundation project 200021-100539/1, "Approximation Algorithms for Machine Scheduling Through Theory and Experiments". This paper contains ideas obtained while the author stayed at Università degli Studi di Roma "Tor Vergata" in Italy and was supported by the European Union under the RTN Project ARACNE.
** Partially supported by the Swiss Federal Office for Education and Science under the Project "Highly Available Scalable Distributed Data Structures" NF 21-66768.

V. Diekert and M. Habib (Eds.): STACS 2004, LNCS 2996, pp. 211–221, 2004.
© Springer-Verlag Berlin Heidelberg 2004

the cache even before it is actually requested. But prefetching a page too early can cause the eviction of a page which is requested shortly.

Integrated prefetching and caching on single disk systems was introduced by Cao et al. in [5]. They developed the first approximation algorithms to tackle the problem. Kimbrel and Karlin [11] extended the single disk model to multiple disks and proposed approximation algorithms for finding a prefetch/caching schedule for parallel disk systems with minimum stall time. Both theoretical and experimental studies were presented in numerous publications, e.g. [1,2,3,5,6,7, 8,9,10,11]. However, determining the complexity for the multiple disk problem remained open until now.

Model Definition – Parallel Prefetching and Caching

In our model, the computer system consists of D disks and one cache which can hold k pages. Every disk contains a set of distinct pages. The cache initially holds a subset of pages from the disks. Additionally, there is a sequence of requests $\sigma = \sigma_1 \sigma_2 \ldots \sigma_r$. Each of them is denoted by a reference to one page. The task is to satisfy all the requests of σ in turn. If a requested page is in the cache it can be accessed immediately. This takes one time unit. Otherwise it has to be fetched, which takes F time units. It is possible to prefetch a page before it is requested. At any time, at most one fetch operation per disk can be processed. If the cache is completely filled, it is necessary to evict a page in order to fetch a new one. While the fetch operation is in progress, neither the incoming nor the evicted page is available for access. When a requested page is not in the cache, the system stalls until the page arrives. The goal is to find a prefetch/caching schedule that minimizes the stall time of the system.

Approximation algorithms for this problem can be evaluated either by the stall time or by the elapsed time. Computing the optimum of these two measures is equivalent, but approximating the stall time is more difficult than approximating the elapsed time.

Example

We consider a system with two disks $D_1 = \{A, B\}$, $D_2 = \{c, d\}$, a cache of size two holding $C = [A, B]$ initially, and a sequence $\sigma = (B, A, c, d, B)$ of requests. It takes $F = 2$ time to fetch a page from a disk. The stall time for the schedule depicted in Figure 1 is two. The first page missing is c. The prefetch operation for c starts at time $t = 1$ evicting page B after its requested. Because Disk D_2 is busy until $t = 3$, the prefetch of page d evicting A cannot start before $t = 3$. After processing page c at time $t = 4$ a prefetch operation is started to refetch page B.

There are two graphical representations for the schedule, both displayed in Figure 1. The first one uses the cache state, the second one the operations of every disk. We are going to use the disk representation.

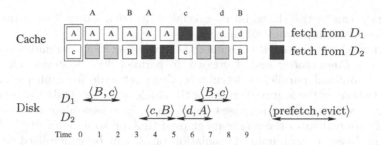

Fig. 1. Example for two disks.

Previous Work

For integrated prefetching and caching on single disk systems, Cao et al. [5] introduced two algorithms called *Conservative* and *Aggressive*. They also proved that on single disk systems, there always exists an optimal schedule which fulfills the following four basic rules.

1. *Optimal Prefetch:* Always fetch the missing page that will be requested soonest.
2. *Optimal Eviction:* Always evict the page in the cache whose next request is furthest in the future.
3. *Do No Harm:* Never evict a page A to fetch page B when A's next request is before B's next request.
4. *First Opportunity:* Never evict page A to fetch page B when the same thing could have been done one time unit earlier.

The first two rules specify which page to prefetch and to evict. The last two rules indicate the time at which a prefetch operation should be initiated. However, these rules do not uniquely determine a prefetch/caching schedule. Nevertheless they provide some guidance how to design algorithms.

The algorithm *Conservative* performs exactly the same fetch operations as the optimum offline paging algorithm MIN [4] and starts these operations as soon as possible. The elapsed time of a *Conservative* schedule is at most twice the elapsed time of an optimum schedule. The *Aggressive* algorithm starts prefetch operations as soon as possible, following the four basic rules. Cao et al. proved that the approximation ratio, with respect to the elapsed time, is at most $\min\{1 + \frac{F}{k}, 2\}$. Recently, Albers and Büttner [1] improved this ratio to $\min\{1 + F/(k + \lfloor\frac{k}{F}\rfloor - 1), 2\}$. They also presented a new family of algorithms called *Delay(d)*, which delays the next possible fetch operation for d time units. They could prove that *Delay(d)* combined with *Aggressive* has a better approximation ratio than the two previously known algorithms. Experimental studies on the performance of these algorithms were presented in [5] and [10].

It was proven in [2] that an optimal prefetching/caching schedule for a sequence of requests on a single disk system can be computed in polynomial time using a linear programming formulation. In [3] it was shown that this linear program can be translated into a special multi-commodity flow instance which can be solved in polynomial time.

Kimbrel and Karlin [10] extended the single disk model to multiple disks and analyzed *Conservative* and *Aggressive* in parallel disks systems. They showed that an optimal parallel prefetching/caching schedule for multiple disks does obey to three of the four basic rules for the single disk case. Only the *Do No Harm* rule gets violated. They proposed the *Reverse Aggressive* algorithm and showed that it approximates the minimum elapsed time up to a factor of $1 + DF/k$.

The linear programming formulation of [2] can be generalized to multiple disks and achieves a D-approximation for the stall time of the system with $D-1$ additional pages in cache. Recently, Albers and Büttner [1] gave an algorithm for integrated prefetching and caching on multiple disks which achieves the same optimal stall time, but uses up to $3(D-1)$ extra cache positions.

In [13], Vitter and Shriver describe an alternative model for parallel disk systems. For their model, Kallahalla and Varman [8] have shown that an optimal schedule can be found in time $O(n \log(k))$.

Notation

A prefetching instance $\mathcal{P}$ is a 4−tuple $(\mathcal{D}, C, F, \sigma)$. By $\mathcal{D} = \{D_1, D_2, \ldots D_m\}$ we denote the set of m disks. C represents the cache. F is the time needed to fetch a page from a disk to the cache and $\sigma = \sigma_1 \sigma_2 \ldots \sigma_n$ the sequence of requests to pages. We say a page is *active* at time t if it is in cache or it is being fetched. We denote a fetch operation in which page b gets evicted in order to fetch page a by $\langle a, b \rangle$.

For a sequence σ of requests let σ_t be the t-th request. The *gap* of a page p at σ_t is the number request to pages different from p until the next request to p. Hence, the gap of p at σ_t, if the next request to p is $\sigma_{t'}$, is $t' - t - 1$. Finally, we will refer to a schedule with at most ℓ stall times as an ℓ-*schedule*.

2   MinDel2Sat and Monotone MinDel2Sat Are APX-Hard

In this section we prove that MINDEL2SAT is $\mathcal{APX}$-hard. This result will be used to prove the $\mathcal{APX}$ hardness of MONOTONE MINDEL2SAT. In turn, this result will be used in the next section to show that minimizing the stall time of a prefetching instance is $\mathcal{APX}$-hard.

The MINDEL2SAT problem is very similar to MAX2SAT. The only difference is that the objective is to minimize the number of unsatisfied clauses. In the MONOTONE MINDEL2SAT problem, only monotone 2SAT formulas are allowed. A 2SAT formula $\mathcal{F}$ is called monotone if no clause contains both positive and negative literals.

Lemma 1. MINDEL2SAT *is $\mathcal{APX}$-hard.*

Proof. It was shown in [12] that for a MAX2SAT instance it is $\mathcal{NP}$-hard to decide whether at least a fraction of $\frac{56}{80}$ of the clauses, or if at most a fraction of $\frac{55}{80}$ of the clauses can be satisfied. From these factors we can conclude that it is $\mathcal{NP}$-hard to decide if at least a fraction of $\frac{25}{80}$ of the clauses, or if at most a fraction of $\frac{24}{80}$ of the clauses have to be unsatisfied. It is hard to approximate MINDEL2SAT within a factor of $\frac{25}{24} - \varepsilon$.   □

Lemma 2. MONOTONE MINDEL2SAT *is* $\mathcal{APX}$-*hard.*

Proof. The proof is done by a gap preserving reduction from MINDEL2SAT: For any variable x that appears in the formula $\mathcal{F}$, we introduce a new variable $\hat{x}$ that represents the negative of x. The new formula is obtained by replacing all appearances of $\neg x$ in $\mathcal{F}$ by $\hat{x}$ and adding to $\mathcal{F}$ for each variable m copies of the two clauses $(x \vee \hat{x})$ and $(\neg x \vee \neg \hat{x})$. If m is chosen equal to the number of clauses in $\mathcal{F}$, obviously in an optimal solution, all the added clauses will be fulfilled. It is easy to see that this reduction is gap-preserving and that MONOTONE MINDEL2-SAT is hard to approximate within a factor of $\frac{25}{24} - \varepsilon$.   □

3 Approximation the Stall Time for ParPrefetch Is APX-Hard

We consider the following problem:

PARPREFETCH: Given a prefetching instance $\mathcal{P} = (\mathcal{D}, C, F, \sigma)$. Find the minimum ℓ for which there exists an ℓ-schedule for $\mathcal{P}$.

Theorem 1. PARPREFETCH *is* $\mathcal{APX}$-*hard. Hence, there exists no PTAS unless* $\mathcal{P} = \mathcal{NP}$.

The proof is done by a gap preserving reduction from MONOTONE MINDEL2SAT. For a given monotone 2-SAT formula $\mathcal{F}$, we construct an instance $\mathcal{I}$ of PARPREFETCH such that there exists a prefetching schedule for $\mathcal{I}$ with stall time at most 2ℓ if and only if there exists a truth assignment that leaves at most ℓ clauses unsatisfied. Let $\mathcal{F}$ be a monotone 2-SAT formula composed of n variables $x_1, x_2, \ldots x_n$ and m monotone clauses $C_1, C_2, \ldots C_m$. Note that we can assume $\ell \leq m$.

The instance $\mathcal{I}$ will have $n + 1$ disks. For every variable x_i in $\mathcal{F}$, there will be a disk D_i on which the pages a_i, b_i, c_i, d_i, and e_i are stored. These disks and pages are called *variable disks* and *variable pages*. Additionally, there is a disk called P, which contains the page p. The cache has $4n + 1$ slots. Initially, it contains all pages except d_i, $1 \leq i \leq n$.

The request sequence σ is composed of $2m + 4$ rounds, starting with round 0. Every round contains exactly $5(4n + 4m)$ requests. A round is composed of five blocks, each having $4n + 4m$ requests. We will often refer to them as xy-blocks, with $xy \in \{ea, ab, bc, cd, de\}$. As with the rounds, the first block of σ will be called block 0. The fetch time is $F = 2(4n + 4m)$. Observe that the fetch time F is exactly the length of two blocks.

For each clause C_j in $\mathcal{F}$, there is one round implemented by a *clause gadget* σ_{C_j}. The remaining rounds will be implemented by so-called *bridge rounds* σ_B.

The basic idea of the reduction is the following. The PARPREFETCH instance $\mathcal{I}$ is chosen such that for each variable disk D_i, there are exactly two ways how its pages can be loaded into the cache without stalling the system for more than 2ℓ units. It all depends on which page of D_i is evicted first. We will call these two ways *policy* T and *policy* F. The policy of a variable disk D_i can be interpreted as a truth assignment of the corresponding variable x_i in $\mathcal{F}$. In every clause gadget σ_{C_j}, it is checked whether the chosen policies satisfy the corresponding clause C_j in $\mathcal{F}$, incurring two units of stall time if it does not.

Let us start with the definition of σ_B:

$$
\sigma_B := \begin{array}{l}
e_1 a_1 \ pp \ e_2 a_2 \ pp \ \cdots \ e_n a_n \ pp \ \overbrace{p \ldots p}^{\alpha := 4m} \oplus \\
a_1 b_1 \ pp \ a_2 b_2 \ pp \ \cdots \ a_n b_n \ pp \ p \ldots p \oplus \\
b_1 c_1 \ pp \ b_2 c_2 \ pp \ \cdots \ b_n c_n \ pp \ p \ldots p \oplus \\
c_1 d_1 \ pp \ c_2 d_2 \ pp \ \cdots \ c_n d_n \ pp \ p \ldots p \oplus \\
d_1 e_1 \ pp \ d_2 e_2 \ pp \ \cdots \ d_n e_n \ pp \ p \ldots p
\end{array}
\tag{1}
$$

$\oplus$ denotes a concatenation. Notice that each row of (1) corresponds to a block. For space considerations in the figures, we introduce $\alpha := 4m$. In the following, we describe how the sequence λ of (2) can be served with stall time at most 2ℓ.

$$
\lambda := \underbrace{\sigma_B \oplus \sigma_B \oplus \cdots \oplus \sigma_B}_{2m+4}
\tag{2}
$$

In a 2ℓ-schedule of λ, every disk D_i is either on policy T or policy F. In both policies, each page has exactly four active pages at the end of each block. If a page D_i is on policy T, then the set of active pages does not change within odd rounds. Hence, during odd rounds, no fetch operation that involves a page of D_i is initiated. On the other hand, in every even block, the initially inactive page of D_i has to be fetched, while exactly one of the active pages of D_i is evicted. Remember that the first block of λ is block 0, and hence is even. For a disk D_i on policy F, the fetch operations start in the odd blocks, whereas no operations involving pages from D_i begin in even blocks.

Figure 2 describes the two policies by stating which pages are fetched and evicted in the corresponding blocks. The nodes in Figure 2 represent the five different kinds of blocks. Their circular ordering in λ is indicated by the dotted arrows. In an xy-block, only the x_i pages can get evicted. The pages which are fetched are denoted by the arc leaving the xy-node. The only exception is block 0. Although it is a ea-block, the page fetched in this case is d_i.

The following Figures 3 – 5 show how λ can be served with zero stall time. The two policies for each variable disk are indicated. Policy F is the one with the dashed arcs. Figure 3 shows the two policies in round 0. Figure 4 and 5 display how the policies look like in even and odd rounds of λ, respectively.

The following request sequence σ completes our reduction.

$$
\sigma := \sigma_B \oplus \sigma_B \oplus \bigoplus_{i=1}^{m} \begin{cases} \sigma_{C_j} \oplus \sigma_B & \text{if } C_j \text{ positive} \\ \sigma_B \oplus \sigma_{C_j} & \text{if } C_j \text{ negative} \end{cases} \oplus \sigma_B \oplus \sigma_B
$$

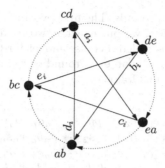

Fig. 2. The fetch/evict cycle of D_i.

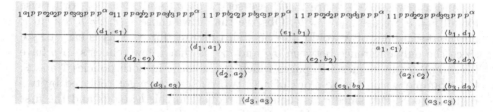

Fig. 3. The two policies per variable in round 0.

Fig. 4. The two policies per variable in even rounds of λ and σ.

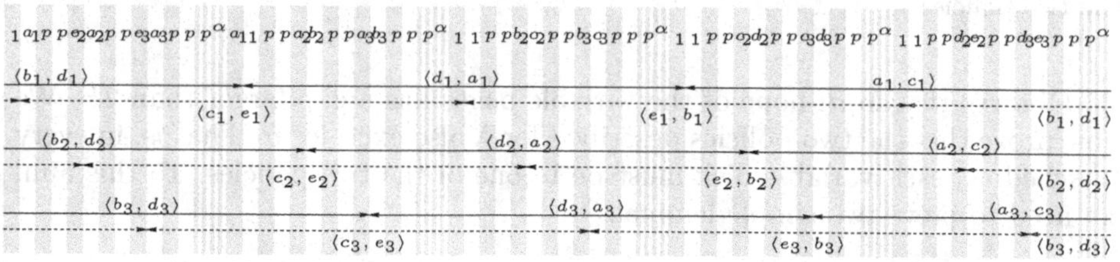

Fig. 5. The two policies per variable in odd rounds of λ and σ.

Also σ consists of $2m+4$ rounds. The first two and the last two rounds are σ_B rounds. Then for each clause, we put exactly two rounds. For a positive clause, we put $\sigma_{C_j}\sigma_B$, where σ_{C_j} is called a clause gadget for C_j. For a negative clause, we put $\sigma_B\sigma_{C_j}$. Note that σ_{C_j} is an even round of σ if and only if C_j is positive. The σ_{C_j} rounds are defined as follows.

$$
\sigma_{C_j} :=
\begin{array}{llllllll}
e_1a_1 & pp & e_2a_2 & pp & \cdots & e_na_n & pp & \overbrace{p\ldots p}^{\alpha:=4m} & \oplus \\
a_1b_1 & \mathbf{r_1s_1} & a_2b_2 & \mathbf{r_2s_2} & \cdots & a_nb_n & \mathbf{r_ns_n} & b_n\ldots b_n & \oplus \\
b_1c_1 & c_1c_1 & b_2c_2 & c_2c_2 & \cdots & b_nc_n & c_nc_n & c_n\ldots c_n & \oplus \\
c_1d_1 & d_1d_1 & c_2d_2 & d_2d_2 & \cdots & c_nd_n & d_nd_n & p\ldots p & \oplus \\
d_1e_1 & pp & d_2e_2 & pp & \cdots & d_ne_n & pp & p\ldots p &
\end{array}
$$

The bold requests denoted by r_i and s_i depend on the variables in C_j. If x_u and x_v (with $u < v$) are in C_j, we set $r_v := a_v$ and $s_v := a_u$, otherwise for all $i \neq v$, we use $s_i, r_i := b_i$. Observe that if we chose $s_i, r_i := b_i$ for all i, all the 0-schedules of λ would also be stall time free for σ. This is easy to see since the only difference between σ_B and σ_{C_j} is that a few requests to p have been replaced by requests to pages which are in cache in both policies T and F. For example within the bc-block of σ_{C_j}, two requests to p got replaced by two requests to c_1. But since c_1 is the second request in this bc-block and the first request of the subsequent cd-block, it will be in cache for sure.

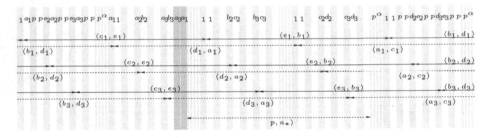

Fig. 6. Clause Gadget for $(x_1 \vee x_3)$. Some requests are omitted here, since they are easy to serve in both policies. The picture for $(\neg x_1 \vee \neg x_3)$ can be obtained by interchanging the two policies.

Observe that in σ, none of the variable pages has a gap larger than $2F$. We now prove that the two policies described for λ also exist for σ. That is, in every 2ℓ-schedule, each variable disk must be in one of the two policies. To this aim, we need to prove two simple lemmas.

Lemma 3. *In a 2ℓ-schedule of σ, the following holds. At the end of each block, page p is active and there are exactly four active pages per variable disk.*

Proof. First consider page p. With the exception of the ac-block and the bc-block in a round σ_{C_j}, the last request of a block is always to p. Hence, p certainly is active at the end of such a block. In the two exceptional cases, its gap is at most $F - 4m < F - 2\ell$. From this we can conclude that p needs to be active there as well.

Concerning the variable pages, note that at the end of each block, the gap of all variable pages is at most $2F - 4m$. Therefore, if a page has less than four active pages, we will incur stall time larger than $4m \geq 2\ell$. Since p is active at the end of each block and there are exactly $4n + 1$ cache slots, all variable disks have exactly four active pages. □

Lemma 4. *In a 2ℓ-schedule, a page s_i from a disk D_i with at most four active pages can be evicted only if the gap of the non-active page of D_i or the gap of s_i is at least $2F - 2\ell$.*

Proof. If both pages of D_i have gap smaller than $2F - 2\ell$, we have to fetch two pages within less than $2F$ time units to prevent more than 2ℓ stall times. Since the two pages are from the same disk, this is not possible. □

Lemma 5. *In a 2ℓ-schedule, every page is on one of the two policies.*

Proof. We use induction on the blocks in order to prove the lemma. For the base case, consider the first two blocks. Until the end of the second block, all disks must be fetching their d_i page. Clearly, p cannot be evicted in the first two blocks. Hence, every variable disk has to evict one of its pages in the first two rounds. From Lemma 4, we can conclude that there are only two options per disk, namely either e_i during the first block or a_i during the second block.

For the induction step, let us consider block $\beta > 2$. W.l.o.g. let it be an ab-block. Then the block $\beta - 2$ is a de-block and block $\beta + 2$ is a cd-block.

Let us first consider the case where a page was fetched from disk D_i in block $\beta - 2$. By the induction hypothesis, its d_i page was evicted and d_i was not fetched in block $\beta - 2$ and $\beta - 1$. Thus, its gap at the end of block β will be smaller than $F - 2\ell$. Hence page d_i needs to be fetched in block β. Because of Lemma 3, a page of disk D_i must be evicted in block β. By Lemma 4, we obtain that only a_i can be evicted.

Concerning the disks that evicted and fetched a page in block $\beta - 1$, we now prove that they cannot do so in block β: Let D_i be a disk that fetched a page in block $\beta - 1$. This fetch operation will terminate not before the last 2ℓ requests of block β. But at this point, all the pages of D_i have a gap smaller than $2F - 2\ell$. Hence, none of them can be evicted and therefore, because of Lemma 3, D_i cannot fetch a page either. □

Lemma 6. *The PARPREFETCH instance $\mathcal{I}$ can be processed with at most 2ℓ units of stall time if and only if there exists a truth assignment for $\mathcal{F}$ that leaves at most ℓ clauses unsatisfied.*

Proof. Since we know that every variable disk must be on one of the two policies, there is not much freedom left. Basically, the schedules will look like the one for λ described in the Figures 3–5. The only difference is within the clause gadgets, where p can be evicted.

Let us first analyze the behavior of a positive clause gadget $C_j = (x_u \vee x_v)$ (the proofs for negative clauses are very similar). Figure 6 will be used as an instructive example.

If both disks D_u and D_v ($u < v$) are on policy F, consider σ_{C_j} just after the request r_v in the ab-block. In Figure 6, this corresponds to the first request in the dark shaded area. Consider those disks from $\{D_1, D_2, \ldots, D_v\}$ which are on policy F. Let $\mathcal{M}$ be the set of the a_i pages stored on these disks.

Until just after r_v, the only pages that can have been evicted in this block in order to fetch d_i pages is page p and those in $\mathcal{M} \setminus \{a_u, a_v\}$. Hence, there is at least one d_i page from a disk in $\mathcal{M}$ which is not fetched by now. Since this page has gap at most $F - 2$, there will be at least two stall times.

Indeed, there is always a solution that produces two stall times. Namely for all $i \neq u$, the operation $\langle d_i, a_i \rangle$ is executed as soon as possible. Hence, $\langle d_v, a_v \rangle$ will be two time units late. Concerning d_u, the operation $\langle d_u, p \rangle$ starts right after the first request to a_u in the ab-block. And $\langle p, a_u \rangle$ starts after the second request to a_u. In Figure 6, this means that the operation $\langle d_1, a_1 \rangle$ gets replaced by $\langle d_1, p \rangle$. Later, p is refetched by $\langle p, a_1 \rangle$ right after dark shaded requests (indicated by $\langle p, a_* \rangle$). Since $\langle d_3, a_3 \rangle$ cannot start before the request to a_3 in the dark shaded area, we will incur two stall times waiting for d_3 to arrive in cache in the next cd-block.

If at most one of D_u, D_v is on policy F, by the use of the cache slot containing p, we do not incur any stall time during σ_{C_j}: Assume that D_v is on policy F. Then we evict p just after the first request to a_v in the ab-block in order to fetch d_v. After the second request to a_v in the ab-block, we can now evict a_v in order to refetch p.

With the above findings, we can now conclude the proof: If there is no truth assignment of $\mathcal{F}$ such that at most ℓ clauses remain unsatisfied, there cannot be a schedule with less than 2ℓ stall time. This holds since every disk must be in one of the two policies and since there are two units of stall time in σ_{C_j} whenever the two disks appearing in the C_j are on the wrong policy. On the other hand, a truth assignment with at most ℓ unsatisfied clauses can be translated in a schedule with at most 2ℓ stall times by running disk D_i on policy T if and only if $x_i = \texttt{true}$. □

With the previous lemmas, the main theorem follows easily.

Proof of Theorem 1. The instance $\mathcal{I}$ can be constructed in polynomial time. From Lemma 6, it follows that $\mathcal{I}$ has a 2ℓ-schedule if and only if there is a truth assignment for $\mathcal{F}$ in which ℓ clauses are unsatisfied. Obviously, the reduction is gap preserving and therefore the theorem is proven. A simple calculation shows an inapproxmability factor of $\frac{25}{24} - \varepsilon$. □

4   Open Problems and Acknowledgments

There are many ways to extend our result. First of all, our result only shows that the stall time is hard to approximate. Concerning the elapsed time, we can only prove $\mathcal{NP}$-hardness. An interesting open question is to decide whether there exists a PTAS for this variant.

If the number of cache slots is bounded, PARPREFETCH can be solved in polynomial time, since the number of cache states then is polynomial. It would be very interesting to know whether polynomial time algorithm exists also for bounded number of disks or bounded fetch time.

We are grateful to Riko Jacob for proof reading and Sebastian Seibert for clarifying discussions.

References

1. S. Albers and M. Büttner. Integrated prefetching and caching in single and parallel disk systems. In *Proc. 15th Annual ACM Symposium on Parallelism in Algorithms and Architectures (SPAA)*. ACM Press, 2003.
2. S. Albers, N. Garg, and S. Leonardi. Minimizing stall time in single and parallel disk systems. *Journal of the ACM (JACM)*, 47(6):969–986, 2000. Preliminary version in STOC98.
3. S. Albers and C. Witt. Minimizing stall time in single and parallel disk systems using multicommodity network flows. In *Proc. 4th International Workshop on Approximation Algorithms for Combinatorial Optimization Problems (APPROX01)*, pages 12–23. Springer-Verlag LNCS 1665, 2001.
4. L.A. Belady. A study of replacement algorithms for virtual-storage computer. *IBM Systems Journal*, 5(2), 1966.
5. P. Cao, E.W. Felten, A.R. Karlin, and K. Li. A study of integrated prefetching and caching strategies. In *Proc ACM International Conference on Measurement and Modeling of Computer Systems (SIGMETRICS)*, pages 188–197, 1995.
6. A. Gaysinsky, A. Itai, and H. Shachnai. Strongly competitive algorithms for caching with pipelined prefetching. In *Proc. 9th Annual European Symposium on Algorithms (ESA01)*, pages 49 –61. Springer-Verlag LNCS 2161, 2001.
7. D.A. Hutchinson, P. Sanders, and J.S. Vitter. Duality between prefetching and queued writing with parallel disks. In *Proc. 9th Annual European Symposium on Algorithms (ESA01)*, pages 62–73. Springer-Verlag LNCS 2161, 2001.
8. M. Kallahalla and P.J. Varman. Optimal prefetching and caching for parallel i/o systems. In *Proc. 13th Annual ACM Symposium on Parallelism in Algorithms and Architectures (SPAA)*, pages 219–228. ACM Press, 2001.
9. T. Kimbrel. *Parallel Prefetching and Caching*. PhD thesis, University of Washington, 1997.
10. T. Kimbrel, P. Cao, E.W. Felten, A.R. Karlin, and K. Li. Integrated parallel prefetching and caching. In *Proc ACM International Conference on Measurement and Modeling of Computer Systems (SIGMETRICS)*, pages 262–263, 1996.
11. T. Kimbrel and A.R. Karlin. Near-optimal parallel prefetching and caching. *SIAM Journal on Computing*, 29(4):1051–1082, 2000. Preliminary version in FOCS96.
12. E. W. Mayr, H. J. Prömel, and A. Steger, editors. *Lectures on Proof Verification and Approximation Algorithms*. Springer-Verlag LNCS 1367, 1998.
13. J.S. Vitter and E.A.M. Shriver. Algorithms for parallel memory, I: Two-level memories. *Algorithmica*, 12(2-3):110–147, 1994.

Strongly Stable Matchings in Time $O(nm)$ and Extension to the Hospitals-Residents Problem

Telikepalli Kavitha[1*], Kurt Mehlhorn[1*], Dimitrios Michail[1*], and Katarzyna Paluch[2**]

[1] Max-Planck-Institut für Informatik, Saarbrücken, Germany.
{kavitha,mehlhorn,michail}@mpi-sb.mpg.de
[2] Institute of Computer Science, University of Wroclaw, Poland.
abraka@ii.uni.wroc.pl.

Abstract. An instance of the stable marriage problem is an undirected bipartite graph $G = (X \cup W, E)$ with linearly ordered adjacency lists; ties are allowed. A matching M is a set of edges no two of which share an endpoint. An edge $e = (a, b) \in E \setminus M$ is a *blocking edge* for M if a is either unmatched or strictly prefers b to its partner in M, and b is either unmatched or strictly prefers a to its partner in M or is indifferent between them. A matching is strongly stable if there is no blocking edge with respect to it. We give an $O(nm)$ algorithm for computing strongly stable matchings, where n is the number of vertices and m is the number of edges. The previous best algorithm had running time $O(m^2)$.

We also study this problem in the hospitals-residents setting, which is a many-to-one extension of the above problem. We give an $O(m(|R| + \sum_{h \in H} p_h))$ algorithm for computing a strongly stable matching in the hospitals-residents problem, where $|R|$ is the number of residents and p_h is the quota of a hospital h. The previous best algorithm had running time $O(m^2)$.

1 Introduction

An instance of the *stable marriage problem* is an undirected bipartite graph $G = (X \cup W, E)$ where the adjacency lists of vertices are linearly ordered with ties allowed. As is customary, we call the vertices of the graph men and women, respectively.[1] Each person seeks to be assigned to a person of the opposite sex and his/her preference is given by the ordering of his/her adjacency list. In a's list, if the edges (a, b) and (a, b') are tied, we say that a is indifferent between b and b' and if the edge (a, b) strictly precedes (a, b'), we say that a prefers b to b'. We use n for the number of vertices and m for the number of edges. A stable

---

* Partially supported by the Future and Emerging Technologies programme of the EU under contract number IST-1999-14186 (ALCOM-FT).

** Work done while the author was at MPII supported by Marie Curie Doctoral Fellowship.

[1] We use x, x', x'' to denote men and w, w', w'' to denote women, and a, a', b, b' to denote persons of either sex.

V. Diekert and M. Habib (Eds.): STACS 2004, LNCS 2996, pp. 222–233, 2004.
© Springer-Verlag Berlin Heidelberg 2004

marriage problem is called *complete* if there are an equal number of men and women and G is the complete bipartite graph; thus $m = (n/2)^2$.

A matching M is a set of edges no two of which share an endpoint. If $(a, b) \in M$ we call b the partner of a and a the partner of b. A matching M is *strongly stable* if there is no edge $(a, b) \in E \setminus M$ (called *blocking edge*) such that by becoming matched with to each other, one of a and b (say, a) is better off and b is not worse off. For a being better off means that it is either unmatched in M or strictly prefers b to his/her partner in M, and a being not worse off means that it is either better off or is indifferent between b and his/her partner in M. In other words, a would prefer to match up with b and b would not object to the change.

In this paper, we consider the problem of computing a strongly stable matching. One of the motivations for this form of stability is the following. Suppose we have a matching M and there exists a blocking edge (a, b). Suppose it is a that becomes better off by becoming matched to b. It means that a is willing to take some action to improve its situation and as b's situation would not get worse, it might yield to a. If there exists no such edge, then M can be considered to be reasonably stable since no two vertices a and b such that (a, b) in $E \setminus M$ gain by changing their present state and getting matched with each other. Observe that not every instance of the stable marriage problem has a strongly stable solution.

There are two more notions of stability in matchings. The matching M is said to be weakly stable (or, super strongly stable) if there does not exist a pair $(a, b) \in E \setminus M$ such that by becoming matched to each other both a and b are better off (respectively, neither of them is worse off). The problem of finding a weakly stable matching of maximum size was recently proved to be NP-hard [7]. There is a simple $O(n^2)$ algorithm [6] to determine if a super strongly stable matching exists or not and it computes one, if it exists.

The stable marriage problem can also be studied in the more general context of hospitals and residents. This is a many-to-one extension of the classical men-women version. An instance of the hospitals-residents problem is again an undirected bipartite graph $(R \mathbin{\dot{\cup}} H, E)$ with linearly ordered (allowing ties) adjacency lists. Each resident $r \in R$ seeks to be assigned to exactly one hospital, and each hospital $h \in H$ has a specified number p_h of posts, referred to as its *quota*. A matching M is a valid assignment of residents to hospitals, defined more formally as a set of edges no two of which share the same resident and at most p_h of the edges in M can share the hospital h.

A blocking edge to a matching is defined similarly as in the case of men-women. An edge $(a, b) \in E \setminus M$ is a blocking edge to M if a would prefer to match up with b and b would not object to the change. A matching is strongly stable if there is no blocking edge with respect to it. We also consider the problem of computing a strongly stable matching in this setting. Observe that the classical stable marriage problem is a special case of this general problem by setting $p_h = 1$ for all hospitals.

Our Contributions: In this paper we give an $O(nm)$ algorithm to determine a strongly stable matching for the classical stable marriage problem. We also give an $O(m(|R| + \sum_{h \in H} p_h))$ algorithm to compute a strongly stable matching in the hospitals-residents problem. The previous results for computing strongly stable matchings are as follows. Irving [6] gave an $O(n^4)$ algorithm for computing strongly stable matchings for men-women in complete instances. In [8] Manlove extended the algorithm to incomplete bipartite graphs; the extended algorithm has running time $O(m^2)$. In [4] an $O(m^2)$ algorithm was given for computing a strongly stable matching for the hospitals-residents problem.

Our new algorithm for computing a strongly stable matching for the classical stable marriage problem can be viewed as a specialisation of Irving's algorithm, i.e., every run of our algorithm is a run of his, but not vice versa. We obtain the improved running time by introducing the concept of *levels*. Every vertex has a level associated with it, the level of a vertex can change during the algorithm. We use the levels of vertices to search for special matchings which are *level-maximal* and this reduces the running time of the algorithm to $O(nm)$. We also use the above ideas in the hospitals-residents problem and obtain an improvement over [4].

The stable marriage problem has great practical significance [5,9], [1]. The classical results in stable marriage (no ties and the lists are complete) are the Gale/Shapley theorem and algorithm [2]. Gusfield and Irving [3] covers plenty of results obtained in the area of stable matchings.

Organisation of the paper: In Section 2 we present our $O(nm)$ algorithm for strongly stable matchings for the classical stable marriage problem. In Section 3 we present our $O(m(|R| + \sum_{h \in H} p_h))$ algorithm for the hospitals-residents problem.

2   The Algorithm for Strongly Stable Marriage

We review a variant of Irving's algorithm [6] in Section 2.1 and then describe our modifications in Section 2.2. Figure 1 contains a concise write-up of our algorithm.

2.1   Irving's Algorithm

We review a variant of Irving's algorithm for strongly stable matchings. The algorithm proceeds in phases and maintains two graphs G' and G_c; G' and G_c are subgraphs of G. G_c is the current graph in which we compute maximum matchings and G' is the graph of edges E' not considered relevant yet. In each phase, a certain subset of the edges of G' is moved to G_c. Also edges get deleted from G' and G_c. We use $\mathcal{E}_i$ to denote the edges moved in phase i and $\mathcal{E}_{\leq i}$ to denote the edges moved in the first i phases. Initially, we have $G' = G$ and $E_c = \emptyset$.

At the beginning of phase i, $E_c \subseteq \mathcal{E}_{<i}$ and we have a maximum matching M in G_c. Also, if a man is free with respect to M, then no edges of E_c are incident to it. Let $\mathcal{E}_i$ consist of the top choices[2] in E' of each free man. We say, that every free man proposes to all women currently at the top of his list. When a woman

---

[2] Recall that $E' \subseteq E$ and that adjacency lists are linearly ordered with ties allowed. The top choices for a man x are the set of women tied for first place.

receives a proposal from a man x, she deletes all strict successors of x from E' and E_c. This may also remove edges in M.

Observe, that the rules for adding and deleting edges guarantee that if $(a, b) \in E_c$ and $(a, b') \in E_c$ then a is indifferent between b and b'. For a free man x, all his top choices are moved to E_c and hence edges in E' go to strictly inferior women. A woman keeps only the best proposals made to her and hence edges in E' go either to strictly superior men or to men tied with her choices in E_c.

Next we extend M to a maximum matching in E_c. During this process, further edges may be deleted. We iterate over the free men in arbitrary order. Let x be any free man. If there is an augmenting path starting at x, we use it to increase the cardinality of the matching. Otherwise, let Z be the set of men reachable from x by alternating paths and let $N(Z)$ be the set of women adjacent to Z in E_c. For each woman $w \in N(Z)$ we delete[3] all lowest ranked edges in $E_c \cup E'$ incident to it. This is at least one edge $(x, w) \in E_c$ and zero or more edges $(x', w) \in E'$.

At the end of the phase, we have a maximum matching in E_c. Also, every free man is isolated in G_c since the edges incident to it were removed when we searched for an augmenting path starting from it.

The algorithm terminates when all free men have run out of proposals. Let M be the final matching and let G_c be the final graph. Then M is a maximum matching in G_c and all free men are isolated in G_c and G'. M is a strongly stable matching in G if no woman that was ever non-isolated in G_c during the execution of the algorithm is free with respect to M. [4]

We refer the reader to [6,8] for the proof of correctness of this algorithm. The algorithm runs in $O(m^2)$ time since the cost summed over all phases is $O(m \cdot (1 + \text{number of successful augmenting path computations}))$ and since the number of augmenting path computations is at most m. The latter claim follows from the fact that a matched man becomes free only if the matching edge incident to it is deleted.

2.2   The New Algorithm

We now show how to modify the algorithm so that it runs in time $O(nm)$. Our method maintains *level-maximal* matchings and uses level-maximal augmenting paths.

The running time of the algorithm for a strongly stable matching is actually the time spent on looking for augmenting paths. The notion of the level of an edge and the level of a vertex help us to search for augmenting paths in a streamlined manner. The vertices with higher levels are given precedence when searching for augmenting paths. When we search for augmenting paths with this precedence and we succeed in finding one, then we can show that the level numbers of all the edges traversed are at least the level number of the unmatched vertex at the

---

[3] It is here, where we slightly deviate from Irving's algorithm. We delete edges whenever we identify a free man which cannot be matched. Irving first computes a maximum matching in E_c and then deletes edges.

[4] For complete instances, it is particularly easy to decide whether the final matching M is stable. M is stable if it is a perfect matching in G.

Set phase number $i = 1$, $E' = E$ and $E_c = \emptyset$.
$M = \emptyset$
repeat
  while $\exists$ a free man x **do**
    move all top choice edges $e = (x, w)$ of x in E' to E_c and delete all edges
    (x', w) from $E' \cup E_c$ which w ranks strictly after e.
  end while
  Let $\mathcal{E}_i$ be the edges moved to E_c.
  for all free men x w.r.t. M **do**
    if an alternating path from x to a free woman exists **then**
      let w be a free woman [*of maximal level*] reachable from x by an alter-
      nating path and let p be an alternating path from x to w
      $M = M \oplus p$
    else
      let Z be the set of men reachable from x by alternating paths and let
      $N(Z)$ be the women adjacent to them in E_c;
      for all women $w \in N(Z)$ **do**
        delete all lowest ranked edges in $E_c \cup E'$ incident to w;
      end for
    end if
  end for
  $i = i + 1$
until (all free men have run out of proposals)
declare M strongly stable if every woman that was ever non-isolated in G_c
during the execution of the algorithm is matched in M. Otherwise, there is no
strongly stable matching.

Fig. 1. Two algorithms for strongly stable marriage. The algorithms differ by the phrase [*of maximal level*]. Without the phrase, the algorithm may augment the current matching along any augmenting path and the running time is $O(m^2)$. With the phrase, an augmenting path to a woman of maximal level (see Section 2.2) must be used. The running time improves to $O(nm)$.

end of the augmenting path. This allows us to bound the total number of edges traversed in our search for augmenting paths.

Definition 1. *Let $\mathcal{E}_i$ be the edges added to G_c in phase i and define the level $l(e)$ of an edge to be the phase when this edge was first added to G_c. Edges never added to G_c have no level assigned to them.*

So, the set of edges ever added to G_c consists of the disjoint union $\mathcal{E}_1 \cup \mathcal{E}_2 \cup \ldots \mathcal{E}_r$, where r is the total number of phases in the algorithm. Note that r can be as large as m.

Definition 2. *Define the level $l(v)$ of a vertex v to be the minimum level of the edges in G_c incident to v. The level of an isolated vertex is undefined.*

Definition 3. *The level $l(M)$ of a matching M is the sum of the levels of the matched women. A matching M is level-maximal if $l(M) \geq l(M')$ for any matching M' which matches the same men.*

Lemma 1. *For a man all incident edges in G_c have the same level. All women adjacent to a man of level i have level at most i. When a woman loses an incident edge in E_c she loses all her incident edges in E_c.*

Proof. Obvious.

Lemma 2. *A matching M is level-maximal iff there is no alternating path from a free woman to a woman of lower level.*

Proof. Observe that the endpoint of the path is a matched woman. Augmentation increases the level of the matching and does not change the set of matched men.

For the converse, assume that M is not level-maximal. Let M' be level-maximal and matching the same men. Then $M \oplus M'$ is a set of alternating paths and cycles. Augmenting a cycle does not change the level sum. Thus there must be at least one path whose augmentation to M increases the level sum. Since the degree of every man in $M \oplus M'$ is either zero or two, the path must connect two women, one free in M and one free in M'.

Lemma 3. *If M is level-maximal, x is a free man with respect to M, w is a woman of maximal level reachable from x by an augmenting path and p is an augmenting path from x to w, then $N = M \oplus p$ is level-maximal.*

Proof. Let us look at an alternating path p' from a free woman w' to a matched woman w'' (all with respect to N). We will show that $l(w') \leq l(w'')$ and thereby by Lemma 2 that N is level-maximal.

If p' does not contain any edge from p, then p' was an alternating path from a free woman w' to a matched woman w'' in M. Since M is level-maximal, by Lemma 2, $l(w') \leq l(w'')$.

Let us then assume, that p' contains some edge(s) from p.

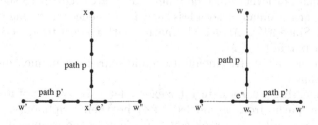

Fig. 2. The thick edges belong to the matching N

Let x' denote the first vertex on the path p' that belongs to p, which we meet while traversing p' from w'. Let e' denote the first edge belonging to p (Figure 2). The vertex x' must be a man, because all edges incident to vertices on p and not belonging to p, cannot belong to the matching N and we started the traversal of p' from the unmatched woman. So, e' is matched. Let us now look at this part of p that has x' at its one end and does not contain e'. It has the man x at its other end, that was free in M. Since $M \oplus p = N$, the matched edges of path p were exactly vice versa before the augmentation, in the sense that those edges, that are now present in the matching N, were not present in the matching M previously and the other way round. It means that w' was reachable by an alternating path from x in M. Thus $l(w') \leq l(w)$.

Analogously, let w_2 denote the first vertex on the path p'' that belongs to p which we meet when we traverse p' beginning from the matched woman w''. Let e'' denote the first edge belonging to p (Figure 2). It is not difficult to notice that w_2 must be a woman. Now, if we look at that part of p, that has w_2 at its one end and does not contain e'', we will notice that it has the woman w at its other end. Thus in M there existed an alternating path from the free woman w to the matched woman w'' and hence, by Lemma 2, $l(w) \leq l(w'')$.

Combining the observations, we get that $l(w') \leq l(w'')$.

Lemma 4. *M is a level-maximal matching at all times of the execution.*

Proof. We use induction on time. Initially, M is empty and therefore level-maximal. For the induction step assume that M is level-maximal at the beginning of phase i.

First, every free man proposes to the women at the top of his list. This introduces the edge set $\mathcal{E}_i$. The level of non-isolated women does not change, the level of women previously isolated and not isolated anymore is set to i. M is still level-maximal. Assume otherwise, then there must be an alternating path from a free woman to a woman of lower level. This path must use one of the new edges. The new edges are incident to free men, a contradiction.

Every woman keeps only her best proposals. For a particular woman w this has one of two effects: either she does not drop any incident edge or she keeps only edges in $\mathcal{E}_i$ (not necessarily all of them). The matching M may be reduced in size. Let us use M' to denote the resulting matching. We claim that it is level-maximal. Assume otherwise, then there must an alternating path p from a free woman to a woman of lower level. It cannot use any of the new edges since new edges are incident to free men. Thus p can use only old edges. Also p cannot start at a woman of level i since only new edges are incident to such a woman. Thus p starts at a woman of level less than i and hence the woman is free with respect to M. Since $M' \subseteq M$, p is alternating with respect to M, a contradiction to the level-maximality of M.

Next, we consider the free men in turn and search for augmenting paths. Let x be a free man.

If no augmenting path starting at x exists, let Z be the set of men reachable by alternating paths from x and let $N(Z)$ be their neighbours. Then $|Z| > |N(Z)|$. We delete all lowest rank edges incident to the women in $N(Z)$. This may decrease the size of the matching. The matching clearly stays level-maximal.

If an augmenting path exists, let p be an augmenting path to a woman of maximal level. We use p to increase the cardinality of the matching. By Lemma 3, the resulting matching is level-maximal.

2.3   The Search for Augmenting Paths and the Analysis

We come to the implementation of the search for augmenting paths and the analysis.

Let x be a free man. We need to determine a maximal level free woman w reachable from x and an augmenting path from x to w. Let p be such an augmenting path. Then all women on this path have level at least $l(w)$ by Lemma 2. Note that $l(w) \leq l(x)$. This is because all the women adjacent to x have level at most $l(x)$, so if w is adjacent to x, then $l(w) \leq l(x)$. If w is not adjacent to x and if $l(w) > l(x)$, then p contains an alternating path from a free woman of higher level (that is, w) to a matched woman of lower level (the neighbour of x). This contradicts the level-maximality of the matching.

We organise the search in rounds $l(x)$, $l(x) - 1$, $l(x) - 2$, ... In round j, we explore all augmenting paths starting in x and exploring only edges out of vertices of level j or larger. We stop in round j when a free woman of level j is reached by the search or if the Hungarian tree rooted at x has reached its full size. In the former case, j is the maximal level of a woman reachable from x by an augmenting path. In the latter case, no free woman is reachable from x. If the search has not stopped yet, the frontier of the search consists of women of level less than j. In the next round, we continue the search from all women of level $j - 1$ in the frontier.

In order to find these women, we maintain an array A of buckets ($=$ linear lists) which implements a simple priority queue. All buckets are initially empty. At the beginning of round j, bucket B_l, $l \leq j$ contains the women of level l in the frontier. We also keep an (unsorted) list of the non-empty buckets and the total number of women contained in the buckets. We initialise the bucket structure by putting the neighbours of x into the appropriate buckets and setting j to $l(x)$. In round j, we continue the search from the women in bucket j. If the bucket is empty and the number of unexplored women is positive, we decrease j by one. If the bucket is empty and the number of unexplored women is zero, we stop. There is no augmenting path starting at x (failure). If the bucket is non-empty, let w be a woman in the bucket. We remove w from the bucket. If w is free, we stop (success): w is the highest ranked woman reachable from x. If w is matched, we explore alternating paths from w (starting with matched edges) until a woman of level less than j is reached. These women are then added to their appropriate buckets. When the search stops, we empty all buckets using the list of non-empty buckets.

Let $j(x)$ be the minimal bucket index from which we remove a woman. In the case of failure this is the minimal level of a woman reachable from x and in the case of success this is the maximum level of a woman reachable from x by an augmenting path.

The time for the search from x is proportional to the number k of edges explored in the search plus $l(x) - j(x) + 1$. We charge this cost as follows:

In the case of failure we charge one unit each to each edge deleted (this accounts for k) and we charge $l(x) - j(x) + 1$ to the minimum level woman w reachable from x. The first kind of charges adds up to m since every edge is deleted at most once. The second kind of charge is less than the difference of the current level of w and the next level of w. Thus for a single woman the total charge of the second kind is bounded by m. We conclude that the total cost of unsuccessful searches is $O(nm)$.

In the case of success, we charge both costs to w. Observe that all edges explored have level at least $l(w)$ $(= j(x))$ and at most i $(=$ the phase number) and that the level of w jumps to at least $i + 1$ if it ever becomes free again. Thus every edge can be assigned at most once to w. Also $l(x) - j(x) + 1$ is bounded by the difference between the current level of w and the next level of w. Thus the total charge to w is bounded by m. The total cost of successful searches is therefore bounded by $O(nm)$.

Theorem 1. *Strongly stable matchings for the classical stable marriage problem can be computed in time $O(nm)$.*

Note that the running time of our strongly stable matching algorithm is actually $O(|W|m)$ since the total cost of all unsuccessful searches and augmentations is shared by women and the cost charged to a single woman sums to at most m over all phases. So, if $|W| \ll |X|$ or $|X| \ll |W|$ (then we reverse the roles of men and women and it is free women who propose in every phase and it is men who pay for the augmentations), then we can bound the running time of our algorithm by $O(\min(|X|, |W|) \cdot m)$.

3   Extension to Hospitals-Residents

Recall that the hospitals-residents problem is a many-to-one extension of the classical stable marriage problem. We give an $O(m(|R| + \sum_{h \in H} p_h))$ algorithm for computing a strongly stable matching for the hospitals-residents problem. Our algorithm is based on the algorithm in [4] which is an $O(m^2)$ algorithm. We obtain the improved running time by restricting again all augmentations to result in level-maximal matchings. We give an outline of our approach here and the full version of the paper has all the proofs and details.

3.1   The Algorithm in [4]

We first review a variant of the algorithm in [4] and then present our modified algorithm. The algorithm in [4] generalises the ideas used for computing strongly stable matchings in [6] to the hospitals-residents problem.

As in the case of the stable marriage problem, the algorithm proceeds in phases. In any phase, every free resident proposes to all hospitals currently at the top of his list and residents become *provisionally assigned* to hospitals. Each hospital h can accommodate up to p_h residents, and it needs to keep only the best p_h proposals made to it but if there is a tie in the last place of its list (called the *tail*), then h can be provisionally assigned to $> p_h$ residents. We introduce a few terms:

- A hospital is said to be *over-subscribed, under-subscribed* or *fully subscribed* according as it is provisionally assigned a number of residents greater than, less than, or equal to, its quota.
- A resident r who is provisionally assigned to a hospital h is said to be *bound* to h if h is not over-subscribed or r is not in h's tail (or both).
- A resident r is *dominated* in a hospital h's list if h prefers to r at least p_h residents who are provisionally assigned to it.

The algorithm maintains two graph G' and G_c which are subgraphs of G. G_c is called the provisional assignment graph with edge set E_c and G' is the graph of edges E' not considered yet. During the execution of the algorithm, residents become provisionally assigned to hospitals which means that edges are moved from G' to G_c. The algorithm proceeds in the same way, as the algorithm for strongly stable marriage, by deleting edges $e = (r, h)$ which cannot belong to any strongly stable matching.

Reduced Assignment Graph: We maintain a graph $G_r \subseteq G_c$, called the *reduced assignment graph*. The residents who appear in G_r are those that are not bound to any hospital (we call such residents unbound). So, for any hospital h, the edges incident to h in G_r are to the unbound residents, and hence are at the tail of h's list. Each hospital h has a reduced quota p'_h in the reduced assignment graph, which is the difference between the original quota p_h and the number of residents bound to h. So, the vertices of G_r are the set of unbound residents and the set of hospitals which are the neighbours of the unbound residents. The reduced assignment graph of phase i is denoted as $G_r^{(i)}$.

Now the algorithm is very similar to the algorithm for strongly stable marriage, except that we compute maximum matchings in the reduced assignment graph. Initially, $G' = G$; $E_c = \emptyset$; all the residents are free and $G_r^{(0)}$ is the empty graph. At the beginning of phase i, we have a maximum matching M in $G_r^{(i-1)}$. If a resident is free with respect to M, then he is isolated in $G_r^{(i-1)}$. Then we move the edges corresponding to the top most choices of every free resident from E' to E_c. This denotes free residents being provisionally assigned to hospitals. Whenever a hospital h becomes fully or over-subscribed, then we delete all edges (r, h), where r is dominated on h's list, from G' and G_c. The reduced assignment graph $G_r^{(i)}$ is computed from $G_r^{(i-1)}$. Observe that an edge (r, h) can change state from bound (r is bound to h) to unbound (r is not bound to h) but not vice-versa. If a new edge that gets added to G_c corresponding to one of the top choices of a free resident in $G_r^{(i-1)}$ is a bound edge, then it could cause some bound edges to become unbound or it could cause some edges to get deleted. Any edge of $G_r^{(i-1)}$ that is not deleted from G_c continues to remain in $G_r^{(i)}$. The change of state of an edge (r, h) from bound to unbound need not make the resident r unbound unless (r, h) was the only bound edge incident to r and now (r, h) has changed state to unbound. Then r, which was not present in $G_r^{(i-1)}$, starts appearing in $G_r^{(i)}$. Then we extend M in $G_r^{(i)}$ to match all the unmatched residents.

Augmenting path: In the hospitals-residents setting, a hospital h is considered free in G_r if it is not matched up to its reduced quota p'_h. An alternating path from a free resident to a hospital that is not filled up to its quota is considered an augmenting path.

We iterate over the free residents in arbitrary order. Let r be any free resident. If there is an augmenting path starting at r, we use it to increase the cardinality of the matching. Otherwise, let Z be the set of residents reachable from r by alternating paths and let $N(Z)$ be the set of hospitals adjacent to Z in E_c. For each hospital $h \in N(Z)$ we delete all lowest ranked edges in $E_c \cup E'$ incident to it.

At the end of the phase, we have a maximum matching M in $G_r^{(i)}$. Also, every free resident is isolated in G_c since the edges incident to it were removed when we searched for an augmenting path starting from it. When all free residents have run out of proposals, we need to find a *feasible* matching M' in G_c which contains the maximum matching M in G_r and matches every bound resident r to a hospital that r is bound to. M' is a strongly stable matching if a hospital that was fully or over-subscribed at some point in the execution of the algorithm is fully matched in M' or a hospital that was always under-subscribed has assignees in M' equal to its degree in G_c. We refer the reader to [4] for the proof of correctness of this algorithm.

3.2   Our Modifications

Let us extend our definitions in order to capture the somehow different structure of the hospitals-residents problem.

Definition 4. *Define the level of an edge e, $l(e)$, to be the phase that e is added to the reduced assignment graph G_r.* [5]

Definition 5. *Define the level of a vertex v, $l(v)$, to be the minimum level of the edges incident to v. If v does not belong to G_r, its level is undefined.*

Definition 6. *Define the level of a matching M, $l(M)$, to be the sum over all hospitals of the level of a hospital multiplied by the number of edges that this hospital is matched with.*

Definition 7. *A matching M is level-maximal if $l(M) \geq l(M')$ for any matching M' which matches the same residents.*

The following lemmas show how to maintain a level maximal matching. The proofs are available in the full version of this paper.

Lemma 5. *A matching M is level-maximal iff there is no alternating path starting with an unmatched edge from a free hospital to a hospital of lower level.*

Lemma 6. *If M is level-maximal, r is a free resident with respect to M, h is a hospital of maximal level reachable from r by an augmenting path and p is an augmenting path from r to h, then $N = M \oplus p$ is level-maximal.*

Lemma 7. *M is a level-maximal matching at all times of the execution.*

---

[5] Note that an edge appears in G_r at some phase which might not necessarily be the phase that this edge appeared in G_c.

3.3   The Running Time

The search for augmenting paths in G_r is implemented as in the classical stable marriage problem. Using similar arguments, one can see that the cost of unsuccessful searches is $O(m)$ and of successful searches is $O((\sum_{h \in H} p_h)m)$. Furthermore, with an appropriate representation of the graphs, all changes of G_r can be done in time $O(|R|m)$.

Theorem 2. *Strongly stable matchings for the hospitals-residents problem can be computed in time* $O(m(|R| + \sum_{h \in H} p_h))$.

We conclude that in the worst case $\sum_{h \in H} p_h$ can be as large as m, in which case we get a running time of $O(m^2)$, but in any practical application, we expect that $\sum_{h \in H} p_h = |R|$, in which case we get a total running time $O(|R|m)$.

References

1. Canadian Resident Matching Scheme. How the matching algorithm works. http : //www.carms.ca/matching/algorith.htm
2. D. Gale and L.S. Shapley. College admissions and the stability of marriage. *American Mathematical Monthly*, 69, pages 9–15, 1962.
3. D. Gusfield and R.W. Irving. The Stable Marriage Problem: Structure and Algorithms. (MIT Press, Boston, MA, 1989).
4. R.W. Irving, D.F. Manlove, and S. Scott. Strong stability of the hospitals/residents problem. In *STACS* , LNCS 2607, pages 439–450. Springer Verlag, 2003.
5. R. W. Irving. Matching medical students to pairs of hospitals: a new variation of a well-known theme. In *ESA, LNCS 1461*, pages 381–392. Springer Verlag, 1998.
6. R.W. Irving. Stable marriage and indifference. *Discrete Applied Mathematics*, pages 261–272, 1994.
7. K. Iwama, D. Manlove, S. Miyazaki, and Y. Morita. Stable Marriage with incomplete lists and ties. In *ICALP* , LNCS 1644, pages 443–452. Springer Verlag, 1999.
8. D.F. Manlove. Stable marriage with ties and unacceptable partners. Technical report, University of Glasgow, 1999.
9. A. E. Roth. The evolution of the labor market for medical interns and residents: a case study in game theory. *Journal of Political Economy*, 92(6), pages 991–1016, 1984.

Approximation Algorithms for Minimizing Average Distortion

Kedar Dhamdhere[*1], Anupam Gupta[1], and R. Ravi[**2]

[1] School of Computer Science, Carnegie Mellon University.
{kedar,anupamg}@cs.cmu.edu
[2] Graduate School of Industrial Administration, Carnegie Mellon University.
ravi@cmu.edu

Abstract. We study the problem of embedding arbitrary finite metrics into a line metric in a non-contracting fashion to approximate the minimum average distortion. Since a path metric (or a line metric) is quite restricted, these embeddings could have high average distortions ($\Omega(n)$), where n is the number of points in the original metric). Furthermore, we prove that finding best embedding of even a tree metric into a line to minimize average distortion is NP-hard. Hence, we focus on *approximating* the best possible embedding for given input metric.

We give a constant-factor approximation for the problem of embedding general metrics into the line metric. For the case of the metrics which can be represented as trees, we provide improved approximation ratios in polynomial time as well as a QPTAS (Quasi-Polynomial Time Approximation Scheme).

1 Introduction

Metric embeddings have recently attracted much attention in theoretical computer science because of their many algorithmic applications. These range from simplifying the structure of the input data for approximation and online problems [5,8,9,15,18,24], serving as a well-roundable relaxation of important NP-hard problems [7,11,12,13,17,27] or simply by being the object of study [1,16] arising from applications such as computational biology. Embedding techniques have thus become an indispensable addition to the algorithms toolbox, providing powerful and elegant solutions to many algorithmic problems (see, e.g., [29, Chapter 15] and [22]).

An embedding of a metric (V, d) into a "simpler" host metric (H, δ) is a map $f : V \to H$; the embedding is a good one if the distances between points in d closely resemble those between their images in δ. An embedding is called *non-contracting* if the map does not decrease any distances, i.e., $d(x, y) \leq \delta(f(x), f(y))^1$ for all $x, y \in V$. We restrict ourselves to non-contracting

---

[*] Supported by NSF ITR grants CCR-0085982 and CCR-0122581.
[**] Supported in part by NSF grant CCR-0105548 and ITR grant CCR-0122581.
[1] In the sequel, we will abbreviate $\delta(f(x), f(y))$ to $\delta(x, y)$.

V. Diekert and M. Habib (Eds.): STACS 2004, LNCS 2996, pp. 234–245, 2004.
© Springer-Verlag Berlin Heidelberg 2004

embeddings in this paper. Perhaps the most popular and useful measure of the quality of an embedding f is the distortion $\alpha = \alpha(f)$, which is:

$$\text{distortion } \alpha = \max_{x,y \in V} \frac{\delta(x,y)}{d(x,y)}.$$

A closely related measure is that of *average distortion*, which is

$$\text{average distortion } \rho(f) = \frac{\sum_{x,y \in V} \delta(x,y)}{\sum_{x,y \in V} d(x,y)}.$$

While many embedding techniques and algorithms are known, the analyses for these embeddings usually only offer uniform bounds on the distortion of the embeddings; few results which *approximate* the distortion of the embeddings to better than these uniform bounds. This is best shown by a concrete example: Matoušek [28] proved that *any* metric (V, d) can be embedded into the real line with distortion $O(|V|)$; furthermore, the result is existentially tight, as the n-cycle cannot be embedded into the line with distortion $o(|V|)$ (see, e.g., [31,21]). However, no algorithm is known which offers *per-instance* guarantees; hence, while it may be possible to embed (X, d) into $\mathbb{R}$ with distortion $\alpha = O(1)$, no algorithms are known which give us embeddings with distortion, say, that is within $O(|V|^{1-\epsilon})$ times ρ! No results are known even when we replace distortion α by average distortion ρ as the measure of goodness[2].

1.1 Our Results

In this paper, we prove results for approximating the average distortion when embedding metrics into the line $\mathbb{R}$ (while ensuring that the map is non-contracting). We can think of embeddings into a line as defining a tour on the nodes of the original metric. Note that for an embedding to be non-contracting, it is necessary and sufficient to have the distance between adjacent pair of vertices in the tour to be the same as their distance in the input metric. Our results demonstrate a close relationship between minimizing average distortion and the problems of finding short TSP tours [25], minimum latency tours [10,20,4], and optimal k-repairmen solutions[14]. In particular, we prove the following results.

– **Hardness for average distortion:** We prove that the problem of finding a minimum average distortion non-contracting embedding of finite metrics into the line is NP-hard, *even when the input metric is a tree metric*. This is proved via a reduction from the Minimum Latency Problem on trees [33].
– **Constant-factor approximations:** We give an algorithm that embeds any metric (V, d) into the line with average distortion that is within a constant of the minimum possible over all non-contracting embeddings. In fact, we prove a slightly more general bound on non-contracting embeddings into k-spiders (i.e., homeomorphs of stars with k leaves). This result uses a lower

---

[2] One notable exception is the remark of Linial et al. [27] that the optimal embedding of any finite metric into (unbounded dimensional) Euclidean spaces to minimize distortion can be computed as a solution to a semi-definite program.

bound on the minimum average distortion of a non-contracting embedding into a k-spider in terms of the minimum k-repairmen tour [14] on the metric. We also show a tightened result for the case of 2-spiders using ideas from constructing minimum latency tours [20].

- **QPTAS on trees:** For tree metrics on n nodes, we give an algorithm for finding a $(1 + \epsilon)$-approximation to the minimum average distortion non-contracting embedding into a line in $n^{O(\log n/\epsilon^2)}$ time. Our algorithm uses a lower bound on the minimum average distortion related to the TSP tour length and latencies of appropriately chosen segments of an optimal tour. In this way, it extends the ideas of Arora & Karakostas [6] for minimizing latency on trees to the more general time-dependent TSPs [10] to provide a QPTAS for the latter problem as well.

Given a tree metric as input, if the minimum average distortion is measured only over the endpoints of the edges of the tree (we call this objective the average tree-edge distortion), we can prove that an embedding following an Euler tour of the tree is optimal. This tour can be found in polynomial time by dynamic programming. We omit the description of this algorithm due to lack of space.

1.2   Related Work

The definition of average distortion is by no means new; e.g., Alon et al. [2] study the question of embedding a metric into a tree with low average distortion. In recent work on average distortion that is closer to our work, Rabinovich [30] proves bounds on average distortion of *non-expanding* embeddings into a line and shows the close connection between this and the max-flow min-cut ratio for concurrent multicommodity flow with applications to finding quotient cuts in graphs [26].

Our problem is similar to that of finding the Minimum Linear Arrangement (MLA), for which Rao & Richa [32] gave an $O(\log n)$ approximation using the notion of spreading metrics. However, while the MLA problem involves minimizing the average stretch of the edges $\sum_{\{u,v\} \in E} |\pi(u) - \pi(v)|$ under all maps $\pi : V \to [n]$, the mappings in our problem are $f : V \to \mathbb{R}$, and must ensure that $|f(u) - f(v)| \geq d(u, v) \ \forall \{u, v\} \in V \times V$.

The problem of finding Minimum Latency tours (a.k.a. the traveling repairman problem) is most relevant to our discussion in terms of techniques used. This problem requires a repairman who starts from a depot on a given finite metric to visit n customers, one at each node of the metric; his goal is to minimize the *average waiting time* or *latency* of the customers, where the waiting time of a customer is the sum of the distances of all edges traversed by the repairman before visiting this customer. The version of this problem with only one repairman (also called the Minimum Latency Problem) is known to be NP-hard even on trees [33] and MAX-SNP hard in general [10]. The first constant-factor approximation for this problem was given by Blum *et al.*[10], which was subsequently improved by Goemans and Kleinberg [20] to the currently best-known bound of 7.18. Recently, Archer, Levin and Williamson [4,3] gave faster algorithms obtaining very similar approximation guarantees. For the special cases of the latency problem on trees, and in $\mathbb{R}^d$ for fixed dimension d, Arora and Karakostas [6] gave quasi-polynomial time approximation schemes (QPTAS). The extension of the latency problem to more than one repairmen was recently studied in [14] where the authors show a 16.994-approximation for the general k-repairman case.

Finally, a problem that generalizes both the cost of a tour as well as its latency into one objective is that of finding time dependent TSP tours. A constant factor approximation algorithm is also known for this problem [10].

Outline: The rest of the paper is organized as follows. In Section 2, we argue that the embedding problem is NP-hard, and give the constant-factor approximation algorithm for embedding metrics into the line with constant average distortion. Section 3 shows the QPTAS for the case of trees metrics as inputs.

2   Embedding Arbitrary Metrics into the Line

In this section, we show that we can approximate the average distortion into a line for a given metric to within a constant; to this end, we show that the problem is closely related to that of finding the minimum latency tours and its generalizations in a finite metric space. We omit the proof of the following theorem; the reduction is from Minimum Latency on trees.

Theorem 1. *It is NP-hard to find a non-contracting embedding of a given metric induced by a tree into a line that minimizes the average distortion.*

First, we show a simple 2-approximation for embedding a finite metric into a special kind of tree metric, namely a *k-spider*. (A k-spider is a tree with all vertices except the *center* having degrees 1 or 2, and hence is a homeomorph of the star with k leaves). The case of a n-spider or a complete star is more natural to argue about, while the 2-spider is a path giving our main result.

Embeddings into trees. Consider the problem of embedding the given metric d into a tree metric δ to minimize average distortion. Let $\Delta = \sum_{x,y \in V} d(x,y)$ denote the sum of all the distances in the metric d, and hence $\text{av}(d) = \Delta/n^2$ is the average distance in d. The *median* of the metric d is the point $v \in V$ that minimizes $\Delta_v = \sum_{w \in V} d(v,w)$, and will be denoted by *med*. Note that we can decompose Δ as follows:

$$\Delta = \sum_{u,v \in V} d(u,v) = \sum_{u \in V}(\sum_{v \in V} d(u,v)) = \sum_{u \in V} \Delta_u \geq n\,\Delta_{med} \quad (1)$$

since $\Delta_{med} \leq \Delta_v$ for all $v \in V$. Consider a shortest-path tree T (which is a star in a general metric d) rooted at *med*, and let d_T denote the metric induced by this shortest path tree. Then the total distance in this tree T is

$$\Delta_T = n^2 \cdot \text{av}(d_T) = \sum_{u,v \in V} d_T(u,v) \leq \sum_{u,v \in V} d_T(\text{med}, u) + d_T(\text{med}, v)$$
$$= \sum_{u,v \in V} d(\text{med}, u) + d(\text{med}, v) = 2n\Delta_{med}$$

where the inequality in the second step is just the triangle inequality. This implies that $n\Delta_{med} \leq \Delta \leq \Delta_T \leq 2n\Delta_{med}$, and thus:

Lemma 1 (See also [34]). *Given any graph, the average distance Δ_T for the tree rooted at the median is at most 2Δ, and is a 2-approximation for the problem of embedding the graph into trees.*

Note here that the bound of 2 above is an *absolute* bound on the worst-case ratio between the average distance in the output tree and the graph, and is in the same flavor as the more traditional results on bounding the maximum distortion of embeddings. We next move toward an approximation approach by restricting the class of trees into which we embed.

Embeddings into spiders. We now generalize the previous result to the case of embeddings into k-spiders. The vertex of degree k is called the *center* of the spider, and the components obtained by removing the center are called its *legs* [23].

Let d_k^* denote the optimal k-spider embedding. We decompose the sum of distances in d_k^* as the sum of k-repairman paths rooted at each vertex. Recall that, in k-traveling repairman problem, we are given k repairmen starting at a common depot s. The k repairmen are to visit n customers sitting one per node of the input metric space. The goal is to find tours on which to send the repairmen so as to minimize the total time customers have to wait for a repairman to arrive [14].

Let c be the center of the spider in the optimal k-spider embedding. To construct a k-repairman paths starting from a vertex r, we do the following. We send one repairman away from the center along the leg of the spider which contains r. The other $k-1$ repairmen travel toward the center c of the spider. From the center, they go off, one per remaining leg of the spider. The cost of this k-repairman tour is $\Delta_r^* = \sum_j d_k^*(r,j)$. Summing over all choices of the root we see that this is same as the sum of distances in the embedding d_k^*.

$$\sum_{v \in V} \Delta_v^* = n^2 \cdot \mathrm{av}(d_k^*)$$

Hence, n times the cost of the cheapest k-repairman tour over all choices of the depots (denoted by Δ^{opt}), is a lower bound on the sum of all the distances. i.e.,

$$\sum_{u,v \in V} d_k^*(u,v) \geq n \cdot \min_r \{\Delta_r^{opt}\}.$$

Consider the cheapest k-repairman tour over all choices of centers. Let it be centered at a vertex c. This tour defines a non-contracting embedding into a k-spider with c at the center of the spider. Let $d^c(u)$ denote the distance of vertex u from the center c in the tour. We can bound the sum of distances in this embedding as follows:

$$\sum_{u,v \in V} d_k^c(u,v) \leq \sum_{u,v \in V} d^c(u) + d^c(v) \leq 2n \sum_{u \in V} d^c(u) \leq 2 \sum_{u,v \in V} d_k^*(u,v).$$

Thus, if we could compute the optimal k-repairman tour centered at c exactly, we would obtain a 2-approximation to the problem of embedding the metric into k-spiders. Although the problem of finding an optimal k-repairman tour is NP-hard, the argument above proves the following.

Theorem 2. *Given a γ-approximation for the minimum k-repairmen problem on a metric d, we can obtain a 2γ-approximation for embedding the metric d into a k-spider in a non-contracting fashion to minimize the average distortion.*

The current best known approximation factor for the k-repairman problem is about 17 (due to Fakcharoenphol et al. [14]), leading to the following corollary.

Corollary 1. *There is a 34-approximation for minimizing the average distortion of a non-contracting embedding of a given finite metric into a k-spider.*

Embeddings into a line: Improved guarantee. We can get a better approximation factor for embeddings into the line by employing a slightly different strategy. Instead of using the result of Fakcharoenphol *et al.* as a black box, we instead give an algorithm to find a 1-repairman tour (i.e., a minimum latency tour) that is within a factor of 14.36 of the optimum 2-repairmen tour in the given metric. Since a 1-repairman tour is also a 2-repairmen tour (with the second repairman doing nothing), we can then apply Theorem 2 to bring down the overall approximation ratio to 28.72.

The idea behind the algorithm is the same as in scaled search, due to Blum *et al.* [10]; here is an outline. To find a 1-repairman solution centered at r:

> **for** $j = 0, 1, 2, 3, \ldots,$ **do**
> $T_j \leftarrow$ tree rooted at r spanning the most vertices among those
>   with cost $\leq 2^{j+2}$.
> Concatenate Euler tours of the trees T_j (in increasing order of j), to form a 1-repairman path.

Lemma 2. *The cost of the 1-repairman tour produced by the preceding algorithm is within a factor 32 of the cheapest 2-repairman tour.*

Proof. Let vertex v be the ith closest vertex to root r in the optimal 2-repairman tour. Let the distance of v from the root r in the tour be between $[2^j, 2^{j+1})$ in the optimal solution. Consider the tree T_j of cost 2^{j+2} constructed by our algorithm. We claim that T_j spans at least i vertices. Thus cost of ith vertex in our tour has latency at most

$$\sum_{i=0}^{j}(\text{cost of } i^{\text{th}} \text{ tour}) \leq \sum_{i=0}^{j} 2 \cdot 2^{i+2} \leq 2^{j+4}$$

Hence, the distance of the ith vertex in our 1-repairman tour is at most 16 times its counterpart in the optimal 2-repairmen tour.

Although the problem of finding the largest tree with cost at most 2^{j+2} is NP-hard, we can find a tree having as many vertices as the the this optimal tree instead (but with cost at most $2 \cdot 2^{j+2}$ using Garg's [19] algorithm for i-MST. This increases the overall approximation factor to $16 \cdot 2 = 32$.

Lemma 3. *We can find a 1-repairman tour with cost ≤ 14.36 times the cost of the cheapest 2-repairman tour.*

Proof. (Sketch) Let b be a real number greater than 1 to be chosen later. Let $c = b^U$, where U is a real number chosen uniformly at random from the interval $[0, 1]$. Instead of finding the trees of cost $2, 4, 8, \ldots$ which cover the most vertices, we will find the trees of cost at most $2c, 2cb, 2cb^2, \ldots$ which cover the most vertices. Using the methods of Goemans and Kleinberg, we can show that the approximation ratio of the previous proof can be improved to 14.36.

Note that this improves on the result of Fakcharoenphol et al. [14] for the special case of the 2-repairman problem. An application of Theorem 2 now gives us the following:

Theorem 3. *There exists a 28.72-approximation algorithm to embed a given (weighted) metric it into a line in a non-contracting fashion to minimize the average distortion.*

As a consequence of the analysis in Lemma 2, we also get the following result:

Lemma 4. *For $l \leq k$, we can find an l-repairman tour with cost at most $17\,(k/l)$ times that of the optimal k-repairman tour.*

We note that the factor $\frac{k}{l}$ in the above Lemma is necessary as demonstrated by the metric induced by an unweighted star graph. Compare the above result to that of Fakcharoenphol et al. [14] which outputs a k-repairmen tour of cost $O(\frac{k}{l})$ times the minimum l-repairmen tour for $k \geq l$ (where the factor $\frac{k}{l}$ is not necessary since the algorithm delivers a solution with more repairmen than the optimal compared against).

3   Approximation Schemes for Trees

In this section, we restrict our attention to the special case of tree metrics. We give a quasi-polynomial time approximation scheme for minimizing the average distortion for embeddings into the line metric. Our algorithm is based on the QPTAS given by Arora and Karakostas for the minimum latency problem [6]. They proved that a near-optimal latency tour can be constructed by concatenating $O(\log |V|/\epsilon)$ optimal TSP subtours, and the best such solution can be found by dynamic programming.

For an embedding $f : V \to \mathbb{R}$ into the line, let the *span* of the embedding be defined as $\max_{x,y} |f(x) - f(y)|$, the maximum distance between two points on the line. We note that an embedding with the shortest span is just the optimal TSP tour. While embedding a given metric into the line metric, minimizing the span of the embedding could result in very high average distortion. However, we show that it suffices to minimize the span locally to find near optimal embedding. In particular, our solution within $(1 + \epsilon)$ of optimal minimum average distortion is to find an embedding that is the union of $O(\log|V|/\epsilon^2)$ TSP tours with geometrically decreasing number of vertices.

In the sequel, we use n to denote $|V|$, the number of vertices. For our algorithm, we assume that all the edge lengths are in the range $[1, n^2/\epsilon]$. Indeed, if D is the diameter of the metric space and u and v are two vertices such that $d(u, v) = D$, then $\sum_{x,y \in V} d(x, y) \geq \sum_{x \in V} d(x, u) + d(x, v) \geq nD$. We can then merge all pairs of nodes with inter-node distance at most $\epsilon D/n^2$, which affects the sum of distance by at most ϵnD. Hence the ratio of maximum to minimum nonzero distance in the metric can be assumed to be n^2/ϵ.

Relation to TDTSPs. We first show that the Arora-Karakostas QPTAS works also for the case of Time Dependent Traveling Salesman Problem (TDTSP) defined by Blum et al.. In the TDTSP, the objective is to minimize a positive linear combination of the TSP tour value and the total latency of the tour. The intuition behind this is that adding a component of TSP in the objective value preserves the property that the tour composed of TSP tours continues to remain near-optimal.

We now describe how to break up an optimal tour into locally optimal segments. Let $\mathcal{T}$ denote the optimal tour for the objective function $\alpha TSP + \beta LAT$ where TSP and LAT denote the span and latency objective values of the tour respectively. We break this tour into k segments (k depends on the input parameter ϵ). In segment i we visit n_i nodes, where

$$n_i = \lceil (1 + \epsilon)^{k-1-i} \rceil \text{ for } i = 1, \ldots, k - 1; \qquad n_k = \lceil 1/\epsilon \rceil$$

Note that these n_i's are chosen in such a way that $n_i \leq \epsilon \sum_{j>i} n_j$. Denote $\sum_{j>i} n_j$ by r_i. Replace the optimal tour in each segment, except the last one, by the minimum-distance traveling salesman tour for that segment. The new tour now consists of the concatenation of $O(\log n/\epsilon)$ locally optimal TSP tours. This gives us the following lemma.

Lemma 5. *There is a tour that is a concatenation of $O(\log n/\epsilon)$ TSP tours that has $\alpha TSP + \beta LAT$ objective value at most $(1 + \epsilon)$ times the minimum.*

We now use the Lemma 5 to show the following theorem for average distance.

Theorem 4. *Any finite metric has a non-contracting embedding into a line that is composed of $O(\log n/\epsilon^2)$ minimum TSP tour segments with average distortion no more that $(1 + \epsilon)$ times the minimum possible over all such embeddings.*

Proof. Our strategy is same as in Lemma 5. Consider the optimal embedding of the input tree into a line. We break this embedding up into $O(\log n/\epsilon)$ segments. Let n_i be the size of ith segment defined as before. We now divide the objective function value according to the segments, so that only the share C_i of segment i changes, if we replace the embedding of segment i with a different embedding.

Let T_i be the length of the embedding of segment i. If i_0 is the left-most node in the embedding of the segment i, then let $L_i = \sum_{j \in n_i} l(i_0, j)$ be the sum of the distances of all nodes in segment i from node v. Note that L_i is the total latency of vertices in segment i with i_0 as root. And let $D_i = \sum_{u,v \in n_i} l(u,v)$ be the sum of all the pairwise distances in segment i.

Let $q_i = \sum_{j<i} n_j$ and $r_i = \sum_{j>i} n_j$ be the number of total nodes to the left and right of segment i respectively.

The contribution of the segment i to the objective comes from the following distinct terms.

1. If a vertex u is to the left of the segment i and a vertex v is to the right, then the segment i adds T_i to the distance between them.
2. If a vertex u is to the left and w is in the segment i, then the contribution is $l(i_0, w) =$ the distance from the left most vertex i_0 of the segment i to w.
3. If a vertex v is to the right and w is in the segment i, then the contribution is $T_i - l(i_0, w)$.
4. If both the vertices w and w' are in the segment i, then the contribution is $l(w, w')$.

These contributions, when summed up over all pairs of vertices, give:

$$C_i = q_i r_i T_i + q_i L_i + r_i(n_i T_i - L_i) + D_i \qquad (2)$$

Note that $D_i \le n_i^2 T_i$. For $i = 2, \ldots, k$, we know that $n_i \le q_i$ and $n_i \le \epsilon \cdot r_i$. Hence, comparing D_i with the first term in (2), we get

$$(1 + \epsilon)(q_i r_i T_i + q_i L_i + r_i(n_i T_i - L_i)) \ge C_i \ge q_i r_i T_i + q_i L_i + r_i(n_i T_i - L_i) \quad (3)$$

To prove the statement in Theorem 4, it suffices to find a tour that is within $(1 + \epsilon)$ of the lower bound in the RHS of the above inequality 3. The expression for the lower bound on the RHS of inequality 3 is a linear combination of TSP and Latency values of the tour in segment i. We can apply Lemma 5 to obtain a tour composed of $O(\log n_i/\epsilon)$ TSP tours. This tour is within $(1 + \epsilon)$ factor of the lower bound on C_i.

A technical detail in this argument is that the coefficient of L_i could be negative. Lemma 5 does not handle this case. But note that $n_i T_i - L_i$ is the total "reverse" latency in segment i with the rightmost endpoint being the root. Thus we can rewrite the lower bound as a linear combination of T_i and $n_i T_i - L_i$ with positive coefficients.

We can thus replace each segment i, with a concatenation of $O(\log n_i/\epsilon)$ TSP tours, without increasing the cost by more than a factor of $(1 + \epsilon)$. Since there are $O(\log n/\epsilon)$ segments in all, it follows that there is an embedding consisting of $O(\log^2 n/\epsilon^2)$ shortest TSP tours.

Finally, we show how to reduce this number down to $O(\log n/\epsilon^2)$. Let us rewrite the lower bound in (3) as $(q_i - r_i)L_i + (q_i + n_i)r_i T_i$. Note that $L_i \le n_i T_i$. This gives us that the term $(q_i - r_i)L_i$ is at most $\epsilon \cdot (q_i + n_i)r_i T_i$, whenever $q_i - r_i$ is positive. Hence, if we replace the segment i with a shortest TSP tour on those vertices, the cost will be within $(1 + \epsilon)$ of the lower bound in (3). It is easy to check that, for $i \ge 1/\epsilon$, we have $q_i \ge r_i$. Hence for $i = 1, \ldots, 1/\epsilon$, using

Lemma 5, we replace each segment by a concatenation of $O(\log n/\epsilon)$ tours each. Then for the segments i and above, we use only one minimum TSP tour. Overall this results in a concatenation of $O(\log n/\epsilon^2)$ tours with near-optimal average distortion.

Note that, an optimal TSP tour of the tree is an Euler tour. In other words, each edge is crossed exactly twice, once in each direction. As a consequence, we have the following.

Theorem 5. *There exists a non-contracting embedding of a tree metric into a line with average distortion at most $(1 + \epsilon)$ times the minimum possible that, when viewed as a walk, crosses every tree edge $O(\log n/\epsilon^2)$ times.*

Now using dynamic programing using these structural results proves the following theorem.

Theorem 6. *For any given $\epsilon > 0$, there is an algorithm that runs in time $n^{O(\log n/\epsilon^2)}$ and computes a non-contracting embedding of a given input tree metric into a line with average distortion at most $(1 + \epsilon)$-times the minimum.*

Proof. (Sketch)
We now describe the quasi-polynomial-time approximation scheme based on dynamic programming. Theorem 5 can be restated in terms of crossings of vertices. Consider a separator vertex for the tree. We will denote the partition of the tree at the centroid as the left and right parts. There exists a near optimal embedding that, when viewed as a tour, crosses the separator node from left half to right half $O(\log n/\epsilon^2)$ times.

We develop a dynamic program based on the above observation. Given the input tree, we try each vertex as the starting point of our tour. In order to compute the tour, we first find a separator node in the tree. For the dynamic program, we maintain the following state space. Consider the sub-tours formed between successive places where we cross the separator node. We guess the number of nodes and the length for each of these sub-tours. Note that since there are only $O(\log n/\epsilon^2)$ crossings, there are only $n^{O(\log n/\epsilon^2)}$ choices for the number of nodes. Moreover, the length of each tour can take at most $O(\log n/\epsilon)$ different values. Thus the number of choices for the length are bounded by about $O((\log n)^{\log n})$. Thus the total size of state space is $n^{O(\log n/\epsilon^2)}$. Finding the best tour given the lengths of sub-tours can be done by recursing on the left and right parts independently. For each of these sub-tours, we want to visit all the vertices while staying on one side throughout. The total running time of this procedure is $n^{O(\log n/\epsilon^2)}$.

4   Open Problems and Discussion

It is important to note that a non-contracting embedding can be converted to a non-expanding embedding by scaling down all the distances. However, the converse is not true, since in non-expanding embeddings, the host metric could be a semi-metric. In other words, mapping two points in the guest metric to the same point in the host metric is allowed. This represents a crucial difference between the two problems.

For the case of non-contracting embeddings considered in the paper, here are some open questions :

(1) Is there a simpler and better approximation algorithm for minimizing average distortion in trees?

(2) Can the Quasi-PTAS be extended to (outer)planar graphs?

(3) A different but related objective function is sum of the distortions of all pairs over all non-contracting embeddings. Are there approximation algorithms for this objective?

(4) For the case of weighted average distance, we can write a linear program based on the spreading metric LP for minimum linear arrangement (á la Rao & Richa [32]). However, the integrality gap of this LP is as yet unknown.

References

1. Richa Agarwala, Vineet Bafna, Martin Farach, Babu O. Narayanan, Mike Paterson, and Mikkel Thorup. On the approximability of numerical taxonomy (fitting distances by tree metrics). In *SODA*, pages 365–372, 1996.

2. Noga Alon, Richard M. Karp, David Peleg, and Douglas West. A graph-theoretic game and its application to the k-server problem. *SIAM J. Comput.*, 24(1):78–100, 1995.

3. Aaron Archer, Asaf Levin, and David P. Williamson. A faster, better approximation algorithm for the minimum latency problem. In *Cornell ORIE Technical Report number 1362*, 2003.

4. Aaron Archer and David P. Williamson. Faster approximation algorithms for the minimum latency problem. In *SODA*, 2003.

5. Sanjeev Arora. Polynomial time approximation schemes for Euclidean traveling salesman and other geometric problems. *Journal of the ACM*, 45(5):753–782, 1998.

6. Sanjeev Arora and George Karakostas. Approximation schemes for minimum latency problems. In *Proceedings of the ACM STOC*, pages 688–693, 1999.

7. Yonatan Aumann and Yuval Rabani. An o(log k) approximate min-cut max-flow theorem and approximation algorithm. *SIAM J. Comput.*, 27(1):291–301, 1998.

8. Yair Bartal. Probabilistic approximations of metric spaces and its algorithmic applications. In *IEEE FOCS*, pages 184–193, 1996.

9. Yair Bartal, Avrim Blum, Carl Burch, and Andrew Tomkins. A polylog(n)-competitive algorithm for metrical task systems. In *Proceedings of STOC*, pages 711–719, 1997.

10. Avrim Blum, Prasad Chalasani, Don Coppersmith, Bill Pulleyblank, Prabhakar Raghavan, and Madhu Sudan. The minimum latency problem. In *Proceedings of the ACM STOC*, pages 163–171, 1994.

11. Avrim Blum, Goran Konjevod, R. Ravi, and Santosh Vempala. Semi-definite relaxations for minimum bandwidth and other vertex-ordering problems. In *Proceedings of the 30th ACM STOC*, pages 100–105, 1998.

12. J. Bourgain. On lipshitz embedding of finite metric spaces in hilbert space. *Israel J. Math.*, 52:46–52, 1985.

13. Gruia Calinescu, Howard J. Karloff, and Yuval Rabani. Approximation algorithms for the 0-extension problem. In *SODA*, pages 8–16, 2001.
14. Jittat Fakcharoenphol, Chris Harrelson, and Satish Rao. The k-traveling repairman problem. In *SODA: 14thACM-SIAM Symposium on Discrete Algorithms*, 2003.
15. Jittat Fakcharoenphol, Satish Rao, and Kunal Talwar. A tight bound on approximating arbitrary metrics by tree metrics. In *Proceedings of the 35th Annual ACM STOC*, pages 448–455, 2003.
16. Martin Farach, Sampath Kannan, and Tandy Warnow. A robust model for finding optimal evolutionary trees. *Algorithmica*, 13(1/2):155–179, 1995.
17. Uriel Feige. Approximating the bandwidth via volume respecting embeddings (extended abstract). In *Proc. 30th ACM STOC*, pages 90–99, 1998.
18. Garg, Konjevod, and Ravi. A polylogarithmic approximation algorithm for the group steiner tree problem. In *SODA*, 1998.
19. N. Garg. Personal communication, Spetember 2000.
20. Goemans and Kleinberg. An improved approximation ratio for the minimum latency problem. In *SODA*, 1996.
21. Anupam Gupta. Steiner nodes in trees don't (really) help. In *SODA*, 2001.
22. Piotr Indyk. Algorithmic aspects of geometric embeddings. In *IEEE FOCS*, 2001.
23. Philip N. Klein and R. Ravi. A nearly best-possible approximation algorithm for node-weighted steiner trees. *J. Algorithms*, 19(1):104–115, 1995.
24. Jon M. Kleinberg and Eva Tardos. Approximation algorithms for classification problems with pairwise relationships: Metric labeling and markov random fields. In *IEEE FOCS*, pages 14–23, 1999.
25. E. L. Lawler, J. K. Lenstra, A. H. G. Rinnooy Kan, and editors D. B. Shmoys. *The Traveling Salesman Problem*. John Wiley & Sons, 1985.
26. F. T. Leighton and S. Rao. An approximate max-flow mincut theorem for uniform multicommodity flow problems with applications to approximation algorithms. In *Proc. of the 29th IEEE FOCS*, pages 422–431, 1988.
27. Nathan Linial, Eran London, and Yuri Rabinovich. The geometry of graphs and some of its algorithmic applications. *Combinatorica*, 15:215–245, 1995.
28. J. Matoušek. Bi-lipschitz embeddings into low dimensional euclidean spaces. *Comment. Math. Univ. Carolinae*, 31(3):589–600, 1990.
29. J. Matoušek. *Lectures on Discrete Geometry*. Springer-Verlag, 2002.
30. Y. Rabinovich. On average distortion of embedding metrics into l_1 and into the line. In *35th Annual ACM STOC*, 2003.
31. Y. Rabinovich and R. Raz. Lower bounds on the distortion of embedding finite metric spaces in graphs. *GEOMETRY: Discrete & Computational Geometry*, 19, 1998.
32. Satish Rao and Andrea Richa. New approximation techniques for some ordering problems. In *SODA*, 1998.
33. R.A. Sitters. The minimum latency problem is np-hard for weighted trees. In *W.J. Cook, A.S. Schulz (eds.), Integer Programming and Combinatorial Optimization, Lecture Notes in Computer Science 2337*, pages 230–239, 2002.
34. R.T. Wong. Worst-case analysis of network design problem heuristics. *SIAM Journal Alg. Disc. Math*, 1(1):51–63, 1980.

Digraphs Exploration with Little Memory

Pierre Fraigniaud and David Ilcinkas

CNRS, LRI, Université Paris-Sud, 91405 Orsay, France.
{pierre,ilcinkas}@lri.fr

Abstract. Under the robot model, we show that a robot needs
$\Omega(n \log d)$ bits of memory to perform exploration of digraphs with n
nodes and maximum out-degree d. We then describe an algorithm that
allows exploration of any n-node digraph with maximum out-degree d
to be accomplished by a robot with a memory of size $O(nd \log n)$ bits.
Under the agent model, we show that digraph exploration cannot be
achieved by an agent with no memory. We then describe an exploration
algorithm for an agent with a constant-size memory, using a whiteboard
of size $O(\log d)$ bits at every node of out-degree d.

1 Introduction

A mobile entity (e.g., a software agent or a robot) has to *explore* a graph by
visiting all its nodes and traversing all edges, without any a *priori* knowledge
of the topology of the graph nor of its size. Once exploration is completed,
the mobile entity has to stop. We also consider the more demanding task of
exploration with return in which the entity has to return to its original position,
and the auxiliary easier task of *perpetual exploration* in which the entity has to
traverse all edges of the graph but is not required to stop. The task of visiting all
nodes of a network is fundamental in searching for data stored at unknown nodes
of a network, and traversing all edges is often required in network maintenance
and when looking for defective components. Perpetual exploration may be of
independent interest, e.g., if regular control of a network for the presence of
faults is required, and all edges must be periodically traversed over long periods
of time.

If nodes and edges have unique labels, exploration can be easily done (e.g., by
depth-first search). However, in some navigation problems in unknown environments such unique labeling may not be available, or limited sensory capabilities
of the mobile entity may prevent it from perceiving such labels. Hence it is important to be able to program the entity to explore *anonymous* graphs, i.e., graphs
without unique labeling of nodes or edges. Arbitrary graphs cannot be explored
under such weak assumptions, as witnessed by the case of a cycle: without any
labels of nodes and without the possibility of putting marks on them, it is clearly
impossible to explore a cycle of unknown size and stop. Hence, we assume, as
in [5,6,11], some ability of marking nodes. More precisely we consider two different models. In the *robot model*, the mobile entity is given the ability of dropping
and removing indistinguishable *pebbles* at nodes. This model aims to capture the

V. Diekert and M. Habib (Eds.): STACS 2004, LNCS 2996, pp. 246–257, 2004.

behavior of a robot in a labyrinth. In the *agent model*, the mobile entity is given the ability to read and write messages at memory locations available at each node, called *whiteboards*. This model aims to capture the behavior of a software agent in a computer network. Observe that the robot model is weaker than the agent model since a robot that is given k pebbles acts as a software agent in a network with whiteboards of size one bit, in which at most k whiteboards can simultaneously contain a 1.

Clearly the robot has to be able to *locally* distinguish ports at a node: otherwise it is impossible to explore even the star with 3 leaves (after visiting the second leaf the robot cannot distinguish the port leading to the first visited leaf from that leading to the unvisited one). Hence we make a natural assumption that all ports at a node are locally labeled $1, \ldots, d$, where d is the degree of the node. No coherence between those local labelings is assumed.

In many applications, robots and mobile agents are meant to be simple, often small, and inexpensive devices which limits the amount of memory with which they can be equipped. As opposed to numerous papers that imposed no restrictions on the memory of the robot and sought exploration algorithms minimizing time, i.e., the number of edge traversals, we investigate the minimum size of the memory of the robot that allows exploration of graphs of given (unknown) size, regardless of the time of exploration. That is, we want to find an algorithm for a mobile entity performing exploration using as little memory as possible, i.e., we want to minimize the memory of the robot in the robot model, and we want to minimize both the amount of information transported by the agent and the size of the whiteboards in the agent model. In the latter case, our specific goal is to design an exploration algorithm for an agent with constant memory size, using small whiteboards.

1.1   Our Results

Under the robot model, we first prove a lower bound of $\Omega(n \log d)$ bits of memory for perpetual exploration of n-node digraphs with maximum out-degree d. This lower bound holds even if the robot is given a linear amount of pebbles. We then present two algorithms for exploration with stop in digraphs. One requires $O(nd \log n)$ bits of memory, and uses one pebble. This algorithm is only $O(\log n)$ away from the optimal in constant-degree digraphs. Its time performance is however exponential (again, time is measured by the number of edge traversals). Hence, we also describe another algorithm, which performs exploration with stop in polynomial time, but requires $O(n^2 d \log n)$ bits of memory, and uses $O(\log \log n)$ pebbles. This latter algorithm is a variant of the algorithm in [5], designed for the purpose of compressing the robot memory. Note that it has been proved [5] that $\Omega(\log \log n)$ pebbles are required to explore in polynomial time, thus our algorithm is optimal with regard to the number of pebbles.

Under the agent model, we first prove that exploration with stop cannot be achieved by an oblivious agent, i.e., an agent carrying no information when moving from one node to another. However, we describe an algorithm for an agent with constant size memory. It performs exploration with return in all digraphs, using a whiteboard of size $O(\log d)$ at every node of out-degree d. Note that $\Omega(\log d)$ bits is a lower bound for the size of the whiteboards when using an agent with constant-size memory. Indeed, an agent with a memory of size $k = O(1)$ and a whiteboard of size $k' = o(\log d)$ generate at most $2^{k+k'} < d$ states, and hence not all out-going edges can be distinguished. Our algorithm is also optimal according to the following criteria. We mentioned before the lower bound of $\Omega(n \log d)$ bits of memory for exploration in digraphs under the robot model. Therefore our algorithm under the agent model demonstrates that the memory of the robot can be optimally distributed among the n nodes of the digraph. This is in contrast with other contexts (e.g., compact routing) in which there is a penalty for the distribution of a centralized data structure.

1.2   Related Work

Exploration and navigation problems for robots in an unknown environment have been extensively studied in the literature (cf. [14]). There are two groups of models for these problems. In one of them a particular geometric setting is assumed. Another approach is to model the environment as a graph, assuming that the robot may only move along its edges. The graph setting can be further specified in two different ways. In [1,5,6,9] the robot explores strongly connected directed graphs and it can move only in the direction from head to tail of an edge, not vice-versa. In [2,7,10,11,12,16] the explored graph is undirected and the robot can traverse edges in both directions. (See also [13] an the references therein where parallel search is investigated.) In the graph setting it is often required that apart from completing exploration the robot has to draw a map of the graph, i.e., output an isomorphic copy of it.

Graph exploration scenarios considered in the literature differ in an important way: it is either assumed that nodes of the graph have unique labels which the robot can recognize, or it is assumed that nodes are anonymous. It is impossible to explore arbitrary anonymous graphs if no marking of nodes is allowed. Hence the scenario adopted in [5,6] was to allow *pebbles* which the robot can drop on nodes to recognize already visited ones, and then remove them and drop in other places. The authors concentrated attention on the minimum number of pebbles allowing efficient exploration and mapping of arbitrary directed n-node graphs. (In the case of undirected graphs, one pebble suffices for efficient exploration [11].) In [6] the authors compared exploration power of one robot with pebbles to that of two cooperating robots. In [5] it was shown that, to perform exploration in polynomial time, one pebble is enough if the robot knows an upper bound on the size of the graph. However, without the knowledge of any bound on the size of the graph, $\Theta(\log \log n)$ pebbles are necessary and sufficient for exploration in polynomial time.

The efficiency measure adopted in most papers dealing with graph exploration is the completion time of this task, measured by the number of edge traversals. On the other hand, there are no restrictions imposed on the memory of the robot. Minimizing the memory of the robot for the exploration of anonymous non-directed graphs has been addressed in, e.g., [8,10,16,17]. Most of previous works deal with perpetual exploration. For instance, it is shown in [17] that, with no pebble, no finite set of finite automata can perform perpetual exploration of all cubic planar graphs. Using a pebble, exploration with stop of undirected graphs is much facilitated by the ability of backtracking. In particular, it is easy to design an exploration algorithm for a robot with $O(D \log d)$ bits of memory, where D denotes the diameter of the graph. Also, a simple variant of the algorithm in [11] yields a bound $O(n \log d)$ bits. Better bounds are known for specific families of graphs. For instance, it is shown in [10] that exploration with stop in n-node trees requires a robot with memory size $\Omega(\log \log \log n)$, and that exploration with return in n-node trees can be achieved by a robot with $O(\log^2 n)$ bits of memory. Our paper focuses on directed graphs.

It is worth mentioning that our work has connections with derandomized random walks (cf. [10] and the references therein). There, the objective is to produce an explicit universal traversal sequence (UTS), i.e., a sequence of port labels, such that the path guided by this sequence visits all edges of any graph. However, without the a priori knowledge of n, non of these UTS allows the robot to stop. Moreover, even if bounds on the length of these sequences have been derived, they provide little knowledge on the minimum number of states for graph exploration by a robot. For instance, sequences of length $\Omega(n \log n)$ are required to traverse all degree 2 graphs with n nodes [3], although a 2-state robot can explore all degree-2 graphs.

2   Terminology and Models

An anonymous graph (resp., digraph) with locally labeled ports is a connected graph (resp., strongly connected digraph) whose nodes are unlabeled, and edges incident to a node v have distinct labels $1,...,d$, where d is the degree of v. Thus every undirected edge $\{u, v\}$ has two labels which are called its port numbers at u and at v. Port numbering is local: there is no relation between labels at u and at v. In digraphs, edges out-going from a node v have distinct labels $1,...,d$, where d is the out-degree of v. Edges incoming to a node v are not labeled at v.

We are given a mobile entity traveling in an anonymous (di)graph with locally labeled ports. The graph and its size are a priori unknown to the entity. We consider the two following models.

Robot model. The mobile entity is called a *robot*. A robot with k-bit memory is a finite automaton of $K = 2^k$ states among which a specified state S_0 is called *initial* and some specified states are called *final*. The robot is originally given a source of indistinguishable pebbles. If the robot is in a node v in a non-final state S, this state determines a local port number p, and the decision of dropping a pebble at v, removing a pebble from v (if such a pebble is currently present at v), or doing nothing. Then the robot leaves the node by port p. Upon traversing the corresponding edge, the behavior of the robot differs depending whether the graph is directed or not.

In graphs, the robot reads the port number i at the node it enters, and the degree d of this node. It also detect the presence or not of a pebble at this node,

$b = 0$ if no pebble, and $b = 1$ otherwise. The triple (i, d, b) is an input symbol that causes the transition from state S to S'.

In digraphs, the robot reads the out-degree d of the node it enters, and check the presence or not of a pebble at this node. The pair (d, b) is an input symbol that causes the transition from state S to S'.

In both cases, the robot continues moving in this way until it enters a final state for the first time. Then it stops.

Agent model. The mobile entity is called *agent*. An agent with k-bit memory is a pair $(\mathcal{P}, \mathcal{M})$ where $\mathcal{P}$ is a constant size program, and $\mathcal{M}$ is a memory of size k bits. In the agent model, every node is given computing facilities, including CPU and q bits of local memory. The local memory is called *whiteboard*. Initially, all whiteboards are empty, and the agent memory contains an *initial* k-bit binary string s_0. Every pair agent-node forms a system that acts as a finite automaton of 2^{k+q} states. A state of the system is a pair $S = (s, \omega)$ where s is the content of the agent memory, and ω is the content of the whiteboard. This includes some specified states called *final*. When the system is in a non-final state S, the agent is operated as follows. The state S determines a local port number p, a k-bit binary string s, and a q-bit binary string ω. Then ω is written on the whiteboard, s is stored in the agent memory, and the agent is sent through port p. Upon reception of the agent by a node, the operation performed by that node differs depending whether the graph is directed or not.

In graphs, let i be the port number through which the agent enters the current node. Let d be the degree of that node, and let s and ω be the current contents of the agent memory and the node whiteboard. The pair (i, d) is an input symbol that causes transition of the system from state $S = (s, \omega)$ to $S' = (s', \omega')$ by application of program $\mathcal{P}$.

In digraphs, the out-degree d is an input symbol that causes the transition from state $S = (s, \omega)$ to $S' = (s', \omega')$ by application of program $\mathcal{P}$. (There is no access to the input port number.)

In both cases, the agent continues moving in this way until it enters a final state for the first time. Then it stops.

Remark. Most of our exploration algorithms under the robot model actually perform in the weakest version of the model, i.e., when the robot is given a unique pebble.

We consider three tasks of increasing difficulty: *perpetual exploration* in which the mobile entity has to traverse all edges of the (di)graph but is not required to stop, *exploration with stop* (often simply called *exploration* in this paper) in which starting at any node of the graph, the entity has to traverse all edges and stop at some node, and *exploration with return* in which starting at any node of the graph, the entity has to traverse all edges and stop at the starting node. An entity is said to perform one of the above tasks in a (di)graph, if starting at *any* node of this graph in the initial state, it completes this task in finitely many steps. (Notice that in the case of perpetual exploration, completing this task after finitely many steps means only traversing all edges, not necessarily stopping after it.) We compute the memory requirement of an exploration algorithm by measuring either the size of the robot memory in the robot model, or both the size of the agent memory and the size of the whiteboards in the agent model.

Terminology. A one-to-one and onto mapping f between the two sets of nodes V and V' of two edge-labeled graphs $G = (V, E)$ and $G' = (V', E')$ is an *isomorphism* if, for every two nodes x and y in V: $(x, y) \in E \Leftrightarrow (f(x), f(y)) \in E'$, and the two edges have the same label. In the *map drawing* problem, the robot (resp., the agent) has to compute an edge-labeled graph G such that G is isomorphic to X where X is the unknown edge-labeled graph that the robot (resp., the agent) is exploring. Given two digraphs G and X, and two nodes u and x of G and X, respectively, we note $(G, u) \cong (X, x)$ if there exists an isomorphism f between G and X, such that $f(u) = x$.

3 Exploration of Directed Graphs under the Robot Model

We first prove a lower bound on the size of the robot memory. The proof uses the digraph *combination lock* (see, e.g., [15]) defined as follows.

Definition 1. *The* combination lock $L_{d,n}$ *is a regular digraph of out-degree d, and order n. The n nodes $u_0, u_1, \ldots, u_{n-1}$ are connected as follows. For every $i < n - 1$, node u_i has one out-going edge pointing to u_{i+1}, and $d - 1$ out-going edges pointing to u_0. Node u_{n-1} has all its d out-going edges pointing to u_0.*

Theorem 1. *Perpetual exploration in n-node digraphs of maximum out-degree $d > 2$ cannot be accomplished by a robot with less than $\Omega(n \log d)$ bits of memory, even if it is given up to n pebbles. For $d = 2$, the result holds even if the robot is given up to $n/2$ pebbles.*

Proof. Let us given d and n, and a robot able to explore all n-node digraphs of maximum out-degree d, thus including all distinct edge-labeled combination locks $L_{d,n}$. Assume that the robot is given k pebbles, $k \geq 1$. A *full run* of the robot in $L_{d,n}$ is a run of the robot along the path $u_0, u_1, \ldots, u_{n-1}$. For every edge-labeled combination lock, place the robot at node u_0, and let us consider the state of the robot at u_0 before its first full run. (For each exploration, there are at least d full runs since node u_{n-1} must be reached at least d times to traverse its d out-going edges.) Since the n nodes u_i, $i = 0, \ldots, n - 1$, look identical to the robot up to the presence of a pebble, the ability to perform a full run is determined by the state of the robot just before leaving node u_0, and by the positions of the k pebbles. There are d^{n-1} different labelings of the edges (u_i, u_{i+1}), $i = 0, \ldots, n - 2$, and $p = \sum_{i=0}^{k} \binom{i}{n}$ possible positions for the pebbles. Therefore, the robot must be able to be in at least d^{n-1}/p different states at u_0. Thus it must have at least $\lceil (n-1) \log d - \log p \rceil$ bits of memory. Since $p \leq 2^n$, the result follows for $d > 2$. For $d = 2$, we use the fact that $\binom{a}{b} \leq (\frac{ae}{b})^b$ for $0 < a < b$, where $\ln e = 1$. Since $k \leq n/2$, we have $p \leq k(\frac{ke}{n})^n$, and thus $\log p \leq \log k + n \log(\frac{ke}{n})$. We have $k \leq n/2 < 2n/e$, thus $\log p < \log n + \alpha n$ with $\alpha < 1$, which completes the proof. $\qquad\square$

Note that our exploration algorithms use much less than $O(n)$ pebbles. One of them uses only one pebble, and the other uses $O(\log \log n)$ pebbles. We first sketch the description of an exploration algorithm, called Test-all-maps, satisfying the following:

Theorem 2. *Under the robot model, Algorithm* Test-all-maps *accomplishes exploration with stop in any digraph with a robot using one pebble, and whose memory does not exceed $O(nd \log n)$ bits in n-node digraphs of maximum out-degree d.*

We first sketch the description of Algorithm Test-all-maps and later prove that it satisfies the statement of Theorem 2.

Algorithm Test-all-maps. The robot successively tries every value for n, starting at $n = 1$. For a fixed n, the robot tries all possible maps of edge-labeled digraphs of order n. For a given map $G = (V, E)$, with $V = \{v_1, \ldots, v_n\}$, the robot proceeds as follows. Let x be the current position of the robot in the unknown digraph X, and assume that the robot holds the pebble. The robot chooses node $v_1 \in V$, and tests whether it is standing on node v_1 of G, i.e., whether $(G, v_1) \cong (X, x)$. This is done thanks to the use of Procedure Check-Consistency that will be detailed later in the text. This procedure takes as input a graph G and a node v of G, and tests whether the robot is currently standing at v in G. If the test succeeds, then the exploration stops. Otherwise, the robot chooses another node $v_2 \in V$, and tests whether $(G, v_2) \cong (X, x)$. Observe that during Procedure Check-Consistency, the robot moves in the graph X, and thus, since the procedure failed for v_1, there is no guarantee that the robot is yet standing at node x of X. Hence, the robot uses a linear array position, of size n, such that position[i] is the index j of the node $v_j \in V$ where the robot would be now standing *if* the original position x of the robot would satisfy $x = v_i$. Assuming x is node v_2 of G, the robot would now stand on node v_j, $j = $ position[2]. The robot thus executes procedure Check-Consistency with input (G, v_j). If the procedure succeeds, then the exploration stops. Otherwise, the robot chooses the next node v_3, and tests whether $(G, v_3) \cong (X, x)$. The robot thus executes procedure Check-Consistency with input (G, v_j) where $j = $ position[3]. This process is carried on until either a test is eventually satisfied, or all nodes of G have been exhausted. In the latter case, the robot picks the next map, and repeats the same scenario until if finds the map of the a *priori* unknown explored digraph. Now, we describe procedure Check-Consistency.

Procedure Check-Consistency(G, u). Given the map of an edge-labeled graph $G = (V, E)$, with n nodes and maximum out-degree d, and given a node u of G, Procedure Check-Consistency checks whether the robot is currently standing at node u of G, i.e., whether $(G, u) \cong (X, x)$ where x is the current position of the robot in the unknown digraph X. The procedure borrows from [5] the technique of marking nodes of a cycle. However, this technique is implemented without the use of a large data-structure. More precisely, the robot assigns numbers, from 1 to

m, to all the $m \leq nd$ edges of the map G, with the additional condition that the edge labeled 1 is out-going from u, and the edge labeled m is incoming to u (such an edge does exist because G is strongly connected). Thus $E = \{e_1, \ldots, e_m\}$. For every $i \in \{1, \ldots, m-1\}$, the robot computes a shortest path P_i in the map G starting from the head of edge e_i to the tail of edge e_{i+1}. During Procedure Check-Consistency, the paths P_i's are computed on-line, and at most one path is stored at any given time in the robot memory. Let C be the following closed walk starting and ending at u: $C = e_1, P_1, \ldots, e_{m-1}, P_{m-1}, e_m$. This walk will be traversed several times during the execution of Procedure Check-Consistency. C is thus recomputed several times by the robot, and when P_i is computed, the robot forgets about path P_{i-1}.

There are at most n phases in Procedure Check-Consistency, one for every node of G. (The procedure assumes that the robot holds the pebble. Otherwise, the robot runs Procedure Find-Pebble described later.) For every phase there is a new *considered* node. During Phase i, the robot leaves u with the pebble, and follows the edges of C until it visits a node v in G that has not yet been *considered* during the $i - 1$ previous phases. This node is marked *considered* on the map of G, and the pebble is dropped there. (Hence the first considered node is node u.) Then the robot carries on its walk guided by C until, according to the map, it is back at u. Now, the robot traverses C again. During its way along C, it checks the following property $\mathcal{P}$: the token is at the current node x if and only if x is the considered node v, according to the map of G. If property $\mathcal{P}$ is satisfied for every node of C, then the robot follows C once again to bring the pebble back to u. If there is yet another node to be considered, then the next phase proceeds with this node. Otherwise the robot completes Procedure Check-Consistency as follows. It executes a last journey along C to check whether there is equality between the degree of each node in the map G, and the degree of the corresponding node in the explored graph X. If so, the robot returns success. The robot turns into state failure as soon as it detects a problem at any step (e.g., the pebble is not where it should be, the pebble is where it should not be, the degree-sequences are different in the map and in the explored graph, etc.). As in [5], we have:

Lemma 1. *Given a robot at node x of an anonymous digraph X, Procedure* Check-Consistency *returns* success *for* (G, u) *if and only if* $(G, u) \cong (X, x)$.

If the robot loses the pebble during the execution of Procedure Check-Consistency(G, u), then either the map G is not correct, or it is correct but the robot was not at u. The robot then looks for the pebble by running the following procedure:

Procedure Find-Pebble. The robot computes a (non necessarily simple) closed path P in the map G, visiting all nodes $\{v_1, \ldots, v_n\}$ of G. P is computed on-line, e.g., P is a sequence of sub-paths P_i from v_i to v_{i+1}, $i = 1, \ldots, n-1$, and the P_i's are computed one after the other. The robot traverses the path P several times, successively assuming that it starts from a node v_i of the map, $i = 1, \ldots, n$, and using an array position as in Procedure Test-all-maps. If the robot does not find the pebble, then the current map G is for sure not a map of the explored digraph X. Therefore the robot considers the next map, and looks for the pebble in this new map using the same strategy as above. The robot proceeds this way until it finds the pebble when considering some map H. Once the pebble is found, the robot returns to the execution of Procedure Test-all-maps, and tests the current map H.

Proof of Theorem 2. We prove that the algorithm Test-all-maps can be implemented so not to use more than $O(nd \log n)$ bits of memory in n-node digraphs of maximum out-degree d. It is easy to list all edge-labeled digraphs with at most n nodes and maximum out-degree d using an array of $O(nd \log n)$ bits. Since the cycle $C = e_1, P_1, e_2, P_2, \ldots, e_{m-1}, P_{m-1}, e_m$ visiting all edges of a given map is computed on the fly, and since any path P_i can be encoded by a sequence of at most D labels, where D is the diameter of G, we get that Procedure Check-Consistency requires $O(D \log d) \leq O(n \log d)$ bits of memory for the storage of C. The same holds in Procedure Find-Pebble for the storage of P. Thus the robot does not use more than $O(nd \log n)$ bits of memory in total.   □

The algorithm Test-all-maps performs exploration in exponential time in the worst case (recall that time is counted as the number of edge traversals). Nevertheless, we can describe a variant of Algorithm Explore-and-Map presented in [5]. Although polynomial in time, Explore-and-Map is costly in term of memory space: a rough analysis shows that it requires a memory of $O(n^5 d \log n)$ bits. Our variant is called Compacted-Explore-and-Map. We summarize its performances by the following:

Theorem 3. *For any n-node digraph of maximum out-degree d, Algorithm Compacted-Explore-and-Map accomplishes exploration with stop in polynomial time under the robot model, with a robot using $O(\log \log n)$ pebbles and a memory of size $O(n^2 d \log n)$ bits.*

4   Exploration of Directed Graphs under the Agent Model

This section is dedicated to the agent model, i.e., nodes are given whiteboards on which the agent can read, erase, and write messages. The goal is to limit the sizes of both the agent memory, and the nodes' whiteboards. We first observe that exploration is impossible with an agent that performs obliviously, that is carrying no information from node to node.

Theorem 4. *Under the agent model, exploration with stop cannot be achieved by an agent with zero bit of memory.*

Proof. Assume for the purpose of contradiction that exploration with stop can be achieved by an agent with zero bit of memory. Then consider regular digraphs of out-degree $d \geq 2$. The content ω_i of the whiteboard of a node u at the ith visit of that node by the agent is independent of u. Therefore $\omega_{i+1} = f(\omega_i)$, where f is a function that is uniquely defined by the program $\mathcal{P}$ of the agent. Thus the decision to stop depends only of the number of times the agent visits the same node. Let k be the smallest integer such that ω_k is a final state. Let $L_{d,k+1}$ be the combination lock of out-degree d and order $k + 1$. To traverse all edges incoming to the first node u_0 of $L_{d,k+1}$, the agent must visit node u_0 at least $k + 1$ times. Since it stops at the kth visit, not all edges have been traversed, and thus exploration is not completed, a contradiction.   □

Theorem 5. *Under the agent model, Algorithm* DFS *accomplishes exploration with return in any digraph using an agent with* $O(1)$ *bits of memory.* DFS *uses* $O(\log d)$ *bits of memory per node of out-degree* d.

We first describe Algorithm Next-Port that performs perpetual exploration in any digraph.

Algorithm Next-Port.

1. If the current node whiteboard is empty, then the agent writes 1 on it, and leaves the node through port 1;
2. Otherwise let i be the integer written on the whiteboard, and let d be the out-degree of the node. The program erases the whiteboard, writes $j = (i \bmod d) + 1$ on it, and the agent leaves the node through port j;

Lemma 2. *Algorithm* Next-Port *accomplishes perpetual exploration of any digraph using an agent with zero bit of memory, and uses* $O(\log d)$ *bits of memory per node of out-degree* d.

Remark. Algorithm Next-Port is used several times as a sub-routine in Algorithm DFS, and thus will be called with non-empty whiteboards. Nevertheless, it was shown [4] that Algorithm Next-Port is self-stabilizing and thus does not require the whiteboards to be initially empty to eventually perform correctly.

Algorithm DFS. Algorithm DFS performs a depth-first search (DFS) in the graph, using Algorithm Next-Port as a sub-routine. Nodes visited during the DFS are marked visited on their whiteboards. The last visited node is marked last. There is at most one node marked last during the execution of DFS. When exploration starts, the node on which is placed the agent is marked visited and last. It is also marked root. The path from the root to the last node is maintained thanks to port numbers that are stored on the whiteboards during the exploration. This path is called the *main path*. The agent leaves the root through port number 1. The DFS will proceeds by successively traversing incident edges of any node u in order $1, 2, \ldots, d$ where d is the out-degree of u. Before leaving the last node u, the port number through which the agent leaves is stored on u's whiteboard. Assume that the agent then reaches node v. There are two cases, depending on whether node v has been visited or not.

If v has not yet been visited, it is marked visited. The agent then starts Algorithm Next-Port to find the root. From Lemma 2, this task will eventually succeed. From the root, the agent follows the main path and eventually reaches the last node u. There, the mark last is erased from u's whiteboard. The agent then leaves u by the port whose number is stored on u's whiteboard, to reach v again. Node v is marked last. This sequence of instructions is repeated until the agent reaches a node v that has been previously visited during the DFS.

If the agent reaches a node v that is marked visited, it runs Algorithm Next-Port to find the root, and follows the main path from the root to the last node u. Once back at u, there are two sub-cases. If the port number p of the edge leading to v is smaller than the out-degree d of u, then the agent leaves u through port $p+1$, and repeats the same sequence of instructions as described before. If $p = d$, then the agent aims to backtrack. For that purpose, it runs Algorithm Next-Port to return to the root. The goal of the agent is to find the node of the main path that stands just before the node marked last. It marks the root as next, and proceed as follows. From the node marked next, the agent goes down one step along the main path to reach some node w. If w is not marked last, the agent goes back to the root, follows the main path to the node marked next, erases next from the whiteboard of that node, moves to w, and mark w as next. This is repeated until the agent finds the last node. Then it erases the mark last from the whiteboard of that node, goes back to the root using Next-Port, follows the main path until the node marked next, and replaces the mark next by last.

The process above is repeated until all edges out-going from the root have been visited, and the last backtrack leads to the root. Then the robot stops.

Proof of Theorem 5. During the execution of Algorithm DFS, the agent is clearly in a constant number of different states, hence a memory of $O(1)$ bits is enough for the agent. There is a constant number of marks written on each whiteboards. However, the storage of the port numbers of the main path, as well as the local storage used by Algorithm Next-Port (cf. Lemma 2) require whiteboards of size $O(\log d)$ bits.   □

Remark. It is possible to call Algorithm Next-Port only once (amortized), and to use it to construct a tree whose edges are pointing toward the root. Then returning to the root in Algorithm DFS takes a linear time after the first run of Algorithm Next-Port.

5   Conclusion and Further Works

Our algorithm Test-all-maps requires the storage of a test map of the unknown explored digraph. Graph exploration is however a weaker task than map drawing. One may thus expect to find an algorithm using a memory smaller than the size of a map. Another interesting direction of research is the investigation of compact exploration under the constraint that the algorithm must perform in polynomial time (i.e., the mobile entity must perform a polynomial number of edge-traversals). We described an algorithm for polynomial-time exploration, using a robot with a memory of size $O(n^2 d \log n)$ bits. This is however far from the $\Omega(n \log d)$ lower bound, and it would be interesting to determine the exact trade-off between time and memory space for graph exploration.

Acknowledgement. Both authors are supported by the Actions Spécifiques CNRS "Dynamo" and "Algorithmique des grands graphes", and by the project "PairAPair" of the ACI Masses de Données.

References

1. S. Albers and M. R. Henzinger, Exploring unknown environments, SIAM Journal on Computing 29:1164-1188, 2000.
2. B. Awerbuch, M. Betke, R. Rivest and M. Singh, Piecemeal graph learning by a mobile robot, Proc. 8th Conf. on Comput. Learning Theory, pages 321-328, 1995.
3. A. Bar-Noy, A. Borodin, M. Karchmer, N. Linial, and M.Werman, Bounds on universal sequences, SIAM J. Computing, 18(2):268-277, 1989.
4. J. Beauquier, T. Hérault, and E. Schiller, Easy stabilization with an agent, In 5th Workshop on Self-Stabilizing Systems (WSS), Vol. 2194 of LNCS, pages 35-51, Springer-Verlag, 2001.
5. M. Bender, A. Fernandez, D. Ron, A. Sahai and S. Vadhan, The power of a pebble: Exploring and mapping directed graphs, Proc. 30th Ann. Symp. on Theory of Computing (STOC), pages 269-278, 1998.
6. M. Bender and D. Slonim, The power of team exploration: Two robots can learn unlabeled directed graphs, Proc. 35th Ann. Symp. on Foundations of Computer Science (FOCS), pages 75-85, 1994.
7. M. Betke, R. Rivest and M. Singh, Piecemeal learning of an unknown environment, Machine Learning 18:231-254, 1995.
8. L. Budach. Automata and labyrinths. Math. Nachrichten 86:195-282, 1978.
9. X. Deng and C. H. Papadimitriou, Exploring an unknown graph, Journal of Graph Theory 32:265-297, 1999.
10. K. Diks, P. Fraigniaud, E. Kranakis, and A. Pelc. Tree Exploration with Little Memory. To appear in Journal of Algorithms (see also proceedings of the 13th Annual ACM-SIAM Symp. on Discrete Algorithms (SODA), pages 588-597, 2002).
11. G. Dudek, M. Jenkins, E. Milios, and D. Wilkes. Robotic Exploration as Graph Construction. IEEE Transaction on Robotics and Automation 7(6):859-865, 1991.
12. C. Duncan, S. Kobourov and V. Kumar, Optimal constrained graph exploration. In 12th Ann. ACM-SIAM Symp. on Discrete Algorithms (SODA), pages 807-814, 2001.
13. P. Fraigniaud, L. Gasieniec, D. Kowalski, and A. Pelc. Collective Tree Exploration. In 6th Latin American Theoretical Informatics Symposium (LATIN), Buenos Aires, April 2004.
14. A. Hemmerling. Labyrinth Problems. Teubner-Texte zur Mathematik, Bd. 114, Leipzig, 1989.
15. E. Moore. Gedanken-Experiments on Sequential Machines. In Automata Studies, pages 129-153, C. Shannon and J. McCarthy (Eds.), Princeton University Press, 1956.
16. P. Panaite and A. Pelc, Exploring unknown undirected graphs, Journal of Algorithms 33:281-295, 1999.
17. H.-A. Rollik. Automaten in planaren graphen. Acta Informatica 13:287-298, 1980.

Approximate Path Coloring with Applications to Wavelength Assignment in WDM Optical Networks*

Ioannis Caragiannis and Christos Kaklamanis

Research Academic Computer Technology Institute and
Department of Computer Engineering and Informatics
University of Patras, 26500 Rio, Greece

Abstract. Motivated by the wavelength assignment problem in WDM optical networks, we study path coloring problems in graphs. Given a set of paths P on a graph G, the path coloring problem is to color the paths of P so that no two paths traversing the same edge of G are assigned the same color and the total number of colors used is minimized. The problem has been proved to be NP-hard even for trees and rings.

Using optimal solutions to fractional path coloring, a natural relaxation of path coloring, on which we apply a randomized rounding technique combined with existing coloring algorithms, we obtain new upper bounds on the minimum number of colors sufficient to color any set of paths on any graph. The upper bounds are either existential or constructive.

The existential upper bounds significantly improve existing ones provided that the cost of the optimal fractional path coloring is sufficiently large and the dilation of the set of paths is small. Our algorithmic results include improved approximation algorithms for path coloring in rings and in bidirected trees. Our results extend to variations of the original path coloring problem arizing in multifiber WDM optical networks.

1 Introduction

We study path coloring problems in graphs. Let P be a set of paths on a graph G and $k > 0$ be an integer. The paths of P and the edges of G may be directed or undirected. The path k-coloring problem (or, simply, path coloring when $k = 1$) is to assign colors to the paths of P in such a way that at most k paths with the same color share an edge of the graph and the total number of colors is minimized. The problem has been proved to be NP-hard, even for $k = 1$ and even for the simplest topologies of rings and trees. Thus, approximation algorithms are essential.

The problem has application to Wavelength Division Multiplexing (WDM) optical networks [18]. Such networks consist of nodes connected with fibers. Connection requests are pairs of nodes to be thought of as transmitter-receiver

---

* This work was partially funded by the European Union under IST FET Project ALCOM–FT, IST FET Project CRESCCO and RTN Project ARACNE.

V. Diekert and M. Habib (Eds.): STACS 2004, LNCS 2996, pp. 258–269, 2004.
© Springer-Verlag Berlin Heidelberg 2004

pairs. For each connection request, WDM technology routes the request through a transmitter-receiver path and assigns this path a wavelength, in such a way that paths going through the same fiber are assigned different wavelengths. Recently, the multifiber WDM network model was introduced [6,15,12]. In these networks each fiber of the standard model is replaced by k identical "parallel" fibers.

For path coloring problems, bounds on the number of colors are usually expressed as a function of the load of the set of paths given as input, i.e., the maximum number of paths going through any edge of the graph. Erlebach et al. [5] present an algorithm that colors any set of paths of load L on a bidirected tree with at most $5L/3$ colors. Auletta et al. [1] present a randomized algorithm that colors any set of paths of load L on a bidirected binary tree of depth $o(L^{1/3})$ with at most $7L/5 + o(L)$ colors, with high probability. In rings, Tucker's algorithm [19] colors any set of paths of load L with $2L$ colors or with $\lceil \frac{l-1}{l-2} L \rceil + 1$ colors where l is the minimum number of paths necessary to cover the ring, as shown recently in [13,20]. The interested reader may refer to [2] for a survey on path coloring results motivated by WDM optical networks.

Upper bounds of $(1 + 1/k)\frac{L}{k} + c_k$ (where c_k depends only on k) for path k-coloring in rings are presented in [15,12]. The results in [5,1] can be trivially modified to give $\lceil \frac{5L}{3k} \rceil$ and $\frac{7L}{5k} + o(L/k)$ upper bounds for path k-coloring in arbitrary and binary bidirected trees, respectively. Note that L/k is a lower bound on the minimum number of colors necessary to k-color any set of paths of load L. Thus, by dividing the upper bound on the number of colors achieved by an algorithm by L/k we obtain an upper bound on its approximation ratio.

Another approach is to design approximation path coloring algorithms which use optimal fractional colorings to obtain provably good approximations of the optimal path coloring. Given a set of paths on a graph, we may think of the path k-coloring problem as the problem of covering the paths by as few as possible k-independent sets of paths, i.e., sets of paths in which at most k paths share an edge of the graph. This can be captured by the following integer linear program

$$\text{minimize } \sum_{I \in \mathcal{I}} x(I)$$
$$\text{subject to } \sum_{I \in \mathcal{I}: p \in I} x(I) \geq 1 \; p \in P$$
$$x(I) \in \{0, 1\} \qquad I \subset \mathcal{I}$$

where $\mathcal{I}$ denotes the set of the k-independent sets of P. This formulation has a natural linear programming relaxation by substituting the integrality constraint by $x(I) \geq 0$. The corresponding combinatorial problem is called the fractional (path) k-coloring problem [3,8] and any feasible solution to the linear program is called a fractional k-coloring of P. Given a set of paths P on a graph G, we denote by $w_k(P, G)$ and $f_k(P, G)$ the cost of the optimal solution of the integer linear program and its relaxation, respectively. Alternatively, one may see the (fractional) path coloring problem for a set of paths P on a graph G as a (fractional) graph coloring problem on the conflict graph of P, i.e., the graph which has a node for each path of P and an edge between two nodes if the corresponding paths traverse the same edge on G.

In general, fractional path coloring is hard to approximate while it can be approximated within α in polynomial time provided that α-approximate indepedent sets can be computed efficiently [8,9,10]. The techniques of [8,9,10] can be applied to fractional path k-colorings as well. However, they constitute general ways for approximating the optimal objective value of the corresponding linear program with an exponential number of variables while, in approximation algorithms for path coloring, a provably good solution for fractional path coloring (the values of the variables of the corresponding linear program) is rounded to an integral one which gives a path coloring. So, previous work (as well as this paper) seeks for formulations of fractional path coloring as a linear program with a polynomial number of variables.

The work of Kumar [11] on the path coloring problem in rings (also known as circular arc coloring problem) uses a reduction to instances of integral multicommodity flow due to Tucker [19]. Kumar solves the relaxation of the multicommodity flow problem optimally (this is equivalent to computing the optimal fractional coloring almost exactly) and then performs randomized rounding [17] to obtain the path coloring. The resulting path coloring is proved to be within $1.37 + o(1)$ of the optimal number of colors.

In [3], it is shown that the fractional path coloring can be solved in polynomial time in bounded-degree bidirected trees. By applying a randomized rounding method similar to that used by Kumar and using the algorithm of Erlebach et al. [5] as a subroutine, a $(1.613 + o(1))$-approximation algorithm is obtained.

The contribution of this paper can be summarized as follows:

- We introduce a new randomized rounding method applied to fractional path k-colorings. For the analysis, we study a generalization of a classical occupancy problem which may be of interest in other applications as well.
- Using the randomized rounding we obtain new existential upper bounds on the minimum number of colors sufficient to k-color any set of paths provided that the cost of the optimal fractional coloring is sufficiently large and the dilation (i.e., the length of the longest path) is small. Existential upper bounds for arbitrary k are also obtained for arbitrary trees and rings.
- We also discuss two algorithmic applications of the method. For constant k, we present polynomial time approximation path k-coloring algorithms in bidirected trees of bounded-degree and in rings. Our algorithms improve existing ones provided that the load is not small. The same restriction exists in previous results [3,11]. For WDM networks, this is a realistic assumption.
  - We give a method which computes an almost optimal fractional k-coloring of a set of paths on a bounded-degree bidirected tree. For $k = 1$, this method is slightly weaker than the method in [3] but it is suitable for our purposes. The fractional k-coloring is then used to perform randomized rounding and, using the algorithms in [5] and [1] as subroutines, we obtain $(1.511 + o(1))$- and $(1.336 + o(1))$-approximation algorithms for path k-coloring in bounded-degree and binary trees, respectively.
  - In rings, we present a reduction of path k-coloring to instances of an integral constrained multicommodity flow problem, generalizing in this way Tucker's reduction for $k > 1$. This reduction is used for computing almost optimal fractional k-colorings, which, combined with randomized rounding and existing algorithms [12,13,15,19,20], give better approximation algorithms for path k-coloring ($k \geq 2$) and for special instances of path coloring.

The strength of our randomized rounding technique is that it uses a parameter which can be adjusted according to the approximation ratio of the k-coloring algorithm used as a subroutine. It can be used to give path k-coloring algorithms with improved approximation ratio in any graph (directed or undirected) where the best known upper bound is expressed in terms of the load, provided that an almost optimal fractional k-coloring can be computed efficiently.

The rest of the paper is structured as follows. In Section 2, we present the occupancy problem and study the behavior of related random variables. We present the randomized rounding technique in Section 3 together with its analysis and applications. We devote Section 4 to describe how to compute almost optimal fractional k-colorings in bidirected trees and in rings and how to perform randomized rounding according to them. Due to lack of space, most of the proofs have been omitted. They will be included in the final version of the paper.

2   An Occupancy Problem

In this section, we study the behavior of random variables in a new occupancy problem which generalizes classical "balls-to-bins" processes [16]. This will be very useful for analyzing the performance of our randomized rounding method.

Let $k \geq 1$ be an integer, $n > 0$ be an integer multiple of k and $q > 0$. Consider the following "balls-to-bins" process. We have n/k balls and n bins. Associated with each ball i and each subset of bins s_j of size k is a non-negative number p_{ij} such that $\sum_j p_{ij} = 1$ for any ball i, and $\sum_{i=1}^{n/k} \sum_{j:\ell \in s_j} p_{ij} = 1$ for each bin ℓ. For each ball $i = 1, ..., n/k$, we toss a coin with $\Pr[\text{HEADS}] = q - \lfloor q \rfloor$. On HEADS, we execute $\lfloor q \rfloor + 1$ rounds, otherwise we execute $\lfloor q \rfloor$ rounds. In each round executed for ball i, a subset of bins of size k is selected randomly among all possible subsets according to the probabilities p_{ij}, and one copy of ball i is thrown to each bin of the selected set. We denote by $\mathcal{Q}$ the random variable representing the number of empty bins after the execution of the process and by $\mathcal{R}$ the random variable representing the total number of rounds executed.

Lemma 1

a. $E[\mathcal{Q}] \leq ne^{-q}$

b. For any $\lambda > 0$, $\Pr[|\mathcal{Q} - E[\mathcal{Q}]| > \lambda] \leq 2 \exp\left(-\frac{\lambda^2}{2\lceil q \rceil nk}\right)$

c. $E[\mathcal{R}] = qn/k$

d. If q is not integer, then for any $\lambda > 0$, $\Pr[\mathcal{R} - E[\mathcal{R}] > \lambda] \leq \exp\left(-\frac{\lambda^2 k}{4(q - \lfloor q \rfloor)n}\right)$

3   The Randomized Rounding Technique

In this section we present the randomized rounding technique. The technique is applied to normal sets of paths. A set of (directed) paths P on a network G is called normal if it has the same load on every (directed) edge of G.

The main idea is to round a fractional k-coloring of the set of paths P and obtain a k-coloring of some of the paths of P. In particular, we use a family of fractional k-coloring functions as a representation of a fractional k-coloring.

Definition 2 *Let P be a normal set of paths of load kZ (where Z is an integer). A set of non-negative weight functions x_j for $j = 1, ..., Z$ on the k-independent sets of P is called a family of fractional k-coloring functions for P if*

$$\sum_{I \in \mathcal{I}: p \in I} \sum_{j=1}^{Z} x_j(I) = 1, \text{ for any path } p \in P, \text{ and}$$

$$\sum_{I \in \mathcal{I}} x_j(I) = 1, \text{ for any } j = 1, ..., Z,$$

where $\mathcal{I}$ is the set of the k-independent sets of P.

Observe that if a set of paths P of load kZ (where Z is an integer) on a graph G has a family of fractional k-coloring functions, then it has a fractional k-coloring of cost exactly Z since the weight function x defined as $x(I) = \sum_{i=1}^{Z} x_i(I)$ for $I \in \mathcal{I}$, is a fractional k-coloring of P of cost Z. The opposite also holds as the following lemma states.

Lemma 3 *Let $k \geq 1$ be an integer constant and let P be a normal set of paths of load kZ (where Z is integer) on a graph G. Given a fractional k-coloring x of P of cost Z, we can construct a family of fractional k-coloring functions y_j for $j = 1, ..., Z$.*

The following lemma implies that, for any set of paths, there exists a superset which has a family of fractional k-coloring functions.

Lemma 4 *Let $k > 0$ be an integer and let P be a set of paths on a graph G. Consider the normal set of paths P' of load $k(1 + \lceil f_k(P, G) \rceil)$ on G obtained by adding single-hop paths to P. It is $f_k(P', G) = 1 + \lceil f_k(P, G) \rceil$.*

We are now ready to describe the randomized rounding technique. The technique applies to normal sets of paths having a family of fractional k-coloring functions. On input a set of paths P of load $kf_k(P, G)$ (where $f_k(P, G)$ is integer) on a graph G, the randomized rounding technique uses a parameter $q > 0$ and a family of fractional k-coloring functions x_i, $i = 1, ..., f_k(P, G)$ for P to properly k-color some of the paths of P as follows. Initially, all paths of P are uncolored. For each $i = 1, ..., f_k(P, G)$, randomized rounding proceeds by tossing a coin with $\Pr[\text{HEADS}] = q - \lfloor q \rfloor$. On HEADS, it executes $\lfloor q \rfloor + 1$ rounds, otherwise it executes $\lfloor q \rfloor$ rounds. In each round associated with some i, a k-independent set is selected by casting a die with a face for each k-independent set with $x_i(I) > 0$ and probability $x_i(I)$ associated with the face corresponding to the k-independent set I. At the end of the round, all the paths of the selected k-independent set which are still uncolored are colored with a new color.

In the rest of this section we will use the randomized rounding technique either to prove existential upper bounds on the minimum number of colors sufficient to k-color a set of paths or to obtain polynomial time approximation algorithms for k-coloring sets of paths using a provably small number of colors.

3.1   Existential Upper Bounds

An upper bound of $f_k(P,G)(1+\ln(km))$ for $w_k(P,G)$ can be obtained by using the techniques of Lovász [14]. In the following we give better upper bounds for $w_k(P,G)$ provided that $f_k(P,G)$ is sufficiently large.

Lemma 5 *Let P be a set of paths on a graph G with $m > 3$ edges, $k > 0$ be an integer and β be such that*

$$\beta \geq \max_{P'\subseteq P}\left\{\frac{kw_k(P',G)}{L(P',G)}\right\}$$

where $L(P',G)$ denotes the load of the set of paths P' on G. If $f_k(P,G) = \Omega\left(\frac{\beta^2\ln m}{\ln\beta}\right)$, then $w_k(P,G) \leq f_k(P,G)O(\ln\beta)$, and, if $f_k(P,G) = \omega\left(\frac{\beta^2\ln m}{\ln\beta}\right)$, then $w_k(P,G) \leq f_k(P,G)(1+\ln\beta+o(1))$.

Proof. Let P' be the normal set of paths of load $k(1 + \lceil f_k(P,G)\rceil)$ obtained by adding single-hop paths to P. By Lemma 4, it is $f_k(P',G) = 1 + \lceil f_k(P,G)\rceil$ and P' has a family of fractional k-coloring functions x_i for $i = 1, ..., 1 + \lceil f_k(P,G)\rceil$. We apply randomized rounding to P' with $q = \ln\beta$ using the family of fractional k-coloring functions x_i. We define $Z = 1 + \lceil f_k(P,G)\rceil$.

Let $\mathcal{R}$ be the random variable denoting the number of rounds, e be an edge of G and $\mathcal{Q}_e$ be the random variable representing the number of paths traversing e which are left uncolored after the application of randomized rounding. We may view the randomized rounding as a balls-to-bins process like the one described in Section 2. The random variable $\mathcal{R}$ corresponds to the number of rounds in the balls-to-bins process. The paths traversing edge e are the bins and the paths of the k-independent set traversing e which are selected during a round correspond to copies of a ball thrown into the k corresponding bins. The probabilities on the sets of k bins where copies of balls are thrown in the corresponding balls-to-bins process are defined by the family of fractional k-coloring functions. Thus, the random variable $\mathcal{Q}_e$ corresponds to the number of empty bins in the balls-to-bins process.

By Lemma 1, we obtain that $E[\mathcal{R}] = Z\ln\beta$ and that, for any $\lambda > 0$, the probability that $\mathcal{R} \geq E[\mathcal{R}] + \lambda$ is at most $\exp\left(-\frac{\lambda^2}{4Z}\right)$. By setting $\lambda = 2\sqrt{Z\ln m}$, we have that the probability that the number of colors used during rounding exceeds $Z\ln\beta + 2\sqrt{Z\ln m}$ is at most $1/m$.

Using Lemma 1, we obtain that $E[\mathcal{Q}_e] \leq \frac{kZ}{\beta}$ and that, for any $\lambda > 0$, the probability that $\mathcal{Q}_e \geq E[\mathcal{Q}_e] + \lambda$ is at most $2\exp\left(-\frac{\lambda^2}{2k^2Z\lceil\ln\beta\rceil}\right)$. By setting $\lambda = 2k\sqrt{Z\lceil\ln\beta\rceil\ln m}$, we have that the probability that $\mathcal{Q}_e$ exceeds $\frac{kZ}{\beta} + 2k\sqrt{Z\lceil\ln\beta\rceil\ln m}$ is less than $2/m^2$. Since there are m edges in G, the load of the paths left uncolored after the application of the randomized rounding technique is at most $\frac{kZ}{\beta} + 2k\sqrt{Z\lceil\ln\beta\rceil\ln m}$, with probability at least $1 - 2/m$.

Now, using the definition of β, it can be easily verified that, since the set of paths left uncolored after rounding consists of a subset of the original set of paths P and (possibly) some additional single-hop paths, it can be k-colored with at most β/k times its load colors.

Hence, with probability at least $1 - 3/m > 0$, the total number of colors is at most

$$Z \ln \beta + 2\sqrt{Z \ln m} + Z + 2\beta \sqrt{Z \lceil \ln \beta \rceil} \ln m.$$

The proof completes by observing that if $f_k(P, G) = \Omega\left(\frac{\beta^2 \ln m}{\ln \beta}\right)$ (resp. $\omega\left(\frac{\beta^2 \ln m}{\ln \beta}\right)$), then the sum of the second and the fourth term in the above expression is of order $O(f_k(P, G) \ln \beta)$ (resp. $o(f_k(P, G) \ln \beta)$). $\quad\square$

We will apply Lemma 5 to obtain existential upper bounds for $w_k(P, G)$ in general (directed or undirected graphs) and in bidirected trees.

Theorem 6 *Let P be a set of paths on a graph G with dilation D and $k > 0$ be an integer. If $f_k(P, G) = \Omega\left(\frac{D^2 \ln m}{\ln D}\right)$, then $w_k(P, G) \leq f_k(P, G) O(\ln D)$, and, if $f_k(P, G) = \omega\left(\frac{D^2 \ln m}{\ln D}\right)$, then $w_k(P, G) \leq f_k(P, G)(1 + \ln D + o(1))$.*

Proof. Observe that the conflict graph of any set of paths of dilation D and load L has degree at most $D(L - 1)$ and, hence, can be k-colored with at most $\lceil \frac{DL - D + 1}{k} \rceil$ colors. The proof completes by applying Lemma 5 with $\beta = D$. $\quad\square$

Theorem 7 *Let $k > 0$ be an integer and P be a set of paths of load $\omega(k \ln m)$ on a bidirected tree T with m directed edges. It holds that $w_k(P, T) \leq (1.511 + o(1)) f_k(P, T)$.*

Proof. Erlebach et al. [5] present an algorithm which colors any set of paths of load L on a bidirected tree with at most $5L/3$ colors. Clearly, it can be slightly modified to k-color any set of paths of load L with at most $\lceil \frac{5L}{3k} \rceil$ colors. Thus, we may apply Lemma 5 with $\beta = \frac{5}{3} + \frac{1}{\ln m}$ (observe that the lower bound on the load implies that $f_k(P, T) = \omega(\ln m)$) and obtain the desired bound. $\quad\square$

3.2 Algorithmic Applications

Observe that the path k-coloring algorithm we used in the proof of Lemma 5 would run in polynomial time on input a set of paths P on a graph G if (1) a normal superset P' of P of load $k\lceil f_k(P, G) \rceil$ on G can be computed in polynomial time, (2) die-casting according to a family of fractional k-coloring functions implied by the fractional k-coloring of P' can be performed in polynomial time, and (3) for any set of paths P, a k-coloring of the paths in P with at most β/k times the load of P colors can be computed in polynomial time. Although in both Theorems 6 and 7 property (3) is guaranteed by a polynomial time algorithm, (1) and (2) are infeasible in general unless $P = NP$. This is due to the fact that fractional path coloring is as hard to approximate as fractional graph coloring (it is easy to see that for any graph H, we can construct a set of paths on a graph G having H as its conflict graph) which, in turn, is almost as hard to approximate as graph coloring [8,14]. Moreover, a family of fractional k-coloring functions x_i may have $x_i(I) > 0$ for exponentially many k-independent sets of P.

In Section 4, given a set of paths P on a graph G which is either a bidirected tree of bounded degree or a ring, we show how to construct a normal superset of P of load kZ having a fractional k-coloring of integer cost $Z \leq 1 + \lceil f_k(P,G) \rceil$ and how to perform die-casting according to a family of fractional k-coloring functions implied by this fractional k-coloring, both in polynomial time when $k > 0$ is an integer constant.

For bidirected trees of bounded degree, following this approach, applying randomized rounding with $q = \ln \frac{5}{3} \approx 0.511$, and using the algorithm of Erlebach et al. [5] to k-color the paths left uncolored after the application of randomized rounding, we obtain the following result.

Theorem 8 *Let $k \geq 1$ be an integer constant. There exists a polynomial-time algorithm which, on input a set of paths P of load $\omega(\ln m)$ on a bounded-degree bidirected tree with m directed edges, computes a $(1.511 + o(1))$-approximate k-coloring of P, with high probability.*

For sets of paths of load L on binary trees of depth $o(L^{1/3})$, there exists a randomized algorithm that colors them using at most $7L/5 + o(L)$ colors, with high probability [1]. Thus, we may follow the same approach used for bounded-degree trees, apply randomized rounding with $q = \ln \frac{7}{5} \approx 0.336$, and use this randomized algorithm to k-color the paths left uncolored to obtain the following result.

Theorem 9 *Let $k \geq 1$ be an integer constant. There exists a polynomial-time algorithm which, on input a set of paths P of load $\omega(\ln m)$ on a binary bidirected tree with m directed edges and of depth $o(L^{1/3})$, computes a $(1.336 + o(1))$-approximate k-coloring of P, with high probability.*

We now present an improved approximation for some instances of the path coloring problem in rings. On input a set of paths P on a ring, we use randomized rounding with $q = \ln \frac{l-1}{l-2}$ where l is the minimum number of paths of P necessary to cover the ring, and Tucker's algorithm [19] to color the paths left uncolored after randomized rounding. Li and Simha [13] and, independently, Valencia-Pabon [20] show that Tucker's algorithm colors P with at most $\lceil \frac{l-1}{l-2} L \rceil + 1$ colors. We obtain the following result.

Theorem 10 *There exists a polynomial-time algorithm which, on input a set of paths P of load $\omega(\ln m)$ on a ring with m edges, computes a $\left(1 + \ln \frac{l-1}{l-2} + o(1)\right)$-approximate coloring of P, with high probability, where l is the minimum number of paths in P necessary to cover the ring.*

For sets of paths with $l \geq 5$, the approximation ratio of our algorithm is better than the approximation ratio of the algorithms in [11], [20], and [13].

We can also improve the best known approximation ratio for k-coloring of sets of paths in rings by using randomized rounding with $q = \ln(1 + 1/k)$ and an algorithm presented in [15,12] to complete the k-coloring. This algorithm k-colors any set of paths of load L on a ring using at most $\left(1 + \frac{1}{k}\right) \frac{L}{k} + c_k$ colors (where c_k may depend on k). We obtain the following result.

Theorem 11 *Let $k \geq 2$ be an integer constant. There exists a polynomial-time algorithm which, on input a set of paths P of load $\omega(\ln m)$ on a ring with m edges, computes a $(1 + \ln(1 + 1/k) + o(1))$-approximate k-coloring of P, with high probability.*

4   Computing Families of Fractional k-Coloring Functions

In this section, given a set of paths P on a bounded-degree tree or on a ring, we show how to compute normal supersets of P of load kZ which have a fractional k-coloring of integer cost $Z \leq 1 + \lceil f_k(P, G) \rceil$.

In both cases, we follow the same augmentation procedure. Starting with a set of paths P of load L on a network G, we construct a normal superset P_0 of P having load the first multiple of k greater or equal to L (i.e., $k\lceil L/k \rceil$). This is done by adding single-hop paths traversing the edges of the tree which are not fully loaded. We run a procedure called checker on the set of paths P_0. The checker returns YES if the set of paths taken as input has a fractional k-coloring of cost equal to its load over k; it returns NO otherwise. If the checker returns NO, we continue this procedure for $i = 1, 2, ...$, by constructing a normal superset P_i of P of load $k(i + \lceil L/k \rceil)$ and running the checker on P_i, until it returns YES.

By Lemma 4, we know that the augmentation procedure terminates after at most $2 + \lceil f_k(P, G) \rceil - \lceil L/k \rceil$ executions of the checker. Clearly, $\lceil f_k(P, G) \rceil$ is polynomial in L and the size of the graph. Furthermore, the load of the set of paths given as input to the checker in each execution is also polynomial in L and the size of the graph. In what follows, we will describe how the checker works in bounded-degree bidirected trees and in rings and we will claim that it runs in polynomial time in terms of the load of the set of paths taken as input and the size of the graph. As a result, we will obtain that the whole augmentation procedure runs in polynomial time. In both cases, we can also show how to use the fractional k-coloring computed during the last execution of the checker to perform die-casting in polynomial time according to a family of fractional k-coloring functions implied by this fractional k-coloring. Due to lack of space, formal proofs have been omitted. They will be included in the final version of the paper.

4.1   Bidirected Trees

In this section, we will describe the checker TREE-k-CHECKER for checking whether a normal set of paths P of load L which is a multiple of k on a bidirected tree T has a fractional k-coloring of cost L/k.

Given a non-leaf node v of the tree, consider the subset P_v of P containing the paths that touch node v. We denote by $\mathcal{I}(P_v)$ the set of all k-independent sets of paths of P_v which have full load k on each directed edge adjacent to v. TREE-k-CHECKER constructs the linear program described in the following:

The linear program has a non-negative weight $x(I)$ for each k-independent set of $\mathcal{I}(P_v)$, for any non-leaf node v of the tree. The objective is to maximize the sum of the weights of the k-independent sets of $\mathcal{I}(P_r)$, where r is a specific non-leaf node of T. There are constraints of two types. The first type of constraints is that, for each path $p \in P$ and for each non-leaf node v it touches, the sum of the weights of the k-independent sets of $\mathcal{I}(P_v)$ it belongs to is constrained to be at most 1. The second type of contraints is that, for any pair of adjacent non-leaf nodes v and u of the tree, and any set of k paths $p_1, ..., p_k$ traversing the directed edge (v, u) and any set of k paths $q_1, ..., q_k$ traversing the opposite directed edge (u, v), the sum of the weights of the k-independent sets of $\mathcal{I}(P_u)$ that contain $p_1, ..., p_k, q_1, ...q_k$ is constrained to be equal to the sum of weights of the k-independent sets of $\mathcal{I}(P_v)$ that contain $p_1, ..., p_k, q_1, ...q_k$.

TREE-k-CHECKER solves the above linear program and returns YES if it has a solution of cost L/k. Otherwise, it returns NO.

Lemma 12 *Let $k > 0$ be an integer constant. On input a normal set of paths P of load L which is a multiple of k on a bidirected tree T of bounded degree, TREE-k-CHECKER runs in polynomial time and returns YES iff P has a fractional k-coloring of cost L/k.*

Now consider the application of the augmentation procedure on the original set of paths P of load L on the tree T using TREE-k-CHECKER as checker. We denote by $P_{Z-\lceil L/k \rceil}$ the normal set of paths of load kZ (where Z is an integer) produced when the augmentation procedure terminates. By the definition of the augmentation procedure and by Lemma 12, it is clear that $Z = \lceil f_k(P_{Z-\lceil L/k \rceil}, T) \rceil$ which, by Lemma 4, is at most $1 + \lceil f_k(P, T) \rceil$.

When the augmentation procedure terminates we use the solution of the linear program to implicitly build a family of fractional k-coloring functions and perform die-casting according them. We can show that this can be done in polynomial time.

4.2   Rings

In this section, we describe the checker RING-k-CHECKER. It receives as input a normal set of paths P of load L which is a multiple of k on a ring C with m edges and checks whether P has a fractional k-coloring of cost L/k.

We denote by $e_0, e_1, ..., e_{m-1}$ the edges of the ring C (edges e_i and $e_{i+1 \bmod m}$ are consecutive), by P_{e_i} the subset of P consisted of the paths of P traversing edge e_i, and by $\mathcal{I}(P_{e_i})$ the set of all subsets of P_{e_i} of size k. Note that each set of paths in $\mathcal{I}(P_{e_i})$ is a k-independent set. RING-k-CHECKER considers the following multicommodity flow network $H(P, C)$.

The network has $m + 1$ levels of nodes. Levels $0, ..., m - 1$ correspond to the edges $e_0, e_1, ..., e_{m-1}$ of the ring C while level m corresponds to edge e_0 of C as well. In each of these levels corresponding to the edge e_i, the network has $N = \binom{L}{k}$ nodes; one node per each k-independent set of $\mathcal{I}(P_{e_i})$. For each node u of level $i < m$ corresponding to a k-independent set I, we define the forward set of u to be the set of paths of I which traverse edge $e_{i+1 \bmod m}$. For each node u of level $i > 0$ corresponding to a k-independent set I, we define the backward set of u to be the set of paths of I which traverse edge e_{i-1}. The network $H(P,C)$ has a directed edge from a node u of level i to a node v of level $i + 1$ iff the forward set of u is the same with the backward set of v. The network $H(P,C)$ has N commodities. Each node of level 0 is the source of a commodity. The sink for each commodity is located at the node of level m which corresponds to the same k-independent set of $\mathcal{I}(P_{e_0})$ with its source.

RING-k-CHECKER solves the maximum multicommodity flow problem on the network $H(P,C)$ under the constraint that for each path p of P, and for each edge e_i traversed by p, the total flow entering (leaving) all the nodes of $H(P,C)$ of level i corresponding to k-independent sets of $\mathcal{I}(P_{e_i})$ that contain the path p is at most 1. RING-k-CHECKER returns YES if there is a total flow of size L/k. Otherwise, it returns NO.

Lemma 13 *Let $k > 0$ be an integer constant. On input a normal set of paths P of load L which is a multiple of k on a ring C, RING-k-CHECKER runs in polynomial time and returns YES iff P has a fractional k-coloring of cost L/k.*

Now consider the application of the augmentation procedure on the original set of paths P of load L on the ring C using RING-k-CHECKER as checker. We denote by $P_{Z-\lceil L/k\rceil}$ the normal set of paths of load kZ (where Z is an integer) produced when the augmentation procedure terminates. By the definition of the augmentation procedure and by Lemma 13, it is clear that $Z = \lceil f_k(P_{Z-\lceil L/k\rceil}, C)\rceil$ which, by Lemma 4, is at most $1 + \lceil f_k(P,C)\rceil$.

When the augmentation procedure terminates, we use the solution to the multicommodity flow problem on the network $H(P_{Z-\lceil L/k\rceil}, C)$ to obtain a fractional k-coloring x. This is done by decomposing the flow for each commodity on $H(P_{Z-\lceil L/k\rceil}, C)$ into flow paths, mapping the flow paths into k-independent sets of $P_{Z-\lceil L/k\rceil}$, and assigning to each of these k-independent sets I weight $x(I)$ equal to the flow carried by the corresponding flow path. Using x, we can obtain a family of fractional k-coloring functions y_j for $P_{Z-\lceil L/k\rceil}$ and perform die-casting according them. Again, we can show that this can be done in polynomial time.

References

1. V. Auletta, I. Caragiannis, C. Kaklamanis, P. Persiano. Randomized Path Coloring on Binary Trees. *Theoretical Computer Science*, Vol. 289(1), pp. 355–399, 2002.
2. B. Beauquier, J.-C. Bermond, L. Gargano, P. Hell, S. Perennes, U. Vaccaro. Graph Problems arising from Wavelength-Routing in All-Optical Networks. In *Proc. of the 2nd Workshop on Optics and Computer Science (WOCS '97)*, 1997.
3. I. Caragiannis, A. Ferreira, C. Kaklamanis, S. Perennes, H. Rivano. Fractional Path Coloring with Applications to WDM Networks. In *Proc. of the 28th International Colloquium on Automata, Languages, and Programming (ICALP '01)*, LNCS 2076, Springer, pp. 732–743, 2001.

4. T. Erlebach and K. Jansen. The Complexity of Path Coloring and Call Scheduling. *Theoretical Computer Science*, Vol. 255(1-2), pp. 33-50, 2000.
5. T. Erlebach, K. Jansen, C. Kaklamanis, M. Mihail, and P. Persiano. Optimal Wavelength Routing in Directed Fiber Trees. *Theoretical Computer Science*, Vol. 221(1-2), pp. 119-137, 1999.
6. A. Ferreira, S. Perennes, A.W. Richa, H. Rivano, and N. Stier Moses. Models, Complexity and Algorithms for the Design of Multifiber WDM Networks. *Telecommunication Systems*, Vol. 24(2), 123-138, 2003.
7. M.R. Garey, D.S. Johnson, G.L. Miller, and C.H. Papadimitriou. The Complexity of Coloring Circular Arcs and Chords. *SIAM Journal on Alg. Disc. Math.*, Vol. 1(2), pp. 216-227, 1980.
8. M. Grötschel, L. Lovász, and A. Schrijver. The Ellipsoid Method and its Consequences in Combinatorial Optimization. *Combinatorica*, Vol. 1, pp. 169-197, 1981.
9. K. Jansen. Approximate Strong Separation with Application in Fractional Graph Coloring and Preemptive Scheduling. *Theoretical Computer Science*, Vol. 302(1-3), pp. 239-256, 2003.
10. K. Jansen and L. Porkolab. On Preemptive Resource Constrained Scheduling: Polynomial-Time Approximation Schemes. In *Proc. of the 9th International Conference on Integer Programming and Combinatorial Optimization (IPCO '02)*, LNCS 2337, Springer, pp. 329-349, 2002.
11. V. Kumar. An Approximation Algorithm for Circular Arc Coloring. *Algorithmica*, Vol. 30(3), pp. 406-417, 2001.
12. G. Li and R. Simha. On the Wavelength Assignment Problem on Multifiber WDM Star and Ring Networks. *IEEE/ACM Transactions on Networking*, Vol. 9(1), pp. 60-68, 2001.
13. G. Li and R. Simha. On Bounds for the Wavelength Assignment Problem on Optical Ring Networks. *Journal of High-Speed Networks*, Vol. 8(4), pp. 303-309, 1999.
14. L. Lovász. On the Ratio of Optimal Integral and Fractional Covers. *Discrete Mathematics*, Vol. 13, pp. 383-390, 1975.
15. L. Margara and J. Simon. Wavelength Assignment Problem on All–Optical Networks with k Fibers per Link. In *Proc. of the 27th International Colloquium on Automata, Languages, and Programming (ICALP '00)*, LNCS 1853, Springer, pp. 768–779, 2000.
16. R. Motwani, P. Raghavan. Randomized Algorithms. *Cambridge University Press*, 1995.
17. P. Raghavan, C.D. Thompson. Randomized Rounding: A Technique for Provably Good Algorithms and Algorithmic Proofs. *Combinatorica*, 7, pp. 365–374, 1987.
18. R. Ramaswami, K. Sivarajan. Optical Networks: A Practical Perspective. *Morgan Kauffman Publishers*, 1998.
19. A. Tucker. Coloring a Family of Circular Arcs. *SIAM Journal of Applied Mathematics*, Vol. 29(3), pp. 493–502, 1975.
20. M.E. Valencia–Pabon. Revisiting Tucker's Algorithm to Color Circular–Arc Graphs. *Electronic Notes on Discrete Mathematics*, 2000.

An Algorithmic View on OVSF Code Assignment*

Thomas Erlebach[1], Riko Jacob[2], Matúš Mihaľák[1], Marc Nunkesser[2],
Gábor Szabó[2], and Peter Widmayer[2]

[1] Department of Information Technology and Electrical Engineering, ETH Zürich,
{erlebach,mihalak}@tik.ee.ethz.ch
[2] Department of Computer Science, ETH Zürich,
{jacob,nunkesser,szabog,widmayer}@inf.ethz.ch

Abstract. The combinatorial core of the OVSF code assignment problem that arises in UMTS is to assign some nodes of a complete binary tree of height h (the code tree) to n simultaneous connections, such that no two assigned nodes (codes) are on the same root-to-leaf path. Each connection requires a code on a specified level. The code can change over time as long as it is still on the same level. We consider the one-step code assignment problem: Given an assignment, move the minimum number of codes to serve a new request. Minn and Siu proposed the so-called DCA-algorithm to solve the problem optimally. We show that DCA does not always return an optimal solution, and that the problem is NP-hard. We give an exact $n^{O(h)}$-time algorithm, and a polynomial time greedy algorithm that achieves approximation ratio $\Theta(h)$. Finally, we consider the online code assignment problem for which we derive several results.

1 Introduction

Recently UMTS[1] has received a lot of attention, and also raised new algorithmic problems. In this paper we focus on a specific aspect of its air interface W-CDMA[2] that turns out to be algorithmically interesting, more precisely on its multiple access method DS-CDMA.[3] The purpose of this access method is to enable all users in one cell to share the common resource, i.e. the bandwidth. In DS-CDMA this is accomplished by a spreading and scrambling operation. Here we are interested in the spreading operation that spreads the signal and separates the transmissions from the base-station to the different users. More precisely, we consider spreading by Orthogonal Variable Spreading Factor (OVSF-) codes [1, 14]. These codes are derived from a code tree. The OVSF-code tree is a complete binary tree of height h that is constructed in the following way: The root is

---

* Research partially supported by TH-Project TH-46/02-1 (Mobile phone antenna optimization: theory, algorithms, engineering, and experiments).
[1] Universal Mobile Telecommunications System, for more details see [14,17].
[2] Wideband Code Division Multiple Access
[3] Direct Sequence Code Division Multiple Access

V. Diekert and M. Habib (Eds.): STACS 2004, LNCS 2996, pp. 270–281, 2004.
© Springer-Verlag Berlin Heidelberg 2004

labeled with the vector (1), the left child of a node labeled a is labeled with (a, a), and the right child with $(a, -a)$. Each user in one cell is assigned a different OVSF-code. The key property that separates the signals sent to the users is the *mutual orthogonality* of the users' codes. All assigned codes are mutually orthogonal if and only if there is at most one assigned code on each leaf-to-root path. In DS-CDMA users request different data rates and get OVSF-codes of different levels. (The data rate is inversely proportional to the length of the code.) In particular, it is irrelevant which code on a level a user gets, as long as all assigned codes are mutually orthogonal. We say that an assigned code in a node in the tree *blocks* all codes in the subtree below it and all codes on the path to the root, see Fig. 1 for an illustration.

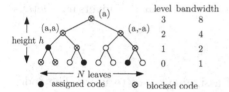

Fig. 1. A code assignment and blocked codes

Fig. 2. A code insertion on level 2 into a single code tree T

As users connect to and disconnect from a given base station, i.e. request and release codes, the code tree can get fragmented. Then it can happen that a code request for a higher level cannot be served at all, because lower level codes block *all* codes on this level. For example in Fig. 1 no code can be inserted on level 2 without reassigning another code, even though there is enough available bandwidth. This problem is known as *code blocking* or *code-tree fragmentation* [17,18]. One way of solving this problem is to reassign some codes in the tree (more precisely, to assign alternative OVSF-codes of the same level to some users in the cell). In Fig. 2 some user requests a code on level two, where all codes are blocked. Still, after reassigning some of the assigned codes as indicated by the dashed arrows, the request can be served. Here and in many of the following figures we only depict the relevant parts (subtrees) of the single code tree.

The process of reassigning codes necessarily induces signaling overhead from the base station to the users whose codes change. This overhead should be kept small. Therefore, a natural objective already stated in [18,19] is to serve all code requests as long as this is possible, while keeping the number of reassignments as small as possible. (In fact, as long as the bandwidth of all simultaneously active code requests does not exceed the total available bandwidth, it is always possible to serve them.) The problem has been studied before with focus on simulations. In [18] the problem of reassigning the codes for a single additional request is introduced. The Dynamic Code Assignment (DCA) algorithm is presented and claimed to be optimal. In this paper we prove that this algorithm is not always optimal and analyze natural versions of the underlying code assignment (CA) problem. Our intention is to present a first rigorous analysis of this problem.

First, we give a counterexample to the optimality of the DCA-algorithm in Sect. 2, then prove the original problem stated by Minn and Siu to be *NP*-hard for a natural input encoding in Sect. 3. In Sect. 4 we give a dynamic programming algorithm that solves the problem with running time $n^{O(h)}$, where n is the number of assigned codes in the tree. In Sect. 5 we give a sketch of an involved analysis showing that a natural greedy algorithm already mentioned in [18] achieves approximation ratio h for one step. Finally, we tackle the online-problem in Sect. 6, which is a more natural version of the problem. We present a $\Theta(h)$-competitive algorithm and show that the greedy strategy that minimizes the number of reassignments in every step is not better than $\Omega(h)$-competitive. We also give an online-algorithm with constant competitive ratio that uses resource augmentation, i.e. we give it one more level than the adversary. Details omitted in this paper can be found in [9].

1.1   Problem Definition

We consider the combinatorial problem of assigning codes to users. The codes are the nodes of an (OVSF-) code tree $T = (V, E)$. Here T is a complete binary tree of height h. The set of all users using a code at a given moment in time can be modelled by a *request vector* $r = (r_0 \ldots r_h) \in \mathbb{N}^{h+1}$, where r_i is the number of users requesting a code on level i (with bandwidth 2^i). The levels of the tree are counted from the leaves to the root starting at level 0. We denote by $l(v)$ the level of node v. Each request is assigned to a node in the tree, such that for all levels $i \in \{0 \ldots h\}$ there are exactly r_i codes on level i, and on every path p_j from a leaf j to the root there is at most one code assigned. We call every set of positions $F \subset V$ in the tree T that fulfills these properties a *code assignment*. For ease of presentation we also call F the set of *codes*. Throughout this paper, a code tree is the tree together with a code assignment F. If a user connects to the base station, the resulting additional request for a code represents a *code insertion* (on a given level). If some user disconnects, this represents a *deletion* (in a given position). A new request is dropped if it cannot be served. This is the case, if its acceptance would exceed the total bandwidth. By N we denote the number of leaves of T and by n the number of assigned codes $|F|$. After an insertion on level l_t at time t, any CA-algorithm must change the code assignment F_t for request vector r into F_{t+1} for the new request vector $r' = (r_0, \ldots, r_{l_t} + 1, \ldots, r_h)$. The size $|F_{t+1} \setminus F_t|$ corresponds to the number of *reassignments*. Therefore, for an insertion, the new assignment is counted as a reassignment. We define the cost function as the number of reassignments. Deletions are not considered in the cost function. When we want to emphasize the combinatorial side of the problem we call a reassignment a *movement* of a code. We state the original CA problem studied by Minn and Siu together with some of its natural variants:

One-step offline CA. Given a code assignment F for a request vector r and a code request for level l. Find a code assignment F' for the new request vector $r' = (r_0, \ldots, r_l + 1, \ldots, r_h)$ with minimum number of reassignments.

General offline CA. Given a sequence S of code insertions and deletions of length m. Find a sequence of code assignments $\{F_t\}_{t=1}^m$ so that the total number of reassignments is minimum, assuming the initial code tree is empty.

Online CA. This is the same problem as the general offline CA, except that the future requests of S are not known in advance.

1.2 Related Work

It was a paper by Minn and Siu [18] that originally drew our attention to this problem. There the one-step offline version is defined together with an algorithm that is claimed to solve it optimally. As we show in Sect. 2 this claim is not correct. Many of the follow-up papers like [3,5,6,11,12,16,19] acknowledge the original problem to be solved by Minn and Siu and study some other aspects of it. Assarut et al. [3] evaluate the performance of Minn and Siu's DCA-algorithm, and compare it to other schemes. Moreover, a different algorithm is proposed for a more restricted setting in [2]. Other authors use additional mechanisms like time multiplexing or code sharing on top of the original problem setting in order to mitigate the code blocking problem [5,19]. Dell'Amico et al. [8] present a tree partitioning policy resembling the compact representation algorithm of Sect. 6. A different direction is to use a heuristic approach that tackles the problem for small input instances [5]. Kam, Minn and Siu [16] address the problem in the context of bursty traffic and different QoS.[4] They present a notion of "fairness" and also propose to use multiplexing. Priority based schemes for different QoS classes can be found in [7], similar in perspective are [11,12].

Fantacci and Nannicini [10] are among the first to express the problem in its online version, although they have quite a different focus. They present a scheme that is similar to the compact-representation scheme in Sect. 6, without focusing on the number of reassignments. Rouskas and Skoutas [19] propose a greedy online-algorithm that minimizes in each step the number of additionally blocked codes, and provide simulation results but no analysis.

2   Non-optimality of Greedy Algorithms

Here we look at possible greedy algorithms for the one-step offline CA. A straightforward greedy approach is to select for a code insertion a subtree with minimum cost (that is not blocked by a code above the requested level), according to some cost function. All codes in the selected subtree must then be reassigned. So in every step a top-down greedy algorithm chooses the maximum bandwidth code that has to be reassigned, places it at the root of a minimum cost subtree, takes out the codes in that subtree and proceeds recursively. The DCA-algorithm in [18] works in this way. The authors propose different cost functions, among which the "topology search" cost function is claimed to solve the one-step offline CA optimally. Here we show the following theorem:

---

[4] Quality of Service

Theorem 1. *Any top-down greedy algorithm A_{tdg} whose cost function depends only on the current assignment of the considered subtree is not optimal.*

As all proposed cost functions in [18] depend only on the current assignment of the considered subtree, this theorem implies the non-optimality of the DCA-algorithm.

Proof. Our construction considers the subtrees in Fig. 3 and the assignment of a new code to the root of the tree T_0. The tree T_0 has a code with bandwidth $2k$ on level l and depending on the cost function has or does not have a code with bandwidth k on level $l-1$. The subtree T_1 contains $k-1$ consecutive codes at

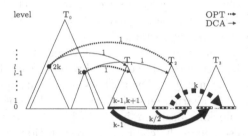

Fig. 3. Example for the proof of Thm. 1

leaf level and the rest of the subtree is empty. The subtrees T_2 and T_3 contain k codes at leaf level interleaved with k free leaves. All other subtrees, in particular, the sibling trees of T_1, T_2 and T_3 (omitted from the figure) have all the leaves assigned. This pairing rules out all cost functions that do not put the initial code at the root of T_0. We are left with two cases:

Case 1: The cost function evaluates T_2 and T_3 as cheaper than T_1. In this case we let the subtree T_0 contain only the code with bandwidth $2k$. Algorithm A_{tdg} reassigns the code with bandwidth $2k$ to the root of the subtree T_2 or T_3, which causes one more reassignment than assigning it to the root of T_1, hence the algorithm fails to produce the optimal solution.

Case 2: The cost function evaluates T_1 as cheaper than T_2 and T_3. In this case we let the subtree T_0 have both codes. A_{tdg} moves the code with bandwidth $2k$ to the root of T_1 and the code with bandwidth k into the tree T_2 or T_3, see solid lines in Fig. 3. The number of reassigned codes is $3k/2 + 2$. But the minimum number of reassignments is $k+3$, achieved when the code with bandwidth k is moved into the empty part of T_1 and the code with bandwidth $2k$ is moved to the root of T_2 or T_3, see dashed lines in Fig. 3.   □

3   *NP*-Hardness of One-Step Offline CA

We prove the decision variant of the one-step offline CA to be *NP*-complete. It asks, if a new insertion can be handled with cost less or equal to $c_{\max}$, which is part of the input. Trivially, the decision variant is in *NP*. *NP*-completeness is established by a reduction from the three-dimensional matching problem.

Problem 1 (3DM). Given a set $M \subseteq W \times X \times Y$, where W, X and Y are disjoint sets having the same number q of elements. Does M contain a matching, i.e., a subset $M' \subseteq M$ such that $|M'| = q$ and no two elements of M' agree in any coordinate? [13]

Let us index the elements of the ground sets W, X, Y from 1 to q. We introduce the *indicator vector* of a triplet (w_i, x_j, y_k) as a zero-one vector of length $3q$ that is all zero except at the indices $i, q+j$ and $2q+k$. The idea of the reduction is to see the triplets as such indicator vectors and to observe that the problem 3DM is equivalent to finding a subset of q indicator vectors from M that sum up to the all-one vector.

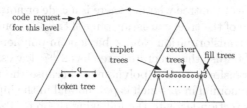

Fig. 4. Sketch of the construction

Figure 4 shows an outline of the construction that we use for the reduction. An input to 3DM is transformed into an initial feasible assignment that consists of a token tree on the left side and different smaller trees on the right. The construction is set up in such a way that the code insertion forces the q codes in the token tree to move to the right side. Then these codes must be assigned to the roots of some *triplet trees*. The choice of the q triplet trees reflects the choice of the corresponding triplets of a matching. All codes in the chosen triplet trees find a place without any additional reassignment, if and only if these triplets represent a 3D matching.

The token tree consists of q codes positioned arbitrarily on level l_{start} with sufficient depth. The triplet trees have their roots on the same level l_{start}. They are constructed from the indicator vectors of the triplets. For each of the $3q$ positions of the vector such a tree has four levels together called a *layer* that encode either zero or one, where the encodings of zero and one are shown in Fig. 5(a) and (b). Figure 5(c) shows how layers are stacked using *sibling trees*.

The receiver trees are supposed to receive all codes moved out of triplet trees. We construct them such that they can absorb from every layer exactly one one-tree and $q - 1$ zero trees and the sibling trees. The codes fit exactly in the free positions, iff the chosen triplets form a 3DM. The exact proof of this statement together with the details of the construction can be found in [9].

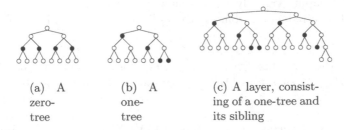

(a) A zero-tree   (b) A one-tree   (c) A layer, consisting of a one-tree and its sibling

Fig. 5. Encoding of zero and one

An interesting question is, whether the transformation from 3DM to the one-step offline CA can be done in polynomial time. This depends on the input encoding of our problem. Two encodings seem natural: a zero-one vector that specifies for every node of the tree whether there is a code or not; or alternatively a sparse representation of the tree, consisting only of the positions of the assigned codes. Obviously, the transformation cannot be done in polynomial time for the first input encoding, because the generated tree has $2^{\mathcal{O}(q)}$ leaves. For the second input encoding the transformation is polynomial, because the total number of generated codes is polynomial in q, which is polynomial in the input size of 3DM. The discussion in this section leads to the following theorem. Its complete proof can be found in [9].

Theorem 2. *The decision variant of the one-step offline CA is NP-complete for an input given by a list of positions of the assigned codes and the code insertion level.*

4   Exact $n^{\mathcal{O}(h)}$ Dynamic Programming Algorithm

In this section we solve the one-step offline CA problem optimally using a dynamic programming approach. The key idea of the algorithm is to store the right information in the nodes of the tree and to build it up in a bottom-up fashion.

We define the *signature* of a subtree T_v with root v as a $l(v) + 1$-dimensional vector $s^v = (s_0^v, \ldots, s_{l(v)}^v)$, in which s_i^v is the number of codes in T_v on level i. A signature s is *feasible* if there exists a subtree T_v with a code assignment that has signature s. The information stored in every node v of the tree consists of a table, in which all possible feasible signatures of an arbitrary tree of height $l(v)$ are stored together with their *cost for T_v*. Here the cost of such a signature s for T_v (usually $s \neq s^v$) is defined as the minimum number of codes in T_v that have to move away from their old position in order to attain some tree T_v' with signature s. To attain T_v' it might be necessary to move codes also into T_v from other subtrees but we do not count these movements for the cost of s for T_v.

Given a code tree T with all these tables computed, one can compute the cost of any single code insertion from the table at the root node r: Let $s^r =$

$(s_0^r, \ldots, s_h^r)$ be the signature of the whole code tree before insertion, then the cost of the insertion on level l is the cost of the signature $(s_0^r, \ldots, s_l^r + 1, \ldots, s_h^r)$ in this table plus one. This follows because the minimum number of codes that are moved away from their positions in T is equal to the number of reassignments minus one.

The computation of the tables starts at the leaf level, where the cost of the one-dimensional signatures is trivially defined. At any node v of level $l(v)$ the cost $c(v, s)$ of signature s for T_v is computed from the cost incurred in the left subtree T_l of v plus the cost incurred in the right subtree T_r plus the cost at v. The costs $c(l, s')$ and $c(r, s'')$ in the subtrees come from two feasible signatures with the property $s = (s_0' + s_0'', \ldots, s_{l(v)-1}' + s_{l(v)-1}'', s_{l(v)})$. Any pair (s', s'') of such signatures corresponds to a possible configuration after the code insertion. The best pair for node v gives $c(v, s)$. Let $s^v = (s_0^v, \ldots, s_{l(v)}^v)$ be the signature of T_v, then it holds that

$$c(v, s) = \begin{cases} c(l, (0, \ldots, 0)) + c(r, (0, \ldots, 0)) & \text{for } s_{l(v)} = 1 \\ \min_{\{s', s'' \mid (s', 0) + (s'', 0) = s\}} (c(l, s') + c(r, s'')) & \text{for } s_{l(v)} = 0, s_{l(v)}^v = 0 \\ 1 & \text{for } s_{l(v)} = 0, s_{l(v)}^v = 1. \end{cases}$$

The costs of all signatures s for v can be calculated simultaneously by combining the two tables in the left and right children of v. Observe for the running time that the number of relevant feasible signatures is bounded by $(n + 1)^h$ because there cannot be more than n codes on any level. The time to combine two tables is $\mathcal{O}(h \cdot n^{2h})$, thus the total running time is bounded by $\mathcal{O}(2^h h \cdot n^{2h})$.

Theorem 3. *The one-step offline CA can be solved optimally in time* $\mathcal{O}(2^h h \cdot n^{2h})$ *and space* $\mathcal{O}(2^h \cdot n^h)$.

5   An h-Approximation for One-Step Offline CA

We analyze a greedy algorithm A_g for one-step offline CA based on the greedy strategy from Sect. 2, where the cost function of the considered subtree is the number of codes in it. The details of its analysis can be found in [9].

We are interested in the approximation ratio of A_g. Let opt denote the number of reassigned codes of an optimal algorithm A_{opt}. For the upper bound we compare A_g to A_{opt}. Let us call the set of subtrees to the root of which A_{opt} moves codes $\mathcal{T}_{opt}$, and the arcs that show how A_{opt} moves the codes the opt-arcs. A sketch of the proof is as follows. First, we show that in every step t A_g has the possibility to assign the codes C_t that remain to be reassigned into $\mathcal{T}_{opt}$. This possibility can be expressed by a code mapping $\phi_t : C_t \to \mathcal{T}_{opt}$. The key-property is that in every step there is the theoretical choice to complete the current assignment using the code mapping ϕ and the opt-arcs as follows: Use ϕ to assign the codes in C_t into positions in $\mathcal{T}_{opt}$ and then use the opt-arcs to move codes out of the subtrees of $\mathcal{T}_{opt}$ to produce a feasible code assignment. This property is enough to ensure that A_g incurs a cost of no more than opt on each level.

For the lower bound there is an example, where the optimal assignment for level l chooses a subtree with 3 leaf codes, whereas A_g always chooses a subtree with 2 codes on level $l-1$. Doing this recursively for every level, we get the lower bound $\Omega(h)$ for the approximation ratio.

Theorem 4. *The algorithm A_g has approximation ratio h.*

6   Online Code Assignment

Here we study the online CA problem. In an *online problem* the input is received in an online manner and the output must be produced online [4]. In the case of the online CA problem the requests for code insertions and deletions must be handled one after another, i.e., the ith request must be served before the $i+1$st request is known. An online algorithm ALG for the CA problem is *c-competitive* if for all finite input sequences I, $\text{ALG}(I) \leq c \cdot \text{OPT}(I)$. In this case the *competitive ratio* of ALG is c.

We give a lower bound on the competitive ratio, analyze an $\mathcal{O}(h)$-competitive algorithm and present a resource augmented algorithm with constant competitive ratio.

Theorem 5. *No deterministic algorithm A for the online CA problem can be better than 1.5-competitive.*

Proof. Let A be any deterministic algorithm for the problem. Consider N leaf insertions. The adversary deletes every other code. Then a code insertion on level $h-1$ causes $N/4$ code reassignments. We proceed with the subtree of full leaf codes recursively and repeat this process $\log_2 N - 1$ times. The optimal algorithm A_{opt} assigns the leaves in such a way that it does not need any extra reassignment at all. Thus, A_{opt} needs $N + \log_2 N - 1$ reassignments, whereas algorithm A needs $3N/2 + \log_2 N - 2$ reassignments. The cost ratio tends to 1.5 as N goes to infinity.   □

One can show that all greedy algorithms for the online problem that minimize the number of code reassignments for every insertion/deletion individually are $\Omega(h)$-competitive [9]. In the following we show an algorithm that achieves competitive ratio $\Theta(h)$ and is easy to implement.

6.1   Compact Representation Algorithm

The algorithm A_{compact} keeps the codes in the tree T ordered from left to right by increasing level of the codes and compact (i.e., no code can be shifted to the left without violating the order constraint).

In the following we show that A_{compact} is $\theta(h)$-competitive. To see this, consider an arbitrary insertion on level l (deletions are handled similarly). A_{compact} inserts the code in the position on level l that is the first after all assigned codes on levels $0, \ldots, l$. This position can be blocked by at most one code from above. A_{compact} takes the code from this position away and assigns it recursively. At most one code per level is reassigned (see Fig. 6).

For the lower bound we consider an example with 2 leaf codes and one code on every higher level. Deleting the level $h-1$ code and inserting a code on level 0,

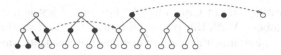

Fig. 6. Reassignment strategy of Algorithm A_{compact}

the algorithm has to move every non leaf code to the right, i.e., it moves $h - 2$ codes. Deleting the 3rd leaf code and inserting the level $h-1$ code, the algorithm has to move all the codes back. Thus the following holds.

Theorem 6. *Algorithm* A_{compact} *is* $\theta(h)$*-competitive.*

6.2   Resource Augmented Online Algorithm

Here we present the online-strategy *3-gap* and study it by a resource-augmented competitive analysis. This type of analysis was introduced in 1995 by Kalyana-sundaram and Pruhs [15]. In a resource-augmented competitive analysis one compares the value of the solution found by the online algorithm when it is provided with more resources to the value of the optimal offline adversary using the original resources. In the case of the OVSF online code assignment problem the resource is the total assignable bandwidth. The strategy *3-gap* uses a tree T' of bandwidth $2b$ to accommodate codes whose total bandwidth is b. By the nature of the code assignment we cannot add a smaller amount of additional resource.

A *gap* is a subtree with no code assigned in it and above it. Algorithm *3-gap* is similar to the compact representation algorithm of Sect. 6.1 (insisting on the ordering of codes according to their level), only that it allows for up to 3 gaps at each level l (instead of only one for aligning), to the right of the assigned codes on l. The algorithm for inserting a code at level l is to place it at the leftmost gap of l. If no such gap exists, we reassign the leftmost code of the next higher level $l + 1$, creating 2 gaps (one of them is filled immediately by the new code) at l. We repeat this procedure toward the root. We reject an insertion if the nominal bandwidth b is exceeded. For deleting a code c on level l we reassign the rightmost code on level l to c, keeping all codes at level l left of the gaps of l. If this results in 4 consecutive gaps, we reassign the rightmost code of $l + 1$, in effect replacing two gaps of l by one of $l + 1$. Again we proceed toward the root. More precisely, we keep for every level a range of codes (and gaps) that are assigned to this level. In every range there are at most 3 gaps allowed. If we run out of space or if there are too many gaps, we move the boundary between two consecutive levels, affecting two places on the lower level and one on the upper level. This notion of a range is in particular important for levels without codes. The levels close to the root are handled differently, to avoid an excessive space usage. The root-code of T' has bandwidth $2b$, it is never used. The bandwidth b code can only be used if no other code is used, there is no interaction with other codes. The $b/2$ codes are kept compactly to the right. In general there is some unused bandwidth between the $b/4$ and the $b/2$ codes, which is not considered a gap. For all other levels ($\leq b/8$ codes) we define a potential-function by counting the number of levels without gaps, and the number of levels having 3 gaps, and adding these numbers. With this potential function it is clear that it is sufficient to charge two (re-)assignments to every insertion or deletion, one for placing the code (filling the gap), and one for the potential function or for moving a $b/4$-bandwidth code. The initial configuration is the empty tree, where the leaf-level has two gaps, and all other levels have precisely one gap (only the close-to-root levels are as described above).

It remains to show that our algorithm manages to host codes as long as the total bandwidth used does not exceed b. To do this, we calculate the bandwidth wasted by gaps, which is at most $3(\frac{b}{8} + \frac{b}{16} + \cdots) \leq 3b/4$. Hence the total bandwidth used in T' is at most $7b/4 < 2b$.

Theorem 7. *Let σ be a sequence of m code insertions and deletions for a code-tree of height h, such that at no time the bandwidth is exceeded. Then the above online-strategy uses a code-tree of height $h + 1$ and performs at most $2m$ code assignments and reassignments.*

Corollary 1. *The above strategy is 4-competitive for resource augmentation by a factor of 2.*

Proof. Any sequence of m operations contains at least $m/2$ insert operations. Hence the optimal offline solution needs at least $m/2$ assignments, and the above resource augmented online-algorithm uses at most $2m$ (re-)assignments, leading to a competitive factor of 4. ☐

This approach might prove to be useful in practice, particularly if the code insertions only use half the available bandwidth.

7   Conclusions and Future Work

In this paper we bring an algorithmically interesting problem from the mobile telecommunications field closer to the theoretical computer science community. We are the first to analyze the computational complexity of the OVSF code assignment problem. Future research on CA could concentrate on the following open problems.

- Is there a constant approximation algorithm for the one-step offline CA?
- Can the gap between the lower bound of 1.5 and the upper bound of $\mathcal{O}(h)$ for the competitive ratio of the online CA be closed?
- Can an optimal algorithm for general offline CA be forced to reassign more than an amortized constant number of codes per insertion or deletion?
- What is the complexity of the general offline CA problem?

References

1. F. Adashi, M. Sawahashi, and K. Okawa. Tree structured generation of orthogonal spreading codes with different length for forward link of DS-CDMA mobile radio. *Electronics Letters*, 33(1):27–28, January 1997.

2. R. Assarut, M. G. Husada, U. Yamamoto, and Y. Onozato. Data rate improvement with dynamic reassignment of spreading codes for DS-CDMA. *Computer Communications*, 25(17):1575–1583, 2002.
3. R. Assarut, K. Kawanishi, R. Deshpande, U. Yamamoto, and Y. Onozato. Performance evaluation of orthogonal variable-spreading-factor code assignment schemes in W-CDMA. In *Proceedings of the IEEE International Conference on Communications (ICC)*, 2002.
4. A. Borodin and R. El-Yaniv. *Online Computation and Competitive Analysis*. Cambridge University Press, 1998.
5. H. Çam. Nonblocking OVSF codes and enhancing network capacity for 3G wireless and beyond systems. *Computer Communications*, 26(17):1907–1917, 2003.
6. W. T. Chen and S. H. Fang. An efficient channelization code assignment approach for W-CDMA. In *IEEE Conference on Wireless LANs and Home Networks*, 2002.
7. W. T. Chen, Y. P. Wu, and H. C. Hsiao. A novel code assignment scheme for W-CDMA systems. In *Proceedings of the 54th IEEE Vehicular Technology Conference (VTC)*, volume 2, pages 1182–1186, 2001.
8. M. Dell'Amico, F. Maffioli, and M. Merani. A tree partitioning dynamic policy for OVSF codes assignment in WCDMA. *IEEE Transaction on Wireless Communications*, to appear.
9. T. Erlebach, R. Jacob, M. Mihal'ák, M. Nunkesser, G. Szabó, and P. Widmayer. An algorithmic view on OVSF code assignment. TIK-Report 173, Computer Engineering and Networks Laboratory (TIK), ETH Zürich, August 2003. Available electronically at ftp://ftp.tik.ee.ethz.ch/pub/publications/TIK-Report173.pdf.
10. R. Fantacci and S. Nannicini. Multiple access protocol for integration of variable bit rate multimedia traffic in UMTS/IMT-2000 based on wideband CDMA. *IEEE Journal on Selected Areas in Communications*, 18(8):1441–1454, August 2000.
11. C. E. Fossa Jr. *Dynamic Code Sharing Algorithms for IP Quality of Service in Wideband CDMA 3G Wireless Networks*. PhD thesis, Virginia Polytechnic Institute and State University, April 2002.
12. C. E. Fossa Jr and N. J. Davis IV. Dynamic code assignment improves channel utilization for bursty traffic in 3G wireless networks. In *Proceedings of the IEEE International Conference on Communications (ICC)*, pages 3061–3065, 2002.
13. M. R. Garey and D. S. Johnson. *Computers and Intractability*. Freeman, 1979.
14. H. Holma and A. Toskala. *WCDMA for UMTS*. Wiley, 2001.
15. B. Kalyanasundaram and K. Pruhs. Speed is as powerful as clairvoyance. In *Proceedings of the 36th IEEE Symposium on Foundations of Computer Science*, pages 214–221, 1995.
16. A. C. Kam, T. Minn, and K.-Y. Siu. Supporting rate guarantee and fair access for bursty data traffic in W-CDMA. *IEEE Journal on Selected Areas in Communications*, 19(11):2121–2130, November 2001.
17. J. Laiho, A. Wacker, and T. Novosad. *Radio Network Planning and Optimisation for UMTS*. Wiley, 2002.
18. T. Minn and K. Y. Siu. Dynamic assignment of orthogonal variable-spreading-factor codes in W-CDMA. *IEEE Journal on Selected Areas in Communications*, 18(8):1429–1440, 2000.
19. A. N. Rouskas and D. N. Skoutas. OVSF codes assignment and reassignment at the forward link of W-CDMA 3G systems. In *Proceedings of the 13th IEEE International Symposium on Personal, Indoor and Mobile Radio Communications*, 2002.

The Syntactic Graph of a Sofic Shift

Marie-Pierre Béal, Francesca Fiorenzi, and Dominique Perrin

Institut Gaspard-Monge, Université de Marne-la-Vallée
77454 Marne-la-Vallée Cedex 2, France
{beal,perrin}@univ-mlv.fr, fiorenzi@mat.uniroma1.it

Abstract. We define a new invariant for the conjugacy of irreducible sofic shifts. This invariant, that we call the syntactic graph of a sofic shift, is the directed acyclic graph of characteristic groups of the non null regular $\mathcal{D}$-classes of the syntactic semigroup of the shift.

Keywords: Automata and formal languages, symbolic dynamics.

1 Introduction

Sofic shifts [17] are sets of bi-infinite labels in a labeled graph. If the graph can be chosen strongly connected, the sofic shift is said to be irreducible. A particular subclass of sofic shifts is the class of shifts of finite type, defined by a finite set of forbidden blocks. Two sofic shifts X and Y are conjugate if there is a bijective block map from X onto Y. It is an open question to decide whether two sofic shifts are conjugate, even in the particular case of irreducible shifts of finite type.

There are many invariants for conjugacy of subshifts, algebraic or combinatorial, see [13, Chapter 7], [6], [12], [3]. For instance the entropy is a combinatorial invariant which gives the complexity of allowed blocks in a shift. The zeta function is another invariant which counts the number of periodic orbits in a shift.

In this paper, we define a new invariant for irreducible sofic shifts. This invariant is based on the structure of the syntactic semigroup of the language of finite blocks of the shift. Irreducible sofic shifts have a unique (up to isomorphisms of automata) minimal deterministic presentation, called the right Fischer cover of the shift. The syntactic semigroup S of an irreducible sofic shift is the transition semigroup of its right Fischer cover.

In general, the structure of a finite semigroup is determined by the Green's relations (denoted $\mathcal{R}, \mathcal{L}, \mathcal{H}, \mathcal{D}, \mathcal{J}$) [16]. Our invariant is the acyclic directed graph whose nodes are the characteristic groups of the non null regular $\mathcal{D}$-classes of S. The edges correspond to the partial order $\leq_{\mathcal{J}}$ between these $\mathcal{D}$-classes. We call it the syntactic graph of the sofic shift. The result can be extended to the case of reducible sofic shifts.

The proof of the invariant is based on Nasu's Classification Theorem for sofic shifts [15] that extends William's one for shifts of finite type. This theorem says that two irreducible sofic shifts X, Y are conjugate if and only if there is a sequence of transition matrices of right Fischer covers $A = A_0, A_1, \ldots, A_{l-1}, A_l = B$, such that A_{i-1}, A_i are elementary strong

V. Diekert and M. Habib (Eds.): STACS 2004, LNCS 2996, pp. 282–293, 2004.
© Springer-Verlag Berlin Heidelberg 2004

shift equivalent for $1 \le i \le l$, where A and B are the transition matrices of the right Fischer covers of X and Y, respectively. This means that there are transition matrices U_i, V_i such that, after recoding the alphabets of A_{i-1} and A_i, we have $A_{i-1} = U_i V_i$ and $A_i = V_i U_i$. A bipartite shift is associated in a natural way to a pair of elementary strong shift equivalent and irreducible sofic shifts [15].

The key point in our invariant is the fact that an elementary strong shift equivalence relation between transition matrices implies some conjugacy relations between the idempotents in the syntactic semigroup of the bipartite shift.

We show that particular classes of irreducible sofic shifts can be characterized with this syntactic invariant: the class of irreducible shifts of finite type and the class of irreducible aperiodic sofic shifts.

Basic definitions related to symbolic dynamics are given in Section 2.1. We refer to [13] or [9] for more details. See also [10], [11], [4] about sofic shifts. Basic definitions and properties related to finite semigroups and their structure are given Section 2.2. We refer to [16, Chapter 3] for a more comprehensive expository. Nasu's Classification Theorem is recalled in Section 2.3. We define and prove our invariant in Section 3. A comparison of this syntactic invariant to some well known other ones is given in Section 4. Proofs of Propositions 1 and 2 are omitted. The extension to the case of reducible sofic shifts is discussed at the end of Section 3.

2   Definitions and Background

2.1   Sofic Shifts and Their Presentations

Let $\mathcal{A}$ be a finite alphabet, i.e. a finite set of symbols. The shift map $\sigma : \mathcal{A}^{\mathbb{Z}} \to \mathcal{A}^{\mathbb{Z}}$ is defined by $\sigma((a_i)_{i \in \mathbb{Z}}) = (a_{i+1})_{i \in \mathbb{Z}}$, for $(a_i)_{i \in \mathbb{Z}} \in \mathcal{A}^{\mathbb{Z}}$. If $\mathcal{A}^{\mathbb{Z}}$ is endowed with the product topology of the discrete topology on $\mathcal{A}$, a *subshift* is a closed σ-invariant subset of $\mathcal{A}^{\mathbb{Z}}$.

If X is a subshift of $\mathcal{A}^{\mathbb{Z}}$ and n a positive integer, the nth *higher power* of X is the subshift of $(\mathcal{A}^n)^{\mathbb{Z}}$ defined by $X^n = \{(a_{in}, \dots, a_{in+n-1})_{i \in \mathbb{Z}} \mid (a_i)_{i \in \mathbb{Z}} \in X\}$.

A finite *automaton* is a finite multigraph labeled on $\mathcal{A}$. It is denoted $\mathsf{A} = (Q, E)$, where Q is a finite set of states, and E a finite set of edges labeled on $\mathcal{A}$. It is equivalent to a *symbolic adjacency* $(Q \times Q)$-*matrix* A, where A_{pq} is the finite formal sum of the labels of all the edges from p to q. A *sofic shift* is the set of the labels of all the bi-infinite paths on a finite automaton. If A is a finite automaton, we denote by X_A the sofic shift defined by the automaton A. Several automata can define the same sofic shift. They are also called *presentations* or *covers* of the sofic shift. We will assume that all presentations are *essential*: all states have at least one outgoing edge and one incoming edge. An automaton is *deterministic* if for any given state and any given symbol, there is at most one outgoing edge labeled with this given symbol. A sofic shift is *irreducible* if it has a presentation with a strongly connected graph. Irreducible sofic shifts have a unique (up to isomorphisms of automata) minimal deterministic presentation called the *right Fischer cover* of the shift.

Let $A = (Q, E)$ be a finite deterministic (essential) automaton on the alphabet $\mathcal{A}$. Each finite word w of $\mathcal{A}^*$ defines a partial function from Q to Q. This function sends the state p to the state q, if w is the label of a path form p to q. The semigroup generated by all these functions is called the *transition semigroup* of the automaton. When X_A is not the full shift, the semigroup has a null element, denoted 0, which corresponds to words which are not factors of any bi-infinite word of X_A. The *syntactic semigroup* of an irreducible sofic shift is defined as the transition semigroup of its right Fischer cover.

Example 1. The sofic shift presented by the automaton of Figure 1 is called the *even shift*. Its syntactic semigroup is defined by the table in the right part of the figure.

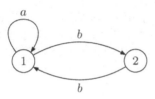

	1	2
a	1	–
b	2	1
ab	2	–
ba	–	1
bb	1	2
bab	–	2
aba	–	–

Fig. 1. The right Fischer cover of the even shift and its syntactic semigroup. Since aa and a define the same partial function from Q to Q, we write $aa = a$ in the syntactic semigroup. We also have $aba = 0$, or $ab^{2k+1}a = 0$ for any nonnegative integer k. The word bb is the identity in this semigroup.

2.2   Structure of Finite Semigroups

We refer to [16] for more details about the notions defined in this section.

Given a semigroup S, we denote by S^1 the following monoid: if S is a monoid, $S^1 = S$. If S is not a monoid, $S^1 = S \cup \{1\}$ together with the law $*$ defined by $x * y = xy$ if $x, y \in S$ and $1 * x = x * 1 = x$ for each $x \in S^1$.

We recall the *Green's relations* which are fundamentals equivalence relations defined in a semigroup S. The four equivalence relations $\mathcal{R}$, $\mathcal{L}$, $\mathcal{H}$, $\mathcal{J}$ are defined as follows. Let $x, y \in S$,

$$x\mathcal{R}y \Leftrightarrow xS^1 = yS^1,$$
$$x\mathcal{L}y \Leftrightarrow S^1x = S^1y,$$
$$x\mathcal{J}y \Leftrightarrow S^1xS^1 = S^1yS^1,$$
$$x\mathcal{H}y \Leftrightarrow x\mathcal{R}y \text{ and } x\mathcal{L}y.$$

Another relation $\mathcal{D}$ is defined by:

$$x\mathcal{D}y \Leftrightarrow \exists z \in S \; x\mathcal{R}z \text{ and } z\mathcal{L}y.$$

In a finite semigroup $\mathcal{J} = \mathcal{D}$. We recall the definition of the quasi-order $\leq_{\mathcal{J}}$:

$$x \leq_{\mathcal{J}} y \Leftrightarrow S^1 x S^1 \subseteq S^1 y S^1.$$

An $\mathcal{R}$-*class* is an equivalence class for a relation $\mathcal{R}$ (similar notations hold for the other Green's relations). An *idempotent* is an element $e \in S$ such that $ee = e$. A *regular* class is a class containing an idempotent. In a regular $\mathcal{D}$-class, any $\mathcal{H}$-class containing an idempotent is a maximal subgroup of the semigroup. Moreover, two regular $\mathcal{H}$-classes contained in a same $\mathcal{D}$-class are isomorphic (as groups), see for instance [16, Proposition 1.8]. This group is called the *characteristic group* of the regular $\mathcal{D}$-class. The quasi-order $\leq_{\mathcal{J}}$ induces a partial order between the $\mathcal{D}$-classes (still denoted $\leq_{\mathcal{J}}$). The structure of the transition semigroup S is often described by the so called "egg-box" pictures of the $\mathcal{D}$-classes.

We say that two elements $x, y \in S$ are conjugate if there are elements $u, v \in S^1$ such that $x = uv$ and $y = vu$. Two idempotents belong to a same regular $\mathcal{D}$-class if and only if they are conjugate, see for instance [16, Proposition 1.12].

Let S be a transition semigroup of an automaton $\mathsf{A} = (Q, E)$ and $x \in S$. The *rank* of x is the cardinal of the image of x as a partial function from Q to Q. The *kernel* of x is the partition induced by the equivalence relation $\sim$ over the domain of x where $p \sim q$ if and only p, q have the same image by x. The kernel of x is thus a partition of the domain of x. We describe the egg-box pictures with Example 1 continued in Figure 2.

Fig. 2. The syntactic semigroup of the even shift of Example 1 is composed of three $\mathcal{D}$-classes D_1, D_2, D_3, of rank 2, 1 and 0, respectively, represented by the above tables from left to right. Each square in a table represents an $\mathcal{H}$-class. Each row represents an $\mathcal{R}$-class and each column an $\mathcal{L}$-class. The common kernel of the elements in each row is written on the left of each row. The common image of the elements in each column is written above each column. Idempotents are marked with the symbol $*$. Each $\mathcal{D}$-class of this semigroup is regular. The characteristic groups of D_1, D_2, D_3 are $\mathbb{Z}/2\mathbb{Z}$, the trivial group $\mathbb{Z}/\mathbb{Z}$ and $\mathbb{Z}/\mathbb{Z}$, respectively.

Let X be an irreducible sofic shift and S its syntactic semigroup. It is known that S has a unique $\mathcal{D}$-class of rank 1 which is regular (see [4] or [5], see also [8]).

We define a finite directed acyclic graph (DAG) associated with X as follows. The set of vertices of the DAG is the set of non null regular $\mathcal{D}$-classes of S, but the regular $\mathcal{D}$-class of null rank, if there is one. Each vertex is labeled with the rank of the $\mathcal{D}$-class and its characteristic group. There is an edge from the vertex associated with a $\mathcal{D}$-class D to the vertex associated with a $\mathcal{D}$-class D' if and only if $D' \leq_{\mathcal{J}} D$. We call this acyclic graph the *syntactic graph* of X (see Figure 3 for an example). Note that the regular $\mathcal{D}$-class of null rank, if there is one, is not taken into account in a syntactic graph. This is linked to the fact that a full shift (i.e. the set of all bi-infinite words on a finite alphabet) can be conjugate to a non full shift.

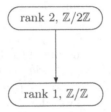

Fig. 3. The syntactic graph of the even shift of Example 1. We have $D_2 \leq_{\mathcal{J}} D_1$ since, for instance, $S^1 abS^1 \subseteq S^1 bS^1$.

2.3   Nasu's Classification Theorem for Sofic Shifts

In this section, we recall Nasu's Classification Theorem for sofic shifts [15] (see also [13, p. 232]), which extends William's Classification Theorem for shifts of finite type (see [13, p. 229]).

Let $X \subseteq \mathcal{A}^{\mathbb{Z}}, Y \subseteq \mathcal{B}^{\mathbb{Z}}$ be two subshifts and m, a be nonnegative integers. A map $\phi : X \to Y$ is a (m, a)-*block map* (or (m, a)-*factor map*) if there is a map $\delta : \mathcal{A}^{m+a+1} \to \mathcal{B}$ such that $\phi((a_i)_{i \in \mathbb{Z}}) = (b_i)_{i \in \mathbb{Z}}$ where $\delta(a_{i-m} \ldots a_{i-1} a_i a_{i+1} \ldots a_{i+a}) = b_i$. A *block map* is a (m, a)-*block map* for some nonnegative integers m, a. The well known theorem of Curtis, Hedlund and Lyndon [7] asserts that continuous and shift-commuting maps are exactly block maps. A *conjugacy* is a one-to-one and onto block map (then, being a shift compact, its inverse is also a block map).

Let A be a symbolic adjacency $(Q \times Q)$-matrix of an automaton A with entries in a finite alphabet $\mathcal{A}$. Let $\mathcal{B}$ be a finite alphabet and f a one-to-one map from $\mathcal{A}$ to $\mathcal{B}$. The map f is extended to a morphism from finite formal sums of elements of $\mathcal{A}$ to finite formal sums of elements of $\mathcal{B}$. We say that f *transforms* A into an adjacency $(Q \times Q)$-matrix B if $B_{pq} = f(A_{pq})$.

We now define the notion of strong shift equivalence between two symbolic adjacency matrices.

Let $\mathcal{A}$ and $\mathcal{B}$ be two finite alphabets. We denote by $\mathcal{AB}$ the set of words ab with $a \in \mathcal{A}$ and $b \in \mathcal{B}$.

Two symbolic adjacency matrices A, with entries in $\mathcal{A}$, and B, with entries in $\mathcal{B}$, are *elementary strong shift equivalent* if there is a pair of symbolic adjacency matrices (U, V) with entries in disjoint alphabets $\mathcal{U}$ and $\mathcal{V}$ respectively, such that there is a one-to-one map from $\mathcal{A}$ to $\mathcal{UV}$ which transforms A into UV, and there is a one-to-one map from $\mathcal{B}$ to $\mathcal{VU}$ which transforms B into VU.

Two symbolic adjacency matrices A and B are *strong shift equivalent within right Fischer covers* if there is a sequence of symbolic adjacency matrices of right Fischer covers

$$A = A_0, A_1, \ldots, A_{l-1}, A_l = B$$

such that for $1 \leq i \leq l$ the matrices A_{i-1} tand A_i are elementary strong shift equivalent.

Theorem 1 (Nasu). *Let X and Y be irreducible sofic shifts and let A and B be the symbolic adjacency matrices of the right Fischer covers of X and Y, respectively. Then X and Y are conjugate if and only if A and B are strong shift equivalent within right Fischer covers.*

Example 2. Let us consider the two (conjugate) irreducible sofic shifts X and Y defined by the right Fischer covers $\mathsf{A} = (Q, E)$ and $\mathsf{B} = (Q', E')$ in Figure 4.

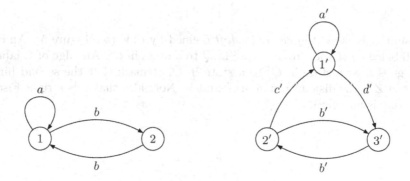

Fig. 4. Two conjugate shifts X and Y.

The symbolic adjacency matrices of these automata are respectively

$$A = \begin{bmatrix} a & b \\ b & 0 \end{bmatrix}, \quad B = \begin{bmatrix} a' & 0 & d' \\ c' & 0 & b' \\ 0 & b' & 0 \end{bmatrix}.$$

Then A and B are elementary strong shift equivalent with

$$U = \begin{bmatrix} u_1 & 0 & u_2 \\ 0 & u_2 & 0 \end{bmatrix}, \quad V = \begin{bmatrix} v_1 & 0 \\ v_2 & 0 \\ 0 & v_2 \end{bmatrix}.$$

Indeed,

$$UV = \begin{bmatrix} u_1 v_1 & u_2 v_2 \\ u_2 v_2 & 0 \end{bmatrix}, \quad VU = \begin{bmatrix} v_1 u_1 & 0 & v_1 u_2 \\ v_2 u_1 & 0 & v_2 u_2 \\ 0 & v_2 u_2 & 0 \end{bmatrix}.$$

The one-to-one maps from $\mathcal{A} = \{a, b\}$ to $\mathcal{UV}$ and from $\mathcal{B} = \{a', b', c', d'\}$ to $\mathcal{VU}$ are described in the tables below.

a	$u_1 v_1$
b	$u_2 v_2$

a'	$v_1 u_1$
b'	$v_2 u_2$
c'	$v_2 u_1$
d'	$v_1 u_2$

An elementary strong shift equivalence enables the construction of an irreducible sofic shift Z on the alphabet $\mathcal{U} \cup \mathcal{V}$ as follows. The sofic shift Z is defined by the automaton $\mathsf{C} = (Q \cup Q', F)$, where the symbolic adjacency matrix C of C is

$$\begin{array}{c} \quad Q \;\; Q' \\ \begin{array}{c} Q \\ Q' \end{array} \begin{bmatrix} 0 & U \\ V & 0 \end{bmatrix}. \end{array}$$

The shift Z is called the *bipartite shift* defined by U, V (see Figure 5). An edge of C labeled on $\mathcal{U}$ goes from a state in Q to a state in Q'. An edge of C labeled on $\mathcal{V}$ goes from a state in Q' to a state in Q. Remark that the second higher power of Z is the disjoint union of X and Y. Note also that C is a right Fischer cover (i.e. is minimal).

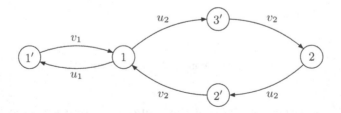

Fig. 5. The bipartite shift Z.

3   A Syntactic Invariant

In this section, we define a syntactic invariant for the conjugacy of irreducible sofic shifts.

Theorem 2. *Let X and Y be two irreducible sofic shifts. If X and Y are conjugate, then they have the same syntactic graph.*

We give a few lemmas before proving Theorem 2.

Let X (respectively Y) be an irreducible sofic shift whose symbolic adjacency matrix of its right Fischer cover is a $(Q \times Q)$-matrix (respectively $(Q' \times Q')$-matrix) denoted by A (respectively by B). We assume that A and B are elementary strong shift equivalent through a pair of matrices (U, V). The corresponding alphabets are denoted $\mathcal{A}$, $\mathcal{B}$, $\mathcal{U}$, and $\mathcal{V}$ as before. We denote by f a one-to-one map from $\mathcal{A}$ to $\mathcal{UV}$ which transforms A into UV and by g a one-to-one map from $\mathcal{B}$ to $\mathcal{VU}$ which transforms B into VU. Let Z be the bipartite irreducible sofic shift associated to U, V. We denote by S (respectively T, R) the syntactic semigroup of X (respectively Y, Z).

Let $w \in R$. If w is non null, the bipartite nature of Z implies that w is a function from $Q \cup Q'$ to $Q \cup Q'$ whose domain is included either in Q or in Q', and whose image is included either in Q or in Q'. If $w \neq 0$ with a domain included in P and an image included in P', we say that w has the *type* (P, P'). Remark that w has type (Q, Q) if and only if $w \neq 0$ and $w \in (f(\mathcal{A}))^*$, and w has type (Q', Q') if and only if $w \neq 0$ and $w \in (g(\mathcal{B}))^*$.

Lemma 1. *Elements of R in a same non null $\mathcal{H}$-class have the same type.*

Proof We show the property for the (Q, Q)-type. Let $w \in H$ and w of type (Q, Q). If $w = w'v$ with $w', v \in R$, then w' has type $(Q, *)$. If $w = zw'$ with $z, w' \in R$, then w' has type $(*, Q)$. Thus, $w\mathcal{H}w'$ implies that w' has type (Q, Q). $\square$

The $\mathcal{H}$-classes of R containing elements of type (Q, Q) (respectively (Q', Q')) are called (Q, Q)-$\mathcal{H}$-*classes* (respectively (Q', Q')-$\mathcal{H}$-*classes*).

Let $w = a_1 \ldots a_n$ be an element of S, we define the element $f(w)$ as $f(a_1) \ldots f(a_n)$. Note that this definition is consistent since if $a_1 \ldots a_n = a'_1 \ldots a'_m$ in S, then $f(a_1) \ldots f(a_n) = f(a'_1) \ldots f(a'_m)$ in R. Similarly we define an element $g(w)$ for any element w of T.

Conversely, let w be an element of R belonging to $f(\mathcal{A})^*$ ($\subseteq (\mathcal{UV})^*$). Then $w = f(a_1) \ldots f(a_n)$, with $a_i \in \mathcal{A}$. We define $f^{-1}(w)$ as $a_1 \ldots a_n$. Similarly we define $g^{-1}(w)$. Again these definitions and notations are consistent. Thus f is a semigroup isomorphism from S to the subsemigroup of R of transition functions defined by the words in $(f(\mathcal{A}))^*$. Notice that $f(0) = 0$ if $0 \in S$. Analogously, g is a semigroup isomorphism from T to the subsemigroup of R of transition functions defined by the words in $(g(\mathcal{B}))^*$.

Lemma 2. *Let $w, w' \in R$ of type (Q, Q). Then $w\mathcal{H}w'$ in R if and only if $f^{-1}(w)\mathcal{H}f^{-1}(w')$ in S.*

Proof Let $w = f(a_1) \dots f(a_n)$ and $w' = f(a'_1) \dots f(a'_m)$, with $a_i, a'_j \in \mathcal{A}$. We have $w = w'v$ with $v \in R$ if and only if $v = f(\bar{a}_1) \dots f(\bar{a}_r)$ with $\bar{a}_i \in \mathcal{A}$ and $f(a_1) \dots f(a_n) = f(a'_1) \dots f(a'_m) f(\bar{a}_1) \dots f(\bar{a}_r)$. This is equivalent to $a_1 \dots a_n = a'_1 \dots a'_m \bar{a}_1 \dots \bar{a}_r$, that is $f^{-1}(w)R^1 \subseteq f^{-1}(w')R^1$. Analogously, we have $w' = wv'$ with $v' \in R$, if and only if $f^{-1}(w')R^1 \subseteq f^{-1}(w)R^1$. This proves that $w\mathcal{R}w'$ in R if and only if $f^{-1}(w)\mathcal{R}f^{-1}(w')$ in S. In the same way, one can prove the same statement for the relation $\mathcal{L}$ and hence for the relation $\mathcal{H}$. $\square$

A similar statement holds for (Q', Q')-$\mathcal{H}$-classes.

Lemma 3. *Let $w, w' \in R$ of type (Q, Q). Then $w \leq_{\mathcal{J}} w'$ in R if and only if $f^{-1}(w) \leq_{\mathcal{J}} f^{-1}(w')$ in S. This implies that $w\mathcal{J}w'$ in R if and only if $f^{-1}(w)$ $\mathcal{J}$ $f^{-1}(w')$ in S.*

Proof The first statement can be prooved as in the previous lemma. $\square$

Similar results hold between T and R. As a consequence we get the following lemma.

Lemma 4. *The bijection f between S and the elements of R belonging to $(f(\mathcal{A}))^*$, induces a bijection between the non null $\mathcal{H}$-classes of S and the (Q, Q)-$\mathcal{H}$-classes of R. Moreover this bijection keeps the relations $\mathcal{J}$, $\leq_{\mathcal{J}}$ and the rank of the $\mathcal{H}$-classes.*

A similar statement holds for the bijection g.

We now come to the main lemma, which shows the link between the elementary strong shift equivalence of the symbolic adjacency matrices and the conjugacy of some idempotents in the semigroup. This link is the key point of the invariant.

Lemma 5. *Let H be a regular (Q, Q)-$\mathcal{H}$-class of R. Then there is a regular (Q', Q')-$\mathcal{H}$-class in the same $\mathcal{D}$-class as H.*

Proof Let $e \in R$ be an idempotent element of type (Q, Q). Let $u_1 v_1 \dots u_n v_n$ in $(\mathcal{U}\mathcal{V})^*$ such that $e = u_1 v_1 \dots u_n v_n$. We define $\bar{e} = v_1 \dots u_n v_n u_1$. Thus $eu_1 = u_1 \bar{e}$ in R. Remark that $\bar{e}$ depends on the choice of the word $u_1 v_1 \dots u_n v_n$ representing e in R.

If w denotes $v_1 \dots u_n v_n$ and v denotes u_1, we have $e = vw$ and $\bar{e} = wv$. It follows that e and $\bar{e}$ are conjugate, thus $e^2 = e$ and $\bar{e}^2$ are conjugate. Moreover

$$\bar{e}^3 = wvwvwv = weev = wev = wvwv = \bar{e}^2.$$

Thus $\bar{e}^2$ is an idempotent conjugate to the idempotent e. As a consequence e and $\bar{e}^2$ belong to a same $\mathcal{D}$-class of R (see Section 2), and $\bar{e}^2 \neq 0$. The result follows since $\bar{e}^2$ is of type (Q', Q'). $\square$

Note that the number of regular (Q, Q)-$\mathcal{H}$-classes and the number of regular (Q', Q')-$\mathcal{H}$-classes in a same $\mathcal{D}$-class of R, may be different in general.

We now prove Theorem 2.

Proof[of Theorem 2] By Nasu's Theorem [15] we can assume, without loss of generality, that the symbolic adjacency matrices of the right Fischer covers of X and Y are elementary strong shift equivalent. We define the bipartite shift Z as above. We denote by S, T and R the syntactic semigroups of X, Y and Z respectively.

Let D be a non null regular $\mathcal{D}$-class of S. Let H be a regular $\mathcal{H}$-class of S contained in D. Let $H'' = f(H)$. By Lemma 4, the groups H and H'' are isomorphic. Let D'' the $\mathcal{D}$-class of R containing H''. By Lemma 5, there is at least one regular (Q', Q')-$\mathcal{H}$-class K'' in D'', which is isomorphic to H''. Let $H' = g^{-1}(K'')$ and let D' be the $\mathcal{D}$-class of T containing H'. By Lemma 4, the groups H' and K'' are isomorphic. Hence the groups H and H' are isomorphic.

By Lemmas 4 and 5, we have that the above construction of D' from D is a bijective function φ from the non null regular $\mathcal{D}$-classes of S onto the non null regular $\mathcal{D}$-classes of T. Moreover the characteristic group of D is isomorphic to the characteristic group of $\varphi(D)$ and, by Lemma 4, the rank of D is equal to the rank of $\varphi(D)$.

We now consider two non null regular $\mathcal{D}$-classes D_1 and D_2 of S. By Lemma 4 and Lemma 5, $D_1 \leq_{\mathcal{J}} D_2$ if and only if $\varphi(D_1) \leq_{\mathcal{J}} \varphi(D_2)$. It follows that the syntactic graphs of S and T are isomorphic through the bijection φ. $\square$

Nasu's Classification Theorem holds for reducible sofic shifts by the use of right Krieger covers instead of right Fischer covers [15]. This enables the extension of our result to the case of reducible sofic shifts. This extension is not described in this short version of the paper.

4   How Dynamic Is This Invariant?

We briefly compare the syntactic conjugacy invariant with other classical conjugacy invariants. We refer to [13] for the definitions and properties of these classical invariants.

First, on can remark that the syntactic invariant does not capture all the dynamic. Two sofic shifts can have the same syntactic graph and a different entropy, see the example given in Figure 6.

The comparison with the zeta function is more interesting. Recall that the zeta function of a shift X is $\zeta(X) = \exp \sum_{n \geq 1} p_n \frac{z^n}{n}$, where p_n is the number of bi-infinite words $x \in X$ such that $\sigma^n(x) = x$. We give in Figure 7 an example of two irreducible sofic shifts which have the same zeta function and different syntactic graphs.

Irreducible shifts of finite type can be characterized with this syntactic invariant. Other equivalent characterizations of finite type shifts can be found in [14] and in [8].

Proposition 1. *An irreducible sofic shifts is of finite type if and only its syntactic graph is reduced to one node of rank 1 representing the trivial group.*

Fig. 6. The two above sofic shifts X, Y have the same syntactic graph and a different entropy. Indeed, we have $b = c$ in the syntactic semigroup of Y. Hence the shifts X and Y have the same syntactic semigroup.

Another interesting class of irreducible sofic shifts can be characterized with the syntactic invariant. It is the class of aperiodic sofic shifts [1].

Let $x \in X$, we denote by period(x) the least positive integer n such that $\sigma^n(x) = x$ if such an integer exists. It is equal to ∞ otherwise.

Let X, Y be two subshifts and let $\phi : X \to Y$ be a block map. The map is said *aperiodic* if period(x) = period($\phi(x)$) for any $x \in X$. Roughly speaking, such a factor map ϕ does not make periods decrease.

A sofic shift X if *aperiodic* if it is the image of a shift of finite type by an aperiodic block map. A characterization of irreducible aperiodic sofic shifts is the following.

Proposition 2. *An irreducible sofic shift is aperiodic if and only if its syntactic graph contains only trivial groups.*

Schützenberger's characterization of aperiodic languages (see for instance [16, Theorem 2.1]) asserts that the set of blocks of an aperiodic sofic shift is a regular star free language.

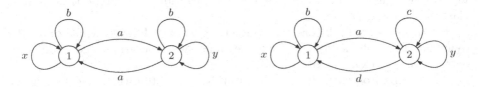

Fig. 7. Two sofic shifts X, Y which have the same zeta function $\frac{1}{1-4z+z^2}$ (see for instance [13, Theorem 6.4.8], or [2] for the computation of the zeta function of a sofic shift), and different syntactic invariants. Indeed the syntactic graph of X is (rank 2, $\mathbb{Z}/2\mathbb{Z}$) $\to$ (rank 1, $\mathbb{Z}/\mathbb{Z}$) while the syntactic graph of Y has only one node (rank 1, $\mathbb{Z}/\mathbb{Z}$). Thus they are not conjugate. Notice that Y is a shift of finite type.

References

1. M.-P. BÉAL, *Codage Symbolique*, Masson, 1993.
2. M.-P. BÉAL, *Puissance extérieure d'un automate déterministe, application au calcul de la fonction zêta d'un système sofique*, RAIRO Inform. Théor. Appl., 29 (1995), pp. 85–103.
3. M.-P. BÉAL, F. FIORENZI, AND F. MIGNOSI, *Minimal forbidden patterns of multidimensional shifts*. To appear in Internat. J. Algebra Comput., 2003.
4. D. BEAUQUIER, *Minimal automaton for a factorial transitive rational language*, Theoret. Comput. Sci., 67 (1989), pp. 65–73.
5. J. BERSTEL AND D. PERRIN, *Theory of Codes*, Academic Press, New York, 1985.
6. M. BOYLE, *Algebraic aspects of symbolic dynamics*, in Topics in symbolic dynamics and applications (Temuco 97), vol. 279 of London Math. Soc. Lecture Notes Ser., Cambridge University Press, Cambridge, 2000, pp. 57–88.
7. G. A. HEDLUND, *Endomorphisms and automorphisms of the shift dynamical system*, Math. Systems Theory, 3 (1969), pp. 320–337.
8. N. JONOSKA, *A conjugacy invariant for reducible sofic shifts and its semigroup characterizations*, Israel J. Math., 106 (1998), pp. 221–249.
9. B. P. KITCHENS, *Symbolic Dynamics: one-sided, two-sided and countable state Markov shifts*, Springer-Verlag, 1997.
10. W. KRIEGER, *On sofic systems. I*, Israel J. Math., 48 (1984), pp. 305–330.
11. ——, *On sofic systems. II*, Israel J. Math., 60 (1987), pp. 167–176.
12. ——, *On a syntactically defined invariant of symbolic dynamics*, Ergodic Theory Dynam. Systems, 20 (2000), pp. 501–516.
13. D. A. LIND AND B. H. MARCUS, *An Introduction to Symbolic Dynamics and Coding*, Cambridge, 1995.
14. A. D. LUCA AND A. RESTIVO, *A characterization of strictly locally testable languages and its applications to subsemigroups of a free semigroup*, Inform. and Control, 44 (80), pp. 300–319.
15. M. NASU, *Topological conjugacy for sofic systems*, Ergodic Theory Dynam. Systems, 6 (1986), pp. 265–280.
16. J.-E. PIN, *Varieties of formal languages*, Foundations of Computer Science, Plenum Publishing Corp., New York, 1986.
17. B. WEISS, *Subshifts of finite type and sofic systems*, Monats. für Math., 77 (1973), pp. 462–474.

Periodicity and Unbordered Words
A Proof of Duval's Conjecture

Tero Harju and Dirk Nowotka

Turku Centre for Computer Science (TUCS)
Department of Mathematics, University of Turku, Finland
{harju,nowotka}@utu.fi

Abstract. The relationship between the length of a word and the maximum length of its unbordered factors is investigated in this paper.
A word is bordered, if it has a proper prefix that is also a suffix of that word. Consider a finite word w of length n. Let $\mu(w)$ denote the maximum length of its unbordered factors, and let $\partial(w)$ denote the period of w. Clearly, $\mu(w) \leq \partial(w)$.
We establish that $\mu(w) = \partial(w)$, if w has an unbordered prefix of length $\mu(w)$ and $n \geq 2\mu(w) - 1$. This bound is tight and solves a 21 year old conjecture by Duval. It follows from this result that, in general, $n \geq 3\mu(w)$ implies $\mu(w) = \partial(w)$ which gives an improved bound for the question asked by Ehrenfeucht and Silberger in 1979.

1 Introduction

Periodicity and borderedness are two properties of words which are investigated in this paper. These concepts are foundational and play a rôle (explicitly or implicitly) in many areas of computer science. Just a few of those areas are pattern matching algorithms [15,3,7], data compression [19,6], and codes [2], which are classical examples, but also computational biology, e.g., sequence assembly [17] or superstrings [4], and serial data communications systems [5] are areas among others where periodicity and borderedness of words (sequences) are important concepts. It is well known that these two word properties do not exist independently from each other. However, it is somewhat surprising that no clear relation has been established so far, despite the fact that this basic question has been around for more than 20 years.

Let us consider a finite word (a sequence of letters) w. We denote the length of w by $|w|$ and call a subsequence of consecutive letters of a word *factor*. The period of w, denoted by $\partial(w)$, is the smallest positive integer p such that the i-th letter equals the $(i+p)$-th letter for all $1 \leq i \leq |w| - p$. Let $\mu(w)$ denote the length of the longest unbordered factor of w. A word is bordered, if it has a proper prefix that is also a suffix, where we call a prefix proper, if it is neither empty nor contains the entire word. For the investigation of the relationship between $|w|$ and the maximality of $\mu(w)$, that is, $\mu(w) = \partial(w)$, we consider the special case where the longest unbordered prefix of a word is of the maximum length, that is, no unbordered factor is longer than that prefix. Let w be an unbordered

V. Diekert and M. Habib (Eds.): STACS 2004, LNCS 2996, pp. 294–304, 2004.
© Springer-Verlag Berlin Heidelberg 2004

word. Then a word wu is a *Duval extension* (of w), if every unbordered factor of wu has at most length $|w|$, that is, $\mu(wu) = |w|$. We call wu *trivial* Duval extension, if $\partial(wu) = |w|$. For example, let $w = abaabb$ and $u = aaba$. Then $wu = abaabbaaba$ is a nontrivial Duval extension of w since (i) w is unbordered, (ii) all factors of wu longer than w are bordered, that is, $|w| = \mu(wu) = 6$, and (iii) the period of wu is 7, and hence, $\partial(wu) > |w|$. Note, that this example satisfies $|u| = |w| - 2$.

In 1979 Ehrenfeucht and Silberger initiated a line of research [10,1,8] exploring the relationship between the length of a word w and $\mu(w)$. In 1982 these efforts culminated in Duval's result: If $|w| \geq 4\mu(w) - 6$ then $\partial(w) = \mu(w)$. However, it was conjectured in [1] that $|w| \geq 3\mu(w)$ implies $\partial(w) = \mu(w)$ which follows if Duval's conjecture [8] holds true.

Conjecture 1. If wu is a Duval nontrivial extension of w, then $|u| < |w|$.

After that, no progress was recorded, to the best of our knowledge, for 20 years. However, the topic remained popular, see for example Chapter 8 in [16]; for recent results see [18] and [9]. Recently, a first improvement of Duval's result was introduced in [11] where it was shown that a Duval extension of w longer than $5\mu(w)/2 - 1$ is trivial. However, the main result of our contribution here is a final characterization of this border by proving an improved version of Conjecture 1.

Theorem 2. *If wu is a Duval nontrivial extension of w, then $|u| < |w| - 1$.*

The example mentioned above shows that this bound on the length of a nontrivial Duval extension is tight. Theorem 2 implies the truth of Duval's conjecture, as well as, the following corollary (for any word w).

Corollary 3. *If $|w| \geq 3\mu(w)$, then $\partial(w) = \mu(w)$.*

This corollary confirms the conjecture by Assous and Pouzet in [1] about a question asked by Ehrenfeucht and Silberger in [10].

Our main result, Theorem 2, is presented in Section 4, which uses the notations introduced in Section 2 and preliminary results from Section 3. We conclude with Section 5.

2   Notations

In this section we introduce the notations of this paper. We refer to [16] for more basic and general definitions.

We consider a finite alphabet A of letters. Let A^* denote the set of all finite words over A including the empty word, denoted by ε. Let $w = w_{(1)}w_{(2)} \cdots w_{(n)}$ where $w_{(i)}$ is a letter, for every $1 \leq i \leq n$. We denote the length n of w by $|w|$. An integer $1 \leq p \leq n$ is a *period* of w, if $w_{(i)} = w_{(i+p)}$ for all $1 \leq i \leq n - p$. The smallest period of w is called the *minimum period* (or simply, the period) of w, denoted by $\partial(w)$. A nonempty word u is called a *border* of a word w, if $w = uv = v'u$ for some suitable words v and v'. We call w *bordered*, if it has a border that is shorter than w, otherwise w is called *unbordered*. Note, that every bordered word w has a minimum border u such that $w = uvu$, where u is unbordered. Let $\mu(w)$ denote the maximum length of unbordered factors of w.

Suppose $w = uv$, then u is called a *prefix* of w, denoted by $u \leq w$, and v is called a *suffix* of w, denoted by $v \preccurlyeq w$. Let $u, v \neq \varepsilon$. Then we say that u *overlaps* v *from the left* or *from the right*, if there is a word w such that $|w| < |u| + |v|$, and $u \leq w$ and $v \preccurlyeq w$, or $v \leq w$ and $u \preccurlyeq w$, respectively. We say that u *overlaps* (intersects) with v, if either v is a factor of u or u is a factor of v or u overlaps v from the left or right.

Let us consider the following examples. Let $A = \{a, b\}$ and $u, v, w \in A^*$ such that $u = abaa$ and $v = baaba$ and $w = abaaba$. Then $|w| = 6$, and 3, 5, and 6 are periods of w, and $\partial(w) = 3$. We have that a is the shortest border of u and w, whereas ba is the shortest border of v. We have $\mu(w) = 3$. We also have that u and v overlap since $u \leq w$ and $v \preccurlyeq w$ and $|w| < |u| + |v|$.

We continue with some more notations. Let w and u be nonempty words where w is also unbordered. We call wu a *Duval extension* of w, if every factor of wu longer than $|w|$ is bordered, that is, $\mu(wu) = |w|$. A Duval extension wu of w is called *trivial*, if $\partial(wu) = \mu(wu) = |w|$. A nontrivial Duval extension wu of w is called *minimal*, if u is of minimal length, that is, $u = u'a$ and $w = u'bw'$ where $a, b \in A$ and $a \neq b$.

Example 4. Let $w = abaabbabaaababb$ and $u = aaba$. Then

$$w.u = abaabbabaaababb.aaba$$

(for the sake of readability, we use a dot to mark where w ends) is a nontrivial Duval extension of w of length $|wu| = 18$, where $\mu(wu) = |w| = 14$ and $\partial(wu) = 15$. However, wu is not a minimal Duval extension, whereas

$$w.u' = abaabbabaaababb.aa$$

is minimal, with $u' = aa \leq u$. Note, that wu is not the longest nontrivial Duval extension of w since

$$w.v = abaabbabaaababb.abaaba$$

is longer, with $v = abaaba$ and $|wv| = 20$ and $\partial(wv) = 17$. One can check that wv is a nontrivial Duval extension of w of maximum length, and at the same time wv is also a minimal Duval extension of w.

Let an integer p with $1 \leq p < |w|$ be called *point* in w. Intuitively, a point p denotes the place between $w_{(p)}$ and $w_{(p+1)}$ in w. A nonempty word u is called a *repetition word* at point p if $w = xy$ with $|x| = p$ and there exist x' and y' such that $u \preccurlyeq x'x$ and $u \leq yy'$. For a point p in w, let

$$\partial(w, p) = \min\{|u| \mid u \text{ is a repetition word at } p\}$$

denote the *local period* at point p in w. Note, the repetition word of length $\partial(w, p)$ at point p is necessarily unbordered, and moreover, $\partial(w, p) \leq \partial(w)$. A factorization $w = uv$, with $u, v \neq \varepsilon$ and $|u| = p$, is called *critical*, if $\partial(w, p) = \partial(w)$, and, if this holds, then p is called *critical point*.

Example 5. The word

$$w = ab.aa.b$$

has the period $\partial(w) = 3$ and two critical points, 2 and 4, marked by dots. The shortest repetition words at the critical points are aab and baa, respectively. Note, that the shortest repetition words at the remaining points 1 and 3 are ba and a, respectively.

3   Preliminary Results

We state some auxiliary and well-known results about repetitions and borders in this section which will be used to prove Theorem 2, in Section 4. The proofs of these auxiliary results are straightforward and not given in this extended abstract. Results taken from the literature are referenced to.

Lemma 6. *Let* $zf = gzh$ *where* $f, g \neq \varepsilon$. *Let* az' *be the maximum unbordered prefix of* az. *If* az *does not occur in* zf, *then* agz' *is unbordered.*

Lemma 7. *Let* w *be an unbordered word and* $u \leq w$ *and* $v \preccurlyeq w$. *Then* uw *and* wv *are unbordered.*

The following lemma was proven in [4].

Lemma 8. *Let* $w = uv$ *be unbordered and* $|u|$ *be a critical point of* w. *Then* u *and* v *do not overlap.*

The next result follows directly from Lemma 8.

Lemma 9. *Let* $u_0 u_1$ *be unbordered and* $|u_0|$ *be a critical point of* $u_0 u_1$. *Then for any word* x, *we have* $u_i x u_{i+1}$, *where the indices are modulo 2, is either unbordered or has a minimum border* g *such that* $|g| \geq |u_0| + |u_1|$.

The following Lemmas 10, 11 and 12 and Corollary 13 are given in [8]. Let $a_0, a_1 \in A$, with $a_0 \neq a_1$, and $t_0 \in A^*$. Let the sequences (a_i), (s_i), (s_i'), (s_i''), and (t_i), for $i \geq 1$, be defined by

- $a_i = a_{i \pmod 2}$, that is, $a_i = a_0$ or $a_i = a_1$, if i is even or odd, respectively,
- s_i such that $a_i s_i$ is the shortest border of $a_i t_{i-1}$,
- s_i' such that $a_{i+1} s_i'$ is the longest unbordered prefix of $a_{i+1} s_i$,
- s_i'' such that $s_i' s_i'' = s_i$,
- t_i such that $t_i s_i'' = t_{i-1}$.

For any parameters of the above definition, the following holds.

Lemma 10. *For any* a_0, a_1, *and* t_0 *there exists an* $m \geq 1$ *such that*

$$|s_1| < |s_2| < \cdots < |s_m| = |t_{m-1}| \leq \cdots \leq |t_1| \leq |t_0|$$

and $s_i \leq s_{i+1}$, *for all* $1 \leq i < m$, *and* $s_m = t_{m-1}$ *and* $|t_0| \leq |s_m| + |s_{m-1}|$.

Lemma 11. *Let* $z \leq t_0$ *such that* $a_0 z$ *and* $a_1 z$ *do not occur in* t_0. *Let* $a_0 z_0$ *and* $a_1 z_1$ *be the longest unbordered prefixes of* $a_0 z$ *and* $a_1 z$, *respectively. Let* m *be the smallest integer such that* $s_m = t_{m-1}$. *Then*

1. *if* $m = 1$ *then* $a_1 t_0$ *is unbordered,*
2. *if* $m > 1$ *is odd, then* $a_1 s_m$ *is unbordered and* $|t_0| \leq |s_m| + |z_0|$,
3. *if* $m > 1$ *is even, then* $a_0 s_m$ *is unbordered and* $|t_0| \leq |s_m| + |z_1|$.

Lemma 12. *Let* v *be an unbordered factor of* w *of length* $\mu(w)$. *If* v *occurs twice in* w, *then* $\mu(w) = \partial(w)$.

Corollary 13. *Let* wu *be a Duval extension of* w. *If* w *occurs twice in* wu, *then* wu *is a trivial Duval extension.*

4   Main Results

The first theorem in this section states a basic fact about minimal Duval extensions which is also used in the proof of Theorem 2. We omit the proof of it because of space limitations.

Theorem 14. *Let wu be a minimal Duval extension of w. Then au occurs in w where $a \preccurlyeq w$ and $a \in A$.*

We come now to the main result of this paper that we already mentioned in the introduction. It proves Duval's conjecture.

Theorem 2. *If wu is a nontrivial Duval extension of w, then $|u| < |w| - 1$.*

Proof (sketch). Recall that every factor of wu which is longer than $|w|$ is bordered since wu is a Duval extension of w. Let z be the longest suffix of w that occurs twice in zu.

If $z = \varepsilon$ then $a \preccurlyeq w$ where $a \in A$ and a does not occur in u. Let $w = u'bw''$ and $u = u'cu''$ such that $b, c \in A$ and $b \neq c$. Then $w = w'_0 au'cw'_1$ by Theorem 14. Consider the factor $au'cw'_1 u$ which has to be bordered with a shortest border g such that $|au| \leq |g|$ and g occurs in w. Hence, $|u| < |w| - 1$.

So, assume $z \neq \varepsilon$. We have $z \neq w$ since wu is otherwise trivial by Corollary 13. Let $a, b \in A$ be such that

$$w = w'az \qquad \text{and} \qquad u = u'bzr$$

and z occurs in zr only once, that is, bz matches the rightmost occurrence of z in u. Note, that bz does not overlap az from the right, by Lemma 7, and therefore u' exists, although it might be empty. Naturally, $a \neq b$ by the maximality of z, and $w' \neq \varepsilon$, otherwise $azu'bz \leq wu$ has either no border or w is bordered (if $azu'bz$ has a border not longer than z) or az occurs in zu (if $azu'bz$ has a border longer than z); a contradiction in any case.

Let az_0 and bz_1 denote the longest unbordered prefix of az and bz, respectively. Let $a_0 = a$ and $a_1 = b$ and $t_0 = zr$ and the integer m be defined as in Lemma 11. We have then a word s_m, with its properties defined by Lemma 10 and 11, such that

$$t_0 = s_m t' \ .$$

Consider $azu'bz_0$. We have that az and $azu'bz_0$ are both prefixes of $a_0 zu$, and bz_0 is a suffix of $azu'bz_0$ and az does not occur in $zu'bz_0$. It follows from Lemma 6 that $azu'bz_0$ is unbordered, and hence,

$$|azu'bz_0| \leq |w| \ . \tag{1}$$

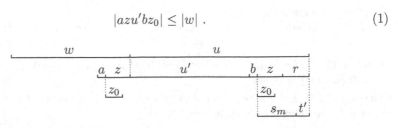

Case: m is even. Then we have $m \geq 2$ and as_m $(= a_m s_m)$ is unbordered and $|t_0| \leq |s_m| + |z_1|$ by Lemma 11.

Suppose $|t_0| = |s_m| + |z_1|$ and $z_1 = z$. Then $|z| \leq |s_{m-1}|$ by Lemma 10. Note, that we have an immediate contradiction, if $m = 2$ since then $|t_0| = |t_1| + |s_1''|$ where $t_1 = s_2$ and $|s_1''| = |z| - |z_0|$, by the definition of (s_i) and (t_i), and hence, $z_0 = \varepsilon$ and $z = a^k$, for some $k \geq 1$, and $c \leq r$, for some $c \in A$ and $a \neq c$ otherwise az occurs in u, and finally, $azu'bzc$ is unbordered, and hence, $|u| < |w| - 1$. So, assume $m > 2$. But now, bz occurs in t_0 since bs_{m-1} is a border of bt_{m-2} and $t_i \leq t_0$, for all $0 \leq i < m$, which is a contradiction.

So, assume that $|t_0| < |s_m| + |z_1|$ or $|z_1| < |z|$. Then $|t'| < |z|$.

Subcase: $|s_m| \leq |z_0|$. Then $|azu'bz_0| \leq |w|$ and

$$
\begin{aligned}
|u| &= |azu| - |z| - 1 \\
&= |azu'bz_0| - |z_0| + |t_0| - |z| - 1 \\
&< |azu'bz_0| - |z_0| + |s_m| + |z_1| - |z| - 1 \\
&\leq |w| + |z_1| - |z| - 1 \\
&\leq |w| - 1
\end{aligned}
$$

if $|t_0| < |s_m| + |z_1|$, or

$$
\begin{aligned}
|u| &= |azu| - |z| - 1 \\
&= |azu'bz_0| - |z_0| + |t_0| - |z| - 1 \\
&\leq |azu'bz_0| - |z_0| + |s_m| + |z_1| - |z| - 1 \\
&\leq |w| + |z_1| - |z| - 1 \\
&< |w| - 1
\end{aligned}
$$

if $|z_1| < |z|$. We have $|u| < |w| - 1$ in both cases.

Subcase: $|s_m| > |z_0|$. Then we have that as_m is unbordered, and since az_0 is the longest unbordered prefix of az, we have that az is a proper prefix of as_m, and hence, $|z| < |s_m|$. Now, $azu'bs_m$ is unbordered otherwise its shortest border is longer than az, since no prefix of az is a suffix of as_m, and az occurs in u; a contradiction. So, $|azu'bs_m| \leq |w|$ and $|u| < |w| - 1$ since $|t'| < |z|$.

Case: m is odd. Then bs_m $(= a_m s_m)$ is unbordered and $|t_0| \leq |s_m| + |z_0|$; see Lemma 11. Note, that $t_0 = s_m$ and $t' = \varepsilon$, if $m = 1$ by Lemma 11. Surely $s_m \neq \varepsilon$. Note, in particular

$$|t'| \leq |z_0| \,.$$

If $|s_m| < |z|$, then $|u| < |w| - 1$ since

$$|u| = |azu'bz_0| - |bz_0| + |bt_0| - |az|$$

and $|azu'bz_0| \leq |w|$, by (1), and $|t_0| \leq |s_m| + |z_0|$.

Assume $|s_m| \geq |z|$. From $|bs_m| \geq 2$ it follows that there exists a critical point p in bs_m such that $bs_m = v_0 v_1$, where $|v_0| = p$, by the critical factorization theorem; see [16].

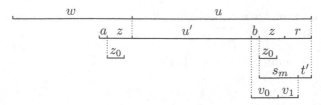

From this follows

$$bz \leq v_0 v_1 \ . \tag{2}$$

Note, that if $s_m = z$ then $|u| < |w| - 1$ since we have $|t_0| \leq |s_m| + |s_{m-1}|$ and $|s_{m-1}| < |s_m|$, by Lemma 10, and

$$
\begin{aligned}
|u| &= |azu| - |z| - 1 \\
&= |azu'bz| - |z| + |t_0| - |z| - 1 \\
&\leq |azu'bz| - |z| + |s_m| + |s_{m-1}| - |z| - 1 \\
&\leq |w| + |s_{m-1}| - |z| - 1 \\
&< |w| - 1 \ .
\end{aligned}
$$

We have therefore in general

$$|z_0| < |v_0 v_1| - 1 \ . \tag{3}$$

Let

$$u = u_0' v_0 v_1 u_1$$

be such that $v_0 v_1$ does not occur in u_0'. Note, that $v_0 v_1$ does not overlap with itself since it is unbordered, and v_0 and v_1 do not overlap by Lemma 8. Consider the prefix $w u_0' bz$ of wu which is bordered and has a shortest border h longer than z, and hence, $bz \preceq h$, otherwise w is bordered since $z \preceq w$. So, bz occurs in w. Let

$$w = w_0 bz w_1$$

such that bz occurs in $w_0 bz$ only once, that is, we consider the leftmost occurence of bz in w. Note, that

$$|w_0 bz| \leq |h| \leq |u_0' bz| \tag{4}$$

where the first inequality comes from the definition of w_0 above and the second inequality from the fact that $|u_0' bz| < |h|$ implies that w is bordered. Let

$$f = bz w_1 u_0' v_0 v_1 \ .$$

If f is unbordered. Then $|f| \leq |w|$, and hence, $|u_0' v_0 v_1| \leq |w_0|$. Now, we have $|u_0'| < |w_0|$ which contradicts (4).

Assume f is bordered, and let h' be its shortest border.

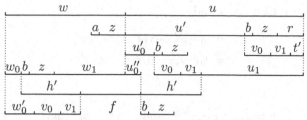

Surely, $|bz| < |h'|$ otherwise v_0v_1 is bordered by (2). So, $bz \le h'$. Moreover, $|v_0v_1| \le |h'|$ otherwise bz occurs in s_m contradicting our assumption that bzr marks the rightmost occurence of bz in u. So, $v_0v_1 \preccurlyeq h'$, and v_0v_1 occurs in w since $w_0h' \le w$ by (4). Let

$$w_0bzv' = w_0h' = w_0'v_0v_1 .$$

Note, that v_0v_1 does not occur in w_0' otherwise it occurs in u_0' contradicting our assumption. Moreover, we have $h' = bzv' \preccurlyeq u_0'v_0v_1$. Let $u_0'v_0v_1 = u_0''h'$. Consider

$$f' = wu_0''bz$$

which has a shortest border h''.

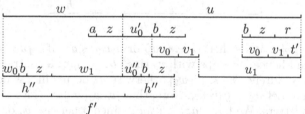

Surely, $bz \preccurlyeq h''$ otherwise w is bordered with a suffix of z. Moreover, we have $|w_0bz| \le |h''| \le |u_0''bz|$ since bz does not occur in w_0 and w is unbordered. From that and $w_0h' = w_0'v_0v_1$ and $u_0''h' = u_0'v_0v_1$ follows now $|w_0'| \le |u_0'|$ and

$$u_0'v_0v_1 = u_0''bzv' \text{ and } w_0 \text{ occurs in } u_0''. \tag{5}$$

Let now

$$w = w_0'v_0v_1w_i' \cdots v_0v_1w_2'v_0v_1w_1'v_0v_1w_2$$

and

$$u = u_0'v_0v_1u_j' \cdots v_0v_1u_2'v_0v_1u_1'v_0v_1t'$$

such that v_0v_1 does not occur in w_k', for all $0 \le k \le i$, or v_ℓ', for all $0 \le \ell \le j$. Note, that this factorization of w and u is unique.

We claim that $i = j$ and $w_k' = u_k'$, for all $1 \le k \le i$. However, we omit the proof here for lack of space. The left out part of the proof first proceeds by induction on $k' = \min\{i, j\}$ showing that $w_k' = u_k'$, for all $1 \le k \le k'$, and then consideres the two cases $i < j$ and $j < i$ deriving a contradiction in each of them.

So assume, we have $i = j$ and

$$\bar{v} = v_0 v_1 w_i' \cdots v_0 v_1 w_2' v_0 v_1 w_1'$$
$$= v_0 v_1 u_i' \cdots v_0 v_1 u_2' v_0 v_1 u_1'$$

and

$$w = w_0' \bar{v} v_0 v_1 w_2 \quad \text{and} \quad u = u_0' \bar{v} v_0 v_1 t' \ .$$

Consider

$$f_0 = v_1 w_2 u_0' \bar{v} v_0 \ .$$

Subcase: f_0 is bordered. Then it has a shortest border $h_0 = v_1 g_0 v_0$ (where g_0 is possibly empty).

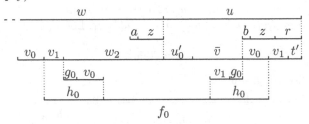

Recall, that $w_2 \neq \varepsilon$ and either $az \preccurlyeq v_1 w_2$ or $v_1 w_2 \preccurlyeq az$. If $|v_1 w_2| < |az|$ then v_1 occurs in z, and hence, overlaps with v_0 since $bz \le v_0 v_1$; a contradiction. So, we have $az \preccurlyeq v_1 w_2$. Surely, $|h_0| < |v_1 w_2|$ otherwise az occurs in u which contradicts our assumption. Let $w_2 = g_0 v_0 w_3$. Note, that $|v_0 w_3| \neq |az|$ since az and v_0 begin with different letters. We have $|az| < |v_0 w_3|$ since otherwise v_0 occurs in z, and hence, overlaps with v_1 which is a contradiction. Consider now,

$$f_1 = v_0 w_3 u_0' \bar{v} v_0 v_1 \ .$$

If f_1 is unbordered, then $|u| < |w| - 1$.

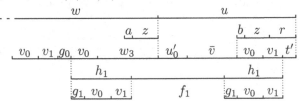

If f_1 is bordered, then it has a shortest border $h_1 = g_1 v_0 v_1$ with $|az| < |h_1|$, otherwise az occurs in u. Let $v_0 w_3 = g_1 v_0 v_1 w_4$. But, now

$$w = w_0' \bar{v} v_0 v_1 g_0 g_1 v_0 v_1 w_4$$

which contradicts our assumption that $w = w_0' \bar{v} v_0 v_1 w_2$ and $v_0 v_1$ does not occur in w_2.

Subcase: f_0 is unbordered. Then $|f_0| \le |w|$, and hence, $|w_0'| \ge |u_0'|$. But, we also have $|w_0'| \le |u_0'|$; see (5). That implies $|w_0'| = |u_0'|$. Moreover, the factors

w_0 and bzv' have both nonoverlaping occurences in $u_0'v_0v_1$ by (5). Therefore, $w_0' = u_0'$. Now,

$$w = xaw_2' \quad \text{and} \quad u = xbt''$$

where $w_0'\bar{v}v_0v_1 \leq x$ and $a, b \in A$ and $a \neq b$ and $w_2' \preccurlyeq w_2$ and $t'' \preccurlyeq t'$. We have that xb occurs in w by Theorem 14. Since xb is not a prefix of w and v_0v_1 does not overlap with itself, we have $|xb| + |v_0v_1| \leq |w|$. From $|t'| \leq |z_0| < |v_0v_1| - 1$ we get $|u| < |w| - 1$ and the claim follows. $\square$

Note, that the bound $|u| < |w| - 1$ on the length of a nontrivial Duval extension wu of w is tight, as the example given in the introduction shows. Theorem 2 also implies a new bound on the length of any word w auch that $\partial(w) = \mu(w)$ must hold.

Corollary 3. *If $|w| \geq 3\mu(w) - 2$ then $\partial(w) = \mu(w)$.*

5   Conclusions

In this paper we have given a confirmative answer to a long standing conjecture [8] by proving that a Duval extension wu of w longer than $2|w| - 2$ is trivial. This bound is thight and also gives a new bound on the relation between the length of an arbitrary word w and its longest unbordered factors $\mu(w)$, namely that $|w| \geq 3\mu(w) - 2$ implies $\partial(w) = \mu(w)$ as conjectured by Assous and Pouzet in [1]. Assous and Pouzet also gave the following example

Example 15. Let $\qquad w = a^nba^{n+1}ba^nba^{n+2}ba^nba^{n+1}ba^n$.
with $|w| = 7n + 10$ and $\mu(w) = 3n + 6$ and $\partial(w) = 4n + 7$.
We have that the precise bound for the length of a word that implies $\partial(w) = \mu(w)$ is larger than $7/3\mu(w) - 4$ and smaller than $3\mu(w) - 1$. The characterization of the precise bound of the length of a word as a function of its longest unbordered factor is still an open problem.

Finally, we would like to mention that after our proof was first made public in [12] an alternative proof of Conjecture 1 [13] and finally also of Theorem 2 [14] was proposed by Štěpán Holub. Those proofs use a different technique relying on lexicographic orders and is shorter than the original one presented here.

We think that our poof provides a more detailed insight into the structure of a nontrivial Duval extension by examining those words closely, and might therefore be useful for answering further questions on this subject.

Acknowledgements. We would like to thank the anonymous referees for their detailed comments on this paper.

References

[1] R. Assous and M. Pouzet. Une caractérisation des mots périodiques. Discrete Math., 25(1):1–5, 1979.

[2] J. Berstel and D. Perrin. *Theory of codes*, volume 117 *Of Pure and Applied Mathematics*. Academic Press Inc., Orlando, FL, 1985.

[3] R. S. Boyer and J. S. Moore. A fast string searching algorithm. *Commun. ACM*, 20(10):762–772, October 1977.

[4] D. Breslauer, T. Jiang, and Z. Jiang. Rotations of periodic strings and short superstrings. *J. Algorithms*, 24(2), 1997.

[5] P. Bylanski and D. G. W. Ingram. *Digital transmission systems*. Number 4 in Telecommunications Series. IEE, 1980.

[6] M. Crochemore, F. Mignosi, A. Restivo, and S. Salemi. Text compression using antidictionaries. In *26th Internationale Colloquium on Automata, Languages and Programming (ICALP)*, Prague, volume 1644 of *Lecture Notes in Comput. Sci.*, pages 261–270. Springer, Berlin, 1999.

[7] M. Crochemore and D. Perrin. Two-way string-matching. *J. ACM*, 38(3):651–675, 1991.

[8] J.-P. Duval. Relationship between the period of a finite word and the length of its unbordered segments. *Discrete Math.*, 40(1):31–44, 1982.

[9] J.-P. Duval, T. Harju, and D. Nowotka. Unbordered factors and Lyndon words. submitted.

[10] A. Ehrenfeucht and D. M. Silberger. Periodicity and unbordered segments of words. *Discrete Math.*, 26(2):101–109, 1979.

[11] T. Harju and D. Nowotka,. About Duval's conjecture. In Z. Esik and Z. Fülöp, editors, *DLT 2003 (Szeged)*, volume 2710 of *Lecture Notes in Comput. Sci.*, pages 316–324, Berlin, 2003. Springer-Verlag.

[12] T. Harju and D. Nowotka. Periodicity and unbordered words. TUCS Tech. Rep. 523, Turku Centre of Computer Science, Finland, April 2003.

[13] S. Holub. A proof of Duval's conjecture. In T. Harju and J. Karhumäki, editors, *WORDS 2003 (Turku)*, volume 27 of *TUCS General Publications*, pages 398–399, Finland, August 2003. Turku Centre of Computer Science.

[14] S. Holub. Unbordered words and lexicographic orderings. personal communication, July 2003.

[15] D. E. Knuth, J. H. Morris, and V. R. Pratt. Fast Pattern matching in strings. *SIAM J. Comput.*, 6(2):323–350, 1977.

[16] M. Lothaire. *Algebraic Combinatorics on Words*, volume 90 of *Encyclopedia of Mathematics and its Applications*. Cambridge University Press, Cambridge, United Kingdom, 2002.

[17] D. Margaritis and S. Skiena. Reconstructing strings from substrings in rounds. In *36th Annual Symposium on Foundations of Computer Science (FOCS)*, pages 613–620, Milwaukee, WI, 1995. IEEE Computer Society.

[18] F. Mignosi and L. Q. Zamboni. A note on a conjecture of Duval and Sturmian words. *Theor. Inform. Appl.*, 36(1):1–3, 2002.

[19] J. Ziv and A. Lempel. A universal algorithm for sequential data compression. *IEEE Trans. Information Theory*, 23(3):337–343, 1977.

Desert Automata and the Finite Substitution Problem*

(Extended Abstract)**

Daniel Kirsten

LIAFA, Université Denis Diderot – Case 7014, 2 place Jussieu,
F-75251 Paris Cedex 05, France

Abstract. We give a positive solution to the so-called finite substitution problem which was open for more than 10 years [11]: given recognizable languages K and L, decide whether there exists a finite substitution σ such that $\sigma(K) = L$. For this, we introduce a new model of weighted automata and show the decidability of its limitedness problem by solving the underlying Burnside problem.

1 Introduction

The present paper is the first one in a series of papers in which we will introduce new models of weighted automata to solve important decision problems in the theory of recognizable languages. The problems we address include the so-called limitedness problem, solved independently by K. HASHIGUCHI, H. LEUNG, and I. SIMON [1,7,13], Burnside type problems in semigroup theory, and the so-called finite substitution problem, which was open for more than 10 years [11]: given recognizable languages K and L, decide whether there exists a finite substitution σ such that $\sigma(K) = L$. Our main result is a solution to this problem.

Our tools rely on the approach by H. LEUNG and I. SIMON involving distance automata [7,8,12,13]. However, this concept proved to be insufficient for our purpose and led us to introduce a different class of automata, the *desert automata* which are non-deterministic finite automata with a set of marked transitions. The weight of a path is defined as the length of a longest subpath which does not contain a marked transition. The weight of a word is the minimum of the weights of all successful paths of the word. The second main result of the paper states that it is decidable whether the range of the mapping of a desert automaton is finite which is a counterpart of the corresponding result for distance automata [1,7,13]. Finally, we obtain some partial results on the complexity.

* Supported by the grant KI 822/1–1 of the German Research Community (DFG). On leave from Institute of Algebra, Dresden University of Technology, Germany.
** See www.math.tu-dresden.de/~kirsten for a complete version [4].

V. Diekert and M. Habib (Eds.): STACS 2004, LNCS 2996, pp. 305–316, 2004.
© Springer-Verlag Berlin Heidelberg 2004

2 Overview

2.1 Preliminaries

For sets M, we denote by $\mathcal{P}(M)$ the power set of M, and we denote by $\mathcal{P}_f(M)$ the set of all finite subsets of M.

Within the entire paper, we fix some $n \geq 1$ which is used as the dimension of matrices. Whenever we do not explicitly state the range of a variable, then we assume that it ranges over the set $\{1, \ldots, n\}$. For example, a phrase like "for every i, j" is understood as "for every $i, j \in \{1, \ldots, n\}$".

2.2 Distance Automata

K. HASHIGUCHI introduced the notion of a distance automaton motivated by his research on the star height hierarchy in 1982 [1]. A *distance automaton* is a tuple $\mathcal{A} = [Q, E, I, F, \Delta]$, where $[Q, E, I, F]$ is a non-deterministic finite automaton and $\Delta : E \to \{0, 1\}$ is a mapping called *distance function*. Let $\mathcal{A} = [Q, E, I, F, \Delta]$ be a distance automaton. The distance function is extended to paths: the distance of a path π is defined as the sum of the distances of all transitions in π and denoted by $\Delta(\pi)$. The distance of a word $w \in \Sigma^*$ is denoted by $\Delta(w)$ and defined as the minimum over the distances of all successful paths labeled with w.

A distance automaton is *limited* if there is a $d \in \mathbb{N}$ such that $\Delta(w) \leq d$ for every $w \in L(\mathcal{A})$. The problem whether a distance automaton is limited is decidable [1,3,7,8,13] and PSPACE-complete [9].

2.3 Desert Automata

A *desert automaton* is a tuple $\mathcal{A} = [Q, E, I, F, E^\curlyvee]$ where $[Q, E, I, F]$ is a non-deterministic finite automaton and $E^\curlyvee \subseteq E$ are called *water transitions*. Let $\mathcal{A} = [Q, E, I, F, E^\curlyvee]$ be a desert automaton. Its language $L(\mathcal{A})$ is defined as the language of $[Q, E, I, F]$. We call $\mathcal{A}$ *unambiguous* (resp. *deterministic*) if $[Q, E, I, F]$ is unambiguous (resp. deterministic).

Let π be a path in $\mathcal{A}$. We call π' a *subpath* of π if there are paths π_1, π_2 in $\mathcal{A}$ satisfying $\pi = \pi_1 \pi' \pi_2$. We denote by $\Delta(\pi)$ the length of a longest subpath of π which does not contain any water transition. The intuition behind this definition is that we imagine π as a path through a desert. We intend to walk along π. We carry a water tank, but this tank does not last the entire path. Whenever we come along a water transition, we can fill up the tank, and the tank has to last until we meet the next water transition. We can understand $\Delta(\pi)$ as the required capacity of the tank to walk along the path π.

For every $w \in \Sigma^*$, let $\Delta(w) = \min\{\Delta(\pi) \mid p \in I, q \in F, \pi \in p \overset{w}{\leadsto} q\}$, where $p \overset{w}{\leadsto} q$ denotes the set of all paths from p to q with the label w. A desert automaton is *limited* if there is a $d \in \mathbb{N}$ such that $\Delta(w) \leq d$ for every $w \in L(\mathcal{A})$.

Example 1. Consider the desert automaton $\mathcal{A}_1$ with $Q_1 = I_1 = F_1 = \{q_1\}$, $E_1 = \{(q_1, a, q_1), (q_1, b, q_1)\}$, and $E_1^\curlyvee = \{(q_1, b, q_1)\}$. For every $w \in \Sigma^*$, $\Delta_1(w)$ is the largest k such that $w \in \Sigma^* a^k \Sigma^*$. Similarly, there is a desert automaton $\mathcal{A}_2$ such that for every $w \in \Sigma^*$, $\Delta_2(w)$ is the largest k such that $w \in \Sigma^* b^k \Sigma^*$.

The disjoint union of $\mathcal{A}_1$ and $\mathcal{A}_2$ yields a desert automaton $\mathcal{A}$ such that for every $w \in \Sigma^*$, $\Delta(w) = \min(\Delta_1(w), \Delta_2(w))$. For every $k \in \mathbb{N}$, we have $\Delta(a^k b^k) = k$, and thus, $\mathcal{A}$ is not limited. However, for every $u, v, w \in \Sigma^*$, $k \in \mathbb{N}$, we have $\Delta(uv^k w) \leq |uvw|$, i.e., the sequence $(\Delta(uv^k w))_{k \geq 1}$ is bounded.

By Example 1, a pumping condition does not suffice to guarantee limitedness of desert automata. On the other hand, a pumping condition is sufficient to guarantee limitedness of unambiguous desert automata, and thus, the mapping Δ in Example 1 cannot be computed by an unambiguous desert automaton. In [4], we show by a bounded variation argument, that there are mappings which can be computed by unambiguous but not by deterministic desert automata. Consequently, the classes of mappings which are computable by deterministic, unambiguous, resp. arbitrary desert automata form a strict hierarchy.

Another difficulty in the research on desert automata is that in contrast to distance automata, the distance of a path $\pi = \pi_1 \pi_2$ cannot be calculated from $\Delta(\pi_1)$ and $\Delta(\pi_2)$. We just have $\max(\Delta(\pi_1), \Delta(\pi_2)) \leq \Delta(\pi) \leq \Delta(\pi_1) + \Delta(\pi_2)$. Thus, we cannot use the tropical semiring [13] and we develop the notion of word matrices and related results in Section 3. As a main result we show:

Theorem 1. *It is decidable and PSPACE-hard whether a desert automaton is limited.*

Here, we just prove the decidability. The proof of PSPACE-hardness is an easy adaptation of H. LEUNG's proof of the same result for distance automata [4,7].

3   An Algebraic Framework for the Limitedness Problem

We develop an algebraic framework to show the decidability of the limitedness problem of desert automata. For the rest of the paper, let $\mathcal{A} = [Q, E, I, F, E^\curlyvee]$ be a desert automaton, let $n = |Q|$, and assume $Q = \{1, \ldots, n\}$.

3.1   Finite Semigroup Theory

We assume that the reader is familiar with basic notions on semigroups [10]. Let S be a finite semigroup. The sets of *idempotent* (resp. *regular*) elements of S are denoted by $\mathsf{E}(S)$ (resp. $\mathsf{Reg}(S)$). For every $m \geq 1$, we call $a_1, \ldots, a_m \in S$ a *smooth product* if $a_1 \Rrightarrow \ldots \Rrightarrow a_m \Rrightarrow (a_1 \ldots a_m) \in \mathsf{Reg}(S)$.

We call a mapping $\sharp : \mathsf{E}(S) \to \mathsf{E}(S)$ *consistent* if we have for every $e, f \in \mathsf{E}(S)$, $a, b \in S$ satisfying $e \Rrightarrow f$ and $f = aeb$, $f^\sharp = ae^\sharp b$. It is shown in [4] that a mapping is consistent iff we have for every $a, b \in S$ with $ab, ba \in \mathsf{E}(S)$ $(ab)^\sharp = a(ba)^\sharp b$. It was already observed in [7] that every consistent mapping $\sharp$ admits an extension to $\sharp : \mathsf{Reg}(S) \to \mathsf{Reg}(S)$ by setting for every $e \in \mathsf{E}(S)$ and $c, d \in S$ satisfying $e \Rrightarrow ced$, $(ced)^\sharp = ce^\sharp d$.

Let $a \in \mathsf{Reg}(S)$. There are $e, f \in \mathsf{E}(S)$ with $e \Rrightarrow_R a \Rrightarrow_L f$, i.e., $ea = a = af$. Thus, $e^\sharp a = a^\sharp = af^\sharp$, and moreover $a^\sharp \leq_L a$ and $a^\sharp \leq_R a$.

If $a, b \in S$ are a smooth product, then $(ab)^\sharp = a^\sharp b^\sharp = a^\sharp b = ab^\sharp$ [4].

3.2   The Semigroup of Word Matrices

As observed above, we cannot describe desert automata by matrices over the tropical semiring. Thus, we develop the notion of word matrices.

Consider the alphabet $D = \{\Upsilon, \mathbb{M}\}$. The symbol Υ (resp. $\mathbb{M}$) should be pronounced "water" (resp. "desert"). The words over D represent paths in desert automata. Consider the semiring $\mathbb{D} = \big(\mathcal{P}_f(D^+) \cup \{\omega\}, \cup, \cdot\big)$, where ω is a new element and $\cup$ and $\cdot$ are extended from $\mathcal{P}_f(D^+)$ by setting for every $X \in \mathbb{D} \setminus \{\emptyset\}$, $\omega \cdot X = X \cdot \omega = \omega$, $\omega \cup X = X \cup \omega = X$, and further, $\emptyset \cdot \omega = \omega \cdot \emptyset = \emptyset$, $\emptyset \cup \omega = \omega \cup \emptyset = \omega$. The natural ordering on $\mathbb{D}$ is set inclusion extended from $\mathcal{P}_f(D^+)$ in a way that ω is between the empty set and the singletons.

We call a matrix A with entries in $\mathbb{D}$ a *word matrix* if there is some k such that every word in A has the length k, i.e., for every i, j and every $\pi \in A[i, j]$ we have $|\pi| = k$. We denote by $\mathbb{D}_{n \times n}$ the semigroup of all $n \times n$ word matrices. Note that $\mathbb{D}_{n \times n}$ is not closed under $\cup$.

Later, we will use the free semigroup $\mathbb{D}_{n \times n}^+$ over $\mathbb{D}_{n \times n}$. We denote by α the natural homomorphism from $\mathbb{D}_{n \times n}^+$ onto $\mathbb{D}_{n \times n}$.

3.3   On the Semantics of Desert Automata

We give another method to define the semantics of desert automata using word matrices. We define a homomorphism $\theta : E^+ \to D^+$, by setting for every transition $e \in E$, $\theta(e) = \Upsilon$ (resp. $\mathbb{M}$) if e is a water transition (resp. e is not a water transition). We can assign every word $w \in \Sigma^+$ a matrix $\theta(w) \in \mathbb{D}_{n \times n}$ by setting $\theta(w)[i, j] = \theta(i \overset{w}{\leadsto} j)$. Clearly, $\theta : \Sigma^+ \to \mathbb{D}_{n \times n}$ is a homomorphism.

For two paths π, π' with $\theta(\pi) = \theta(\pi')$, we have $\Delta(\pi) = \Delta(\pi')$. Hence, we can define Δ on D^+ by $\Delta(\pi) = \max\{l \in \mathbb{N} \mid \pi \in D^* \mathbb{M}^l D^*\}$ and we have for every path π, $\Delta(\pi) = \Delta(\theta(\pi))$. We extend Δ from D^+ to $\mathbb{D}$ by setting $\Delta(X) = \min\{\Delta(\pi) \mid \pi \in X\}$ for $X \neq \omega$ and $\Delta(\omega) = \omega$.

We have another definition of the semantics of desert automata by setting for every $w \in \Sigma^+$, $\Delta(w) = \min\big\{ \Delta\big(\theta(w)[i, j]\big) \mid i \in I, j \in F \big\}$. This definition is equivalent to the definition in Section 2.3 up to the empty word.

3.4   The Small Desert Semiring

Let $\mathcal{D} = \{\Upsilon, \mathbb{M}, \omega, \infty\}$. Intuitively, $\mathbb{M}$ represents a path without water, Υ represents a path with water, and ∞ means that there is no path. We define on $\mathcal{D}$ an operation $\cdot$ as the maximum over the ordering $\mathbb{M} \sqsubseteq \Upsilon \sqsubseteq \omega \sqsubseteq \infty$. This operation corresponds to the concatenation of paths. Clearly, $\cdot$ is idempotent, and $(\mathcal{D}, \cdot)$ is a monoid with identity $\mathbb{M}$ and zero ∞.

We define an operation $\min$ on $\mathcal{D}$ over the ordering $\Upsilon \leq \mathbb{M} \leq \omega \leq \infty$. Clearly, $(\mathcal{D}, \min, \cdot)$ is a semiring. We denote by $\mathcal{D}_{n \times n}$ the semiring of all $n \times n$-matrices over $\mathcal{D}$. Consider the homomorphism $\Psi : (\mathbb{D}, \cup, \cdot) \to (\mathcal{D}, \min, \cdot)$ defined by

$$
\Psi(X) = \begin{cases}
\Upsilon & \text{if } X \cap \{\Upsilon, \mathbb{M}\}^* \Upsilon \{\Upsilon, \mathbb{M}\}^* \neq \emptyset, \\
\mathbb{M} & \text{if } X \text{ is a nonempty subset of } \mathbb{M}^+, \\
\omega & \text{if } X = \omega, \\
\infty & \text{if } X = \emptyset.
\end{cases}
$$

It extends to a homomorphism $\Psi : (\mathbb{D}_{n \times n}, \cdot) \to (\mathcal{D}_{n \times n}, \cdot)$.

3.5 Strange Limits

We define the notion of a Ψ-*limit*. It is not a classic limit notion, because it is not based on a metric and the limit of a sequence does not belong to the same algebraic structure as the members of the sequence. A Ψ-limit of some sequence over $\mathbb{D}$ describes in terms of $\mathcal{D}$ how the sequence is bounded. We will extend this notion in a natural way to word matrices, and we prove some results which enable us to use Ψ-limits in the same way as traditional limit concepts.

Recall that some sequence $(q_k)_{k\geq 1}$ is a *subsequence of* $(p_k)_{k\geq 1}$ if there is a strictly increasing mapping $f : \mathbb{N} \to \mathbb{N}$ such that $q_k = p_{f(k)}$ for every $k \geq 1$.

A sequence $(x_k)_{k\geq 1} \in (\mathbb{N} \cup \{\infty\})$ is said to be *bounded*, if there are $l, K \geq 1$ such that $x_k \leq K$ for every $k \geq l$. It *tends to infinity*, if for every $K \geq 1$ there is some $l \geq 1$ such that for every $k \geq l$ we have $x_k \geq K$.

Let $(X_k)_{k\geq 1} \in \mathbb{D}$ be a sequence. We define the Ψ-limit $\overline{\Psi}$ of $(X_k)_{k\geq 1}$.

L1. If there is an $l \geq 1$ such that $X_k = \emptyset$ for every $k \geq l$, then $\overline{\Psi}(X_k)_{k\geq 1} = \infty$.
In this case, we call $(X_k)_{k\geq 1}$ an ∞-*sequence*.

For every $z \in \{\Upsilon, \mathbb{M}\}$, $X \in \mathbb{D}$, let $\Delta(X, z) = \min\{\Delta(\pi) \mid \pi \in X, \Psi(\pi) = z\}$, where $\min \emptyset = \infty$. We denote the sequence $(\Delta(X_k, z))_{k\geq 1}$ by $\Delta(X_k, z)_{k\geq 1}$.

Assume that there an $l \geq 1$ such that $X_k \neq \emptyset$ for every $k \geq l$. We define

L2. If $\Delta(X_k, \Upsilon)_{k\geq 1}$ is bounded, then we define $\overline{\Psi}(X_k)_{k\geq 1} = \Upsilon$.
L3. If $\Delta(X_k, \Upsilon)_{k\geq 1}$ tends to infinity and $\Delta(X_k, \mathbb{M})_{k\geq 1}$ is bounded, then we define $\overline{\Psi}(X_k)_{k\geq 1} = \mathbb{M}$.
L4. If $\Delta(X_k, \Upsilon)_{k\geq 1}$ and $\Delta(X_k, \mathbb{M})_{k\geq 1}$ tend to infinity, then $\overline{\Psi}(X_k)_{k\geq 1} = \omega$.

If we can apply one of these four definitions to a sequence $(X_k)_{k\geq 1}$, then we call $(X_k)_{k\geq 1}$ a *convergent sequence*. Otherwise, $\overline{\Psi}(X_k)_{k\geq 1}$ is not defined. We denote the set of all convergent sequences by $\mathfrak{C}(\mathbb{D})$. Every sequence contains a convergent subsequence. Every constant sequence $(X_k)_{k\geq 1}$ is convergent and we have $\overline{\Psi}(X_k)_{k\geq 1} = \Psi(X_1)$. For sequences over $\mathbb{D}$, we define $\cup$ and $\cdot$ componentwise.

Lemma 1. [4] *1. Every subsequence of a convergent sequence is convergent and converges to the same Ψ-limit.*
2. The set of convergent sequences is closed under componentwise $\cup$ and $\cdot$, and $\overline{\Psi} : (\mathfrak{C}(\mathbb{D}), \cup, \cdot) \to (\mathcal{D}, \min, \cdot)$ is a homomorphism.

The notion of a Ψ-limit and a convergent sequence extends naturally to matrices. By Lemma 1(2), $\overline{\Psi} : \mathfrak{C}(\mathbb{D}_{n\times n}) \to \mathcal{D}_{n\times n}$ is a homomorphism.

For every subset $T \in \mathbb{D}_{n\times n}$ we denote by $\overline{\Psi}\langle T\rangle$ the set of all Ψ-limits of all convergent sequences over $\langle T\rangle$. We have $\Psi(\langle T\rangle) \subseteq \overline{\Psi}\langle T\rangle$. We formulate the limitedness problem of desert automata by using the notions of a Ψ-limit.

Proposition 1. *Let $\mathcal{A} = [Q, E, I, F, E^{\Upsilon}]$ be a desert automaton and $T = \theta(\Sigma)$. The following assertions are equivalent:*

1. *$\mathcal{A}$ is not limited.*
2. *There is a matrix $a \in \overline{\Psi}\langle T\rangle$ such that $\min\{a[i, j] \mid i \in I, j \in F\} = \omega$.*

Proof (sketch). (2)⇒(1) There is a sequence $(w_k)_{k\geq 1}$ such that $\overline{\Psi}(\theta(w_k))_k = a$. For every $K \in \mathbb{N}$, there is a large $k \in \mathbb{N}$ with $w \in L(\mathcal{A})$ and $\Delta(w_k) \geq K$.

(1)⇒(2) Let $(w_k)_{k\geq 1} \in L(\mathcal{A})$ such that $\Delta(w_1) < \Delta(w_2) < \ldots$ Let $(B_k)_{k\geq 1}$ be some arbitrary convergent subsequence of $(\theta(w_k))_{k\geq 1}$ and $a = \overline{\Psi}(B_k)_{k\geq 1}$.

Clearly, Prop. 1 is rather another formulation of the limitedness problem of desert automata than a solution. To give an algorithm for the limitedness problem of desert automata, we show some method to compute $\overline{\Psi}\langle T \rangle$ by avoiding to examine the possibly uncountable set $\mathfrak{C}\langle T \rangle$.

4   The Solution of the Burnside Problem

In this section, we solve the Burnside problem for word matrices. Our main strategy follows H. Leung's approach [8] to a similar problem for the tropical semiring. However, there are great differences in the proof details, because we consider a more involved semiring and another notion of stabilization.

4.1   Stabilization

We define a mapping $\sharp : \mathsf{E}(\mathcal{D}_{n\times n}) \to \mathcal{D}_{n\times n}$ which we call *stabilization*. For every $e \in \mathsf{E}(\mathcal{D}_{n\times n})$ and i, j let

$$e^{\sharp}[i,j] = \begin{cases} \infty & \text{if } e[i,j] = \infty \\ \curlyvee & \text{if there is some } l \text{ such that } e[i,l] = e[l,l] = e[l,j] = \curlyvee \\ \omega & \text{otherwise.} \end{cases}$$

Remark 1. Let i, l such that $e[i,l] = \curlywedge$ and $e[l,l] = \curlyvee$. Then, $e^2[i,l] = \curlyvee \neq e[i,l]$. Thus, such i and l cannot exist, and similarly, it is impossible that for some l, j, $e[l,l] = \curlyvee$ and $e[l,j] = \curlywedge$.

If for some i, j $e[i,j]^{\sharp} = \curlyvee$, then $e[i,j] = e^3[i,j] = \curlyvee$.

Lemma 2. *Let $e \in \mathsf{E}(\mathcal{D}_{n\times n})$. If $e[i,j] \neq \curlywedge$ for every i, j, then $e = e^{\sharp}$.*

Proof. Let i, j be arbitrary. If $e[i,j] \in \{\omega, \infty\}$, then $e[i,j] = e^{\sharp}[i,j]$.

Assume $e[i,j] = \curlyvee$. By $e^{n+2} = e$, there are $i = i_0, \ldots, i_{n+2} = j$, such that for $l \in \{1, \ldots, n+2\}$ we have $e[i_{l-1}, i_l] \in \{\curlyvee, \curlywedge\}$, i.e., $e[i_{l-1}, i_l] = \curlyvee$. There are $p < q \in \{1, \ldots, n+1\}$ satisfying $i_p = i_q$. Then, we have $e[i, i_p] = e[i_p, i_p] = e[i_p, j]$ and $e^{\sharp}[i,j] = \curlyvee$.

We state the main result of Section 4. For subsets $M \subseteq \mathcal{D}_{n\times n}$ we define $\langle M \rangle^{\sharp}$ as the least subset of $\mathcal{D}_{n\times n}$ which contains M and is closed both under matrix multiplication and stabilization $\sharp$ of idempotent matrices.

Theorem 2. *Let $T \subseteq \mathbb{D}_{n\times n}$ be finite. We have $\overline{\Psi}\langle T \rangle = \langle \Psi(T) \rangle^{\sharp}$.*

4.2   Stabilization Is a Consistent Mapping

We establish a first connection between stabilization and Ψ-limits of sequences.

Proposition 2. *Let* $E \in \mathbb{D}_{n \times n}$ *such that* $\Psi(E) \in \mathsf{E}(\mathcal{D}_{n \times n})$. *The sequence* $(E^k)_{k \geq 1}$ *is convergent and* $\overline{\Psi}(E^k)_{k \geq 1} = \Psi(E)^\sharp$.

Proof (sketch). Let $e = \Psi(E)$. Let i, j be arbitrary.

If $e^\sharp[i, j] = \infty$, then for every $k \geq 1$, $e^k[i, j] = \infty$ and $E^k[i, j] = \emptyset$, and thus, $\overline{\Psi}(E^k)_{k \geq 1} = \infty$. In the rest of the proof, we assume $e^\sharp[i, j] \neq \infty$, i.e., $E^k[i, j] \neq \emptyset$ for every $k \geq 1$.

At first, we show that if $e^\sharp[i, j] = \curlyvee$ then $\Delta(E^k[i, j], \curlyvee)_{k \geq 1}$ is bounded, and thus, $\overline{\Psi}(E^k[i, j])_{k \geq 1} = \curlyvee$. Since $e^\sharp[i, j] = \curlyvee$, there is some l with $e[i, l] = e[l, l] = e[l, j] = \curlyvee$. There are $\pi_1 \in E[i, l]$, $\pi_2 \in E[l, l]$, $\pi_3 \in E[l, j]$ such that $\Psi(\pi_1) = \Psi(\pi_2) = \Psi(\pi_3) = \curlyvee$. For every $k \geq 2$, we have $\pi_1(\pi_2)^{k-2}\pi_3 \in E^k[i, j]$ and $\Delta(\pi_1(\pi_2)^{k-2}\pi_3) < |\pi_1\pi_2\pi_3|$. Thus, $\Delta(E^k[i, j], \curlyvee)_{k \geq 1}$ is bounded.

Finally, we deal with the case $e^\sharp[i, j] = \omega$. We assume by contradiction that $\Delta(E^k[i, j], \curlyvee)_{k \geq 1}$ does not tend to infinity. There is some $K \in \mathbb{N}$ such that we have $\Delta(E^k[i, j], \curlyvee) = K$ for infinitely many k. Choose some $k \geq (K+1)(n+1)+1$ with $\Delta(E^k[i, j], \curlyvee) = K$. Let $\pi \in E^k[i, j]$ with $\Delta(\pi) = K$ and $\Psi(\pi) = \curlyvee$. By counting arguments, there are $0 < p < q < k$ and l with $(p + K) < q$ such that $\pi \in E^p[i, l]\, E^{q-p}[l, l]\, E^{k-q-p}[l, j]$, i.e., we can factorize π into π_1, π_2, π_3 which belong to $E^p[i, l]$, $E^{q-p}[l, l]$, $E^{k-q-p}[l, j]$, respectively. We have $|\pi_2| > K$, and since $\Delta(\pi) = K$, π_2 contains a water transition. Thus, $\curlyvee = e^{q-p}[l, l] = e[l, l]$. Similarly, we obtain $e[i, l], e[l, j] \in \{\curlyvee, \text{\Finv}\}$, and by Remark 1, we have $e[i, l] = e[l, l] = e[l, j] = \curlyvee$, i.e., $e^\sharp[i, j] = \curlyvee$, which is a contradiction.

For every $k \geq 1$, we have $\Delta(E^k[i, j], \text{\Finv}) \geq k$, because every word in E^k is at least of length k. Thus, $\Delta(E^k[i, j], \text{\Finv})_{k \geq 1}$ tends to infinity. To sum up, if $e^\sharp[i, j] = \omega$, then $\overline{\Psi}(E^k[i, j])_{k \geq 1} = \omega$.

Lemma 3. *Let* $T \subseteq \mathbb{D}_{n \times n}$ *be finite. For every idempotent* $e \in \overline{\Psi}\langle T \rangle$, *we have* $e^\sharp \in \overline{\Psi}\langle T \rangle$.

Proof. There is a sequence $(w_k)_{k \geq 1} \in T^+$ with $e = \overline{\Psi}(\alpha(w_k))_{k \geq 1}$. By subsequence selection, it suffices to consider the cases that $(w_k)_{k \geq 1}$ is strictly length increasing and that $w_1 = w_2 = \ldots$ If $(w_k)_{k \geq 1}$ is strictly length increasing, then \text{\Finv} does not occur in $e^\sharp$, and by Lemma 2, $e^\sharp = e \in \overline{\Psi}\langle T \rangle$. If $w_1 = w_2 = \ldots$, then let $E = \alpha(w_1) \in \langle T \rangle$. By Prop. 2, we have $e^\sharp = \overline{\Psi}(E^k)_{k \geq 1} \in \overline{\Psi}\langle T \rangle$.

Lemma 4. *Stabilization* $\sharp$ *is a consistent mapping.*

Proof. Let $e \in \mathsf{E}(\mathcal{D}_{n \times n})$. Let $E \in \mathbb{D}_{n \times n}$ with $\Psi(E) = e$. By Prop. 2 and Lemma 1, $e^\sharp e^\sharp = \overline{\Psi}(E^k)_{k \geq 1} \overline{\Psi}(E^k)_{k \geq 1} = \overline{\Psi}(E^k E^k)_{k \geq 1} = \overline{\Psi}(E^k)_{k \geq 1} = e^\sharp$, i.e., $e^\sharp \in \mathsf{E}(\mathcal{D}_{n \times n})$. Let $a, b \in \mathcal{D}_{n \times n}$ with $ab, ba \in \mathsf{E}(\mathcal{D}_{n \times n})$. Let $A, B \in \mathbb{D}_{n \times n}$ with $a = \Psi(A)$, $b = \Psi(B)$. Then, $(ab)^\sharp = \overline{\Psi}((AB)^k)_{k \geq 1} = a\overline{\Psi}((BA)^k)_{k \geq 1} b = a(ba)^\sharp b$.

Lemma 5. *Let* $a \in \mathsf{Reg}(\mathcal{D}_{n \times n})$ *and* i, j *be arbitrary. We have* $a^\sharp[i, j] \neq \text{\Finv}$. *If* $a[i, j] \in \{\omega, \infty\}$, *then* $a^\sharp[i, j] = a[i, j]$. *If* $a[i, j] = \curlyvee$, *then* $a^\sharp[i, j] \in \{\curlyvee, \omega\}$. *If* $a[i, j] = \text{\Finv}$, *then* $a^\sharp[i, j] = \omega$.

Proof (sketch). Let $e \in \mathsf{E}(\mathcal{D}_{n \times n})$ with $e =_{\mathcal{L}} a$, i.e., $a = ae$, $a^\sharp = ae^\sharp$. The proof follows by an examination of the product $a\, e^\sharp$ and Remark 1.

4.3   On the Growth of Entries

We call $w = A_1 \ldots A_{|w|} \in \mathbb{D}^+_{n \times n}$ a *smooth product* if $\Psi(A_1), \ldots, \Psi(A_{|w|})$ is a smooth product. We extend the distance function Δ.

1. For $A \in \mathbb{D}_{n \times n}$, let $\Delta(A) = \max_{i,j,\, A[i,j] \notin \{\omega, \emptyset\}} \Delta(A[i,j])$.
2. For $w = A_1 \ldots A_{|w|} \in \mathbb{D}^+_{n \times n}$, let $\Delta(w) = \max_{l \in \{1,\ldots,|w|\}} \Delta(A_l)$.
3. For $T = \{w_1, \ldots, w_{|T|}\} \subseteq \mathbb{D}^+_{n \times n}$, let $\Delta(T) = \max_{l \in \{1,\ldots,|T|\}} \Delta(w_l)$.

Proposition 3. *Let $w \in \mathbb{D}^+_{n \times n}$ be a smooth product and i, j be arbitrary.*

1. *If $\Psi(\alpha(w))^\sharp[i,j] = \curlyvee$, then $\Delta(\alpha(w)[i,j]) \leq 2 \cdot \Delta(w)$.*
2. *If $\Psi(\alpha(w))^\sharp[i,j] = \omega$, then $\Delta(\alpha(w)[i,j]) \geq \frac{|w|}{4^{n^2}n} - 1$.*

Proof (sketch). Let $w = A_1 \ldots A_{|w|}$ and $a_l = \Psi(A_l)$ for every $l \in \{1, \ldots, |w|\}$.

(1) We have $\curlyvee = (a_1 \ldots a_{|w|})^\sharp[i,j] = (a_1^\sharp \ldots a_{|w|}^\sharp)[i,j]$. There are $i = i_0, \ldots,$ $i_{|w|} = j$ such that for every $l \in \{1, \ldots, |w|\}$ $a_l^\sharp[i_{l-1}, i_l] \in \{\curlyvee, \curlywedge\}$. By Lemma 5, we can conclude for every $l \in \{1, \ldots, |w|\}$ $a_l^\sharp[i_{l-1}, i_l] = a_l[i_{l-1}, i_l] = \curlyvee$. Choose $\pi_l \in A_l[i_{l-1}, i_l]$ such that $\Delta(\pi_l)$ is minimal. Since $a_l[i_{l-1}, i_l] = \curlyvee$ and because the words in $A_l[i_{l-1}, i_l]$ are of the same length, we have $\Psi(\pi_l) = \curlyvee$, and of course $\Delta(\pi_l) \leq \Delta(w)$. Thus, $\Delta(\pi_1 \ldots \pi_{|w|}) \leq 2 \cdot \Delta(w)$ which proves (1).

(2) We assume $|w| > 4^{n^2}n$. Let $\pi \in \alpha(w)[i,j]$. By a counting argument, there are $1 \leq k < l \leq |w|$ and p such that $(l - k) \geq \frac{|w|}{4^{n^2}n} - 1$, $a_{k+1} \ldots a_l \in \mathsf{E}(\mathcal{D}_{n \times n})$, and we can factorize π into $\pi = \pi_1 \pi_2 \pi_3$ for some $\pi_1 \in (A_1 \ldots A_k)[i,p]$, $\pi_2 \in (A_{k+1} \ldots A_l)[p,p]$, and $\pi_3 \in (A_{l+1} \ldots A_{|w|})[p,j]$. If $\Psi(\pi_2) = \curlyvee$, then we have $\Psi(\alpha(w))^\sharp[i,j] \neq \omega$. Thus, $\pi_2 \in \curlywedge^+$, i.e., $\Delta(\pi) \geq \Delta(\pi_2) = |\pi_2| = l - k \geq \frac{|w|}{4^{n^2}n} - 1$. $\qquad \square$

4.4   The Proof of Theorem 2

In order to complete the proof of Theorem 2 by showing $\overline{\Psi}\langle T \rangle \subseteq \langle \Psi(T) \rangle^\sharp$, we define a relation to compare word matrices. Let $K \geq 1$. Let $X, Y \in \mathbb{D}$. We denote $X \preceq_K Y$ if we have the following assertions:

1. If $X = \emptyset$, then $Y = \emptyset$.
2. If $X \neq \emptyset$, then $X \supseteq Y \neq \emptyset$.
3. X and Y "agree in their bounded words", i.e., $\{\pi \in X \mid \Delta(\pi) \leq K\} \subseteq Y$.

In particular, for $X \in \mathbb{D}$ with $X \neq \emptyset$ and $\Delta(X) > K$, we have $X \preceq_K \omega$, but we do not have $X \preceq_K \emptyset$. We generalize $\preceq_K$ componentwise to matrices in $\mathbb{D}_{n \times n}$. It is easy to prove that $\preceq_K$ is stable w.r.t. matrix multiplication.

We extend stabilization to word matrices. For matrices $A \in \mathbb{D}_{n \times n}$, we define the stabilization $A^\sharp$ if $\Psi(A) \in \mathsf{Reg}(\mathcal{D}_{n \times n})$ as follows:

$$A^\sharp[i,j] = \begin{cases} A[i,j] & \text{if } \Psi(A)^\sharp[i,j] = \Psi(A)[i,j] \\ \omega & \text{if } \Psi(A)^\sharp[i,j] = \omega. \end{cases}$$

This definition is correct by Lemma 5. Note that if $A^\sharp$ is defined, then $A^\sharp \in \mathbb{D}_{n \times n}$ and we have $\Psi(A^\sharp) = \Psi(A)^\sharp$ and $\Psi(A^\sharp)[i,j] \neq \curlywedge$ for every i, j.

Proposition 4. *Let $K \geq 2$. Let T be some finite subset of $\mathbb{D}_{n \times n}$. There is some $x_K \geq 1$ such that for every $w \in T^+$ there is a $B \in \mathbb{D}_{n \times n}$ satisfying $\Psi(B) \in \langle \Psi(T) \rangle^\sharp$, $\alpha(w) \preceq_K B$, and $\Delta(B) \leq x_K$.*

We should spend some attention to the conditions $\Delta(B) \leq x_K$ and $\alpha(w) \preceq_K B$. Let i, j be arbitrary. If $\alpha(w)[i,j] \in \{\omega, \emptyset\}$, then $\alpha(w)[i,j] = B[i,j]$. If we have $\Delta(\alpha(w)[i,j]) \leq K$, then $\alpha(w)[i,j] \supseteq B[i,j]$ but $\alpha(w)[i,j]$ and $B[i,j]$ agree in their bounded words (cf. 2, 3 in the definition of $\preceq_K$). If $\Delta(\alpha(w)[i,j]) > x_K$, then $\alpha(w) \preceq_K B$ and $\Delta(B) \leq x_K$ together imply $B[i,j] = \omega$.

We establish the following lemma to prove Prop. 4.

Lemma 6. *Let $K \geq 2$ and $x \geq 1$ be arbitrary. Let $I' \subsetneq I \subseteq \langle \Psi(T) \rangle^\sharp$ be two ideals of $\langle \Psi(T) \rangle^\sharp$ such that $I \setminus I'$ is a J-class of $\langle \Psi(T) \rangle^\sharp$. There is some $x' \geq 1$ such that for every $w = A_1 \ldots A_{|w|} \in \mathbb{D}_{n \times n}^+$ satisfying*

- **A1.** $\Psi(A_1), \ldots, \Psi(A_{|w|}) \in \langle \Psi(T) \rangle^\sharp$,
- **A2.** $\Delta(w) \leq x$,
- **A3.** *For every $l \in \{1, \ldots, |w| - 1\}$, $\Psi(A_l A_{l+1}) \in I$,*

there is some $v = B_1 \ldots B_{|v|} \in \mathbb{D}_{n \times n}^+$ satisfying $\alpha(w) \preceq_K \alpha(v)$ and

- **C1.** $\Psi(B_1), \ldots, \Psi(B_{|v|}) \in \langle \Psi(T) \rangle^\sharp$,
- **C2.** $\Delta(v) \leq x'$,
- **C3.** *For every $l \in \{1, \ldots, |v| - 1\}$, $\Psi(B_l B_{l+1}) \in I'$.*

In particular, this assertion is true for $x' = 2 \cdot 4^{n^2} n(K+2)x$.

At first, note the similarity between the assumptions (A1), (A2), (A3) and the claims (C1), (C2), (C3). This similarity enables us to apply Lemma 6 inductively on a chain of ideals $\emptyset \subsetneq \ldots \subsetneq I_2 \subsetneq I_1 \subseteq \langle \Psi(T) \rangle^\sharp$ to prove Prop. 4. In the last step of this induction, I' is empty, and thus, claim (C3) implies that v has the length 1, and v is exactly the matrix B which we require to prove Prop. 4.

Proof (Lemma 6). Let K, x, and w as in the lemma.

We factorize w into words $v_1, v_2, \ldots, v_m$. If $\Psi(A_1) \in I'$, then let $v_1 = A_1$ and proceed with $A_2 \ldots A_{|w|}$. If $\Psi(A_1) \notin I'$, then let v_1 be the longest prefix of w satisfying $\Psi(\alpha(v_1)) \notin I'$ and proceed with the remaining part of w.

In this way, we achieve some $m \geq 1$ and $v_1, \ldots, v_m \in \mathbb{D}_{n \times n}^+$ such that

1. $A_1 \ldots A_{|w|} = v_1 \ldots v_m$ (concatenation of words)
2. $\Psi(\alpha(v_1)), \ldots, \Psi(\alpha(v_m)) \in \langle \Psi(T) \rangle^\sharp$
3. For every $l \in \{1, \ldots, m - 1\}$, $\Psi(\alpha(v_l v_{l+1})) \in I'$ (by construction of v_l)
4. For every $l \in \{1, \ldots, m\}$ with $|v_l| > 1$, we have $\Psi(\alpha(v_l)) \in I \setminus I'$.

Let $l \in \{1, \ldots, m\}$ be arbitrary.

Case 1: $|v_l| < 2 \cdot 4^{n^2} n(K+2)$

We set $B_l = \alpha(v_l)$. Then, $\alpha(v_l) \preceq_K B_l$ and B_l satisfies (C1). Moreover, $\Delta(B_l) \leq |v_l| \cdot \Delta(v_l) \leq |v_l| \cdot \Delta(w) = x'$, i.e., B_l satisfies (C2).

Case 2: $|v_l| \geq 2 \cdot 4^{n^2} n(K+2)$

We set $B_l = \alpha(v_l)^\sharp$. However, we have to ensure $\Psi(\alpha(v_l)) \in \mathsf{Reg}(\langle \Psi(T) \rangle^\sharp)$. We denote v_l as $v_l = V_1 \ldots V_{|v_l|}$. We transform v_l into a word u. If $|v_l|$ is even, then we set $u = \alpha(V_1 V_2)\alpha(V_3 V_4) \ldots \alpha(V_{|v_l|-1} V_{|v_l|})$. Otherwise, $u = \alpha(V_1 V_2)\alpha(V_3 V_4) \ldots \alpha(V_{|v_l|-2} V_{|v_l|-1} V_{|v_l|})$. Clearly, $\alpha(v_l) = \alpha(u)$.

We have $|u| \geq (4^{n^2} n+1)(K+2)$. We denote the letters of u by $u = U_1 \ldots U_{|u|}$. By (A3), we have for every $k \in \{1, \ldots, |u|\}$ $\Psi(U_k) \in I$. If $\Psi(U_k) \in I'$, then $\Psi(\alpha(u)) \in I'$ and $\Psi(\alpha(u)) = \Psi(\alpha(v_l)) \in I'$ which contradicts (4), above. Hence, $\Psi(U_k) \in I \setminus I'$ for every $k \in \{1, \ldots, |u|\}$. Thus, $I \setminus I'$ is a regular J-class of $\langle \Psi(T) \rangle^\sharp$, and hence, u is a smooth product. Moreover, $\Psi(\alpha(u)) = \Psi(\alpha(v_l)) \in \mathsf{Reg}(\langle \Psi(T) \rangle^\sharp)$, i.e., $\alpha(v_l)^\sharp$ is defined, and $\Psi(B_l) = \Psi(\alpha(v_l)^\sharp) = \Psi(\alpha(v_l))^\sharp \in \langle \Psi(T) \rangle^\sharp$.

We show $\alpha(u) \preceq_K \alpha(u)^\sharp$. We know that $\alpha(u)$ and $\alpha(u)^\sharp$ are only different in entries i, j for which $\Psi(\alpha(u))^\sharp[i, j] = \omega$. Let i, j with $\Psi(\alpha(u))^\sharp[i, j] = \omega$. By Prop. 3(2) and $|u| \geq (4^{n^2} n+1)(K+2)$, we get $\Delta(\alpha(u)[i, j]) \geq \frac{|u|}{4^{n^2} n} - 1 > K$, and thus, $\alpha(u) \preceq_K \alpha(u)^\sharp$, i.e., $\alpha(v_l) = \alpha(u) \preceq_K \alpha(u)^\sharp = \alpha(v_l)^\sharp = B_l$.

Now, we take care on (C2) for B_l. Let i, j be arbitrary. Assume that $B_l[i, j]$ contains some path. By $B_l = \alpha(u)^\sharp$, $B_l[i, j]$ contains some water transition, i.e., $\Psi(B_l)[i, j] = \Upsilon$. By Prop. 3(1) and $\Delta(u) \leq 3 \cdot \Delta(w)$, we obtain $\Delta(B_l[i, j]) = \Delta(\alpha(u)[i, j]) < x'$. Hence, B_l satisfies (C2).

We show (C3). By (3), $\Psi(\alpha(v_l))\Psi(\alpha(v_{l+1})) \in I'$ for every $l \in \{1, \ldots, m-1\}$. By the definition of B_l, we have $\Psi(B_l) \leq_L \Psi(\alpha(v_l))$ and $\Psi(B_{l+1}) \leq_R \Psi(\alpha(v_{l+1}))$, i.e., $\Psi(B_l B_{l+1}) = \Psi(B_l)\Psi(B_{l+1}) \leq_J \Psi(\alpha(v_l))\Psi(\alpha(v_{l+1})) \in I'$.

We show $\alpha(w) \preceq_K \alpha(v)$. In both case 1 and 2, we have seen $\alpha(v_l) \preceq_K \alpha(B_l)$. By the stability of $\preceq_K$ w.r.t. matrix multiplication it follows $\alpha(w) \preceq_K \alpha(v)$.

Proof (Prop. 4.). Let $z \leq 4^{n^2}$ be the number of J-classes of $\langle \Psi(T) \rangle^\sharp$.

Let $w \in T^+$. We apply Lemma 6 z times over a chain of ideals $\langle \Psi(T) \rangle^\sharp = I_1 \supsetneq \cdots \supsetneq I_z \supsetneq I_{z+1} = \emptyset$. Initially, $x = \Delta(T)$ and (A1, A2, A3) are satisfied.

In the last application of Lemma 6 we achieved a word v with $|v| = 1$ by (C3). We set $B = v$ and $x_K = x'$ (x' from the last application of Lemma 6).

Proof (Theorem 2). We show $\langle \Psi(T) \rangle^\sharp \subseteq \overline{\Psi}\langle T \rangle$. We have $\Psi(T) \subseteq \overline{\Psi}\langle T \rangle$, because for every $A \in T$, $\Psi(A)$ is the Ψ-limit of $(A)_{k \geq 1}$. Moreover, $\overline{\Psi}\langle T \rangle$ is closed under multiplication (Lemma 1) and stabilization of idempotents (Prop. 3).

We show $\overline{\Psi}\langle T \rangle \subseteq \langle \Psi(T) \rangle^\sharp$. Let $(w_k)_{k \geq 1} \in T^+$. We assume $(\alpha(w_k))_{k \geq 1} \in \mathfrak{C}\langle T \rangle$ and denote $a = \overline{\Psi}(\alpha(w_k))_{k \geq 1}$. We have to show $a \in \langle \Psi(T) \rangle^\sharp$.

By subsequence selection, there is a $K \geq 1$ such that for every i, j and $l \geq 1$:

1. If $a[i, j] = \infty$, then $\alpha(w_l)[i, j] = \emptyset$, i.e., $\Psi(\alpha(w_l))[i, j] = \infty$.
2. If $a[i, j] \in \{\Upsilon, \mathbb{M}\}$, then $\Delta(\alpha(w_l)[i, j]) \leq K$ and $\Psi(\alpha(w_l))[i, j] = a[i, j]$.

Let x_K be from Prop. 4. There is a word w in $(w_k)_{k \geq 1}$ such that for every i, j with $a[i, j] = \omega$, we have $\Delta(\alpha(w)[i, j]) > x_K$. We apply Prop. 4 on w and obtain $B \in \mathbb{D}_{n \times n}$. Let i, j be arbitrary.

Assume $a[i, j] = \Upsilon$. By (2), there is some $\pi \in \alpha(w)[i, j]$ with $\Psi(\pi) = \Upsilon$ and $\Delta(\pi) \leq K$. By $\alpha(w) \preceq_K B$, we have $\pi \in B[i, j]$, i.e., $\Psi(B[i, j]) = \Upsilon = a[i, j]$.

Assume $a[i,j] = \mathbb{M}$. As above, there is a $\pi \in B[i,j]$ with $\Psi(\pi) = \mathbb{M}$ and $\Delta(\pi) \leq K$, i.e., $B[i,j] \in \{\Upsilon, \mathbb{M}\}$. If $B[i,j] = \Upsilon$, then we have (by $\alpha(w) \preceq_K B$) $\Psi(\alpha(w))[i,j] = \Upsilon$ which contradicts (2). Hence, $\Psi(B[i,j]) = \mathbb{M} = a[i,j]$.

Assume $a[i,j] = \omega$. By (1), $\alpha(w)[i,j] \neq \emptyset$. By the choice of w, we have $\Delta(\pi) > x_K$ for every $\pi \in \alpha(w)[i,j]$. Consequently, $\alpha(w) \preceq_K B$ and $\Delta(B) \leq x_K$ imply $B[i,j] = \omega$, i.e., $\Psi(B[i,j]) = \omega = a[i,j]$.

Finally, if $a[i,j] = \infty$, then we have $\Psi(B[i,j]) = \infty = a[i,j]$ in the same way.

To sum up, we have $\overline{\Psi}(\alpha(w_k))_{k \geq 1} = a = \Psi(B) \in \langle \Psi(T) \rangle^{\sharp}$.

Proof (Theorem 1.). We combine Prop. 1 and Theorem 2.

5   On the Finite Substitution Problem

To simplify some technical details, we forbid the empty word. In [4], we show the same result for free monoids. Let Σ_1 and Σ_2 be two alphabets. A mapping $\sigma : \Sigma_1 \to \mathcal{P}_f(\Sigma_2^+)$ is called a *finite substitution*. Every finite substitution extends to a homomorphism $\sigma : \mathcal{P}(\Sigma_1^+) \to \mathcal{P}(\Sigma_2^+)$.

Theorem 3. *It is decidable whether for two given recognizable languages $K \subseteq \Sigma_1^+$ and $L \subseteq \Sigma_2^+$, there exists a finite substitution σ such that $\sigma(K) = L$.*

Proof. Let $\eta : \Sigma_2^+ \to S(L)$ be the syntactic morphism of L. We call every homomorphism $\tau : \mathcal{P}(\Sigma_1^+) \to \mathcal{P}(S(L))$ with $\tau(K) = \eta(L)$ a *type*. There are just finitely many types, and there is an algorithm which computes the list of all types. A substitution σ is of type τ if $\eta(\sigma(a)) \subseteq \tau(a)$ for every $a \in \Sigma_1$. Every finite substitution σ with $\sigma(K) = L$ is of the type $\eta \circ \sigma$. Hence, it suffices to decide the existence of a finite substitution σ of a given type τ with $\sigma(K) = L$.

Let $\mathcal{A}_K = [Q_K, E_K, I_K, F_K]$ be an automaton which recognizes K. For every $t = (p,a,q) \in E$, we construct a desert automaton $\mathcal{A}_t = [Q_t, E_t, p, q', E_t^{\Upsilon}]$ with $L(\mathcal{A}_t) = \eta^{-1}(\tau(a))$, $E_t \subseteq (Q_t \backslash q') \times \Sigma_2 \times (Q_t \backslash p)$, and $E_t^{\Upsilon} = E_t \cap (Q_t \times \Sigma_2 \times q')$.

We define $\mathcal{A} = [Q, E, I_K, F_K, E^{\Upsilon}]$. We replace in $\mathcal{A}_K$ every $t = (p,a,q) \in E_K$ by $\mathcal{A}_t$ and identify p and q with the initial and accepting state of $\mathcal{A}_t$. The key argument is that there is a finite substitution with $\sigma(K) = L$ if and only if $L = L(\mathcal{A})$ and $\mathcal{A}$ is limited [4]. $\qquad\square$

6   Next Research Steps

The next step is to develop an automata concept which includes desert and distance automata as two extremal cases and to solve the limitedness problem of the new automata concept which allows a new proof for the decidability of the star height one problem [2,5].

Finally, we would like to address two problems on desert automata.

Is the limitedness problem for desert automata in PSPACE? Prop. 1 and Theorem 2 give an algorithm with time complexity $2^{\mathcal{O}(n^2)}$, where n is the number of states. One of the mostly examined problems on distance automata is to find a sharp upper bound on the range of the distance function of limited distance automata. The bound shown in [3] and recently improved in [9] allows to show that the limitedness problem for distance automata is in PSPACE [9]. The hope is to find such a bound for desert automata.

It is undecidable whether two given distance automata compute the same mapping [6], but this problem is open for desert automata.

Acknowledgments. The author acknowledges the discussions with JEAN-ERIC PIN on the paper.

References

1. K. Hashiguchi. Limitedness theorem on finite automata with distance functions. *Journal of Computer and System Sciences*, 24:233–244, 1982.
2. K. Hashiguchi. Regular languages of star height one. *Information and Control*, 53:199–210, 1982.
3. K. Hashiguchi. New upper bounds to the limitedness of distance automata. *Theoretical Computer Science*, 233:19–32, 2000.
4. D. Kirsten. Desert automata I. A Burnside problem and its solution. LIAFA Technical Report 2003-020, Paris, 2003.
5. D. Kirsten. Distance desert automata and the star height one problem. In I. Walukiewicz, ed., *FoSSaCS'04 Proc.*, LNCS, Springer-Verlag, to appear in 2004.
6. D. Krob. The equality problem for rational series with multiplicities in the tropical semiring is undecidable. *Int. J. of Algebra and Computation*, 4(3):405–425, 1994.
7. H. Leung. *An Algebraic Method for Solving Decision Problems in Finite Automata Theory*. PhD thesis, Pennsylvania State Univ., Dep. of Computer Science, 1987.
8. H. Leung. The topological approach to the limitedness problem on distance automata. In J. Gunawardena, ed., *Idempotency*, p. 88–111. Cambridge Univ., 1998.
9. H. Leung and V. Podolskiy. The limitedness problem on distance automata: Hashiguchi's method revisited. *Theor. Comp. Science*, 310(1-3):147–158, 2004.
10. J.-E. Pin. *Varieties of Formal Languages*. North Oxford Academic Publ., 1986.
11. J.-E. Pin. Personal communication, 2003.
12. I. Simon. Limited subsets of a free monoid. In *Proceedings of the 19th IEEE Annual Symposium on Foundations of Computer Science*, p. 143–150. 1978.
13. I. Simon. On semigroups of matrices over the tropical semiring. *Informatique Théorique et Applications*, 28:277–294, 1994.

Satisfiability Problems Complete for Deterministic Logarithmic Space

Jan Johannsen

Institut für Informatik
Ludwig-Maximilians-Universität München
jjohanns@informatik.uni-muenchen.de

Abstract. The satisfiability and not-all-equal satisfiability problems for boolean formulas in CNF with at most two occurrences of each variable are complete for deterministic logarithmic space.

1 Introduction

The satisfiability problem (SAT) for formulas of propositional logic in conjunctive normal form (CNF) is the canonical complete problem for the complexity class **NP** [1] of nondeterministic polynomial time. Similarly, SAT problems restricted to several subclasses of CNF formulas are complete for smaller complexity classes.

For Horn formulas, i.e., CNF formulas where every clause contains at most one positive literal, satisfiability is complete for deterministic polynomial time **P** [2]. For formulas in 2-CNF, i.e., formulas where every clause contains at most two literals, satisfiability is complete for nondeterministic logarithmic space **NL** [3]. We exhibit the first known natural special cases of SAT that are complete for deterministic logarithmic space **L**.

Let CNF(2) be the class of formulas $F \in$ CNF such that every variable occurs at most twice in F, and let SAT(2) be the problem SAT restricted to instances in CNF(2). It is well-known that SAT(2) can be decided in linear time (see e.g. the book by Kleine Büning and Lettmann [4]). We will show that SAT(2) is complete for **L**.

The not-all-equal-satisfiability problem (NAE-SAT) is a variant of SAT that is studied in many contexts. Given a formula in CNF, the question is whether there is a satisfying assignment that also falsifies at least one literal in every clause.

In general, NAE-SAT is **NP**-complete for those classes of CNF-formulas for which also SAT is **NP**-complete. NAE-SAT restricted to formulas in 2-CNF is complete for symmetric logarithmic space **SL** [3,5]. Recently, Porschen et al. [6] have shown that NAE-SAT(2), defined analogously to SAT(2), is solvable in linear time, and is in the parallel complexity class **NC**, their proof actually shows it is computable in parallel logarithmic time by a nearly linear number of processors, and thus is in **AC**^{1}. We will show here that NAE-SAT(2) is in, and in fact complete for **L**.

V. Diekert and M. Habib (Eds.): STACS 2004, LNCS 2996, pp. 317–325, 2004.
© Springer-Verlag Berlin Heidelberg 2004

It should be noted that our logarithmic space algorithms, in contradistinction to the algorithms mentioned above, only solve the decision problems SAT(2) and NAE-SAT(2), they do not give a witnessing assignment in case of a positive answer. However, after a draft of this paper was circulated, Stephen Cook (personal communication) and Mark Braverman [7] have given algorithms to construct satisfying assignments for satisfiable CNF(2)-formulas in logarithmic space.

It is easily checked that all the reductions we construct can be written as first-order reductions, given the usual encoding of the problem instances as logical structures (see Immerman [8] for background on these notions.) Therefore, all our reductions are uniform $\mathbf{AC}^0$ many-one reductions.

2   Satisfiability

In this section we show the **L**-completeness of SAT(2). To this end, we reduce SAT(2) to a problem on a certain class of graphs:

A *tagged graph* $G = (V, E, T)$ is an undirected multigraph (V, E) with a distinguished set $T \subseteq V$ of vertices. We refer to the vertices in T as the *tagged* vertices.

We call a connected component in G tagged, if it contains at least one tagged vertex, and untagged otherwise.

From a formula $F \in \mathrm{CNF}(2)$, we construct a tagged graph $G(F)$ as follows:

- $G(F)$ has a vertex v_C for every clause C in F.
- If clauses C and D contain a pair of complementary literals x and $\bar{x}$, then there is an edge e_x between v_C and v_D.
- If C contains a pure literal, i.e., a literal a such that the complementary literal $\bar{a}$ does not occur in F, then v_C is tagged.

Note that there can be parallel edges between clauses containing more than one pair of complementary literals.

The assignment of a value to a variable x in F corresponds to giving the edge e_x in $G(F)$ a direction, from the clause containing the literal among x, $\bar{x}$ that gets the value 1 to the one that gets the value 0. Thus a clause C is satisfied by an assignment if v_C has nonzero outdegree.

Since clauses that contain pure literals can always be satisfied, the following characterization of satisfiability is rather obvious:

Proposition 1. *A formula $F \in \mathrm{CNF}(2)$ is satisfiable iff the edges in $G(F)$ can be directed so that in the resulting directed graph, there is no untagged sink.*

This characterization leads us to the following lemma:

Lemma 2. *A formula $F \in \mathrm{CNF}(2)$ is satisfiable iff every connected component in $G(F)$ contains a tagged vertex or a cycle.*

Proof. It suffices to show that the condition on the right-hand side is equivalent to the condition from Proposition 1. Since it is obviously necessary, we only need to show it is sufficient.

Let a connected component C of $G(F)$ contain a tagged vertex v. Perform a depth-first-search of C starting from v, and direct every edge in the resulting tree towards the root v. This way, every vertex in C other than v will have an outgoing edge, so the only sink is v, which is tagged. The back-edges can be directed arbitrarily.

If a connected component C contains a cycle $v_1, v_2, \ldots, v_k$, then we direct the edges around the cycle. To obtain the direction of the other edges, perform a depth-first-search starting from $v_1, v_2, \ldots, v_k$ in order, but during the search from v_i, do not visit the vertices v_j for $j > i$. In the resulting forest, direct as above all edges in every tree towards the root v_i. This way, every vertex in C will have an outgoing edge, and the remaining edges can be directed arbitrarily. □

In other words, F is unsatisfiable iff $G(F)$ contains a connected component that is an untagged tree.

Theorem 3. SAT(2) *is in* **L**.

Proof. It suffices to show that the condition in Lemma 2 can be verified in logarithmic space. We employ a technique that was used by Cook and McKenzie [9] to test in logarithmic space whether a graph is acyclic.

For a tagged graph $G = (V, E, T)$, let $D(G) := \{(v, e)\,;\, e \text{ incident on } v\}$ be the set of darts of G, i.e., the ends of edges in G. For a dart $d = (v, e) \in D(G)$, we denote v by $v(d)$ and e by $e(d)$. We consider permutations of the set $D(G)$. The disjoint-cycle representations of the following two permutations can be easily constructed from G:

ρ_G is the product of the cycles $((v, e_1) \ldots (v, e_k))$ for every vertex v, where $e_1, \ldots, e_k$ are all the edges incident on v.

σ_G is the product of the transpositions $((v, e)\,(u, e))$ for every edge e, where e is an edge between vertices u and v.

By a result of Cook and McKenzie [9], from the disjoint-cycle representations of two permutations, one can compute the representation of their product in logarithmic space.

Hence we can obtain the disjoint-cycle representation of the product $\pi_G = \rho_G \circ \sigma_G$. We will show how, using this representation of π_G, we can decide whether G contains a connected component that is an untagged tree.

We start a search from every dart $d \in D(G)$. If the search is successful for every d, then we accept, otherwise we reject.

The search procedure performs two nested walks of the graph along the orbits of π_G. The outer walk is started at $w_1 := d$, then the inner walk is started at $w_2 := w_1$. It repeatedly remembers $e' := e(w_2)$, and then sets $w_2 := \pi_G(w_2)$, until either a tagged vertex is found, i.e., $v(w_2) \in T$, or the walk returns to w_1, i.e., $v(w_2) = v(w_1)$. In the first case, the search terminates successfully. In the second case, the search is successful if the walk did not return to $v(w_1)$ through $e(w_1)$, i.e., $e' \neq e(w_2)$.

If none of these cases occur, then the outer walk is continued by updating $w_1 := \pi_G(w_1)$. If $w_1 = d$, then the search terminates unsuccessfully, otherwise the inner walk is started again.

Note that the algorithm only stores two darts and one edge, so it runs in logarithmic space. The problem is therefore in **L**, since logarithmic space functions are closed under composition. To verify the correctness of the algorithm, we need to prove the following claim:

Claim. For every dart $d \in D(G)$, the search from d terminates unsuccessfully if and only if the connected component of G containing $v(d)$ is an untagged tree.

The "if" direction is obvious. For the other direction, we use the following observation: if for every d' in the orbit of d, the walk along π_G returns to $v(d')$ through the edge $e(d')$, then the component of $v(d)$ is a tree, which is seen as follows:

If a vertex is reached through the edge $e = e_1$, then the walk will traverse every other edge leaving v before returning on e. In fact, if

$$((v, e_1)\,(v, e_2) \ldots (v, e_k))$$

is the orbit of (v, e_1) in ρ_G, then the walk will traverse the edges $e_2, \ldots e_k$ in that order before returning on e_1: if u_i is the other vertex incident with e_i, then $\pi_G((u_i, e_i)) = (v, e_{i+1})$.

It follows inductively that the walk visits the entire component of $v(d)$. It also follows that the component contains no cycle, by the following argument of Cook and McKenzie [9]:

Let $v_1, \ldots, v_k, v_{k+1} = v_1$ be a cycle, with edges e_i between v_i and v_{i+1}, and with v_1 reached first through edge e_0. By the above observation, for every i, at v_{i+1} the walk would traverse e_{i+1} before returning on e_i. Therefore, the walk returns through $v_1 = v_{k+1}$ through $e_k \neq e_1$, in contradiction to the assumption.

Therefore, if the search from d is unsuccessful, the component of $v(d)$ is a tree, which is untagged, since the walk would have encountered any tagged vertices present.   □

Let $\mathrm{SAT}(2)^-$ be the restriction of $\mathrm{SAT}(2)$ to instances that contain no pure literals, and let TF (tree-freeness) denote the following problem:

TF: Given an undirected graph G, does every connected component in G contain a cycle?

As a consequence of Lemma 2, we obtain the following equivalence:

Proposition 4. $\mathrm{SAT}(2)^-$ *is equivalent to* TF.

Proof. One direction is given by the construction above, which produces no tagged vertices when F contains no pure literals.

For the other direction, we can reverse the reduction as follows: For an undirected graph $G = (V, E)$, we construct a formula $F(G)$ as follows: we introduce one variable x_e for every edge $e \in E$, and for each vertex $v \in V$, we construct a clause C_v that contains one literal for each edge e incident to v. This literal is x_e, if e connects v to a higher numbered vertex, and $\bar{x}_e$ otherwise.

Obviously, $F(G)$ is a formula in CNF(2) with no pure literals, and $G(F(G)) = G$, so by Lemma 2, the construction is a reduction from TF to SAT(2)$^-$. □

Proposition 5. TF *is* L-*complete.*

Proof. TF is in L by Proposition 4 and Theorem 3. Its L-hardness remains to be shown.

We reduce the following problem $\overline{\text{UFA}}$, which is known to be complete for L [9], to TF: Given an undirected forest G consisting of exactly two trees, and vertices u and v in G, are u and v in different trees?

The reduction adds two new vertices to G, and connects them both by edges to u and v, as shown below, giving G'.

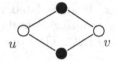

Now if u and v are in the same tree, then the other tree is still a tree in G'. If u and v are on different trees, then G' has only one connected component, which contains a cycle. Thus the construction reduces $\overline{\text{UFA}}$ to TF. □

From Propositions 5 and 4 above, we get that SAT(2)$^-$ is L-hard, therefore also SAT(2) is L-hard. Together with Theorem 3, this proves the main result of this section:

Theorem 6. SAT(2) *is* L-*complete.*

3   Not-All-Equal-Satisfiability

We are now going to show the L-completeness of NAE-SAT(2). We first consider the problem for the special case of monotone formulas, which turns out to be equivalent to another problem on tagged graphs.

Let an *isolated* clause be a unit clause such that the variable in this clause does not occur in any other clause. In this section we assume w.l.o.g. that formulas do not contain isolated clauses. This is possible, since no formula with an isolated clause is in NAE-SAT, and on the other hand such formulas are easily recognized.

Let mCNF(2) be the class of monotone formulas in CNF(2), i.e., formulas that contain only positive literals, and let mNAE-SAT(2) be the restriction of NAE-SAT(2) to instances in mCNF(2). Whereas satisfiability is trivial, NAE-SAT is **NP**-complete even for monotone formulas.

For a formula $F \in \mathrm{mCNF}(2)$, we define the tagged graph $G'(F)$ by

- $G'(F)$ has a vertex v_C for every clause C in F.
- If clauses C and D contain the same literal x, then there is an edge e_x between v_C and v_D.
- If C contains a literal, that does not occur in another clause, then v_C is tagged.

Let E2C (edge-2-colorability) denote the following problem:

E2C: given a tagged graph $G = (V, E, T)$, can the edges in G be colored by two colors such that every untagged vertex $v \in V \setminus T$ has incident edges of both colors.

The following characterization of mNAE-SAT(2) is rather obvious.

Proposition 7. *A formula $F \in \mathrm{mCNF}(2)$ is in* NAE-SAT *iff $G'(F)$ is in* E2C.

Note that for a formula F with an isolated clause, the graph $G'(F)$ contains a tagged isolated vertex. If an isolated clause is added to a formula $F \in \mathrm{NAE\text{-}SAT}(2)^-$, then the resulting formula F' is no longer not-all-equal satisfiable, whereas $G'(F')$ is in E2C. Thus our assumption is needed for the equivalence to hold.

In fact, we can show that the two problems are equivalent.

Proposition 8. mNAE-SAT(2) *is equivalent to* E2C.

Proof. One direction is Proposition 7. For the other direction, given a tagged graph $G = (V, E, T)$, we define a formula $F(G) \in \mathrm{mCNF}(2)$ as follows: for every edge $e \in E$, there is a variable x_e. For every vertex we form a clause C_v containing the variables x_e for the edges e incident on v. Finally, for every tagged vertex $v \in T$, we add a variable x_v to the clause C_v. It is easily seen that $G'(F(G)) = G$, and hence by Proposition 7, the construction reduces E2C to mNAE-SAT(2). $\square$

Lemma 9. *An undirected graph G is in* E2C *iff the following two conditions hold:*

1. *every untagged vertex has degree at least two, and*
2. *there is no untagged connected component that is a simple odd length cycle.*

Proof. Both conditions are obviously necessary. To see that they are sufficient, we first show the following claim:

Claim. If the conditions above hold, then every untagged component C contains either an even length cycle, or two edge-disjoint odd cycles.

Start a walk from some vertex on C, that never leaves a vertex on the same edge it came from, which is possible by condition 1. Since C is finite, we must find a cycle Z that way. Either Z is of even length, or else by condition 2 there must be a vertex v on Z of degree at least 3. Start another walk leaving v on an edge not on Z. Again, this walk must end in a cycle Z'. Now either Z' is of even length, or otherwise it either is edge-disjoint from Z, or it shares a common part with Z. But in the latter case, the cycle following Z and Z', leaving out the common part, is of even length.

The task to show that a graph satisfying the two conditions can be edge-colored, can now be split into three subtasks, to show how to color each type of connected component.

Claim. Every tagged component can be edge-colored.

This is shown by induction on the number of vertices in the component. The induction basis is trivial.

For the induction step, let a tagged component C be given, and let v be a tagged vertex in C. We modify C by deleting v and all incident edges, and by tagging all neighbors of v. The result C' is a union of several smaller tagged components, which can be colored by the induction hypothesis. This coloring can be extended to a coloring of C: if for a neighbor u of v, all incident edges in C' receive the same color, then we give the edge between u and v the other color. By induction, any tagged component can be colored.

Claim. A component C that contains an even length cycle can be edge-colored.

We color the edges around the cycle by alternating colors. For a vertex on the cycle, the incident edges other than the two cycle edges can now be colored arbitrarily. We therefore modify C by deleting the edges in the cycle, and by tagging the vertices on the cycle. The result is a union of tagged components, which can be colored by the previous case. Thus we can color all of C.

Claim. A component C that contains two edge-disjoint odd length cycles Z_1 and Z_2 can be edge-colored.

Choose vertices v_1 on Z_1 and v_2 on z_2 that are connected by a simple path P (possibly of length 0.) As in the previous claim, it suffices to color the edges on Z_1, Z_2 and P. We color the two edges on Z_1 incident with v_1 by the same color χ, and the two edges on Z_2 incident with v_2 by χ', where $\chi = \chi'$ if P is of odd length, and $\chi \neq \chi'$ otherwise.

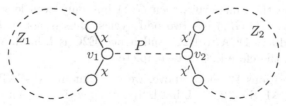

The coloring can now be completed by coloring P and the rest of Z_1 and Z_2 by alternating colors.   □

From this characterization we see that E2C $\in$ **L**, by the following algorithm: First check that condition 1 holds, which is easy. Then for every dart $d = (v, e) \in D(G)$, start a walk leaving v via e as in the above proof, until either a tagged vertex or a vertex of degree at least 3 is found, in which case the walk terminates successfully. If neither happens before the walk returns to v, then v lies on a simple cycle, thus we count the number of steps in the walk to decide whether the cycle is of even or odd length, and terminate with success or not accordingly.

By Proposition 8, we obtain the following result:

Proposition 10. mNAE-SAT(2) *is in* **L**.

We now show that the general case is in **L** as well:

Theorem 11. NAE-SAT(2) *is in* **L**.

Proof. We reduce NAE-SAT(2) to E2C. The definition of $G'(F)$ is extended to non-monotone formulas in CNF(2) by adding the clause:

- if C and D contain complementary literals x and $\bar{x}$, then we add a new vertex v_x and connect it to v_C and v_D as shown below.

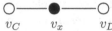

$$v_C \qquad v_x \qquad v_D$$

The presence of the vertex v_x enforces that the two edges get different colors, therefore $F \in \text{CNF}(2)$ is in NAE-SAT iff $G'(F)$ is in E2C. $\qquad \square$

Proposition 12. E2C *is* **L**-*complete*.

Proof. We reduce the following problem DCA, which is **L**-complete by a result of Cook and McKenzie [9], to E2C: given a permutation π, and two points a and b, do a and b lie on the same orbit of π?

The reduction produces a graph $G(\pi)$ as follows: there are two vertices c and c' for each point c, plus two extra vertices a'' and b''. In the graph $G(\pi)$, every c other than a, b is connected to $\pi(c)$ by a path of length 2 going through c', as shown below. Similarly, a is connected to $\pi(a)$ by a path of length 3 going through a' and a'', as shown below, and analogously for b.

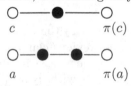

$$c \qquad\qquad\qquad \pi(c)$$

$$a \qquad\qquad\qquad \pi(a)$$

Note that $G(\pi)$ consists of disjoint cycles corresponding to the orbits of π. Now if a and b lie on the same orbit, then $G(\pi)$ has only even length cycles, thus is in E2C. Otherwise $G(\pi)$ has two odd cycles, thus is not in E2C. Thus the construction reduces DCA to E2C, and hence E2C is **L**-hard. We have shown E2C $\in$ **L** above, therefore E2C is **L**-complete. $\qquad \square$

From Propositions 12 and 8 above, we get that mNAE-SAT(2) is **L**-hard, therefore also NAE-SAT(2) is **L**-hard. Together with Theorem 11, this proves the main result of this section:

Theorem 13. NAE-SAT(2) *is* **L**-*complete*.

Acknowledgments. I would like to thank Albert Atserias and Jacobo Torán for helpful conversations about the subject.

References

1. Cook, S.A.: The complexity of theorem proving procedures. In: Proc. 3rd ACM Symposium on Theory of Computing. (1971) 151–158
2. Plaisted, D.A.: Complete problems in the first-order predicate calculus. Journal of Computer and System Sciences **29** (1984) 8–35
3. Jones, N.D., Lien, Y.E., Laaser, W.T.: New problems complete for nondeterministic log space. Mathematical Systems Theory **10** (1976) 1–17
4. Kleine Büning, H., Lettman, T.: Aussagenlogik: Deduktion und Algorithmen. Teubner, Stuttgart (1994)
5. Lewis, H.R., Papadimitriou, C.H.: Symmetric space-bounded computation. Theoretical Computer Science **19** (1982) 161–187
6. Porschen, S., Randerath, B., Speckenmeyer, E.: Linear time algorithms for some not-all-equal satisfiability problems. In: Proc. 6th International Conference on Theory and Applications of Satisfiability Testing, Springer LNAI (2003)
7. Braverman, M.: Witnessing SAT(2) and NAE-SAT(2) in L. Unpublished notes (November 2003)
8. Immerman, N.: Descriptive Complexity. Springer (1999)
9. Cook, S.A., McKenzie, P.: Problems complete for deterministic logarithmic space. Journal of Algorithms **8** (1987) 385–394

A Logspace Approximation Scheme for the Shortest Path Problem for Graphs with Bounded Independence Number

Till Tantau*

International Computer Science Institute
1947 Center Street
Berkeley, CA 94704, USA
tantau@icsi.berkeley.edu

Abstract. How difficult is it to find a path between two vertices in finite directed graphs whose independence number is bounded by some constant k? The independence number of a graph is the largest number of vertices that can be picked such that there is no edge between any two of them. The complexity of this problem depends on the exact question we ask: Do we only wish to tell whether a path exists? Do we also wish to construct such a path? Are we required to construct the shortest path? Concerning the first question, it is known that the reachability problem is first-order definable for all k. In contrast, the corresponding reachability problems for many other types of finite graphs, including dags and trees, are not first-order definable. Concerning the second question, in this paper it is shown that not only can we construct paths in logarithmic space, but there even exists a logspace approximation scheme for this problem. It gets an additional input $r > 1$ and outputs a path that is at most r times as long as the shortest path. In contrast, for directed graphs, undirected graphs, and dags we cannot construct paths in logarithmic space (let alone approximate the shortest one), unless complexity class collapses occur. Concerning the third question, it is shown that even telling whether the shortest path has a certain length is NL-complete and thus as difficult as for arbitrary directed graphs.

1 Introduction

Finding paths in graphs is one of the most fundamental problems in graph theory. The problem has both practical and theoretical applications in many different areas. For such problems we are given a graph G and two vertices s and t, the *source* and the *target*, and we are asked to find a path from s to t. This problem comes in different versions: The most basic one is the *reachability problem*, which just asks whether such a path *exists*. This problem is also known as 'accessibility problem' or 's-t-connectivity problem'. The *construction problem*

---

* Supported by a postdoc research fellowship grant of the German academic exchange service (DAAD). Work done in part at the Technical University of Berlin.

V. Diekert and M. Habib (Eds.): STACS 2004, LNCS 2996, pp. 326–337, 2004.

asks us to *construct* a path, provided one exists. The *optimization problem* asks us to construct not just any path, but the *shortest* one. Closely related to the optimization problem is the *distance problem*, which asks us to decide whether the distance of s and t is bounded by a given number. If the optimization problem is difficult to solve, we can consider the *approximation problem*, which asks us to construct a path that is not necessarily a shortest path, but that is only a constant factor longer than the distance of s and t.

In this paper it is shown that for directed graphs whose independence number is bounded by some constant k the reachability problem, the construction problem, and the optimization problem have fundamentally different computational complexities. The paper extends a previous paper [18] that treated only the reachability problem. The main contribution of the present paper is a logspace approximation scheme for the optimization problem and a proof that the distance problem is NL-complete. This paper presents the first example of an optimization problem that cannot be solved optimally in logarithmic space (unless L = NL), but that can be approximated well in logarithm space. Approximation theory has traditionally focused on polynomial-time computations; mostly because approximation algorithm are typically only sought for if computing optimal solutions turns out to be NP-hard, but also because computing *any* solution and computing an *optimal* solution seemed to have the same complexity for the problems considered in small space complexity theory.

The *independence number* $\alpha(G)$ of a graph G is the maximum number of vertices that can be picked from G such that there is no edge between any two of these vertices. The most prominent examples of graphs with bounded independence number are *tournaments* [17,20], which are directed graphs with exactly one edge between any two vertices. Their independence number is 1. The reachability problem for tournaments arises naturally if we try to rank or sort objects according to a comparison relation that tells us for any two objects which 'beats' the other, but that is not necessarily acyclic.

A different example of graphs with bounded independence number, studied in [5], are directed graphs $G = (V, F)$ whose underlying undirected graph is claw free, i. e., does not contain the $K_{1,m}$ for some constant m, and whose minimum degree is at least $|V|/3$. Their independence number is at most $3m - 3$.

To get an intuition on the behaviour of the independence number function, first note that independence is a monotone graph property: adding edges to a graph can only increase, deleting only decrease the independence number. Given two graphs with the same vertex set and independence numbers α and α', the independence number of their union is at most the minimum of α and α' and the independence number of their disjoint union is $\alpha + \alpha'$. Thus if a graph consists of, say, four disjoint tournaments with arbitrary additional edges connecting these tournaments, its independence number would be at most 4. Intuitively, a graph with a low independence number must have numerous edges and, indeed, at least $\binom{n}{2} / \binom{\alpha(G)+1}{2}$ edges must be present in any n-vertex graph G. This abundance of edges might suggest that if paths between two given vertices exist, there should also exist a short path between them. While this is true for the undirected case, in the directed case (which we are interested in in this paper) the distance between two vertices can become as large as $n-1$ even in n-vertex tournaments.

1.1 How Difficult Is It to Tell Whether a Path Exists?

The reachability problem for finite directed graphs, which will be denoted REACH in the following, is well-known to be NL-complete [11,12] and thus easy from a computational point of view. The complexity of the reachability problem drops if we restrict the type of graphs for which we try to solve it. The reachability problem REACH$_u$ for finite undirected graphs is SL-complete [14] and thus presumably easier to solve. The even more restricted problem REACH$_{forest}$ for undirected forests and the problem REACH$_{out\leq 1}$ for directed graphs in which all vertices have out-degree at most 1 are L-complete [4]. Here and in the following 'completeness' always refers to completeness with respect to the restrictive $\leq_m^{AC^0}$-reductions, i.e., many-to-one reductions that can be computed by a family of logspace-uniform constant-depth circuits with unbounded fan-in and fan-out [2,3].

The complexity of the reachability problem for finite directed graphs whose independence number is bounded by a constant k is much lower: somewhat surprisingly, this problem is first-order definable for all k, as shown in [18]. Formally, for each k the language REACH$_{\alpha\leq k} :=$ REACH $\cap \{\langle G,s,t\rangle \mid \alpha(G) \leq k\}$ is first-order definable, where $\langle\rangle$ denotes a standard binary encoding. Languages whose descriptive complexity is first-order are known to be very simple from a computational point of view. They can be decided by a family of logspace-uniform AC^0-circuits [15], in constant parallel time on concurrent-read, concurrent-write parallel random access machines (CRCW-PRAMs) [15], and in logarithmic space. Since it is known that L-hard sets cannot be first-order definable [1,6], REACH$_{\alpha\leq k}$ is *unconditionally* easier to solve than REACH, REACH$_u$, and REACH$_{forest}$.

When studying the complexity of a graph problem, one usually assumes (as done above) that the input graph is encoded as a binary string 'in some standardized way'. Which particular way of encoding is chosen is of little or no concern for the computational complexity of the problem. This is no longer true if the input graphs are encoded *succinctly*, as is often the case for instance in hardware design. Succinctly represented graphs are given indirectly via a program or a circuit that decides the edge relation of the graph. Papadimitriou, Yannakakis, and Wagner [19,23,24] have shown that the problems SUCCINCT-REACH, SUCCINCT-REACH$_u$, SUCCINCT-REACH$_{forest}$, and SUCCINCT-REACH$_{out\leq 1}$ are all PSPACE-complete. Opposed to this, SUCCINCT-REACH$_{\alpha\leq k}$ is Π_2^P-complete for all k, see [18] once more.

1.2 How Difficult Is It to Construct a Path?

The low complexity of the reachability problem seemingly settles the complexity of finding paths in graphs with bounded independence number. At first sight, the path construction problem appears to reduce to the reachability problem via a simple algorithm: Starting at the source vertex, for each successor of the current vertex check whether we can reach the target from it (for at least one successor this test will be true); make that successor the current vertex; and repeat until we have reached the target. Unfortunately, this algorithm is flawed since it can lead us around in endless cycles for graphs that are not acyclic. A correct algorithm does not move to any successor, but to the successor that is *nearest* to the target. This corrected algorithm does not only produce *some* path, but the shortest one. However, the algorithm now needs to compute the distance between two vertices internally, which is conceptually a more difficult problem than deciding whether two vertices are connected.

Nevertheless, we shall see that a path between any two connected vertices can be constructed in logarithmic space in graphs with bounded independence number. There even exists a *logspace approximation scheme* for this problem. This means that for each $r > 1$ and each k there exists a logspace-computable function that maps an input $\langle G, s, t \rangle$ with $\alpha(G) \leq k$ to a path from s to t of length at most r times the distance of s and t. If no path exists, the function outputs 'no path exists'.

1.3   How Difficult Is It to Construct the Shortest Path?

How difficult is it to construct the shortest path in a graph with bounded independence number? We show that, again surprisingly, even for tournaments this problem is as difficult as constructing the shortest path in an arbitrary graph. As pointed out above, the complexity of constructing the shortest path hinges on the complexity of the *distance problem* DISTANCE$_{\text{tourn}}$:= $\big\{ \langle G, s, t, d \rangle \mid G$ is a tournament in which there is a path from s to t of length at most $d \big\}$. This problem is shown to be NL-complete. Thus DISTANCE and DISTANCE$_{\text{tourn}}$ are $\leq_{\text{m}}^{\text{AC}^0}$-equivalent, but REACH and REACH$_{\text{tourn}}$ are not. The succinct version of DISTANCE$_{\text{tourn}}$ is shown to be PSPACE-complete.

1.4   Organization of This Paper

This paper is organized as follows. In Section 2 graph-theoretic terminology and known results on the reachability problem for graphs with bounded independence number are reviewed. In Section 3 a logspace approximation scheme for the shortest path problem for graphs with bounded independence number is presented. In Section 4 the distance problem for tournaments is shown to be NL-complete and its succinct version is shown to be PSPACE-complete.

2   Review of Known Results

In this section graph-theoretic terminology and known results on the reachability problem in graphs with bounded independence number are reviewed.

A *(directed) graph* is a nonempty set V of vertices together with a set $E \subseteq V \times V$ of directed edges. A graph is *undirected* if its edge relation is symmetric. A *tournament* is a graph with exactly one edge between any two different vertices and $(v, v) \notin E$ for all $v \in V$. A *forest* is an undirected, acyclic graph. A *tree* is a connected forest.

A *path of length* ℓ in a graph $G = (V, E)$ is a sequence $(v_0, \ldots, v_\ell)$ of distinct vertices with $(v_i, v_{i+1}) \in E$ for $i \in \{0, \ldots, \ell - 1\}$. A vertex t is *reachable* from a vertex s if there is a path from s to t. The *distance* $d(s, t)$ of two vertices is the length of the shortest path between them or ∞, if no path exists. For $i \in \mathbb{N}$, a vertex $u \in V$ is said to i-*dominate* a vertex $v \in V$ if there is a path from u to v of length at most i. A set $U \subseteq V$ is an i-*dominating set for* G if every vertex $v \in V$ is i-dominated by some vertex $u \in U$. The i-*domination number* $\beta_i(G)$ is the minimal size of an i-dominating set for G. A set $U \subseteq V$ is an *independent set* if there is no edge in E connecting vertices in U. The maximal size of independent sets in G is its *independence number* $\alpha(G)$.

Fact 2.1 ([18]). *Let* $G = (V, E)$ *be a finite graph with at least two vertices,* $n := |V|$, $\alpha := \alpha(G)$, *and* $c := (\alpha^2 + \alpha)/(\alpha^2 + \alpha - 1)$. *Then*

1. $\beta_1(G) \leq \lceil \log_c n \rceil$ *and*
2. $\beta_2(G) \leq \alpha$.

For tournaments G, Fact 2.1 yields $\beta_1(G) \leq \lceil \log_2 n \rceil$ and $\beta_2(G) = 1$. The first result was first proved by Megiddo and Vishkin in [16], where it was used to show that the dominating set problem for tournaments is not NP-complete, unless NP $\subseteq$ DTIME$[n^{O(\log n)}]$. The second result is also known as the Lion King Lemma, which was first noticed by Landau [13] in the study of animal societies, where the dominance relations on prides of lions form tournaments. It has applications in the study of P-selective sets [9] and many other fields.

The next fact states that the complexity of the reachability problem for graphs with bounded independence number is low: REACH$_{\alpha \leq k}$ is first-order definable for all k. *First-order definability* is a language property studied in descriptive complexity theory. It can be defined as follows for the special case of languages $A \subseteq \{\langle V, E, s, t \rangle \mid (V, E) \text{ is a finite graph}, s, t \in V\}$: Let $\tau = (\mathrm{E}^2, \mathrm{s}, \mathrm{t})$ be the *signature of graphs with two designated vertices*. A first-order τ-*formula* is a first-order formula that contains, other than quantifiers, variables, and connectives, only the binary relation symbol E and the constant symbols s and t. An example is the formula $\exists x [\mathrm{E}(\mathrm{s}, x) \wedge \mathrm{E}(x, \mathrm{t})]$. A τ-*structure* is a tuple (V, E, s, t) consisting of a graph (V, E) and two vertices $s, t \in V$. A τ-structure is a *model* of a τ-formula if the formula holds when we interpret the relation symbol E as the edge relation E and the constant symbols s and t as the vertices s and t. For example, the τ-formula $\exists x [\mathrm{E}(\mathrm{s}, x) \wedge \mathrm{E}(x, \mathrm{t})]$ is a model of every τ-structure (V, E, s, t) in which there is a path from s to t in the graph (V, E) of length exactly 2. The language A is *first-order definable* if there exists a τ-formula ϕ such that $\langle V, E, s, t \rangle \in A$ iff (V, E, s, t) is a model of ϕ.

Fact 2.2 ([18]). *For each* k, REACH$_{\alpha \leq k}$ *is first-order definable.*

The complexity of the reachability problem for graphs with bounded independence number is also interesting in the succinct setting. Succinctly represented graphs are given implicitly via a description in some description language. Since succinct representations allow the encoding of large graphs into small codes, numerous graph properties are (provably) harder to check for succinctly represented graphs than for graphs coded in the usual way. Papadimitriou et al. [19,24] have shown that most interesting problems for succinctly represented graphs are PSPACE-complete or even NEXP-complete. The following formalization of succinct graph representations follows Galperin and Wigderson [7], but others are also possible [24,8].

Definition 2.1. *A succinct representation of a graph* $G = (\{0,1\}^n, E)$ *is a $2n$-input circuit C such that for all $u,v \in \{0,1\}^n$ we have $(u,v) \in E$ iff $C(uv) = 1$.*

The circuit tells us for any two vertices of the graph whether there is a directed edge between them or not. Note that C will have size at least $2n$ since it has $2n$ input gates.

Definition 2.2. *Let $A \subseteq \{\langle G, s, t \rangle \mid G = (V, E)$ is a finite graph, $s, t \in V\}$. Then* SUCCINCT-A *is the set of all codes $\langle C, s, t \rangle$ such that C is a succinct representation of a graph G with $\langle G, s, t \rangle \in A$.*

Fact 2.3 ([18]). *For each k,* SUCCINCT-REACH$_{\alpha \leq k}$ *is Π_2^P-complete.*

3   Complexity of the Approximation Problem

In this section it is shown that for graphs with bounded independence number we can not only tell in logarithmic space whether a path exists between two vertices, but we can also construct such a path. While it seems difficult to construct the *shortest* path in logarithmic space (by the results of the next section this is impossible unless L = NL), it is possible to find a path that is *approximately* as long as the shortest path. Even better, there exists a *logspace approximation scheme* for constructing paths whose length is as close to the length of the shortest path as we would like:

Theorem 3.1. *For all k there exists a deterministic Turing machine M with read-only access to the input tape and write-only access to the output tape such that:*

1. *On input $\langle G, s, t, m \rangle$ with $\langle G, s, t \rangle \in$ REACH$_{\alpha \leq k}$ and $m \geq 1$, it outputs a path from s to t of length at most $(1 + 1/m)\,d(s,t)$.*
2. *On input $\langle G, s, t, m \rangle$ with $\langle G, s, t \rangle \notin$ REACH$_{\alpha \leq k}$ it outputs 'no path exists'.*
3. *It uses space $O(\log m \log n)$ on the work tapes, where n is the number of vertices in G.*

For the proof of the theorem we need two lemmas. The second lemma is a 'constructive version' of Savitch's theorem [21].

Lemma 3.2. *There exists a function in* FL *that maps every input $\langle G, s, t \rangle \in$ REACH$_{forest}$ to the shortest path from s to t in G and all other inputs to 'no path exists'.*

Proof. The problem REACH$_{\text{forest}}$ is L-complete as shown in [4]. In order to compute the shortest path from s to t we iterate the following procedure, starting at s: For each neighbour v of the current vertex, we check whether t is reachable from v in the forest obtained by removing the edge connecting the current vertex and v. There is exactly one vertex for which this test succeeds. We output this vertex, make it the new current vertex, and repeat the procedure until we reach t. $\qquad\square$

Lemma 3.3. *There exists a deterministic Turing machine M with read-only access to the input tape and write-only access to the output tape such that:*

1. *On input $\langle G, s, t\rangle \in$ REACH it outputs a shortest path from s to t and uses space $O\big(\log \mathrm{d}(s,t) \log n\big)$ on the work tapes, where n is the number of vertices in G.*
2. *On input $\langle G, s, t\rangle \notin$ REACH it outputs 'no path exists'. It uses space $O(\log^2 n)$ on the work tapes, where n is the number of vertices in G.*

Proof. We augment Savitch's algorithm [21] by a construction procedure that outputs paths. If there are several paths, the procedure 'decides on one of them' and does so 'within the recursion'.

Let *reachable*(u, v, ℓ) be Savitch's procedure for testing whether there is a path from u to v of length at most ℓ: For $\ell = 1$, it checks whether $(u, v) \in E$ or $u = v$. For larger ℓ, it checks whether for some vertex z both the calls *reachable*$(u, z, \lfloor \ell/2 \rfloor)$ and *reachable*$(z, v, \ell - \lfloor \ell/2 \rfloor)$ succeed. As noted by Savitch, we can compute *reachable*(u, v, ℓ) in space $O(\log \ell \log n)$ since we can reuse space.

We next define a procedure *construct*(u, v, ℓ) that writes a path of length ℓ from u to v onto an output tape, provided *reachable*(u, v, ℓ) holds. In order to simplify the assemblage of outputs of different calls to *construct*, the last vertex of the path, i.e., the vertex v, will be omitted. For $\ell = 1$, *construct* simply outputs u. For larger ℓ, it finds the first vertex z for which both the calls *reachable*$(u, z, \lfloor \ell/2 \rfloor)$ and *reachable*$(z, v, \ell - \lfloor \ell/2 \rfloor)$ succeed. For this vertex z it first calls *construct*$(u, z, \lfloor \ell/2 \rfloor)$ and then *construct*$(z, v, \ell - \lfloor \ell/2 \rfloor)$.

The machine M iteratively calls *reachable*(s, t, ℓ) for increasing values of ℓ. For the first value ℓ for which this test succeeds, it calls *construct*(s, t, ℓ), appends the missing vertex t, and quits. If the tests do not succeed for any $\ell \leq n$, it outputs 'no path exists'. $\qquad\square$

Proof (of Theorem 3.1). Let an input $\langle G, s, t, m\rangle$ be given. Let $G = (V, E)$ and $n := |V|$. For a set U of vertices let $\mathrm{d}(U, t) := \min\{\mathrm{d}(u, t) \mid u \in U\}$.

We first check, in space $O(\log n)$, whether $\langle G, s, t\rangle \in$ REACH$_{\alpha \leq k}$ holds and output 'no path exists' if this is not the case. Otherwise we enter a loop in which we construct a sequence $U_1, U_2, \ldots, U_\ell \subseteq V$ of vertex sets with $U_1 = \{s\}$ and $U_\ell = \{t\}$. For the construction of U_{i+1} we access only U_i and use space $O(\log m \log n)$. Once we have constructed U_{i+1} we erase U_i and reuse the space it occupied.

The set U_i is obtained from U_{i-1} as follows: If $\mathrm{d}(U_{i-1}, t) \leq 2m + 1$, let $U_i := \{t\}$. Otherwise let $S_i := \{v \in V \mid \mathrm{d}(U_{i-1}, v) = 2m + 2\}$ and choose $U_i \subseteq S_i$

as a 2-dominating, size-k vertex subset the graph $G' := (S_i, E \cap (S_i \times S_i))$ induced on the vertices in S_i. Since $\alpha(G') \leq \alpha(G) \leq k$, such a 2-dominating set U_i exists by Fact 2.1. We can obtain it in space $O(\log m \log n)$ since the question '$v \in S_i$?' can be answered in space $O(\log m \log n)$ using the procedure *reachable* from Lemma 3.3.

The sets U_i have the following properties for $i \in \{2, \ldots, \ell - 1\}$:

1. All elements of U_i are reachable from s.
2. $|U_i| \leq k$.
3. $d(U_{i-1}, u) = 2m + 2$ for all $u \in U_i$.
4. $d(U_i, t) \leq d(U_{i-1}, t) - 2m$ and hence $d(U_i, t) \leq d(s, t) - 2m(i - 1)$.

To see that the last property holds, note that $d(U_i, t) \leq d(S_i, t) + 2$ and that $d(S_i, t) = d(U_{i-1}, t) - 2m - 2$. For $i = \ell$, the first two properties are also true and the third one becomes $d(U_{i-1}, t) \leq 2m + 1$.

Intuitively, in each iteration we reduce the distance between U_i and t by at least $2m$ and each U_{i-1} can be connected to the next U_i by a path of length $2m + 2$. It remains to explain how to connect the U_i's correctly.

In order to output the desired path from s to t of length at most $(1 + 1/m)\, d(s, t)$, we first construct a forest that contains this path. The forest is not actually written down anywhere (we are allowed only a logarithmic amount of space). Rather, as in the proof of FL being closed under composition, the forest's code is dynamically recalculated in space $O(\log m \log n)$ whenever one of its bits is needed. Finding the shortest path in a forest can be done in logarithmic space by Lemma 3.2, and the shortest path in the forest will be the desired path.

To define the forest F, for each $i \in \{2, \ldots, \ell\}$ we first define a 'small' forest F_i as follows: For each $u \in U_i$ it contains the vertices and edges of the shortest path from U_{i-1} to u. This path is constructed by calling the machine M from Lemma 3.3 on input $\langle G, u', u \rangle$ for the first vertex $u' \in U_{i-1}$ for which $d(u', u)$ is minimal. Since $d(u', u) \leq 2m + 2$, this call needs space $O(\log m \log n)$. The graph F_i is, indeed, a forest since if two paths output by M for the same source vertex split at some point, they split permanently. Let F be the union of all the forests F_i constructed during the run of the algorithm. This union is a forest since every tree in a forest F_i has at most one vertex in common with any other tree in a forest F_j with $j \neq i$.

Consider the shortest path from s to t in the forest F. This path passes through all U_i. For $i \in \{1, \ldots, \ell\}$ let $u_i \in U_i$ be the last vertex of U_i on this path. The total length of the path is given by $\sum_{i=1}^{\ell-1} d(u_i, u_{i+1})$. We have $d(u_i, u_{i+1}) = 2m + 2$ for $i \in \{1, \ldots, \ell - 2\}$. Thus the total length is

$$
\begin{aligned}
(2m + 2)(\ell - 2) + d(u_{\ell-1}, t) &= (2m + 2)(\ell - 2) + d(U_{\ell-1}, t) \\
&\leq (2m + 2)(\ell - 2) + d(s, t) - 2m(\ell - 2) \\
&= d(s, t) + 2(\ell - 2) \leq d(s, t) + d(s, t)/m.
\end{aligned}
$$

For the two inequalities, we both times used the last property of $U_{\ell-1}$, by which $d(U_{\ell-1}, t) \leq d(s, t) - 2m(\ell - 2)$ and hence also $2(\ell - 2) \leq d(s, t)/m$.   □

The space bound from Theorem 3.1 is optimal in the following sense: Suppose we could construct a machine M' that uses space $O(\log^{1-\epsilon} m \log n)$ and achieves the same as M. Then DISTANCE$_{\text{tourn}} \in$ DSPACE$[\log^{2-\epsilon} n]$, because M' outputs the *shortest* path for $m = n + 1$. The results of the next section show that this would imply NL $\subseteq$ DSPACE$[\log^{2-\epsilon} n]$.

4   Complexity of the Distance Problem

In this section we study the complexity of the distance problem for graphs with bounded independence number. This problem asks us to decide whether the distance of two vertices in a graph is smaller than a given input number. It is shown that this problem is NL-complete even for tournaments and that the succinct version is PSPACE-complete.

The distance problem is closely linked to the problem of constructing the shortest path in a graph: As argued in the introduction, we can *construct* the shortest path in graph if we have oracle access to the distance problem for this graph. The other way round, we can easily solve the distance problem if we have oracle access to an algorithm that constructs shortest paths. Because of this close relationship, the completeness result bashes any hope of finding a logspace algorithm for constructing shortest path in tournaments, unless L = NL.

Theorem 4.1. *The problem* DISTANCE$_{\text{tourn}}$ *is NL-complete.*

Proof. We show REACH $\leq_m^{\text{AC}^0}$ DISTANCE$_{\text{tourn}}$. Let an input $\langle G, s, t \rangle$ be given. Let $G = (V, E)$ and $n := |V|$. The tournament $G' = (V', E')$ is constructed as follows: The vertex set V' is $\{1, \ldots, n\} \times V$. We can think of this vertex set as a grid consisting of n rows and n columns. There is an edge in G' from a vertex (r_1, v_1) to a vertex (r_2, v_2) iff one of the following conditions holds:

1. $r_2 = r_1 + 1$ and $(v_1, v_2) \in E \cup \{(v, v) \mid v \in V\}$, i.e., if v_1 and v_2 are connected in G or if $v_1 = v_2$, then there is an edge leading 'downward' between them on adjacent rows.
2. $r_1 = r_2$ and $v_1 < v_2$, where $<$ is some linear ordering on V, i.e., the vertices on the same row are ordered linearly.
3. $r_2 = r_1 - 1$ and $(v_1, v_2) \notin E \cup \{(v, v) \mid v \in V\}$, i.e., if v_1 and v_2 are not connected in G and if they are not identical, then there is an edge leading 'upward' between them on adjacent rows.
4. $r_2 \leq r_1 - 2$, i.e., all edges spanning at least two rows point 'upward'.

The reduction machine poses the query 'Is there a path from $s' = (1, s)$ to $t' = (n, t)$ in G' of length at most $n - 1$?' Clearly this query can be computed by a logspace-uniform family of AC^0-circuits.

To see that this reduction works, first assume that there exists a path from s to t in G of length $m \leq n - 1$. Let $(s, v_2, \ldots, v_m, t)$ be this path. Then $((1, s), (2, v_2), \ldots, (m, v_m), (m + 1, t), \ldots, (n, t))$ is a path in G' of length $n - 1$. Second, assume that there exists a path from s' to t' in G' of length $m \leq n - 1$.

Then $m = n - 1$ since any path from the first row to the last row must 'brave all rows'—there are no edges that allow us to skip a row. Let $(v_1', \ldots, v_n')$ be this path. Then $v_i' = (i, v_i)$ for some vertices $v_i \in V$. The sequence $(v_1, \ldots, v_n)$ is 'almost' a path from s to t in G: For each $i \in \{1, \ldots, n-1\}$ we either have $v_i = v_{i+1}$ or $(v_i, v_{i+1}) \in E$. Thus, by removing consecutive duplicates and loops, we obtain a path from s to t in G.   □

By the above theorem, DISTANCE and DISTANCE$_{tourn}$ are $\leq_m^{AC^0}$-equivalent, while REACH and REACH$_{tourn}$ are not. The 'complexity jump' from REACH$_{tourn}$ to DISTANCE$_{tourn}$ is reflected by a similar jump for the succinct versions.

Definition 4.2. *Let* SUCCINCT-DISTANCE$_{tourn}$ *denote the language that contains all coded tuples* $\langle C, s, t, d \rangle$, *where* C *is a circuit,* s *and* t *are bitstrings, and* d *is a positive integer, such that* C *is a succinct representation of a graph* G *with* $\langle G, s, t, d \rangle \in$ DISTANCE$_{tourn}$.

Theorem 4.3. SUCCINCT-DISTANCE$_{tourn}$ *is PSPACE-complete.*

Proof. Since DISTANCE$_{tourn} \in$ NL, we have

$$\text{SUCCINCT-DISTANCE}_{tourn} \in \text{NPSPACE} = \text{PSPACE}.$$

For the hardness, let $A \in$ PSPACE be an arbitrary language and let M be a polynomial-space machine that accepts A. We show that A is $\leq_m^{AC^0}$-reducible to SUCCINCT-DISTANCE$_{tourn}$. For an input x, let G denote the configuration graph of M on input x, let s be the initial configuration, let t be the (unique) accepting configuration, and let d be an (exponential) bound on the running time of M on input x. Let G' be the tournament constructed in Theorem 4.1 and let C be an appropriate circuit that represents G'. Then $x \in A$ iff $\langle C, s, t, d \rangle \in$ SUCCINCT-DISTANCE$_{tourn}$.

The representing circuit C can be constructed by a logspace-uniform family of AC^0-circuits. To see this, first note that the circuit C can easily be constructed in logarithmic space since G' is highly structured. For an appropriate construction, C will depend on x only in a very limited way: For each bit of x there is a constant gate in C that 'feeds' this bit to the rest of the circuit, which does not depend on x at all. Thus we can hardwire almost all of C into the AC^0-circuit that computes it, only C's constant gates must be setup depending on x.   □

5 Conclusion

The results of this paper extend the answer to the question 'How difficult is it to find paths in graphs with bounded independence number?' in two different ways. It was previously known that checking whether a path *exists* in a given graph can be done using AC^0-circuits. In this paper it was shown that *constructing* a path between two vertices can be done in logarithmic space. Constructing the *shortest* path in logarithmic space was shown to be impossible, unless L = NL.

These results settle the approximability of the (logspace) optimization problem 'shortest paths in graphs with bounded independence number'. This minimization problem cannot be solved exactly in logarithmic space (unless $L = NL$), but it can be approximated well: there exists a logspace approximation scheme for it. As we saw, the space $O(\log m \log n)$ needed by the scheme for a desired approximation ratio of $1 + 1/m$ is essentially optimal—any approximation scheme that does substantially better could be used to show unlikely inclusions like $NL \subseteq DSPACE[\log^{2-\epsilon} n]$. Thus it seems appropriate to call the scheme a '*fully* logspace approximation scheme' in analogy to 'fully polynomial-time approximation schemes'.

The shortest path problem for tournaments is not the only logspace optimization problem with surprising properties: In [22] it is shown that the distance problem for *undirected* graphs is also NL-complete, while the reachability problem is SL-complete. On the other hand, the distance problem for directed graphs is just as hard as the reachability problem for directed graphs. This shows that, just as in the polynomial-time setting, logspace optimization problems can have different approximation properties, although their underlying decision problems have the same complexity.

References

1. M. Ajtai. Σ_1^1 formulae on finite structures. *Annals of Pure and Applied Logic*, 24:1–48, 1983.
2. A. Chandra, L. Stockmeyer, and U. Vishkin. Constant depth reducibilities. *SIAM J. Comput.*, 13(2):423–439, 1984.
3. S. Cook. A taxonomy of problems with fast parallel algorithms. *Inform. Control*, 64(1–3):2–22, 1985.
4. S. Cook and P. McKenzie. Problems complete for deterministic logarithmic space. *J. Algorithms*, 8(3):385–394, 1987.
5. R. Faudree, R. Gould, L. Lesniak, and T. Lindquester. Generalized degree conditions for graphs with bounded independence number. *J. Graph Theory*, 19(3):397–409, 1995.
6. M. Furst, J. Saxe, and M. Sipser. Parity, circuits, and the polynomial-time hierarchy. *Math. Systems Theory*, 17(1):13–27, 1984.
7. H. Galperin and A. Wigderson. Succinct representations of graphs. *Inform. Control*, 56(3):183–198, 1983.
8. G. Gottlob, N. Leone, and H. Veith. Succinctness as a source of complexity in logical formalisms. *Annals of Pure and Applied Logic*, 97:231–260, 1999.
9. L. Hemaspaandra and L. Torenvliet. Optimal advice. *Theoretical Comput. Sci.*, 154(2):367–377, 1996.
10. N. Immerman. *Descriptive Complexity*. Springer-Verlag, 1998.
11. N. Jones. Space-bounded reducibility among combinatorial problems. *J. Comput. Syst. Sci.*, 11(1):68–85, 1975.
12. N. Jones, Y. Lien, and W. Laaser. New problems complete for nondeterministic log space. *Math. Systems Theory*, 10:1–17, 1976.
13. H. Landau. On dominance relations and the structure of animal societies, III: The condition for secure structure. *Bull. Mathematical Biophysics*, 15(2):143–148, 1953.

14. H. Lewis and C. Papadimitriou. Symmetric space-bounded computation. *Theoretical Comput. Sci.*, 19(2):161–187, 1982.
15. S. Lindell. A purely logical characterization of circuit uniformity. In *Proc. 7th Struc. in Complexity Theory Conf.*, pages 185–192, 1992. IEEE Computer Society Press.
16. N. Megiddo and U. Vishkin. On finding a minimum dominating set in a tournament. *Theoretical Comput. Sci.*, 61:307–316, 1988.
17. J. Moon. *Topics on Tournaments.* Holt, Rinehart, and Winston, 1968.
18. A. Nickelsen and T. Tantau. On reachability in graphs with bounded independence number. In O. H. Ibarra and L. Zhang, editors, *Proc. 8th Annual International Computing and Combinatorics Conf.*, volume 2387 of *Lecture Notes on Comput. Sci.*, pages 554–563. Springer-Verlag, 2002.
19. C. Papadimitriou and M. Yannakakis. A note on succinct representations of graphs. *Inform. Control*, 71(3):181–185, 1986.
20. K. Reid and L. Beineke. *Selected Topics in Graph Theory*, chapter Tournaments, pages 169–204. Academic Press, 1978.
21. W. Savitch. Relationships between nondeterministic and deterministic tape complexities. *J. Comput. Syst. Sci.*, 4(2):177–192, 1970.
22. T. Tantau. Logspace optimisation problems and their approximation properties. Technical report TR03-077, Electronic Colloquium on Computational Complexity, 2003.
23. K. Wagner. The complexity of problems concerning graphs with regularities. In *Proc. 7th Symposium on Math. Foundations of Comput. Sci.*, volume 176 of *Lecture Notes in Comput. Sci.*, pages 544–552. Springer-Verlag, 1984.
24. K. Wagner. The complexity of combinatorial problems with succinct input representation. *Acta Informatica*, 23(3):325–356, 1986.

The Minimal Logically-Defined NP-Complete Problem

Régis Barbanchon and Etienne Grandjean

GREYC, Université de Caen, 14032 Caen Cedex, France
{regis.barbanchon,etienne.grandjean}@info.unicaen.fr

Abstract. We exhibit an NP-complete problem defined by an existential monadic second-order (EMSO) formula over *functional structures* that is:

1. *minimal* under several syntactic criteria (i.e., any EMSO formula that further strengthens any criterion defines a PTIME problem even if all other criteria are weakened);
2. *unique* for such restrictions, up to renamings and symmetries.

Our reductions and proofs are surprisingly very elementary and simple in comparison with some recent similar results classifying existential second-order formulas over *relational structures* according to their ability either to express NP-complete problems or to express only PTIME ones.

Keywords: Computational complexity, descriptive complexity, finite model theory, second-order logic, NP-completeness, parsimony.

1 Introduction and Main Results

1.1 Which Formulas Express NP-Complete Problems?

In the line of Fagin's Theorem [5] which states that *existential second order logic* (ESO) captures the class NP, this paper studies the following natural question: what is (are) the most simple ESO sentence(s) that define(s) some NP-complete problem(s)? This question is somewhat related to two recent papers [7,4] that completely classified prefix classes of ESO over strings and graphs (and more generally over *relational structures*) with respect to their ability to express either some NP-complete problems or only tractable (i.e., PTIME) ones. For example, it is easy to express an NP-complete problem over graphs, such as 3-colourability, in *existential monadic second-order logic* (EMSO) with only *two* first-order variables. In contrast, one notices that ESO formulas that use only *relation* ESO variables and only *one* first-order variable can only define easy (degenerate) properties on *relational structures*. The situation completely changes if *function* symbols are allowed either in the input signature or among the ESO symbols. For example, ESO formulas with *only one first-order variable* x of one of the forms (1-2)

$$(1) \quad \langle D, E \rangle \models \quad \exists \overline{f} \, \forall x \quad \psi(x, \overline{f}, E)$$
$$(2) \quad \langle D, \overline{f} \rangle \models \quad \exists \overline{U} \, \forall x \quad \psi(x, \overline{f}, \overline{U})$$

V. Diekert and M. Habib (Eds.): STACS 2004, LNCS 2996, pp. 338–349, 2004.
© Springer-Verlag Berlin Heidelberg 2004

(where x is quantified over the finite domain D, E is a binary relation symbol, $\overline{f}$ and $\overline{U}$ are lists of unary function symbols and of monadic relation symbols respectively, and ψ is quantifier-free) can express some NP-complete problems. More precisely, [9] has recently proved that formulas of form (1) exactly define graph problems (such as the Hamiltonian cycle problem) that are recognizable in nondeterministic linear time $O(n)$ where n is the number of vertices in the graph, and [1] states that any problem is linearly reducible to SAT iff it is linearly reducible to some problem expressible by some formula of the form (2) (see also [12]). Moreover, as proved in [1], it can be assumed that the unary functions $\overline{f}$ of the input structures are permutations: the class of such problems are called LIN-LOCAL since they are linearly reducible to *local* problems.

In this paper, we exhibits a formula of the form (2) over *functional structures* that defines some NP-complete problem and is *minimal* for several criteria over the signature of input structures, the prefix and the matrix of the formula; more precisely, the further strengthening of any criterion makes the problem fall in PTIME even if all others criteria are weakened. Moreover, this problem is essentially *unique*, up to renamings and symmetries.

Finally, in contrast with our results about *functional structures*, notice that the similar question of determining the minimal ESO formulas (with two first-order variables) that define NP-complete problems over *relational structures* is, to our knowledge, widely open and seems rather difficult to us: e.g., the unicity of such a formula is very dubious.

1.2   Minimal Formulas for NP-Complete Problems

We study the problem MIN_0 defined by the *very simple* EMSO formula φ_0 of the particular form (2) that follows.

Notation 1. *Let* φ_0 *denote the* $\{f, g\}$-*formula in* conjunctive normal form *(CNF)*

$$\varphi_0: \quad \exists U \; \forall x \quad \psi_0(x) \qquad \text{where } \psi_0 \text{ is the conjunction}$$
$$\psi_0: \quad (Ux \vee Ufx) \wedge (\neg Ux \vee \neg Ufx \vee \neg Ugx),$$

and f, g *are unary function symbols. Let* δ_0 *denote the following formula in* disjunctive normal form *(DNF) which is logically equivalent to* φ_0

$$\delta_0: \quad \exists U \; \forall x \quad (Ux \wedge \neg Ufx) \vee (Ux \wedge \neg Ugx) \vee (\neg Ux \wedge Ufx).$$

The problem MIN_0 *is defined as the set of finite models* $\langle D, f, g \rangle$ *of* φ_0 *(or of* δ_0*).*

We shall also study the following subproblems of MIN_0:

Notation 2. *Define* MIN_1 *as the set of finite models* $\langle D, f, g \rangle$ *of* φ_0, *where* f *and* g *are permutations of* D. *For some functional structure* $\langle D, f, g \rangle$, *let* $G(D, f, g)$ *denote the graph* (V, E) *defined by* $V = D$ *and* $E = \{(x, fx) : x \in D\} \cup \{(x, gx) : x \in D\} \cup \{(fx, gx) : x \in D\}$. *Define* MIN_2 *as the set of finite models* $\langle D, f, g \rangle$ *of* φ_0, *where* f *and* g *are permutations of* D *and* $G(D, f, g)$ *is planar.*

Our main results use the following notations:

Notation 3. *The* atoms *of a formula are its atomic subformulas. In particular, the distinct atoms of* φ_0 *(or* δ_0*) are* Ux, Ufx *and* Ugx. *The* length *of a formula* *is the total number of occurrences of atoms in it. The disjuncts of a DNF formula are called its* anticlauses.

Theorem 1 (NP-completeness). MIN_0, MIN_1 *and* MIN_2 *are NP-complete.*

Theorem 2 (Minimality). *If* $P \neq NP$, φ_0 *(resp.* δ_0*) is, for the syntactic criteria enumerated in the table below, a* minimal *EMSO formula in CNF (resp. in DNF) of the form* $\exists \overline{U} \, \forall \overline{x} \, \psi$ *(where* ψ *is quantifier-free and* $\overline{x}$ *is a list of first-order variables) that defines an NP-complete problem over functional structures.*

input signature	2 unary functions		distinct atoms	3
EMSO symbols	1		clauses in CNF φ_0	2
FO variables	1		length of CNF φ_0	5
compositions of functions	0		anticlauses in DNF δ_0	3
equalities	0		length of DNF δ_0	6

That means that if any of these criteria is strenghtened and the other criterias are weakened then the problem so defined is PTIME; e.g, any formula of the form $\exists \overline{U} \, \forall \overline{x} \, \psi$ with length of $\psi < 5$ in CNF defines a PTIME problem.

Theorem 3 (Unicity). *If* $P \neq NP$, φ_0 *(resp.* δ_0*) is – up to symmetries – the* unique *minimal EMSO formula in CNF (resp. in DNF) of the form* $\exists \overline{U} \, \forall \overline{x} \, \psi$ *(where* ψ *is quantifier-free) that defines an NP-complete problem over functional structures. The symmetrical formulas are obtained by any permutation of the terms* x, fx *and* gx *and by swap of* U *and* $\neg U$ *in* φ_0 *(resp.* δ_0*).*

More precisely, all the symmetrical formulas of φ_0 essentially define the *same* minimal NP-complete problem over *permutations* (resp. planar permutations) structures. In case of (general) *functional* structures, one obtains essentially *two* minimal NP-complete problems: the one defined by φ_0 itself, and the one defined by the following formula φ_0', that is φ_0 with terms x and gx permuted:

$$\varphi_0' : \quad \exists U \quad \forall x \quad (Ugx \lor Ufx) \land (\neg Ugx \lor \neg Ufx \lor \neg Ux)$$

1.3   Minimal Formulas for #P-Complete Problems

Besides NP-completeness, another important concept of the theory of complexity is #P-completeness [14]. It is also natural to look for a minimal logical formula that defines some #P-complete problem. In this regard, it is well known that the generic reduction from any NP problem to SAT can (easily) be made parsimonious with a bijective and PTIME-computable correspondence between solutions. That means that the problem SAT not only "simulates" the decision process of any problem in NP but also "reproduces" the number of its solutions and the "structure" of this set of solutions.

Notation 4. *For any problem* A *in NP, let us denote by* #A *the "natural" counting problem associated to* A, *i.e., the problem of counting the "natural" solutions of the instances of* A. #P *is the class of such counting problems; e.g.,* #SAT *is the function which maps each propositional formula* F *to the number of assignments* I *over the variables of* F *such that* $I \models F$; *similarly,* $\#\text{MIN}_1$ *is the function which maps each permutation structure* $S = \langle D, f, g \rangle$ *to the number of predicates* U *such that* $(S, U) \models \forall x \, \psi_0(x)$.

We say that an ordered pair (ρ, μ) is a *weakly parsimonious* reduction from #A to #B if ρ is a PTIME reduction from A to B, μ is a PTIME-computable function valued in positive integers such that for each instance w of A we have #{solutions of A for w} = $\mu(w) \times$ #{solutions of B for $\rho(w)$}. If furthermore $\mu = 1$, then ρ is called a *parsimonious reduction*. We conjecture that:

Conjecture 1. *There exists no* parsimonious *reduction from problem* #SAT *to problems* #MIN$_1$ *or* #MIN$_2$.

Nevertheless, we prove in this paper that:

Theorem 4. *There exists* weakly parsimonious *reductions from problem* #SAT *to problems* #MIN$_1$ *and* #MIN$_2$.

In regard to Conjecture 1 concerning Formula φ_0, it is natural to look for another simple EMSO formula defining a problem to which SAT (and hence any NP problem) *parsimoniously* reduces. Let φ_{nand} denote the $\{f, g\}$-formula

$$\varphi_{\mathrm{nand}} : \quad \exists U \; \forall x \;\; \psi_{\mathrm{nand}}(x) \qquad\qquad \text{where } \psi_{\mathrm{nand}} \text{ is}$$
$$\psi_{\mathrm{nand}} : \quad Ux \iff \neg(Ufx \wedge Ugx) \qquad \text{or equivalently in CNF}$$
$$\psi_{\mathrm{nand}} : \quad (Ux \vee Ufx) \wedge (Ux \vee Ugx) \wedge (\neg Ux \vee \neg Ufx \vee \neg Ugx).$$

Clearly, ψ_{nand} (resp. φ_{nand}) implies ψ_0 (resp. φ_0). The formula φ_{nand} defines the following problems:

Notation 5. *Define* NAND$_1$ *as the set of finite models* $\langle D, f, g \rangle$ *of* φ_{nand} *where* f *and* g *are permutations of* D. *Define* NAND$_2$ *as the set of finite models* $\langle D, f, g \rangle$ *of* φ_{nand} *where* f *and* g *are permutations of* D *and* $G(D, f, g)$ *is planar.*

In contrast to Conjecture 1, we can prove that:

Theorem 5. (i) *#SAT parsimoniously reduces to* #NAND$_1$ *(resp.* #NAND$_2$*).* **(ii)** *If Conjecture 1 holds and* $P \neq NP$, *then* φ_{nand} *is (up to symmetries) the* unique minimal *EMSO formula for which (i) holds, i.e., that defines a problem over permutation structures* $\langle D, f, g \rangle$ *to which* #SAT *parsimoniously reduces.*

Surprisingly, our proofs of completeness are rather simple and the reductions involved in Theorems 1 and 5 are essentially the same one reduction $\rho : F \mapsto \mathcal{S}(F)$ described in the next section.

2   Proofs of Our Results

2.1   The Structures Involved

Let us recall the three kinds of instances of our problems.

Definition 1. *A function structure is a finite structure* $\langle D, f, g \rangle$ *where* $f, g : D \longrightarrow D$ *are unary functions. A function structure* $\langle D, f, g \rangle$ *is a* permutation structure *(resp. is a planar permutation structure) if* f, g *are permutations of* D *(resp. are permutations of* D *such that the graph* $G(D, f, g)$ *is planar).*

Remark 1. *A permutation structure* $\langle D, f, g \rangle$ *is naturally given by its* f- *and* g-circuits, *where an* f-circuit of length k *is an orbit* $a, fa, f^2a, \cdots, f^k a = a$.

Definition 2 (Planar formula and PLAN-SAT). *Let F be a propositional formula in CNF. Let $G(F)$ denote the following bipartite graph (V, E) where V is the disjoint union of the set of variables and the set of clauses of F, and E is the set of pairs (v, C) such that v is a variable that occurs in clause C. F is a planar formula if $G(F)$ is a planar graph, and PLAN-SAT is defined as the satisfiability problem of planar formulas.*

Our proofs of completeness use the NP-complete problem PLAN-SAT [13].

2.2   A Gadget Structure

We are going to describe a reduction $\rho : F \mapsto \mathcal{S}(F)$ that associates to each SAT (resp. PLAN-SAT) instance F a permutation structure $\mathcal{S}(F)$ that contains as substructures many occurrences of the following gadget denoted True whose role is essential in our reduction.

Definition 3. *True or* $\mathrm{True}(\alpha, \beta, \gamma)$ *is the gadget depicted on the left of Fig. 1.*

The symbolization means that the gadget True plays the role of the Boolean constant "true" (or "1"). More formally, the following lemma expresses that in any case, $U(\gamma)$ can and *should* be true whereas the value of $U(g\gamma)$ (reached via the "pending" outgoing g-edge of γ) is *free*.

Lemma 1. *Let* $\mathrm{True}(\alpha, \beta, \gamma)$ *be a gadget included in a permutation structure* $\mathcal{S} = \langle D, f, g \rangle$ *and* $U : D \longrightarrow \{0, 1\}$ *be a monadic predicate[1].*

1. *If* $(\mathcal{S}, U) \models \varphi_0$ *then we have* $U(\alpha) = 1$, $U(\beta) = 0$ *and* $U(\gamma) = 1$;
2. *Conversely: if* $U(\alpha) = 1$, $U(\beta) = 0$ *and* $U(\gamma) = 1$, *then the structure* $(True, U)$ *satisfies* $\forall x \; \psi_{\mathrm{nand}}$ *(and hence* $\forall x \; \psi_0$*); in other words,* $\psi_{\mathrm{nand}}(x)$ *is satisfied by each element* $x = \alpha, \beta, \gamma$ *independently of the value of* $U(g\gamma)$.

Proof. Easy and left to the reader.   □

2.3   Our Reduction

Let us now construct our reduction $\rho : F \mapsto \mathcal{S}(F)$ where F is a SAT (resp. PLAN-SAT) instance, i.e., a conjunction of clauses $F = C_1 \wedge C_2 \wedge \cdots \wedge C_q$. In the description of the permutation structure $\mathcal{S}(F)$, we freely make use of the following notation:

Notation 6. *Whenever there exists some gadget* $True(\alpha, \beta, \gamma)$ *such that* $g(x) = \gamma$ *and* $g(\gamma) = y$, *we will often write* $g(x) = True$ *and* $g(True) = y$ *by commodity.*

Let us now describe the f- and g-circuits of our permutation structure $\mathcal{S}(F)$:

- Construct a f-circuit $(x_i^1, nx_i^1, x_i^2, nx_i^2, \cdots, x_i^{r-1}, nx_i^{r-1}, x_i^r, nx_i^r)$ for each variable x_i with r occurrences in F. Vertices x_i^k, nx_i^k correspond to the kth occurrence of x_i in F.

---

[1] For convenience, we confuse truth values "true" and "false" with 0 and 1 and assimilate a monadic predicate $U \subseteq D$ to its characteristic function $U : D \longrightarrow \{0, 1\}$.

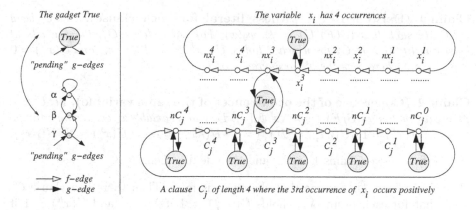

Fig. 1. The gadget True and the reduction around variable x_i and clause C_j

- Construct a f-circuit $(nC_j^\ell, C_j^\ell, nC_j^{\ell-1}, C_j^{\ell-1}, \cdots, nC_j^1, C_j^1, nC_j^0)$ of odd length for each clause $C_j = \lambda_1 \vee \cdots \vee \lambda_\ell$ in F, where the C_j^k and nC_j^k are new elements corresponding to the "prefix" of length k of the clause C_j defined as $\text{prefix}_k(C_j) = \lambda_1 \vee \cdots \vee \lambda_k$; also construct the $\ell + 1$ g-circuits (nC_j^k, True) for $0 \le k \le \ell$ using $\ell + 1$ new gadgets True.

- If the kth literal of C_j is the hth occurrence – resp. negation of the hth occurrence – of x_i, construct the g-circuits $(C_j^k, nx_i^h, \text{True})$ and (x_i^h, True) – resp. $(C_j^k, x_i^h, \text{True})$ and (nx_i^h, True) – using two new gadgets True.

This completes the description of $\mathcal{S}(F)$ which is represented on the right of Fig. 1. The following lemma, that is obvious by the construction of $\mathcal{S}(F)$, means that our reduction preserves planarity.

Lemma 2. F is a planar formula iff $\mathcal{S}(F)$ is a planar permutation structure.

2.4   Properties of the Reduction

Lemmas 3 and 4 that follow mean together that $\rho : F \mapsto \mathcal{S}(F)$ is a reduction (resp. parsimonious reduction) from SAT to the problem defined by φ_0 (resp. φ_{nand}). First, the following fact whose proof is straightforward will be useful in our study of the f-circuits of $\mathcal{S}(F)$.

Fact 1. Let $\mathcal{S} = \langle D, f, g \rangle$ be a permutation structure and $U : D \longrightarrow \{0, 1\}$ be a monadic predicate such that $(\mathcal{S}, U) \models \forall x \; \psi_0(x)$. Then, for every $a \in D$ such that $(\mathcal{S}, U) \models U(ga)$ (i.e., $U(ga) = 1$), it holds $U(a) = 1 - U(fa)$.

Here is the first implication involved in the equivalence to be proved, i.e., $\mathcal{S}(F) \models \varphi_0$ (resp. φ_{nand}) iff F is satisfiable.

Lemma 3. If $\mathcal{S}(F)$ satisfies φ_0 then F is satisfiable.

In order to prove Lemma 3, we need the following two claims:

Claim 1 (Existence of a witness literal for each clause). *Let U be a predicate such that $(\mathcal{S}(F), U) \models \forall x \; \psi_0(x)$. For each clause C_j, there exists at least one literal λ in C_j for which it holds: $U(nx_i^h) = 0$ if $\lambda = x_i$, and $U(x_i^h) = 0$ if $\lambda = \neg x_i$, where λ is the hth occurrence of x_i.*

Claim 2 (Coherence of the occurrences of the same variable). *Let U be a predicate such that $(\mathcal{S}(F), U) \models \forall x \; \psi_0(x)$. For each variable x_i occurring r times, it holds: $U(x_i^1) = 1 - U(nx_i^1) = U(x_i^2) = 1 - U(nx_i^2) = \cdots = U(x_i^r) = 1 - U(nx_i^r)$.*

We first prove Claims 1 and 2, and then deduce Lemma 3.

Proof (of Claim 1). Assume that the claim is false. Then there is a clause C_j such that for each literal λ, it holds $U(nx_i^h) = 1$ if $\lambda = x_i$ and $U(x_i^h) = 1$ if $\lambda = \neg x_i$. This implies $U(ga) = 1$ for each element a of the f-circuit of C_j, and hence $U(a) = 1 - U(fa)$ by Fact 1, which is impossible since the length of this f-circuit is odd.   □

Proof (of Claim 2). Immediate consequence of Fact 1 applied to each element a of the f-circuit of x_i since we always have $g(a) =$ True and thus $U(ga) = 1$.   □

Proof (of Lemma 3). Define the assignment I of the variables F as $I(x_i) = U(x_i^h) = 1 - U(nx_i^h)$, for each variable x_i and any $1 \leq h \leq r$, which is coherent by Claim 2. Claim 1 ensures that in each clause C_j of F, there is some literal λ such that $I(\lambda) = 1$. Hence, $I \models C_j$ and $I \models F$.   □

Lemma 4 states the most precise property of our reduction $\rho : F \mapsto \mathcal{S}(F)$.

Lemma 4. *There is a bijective correspondence $I \mapsto U_I$ of the set of satisfying assignments $\{I : I \models F\}$ onto the set of monadic predicates $\{U : (\mathcal{S}(F), U) \models \forall x \; \psi_{\text{nand}}(x)\}$. That means that $\rho : F \mapsto \mathcal{S}(F)$ is a parsimonious reduction from* SAT *to the problem defined by φ_{nand}.*

Proof (of Lemma 4). For each I such that $I \models F$, let us construct its associated monadic predicate U_I, on the domain D of $\mathcal{S}(F)$. The correction will be ensured by Claim 3 and its converse Claim 4:

• Set $U_I(\alpha) = 1$, $U_I(\beta) = 0$ and $U_I(\gamma) = 1$ for each gadget True(α, β, γ) in $\mathcal{S}(F)$: this is justified by Lemma 1;

• Set $U_I(x_i^h) = I(x_i)$ and $U_I(nx_i^h) = 1 - I(x_i)$ for each variable x_i occurring r times in F and each $1 \leq h \leq r$;

• For each clause $C_j = \lambda_j^1 \vee \cdots \vee \lambda_j^\ell$, set $U_I(nC_j^0) = 1$, and for $k = 1, \cdots, \ell$, set $U_I(C_j^k) = \text{value}(\text{prefix}_k(C_j), I)$, and $U_I(nC_j^k) = 1 - \text{value}(\text{prefix}_k(C_j), I)$, where $\text{prefix}_k(C_j) = \lambda_j^1 \vee \cdots \vee \lambda_j^k$ and in particular $C_j = \text{prefix}_\ell(C_j)$.

In the following, we essentially use the well-known fact that all the Boolean connectives can be expressed by means of the NAND one only. More precisely, $1 - v = \text{NAND}(v, 1)$ and $\text{OR}(v, v') = \text{NAND}(1 - v, 1 - v')$.

Claim 3. $(\mathcal{S}(F), U_I) \models \forall x \; \psi_{\text{nand}}(x)$.

Proof (of Claim 3). For each element a of the f-circuit of any variable x_i, we have $U_I(ga) = 1$ and $U_I(a) = 1 - U_I(fa)$, and hence $(\mathcal{S}(F), U_I) \models U(a) \iff \text{NAND}(U(fa), U(ga))$. For every clause C_j of length ℓ, one easily obtains the following equalities for $1 \le k \le \ell$ if $C_j^k = C_j^{k-1} \vee x_i^h$:

- $U_I(nC_j^k) = 1 - U_I(C_j^k) = \text{NAND}(U_I(C_j^k), 1)$, and
- $U_I(C_j^k) = \text{NAND}(U_I(nC_j^{k-1}), U_I(nx_i^h))$;

and similarly in the case $C_j^k = C_j^{k-1} \vee \neg x_i^h$. This proves $(\mathcal{S}(F), U_I) \models \psi_{\text{nand}}(a)$ for every element $a \ne nC_j^0$ in the f-circuit of C_j. Finally, this also holds for $a = nC_j^0$ since $U_I(nC_j^\ell) = \text{value}(\neg C_j, I) = 0$ and, as a consequence, $U_I(nC_j^0) = 1 = \text{NAND}(U_I(nC_j^\ell), 1)$ as required. This completes the proof of Claim 3.   □

It remains to prove the converse of Claim 3.

Claim 4. *Let U be a monadic predicate such that $(\mathcal{S}(F), U) \models \forall x \; \psi_{\text{nand}}(x)$. Then there is an assignment I, of course unique, such that $U = U_I$ and $I \models F$.*

Proof (of Claim 4). It is a variant of the proof of Lemma 3 and is left to the reader. This completes the proof of Lemma 4.   □

Lemmas 2, 3 and 4 together imply the following:

Corollary 1. **(i)** SAT *(resp.* PLAN-SAT*) reduces to problem* MIN₁ *(resp.* MIN₂*) by the reduction* $\rho : F \mapsto \mathcal{S}(F)$. **(ii)** #SAT *(resp.* #PLAN-SAT*) parsimoniously reduces to problem* #NAND₁ *(resp.* #NAND₂*) by the same reduction.*

So, we have proved Theorems 1 and 5(i), by making use of the known result that #SAT parsimoniously reduces to #PLAN-SAT [13]. A careful analysis of our reduction $\rho : F \mapsto \mathcal{S}(F)$ from SAT (PLAN-SAT) to MIN₁ (MIN₂) shows that the only part of $\mathcal{S}(F)$ where this reduction is not parsimonious are the f-circuits of the clauses of F when at least two literals of some clause of F are true together. On the other hand, it is known that the problem $\frac{1}{3}$-SAT (also denoted one-in-three-SAT, see [6]) and its planar restriction PLAN-$\frac{1}{3}$-SAT defined below are equivalent to SAT and PLAN-SAT under parsimonious reductions (see [10]).

Definition 4. *Let $\frac{1}{3}$-SAT (resp.* PLAN-$\frac{1}{3}$-SAT*) denote the satisfiability problem of a conjunction of $\frac{1}{3}$-clauses (resp. planar $\frac{1}{3}$-clauses) of the form $\frac{1}{3}(a, b, c)$ whose meaning is "exactly one of the three variables a, b, c is true".*

Theorem 4 is a straightforward consequence of the following lemma:

Lemma 5. #$\frac{1}{3}$-SAT *(resp.* #PLAN-$\frac{1}{3}$-SAT*) reduces to* #MIN₁ *(resp.* #MIN₂*) under a weakly parsimonious reduction.*

Proof. Let $F \mapsto F'$ be the trivial parsimonious and planarity-preserving reduction from $\frac{1}{3}$-SAT (resp. PLAN-$\frac{1}{3}$-SAT) to SAT (resp. PLAN-SAT) that replaces every $\frac{1}{3}$-clause $\frac{1}{3}(a, b, c)$ by the logically equivalent conjunction $(a \vee b \vee c) \wedge (\neg a \vee \neg b) \wedge (\neg b \vee \neg c) \wedge (\neg c \vee \neg a)$. One notices that in each clause of this conjunction, except one 2-clause, e.g., $C = \neg a \vee \neg b$, exactly one literal is true and both literals of C are true. Let us now consider the composed reduction $\rho' : F \mapsto \mathcal{S}(F')$ from $\frac{1}{3}$-SAT (PLAN-$\frac{1}{3}$-SAT) to MIN₁ (MIN₂). If F contains q $\frac{1}{3}$-clauses then it holds $\#\{U : (\mathcal{S}(F'), U) \models \forall x \; \psi_0(x)\} = 2^q \times \#\{I : I \models F\}$.

This is easily justified by a careful analysis of the f-circuits of clauses (of F') in $\mathcal{S}(F')$: one sees that each $\frac{1}{3}$-clause of F gives exactly 2 "local configurations" of the (union of four) f-circuits of the four corresponding clauses of F'.   □

2.5 Minimality of φ_0 and δ_0 in Theorem 2

We consider EMSO formulas of the form: $\varphi : \exists \overline{U} \, \forall \overline{x} \, \psi$, where $\overline{U}$ (resp. $\overline{x}$) is a list of monadic relation symbols (resp. first-order variables) and ψ is quantifier-free.

Proof. There is nothing to prove about the absence of composition of functions and the absence of equality. We prove the minimality of:

• *the input signature* (= 2 unary function symbols)*:* a famous theorem of Courcelle [2], asserts that any MSO property of bounded tree-width structures can be checked in deterministic linear time. In particular, any EMSO property of σ-structures with $\sigma = \{f, U_1, \cdots, U_k\}$ where f is a unary function symbol and $U_1, \cdots, U_k$ are monadic relation symbols is checkable in linear time.

• *the number of EMSO symbols* (= 1)*:* immediate since any first-order (FO) property is AC_0 and thus is PTIME.

• *the number of FO symbols* (= 1)*:* trivial.

• *the number of clauses in φ_0* (= 2)*:* assume φ is an ESO formula in CNF with only one clause. If some ESO symbol occurs in φ then φ defines a trivial "yes"-problem. Otherwise, φ defines a first-order property.

• *the length of φ_0* (= 5)*:* if the length of φ in CNF is ≤ 4 then φ either: (*i*) contains only clauses of length ≤ 2, or (*ii*) contains only one clause (of length 3 or 4), or (*iii*) contains exactly one 3-clause and one unit clause. In case (*i*), φ is ESO-Krom and, as a consequence, defines a PTIME problem [8]. In case (*ii*), φ defines a PTIME problem as it was noticed above. Finally, in case (*iii*), one observes that the 3-clause either contains ≤ 1 positive literal or contains ≤ 1 negative literal. Hence, φ is either ESO-Horn or ESO-Anti-Horn, and thus defines a PTIME problem [8].

• *the number of distinct atoms* (= 3)*:* if φ in CNF contains ≤ 2 distinct atoms, then its clauses are trivially of length ≤ 2, and φ is ESO-Krom.

• *the number of anticlauses in δ_0* (= 3)*:* notice that any formula φ in DNF that contains ≤ 2 disjuncts is equivalent to a CNF formula that consists of clauses of length ≤ 2.

• *the length of δ_0 in DNF* (= 6)*:* w.l.g., assume that φ in DNF is of the form $\varphi : \exists \overline{U} \, \forall \overline{x}(\psi_0 \vee \psi_1)$, where ψ_0 (resp. ψ_1) is a disjunction of anticlauses in each of which no (resp. at least one) EMSO symbol occurs. If ψ_1 contains a unit anticlause, then φ defines a trivial "yes"-problem. Moreover, if the number of anticlauses in ψ_1 is ≤ 2, then φ defines a PTIME problem. Thus, if φ defines an NP-complete problem then ψ_1 consists of at least 3 anticlauses of length ≥ 2. □

2.6 Unicity up to Symmetries of φ_0 and δ_0 in Theorem 3

Let us prove the unicity of φ_0 (the proof of δ_0 is similar). Let φ be an EMSO formula in CNF that satisfies the conditions of the table of Thereom 2 and defines an NP-complete problem over functional structures $\langle D, f, g \rangle$. The list of atoms that occur in φ is Ux, Ufx, Ugx, and φ is of the form $\exists U \, \forall x \, \psi(f, g, U, x)$, where ψ is a conjunction of two clauses C_1 and C_2 with $|C_1| + |C_2| = 5$ and $|C_1| < |C_2| \leq 3$. That implies $|C_1| = 2$ and $|C_2| = 3$.

Proof. One notices that one clause consists of positive literals and the other one consists of negative literals: otherwise, φ would define a trivial "yes"-problem. That implies that φ has one of the following two forms φ_0 or φ_0' as defined in Subsection 1.2, up to permutations of f and g and swap of U and $\neg U$:

Formulas φ_0 and φ_0' essentially define the same problem over (planar) permutation structures $\langle D, f, g \rangle$: By replacing x by $g^{-1}x$ in the matrix of the formula φ_0, we immediately get $\langle D, f, g \rangle \models \varphi_0(f, g)$ iff $\langle D, f', g' \rangle \models \varphi_0'(f', g')$, where $f' = g^{-1}$ and $g' = fg^{-1}$. This also makes sense for planar permutation structures since $G(D, f, g)$ is planar iff $G(D, f', g')$ is planar.   □

It remains to prove Theorem 5(*ii*), more precisely reformulated as follows: assume Conjecture 1 and P $\neq$ NP. Then φ_{nand} is (up to permutations of x, fx, gx and swap of U and $\neg U$) the *unique minimal* EMSO $\{f, g\}$-formula in CNF of the form $\exists U \, \forall x \, \psi(x)$ with the only atoms Ux, Ufx and Ugx that defines a problem over permutation structures to which #SAT *parsimoniously* reduces. More precisely, φ_{nand} has a minimal number of clauses ($= 3$), and a minimal length ($= 7$).

2.7   Minimality of φ_{nand} in Theorem 5(ii)

Proof. We prove the minimality of:
- *the number of clauses* ($= 3$): clearly, any EMSO formula φ of the required form that defines an NP-complete problem (over permutation structures) with exactly two clauses has exactly one purely negative clause and one purely positive clause, and has at least one 3-clause and no unit clause[2]; so, the other one has length 2 or 3. This gives only two possible forms: our minimal formula φ_0 (and its symmetrical variants), and φ_{nae} defined as:

φ_{nae} : $\exists U \, \forall x \, \psi_{nae}(x)$ where ψ_{nae} is the "not-all-equal" formula
ψ_{nae} : $(Ux \vee Ufx \vee Ugx) \wedge (\neg Ux \vee \neg Ufx \vee \neg Ugx)$.

One easily sees that for any function structure $\mathcal{S}$, the number $\#\{U : (\mathcal{S}, U) \models \forall x \, \psi_{nae}(x)\}$ is *even* because ψ_{nae} is invariant by inversion of U and $\neg U$. So, no reduction from SAT to the problem defined by φ_{nae} (if such a polynomial reduction exists) can be parsimonious with the standard way of counting solutions.
- *the length* ($= 7$): it is a consequence of the fact that there should be at least three clauses of length ≥ 2 with at least one of length 3.   □

2.8   Unicity of φ_{nand} in Theorem 5(ii)

Proof. Clearly, any formula that meets our minimality conditions, i.e., that has three clauses and length 7, has exactly one 3-clause and two 2-clauses. Moreover:
(i) At least one clause is purely positive and at least one is purely negative;
(ii) No 2-clause subsumes the 3-clause;

---

[2] If φ contained a unit clause, then it would define either a trivial "yes"-problem or a trivial "no"-problem.

(**iii**) Each 2-clause must disagree with the 3-clause on the sign of every literal: otherwise, if we write the 3-clause as $(\ell_1 \vee \ell_2 \vee \ell_3)$, either the 2-clause is of the form $(\ell_1 \vee \ell_2)$ and then its subsumes the 3-clause, or the 2-clause is of the form $(\overline{\ell_1} \vee \ell_2)$ and then a resolution step over ℓ_1 induces the 2-clause $(\ell_2 \vee \ell_3)$ that in turn subsumes the 3-clause. This contradicts (*ii*);

(**iv**) The 2-clauses have exactly one atom in common: they clearly have at least one since there are only three atoms available. Now, if they have two, they disagree on the sign of either one literal or two literals. If we have $(\ell_1 \vee \ell_2) \wedge (\ell_1 \vee \overline{\ell_2})$, then a resolution step over ℓ_2 induces the unit clause (ℓ_1). If we have $(\ell_1 \vee \ell_2) \wedge (\overline{\ell_1} \vee \overline{\ell_2})$, then $\ell_1 \iff \overline{\ell_2}$ and the 3-clause reduces either to a 2-clause or to "true" by replacing ℓ_1 by $\overline{\ell_2}$;

(**v**) The 3-clause must be monotone. Otherwise, by (*i*), the two 2-clauses must be monotone of opposite sign: Let then ε be the majoritary sign of the 3-clause. The 2-clause of sign ε cannot disagree on the sign of every literal with the 3-clause, since this latter has only one literal of sign $\overline{\varepsilon}$. This contradicts (*iii*);

(**vi**) Both 2-clauses are monotone, of the same sign, opposite to the sign of the 3-clause: This is a direct consequence of (*iii*) and (*v*).

Clearly, Remarks (*iv*), (*v*) and (*vi*) together leave exactly ψ_{nand} and its symmetrical variants as the only candidates.   □

3   Conclusion and Open Problems

Exhibiting "the" minimal EMSO formula that defines an NP-complete problem over functional structures is the main contribution of this paper. The "minimality" is also strengthened by the fact that this main result also holds when restricted to permutation structures or even to planar permutation structures which seem to be the simplest functional structures. A striking point is the unicity (up to symmetries) of our formula. More precisely, we have seen that all the symmetrical forms of our minimal formula essentially define only *two* distinct NP-complete problems over functional structures (see formulas φ_0 and φ_0' in Section 2.6) and only *one* such problem over permutation (resp. planar permutation) structures. This delineates a very neat frontier in logic between NP-complete problems and tractable ones. Several open problems remain:

The first one is the analogous minimality question over relational structures. The second one is Conjecture 1 and its analogue for function structures: is there a parsimonious reduction from #SAT to #MIN$_0$? A difficulty in counting complexity is to define a relevant notion of reduction. Recently, Durand et al [3] have defined an interesting reduction, callled subtractive reduction, under which #P and other counting complexity classes are closed and have significant complete problems. If positively answered, the following question may be easier and more relevant than Conjecture 1: is there a subtractive reduction from #SAT to #MIN$_1$ and #MIN$_2$ (i.e., are the latter #P-complete under such reductions)?

Another interesting objective consists in looking for a necessary and sufficient decidable condition for which any EMSO formula of the form $\exists \overline{U} \, \forall \overline{x} \, \psi(\overline{U}, \overline{f}, \overline{x})$

and of unary signature $\overline{f}$ expresses an NP-complete problem over $\overline{f}$-structures (resp. over permutation $\overline{f}$-structures, or over planar permutation $\overline{f}$-structures.)

Finally, does the EMSO formula φ_{nae} of subsection 2.7 define a PTIME or NP-complete problem over permutation structures? Notice that φ_{nae} defines a PTIME problem over planar permutation structures since the problem NAE-SAT is PTIME for planar instances [11].

Acknowledgments. The authors thank the referees for their helpful comments that contributed to improve the presentation.

References

[1] R. Barbanchon and E. Grandjean. Local problems, planar local problems and linear time. In *Computer Science Logic*, volume 2471 of *LNCS*, pages 397–411, 2002.

[2] B. Courcelle. On the expression of graph properties in some fragments of monadic second-order logic. In N. Immermann and P. Kolaitis, editors, *Descriptive Complexity and Finite Models*, pages 33–62. American Mathematical Society, 1997.

[3] A. Durand, M. Hermann, and P. Kolaitis. Subtractive reductions and complete problems for counting complexity classes. *Theoretical Computer Science (to appear)*, 2003.

[4] T. Eiter, G. Gottlob, and Y. Gurevitch. Existential second order logic over strings. *Journal of the ACM*, 41(1):77–131, 2000.

[5] R. Fagin. Generalized first-order spectra and polynomial-time recognizable sets. *Complexity and Computation*, 7:43–73, 1974.

[6] M. R. Garey and D. S. Johnson. *Computers and Intractability*. W.H. Freeman and Co., 1979.

[7] G. Gottlob, P. G. Kolaitis, and T. Schwentick. Existential second-order logic over graphs: Charting the tractability frontier. *Foundations Of Computer Science*, pages 664–674, 2000.

[8] E. Grädel. Capturing complexity classes by fragments of second order logic. *Theoretical Computer Science*, 101(1):35 57, 1991.

[9] E. Grandjean and F. Olive. Graph properties checkable in linear time in the number of vertices. *Journal of Compter System Sciences (to appear)*, 2004.

[10] H. B. Hunt III, M. V. Marathe, V. Radhakrishnan, and R. E. Stearns. The complexity of planar counting problems. *SIAM Journal on Computing*, 27(4):1142–1167, 1998.

[11] J. Kratochvíl and Z. Tuza. On the complexity of bicoloring clique hypergraphs of graphs. *Symposium On Discrete Algorithms*, pages 40–41, 2000.

[12] C. L. Lautemann and B. Weinzinger. Monadic-NLIN and quantifier-free reductions. In *Computer Science Logic*, volume 1683 of *LNCS*, pages 322–337, 1999.

[13] D. Lichtenstein. Planar formulae and their uses. *SIAM Journal on Computing*, 11(2):329–343, 1982.

[14] L. G. Valiant. The complexity of computing the permanent. *Theoretical Computer Science*, 8(2):189–201, 1979.

Solving the 2-Disjoint Paths Problem in Nearly Linear Time

Torsten Tholey

Institut für Informatik
Johann Wolfgang Goethe-Universität Frankfurt
D-60054 Frankfurt am Main, Germany
tholey@cs.uni-frankfurt.de

Abstract. Given four distinct vertices s_1, s_2, t_1, and t_2 of a graph G, the 2-disjoint paths problem is to determine two disjoint paths, p_1 from s_1 to t_1 and p_2 from s_2 to t_2, if such paths exist. Disjoint can mean vertex- or edge-disjoint.
Both, the edge- and the vertex-disjoint version of the problem, are $\mathcal{NP}$-hard in the case of directed graphs. For undirected graphs, we show that the $O(mn)$-time algorithm of Shiloach can be modified so as to solve the 2-(vertex-)disjoint paths problem in $O(n + m\alpha(m, n))$ time, where m is the number of edges in G, n is the number of vertices in G, and α denotes the inverse of the Ackermann function. Our result also improves the running time for the 2-edge-disjoint paths problem on undirected graphs as well as the running times for the decision versions of the 2-vertex- and the 2-edge-disjoint paths problem on dags.

1 Introduction

In the k-disjoint paths problem ($k \in \mathbb{N}$) we have $2k$ pairwise distinct vertices $s_1, \ldots, s_k, t_1, \ldots, t_k$ of a graph $G = (V, E)$, and we want to output k pairwise disjoint paths p_i from s_i to t_i ($1 \leq i \leq k$), if such paths exist. For short, we will subsequently refer to the k-disjoint paths problem as k-DPP or, more precisely, as k-VDPP if disjoint means vertex-disjoint, and as k-EDPP if disjoint means edge-disjoint. For time bounds, we let $n = |V|$ and $m = |E|$.

The k-DPP arises in the context of VLSI-design, routing problems, and network reliability (see [1] and [15]) and has been extensively studied. A short overview is given in this introduction. Further overviews can be found in [2], [21], and [22]. We will also consider the *decision version* of the k-DPP in which we only want to test the existence of k disjoint paths p_i from s_i to t_i ($1 \leq i \leq k$). Given an $O(T(n, m))$-time algorithm for the decision version of the k-DPP, the disjoint paths, if they exist, can be computed within $O(n + mT(m, n))$ time using the following algorithm: Step through all edges of the input graph G, and, for each edge e considered, if there are k pairwise disjoint paths connecting s_i to t_i for $1 \leq i \leq k$ in the graph $G - \{e\}$,[1] delete e from G before considering the next

---

[1] For short, given a graph $G = (V, E)$ and a set $W \subseteq V$ we define $G - W$ to be the graph $(V - W, E \cap \{\{u, v\} \mid u, v \in V - W\})$, and, similarly, for each set $F \subseteq E$ we let $G - F$ be the graph $(V, E - F)$.

V. Diekert and M. Habib (Eds.): STACS 2004, LNCS 2996, pp. 350–361, 2004.

edge. After having considered all edges the resulting graph consists of exactly k disjoint paths connecting s_i to t_i for $1 \leq i \leq k$. The paths themselves can be output with a depth-first search in the case of the k-VDPP. In the case of the k-EDPP the construction of the paths is more complicated. It can be done in $O(n + mT(n, m))$ time, but we will not show this here.

Previous results. For directed graphs, the decision versions of the k-EDPP and the k-VDPP are $\mathcal{NP}$-complete, even for $k = 2$, as shown by Fortune, Hopcroft, and Wyllie [5]. However, in [17] Perl and Shiloach presented an $O(mn)$-time algorithm for solving the 2-VDPP on dags (directed acyclic graphs). Fortune, Hopcroft, and Wyllie [5] generalized this result of Perl and Shiloach to a polynomial-time algorithm for the k-VDPP on dags. Lucchesi and Giglio [13] gave a linear-time reduction from the decision version of the 2-VDPP on dags to the 2-VDPP on undirected graphs. Solving the latter problem with the previously best known algorithm for the 2-VDPP on undirected graphs leads to an improved running time of $O(n^2)$ for the decision version of the 2-VDPP on dags. This bound holds also for the decision version of the 2-EDPP as we will show in Sect. 3 of this paper by using an $O(n + m \log_{2+m/n} n)$-time reduction from the 2-EDPP to the 2-VDPP. As an application Schrijver [20] described an air plane routing problem that can be solved with an algorithm for the k-EDPP on dags.

If k is not fixed, as defined above, but part of the input, the problem of testing whether there are k disjoint paths p_i from s_i to t_i ($1 \leq i \leq k$) is $\mathcal{NP}$-complete also for undirected graphs. This was shown by Knuth, cf. [10], and Lynch [14] for the VDPP and by Even, Itai, and Shamir [4] for the EDPP.

The first polynomial-time algorithms for the 2-DPP on undirected graphs were given by Ohtsuki [15], Seymour [23], Shiloach [24], and Thomassen [26]. More precisely, Seymour gave only a solution for the decision version of the 2-DPP, but for both, the 2-EDPP and the 2-VDPP. Ohtsuki, Shiloach, and Thomassen considered only the 2-VDPP. However, with the reductions described in [17] their algorithms can also be used for solving the 2-EDPP without increasing the running time of $O(nm)$ of Ohtsuki's and Shiloach's algorithms. Later, Khuller, Mitchell, and Vazirani implicitly showed in [11] that the algorithm of Shiloach can be modified so as to run in $O(n^2)$ time. Using an appropriate reduction, one can also show that the 2-EDPP can be solved within the same time bound (see Sect. 5 for an example of such a reduction). Finally, in [7] Gustedt described an $O(n + m \log n)$-time algorithm for the 2-VDPP on undirected graphs. Unfortunately, since some of the lemmas in [7] fail for certain types of graphs, the current version of Gustedt's algorithm does not work on all graphs. But, for all instances of the 2-VDPP for which G is a triconnected graph such that there is no vertex v of G with $v \notin \{s_1, s_2, t_1, t_2\}$ that can be separated from $\{s_1, s_2, t_1, t_2\}$ by a separator of size three, the lemmas of [7] mentioned above hold and, as a byproduct of this paper, we prove that the 2-VDPP can be reduced to the 2-VDPP on this restricted set of graphs. Concerning the more general k-DPP, Robertson and Seymour [18] showed that the decision version of the undirected k-VDPP is solvable in $O(n^3)$ time. Finally, Perković and Reed [16] improved the running time to $O(n^2)$, which is currently the best known time bound for the decision version of the k-DPP on undirected graphs, for all $k \geq 3$. For some kinds of graphs, the 2-DPP or the general k-DPP are solvable in linear time (see [17], [6], [12], and [19]).

New results. In this paper we present an algorithm for solving the 2-VDPP on undirected graphs in $O(n + m\alpha(m, n))$ time, which improves the previously best known time bound of $O(n^2)$ to $O(\min\{n^2, n + m\alpha(m, n)\})$. α denotes the inverse of the Ackermann function. Applying some well-known reductions or slightly modified versions thereof, we will also show that our result also leads to an $O(m\alpha(m, n) + n \log n)$ time bound for the 2-EDPP on undirected graphs, an $O(n + m\alpha(m, n))$ time bound for the decision version of the 2-VDPP on dags, and finally an $O(n + m \log_{2+m/n} n)$ time bound for the decision version of the 2-EDPP on dags.

The paper is organized as follows. In Sect. 2 we discuss Shiloach's algorithm for the 2-VDPP on undirected graphs. We will see that the 2-VDPP can be reduced to a problem that basically consists in eliminating, without changing the solvability of the problem, all vertices of an instance of the 2-VDPP that can be separated from s_1, s_2, t_1, and t_2 by a separator consisting of three or fewer vertices. Following the presentation, in Sect. 3, of some simple definitions concerning the k-vertex-connectivity, the problem above is solved in Sect. 4. Other versions of the 2-DPP are discussed in Sect. 5.

2   Shiloach's Algorithm

In this section we consider Shiloach's algorithm for the 2-VDPP on undirected graphs. For an instance $I = (G, s_1, s_2, t_1, t_2)$ of the 2-VDPP, if there exist two vertex-disjoint paths p_1 from s_1 to t_1 and p_2 from s_2 to t_2, we say that I *has a solution* and that p_1 *and* p_2 *solve* I. Given two instances $I_1 = (G, s_1, s_2, t_1, t_2)$ with $G = (V, E)$ and $I_2 = (G', s_1', s_2', t_1', t_2')$ with $G' = (V', E')$ of the 2-VDPP, let us say that I_1 is *2-paths reducible* (or for short *2P-reducible*) to I_2 if the following conditions hold: First, I_1 has a solution iff I_2 has a solution; second, $|V'| = O(|V|)$; third, $|E'| = O(|E|)$; and finally, fourth, given a solution of I_2 we can solve I_1 in $O(|V| + |E|)$ time. If we replace an instance I_1 of the 2-VDPP by another instance I_2 such that I_1 is 2P-reducible to I_2 we also say that I_1 is *2P-reduced* to I_2.

In [24] Shiloach outlined a proof of Itai according to which we can assume w.l.o.g. that the input graph $G = (V, E)$ of an instance $I = (G, s_1, s_2, t_1, t_2)$ of the 2-VDPP is triconnected. On a triconnected graph the algorithm of Shiloach proceeds as follows: If G is planar, the problem instance I is solved with the algorithm of Perl and Shiloach [17]. Otherwise I is 2P-reduced to an instance $I' = (G', s_1, s_2, t_1, t_2)$ of the 2-VDPP with $G' = (V', E')$ a triconnected graph such that there are four vertex-disjoint paths from s_1, s_2, t_1, and t_2 to any other set $S \subseteq V' - \{s_1, s_2, t_1, t_2\}$ with at most four vertices (if $|S| < 4$ the end points of the paths in S may overlap). According to Shiloach, the 2-VDPP on such an instance $I' = (G', s_1, s_2, t_1, t_2)$ can be solved as follows: First extract a subgraph of G' homeomorphic to K_5 or $K_{3,3}$. If no such subgraphs exist, G' is planar and

I' can be solved with the algorithm of Perl and Shiloach [17]. Otherwise, if there is a subgraph homeomorphic to K_5, two disjoint paths from s_1 to t_1 and from s_2 to t_2 can be found with an algorithm of Watkins [27]. For the remaining case, Shiloach proved that using some further reductions two disjoint paths from s_1 to t_1 and from s_2 to t_2 can be constructed in linear time.

Concerning the complexity of the algorithm above, Shiloach showed that nearly all steps of the algorithm run in $O(m + n)$ time. Only two bottlenecks were not solved in $O(m + n)$ time by Shiloach: The first one is the reduction from I to I', and the second one is the extraction of a subgraph homeomorphic to $K_{3,3}$ or K_5. But Williamson [28] gave a linear-time algorithm for the latter problem. Thus, for solving the 2-VDPP in $O(n + m\alpha(m,n))$ time, we only need to show that, given an instance $I = (G, s_1, s_2, t_1, t_2)$ of the 2-VDPP, where G is a triconnected graph, it is possible to construct, in $O(m\alpha(m,n))$ time, an instance $I' = (G', s_1, s_2, t_1, t_2)$ of the 2-VDPP, where $G' = (V', E')$ is a triconnected graph such that in G' there are four disjoint paths from s_1, s_2, t_1, and t_2 to any other set $S \subseteq V' - \{s_1, s_2, t_1, t_2\}$ with $|S| \leq 4$, and I is 2P-reducible to I'. This is exactly what we will do in Sect. 4.

3 k-Vertex-Connectivity – Facts and Definitions

The following facts and definitions related to k-vertex-connectivity will be useful for understanding the correctness of our algorithm for the 2-VDPP in Sect. 4. Let $G = (V, E)$ be an undirected graph and let $s, t \in V$ with $s \neq t$. We say that s and t are k-vertex-connected (or that s is k-vertex-connected to t), iff there are k internally vertex-disjoint paths from s to t. By internally vertex-disjoint we mean that every pair of the k disjoint paths has no vertex in common, except s and t. We say that G is k-vertex-connected if all pairs of vertices of G are k-vertex-connected. If two distinct vertices s and t of a graph $G = (V, E)$ with $\{s, t\} \notin E$ are not $(k + 1)$-vertex-connected, they can be separated by a k-separator:

Definition 1. *Let* $G = (V, E)$ *be an undirected graph. Then we call a subset* $S \subseteq V$ *with* $|S| = k$ *a (k-)separator (of G) iff the graph* $G^* = G - S$ *is not connected. If two vertices* s, t *of* G^* *are not connected in* G^*, *we say that* S *separates* s *and* t *(in G). If, for a vertex* s *and a set* $T \subseteq V$, *the connected component of* G^* *containing* s *does not contain any vertex of* T, *we say that* s *can be separated from* T *by* S *(in G) or that* S *separates* s *from* T *(in G).*

For an undirected graph $G = (V, E)$ and two distinct vertices $s, t \in V$, let us define $\kappa(s, t)$ as the size of a smallest separator S (containing neither s nor t) that separates s and t if $\{s, t\} \notin E$, and as one plus the size of a smallest separator S (containing neither s nor t) that separates s and t in $G - \{\{s, t\}\}$ if $\{s, t\} \in E$. Then there is an alternative characterization of k-vertex-connectivity:

Lemma 2. *Two vertices* s *and* t *of an undirected graph* $G = (V, E)$ *are* k-*vertex-connected iff* $\kappa(s, t) \geq k$. G *is* k-*vertex-connected iff* $\kappa(s, t) \geq k$ *for all* $s, t \in V$.

One can also show:

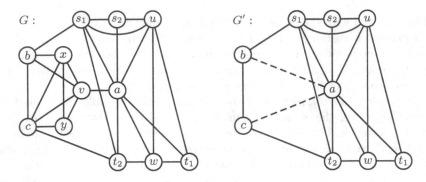

Fig. 1. A graph G and the Δ-replacement G' of G by the triangular cut $S = \{a, b, c\}$. The dashed lines represent newly inserted edges.

Lemma 3. *Let S be a k-separator that separates two vertices v and w of an undirected graph G and let $p_1, p_2, \ldots, p_k$ be k internally vertex-disjoint paths from v to w. Then, every path p_i with $1 \leq i \leq k$ contains exactly one vertex of S.*

In the following, we use "biconnected" and "triconnected" as synonyms for "2-vertex-connected" and "3-vertex-connected", respectively. Moreover, queries, referred to as k-connectivity queries, ask whether two given vertices v and w are k-vertex-connected. Finally, in the following section, disjoint will always mean vertex-disjoint and k-connected will mean k-vertex-connected.

4   An $O(n + m\alpha(m, n))$-Time Algorithm for the 2-VDPP

As we have already seen in Sect. 2, for solving the 2-VDPP in $O(n + m\alpha(m, n))$ time on undirected graphs, we only need to show that, given an instance $I = (G, s_1, s_2, t_1, t_2)$ of the 2-VDPP, where G is a triconnected graph, it is possible to construct, in $O(m\alpha(m, n))$ time, an instance $I' = (G', s_1, s_2, t_1, t_2)$ of the 2-VDPP, where $G' = (V', E')$ is a triconnected graph such that there are four disjoint paths from s_1, s_2, t_1, and t_2 to any other set $S \subseteq V' - \{s_1, s_2, t_1, t_2\}$ with at most four vertices (except that the end points in S may overlap), and I is 2P-reducible to I'. For this we will make use of so-called triangle-replacements:

Suppose we are given an instance $I = (G, s_1, s_2, t_1, t_2)$ of the 2-VDPP such that there exists a vertex v in G that is separated from $\{s_1, s_2, t_1, t_2\}$ by a 3-separator $S = \{a, b, c\}$. Then, like Gustedt in [7], we call S a *triangular cut of G* and the graph G' obtained from G by deleting all vertices of the connected component of $G - S$ containing v together with their adjacent edges and by inserting edges between all pairs of vertices of S that are not already connected by an edge the *triangle-replacement of G by S (removing vertex v)* or, for short, the *Δ-replacement of G by S* (see Fig. 1). Sometimes we also call the replacement step that replaces G by G' a *Δ-replacement*.

Shiloach [24] showed that if G contains no triangular cut separating a vertex v from $\{s_1, s_2, t_1, t_2\}$, then there are four disjoint paths from s_1, s_2, t_1, and t_2 to any other set $S \subseteq V - \{s_1, s_2, t_1, t_2\}$ with at most four vertices. Thus, if for an instance $I = (G, s_1, s_2, t_1, t_2)$ the graph G does not contain a triangular cut, we already know that we can solve the 2-VDPP in linear time. Otherwise, we just eliminate all triangular cuts from G. More precisely, we repeatedly search for a vertex v of G that is separated from $\{s_1, s_2, t_1, t_2\}$ by a triangular cut S and replace I by $I^* = (G^*, s_1, s_2, t_1, t_2)$, where G^* is the Δ-replacement of G by S removing v. We stop if, for the resulting instance $I' = (G', s_1, s_2, t_1, t_2)$ after all Δ-replacements, G' has no triangular cut S separating a vertex v from $\{s_1, s_2, t_1, t_2\}$.

One can easily show that the Δ-replacements do not change the solvability of the problem (see [24] for example).

Lemma 4. *Let $I = (G, s_1, s_2, t_1, t_2)$ be an instance of the 2-VDPP such that G is a triconnected graph and let G^* be a Δ-replacement of G. Then G^* is also a triconnected graph and $I^* = (G^*, s_1, s_2, t_1, t_2)$ has a solution iff I has a solution.*

Moreover, Shiloach [24] showed that if I is our original instance before the first Δ-replacement and I' is the instance of the 2-VDPP after the last Δ-replacement, then the following holds:

Lemma 5. *I is 2P-reducible to I'. In particular, given two paths p_1' and p_2' that solve I', one can construct, in linear time, two paths p_1 and p_2 that solve I.*

Concerning the running time of the reduction from I to I' one can show:

Lemma 6. *Given an instance $I = (G, s_1, s_2, t_1, t_2)$ of the 2-VDPP, where $G = (V, E)$ is triconnected graph, a triangular cut S of G, and a vertex $v \in V$ that is separated from $\{s_1, s_2, t_1, t_2\}$ by S, the Δ-replacement $G^* = (V^*, E^*)$ of G by S removing v can be constructed in $O(|E - E^*|)$ time.*

Proof. Just start a depth-first search on $G - S$ with v as the source node and stop after the depth-first search tree T with root v is complete. Then G^* is the graph obtained from G by deleting all vertices of T and all their adjacent edges in G and by inserting a constant number of edges between vertices of S, if necessary. Since the set of vertices of T is a subset of $V - V^*$, it is easy to see that the construction of T and the deletion of the vertices and edges from G can be done in $O(|E - E^*|)$ time. □

From Lemma 6 we can conclude that, beside the time needed for finding a vertex v that can be separated from $\{s_1, s_2, t_1, t_2\}$ by a triangular cut and the time needed for finding such a triangular cut, the construction of our final instance I' without any triangular cut takes linear time. Thus, we just need to search for an efficient algorithm for determining a vertex v and a triangular cut S such that v is separated from $\{s_1, s_2, t_1, t_2\}$ by S. The main difference between the algorithm of this paper and Shiloach's algorithm is the computation of such vertices and triangular cuts. While not searching explicitly for triangular cuts

Shiloach's algorithm is occasionally unable to proceed due to the presence of such a cut. The cut is then removed by a Δ-replacement. After the Δ-replacement Shiloach's algorithm is restartet on the resulting graph. Since this my happen $\Theta(n)$ times, the running time of Shiloach's algorithm is bounded by only $O(mn)$.

Here, in contrast, we systematically remove all triangular cuts separating a vertex v from $\{s_1, s_2, t_1, t_2\}$ efficiently. For identifying such a vertex v, the following lemma will be very useful.

Lemma 7. *Let $G = (V, E)$ be an undirected triconnected graph containing four vertices s_1, s_2, t_1, and t_2, and let $G_x = (V_x, E_x)$ be the graph that is obtained from G by adding a new vertex x to V and new edges $\{x, s_1\}, \{x, s_2\}, \{x, t_1\}$, and $\{x, t_2\}$ to E. Then, a vertex $v \in V - \{s_1, s_2, t_1, t_2\}$ can be separated from $\{s_1, s_2, t_1, t_2\}$ by a set $S \subseteq V$ with $|S| \leq 3$ in G iff S separates v and x in G_x.*

Proof. Every path from v to x in G_x must visit a vertex $w \in \{s_1, s_2, t_1, t_2\}$ before reaching x. Hence, if S is a 3-separator separating v from $\{s_1, s_2, t_1, t_2\}$ in G, every path from v to x must visit a vertex in S before (or exactly when) visiting a vertex in $\{s_1, s_2, t_1, t_2\}$. Thus, S separates v and x in G_x.

Conversely, if S is a 3-separator separating x and v in G_x, then the vertices of $\{s_1, s_2, t_1, t_2\}$ are contained either in S or in the connected component of $G_x - S$ containing x. It follows that the connected component of $G_x - S$ containing v does not contain any vertex of $\{s_1, s_2, t_1, t_2\}$ and that the same is true of the graph $G - S$. Hence, v is separated from $\{s_1, s_2, t_1, t_2\}$ in G by S. $\square$

Now, for an instance $I = (G, s_1, s_2, t_1, t_2)$ of the 2-VDPP, like in Lemma 7, let G_x be the graph obtained from G, by adding a new vertex x and edges $\{x, s_1\}, \{x, s_2\}, \{x, t_1\}$, and $\{x, t_2\}$ to G. Then, if G is triconnected, the same is true of G_x, and s_1, s_2, t_1, t_2 are 4-connected to x. Lemma 7 implies that in each reduction step, replacing an instance $I = (G, s_1, s_2, t_1, t_2)$ by an instance $I^* = (G^*, s_1, s_2, t_1, t_2)$ such that G^* is a Δ-replacement of G, for identifying a vertex $v \notin \{s_1, s_2, t_1, t_2\}$ that can be separated from $\{s_1, s_2, t_1, t_2\}$ by a triangular cut, we only need to look for a vertex v that is not 4-connected to x in G_x (note that v is not adjacent to x). To find such a vertex we could step through all vertices of V and test, for each vertex, whether it is 4-connected to x (we will later see efficient implementations for answering 4-connectivity queries). But, if we recompute the set of all vertices that are not 4-connected to x after each update of G, we might have to answer up to $\Omega(n^2)$ connectivity queries for the whole sequence of all reduction steps. The following lemma will help us to reduce the number of connectivity queries.

Lemma 8. *Let $I = (G, s_1, s_2, t_1, t_2)$ be an instance of the 2-VDPP such that $G = (V, E)$ is a triconnected graph, let S be a triangular cut of G, let v be a vertex of G that is separated from $\{s_1, s_2, t_1, t_2\}$ by S, and, finally, let G^* be the Δ-replacement of G by S removing v. Then, if two distinct vertices $a \in V^* - S$ and $b \in V^*$ are 4-connected in G, they are also 4-connected in G^*.*

Proof. Let $a \in V^* - S$, $b \in V^*$ be two distinct vertices that are 4-connected in G, and let p_1, p_2, p_3, and p_4 be pairwise internally vertex-disjoint simple paths connecting a and b.

If $b \in V^* - S$, only one path p out of our four paths can visit a vertex in $V - V^*$, and such a path must visit at least two vertices of S. Let us define c to be the first vertex on p in S, and d to be the last vertex on p in S. Now, if we replace the sub-path of p from c to d by the edge $\{c, d\}$, p and the other three paths of p_1, p_2, p_3, and p_4 are four internally vertex-disjoint paths in G^*.

If $b \in S$, no more than two of the paths p_1, p_2, p_3, and p_4 can visit a vertex in $V - V^*$. If they do so, they also visit a vertex in $S - \{b\}$. Then we follow these paths up to a first node $c \in S - \{b\}$, and then use the edge $\{c, b\}$ to reach b. After this replacement, the four paths are pairwise internally vertex-disjoint in G^*. □

Hence, having replaced G by a new graph G^*, if we search for a vertex v that is not 4-connected to x, we can exclude all vertices for which, in a previous reduction step, we have already tested whether they are 4-connected to x. If such a vertex was 4-connected to x, it remains 4-connected to x, and, otherwise, it was deleted from G. Thus, the number of 4-connectivity-queries is reduced to $O(n)$.

For efficiently supporting 4-connectivity queries, we might consider using a *dynamic data structure*. This is a data structure that supports two kinds of operations: update operations, which in case of graph problems usually consist of edge insertions and edge deletions, and queries, which in our case will be 4-connectivity queries. The idea behind dynamic data structures for graph problems is that, using the knowledge about a graph before an edge insertion or edge deletion, possibly queries can be answered faster than without such knowledge. Unfortunately, there is no known dynamic data structure supporting all of the operations above in nearly constant time. However, Kanevsky, Tamassia, Di Battista, and Chen [9] presented a very efficient *incremental dynamic data structure* supporting only edge insertions and 4-connectivity queries. This data structure can be initialized, in $O(m\alpha(m, n))$ time, with a triconnected graph containing m edges and n vertices, and, after this initialization, it supports $O(m)$ queries and insertions in $O(m\alpha(m, n))$ time. With a simple trick we can make use of this data structure: In addition to G_x, we also maintain a graph H_x. that, before the first Δ-replacement, is initialized with a copy of G_x. In a reduction step replacing G_x by a Δ-replacement G_x^* of G, we do not delete any vertex or edge of H_x, but insert in H_x the same edges that are inserted in G_x. Now, if we want to test whether a vertex of G_x is 4-connected to x in G_x, we only need to ask whether it is 4-connected to x in H_x, as shown by Lemma 9. Queries in H_x can now be answered with the data structure of Kanevsky et al..

Lemma 9. *A vertex w of G_x is 4-connected to x in G_x iff it is 4-connected to x in H_x.*

Proof. Let us define a set of k-paths $p_1, p_2, \ldots, p_k$ to be *quasi internally disjoint* (or, for short, *q.i. disjoint*) if, for all pairs (i, j) with $i, j \in \{1, \ldots, k\}$ and $i \neq j$, no inner vertex of p_i appears on p_j. We first show that, before and after each reduction step – i.e. Δ-replacement of G_x – transforming $G_x = (V_{G_x}, E_{G_x})$ and $H_x = (V_{H_x}, E_{H_x})$ into new graphs, the following invariant holds: If, in H_x, there are k q.i. disjoint simple paths p_i $(1 \leq i \leq k)$ connecting x to a vertex

$v_i \in V_{H_x} \cap V_{G_x}$, where $v_1, v_2, \ldots, v_k$ need not necessarily be distinct, there are also k q.i. disjoint paths q_i $(1 \leq i \leq k)$ connecting x to v_i in G_x such that the set of the vertices visited by q_i is a subset of the vertices visited by p_i. The invariant holds before the first reduction step, since H_x is initialized with G_x. Let us now assume that, for an $l \in \mathbb{N}$, after l reduction steps, there are k q.i. disjoint paths p_i $(1 \leq i \leq k)$ in H_x connecting x to a vertex $v_i \in V_{H_x} \cap V_{G_x}$. Moreover, let S be the triangular cut used for the first Δ-replacement of our algorithm, i.e. in the first reduction step of our algorithm. If one path p of the paths $p_1, \ldots, p_k$ uses an edge $\{a, b\}$ that is deleted from G_x after the first Δ-replacement, this path must also visit a vertex $c \in S$ before following edge $\{a, b\}$ and a vertex $d \in S$ after having reached edge $\{a, b\}$. We can now replace the sub-path of p between c and d by edge $\{c, d\}$. It is easy to see that, after this replacement, the paths $p_1, \ldots, p_k$ remain pairwise q.i. disjoint. We eventually must repeat this step to obtain k pairwise q.i. disjoint paths $p'_1, \ldots, p'_k$ such that no path uses an edge that is deleted from G_x after the first Δ-replacement, and such that the vertices visited by p'_i are a subset of the vertices visited by p_i. In the same way, we can replace all edges of any path in $p'_1, \ldots, p'_k$ that are deleted from G_x after the second, third, $\ldots$ Δ-replacement until the resulting paths use only edges that are not deleted from G_x after l reduction steps.

The invariant above implies that, if, after an arbitrary number of reduction steps, x is 4-vertex-connected to a vertex $v \in V_{G_x} \cap V_{H_x}$ in H_x, the same is true in G_x. The reverse direction is trivial.   □

Given a vertex v of G_x that is not 4-connected to x, we still have to show how we can determine a 3-separator S that separates v and x. Once again, instead of searching for a 3-separator in G_x, we search for a 3-separator in H_x:

Lemma 10. *Let v be a vertex of G_x and let S be a 3-separator separating v and x in H_x. Then S is also a 3-separator separating v and x in G_x.*

Proof. Assume that the lemma above is not true. Let us consider the first replacement of $G_x = (V_{G_x}, E_{G_x})$ by a graph $G_x^* = (V_{G_x^*}, E_{G_x^*})$, and of $H_x = (V_{H_x}, E_{H_x})$ by a graph $H_x^* = (V_{H_x^*}, E_{H_x^*})$ such that the assertion of the lemma holds before, but not after, the replacement. It is clear that every 3-separator $T \subseteq V_{G_x^*}$ in H_x^* that separates a vertex $w \in V_{G_x^*}$ and x also separates w and x in G_x^*, since G_x^* is a subgraph of H_x^*. Thus, if the lemma does not hold for G_x^* and H_x^*, there must be a 3-separator T with $T \not\subseteq V_{G_x^*}$ that separates a vertex $w \in V_{G_x^*}$ and x in H_x^*. Since H_x^* is triconnected, there are three pairwise internally vertex-disjoint paths from x to w in H_x^*. Then, as shown in the proof of Lemma 9, there also exist three pairwise internally vertex-disjoint paths q_1, q_2, and q_3 from x to w in H_x^* that do not visit any vertex outside G_x^*. Hence, at least one vertex of T is not visited by q_1, q_2, and q_3. But this contradicts Lemma 3.   □

For determining a 3-separator of H_x separating a vertex v and x, we can again use the data structure of Kanevsky et. al.. This data structure also maintains, in $O(\alpha(m, n))$ amortized time per edge insertion, a special decomposition tree from which, for any given pair of two non-4-connected vertices u and w, one can construct, in constant time, two sets S_1 and S_2 such that one of these sets is a 3-separator separating u and w (see [9] for more details). Now, for two sets S_1 and S_2 with one of them being a 3-separator separating v and x, we start two interleaved depth-first searches on $G_x - S_1$ and on $G_x - S_2$ with v as the source node; and we continue until one of the two depth-first searches has completed its depth-first search tree containing vertex v without having visited vertex x. Depending on whether this happens to the depth-first search on $G_x - S_1$ or to that on $G_x - S_2$, either S_1 (in the first case) or S_2 (in the second case) is a 3-separator separating v and x. Since the running time of the subroutine above is dominated by that of the depth-first search that detects a 3-separator $S = S_1$ or $S = S_2$, and, after identifying S, all vertices and edges visited by this depth-first search will be deleted from G_x in order to complete the reduction step replacing G_x by the Δ-replacement G_x^* of G by S, the extra running time for determining 3-separators of two possible candidates can be bounded by $O(m)$, taken over all reduction steps.

Let us now analyze the complexity of the whole algorithm. For answering all 4-connectivity queries and identifying 3-separators separating a vertex v and x, we need only $O(m\alpha(m, n))$ time using the data structure of Kanevsky et. al., since this data structure can be initialized in $O(m\alpha(m, n))$ time and our algorithm consists of only $O(n)$ edge insertions and 4-connectivity queries (note that $n \leq m$, since G is triconnected). Since we have already shown that the remaining parts of our algorithm for identifying triangular cuts run in linear time, we can conclude that the following lemma holds:

Theorem 11. *Let* $I = (G, s_1, s_2, t_1, t_2)$ *be an instance of the 2-VDPP, where* $G = (V, E)$ *is an undirected triconnected graph. Then, in* $O(m\alpha(m, n))$ *time, an instance* $I' = (G', s_1, s_2, t_1, t_2)$ *of the 2-VDPP can be constructed such that I is 2P-reducible to I', and such that $G' = (V', E')$ is an undirected triconnected graph not containing any vertex* $v \notin \{s_1, s_2, t_1, t_2\}$ *that can be separated from* $\{s_1, s_2, t_1, t_2\}$ *by a triangular cut.*

With the results of Sect. 2 we can conclude:

Theorem 12. *The 2-VDPP can be solved in* $O(n + m\alpha(m, n))$ *time.*

5   Extensions

Perl and Shiloach [17] showed that the 2-EDPP on undirected graphs can be reduced to the 2-VDPP on undirected graphs as follows: If, for an instance (G, s_1, s_2, t_1, t_2) of the 2-EDPP, there are two vertex-disjoint paths from s_1 to t_1 and from s_2 to t_2, just output two such paths with an algorithm for the 2-VDPP. Otherwise, add a new vertex x and edges $\{x, s_1\}, \{x, s_2\}, \{x, t_1\}$ and $\{x, t_2\}$ to G. Then, there are two edge- (but not vertex-)disjoint paths from s_1 to t_1 and from s_2 to t_2, if and only if there is a vertex u of G that is 4-edge-connected to x. Given such a vertex u, one can use network-flow techniques to determine, in $O(m)$ time, four edge-disjoint paths from u to s_1, s_2, t_1, and t_2, and by concatenating two of these paths it is easy to construct, in linear time, two edge-disjoint paths from s_1 to t_1 and s_2 to t_2. In [17] the problem of determining a vertex u that is 4-edge-connected to x was solved by n applications of network-flow techniques, which yields a running time of $O(mn)$. But, as shown by Dinitz and Westbrook [3], a sequence of q 4-edge-connectivity queries in an undirected graph with n vertices and m edges can be answered in $O(q + m + n \log n)$ total time. Hence, the 2-EDPP on undirected graphs can be solved in $O(m\alpha(m, n) + n \log n)$ time.

In [13] Lucchesi and Giglio presented a linear-time algorithm that, given an instance $I = (G, s_1, s_2, t_1, t_2)$ of the decision version of the 2-VDPP on dags with $G = (V, E)$, constructs an instance $I' = (G', s_1, s_2, t_1, t_2)$ of the decision version of the 2-VDPP for undirected graphs with $G' = (V', E')$ such that $|E'| \leq |E|$, $|V'| \leq |V|$, and there are two disjoint paths from s_1 to t_1 and from s_2 to t_2 in G iff the same is true of G'. Thus, there is an $O(m\alpha(m, n) + n)$-time algorithm for solving the decision version of the 2-VDPP on dags. Finally, similarly to the reduction of the 2-EDPP to the 2-VDPP on undirected graphs, for the 2-EDPP on a dag, either two disjoint paths can be found with an algorithm for the 2-VDPP, or we add two vertices x and y and directed edges $(x, s_1), (x, s_2), (t_1, y)$, and (t_2, y) to our input graph. In the latter case, there are two edge- (but not vertex-)disjoint paths, p_1 from s_1 to t_1 and p_2 from s_2 to t_2, iff there is a vertex u such that there are two edge-disjoint paths leading from x to u as well as two edge-disjoint paths from u to y. u, if it exists, can be determined in $O(n + m \log_{2+m/n} n)$ time with a data structure of Suurballe and Tarjan [25]. Hence, the decision version of the 2-EDPP on dags is solvable in $O(n + m \log_{2+m/n} n)$ time.

Acknowledgements. My special thanks go to Jens Gustedt for his contributions to our email discussion on the 2-disjoint paths problem. The feedback and friendly support I received from Jens Gustedt have been a constant encouragement for me to pursue my objective and solve the 2-VDPP in nearly linear time. I am indebted to Torben Hagerup for his advice and many helpful comments on preversions of this paper.

References

1. A. Aggarwal, J. Kleinberg, and D. P. Williamson, Node-disjoint paths on the mesh and a new trade-off in VLSI layout, *SIAM J. Comput.* **29** (2000), pp. 1321–1333.
2. J. Bang-Jensen and G. Gutin, *Digraphs: Theory, Algorithms and Applications*, Springer, London, 2001.
3. Y. Dinitz and J. Westbrook, Maintaining the classes of 4-edge-connectivity in a graph on-line, *Algorithmica* **20** (1998), pp. 242–276.
4. S. Even, A. Itai, and A. Shamir, On the complexity of timetable and multicommodity flow problems, *SIAM J. Comput.* **5** (1976), pp. 691–703.
5. S. Fortune, J. Hopcroft, and J. Wyllie, The directed subgraph homeomorphism problem, *Theoret. Comput. Sci.* **10** (1980), pp. 111–121.
6. C. P. Gopalakrishnan and C. Pandu Rangan, Edge-disjoint paths in permutation graphs, *Discuss. Math. Graph Theory* **15** (1995), pp. 59–72.

7. J. Gustedt, The general two-path problem in time $O(m \log n)$ (extended abstract), Report No. 394/1994, TU Berlin, FB Mathematik, 1994.
8. D. Jungnickel, *Graphen, Netzwerke und Algorithmen*, B. I. Wissenschaftsverlag, Mannheim, 1994.
9. A. Kanevsky, R. Tamassia, G. Di Battista, and J. Chen, On-line maintenance of the four-connected components of a graph, Proc. 32nd Annual IEEE Symposium on Foundations of Computer Science (FOCS 1991), pp. 793–801.
10. R. M. Karp, On the computational complexity of combinatorial problems, *Networks* **5** (1975), pp. 45–68.
11. S. Khuller, S. G. Mitchell, and V. V. Vazirani, Processor efficient parallel algorithms for the two disjoint paths problem and for finding a Kuratowski homeomorph, *SIAM J. Comput.* **21** (1992), pp. 486–506.
12. E. Korach and A. Tal, General vertex disjoint paths in series-parallel graphs, *Discrete Appl. Math.* **41** (1993), pp. 147–164.
13. C. L. Lucchesi and M. C. M. T. Giglio, On the irrelevance of edge orientations on the acyclic directed two disjoint paths problem, IC Technical Report DCC-92-03, Universidade Estadual de Campinas, Instituto de Computação, 1992.
14. J. F. Lynch, The equivalence of theorem proving and the interconnection problem, *(ACM) SIGDA Newsletter,* **5** (1975), pp. 31–36.
15. T. Ohtsuki, The two disjoint path problem and wire routing design, Proc. Symposium on Graph Theory and Applications, Lecture Notes in Computer Science, Vol. 108, Springer, Berlin, 1981, pp. 207–216.
16. L. Perković and B. Reed, An improved algorithm for finding tree decompositions of small width, *International Journal of Foundations of Computer Science (IJFCS)* **11** (2000), pp. 365–372.
17. Y. Perl and Y. Shiloach, Finding two disjoint paths between two pairs of vertices in a graph, *J. ACM* **25** (1978), pp. 1–9.
18. N. Robertson and P. D. Seymour, Graph minors. XIII. The disjoint paths problem, *J. Comb. Theory, Ser. B,* **63** (1995), pp. 65–110.
19. P. Scheffler, A practical linear time algorithm for disjoint paths in graphs with bounded tree-width, Report No. 396/1994, TU Berlin, FB Mathematik, 1994.
20. A. Schrijver, A group-theoretical approach to disjoint paths in directed graphs, *CWI Quarterly* **6** (1993), pp. 257–266.
21. A. Schrijver, *Combinatorial optimization – Polyhedra and Efficiency Vol. C,* Springer, Berlin, 2002.
22. A. Schwill, Nonblocking graphs: greedy algorithms to compute disjoint paths, Proc. 7th Annual Symposium on Theoretical Aspects of Computer Science (STACS 1990), Lecture Notes in Computer Science Vol. 415, Springer-Verlag, Berlin, 1990, pp. 250-262.
23. P. D. Seymour, Disjoint paths in graphs, *Discrete Math.* **29** (1980), pp. 293–309.
24. Y. Shiloach, A polynomial solution to the undirected two paths problem, *J. ACM* **27** (1980), pp. 445–456.
25. J. W. Suurballe and R. E. Tarjan, A quick method for finding shortest pairs of disjoint paths. *Networks* **14** (1984), pp. 325-336.
26. C. Thomassen, 2-linked graphs, *Europ. J. Combinatorics* **1** (1980), pp. 371–378.
27. M. E. Watkins, On the existence of certain disjoint arcs in graphs, *Duke Math. J.* **35** (1968), pp. 231–246.
28. S. G. Williamson, Depth-first search and Kuratowski subgraphs, *J. ACM* **31** (1984), pp. 681–693.

Simpler Computation of Single-Source Shortest Paths in Linear Average Time

Torben Hagerup

Institut für Informatik, Universität Augsburg, D–86135 Augsburg, Germany
hagerup@informatik.uni-augsburg.de

Abstract. Meyer as well as Goldberg recently described algorithms that solve the single-source shortest-paths problem in linear average time on graphs with random edge lengths drawn from the uniform distribution on $[0, 1]$. This note points out that the same result can be obtained through simple combinations of standard data structures and with a trivial probabilistic analysis.

1 Introduction

The classic *single-source shortest-paths* (*SSSP*) problem asks, given a network $\mathcal{N}$ with real-valued edge lengths and a distinguished vertex s in $\mathcal{N}$, called the *source*, for shortest paths in $\mathcal{N}$ from s to all vertices in $\mathcal{N}$ for which such shortest paths exist. This paper considers the important special case of the SSSP problem in which all edge lengths are nonnegative, and which can be solved with *Dijkstra's algorithm* [2,3,10]. The running time of Dijkstra's algorithm depends on the implementation of a priority-queue data structure used by the algorithm. Realizing the priority queue by means of a *Fibonacci heap*, Fredman and Tarjan [4] achieved a time bound of $O(m + n \log n)$ for input networks with n vertices and m edges. Faster algorithms, some of them randomized, are known for the case of integer edge lengths (see [9]). None of these algorithms guarantees a linear (expected) running time in all circumstances, however, for which reason some researchers left the worst-case scenario and tried to obtain good average performance on networks drawn at random. Meyer [7,8] showed that on arbitrary directed graphs equipped with random edge lengths drawn independently from the uniform distribution on the interval $[0, 1]$, the SSSP problem can be solved in linear average time; moreover, a linear time bound holds with high probability. Meyer's algorithm is somewhat involved, and his probabilistic analysis is complicated. Subsequently Goldberg [5] gave a simpler analysis of an algorithm with the same properties and observed that independence of the edge weights is not needed for a linear average time bound. This note points out that essentially the same result can be obtained through simple combinations of standard data structures and with a trivial probabilistic analysis. A generic algorithm is introduced and proved correct, after which two concrete instantiations of the generic algorithm, Algorithm A and Algorithm B, are presented and analyzed. Algorithm A uses the Fibonacci-heap data structure and is, arguably,

V. Diekert and M. Habib (Eds.): STACS 2004, LNCS 2996, pp. 362–369, 2004.
© Springer-Verlag Berlin Heidelberg 2004

simpler to describe than Algorithm B, which replaces the Fibonacci heap by a standard binary heap. For the most part, the new algorithms can be viewed as simplifications of both previous algorithms due to Meyer and Goldberg.

2   The Generic Algorithm

Our goal is to give new proofs of the theorem below, which also follows from the work of Meyer [7,8] and Goldberg [5]. The model of computation is assumed to allow real numbers to be compared, added, multiplied, divided and rounded to their integer parts in constant time.

Theorem 1. *There is an algorithm $\mathcal{A}$ with the following properties: Given an arbitrary directed graph $G = (V, E)$ with n vertices and m edges and a source $s \in V$, if the edges in G are equipped with random edge lengths drawn from the uniform distribution on $[0, 1]$, then $\mathcal{A}$ solves the instance of the SSSP problem defined by the resulting network in $O(n + m)$ average time and $O(n + m)$ space. If, moreover, the edge lengths are mutually independent and $m \geq 2$, the running time of $\mathcal{A}$ is $O(n + m)$ with probability at least $1 - 2^{-Cm/\log m}$, for every constant $C > 0$.*

Let us fix a directed graph $G = (V, E)$ with n vertices and m edges and a source $s \in V$. In proving the theorem, we can assume without loss of generality that all vertices in V are reachable from s in G and that $m \geq 2$. Let $\mathcal{N}$ be the instance of the SSSP problem obtained by giving each edge $e \in E$ a length $c(e) \in [0, 1]$.

For all $v \in V$, denote by $\delta(v)$ the length of a shortest path in $\mathcal{N}$ from s to v. It is well-known that knowledge of $\delta(v)$ for all $v \in V$ allows us, in $O(n + m)$ time, to construct a *shortest-path tree* of $\mathcal{N}$ rooted at s, i.e., a tree that is the union, over all $v \in V$, of a shortest path in $\mathcal{N}$ from s to v (see, e.g., [1, Section 4.3]), so our task is to compute $\delta(v)$ for all $v \in V$. When f is a function and x belongs to the domain of f, we call $f(x)$ the f *value* of x.

Define $k = \lfloor \log_2 m \rfloor$ and $\Delta = 1/k$, let V_1 be the set of vertices in V that have one or more incoming edges of length smaller than Δ, and take $V_2 = V \setminus V_1$. Similarly to many other SSSP algorithms, the generic algorithm manipulates an upper bound $d(v)$ on $\delta(v)$ for each $v \in V$. For brevity, let us define $\widehat{d}(v) = d(v)$ for all $v \in V_1$ and $\widehat{d}(v) = \lfloor d(v)/\Delta \rfloor \Delta$ for all $v \in V_2$. For all $v \in V$, we have $d(v) - \Delta < \widehat{d}(v) \leq d(v)$. The generic algorithm is shown in Fig. 1.

When a vertex u is chosen in line (5), we will say that u is *selected*. The operation $d(v) := \min\{d(v), d(u) + c(u, v)\}$ carried out in line (8) is called a *relaxation* of the edge (u, v). After the initialization in lines (1)–(3), the algorithm selects the vertices in V one by one, always choosing the next vertex as a remaining vertex with minimal $\widehat{d}$ value, and relaxes the edges leaving the selected vertex one by one. At this level of abstraction, the only difference to Dijkstra's algorithm is that line (5) chooses u to minimize $\widehat{d}(u)$ rather than $d(u)$.

Standard arguments show the correctness of the algorithm. Immediately after the execution of line (2), d is an upper bound on δ, as every vertex in V is

---

(1) $d(s) := 0$;
(2) **for all** $v \in V \setminus \{s\}$ **do** $d(v) := n - 1$;
(3) $U := V$;
(4) **while** $U \neq \emptyset$ **do**
(5)   Choose $u \in U$ such that $\widehat{d}(u)$ is minimal;
(6) $U := U \setminus \{u\}$;
(7)   **for all** $v \in V$ with $(u, v) \in E$ **do**
(8) $d(v) := \min\{d(v), d(u) + c(u, v)\}$;

Fig. 1. The generic SSSP algorithm.

reachable from s via a path with at most $n - 1$ edges and therefore of length at most $n - 1$. Since d is subsequently changed only through edge relaxations, it is easy to see with induction that it remains an upper bound on δ. Because $d(w)$ never increases after the execution of line (2), it suffices to prove that $d(w) = \delta(w)$ holds for every $w \in V$ when w is selected.

Assume, by way of contradiction, that w is the first vertex to be selected when $d(w) > \delta(w)$. Let (u, v) be an edge on a shortest path in $\mathcal{N}$ from s to w such that just before the selection of w, v belongs to U, but u does not. Since $s \notin U$ and $w \in U$ at the time under consideration, such an edge exists. The selection of u takes place before that of w. Therefore, by assumption, $d(u) = \delta(u)$ holds when u is selected, and just after the relaxation of (u, v), we have $d(v) \leq d(u) + c(u, v) = \delta(u) + c(u, v) = \delta(v)$. The relation $d(v) = \delta(v)$ still holds when w is selected; in particular, $v \neq w$.

Since all edge lengths are nonnegative, we have $\delta(w) \geq \delta(v)$. If $w \in V_2$, moreover, $\delta(w) \geq \delta(v) + \Delta$. When w is selected, we therefore have $d(w) > \delta(w) \geq \delta(v) = d(v)$ and, if $w \in V_2$, $d(w) > \delta(w) \geq \delta(v) + \Delta = d(v) + \Delta$. Whether or not $w \in V_2$, we find $\widehat{d}(w) > \widehat{d}(v)$. Since $v \in U$ when w is selected, this contradicts the selection of w as a vertex in U whose $\widehat{d}$ value is minimal.

3   Algorithm A

Algorithm A stores the vertices in $U \cap V_1$ in a Fibonacci heap [4] with their $\widehat{d}$ values as keys. For $i = 0, \ldots, nk - 1$, the vertices v in $U \cap V_2$ with $\widehat{d}(v) = i\Delta$ are stored in a set L_i implemented as a doubly-linked list, known as a *bucket*, so that insertions, deletions, and emptyness tests can all be carried out in constant time. Moreover, for $j = 0, \ldots, n - 1$, the set $I_j = \{i \mid jk \leq i < (j+1)k$ and $L_i \neq \emptyset\}$ is stored in a data structure D_j that supports the following operations in constant time: Insertion, deletion, test of $I_j = \emptyset$ and, if $I_j \neq \emptyset$, the computation of $\min I_j$. Note that, for $j = 0, \ldots, n - 1$, $I_j \neq \emptyset$ exactly if $U \cap V_2$ contains at least one vertex v with $j \leq \widehat{d}(v) < j + 1$.

Because $k \leq \log_2 m$, D_j can be represented as a single integer. For ease of discussion, consider the case $j = 0$. A set $I \subseteq \{0, \ldots, k-1\}$ is represented through the integer $\sum_{i \in I} 2^{k-1-i} \in \{0, \ldots, m-1\}$. To insert an element i (which is not already present), add 2^{k-1-i} to D_j. To delete an element i (which is present), subtract 2^{k-1-i} from D_j. I_j is empty exactly if $D_j = 0$. And to find $\min I_j$ when $I_j \neq \emptyset$, finally, compute $k - 1 - \lfloor \log_2 D_j \rfloor$. If the available instruction set does not allow constant-time computation of 2^{k-1-i} from i or of $\lfloor \log_2 D_j \rfloor$ from D_j, these mappings are easily realized via lookup in tables of size $O(m)$ that can be constructed in $O(m)$ time and shared among $D_0, \ldots, D_{n-1}$.

A final variable is an integer j^* that, logically, points to one of the sets I_j and that is initialized to 0 (i.e., pointing to I_0). The complete representation of the vertices in $U \cap V_2$ is illustrated in Fig. 2.

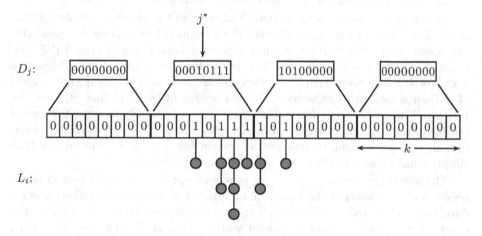

Fig. 2. The representation of $U \cap V_2$.

We now discuss the implementation of the generic algorithm using the data structures introduced above. Line (5) of the generic algorithm is refined as shown in Fig. 3.

(5.1) $x := \min(\{\widehat{d}(v) \mid v \in U \cap V_1\} \cup \{\infty\})$;
(5.2) **while** $I_{j^*} = \emptyset$ and $j^* + 1 \leq x$ **do** $j^* := j^* + 1$;
(5.3) $i^* := \min(I_{j^*} \cup \{\infty\})$;
(5.4) **if** $i^* \Delta \leq x$
(5.5) **then** choose $u \in L_{i^*}$ arbitrarily
(5.6) **else** choose $u \in U \cap V_1$ with $\widehat{d}(u) = x$;

Fig. 3. The refinement of line (5) in Algorithm A.

Line (5.1) computes x as the smallest $\widehat{d}$ value of a vertex in $U \cap V_1$, or as the dummy value ∞ if $U \cap V_1 = \emptyset$. If $j^* \leq x$, line (5.2) repeatedly increments j^*

until some vertex in U has a $\widehat{d}$ value in $[j^*, j^* + 1)$. We claim that subsequently $\min\{\widehat{d}(v) \mid v \in U\} \in [j^*, j^* + 1)$. This would be trivial if j^* were set to 0 prior to the execution of line (5.2). In reality, however, j^* keeps the value that it acquired in the last execution of line (5.2), if any, and the "search" takes place only from there. That this is also correct follows from the easily verifiable fact that the $\widehat{d}$ values of the selected vertices, in the order in which the vertices are selected, form a nondecreasing sequence—the relaxation of an edge (u, v) cannot give v a smaller $\widehat{d}$ value than that of u, not even if $u \in V_1$ and $v \in V_2$. Line (5.3) computes the integer i^* such that the smallest $\widehat{d}$ value of a vertex in $U \cap V_2$ is $i^*\Delta$, or ∞ if $I_{j^*} = \emptyset$ (which may happen even if $U \cap V_2 \neq \emptyset$). Finally the vertex u is chosen in line (5.5) or (5.6) based on a direct comparison between $i^*\Delta$ and x.

At this point, the implementation of all steps of the algorithm is straightforward: The initialization in line (3) calls the Fibonacci-heap operation *insert* $|V_1|$ times and inserts $|V_2|$ vertices in appropriate buckets. Lines (5.1) and (5.6) are realized through the *findmin* operation of the Fibonacci heap. Line (6) involves a call of the Fibonacci-heap operation *deletemin* if $u \in V_1$, and the removal of u from some bucket otherwise. The relaxation of (u, v) in line (8) calls the Fibonacci-heap operation *decreasekey* if $v \in V_1$, and possibly moves v from some bucket to another one otherwise. Finally, since the set U is not explicitly maintained, it is convenient to replace the test in line (4) by a construction that simply causes lines (5)–(8) to be executed exactly n times.

The algorithm works in $O(n + m)$ space, except that, as described so far, it needs to store headers of the lists L_i in an array A of size nk. The following standard observation reduces the overall space requirements to $O(n + m)$: Because every edge "spans" at most k "bucket widths" (i.e., its length is at most $k\Delta$), all nonempty buckets, except for the single bucket that contains vertices v with $d(v) = n - 1$, at all times belong to a (varying) set of $k + 1$ consecutive buckets. Therefore A can be replaced by a "sliding window" of size $k + 1$, i.e., an array of size $k + 1 = O(\log n)$ thought of as cyclic, but cut at a moving position, that always represents the segment of A of current interest.

Outside of calls of Fibonacci-heap operations and of line (5), the time spent by the algorithm is easily seen to be $O(n + m)$. Since the Fibonacci-heap operation *findmin* works in constant time, a single execution of line (5) takes $O(1 + h)$ time, where h is the resulting increase in j^*. j^* remains bounded by $n - 1$ and line (5) is executed n times, so the total time spent in line (5) is $O(n)$. The algorithm executes exactly $|V_1|$ calls of each of the Fibonacci-heap operations *insert* and *deletemin* and at most m calls of *decreasekey*. Since the Fibonacci heap has a constant amortized time bound for *insert* and *decreasekey* and a logarithmic amortized bound for *deletemin*, the total time spent in Fibonacci-heap operations and altogether is $O(n + m + |V_1| \log n)$.

The quantity $|V_1|$ is clearly upper-bounded by the number S of edges in E of length smaller than Δ. If the edge lengths are drawn from the uniform distribution on $[0, 1]$, the expected value $E(S)$ of S is $m\Delta$, so that the average running time of the algorithm is $O(n + m + m\Delta \log n) = O(n + m)$. If, moreover, the edge lengths are mutually independent, S is binomially distributed. By the

Chernoff bound [6, Eq. (8)], $\Pr(S \geq r) \leq 2^{-r}$ then holds for every $r \geq 6E(S)$. Using this with $r = Cm/\log_2 m$ for arbitrary constant $C \geq 12$, we can conclude that the running time is $O(n+m)$ with probability at least $1 - 2^{-Cm/\log_2 m}$. This ends the proof of Theorem 1.

4   Algorithm B

Because the Fibonacci heap is occasionally viewed with suspicion, in terms of its practical performance, this section presents an alternative instantiation of the generic algorithm that allows the Fibonacci heap to be replaced by a standard binary heap.

In Algorithm B, the vertices in V_1, rather than being stored separately in a Fibonacci heap, are stored together with the vertices in V_2 in the lists L_i, every vertex $v \in V$ belonging to $L_{\lfloor d(v)/\Delta \rfloor}$. The only exception is that the *current bucket*, L_{i^*}, is instead represented via a binary heap H and a list L, both initialized to be empty. Line (5) of the generic algorithm is refined as shown in Fig. 4 below. In the interest of succinctness, the symbols "H" and "L" are used to denote also the sets of vertices stored in the corresponding data structures.

(5.1) **if** $H \cup L = \emptyset$ **then**
(5.2)   **while** $I_{j^*} = \emptyset$ **do** $j^* := j^* + 1$;
(5.3) $i^* := \min I_{j^*}$;
(5.4)   Represent $L_{i^*} \cap V_1$ in H and $L_{i^*} \cap V_2$ in L;
(5.5) **if** $L \neq \emptyset$
(5.6) **then** choose $u \in L$ arbitrarily
(5.7) **else** choose $u \in H$ such that $\widehat{d}(u)$ is minimal;

Fig. 4. The refinement of line (5) in Algorithm B.

Line (5.1) tests whether the current bucket has been exhausted. If so, lines (5.2) and (5.3) establish a new current bucket in a way familiar from Algorithm A. We already noted earlier that, whenever the current bucket is nonempty, it contains a vertex in U with minimal $\widehat{d}$ value.

In line (5.4), the new current bucket is converted from the list representation to the representation in H and L: Those vertices in L_{i^*} that belong to V_1 are stored in H (with their $\widehat{d}$ values as keys), and those belonging to V_2 are stored in L (H and L are empty before this step). Future operations on (vertices in) the current bucket are executed on H and L. Lines (5.5)–(5.7), finally, choose u from L, if possible, and otherwise from H. Since $\widehat{d}(u) \leq \widehat{d}(v)$ for all $u \in V_2$ and $v \in V_1$ with $\lfloor d(u)/\Delta \rfloor = \lfloor d(v)/\Delta \rfloor$, this implements line (5) of the generic algorithm correctly.

The relaxation of an edge (u, v) may cause v to enter the current bucket, or may decrease $\widehat{d}(v)$ while v belongs to the current bucket. The important thing to note, however, is that this can happen only if $c(u,v) < \Delta$, and therefore not at all if $v \in V_2$. This shows that over the whole execution, H must support at most S *decreasekey* operations, where S is the number of edges in E of length smaller than Δ, in addition to exactly $|V_1|$ insertions, $|V_1|$ *deletemin* operations, and n emptiness tests. This needs $O((S + |V_1|)\log n) = O(S \log n)$ time. Moreover, L must support exactly $|V_2|$ insertions, $|V_2|$ deletions, and $2n$ emptiness tests, which takes $O(n)$ time. Referring to the old analysis of the probability distribution of S, we obtain a new proof of Theorem 1.

5 Concluding Remarks

The bound of $2^{-Cm/\log_2 m}$ on the probability of exceeding the time bound of $O(n+m)$ established in Theorem 1, for arbitrary fixed C, is not quite as good as the bound of 2^{-Cm} that holds for the approaches of Meyer [7,8] and Goldberg [5], but certainly amply suffices for all practical purposes.

As described, the algorithms cannot cope with arbitrary nonnegative edge lengths. This is easily remedied: Letting M be an upper bound on the maximum finite distance of a vertex in V from s (such as $n-1$ times the maximum edge length), initialize $d(v)$ to M instead of to $n-1$ for all $v \in V \setminus \{s\}$, redefine Δ as $M/((n-1)k)$ and use nk buckets as before (or take $\Delta = M/(mk)$ and use $(m+1)k$ buckets). Slightly more elaborate algorithms work in linear time if there is a (possibly unknown) constant $\epsilon > 0$ so that the number of edges of length smaller than $\epsilon M/(m\log_2 m)$ is bounded by $m/(\epsilon \log_2 m)$.

The algorithms adapt easily to the case of edge lengths drawn from the uniform distribution on some set $\{a, a+1, \ldots, b\}$ of consecutive integers with $0 \le a \le b$. The only nonobvious fact to note is that if $\Delta \le 1$, then the Fibonacci heap (in Algorithm A) and the binary heap (in Algorithm B) should be ignored, i.e., all vertices in V should be considered to belong to V_2.

Algorithm A deteriorates gracefully for unfavorable edge lengths towards a worst-case running time of $O(m + n\log n)$ without any need for it to be run in parallel with a separate algorithm with good worst-case behavior. If a smaller probability of exceeding the time bound or, for integer edge lengths, a better asymptotic worst-case running time are desired, these can be achieved by replacing the data structures D_j and/or the Fibonacci heap by more efficient but more complicated data structures.

References

1. R. K. Ahuja, T. L. Magnanti, and J. B. Orlin, *Network Flows: Theory, Algorithms, and Applications*, Prentice-Hall, Englewood Cliffs, NJ, 1993.
2. G. B. Dantzig, On the shortest route through a network, *Management Sci.* **6** (1960), pp. 187–190.
3. E. W. Dijkstra, A note on two problems in connexion with graphs, *Numer. Math.* **1** (1959), pp. 269–271.
4. M. L. Fredman and R. E. Tarjan, Fibonacci heaps and their uses in improved network optimization algorithms, *J. ACM* **34** (1987), pp. 596–615.

5. A. V. Goldberg, A simple shortest path algorithm with linear average time, Proc. 9th Annual European Symposium on Algorithms, (ESA 2001), Lecture Notes in Computer Science, Springer, Berlin, Vol. 2161, pp. 230–241.

6. T. Hagerup and C. Rüb, A guided tour of Chernoff bounds, *Inform. Proc. Lett.* **33** (1990), pp. 305–308.

7. U. Meyer, Single-source shortest-paths on arbitrary directed graphs in linear average-case time, Proc. 12th Annual ACM-SIAM Symposium on Discrete Algorithms (SODA 2001), pp. 797–806.

8. U. Meyer, Average-case complexity of single-source shortest-paths algorithms: lower and upper bounds, *J. Algorithms* **48** (2003), pp. 91–134.

9. M. Thorup, Integer priority queues with decrease key in constant time and the single source shortest paths problem, Proc. 35th Annual ACM Symposium on Theory of Computing (STOC 2003), pp. 149–158.

10. P. D. Whiting and J. A. Hillier, A method for finding the shortest route through a road network, *Oper. Res. Quart.* **11** (1960), pp. 37–40.

Lattices with Many Cycles Are Dense

Mårten Trolin

Department of Numerical Analysis and Computer Science,
Royal Institute of Technology, Stockholm, Sweden
marten@nada.kth.se

Abstract. We give a method for approximating any n-dimensional lattice with a lattice Λ whose factor group $\mathbb{Z}^n/\Lambda$ has $n-1$ cycles of equal length with arbitrary precision. We also show that a direct consequence of this is that the Shortest Vector Problem and the Closest Vector Problem cannot be easier for this type of lattices than for general lattices.

Keywords: lattices, shortest vector problem, closest vector problem

1 Introduction

The interest in the computational complexity of lattice problems started in the beginning of the 1980s, when van Emde Boas published the first **NP**-completeness result for lattice problems [16]. Several hardness results for different variants of this problems and for different subsets of lattices have followed. One such way of classifying lattices is according to the cycle structure of Abelian group $\mathbf{Z}^n/\Lambda$, which is the main focus of this paper. Previous results on the complexity of lattice problems that either explicitly or implicitly consider lattices with a certain cycle structure include [1,3,13,14].

There are two reasons to study the hardness of certain lattice problems in different subclasses of lattices rather than for general lattices. The first reason is purely theoretical — it gives us a better understanding of how the computational complexity of lattice problems behaves if we restrict ourselves to certain lattice classes. The second reason is more practical — most hardness results are worst-case results for general lattices. The lattices that appear in many applications may have certain structural properties. It would be desired to have results that show that these properties cannot be used to solve lattice problem more efficiently.

The first result on the cycle structure was published by Paz and Schnorr [13]. In that paper it is shown that any lattice can be approximated arbitrarily well by a lattice with one cycle. In other words, the lattices with one cycle form a hard core. On the other hand, the lattices Cai and Nerurkar [3] prove to be hard in the improved version of Ajtai [1] have up to n/c cycles. Although the results are different in nature (the latter is not an **NP**-hardness result), it is interesting to note that they give hardness results for lattices with different cycle structure. This gives rise to the question of the role of the cycle structure in the complexity of lattice problems.

V. Diekert and M. Habib (Eds.): STACS 2004, LNCS 2996, pp. 370–381, 2004.

The influence of the cycle structure on the hardness of lattice problems has practical implications. For some crypto systems (e.g., NTRU [6]) there are attacks based on finding short vectors in certain lattices. The lattices used in some of these attacks have a cycle structure that differs from the cycle structure of the lattices that previously have been shown to be **NP**-hard.

Since a lattice with n cycles always can be transformed into a lattice with fewer cycles by a simple rescaling, the maximum number of cycles that is meaningful to analyze is $n - 1$. Trolin showed that the exact version SVP under the max-norm is **NP**-complete for n-dimensional lattices with $n - 1$ cycles of equal length [14].

In this paper we investigate the importance of the cycle structure further. Our main result is a polynomial-time transformation that with arbitrary precision approximates any n-dimensional lattice with a lattice that has $n - 1$ cycles of equal length, showing that these lattices form a hard core. A consequence of this is that short vectors and close vectors cannot be computed more efficiently in this class of lattices than in general lattices, except possibly for a polynomial factor. As our transformation only changes the size of the coordinates of the basis vectors and not the dimension of the lattice, the transformation is rather tight.

2 Background

2.1 Lattices

A *lattice* is a discrete additive subgroup $\Lambda \subseteq \mathbb{R}^n$. A lattice Λ can be defined by its basis, a set of independent vectors $\{\mathbf{b_1}, \mathbf{b_2}, \ldots, \mathbf{b_m}\}$, $\mathbf{b_i} \in \mathbb{R}^n$, such that $\mathbf{u} \in \Lambda$ if and only if there exist integers $t_1, t_2, \ldots, t_m$ such that $\mathbf{u} = \sum_{i=1}^{m} t_i \mathbf{b_i}$. If $m = n$ the lattice is said to be full-dimensional. Only lattices that are subsets of $\mathbb{Q}^n$ (and often $\mathbb{Z}^n$) are considered in this paper. For each vector $\mathbf{v} \in \mathbb{R}^n$ and $p \geq 1$ the ℓ_p-norm is defined as $\|\mathbf{v}\|_p = \sqrt[p]{\sum_{i=1}^{n} |v_i|^p}$. The ℓ_∞-norm, also called the maximum norm, is defined as $\|\mathbf{v}\|_\infty = \max_{i=1}^{n} |v_i|$. When no index is given, $\|\mathbf{v}\| = \|\mathbf{v}\|_2$.

A *basis matrix* of a lattice is a matrix whose rows form a basis of the lattice. The *determinant* of a lattice is the absolute value of the determinant of a basis matrix. For lattices that are not full-dimensional, the determinant is defined as $\det(\Lambda) = \sqrt{\det(\mathbf{B}\mathbf{B}^T)}$. It is not difficult to see that the determinant is independent of the choice of basis.

2.2 Basis Representations

In different situations different bases may be suitable. Two such representations are the Hermite Normal Form and LLL-reduced bases.

A basis $\{\mathbf{b_1}, \mathbf{b_2}, \ldots, \mathbf{b_n}\}$ is said to be on Hermite Normal Form (HNF) if the basis matrix is upper triangular, and $b_{ii} > b_{ji} \geq 0$ for $j < i$. The Hermite Normal Form can be computed efficiently [7]. In [11] Micciancio gives some results on the use of HNF in cryptographic applications.

An LLL-reduced basis is defined as follows. Every lattice basis $\{\mathbf{b_1}, \mathbf{b_2}, \ldots, \mathbf{b_m}\}$ has an associated *orthogonal* basis $\{\hat{\mathbf{b}}_1, \hat{\mathbf{b}}_2, \ldots, \hat{\mathbf{b}}_m\}$ defined by

$$\hat{\mathbf{b}}_i = \mathbf{b}_i - \sum_{j=1}^{i-1} \mu_{ij} \hat{\mathbf{b}}_i$$

where $\mu_{ij} = \langle \mathbf{b_i}, \hat{\mathbf{b}}_\mathbf{j} \rangle / \left\| \hat{\mathbf{b}}_\mathbf{j} \right\|^2$ for $i > j$. Extending the definition, we let $\mu_{ii} = 1$ and $\mu_{ij} = 0$ for $i < j$. It holds that $\prod_{i=1}^{m} \left\| \hat{\mathbf{b}}_\mathbf{i} \right\| = \det(\Lambda)$. A lattice basis is called *LLL-reduced* (after Lenstra, Lenstra and Lovász) with δ, $1/4 \leq \delta < 1$, if $|\mu_{ij}| \leq 1/2$ for $1 \leq j < i \leq m$ and $\delta \left\| \hat{\mathbf{b}}_{\mathbf{i-1}} \right\|^2 \leq \left\| \hat{\mathbf{b}}_\mathbf{i} \right\|^2 + \mu_{i,i-1}^2 \left\| \hat{\mathbf{b}}_{\mathbf{i-1}} \right\|^2$ for $i = 2, \ldots, m$. An LLL-reduced basis can be found in polynomial time [10].

The two most studied lattice problems are the closest vector problem, CVP, and the shortest vector problem, SVP. The input to the closest vector problem is a lattice Λ, $\mathbf{y} \in \mathbb{R}^n$ and $d > 0$. The problem is to determine whether or not there exists $\mathbf{x} \in \Lambda$ such that $\|\mathbf{y} - \mathbf{x}\| < d$. SVP is the homogeneous variant of the same problem, where we want to determine whether or not there exists $\mathbf{x} \in \Lambda$ such that $0 < \|\mathbf{x}\| < d$. As a matter of fact, these are both families of problems, since every norm gives a different problem.

It is known that CVP is **NP**-complete for any ℓ_k-norm (including the max-norm, ℓ_∞) [16]. It is also known that SVP is **NP**-complete in the ℓ_∞-norm [9] and under randomized reductions also for any ℓ_k-norm [2]. It has been shown that SVP is **NP**-hard to approximate within any factor smaller than $\sqrt{2}$ under randomized reductions [12]. Khot has improved that inapproximability bound in ℓ_p-norm to $p^{1-\varepsilon}$ for large values of p under randomized reductions [8] and Dinur has improved the bound for ℓ_∞-norm to $n^{1/\log\log n}$ [4].

2.3   The Cycle Structure

In this paper we focus on the role of the *cycle structure* of a lattice in the complexity of lattice problems. The cycle structure is defined as the algebraic structure of the group $\mathbb{Z}^n/\Lambda$ for a full-dimensional lattice Λ.

Definition 1 (Cycle structure). *A lattice Λ is said to have the* cycle structure $k_1 \times k_2 \times \cdots \times k_m$, *if the additive factor group* $\mathbb{Z}^n/\Lambda \sim \mathbb{Z}_{k_1} \times \mathbb{Z}_{k_2} \times \cdots \times \mathbb{Z}_{k_m}$ *and k_i divides k_{i+1} for $i = 1, 2, \ldots, m - 1$.*

Cycles of length one are called trivial. In the cases where it is not clear from the context we specify whether non-trivial cycles should be considered. A lattice with only one non-trivial cycle is called *cyclic*. Depending on context, it may be more convenient to number the cycle lengths in increasing or decreasing order.

Another way to describe the number of cycles of a lattice is to use a different representation of the lattice, namely as a set of modular equations. Every lattice can be described in this way.

Theorem 1. *Let $\Lambda \subseteq \mathbb{Z}^n$ be a lattice. Then there exist n-dimensional vectors $\mathbf{a_1}, \mathbf{a_2}, \ldots, \mathbf{a_m}$ and integers $b_1, b_2, \ldots, b_m$, $b_i > 1$, such that*

$$\Lambda = \{\mathbf{x} : \langle \mathbf{a_1}, \mathbf{x} \rangle \equiv 0 \bmod b_1 \land \langle \mathbf{a_2}, \mathbf{x} \rangle \equiv 0 \bmod b_2 \land \ldots \land \langle \mathbf{a_m}, \mathbf{x} \rangle \equiv 0 \bmod b_m \} \ .$$

The essence of this theorem is that any lattice can be expressed as a system of modular linear equations whose solutions form the lattice.

The connection to the cycle structure is that the number of nontrivial cycles is m, and the length of cycle i is b_i, provided that the system of equations has been reduced to minimize the number of equations and that the gcd of the coefficients and the modulus is 1 in each equation.

In the transformations we approximate lattices in $\mathbb{Z}^n$ with lattices in $\mathbb{Q}^n$. The standard definition of cycle structure cannot be applied to general lattices in $\mathbb{Q}^n$. Since multiplication by a constant does not affect lattice problems such as SVP and CVP, we will define the cycle structure of a lattice $\Lambda \subset \mathbb{Q}^n$ as the cycle structure of $k\Lambda$, where k is the smallest integer such that $k\Lambda \subseteq \mathbb{Z}^n$.

We now state three simple lemmas (proofs omitted) on the cycle structure.

Lemma 1. *Let $\Lambda \subseteq \mathbb{Z}^n$ be a lattice with cycle structure $k_1 \times k_2 \times \cdots \times k_m$. Then $\det(\Lambda) = \prod_{i=1}^m k_i$.*

Lemma 2. *Let $\Lambda \subseteq \mathbb{Z}^n$ be a lattice with cycle structure $k_1 \times k_2 \times \cdots \times k_n$ (not necessarily all nontrivial). Then the lattice $t \cdot \Lambda$ has cycle structure $t \cdot k_1 \times t \cdot k_2 \times \cdots \times t \cdot k_n$*

Lemma 3. *Let $\Lambda \subseteq \mathbb{Z}^n$ be a lattice with cycle structure $k_1 \times k_2 \times \cdots \times k_n$, $k_1 \geq k_2 \geq \cdots \geq k_n$. Then the lattice $\frac{1}{k_n} \cdot \Lambda$ has cycle structure $\frac{k_1}{k_n} \times \frac{k_2}{k_n} \times \cdots \times \frac{k_n}{k_n}$.*

Because of the divisibility requirement, the lattice $\frac{1}{k_n} \Lambda$ in Lemma 3 is in $\mathbb{Z}^n$. Should k_n be greater than one, we can always remove it as shown in the theorem. Hence we can assume without loss of generality that the number of cycles is less than n.

2.4   Previous Results on the Cycle Structure

In [13] the following theorem is proved.

Theorem 2. *Let $\Lambda \subseteq \mathbb{Z}^n$ be a lattice. Then for every $\varepsilon > 0$ we can efficiently construct a linear transformation $\sigma_{\Lambda,\varepsilon} : \Lambda \to \mathbb{Z}^n$ such that $\sigma_{\Lambda,\varepsilon}(\Lambda)$ is a lattice and for some integer k*

1. $\forall \mathbf{u} \in \Lambda : \|\mathbf{u} - \sigma_{\Lambda,\varepsilon}(\mathbf{u})/k\| \leq \varepsilon \|\mathbf{u}\|$
2. $\sigma_{\Lambda,\varepsilon}(\Lambda)$ is cyclic.

This theorem implies that if we can solve a lattice problem for cyclic lattices, we can get an approximative solution for the same problem for any with arbitrary precision. In other words, the cyclic lattices form a hard core.

In his celebrated paper [1], Ajtai showed how to generate lattices with a connection between the average case and the worst case of variants of SVP. The lattices in the constructions in Cai's and Nerurkar's improved version of Ajtai's result [3] have n/c cycles. Although this result is not an **NP**-hardness result, it raises the question of whether the hardness of lattice problems does or does not in general decrease with a higher number of cycles. In [14] it is shown that SVP in the maximum norm is **NP**-complete for lattices with $n-1$ cycles, giving further evidence that hardness results of lattice problems extend to many cycle structures. The result of the current paper gives the main result of [14] as a consequence.

3   The Approximation

Let $\Lambda \subseteq \mathbb{Z}^n$ be an arbitrary lattice. To adapt this into a lattice with $n-1$ cycles that is arbitrarily close to the original lattice we go through the following five steps:

1. Inflate the lattice by a factor k and perturb to achieve a lattice with Hermite Normal Form of a certain form.
2. Reduce the sublattice spanned by the first $n-1$ vectors of the Hermite Normal Form using the LLL algorithm.
3. Factor the partly reduced basis matrix into two matrices, where the second has its determinant equal to one.
4. Perform modifications to the first matrix to give it $n-1$ cycles of equal length.
5. Multiply the two matrices to get a basis for an $(n-1)$-cyclic lattice that is close to the original lattice.

In Sections 3.1 to 3.4 these steps are described in detail. It is also shown that the modifications have the desired effect on the cycle structure. In Section 3.5 we analyze the disturbance from the perturbation and show that it does not move a lattice vector more than a small multiple of the original length. All the transformations are linear, and extend through linearity to any point in $\mathbb{R}^n$.

Many of the proofs are omitted in this extended abstract. The interested reader can find them in the full version of the paper.

3.1   Acquiring a Lattice with a Good Hermite Normal Form

For the modification to work we need the lattice to have a Hermite Normal Form of a certain form. In this section we describe how we efficiently can modify a general lattice slightly to get the Hermite Normal Form we need.

Let $\Lambda \subseteq \mathbb{Z}^n$ be a lattice, and let $\mathbf{H}$ be its basis in Hermite Normal Form. For the coming steps, we need the basis of the lattice to be of the following form:

$$\mathbf{B} = \begin{pmatrix} 1 & 0 & \cdots & 0 & a_1 \\ 0 & 1 & \cdots & 0 & a_2 \\ \vdots & \vdots & \ddots & \vdots & \vdots \\ 0 & 0 & \cdots & 1 & a_{n-1} \\ 0 & 0 & \cdots & 0 & d \end{pmatrix} \tag{1}$$

where $d = \det(\Lambda)$ and $0 \le a_i < d$. We show how to perturb Λ so that we get a lattice whose Hermite Normal Form as is in equation (1). The method we use is based on the following theorem whose proof can be found in the full version [15].

Lemma 4. *Let $\mathbf{H}$ be a matrix on Hermite Normal Form, i.e.,*

$$
\mathbf{H} = \begin{pmatrix}
h_{11} & h_{12} & h_{13} & \cdots & h_{1(n-1)} & h_{1n} \\
0 & h_{22} & h_{23} & \cdots & h_{2(n-1)} & h_{2n} \\
0 & 0 & h_{33} & \cdots & h_{3(n-1)} & h_{3n} \\
\vdots & \vdots & \vdots & \ddots & \vdots & \vdots \\
0 & 0 & 0 & \cdots & h_{(n-1)(n-1)} & h_{(n-1)n} \\
0 & 0 & 0 & \cdots & 0 & h_{nn}
\end{pmatrix} .
$$

Then the matrix $\tau(\mathbf{H})$ given by

$$
\tau(\mathbf{H}) = \begin{pmatrix}
h_{11} & h_{12} & h_{13} & \cdots & h_{1(n-1)} & h_{1n} \\
1 & h_{22} & h_{23} & \cdots & h_{2(n-1)} & h_{2n} \\
0 & 1 & h_{33} & \cdots & h_{3(n-1)} & h_{3n} \\
\vdots & \vdots & \vdots & \ddots & \vdots & \vdots \\
0 & 0 & 0 & \cdots & h_{(n-1)(n-1)} & h_{(n-1)n} \\
0 & 0 & 0 & \cdots & 1 & h_{nn}
\end{pmatrix} \tag{2}
$$

has a Hermite Normal Form as in equation (1). The transformation can be computed in time polynomial in the size of the input data.

We also define the transformation when the input is a vector as

$$
\tau_{\Lambda,k}\left(\sum_{i=1}^{n} t_i \mathbf{u_i}\right) = \sum_{i=1}^{n} t_i \mathbf{u'_i} \tag{3}
$$

where $\mathbf{u_1}, \mathbf{u_2}, \ldots, \mathbf{u_n}$ are the rows of $\mathbf{U}$ and $\mathbf{u'_1}, \mathbf{u'_2}, \ldots, \mathbf{u'_n}$ are the rows of $\tau(k\mathbf{U})$.

As the reader may have noticed, this step actually implies the result from [13], although we not only achieve a cyclic lattice, but a lattice whose Hermite Normal Form is as defined above.

3.2 Factoring the Basis

Now that we have a basis with the Hermite Normal Form we need, we proceed by finding a more orthogonal basis and factoring the basis matrix.

Let the operation $\rho(\mathbf{B})$ be defined as follows: First the LLL-reduction is applied to the first $n - 1$ vectors of $\mathbf{B}$ using $\delta = 3/4$, keeping the last vector unchanged. Let us call this intermediate step ρ'. Assuming that the input is a basis matrix $\mathbf{B}$ of the form (1), this gives a matrix of the form

$$
\rho'(\mathbf{B}) = \begin{pmatrix}
b_{11} & b_{12} & \cdots & b_{1(n-1)} & b_{1n} \\
b_{21} & b_{22} & \cdots & b_{2(n-1)} & b_{2n} \\
\vdots & \vdots & \ddots & \vdots & \vdots \\
b_{(n-1)1} & b_{(n-1)2} & \cdots & b_{(n-1)(n-1)} & b_{(n-1)n} \\
0 & 0 & \cdots & 0 & d
\end{pmatrix} . \tag{4}
$$

From the LLL-reduced basis the $(n-1)$'th vector is placed first, keeping the internal order of the other vectors. The complete transformation is called ρ. The matrix $\rho(\mathbf{B})$ can be factored into

$$
\begin{pmatrix}
1 & 0 & 0 & \cdots & 0 & 0 \\
0 & 1 & 0 & \cdots & 0 & 0 \\
0 & 0 & 1 & \cdots & 0 & 0 \\
\vdots & \vdots & \vdots & \ddots & \vdots & \vdots \\
0 & 0 & 0 & \cdots & 1 & 0 \\
0 & 0 & 0 & \cdots & 0 & d
\end{pmatrix}
\cdot
\begin{pmatrix}
b_{(n-1)1} & b_{(n-1)2} & \cdots & b_{(n-1)n} \\
b_{11} & b_{12} & \cdots & b_{1n} \\
b_{21} & b_{22} & \cdots & b_{2n} \\
\vdots & \vdots & \ddots & \vdots \\
b_{(n-2)1} & b_{(n-2)2} & \cdots & b_{(n-2)n} \\
0 & 0 & \cdots & 1
\end{pmatrix}
\tag{5}
$$

Since the determinant of the right factor is 1, the cycle structure of the product only depends on the left factor. This follows since, as pointed out in [13], unimodular transformations do not change the cycle structure.

3.3   Modifying the Cycle Structure

Let $\mathbf{B}_l$ be the left factor in the basis factorization (5) and $\mathbf{B}_r$ the right factor. We create a new lattice Λ' by inflating the lattice spanned by $\mathbf{B}_l$ by a factor d^{n-2}. Put differently, the matrix $d^{n-2} \cdot \mathbf{B}_l$ is a basis matrix of Λ'. By Lemma 2, this lattice has $n-1$ cycles of length d^{n-2} and one cycle of length d^{n-1}.

By modifying the lattice Λ' slightly, we get a new lattice that has $n-1$ cycles of length d^{n-1}. We call the new lattice Λ''. The modification is defined by the function γ':

$$
\gamma'_n(d) =
\begin{pmatrix}
d^{n-2} & d^{n-3} & d^{n-4} & \cdots & d^2 & d & 1 & 0 \\
0 & d^{n-2} & d^{n-3} & \cdots & d^3 & d^2 & d & 0 \\
0 & 0 & d^{n-2} & \cdots & d^4 & d^3 & d^2 & 0 \\
\vdots & \vdots & \vdots & \ddots & \vdots & \vdots & \vdots & \vdots \\
0 & 0 & 0 & \cdots & d^{n-2} & d^{n-3} & d^{n-4} & 0 \\
0 & 0 & 0 & \cdots & 0 & d^{n-2} & d^{n-3} & 0 \\
0 & 0 & 0 & \cdots & 0 & 0 & d^{n-2} & 0 \\
0 & 0 & 0 & \cdots & 0 & 0 & 0 & d^{n-1}
\end{pmatrix} .
$$

Theorem 3. *The lattice Λ'' with basis matrix $\gamma'_n (\det(\mathbf{B}_l))$ has $n-1$ nontrivial cycles, each of which has length d^{n-1}.*

The proof is given in the full version.

3.4   Returning to the Original Representation

Returning to the original representation is just a matter of multiplying by $\mathbf{B}_r$. Since this does not change the cycle structure ($\mathbf{B}_r$ is unimodular), we still have a lattice with the required cycle structure.

We denote the transformation described in Sections 3.2 to 3.4 by γ. More precisely,

$$
\gamma(\mathbf{B}) = \gamma'_n (\det(\mathbf{B}_l)) \cdot \mathbf{B}_r
$$

where $\mathbf{B}_l$ and $\mathbf{B}_r$ are the left and right factors of $\rho(\mathbf{B})$ as in (5) and n is the dimension of the lattice.

We also define the transformation when applied to a vector $\mathbf{v} = \sum_{i=1}^{n} t_i \mathbf{b}_i$ in a lattice Λ where $\mathbf{b_1}, \mathbf{b_2}, \ldots, \mathbf{b_n}$ is a basis. The transformation is then defined as

$$\gamma_\Lambda(\mathbf{v}) = \sum_{i=1}^{n} t_i \mathbf{b'_i}$$

where $\mathbf{b'_1}, \mathbf{b'_2}, \ldots, \mathbf{b'_n}$ are the rows of $\gamma(\mathbf{B})$.

Since LLL-reduction can be performed in polynomial time ρ can be computed in polynomial time. It is obvious that also γ' and the factorization in $\mathbf{B}_l$ and $\mathbf{B}_r$ require at most polynomial time. Hence γ can be computed in time polynomial in the size of the input data.

3.5 Completing the Approximation

Now we have the necessary steps to complete the approximation. Let $\Lambda \subseteq \mathbb{Z}^n$ be a lattice. Our goal is to prove that for any $\varepsilon > 0$ there exist a transformation $\sigma_{\Lambda,\varepsilon}$ and an integer k such that

1. $\forall \mathbf{u} \in \mathbb{Z}^n : \|\mathbf{u} - \sigma_{\Lambda,\varepsilon}(\mathbf{u})/k\| \leq \varepsilon \|\mathbf{u}\|$.
2. $\sigma_{\Lambda,\varepsilon}(\Lambda)$ has $n - 1$ non-trivial cycles of equal length.

The transformations we use are $\tau_{\Lambda,k}$ and γ_Λ as described above. Since the displacement for these transformations (as we will see) depends on the determinant, we need to find an appropriate k that makes the determinant large enough. In the final approximation we will begin by applying τ and then apply γ. This composed transformation is called $\sigma_{\Lambda,\varepsilon}(\mathbf{u})$ and can be computed in polynomial time since both τ and γ can be computed in polynomial time.

We bound the displacement introduced by the two transformations τ and γ described above.

Lemma 5. *Let Λ be a lattice and let $\tau_{\Lambda,k}$ be defined as in (3). Then $\forall \mathbf{u} \in \mathbb{Z}^n$: $\|\mathbf{u} - \frac{1}{k}\tau_{\Lambda,k}(\mathbf{u})\| \leq \frac{1}{k}2^n \|\mathbf{u}\|$.*

The proof of this lemma follows the proof in [13] closely and is given in the full version.

We need some bounds on the basis (4) before we can complete the proof. We give these bounds as two lemmas. The first lemma shows that the coordinates of a vector are bounded in a way similar to Lemma 5, and the second that the basis vectors are bounded. The full proofs are omitted from this extended abstract.

Lemma 6. *Let $\mathbf{B}$ be the basis matrix of Λ given on the form (4), let $\mathbf{b_1}, \mathbf{b_2}, \ldots, \mathbf{b_n}$ be its rows. Assume $\mathbf{u} = \sum_{i=1}^{n} t_i \mathbf{b_i}$. Then*

$$|t_i| \leq 2^{\frac{3}{2}n - i} \|\mathbf{u}\| \tag{6}$$

for $i < n$ and for any ℓ_k-norm (including ℓ_∞).

Lemma 7. *Let* $\mathbf{B}$ *be a basis matrix of the form (1), and let* $\mathbf{b_i}$ *be the row vectors of the matrix* $\rho(\mathbf{B})$. *Then it holds that*

$$\|\mathbf{b_i}\| \le n2^{\frac{n^2}{8}}\sqrt[4]{d^2 n}$$

for $i = 2, 3, \ldots, n-1$.

The idea of the proof is that in an LLL-reduced basis $\mathbf{B}$ the length of every vector except the last one has an upper bound of the order $\sqrt{\det(\mathbf{B})}$. We then need to renumber the vectors since the can only afford the first vector to remain unbounded in order to bound $\gamma(\mathbf{B})$. It is essential that the bound is $o(\det(\mathbf{B}))$ because of the displacement of γ.

Now we have the necessary tools to find a bound for the transformation γ_Λ.

Lemma 8. *Let* Λ *be an* n-*dimensional lattice and let* γ_Λ *be as defined in Section 3.4. Then* $\forall \mathbf{u} \in \mathbb{Z}^n$

$$\left\| \mathbf{u} - \frac{1}{\det(\Lambda)^{n-2}}\gamma_\Lambda(\mathbf{u}) \right\| \le \frac{n^{9/4}2^{\frac{3}{2}n+\frac{n^2}{8}}}{\sqrt{\det(\Lambda)}}\|\mathbf{u}\|$$

for $\det(\Lambda) = \Omega\left(2^{n^2}\right)$.

Now we combine these two lemmas in order to show a bound for the composed transformation $\sigma_{\Lambda,\varepsilon}$. The proof is omitted.

Theorem 4. *Let* Λ *be an* n-*dimensional lattice. For every choice of* $\varepsilon > 0$ *there exist integers* k *and* s, *at most of size polynomial in* $\log\left(\varepsilon^{-1}\right)$ *and* n, *such that the transformation* $\sigma_{\Lambda,\varepsilon} = \gamma_{\tau_s(\Lambda)} \circ \tau_{\Lambda,s}$ *generates a lattice with* $n-1$ *cycles of equal length and for any vector* $\mathbf{u}$

$$\left\| \mathbf{u} - \frac{1}{k}\sigma_{\Lambda,\varepsilon}(\mathbf{u}) \right\| \le \varepsilon\|\mathbf{u}\|$$

4   Applications to CVP and SVP

In this section we will outline how the transformation can be used to find a solution to CVP and SVP, should these problems be easier to solve in lattices with many cycles.

In CVP our goal, given a lattice $\Lambda \subseteq \mathbb{Z}^n$ and a point $\mathbf{y} \in \mathbb{Z}^n$, is to find $\mathbf{x} \in \Lambda$ such that $\|\mathbf{x} - \mathbf{y}\|_p$ is minimized in some ℓ_p-norm. If (a slightly perturbed) $\mathbf{x}$ remains the lattice point closest to (a slightly perturbed) $\mathbf{y}$ after the transformation, we can reduce the instance of CVP to an instance of CVP in a lattice with many cycles. The following theorem shows how to choose the transformation parameters. The proof is given in the full version.

Theorem 5. *Let $\Lambda \subseteq \mathbb{Z}^n$, and let $\mathbf{y} \in \mathbb{Z}^n$. Let $\mathbf{x} \in \Lambda$ and $\mathbf{z} \in \Lambda$. Assume that all coordinates are in the interval $0, \ldots, \det(\Lambda) - 1$. It holds that if*

$$\|\mathbf{x} - \mathbf{y}\|_p < \|\mathbf{z} - \mathbf{y}\|_p$$

then

$$\left\| \frac{1}{k}\sigma_{\Lambda,\varepsilon}(\mathbf{x}) - \frac{1}{k}\sigma_{\Lambda,\varepsilon}(\mathbf{y}) \right\|_p < \left\| \frac{1}{k}\sigma_{\Lambda,\varepsilon}(\mathbf{z}) - \frac{1}{k}\sigma_{\Lambda,\varepsilon}(\mathbf{y}) \right\|_p$$

for

$$0 < \varepsilon < \left(2pn^{1+1/p} \det(\Lambda)^{p+1} \right)^{-1}$$

and any number p where k is polynomial in ε^{-1}.

The following two lemmas show how to use Theorem 5 to reduce CVP to a lattice with $n - 1$ cycles. The first lemma follows directly from the fact that every lattice repeats itself in cubes with side $\det(\Lambda)$.

Lemma 9. *Let $(\Lambda \subseteq \mathbb{Z}^n, \mathbf{y} \in \mathbb{Z}^n)$ be an instance of CVP. Then for any $\mathbf{u} \in \mathbb{Z}^n$ $\mathbf{x} \in \Lambda$ is a solution if and only if $\mathbf{x} - \det(\Lambda) \cdot \mathbf{u}$ is a solution of the instance $(\Lambda, \mathbf{y} - \det(\Lambda) \cdot \mathbf{u})$.*

Lemma 10. *Let $(\Lambda \subseteq \mathbb{Z}^n, \mathbf{y} \in \mathbb{Z}^n)$ be an instance of CVP such that $0 \le y_i < \det(\Lambda)$. Then $\mathbf{x} \in \Lambda$ is a solution if and only if $\frac{1}{k}\sigma_{\Lambda,\varepsilon}(\mathbf{x})$ is a solution of the instance $\left(\frac{1}{k}\sigma_\varepsilon(\Lambda), \frac{1}{k}\sigma_{\Lambda,\varepsilon}(\mathbf{y}) \right)$ for k and ε^{-1} polynomial in $\det(\Lambda)$ and n.*

Proof. The lemma follows directly from Theorem 5. Using the two lemmas, we can construct the reduction by first reducing the target vector modulo $\det(\Lambda)$ and then apply the transformation with the appropriate value of ε.

Obviously the same technique can be used to achieve a similar result for SVP. The following lemma follows directly from the above lemmas.

Lemma 11. *Let $\Lambda \subseteq \mathbb{Z}^n$ be an instance of SVP. Then $\mathbf{x} \in \Lambda$ is a solution if and only if $\frac{1}{k}\sigma_{\Lambda,\varepsilon}(\mathbf{x})$ is a solution of the instance $\frac{1}{k}\sigma_\varepsilon(\Lambda)$ for k and ε^{-1} polynomial in $\det(\Lambda)$ and n.*

This leads to the following theorem.

Theorem 6. *SVP is **NP**-hard to approximate within $\sqrt{2} - \varepsilon$ in ℓ_2-norm for n-dimensional lattices with $n - 1$ non-trivial cycles of equal length.*

5   Conclusions

We have constructed a transformation that given an n-dimensional lattice of any cycle structure produces a lattice with $n - 1$ cycles that is arbitrarily close to the original lattice. This closes the question of whether SVP and CVP can be easier to solve in lattices with many cycles. Using the presented result, such a solution would give a solution for the general case that is at most a polynomial factor slower in running time. Also the known inapproximability results for SVP and CVP extend to lattices with $n - 1$ cycles.

By previous results, we know that any lattice can be approximated arbitrarily well with a cyclic lattice, and hence that SVP and CVP cannot be easier to solve in cyclic lattices than in general lattices, except possibly for a polynomial factor. We now have the two extremes, for one cycle and for $n - 1$ cycles.

From Ajtai's and other papers we have a hardness result also for lattices with n/c cycles. Together with the results of the current paper, this gives evidence to the general hypothesis that the cycle structure have little importance in deciding the hardness of a certain lattice.

Although it does seem likely that also lattices with m non-trivial cycles form a hard core for $2 \leq m \leq n - 2$, we don't have a proof for this. The current proof does not easily extend to these cycle structures. Since our method relies on inflating the lattice by a factor d^t to get a lattice with determinant d^{nt+1} and then making changes to achieve m cycles, the length of each cycle is $d^{(nt+1)/m}$. Naturally t must be chosen so that $(nt + 1)/m$ is an integer. In our case, we achieve this by setting $t = n - 2$ and $m = n - 1$. Since the value of t would depend on m and for certain relations between m and n no such t exists at all, our method cannot directly be generalized to create any cycle structure where the non-trivial cycles have equal length.

Even if a transformation into m cycles of equal length for $1 \leq m \leq n-1$ were found it would still be an open question whether other cycle structures, where the cycles have different lengths, remain easy. Still the current result seems to be a strong indication that the cycle structure does not play an important role for the computational complexity of lattice problems.

Acknowledgments. I would like to thank Johan Håstad for valuable tips and ideas in several of the proofs, as well as the anonymous referees for pointing out possible improvements.

References

1. M. Ajtai. Generating Hard Instances of Lattice Problems. *Proc. 28th ACM Symposium on Theory of Computing*, pages 99–108, 1996.
2. M. Ajtai. The shortest vector problem in ℓ_2 is **NP**-hard for randomized reductions. *Proc. 30th ACM Symposium on the Theory of Computing*, pages 10–19, 1998.
3. J-Y. Cai and A. Nerurkar. An Improved Worst-Case to Average-Case Connection for Lattice Problems. *Proc. 38th IEEE Symposium on Foundations of Computer Science*, pages 468–477, 1997.
4. I. Dinur. Approximating SVP_∞ to within almost polynomial factors is NP-hard. *CIAC 2000, volume 1767 of LNCS*, pages 263–276, 2000.
5. O. Goldreich and S. Goldwasser. On the limits of non-approximability of lattice problems. *Journal of Computer and System Sciences*, Academic Press, 60(3):540–563, 2000. Can be obtained from http://www.eccc.uni-trier.de/eccc.
6. J. Hoffstein, J. Pipher, and J.H. Silverman. NTRU: a ring based public key cryptosystem. *Proc. of ANTS III, volume 1423 of LNCS*, pages 267–288, 1998.
7. R. Kannan and A. Bachem. Polynomial Algorithms for Computing of the Smith and Hermite Normal Forms of an Integer Matrix. *SIAM Journal of Computing*, 8:499–507, 1979.

8. S. Khot. Hardness of Approximating the Shortest Vector Problem in High L_p Norms. *Proc. 44th IEEE Symposium on Foundations of Computer Science*, pages 290–297, 2003.

9. J.C. Lagarias. The Computational Complexity of Simultaneous Diophantine Approximation Problems. *SIAM Journal of Computing*, 14:196–209, 1985.

10. A.K. Lenstra, H.W. Lenstra and L. Lovász. Factoring Polynomials with Rational Coefficients. *Mathematische Annalen* 261:515–534, 1982.

11. D. Micciancio. Improving Lattice Based Cryptosystems Using the Hermite Normal Form. *CaLC 2001, volume 2146 of LNCS*, pages 126–145, 2001.

12. D. Micciancio. The Shortest Vector in a Lattice is Hard to Approximate within Some Constant. *SIAM Journal of Computing*, 30:2008–2035, 2001.

13. A. Paz and C.P. Schnorr. Approximating Integer Lattices by Lattices with Cyclic Lattice Groups. *Automata, languages and programming (Karlsruhe)*, pages 386–393, 1987.

14. M. Trolin. The Shortest Vector Problem in Lattices with Many Cycles. *CaLC 2001, volume 2146 of LNCS*, pages 194–205, 2001.

15. M. Trolin. Lattices with Many Cycles are Dense (full version). Can be obtained from http://www.nada.kth.se/~marten.

16. P. van Emde Boas. Another **NP**-complete partition problem and the complexity of computing short vectors in lattices. Technical Report 81-04. Mathematics Department, University of Amsterdam, 1981. Can be obtained from http://turing.wins.uva.nl/~peter.

Automata-Based Analysis of Recursive Cryptographic Protocols*

Ralf Küsters[1] and Thomas Wilke[2]

[1] Stanford University
kuesters@theory.stanford.edu
[2] Christian-Albrechts-Universität zu Kiel
wilke@ti.informatik.uni-kiel.de

Abstract. Cryptographic protocols can be divided into (1) protocols where the protocol steps are simple from a computational point of view and can thus be modeled by simple means, for instance, single rewrite rules—we call these protocols *non-looping*—and (2) protocols, such as group protocols, where the protocol steps are complex and typically involve an iterative or recursive computation—we call them *recursive*. While much is known on the decidability of security for non-looping protocols, only little is known for recursive protocols. In this paper, we prove decidability of security (w.r.t. the standard Dolev-Yao intruder) for a core class of recursive protocols and undecidability for several extensions. The key ingredient of our protocol model are specifically designed tree transducers which work over infinite signatures and have the ability to generate new constants (which allow us to mimic key generation). The decidability result is based on an automata-theoretic construction which involves a new notion of regularity, designed to work well with the infinite signatures we use.

1 Introduction

In most cryptographic protocols, principals are described by a fixed sequence of what we call *receive-send actions*. When performing such an action, a principal receives a message from the environment and, after some internal computation, reacts by returning a message to the environment. Research on automatic protocol analysis [23,3,5,19] has concentrated on protocols where a receive-send action can basically be described by a single rewrite rule of the form $t \rightarrow t'$: When receiving a message m, the message $\sigma(t')$ is returned as output provided that σ is the matcher for t and m, i.e., $\sigma(t) = m$. In other words, an input message is processed by applying the rewrite rule *once* on the top-level. We call receive-send actions of this kind and protocols based on such receive-send actions *non-looping*. It has been proved that for non-looping protocols when analyzed w.r.t. a finite number of receive-send actions and the standard Dolev-Yao intruder where the message size is not bounded, security (more precisely, secrecy) is decidable even when principals can perform equality tests on arbitrary messages [23,3,5,19],

---

* This work was partially supported by PROCOPE. The first author was also supported by the Deutsche Forschungsgemeinschaft (DFG).

V. Diekert and M. Habib (Eds.): STACS 2004, LNCS 2996, pp. 382–393, 2004.
© Springer-Verlag Berlin Heidelberg 2004

complex keys are allowed [23,5,19], and the free term algebra assumption is relaxed by algebraic properties of XOR and Diffie-Hellman Exponentiation [8,12, 9].

The main question we are concerned with in this paper is in how far security is decidable for protocols where receive-send actions are complex and typically involve an iterative or recursive computation; we call such receive-send actions and protocols containing such actions *recursive*. The answer to this question is not at all obvious since protocol models for non-looping protocols do not capture recursive protocols and there are almost no decidability results for recursive protocols (see the related work).

To illustrate the kind of receive-send actions which are performed in recursive protocols, let us consider the key distribution server S of the Recursive Authentication (RA) Protocol [7] (see also Section 4). In this protocol, the server S needs to perform the following *recursive* receive-send action: The server S first receives an a priori unbounded sequence of requests of pairs of principals who want to share session keys. Then, S generates sessions keys, and finally sends a sequence of certificates (corresponding to the requests) containing the session keys. Receive-send actions of this kind are typical for group protocols, but also occur in protocols such as the Internet Key Exchange protocol (IKE)—see [18] for a description of some recursive protocols. As pointed out by Meadows [18] and illustrated in [25,14], modeling recursion is security relevant.

A natural way to describe recursive receive-send actions is by tree transducers, which extend the class of transductions expressible by single rewrite rules (with linear left-hand side). More precisely, to study decidability, in Section 2 we introduce non-deterministic top-down tree transducers (TTACs) with lookahead and epsilon transitions which work on a signature containing an *infinite* set of what we call *anonymous constants* (ACs), over which the TTACs has only very limited control. TTACs can generate new (anonymous) constants, a feature often needed to model recursive receive-send actions; in the RA protocol for instance, the key distribution server needs to generate (an a priori unbounded number of) session keys.

The main result of this paper is that i) security (for a finite number of receive-send actions, atomic keys, and the standard Dolev-Yao intruder where the message size is not bounded) is decidable if receive-send actions are modeled by TTACs (Section 5), and that ii) certain features of models for non-looping protocols cannot be added without losing decidability: As soon as TTACs are equipped with the ability to perform equality tests between arbitrary messages, complex keys are allowed, or the free term algebra assumption is relaxed by adding XOR or Diffie-Hellman Exponentiation security is undecidable (Section 6).

The undecidability results are obtained by reductions from Post's Correspondence Problem. The decidability result is obtained in two steps. First, we show that TTACs are powerful enough to simulate the intruder. This allows us to describe attacks as the composition of transducers. We can then reduce the security problem to the iterated pre-image word problem for a composition of TTACs, which we show to be decidable (Section 2.3): Given a term t, a "regular set" R of terms, and a sequence of TTACs, the *iterated pre-image word problem* asks whether on input t the composition of TTACs can produce an output in R.

Here, "regular set" means the set of terms recognizable by a new kind of tree automata, *tree automata over signatures with anonymous constants* (TAACs), which can compare anonymous constants for equality.

See our technical report [16] for detailed proofs of all results presented here.

Related work. Recursive protocols have been analyzed manually [22] and semiautomatically using theorem provers or special purpose tools [21,6,17].

Decidability for recursive protocols has initially been investigated in a previous paper [15]. However, there are several significant differences to the present paper. Among others, in [15] *word* transducers, as opposed to *tree* transducers, were considered which do not allow generating new constants (e.g., session keys), a common cause for undecidability of security (see, e.g., [2] and references therein). Also, the proof techniques employed are completely different (see [16] for more details).

In various papers, automata-theoretic techniques have been applied to the analysis of cryptographic protocols (see, e.g., [2] and references therein). However, these works aim at non-looping protocols and do not seem to be applicable to recursive protocols in an obvious way. To the best of our knowledge, the work in [15] and the present work are the first to employ transducers (over infinite signatures) for protocol analysis. Automata and transducers over infinite signatures (although different from those considered here) have been studied in the context of type checking and type inference for XML queries with data values (see, e.g., [1,20]).

Basic definitions and notation. If Σ is a signature, let Σ_n denote the set of symbols in Σ of arity n. The set of terms over Σ is denoted T_Σ. For a set C of constant symbols (symbols of arity 0) disjoint from Σ let $T_\Sigma(C) = T_{\Sigma \cup C}$. We fix an infinite supply X of variables among which we find x_0, x_1, x_2, ... For $n \geq 0$, we write T_Σ^n for the set of all terms in $T_\Sigma(\{x_0, \ldots, x_{n-1}\})$. When $t \in T_\Sigma^n$ and $t_0, \ldots, t_{n-1}$ are arbitrary terms, we write $t[t_0, \ldots, t_{n-1}]$ for the term which is obtained from t by simultaneously substituting t_i for x_i, for every $i < n$. A term $t \in T_\Sigma^n$ is *linear* if every x_i with $i < n$ occurs exactly once in t. A substitution over Σ is a function $\sigma : T_\Sigma(X) \to T_\Sigma(X)$ such that for each term t, $\sigma(t)$ is obtained from t by simultaneously substituting $\sigma(x)$ for x for every $x \in X$. A subset τ of $T_\Sigma \times T_\Sigma$ is called a *transduction* over Σ. For $t \in T_\Sigma$, we define $\tau(t) = \{t' \mid (t, t') \in \tau\}$. If τ and τ' are transductions over Σ, then their *composition* $\tau \circ \tau'$ is defined as expected, where the composition is read from right to left. Given a transduction τ over Σ and a set $R \subseteq T_\Sigma$, the *pre-image* of R under τ is the set $\tau^{-1}(R) = \{t \mid \exists t'(t' \in R \wedge (t, t') \in \tau)\}$.

2   Tree Automata and Transducers with Anonymous Constants

In this section we describe the models of tree automata and transducers that we use, completely independent of the application we have in mind, as they are of general interest. (See [11] for more information on tree automata and transducers.)

A pair (Σ, C) consisting of a finite signature Σ, the set of *regular symbols*, and an arbitrary *infinite* set C of constant symbols, the set of *anonymous constants*, disjoint from Σ is called a *signature with anonymous constants*. When we speak of a *term over* (Σ, C) we mean a term over $\Sigma \cup C$. In what follows, let $occ_C(t)$ $(occ_C(S))$ denote the set of elements from C that occur in the term t (the set of terms S).

2.1 Tree Automata over Signatures with Anonymous Constants

Our tree automata are non-deterministic bottom-up tree automata that accept trees over signatures with anonymous constants; they have full control over the regular symbols but only very limited control over the anonymous constants. These automata are designed in such a way that they are powerful enough to recognize tree languages such as the one defined in Example 1 (which is needed for our cryptographic application) and such that they fit well with the tree transducers introduced in Section 2.2, in the sense that we can prove Theorem 1.

Formally, a *tree automaton (TAAC) over a signature* (Σ, C) *with anonymous constants* is a tuple $\mathbf{A} = (Q, q^d, q^s, \Delta, F)$ where Q is a non-empty finite *set of states*, $q^d \in Q$ is the *default state*, $q^s \in Q$ is the *selecting state*, Δ is a finite *set of transitions* as specified below, and $F \subseteq Q$ is a *set of final states*. The latter can be omitted; in this case, we speak of a *semi TAAC*.

There are two types of transitions: a *consuming transition* is of the form $f(q_0, \ldots, q_{n-1}) \to q$ where $f \in \Sigma_n$, $q, q_0, \ldots, q_{n-1} \in Q$; an *epsilon transition* is of the form $q' \to q$ where $q', q \in Q$.

Each TAAC over a signature with anonymous constants (Σ, C) defines a set of terms (also called trees) from $T_\Sigma(C)$. To describe this set, we view the set Q as a set of constants and introduce the notion of a permitted substitution. A *permitted substitution* σ is a function $\sigma \colon C \to \{q^d, q^s\}$ where at most one element of C, the *selected element*, gets assigned q^s and all the others get assigned q^d, the *default value*. For $t \in T_\Sigma(Q)$ (which does not contain anonymous constants), we define $[t]_\mathbf{A}$ inductively as follows: The set $[t]_\mathbf{A}$ is the smallest set such that if $t \in Q$, then $t \in [t]_\mathbf{A}$; if $t = f(t_0, \ldots, t_{n-1})$ and there exist $q_0, \ldots, q_{n-1}$ such that $f(q_0, \ldots, q_{n-1}) \to q \in \Delta$ and $q_i \in [t_i]_\mathbf{A}$ for every $i < n$, then $q \in [t]_\mathbf{A}$; if $q \in [t]_\mathbf{A}$ and $q \to q' \in \Delta$, then $q' \in [t]_\mathbf{A}$. For every term $t \in T_\Sigma(C \cup Q)$ (which may contain anonymous constants), the set $[t]_\mathbf{A}$ of states which the automaton reaches after having read the term t is defined to be the union of all sets $[\sigma(t)]_\mathbf{A}$ where the union is taken over all permitted substitutions σ. Now, the *tree language recognized* by $\mathbf{A}$ is the language $T(\mathbf{A}) = \{t \in T_\Sigma(C) \mid F \cap [t]_\mathbf{A} \neq \emptyset\}$. We say a tree language over (Σ, C) is *TAAC recognizable* over (Σ, C) if it is recognized by some TAAC over (Σ, C).

Example 1. Assume $\Sigma_2 = \{f\}$ and $\Sigma_i = \emptyset$ for every $i \neq 2$. Let $T_= = \{f(c, c) \mid c \in C\}$. This language is recognized by a TAAC with only three states, say q_0, q_1, and q_2. We choose $q^d = q_0$, $q^s = q_1$, $F = \{q_2\}$, and we have only one transition, namely $f(q_1, q_1) \to q_2$.

We will also use what we call a *weak TAAC (WTAA)* which does not have a selecting state, i.e., the default state is assigned to all anonymous constants. WTAAs are really weaker because it is easy to see that, for instance, $T_=$ is not WTAAC recognizable over (Σ, C). We can prove the following basic properties of TAACs and WTAACs.

Lemma 1. *Let (Σ, C) be a signature with an infinite set C of anonymous constants. The set of TAAC recognizable tree languages over (Σ, C) is closed under union. It is closed under intersection/complementation over (Σ, C) iff $\Sigma = \Sigma_0 \cup \Sigma_1$. The word problem and the emptiness problem for TAACs are decidable. The set of WTAAC recognizable tree languages over (Σ, C) is closed under union, intersection, and complementation.*

2.2   Tree Transducers over Signatures with Anonymous Constants

As mentioned in the introduction, we use non-deterministic top-down tree transducers with epsilon transitions which have the following specific features: a WTAAC look-ahead; generation of new (!) anonymous constants; a register for one anonymous constant.

To define our transducers we need some notation. We fix a signature (Σ, C) with anonymous constants and a finite set S of states, whose elements we view as *binary* symbols. We assume that we are given a set $V = \{v_R, v_N\}$ of two variables for anonymous constants: v_R represents the aforementioned register, v_N refers to a newly generated anonymous constant. A *state term* is of the form $s(z, t)$ for $s \in S$, $z \in V \cup C \cup \{*\}$, and $t \in T_\Sigma(C \cup X)$. The term t is then called the *core term* of this term. If z belongs to some set $D \subseteq V \cup C \cup \{*\}$, then we say $s(z, t)$ is a *D-state term*. Intuitively, a state term of the form $s(*, t)$ or $s(c, t)$ with $c \in C$ is part of a configuration of a transducer and means that the transducer is about to read t starting in state s where the register does not store a value or stores the anonymous constant c, respectively. To describe transitions we use state terms of the form $s(v_R, t)$, $s(v_N, t)$, and again $s(*, t)$, but not $s(c, t)$ (see below).

Formally, a *tree transducer (TTAC)* over a signature (Σ, C) *with anonymous constants* is a tuple $\mathbf{T} = (S, I, \mathbf{A}, \Gamma)$ where S is a finite set of *states*, $I \subseteq S$ is a set of *inital states*, $\mathbf{A}$ is a semi WTAAC over (Σ, C), and Γ is a finite set of transitions. A *transition* is of the form

$$s(z, t) \to^q t'[v_R, v_N, t'_0, \ldots, t'_{r-1}] \tag{1}$$

where $q \in Q$ is the *look-ahead*, $s(z, t)$ is a $\{v_R, *\}$-state term (recall that this means that $z = v_R$ or $z = *$) with $t \in T_\Sigma^n$ and t linear, $t' \in T_\Sigma^{r+2}$ (not necessarily linear), and each t'_i is either a variable x_j with $j < n$ or a $\{z, v_N, *\}$-state term with the core term being a subterm of t. If $z = *$, we require that v_R does not occur in $t'[v_R, v_N, t'_0, \ldots, t'_{r-1}]$. If v_N occurs in this term, the transition is called *generative* and *non-generative* otherwise.

The computation the TTAC carries out is described by a sequence of rewrite steps. The corresponding rewrite relation $\vdash_U$ is defined w.r.t. a subset $U \subseteq C$ of anonymous constants to ensure that newly generated constants do not belong to U. Later, U will be the set of anonymous constants in the input term, which then ensures that the anonymous constants generated by the TTAC are different from those occurring in the input. To define $\vdash_U$, assume we are given a term $u_0 = u_1[s(c, u_2)]$ where $c \in C$, a term $u_2 = t[t_0, \ldots, t_{n-1}] \in T_{\Sigma}(C)$, a transition T as in (1) with $z = v_R$, and assume u_1 is linear. Let σ be the substitution defined by $\sigma(x_i) = t_i$. Then, for every $c' \in C \setminus (occ_C(u_0) \cup U)$, if $q \in [u_2]_A$ we define $u_0 \vdash_U u_1[t'[c, c', \sigma(t'_0), \ldots, \sigma(t'_{r-1})]]$. (Observe that if T is non-generative, v_N and U are irrelevant.) Note that the newly generated anonymous constant c' does not occur in U and the output term computed so far. The rewrite step in case $u_0 = u_1[s(*, u_2)]$ is defined analogously where transitions as in (1) can only be applied if $z = *$.

Let $\vdash_U^*$ denote the reflexive transitive closure of $\vdash_U$. The transduction over (Σ, C) defined by the TTAC is

$$\tau_{\mathbf{T}} = \{(t, t') \in T_{\Sigma}(C) \times T_{\Sigma}(C) \mid \exists s(s \in I \wedge s(*, t) \vdash_{occ_C(t)}^* t')\} \ .$$

A transduction τ on (Σ, C) is called *TTAC realizable* if there exists a TTAC $\mathbf{T}$ such that $\tau_{\mathbf{T}} = \tau$. Just as for classical non-deterministic top-down tree transducers [11], it is easy to see that the set of TTAC realizable transductions is not closed under composition.

2.3   The Iterated Pre-image Word Problem

The iterated pre-image word problem is defined as follows:

ITERATEDPREIMAGE. Given a term t over (Σ, C), a TAAC $\mathbf{B}$ over (Σ, C), and a sequence of TTACs $\mathbf{T_0}, \ldots, \mathbf{T_{l-1}}$ over (Σ, C) with $\tau = \tau_{T_0} \circ \cdots \circ \tau_{T_{l-1}}$, decide whether $t \in \tau^{-1}(T(\mathbf{B}))$.

The key for proving decidability of this problem is:

Theorem 1. *The pre-image of a TAAC recognizable tree language under a TTAC realizable transduction is a TAAC recognizable tree language. Moreover, an appropriate TAAC can be constructed effectively.*

To prove this theorem, given a TAAC $\mathbf{B}$ and a TTAC $\mathbf{T}$, we provide an exponential time construction of a TAAC recognizing $\tau_{\mathbf{T}}^{-1}(T(\mathbf{B}))$. Using Theorem 1 and Lemma 1 (decidability of the word problem), we obtain:

Corollary 1. ITERATEDPREIMAGE *is decidable.*

3   The Tree Transducer-Based Protocol Model

We now define our tree transducer-based protocol model by specifying messages, the intruder, protocols, and attacks. As mentioned in the introduction, the main difference between the model presented here and decidable models for non-looping protocols is the way receive-send actions are described—instead of single rewrite rules, we use TTACs. These transducers have two important features necessary to model recursive receive-send actions, but missing in decidable models for non-looping protocols: First, they allow to apply a set of rewrite rules recursively to a term. Second, they allow to generate new constants—a feature not necessary for non-looping protocols when analyzed w.r.t. a finite number of receive-send actions.

Due to the space limit, the exposition below is slightly simplified. For details, the reader is referred to [16].

3.1   Messages

The definition of messages we use here is rather standard, except that we allow an infinite number of (anonymous) constants. As mentioned, we assume keys to be atomic.

More precisely, messages are defined as terms over the signature (Σ_A, C) with anonymous constants. The set C is some *infinite* set of anonymous constants, which in this paper will be used to model session keys (Section 4). The finite signature Σ_A is defined relatively to a *finite* set A of constants, the set of *atomic messages*, which may for instance contain principal names and (long-term) keys. It also contains a subset $K \subseteq A$ of public and private keys which is equipped with a bijective mapping $\cdot^{-1}$ assigning to a public (private) key $k \in K$ its corresponding private (public) key $k^{-1} \in K$. Now, Σ_A denotes the (finite) signature consisting of the constants A, the unary symbols hash_a (*keyed hash*) and enc_a^s (*symmetric encryption*) for every $a \in A$, enc_k^a (*asymmetric encryption*) for every $k \in K$, and the binary symbol $\langle\rangle$ (*pairing*). Instead of $\langle\rangle(t, t')$ we write $\langle t, t'\rangle$. We point out that $\mathsf{hash}_a(m)$ shall represent the keyed hash of m under the key a plus m itself. Note that anonymous constants are not allowed as keys (see also Section 3.4 and 7). The set of *messages* over (Σ_A, C) is denoted $\mathcal{M} = T_{\Sigma_A}(C)$.

3.2   Receive-Send Actions, Principals, and Protocols

A *receive-send action* is a TTAC over (Σ_A, C). Roughly speaking, a *principal* is defined to be a finite sequence of receive-send actions, where the last action may or may not be marked to be what we call a *challenge output action* (see [16] for a precise definition of principals). The purpose of challenge output actions is explained below. A protocol is a tuple consisting of a finite family of principals and a finite set $S \subseteq \mathcal{M}$, the *initial intruder knowledge*.

3.3   The Intruder

As in the case of models for non-looping protocols, our intruder model is based on the well-known and widely used Dolev-Yao intruder [13]. That is, an intruder has complete control over the network and can derive new messages from his current knowledge by composing, decomposing, encrypting, decrypting, and hashing messages. We do not impose any restrictions on the size of messages.

The (possibly infinite) set of messages $\mathsf{d}(\mathcal{S})$ the intruder can derive from some set $\mathcal{S} \subseteq \mathcal{M}$ is the smallest set satisfying the following conditions: $\mathcal{S} \subseteq \mathsf{d}(\mathcal{S})$; if $\langle m, m' \rangle \in \mathsf{d}(\mathcal{S})$, then $m, m' \in \mathsf{d}(\mathcal{S})$ (decomposition); if $\mathsf{enc}_a^s(m) \in \mathsf{d}(\mathcal{S})$ and $a \in \mathsf{d}(\mathcal{S})$, then $m \in \mathsf{d}(\mathcal{S})$ (symmetric decryption); if $\mathsf{enc}_k^a(m) \in \mathsf{d}(\mathcal{S})$ and $k^{-1} \in \mathsf{d}(\mathcal{S})$, then $m \in \mathsf{d}(\mathcal{S})$ (asymmetric decryption); if $\mathsf{hash}_a(m) \in \mathsf{d}(\mathcal{S})$, then $m \in \mathsf{d}(\mathcal{S})$ (obtaining hashed messages); if $m, m' \in \mathsf{d}(\mathcal{S})$, then $\langle m, m' \rangle \in \mathsf{d}(\mathcal{S})$ (composition); if $m \in \mathsf{d}(\mathcal{S})$ and $a \in \mathcal{A} \cap \mathsf{d}(\mathcal{S})$, then $\mathsf{enc}_a^s(m), \mathsf{hash}_a(m) \in \mathsf{d}(\mathcal{S})$ (symmetric encryption and keyed hash); and if $m \in \mathsf{d}(\mathcal{S})$ and $k \in \mathcal{K} \cap \mathsf{d}(\mathcal{S})$, then $\mathsf{enc}_k^a(m) \in \mathsf{d}(\mathcal{S})$ (asymmetric encryption).

We note that although principals have the ability to generate new (anonymous) constants, as they are defined in terms of TTACs, for the intruder adding this ability is not necessary since it would *not* increase his power to attack protocols (see [16] for more details).

3.4 Attacks on Protocols

In a (successful) attack on a protocol P, the intruder chooses an interleaving $\mathbf{T}_0, \ldots, \mathbf{T}_{l-1}$ of the receive-send actions of the principals in P (i.e., a total ordering of these receive-send actions) in such a way that i) the last receive-send action $\mathbf{T}_{l-1}$ in this interleaving is a challenge output action, ii) the intruder can produce the input m_i for the receive-send actions, and iii) from the messages m'_i returned by the receive-send actions and his initial knowledge $\mathcal{S}$ he can derive a secret message. The secret message m'_{l-1} the intruder tries to derive is a regular or anonymous constant determined by the challenge output action $\mathbf{T}_{l-1}$ and it is presented to the intruder as a challenge but *not* added to his knowledge. In the following definition of attack, due to space limitations and for simplicity of notation, in this extended abstract we assume that the interleaving of receive-send actions is given beforehand. Since the number of possible interleavings is finite, from a decidability point of view this is not a restriction (see [16] for a full definition of attack). The second condition in the following definition ensures that new anonymous constants generated in the ith receive-send action are also new w.r.t. the knowledge of the intruder before the ith action is performed.

ATTACK. *Given a finite set $\mathcal{S} \subseteq \mathcal{M}$ (the initial intruder knowledge), TTACs $\mathbf{T}_0, \ldots, \mathbf{T}_{l-1}$ (the interleaving of receive-send actions) with $\mathbf{T}_i = (S_i, I_i, \mathbf{A}_i, \Gamma_i)$ for $i < l$, decide whether there exist messages $m_i, m'_i \in \mathcal{M}$, $i < l$, such that*

1. $(m_i, m'_i) \in \tau_{\mathbf{T}_i}$ *for every $i < l$,*
2. $(occ_{\mathcal{C}}(m'_i) \setminus occ_{\mathcal{C}}(m_i)) \cap occ_{\mathcal{C}}(\mathcal{S}_i) = \emptyset$ *for every $i < l$,*
3. $m_i \in \mathsf{d}(\mathcal{S}_i)$ *for every $i < l$, and*
4. $m'_{l-1} \in \mathsf{d}(\mathcal{S}_{l-1}) \cap (\mathcal{A} \cup \mathcal{C})$. *(Can the intruder derive the challenge?)*

where $\mathcal{S}_i = \mathcal{S} \cup \{m'_0, \ldots, m'_{i-1}\}$ is the intruder's knowledge before the ith receive-send action is performed.

We write $(\mathcal{S}, \mathbf{T}_0, \ldots, \mathbf{T}_{l-1}) \in$ ATTACK if all the above conditions are satisfied.

The use of challenge output actions, as presented above, allows to determine secrets dynamically, depending on the protocol run. This is for example needed when asking whether the intruder is able to derive a session key (an anonymous constant, which may change from one protocol run to another) generated by a key distribution server. Challenge output actions are somewhat related to the way security is defined in computational models for key distribution protocols where at the end of an attack, the intruder is presented a string for which he needs to decide whether it is an actual session key or just some random string [4]. In [16], we discuss alternatives to challenge output actions.

4   Modeling Recursive Cryptographic Protocols

To illustrate the TTAC-based protocol model, we now present a formal description of the key distribution server, called S in the following, of the Recursive Authentication (RA) Protocol [7] (see [16] for a complete description and a more detailed account of the RA protocol). In what follows, we abbreviate messages of the form $\langle m_0, \ldots, \langle m_{n-1}, m_n \rangle \cdots \rangle$ by $m_0, \ldots, m_n$.

The server S shares a long-term (symmetric) key with every principal and performs only one (recursive) receive-send action in a protocol run. In this receive-send action, S receives an a priori unbounded sequence of requests of pairs of principals who want to obtain session keys for secure communication and has to generate certificates for the principals containing the session keys. An example of the kind of message S receives is

$$m = \mathsf{hash}_{K_c}(C, S, N_c, \mathsf{hash}_{K_b}(B, C, N_b, \mathsf{hash}_{K_a}(A, B, N_a, -)))$$

where N_c, N_b, and N_a are nonces generated by C, B, and A respectively, and K_c, K_b, and K_a are the long-term keys shared between the server S and the principals C, B, and A, respectively. The above message consists of three requests and indicates that C wants to share a session key with S, B with C, and A with B. The symbol "$-$" marks the end of the sequence of requests. It is important to note that messages sent to S may contain an arbitrary number of requests— which must be processed by S recursively. Now, given m, S processes the requests starting from the outermost. First, S generates two certificates for C, namely, $\mathsf{enc}^s_{K_c}(K_{cs}, C, N_c)$ and $\mathsf{enc}^s_{K_c}(K_{cb}, B, N_c)$, where K_{cs} and K_{cb} are session keys generated by S and intended to be used by C for communication with S and B, respectively. In the same way, certificates for B and A are generated, where A only obtains one certificate (containing the session key for communication with B).

We now describe S by the TTAC $\mathbf{T}_S$. Let $P_0, \ldots, P_n$ be the principals participating in the RA protocol. We assume that $P_n = S$ is the server. Every P_i, $i < n$, shares a long-term key K_i with S. The transducer $\mathbf{T}_S$ has two states, start and read, and does not need a look-ahead—we will need a look-ahead to model the intruder in terms of a TTAC (Section 5). In state start, the initial state, $\mathbf{T}_\mathbf{S}$ checks whether the first request is addressed to S and initializes the process of reading the requests by generating one session key which is stored in the register. In state read, the requests are processed. In this phase, the register is used to store a session key while moving from one request to the next.

The transitions of $\mathbf{T}_S$ are specified as follows:

$$\mathsf{start}(*, \mathsf{hash}_{K_i}(P_i, P_n, x_0, x_1)) \rightarrow \mathsf{read}(v_N, \mathsf{hash}_{K_i}(P_i, P_n, x_0, x_1))$$
$$\mathsf{read}(v_R, \mathsf{hash}_{K_i}(P_i, P_j, x_0, -)) \rightarrow \mathsf{enc}^s_{K_i}(v_R, P_j, x_0)$$
$$\mathsf{read}(v_R, \mathsf{hash}_{K_i}(P_i, P_j, x_0, \mathsf{hash}_{K_{i'}}(P_{i'}, P_i, x_1, x_2))) \rightarrow \mathsf{enc}^s_{K_i}(v_R, P_j, x_0),$$
$$\mathsf{enc}^s_{K_i}(v_N, P_{i'}, x_0),$$
$$\mathsf{read}(v_N, \mathsf{hash}_{K_{i'}}(P_{i'}, P_i, x_1, x_2))$$

where $i, i', j \leq n$ and x_0, x_1, x_2 are variables which take arbitrary messages, and v_R and v_N are the variables for the register and the new anonymous constants, respectively.

5   The Decidability Result

The main result of this section is the following:

Theorem 2. ATTACK *is decidable.*

The proof of this theorem proceeds in two steps. In the first step, we show that the intruder can be simulated by a TTAC, which we call $\mathbf{T}_{der}$. We point out that for the construction of $\mathbf{T}_{der}$ the use of a look-ahead is necessary to gather all information about which keys can be accessed in a given message. In the second step of the proof of Theorem 2, we describe attacks as composition of transducers $\mathbf{T}_{der}, \mathbf{T}_{l-1}, \mathbf{T}_{der}, \mathbf{T}_{l-2}, \mathbf{T}_{der}, \cdots \mathbf{T}_{der}, \mathbf{T}_0, \mathbf{T}_{der}$ (applied from right to left). More accurately, these transducers need to be slightly modified to pass on the intruder's knowledge from one transducer to the next. The (slightly modified) transducer $\mathbf{T}_{l-1}$ will produce a pair $\langle m, m'_{l-1} \rangle$ where m represents the intruder's current knowledge $\mathcal{S}_{l-1}$ and m'_{l-1} is the challenge. Given $\langle m, m'_{l-1} \rangle$, the transducer $\mathbf{T}_{der}$ (again slightly modified in a similar fashion as above) will now try to transform m into m'_{l-1}, i.e., try to derive the challenge from m, without using m'_{l-1}. In other words, in the last step $\mathbf{T}_{der}$ tries to produce a pair in the set $R = \{\langle a, a \rangle \mid a \in \mathcal{A}\} \cup \{\langle c, c \rangle \mid c \in \mathcal{C}\}$. Using Example 1, it is easy to see that R is TAAC recognizable over $(\Sigma_\mathcal{A}, \mathcal{C})$. The following lemma formalizes the reduction from ATTACK to ITERATEDPREIMAGE where τ is the transduction obtained from the composition of transducers just described and $m_\mathcal{S} = \langle u_0, \langle \cdots \langle u_{n-2}, u_{n-1} \rangle \cdots \rangle$ represents the intruder's initial knowledge $\mathcal{S} = \{u_0, \ldots, u_{n-1}\}$. This lemma, together with Corollary 1, immediately implies Theorem 2.

Lemma 2. *We have* $(\mathcal{S}, \mathbf{T}_0, \ldots, \mathbf{T}_{l-1}) \in \text{ATTACK}$ *if and only if* $m_\mathcal{S} \in \tau^{-1}(R)$.

6   Adding Features of Models for Non-looping Protocols and Undecidability Results

In the TTAC-based protocol model as introduced in Section 3, many non-looping protocols can be analyzed with the same precision as in decidable models for non-looping protocols with atomic keys (see, e.g., [3]). More precisely, this is the case for protocols where a) the receive-send actions can be described by rewrite rules with linear left-hand side, since TTACs can simulate *all* such rewrite rules, and b) only a finite amount of information needs to be conveyed from one receive-send action to the next. This includes for instance many of the protocols in the Clark-Jacobs library [10] (see [16] for a formal TTAC-based model of the Needham-Schroeder Public Key Protocol).

However, some features present in decidable models for non-looping protocols are missing in the TTAC-based protocol model: i) Equality tests for messages of arbitrary size, which are possible when left-hand sides of rewrite rules may be non-linear (this corresponds to allowing non-linear left-hand sides in transitions of TTACs) or arbitrary messages can be conveyed from one receive-send action to another and can then be compared with other messages [3,23,19,5]; ii) complex keys, i.e., keys that may be arbitrary messages [23,19,5]; and iii) relaxing the free term algebra assumption by adding the XOR operator [8,12] or Diffie-Hellman Exponentiation [9]. The main result of this section is that these features cannot be added without losing decidability (see [16] for a formal statement and the proof, in which we present reductions from Post's Correspondence Problem):

Theorem 3. ATTACK *is undecidable when one (or more) of the above features is added to the TTAC-based protocol model.*

7   Conclusion

The main goal of this paper was to shed light on the feasibility of automatic analysis of recursive cryptographic protocols. The results obtained here trace a fairly tight boundary of the decidability of security for such protocols. To obtain our results we introduced tree automata (TAACs) and transducers (TTACs) over signatures with an infinite set of (anonymous) constants and proved that for TTACs the iterated pre-image word problem is decidable. We believe that the study of TAACs and TTACs started here is of independent interest.

Our decision procedure for finding attacks on protocols is non-elementary and the problem can easily be seen to be EXPTIME-hard. Thus, one open problem is to establish tight complexity bounds. While so far we do not allow anonymous constants as keys, this would be an interesting extension of our model. In this paper, we have identified the computation of pre-images as a means to analyze protocols. It is worthwhile to investigate to what extent this method is practical and whether it could be an altnerative to constraint solving approaches usually employed for the analysis of (non-looping) protocols.

References

1. N. Alon, T. Milo, F. Neven, D. Suciu, and V. Vianu. XML with Data Values: Typechecking Revisited. In *JCSS 66(4): 688-727 (2003)*.
2. R.M. Amadio and W. Charatonik. On Name Generation and Set-Based Analysis in the Dolev-Yao Model. In *CONCUR 2002*.

3. R.M. Amadio, D. Lugiez, and V. Vanackere. On the symbolic reduction of processes with cryptographic functions. *Theoretical Computer Science*, 290(1):695–740, 2002.
4. M. Bellare and P. Rogaway. Provably secure session key distribution: the three party case. In *STOC'95*, pages 57–66. ACM, 1995.
5. M. Boreale. Symbolic trace analysis of cryptographic protocols. In *ICALP 2001*, pages 667–681. Springer, 2001.
6. J. Bryans and S.A. Schneider. CSP, PVS, and a Recursive Authentication Protocol. In *DIMACS Workshop on Formal Verification of Security Protocols*, 1997.
7. J.A. Bull and D.J. Otway. The authentication protocol. Technical Report DRA/CIS3/PROJ/CORBA/SC/1/CSM/436-04/03, Defence Research Agency, Malvern, UK, 1997.
8. Y. Chevalier, R. Küsters, M. Rusinowitch, and M. Turuani. An NP Decision Procedure for Protocol Insecurity with XOR. In *LICS 2003*.
9. Y. Chevalier, R. Küsters, M. Rusinowitch, and M. Turuani. Deciding the Security of Protocols with Diffie-Hellman Exponentiation and Products in Exponents. In *FSTTCS 2003*.
10. J. Clark and J. Jacob. *A Survey of Authentication Protocol Literature*, 1997. Web Draft Version 1.0 available from http://citeseer.nj.nec.com/.
11. H. Comon, M. Dauchet, R. Gilleron, F. Jacquemard, D. Lugiez, S. Tison, and M. Tommasi. Tree Automata Techniques and Applications, 1997. Available from `http://www.grappa.univ-lille3.fr/tata`.
12. H. Comon-Lundh and V. Shmatikov. Intruder deductions, constraint solving and insecurity decision in presence of exclusive or. In *LICS 2003*.
13. D. Dolev and A.C. Yao. On the Security of Public-Key Protocols. *IEEE Transactions on Information Theory*, 29(2):198–208, 1983.
14. N. Ferguson and B. Schneier. A Cryptographic Evaluation of IPsec. Technical report, 2000. Available from http://www.counterpane.com/ipsec.pdf.
15. R. Küsters. On the decidability of cryptographic protocols with open-ended data structures. In *CONCUR 2002*, LNCS 2421, pages 515–530. Springer, 2002.
16. R. Küsters and Th. Wilke. Automata-based Analysis of Recursive Cryptographic Protocols. Technical Report IFI 0311, CAU Kiel, 2003. Available from http://www.informatik.uni-kiel.de/reports/2003/0311.html
17. C. Meadows. Extending formal cryptographic protocol analysis techniques for group protocols and low-level cryptographic primitives. In *WITS 2000*.
18. C. Meadows. Open issues in formal methods for cryptographic protocol analysis. In *DISCEX 2000*, pages 237–250. IEEE Computer Society Press, 2000.
19. J. K. Millen and V. Shmatikov. Constraint solving for bounded-process cryptographic protocol analysis. In *CCS 2001*, pages 166–175. ACM Press, 2001.
20. F. Neven, Th. Schwentick, and V. Vianu. Towards regular languages over infinite alphabets. In *MFCS 2001*, LNCS 2136, pages 560–572. Springer, 2001.
21. L.C. Paulson. Mechanized Proofs for a Recursive Authentication Protocol. In *CSFW-10*, pages 84–95. IEEE Computer Society Press, 1997.
22. O. Pereira and J.-J. Quisquater. A Security Analysis of the Cliques Protocols Suites. In *CSFW-14*, pages 73–81. IEEE Computer Society Press, 2001.
23. M. Rusinowitch and M. Turuani. Protocol Insecurity with Finite Number of Sessions is NP-complete. In *CSFW-14*, pages 174–190. 2001.
24. H. Seidl. Haskell overloading is DEXPTIME-complete. *Information Processing Letters*, 52(2), 1994.
25. J. Zhou. Fixing a security flaw in IKE protocols. *Electronic Letter*, 35(13):1072–1073, 1999.

On Minimum Circular Arrangement*

Murali K Ganapathy[1][**] and Sachin P Lodha[2]

[1] Dept. of Computer Science, University of Chicago, Chicago, Illinois, USA.
[2] Tata Research Development and Design Centre, Pune, Maharashtra, India.
{gmkrishn@cs.uchicago.edu, sachin.lodha@tcs.com}

Abstract. Motivated by a scheduling problem encountered in multicast environments, we study a vertex labelling problem, called Minimum Circular Arrangement (MCA), that requires one to find an embedding of a given weighted directed graph into a discrete circle which minimizes the total weighted arc length. Its decision version is already known to be NP-complete when restricted to sparse weighted instances. We prove that the decision version of even un-weighted MCA is NP-complete in case of sparse as well as dense graphs.

We also consider complementary version of MCA, called MaxCA. We prove that it is MAX-SNP[π] complete and, therefore, has no PTAS unless P=NP. A similar proof technique shows that MCA is MAX-SNP[π]-Hard and hence admits no PTAS as well. Then we prove a conditional lower bound of $\sqrt{2} - \epsilon$ for MCA approximation under some hardness assumptions, and conclude with a PTAS for MCA on dense instances.

Keywords: Computational complexity, hardness of approximation, polynomial time approximation scheme, scheduling, multicast.

1 Introduction

Availability of very high-speed and large bandwidth networks, explosion in inter-networking, and advent of cheap, low-power, portable computing devices have given rise to one-to-many asymmetric communication networks and huge client populations having commonality of interests [1]. In such environments, servers are endowed with much more computing power and have access to much larger bandwidth than clients. Therefore, it becomes cost effective to *push* data from server side rather than follow traditional client-server based *pull* model. This can be achieved using *multicast* where a server needs to send a data unit only once to reach arbitrary number of clients.

A common way to use multicast in data dissemination is to use server initiated *repetitive* multicast where a server cyclically multicasts data to a large

---

* Full version of the paper is available online [12].
** This work was done when the author was visiting Tata Research Development and Design Centre as a summer intern in 2003.

V. Diekert and M. Habib (Eds.): STACS 2004, LNCS 2996, pp. 394–405, 2004.
© Springer-Verlag Berlin Heidelberg 2004

client population. This finds application in many diverse domains, *e.g.*, high-throughput database systems [15], data management in broadcast disks [1], in solving scalability problems of heavily loaded Web servers [3], content delivery networks (CDNs) [22], etc.

A fundamental question is the order in which the server should multicast data, that is, *scheduling*. In general, clients are seldom interested in individual data items, and attempt to download multiple items. For example, Web clients hardly ever access only one HTML resource, but access almost always the HTML document along with all its embedded images [17]. Database clients often access multiple items to complete a read transaction [24]. Thus client access patterns often show dependencies between consecutive requests, so that the request for a data unit will make it more likely or less likely that certain data unit will be requested next. These access patterns must be taken into account while designing a good cyclic multicast schedule that has low client-perceived latency while accessing multi-item objects [19].

One way to model this scenario is to treat the server data set as a weighted directed graph where nodes represent server data units and arc weights represent the strength of the dependency. Then the scheduling problem becomes following question in combinatorial optimization:

Minimum Circular Arrangement (MCA): Given a directed weighted graph $G = (V, E, w)$ with non-negative weights, find a surjection $f : V \mapsto \{0, 1, \ldots, n-1\}$ which minimizes $\sum_{e \in E} w(e)\ell(e)$, where $\ell(e) = (f(v) - f(u)) \mod n$, for $e = (u, v)$. Note that $\ell(e)$ is called the latency of the edge e in the arrangement f.

1.1 Related Problems

The MCA problem first appeared in work of Liberatore [19]. It falls under the class of vertex labelling problems where the question is to find a labelling of the vertices which optimizes some cost function. This class includes many interesting practical problems [7], *e.g.*, optimal linear arrangement problem, directed optimal linear arrangement problem, minimum bandwidth problem, folding labelling (also called minimum cut linear arrangement) problem, etc. We give more consideration to optimal linear arrangement problem and directed optimal linear arrangement problem since MCA is very closely related to them.

Optimal Linear Arrangement (OLA): Given an undirected weighted graph $G = (V, E, w)$ with non-negative weights, find a surjection $f : V \mapsto \{0, 1, \ldots, n-1\}$ which minimizes $\sum_{e \in E} w(e)\ell(e)$, where $\ell(e) = |f(v) - f(u)|$, for $e = (u, v)$.

OLA problem naturally arose from applications in VLSI design. Garey, Johnson and Stockmeyer [14] proved NP-completeness of the decision version of OLA. Today we know how to solve OLA problem exactly for some special cases of graphs, *e.g.*, un-weighted trees [25,8], outer planar graphs [10], cycles, wheels, complete bipartite graphs [16], etc. For arbitrary graphs, the currently best known guarantee of $O(\log n)$-approximation is due to Rao and Richa [23]. Meanwhile, there has also been some work done on polynomial time approximation schemes for un-weighted OLA of dense graphs, namely, [4] and [11].

Directed Optimal Linear Arrangement (DOLA): Given a directed acyclic weighted graph $G = (V, E, w)$ with non-negative weights, find a surjection $f : V \mapsto \{0, 1, \ldots, n-1\}$ such that $(u, v) \in E \implies f(u) < f(v)$, i.e. a topological sort, which minimizes $\sum_{e \in E} w(e)\ell(e)$, where $\ell(e) = f(v) - f(u)$, for $e = (u, v)$.

Not much is known about DOLA. Its decision version was shown to be NP-complete by Even and Shiloach [9]. On the algorithmic front, Adolphson and Hu [2] gave an $O(n \log n)$-time algorithm to solve DOLA exactly on rooted trees, where all the edges are oriented towards (or away from) the root. Otherwise neither any approximation algorithms nor any hardness of approximation results are known for it.

1.2   Current Status

The MCA problem is pretty recent [19]. Very few theoretical results are known about it. One of them is the proof of NP-completeness for the decision version of MCA problem restricted to sparse weighted graphs by Liberatore [18]. He also demonstrates an $\tilde{O}(\sqrt{n})$-approximation algorithm on any arbitrary graph instance using divide-and-conquer strategy in [18]. This result has recently been improved by Naor and Schwartz in [20] where they present $O(\log n \log \log n)$-approximation algorithm for the MCA problem.

1.3   Our Results

In this paper, we start out by proving some preliminary lemmas in section 3 that bound MCA cost. In section 4, we draw comparison between MCA cost and OLA cost (DOLA cost), throwing light on the relative hardness of these problems.

We prove that the decision version of even un-weighted MCA is NP-complete in case of sparse as well as dense graphs (section 5), a stronger result than [18]. We also consider complementary version of MCA, called MaxCA in section 6. We prove that it is MAX-SNP[π] complete [21] and, therefore, has no PTAS unless P=NP [5]. A similar proof technique would then show that MCA is MAX-SNP[π]-Hard and hence there is no PTAS for MCA too [5]. In section 7, we prove a conditional lower bound of $\sqrt{2} - \epsilon$ for MCA approximation under the assumption that DOLA does not admit constant factor approximation. Finally we conclude with a PTAS for MCA on dense instances in section 8.

2   Notation

By a graph G, we mean a directed graph without parallel edges and loops. V and E, as always, stand for vertex-set and edge-set of G respectively. $|V| = n$. An un-weighted graph is considered as a graph with edges of unit weight. When we talk about the OLA problem on a directed graph we mean the OLA problem on the underlying undirected graph.

Definition 1. *A graph G is **dense** if $|E| = \Omega(n^2)$. More specifically, G is δ-**dense** if $|E| \geq \delta n^2$. Similarly G is **sparse** if $|E| = O(n)$.*

Consider a graph G and $f : V \mapsto \{1, \ldots, n\}$ an arrangement of G.

Definition 2. *An edge $e = (u, v)$ of G is said to be a **forward edge with respect to** f if $f(u) < f(v)$. Similarly e is a **backward edge with respect to** f if $f(u) > f(v)$. Note that the forward/backward status of an edge can be changed by rotating f.*

Let $\mathrm{MCOST}(f)$, $\mathrm{LCOST}(f)$ and $\mathrm{DCOST}(f)$ respectively denote the circular, linear and the directed linear cost of the arrangement f as defined in the problem definitions. For an edge e, $\mathrm{MCOST}_e(f)$ denotes the cost of the edge e in the arrangement f. Similarly for $\mathrm{DCOST}_e(f)$ and $\mathrm{LCOST}_e(f)$. Set $\mathrm{DCOST}_e(f) = \mathrm{DCOST}(f) = \infty$, if any edge $e = (u, v)$ is a backward edge.

Definition 3. *Let g be a circular arrangement of G. By $\mathrm{ROT}(g)$ we mean an arrangement h obtained by rotating g so that the total weight of the backward edges is minimized. Note that $\mathrm{MCOST}(\mathrm{ROT}(g)) = \mathrm{MCOST}(g)$.*

Let $\mathrm{MCA}(G)$ be the set of all optimal circular arrangements of G. Similarly define $\mathrm{OLA}(G)$ and $\mathrm{DOLA}(G)$. Sometimes, by abuse of notation, $\mathrm{MCA}(G)$ also stands for some optimal circular arrangement. Similarly for $\mathrm{OLA}(G)$ and $\mathrm{DOLA}(G)$. Finally, let $\mathrm{MCOST}(G) := \mathrm{MCOST}(\mathrm{MCA}(G))$ denote the cost of the optimal arrangement. Similarly for $\mathrm{LCOST}(G)$ and $\mathrm{DCOST}(G)$.

By P_m we mean a directed path $p_1, \ldots, p_{m+1}$ of length m (on $m+1$ vertices), with unit weight edges. By $\overrightarrow{K}_n$ we mean the complete directed acyclic graph on n vertices, i.e. for $1 \leq i < j \leq n$, there is an edge (i, j) of unit weight.

By $\overleftarrow{G}$ we mean the graph *anti-parallel* to G, that is, $V(\overleftarrow{G}) = V(G)$ and $E(\overleftarrow{G}) = \{(v, u) | (u, v) \in E\}$. The edges in $\overleftarrow{G}$ carry same weight as their counterparts in G.

If G and H are two graphs, then $G + H$ is the graph which has G and H as its two components.

3   Bounding MCA Cost

In this section we show some upper and lower bounds on MCA cost and highlight its peculiar features that would help us derive our hardness results.

Proposition 1. *The total weight of the backward edges of $\mathrm{ROT}(g) \leq \frac{\mathrm{MCOST}(g)}{n}$.*

Proposition 2. *Let $G = H_1 + \cdots + H_k$ be a graph with k components. Put $n = |V(G)|$ and $n_i = |V(H_i)|$. Then $\sum_{i=1}^{k} \mathrm{MCOST}(H_i) \leq \mathrm{MCOST}(G) \leq n \sum_{i=1}^{k} \mathrm{MCOST}(H_i)/n_i$. Moreover these inequalities are tight.*

Proof (sketch). For $1 \leq i \leq k$, let $f_i \in \mathrm{MCA}(H_i)$ and consider $g = \mathrm{ROT}(f_1) \circ \cdots \circ \mathrm{ROT}(f_k)$. $\qquad\square$

This behavior of MCA (with components) enables us to derive our hardness results. The fundamental difference between MCA and OLA (or DOLA) is the issue of connectedness. In case of a graph with more than one component it is easy to the see that the optimal arrangement (in case of OLA and DOLA) is obtained by concatenating the optimal arrangements of the components. However, such is not the case with MCA. If there are any backward edges in the optimal circular arrangement of one of the components, then the latency of that edge is increased due to the presence of the other components.

Definition 4. *Let G be a weighted directed graph. For a vertex u, let $w_1 \geq \cdots \geq w_d$ denote the weights of the outgoing edges from u. Define $X^+(u) = \sum_i i w_i$, and $X^+(G) = \sum_{v \in V(G)} X^+(v)$. Similarly define $X^-(u)$ and $X^-(G)$ by replacing outgoing with incoming.*

Proposition 3. $\mathrm{MCOST}(G) \geq \max\{X^+(G), X^-(G)\}$.

4   Comparison of MCA with OLA and DOLA

4.1   Comparison with OLA

Proposition 4. *For any graph G, $\mathrm{LCOST}(G) \leq 2(1 - 1/n) \cdot \mathrm{MCOST}(G)$.*

Proof (sketch). Let $f \in \mathrm{MCA}(G)$ be an optimal circular arrangement. Denote by f_i the arrangement got by rotating f by i-positions. Now consider any edge $e = (u, v)$ of weight w with latency p with respect to the f ordering. The cost of this edge in the linear arrangement f_i is pw if $f_i(u) < f_i(v)$ and $(n - p)w$ if $f_i(u) > f_i(v)$. Averaging over all n rotations settles the claim.   □

To see that the above result is tight, consider $G = C_n$, a directed cycle. On the other hand, $\mathrm{MCOST}(G) \leq (n - 1)\mathrm{LCOST}(G)$ trivially. By considering appropriately directed sunflowers, one can show examples [12] which achieve $\mathrm{MCOST}(G) \geq (n/12)\mathrm{LCOST}(G)$.

4.2   Comparison with DOLA

From the definition, any legal DOLA arrangement is a legal MCA arrangement. Hence we trivially have $\mathrm{MCOST}(G) \leq \mathrm{DCOST}(G)$. On the other hand, $\mathrm{DCOST}(G)$ is trivially $\leq (n - 1)\mathrm{MCOST}(G)$. In case of weighted graphs this is optimal as shown in [19]. We can get little more sophisticated bound if we restrict ourselves to un-weighted graphs.

Proposition 5. *Let G be an un-weighted directed acyclic graph and f be any DOLA arrangement of G. Then $\mathrm{DCOST}(f) \leq |E|n - \frac{2\sqrt{2}}{3}|E|\sqrt{|E|} + \frac{7}{3}|E|$. Moreover for interesting E (i.e. $|E| \geq 28$), $\mathrm{DCOST}(f) \leq |E|n - |E|\sqrt{|E|}/2$.*

Proof (sketch). Note that in any legal DOLA arrangement of G, there can be at most $n - i$ edges with latency i for each i.   □

Corollary 1. *For any un-weighted directed acyclic graph G,*

$$\text{DCOST}(G) \leq \text{MCOST}(G) \cdot \frac{n(2n - \sqrt{|E|})}{|E| + n}.$$

Thus in order to get a $\Omega(n)$ separation between $\text{DCOST}(G)$ and $\text{MCOST}(G)$, we only need to look at sparse graphs in the un-weighted case. Moreover any approximation algorithm for DOLA on dense graphs automatically yields an approximation algorithm for MCA on dense graphs. However an approximation algorithm for MCA does not apriori give rise to a DOLA approximation algorithm since an MCA arrangement need not be a legal DOLA arrangement.

5 NP Completeness

Theorem 1 (Proposition 3.1 in [18]). *The decision version of the MCA problem is NP-complete.*

Liberatore [18] proves that *weighted* MCA problem is NP-complete by a reduction from an un-weighted DOLA. Since the MCA instance in his proof has $|E| = O(|V|)$, we infer that MCA is NP-complete even when restricted to sparse graphs. In this section we prove that even *un-weighted* MCA is NP-complete in case of sparse as well as dense graphs, stronger result than Liberatore [18]. We too make use of reduction from an un-weighted DOLA.

5.1 Straightening Algorithm

We start with an algorithm which allows us to normalize optimal solutions in a special case.

Theorem 2 (Straightening Algorithm). *Let G be a weighted directed graph, and $m > 2$. Let f be any circular arrangement of $G + P_m$. We can transform f (in time polynomial in $m + n$) to an arrangement g in which all the vertices in P_m appearing in the order $p_1, \ldots, p_{m+1}$. Moreover $\text{MCOST}(g) \leq \text{MCOST}(f)$.*

Proof (sketch). For this proof it is more convenient to think of an arrangement as a mapping from $[n]$ to V or as an ordered list of vertices, rather than the other way around. Let f be any circular arrangement of $G + P_m$. We define a sequence of arrangements $g_1, \ldots, g_{m+1}$ with the following properties:

- $g_i(j) = p_j$ for all $1 \leq j \leq i \leq m + 1$
- $\text{MCOST}(g_{i+1}) \leq \text{MCOST}(g_i)$ for $1 \leq i \leq m$

Thus $g = g_{m+1}$ is the required arrangement. To start, let $g_1 = f$ suitably rotated so that $g_1(1) = p_1$. Note that $\text{MCOST}(g_1) = \text{MCOST}(f)$. Assume we know g_i and $i \leq m$ (else we are done). If $g_i(i+1) = p_{i+1}$, then set $g_{i+1} = g_i$ and continue with the next i.

Suppose $g_i(i + 1) \neq p_{i+1}$. Let $i + \ell$ denote the position of the vertex p_{i+1} $(2 \leq \ell \leq m + n - i)$. Partition the vertices as follows: $L = \{p_1, \ldots, p_i\}$, $M = \{g_i(i + 1), \ldots, g_i(i + \ell - 1)\}$, $R = \{g_i(i + \ell + 1), \ldots, g(m + n + 1)\}$. Thus the arrangement g_i is $L M p_{i+1} R$.

Let W_{MR} be the total weight of all the edges going from M to R and W_{RM} be the total weight of all edges going from R to M. Define

$$g_{i+1} = \begin{cases} L p_{i+1} M R & \text{if } W_{MR} \geq W_{RM} \\ L p_{i+1} R M & \text{if } W_{MR} < W_{RM} \end{cases}$$

The verification that $\mathrm{MCOST}(g_{i+1}) \leq \mathrm{MCOST}(g_i)$ is left to the reader.   □

Note that $g = p_1 p_2 \ldots p_{m+1} \circ \mathrm{ROT}(f|G)$, where $f|G$ is the arrangement f restricted to vertices in G. Hence this transformation can be implemented in time $O(m + n^3)$. A generalization of this is proved in [18].

Proposition 6 (Lemma 3.4 of [18]). *Let $G = H_1 + \cdots + H_k$ be a directed graph with k components. Then there is an optimal circular arrangement of G which can be obtained by concatenating (not necessarily optimal) circular arrangements of H_i.*

We now have a corollary of Theorem 2 which gives us a technique to force an optimal MCA arrangement to have only forward edges.

Corollary 2. *Let G be an un-weighted directed acyclic graph, $m \geq \mathrm{DCOST}(G)$. Let g be the circular arrangement obtained by concatenating P_m with the optimal DOLA arrangement of G. Then $\mathrm{MCOST}(G + P_m) = \mathrm{DCOST}(G) + m = \mathrm{MCOST}(g)$, i.e. g is an optimal circular arrangement.*

Proof (sketch). First note that $\mathrm{MCOST}(g) = \mathrm{DCOST}(G) + m \leq 2m$. Moreover, G cannot have any backward edges in the *straightened* optimal circular arrangement of $G + P_m$, for that implies the cost of the arrangement is $> 2m$.   □

We conclude this section with a couple of NP Completeness proofs of un-weighted MCA.

Theorem 3. *The decision version of the un-weighted MCA problem is NP-complete.*

Proof. Proof by reduction from un-weighted DOLA. Let (G, K) be a DOLA instance. Let $m = n^3$ be an upper bound for cost of optimal DOLA arrangement. By Corollary 2, $\mathrm{MCOST}(G + P_m) = DOLA(G) + m$. So if $G' = G + P_m$ and $K' = K + m$, we have $DOLA(G) \leq K \iff \mathrm{MCOST}(G + P_m) \leq K'$.   □

Since the MCA instance in this proof has $|E| = O(|V|)$, we infer that un-weighted MCA is NP-complete even when restricted to sparse graphs. We now prove a generalization of Corollary 2 and use it to show that un-weighted MCA is NP-complete even when restricted to dense instances.

Proposition 7. *Let G and H be un-weighted directed acyclic graphs such that $|V(H)| = m \geq \mathrm{DCOST}(G)$. Assume further that there is an optimal MCA arrangement h of H which does not contain any backward edges. Let g be the circular arrangement obtained by concatenating h with the optimal DOLA arrangement of G. Then $\mathrm{MCOST}(G + H) = \mathrm{DCOST}(G) + \mathrm{DCOST}(H) = \mathrm{MCOST}(g)$, i.e. g is an optimal circular arrangement.*

Proof (sketch). First apply Proposition 6 to separate out vertices of G and H in the optimal arrangement. Then rearrange the H portion to be h, since h has no backward edges. Then proceed as in Corollary 2 to show that G cannot have any backward edges.   □

Theorem 4. *Decision version of the un-weighted MCA is NP-complete even when restricted to dense instances.*

Proof (sketch). Proof by reduction from un-weighted DOLA. Let (G, K) be a DOLA instance. Let $m = n^3$ be an upper bound for cost of optimal DOLA arrangement. Then consider MCA instance $G' = G + \vec{K}_m$, where $\vec{K}_m$ is the complete DAG on m vertices, and use proposition 7!   □

6   MAX-SNP[π] and PTAS

Papadimitriou and Yannakakis [21] show that the complementary version of OLA, called Maximum Linear Arrangement, is in MAX-SNP[π]. We show that same is true for the following complementary version of MCA as well.

MaxCA Given a directed graph G, find an arrangement f that maximizes $\mathrm{MCOST}(f)$.

Theorem 5. *MaxCA is in MAX-SNP[π].*

Proof (sketch). To show that MaxCA is in MAX-SNP[π], consider the first-order quantifier-free predicate $\psi(\pi, u, w, v, G) := B(u, w, v) \wedge ((u, v) \in E(G))$, where $B(u, w, v)$ is true when $w = v$, or w occurs in between u and v in π order (considered cyclically).   □

6.1   MAX-SNP[π] Completeness of MaxCA

We prove that MaxCA is complete for MAX-SNP[π] by showing a L-reduction [21] from the following MAX-SNP[π] complete problem. This problem is, in fact, the complementary version of minimum feedback arc set problem [13] and it does not admit a PTAS unless P=NP as shown in [5].

MAX SUBDAG: Given a directed graph $G = (V, E)$, find a subset $E' \subseteq E$ of maximum cardinality for which (V, E') is acyclic.

In [12], we prove the following theorem.

Theorem 6. *MaxCA is MAX-SNP[π] complete.*

6.2   MCA Is MAX-SNP[π] Hard

We now show that MCA cannot have a PTAS by showing a similar reduction from MAX SUBDAG. In fact, this reduction can be easily modified into a L-reduction. It, then, proves that MCA is MAX-SNP[π]-Hard problem. But we prefer to put the proof in algorithmic form, since our main goal is to prove that MCA has no PTAS unless P=NP.

Theorem 7. *MCA does not have a PTAS unless P=NP.*

Proof (sketch). Suppose $\mathcal{M}$ is a $(1 + \epsilon)$-approximation algorithm for MCA for some $0 < \epsilon < 1/3$.

Require: A directed graph G.
Ensure: $F \subseteq E$ for which (V, F) is acyclic.
  1: $m \Leftarrow \frac{4n}{\epsilon}$.
  2: $G' \Leftarrow \hat{G} + P_m$.
  3: $f \Leftarrow \mathcal{M}(G')$.
  4: $f' \Leftarrow \mathcal{SA}(f)$. ($\mathcal{SA}$ is the straightening algorithm)
  5: $F \Leftarrow$ edges of G which are forward edges in the arrangement f'.
  6: Output F.

It can now be shown that $|F| \geq (1 - 3\epsilon)|F^*|$, where $F^* \subseteq E$ denotes the optimal solution to the MAX SUBDAG problem. This gives us a $(1 - 3\epsilon)$-approximation for MAX SUBDAG. Thus a PTAS for MCA gives a PTAS for the MAX SUBDAG. In the light of [5], this implies P=NP.   □

7   Hardness of Approximation

We now turn to hardness of approximation. We use the straightening algorithm to prove a curious hardness result for MCA.

Proposition 8. *Suppose that un-weighted DOLA has a polynomial time α - approximation algorithm and un-weighted MCA has a polynomial time $(1 + \delta)$-approximation algorithm ($\delta < 1$). Then un-weighted DOLA has a polynomial time $\mu(\alpha)$-approximation algorithm, where*

$$\mu(p) = (1 + \delta) + \frac{\delta(1 + \delta)}{1 - \delta} p.$$

Proof (sketch). Let $\mathcal{D}$ denote the α-approximation algorithm for un-weighted DOLA, and $\mathcal{M}$ denote the $(1 + \delta)$-approximation algorithm for un-weighted MCA. Let $\mathcal{SA}$ denote the straightening algorithm of Theorem 2. Put $\theta = (1 + \delta)/(1 - \delta)$.

Require: Input un-weighted directed graph G.
Ensure: g is a β-approximate DOLA arrangement of G.
  1: $\mathtt{f} \Leftarrow \mathcal{D}(G)$.
  2: $\mathtt{m} \Leftarrow \theta \cdot \mathrm{DCOST}(f)$.

3: g1 ⇐ $\mathcal{M}(G + P_m)$.
4: g2 ⇐ $\mathcal{SA}(g_1)$.
5: g ⇐ g2 restricted to G.
6: Output g.

It can be shown that $\mathrm{DCOST}(G) \leq \mathrm{DCOST}(\mathbf{g}) \leq \mu(\alpha) \cdot \mathrm{DCOST}(G)$.   □

One can view the above algorithm as a way of generating a $\mu(\alpha)$-approximate arrangement given the cost (we don't need the arrangement) of an α-approximate arrangement. This leads to the following theorem. See [12] for complete proof.

Theorem 8 (Bootstrapping). *Suppose that un-weighted MCA has a poly-nomial time $(1 + \delta)$-approximation algorithm for some $\delta < \sqrt{2} - 1$. Put $\Gamma(\delta) = 1 + \frac{2\delta}{1-2\delta-\delta^2}$. Then for every $\epsilon > 0$, there is a polynomial time $(\Gamma(\delta)+\epsilon)$-approximation algorithm for un-weighted DOLA.*

As a corollary we have the following conditional hardness result.

Corollary 3. *For all $\eta \in (0, \sqrt{2} - 1)$, there is a constant c_η such that it is NP-hard to approximate un-weighted MCA to within $\sqrt{2} - \eta$ if it is NP-hard to approximate un-weighted DOLA within c_η.*

8   Polynomial Time Approximation Scheme

We conclude with a PTAS for un-weighted MCA on dense graphs. Arora, Frieze and Kaplan [4] give a PTAS for OLA on dense graphs. We show how the same algorithm with minor modifications works for MCA as well. The algorithm gives an arrangement which is at most ηn^3 away from the optimal solution. If the graph is dense, then Proposition 3 shows that the optimum value is $\Omega(n^3)$.

Definition 5. *For constant t, let $I_1, \ldots, I_t$ be a partition of $[n] := \{1, \ldots, n\}$ into consecutive equal sized intervals, such that $I_i = \{it, \ldots, (i + 1)t - 1\}$. A placement is a mapping from the vertex set to the set $\{I_1, \ldots, I_t\}$. A placement f' is proper if $|f'^{-1}(I_i)| = |I_i|$ for each i. Given any mapping $f : V \mapsto [n]$, we denote by f' the induced placement. The cost of a placement f', denoted by $\mathrm{CP}(f')$ is defined to be $\sum_{(u,v)\in E}(f'(v) - f'(u) \mod t)$.*

Proposition 9. *If f is any arrangement, $|\mathrm{MCOST}(f) - \mathrm{CP}(f')n/t| \leq n^3/t$.*

Proof (sketch). Consider any edge which crosses an interval. If it has latency x w.r.t the arrangement f, then it has latency $\lfloor xt/n \rfloor$ or $\lfloor xt/n+1 \rfloor$ in the placement f'. This observation together with a generous upper bound on the number edges within an interval gives the result.   □

Proposition 10. *If f and g are arrangements such that $|\mathrm{CP}(f') - \mathrm{CP}(g')| \leq \epsilon n^2$, then $|\mathrm{MCOST}(f) - \mathrm{MCOST}(g)| \leq (2 + \epsilon)n^3/t$.*

Now proceed just like in [4]. See proof details in [12].

9   Discussion

We studied the MCA problem in this paper. Its motivation came from a problem related to design of cyclic multicast schedule. Considering current trend in technologies and applications, cyclic multicast that pays heed to data dependencies should play a pivotal role in the future [6].

Our research pointed out certain negative aspects of the MCA problem, namely, it does not have a polynomial time algorithm and it does not even admit a polynomial time approximation scheme for arbitrary graph instance (unless P=NP). Yet it is possible that MCA problem might be tenable if restricted to certain special kinds of graphs that have practical significance. Literature has many such instances of polynomial time algorithms for OLA problem, *e.g.*, unweighted trees [25,8], outer planar graphs [10], wheels, complete bipartite graphs [16], etc. Can one hope for the same in case of MCA? Or is it also *too hard*?

Assuming DOLA to be non-approximable within any constant factor, we could show a lower bound of $\sqrt{2} - \epsilon$ for MCA approximation. We believe it to be far from being tight. In fact, there is a conspicuous lack of hardness of approximation results even for OLA and DOLA. They stand as natural open problems.

Liberatore provides few heuristics [19,18] and a $\widetilde{O}(\sqrt{n})$-approximation algorithm [18] to solve MCA problem on arbitrary graphs. Similarly Naor and Schwartz present $O(\log n \log \log n)$-approximation algorithm in [20]. But these algorithms suffer either from no performance guarantee or from inherent inefficiency. Therefore it is an interesting open question to design an efficient approximation algorithm for MCA problem.

References

1. S Acharya. *Broadcast Disks: Dissemination-based Data Management for Assymetric Communication Environments*. PhD thesis, Brown University, May 1998.
2. D Adolphson and T C Hu. Optimal linear ordering. *SIAM Journal on Applied Mathematics*, 25(3):403–423, 1973.
3. K C Almeroth, M H Ammar, and Z Fei. Scalable delivery of web pages using cyclic best-effort multicast. In *IEEE INFOCOM*, pages 1214–1221, March 1998.
4. S Arora, A Frieze, and H Kaplan. A new rounding procedure for the assignment problem with applications to dense graph arrangement problems. In *37th Annual IEEE Symposium on Foundations of Computer Science*, pages 21–30, October 1996.
5. S Arora, C Lund, R Motwani, M Sudan, and M Szegedy. Proof verification and hardness of approximation problems. In *33rd Annual IEEE Symposium on Foundations of Computer Science*, pages 14–23, October 1992.
6. P K Chrysanthis, V Liberatore, and K Pruhs. Middleware support for multicast-based data dissemination: A working reality, 2001. White paper.
7. F R K Chung. *Theory and Applications of Graphs*, chapter Some Problems and Results in Labelings of Graphs, pages 255–264. John Wiley & Sons, New York, 1981.

8. F R K Chung. On optimal linear arrangements of trees. *Comp. & Maths with Applications*, 10(1):43–60, 1984.

9. S Even and Y Shiloach. NP-Completeness of several arrangement problems. Technical Report 43, Isreal Institute of Technology, 1975.

10. G N Frederickson and S E Hambrusch. Planar linear arrangements of outerplanar graphs. *IEEE Transactions on Circuits and Systems*, 35(3):323–332, 1988.

11. A M Frieze and R Kannan. Quick approximation to matrices and applications. *Combinatorica*, 19(2):175–220, 1999.

12. M K Ganapathy and S Lodha. On minimum circular arrangement, 2003. URL: http://www.research.rutgers.edu/~lodha/research/ps/mca.ps.

13. M R Garey and D S Johnson. *Computers and Intractability: A guide to the theory of NP-Completeness*. W H Freeman and Company, 2nd edition, 1979.

14. M R Garey, D S Johnson, and L Stockmeyer. Some simplified NP-Complete graph problems. *Theoretical Computer Science*, 3(1):237–267, 1976.

15. G Herman, G Gopal, K C Lee, and A Weinrib. The datacycle architecture for very high throughput data systems. In *ACM SIGMOD International Conference on Management of Data*, pages 97–103, May 1987.

16. M Juvan and B Mohar. Optimal linear labelings and eigenvalues of graphs. *Discrete Applied Mathematics*, 36:153–168, 1992.

17. B Krishnamurthy and J Rexford. *Web Protocols and Practice*. Addison-Wesley, Boston, 2001.

18. V Liberatore. Circular arrangements. In *ICALP*, pages 1054–1066, 2002.

19. V Liberatore. Multicast scheduling for list requests. In *IEEE INFOCOM*, pages 1129–1137, June 2002.

20. J Naor and R Schwartz. The directed circular arrangement problem. In *15th Annual ACM-SIAM Symposium on Discrete Algorithms*, January 2004. To appear.

21. C H Papadimitriou and M Yannakakis. Optimmization, approximation and complexity classes. *Journal of Computer and System Sciences*, 43:425–440, 1991.

22. M Rabinovich. Resource management issues in content delivery networks (CDNs). In *DIMACS Workshop on Resource Management and Scheduling in Next Generation Networks*, 2001.

23. S Rao and A W Richa. New approximation techniques for some ordering problems. In *9th Annual ACM-SIAM Symposium on Discrete Algorithms*, pages 211–218. ACM-SIAM, January 1998.

24. J Shanmugasundaram, A Nithrakashyap, R Sivasankaran, and K Ramamritham. Efficient concurrency control for broadcast environments. In *ACM SIGMOD International Conference on Management of Data*, pages 85–96, June 1999.

25. Y Shiloach. A minimum linear arrangement algorithm for undirected trees. *SIAM Journal of Computing*, 8(1):15–32, 1979.

Integral Symmetric 2-Commodity Flows

Aubin Jarry

I3S/INRIA Project Mascotte
2004, route des Lucioles – BP 93 – F-06902 Sophia Antipolis Cedex – FRANCE
Aubin.Jarry@sophia.inria.fr

Abstract. We study integral 2-commodity flows in networks with a special characteristic, namely symmetry. We show that the Symmetric 2-Commodity Flow Problem is in P, by proving that the cut criterion is a necessary and sufficient condition for the existence of a solution. We also give a polynomial-time algorithm whose complexity is $6C_{flow} + O(|A|)$, where C_{flow} is the time complexity of your favorite flow algorithm (usually in $O(|V| \times |A|)$). Our result closes an open question in a surprising way, since it is known that the Integral 2-Commodity Flow Problem is NP-complete for both directed and undirected graphs. This work finds application in optical telecommunication networks.

1 Introduction

Given a graph $G = (V, A)$, a capacity $\kappa : A \to \mathbb{N}$ and a request set $R \in (V \times V \times \mathbb{N})$, the Multi-Commodity Flow Problem (MCF) consists in finding $|R|$ flows corresponding to the request set and with respect to the capacity constraints on the graph. MCF has been widely studied, as it arises naturally from many classical problems such as routing problems. The Fractional Problem (allowing fractional flows) can be solved in polynomial time by using linear programming ([9]). However, the Integral Problem (not allowing fractional flows) is also of interest when we have non-splittable units of traffic, or non-splittable routes to find (e.g. for synchronous communications).

The integral MCF is NP-complete in the general case ([4] and [6]), and many variants have been studied, depending on the properties of G, R and $G + R$ ($G + R$ is the multigraph obtained from G by adding an arc for each request in R). They divide themselves between NP-complete and tractable problems. One variant is the Disjoint Paths Problem which consists in finding $|R|$ disjoint paths corresponding to the request set (with $R \subset (V \times V)$). The other main variants depend on the structure of G or R or both: whether G is directed or undirected, whether G or $G + R$ is planar, whether G or $G + R$ is Eulerian, etc... For a planar and Eulerian graph G and demands on the boundary, the problem has been proven polynomial ([7]) and a linear time algorithm has been found ([12]).

Since G is also Eulerian, the integral symmetric MCF would appear to be a particular case of the directed Eulerian variant, except that usually $G + R$ is assumed to be Eulerian (and not only G). On this variant, C.Nash-Williams proved in 1965 (one can find a proof in [10]) that with $|R| = 2$ the problem was

V. Diekert and M. Habib (Eds.): STACS 2004, LNCS 2996, pp. 406–417, 2004.

polynomial, whereas with $|R| \geq 3$ the problem was NP-complete ([11]). In the general directed case, the Disjoint Paths Problem is NP-complete with $|R| = 2$ ([4]).

MCFs in Symmetric Digraphs are motivated by routing in optical networks, since optical networks are best represented by symmetric digraphs. Hence, the interconnection graph $G = (V, A)$ is symmetric directed (i.e. $(x, y) \in A \Rightarrow (y, x) \in A$), and the capacity function is symmetric (i.e. $\forall (x, y) \in A$, $\kappa(x, y) = \kappa(y, x)$). Such restrictions apply also to many other telecommunication networks.

In this paper, we will more specifically study the problem with symmetric requests (so $G + R$ is indeed Eulerian, but $|R| = 4$). One can observe that a symmetric digraph with symmetric requests has the same knowledge structure as an undirected graph with undirected requests, and that an undirected solution would perfectly fit for the symmetric problem. While this is true, the symmetric problem allows also more solutions and is more tractable : [2] proved that the Integral Undirected 2-Commodity (i.e. $|R| = 2$) Flow Problem was NP-complete even with a value of 1 for the first commodity. In this paper we will prove that the Integral Symmetric (i.e. with a symmetric capacity and symmetric requests) 2-Commodity Flow Problem is polynomial.

In the course of our algorithm, we use standard cut considerations to build or ensure the existence of simple flows. We also exploit the symmetry of the problem to swap opposite flows without breaking the constraints. We give below a diagram of the complexity of flow and paths problems. We denote the number of vertices and arcs by N and M, respectively.

Problem	Graph		
	Directed	Undirected	Directed Symm.
Disjoint paths			
1 request [Dijkstra]	$O(M + NlogN)$	$O(M + NlogN)$	$O(M + NlogN)$
2+ req.	NP-hard [4]	$O(N^3)$ [8]	$O(N^3)$ [5]
k req.	NP-hard [6]	NP-hard [6]	NP-hard [1]
Integral MCF			
1 req. [3]		C_{flow}	C_{flow}
2 req.		NP-hard [2]	??
3+ req.		NP-hard	NP-hard [2]
1 pair of symm. req.	NP-hard	-	C_{flow} [1]
2 pairs of symm. req.	NP-hard	-	$\mathbf{6C}_{flow} + \mathbf{O(M)}$
3+ pairs of symm. req.	NP-hard	-	??

In section 2 we introduce our notations and our problem. In section 3 we consider related works. In section 4 we give our algorithm and prove it, thus proving our main theorem:

Theorem 1 (symmetric 2-commodity flow). *The symmetric cut criterion is a necessary and sufficient condition for the existence of a solution to the Integral Symmetric 2-Commodity Flow Problem. A solution can be found in $6C_{flow} + O(M)$ steps, where C_{flow} is the time complexity of a chosen flow algorithm.*

2   Standard Notations

In the following, we present some notations that will be used throughout this paper.

Note that the standard definition of a flow allows for the existence of loops and we shall specify "flow without loops" when required. A k-commodity flow $(f_1, \ldots, f_k)$ is a collection of flows sharing the capacity κ of the support graph.

One of the main notion related to flows et MCFs is the cut criterion. Such a criterion express some global constraints on the quantities of flow, with respect capacities of the support graph.

Definition 1 (cut criterion). *Let $\kappa : A \to \mathbb{N}$ be a capacity on $G = (V, A)$. Let $s_1, ..s_k, t_1, ..t_k \in V$. Let $v_1, ..v_k \in \mathbb{N}$. The cut criterion for $(\kappa, (s_1, t_1, v_1), .. (s_k, t_k, v_k))$ is : for all cut $C \subset V$, for all $I \subset \{1, ..k\}$ we have : $(\forall i \in I, s_i \in C$ and $t_i \notin C) \Rightarrow \kappa(C) \geq (\Sigma_{i \in I} v_i)$.*

In the following, we define some symmetric notions related to the properties of symmetric digraphs.

Definition 2 (symmetric function). *Let $G = (V, A)$ be a symmetric digraph, and let f be a function from A to $\mathbb{N}$. We say that f is symmetric if for all $(x, y) \in A$, $f(x, y) = f(y, x)$.*

Note that, in the MCF on symmetric digraphs, the capacity is assumed to be symmetric. Now we introduce reverse functions.

Definition 3 (f^r, reverse). *Let $f : A \to \mathbb{N}$. The reverse function of f, $f^r : A \to \mathbb{N}$ is the function defined by $\forall (x, y) \in A$, $f^r(x, y) = f(y, x)$*

To finish with the use of symmetric digraphs, we add a last operation on functions:

- simplification: given a function f from A to $\mathbb{N}$, $|f| : A \to \mathbb{N}$ is the function defined by $\forall (x, y) \in A$, if $f(x, y) \geq f(y, x)$, then $|f|(x, y) = f(x, y) - f(y, x)$, otherwise $|f|(x, y) = 0$.

Symmetric 2-commodity flows. If an undirected 2-Commodity Flow represents the solution of a communication instance between two pair of nodes, then for each pair of nodes the same set of paths is used for both directions. When we relax the problem, i.e. when we allow the "returning" messages to use another set of paths than the "incoming" messages, then we have a symmetric 2-commodity flow.

Definition 4 (symmetric 2-commodity flow). *Let $(f_1, f_{-1}, f_2, f_{-2})$ be a 4-commodity flow from (s_1, t_1, s_2, t_2) to (t_1, s_1, t_2, s_2) of value (v_1, v_1, v_2, v_2). $(f_1, f_{-1}, f_2, f_{-2})$ is also called symmetric 2-commodity flow from (s_1, s_2) to (t_1, t_2) of value (v_1, v_2).*

For the Symmetric 2-Commodity Flow Problem, we use a specific cut criterion, called symmetric.

Definition 5 (symmetric cut criterion). *Let* $\kappa : A \to \mathbb{N}$ *be a symmetric capacity. Let* $s_1, t_1,\ s_2, t_2 \in V$. *Let* v_1 *and* v_2 *be two positive integers. The symmetric cut criterion for* $(\kappa, (s_1, t_1, v_1), (s_2, t_2, v_2))$ *is the cut criterion for* $(\kappa, (s_1, t_1, v_1), (t_1, s_1, v_1), (s_2, t_2, v_2), (t_2, s_2, v_2))$.

3   Related Flow Formulations

The main result we will use in this paper is a straightforward corollary of Menger's theorem.

Theorem 2 (Menger). *The cut criterion is a necessary and sufficient condition for the existence of a solution to the Integral Flow Problem.*

Corollary 1. *The cut criterion is a necessary condition for the existence of a solution to the Integral k-Commodity Flow Problem.*

This corollary implies for instance that the symmetric cut criterion is a necessary condition for the Symmetric 2-Commodity Flow Problem.

3.1   Complexity of Some Integral Multi-commodity Flow Problems

As we said in the Introduction, our problem is a particular case of the general Integral MCF. Since the result of Fortune, Hopcroft and Willie [4] we know that the Disjoint Paths Problem is NP-complete with only two requests ($|R| = 2$).

More specifically, we know that in Eulerian digraphs ($G + R$ is Eulerian), the problem is polynomial with 2 commodities ($|R| = 2$). This is because if one finds a flow for the first request, and removes the used capacities along with the request in $G + R$, then the remaining request is part of some cycles in $G + R$, so there is solution for it. This property no longer holds if there is two requests left. The problem is NP-hard with three ($|R| = 3$). In our problem, we have not less than four requests $|R| = 4$.

Concerning undirected graphs, it is noteworthy that the Disjoint Paths Problem is polynomial with a bounded number of requests ($|R| \leq k$) [8], like in symmetric digraphs, but the 2-Commodity Flow Problem (with $|R| = 2$) is NP-complete even if one of the requested flows should be of value 1 (with $R = \{(x, y, 1), (x', y', v)\}$) [2], unlike in symmetric digraph (see below).

3.2   The 2-Commodity Flow Problem in a Symmetric Digraph

In symmetric digraphs, we already know that the Disjoint Path Problem is NP-complete [1] in general, but that it is polynomial with a bounded number of requests [5]. For the MCF, we prove in the following theorem that the 2-Commodity Flow Problem is polynomial with a value of $(1, v)$ (with $R = \{(x, y, 1), (x', y', v)\}$).

Theorem 3. *The 2-Commodity Flow Problem is polynomial in symmetric digraphs if the value is* $(1, v)$.

Proof. We assume that the cut criterion is true (it can be checked in polynomial time), then find the flow of value v, and last find the flow of value 1.
The input is:

- a symmetric capacity $\kappa : A \to \mathbb{N}$;
- the source and target of the requested 2-commodity flow (s_1, s_2), (t_1, t_2) $\in V^2$;
- the value of the requested 2-commodity flow $(1, v) \in \mathbb{N}^2$.

We first find a flow without loops $f_2 \leq \kappa$ from s_2 to t_2 of value v. If the cut criterion is true, then f_2 can be found using any polynomial time flow algorithm. Now we prove that the cut criterion is true for $((\kappa - f_2), (s_1, t_1, 1))$. Let $C \subset V$ be a cut such that $s_1 \in C$ and $t_1 \notin C$. Two cases are possible:

- if $s_2 \in C$ and $t_2 \notin C$, then $\kappa(C) \geq (1 + v)$. If $f_2(C) \geq v + 1$, then there is $x \in C$ and $y \notin C$ with $(x, y) \in A$ such that $f_2(y, x) \geq 1$ so $f_2(x, y) = 0$: $(\kappa - f_2)(C) \geq 1$
- otherwise, $\kappa(C) \geq 1$. If $f_2(C) \geq 1$, then there is $x \in C$ and $y \notin C$ with $(x, y) \in A$ such that $f_2(y, x) \geq 1$ so $f_2(x, y) = 0$: $(\kappa - f_2)(C) \geq 1$

The cut criterion is true, so according to Theorem 2, we can find a flow $f_1 \leq (\kappa - f_2)$ from s_1 to t_1 of value 1.

The 2-Commodity Flow Problem in a Symmetric Digraph is closely related to our problem, though its formulation breaks somehow the symmetry of the model. Here we give few remarks on it.
The cut criterion is not a sufficient condition for the 2-Commodity Flow Problem, though it is necessary according to Theorem 2. Here is an example (see Figure 1) showing that the cut criterion is not sufficient:

- the vertex set is $V = \{s_1, s_2, t_1, t_2\}$;
- the arc set is $A = \{(s_1, s_2), (s_2, s_1), (s_2, t_1), (t_1, s_2), (s_1, t_2), (t_2, s_1),$ $(t_2, t_1), (t_1, t_2)\}$;
- we consider the symmetric digraph $G = (V, A)$;
- the capacity on G is $\kappa : A \to \mathbb{N}$ such that

$$\kappa(s_1, s_2) = \kappa(s_2, s_1) = 1 \ \kappa(s_2, t_1) = \kappa(t_1, s_2) = 1$$
$$\kappa(s_1, t_2) = \kappa(t_2, s_1) = 3 \ \kappa(t_2, t_1) = \kappa(t_1, t_2) = 1.$$

The cut criterion is true for $(\kappa, (s_1, t_1, 2), (s_2, t_2, 2))$, but there is no 2-commodity flow from (s_1, s_2) to (t_1, t_2) of value $(2, 2)$.
However, observe that the symmetric cut criterion is false when we study the example given before: the cut $\{s_1, t_2\}$ is of value 2 though s_1 and t_2 are in the same side of this cut.
A direct consequence of our main theorem (Theorem 1) is that the symmetric cut criterion is sufficient for the 2-Commodity Flow Problem. Observe that it is not necessary, as shown with the following example (see Figure 2):

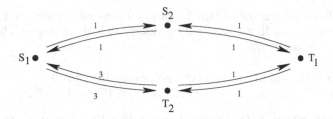

Fig. 1. There is no 2-commodity flow from (s_1, s_2) to (t_1, t_2) of value $(2, 2)$.

- the vertex set is $V = \{x, y\}$; the arc set is $A = \{(x, y), (y, x)\}$;
- we consider the symmetric digraph $G = (V, A)$;
- the capacity on G is $\kappa : A \to \mathbb{N}$ with $\kappa(x, y) = \kappa(y, x) = 1$;
- we define a flow $f \leq \kappa$ by $f(x, y) = 1$ and $f(y, x) = 0$.

The symmetric cut criterion is false for $(\kappa, (x, y, 1), (y, x, 1))$, but (f, f^r) is a 2-commodity flow from (x, y) to (y, x) of value $(1, 1)$.

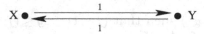

Fig. 2. There is a 2-commodity flow from (x, y) to (y, x) of value $(1, 1)$.

4   Solution to the Symmetric 2-Commodity Flow Problem

In this section, we consider a symmetric digraph $G = (V, A)$ with a symmetric capacity $\kappa : A \to \mathbb{N}$. We also consider two pair of vertices (s_1, t_1) and (s_2, t_2), and two positive integers v_1 and v_2. The goal of this section is to prove the following theorem by construction.

Theorem 1 (symmetric 2-commodity flow). *The symmetric cut criterion is a necessary and sufficient condition for the existence of a solution to the Integral Symmetric 2-Commodity Flow Problem. A solution can be found by Algorithm 1 in $6C_{flow} + O(|A|)$ steps.*

We give an algorithm (Algorithm 1), that solves the symmetric 2-commodity flow problem. This algorithm is divided into three parts, which are explained in the three next subsections.

In Section 4.1 we give the first part of our algorithm (Algorithm 3(first step)) which gives a flow for the first commodity which does not alter the cut criterion for the second commodity. Note however that this intermediate flow is not part of the final solution. Then, in Section 4.2 we compute the flows for the second commodity (Algorithm 4(second step)), reusing the partial solution of Algorithm 3.

These two flows are part of the final solution. Eventually, (Section 4.3) we compute the flows for the first commodity (Algorithm 5(third step)). This last part is quite straightforward.

Algorithm 1 (integral symmetric 2-commodity flow)
Input : $G = (V, A)$; $\kappa : A \to \mathbb{N}$; $s_1, t_1, s_2, t_2 \in V$; $v_1, v_2 \in \mathbb{N}$.

- using **Algorithm 3 (first step)**, compute a flow f from s_1 to t_1 of value v_1 such that the cut criterion is true for $((\kappa - f), (s_2, t_2, v_2), (t_2, s_2, v_2))$
- using **Algorithm 4 (second step)** and f, compute two flows f_2 from s_2 to t_2 of value v_2 and f_{-2} from t_2 to s_2 of value v_2 such that $(f_2 + f_{-2}) \leq \kappa$ and such that the cut criterion is true for $((\kappa - f_2 - f_{-2}), (s_1, t_1, v_1))$.
- using **Algorithm 5 (third step)**, compute two flows f_1 from s_1 to t_1 of value v_1 and f_{-1} from t_1 to s_1 of value v_1 such that $(f_1 + f_{-1} + f_2 + f_{-2}) \leq \kappa$.

Output : $f_1 : A \to \mathbb{N}$; $f_{-1} : A \to \mathbb{N}$; $f_2 : A \to \mathbb{N}$; $f_{-2} : A \to \mathbb{N}$.

In the course of the following section, we will need a subroutine (Algorithm 2) which, split a flow f of even value on a directed graph $G = (V, A)$ in two flows g and g' (this means that $g + g' = f$) so that $2g \leq (f + 1)$ and $2g' \leq (f + 1)$. In other words, it computes a flow g such that $(f - 1) \leq 2g \leq (f + 1)$ (by 1, we mean the function such that $\forall a \in A, 1(a) = 1$).

Algorithm 2 (finding g such that $(f - 1) \leq 2g \leq (f + 1)$)
Input : $G = (V, A)$; $f : A \to \mathbb{N}$.
Variables : $f' : A \to \mathbb{N}$; $x \in V$.

- $\forall a \in A,\ f'(a) \leftarrow f(a)$
- while there is $(x_{start}, y_{start}) \in A$ such that $f'(x_{start}, y_{start})$ is odd do
  - $f'(x_{start}, y_{start}) \leftarrow f'(x_{start}, y_{start}) + 1$
  - $x \leftarrow y_{start}$
  - while $x \neq x_{start}$ do
    - * if there is $y \in \Gamma^+(x)$ such that $f'(x, y)$ is odd then
      - $\cdot$ $f'(x, y) \leftarrow f'(x, y) + 1$
      - $\cdot$ $x \leftarrow y$
    - * else choose $y \in \Gamma^-(x)$ such that $f'(y, x)$ is odd
      - $\cdot$ $f'(y, x) \leftarrow f'(y, x) - 1$
      - $\cdot$ $x \leftarrow y$
- $\forall a \in A,\ \textbf{define } g(a) = \frac{f'(a)}{2}$

Output : $g : A \to \mathbb{N}$.

Lemma 1 (half flow). *Let f be a flow from s to t of even value $2v$. There is a flow g from s to t of value v such that $(f - 1) \leq 2g \leq (f + 1)$. This flow can be computed by Algorithm 2 in $O(|A|)$ steps.*

The proof of Lemma 1 is technical. It can be found in the full version of this paper.

4.1   Finding a Preliminary Flow

In this subsection, we describe an algorithm that finds a flow f such that the cut criterion is true for $((\kappa - f), (s_2, t_2, v_2), (t_2, s_2, v_2))$.

Algorithm 3 (first step)
$Input$: $G = (V, A)$; $\kappa : A \to \mathbb{N}$; $s_1, t_1, s_2, t_2 \in V$; $v_1, v_2 \in \mathbb{N}$.

  − *compute a flow $h \leq \kappa$ from s_2 to t_2 of value v_2*

Let h^r be the reverse flow from t_2 to s_2 of value v_2 (see definition 3).

  − *compute a flow $g \leq (\kappa + h^r - h)$ from s_1 to t_1 of value v_1*
  − *compute a flow $g' \leq (\kappa + h - h^r)$ from s_1 to t_1 of value v_1*
  − *using **Algorithm 2**, compute a flow f from s_1 to t_1 of value v_1 such that*
    $2f \leq (|g + g'| + 1)$

$Output$: $f : A \to \mathbb{N}$.

Lemma 2 (first step). *Let $\kappa : A \to \mathbb{N}$ be a symmetric capacity. Let s_1, t_1, $s_2, t_2 \in V$ and $v_1, v_2 \in \mathbb{N}$ such that the symmetric cut criterion is true for $(\kappa, (s_1, t_1, v_1), (s_2, t_2, v_2))$. Then there is a flow $f \leq \kappa$ from s_1 to t_1 of value v_1 such that the cut criterion is true for $((\kappa - f), (s_2, t_2, v_2), (t_2, s_2, v_2))$. This flow can be computed by Algorithm 3 in $3C_{flow} + O(|A|)$ steps.*

We divide the proof into two parts : first the algorithm completes, and then the output is correct.

Proposition 1. *If the symmetric cut criterion is true for $(\kappa, (s_1, t_1, v_1), (s_2, t_2, v_2))$, then Algorithm 3 completes in $3C_{flow} + O(|A|)$ steps.*

Proof. In the case of the existence of the flows, then any integral flow algorithm can find them.

  − if the symmetric cut criterion is true, then the flow h does exist.
  − in Ford and Fulkerson's algorithm, the capacity $(\kappa + h^r - h)$ is called the residual capacity once h has been computed. Since the cut criterion is true between $\{s_1, s_2\}$ and $\{t_1, t_2\}$, one can increment the flow between $\{s_1, s_2\}$ and $\{t_1, t_2\}$ by v_1 and so find a flow g from s_1 to t_1 of value v_1 with the residual capacity. That is $g \leq (\kappa + h^r - h)$.
  − in the same manner, $(\kappa + h - h^r)$ is the residual capacity once removed the flow h^r, so g' can be found.
  − according to Lemma 1, f is found by Algorithm 2.

This algorithm computes 3 flows, calls Algorithm 2 one time and computes two capacity functions, so this algorithm takes $3C_{flow} + O(|A|)$ steps.

Proposition 2. *If the symmetric cut criterion is true for $(\kappa, (s_1, t_1, v_1), (s_2, t_2, v_2))$, then the flow f given by Algorithm 3 is such that the cut criterion for $((\kappa - f), (s_2, t_2, v_2), (t_2, s_2, v_2))$ is true.*

Proof. First, observe that $(g + g') \leq 2\kappa$, so we have $f \leq \kappa$. Before considering $(\kappa - f)$, we will give two lower bounds to the function $(\kappa - |g + g'|) : A \to \mathbb{Z}$. Those bounds will enable us to control $(\kappa - f)$ over a cut.

We computed g' in order to have $g' \leq (\kappa + h - h^r)$; thus we have $(\kappa - g') \geq (h^r - h)$ and this leads to $(\kappa - (g + g')) \geq (h^r - h - g)$. Now, consider $(x, y) \in A$ such that $g(y, x) > 0$:

- if $|g + g'|(x, y) = g'(x, y) - g(y, x)$, then $(\kappa - |g + g'|)(x, y) = \kappa(x, y) - g'(x, y) + g(y, x)$ so $(\kappa - |g + g'|)(x, y) \geq (h^r - h + g^r)(x, y)$.
- otherwise, $|g + g'|(x, y) = 0$, so $(\kappa - |g + g'|)(x, y) = \kappa(x, y)$. Since $g \leq \kappa + h^r - h$, we have $\kappa(y, x) \geq g(y, x) + h(y, x) - h(x, y)$, so $(\kappa - |g + g'|)(x, y) \geq (h^r - h + g^r)(x, y)$.

Since $g(x, y)$ and $g(y, x)$ can not be non null at the same time, we have $(\kappa - |g + g'|) \geq (h^r - h - g + g^r)$. By a symmetric argument, we have as well $(\kappa - |g + g'|) \geq (h - h^r - g' + g'^r)$.

With these bounds, we can now consider a cut $C \subset V$ with, for instance, $s_2 \in C$ and $t_2 \notin C$. We will prove that $(\kappa - f)(C) \geq v_2$. We know that $(\kappa - |g + g'|)(C) \geq (h - h^r - g' + g'^r)(C)$, so $(\kappa - |g + g'|)(C) \geq v_2 + (g'^r - g')(C)$.

- if $t_1 \in C$ or $s_1 \notin C$, then $g'(C) \leq g'^r(C)$ and $(\kappa - |g + g'|)(C) \geq v_2$ so $(\kappa - f)(C) \geq v_2)$.
- otherwise, $s_1 \in C$ and $t_1 \notin C$ so $g'(C) = g'^r(C) + v_1$ and $(\kappa - |g + g'|)(C) \geq v_2 - v_1$. In this case we have also $|g + g'|(C) = |g + g'|^r(C) + 2v_1$ and $f(C) = f^r(C) + v_1$, so $f(C) \leq |g + g'|^r(C) + v_1$ which implies $f(C) \leq |g + g'|(C) - v_1$. Thus $(\kappa - f)(C) \geq v_2$

Therefore, the cut criterion is true for $((\kappa - f), (s_2, t_2, v_2))$. By a symmetric argument, it is also true for $((\kappa - f), (t_2, s_2, v_2))$.

4.2   Finding Two of the Four Flows

Although the cut criterion is true for $((\kappa - f), (s_2, t_2, v_2), (t_2, s_2, v_2))$, it may not be sufficient to guarantee the existence of a flow h from s_2 to t_2 of value v_2 and a flow h' from t_2 to s_2 of value v_2 such that $(f + h + h') \leq \kappa$. That is why f is not part of the final solution.

However, f is useful to compute the final flows f_2 and f_{-2} for the second commodity.

Algorithm 4 (second step)
Input : $G = (V, A)$, $\kappa : A \to \mathbb{N}$; $s_2, t_2 \in V$; $v_2 \in \mathbb{N}$; $f : A \to \mathbb{N}$.
Let f^r be the reverse flow from t_1 to s_1 of value v_1.

- compute a flow $h \leq (\kappa - f)$ from s_2 to t_2 of value v_2
- compute a flow $h' \leq (\kappa - f^r)$ from s_2 to t_2 of value v_2
- using **Algorithm 2**, compute a flow f_2 from s_2 to t_2 of value v_2 such that $(|h + h'| - 1) \leq 2f_2 \leq (|h + h'| + 1)$.

Let $f_{-2}^r = (|h + h'| - f_2)$. We call f_{-2} the reverse flow from t_2 to s_2 of value v_2.
Output : $f_2 : A \to \mathbb{N}$; $f_{-2} : A \to \mathbb{N}$.

Lemma 3 (second step). *Let $\kappa : A \to \mathbb{N}$ be a symmetric capacity. Let $s_1, t_1, s_2, t_2 \in V$ and $v_1, v_2 \in \mathbb{N}$. Let $f \leq \kappa$ be a flow from s_1 to t_1 of value v_1 such that the cut criterion is true for $((\kappa - f), (s_2, t_2, v_2), (t_2, s_2, v_2))$. Then there are two flows f_2 from s_2 to t_2 of value v_2 and f_{-2} from t_2 to s_2 of value v_2 such that $(f_2 + f_{-2}) \leq \kappa$ and such that the cut criterion is true for $((\kappa - f_2 - f_{-2}), (s_1, t_1, v_1))$. These two flows can be computed by Algorithm 4 in $2C_{flow} + O(|A|)$ steps.*

We divide the proof into three parts : first the algorithm completes, then $(f_2 + f_{-2}) \leq \kappa$, and finally the cut criterion is true for $((\kappa - f_2 - f_{-2}), (s_1, t_1, v_1))$.

Proposition 3. *If the cut criterion is true for $((\kappa - f), (s_2, t_2, v_2), (t_2, s_2, v_2))$, then Algorithm 4 completes in $2C_{flow} + O(|A|)$ steps.*

Proof. If the cut criterion is true for $((\kappa - f), (s_2, t_2, v_2), (t_2, s_2, v_2))$, then the flows h and h' do exist. $|h + h'|$ is a flow from s_2 to t_2 of value $2 \times v_2$, so according to lemma 1, the flow f_2 can be computed by Algorithm 2. This algorithm computes 2 flows, calls Algorithm 2 and computes 4 functions so it completes in $(2C_{flow} + O(|A|))$ steps.

Proposition 4. *The flows f_2 and f_{-2} given by Algorithm 4 are such that $(f_2 + f_{-2}) \leq \kappa$.*

Proof. We know that $2f_2 \leq (|h + h'| + 1)$ and $2f^r_{-2} \leq (|h + h'| + 1)$. Since $|h + h'| \leq 2\kappa$, we have $f_2 \leq \kappa$ and $f_{-2} \leq \kappa$. Moreover, $(f_2 + f^r_{-2}) = |h + h'|$ implies that $\forall (x, y) \in A$, if $f_2(x, y) > 0$, then $f^r_{-2}(y, x) = 0$, so $f_{-2}(x, y) = 0$. Thus $(f_2 + f_{-2}) \leq \kappa$.

Proposition 5. *If $f \leq \kappa$ is a flow from s_1 to t_1 of value v_1, the flows f_2 and f_{-2} given by Algorithm 4 are such that the cut criterion for $((\kappa - f_2 - f_{-2}), (s_1, t_1, v_1))$ is true.*

Proof. Consider a cut $C \subset V$ such that $s_1 \in C$ and $t_1 \notin C$. First we will prove that $(|h + h'|(C) + |h + h'|(V \backslash C)) \leq (2\kappa(C) - 2v_1)$. This implies $((f_2 + f_{-2})(C) + (f_2 + f_{-2})(V \backslash C)) \leq (2\kappa(C) - 2v_1)$. Then we will prove that $(f_2 + f_{-2})(C) \leq (\kappa(C) - v_1)$.

We split $|h + h'|$ into two functions : g (the part related to h) and g' (the part related to h') so $g = \min(h, |h + h'|)$ and $g' = \min(h', |h + h'|)$. We call r the symmetric function $r = (h + h') - |h + h'|$. Observe that if $g(x, y) > 0$ then $g'(y, x) = 0$ and if $g'(x, y) > 0$ then $g(y, x) = 0$. Moreover, for every (x, y), $g(x, y) + r(x, y) + f(x, y) \leq \kappa(x, y)$ and $g'^r(x, y) + r(x, y) + f(x, y) \leq \kappa(x, y)$, so we are able to conclude that $(g + g'^r + r) \leq (\kappa - f)$. Since h and h'^r are flows that go in opposite directions, we have $(h(C) - h(V \backslash C)) = (h'^r(V \backslash C) - h'^r(C))$. This implies $(h + h'^r)(C) = (h^r + h')(C)$, so $(g + g'^r + 2r)(C) \geq (g^r + g')(C)$. It follows that $(g + g'^r + g^r + g')(C) \leq 2(g + g'^r + r)(C)$, thus $|h + h'|(C) + |h + h'|(V \backslash C) \leq (2\kappa(C) - 2v_1)$.

Since $(f_2 + f^r_{-2}) = |h + h'|$, we have as well $(f_2 + f^r_{-2})(C) + (f_2 + f^r_{-2})(V \backslash C) \leq (2\kappa(C) - 2v_1)$, so $(f_2 + f_{-2})(C) + (f_2 + f_{-2})(V \backslash C) \leq (2\kappa(C) - 2v_1)$.

Like h and h', the flows f_2 and f_{-2} go in opposite directions, so $(f_2 + f_{-2})(C) = (f_2 + f_{-2})(V \backslash C)$. Therefore $(f_2 + f_{-2})(C) \leq (\kappa(C) - v_1)$.

4.3   Finding the Last Two Flows

Once f_2 and f_{-2} have been properly computed, the algorithm to find f_1 and f_{-1} is quite straightforward.

Algorithm 5 (third step)
Input : $G = (V, A)$, $\kappa : A \to \mathbb{N}$; $s_1, t_1 \in V$; $v_1 \in \mathbb{N}$; $f_2 : A \to \mathbb{N}$; $f_{-2} : A \to \mathbb{N}$.

— *compute a flow* $f_1 \leq (\kappa - f_2 - f_{-2})$ *from* s_1 *to* t_1 *of value* v_1

Let $f_{-1} = (\kappa - f_1 - f_2 - f_{-2})$
Output : $f_1 : A \to \mathbb{N}$; $f_{-1} : A \to \mathbb{N}$.

Lemma 4 (third step). *If (f_2, f_{-2}) is a two-commodity flow from (s_2, t_2) to (t_2, s_2) of value (v_2, v_2) such that $(f_2 + f_{-2}) \leq \kappa$, and if the cut criterion is true for $((\kappa - f_2 - f_{-2}), (s_1, t_1, v_1))$, then Algorithm 5 completes in $C_{flow} + O(|A|)$ steps, and its output are two flows f_1 from s_1 to t_1 of value v_1 and f_{-1} from t_1 to s_1 of value v_1 such that $(f_1 + f_{-1} + f_2 + f_{-2}) \leq \kappa$.*

Proof. If the cut criterion is true for $((\kappa - f_2 - f_{-2}), (s_1, t_1, v_1))$, then the flow f_1 does exist. So Algorithm 5 takes $C_{flow} + O(|A|)$ steps. Now observe that the function $(\kappa - f_1 - f_2 - f_{-2}) : A \to \mathbb{N}$ is a flow from t_1 to s_1 of value v_1 (see definition **??**), though it may have some loops (which could be easily removed in C_{flow} more steps).

4.4   Summary

Theorem 1 (symmetric 2-commodity flow). *The symmetric cut criterion is a necessary and sufficient condition for the existence of a solution to the Integral Symmetric 2-Commodity Flow Problem. A solution can be found by Algorithm 1 in $6C_{flow} + O(|A|)$ steps.*

Proof. According to corollary 1, the symmetric cut criterion is a necessary condition for the existence of a solution to our problem. The input is:

— a symmetric digraph $G = (V, A)$;
— a symmetric capacity $\kappa : A \to \mathbb{N}$;
— the source and the target $(s_1, s_2), (t_1, t_2) \in V^2$;
— the value $(v_1, v_2) \in \mathbb{N}^2$.

If the symmetric cut criterion is true for $(\kappa, (s_1, t_1, v_1), (s_2, t_2, v_2))$ then according to Lemma 2, Algorithm 3 takes $3C_{flow} + O(|A|)$ steps ; according to Lemma 3, Algorithm 4 takes $2C_{flow} + O(|A|)$ steps and according to Lemma 4, Algorithm 5 takes $C_{flow} + O(|A|)$ steps ; so Algorithm 1 completes in $6C_{flow} + O(|A|)$ steps.

Moreover according to Lemmas 2, 3 and 4 the 4-commodity flow $(f_1, f_{-1}, f_2, f_{-2})$ computed by Algorithm 1 is a symmetric 2-commodity flow from (s_1, s_2) to (t_1, t_2) of value (v_1, v_2) such that $(f_1 + f_{-1} + f_2 + f_{-2}) \leq \kappa$, so it is a solution to the problem.

5 Conclusion

We have proven that the Integral Symmetric 2-Commodity Flow Problem can be solved in polynomial time. Interesting ways for further research deal with the complexity of the Integral Symmetric MCF (likely NP-complete), and with Integral Symmetric k-Commodity Flow Problems, with $k > 2$.

Further, if the requests are not symmetric, the complexity of Integral k-Commodity Flow Problems in symmetric digraphs (with a symmetric capacity) is also open for $k > 1$.

Acknowledgment. This work was supported in part by the European Union under IST FET Project CRESCO and Improving RTN Project ARACNE.

The colleagues of the author would like to thank him for keeping in mind the meaning of "fullpage" LaTeX package.

References

1. Pascal Chanas. *Réseaux ATM : Conception et optimisation.* PhD thesis, Université de Grenoble, June 1998. France Télécom CNET.
2. S. Even, A. Itai, and A. Shamir. On the complexity of timetable and multicommodity flow problems. *SIAM J. Comput.*, 5(4):691–703, December 1976.
3. L.R. Ford and D.R. Fulkerson. *Flows in Networks.* Princeton University Press, 1962.
4. Steven Fortune, John Hopcroft, and James Wyllie. The directed subgraph homeomorphism problem. *Theoretical Computer Science*, (10):111–121, 1980.
5. A. Jarry and S. Pérennes. Disjoint Paths in Symmetric Digraphs. In *International Colloquium on Structural Information and Communication Complexity – SIROCCO*, pages 211–222, Andros, Greece, June 2002. Carleton.
6. R.M. Karp. On the complexity of combinatorial problems. *Networks*, (5):45–68, 1975.
7. H. Okamura and P.D. Seymour. Multicommodity flows in planar graphs. *Journal of Combinatorial Theory*, B(31):75–81, 1981.
8. N. Robertson and P. D. Seymour. Graph Minors XIII. The Disjoint Paths Problem. *J. Combin. Theory Ser. B 63*, pages 65–110, 1995.
9. E. Tardos. A strongly polynomial algorithm to solve combinatorial linear programs. *Operation Research*, 34:250–256, 1986.
10. Jens Vygen. Disjoint paths. Technical Report 94816, Research Institute for Discrete Mathematics, University of Bonn, February 1994. updated September 1998.
11. Jens Vygen. NP-Completeness of Some Edge-Disjoint Paths Problems. *Discrete Applied Mathematics*, (61):83–90, 1995.
12. D. Wagner and K. Weihe. A linear-time algorithm for edge-disjoint paths in planar graphs. *Combinatorica*, 1(15):135–150, 1995.

Efficient Algorithms for Low-Energy Bounded-Hop Broadcast in Ad-Hoc Wireless Networks

(Extended Abstract)

Christoph Ambühl[1][*], Andrea E.F. Clementi[2], Miriam Di Ianni[2],
Nissan Lev-Tov[3][**], Angelo Monti[4], David Peleg[3][**],
Gianluca Rossi[2][* * *], and Riccardo Silvestri[4]

[1] Instituto Dalle Molle di Studi sull'Intelligenza Artificiale
Galleria 2, 6928 Manno - SWITZERLAND
christoph@idsia.ch

[2] Dipartimento di Matematica, Università degli Studi di Roma "Tor Vergata"
Via della Ricerca Scientifica 1, 00133 Roma - ITALY
{clementi,diianni,rossig}@mat.uniroma2.it

[3] Department of Computer Science and Applied Mathematics,
The Weizmann Institute of Science Rehovot, 76100 - ISRAEL.
{nissan.lev-tov,david.peleg}@weizmann.ac.il

[4] Dipartimento di Informatica, Università degli Studi di Roma "La Sapienza"
Via Salaria 113, 00198 Roma - ITALY
{monti,silver}@dsi.uniroma1.it

Abstract. The paper studies the problem of computing a minimal energy cost range assignment in a *ad-hoc wireless network* which allows a station s to perform a broadcast operation in at most h hops. The general version of the problem (i.e., when transmission costs are arbitrary) is known to be `log`-APX hard even for $h = 2$. The current paper considers the well-studied real case in which n stations are located on the plane and the cost to transmit from station i to station j is proportional to the α-th power of the distance between station i and j, where α is any positive constant. A polynomial-time algorithm is presented for finding an optimal range assignment to perform a 2-hop broadcast from a given source station. The algorithm relies on dynamic programming and operates in (worst-case) time $O(n^7)$. Then, a polynomial-time approximation scheme (PTAS) is provided for the above problem for any fixed $h \geq 1$. For fixed $h \geq 1$ and $\epsilon > 0$, the PTAS has time complexity $O(n^\mu)$ where $\mu = O((\alpha 2^\alpha h^\alpha / \epsilon)^{\alpha^h})$.

[*] Supported by the Swiss National Science Foundation project 200021-100539/1, "Approximation Algorithms for Machine Scheduling Through Theory and Experiments". Results obtained while the author stayed at Università di Roma "Tor Vergata" in Italy supported by the European Union under the RTN Project ARACNE.
[**] Partially supported by a grant from the Israel Ministry of Industry and Commerce.
[* * *] Supported by the European Union under the IST FET Project CRESCCO.

1   Introduction

Multi-hop wireless networks [13] require neither fixed, wired infrastructure nor predetermined interconnectivity. In particular, *ad hoc* networking [11] is the most popular type of multi-hop wireless networks because of its simplicity. An *ad-hoc* wireless network consists of a homogeneous system of radio stations connected by wireless links. In an ad hoc network, every station is assigned a transmission range. The overall range assignment determines a transmission (directed) graph since one station s can transmit to another station t if and only if t is within the transmission range of s. The transmission range of a station depends, in turn, on the energy power supplied to the station. In particular, the power P_s required by a station s to correctly transmit data to another station t must satisfy the inequality

$$\frac{P_s}{\text{dist}(s,t)^\alpha} > \gamma \tag{1}$$

where $\text{dist}(s,t)$ is the Euclidean distance between s and t, $\alpha \geq 1$ is the *distance-power gradient*, and $\gamma \geq 1$ is the *transmission quality* parameter. In an ideal environment (i.e., in empty space) it holds that $\alpha = 2$ but it may vary from 1 to more than 6 depending on the environment conditions at the location of the network (see [14]).

The fundamental problem underlying any phase of a dynamic resource allocation algorithm in ad-hoc wireless networks is the following. Find a transmission range assignment such that (1) the corresponding transmission graph satisfies a given connectivity property Π, and (2) the overall energy power required to deploy the assignment (according to Inequality (1)) is minimized (see for example [9,12]). In [6], the reader may find an exhaustive survey on the previous results related to the above problem.

In this paper we address the case in which Π is defined as follows: *Given a set of stations and a specific source station s, the transmission graph has to contain a directed spanning tree rooted at s (a branching from s) of depth at most h. The relevance of this case is due to the fact that any transmission graph satisfying the above property allows the source station to perform a *broadcast* operation in at most h hops. Broadcast is a task initiated by the source station which transmits a message to all stations in the wireless network. This task constitutes a major part of real life multi-hop radio networks [1,2,9].

Previous results. The broadcast range assignment problem described above is a special case of the following optimization problem, called h-MINIMUM EN-ERGY CONSUMPTION BROADCAST SUBGRAPH (in short, h-MECBS). Given a weighted directed graph $G = (V, E)$ with $|V| = n$ and an edge weight function $w : E \to \mathbb{R}^+$, a *range assignment* for G is a function $r : V \to \mathbb{R}^+$; the *transmission (directed) graph* induced by G and r is defined as $G_r = (V, E')$ where

$$E' = \bigcup_{v \in V} \{(v, u) : (v, u) \in E \land w(v, u) \leq r(v)\}.$$

The h-MECBS problem is then defined as follows. Given a *source node* $s \in V$, find a range assignment r for G such that G_r contains a directed spanning tree of G rooted at s of depth at most h and $\text{cost}(r) = \sum_{v \in V} r(v)$ is minimized.

The h-MECBS problem is NP-hard and, if $P \neq NP$, it is not approximable within a sub-logarithmic factor, even when the problem is restricted to undirected graphs [10] and $h = 2$.

The intractability of the general version of h-MECBS does not necessarily imply the same hardness result for its restriction to wireless networks. In particular, let us consider, for any $d \geq 1$ and $\alpha \geq 1$, the family of graphs N_d^α, called *(d-dimensional) wireless networks*, defined as follows. A complete (undirected) graph G belongs to N_d^α if it can be embedded in a d-dimensional Euclidean space such that the weight of an edge is equal to the α-th power of the Euclidean distance between the two endpoints of the edge itself. The restriction of h-MECBS to graphs in N_d^α is then denoted by h-MECBS[N_d^α]. It is clear that the previously described broadcast range assignment problem in the ideal 2-dimensional environment corresponds to h-MECBS[N_2^2].

Observe that if $\alpha = 1$ (that is, the edge weights coincide with the Euclidean distances), then the optimal range assignment is simply obtained by assigning to s the distance from the node farthest from it and assigning 0 to all other nodes. We then have that, for any $d \geq 1$ and $h \geq 1$, h-MECBS[N_d^1] is solvable in polynomial time. Moreover, it has also been shown that, for any $\alpha \geq 1$, h-MECBS[N_1^α] is solvable in polynomial time [7].

It is also possible to prove that, for any $d \geq 2$, $\alpha > 1$ and $h = n - 1$, h-MECBS[N_d^α] is NP-hard (this version is referred to as the unbounded case). The proof of this result is an adaptation of the one given in [8] to prove the NP-hardness of computing a minimum range assignment that guarantees the strong connectivity of the corresponding transmission graph. This adaptation is described in [4]. In [3,5] it is shown that, as for the unbounded case, whenever $\alpha \geq d$ the MST-based algorithm proposed in [9] achieves constant approximation. Given a graph $G \in N_2^\alpha$ and a specified source node s, the MST-based algorithm first computes a minimum spanning tree T of G (observe that this computation does not depend on the value of α). Subsequently, it makes T directed by rooting it at s. Finally, the algorithm assigns to each vertex v the maximum among the weights of all edges of T outgoing from v.

Our results. Bounding the number of hops in message broadcasting on a wireless network is a crucial issue for the QoS of the network. We thus aim to provide efficient solutions for the h-MECBS[N_2^2] problem when h is a "small" constant (i.e., independent from the network size). In particular, we provide the first polynomial-time algorithm that solves the 2-MECBS[N_2^α] problem for any $\alpha \geq 0$. The algorithm use a crossed dynamic programming to get an optimal solution. The dynamic programming is far from being simple and requires $O(n^7)$ time to fill up the relative matrices.

Then, we derive a polynomial-time approximation scheme (PTAS) that works for the h-MECBS[N_2^α], for any fixed constant $h > 1$. For fixed $h \geq 1$ and $\epsilon > 0$, the PTAS has time complexity $O(n^\mu)$ where $\mu = O((\alpha 2^\alpha h^\alpha / \epsilon)^{\alpha^h})$.

2   A Polynomial-Time Algorithm for the 2-MECBS on the Plane

In this section we describe a polynomial time algorithm for the 2-MECBS problem on the Euclidean plane. The stations are represented by points in the Euclidean plane. Let $\texttt{cost}(c, p)$ be the cost required of station c in order to cover station p with minimum power. We only require $\texttt{cost}$ to be a positive function for which $\texttt{cost}(c, r_1) \leq \texttt{cost}(c, r_2)$ if $\texttt{dist}(c, r_1) \leq \texttt{dist}(c, r_2)$ holds. This also includes the cost function mentioned in the introduction.

The input of the algorithm are n points in the Euclidean plane, a specified source station s and a cost function $\texttt{cost} : \{1, \dots, n\}^2 \mapsto \mathbb{R}$ with the above properties.

Our algorithm is based on a procedure that computes an optimal 2-broadcast range assignment for a fixed range of station s. Since the range of s in an optimal solution is defined by the farthest station f covered by the station s, we only have to invoke this procedure $n - 1$ times and take the best solution in order to solve the 2-MECBS problem.

In the rest of this section, we describe the procedure for a fixed source range. Since the range of s is fixed, we can define $\mathcal{P}$ as the set of stations covered by s. Let $\overline{\mathcal{P}}$ be the set of stations not covered by s. Let us rename the stations of $V \setminus \{s\}$ as $\{1, \dots, n-1\}$ such that the first $m = |\overline{\mathcal{P}}|$ stations are those in $\overline{\mathcal{P}}$, and they are ordered in clockwise order around the source station, starting with an arbitrary station in $\overline{\mathcal{P}}$. (The source station is still denoted by s.)

Definition 1. *Let the interval* $[l, r]$ *denote the set of stations* i *such that* $l \leq i \leq r$.

Definition 2. *For an interval* I, *let* $A(I)$ *be the minimum cost required to cover all the stations in* I *by stations from* $\mathcal{P}$.

According to the above definition, the value we are looking for in our procedure is $A([1, m]) + \texttt{cost}(s, f)$ where f is the station defining the source range. Consider an optimal covering of the interval $[l, r]$ expressed by the ranges of all stations in $\mathcal{P}$. Geometrically, this solution is represented as an arrangement $\mathcal{A}$ of disks, in which every disk represents the range of the station in its center. Denote by Δ the set of points contained in these disks. The disk of a station c in the arrangement is denoted by Δ_c.

An alternative representation of $\mathcal{A}$ is to assign to each station $p \in \overline{\mathcal{P}}$ the station in $\mathcal{P}$ that reaches p. In general, there may be many ways to define such an assignment. We do it by the λ function defined below.

Definition 3. *For* $i \in \overline{\mathcal{P}}$, *let* $\beta(i)$ *be the last point in* Δ *on the ray* $\bar{p}$ *emerging from* s *in the direction of* i. *Define* $\lambda(i)$ *to be the station in* $\mathcal{P}$ *whose disk contains* $\beta(i)$. *If there is more than one, choose an arbitrary one. Let* σ *denote the segment* $s\beta(i)$.

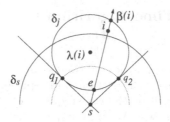

Fig. 1. Point i is always between e and $\beta(i)$

Note that $\beta(i)$ is on the border of some disk in the arrangement, and is not necessarily a station.

In order for λ to be a valid assignment, it is necessary to show the following.

Lemma 1. *In the arrangement $\mathcal{A}$, station i is contained in the range of station $\lambda(i)$.*

Proof. Clearly, $i \in \sigma$. If $s \in \Delta_j$, then the entire segment σ is contained in Δ_j and we are done. Otherwise, consider Fig. 1. Let e be the point in which the ray $\bar{\rho}$ enters Δ_j. We just have to prove that $e \in \Delta_s$. Let q_1 and q_2 be the intersection points of the tangents from s to Δ_j. The lemma follows since $\mathtt{dist}(s, e) \leq \mathtt{dist}(s, q_1) = \mathtt{dist}(s, q_2) \leq \mathtt{dist}(s, j)$ and $j \in \Delta_s$. This also proves that the entire segment σ is contained in Δ. $\square$

If $j = \lambda(i)$, we say that i is λ-*covered* by j. By using the λ-assignment, we now establish the following lemma which states that the cost of $\mathcal{A}$ can be obtained by combining optimal solutions of smaller intervals, thus allowing the use of dynamic programming.

Lemma 2. *There exist stations $c \in \mathcal{P}$, $p \in \overline{\mathcal{P}}$ and subintervals $J_1, \ldots J_t$ of $[l, r]$ such that the cost of $\mathcal{A}$ can be expressed as*

$$\mathtt{cost}(c, p) + \sum_{k=1}^{t} A(J_k).$$

Towards proving the lemma, we identify some properties of the arrangement. Let $D(c, p)$ be a disk of the arrangement with center c and radius $\mathtt{dist}(c, p)$, $c \neq p$. Let $[l, r]$ be the smallest interval that contains all stations that are λ-covered by c. Let I^- be the set of stations in $[l, r]$ that are not λ-covered by c. Let $J_1, \ldots, J_t$ be the partition of I^- into intervals such that i and j are in the same interval if and only if there is no station $q \in [i, j]$ which is λ-covered by c. For $1 \leq k \leq t$, define M_k to be the set of stations in $\mathcal{P}$ which λ-cover some station in J_k. The partitioning $J_1, \ldots, J_t$ has two key properties (whose proof is deferred to the full paper).

Proposition 1.
(P1) For every $1 \leq k \leq t$, no station in J_k is λ-covered by station c.
(P2) $M_i \cap M_j = \emptyset$ for every $1 \leq i < j \leq t$.

Proof of Lemma 2. We clearly have to pay the cost of the range of c, denoted by $\mathrm{cost}(c,p)$. For the second part, consider a set J_k. Let $\mathcal{A}_k$ be the optimal solution for covering the stations in J_k. Assume the cost of $\mathcal{A}_k$ was strictly smaller than the sum of the cost of the stations in M_k. Because of Property (P2), we could remove the ranges of the stations in M_k from $\mathcal{A}$ and add the ranges of $\mathcal{A}_k$. This new solution would be cheaper than the previous one, which is a contradiction to the optimality of $\mathcal{A}$. □

Let $S([l,r],c,p)$ be the set of stations in interval $[r,l]$ which are *not* covered by $D(c,p)$. In order to make use of Lemma 2, we have to solve the problem of finding the $J_1, \ldots, J_t$ for given $[l,r]$, c, and p. This is a kind of one-dimensional set covering problem: We have to find a set $\mathcal{N}$ of subintervals of $[l,r]$ such that any station in $S([l,r],c,p)$ is contained in at least one interval of $\mathcal{N}$ and $\sum_{J \in \mathcal{N}} A(J)$ is minimized.

Let $B([l,r],c,p)$ be the cost of the optimal covering of the stations in $S([l,r],c,p)$. Note that $A(J) \leq A(J')$ if $J \subseteq J'$. This implies that the sets in $\mathcal{N}$ can be chosen such that they do not intersect then $B([l,r],c,p) = B([l+1,r],c,p)$ if $l \in D(c,p)$ and $B([l,r],c,p) = B([l,r-1],c,p)$ if $r \in D(c,p)$. The general case comes from the fact that an optimal partitioning is composed of a first interval $[l,k]$ (which will have $k \in S([l,r],c,p)$) and an optimal partitioning of the remaining interval $[k+1,r]$ then

$$B([l,r],c,p) = \min_{k \in S([l,r],c,p)} \{A([l,k]) + B([k+1,r],c,p)\}.$$

Finally, $B([l,r],c,p) = 0$ for $l > r$ or $S([l,r],c,p) = \emptyset$.

Having $B([l,r],c,p)$ at hand, $A([l,r])$ can be computed considering the optimal partitioning for all pairs of c,p:

$$A([l,r]) = \min_{c \in \mathcal{P}, p \in \overline{\mathcal{P}} \mid l \in D(c,p)} B([l+1,r],c,p) + \mathrm{cost}(c,p).$$

The tables must be filled alternatingly starting with the smallest intervals. Since $B([l,r],c,p)$ might use $A([l,r])$, the latter should be computed first. The optimal value can be found in $A([l,r])$. The running time of the algorithm is $O(n^7)$.

3   A PTAS for Any Constant h

The set of n stations is specified by the set of points $X = \{x_1, \ldots, x_n\}$ in the Euclidean plane, where $x_1 = s$. Without loss of generality assume that the points are ordered by their distance from s, and in particular, x_n is the point farthest from s, and let $R = \mathrm{dist}(s, x_n)$. Every range assignment induces the set of disks

$\{D(x_1), \dots, D(x_n)\}$, each with center x_i and radius $r(x_i)$. If $r(x_i) > 0$, we say that the disk $D(x_i)$ *belongs* to the assignment. For every two points $x_i, x_j \in X$, a *path* from x_i to x_j in the assignment is an ordered set of disks $\{D_1, \dots, D_k\}$ belonging to the range assignment with centers $y_1, \dots, y_k$ respectively, such that $y_1 = x_i$, $x_j \in D_k$ and $y_i \in D_{i-1}$ for each $i = 2, \dots, k$. A *minimum hop path* from x_i to x_j is a path containing a minimum number of disks among all paths from x_i to x_j. In an h-broadcast assignment, the radii must be assigned such that for every $2 \le i \le n$, there exists a path containing at most h disks from s to x_i. Let S^* be an optimal solution to the problem, and denote its cost by C^*.

For every $\epsilon > 0$, let $k = \alpha 2^\alpha h^\alpha / \epsilon$. Define the sequence $\{k_i\}_{i=2}^h$ where $k_2 = k$ and $k_{i+1} = k \cdot k_i^\alpha$ for each $i = 2, \dots, h - 1$.

Notice that in any optimal solution, the disk around any point x_j is of radius $\mathrm{dist}(x_j, x_i)$ for some $1 \le i \le n$. For $2 \le i \le n$, let D_i be the disk of radius $\mathrm{dist}(s, x_i)$ centered at s. A range assignment is called a *principal h-Broadcast* if it consists of one such disk D_i around s, for some $2 \le i \le n$, plus up to k_h^α disks around other points, each of radius at least R/k_h.

Our algorithm operates as follows. For given fixed ϵ and h, if $\epsilon > h^{\alpha-1}$ then the algorithm returns a single disk of radius R centered at s. Otherwise, the algorithm examines all principal h-Broadcasts, and outputs the one attaining the minimal cost.

3.1   Analysis

We first observe that the algorithm is polynomial for fixed ϵ and h. For fixed $h \ge 1$ and $\epsilon > 0$, its time complexity is $O(n^\mu)$ where $\mu = O((\alpha 2^\alpha h^\alpha / \epsilon)^{\alpha^h})$.

Our approximation ratio analysis is based on the observation that the *single disk* solution, obtained by taking a single disk of radius R centered at s, yields a constant approximation to the optimal solution. (The proof is deferred to the full version of the paper.)

Lemma 3. *The single disk solution provides an approximation of ratio $h^{\alpha-1}$, namely, $R^\alpha \le h^{\alpha-1} \cdot C^*$.*

We now prove that the cost of the solution produced by our algorithm is at most $(1+\epsilon)C^*$. Notice that if $\epsilon > h^{\alpha-1}$, then the single disk solution generated by the algorithm attains the desired bound trivially from Lemma 3. Hence hereafter we assume that $\epsilon \le h^{\alpha-1}$.

Consider the disks that belong to the optimal solution S^*. For each such disk $D^*(x)$, define its *level* to be the number of disks in the minimum hop path from s to x. Define a disk $D^*(x)$ of level j, $2 \le j \le h$, to be *large* if $r^*(x) \ge R/k_j$, otherwise it is *small*. For uniformity, define also the disk $D^*(s)$ to be large. For each level $j \ge 1$, let m_j be the number of large disks of level j in the optimal solution S^*. (Always $m_1 = 1$.) Thus the large disks of level j contribute at least $m_j R^\alpha / k_j^\alpha$ to C^*, the cost of the optimal solution. As C^* cannot exceed the cost of the single disk solution, namely R^α, we have the following.

Proposition 2. *For each level $j \ge 2$, $m_j \le k_j^\alpha$.*

Also, noting that every large disk of level $j \geq 2$ has radius at least R/k_h, we have the following.

Proposition 3. S^* *contains at most k_h^α large disks.*

Now, consider the range assignment $\hat{S}$ derived from S^* in the following way. For each large disk $D^*(x)$ in S^*, let $f(x)$ be the farthest point from x of higher level than x for which there is a minimum hop path from x to $f(x)$ that contains only small disks (other than $D^*(x)$). For each large disk $D^*(x)$ in S^*, let $\hat{r}(x) = \mathtt{dist}(x, f(x))$ and let $\varphi(D^*(x))$ be the disk of radius $\hat{r}(x)$ around x. We now take $\hat{S}$ to contain the disk $\varphi(D^*(x))$ for every large disk $D^*(x)$ in S^*.

Since the minimum hop path from x to $f(x)$ contains at most $h - 1$ disks of increasing levels, which are all small to their level, $\mathtt{dist}(x, f(x)) \leq \sum_{\ell=1}^{h-1} \frac{R}{k_{j+\ell}}$, and as $R/k_j > h \cdot R/k_{j+1}$ by the choice of k and the assumption that $\epsilon \leq h^{\alpha-1}$, we have the following.

Proposition 4. *For every large disk $D^*(x)$ in S^* of level j:*

1. *If $2 \leq j \leq h - 1$ then $\hat{r}(x) \leq r^*(x) + 2R/k_{j+1}$.*
2. *If $j = h$ then $\hat{r}(x) = r^*(x)$.*

Lemma 4. *The assignment $\hat{S}$ is a principal h-broadcast.*

Proof. By Proposition 3, $\hat{S}$ contains at most k_h^α disks, all of which (except maybe the one centered at s) have radius at least R/k_h. It remains to argue that every point $x \in X$ is reachable by a path of h or fewer hops. Consider such a point x and suppose a minimum hop path from s to x in S^* is established by the disks $D_1^*, \ldots, D_\ell^*$, where $\ell \leq h$. Note that the minimality of the path ensures that the level of each of the disks D_j^* is exactly j. Each small disk D_i^* in this list is now contained in the large disk $\varphi(D_j^*) \in \hat{S}$ such that D_j^* is the closest large disk in S^* preceding D_i^* in the list. Therefore the number of hops in the path to x in $\hat{S}$ is no greater than in S^*.   □

We thus conclude that the assignment $\hat{S}$ was checked by our algorithm. We now bound the cost of this assignment, denoted $\hat{C}$. For each $j \geq 1$ and $i = 1, \ldots, m_j$, let $r_{i,j}$ be the radii of the large disks of level j. Then $\hat{C}$ satisfies

$$\hat{C} \leq \sum_{j=1}^{h-1} \sum_{i=1}^{m_j} \left(r_{i,j} + \frac{2R}{k_{j+1}} \right)^\alpha + \sum_{i=1}^{m_h} r_{i,h}^\alpha. \tag{2}$$

We rely on the following technical fact (which can be verified, say, by looking at the Taylor expansion of the function $(1 + z)^\alpha$).

Fact 1. *For $\alpha > 1$ and $0 < z \leq 1$, $(1 + z)^\alpha \leq 1 + \alpha z (1 + z)^{\alpha-1}$.*

Proposition 5. $\left(r_{i,j} + \frac{2R}{k_{j+1}} \right)^\alpha \leq r_{i,j}^\alpha + \frac{\alpha 2^\alpha R^\alpha}{k_{j+1}}$.

Proof. Note that $r_{i,j} > 2R/k_{j+1}$ for every i and j, so $z = \frac{2R}{k_{j+1}r_{i,j}}$ satisfies $0 < z < 1$. This allows us to use Fact 1 and get

$$\left(r_{i,j} + \frac{2R}{k_{j+1}}\right)^\alpha \le r_{i,j}^\alpha \left(1 + \frac{2R\alpha}{r_{i,j}k_{j+1}}\left(1 + \frac{2R}{r_{i,j}k_{j+1}}\right)^{\alpha-1}\right)$$
$$= r_{i,j}^\alpha + \frac{2R\alpha}{k_{j+1}}\left(r_{i,j} + \frac{2R}{k_{j+1}}\right)^{\alpha-1} \le r_{i,j}^\alpha + \frac{2R\alpha(2r_{i,j})^{\alpha-1}}{k_{j+1}}.$$

The thesis follows from by observing that $R \ge r_{i,j}$.   □

Combining Inequality (2) with Proposition 5 yields that

$$\hat{C} \le \sum_{i,j} r_{i,j}^\alpha + \sum_{j=1}^{h-1}\sum_{i=1}^{m_j} \frac{\alpha 2^\alpha R^\alpha}{k_{j+1}}.$$

As $C^* \ge \sum_{i,j} r_{i,j}^\alpha$, and using Proposition 2 and the definition of k_j,

$$\hat{C} \le C^* + \sum_{j=1}^{h-1}\left(k_j^\alpha \cdot \frac{\alpha 2^\alpha R^\alpha}{k_{j+1}}\right) < C^* + h\cdot\frac{\alpha 2^\alpha R^\alpha}{k} \le C^* + \epsilon\cdot C^*,$$

where the last inequality is established by the choice of k and Lemma 3. We have thus established the following.

Lemma 5. *The algorithm yields a solution of cost at most $(1+\epsilon)C^*$.*

4   Conclusions and Open Problems

In this paper we investigated the problem of computing a minimal cost range assignment in ad-hoc wireless networks that guarantees the broadcast operation from a given source station in at most h hops. We provide a polynomial-time algorithm for the case $h = 2$ and a PTAS for any constant $h \ge 1$. Nothing is known about the hardness of the case $h > 2$. We conjecture that there exists some constant h for which the problem is NP-hard. This is the main problem left open by this paper. Finally, nothing is known when h is any function of n (but $h = n - 1$).

References

1. R. Bar-Yehuda, O. Goldreich, and A. Itai. On the Time Complexity of Broadcast Operations in Multi-Hop Radio Networks: An Exponential Gap Between Determinism and Randomization. *J. of Computer and Systems Science*, 45:104–126, 1992.
2. R. Bar-Yehuda, A. Israeli, and A. Itai. Multiple Communication in Multi-Hop Radio Networks. *SIAM J. on Computing*, 22:875–887, 1993.

3. G. Călinescu, X.Y. Li, O. Frieder, and P.J. Wan. Minimum-Energy Broadcast Routing in Static Ad Hoc Wireless Networks. In *Proc. 20th Joint Conf. of IEEE Computer and Communications Societies (INFOCOM)*, 1162–1171, 2001.

4. A.E.F. Clementi, P. Crescenzi, P. Penna, G. Rossi, and P. Vocca. A Worst-case Analysis of an MST-based Heuristic to Construct Energy-Efficient Broadcast Trees in Wireless Networks. In *Proc. 3th Workshop on Wireles, Mobile and Ad-Hoc Networks (WMAN-IPDPS)*, 2003.

5. A.E.F. Clementi, P. Crescenzi, P. Penna, G. Rossi, and P. Vocca. On the Complexity of Computing Minimum Energy Consumption Broadcast Subgraphs. In *Proc. 18th Symp. on Theoretical Aspects of Computer Science (STACS)*, 121–131, 2001.

6. A.E.F. Clementi, G. Huiban, P. Penna, G. Rossi, and Y.C. Verhoeven. Some Recent Theoretical Advances and Open Questions on Energy Consumption in Ad-Hoc Wireless Networks. In *Proc. 3rd Workshop on Approximation and Randomization Algorithms in Communication Networks (ARACNE)*, 23–38, 2002.

7. A.E.F. Clementi, M. Di Ianni, and R. Silvestri. The Minimum Broadcast Range Assignment Problem on Linear Multi-Hop Wireless Networks. *Theoretical Computer Science*, 299:751–761, 2003.

8. A.E.F. Clementi, P. Penna, and R. Silvestri. Hardness Results for the Power Range Assignment Problem in Packet Radio Networks. In *Proc. 2nd Int. Workshop on Approximation Algorithms for Combinatorial Optimization Problems (APPROX)*, 197–208, 1999.

9. A. Ephremides, G.D. Nguyen, and J.E. Wieselthier. On the Construction of Energy-Efficient Broadcast and Multicast Trees in Wireless Networks. In *Proc. 19th Joint Conf. of IEEE Computer and Communications Societies (INFOCOM)*, 585–594, 2000.

10. S. Guha and S. Khuller. Improved Methods for Approximating Node Weighted Steiner Trees and Connected Dominating Sets. *Information and Computation*, 150:57–74, 1999.

11. Z. Haas and S. Tabrizi. On Some Challenges and Design Choices in Ad-Hoc Communications. In *Proc. IEEE Military Communication Conf. (MILCOM)*, 1998.

12. L. M. Kirousis, E. Kranakis, D. Krizanc, and A. Pelc. Power Consumption in Packet Radio Networks. *Theoretical Computer Science*, 243:289–305, 2000.

13. G.S. Lauer. *Packet radio routing*, Chapt. 11 of *Routing in communication networks*, M. Streenstrup (ed.), 351–396. Prentice-Hall, 1995.

14. K. Pahlavan and A. Levesque. *Wireless information networks*. Wiley-Interscience, 1995.

15. R. Raz and S. Safra. A Sub-Constant Error-Probability Low-Degree Test, and a Sub-Constant Error-Probability PCP Characterization of NP. In *Proc. 29th ACM Symp. on Theory of Computing (STOC)*, 475–484, 1997.

16. M. Sharir and P.K. Agarwal. *Davenport-Schinzel Sequences and Their Geometric Applications*. Cambridge University Press, Cambridge-New York-Melbourne, 1995.

On the Expressiveness of Deterministic Transducers over Infinite Trees[*]

Thomas Colcombet[1] and Christof Löding[2]

[1] Institute of Informatics, Warsaw University, Poland
thomas.colcombet@laposte.net
[2] Lehrstuhl Informatik VII, RWTH Aachen, Germany
loeding@informatik.rwth-aachen.de

Abstract. We introduce top-down deterministic transducers with rational lookahead (transducer for short) working on infinite terms. We show that for such a transducer $\widetilde{T}$, there exists an MSO-transduction T such that for any graph G, $unfold(T(G)) = \widetilde{T}(unfold(G))$. Reciprocally, we show that if an MSO-transduction T "preserves bisimilarity", then there is a transducer $\widetilde{T}$ such that for any graph G, $unfold(T(G)) = \widetilde{T}(unfold(G))$. According to this, transducers can be seen as a complete method of implementation of MSO-transductions that preserve bisimilarity. One application is for transformations of equational systems.

1   Introduction

The theory of tree transducers has been widely studied since the 1970s (see e.g. [9]). Tree transducers are abstract machines describing relations between finite terms. Among the numerous known families of transducers one happens to be a good compromise between decidability and expressiveness requirements: the top-down tree transducers with regular lookahead [15]. Those transducers are closed by composition, and preserve the regularity of sets of terms by inverse image.

One application of tree transducers is to implement relations between domains different from trees, in particular graphs. The principle is to attach a semantics from tuple of graphs to graphs of correct arity to each symbol and to use this semantic to evaluate any tree build upon those symbols. The resulting object is a graph called the interpretation of the tree. In this context, tree transducers describe relations between graphs through the trees representing them. Engelfriet studied this approach [16] and as it turns out top-down tree transducers with regular lookahead suit particularly well in this setting.

Top-down tree transducers have also been extended to macro tree transducers [18] which are themselves equivalent to so-called tree-to-graph transducers [19]. Those devices are strictly more expressive than top-down tree transducers. Drewes compares them with respect to translations between algebras [13]. The

---

[*] This research has been partially supported by the European Community Research Training Network "Games and Automata for Synthesis and Validation" (GAMES).

V. Diekert and M. Habib (Eds.): STACS 2004, LNCS 2996, pp. 428–439, 2004.
© Springer-Verlag Berlin Heidelberg 2004

representation by monadically definable transformations of those transducers has been studied extensively (see e.g. [17,4]), however, those results cannot be seen as the finite case counterpart of the results presented in this paper.

We describe in the present paper a similar theory for top-down tree transducers, but working on infinite terms. Such infinite terms can be interpreted into infinite objects as investigated first by Courcelle for graphs [10,1,2,7] (technically the interpretation is extended to infinite terms by a limit passing argument). The same need for transducers appears in this context. However, a slightly different point of view can be adopted: each infinite tree can be obtained as the unfolding of a (possibly infinite) graph. To this respect, interpreting the term is equivalent to solving the graph seen as an equational system. For this reason, we investigate how transducers of terms can be compared with transformations of graphs: this approach produces tools for transforming (possibly infinite) equational systems. This approach is extensively used in [8].

In this paper we introduce top-down transducers with rational lookahead — we say simply transducers from now — working on infinite trees. We define the notion of rationality by means of monadic second-order definability: a set of (possibly infinite) trees is rational if it is the set of tree models of some monadic second-order formula. A transducer is a deterministic device with a finite number of states that reads a (possibly infinite) input tree starting from the root and produces a (possibly infinite) output tree. Each transition consists in either consuming the input root symbol, producing an output symbol, or verifying that the input tree belongs to some rational set (this ability is called the 'lookahead').

Major results concerning the finite tree case still hold for those transducers: we show the closure by composition of transducers and the rationality of the inverse image of a rational set by a transducer. However, an extra hypothesis of determinism of the transducer is necessary in our proof. We also investigate the relationships of those transducers with respect to unfolding and monadic second-order transductions (MSO-transductions for short). We establish that the result of a transducer applied to the unfolding of a graph can also be obtained by the successive application of an MSO-transduction followed by an unfolding. We say in this case that the MSO-transduction implements the transducer. Let us note that such an MSO-transduction is by definition bisimilarity preserving. In fact, a converse to this result also holds and is the most involved proof presented in this work: every MSO-transduction implements a transducer provided that it preserves bisimilarity. For this reason transducers can be understood as the tree theoretic counterpart to MSO-transductions.

Among consequences of those results are that regularity of terms (but not rationality of sets of terms) is preserved by transducers. More generally, term solutions of safe higher-order program schemes of level n are closed under application of transducers [20,6,5].

The remainder of the paper is divided as follows. In the next section we give the basic definitions on graphs, MSO-transductions, and transducers. In Section 3 we state some basic properties of deterministic transducers and show that the functions computed by them can also be obtained using MSO-transductions followed by unfolding. In the last section we present the result that MSO-transductions that preserve bisimilarity of graphs can be simulated by deterministic transducers on the unfoldings of the graphs.

2   Definitions

An (edge-labeled) graph G over an alphabet Σ is a pair $G = (V_G, E_G)$ where V_G is the set of vertices and $E_G \subseteq V_G \times \Sigma \times V_G$ is the set of edges. A rooted graph G is of the form $G = (V_G, E_G, r_G)$ where V_G and E_G are as before and $r_G \in V_G$ is the root of G. A directed path in G is a sequence of vertices such that successive vertices u, v in this sequence are connected by an edge $(u, a, v) \in E_G$ for some $a \in \Sigma$. A sequence of vertices is an undirected path if successive vertices u, v in this sequence are connected by an edge $(u, a, v) \in E_G$ or $(v, a, u) \in E_G$. For two vertices $u, v \in V_G$ a connection of u and v is a path from u to v that does not contain any vertex twice.

A (undirected) tree t is a graph such that for each two vertices $u, v \in V_t$ there is exactly one undirected connection between u and v. A rooted tree t is a tree such that for each $v \in V_t$ there is a directed path from the root r_t of t to v. For a rooted graph G we denote by $\mathrm{unfold}(G)$ the rooted tree that is obtained by unfolding G from the root r_G. If we want to unfold G from a vertex v different from the root, then we write this as $\mathrm{unfold}(G, v)$.

For a ranked alphabet $\mathcal{F}$ and $f \in \mathcal{F}$ we write $|f|$ for the arity of f. By $|\mathcal{F}|_{\max}$ we denote the maximal rank of a symbol in $\mathcal{F}$. We represent terms over $\mathcal{F}$ as rooted trees over the alphabet $\Sigma_{\mathcal{F}} = \mathcal{F} \cup \{1, \ldots, |\mathcal{F}|_{\max}\}$. A term over $\mathcal{F}$ is a rooted tree t over $\Sigma_{\mathcal{F}}$ such that

- there is exactly one edge starting from r_t and this edge is labeled with a letter from $\mathcal{F}$,
- if there is an edge $(v, f, v') \in E_t$ for some $f \in \mathcal{F}$, then this is the only edge starting from v and there are exactly $|f|$ edges starting from v' labeled by $1, \ldots, |f|$, respectively, and
- if there is an edge $(v, \ell, v') \in E_t$ with $\ell \in \{1, \ldots, |\mathcal{F}|_{\max}\}$, then there is an edge labeled by a letter from $\mathcal{F}$ starting from v'.

The set of all $\mathcal{F}$-terms is denoted by $\mathcal{T}(\mathcal{F})$.

We say that a rooted graph G represents a term iff $\mathrm{unfold}(G)$ is a term. We are only interested in graphs representing terms. Therefore, in the following an $\mathcal{F}$-graph always means a rooted graph over $\Sigma_{\mathcal{F}}$ that represents a term. So, the $\mathcal{F}$-trees are exactly the $\mathcal{F}$-terms. For two $\mathcal{F}$-graphs G and G' we write $G \sim G'$ if G and G' represent the same term, i.e., if $\mathrm{unfold}(G) = \mathrm{unfold}(G')$. Since $\mathcal{F}$-graphs are deterministic they have the same unfolding iff they are bisimilar. Hence, on $\mathcal{F}$-graphs the relation $\sim$ corresponds to bisimulation equivalence (cf. [22]).

According to the above definition of terms there is a natural partition of the vertices of an $\mathcal{F}$-graph into those vertices being the source of an $\mathcal{F}$-edge and those vertices being the source of edges labeled with natural numbers. We denote the former of these two sets by $V_G^{\mathcal{F}} = \{v \in V_G \mid \exists f \in \mathcal{F}, u \in V_G : (v, f, u) \in E_G\}$. Since the vertices that are not from $V_G^{\mathcal{F}}$ are those that have to be inserted when passing from the usual representation of terms to our representation we call them auxiliary vertices. The vertices from $V_G^{\mathcal{F}}$ are called main vertices.

MSO-Transductions. For the remainder of this article we fix two ranked alphabets $\mathcal{F}$, $\mathcal{F}'$ and write Σ, Σ' instead of $\Sigma_{\mathcal{F}}$ and $\Sigma_{\mathcal{F}'}$. We assume the standard syntax and semantics of MSO logic over graphs, i.e., quantification over individual vertices (first-order quantification) and quantification over sets of vertices (monadic second-order quantification). For an introduction to MSO logic we refer the reader to [14]. An MSO-transduction T is of the form

$$T = (\Sigma, \Sigma', (\phi_{a,i,j}(x, y))_{a \in \Sigma', i,j \in [1,n]}, (\rho_i(x, y))_{i \in [1,n]}, n)$$

with MSO-formulas $\phi_{a,i,j}(x, y)$ and $\rho_i(x, y)$ over the signature $(E_a)_{a \in \Sigma}$, where each E_a is a binary symbol interpreted as the set of a-labeled edges.

In order to obtain a unique root we require that for all $\mathcal{F}$-graphs G and all $v \in V_G$ there is at most one $u \in V_G$ and $i \in [1, n]$ such that $G \models \rho_i(v, u)$. For each $\mathcal{F}$-graph G we define the graph $T(G)$ over Σ' that is obtained by applying T to G as follows. If there are no $u \in V_G$ and $i \in [1, n]$ with $G \models \rho_i(r_G, u)$, then $T(G)$ is undefined. Otherwise,

- $V_{T(G)} = V \times [1, n]$,
- for $a \in \Sigma'$ and $i, j \in [1, n]$ there is an edge $((v, i), a, (u, j))$ in $E_{T(G)}$ iff $G \models \phi_{a,i,j}(v, u)$, and
- $r_{T(G)} = (u, i)$ for the unique u and i with $G \models \rho_i(r_G, u)$.

Note that our definition of MSO-transduction slightly differs from the standard definition (cf. [11]). We are interested in rooted graphs and thus we need the formulas $\rho_i(x, y)$ to define the roots of the transformed graph. Since furthermore, our main interest is on the unfolding of the transformed graphs, we do not need a formula restricting the domain of T. We sometimes write $T(G, v)$ for some vertex v of G to denote the application of T to the graph G with its root changed to v.

The definition of an MSO-transduction does not enforce that $T(G)$ represents an $\mathcal{F}'$-term when applied to a graph G representing an $\mathcal{F}$-term. Furthermore, we are interested in simulating MSO-transductions by transducers working on terms. Thus, we want to consider MSO-transductions that, when applied to two $\mathcal{F}$-graphs representing the same term, yield two $\mathcal{F}'$-graphs again representing the same term. This is captured by the following definition.

We call an MSO-transduction T bisimilarity preserving iff

- $T(G)$ (if it is defined) is an $\mathcal{F}'$-graph for each $\mathcal{F}$-graph G and
- for all $\mathcal{F}$-graphs G and G', if $G \sim G'$, then $T(G)$ is defined iff $T(G')$ is defined and $T(G) \sim T(G')$.

So, bisimilarity preserving MSO-transductions transform $\mathcal{F}$-graphs into $\mathcal{F}'$-graphs and preserve bisimulation equivalence of graphs. In particular, because of the first condition, all the formulas $\phi_{a,i,j}(x,y)$ in a bisimilarity preserving MSO-transduction T must be deterministic in the following sense. For all $\mathcal{F}$-graphs G and $v \in V_G$ there is at most one $u \in V_G$ such that $G \models \phi_{a,i,j}(v,u)$. We call an MSO-transduction with this property deterministic.

Transducers with Rational Lookahead. A top down tree transducer with rational lookahead (transducer for short) is a tuple $\widetilde{T} = (Q, \mathcal{F}, \mathcal{F}', q_0, \Delta)$ with:

- Q a finite set of states,
- $q_0 \in Q$ the initial state, and
- Δ a finite set of rules of one of the following forms:
  (production rule): $q(x) \to g(q_1(x), ..., q_{|g|}(x))$ with $g \in \mathcal{F}'$, x a variable, and $q_1, \ldots, q_{|g|} \in Q$.
  (consumption rule): $q(f(x_1, ..., x_{|f|})) \to q'(x_i)$ with $f \in \mathcal{F}$, $q, q' \in Q$, and $x_1, \ldots, x_{|f|}$ variables.
  (lookahead rule): $q(x \in L) \to q'(x)$ with L a rational set of $\mathcal{F}$-terms (called lookahead set), $q, q' \in Q$, and x a variable.

Each rule of Δ can be interpreted as a rewrite rule. A lookahead rule $q(x \in L) \to q'(x)$ can only be applied to $q(t)$ if t is a term from L. Hence the lookahead rules allow to 'inspect' the input tree and collect some information about it.

A transducer $\widetilde{T} = (Q, \mathcal{F}, \mathcal{F}', q_0, \Delta)$ is deterministic if for each state $q \in Q$ and each $\mathcal{F}$-term t the set of rules that can be applied to $q(t)$

- either consists of lookahead rules with pairwise disjoint lookahead sets, or
- contains exactly one production rule, or
- contains exactly one consumption rule.

According to the above definition we will speak of production states, consumption states, and lookahead states.

The result $\widetilde{T}(t)$ of applying $\widetilde{T}$ to an $\mathcal{F}$-term t is the term that is obtained from t by applying the rewrite rules of $\widetilde{T}$ 'to the limit', starting from $q_0(t)$. In the formal definition of $\widetilde{T}(t)$ we have to be careful because we cannot simply define the image of an infinite term as the limit of a sequence of images of finite terms. Because of the lookahead the functions computed by deterministic transducers need not to be continuous.

Let $\widetilde{T} = (Q, \mathcal{F}, \mathcal{F}', q_0, \Delta)$ be a deterministic transducer and let $\mathcal{F}'_\perp$ be the ranked alphabet $\mathcal{F}'$ augmented by a new symbol $\perp$ of rank 0. By induction on n we define for each state $q \in Q$ and each infinite term $t \in \mathcal{T}(\mathcal{F})$ the term $\delta_n(q,t) \in \mathcal{T}(\mathcal{F}'_\perp)$ as $\delta_0(q,t) = \perp$,

- if $q(x) \to g(q_1(x), \ldots, q_{|g|}(x)) \in \Delta$, then $\delta_{n+1}(q,t) = g(\delta_n(q_1, t), \ldots, \delta_n(q_{|g|}, t))$,
- if $q(f(x_1, ..., x_{|f|})) \to q'(x_i) \in \Delta$, then $\delta_{n+1}(q,t) = \delta_n(q', t_i)$ for $t = f(t_1, \ldots, t_{|f|})$,
- if $q(x \in L) \to q'(x) \in \Delta$ and $t \in L$, then $\delta_{n+1}(q,t) = \delta_n(q', t)$.

If no transition of the transducer can be applied or if the right hand side in the definition of $\delta_{n+1}(q,t)$ is undefined, then $\delta_{n+1}(q,t)$ is undefined.

First note that in each situation at most one rule can be applied because of the determinism of the transducer. Therefore, if $\delta_n(q,t)$ is defined, then it is unique. If we consider the complete partial order $\sqsubseteq$ on $\mathcal{F}'_\perp$-terms with $t' \sqsubseteq t$ if t' is obtained from t by replacing subterms with $\perp$, then one can easily show by induction on n that the sequence $(\delta_n(q,t))_{n \in \mathbb{N}}$ is either increasing (w.r.t $\sqsubseteq$) or undefined from a certain point onward. In the former case we let $\widetilde{T}_q(t)$ be the limit of this sequence and in the latter case $\widetilde{T}_q(t)$ is undefined. Now we can define $\widetilde{T}(t) = \widetilde{T}_{q_0}(t)$.

3   First Results about Transducers

In this section, we establish that the inverse image of a rational set by a transducer is also rational (Lemma 2). We also show that transducers can be implemented by MSO-transductions (Theorem 1).

According to the current definition, it may happen that for some $\mathcal{F}$-term t and some state q the term $\widetilde{T}_q(t)$ still contains the symbol $\perp$. This phenomenon can be a technical burden for the following proofs. We start this section by normalizing transducers in such a way that this situation does not occur anymore.

Formally, let $\widetilde{T}$ be a transducer from $\mathcal{F}$-terms to $\mathcal{F}'$-terms of states Q, we say that $\widetilde{T}$ is *normalized* if for any state $q \in Q$ and any $\mathcal{F}$-term t, $\widetilde{T}_q(t) \neq \perp$.

For $\widetilde{T}$ to be normalized it is sufficient but not necessary to have a production in each of its cycles. Consider for instance a transducer that would remove all the occurrences of a given symbol — say a of arity 1 — provided that this symbol has only a finite number of occurrences in the term. This transducer contains cycles without production since an unbounded number of a can be removed without producing any output symbol. However, by definition this cannot happen infinitely often.

Lemma 1. *Let $\widetilde{T}$ be a transducer from $\mathcal{F}$ to $\mathcal{F}'$ and $\perp'$ be a new symbol of arity 0. There exists effectively a transducer $\widetilde{T}'$ from $\mathcal{F}$-terms to $(\mathcal{F}' \cup \{\perp'\})$-terms such that $\widetilde{T}' = h \circ \widetilde{T}$ where h replaces every occurrence of the symbol $\perp$ in a term by $\perp'$.*

An important property of deterministic transducers is that their domain is rational. More precisely, as stated in Lemma 2, the inverse image of a rational language by a normalized deterministic transducer is rational.

Lemma 2. *Let $\widetilde{T}$ be a deterministic transducer from $\mathcal{F}$-terms to $\mathcal{F}'$-terms. If L is a rational subset of $\mathcal{T}(\mathcal{F}')$, then the set $\widetilde{T}^{-1}(L)$ is also rational.*

Let us notice that in this proof, the determinism of the transducer is explicitly needed and we don't know if the result remains true without this restriction. This was not the case for transducers of finite trees. It also follows directly from this lemma that the domain of a transducer is rational.

Finally, we aim at establishing Theorem 1 which expresses how a transducer can be simulated by an MSO-transduction before unfolding. First of all we need a result relating lookaheads with MSO-logic. It is a particular case of Courcelle's result in [12].

Lemma 3. *For any rational set of $\mathcal{F}$-terms L, there exists an MSO-formula $\phi(x)$ such that for any $\mathcal{F}$-graph G and any vertex $v \in V_G^{\mathcal{F}}$, unfold$(G, v) \in L$ iff $G \models \phi(v)$.*

We can now state the main result of this section.

Theorem 1. *Let $\widetilde{T}$ be a normalized deterministic transducer from $\mathcal{F}$-terms to $\mathcal{F}'$-terms. There exists effectively an MSO-transduction T such that for any $\mathcal{F}$-graph G and any vertex $v \in V_G^{\mathcal{F}}$, $T(G, v)$ is defined iff $\widetilde{T}(\text{unfold}(G, v))$ is defined, and in this case unfold$(T(G, v)) = \widetilde{T}(\text{unfold}(G, v))$.*

The proof consists in using one copy of the graph for each state of the transducer. Then the MSO-formulas put correctly the edges. The Lemmas 2 and 3 combined allow the implementation of lookahead rules.

4   From MSO-Transductions to Transducers

The goal of this section is to show that bisimilarity preserving MSO-transductions can be simulated by deterministic transducers on the unfoldings of graphs. In a first step we use the fact that T is bisimilarity preserving to obtain some kind of normal form for T.

Since rooted graphs are bisimilar to their unfoldings the following simple remark allows us to consider MSO-transductions operating on trees instead of graphs. Formally, this means that if T is a bisimilarity preserving MSO-transduction, then unfold$(T(G)) = \text{unfold}(T(\text{unfold}(G)))$ for every $\mathcal{F}$-graph G.

To simulate an MSO-transduction by a deterministic transducer we would like the MSO-transduction to 'respect' the type (main or auxiliary) of the vertices since transducers only work on main vertices. Furthermore, transducers work in a top-down fashion. Thus, we want to normalize the MSO-transduction in such a way that the new edges go 'downward' if the transduction is applied to a tree. Under this assumption a deterministic transducer can construct the edges defined by the MSO-transduction by going down the term that is represented by t and using its rational lookahead. The following definition formally captures the properties we need to simulate an MSO-transduction by a deterministic transducer.

Definition 1. *An MSO-transduction $T = (\Sigma, \Sigma', (\phi_{a,i,j}(x, y))_{a,i,j}, (\rho_i(x, y))_i, n)$ is in top-down normal form iff for all $\mathcal{F}$-trees t*

(a) $r_{T(t)} = (r_t, 1)$,
(b) *if $t \models \phi_{g,i_1,i_2}(v_1, v_2)$ and $t \models \phi_{\ell,i_2,i_3}(v_2, v_3)$ for $g \in \mathcal{F}'$, $\ell \in \{1, \ldots, |\mathcal{F}'|_{\max}\}$, and $i_1, i_2, i_3 \in [1, n]$, then $v_1 \sqsubseteq v_3$, and*
(c) *for every $\mathcal{F}$-graph G, if $G \models \phi_{g,i,j}(u, v)$ for $g \in \mathcal{F}'$, then $u \in V_G^{\mathcal{F}}$ and $v \notin V_G^{\mathcal{F}}$, and if $G \models \phi_{\ell,i,j}(u, v)$ for $\ell \in \{1, \ldots, |\mathcal{F}'|_{\max}\}$, then $u \notin V_G^{\mathcal{F}}$ and $v \in V_G^{\mathcal{F}}$.*

The following lemma states that we can always ensure condition (a).

Lemma 4. *For each MSO-transduction T there exists an MSO-transduction T' such that $r_{T'(G)} = (r_G, 1)$ and $\mathrm{unfold}(T(G)) = \mathrm{unfold}(T'(G))$ for each rooted graph G.*

The most intricate thing is to establish condition (b) of Definition 1. First, we construct for a given tree t a new graph $\widehat{t}$ on which the MSO-transduction must satisfy condition (b).

Let t be an $\mathcal{F}$-tree. We can assume that $V_t \subseteq \Sigma^*$ by identifying each element v from V_t with the labeling of the unique path leading from r_t to v. We define the $\mathcal{F}$-graph $\widehat{t}$ by

- $V_{\widehat{t}} = \{\langle u_1, \dots, u_n \rangle \mid n > 0, \ u_1, \dots, u_n \in V_t, \text{ and } u_{i-1} \not\sqsubseteq u_i \text{ for all } i \in [2, n]\}$.
- The edges in $E_{\widehat{t}}$ are those of the form $\langle u_1, \dots, u_n \rangle \overset{a}{\to} \langle u_1, \dots, u_n a \rangle$ and $\langle u_1, \dots, u_n, va, v \rangle \overset{a}{\to} \langle u_1, \dots, u_n, va \rangle$.

Figure 1 shows a part of this construction for a term built from a single binary symbol f. The underlined vertices correspond to the vertices of the original term.

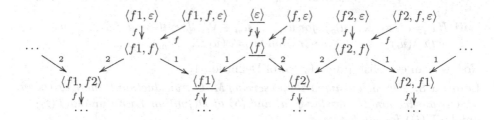

Fig. 1. A part of $\widehat{t}_f$

For $\widehat{u} \in V_{\widehat{t}}$ we denote by $\lambda(\widehat{u})$ the last element in the sequence $\widehat{u}$, i.e., if $\widehat{u} = \langle u_1, \dots, u_m \rangle$, then $\lambda(\widehat{u}) = u_m$. The following properties are easy to derive from the definition of $\widehat{t}$.

Lemma 5. *For each $\mathcal{F}$-tree t and each vertex $\widehat{v} \in V_{\widehat{t}}$:*

(i) $\widehat{t}$ *is a (undirected) tree.*

(ii) *If $\lambda(\widehat{v}) = \varepsilon$, then there are no edges with target $\widehat{v}$ in $\widehat{t}$. Otherwise, $\widehat{v}$ is the target of exactly two edges in $\widehat{t}$ that have the same label as the only edge with target $\lambda(\widehat{v})$ in t.*

(iii) $\widehat{v}$ *is the source of an a-edge in $\widehat{t}$ iff $\lambda(\widehat{v})$ is the source of an a-edge in t.*

(iv) $\mathrm{unfold}(t, v) = \mathrm{unfold}(\widehat{t}, \langle v \rangle)$ *for each $\mathcal{F}$-tree t and vertex v of t.*

An important property of $\widehat{t}$ is that two vertices $\widehat{u}$ and $\widehat{u}'$ with $\lambda(\widehat{u}) = \lambda(\widehat{u}')$ are indistinguishable, i.e., there is an automorphism of $\widehat{t}$ that maps $\lambda(\widehat{u})$ to $\lambda(\widehat{u}')$. This enforces a certain behavior of deterministic MSO-transductions on $\widehat{t}$ that corresponds to the second property of the top-down normal form.

Lemma 6. *Let T be a deterministic MSO-transduction, t an $\mathcal{F}$-tree, and $\widehat{u}, \widehat{v} \in V_{\widehat{t}}$. If $\widehat{t} \models \phi_{a,i,j}(\widehat{u}, \widehat{v})$, then $\lambda(\widehat{u}) \sqsubseteq \lambda(\widehat{v})$.*

As Lemma 6 shows, property (b) of Definition 1 holds on $\widehat{t}$ for MSO-transductions preserving bisimulation equivalence. To transfer this property to t itself we will make use of the concept of tree-like structures (cf. [24,3]).

For a graph G the tree-like structure $G^* = (V_G^*, \text{son}, \text{clone}, E_G^*)$ is the structure over the universe V_G^* with the relations son, clone, and E_G^* defined by son $= \{(w, wv) \mid w \in V_G^*,\ v \in V_G\}$, clone $= \{wvv \mid w \in V_G^*,\ v \in V_G\}$, and $E_G^* = \{(wv, a, wu) \mid w \in V_G^*,\ (v, a, u) \in E_G\}$. The crucial point of the tree-like structure is that monadic second-order properties can be expressed as monadic second order properties of the original structure.

Theorem 2 (cf. [3]). *For each MSO-sentence ϕ there exists an MSO-sentence ϕ^* such that $G^* \models \phi \Leftrightarrow G \models \phi^*$ for all $\mathcal{F}$-graphs G.*

The two structures $\widehat{t}$ and t^* are closely related, $\widehat{t}$ can be interpreted in t^*. This can be used to show a modification of the above result for $\widehat{t}$.

Lemma 7. *For each MSO-formula $\phi(x_1, \dots, x_m)$ there exists an MSO-formula $\phi^*(x_1, \dots, x_m)$ such that for all $\mathcal{F}$-trees t:*

   (i) If $\widehat{t} \models \phi(\widehat{u}_1, \dots, \widehat{u}_m)$, then $t \models \phi^*(\lambda(\widehat{u}_1), \dots, \lambda(\widehat{u}_m))$ for all $\widehat{u}_1, \dots, \widehat{u}_m \in V_{\widehat{t}}$.

   (ii) If $t \models \phi^*(u_1, \dots, u_m)$, for $u_1, \dots, u_m \in V_t$, then there are $\widehat{u}_1, \dots, \widehat{u}_m \in V_{\widehat{t}}$ with $\lambda(\widehat{u}_i) = u_i$ $(1 \le i \le m)$ and $\widehat{t} \models \phi(\widehat{u}_1, \dots, \widehat{u}_m)$.

Now we can establish property (b) of Definition 1.

Lemma 8. *For each bisimilarity preserving MSO-transduction T there exists an MSO-transduction T' satisfying (a) and (b) of Definition 1 with $\text{unfold}(T(t)) = \text{unfold}(T'(t))$ for all $\mathcal{F}$-trees t.*

As a last step in the normalization we have to ensure (c) of Definition 1. Since the MSO-transduction might use copies of auxiliary vertices as targets of $\mathcal{F}$-edges and main vertices as targets of other $\mathcal{F}$-edges we cannot simply redirect the latter ones to main vertices within the same copy. For this reason we have to introduce new copies of the original term and redirect edges with wrong type of source vertex or target vertex to these new copies.

Lemma 9. *For each bisimilarity preserving MSO-transduction T there exists an MSO-transduction T' in top-down normal form with $\text{unfold}(T(t)) = \text{unfold}(T'(t))$ for all $\mathcal{F}$-trees t.*

Having established the top-down normal form the next goal is to simulate MSO-transductions in this normal form by deterministic transducers. We make use of the well-known equivalence between MSO logic and Rabin automata on infinite trees (cf. [23]). This allows us to pass from the formulas defining the edges in the MS transduction to equivalent automata accepting infinite terms with appropriate markings coding the assignment for the free first-order variables in the formulas. We start by defining marked terms and automata running on them. Due to the lack of space we do not give detailed definitions and assume familiarity with the theory of automata on infinite trees (cf. [23]).

For a set Θ, a Θ-marked $\mathcal{F}$-term (t, μ) consists of an $\mathcal{F}$-term t and a marking function $\mu : \Theta \to V_t$. Let $\mathcal{T}(\mathcal{F}, \Theta)$ be the set of all Θ-marked $\mathcal{F}$-terms. For a set $L \subseteq \mathcal{T}(\mathcal{F}, \Theta)$ of marked terms we define $L|_{\mathcal{F}} = \{t \mid \exists \mu . (t, \mu) \in L\}$.

We fix an MSO-transduction $T = (\Sigma, \Sigma', (\phi_{a,i,j}(x, y))_{a,i,j}, (\rho_i(x, y))_i, n)$ in top-down normal form that was obtained from a bisimilarity preserving MSO-transduction as described in the previous subsection. For all $g \in \mathcal{F}'$, all $i \in [1, n]$, and all $j \in [1, n]^{|g|}$ define

$$\psi_{g,i,j}(x, x_1, \dots, x_{|g|}) = \exists y \bigvee_{m \in [1,n]} \left(\phi_{g,i,m}(x, y) \wedge \bigwedge_{\ell \in \{1, \dots, |g|\}} \phi_{\ell, m, j_\ell}(y, x_\ell) \right),$$

where j_ℓ denotes the ℓth component of j, i.e., $j = (j_1, \dots, j_k)$. For $g \in \mathcal{F}'$ we define $\Theta_g = \{g, 1, \dots, |g|\}$. For $(t, \mu) \in \mathcal{T}(\mathcal{F}, \Theta_g)$ we write by abuse of notation $(t, \mu) \models \psi_{g,i,j}$ iff $t \models \psi_{g,i,j}(\mu(g), \mu(1), \dots, \mu(|g|))$. Note that T being in top-down normal form implies that $\mu(g), \mu(1), \dots, \mu(|g|) \in V_t^{\mathcal{F}}$ if $(t, \mu) \models \psi_{g,i,j}$ by Definition 1 (c). This enables us to adapt the usual framework of automata running on infinite trees (cf. [23]) to our representation of marked terms.

Every MSO-formula can be translated into a nondeterministic Rabin tree automaton accepting precisely the models of the formula [21]. Hence, for all $g \in \mathcal{F}'$, all $i \in [1, n]$, and all $j \in [1, n]^{|g|}$ there exists a nondeterministic Rabin tree automaton $\mathcal{A}_{g,i,j} = (Q_{g,i,j}, \mathcal{F} \times 2^{\Theta_g}, Q_{g,i,j}^{\text{in}}, \Delta_{g,i,j}, \Omega_{g,i,j})$ that accepts exactly the Θ_g-marked $\mathcal{F}$-terms (t, μ) with $(t, \mu) \models \psi_{g,i,j}$. We assume that the state sets of these automata are pairwise disjoint. We denote the union of the automata $\mathcal{A}_{g,i,j}$ by the automaton $\mathcal{A} = (Q, \bigcup_{g \in \mathcal{F}'}(\mathcal{F} \times 2^{\Theta_g}), Q_{\text{in}}, \Delta, \Omega)$, where Q, Q_{in}, Δ, and Ω are obtained by taking the union of the respective components of the automata $\mathcal{A}_{g,i,j}$.

The automaton $\mathcal{A}$ is the main ingredient in the construction of the transducer. The idea is to keep track of the states of $\mathcal{A}$ that could have been reached on the input term and to use the rational lookahead to decide which automaton $\mathcal{A}_{g,i,j}$ to use to construct the next edge. We illustrate the work of the transducer with a simple example.

Consider the part of a marked term (t, μ) depicted in the upper left box of Figure 2. The labels g, 1, and 2 on the vertices are the marks. The states q_g, q, q_1, q_2 are part of an accepting run of the automaton $\mathcal{A}_{g,i,j_1,j_2}$ for some i, j_1, j_2. In steps (1) to (5) the work of the transducer is illustrated.

In (1) the transducer is in state $\langle i, C \rangle$. The i indicates in which copy introduced by the MSO-transduction the transducer currently is. The set of states that could have been reached by $\mathcal{A}$ at this point are stored in C. We assume that $q_g \in C$ and using its rational lookahead the transducer can check that the term with the marking depicted in the upper left box is accepted from $\mathcal{A}_{g,i,j_1,j_2}$ with q_g as initial state.

In step (2) the transducer applies a production rule creating the g-edge, the 1-edge, and the 2-edge. Now it has to consume the part of the term until reaching the vertex marked with 1 in the left hand side copy and likewise in the right hand side copy for the vertex marked with 2. To that aim it goes to the

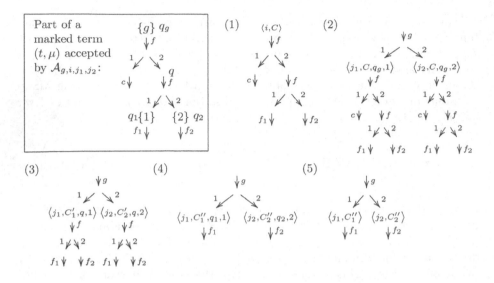

Fig. 2. Illustration of the transducer constructing an edge

states $(j_1, C, q_g, 1)$ and $(j_2, C, q_g, 2)$ in the two corresponding copies of t. The last component of the states indicates for which mark the transducer is waiting.

In step (2) the transducer has reached the two corresponding vertices. Note that in step (3) two independent rewritings of the transducer have been applied in parallel and similarly in step (4). In all these steps the transducer implicitly uses its lookahead to decide in which direction to proceed in the term. In each consumption step the sets storing the reachable states of $\mathcal{A}$ are updated. Having reached the desired vertices the transducer switches back to the mode where it checks which edge to construct next. The formal realization of this idea is rather technical and is omitted here.

Lemma 10. *There exists a deterministic transducer $\widetilde{T}$ such that* $\mathrm{unfold}(T(t)) = \widetilde{T}(t)$ *for each term t.*

Now we can prove the main result of this section.

Theorem 3. *For each bisimilarity preserving MSO-transduction T there exists a deterministic transducer $\widetilde{T}$ such that* $\mathrm{unfold}(T(G)) = \widetilde{T}(\mathrm{unfold}(G))$ *for each $\mathcal{F}$-graph G.*

Proof. Let T be a bisimilarity preserving MSO-transduction. By Lemma 9 there is an MSO-transduction T' in top-down normal form such that $\mathrm{unfold}(T(t)) = \mathrm{unfold}(T'(t))$ for all $\mathcal{F}$-trees t. According to Lemma 10 there is a deterministic transducer $\widetilde{T}$ such that $\mathrm{unfold}(T'(t)) = \widetilde{T}(t)$ for each $\mathcal{F}$-tree t. Let G be an $\mathcal{F}$-graph and let $t_G = \mathrm{unfold}(G)$. Then we get $\mathrm{unfold}(T(G)) = \mathrm{unfold}(T(t_G)) = \mathrm{unfold}(T'(t_G)) = \widetilde{T}(t_G)$.   □

References

1. K. Barthelmann. On equational simple graphs. Technical Report 9, Universität Mainz, Institut für Informatik, 1997.
2. K. Barthelmann. When can an equational simple graph be generated by hyperedge replacement? In *MFCS '98*, volume 1450 of *LNCS*, pages 543–552. Springer, 1998.
3. D. Berwanger and A. Blumensath. The monadic theory of tree-like structures. In E. Grädel, W. Thomas, and T. Wilke, editors, *Automata, Logics, and Infinite Games*, number 2500 in LNCS, chapter 16, pages 285–301. Springer, 2002.
4. R. Bloem and J. Engelfriet. A comparison of tree transductions defined by monadic second order logic and by attribute grammars. *JCSS*, 61(1):1–50, 2000.
5. A. Carayol and S. Wöhrle. The caucal hierarchy of infinite graphs in terms of logic and higher-order pushdown automata. In *FSTTCS 2003*, volume 2914 of *LNCS*, pages 112–123. Springer, 2003.
6. D. Caucal. On infinite terms having a decidable monadic theory. In *MFCS'02*, volume 2420 of *LNCS*, pages 165–176. Springer, 2002.
7. T. Colcombet. On families of graphs having a decidable first order theory with reachability. In *ICALP 2002*, volume 2380 of *LNCS*. Springer, 2002.
8. T. Colcombet. *Propriétés et représentations de structures infinies*. PhD thesis, IRISA, Rennes, 2004. to appear.
9. H. Comon, M. Dauchet, R. Gilleron, F. Jacquemard, D. Lugiez, S. Tison, and M. Tommasi. Tree automata techniques and applications, 1997.
10. B. Courcelle. The monadic second-order logic of graphs II: infinite graphs of bounded tree width. *Mathematical Systems Theory*, 21:187–221, 1989.
11. B. Courcelle. Monadic second-order graph transductions: A survey. In *TCS*, volume 126, pages 53–75. Elsevier, 1994.
12. B. Courcelle. The monadic second order logic of graphs IX: Machines and their behaviours. In *TCS*, volume 151, pages 125–162, 1995.
13. F. Drewes. The use of tree transducers to compute translations between graph algebras. Report 8/94, Univ. Bremen, 1994.
14. H.-D. Ebbinghaus and J. Flum. *Finite Model Theory*. Perspectives in Mathematical Logic. Springer, Berlin, second edition, 1995.
15. J. Engelfriet. Top-down tree transducers with regular lookahead. *Mathematical Systems Theory*, 10:289–303, 1977.
16. J. Engelfriet. Graph grammars and tree transducers. In S. Tison, editor, *CAAP'94*, volume 787 of *LNCS*, pages 15–36. Springer, 1994.
17. J. Engelfriet and S. Maneth. Characterizing and deciding MSO-definability of macro tree transductions. *LNCS*, 1770:542+, 2000.
18. J. Engelfriet and H. Vogler. Macro tree transducers. *JCSS*, 31:71–146, 1985.
19. J. Engelfriet and H. Vogler. The translation power of top-down tree-to-graph transducers. *JCSS*, 49:258–305, 1994.
20. T. Knapik, D. Niwinski, and P. Urzyczyn. Higher-order pushdown trees are easy. In *FOSSACS'02*, volume 2303 of *LNCS*, pages 205–222. Springer, 2002.
21. M. O. Rabin. Decidability of second-order theories and automata on infinite trees. *Transactions of the American Mathematical Society*, 141:1–35, 1969.
22. C. Stirling. *Modal and Temporal Properties of Processes*. Graduate Texts in Computer Science. Springer, 2001.
23. W. Thomas. Languages, automata, and logic. In *Handbook of Formal Language Theory*, volume III, pages 389–455. Springer, 1997.
24. I. Walukiewicz. Monadic second-order logic on tree-like structures. *TCS*, 275:311–346, 2002.

Definability and Regularity in Automatic Structures

Bakhadyr Khoussainov[1], Sasha Rubin[2], and Frank Stephan[3*]

[1] Computer Science Department, The University of Auckland, New Zealand
bmk@cs.auckland.ac.nz
[2] Mathematics Department, The University of Auckland, New Zealand
rubin@math.auckland.ac.nz
[3] National ICT Australia, Sydney Research Laboratory at Kensington, Australia
fstephan@cse.unsw.edu.au

Abstract. An automatic structure $\mathcal{A}$ is one whose domain A and atomic relations are finite automaton (FA) recognisable. A structure isomorphic to $\mathcal{A}$ is called automatically presentable. Suppose R is an FA recognisable relation on A. This paper concerns questions of the following type. For which automatic presentations of $\mathcal{A}$ is (the image of) R also FA recognisable? To this end we say that a relation R is *intrinsically regular* in a structure $\mathcal{A}$ if it is FA recognisable in every automatic presentation of the structure. For example, in every automatic structure all relations definable in first order logic are intrinsically regular. We characterise the intrinsically regular relations of some automatic fragments of arithmetic in the first order logic extended with quantifiers $\exists^{\infty}$ interpreted as 'there exists infinitely many', and $\exists^{(i)}$ interpreted as 'there exists a multiple of i many'.

1 Introduction

This paper investigates the relationship between regularity, that is FA recognisability, and definability in automatic structures. Roots of this topic go back to the results of Büchi and Elgot in the 1960's who proved the equivalence between regularity and weak monadic second order logic. A recasting of this result says that (the coding of) a relation is regular if and only if the relation it is first order definable in the structure $(\mathbb{N}, +, |_k)$, where $+$ is the addition and $n|_k m$ means that n is a power of k and n divides m. Intimately related is the work of Cobham, Semenov, Muchnik, Bruyére and others that investigates the relationship between regular relations of (coded) natural numbers and definability in certain fragments of arithmetic; see [2] for a good exposition. This paper continues and complements these lines of research by initiating the study of the relationship

---

* National ICT Australia is funded by the Australian Government's Department of Communications, Information Technology and the Arts and the Australian Research Council through Backing Australia's Ability and the ICT Centre of Excellence Program.

V. Diekert and M. Habib (Eds.): STACS 2004, LNCS 2996, pp. 440–451, 2004.

between regularity and definability in the general setting of arbitrary automatic structures.

Assume one has a structure $\mathcal{A}$ that can be described by means of finite automata. This is formalised in Definition 2.3 that says that there is an encoding of the elements of the structure under which the domain A of the structure and its atomic relations are all regular. Such a structure is called *automatic*. In this case we say that the coded structure is an *automatic presentation* of $\mathcal{A}$. Automatic presentations of $\mathcal{A}$ can be regarded as finite automata implementations of the structure $\mathcal{A}$. For instance, if $k > 1$, then a least-significant-digit-first base k encoding of the natural numbers gives rise to automatic presentations of $(\mathbb{N}, S)$, $(\mathbb{N}, \leq)$, $(\mathbb{N}, +)$ and $(\mathbb{N}, +, |_k)$. Now assume that $R \subset A^m$ is a relation, not necessarily in the language of $\mathcal{A}$. For example, R may be the reachability relation if $\mathcal{A}$ is a graph, or R may be the dependency relation if $\mathcal{A}$ is a group. It may well be the case that in one automatic presentation of $\mathcal{A}$ the relation R is recognised by a finite automaton, and in another automatic presentation it is not. Thus, automata-theoretic properties of the relation R are dependent on the automata that describe $\mathcal{A}$. Our goal is to study those relations in $\mathcal{A}$ that are regular under *all* automatic presentations of $\mathcal{A}$, and to understand which structures ensure a relation is regular in all automatic presentations and which do not. Formally, we introduce the following definition:

Definition 1.1. See [1]. *A relation R is* intrinsically regular *in an automatic structure $\mathcal{A}$ if for every automatic structure $\mathcal{B}$ isomorphic to $\mathcal{A}$ the image of the relation R in $\mathcal{B}$ is regular. Denote by $IR(\mathcal{A})$ the set of intrinsically regular relations in $\mathcal{A}$.*

Thus the intrinsically regular relations in $\mathcal{A}$ are those for which regularity is invariant under all automatic presentations of $\mathcal{A}$. A natural class of intrinsically regular relations is the class of relations definable in the first order logic. We now single out this class of relations in the following definition:

Definition 1.2. *A relation R is* first order (FO) definable *in $\mathcal{A}$ if there exists a first order formula $\phi(\bar{x}, \bar{c})$ with parameters $\bar{c}$ from $\mathcal{A}$ such that $R = \{\bar{a} \mid \mathcal{A} \models \phi(\bar{a}, \bar{c})\}$. Denote by $FO(\mathcal{A})$ the set of all first order definable relations in $\mathcal{A}$.*

A fundamental result of automatic structures is stated as follows.

Fact 1.3. *Let $\mathcal{A}$ be an automatic structure. There exists an algorithm that from a FO definition ϕ in $\mathcal{A}$ of a relation R produces an automaton recognising R. In particular, $FO(\mathcal{A}) \subset IR(\mathcal{A})$.*

A proof may be found in [6] or [3]; in this paper we will use this fact without explicitly referencing it. Naturally, one asks whether the converse holds. It turns out that although this is sufficient for some structures, for instance $(\mathbb{N}, +)$ and $(\mathbb{N}, +, |_m)$, in general it is not.

Extend the FO predicate logic with quantifiers $\exists^\infty$ and $\exists^{(i)}$, where $i \in \mathbb{N}$, whose interpretations are as follows. The formula $\exists^\infty x\, \phi(x)$ means there are infinitely many x such that $\phi(x)$ holds, and the formula $\exists^{(i)} x\, \phi(x)$ means that there are exactly n elements x such that $\phi(x)$ holds and n is a multiple of i. Denote the logic by $\mathrm{FO}^{\infty,\mathrm{mod}}$. Say that a relation R is $FO^{\infty,\mathrm{mod}}$ *definable* in a structure $\mathcal{A}$ if there is a $\text{FO}^{\infty,\text{mod}}$–formula $\phi(\bar{x}, \bar{a})$, where $\bar{a}$ is a finite tuple of elements, such that $R = \{\bar{c} \mid \mathcal{A} \models \phi(\bar{c}, \bar{a})\}$. Denote by $\text{FO}^{\infty,\text{mod}}(\mathcal{A})$ the set of relations that are $\text{FO}^{\infty,\text{mod}}$ definable in $\mathcal{A}$. Then Fact 1.3 can be extended as follows.

Theorem 3.2. See [3]. [1] *Let $\mathcal{A}$ be an automatic structure. There exists an algorithm that from a $\text{FO}^{\infty,\text{mod}}$ definition ϕ of a relation R produces an automaton recognising R. In particular,*

$$\text{FO}^{\infty,\text{mod}}(\mathcal{A}) \subset \text{IR}(\mathcal{A}).$$

Consequently, there is a neat characterisation of the intrinsically regular relations of $(\mathbb{N}, \leq)$ in terms of $\text{FO}^{\infty,\text{mod}}$:

Theorem 3.3.

$$\text{IR}(\mathbb{N}, \leq) = \text{FO}^{\infty,\text{mod}}(\mathbb{N}, \leq) = \text{FO}(\mathbb{N}, \leq, M^2, M^3, \ldots).$$

In order to show that a particular relation is intrinsically regular in a given automatic structure, one needs to provide a mechanism for extracting an automaton recognising the relation from automatic presentations of the structure. A perfect illustration of this is the subset like construction proof of Theorem 3.2. In order to show that a particular relation is not intrinsically regular, one needs to construct automata that, on the one hand, present the structure; and on the other, preclude the existence of automata recognising the given relation. The following theorem shows that the unary relations M^k are not intrinsically regular for the structure $(\mathbb{N}, S)$.

Theorem 4.1. *For every $k \geq 2$, there is an automatic presentation of $(\mathbb{N}, S)$ in which the image of the set M^k is not regular.*

Consequently we have the following partial result.

Corollary 4.2. *For $R \subset \mathbb{N}$,*

$$R \in \text{IR}(\mathbb{N}, S) \text{ if and only if } R \in \text{FO}^{\infty,\text{mod}}(\mathbb{N}, S).$$

Theorem 4.1 and its proof may be applied to construct automatic structures with pathological properties. The first application is concerned with the reachability problem in automatic graphs. It is known that the reachability problem for automatic graphs is not decidable, see [3]. The underlying reason for this is that such automatic graphs necessarily have infinitely many components. In fact, the reachability problem is decidable if the given graph is automatic and has finitely many components. A natural question is whether or not the reachability relation for automatic graphs with finitely many components can be recognised by finite automata. This is answered in the following corollary:

Corollary 4.3. *There exists an automatic presentation of a graph with exactly two connected components each isomorphic to $(\mathbb{N}, S)$ in which the reachability relation is not regular.*

---

[1] In a personal communication with the first author, A. Blumensath has mentioned having obtained this result.

The second application of Theorem 4.1 is on the structure $(\mathbb{Z}, S)$, where $\mathbb{Z}$ is the set of all integers and S is the successor function. A *cut* is a set of the form $\{x \in \mathbb{Z} \mid x \geq n\}$, where $n \in \mathbb{Z}$ is fixed. In all previously known automatic presentations of $(\mathbb{Z}, S)$ each cut is a regular set. The corollary below states the existence of a counterexample:

Corollary 4.4. *There exists an automatic presentation of $(\mathbb{Z}, S)$ in which no cut is regular.*

Finally, we mention that one of the central topic in modern computable model theory, first initiated by Ash and Nerode in [1], is concerned with understanding the relationship between definability and computability, see [5, Chapter 3] for the current state of the area. For a computable structure $\mathcal{A}$, that is one whose atomic diagram is a computable set, a relation R is *intrinsically recursively enumerable* if in all computable isomorphic copies of $\mathcal{A}$ the relation R is recursively enumerable. In [1] Ash and Nerode show that under some natural conditions put on $\mathcal{A}$, the relation R is intrinsically recursively enumerable if and only if it is definable as an effective disjunction of existential formulas. One may therefore regard the topic of this paper as a refined version of the Ash-Nerode program in which the class of automatic structures is considered rather than the class of all computable structures.

Question 1.4. *Characterise the intrinsically regular relations in $\mathcal{A}$ as those definable in a suitable logic of $\mathcal{A}$.*

The results of this paper suggest that the logic is $\mathrm{FO}^{\infty,\mathrm{mod}}$.

The rest of the paper is organised as follows. The next section contains automata preliminaries including the definition of an automatic structure and a description of simple properties of intrinsically regular relations. The remaining sections contain proofs of some of the results stated in the introduction. Due to space constraints some of the proofs are replaced by sketches or completely omitted. The complete proofs can be found in the full version of this paper which is available as a technical report of the Centre for Discrete Mathematics and Theoretical Computer Science in Auckland.

2 Automata Preliminaries

A thorough introduction to automatic structures can be found in [3] and [6]. In this section, familiarity with the basics of finite automata theory is assumed though for completeness and to fix notations, the necessary definitions are included here. A *finite automaton* $\mathcal{A}$ over an alphabet Σ is a tuple (S, ι, Δ, F), where S is a finite set of *states*, $\iota \in S$ is the *initial state*, $\Delta \subset S \times \Sigma \times S$ is the *transition table* and $F \subset S$ is the set of *final states*. A *computation* of $\mathcal{A}$ on a word $\sigma_1 \sigma_2 \ldots \sigma_n$ ($\sigma_i \in \Sigma$) is a sequence of states, say $q_0, q_1, \ldots, q_n$, such that $q_0 = \iota$ and $(q_i, \sigma_{i+1}, q_{i+1}) \in \Delta$ for all $i \in \{0, 1, \ldots, n-1\}$. If $q_n \in F$, then the computation is *successful* and we say that automaton $\mathcal{A}$ *accepts* the word. The *language* accepted by the automaton $\mathcal{A}$ is the set of all words accepted by $\mathcal{A}$. In general, $D \subset \Sigma^*$ is *finite automaton recognisable*, or *regular*, if D is the language accepted by a finite automaton $\mathcal{A}$.

Classically finite automata recognise sets of words. The following definitions extends recognisability to relations of arity n, called *synchronous n–tape automata*. Informally a synchronous n–tape automaton can be thought of as a one-way Turing machine with n input tapes. Each tape is regarded as semi-infinite having written on it a word in the alphabet Σ followed by an infinite succession of blanks, $\diamond$ symbols. The automaton starts in the initial state, reads simultaneously the first symbol of each tape, changes state, reads simultaneously the second symbol of each tape, changes state, etc., until it reads a blank on each tape. The automaton then stops and accepts the n–tuple of words if it is in a final state. The set of all n–tuples accepted by the automaton is the relation recognised by the automaton. Here is a formalization. Let $\Sigma_\diamond$ be $\Sigma \cup \{\diamond\}$, where $\diamond \notin \Sigma$.

Definition 2.1. *Write $\Sigma_\diamond$ for $\Sigma \cup \{\diamond\}$ where $\diamond$ is a symbol not in Σ. The convolution of a tuple $(w_1, \dots, w_n) \in \Sigma^{*n}$ is the string $\otimes(w_1, \dots, w_n)$ of length $\max_i |w_i|$ over alphabet $(\Sigma_\diamond)^n$ defined as follows. Its k'th symbol is $(\sigma_1, \dots, \sigma_n)$ where σ_i is the k'th symbol of w_i if $k \leq |w_i|$ and $\diamond$ otherwise.*

The convolution *of a relation $R \subset \Sigma^{*n}$ is the relation $\otimes R \subset (\Sigma_\diamond)^{n*}$ formed as the set of convolutions of all the tuples in R. That is $\otimes R = \{\otimes w \mid w \in R\}$.*

Definition 2.2. *An n–tape automaton on Σ is a finite automaton over the alphabet $(\Sigma_\diamond)^n$. An n–ary relation $R \subset \Sigma^{*n}$ is finite automaton recognisable or regular if its convolution $\otimes R$ is recognisable by an n–tape automaton.*

We now relate n–tape automata to structures. A *structure* $\mathcal{A}$ consists of a set A called the *domain* and some relations and operations on A. We may assume that $\mathcal{A}$ only contains relational predicates as the operations can be replaced with their graphs. We write $\mathcal{A} = (A, R_1^A, \dots, R_k^A, \dots)$ where R_i^A is an n_i–ary relation on A. The relation R_i are sometimes called basic or atomic relations. We assume that the function $i \to n_i$ is always a computable one.

Definition 2.3. *A structure $\mathcal{A}$ is automatic over Σ if its domain $A \subset \Sigma^*$ is finite automata recognisable, and there is an algorithm that for each i produces a finite automaton recognising the relation $R_i^A \subset \Sigma^{*n_i}$. An isomorphism from a structure $\mathcal{B}$ to an automatic structure $\mathcal{A}$ is an automatic presentation of $\mathcal{B}$ in which case $\mathcal{B}$ is called automatically presentable (over Σ). A structure is called automatic if it is automatic over some alphabet.*

Consider the word structure $(\{0,1\}^*, L, R, E, \preceq)$, where for all strings $x, y \in \{0,1\}^*$ we have $L(x) = x0$, $R(x) = x1$, $E(x,y)$ iff $|x| = |y|$, and $\preceq$ is the lexicographical order. It is automatic over Σ. The configuration graphs of Turing machines are examples of automatic structures. Write $\mathbb{N}$ for the set of natural numbers including 0. Examples of automatically presentable structures are $(\mathbb{N}, +)$, $(\mathbb{N}, \leq)$, $(\mathbb{N}, S)$, the group $(\mathbb{Z}, +)$, the order on the rationals $(\mathbb{Q}, \leq)$, and the Boolean algebra of finite or co-finite subsets of $\mathbb{N}$.

Thus an automatic structure is one that is explicitly given by finite automata that recognise the domain and the basic relations of the structure. An automatically presentable structure is one that is isomorphic to some automatic structure. Informally, automatically presentable structures are those that have finite automata implementations. The same structure may have different (indeed infinitely many) automatic presentations. One of our goals is to understand the relationships between different automatic presentations of a given structure and understand how the automata-theoretic properties of relations of this structure change when one varies its automatic presentation. We illustrate the introduced concepts with two examples. The first concerns the standard model of Presburger Arithmetic $(\mathbb{N}, +)$.

Example 2.4. For each $m > 1$ consider the presentation $\mathcal{A}_m$ of $\mathbb{N}$ over the alphabet $\Sigma_m = \{0, \ldots, m - 1\}$. Here the natural number $n \in \mathbb{N}$ is represented in A_m as its shortest the least-significant-digit-first base m-representation. The structure $(A_m, +_m)$ is automatic and is isomorphic to $(\mathbb{N}, +)$. Hence, these are automatic presentations of $(\mathbb{N}, +)$. Take any n-ary relation R in $\mathbb{N}$. Assume that R is intrinsically regular. Then the image $R^{(m)}$ of R in $(A_m, +_m)$ is regular. The well-known Cobham-Semenov Theorem, see [2], states that if both $R^{(i)}$ and $R^{(j)}$ are regular for multiplicatively independent i and j, then R is definable in $(\mathbb{N}, +)$. Thus $\mathrm{IR}(\mathbb{N}, +) = \mathrm{FO}(\mathbb{N}, +)$.

The second example concerns an extension of $(\mathbb{N}, +)$.

Example 2.5. Let $|_m$, for $m \geq 2$, be the binary relation where $x|_m y$ if and only if x is a power of m and x divides y. Then the structure $(\mathbb{N}, +, |_m)$ has an automatic presentation $\mathcal{A}_m = (A_m, +_m, D_m)$. So if $R \subset \mathbb{N}^m$ is intrinsically regular for $(\mathbb{N}, +, |_m)$, then its image $R^{(m)}$ is regular in $\mathcal{A}_m$. But a central result of automatic structures is that first order definability in the structure $\mathcal{A}_m$ is equivalent to FA recognisability, see for instance [6]. Hence $R^{(m)}$ is first order definable in $\mathcal{A}_m$, and so R is first order definable in $(\mathbb{N}, +, |_m)$. Thus $\mathrm{IR}(\mathbb{N}, +, |_m) = \mathrm{FO}(\mathbb{N}, +, |_m)$.

3 Intrinsically Regular Relations in $(\mathbb{N}, \leq)$

The linearly ordered set $(\mathbb{N}, \leq)$ has automatic presentations. For example, automatic presentations of $(\mathbb{N}, +)$ are also automatic presentations of $(\mathbb{N}, \leq)$. In this section we study intrinsically regular relations of this structure. Somewhat surprisingly we exhibit intrinsically regular relations of the structure $(\mathbb{N}, \leq)$ that are not definable. We remind the reader that the only first order definable unary relations of $(\mathbb{N}, \leq)$ are finite or co-finite, [4, Theorem 32A].

Let $M^i \subseteq \mathbb{N}$ be the set of all positions in $\mathbb{N}$ that are multiples of i. Then these sets are not definable in $(\mathbb{N}, \leq)$, but are intrinsically regular:

Theorem 3.1. *For every i the unary predicate M^i is intrinsically regular in the structure $(\mathbb{N}, \leq)$.*

Proof. Let $(D, \leq_D)$ be an automatic presentation of $(\mathbb{N}, \leq)$ over Σ. We prove the case when $i = 2$; the case when $i \geq 3$ can be proved in a similar way. Let $E \subseteq D$ be the set of words corresponding to the set of all even natural numbers. Then $x \in E$ iff $\{y \in D \mid y \leq_D x\}$ has odd cardinality. Our goal is to define an automaton over Σ that accepts all such strings x. A rough idea is that the new automaton we want to build calculates the parity of the number of paths in $\mathcal{A}$ with second component fixed at x and accepts x when the parity of the number of successful paths is odd.

Let $\mathcal{A} = (Q_A, \iota_A, \Delta_A, F_A)$ be the automaton over Σ recognising $\leq_D$. We assume that the automaton $\mathcal{A}$ is deterministic. Also, note that since the set $\{y \in D \mid y \leq_D x\}$ is finite for any string $x \in D$, we may assume the following. For each state $s \in Q_A$ there are finitely many strings of the form $(v, \diamond^m)$ that transform the state s into a final state.

Fix a string $x \in D$ and a prefix w of x. For a state $s \in Q_A$ consider all strings v such that $|v| = |w|$ and the automaton $\mathcal{A}$ transforms the string (v, w) to state s from the initial state ι_A. Call these strings (w, s)–strings.

The idea in constructing the desired automaton is this. We use the automaton $\mathcal{A}$. Processing the initial prefix w of x, for each state s, we count the parity of the number of (w, s)–strings. We keep a record of only those states s such that the number of (w, s)–strings is odd. By the time we finish processing the string x we have a record of all states $s_1, \ldots, s_k$ such that for each state s_i there are an odd number of (x, s_i)–strings. For each s_i we count the number n_i of strings of the type $\left(\begin{smallmatrix} v \\ \diamond^m \end{smallmatrix}\right)$, with $m = |v|$, such that the string $\left(\begin{smallmatrix} v \\ \diamond^m \end{smallmatrix}\right)$ transforms s_i into a final state of $\mathcal{A}$. Then whether or not $x \in E$ can be decided based upon the parity of the numbers $n_1, \ldots, n_k$. Here is a formal description of the desired automaton $\mathcal{B} = (Q_B, \iota_B, \Delta_B, F_B)$ over $\Sigma_\diamond$:

1. The set Q_B of states of $\mathcal{B}$ are all subsets of Q_A.
2. The initial state ι_B of $\mathcal{B}$ is $\{\iota_A\}$.
3. $\Delta_B(X, \sigma) = Y$, where Y consists of all states $s \in Q_A$ such that there are an odd number of pairs (s', σ') for which $s = \Delta_A(s', \left(\begin{smallmatrix} \sigma' \\ \sigma \end{smallmatrix}\right))$, $s' \in X$ and $\sigma' \in \Sigma_\diamond$. (Note that Y could be empty).
4. The set of final states F_B is defined as follows. Assume $X = \{s_1, \ldots, s_k\}$ is a subset of Q_A. For each s_i, count the number n_i of all strings of the type $\left(\begin{smallmatrix} v \\ \diamond^m \end{smallmatrix}\right)$, with $v \in \Sigma^*$, $m = |v|$, such that the string $\left(\begin{smallmatrix} v \\ \diamond^m \end{smallmatrix}\right)$ transforms s_i into a final state of $\mathcal{A}$. Then $X \in F_B$ if and only if $X \neq \emptyset$ and the number $n_1 + \ldots + n_k$ is odd.

Let $x = \sigma_0 \ldots \sigma_n$ be an input string for $\mathcal{B}$. Let m be the cardinality of the set $\{y \mid y \leq_D x\}$. Let $X_0 = \{\iota_A\}$, $X_1, \ldots, X_{n+1}$ be a run of $\mathcal{B}$ on x. The automaton has the following property $(*)$ that can be proved by induction on $i \geq 1$:

$(*)$ A state s is in X_i if and only if the number of $(\sigma_0 \ldots \sigma_{i-1}, s)$–strings is odd.

Let $X_{n+1} = \{s_1, \ldots, s_n\}$. For each $s_i \in X_{n+1}$ the number of (s_i, x)–strings is odd. Consider the number n_i of all strings of the type $\left(\begin{smallmatrix} v \\ \diamond^m \end{smallmatrix}\right)$, with $m = |v|$, such that the string $\left(\begin{smallmatrix} v \\ \diamond^m \end{smallmatrix}\right)$ transforms s_i into a final state of $\mathcal{A}$. From the definition of final states for $\mathcal{B}$, and the inductive assumption on X_n, we see that the cardinality of the set $\{y \mid y \leq_D x\}$ is odd if and only if X_n is non-empty and the number $n_1 + n_2 + \ldots + n_k$ is odd. The theorem is proved. $\qquad\square$

As mentioned in the introduction, this proof can be generalised as follows.

Theorem 3.2. *Let $\mathcal{A}$ be an automatic structure. There exists an algorithm that from any $FO^{\infty, \mathrm{mod}}$ definition ϕ of a relation R produces an automaton recognising R. In particular, $FO^{\infty, \mathrm{mod}}(\mathcal{A}) \subset IR(\mathcal{A})$.*

Proof (sketch). Constructing an automata that recognises relation definable by $\exists^{(i)} y\, \psi(\bar{x}, y)$ formula is done in a style similar to the proof of Theorem 3.1. Now note that $\exists^\infty y\, \psi(\bar{x}, y)$ is equivalent to $\forall z \exists y (y \preceq z \,\&\, \phi(\bar{x}, y))$, where $\preceq$ is the length-lexicographic ordering on the domain of $\mathcal{A}$.   □

Theorem 3.3. $IR(\mathbb{N}, \leq) = FO^{\infty, \mathrm{mod}}(\mathbb{N}, \leq) = FO(\mathbb{N}, \leq, M^2, M^3, \ldots)$.

Proof (sketch). By Theorem 3.2, $FO^{\infty, \mathrm{mod}}(\mathbb{N}, \leq) \subset IR(\mathbb{N}, \leq)$. So suppose that a relation R is intrinsically regular for $(\mathbb{N}, \leq)$. Then R is regular in every automatic presentation of $(\mathbb{N}, \leq)$. Consider the structure $(1^*, \leq)$ where $\leq$ stands for the ordering induced by the one on the length: $1^n \leq 1^m$ whenever $n \leq m$. This structure is a (unary) automatic presentation of $(\mathbb{N}, \leq)$ and hence the image of R in this presentation is regular. It is shown in [3] that the regular relations over the unary alphabet coincide with those that are first order definable in structure $(\mathbb{N}, \leq, M^2, M^3, \ldots)$. This can be done, for example, via an analysis of finite automata recognising relations over the unary alphabet. Finally, suppose R is first order definable in $(\mathbb{N}, \leq, M^2, M^3, \ldots)$. Since the M^i are $FO^{\infty, \mathrm{mod}}$ definable in $(\mathbb{N}, \leq)$, then so is R.   □

We end the section with a simple application of Theorem 3.2 which gives a generalization of Theorem 3.1. A *tree* $\mathcal{T} = (T, \preceq)$ is a partially ordered set with a least element (the root) and for which every set of the form $\{y \in T \mid y \preceq x\}$ is a finite linear order. The *level* n of $\mathcal{T}$ is the set of all $x \in T$ such that the cardinality of $\{y \in T \mid y \preceq x\}$ is n.

Corollary 3.4. *Let $(T, \preceq)$ be an automatic tree. Given $n \in \mathbb{N}$, the set $\{x \in T \mid x$ is on level $n \cdot m$ for some $m \in \mathbb{N}\}$ is a regular subset of T.*

4   Intrinsic Regularity in $(\mathbb{N}, S)$

Consider the structure $(\mathbb{N}, S)$, where S is the successor function. Our goal is to show that in this structure, all intrinsically regular unary relations are those that are either finite or co–finite. We are also interested in providing automatic presentations of $(\mathbb{N}, S)$ in which some familiar relations are regular and some not. Recall that the finite or co-finite subsets are the only unary relations of this structure that are first order definable, a property that easily follows from elimination of quantifiers [4, Theorem 31G]. The next theorem shows that the set M^k is not intrinsically regular relation in $(\mathbb{N}, S)$, and so by Theorem 3.1 neither is $\leq$.

Theorem 4.1. *For every $k \geq 2$, there is an automatic presentation of $(\mathbb{N}, S)$ in which the image of the set M^k is not regular.*

Proof. Fix $k \geq 2$ and let $\Sigma = \{0, 1, \ldots, k - 1\}$. We construct an automatic structure (Σ^*, f) isomorphic to $(\mathbb{N}, S)$. To do this, for any given string $x \in \Sigma^*$, we introduce the following auxiliary notations: $ep(x)$ is the string represented by bits of x at even positions; $op(x)$ is the string represented by bits of x at odd positions; n and m are the lengths of strings $ep(x)$ and $op(x)$, respectively. We may also treat $ep(x)$ and $op(x)$ as natural numbers written in least-significant-digit-first base k, and in particular perform addition on them. For example, if

$x = 0111001$ then $ep(x) = 0101$, $op(x) = 110$, $n = 4$ and $m = 3$; note that $m \leq n \leq m+1$ and $|x| = m+n$. We may regard the string x as the ordered pair of strings, written $\langle ep(x), op(x) \rangle$, and think of $op(x)$ as a parameter. Call strings x for which $ep(x) = k^{n-1}$ *midpoints* and strings for which $ep(x) = 0$ modulo k^n *startpoints*. Now we describe rules defining the function f. In brackets [[like this]] we explain the meaning of each rule if needed. We note in advance that all arithmetic is performed modulo k^n. Define an auxiliary function $\text{next}(x) = ep(x) + kop(x) + k - 1$ modulo k^n.

1. If $n \leq 2$ then $f(x)$ is the successor of x with respect to length-lexicographic ordering.
2. If $\langle \text{next}(x), op(y) \rangle$ is neither a midpoint nor a startpoint then $f(x) = y$, where $ep(y) = \text{next}(x)$ and $op(y) = op(x)$. [[This is the generic case according to which the successor of the string x, regarded as the pair $\langle ep(x), op(x) \rangle$, is $\langle \text{next}(x), op(x) \rangle$.]]
3. If $\langle \text{next}(x), op(y) \rangle$ is a midpoint then $f(x) = y$, where $|y| = |x|$, $ep(y) = ep(x) + \text{next}(\text{next}(x))$ modulo k^n and $op(y) = op(x)$. [[This case says that if adding $\text{next}(x)$ to $ep(x)$ produces a midpoint then the midpoint should be skipped. Note that $ep(y) = ep(x) + 2\text{next}(x)$.]]
4. If $\langle \text{next}(x), op(x) \rangle$ is a startpoint then $f(x) = y$, where $|y| = |x|$, $ep(y) = k^{n-1}$ and $op(y) = op(x)$. [[The successor of the endpoint is the midpoint.]]
5. If $\langle ep(x), op(x) \rangle$ is a midpoint and $op(x) < k^m - 1$ then $f(x) = y$, where $|y| = |x|$, $ep(y) = 0$ and $op(y) = op(x) + 1$ modulo k^n. [[This is the case when the parameter $op(x)$ is incremented by 1, and the string $ep(x)$ is initialized to the string consisting of n zeros.]]
6. If $\langle ep(x), op(x) \rangle$ is a midpoint and $op(x) = k^m - 1$ then $f(x) = 0^{n+m+1}$. [[This is the only case when the length of string x increases by one.]]

Now we explain how f acts. Fix $b \in \mathbb{N}$ congruent to $k - 1$ modulo k. For every $a \in \mathbb{N}$ there is a unique number $c \in \{0, 1, \ldots, k^n - 1\}$ such that $a = b \cdot c$ modulo k^n. In other words, every element $c \in \{0, 1, \ldots, k^n - 1\}$ appears exactly once in the sequence $0, b, 2b, 3b, \ldots, (k^n - 1)b$, where elements are taken modulo k^n. Moreover, $k^{n-1}b$ equals k^{n-1} modulo k^n. Hence, $k^{n-1}b$ appears in the middle of this sequence. Let us assume that x is such that $ep(x) = 0$ and let $b = kop(x) + k - 1$. Then by rules 2, 5 and 6, the function f consecutively applied $k^n - 1$ times to $\langle 0, op(x) \rangle$ produces the following sequence:

$$\langle 0, op(x) \rangle, \langle b, op(x) \rangle, \ldots, \langle k^{n-1} - b, op(x) \rangle, \langle k^{n-1} + b, op(x) \rangle,$$
$$\ldots, \langle k^n - b, op(x) \rangle, \langle k^{n-1}, op(x) \rangle.$$

Note that the midpoint $\langle k^{n-1}, op(x) \rangle$ has been removed from the middle of the sequence $\langle 0, op(x) \rangle, \langle b, op(x) \rangle, \ldots, \langle k^n - b, op(x) \rangle$, and placed at the end. Finally rules 3 and 4 imply that f applied to the last string v in the sequence produces the string $\langle 0, op(x) + 1 \rangle$ if $op(x) \neq k^m - 1$; otherwise $f(v) = 0^{n+m+1}$. This completes the description of f.

The function f is FA recognisable because all the rules used in the definition of f be can tested by finite automata. It can be checked that (Σ^*, f) is isomorphic to $(\mathbb{N}, S)$, say via mapping $\pi : \Sigma^* \to \mathbb{N}$.

Our goal is to show that the image of the set $M^k = \{x \mid x$ is a multiple of $k\}$ is not regular in the described automatic presentation of $(\mathbb{N}, S)$. For this we need to have a finer analysis of the isomorphism π from (Σ^*, f) to $(\mathbb{N}, S)$. Denote by x' the string $\langle 0, op(x) \rangle$. One can inductively check the following for the case that $n \geq 3$.

1. The number $\pi(x')$ is congruent to 0 modulo k for all non-empty strings x.
2. There is a unique $u \leq k^n - 1$ such that $ep(x) = u \cdot (kop(x) + k - 1)$ modulo k^n. Moreover:
   a) If $u < k^{n-1}$ then $\pi(x) = \pi(x') + u$.
   b) If $u > k^{n-1}$ then $\pi(x) = \pi(x') + u - 1$.
   c) If $u = k^{n-1}$ then $\pi(x) = \pi(x') + k^n - 1$.
3. If $ep(y) = 0$ and $op(y) = op(x') + 1 \leq k^m - 1$ then $\pi(y) = \pi(x') + k^n$.

Thus, from the above it is easy to see that x is in the image of M^k iff either $u < k^{n-1}$ and u is congruent to 0 modulo k or $u \geq k^{n-1}$ and u is congruent to 1 modulo k. In order to show that the image of M^k is not regular, consider all the strings x such that n is odd, $ep(x) = 1^n$ (its numerical value is $k^{n+1} - 1$), $op(x) = 0^{m-r}1^r$ (its numerical value is $k^{r+1} - 1$, so that $kop(x) + k - 1 = k^{r+2} - 1$), and $n > r + 4$. Then under these premises for every $r \in \mathbb{N}$ the minimal $n \in \mathbb{N}$ for which $x \in \pi(M^k)$ is when $n = 2r + 5$:

Indeed, $(k^{n-1} + k^{r+2} + 1) \cdot (k^{r+2} - 1) = k^{2r+4} - k^{n-1} - 1$ modulo k^n. So under the assumption that $n = 2r + 5$, this is equal to $-1 = ep(x)$ modulo k^n. Hence $u = k^{n-1} + k^{r+2} + 1 > k^{n-1}$ and so by item 2b above conclude that $\pi(x) = \pi(x') + k^{n-1} + k^{r+1}$ and so $x \in \pi(M^k)$.

For the converse, $(k^{r+2} + 1) \cdot (k^{r+2} - 1) = k^{2r+4} - 1$ modulo k^n. Hence under the assumption that $n < 2r + 5$, this is equal to $-1 = ep(x)$ modulo k^n. Now if further $r + 3 < n - 1$, then $u = k^{r+2} + 1 < k^{n-1}$, and so by item 2a above conclude that $\pi(x) = \pi(x') + k^{r+2} + 1$ and so $x \notin \pi(M^k)$.

Now we can check that $\pi(M^k)$ is not regular. Note that in the presence of $n = 2r + 5$ the assumption that $n > r + 4$ is redundant since $n \leq r + 4$ implies that $r \leq -1$ which contradicts that $r \in \mathbb{N}$. So consider the non regular set

$$Y = \{x \in \Sigma^* \mid ep(x) = 1^n, op(x) = 0^{m-r}1^r, n = 2r + 5\}.$$

It can be defined from $\pi(M^k)$ as the set of all $x \in \Sigma^*$ such that $ep(x) = 1^n$, for some odd n, $op(x) = 0^{m-r}1^r$ for some $m, r \in \mathbb{N}$, $n > r + 4$, $x \in \pi(M^k)$ and if $r + 4 < s < n$ then $(1^s, op(x)) \notin \pi(M^k)$. But since Y is not regular, neither is $\pi(M^k)$, as required. □

Corollary 4.2. *A unary relation $R \subset \mathbb{N}$ is intrinsically regular in $(\mathbb{N}, S)$ if and only if it is in $FO^{\infty, \mathrm{mod}}(\mathbb{N}, S)$.*

Proof. The reverse direction is immediate. For the forward direction it is sufficient to prove that if $R \subset \mathbb{N}$ is intrinsically regular in $(\mathbb{N}, S)$ then it is finite or co-finite; in this case it is in $FO(\mathbb{N}, S)$ and so certainly in $FO^{\infty, \mathrm{mod}}(\mathbb{N}, S)$. It can be proved that if R is an eventually periodic set, and if it is infinite and co-infinite, then there is some period p of R such that M_p is first order definable $(\mathbb{N}, S, R)$. Assuming this proceed as follows. Let $R \subset \mathbb{N}$ be intrinsically regular in $(\mathbb{N}, S)$. Since $(1^*, \otimes\{(1^n, 1^{n+1}) \mid n \in \mathbb{N}\})$ is an automatic presentation of $(\mathbb{N}, S)$, R must be eventually periodic. If R is finite or co-finite we are done. Otherwise R is regular in every presentation of $(\mathbb{N}, S)$ and using the fact there exists a period p of R such that M_p is first order definable in $(\mathbb{N}, S, R)$ we get that M_p is also intrinsically regular in $(\mathbb{N}, S)$ contradicting the previous theorem. $\qquad\square$

The first application of the results concerns the reachability relation in automatic graphs. The reachability problem for automatic graphs is undecidable, see [3]. The reason for this is that such automatic graphs necessarily have infinitely many components. In fact for automatic graphs with finitely many components the reachability problem is decidable. A natural question is whether or not the reachability relation for automatic graphs with finitely many components can be recognised by finite automata. To answer this question, consider the following graph $\mathcal{G} = (\{0, 1\}^*, Edge)$, where $Edge(x, y)$ if and only if $f^2(x) = y$ and f is the function defined in the proof of Theorem 4.1 for $k = 2$. The graph $\mathcal{G}$ is automatic with exactly two infinite components each being isomorphic to $(\mathbb{N}, S)$. One of the components coincides with M^2, and so neither component is regular. Hence, we have the following:

Corollary 4.3. *There exists an automatic presentation of a graph with exactly two connected components each isomorphic to $(\mathbb{N}, S)$ for which the reachability relation is not regular.*

A final application of this theorem is on the structure $(\mathbb{Z}, S)$. A *cut* is a set of the form $\{x \in \mathbb{Z} \mid x \geq n\}$, where $n \in \mathbb{Z}$ is fixed.

Corollary 4.4. *There is an automatic presentation of $(\mathbb{Z}, S)$ in which no cut is regular.*

Proof (sketch). It is sufficient to find a presentation of $(\mathbb{Z}, S, 0)$ in which $\{x \in \mathbb{Z} \mid x \geq 0\}$ is not regular since every other cut is first order definable from this one. We modify the presentation in the proof of Theorem 4.1 for $k = 2$, by considering the structure $(\{0, 1\}^*, g)$, where g is defined using the same notation as before. All arithmetic below is performed modulo 2^n.

1. If $n \leq 2$ then $g(x)$ is the length-lexicographic successor of x.
2. If $(ep(x) + 2op(x) + 1, op(x))$ is neither a midpoint nor a startpoint then $g(x) = y$ with $|x| = |y|$ and $ep(y) = ep(x) + 2op(x) + 1$ and $op(y) = op(x)$.
3. If $(ep(x) + 2op(x) + 1, op(x))$ is a midpoint, then
   a) if $op(x) < 2^m - 1$ then $g(x) = y$ with $|x| = |y|$ and $ep(y) = 0$ and $op(y) = op(x) + 1$.
   b) if $op(x) = 2^m - 1$ then $g(x) = y$ with $|y| = |x| + 1$ and $ep(y) = 0$ and $op(x) = 0$.
4. If $(ep(x) + 2op(x) + 1, op(x))$ is a startpoint, then
   a) if $op(x) < 2^m - 1$ then $g(x) = y$ with $|x| = |y|$ and $ep(y) = 2^{n-1}$ and $op(y) = op(x) + 1$.
   b) if $op(x) = 2^m - 1$ then
      i. if $n = 3$ and $m = 2$ then $g(x) = \epsilon$. Otherwise,

ii. if $n = m + 1$ then $g(x) = y$ with $|ep(y)| = n - 1$, $|op(y)| = m$ and $ep(y) = 2^{n-2}$ and $op(y) = 0$.

iii. if $n = m$ then $g(x) = y$ with $|ep(y)| = n$ and $|op(y)| = m - 1$ and $ep(y) = 2^{n-1}$ and $op(y) = 0$.

Thus, $(\{0,1\}^*, g, \epsilon)$ is an automatic presentation of $(\mathbb{Z}, S, 0)$ in which the cut above 0 is exactly those x such that $u < 2^n - 1$. But if this set were regular then so is the image of M^2 in $(\{0,1\}^*, f)$.   □

Finally we mention that there is an automatic presentation of $(\mathbb{N}, S)$ in which $\leq$ is not regular but all the unary relations $M^2, M^3, \ldots$ are regular. This shows that regularity of each of the sets M^i and the successor relation S do not generally imply that the relation $\leq$ is regular. Together with the previous result this theorem says that regularity of $\leq$ is independent of whether or not sets M^i are regular. The proof is available in the full version of this paper.

Theorem 4.5. *The structure* $(\mathbb{N}, S, M^2, M^3, \ldots)$ *has an automatic presentation in which the relation* $\leq$ *is not regular.*   □

Acknowledgment. We would like to thank the referees for their suggestions to improve the presentation of the paper and for their thorough reading.

References

1. Christopher J. Ash and Anil Nerode. Intrinsically recursive relations. In *Aspects of effective algebra* (*Clayton, 1979*), pages 26–41. Upside Down A Book Co. Yarra Glen, 1981.
2. Veronique Bruyère, Georges Hansel, Christian Michaux and Roger Villemaire. Logic and p-recognizable sets of integers. *Bull. Belg. Math. Soc.*, 1:191–238, 1994.
3. Achim Blumensath and Erich Grädel. *Automatic Structures*, Proceedings of 15th Symposium on Logic in Computer Science, LICS 2000.
4. Herbert B. Enderton. *A mathematical introduction to logic*. Academic Press, first edition, 1972.
5. Ershov et al. (eds). Handbook of Recursive Mathematics Volume 1. Studies in Logic and the foundations of Mathematics, Elsevier, 1998.
6. Bakhadyr Khoussainov and Anil Nerode. Automatic presentations of structures. *Lecture Notes in Computer Science*, 960:367–392, 1995.

Active Context-Free Games*

Anca Muscholl[1], Thomas Schwentick[2], and Luc Segoufin[3]

[1] LIAFA, Université Paris VII, 2 pl. Jussieu, F-75251 Paris
[2] Philipps-Universität Marburg, FB Mathematik und Informatik, D-35032 Marburg
[3] INRIA, Parc Club Orsay Univ., ZAC des vignes, 4 rue J. Monod, F-91893 Orsay

Abstract. An *Active* Context-Free Game is a game with two players (ROMEO and JULIET) on strings over a finite alphabet. In each move, JULIET selects a position of the current word and ROMEO rewrites the corresponding letter according to a rule of a context-free grammar. JULIET wins if a string of the regular target language is reached. We consider the complexity of deciding winning strategies for JULIET depending on properties of the grammar, of the target language, and on restrictions on the strategy.

1 Introduction

This work was motivated by implementation issues that arose while developing *active XML* (AXML) at INRIA. Active XML extends the framework of XML for describing semi-structured data by a dynamic component, allowing to cope with e.g. web services and peer-to-peer architectures. For an extensive overview of AXML we refer to [2,3,11].

We briefly describe here the background needed for understanding the motivation of this work. Roughly speaking, an AXML document consists of some explicitly defined data, together with some parts that are defined only intensionally, by means of embedded calls to web services [3,9,7]. An example of an AXML document is given in Figure 1. An important feature is that the call of a web service may return data containing new embedded calls to further web services (see Figure 1). Each web service is specified using an *active* extension of WSDL [17], which defines its input and output type by means of AXML-schemes which in turn are an immediate extension of XML-schemes with additional tags for service calls. For instance, the specification of the service *www.meteo.fr* can be STRING → STRING while the specification of *www.aden.fr* can be ∅ → OPERAS*MOVIES*OUTDOOR* where OPERA, MOVIES, OUTDOOR is either STRING* or a pointer to a web service.

Whenever a user or another application requests some data, the system must decide which data has to be materialized, in order to satisfy the request specification. An important issue is then which services are called and in which order. Assume for instance for our example in Figure 1 that there is a fee for each service call. If the request requires to minimize the overall costs, the system

---

* Work supported by the DAAD and Egide under PROCOPE grant D/0205766.

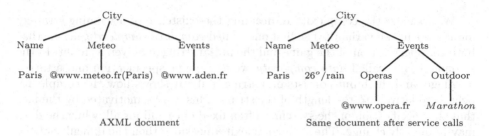

AXML document   Same document after service calls

Fig. 1.

should first call *www.aden.fr* in order to get the list of events and only call the weather forecast if there is some available outdoor event. The requests we are considering in this paper ask for all available data of a given type as specified by an AXML-schema.

The system has access to local data, service specifications and a request specification. This can be modeled as follows (see [12,1,15]): (i) the local data is an AXML document corresponding to a labeled, unranked tree, (ii) the input/output type of a service specification is specified by a regular tree language, and, (iii) the requested data is also modeled by a regular tree language.

As this problem turns out to be computationally difficult, we consider a simpler version. Actually, even this simpler variant is undecidable without any further restrictions. First we assume that services do not have any input. Note that services with a fixed number of different inputs can be modeled by considering several different services, one per input option. Secondly, we assume that the output type consists of finitely many options, that is the regular language is in fact a disjunction of finitely many cases. Finally, we deal with strings instead of trees. This simplifies the combinatorics and allows a better understanding of the problem. Thus, the problem we consider here is stated as follows: given (i) a string, (ii) a set of service specifications of the form $A \ \rangle \ u_1 \mid \cdots \mid u_n$, where A is a letter and the u_i are strings, and (iii) a regular string language, can we decide which services to call and in which order, such that the string eventually obtained belongs to the regular language representing the target? We formalize this problem in terms of games. We discuss extensions of our framework to trees and full regular languages in the last section of the paper.

An *Active Context-Free Game* (CF-game) is played by two players (ROMEO and JULIET) on strings over a finite alphabet. Its rules are defined by a context-free grammar (CFG) and its target by a regular language given by a regular expression (equivalently, a non-deterministic automaton, NFA). In each move, JULIET jumps to a position of the current word and ROMEO rewrites the corresponding letter according to some rule of the grammar. JULIET wins a play if the string obtained belongs to the target language. The intended meaning is obvious: JULIET is the system, ROMEO the environment, the CFG corresponds to the service specification and the target language to the request specification.

We consider the complexity of deciding the existence of a winning strategy for JULIET in two variants. The first one, called *combined complexity*, means that both the specification of the game and the initial string are given as input. In the second variant, called *data complexity*, we fix a game specification and a target language, and the input consists of a string, only. It shows how the complexity behaves relatively to the length of the string. This can be motivated by the fact that the specification of the system is often fixed once and for all, while the data may frequently change. The data complexity measures then the difficulty of the problem after preprocessing the specification.

We show that without any restrictions, there is a fixed CF-game for which data complexity is already undecidable. Thus we consider simpler variants of the problem by restricting the set of rules, the regular target language, or the strategy. The above example already suggests two restrictions. First, both service calls give rise to one new service call tag, only. This means that the underlying CFG is linear. We also consider the more restricted case of unary grammars, where a service call may only return another service call or some data without any service call tag. A more realistic restriction, that is satisfied by the above example and probably by most applications, is that the iterated answer of service calls does not give back a tag with the same service call. This restriction corresponds to non-recursive CFGs and to non-recursive CFGs of given depth (bounded CFGs). The problem is decidable for all these restrictions, although it is intractable in some cases (e.g., EXPSPACE for non-recursive grammars without uniform depth bound). We also consider left-to-right strategies where JULIET has to traverse the string from left to right. In the above scenario this amounts to having a heuristics for parsing the data tree only once, such that if the system decides not to call a service, it never comes back to this service again. This limits drastically the possibilities of the system but also decreases significantly the complexity of the problem. Combined with general CFGs the decision complexity is 2EXPTIME and combined with non-recursive rules it is EXPTIME. But for all other restrictions the complexity is at most PSPACE. This restriction allows for a uniform decision procedure (and very efficient preprocessing as well) as an automaton accepting all winning configurations (strings) can be computed from the CF-game independently from the input string. To further decrease the complexity we also consider games where the specification of the target language is given as a deterministic automaton (DFA). In the case of bounded CFGs, and left-to-right strategies we end up with a tractable PTIME decision procedure. This case seems rather restrictive at first sight, but it is general enough to handle many practical cases and it has been implemented in AXML [11].

Figures 2 and 3 summarize our results. The numbers in brackets refer to the corresponding theorem or lemma, respectively. All complexities are tight.

Related work. For left-to-right strategies there is a tight connection with games on pushdown graphs [16] (see Propositions 1 and 2), which explains the decidability for arbitrary CFGs. A question related to the game problem is that of verifying properties of infinite graphs defined by CF-games (model-checking). Similar questions have been asked, e.g., for automatic graphs [4], process rewrit-

Rules Restriction	Combined Complexity NFA/DFA	Data Complexity
general	undecidable (1)	undecidable (1)
non-recursive	ExpSpace (4)	PSpace (5)
bounded	PSpace (5)	PSpace (5)
linear	ExpTime (5,1)	ExpTime (1)
unary	ExpTime (5,1)	ExpTime (1)

Fig. 2. Unrestricted strategies

Rules Restriction	Combined Complexity NFA	Combined Complexity DFA	Data Complexity
general	2ExpTime (3)	ExpTime (2)	regular (2)
non-recursive	ExpTime (8)	PSpace (9)	regular (2)
bounded	PSpace (6)	PTime (7)	regular (2)
linear	PSpace(10)	PSpace (11)	regular (2)
unary	PSpace (10)	PTime (12)	regular (2)

Fig. 3. Left-to-right strategies

ing graphs [10] and ground tree rewriting graphs [8]. For instance, [8] considers CTL-like versions of the reachability problem in ground tree rewriting graphs. Graphs generated by CFGs on strings can be seen as a special case of ground tree rewriting graphs and therefore the undecidability result obtained in [8] follows from our Theorem 1.

Overview. The paper is organized as follows. Section 2 gives formal definitions and fixes the notation. It also describes a couple of extensions of the basic game which are used in the lower bound proofs. The results on arbitrary CFGs are given in Section 3. Non-recursive and linear CFGs are considered respectively in Section 4 and Section 5. Due to lack of space several proofs are omitted.

2   Definitions

A CF-game is a tuple $G = \langle \Sigma, R, T \rangle$, where Σ is a finite alphabet, $R \subseteq \Sigma \times \Sigma^+$ a finite set of *rules* and T a regular *target language*. Note that the rewriting rules do not allow the empty string on the right-hand side. We call a symbol A of Σ a *non-terminal* if it occurs on the left-hand-side of some rule in R, otherwise a *terminal*.

A *play* of the game G is played by two players, JULIET and ROMEO, which play in *rounds*. In each round, first JULIET selects a position and then ROMEO chooses a rewriting rule associated to the letter of the chosen position.

A *configuration* C of the game is a tuple (w, i, c) where w is a string (*the current word*), $i \leq |w|$ is a number (*the current position*) and c is either pos or rule. A *position choice* in configuration (w, i, pos) consists of selecting a position $j \leq |w|$ resulting in (w, j, rule). A *rule choice* in configuration $(a_1 \cdots a_n, j, \text{rule})$ consists of replacing a_j by a string u such that $a_j \to u$ is a rule of G. The result is $(a_1 \cdots a_{j-1} u a_{j+1} \cdots a_n, j, \text{pos})$. A play starts in an *initial configuration* $C_0 = (w, 1, \text{pos})$, for some string w.

The play stops and JULIET wins if after some round the resulting string is in T. Otherwise it goes on. ROMEO wins immediately, if JULIET chooses a position j, whose corresponding symbol is terminal. As usual, we say that JULIET has a *winning strategy* in configuration (w, i, c) if, no matter how ROMEO plays, T is reached within a finite number of moves.

Note that the winning condition for JULIET is in the first level of the Borel hierarchy (reachability of a set). By Martin's determinacy theorem, CF-games are thus determined i.e., from each configuration one of the two players must have a winning strategy, [6].

We consider the decision problem for JULIET to have a winning strategy in G on a string w. This comes in two flavors, *combined decision problem* and *data decision problem*. The *combined decision problem* is:

[Combined] INPUT: A CF-game $G = \langle \Sigma, R, T \rangle$, a string w
    OUTPUT: True iff JULIET has a winning strategy in G on w.

The *data decision problem* associated with a CF-game G is:

[Data(G)] INPUT: A string w
    OUTPUT: True iff JULIET has a winning strategy in G on w.

We say that JULIET has a *left-to-right winning strategy* if she can always choose a position which is bigger or equal to the position chosen in the preceding move. We call the set R of rules of a game *unary* if each rule is of the form $A \to B$ with $B \in \Sigma$. We call it *linear* if each right-hand side of a rule contains at most one non-terminal. The set R is called *non-recursive* if no symbol A can be derived from A by a non-empty sequence. For a non-recursive set R we call the maximal depth d of a leaf in a derivation tree of R the *depth* of R. A CF-game G is *unary* (resp. *linear, non-recursive*) if its set R of rules is.

Extended games. In the lower bound proofs we make use of several extensions of the basic CF-game in order to simplify reductions. It turns out that the complexity of the decision problems does not change in many cases (we omit the proof of this result in this abstract). These extensions are

- *navigation constraints*: basically regular expressions associated with a rule, which restrict the possible position choices for JULIET in the next move. As an example, JULIET can be forced to choose the next position immediately to the right of the current one;
- *symmetric rule choice*: symbols for which JULIET, instead of ROMEO, chooses the rule;
- *concatenation of games*: games may consist of several successive phases.

For unrestricted strategies, every game G with all these features can be simulated by a usual game G' in polynomial time and every string w can be translated into a string w' such that JULIET wins (G, w) iff she wins (G', w'). Furthermore, unarity, linearity, non-recursiveness and even boundedness are preserved (but not all combinations, e.g. unarity and boundedness are not preserved at the same time). A similar result holds for left-to-right strategies. Navigation constraints behave in an analogous way. For symmetric rule choice, unarity is only preserved if all rules have navigation constraints. Concatenation of games does not seem to work here.

3 Unrestricted Rules

The section is divided into two parts. In the first one we consider unrestricted strategies, while the second one is devoted to left-to-right strategies.

Unrestricted strategies. We prove first that in general, both decision problems are undecidable. We will make use of the following lemma which establishes a close connection between computations and CF-games.

Lemma 1. *Let M be an alternating Turing machine with space bound $s(n)$ and initial state q_0. We can construct in polynomial time a unary game $G = \langle \Sigma, R, T \rangle$ such that the following assertion holds:*

For every input $w = a_1 \cdots a_n$ to M, JULIET has a winning strategy for G on the string $w' = \$(q_0, a_1)a_2 \cdots a_n \sqcup^{s(n)-n} \#$ if and only if $w \in \mathcal{L}(M)$.

The proof idea for the lemma above is to simulate a computation path of the alternating TM by letting JULIET play in existential configurations (symmetric rule choice) and ROMEO in universal configurations. One single transition is simulated by a sequence of game moves, in which we use navigation constraints for forcing the players to rewrite the symbols affected by the transition.

From the theorem below it follows that both decision problems of CF-games are undecidable:

Theorem 1. *There exists a CF-game G for which the data decision problem is undecidable.*

Proof (Sketch): We reduce the *Post correspondence problem (PCP)* to Data(G), for some fixed game G. An instance of PCP is given by two sequences $u_1, \ldots, u_n$ and $v_1, \ldots, v_n$ of finite words over $\{a, b\}^*$ for some $n \in \mathbb{N}$. The problem is to check whether there exist $m > 0$, $i_1, \ldots, i_m$, such that $u_{i_1} \cdots u_{i_m} = v_{i_1} \cdots v_{i_m}$.

The game is played on the string
$w = \$ u_1 \& v_1 \& 01\, u_2 \& v_2 \& 001 \cdots u_n \& v_n \& 0^n 1 \& S \#$. We refer to the prefix of w before S by w_0. The string w encodes the PCP strings, together with their index. The symbol S will generate the solution $i_1, \ldots, i_m$.

The game has two phases. First, JULIET uses (non-linear, recursive) rules $\{S \to S_0 S_1 S, S_0 \to 0, S_1 \to 1, \# \to \sqcup \#\}$ to generate the string $w_0 (0S_1)^{i_1} (S_0 1)^{i_2} \cdots (0S_1)^{i_m} S \sqcup^k \#$. In phase two it is checked that this string encodes a solution to PCP. As a deterministic TM can do this in linear space, Lemma 1 guarantees that it also can be done by a CF-game. $\square$

Left-to-right strategies. In this section we consider only left-to-right strategies. Here, all problems become decidable, but the complexity depends on the representation of the target language. We first show that when the target language is given as a DFA, CF-games are closely related to pushdown games.

We then show that when the target language is given as a NFA that there is an inherent exponential blowup.

A *reachability pushdown game* is played on a graph $G_\mathcal{P}$ associated with an alternating pushdown system $\mathcal{P} = \langle Q = Q_E \cup Q_A, \Gamma, \delta, F \rangle$. The nodes of $G_\mathcal{P}$ are the configurations $(q, u) \in Q \times \Gamma^*$ of $\mathcal{P}$. The set Q of states is partitioned into existential (Q_E, EVE's states) and universal (Q_A, ADAM's states) states, and a node of $G_\mathcal{P}$ is existential (universal, resp.) if its control state is existential (universal, resp.). The transition relation $\delta \subseteq Q \times \Gamma \times Q \times \Gamma^*$ determines the edge relation $(q, u) \vdash (q', u')$ of $G_\mathcal{P}$.

EVE wins the reachability game if whatever ADAM's choices are, she can reach a final configuration. It is known that deciding whether a configuration is winning is EXPTIME-complete, [16]. Moreover, the set of winning configurations can be described by an alternating automaton of exponential size, [5,14].

The next two propositions show the relation between pushdown games and CF-games with left-to-right strategies and DFA target language.

Proposition 1. *Given a game* $G = \langle \Sigma, R, T \rangle$, *where* T *is a DFA with initial state* q_0, *we can construct in polynomial time a pushdown system* $\mathcal{P}$ *such that* JULIET *wins the game* G *on* w *if and only if the configuration* $c = (q_0, w\$)$ *is winning in the reachability pushdown game.*

Proof: Let Q denote the set of states of the DFA T and δ_T its transition function. The states of $\mathcal{P}$ are $Q \cup \bar{Q} \cup \{f\}$, with Q existential states, $\bar{Q}$ universal ones and f the unique final state. The stack symbols are $\Sigma \cup \{\$\}$, where $\$ \notin \Sigma$.

For every pair $q \in Q$, $A \in \Sigma$ we have the transitions $\delta(q, A) = \{(\delta_T(q, A), \text{pop}), (\bar{q}, A)\}$. The transitions correspond to JULIET either skipping the current position (pop), or selecting it and letting ROMEO play next. For every pair $(\bar{q}, A)$ and every rule $A \to u$ of G we have a transition $(q, u) \in \delta(\bar{q}, A)$. These transitions correspond to ROMEO choosing the corresponding rule in R. Finally, we add the transitions $(q, \$, f, \$)$ for every accepting state q of T. □

Proposition 2. *Given a pushdown system* $\mathcal{P}$ *we can construct in polynomial time a game* $G = \langle \Sigma, R, T \rangle$, *where* T *is a DFA, such that for any configuration* $c = (q, A_1 \cdots A_n)$ *of* $\mathcal{P}$, c *is winning in the pushdown game if and only if* JULIET *wins the game* G *on* $w = (q, A_1) A_2 \cdots A_n$.

Proposition 2 is shown by a game simulation using extended games. From propositions 1 and 2 and [16,5,14] we obtain immediately:

Theorem 2. *Given a game* $\langle \Sigma, R, T \rangle$, *where* T *is given as a DFA, it is* EXPTIME-*complete to know whether* JULIET *has a winning left-to-right strategy.*

Moreover the set of input words for which JULIET *has a left-to-right winning strategy is regular and an alternating automaton that recognizes it can be constructed in exponential time from* $\langle \Sigma, R, T \rangle$.

Note 1. Proposition 1 above cannot be extended to CF-games with a non-deterministic target automaton. Indeed consider the following example.

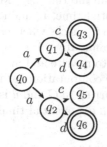

In the game $G = \langle \Sigma, G, \mathcal{A} \rangle$ where $G = \{b \to c \mid d\}$, JULIET has a winning strategy on ab: rewrite b, as both ac and ad are accepting for $\mathcal{A}$. But in the pushdown system as constructed in the proof of Proposition 1, ADAM has a winning strategy on $(q_0, ab\$)$: after reading a, EVE has to commit to state q_1 or to state q_2. Depending on EVE's choice at that state, ADAM will choose respectively d and c for replacing b and thus will end in a non accepting configuration with state respectively q_4 and q_5.

Theorem 3. *Given a game $\langle \Sigma, R, T \rangle$ with T given by an NFA, it is 2EXPTIME-complete to know whether* JULIET *has a winning left-to-right strategy.*

Proof (Sketch): As T can be transformed into an exponential size DFA, the 2EXPTIME upper bound follows immediately from Proposition 1 and the fact that the winner in a pushdown game can be determined in exponential time in the size of the game. The lower bound is shown by simulating the behavior of an alternating exponential space Turing machine M on input x. Starting from $S\&x$, during a first phase the players keep rewriting the leftmost symbol only, generating a sequence of configurations of M. Each configuration is encoded by a sequence of (symbol,position)-pairs, where the position is an exponential size number encoded in binary. The alternation of M is mimicked by alternating between JULIET- and ROMEO-choices (symmetric rule choice). In a second phase, it is checked in a single left-to-right pass, that the outcome of phase 1 really encodes an accepting computation of M on x. That is, ROMEO gets the chance to object each position of the current string, i.e., replace by a special symbol. Then JULIET wins immediately if the objected position is correct, hence she wins the game if there is no error in the outcome of the first phase. It is crucial here that an NFA of polynomial size in n can express that $j \neq i$ and $j \neq i + 1$, for two counter values $i, j < 2^n$. $\square$

4 Non-recursive Rules

In this section we focus on non-recursive games. We also consider *bounded games*, i.e., with depth bounded by some constant d. Non-recursive games are important in practice because many applications do not have recursion in the calls of web services and the nesting of calls is small.

Unrestricted strategies. We first consider non-recursive sets of rules. We stress that the lower bound of the following theorem does not depend on whether the target language is coded as an NFA or as a DFA. Indeed we can show that in general, for unrestricted strategies, a CF-game with a target language given by an NFA can be reduced in polynomial time to a CF-game whose target language is given by a DFA, while preserving unarity, linearity and non-recursiveness.

Theorem 4. *It is* EXPSPACE-*complete to decide whether* JULIET *has a winning strategy in a non-recursive game G on string w.*

Proof (Sketch): We show the upper bound by constructing an alternating TM deciding whether JULIET has a winning strategy in exponential time. It maintains on its tape the current game configuration. At each step it checks whether the string of the current configuration is in the target of the game. If yes it stops and accepts. If not it nondeterministically chooses a position to rewrite and universally branches over all possible rewritings. The time of each computation path is $O(m^d|w|)$, where m is the length of the maximal word occurring in G and d is the depth of G. The lower bound is obtained by simulating an exponential time alternating TM by a game. $\square$

We now consider games with set of rules of depth bounded by some given d. The first lemma is used in lower bound proofs to get down from depth d to depth 1, the second lemma shows that the data decision problem is already hard for $d = 1$ and unary rules.

Lemma 2. *For each $d \geq 1$ there are polynomial-time computable functions $G \mapsto G'$ and $(w, G) \mapsto w'$ transforming any d-bounded CF-game G into a 1-bounded CF-game G', such that JULIET has a winning strategy in (G, w) if and only if she has a winning strategy in (G', w'). Furthermore, linearity, unarity and deterministic target are preserved.*

Lemma 3. *There is a unary CF-game $G = (\Sigma, R, T)$ of depth 1 such that Data(G) is PSPACE-hard.*

Proof (Sketch): We use a reduction from the quantified Boolean satisfaction problem QBS. The input of QBS is a formula Φ in prenex normal form, with the quantifier-free part in 3CNF.

The extended game we construct consists of two phases and is played on a straightforward string encoding of Φ. The first phase is a left-to-right pass in which (i) each variable is rewritten by a truth value - by JULIET for existentially quantified variables and by ROMEO for universally quantified variables, (ii) a clause is selected by ROMEO, and, (iii) a literal in the clause by JULIET(symmetric rule choice). The second phase checks that the literal becomes true by the variable assignment. As R and T have to be independent of Φ, variable names are encoded as binary strings. Therefore, this check has to be done through the game by going back and forth between the value of each variable and the clause in which it is used. $\square$

When d is fixed, $O(m^d|w|)$ is a polynomial bound. Therefore, from the above lemma and the upper bound proof of Theorem 4 we get:

Theorem 5. *For each d, given a CF-game G with rules of depth bounded by d and a string w it is PSPACE-complete to tell whether JULIET has a winning strategy for G on w. Furthermore, there is a game G of depth 1 for which Data(G) is PSPACE-complete.*

Left-to-right strategies. We continue with non-recursive rules of depth bounded by some d, but we now concentrate on left-to-right strategies. Recall

Lemma 3 which shows that the data complexity of non-recursive games for unrestricted strategies is PSPACE-hard. With combined complexity PSPACE-hardness can now be obtained with only one pass.

Lemma 4. *For each $d \geq 1$, it is PSPACE-hard to tell, for a unary game $G = \langle \Sigma, R, T \rangle$ of depth d and a string w, whether JULIET has a left-to-right winning strategy.*

From Lemma 4 and an immediate adaptation of the proof of Theorem 5 for left-to-right strategies we obtain:

Theorem 6. *For each $d \geq 1$, it is PSPACE-complete to tell, for a game $G = \langle \Sigma, R, T \rangle$ of depth d, where T is given by an NFA, and a string w, whether JULIET has a winning left-to-right strategy for G on w.*

When the target language is given as a DFA the decision becomes tractable. The PTIME upper bound of the left-to-right, bounded, DFA target language case was already obtained in [11] using automata theoretical techniques. It is also the framework which has been implemented in AXML [11].

Theorem 7. *For each $d \geq 2$, given a game $G = \langle \Sigma, R, T \rangle$ of depth d and a string w where R is non-recursive and where T is a deterministic automaton, it is PTIME-complete to tell whether JULIET has a winning left-to-right strategy for G on w.*

Proof (Sketch): We prove the upper bound by constructing an alternating Turing machine deciding whether JULIET has a winning left-to-right strategy in logarithmic space. The machine has one pointer per level in the rewriting tree corresponding to a position of the input. Those d pointers are sufficient for the TM to specify the rightmost part of the current configuration which still needs to be processed.

The lower bound is proved by a reduction from the monotone Boolean circuit value problem [13]. Let C be a Boolean circuit. We can assume w.l.o.g. that all paths in C are alternating between **or** and **and** gates, have fan-in two and start/end with **and** gates [13]. From C we construct a DFA which accepts all strings over $\{l, r\}$ which describe paths from the output gate to an input gate which is 1. The extended game is played on a blank string of length depth(C) and JULIET and ROMEO select such a path by rewriting each symbol by l or r. By doing so JULIET selects the predecessor of *or*-gates, ROMEO of *and*-gates. The circuit is 1 iff JULIET can manage to end up in a 1-gate. Notice that the constructed game is also unary. $\square$

In the case of non-recursive rules without a uniform depth bound the combined complexity is one level higher.

Theorem 8. *It is EXPTIME-complete to know whether JULIET has a left-to-right strategy for G on w, for G non-recursive and target given by an NFA.*

Theorem 9. *It is PSPACE-complete to know whether JULIET has a left-to-right strategy for G and w, if G are non-recursive and the target is given by a DFA.*

5   Linear Rules

In this section we focus on linear and unary games. Recall from our example that in practice, service calls often generate a single subsequent call, which motivates linear CFGs.

Unrestricted strategies. From Lemma 1 it follows immediately that the complexity of the data decision problem for *unary* games is EXPTIME-hard. The following lemma shows that the combined decision problem for *linear* games can be done in EXPTIME. Hence, for unary and linear games with unrestricted strategies all decision problems are EXPTIME-complete.

Lemma 5. *Given a game $G = \langle \Sigma, R, T \rangle$ where R is linear, and a string w, one can tell in* EXPTIME *whether* JULIET *has a winning strategy.*

Proof (Sketch): Let k be the number of non-terminal symbols occurring in w. By linearity of R this will be an upper bound on the number of non-terminal symbols during the game. We construct an alternating polynomial space Turing machine that decides whether JULIET has a winning strategy. Alternation is used to mimic the CF-game as usual and memory is used to store the current configuration. For the latter the machine needs only to maintain a sequence $f_1 A_1 f_2 A_2 \cdots A_k f_{k+1}$ where the A_i are the non-terminal letters of the current configuration while the f_i are transition relations of T corresponding to the words between successive non-terminal symbols. This requires space $O(k|Q|^2)$. $\square$

Left-to-right strategies. We now consider left-to-right strategies for unary and linear CF-games.

Theorem 10. *It is* PSPACE-*complete to tell, given a unary (resp. linear) CF-game whether* JULIET *has a left-to-right-winning strategy.*

Proof (Sketch): For the lower bound the unary case suffices, for which it follows from Lemma 4. For the upper bound it is enough to consider the linear case. We check in NPSPACE whether ROMEO has a winning strategy. Hence, we guess the moves of ROMEO and, using backtracking, we cycle through all possible moves of JULIET. I.e., for the first symbol to replace, we first compute what happens if JULIET jumps after one move of ROMEO, then after the second, and so on. In order to do so, we only need to store a polynomial number of game configurations. Each configuration is of polynomial size as in Lemma 5. $\square$

When the target language is given as a DFA the complexity decreases in the unary case, but not in the linear case:

Theorem 11. *It is* PSPACE-*complete to tell, given a linear CF-game with target language given by a DFA whether* JULIET *has a left-to-right-winning strategy.*

Proof (Sketch): The upper bound follows from Theorem 10. We prove the lower bound by simulating the behavior of a polynomial space Turing machine M by a CF-game with linear rules and a deterministic target automaton. Using linear recursive rules of the form $S \rightarrow Sa$ ROMEO produces a sequence of configu-rations of M. When he does a mistake JULIET immediately stops. Therefore the mismatch comes from the previous configuration which is within polynomial distance (recall that M uses only polynomial space) from the beginning of the current string. The target language, a polynomial size DFA, can therefore check the mistake by proper counting and comparing the corresponding positions. □

Theorem 12. *It is* PTIME-*complete to tell, given a unary CF-game with target language given by a DFA whether* JULIET *has a left-to-right-winning strategy.*

Proof (Sketch): The lower bound is done as in the proof of Theorem 7. For the upper bound we construct an alternating Turing machine deciding whether JULIET has a winning strategy in logarithmic space. Because the grammar is unary the length of the word never increases and therefore the input word can be processed letter by letter while reading it. For each letter the TM maintains on its tape a pointer to the current state in the target automaton and a pointer to the current candidate letter for replacing the current position. Looping over the alphabet is avoided by using a counter of logarithmic size. Alternation is used in a standard way to mimic the CF-game. □

6   Discussion

We have seen that in general is it undecidable to tell who wins a CF-game. We have also seen several restrictions on the set of rules and on the strategy which imply decidability. A natural interesting situation not considered in this paper is the case where the target language T is finite. This is often the case in our scenario, as a user may require all data looking exactly like this or that, with no other options. If no ϵ-rules are allowed, the game is obviously decidable in EXPTIME (APSPACE) as no useful configuration can be larger than the size of T. It is open whether this bound is tight. If ϵ-rules are allowed it is not even clear whether the game is decidable.

As mentioned in the introduction the initial motivation of this work was to consider trees and rules defined using *extended* context-free grammars (rules of the form $a \rightarrow R_a$ where R_a is a regular language). For trees each rule would rewrite a leaf labeled a into a finite tree (into a regular language in the extended case). We can show that all the results presented in this paper extend to trees. However the situation is more complex for extended CFG rules. We can extend all our results with left-to-right strategies to these grammars but for unrestricted strategies even the non-recursive case can be shown to be undecidable.

Knowing that there exists a winning strategy is one thing. In practice the system needs to know which web service it should call and in which order. This correspond to extracting a winning strategy of a CF-game when it exists. We can show that this is always possible within the same complexity bounds as for the decision problem.

Acknowledgment. We are grateful to Tova Milo who brought the problem to our attention and to Tova Milo and Omar Benjelloun for the time they spent explaining us the beauty of AXML.

References

1. S. Abiteboul. *Semistructured Data: from Practice to Theory.* In *LICS'01*, IEEE Comp. Soc. 2001.
2. S. Abiteboul, A. Bonifati, G. Cobena, I. Manolescu, and T. Milo. *Dynamic XML documents with distribution and replication.* In *SIGMOD'03*, pages 527-538, ACM 2003.
3. Active XML. *http://www-rocq.inria.fr/verso/Gemo/Projects/axml.*
4. A. Blumensath and E. Grädel. Automatic structures. In *LICS'00*, pages 51–62, IEEE Comp. Soc. 2000.
5. Th. Cachat. *Symbolic Strategy Synthesis for Games on Pushdown Graphs.* In *ICALP'02*, LNCS 2380, pages 704-715, Springer, 2002.
6. E. Grädel, W. Thomas, and Th. Wilke, eds. *Automata, Logics, and Infinite Games.* Springer, 2002.
7. Jelly: Executable XML. *http://jakarta.apache.org/commons/sandbox/jelly.*
8. Ch. Löding. *Infinite graphs generated by tree rewriting.* PhD thesis, RWTH Aachen, 2003.
9. Macromedia Coldfusion MX. *http://www.macromedia.com/.*
10. R. Mayr. *Process rewrite systems.* In *Theoretical computer science* 156(1-2):264-286, 2000.
11. T. Milo, S. Abiteboul, B. Amann, O. Benjelloun, F. Dang Ngoc. *Exchanging Intensional XML Data.* In *SIGMOD'03*, pages 289-300, ACM 2003.
12. F. Neven. *Automata, Logic, and XML.* In *Proc. of CSL'02*, LNCS 2471, pages 2-26, Springer, 2002.
13. C. Papadimitriou. *Computational complexity.* Addison-Wesley, 1994.
14. O. Serre. *Note on winning positions on pushdown games with ω-regular conditions.* In *Information Processing Letters* 85:285-291, 2003.
15. V. Vianu. *A Web Odyssey: From Codd to XML.* In *PODS'01*, ACM 2001.
16. I. Walukiewicz. *Pushdown Processes: Games and Model-Checking.* In *Information and Computation* 164(2), 2001, pages 234-263.
17. Web services. *http://www.w3.org/2002/ws.*

Worst Case Performance of an Approximation Algorithm for Asymmetric TSP

Anna Palbom

KTH – Numerical Analysis and Computer Science
S-100 44 Stockholm, Sweden
annap@nada.kth.se

Abstract. In 1982 Frieze, Galbiati and Maffioli (Networks 12:23-39) published their famous algorithm for approximating the TSP tour in an *asymmetric* graph with triangle inequality. They show that the algorithm approximates the TSP tour within a factor of $\log_2 n$. We construct a family of graphs for which the algorithm (with some implementation details specified by us) gives an approximation which is $\log_2 n/(2+2\epsilon)$ times the optimum solution. This shows that the analysis by Frieze et al. is tight up to a constant factor and can hopefully give deeper understanding of the problem and new ideas in developing an improved approximation algorithm.

1 Introduction

The Travelling Salesman Problem (TSP) is one of the most famous and well-studied combinatorial optimisation problems.

Definition 1. *The (Asymmetric) TSP is the following minimisation problem: Given a collection of cities and a matrix whose entries are interpreted as the non-negative distance from a city to another, find the shortest tour starting and ending in the same city and visiting every city exactly once.*

TSP was proven to be NP-hard already by Karp [5] in 1972. This means that an efficient algorithm for TSP is highly unlikely; hence it is interesting to investigate algorithms that compute *approximate* solutions. However Sahni and Gonzalez [8] showed that in the case of general distance functions it is NP-hard to find a tour with length within exponential factors of the optimum, this is true even if the graph is restricted to be symmetric. When the distance function is symmetric and constrained to satisfy the triangle inequality the best known approximation algorithm is a factor 3/2-approximation algorithm due to Christofides [2]. With a c-approximation algorithm we mean a polynomial time algorithm that outputs a tour with weight at most c times the optimum weight.

We will study the case when the distance function satisfy the triangle inequality but is not limited to be symmetric. This case is much less understood. In 1982 Frieze, Galbiati and Maffioli [3] invented their famous algorithm for *asymmetric* graphs with triangle inequality, which approximates the TSP tour within a

V. Diekert and M. Habib (Eds.): STACS 2004, LNCS 2996, pp. 465–476, 2004.

factor of $\log_2 n$. There is only a miniscule lower bound: Papadimitriou and Vempala [7] recently proved that it is NP-hard to approximate the minimum TSP tour within a factor less than $220/219 - \epsilon$, for any constant $\epsilon > 0$. Obviously, huge improvements can be done either on a better algorithm or a tighter lower bound. Despite a lot of effort during the last twenty years there are only two algorithmic improvements, both very recent. The first by Bläser was announced in 2003 [1]. He improves the algorithm by Frieze et al. and proves a factor $0.999 \cdot \log_2 n$. The second algorithm by Kaplan, Lewenstein, Shafrir and Sviridenko [4] decomposes multigraphs and gives an approximation of $3/4 \log_3 n < 0.842 \log_2 n$. Hence, any new insight regarding the asymmetric TSP is important. One way to achieve such insight is to identify potential "hard" instances for the known approximation algorithms. The algorithms by Bläser and by Kaplan et al. are more complicated than the original algorithm due to Frieze et al. and are hence more difficult to understand. Therefore, we study the original algorithm in this paper. By constructing an explicit family of graphs we establish that the analysis of the algorithm is tight up to a constant factor (Theorem 1). We apply the algorithm by Bläser on the graphs and see that it with certain assumptions gives the same approximation as the original algorithm hence also Bläser's analysis is tight up to a constant factor.

The main idea of the algorithm by Freize et al. is: Find a minimum cycle cover in the graph by linear programming. Choose one node in every cycle and form a subgraph with the same distance function as in the original graph. Find a minimum cycle cover in the subgraph. Continue recursively until there is only one cycle in the cycle cover. The union of the cycle covers form a Eulerian graph. Replace edges in the union with a shortcut edge in the original complete graph to obtain a TSP tour. Since the graph respects the triangle inequality the TSP tour has weight less than or equal to the the sum of the cycle covers.

The description of the algorithm by Frieze et al. [3] leaves some implementation details unspecified. The algorithm chooses one arbitrary node in every cycle to be in the subgraph and shortcuts are made in arbitrary order. In our analysis of the worst case performance we make the following assumptions;

1. The *first* node in every cycle is chosen for the subgraph.
2. The shortcuts are made in a certain specified order.

We have constructed a family of graphs which gives the algorithm by Frieze et al. a worst case performance. This shows that the analysis of the algorithm by Frieze et al. is tight and our main result is:

Theorem 1. *For every ϵ $(0 < \epsilon < 1/n)$, there exists a family of graphs, G_n, such that the approximation algorithm by Frieze et al. [3] with our specifications, gives a TSP tour, T such that*

$$\frac{T}{opt(G_n)} > \frac{\log_2 n}{2 + 2\epsilon}$$

For asymmetric graphs Frieze et al. [3] give another data dependent algorithm which gives a $3\alpha/2$-approximation of the TSP tour, where α is the maximum ratio of $d(v_i, v_j)/d(v_j, v_i)$ for $v_i, v_j \in V$, $v_i \neq v_j$. The idea of the algorithm is to make the graph symmetric and then use the algorithm for symmetric graphs by Christofides [2]. We will not show a worst case behaviour of this algorithm, we just make sure that the class of graphs which has a worst case behaviour of the ordinary algorithm is not guaranteed to be well-approximated by the data dependent algorithm.

2   Notations and Conventions

All graphs in this paper have $n = 2^m$ nodes placed in a circle as in Fig. 1a. When an algorithm operates on an arbitrary node the ordering is modulo 2^m. For example the node before v_0 is v_{2^m-1}. Difference in index for two nodes v_i and v_j is $\min\{|i - j|, n - |i - j|\}$. An interval of node-indexes $[a, b]$ represents if $a < b$ all numbers $a \leq i \leq b$ and if $b < a$ (the complement of $[b, a]$) $\cup \{a, b\}$.

Definition 2. *For an m-bit integer x the we define the function*

$$z_m(x) = \max\{k \in Z_m \mid 2^k \ divides \ x\}$$

In particular $z_m(0) = m - 1$ since all numbers divide zero.

   In words, $z_m(i)$ is, for $i \neq 0$, the position of the least sigificant non-zero bit in the binary representation of i.

2.1   Constructing a Distance Function

Given a strongly connected graph, $G = (V, E)$ with weighted edges, we define the distance between two nodes, $d(v_i, v_j)$, as the weight of the shortest path in G from v_i to v_j. This distance function clearly obeys the triangle inequality.

2.2   Some Terminology

In this paper we often discuss parts of graphs; we therefore introduce some terms describing such parts.

Definition 3. *A cycle cover for a directed graph $G = (V, E)$ is a subgraph of G such that for each node $v \in V$, $indegree(v) = outdegree(v) = 1$. A cycle cover where every cycle has exactly two nodes is called a 2-cover.*

Definition 4. *A directed cactus is a strongly connected, asymmetric graph where each edge is contained in at most (and thus, in exactly) one simple directed cycle [9]. A spanning cactus for an asymmetric graph G is a subgraph of G that is a directed cactus and connects all vertices in G.*

Notations. Throughout the paper, T is a TSP tour, $opt(G)$ is total weight of the minimum TSP tour in the graph G, and C is a cycle cover or a cactus. By cycle we mean simple cycle and a cycle is denoted by the nodes in it; for example (v_i, v_j, v_k) is the directed cycle from v_i to v_j to v_k and back to v_i.

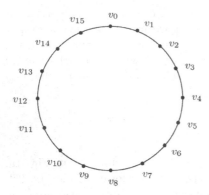
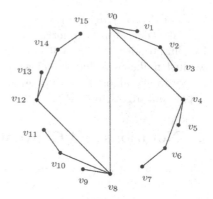

Fig. 1. Left (a): The graph inducing the distance function, $d_{16}(v_i, v_j)$. All edges have weight one. **Right (b)**: The Worst Case Spanning Cactus (*W-cactus*) in the graph G_{16}^1. Each 2-cycle is symbolised with an edge.

3   The Approximation Algorithm

An intuitive description of the approximation algorithm by Frieze et al. [3] is given in the introduction. Their description of the algorithm leaves some implementation details unspecified which we now specify.

To get an upper bound on their algorithm Frieze et al. make the following analysis: In the worst case all cycles in the cycle cover have length two, hence are $\lfloor \log_2 n \rfloor$ cycle covers at most produced. The weight of every cycle cover is less than or equal to $opt(G)$. Thus the spanning cactus formed by the union of the cycle covers has weight at most $opt(G) \cdot \log_2 n$. Since the graph obeys the triangle inequality the TSP tour found from the spanning cactus is shorter than or equal to $opt(G) \cdot \log_2 n$.

In order to analyse the algorithm we need to specify the arbitrary choices in the description by Frieze et al.:

1. An arbitrary node from every cycle in a cycle cover is chosen to be in the next subgraph. We choose the node with lowest index.
2. The shortcuts made to transform the spanning cactus to a TSP tour are in arbitrary order. We use our procedure SHORTCUT below which makes the shortcuts in a specific order.

SHORTCUT(G, C)	**DEPTH-FIRST(G, C, s)**
Input: A graph $G = (V, E)$	Input: A graph $G = (V, E)$
A cactus $C \subset E$	A cactus $C \subset E$
	The present node s
Output: A TSP tour T	Output: The last node added.
begin	begin
global $T \leftarrow \emptyset$;	$t \leftarrow s,\ U \leftarrow U \cup \{s\}$;
global set of visited nodes $U \leftarrow \emptyset$;	$\forall(s, v) \in C : v \notin U$ do

$t \leftarrow$ DEPTH-FIRST (G, C, v_0);	$T \leftarrow T \cup (t, v)$;
$T \leftarrow T \cup (t, v_0)$;	$t \leftarrow$ DEPTH-FIRST(G, C, v);
return T;	end
end	return t;
	end

SHORTCUT makes a depth-first search in C starting at the node v_0 and connects the nodes in the order they are found. If there, in the procedure DEPTH-FIRST, are several edges $(s, v_i) \in C$ such that $v_i \notin U$ from a node s, edges to nodes with higher index i are traversed first. The algorithm with these specifications is called *ATSPS*.

A straightforward analysis shows that the tour produced by the procedure SHORTCUT is a TSP tour. Since the algorithm is independent of the distance function the TSP tour only depends on the structure of the spanning cactus. A comparison with the original algorithm by Frieze et al. shows the following:

Lemma 1. *The TSP tour produced by SHORTCUT on a spanning cactus, with exactly two nodes in every cycle can be produced by the algorithm by Frieze et al. on the same graph.*

4   A Worst Case Approximation

In this section we construct a simple family of graphs to illustrate the algorithm by Frieze et al. and the main ideas of the worst case preformance. Since the graphs are symmetric they can be approximated within 3/2 by the algorithm due to Christofides [2].

4.1   Constructing the Graph

The distance function is induced by a graph (Fig. 1a) defined as follows:

Definition 5. *The distance function, $d_n^1(v_i, v_j)$, is induced by an undirected graph with $n = 2^m$ nodes arranged in a circle. Adjacent nodes are connected by edges of weight one and there are no other edges in the graph.*

Definition 6. *Let G_n^1 be a complete, directed graph with $n = 2^m$ nodes and the distance function $d_n^1(v_i, v_j)$.*

The distance between two nodes in G_n^1 is the difference in index; $d_n^1(v_i, v_j) = \min\{|i - j|, n - |i - j|\}$. The edges are directed even though they have the same distance in both directions. The minimum TSP tour is of course to traverse the nodes in clock-wise order (or counter-clock-wise) and $opt(G_n^1) = n$.

4.2   The Spanning Cactus

The algorithm by Frieze et al. recursively finds a minimum cycle cover in the graph. In a complete, asymmetric graph, the union of all cycle covers recursively produced by the algorithm forms a *spanning cactus*.

To get an intuitive understanding of the algorithm ATSPS and the worst case behaviour of G_n^1 we use a graph with $n = 2^4 = 16$ nodes as an example (Fig. 1b). In the first recursion the minimum cycle cover can consist of one large cycle or eight of weight two. Both have total weight 16. Assume that the 2-cover is chosen. Then the cycle cover consists of $\{(v_0, v_1), (v_2, v_3), (v_4, v_5), (v_6, v_7), (v_8, v_9), (v_{10}, v_{11}), (v_{12}, v_{13}), (v_{14}, v_{15})\}$. Choose the first node in every cycle to be in the set of nodes for the next recursion. In our example this gives the nodes with even index. Now the shortest distance between any nodes in the subgraph G is two. Again the procedure can return one large cycle or four cycles of weight four. Both have the total weight 16 and we assume that the 2-cover is returned. Proceed in the same way until there is just one cycle in the cycle cover. The union of all 2-covers is called a *W-cactus*.

Definition 7. *For a graph G with $n = 2^m$ nodes a Worst Case Spanning Cactus or a* W-cactus *is a subgraph of G such that $E = \{(v_i, v_{i-2^k}), (v_{i-2^k}, v_i) : z_m(i) = k\}$.*

For $n = 16$ nodes the W-cactus looks like in Fig. 1b. It can be seen that a *W-cactus* in G_n^1 has weight $n \log n$.

Lemma 2. *For a W-cactus, C, in a graph G with $n = 2^m$ nodes and an node $s = v_i$ the procedure DEPTH-FIRST returns v_i if i is odd and v_{i+1} if i is even.*

Proof. Every node v_i in a W-cactus with odd index, i.e., such that $z_m(i) = 0$, is by Definition 7 in exactly one cycle (v_i, v_{i-1}). Every node v_i in a W-cactus with even index, i.e., such that $z_m(i) = k \geq 1$, is in least two cycles (v_i, v_{i+1}) and (v_i, v_{i-2^k}). When DEPTH-FIRST is called with an odd node $s = v_i$ as input there is no other cycle $(s, v) \in C$ and the procedure returns $t = s$. If the input node $s = v_i$ is even there may be several cycles $(s, v) \in C$ but the one with smallest difference in index is (v_i, v_{i+1}) and it is the last cycle selected in the loop. The node $v_{i+1} \notin U$ since there is just one cycle connecting the odd node v_{i+1} with the rest of the cactus. After the recursive call to DEPTH-FIRST $t \leftarrow v_{i+1}$. Hence the procedure returns $t = v_{i+1}$ in this case.

To make the notation in some proofs clear we need the following definition:

Definition 8. *For the algorithm ATSPS and the graph $G_n = G_{n,0}$ with n nodes, the subgraph remaining after the first cycle cover is found is denoted by $G_{n,1}$ and the subgraph remaining after the i:th recursion is denoted by $G_{n,i}$.*

Since every cycle in the cycle cover is a 2-cycle of edges with equal weight, we visualize every 2-cycle as an undirected weighted edge. The union of the cycle covers can with this view be seen as a spanning, undirected tree. Since every node is in at least one cycle the tree is spanning and by the construction the cover is cycle-free. The view of the spanning cactus as a spanning tree directly gives that a W-cactus has $n - 1$ cycles.

4.3   The TSP Tour

We proceed by analysing SHORTCUT. The procedure takes a spanning cactus and returnes a TSP tour. It is independent of the distance function and only considers the structure of the spanning cactus. Again we use the graph G^1_{16} as an example to describe the procedure and the spanning cactus is a W-cactus. Initially the TSP tour $T = \emptyset$ and the start node $s = t \leftarrow v_0$. After the first call to DEPTH-FIRST $T \leftarrow (v_0, v_8)$. After some recursive calls to DEPTH-FIRST the graph will look like Fig. 2(a). Then $U = \{v_0, v_8, v_{12}, v_{14}, v_{15}, v_{13}, v_{10}, v_{11}\}$, and T contains the cycles (v_0, v_8), (v_8, v_{12}), (v_{12}, v_{14}), (v_{14}, v_{15}), (v_{15}, v_{13}), (v_{13}, v_{10}), (v_{10}, v_{11}) added in that order and $t = v_{11}$. In the next step $T \leftarrow T \cup (v_{11}, v_9)$.

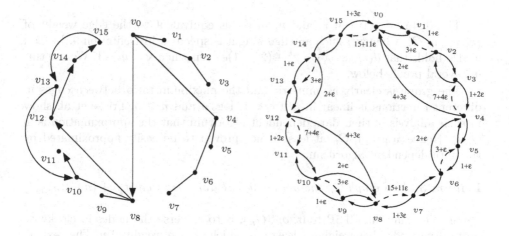

Fig. 2. Left (a): The TSP tour after some steps with the procedure SHORTCUT on a W-cactus with $n = 2^4 = 16$ nodes. Undirected edges represent 2-cycles in the W-cactus and arrows represent edges in the TSP tour. **Right (b):** A graph with induced distance function. The solid lines are edges in G^D_{16} and dashed lines are edges with induced distances. For simplicity weights equal to one are omitted and only some induced edges are shown.

It can be seen that the TSP tour produced by ATSPS with the assumtion that small cycles are prefered in the cycle cover, on the graph G^1_n, has weight larger than $\frac{1}{2} n \log_2 n$. Since the optimum TSP tour has length n, this gives an approximation in $\Omega(\log n)$.

5   A Worst Case Preformance

In this section we construct the family of graphs that gives the worst case preformance of the algorithm ATSPS. The graphs in the previus section have two main disadvantages: That they are symmetric and hence can be approximated by the algorithm due to Christofides and that the minimal cycle cover is not unique. The graphs defined in this section do not have these disadvantages.

Figure 2(b) shows a graph defined as follows:

Definition 9. *The distance function, $d_n(v_i, v_j)$, is induced by a graph G_n^D with $n = 2^m$ nodes arranged in a circle. Edges (v_{i-1}, v_i) in G_n^D have weight $w(v_{i-1}, v_i) = 1 + z_m(i)\epsilon$ where $0 < \epsilon < 1/n$. Edges (v_i, v_{i-2^k}) G_n^D with $z_m(i) = k < m - 1$ have weight $w(v_i, v_{i-2^k}) = 2^k + (2^k - 1)\epsilon$.*

Definition 10. *Let G_n be a complete, asymmetric graph with $n = 2^m$ nodes and distance function $d_n(v_i, v_j)$.*

The distance between v_i and v_j in G_n is equivalent to the edge weight of (v_i, v_j) in G_n^D whenever such an edge weight is specified in Definition 9. In fact, it also holds that $d(v_i, v_{i-2^k}) = 2^k + (2^k - 1)\epsilon$ even when $k = m - 1$. We use this in several proofs below.

The graph is clearly asymmetric and the maximum ratio between edges in different directions is linear in n if $\epsilon < 1/\log_2 n$ and $n \geq 4$. Frieze et al. show in their analysis of their data dependent algorithm that the approximation is in $O(\alpha)$. Hence, a graph G_n at least is not proven to be easily approximated by the data dependent algorithm.

Lemma 3. *In a graph G_n the optimum TSP tour has weight $n + (n - 2)\epsilon$.*

Proof. The minimum TSP tour, $opt(G_n)$, is to traverse the nodes in clockwise order. Every edge has weight at least one which gives a weight of n. The "extra" weight is

$$\sum_{i=1}^{\log_2 n} \left(\frac{n\epsilon}{2^i}\right) - \epsilon = n\epsilon\left(\sum_{i=1}^{\log_2 n} \left(\frac{1}{2^i}\right)\right) - \epsilon = (n - 2)\epsilon$$

and the total weight is $n + (n - 2)\epsilon$.

Is the tour minimal? There are n edges in G_n of weight one. Only half of them can be in a TSP tour since they have opposite direction. There are $n/2$ edges of weight less than two, all induced edges have length greater than 2. The TSP tour consists of the n shortest edges possible in a TSP tour and is hence minimal. $\square$

For the following two lemmas we need a simpler distance function:

Definition 11. *The distance function $d_n^S(v_i, v_j)$ is induced by a symmetric graph G_n^{DS} with $n = 2^m$ nodes arranged in a circle. Adjacent nodes are connected by an edge. The weight of an edge is $w(v_{i-1}, v_i) = 1 + z_m(i)\epsilon$ where $0 < \epsilon < 1/n$. Let G_n^S be a complete, directed graph with $n = 2^m$ nodes and the distance function $d_n^S(v_i, v_j)$.*

The distance function in G_n^S is a "symmetrised" version of the distance function in G_n. The distance of (v_i, v_{i-1}) in G_n^{DS} is equal to the minimum of the weights of (v_i, v_{i-1}) and (v_{i-1}, v_i) in G_n^D (non-existent edges in G_n^D are here given weight ∞). Edges (v_i, v_{i-2^k}) in G_n^S with $z_m(i) = k < m - 1$ are assigned to the induced distance $d(v_i, v_{i-2^k}) = 2^k + (2^k - 1)\epsilon$ which is the minimum of the weights of (v_i, v_{i-2^k}) and (v_{i-2^k}, v_i) in G_n^D. Hence edges in G_n^S are equal to or shorter than edges in G_n. If a cycle cover is minimal in G_n^S and all edges in the cycle cover have the same distance in G_n^S and in G_n then the cycle cover is minimal in G_n as well.

Lemma 4. *For $j < m$ and $n = 2^m$ it holds in G_n^S that $d(v_{i-2^j}, v_i) = 2^j + \epsilon \cdot (2^j - 1 + z_m(i \gg j))$. Here $\gg$ denotes a bitwise shift to the right padded with zeros on the left, i.e., $i \gg j = \lfloor i \cdot 2^{-j} \rfloor$*

Proof. Consider the edge (v_{i-2^j}, v_i) in G_n^S. The path of edges $[i - 2^j, i]$ in G_n^{DS} has weight

$$d(v_{i-2^j}, v_i) = \sum_{t=i-2^j+1}^{i} (1 + z_m(t)\epsilon) = 2^j + \epsilon \cdot \sum_{t=i-2^j+1}^{i} z_m(t)$$

When the j least significant bits in t are zero $z_m(t) = z_m(t \gg j) + j$. The remaining terms sum up to

$$\sum_{t=1}^{2^j-1} z_m(t) = 2^j - 1 - j$$

If $j = m-1$ the path $[i, i-2^j]$ has equal weight to the path $[i-2^j, i]$. If $j < m-1$ the path $[i, i-2^j]$ has weight larger than 2^{m-1}. Since $\epsilon < 1/n$ this is larger than the weight of the path $[i-2^j, i]$. Hence the path $[i-2^j, i]$ is minimal and therefore induces the distance between v_{i-2^j} and v_i in G_n^S. $\square$

An edge (v_{i-2^j}, v_i) with fixed value of j has minimum distance if it is in the W-cactus since edges in the W-cactus has $z_m(i) = j$ which gives $z_m(i \gg j) = 0$ in the lemma above.

Lemma 5. *In the graph G_n the algorithm ATSPS produces a W-cactus as spanning cactus and it has weight at least $n \log_2 n$.*

Proof. First we show by induction that a minimum cycle cover in G_n^S is a W-cactus and has the desired weight. Then we show that the same cover exists in G_n. In the beginning $G_{n,0}^S$ consists of all n nodes v_i and $z_m(i) \geq 0$. Every other edge has length one and every other edge has at least one extra ϵ-distance added and the 2-cover is the unique minimal cycle cover. The edged in the cycles are $(v_i, v_{i-2^0}), (v_{i-2^0}, v_i)$ and the index i is odd or $z_m(i) = 0$. If the first node in every cycle is put in the subgraph, $G_{n,1}^S$ consists of nodes v_i with even index $i : z_m(i) \geq 1$. Suppose $G_{n,j}^S$ consists of all nodes v_i with $z_m(i) \geq j$ and that the cycle covers in $G_{n,r}^S$ for $r < j$ form a subgraph of the W-cactus. Every other edge has by Lemma 4 distance $2^j + (2^j - 1)\epsilon$ and every other has by at least one extra ϵ-distance added. The 2-cover is minimal. Select the first node in every cycle to be in $G_{n,j+1}^S$. Then the cycle cover in $G_{n,j}^S$ is a subgraph of the W-cactus and nodes v_i in $G_{n,j+1}^S$ have $z_m(i) \geq j + 1$. By induction the 2-cover is minimal for every subgraph and it forms a W-cactus.

If there were no ϵ-weights the cactus would have weight $n \log_2 n$. Since all edges in the minimum cycle cover have the same weight in G_n the W-cactus is a minimum cycle cover in G_n as well. $\square$

Now we have a W-cactus as spanning cactus. The procedure SHORTCUT makes a TSP tour from the cactus.

Lemma 6. *In the graph G_n the approximation algorithm ATSPS gives a TSP tour of weight greater than $(n \log_2 n)/2$.*

Proof. For a graph G_n the procedure ATSPS gives by Lemma 5 a W-cactus with weight greater than $n \log n$ as spanning cactus. The procedure SHORTCUT does not depend on the distance function. Hence if the spanning cactus is a W-cactus SHORTCUT will always return the same TSP tour. We show that the TSP tour in G_n^S with a W-cactus as spanning cactus has the desired weight and since every edge in G_n has at least the same weight as in G_n^S the TSP tour in G_n must have at least the same weight.

From the proof of Lemma 5 the algorithm ATSPS given G_n^S, produces a W-cactus of weight greater than $n \log_2 n$. To show that the TSP tour produced by the algorithm has weight larger than half the weight of the W-cactus, we construct an injective function from the cycles in the cactus to the edges in the TSP tour such that each edge in the TSP tour has higher or equal distance than the longest edge in the corresponding cycle.

A cycle in the W-cactus (v_i, v_j) is mapped to an edge (v_t, v_j) in the TSP tour such that either $t = i$ or $t = j + (j - i) + 1$. The value of t is determined by the order in which edges are added to the TSP tour in SHORTCUT. Suppose DEPTH-FIRST is called with some even node s. The first cycle $(s, v) \in C$ processed in the loop is mapped to the edge (s, v). For the remaining iterations in the loop, the cycle (s, v) is mapped to the edge (t, v) where t was obtained from the call to DEPTH-FIRST in the previus iteration of the loop.

The mapping is obviously injective since DEPTH-FIRST visits every node exactly once. The first cycle is mapped to one edge in the cycle. If there are several cycles $(s, v) \in C$ in DEPTH-FIRST, s is even. Consider the cycle $(v_i, v_j) = (v_i, v_{i+2^k})$ which is not the first cycle chosen. The node $v = v_{i+2^{k+1}}$ was sent to DEPTH-FIRST in the previous recursion. Since $i + 2^{k+1}$ is even $t \leftarrow i + 2^{k+1} + 1$ was returned by Lemma 2. Hence, the cycle is mapped to the edge $(v_t, v_j) = (v_{i+2^{k+1}+1}, v_{i+2^k})$. The difference between the indices of the nodes in this edge is $\min\{|t - j|, n - |t - j|\} = 2^k + 1$ which is greater than the corresponding differnce for the cycle (v_i, v_j) since $\min\{|i - j|, n - |i - j|\} = 2^k$. Therefore Lemma 4 implies that $d(v_t, v_j) \geq d(v_i, v_j)$.

Thus for every cycle there is an associated edge with length at least as high as the edges in the cycle and the TSP tour has weight at least half of the W-cactus in G_n^S.   □

By combining Lemma 6 and Lemma 3 we have proved Theorem 1.

6   Conclusions and Future Work

The graphs, G_n, form a family of asymmetric graphs for which the approximation algorithm for asymmetric TSP by Frieze et al., with our specifications, shows a worst case behaviour. The algorithm returns by Theorem 1 a TSP tour of weight greater than $(opt(G_n) \cdot \log_2 n)/(2 + \epsilon)$, $\epsilon > 0$. The analysis of the algorithm by Frieze et al. shows that the algorithm gives a TSP tour with weight less than or equal to $opt(G_n) \cdot \log_2 n$, hence the analysis of the algorithm by Frieze et al. is tight up to a factor of $1/2$. One improvement of the algorithm might be to make the choices data dependent. It would also be interesting to investigate the average behaviour of the algorithm with random choices.

The ratio α between edges in different directions is greater than $n/2$ and the data dependent approximation algorithm by Frieze et al. is then proven to give an approximation better than $3\alpha/2 = 3n/4$ or $O(n)$. When we apply the data dependent algorithm to G_n, there are two possible outcomes. The algorithm converts the asymmetric graph to a symmetric, uses the algorithm due to Christofides [2] and in the end arbitrarily chooses the direction of the found TSP tour. The undirected TSP tour is around the circle. If the direction is chosen to be clockwise the algorithm finds the optimum TSP tour of weight n. If the direction on the other hand is chosen to be anti-clockwise the directed cycle has weight $n \log_2 n$ which is the same as for the original approximation algorithm. Thus with one choice assumed to be bad the data dependent algorithm approximates the asymmetric TSP tour within a factor of $\log_2 n$. The expected approximation is $(\log_2 n)/2$ over the choice of orientation of the tour.

The new algorithm by Bläser is a development of the algorithm by Frieze et al. and is more complicated. When we apply it to our graphs G_n it can return different TSP tours. It turns out that it is possible to specify Bläser's algorithm in such way that it, for the graph G_n, returns the same TSP tour as the algorithm by Frieze et al. Hence, Theorem 1 applies also to Bläser's algorithm.

In their very recent algorithm Kaplan et al. [4] introduce some new ideas. Basically, they compute a fractional cycle cover with certain 2-cycle constraints and use such covers to extract cycle covers with few 2-cycles for the underlying graph. A very interesting direction for future research is to investigate if the graphs G_n defined in this paper—or any other class of graphs—give an approximation ratio Omega(log n) for this new algorithm.

The question by Karp [6] as to whether there is a polynomial time heuristic for which the approximation ratio of asymmetric TSP is bounded by a constant is still open.

Acknowledgements. I thank Lars Engebretsen for great inspiration developing the ideas and support writing the paper and Mikael Goldmann for help writing the paper. Lena Folke and Simon Wigzell have helped me correcting the language – thank you! (All mistakes that still remain are due to me.)

References

1. Markus Bläser A new approximation algorithm for the asymmetric TSP with triangle inequality *Proceedings 14th Ann. ACM-SIAM Symp. on Discrete Algorithms (SODA)*, 638–645, 2003.
2. Nicos Christofides Worst case analysis of a new heuristic for the traveling salesman problem *Tech. Rep.* 388, GSIA, Carnegie Mellon Univerity, 1976.
3. Alan M. Frieze, Giulia Galbiati and Francesco Maffioli On the Worst-Case Performance of Some Algorithms for the Asymmetric Traveling Salesman Problem *Networks* 12:23–39, 1982.
4. Haim Kaplan, Moshe Lewenstein, Nira Shafrir, Maxim Sviridenko Approximation algorithms for Asymmetric TSP by Decomposing Directed Regular Multigraphs *Proceedings of Symposium on Foundations of Computer Science (FOCS)*,56–65, 2003.
5. Richard M. Karp Reducibility among combinatorial problems In Raymond E Miller and James W Thatcher, editors, *Complexity of Computer Computations* 85–103, Plenum Press, New York, 1972.
6. Richard M. Karp The fast approximate solution of hard combinatorial problems *Proceedings 6th South Eastern Conference on Combinatorics, Graph Theory and Computing* 15-21, Utilitas Mathematica, Winnipeg, 1975.
7. Christos H. Papadimitriou and Santosh Vempala On the approximability of the traveling salesman problem Manuscript May 2002.
   http://www.cs.berkeley.edu/~christos/tsp.ps
8. Sartaj K. Sahni and Teofilo Gonzalez P-complete approximation problems *Journal of the Assoc. Comput. Mach.* 23, 3, 555–565, 1976.
9. Günter Schaar Remarks on Hamiltonian properties of powers of digraphs *Discrete Applied Mathematics* 51:181–186, 1994.

On Visibility Representation of Plane Graphs[*]

Huaming Zhang and Xin He

Department of Computer Science and Engineering,
SUNY at Buffalo, Buffalo, NY, 14260, USA

Abstract. In a *visibility representation* (VR for short) of a plane graph G, each vertex of G is represented by a horizontal line segment such that the line segments representing any two adjacent vertices of G are joined by a vertical line segment. Rosenstiehl and Tarjan [11], Tamassia and Tollis [14] independently gave linear time VR algorithms for 2-connected plane graph. Recently, Lin et. al. reduced the width bound to $\lfloor \frac{22n-42}{15} \rfloor$ [10]. In this paper, we prove that any plane graph G has a VR with width at most $\lfloor \frac{13n-24}{9} \rfloor$.
For a 4-connected plane triangulation G, we give a visibility representation of G with height at most $\lceil \frac{3n}{4} \rceil$. In order to show that, we first show that every such graph has a *canonical ordering tree* with at most $\lceil \frac{n+1}{2} \rceil$ leaves instead of the previously known bound $\lfloor \frac{2n+1}{3} \rfloor$, which is of independent interest. All of them can be obtained in linear time.

1 Introduction

A *visibility representation* (VR for short) of a plane graph G is a representation, where the vertices of G are represented by non-overlapping horizontal segments (called *vertex segment*), and each edge of G is represented by a vertical line segment touching the vertex segments of its end vertices. A simple linear time VR algorithm was given in [11,14] for a 2-connected plane graph G. It only uses an *st-orientation* of G and the corresponding *st*-orientation of its dual G^* to construct the VR.

One of the main concerns afterwards for VR is the size of the representation, i.e., the height and width of VR. (The height and width of VR is the height and width of the rectangle in which the VR is drawn into.) Recently, using a more sophisticated greedy algorithm, Lin et. al. reduced the width bound to $\lfloor \frac{22n-42}{15} \rfloor$. In this paper, we prove that every plane graph G has a VR with width at most $\lfloor \frac{13n-24}{9} \rfloor$ by using the simpler algorithms from [11,14].

Canonical ordering tree of plane graphs is another important concept. In many applications of canonical ordering tree T, the number of leaves of T is a crucial parameter. It is known that there exists a plane graph for which every canonical ordering tree has at least $\lfloor \frac{2n+1}{3} \rfloor$ leaves.

We explore the properties of *regular edge labeling* (REL for short) of a 4-connected plane triangulation G and prove: Every 4-connected plane triangulation G has a canonical ordering tree with at most $\lceil \frac{n+1}{2} \rceil$ leaves. Applying this

---

[*] Research supported in part by NSF Grant CCR-0309953.

result, we show that: Every 4-connected plane graph G has a VR with height at most $\lceil \frac{3n}{4} \rceil$. This improves the previously known bound $\lceil \frac{15n}{16} \rceil$ [15].

We summarize related previous results and our results in the following table:

References	Plane graph G	4-Connected plane graph G
[11,14]	Width of VR $\leq (2n - 5)$	Height of VR $\leq (n - 1)$
[7]	Width of VR $\leq \lfloor \frac{3n-6}{2} \rfloor$	
[10]	Width of VR $\leq \lfloor \frac{22n-42}{15} \rfloor$	
[8]		Width of VR $\leq (n - 1)$
[15]	Height of VR $\leq \lceil \frac{15n}{16} \rceil$	
This paper	Width of VR $\leq \lfloor \frac{13n-24}{9} \rfloor$	Height of VR $\leq \lceil \frac{3n}{4} \rceil$

The present paper is organized as follows. Section 2 introduces preliminaries. Section 3 presents the construction of a VR with width at most $\lfloor \frac{13n-24}{9} \rfloor$. Section 4 explores the properties of REL of a 4-connected plane triangulation G and proves: Every 4-connected plane graph G has a VR with height at most $\lceil \frac{3n}{4} \rceil$. It also proves that: Every 4-connected plane triangulation G has a canonical ordering tree with at most $\lceil \frac{n+1}{2} \rceil$ leaves. We refer the readers to the technical reports 2003-06 and 2003-10 of CSE department at SUNY at Buffalo for omitted details. The authors are grateful to the anonymous referees for helpful comments.

2   Preliminaries

In this section, we give definitions and preliminary results. $G = (V, E)$ denotes a graph with $n = |V|$ vertices and $m = |E|$ edges. An embedding of a plane graph divides the plane into a number of two dimensional regions, called *faces*. The unbounded region is the *exterior face*. Other regions are *interior faces*. The vertices and the edges on the exterior face are called *exterior vertices* and *exterior edges*. Other vertices and edges are *interior vertices* and *interior edges*. A *path* P of G is a sequence of distinct vertices $u_1, u_2, \ldots, u_k$ such that $(u_i, u_{i+1}) \in E$ for $1 \leq i < k$. Furthermore, if $(u_k, u_1) \in E$, then $u_1, u_2, \ldots, u_k$ is called a *cycle*. We normally use C to denote a cycle and the set of the edges in it. If C contains k vertices, it is a k-cycle. A *triangle* (*quadrangle*, resp.) is a 3-cycle (4-cycle, resp.) A cycle C of G divides the plane into its interior and exterior regions. If C contains at least one vertex in its interior region, C is called a *separating cycle*. If all facial cycles of G are triangles, G is a *plane triangulation*. G is called a *directed graph* (digraph for short) if each edge of G is assigned a direction. We abbreviate the words "counterclockwise" and "clockwise" as ccw and cw respectively.

The *dual graph* $G^* = (V^*, E^*)$ of a plane graph G is defined as follows: For each face F of G, G^* has a node v_F. For each edge e in G, G^* has an edge $e^* = (v_{F_1}, v_{F_2})$ where F_1 and F_2 are the two faces of G with e on their common boundaries. e^* is called the *dual edge* of e. For each vertex $v \in V$, the dual face of v in G^* is denoted by v^*.

Let G be a 2-connected plane digraph with two specified exterior vertices s and t. G is called an *st-plane graph* if it is acyclic with s as the only source and t as the only sink. The properties of st-plane graphs were studied in [9,11]. In particular, for every face f of G, its boundary cycle consists of two directed paths. The path on its left (right, resp.) side is called the *left (right, resp.) path* of f. There is exactly one source (sink, resp.) vertex on the boundary of f, it is called the source (sink, resp.) of f.

An *orientation* of a graph G is a digraph obtained from G by assigning a direction to each edge of G. We will use G to denote both the resulting digraph and the underlying undirected graph unless otherwise specified. (Its meaning will be clear from the context.) For a plane graph G and an exterior edge (s,t), an orientation of G is called an *st-orientation* if the resulting digraph is an st-plane graph. Note: For an st-orientation, we require that (s,t) is an exterior edge. This is the difference between an st-orientation and an st-plane graph.

Let G be a 2-connected plane graph and (s,t) an exterior edge. An *st-numbering* of G is a one-to-one mapping $\xi : V \to \{1, 2, \cdots, n\}$, such that $\xi(s) = 1$, $\xi(t) = n$, and each vertex $v \neq s,t$ has two neighbors u, w with $\xi(u) < \xi(v) < \xi(w)$, where u (w, resp.) is called a *smaller neighbor (bigger neighbor, resp.)* of v. Given an st-numbering ξ of G, we can orient G by directing each edge in E from its lower numbered end vertex to its higher numbered end vertex. The resulting orientation is called the *orientation derived from ξ* which, obviously, is an st-orientation of G. On the other hand, if $G = (V, E)$ has an st-orientation $\mathcal{O}$, we can define an 1-1 mapping $\xi : V \to \{1, \cdots, n\}$ by topological sort. It is easy to see that ξ is an st-numbering and the orientation derived from ξ is $\mathcal{O}$. From now on, we will interchangeably use the term an st-numbering of G and the term an st-orientation of G, where each edge of G is directed accordingly.

Given an st-orientation $\mathcal{O}$ of G, consider the dual graph G^* of G. For each $e \in G$, we direct its dual edge e^* from the face on the left of e to the face on the right of e when we walk on e along its direction in $\mathcal{O}$. We then reverse the direction of $(s,t)^*$. It was shown in [11,14] that this orientation is an st-orientation of G^* with $(s,t)^*$ as the distinguished exterior edge. We denote the source by $\bar{s}$, and the sink by $\bar{t}$. When we embed G and G^* on plane simultaneously, we fix t^* to be the exterior face of G^*. We will denote this orientation of G^* by $\mathcal{O}^*$ and call it the *corresponding st-orientation* of $\mathcal{O}$.

Lempel et. al. [9] showed that for every 2-connected plane graph G and an exterior edge (s,t), there exists an st-numbering. The following lemma was given in [11,14]:

Lemma 1. *Let G be a 2-connected plane graph. Let $\mathcal{O}$ be an st-orientation of G. A VR of G can be obtained from $\mathcal{O}$ in linear time. The height of the VR is the length of the longest directed path in $\mathcal{O}$. The width of the VR is the length of the longest directed path in the corresponding st-orientation $\mathcal{O}^*$ of G^*.*

Let G be a plane triangulation with $n \geq 3$ vertices and $m = 3n - 6$ edges. Let $v_1, v_2, \cdots, v_n$ be an ordering of the vertices of G where v_1, v_2, v_n are the three exterior vertices of G in ccw order. Let G_k be the subgraph of G induced by $v_1, v_2, \cdots, v_k$ and H_k the exterior face of G_k. Let $G - G_k$ be the subgraph of G obtained by removing $v_1, v_2, \cdots, v_k$.

Definition 1. [4] *An ordering $v_1, \cdots, v_n$ of a plane triangulation G is* canonical *if the following hold for every $k = 3, \cdots, n$:*

1. *G_k is 2-connected, and its exterior face H_k is a cycle containing the edge (v_1, v_2).*
2. *The vertex v_k is on the exterior face of G_k, and its neighbors in G_{k-1} form a subinterval of the path $H_{k-1} - (v_1, v_2)$ with at least two vertices. Furthermore, if $k < n$, v_k has at least one neighbor in $G - G_k$. (Note that the case $k = 3$ is degenerated, and $H_2 - (v_1, v_2)$ is regarded as the edge (v_1, v_2) itself.)*

A canonical ordering of G can be viewed as an order in which G is reconstructed from a single edge (v_1, v_2) step by step. At step k, when v_k is added to construct G_k, let $c_l, c_{l+1}, \cdots, c_r$ be the lower ordered neighbors of v_k from left to right on the exterior face of G_{k-1}. We call (v_k, c_l) the *left edge* of v_k. The collection T of the left edges of the vertices v_j for $3 \le j \le n$ plus the edge (v_1, v_2) is a spanning tree of G and is called a *canonical ordering tree* of G [4,6].

3   Compact Visibility Representation of Plane Graphs

We assume that G is a 2-connected plane graph for now. First, we introduce several concepts and a technical theorem whose proof is omitted.

Definition 2. *Let G be a 2-connected plane graph, $\mathcal{O}$ be an st-orientation of G. Let G^* be the dual graph of G, $\mathcal{O}^*$ be the corresponding st-orientation of $\mathcal{O}$.*

1. *For any vertex $v \ne s, t$ of G, define: $Hand(v) = \{(v, u) \in E \mid u$ is a bigger neighbor of $v\}$; $Foot(v) = \{(u, v) \in E \mid u$ is a smaller neighbor of $v\}$. For $v = s$, define $Foot(s) = \{(s, t)\}$, $Hand(s) = \{(s, u) \in E \mid u \ne t\}$. (Note, the two definitions for the source s are special.)*
2. *For any face $v^* \ne t^*$ of G^*, define: $cover(v^*) = \{e^* \mid e \in Hand(v)\}$; $sheet(v^*) = \{e^* \mid e \in Foot(v)\}$. Note that, for any face $v^* \ne t^*$ of G^* (including s^*), its boundary consists of two directed paths, one is $cover(v^*)$, the other is $sheet(v^*)$.*
3. *For any vertex $v \ne t$ of G, define $score_{\mathcal{O}}(v) = \min\{|Hand(v)|, |Foot(v)|\}$, and $Score_{\mathcal{O}}(G) = \sum_{v \ne t} score_{\mathcal{O}}(v)$.*

Theorem 1. *Let G be a 2-connected plane graph with an st-orientation $\mathcal{O}$. Let $\mathcal{O}^*$ be the corresponding st-orientation of G^*. Then G has a VR with width at most $|E| - Score_{\mathcal{O}}(G)$.*

Thus, in order to shorten the width of VR of a plane graph G, we need to find an *st*-orientation $\mathcal{O}$ of G such that $Score_{\mathcal{O}}(G)$ is as large as possible.

Without loss of generality, we assume that G is a plane triangulation with $n \ge 4$ vertices in the rest of this section. (Otherwise, we triangulate it into a plane triangulation G' by adding edges, a VR of G can be obtained from a VR of G' by deleting the vertical line segments representing the added edges.) First we need to introduce the concept of Schnyder's realizer [12,13]:

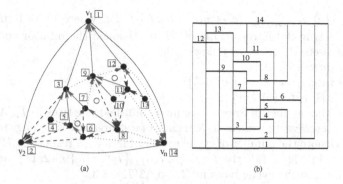

Fig. 1. (a) A plane triangulation G and one realizer $\mathcal{R}$ of G; (b) A VR of G.

Definition 3. *Let G be a plane triangulation with three exterior vertices v_1, v_2, v_n in ccw order. A Schnyder's realizer (realizer in short) $\mathcal{R}$ of G is a partition of the interior edges of G into three sets T_1, T_2, T_n of directed edges such that the following hold:*

- *For each $i \in \{1, 2, n\}$, the interior edges incident to v_i are in T_i and directed toward v_i.*
- *For each interior vertex v of G, the neighbors of v form six blocks U_1, D_n, U_2, D_1, U_n, and D_2 in ccw order around v, where U_j and D_j ($j = 1, 2, n$) are the parent and the children of v in T_j.*

It was shown in [12,13] that every plane triangulation G has a realizer $\mathcal{R}$, which can be obtained in linear time. Each T_i ($i \in \{1, 2, n\}$) is a tree rooted at the vertex v_i containing all interior vertices of G. Fig. 1 (a) shows a realizer of a plane triangulation G. Three trees T_1, T_2, T_n are drawn as solid, dashed, and dotted lines, respectively. (Ignore the small boxes containing integers for now. Their meaning will be explained later.)

The following lemma shows how to obtain st-numberings from a Schnyder's realizer [15].

Lemma 2. *Let G be a plane triangulation and $\mathcal{R} = \{T_1, T_2, T_n\}$ a Schnyder's realizer of G. T_i' be the tree obtained by T_i plus the two exterior edges adjacent to v_i in G. T_i' is rooted at v_i. Then the ccw preordering of the vertices of G with respect to T_i' is an st-numbering of G.*

For example, consider the tree T_1 (rooted at v_1) shown in Fig. 1. The union of T_1 and the two exterior edges (v_2, v_1) and (v_n, v_1) is a tree of G, denote it by T_1'. The ccw preordering of the vertices of G with respect to T_1' are shown in integers inside the small boxes. It is an st-orientation of G by Lemma 2, denoted by $\mathcal{O}_1$. Similarly, we have two other st-orientations $\mathcal{O}_2$, $\mathcal{O}_n$.

Denote the set of interior vertices of G by I. Then for each vertex $v \in I$, $score_{\mathcal{O}_i}(v), i = 1, 2, n$ is always definable. And obviously $Score_{\mathcal{O}_i}(G) = 2 + \sum_{v \in I} score_{\mathcal{O}_i}(v)$. We denote $score_{sum}(v) = \sum_{i=1,2,n} score_{\mathcal{O}_i}(v)$ for each $v \in I$.

Next, we want to find a lower bound of $\sum_{i=1,2,n} Score_{\mathcal{O}_i}(G)$.

Let $inter(v) = \sum_{i=1,2,n}[v\ is\ not\ a\ leaf\ of\ T_i]$, where $[c]$ is 1 (0, resp.) if condition c is true (false, resp.). Lin et. al. partitioned the interior vertices of G into three subsets A, B, C as follows [10]:

$A = \{v|\ inter(v) = 0\}$;

$B = \{v|\ inter(v) = 2,\ deg(v) = 5\}$;

$C = \{v \notin B|\ inter(v) \geq 1\}$.

Let ξ_i be the number of internal (namely, non-leaf) vertices in T_i. An interior face f of G is *cyclic* with respect to $\mathcal{R}$ if each of its three edges belongs to different trees of $\mathcal{R}$. Denote the number of cyclic interior faces with respect to $\mathcal{R}$ by $\Delta(\mathcal{R})$. For example, in Fig. 1 (a), the faces $\{5, 7, 6\}$, $\{7, 9, 8\}$, $\{9, 12, 11\}$ (marked by empty circles) are the cyclic faces in $\mathcal{R}$. So, $\Delta(\mathcal{R}) = 3$.

The following results were proved in [1,10]:

Lemma 3. *Let G be a plane triangulation with $n \geq 4$ vertices. Let v_1, v_2, v_n be the exterior vertices of G in the ccw order. Let $\mathcal{R} = \{T_1, T_2, T_n\}$ be any realizer of G, where T_i, $i \in \{1, 2, n\}$ is rooted at v_i respectively. Let k be the number of connected components of the graph $G[B]$, which is a subgraph of G induced by B.*

1. $\xi_1 + \xi_2 + \xi_n - \Delta(\mathcal{R}) = n - 1$.

2. $\xi_1 + \xi_2 + \xi_n - 3 = \sum_{v \in I} inter(v) \geq 2|B| + |C|$.

3. $score_{sum}(v) \geq 3 + 2 \cdot inter(v) - [v \in B]$, $v \in I$.

4. $|B| - k \leq 2\Delta(\mathcal{R})$.

Now we can prove the following theorem:

Theorem 2. *Let G be a plane triangulation with $n \geq 4$ vertices, $R = \{T_1, T_2, T_n\}$ be any Schnyder's realizer of G. Then $\sum_{i=1,2,n} Score_{O_i}(G) \geq \frac{14n}{3} - 10$.*

Proof. Let $G[B]$ be the subgraph of G induced by B. Suppose that $G[B]$ has k connected components. Let $|B| - k = \delta\Delta(\mathcal{R})$, then we have $0 \leq \delta \leq 2$ by Lemma 3 (4). Let B_t, $t = 1, 2, \cdots, k$ be all the connected components of $G[B]$. Lin et. al. observed that [10]: any two distinct vertices of A are not adjacent in G; and each vertex in A is adjacent to at most one B_t. Thus, we know that the number of the connected components of $G[A \cup B]$ is at least k. Considering $G - (A \cup B)$, each interior face of $G - (A \cup B)$ contains at most one connected component of $G[B]$. We remove edges of $G - (A \cup B)$ until each interior face contains exactly one connected component of $G[B]$, denote this graph by G'. (If $G[B]$ is empty, G' does not have interior face.) Let F_i $(i = 3, 4, \cdots)$ be the set of interior faces of G' with i edges on its boundary. Thus, we have:

$$k = \sum_{i=3}^{\infty} |F_i| \tag{1}$$

For any face in F_i, $i \geq 4$, we can triangulate it into $i - 2$ faces, then by applying Euler's formula to the resulting graph, the number of its interior faces is at most $2(|C| + 3) - 5 = 2|C| + 1$. Thus:

$$\sum_{i=3}^{\infty} (i - 2)|F_i| \leq 2(|C| + 3) - 5 = 2|C| + 1.$$

Therefore:

$$\sum_{i=3}^{\infty} \frac{i-2}{2}|F_i| - \frac{1}{2} \leq |C| \tag{2}$$

Using Equation (1) and (2), we have:

$$|C| \geq \frac{k}{2} + \frac{1}{2}|F_4| + |F_5| + \frac{1}{2}|F_6| - \frac{1}{2} \tag{3}$$

Applying Lemma 3 (1) and (2) and above equation, we have:

$$n + \Delta(\mathcal{R}) - 4 \geq 2|B| + |C| \geq \frac{5}{2}k + 2\delta\Delta(\mathcal{R}) - \frac{1}{2} + \frac{1}{2}|F_4| + |F_5| + \frac{1}{2}|F_6|.$$

Thus, we have:

$$\frac{5}{2}k \leq n + \Delta(\mathcal{R}) - 2\delta\Delta(\mathcal{R}) - \frac{7}{2} - \frac{1}{2}|F_4| - |F_5| - \frac{1}{2}|F_6| \tag{4}$$

Because any vertex in B has degree 5 in G, and an interior face of G' in F_3 contains at least 1 vertex from B in G, so it contains at least 3 vertices from $A \cup B$ in G. Similarly, an interior face of G' in F_4 contains at least 2 vertices from $A \cup B$ in G. An interior face of G' in F_i for $i \geq 5$ contains at least 1 vertices from $A \cup B$ in G. Thus:

$$3|F_3| + 2|F_4| + \sum_{i=5}^{\infty} |F_i| \leq |A| + |B|.$$

Add this to Equation (2), we have:

$$\frac{7}{2}|F_3| + 3|F_4| + \frac{5}{2}|F_5| + 3|F_6| + \sum_{i=7}^{\infty} \frac{i}{2}|F_i| \leq |A| + |B| + |C| + \frac{1}{2} = n - \frac{5}{2}.$$

Combining it with Equation (1), we have:

$$\frac{7}{2}k \leq (\frac{7}{2}|F_3| + 3|F_4| + \frac{5}{2}|F_5| + 3|F_6| + \sum_{i=7}^{\infty} \frac{i}{2}|F_i|) + (\frac{1}{2}|F_4| + |F_5| + \frac{1}{2}|F_6|)$$

$$\leq n - \frac{5}{2} + \frac{1}{2}|F_4| + |F_5| + \frac{1}{2}|F_6| \tag{5}$$

Add Equation (4) and (5), and divide both sides by 6. We have:

$$k \leq \frac{n}{3} + \frac{1}{6}\Delta(\mathcal{R}) - \frac{1}{3}\delta\Delta(\mathcal{R}) - 1 \tag{6}$$

Applying Lemma 3 (2), (3) and above equation, also note that $0 \leq \delta \leq 2$, we have:

$$\sum_{i=1,2,n} Score_{\mathcal{O}_i}(G) = 6 + \sum_{v \in I} score_{sum}(v)$$

$$\geq 6 + \sum_{v \in I} \{3 + 2 \cdot inter(v)\} - |B|$$
$$= 6 + 3(n-3) + 2(n + \Delta(\mathcal{R}) - 4) - |B|$$
$$= 5n + 2\Delta(\mathcal{R}) - 11 - |B|$$
$$= 5n + 2\Delta(\mathcal{R}) - 11 - (|B| - k) - k$$
$$\geq 5n + 2\Delta(\mathcal{R}) - 11 - \delta\Delta(\mathcal{R}) - \frac{1}{3}n - \frac{1}{6}\Delta(\mathcal{R}) + \frac{1}{3}\delta\Delta(\mathcal{R}) + 1$$
$$= \frac{14n}{3} + (\frac{11}{6} - \frac{2}{3}\delta)\Delta(\mathcal{R}) - 10 \geq \frac{14n}{3} - 10 \qquad (7)$$

Theorem 3. *Let G be a plane triangulation with $n \geq 4$ vertices, then G has a VR with width at most $\lfloor \frac{13n-24}{9} \rfloor$. And it can be obtained in linear time.*

Proof. Applying Theorem 2, we have $\sum_{i=1,2,n} Score_{O_i}(G) \geq \frac{14n}{3} - 10$. Thus, one of $Score_{O_i}(G) \geq \lceil \frac{14n-30}{9} \rceil$. Applying Theorem 1 and Lemma 1, the width of the VR is at most $3n - 6 - \lceil \frac{14n-30}{9} \rceil = \lfloor \frac{13n-24}{9} \rfloor$. And it is easy to see that the running time is $O(n)$.

For example, Fig. 1 (b) gives a VR of G, using the st-numbering in Fig. 1 (a).

4   Fewer-Leaf Canonical Ordering Tree and Compact VR of 4-Connected Plane Triangulations

In order to obtain a canonical ordering tree for a 4-connected plane triangulation with fewer leaves, we need another concept and a lemma from [5] as follows:

Definition 4. *Let G' be a plane graph with four vertices v_W, v_S, v_E, v_N in ccw order on its exterior face. A regular edge labeling (REL for short) of G' is a partition of the interior edges of G' into two subsets S_1, S_2 of directed edges such that the following hold:*

1. *For each interior vertex v, the edges incident to v appear in ccw order around v as follows: a set of edges in S_1 leaving v; a set of edges in S_2 entering v; a set of edges in S_1 entering v; a set of edges in S_2 leaving v. Each set is nonempty.*
2. *All interior edges incident to v_N are in S_1 and entering v_N. All interior edges incident to v_W are in S_2 and leaving v_W. All interior edges incident to v_S are in S_1 and leaving v_S. All interior edges incident to v_E are in S_2 and entering v_E. Each block is not empty.*

Lemma 4. *Let G' be a plane graph with four vertices on its exterior face. G' has a REL if and only if the following conditions hold: (1) Every interior face of G' is a triangle and the exterior face of G' is a quadrangle; (2) G' has no separating triangles. A graph satisfying the two conditions in the above lemma will be called a* proper triangulated plane *(PTP for short) graph.*

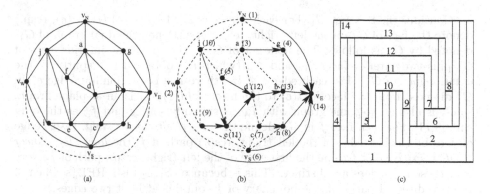

Fig. 2. (a) A 4-connected plane triangulation G and the PTP graph G' after deleting (v_W, v_E), (b) An st-numbering of G, (c) A VR of G.

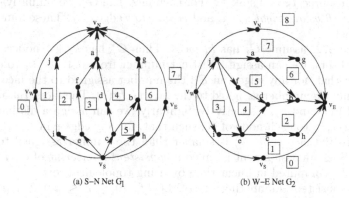

Fig. 3. The S-N net G_1 and the W-E net G_2 for the PTP graph G' in Fig. 2 (a).

Let G be a 4-connected plane triangulation with three exterior vertices v_W, v_E, v_N in ccw order. Delete the edge (v_W, v_E). Denote the new exterior vertex by v_S and the resulting plane graph by G'. (See Fig. 2 (a) for an example.) G' does not have separating triangles, and it has four exterior vertices v_W, v_S, v_E, v_N in ccw order on its own exterior face. Thus, G' is a PTP graph and has a REL (S_1, S_2) according to Lemma 4.

We investigate the properties of the REL of G'. Denote by G_1 the directed subgraph of G' induced by S_1 and the four exterior edges directed as $v_S \rightarrow v_W, v_W \rightarrow v_N, v_S \rightarrow v_E, v_E \rightarrow v_N$. Let E_1 be the edge set of G_1. (E_1 is the union of S_1 and the four exterior edges.) Then G_1 is an st-plane graph with source v_S and sink v_N. Similarly, let G_2 be the directed subgraph of G' induced by S_2 and the four exterior edges directed as $v_W \rightarrow v_S, v_S \rightarrow v_E, v_W \rightarrow v_N, v_N \rightarrow v_E$. Let E_2 be the edge set of G_2. Then G_2 is an st-plane graph with source v_W and sink v_E. We will call G_1 the S-N net and G_2 the W-E net of G' derived from the REL (S_1, S_2). For example, Fig. 3 shows a REL with its derived S-N and W-E nets for the PTP graph G' shown in Fig. 2 (a). (Ignore the small boxes containing integers for now. Their meaning will be explained later.)

Consider the S-N net G_1. For each edge $e \in E_1$, let $left(e)$ ($right(e)$, resp.) denote the face of G_1 on the left (right, resp.) of e. Define the dual graph of G_1, denoted by G_1^* as follows. The node set of G_1^* is the set of the interior faces of G_1 plus two exterior faces f_W and f_E, (which are obtained by "splitting" the exterior face of G_1). For each edge $e \in E_1$, there is a corresponding edge e^* in G_1^* directed from the face $left(e)$ to the face $right(e)$. G_1 is an st-plane graph, so G_1^* is also an st-plane graph with f_W as the only source and f_E as the only sink [9,11]. For each face f in G_1, define the *upper left (upper right, resp.)* edge of f to be the last edge of the left (right, resp.) path of f, the *lower left (lower right, resp.)* edge of f to be the first edge of the left (right, resp.) path of f. Note that these four edges are distinct. (This is because (S_1, S_2) is a REL, so each of the two directed paths on the boundary of f contains at least two edges.)

Similarly, we can define the dual G_2^* for G_2 with the word "left" ("right", resp.) replaced by the word "below" ("above", resp.). G_2^* is also an st-plane graph with source f_S and sink f_N. For each face f in G_2, we similarly define the *left above, left below, right above*, and *right below* edge of f. These four edges are also distinct.

For $i = 1, 2$, assume G_i has k_i faces. Thus G_i^* has $k_i + 1$ nodes. By using topological sort, we can assign a distinct number from $0, 1, \cdots, k_1$ to each node of G_1^* such that, for any edge e in E_1, the number assigned to the face $left(e)$ is smaller than the number assigned to the face $right(e)$. The faces f_W and f_E are numbered by 0 and k_1, respectively. Similarly, we can assign a distinct number from $0, 1, \cdots, k_2$ to each node of G_2^* such that, for any edge e in E_2, the number assigned to the face $below(e)$ is smaller than the number assigned to the face $above(e)$. Such an assignment is called a *consistent numbering* of $G_i, i = 1, 2$ [5]. They can be computed in linear time by using topological sort.

Fix a consistent numbering of G_1. Let f_r ($0 \le r \le k_1$) denote the face numbered by r. We define *the i-th S-N separation path SN_i* to be the directed path in G_1 such that the faces numbered by $0, 1, \cdots, i - 1$ are on its left and the other faces are on its right. (These paths were called path system in [5].) G_1 has exactly k_1 S-N separation paths and all of them are directed from v_S to v_N. Note that SN_{r+1} is obtained from SN_r by deleting the left path of the face f_r and adding the right path of f_r.

The *j-th W-E separation path WE_j* of G_2 is defined similarly. G_2 has exactly k_2 W-E separation paths and all of them are directed paths from v_W to v_E [5].

For example, the faces in Fig. 3 are consistently numbered for G_1 and G_2 (indicated by the integers in small boxes). The 4-th W-E separation path WE_4 in G_2 consists of the vertices v_W, j, e, d, b, v_E. Note that there are 4 vertices (i, c, h, v_S) below it and 4 vertices (f, a, g, v_N) above it.

We have the following technical lemma. The proof is omitted:

Lemma 5. *Let G' be a PTP graph with n vertices. Let G_1 be the S-N net and G_2 be the W-E net derived from a REL (S_1, S_2) of G'. Suppose G_1 has k_1 faces and G_2 has k_2 faces. Then:*

(1) $k_1 + k_2 = n + 1$.

(2) The i-th S-N separation path SN_i has at least $i - 1$ vertices on its left and at least $k_1 - i$ vertices on its right in G_1. The j-th W-E separation path WE_j has at least $j - 1$ vertices below it and at least $k_2 - j$ vertices above it in G_2.

The next theorem shows how to get a canonical ordering tree from the S-N net and the W-E net respectively. We prove that one of the two canonical ordering trees has at most $\lceil \frac{n+1}{2} \rceil$ leaves. The proof is omitted:

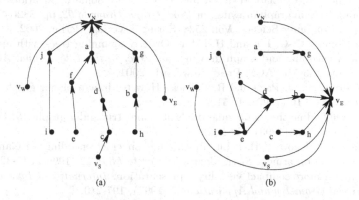

Fig. 4. (a) A canonical ordering tree of G from the S-N net in Fig. 3 (a), (b) A canonical ordering tree of G from the W-E net in Fig. 3 (b).

Theorem 4. *Let G be a 4-connected plane triangulation with three exterior vertices v_W, v_E, v_N in ccw order. Delete the edge (v_W, v_E). Denote the new exterior vertex by v_S and the resulting graph by G'. Let (S_1, S_2) be a REL of G'. Let G_1 be the S-N net and G_2 be the W-E net derived from (S_1, S_2). Then the following statements hold:*

1. *For each vertex $v \neq v_N, v_S$ in G_1, select an outgoing edge in G_1. For v_S, select an outgoing edge not leading to v_W or v_E. Then the set T_1 of the selected edges is a canonical ordering tree of G.*
2. *For each vertex $v \neq v_W, v_E$ in G_2, select an outgoing edge in G_2. For v_W, select the edge (v_W, v_E). Then the set T_2 of the selected edges is a canonical ordering tree of G.*
3. *One of T_1, T_2 has at most $\lceil \frac{n+1}{2} \rceil$ leaves. It can be obtained in linear time.*

Fig. 4 (a) shows the tree described in the statement (1) for the S-N net in Fig. 3 (a). Fig. 4 (b) shows the tree described in the statement (2) for the W-E net in Fig. 3 (b).

We omit the proof of the following theorem:

Theorem 5. *Every 4-connected plane graph G with n vertices has a VR with height at most $\lceil \frac{3n}{4} \rceil$, which can be obtained in linear time.*

Fig. 2 (c) shows a VR of the graph G using the st-numbering in Fig. 2 (b).

References

1. N. Bonichon, B. Le Saëc and M. Mosbah, Wagner's theorem on realizers, in: Proc. ICALP'02, Lecture Notes in Computer Science, Vol. 2380, 1043-1053.
2. H.-L. Chen, C.-C. Liao, H.-I. Lu and H.-C. Yen, Some applications of orderly spanning trees in graph drawing, in *Proc. Graph Drawing'02*, pp. 332-343, Lecture Notes in Computer Science, Vol. 2528, Springer-Verlag, Berlin, 2002.
3. Y.-T. Chiang, C.-C. Lin and H.-I. Lu, Orderly spanning trees with applications to graph encoding and graph drawing, in *Proc. of the 12th Annual ACM-SIAM SODA*, pp. 506-515, ACM Press, New York, 2001.
4. H. de Fraysseix, J. Pach and R. Pollack, How to draw a planar graph on a grid. *Combinatorica* 10 (1990), 41-51.
5. X. He, On finding the rectangular duals of planar triangular graphs. *SIAM Journal on Computing* 22 (1993), 1218-1226.
6. X. He, M.-Y. Kao and H.-I. Lu, Linear-time succinct encodings of planar graphs via canonical orderings. *SIAM Journal Discrete Math* 12 (1999), 317-325.
7. G. Kant, A more compact visibility representation. *International Journal of Computational Geometry and Applications* 7 (1997), 197-210.
8. G. Kant and X. He, Regular edge labeling of 4-connected plane graphs and its applications in graph drawing problems. *Theoretical Computer Science* 172 (1997), 175-193.
9. A. Lempel, S. Even and I. Cederbaum, An algorithm for planarity testing of graphs, in *Theory of Graphs (Proc. of an International Symposium, Rome, July 1966)*, pp. 215-232, Rome, 1967.
10. C.-C. Lin, H.-I. Lu and I-F. Sun, Improved compact visibility representation of planar graph via Schnyder's realizer, in *Proc. 20th Annual Symposium on Theoretical Aspects of Computer Science*, pp. 14-25, Lecture Notes in Computer Science, Vol. 2607, Springer-Verlag, Berlin, 2003.
11. P. Rosenstiehl and R. E. Tarjan, Rectilinear planar layouts and bipolar orientations of planar graphs. *Discrete Comput. Geom.* 1 (1986), 343-353.
12. W. Schnyder, Planar graphs and poset dimension. *Order* 5 (1989), 323-343.
13. W. Schnyder, Embedding planar graphs on the grid, in *Proc. of the First Annual ACM-SIAM Symposium on Discrete Algorithms*, pp. 138-148, SIAM, Philadelphia, 1990.
14. R. Tamassia and I.G.Tollis, An unified approach to visibility representations of planar graphs. *Discrete Comput. Geom.* 1 (1986), 321-341.
15. H. Zhang and X. He, Compact Visibility Representation and Straight-Line Grid Embedding of Plane Graphs, in: Proc. WADS'03, Lecture Notes in Computer Science, Vol. 2748, (Springer, Berlin, 2003) 493-504.

Topology Matters: Smoothed Competitiveness of Metrical Task Systems*

Guido Schäfer and Naveen Sivadasan

Max-Planck-Institut für Informatik, Saarbrücken, Germany,
{schaefer,ns}@mpi-sb.mpg.de

Abstract. We consider *metrical task systems*, a general framework to model online problems. Borodin, Linial and Saks [3] presented a deterministic *work function algorithm* (WFA) for metrical task systems having a tight competitive ratio of $2n - 1$. We present a *smoothed competitive analysis* of WFA. Given an adversarial task sequence, we smoothen the request costs by means of a symmetric additive smoothing model and analyze the competitive ratio of WFA on the smoothed task sequence. We prove upper and matching lower bounds on the smoothed competitive ratio of WFA. Our analysis reveals that the smoothed competitive ratio of WFA is much better than $O(n)$ and that it depends on several topological parameters of the underlying graph G, such as the maximum degree D and the diameter. For example, already for small perturbations the smoothed competitive ratio of WFA reduces to $O(\log n)$ on a clique or a complete binary tree and to $O(\sqrt{n})$ on a line. We also provide the first average case analysis of WFA showing that its expected competitive ratio is $O(\log(D))$ for various distributions.

1 Introduction

Borodin, Linial and Saks [3] introduced a general framework to model online problems, called *metrical task systems*. Many important online problems can be formulated as metrical task systems; for example, the paging problem, the static list accessing problem and the k-server problem.

We are given an undirected and connected graph $G = (V, E)$, with node set V and edge set E, and a positive length function $\lambda : E \to \mathbb{R}^+$ on the edges of G. We extend λ to a metric δ on G. Let $\delta : V \times V \to \mathbb{R}^+$ be a distance function such that $\delta(u, v)$ denotes the shortest path distance (with respect to λ) between any two nodes u and v in G. A *task* τ is an n-vector $(r(v_1), \ldots, r(v_n))$ of *request costs*. The cost to process task τ in node v_i is $r(v_i) \in \mathbb{R}^+ \cup \{\infty\}$. The online algorithm starts from a given initial position $s_0 \in V$ and has to service a sequence $\mathcal{S} = \langle \tau_1, \ldots, \tau_r \rangle$ of tasks, arriving one at a time. If the online algorithm resides after task τ_{t-1} in node u, the cost to service task τ_t in node v is $\delta(u, v) + r_t(v)$; $\delta(u, v)$ is the *transition cost* and $r_t(v)$ is the *processing cost*. The objective is to minimize the total transition plus processing cost.

---

* Partially supported by the Future and Emerging Technologies programme of the EU under contract number IST-1999-14186 (ALCOM-FT).

V. Diekert and M. Habib (Eds.): STACS 2004, LNCS 2996, pp. 489–500, 2004.
© Springer-Verlag Berlin Heidelberg 2004

Table 1. Upper bounds on the competitive ratio of WFA.

Upper Bounds

random tasks	$O\left(\frac{\sigma}{U_{\min}}\left(\frac{U_{\min}}{\sigma}+\log(D)\right)\right)$
arbitrary tasks	$O\left(\frac{Diam}{U_{\min}}\cdot\left(\frac{U_{\min}}{\sigma}+\log(D)\right)\right)$ and $O\left(\sqrt{n\cdot\frac{U_{\max}}{U_{\min}}\left(\frac{U_{\min}}{\sigma}+\log(D)\right)}\right)$
β-elementary tasks	$O\left(\beta\cdot\frac{U_{\max}}{U_{\min}}\left(\frac{U_{\min}}{\sigma}+\log(D)\right)\right)$

Borodin, Linial and Saks [3] gave a deterministic online algorithm, known as the *work function algorithm* (WFA), for metrical task systems. WFA has a competitive ratio of $2n-1$, which is optimal. However, the competitive ratio is often an over-pessimistic estimation of the true performance of an online algorithm.

Based on the idea underlying *smoothed analysis* [7], Becchetti et al. [2] recently proposed *smoothed competitive analysis* as an alternative to worst case competitive analysis of online algorithms. The idea is to randomly perturb, or *smoothen*, an adversarial input instance $\check{S}$ and to analyze the performance of the algorithm on the perturbed instances. Let $\text{ALG}[S]$ and $\text{OPT}[S]$, respectively, be the cost of the online and the optimal offline algorithm on a smoothed instance S obtained from $\check{S}$. The *smoothed competitive ratio* c of ALG with respect to a smoothing distribution f is defined as

$$c := \sup_{\check{S}} \mathbf{E}_{S \leftarrow \check{S}} \left[\frac{\text{ALG}[S]}{\text{OPT}[S]}\right].$$

We use the notion of smoothed competitiveness to characterize the asymptotic performance of WFA. We smoothen the request costs of each task according to an additive symmetric smoothing model. Each cost entry is smoothed by adding a random number chosen from a probability distribution f, whose expectation coincides with the original cost entry. Our analysis holds for various probability distributions, including the uniform and the normal distribution. We use σ to refer to the standard deviation of f. Our analysis reveals that the smoothed competitive ratio of WFA is much better than its worst case competitive ratio suggests and that it depends on certain *topological parameters* of the underlying graph.

Definition of Topological Parameters. In this paper, we assume that the underlying graph G has n nodes, minimum edge length $U_{\min}$, maximum edge length $U_{\max}$, and maximum degree D. Furthermore, we use $Diam$ to refer to the *diameter* of G, i.e., the maximum length of a shortest path between any two nodes. Similarly, a graph has *edge* diameter $diam$ if any two nodes are connected by a path of at most $diam$ edges. Observe that $diam U_{\min} \leq Diam \leq diam U_{\max}$. We emphasize that these topological parameters are defined with respect to G and its length function λ—not with respect to the resulting metric.

Table 2. Lower bounds on the competitive ratio of any deterministic online algorithm.

Lower Bounds

arbitrary tasks

- existential $\Omega\left(\frac{Diam}{U_{\min}} \cdot \left(\frac{U_{\min}}{\sigma} + \log(D)\right)\right)$ and $\Omega\left(\sqrt{n \cdot \frac{U_{\max}}{U_{\min}}} \cdot \left(\frac{U_{\min}}{\sigma} + \log(D)\right)\right)$

- universal $\Omega\left(\frac{U_{\min}}{\sigma} + \frac{U_{\min}}{U_{\max}}\log(D)\right)$ and $\Omega\left(\sqrt{diam \cdot \frac{U_{\min}}{U_{\max}}} \cdot \left(\frac{U_{\min}}{\sigma} + 1\right)\right)$

β-elementary tasks $\Omega\left(\beta \cdot \left(\frac{U_{\min}}{\sigma} + 1\right)\right)$ (existential)

We prove several upper bounds; see also Table 1.

1. We show that if the request costs are chosen randomly from a distribution f, which is non-increasing in $[0, \infty)$, the expected competitive ratio of WFA is

$$O\left(1 + \frac{\sigma}{U_{\min}} \cdot \log(D)\right).$$

   In particular, WFA has an expected competitive ratio of $O(\log(D))$ if $\sigma = \Theta(U_{\min})$. For example, we obtain a competitive ratio of $O(\log(n))$ on a clique and of $O(1)$ on a binary tree.
2. We prove two upper bounds on the smoothed competitive ratio of WFA:

$$O\left(\frac{Diam}{U_{\min}} \cdot \left(\frac{U_{\min}}{\sigma} + \log(D)\right)\right) \quad \text{and} \quad O\left(\sqrt{n \cdot \frac{U_{\max}}{U_{\min}}}\left(\frac{U_{\min}}{\sigma} + \log(D)\right)\right).$$

   For example, if $\sigma = \Theta(U_{\min})$ and $U_{\max}/U_{\min} = \Theta(1)$, WFA has smoothed competitive ratio $O(\log(n))$ on any constant diameter graph and $O(\sqrt{n})$ on any constant degree graph. Note also that on a complete binary tree we obtain an $O(\log(n))$ upper bound.
3. We obtain a better upper bound on the smoothed competitive ratio of WFA if the adversarial task sequence only consists of β-*elementary tasks*. A task is β-elementary if it has at most β non-zero entries. We prove a smoothed competitive ratio of

$$O\left(\beta \cdot \frac{U_{\max}}{U_{\min}}\left(\frac{U_{\min}}{\sigma} + \log(D)\right)\right).$$

   For example, if $\sigma = \Theta(U_{\min})$ and $U_{\max}/U_{\min} = \Theta(1)$, WFA has smoothed competitive ratio $O(\beta \log(D))$ for β-elementary tasks.

We also present lower bounds; see Table 2. All our lower bounds hold for *any* deterministic online algorithm and if the request costs are smoothed according to the additive symmetric smoothing model. We distinguish between *existential* and *universal* lower bounds. An existential lower bound, say $\Omega(f(n))$, means that there *exists* a class of graphs such that *every* deterministic algorithm has smoothed competitive ratio $\Omega(f(n))$ on these graphs. On the other hand, a universal lower bound $\Omega(f(n))$ states that for *any arbitrary* graph, *every* deterministic algorithm has smoothed competitive ratio $\Omega(f(n))$. Clearly, for metrical task systems, the best lower bound we can hope to obtain is $\Omega(n)$. Therefore, if we state a lower bound of $\Omega(f(n))$, we actually mean $\Omega(\min\{n, f(n)\})$.

4. For a large range of values for *Diam* and *D*, we present existential lower bounds that are asymptotically tight to the upper bounds stated in 2.
5. We also prove two universal lower bounds on the smoothed competitive ratio:

$$\Omega\left(\frac{U_{\min}}{\sigma} + \frac{U_{\min}}{U_{\max}} \log(D)\right) \quad \text{and} \quad \Omega\left(\min\left\{diam, \sqrt{diam \cdot \frac{U_{\min}}{U_{\max}} \cdot \left(\frac{U_{\min}}{\sigma} + 1\right)}\right\}\right).$$

Assume that $U_{\max}/U_{\min} = \Theta(1)$. Then, the first bound matches the first upper bound stated in 2 if the edge diameter *diam* is constant, e.g., for a clique. The second bound matches the second upper bound in 2 if $diam = \Omega(n)$ and the maximum degree D is constant, e.g., for a line.
6. For β-elementary tasks, we prove an existential lower bound of

$$\Omega\left(\beta \cdot \left(\frac{U_{\min}}{\sigma} + 1\right)\right).$$

This implies that the bound in 3 is tight up to a factor of $(U_{\max}/U_{\min}) \log(D)$.

Constrained Balls into Bins Game. Our analysis crucially relies on a lower bound on the cost of an optimal offline algorithm. We therefore study the growth of the work function values on a sequence of random requests. It turns out that the increase in the work function values can be modeled by a version of a balls into bins game with dependencies between the heights of the bins, which are specified by a constraint graph. We call this game the *constrained balls into bins game*. We believe that this game is also interesting independently of the context of this paper.

Due to lack of space, we omit the lower bounds and some upper bound proofs from this extended abstract. We refer the reader to [6] for a complete version of this paper.

2   Work Function Algorithm

Let $\mathcal{S} = \langle \tau_1, \ldots, \tau_\ell \rangle$ be a request sequence, and let $s_0 \in V$ denote the initial position. Let $\mathcal{S}_t$ denote the subsequence of the first t tasks of $\mathcal{S}$. For each t, $0 \le t \le \ell$, we define a function $w_t : V \to \mathbb{R}$ such that for each node $u \in V$, $w_t(u)$ is the minimum offline cost to process $\mathcal{S}_t$ starting in s_0 and ending in u. The function w_t is called the *work function* at time t with respect to $\mathcal{S}$ and s_0.

Let OPT denote an optimal offline algorithm. Clearly, the optimal offline cost OPT[$\mathcal{S}$] on $\mathcal{S}$ is equal to the minimum work function value at time ℓ, i.e.,

OPT$[\mathcal{S}] = \min_{u \in V}\{w_\ell(u)\}$. We can compute $w_t(u)$ for each $u \in V$ by dynamic programming:

$$w_0(u) := \delta(s_0, u), \quad \text{and} \quad w_t(u) := \min_{v \in V}\{w_{t-1}(v) + r_t(v) + \delta(v, u)\}. \quad (1)$$

We next describe the online work function algorithm; see also [3,1]. Intuitively, a good strategy for an online algorithm to process task τ_t is to move to a node where OPT would reside if τ_t would be the final task. However, the competitive ratio of an algorithm that solely sticks to this policy can become arbitrarily bad. A slight modification gives a $2n - 1$ competitive algorithm: Instead of blindly (no matter at what cost) traveling to the node of minimum work function value, we additionally take the transition cost into account. Essentially, this is the idea underlying the work function algorithm.

Work Function Algorithm (WFA): Let $s_0, \ldots, s_{t-1}$ denote the sequence of nodes visited by WFA to process $\mathcal{S}_{t-1}$. Then, to process task τ_t, WFA moves to a node s_t that minimizes $w_t(v) + \delta(s_{t-1}, v)$ for all $v \in V$. There is always a choice for s_t such that in addition $w_t(s_t) = w_{t-1}(s_t) + r_t(s_t)$. More formally,

$$s_t := \arg\min_{v \in V}\{w_t(v) + \delta(s_{t-1}, v)\} \quad \text{such that} \quad w_t(s_t) = w_{t-1}(s_t) + r_t(s_t). \quad (2)$$

In the sequel, we use WFA and OPT, respectively, to denote the work function and the optimal offline algorithm. For a given sequence $\mathcal{S} = \langle \tau_1, \ldots, \tau_\ell \rangle$ of tasks, WFA$[\mathcal{S}]$ and OPT$[\mathcal{S}]$ refer to the cost incurred by WFA and OPT on $\mathcal{S}$, respectively. By $s_0, \ldots, s_\ell$ we denote the sequence of nodes visited by WFA.

We state the following facts without proof.

Fact 1. *For any two nodes u and v and any time t, $|w_t(u) - w_t(v)| \leq \delta(u, v)$.*

Fact 2. *At any time t, $w_t(s_t) = w_t(s_{t-1}) - \delta(s_{t-1}, s_t)$.*

Fact 3. *At any time t, $r_t(s_t) + \delta(s_{t-1}, s_t) = w_t(s_{t-1}) - w_{t-1}(s_t)$.*

3 Smoothing Model

Let the *adversarial task sequence* be given by $\check{\mathcal{S}} := \langle \check{\tau}_1, \ldots, \check{\tau}_r \rangle$. We smoothen each task vector $\check{\tau}_t := (\check{r}_t(v_1), \ldots, \check{r}_t(v_n))$ by perturbing each *original cost* entry $\check{r}_t(v_j)$ according to some probability distribution f as follows

$$r_t(v_j) := \max\{0, \check{r}_t(v_j) + \epsilon(v_j)\}, \quad \text{where } \epsilon(v_j) \leftarrow f.$$

That is, to each original cost entry we add a random number which is chosen from f. The obtained *smoothed* task is denoted by $\tau_t := (r_t(v_1), \ldots, r_t(v_n))$. We use μ and σ, respectively, to denote the expectation and the standard deviation of f. We assume that f is symmetric around $\mu := 0$. We take the maximum of zero and the smoothing outcome in order to assure that the smoothed costs are non-negative. Thus, the probability for an original zero cost entry to remain zero is amplified to $\frac{1}{2}$.

A major criticism to the additive model is that zero entries are destroyed. However, one can easily verify that the lower bound proof of $2n - 1$ [3,4,1] on the competitive ratio of any deterministic algorithm for metrical task systems goes through for any smoothing model that does not destroy zeros.

Our analysis holds for a large class of probability distributions, which we call *permissible*. We say f is permissible if (i) f is symmetric around $\mu = 0$ and (ii) f is non-increasing in $[0, \infty)$. For example, the uniform and the normal distribution are permissible. Since the stated upper bounds on the competitive ratio of WFA do not further improve by choosing σ much larger than $U_{\min}$, we assume that $\sigma \leq 2U_{\min}$. Moreover, we use c_f to denote a constant depending on f such that for a random ϵ chosen from f, $\mathbf{P}[\epsilon \geq \sigma/c_f] \geq \frac{1}{4}$.

All our results hold against an *adaptive adversary*. An adaptive adversary reveals the task sequence over time, thereby taking decisions made by the online algorithm in the past into account.

4   A Lower Bound on the Optimal Offline Cost

In this section, we establish a lower bound on the cost incurred by an optimal offline algorithm OPT when run on smoothed task sequences. For the purpose of proving the lower bound, we first investigate an interesting version of a balls into bins experiment, which we call the *constrained balls into bins game*.

4.1   Constrained Balls into Bins Game

We are given n bins $B_1, \ldots, B_n$. In each round, we place a ball independently in each bin B_i with probability p; with probability $1 - p$ no ball is placed in B_i. We define the *height* $h_t(i)$ of a bin B_i as the number of balls in B_i after round t. We have dependencies between the heights of different bins that are specified by an (undirected) *constraint graph* $G_c := (V_c, E_c)$. The node set V_c of G_c contains n nodes $u_1, \ldots, u_n$, where each node u_i corresponds to a bin B_i. All edges in E_c have uniform edge lengths equal to Q. Let D be the maximum degree of a vertex in G_c. Throughout the experiment, we maintain the following invariant.

Invariant: The difference in height between two bins B_i and B_j is at most the shortest path distance between u_i and u_j in G_c.

If the placement of a ball into a bin B_i would violate this invariant, the ball is *rejected*; otherwise we say that the ball is *accepted*. Observe that if two bins B_i and B_j do not violate the invariant in round t, then, in round $t + 1$, B_i and B_j might cause a violation only if one bin, say B_i, receives a ball, and the other, B_j, does not receive a ball; if both receive a ball, or both do not receive a ball, the invariant remains true.

Layer

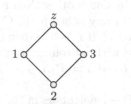
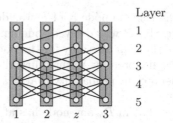

Fig. 1. Illustration of the "unfolding" for $Q = 1$ and $h = 5$. Left: constraint graph G_c. Right: layered dependency graph $\mathcal{D}_h$.

Theorem 1. *Fix any bin B_z. Let R_z be the number of rounds needed until the height of B_z becomes $h \geq \log(n)$. Then, $\mathbf{P}[R_z > c_3 h\,(1 + \log(D)/Q)] \leq 1/n^4$.*

We remark that there are instances, where the above bound is indeed tight.

We next describe how one can model the growth of the height of B_z by an alternative, but essentially equivalent, game on a *layered dependency graph*. A layered dependency graph $\mathcal{D}_h$ consists of h layers, $V_1, \ldots, V_h$, and edges are present only between adjacent layers. The idea is to "unfold" the constraint graph G_c into a layered dependency graph $\mathcal{D}_h$.

We describe the construction for $Q = 1$; the details for $Q > 1$ can be found in [6]. Each layer of $\mathcal{D}_h$ corresponds to a subset of nodes in G_c. Layer 1 consists of z only, the node corresponding to bin B_z. Assume we have constructed layers $V_1, \ldots, V_i, i < h$. Then, V_{i+1} is constructed from V_i by adding all nodes, $\Gamma_{G_c}(V_i)$, that are adjacent to V_i in G_c, i.e., $V_{i+1} := V_i \cup \Gamma_{G_c}(V_i)$. For every pair $(u, v) \in V_i \times V_{i+1}$, we add an edge (u, v) to $\mathcal{D}_h$ if $(u, v) \in E_c$, or $u = v$. See Figure 1 for an example.

Now, the following game on $\mathcal{D}_h$ is equivalent to the balls and bins game. Each node in $\mathcal{D}_h$ is in one of three states, namely UNFINISHED, READY or FINISHED. Initially, all nodes in layer h are READY and all other nodes are UNFINISHED. In each round, all READY nodes toss a coin; each coin independently turns up *head* with probability p and *tail* with probability $1 - p$. A READY node changes its state to FINISHED if the outcome of its coin toss is *head*. At the end of each round, an UNFINISHED node in layer j changes its state to READY, if all its neighbors in layer $j + 1$ are FINISHED.

Note that the nodes in layer V_j are FINISHED if and only if the corresponding bins $B_i, i \in V_j$, have height at least j. Consequently, the number of rounds needed until the root node z in $\mathcal{D}_h$ becomes FINISHED is equal to the number of rounds needed for the height of B_z to become h.

Proof (Theorem 1). Let $\mathcal{D}_h$ be a layered dependency graph constructed from G_c as described above. As argued above, the event $(R_z \leq t)$ is equivalent to the event that the root node becomes FINISHED within t rounds in $\mathcal{D}_h$. Consider the event that the root node z does not become FINISHED after t rounds. Then, there exists a *bad* path $P := (v_1, \ldots, v_h)$ from $z = v_1$ to some node v_h in the bottom layer h such that no node v_i of P was delayed by nodes other than $v_{i+1}, \ldots, v_h$. Put differently, P was delayed independently of any other path. Consider the outcome of the coin flips only for the nodes along P. If P is bad then the number of coin flips, denoted by X, that turned up *head* within t rounds is at most $h-1$. Let $\alpha(t)$ denote the probability that P is bad, i.e., $\alpha(t) := \mathbf{P}[X \le h-1]$. Clearly, $\mathbf{E}[X] = tp$.

Observe that in $\mathcal{D}_h$ any node has at most $D+1$ neighbors in the next larger layer. That is, the number of possible paths from z to any node v in layer h is bounded by $(D+1)^h$.

Thus, $\mathbf{P}[R_z > t] \le \alpha(t)(D+1)^h$. We want to choose t such that this probability is at most $1/n^4$. If we choose $t \ge (32/p)(h + h\log(D))$ and use Chernoff's bound [5] on X, we obtain for $h \ge \log(n)$

$$\alpha(t) = \mathbf{P}[X \le h-1] \le \mathbf{P}[X \le pt/2] \le e^{-pt/8} \le \frac{1}{n^4(D+1)^h}.$$

□

4.2   Lower Bound

We are now in a position to prove the following lemma.

Lemma 1. *Let $\check{S}$ be an adversarial sequence of $\ell := \lceil c_2 n\gamma(U_{\min}/\sigma + \log(D)) \rceil$ tasks, for a fixed constant c_2 and some $\gamma \ge 1$. Then, $\mathbf{P}[\text{OPT}[S] < n\gamma U_{\min}] \le 1/n^3$.*

We relate the growth of the work function values to the balls and bins game as follows. For each node v_i of G we have a corresponding bin B_i. We obtain the constraint graph G_c from G by setting all edge lengths to $Q := \lfloor U_{\min}/\Delta \rfloor$, where $\Delta := \min\{U_{\min}, \sigma/c_f\}$. Since for any v_i and any time t, $\mathbf{P}[r_t(v_i) \ge \sigma/c_f] \ge \frac{1}{4}$, we place a ball into B_i with probability $\frac{1}{4}$. The following lemma establishes a relation between the work function value of v_i and the height $h_t(i)$ of B_i.

Lemma 2. *Consider any node v_i and its corresponding bin B_i. Let $h_t(i)$ denote the number of balls in bin B_i after t rounds. Then, for any $t \ge 0$, $w_t(v_i) \ge h_t(i)\,\Delta$.*

Put differently, the number of rounds needed until a bin B_i has height h stochastically dominates the time t needed until $w_t(v_i) \ge h\Delta$. Applying Theorem 1, we obtain that after $\ell := \lceil c_2 n\gamma(U_{\min}/\sigma + \log(D)) \rceil$ rounds, for an appropriate constant c_2, the probability that there exists a bin of height less than $2n\gamma Q$ is at most $1/n^3$. That is, with probability at least $1 - 1/n^3$, all v_i satisfy $w_\ell(v_i) \ge 2n\gamma Q\Delta \ge n\gamma U_{\min}$. Since $\text{OPT}[S] = \min_{u \in V}\{w_\ell(u)\}$, the theorem follows.

We will use the Lemma 1 several times as follows.

Corollary 1. *Let $\check{S}$ be an adversarial sequence of $\ell := \lceil c_2 n\gamma(U_{\min}/\sigma + \log(D)) \rceil$ tasks, for a fixed constant c_2 and an some $\gamma \ge 1$. Then, the smoothed competitive ratio of WFA is at most $\mathbf{E}[\text{WFA}[S]]/(n\gamma U_{\min}) + o(1)$.*

Proof. Let $\mathcal{S}$ be a random variable denoting a smoothed sequence obtained from $\check{S}$. We define $\mathcal{E}$ as the event that OPT incurs a cost of at least $n\gamma U_{\min}$ on $\mathcal{S}$. By Lemma 1, we have $\mathbf{P}[\neg\mathcal{E}] \leq 1/n^3$. Thus,

$$\mathbf{E}\left[\frac{\mathrm{WFA}[\mathcal{S}]}{\mathrm{OPT}[\mathcal{S}]}\right] = \mathbf{E}\left[\frac{\mathrm{WFA}[\mathcal{S}]}{\mathrm{OPT}[\mathcal{S}]}\,\Big|\,\mathcal{E}\right]\mathbf{P}[\mathcal{E}] + \mathbf{E}\left[\frac{\mathrm{WFA}[\mathcal{S}]}{\mathrm{OPT}[\mathcal{S}]}\,\Big|\,\neg\mathcal{E}\right]\mathbf{P}[\neg\mathcal{E}]$$

$$\leq \frac{\mathbf{E}[\mathrm{WFA}[\mathcal{S}]\,|\,\mathcal{E}]\,\mathbf{P}[\mathcal{E}]}{n\gamma U_{\min}} + \frac{2n-1}{n^3} \leq \frac{\mathbf{E}[\mathrm{WFA}[\mathcal{S}]]}{n\gamma U_{\min}} + o(1),$$

where the second inequality follows from the definition of $\mathcal{E}$ and the fact that the (worst case) competitive ratio of WFA is $2n - 1$. $\qquad\qquad\square$

5   Upper Bounds

5.1   First Upper Bound

We derive the first upper bound on the smoothed competitive ratio of WFA. The idea is as follows. We derive two upper bounds on the smoothed competitive ratio of WFA. The first one is a deterministic bound, and the second one uses the probabilistic lower bound on OPT. We combine these two bounds using the following fact to obtain the theorem stated below.

Fact 4. *Let A, B, and X_i, $1 \leq i \leq m$, be positive quantities. We have*

$$\min\left\{\frac{A\sum_{i=1}^m X_i}{\sum_{i=1}^m X_i^2}, \frac{B\sum_{i=1}^m X_i}{m}\right\} \leq \sqrt{AB}.$$

Consider any deterministic input sequence $\mathcal{K}$ of length ℓ. Let $s_0, s_1, \ldots, s_\ell$ denote the sequence of nodes visited by WFA. Define $C(t) := r_t(s_t)+\delta(s_{t-1}, s_t)$ as the service cost plus the transition cost incurred by WFA in round t. With respect to $\mathcal{K}$ we define T as the set of rounds, where the increase of the work function value of s_{t-1} is at least one half of the transition cost, i.e., $t \in T$ if and only if $w_t(s_{t-1}) - w_{t-1}(s_{t-1}) \geq \delta(s_{t-1}, s_t)/2$. We use $\bar{T}$ to refer to the complement of T. Due to Fact 2 we have $w_t(s_{t-1}) = w_t(s_t) + \delta(s_{t-1}, s_t)$. Therefore, the above definition is equivalent to

$$T := \left\{t : w_t(s_t) - w_{t-1}(s_{t-1}) \geq -\tfrac{1}{2}\delta(s_{t-1}, s_t)\right\}. \tag{3}$$

We first prove that the total cost of WFA on $\mathcal{K}$ is bounded by a constant times the contribution of rounds in T.

Lemma 3. *Let $\mathcal{K}$ be a sufficiently long sequence such that $\mathrm{WFA}[\mathcal{K}] \geq 6Diam$. Then, $\mathrm{WFA}[\mathcal{K}] \leq 8\sum_{t\in T} C(t)$.*

We partition T into T^1 and T^2, where $T^1 := \{t \in T : w_t(s_t) - w_{t-1}(s_t) \leq 4U_{\max} diam\}$, and $T^2 := T \setminus T_1$.

Lemma 4. *Let $\mathcal{K}$ be a sufficiently long sequence such that $\mathrm{OPT}[\mathcal{K}] \geq 2Diam$. There exists a constant b such that*

$$\mathrm{OPT}[\mathcal{K}] \geq \frac{1}{bn}\left(\frac{1}{U_{\max}}\sum_{t\in T^1}C(t)^2 + n\sum_{t\in T^2}C(t)\right).$$

Theorem 2. *The smoothed competitive ratio of* WFA *is $O(\sqrt{n\cdot(U_{\max}/U_{\min})}(U_{\min}/\sigma + \log(D)))$.*

Proof. Let $\check{S}$ be an adversarial task sequence of length $\ell := \lceil c_2 n\gamma(U_{\min}/\sigma + \log(D))\rceil$, and let S be a random variable denoting a smoothed sequence obtained from $\check{S}$. Due to the proof of Corollary 1 it suffices to bound $\mathbf{E}[\mathrm{WFA}[S]/\mathrm{OPT}[S]\,|\,\mathcal{E}]$, where $\mathcal{E}$ is the event $(\mathrm{OPT}[S] \geq n\gamma U_{\min})$. Consider a smoothing outcome S such that the event $\mathcal{E}$ holds. We fix γ sufficiently large such that $\mathrm{OPT}[S] \geq 6Diam$. Observe that $\mathrm{WFA}[S] \geq \mathrm{OPT}[S] \geq 6Diam$.

First, assume $\sum_{t\in T^1}C(t) < \sum_{t\in T^2}C(t)$. Due to Lemma 3 and Lemma 4,

$$\mathrm{WFA}[S] \leq 16\sum_{t\in T^2}C(t) \quad\text{and}\quad \mathrm{OPT}[S] \geq \frac{1}{b}\sum_{t\in T^2}C(t).$$

Hence, $\mathbf{E}[\mathrm{WFA}[S]/\mathrm{OPT}[S]\,|\,\mathcal{E}] = O(1)$.

Next, assume $\sum_{t\in T^1}C(t) \geq \sum_{t\in T^2}C(t)$. By Lemma 3 and Lemma 4 we have

$$\mathrm{WFA}[S] \leq 16\sum_{t\in T^1}C(t) \quad\text{and}\quad \mathrm{OPT}[S] \geq \frac{1}{bn}\left(\frac{1}{U_{\max}}\sum_{t\in T^1}C(t)^2\right). \qquad (4)$$

Thus,

$$\frac{\mathrm{WFA}[S]}{\mathrm{OPT}[S]} \leq 16bnU_{\max}\left(\frac{\sum_{t\in T^1}C(t)}{\sum_{t\in T^1}C(t)^2}\right). \qquad (5)$$

Since $\mathcal{E}$ holds, we also have

$$\frac{\mathrm{WFA}[S]}{\mathrm{OPT}[S]} \leq \frac{16\ell\sum_{t\in T^1}C(t)}{\ell n\gamma U_{\min}} \leq \frac{c}{U_{\min}}\left(\frac{U_{\min}}{\sigma}+\log(D)\right)\left(\frac{\sum_{t\in T^1}C(t)}{|T^1|}\right), \qquad (6)$$

where the last inequality holds for an appropriate constant c and since $\ell \geq |T^1|$. Observe that (6) is well-defined since $\sum_{t\in T^1}C(t) \geq \frac{1}{16}\mathrm{WFA}[S]$ (by (4)) and $\mathrm{WFA}[S] \geq 6Diam$ imply that $|T^1| \geq 1$.

Applying Fact 4 to (5) and (6), these two bounds are combined to the one stated in the theorem. $\qquad\square$

5.2   Second Upper Bound

Our second upper bound easily follows from the proof of Corollary 1 and the following deterministic relation between WFA and OPT.

Lemma 5. *Let $\mathcal{K}$ be any request sequence of length ℓ. Then, $\mathrm{WFA}[\mathcal{K}] \leq \mathrm{OPT}[\mathcal{K}] + Diam\cdot\ell$.*

Theorem 3. *The smoothed competitive ratio of* WFA *is $O((Diam/U_{\min})\cdot(U_{\min}/\sigma + \log(D)))$.*

5.3 Potential Function

The next lemma can be proved using a potential function argument. Intuitively, it states that the expected cost of WFA is bounded by the expected cost of a simple greedy online algorithm.

Lemma 6. *Let $\mathcal{S}$ be a smoothed sequence of ℓ tasks. For each t, $1 \leq t \leq \ell$, and a given node s, define a random variable $\Delta_t(s) := \min_{u \in V}\{r_t(u) + \delta(u, s)\}$. Let $\kappa > 0$. If $\mathbf{E}[\Delta_t(s)] \leq \kappa$ for each $s \in V$ and for each t, $1 \leq t \leq \ell$, then $\mathbf{E}[\text{WFA}[\mathcal{S}]] \leq 4\kappa\ell + Diam$.*

5.4 Random Tasks

We derive an upper bound on the expected competitive ratio of WFA if each request cost is chosen independently from a probability distribution f which is non-increasing in $[0, \infty)$. We need the following fact.

Fact 5. *Let f be a continuous, non-increasing distribution over $[0, \infty)$ with mean μ and standard deviation σ. Then, $\mu \leq \sqrt{12}\sigma$.*

Theorem 4. *If each request cost is chosen independently from a non-increasing probability distribution f over $[0, \infty)$ with standard deviation σ then the expected competitive ratio of WFA is $O(1 + (\sigma/U_{\min}) \cdot \log(D))$.*

Proof. Let $\mathcal{S}$ be a random task sequence of length $\ell := \lceil c_2 n\gamma(U_{\min}/\sigma) + \log(D)) \rceil$, for an appropriate $\gamma \geq U_{\max}$, generated from f. Observe that since $\gamma \geq U_{\max}$, we have $\ell \geq Diam$. For any t and any node s, we have $\Delta_t(s) = \min_{u \in V}\{r_t(u) + \delta(u, s)\} \leq r_t(s)$. Since $r_t(s)$ is chosen from f, Fact 5 implies that $\mathbf{E}[\Delta_t(s)] \leq \kappa := \sqrt{12}\sigma$. Thus, by Lemma 6, we have $\mathbf{E}[\text{WFA}[\mathcal{S}]] = 4\sqrt{12}\sigma\ell + Diam = O(\sigma\ell)$.

Note that we can use the lower bound established in Section 4 to bound the cost of OPT: The generation of $\mathcal{S}$ is equivalent to smoothing (according to f) an adversarial task sequence consisting of all-zero request vectors only. Here, we do not need that the distribution f is symmetric around its mean. The theorem now follows from Corollary 1. $\qquad\square$

5.5 β-Elementary Tasks

We can strengthen the upper bound on the smoothed competitive ratio of WFA if the adversarial task sequence only consists of β-elementary tasks. Recall that in a β-elementary task the number of non-zero request costs is at most β.

Theorem 5. *If the adversarial task sequence only consists of β-elementary tasks then the smoothed competitive ratio of WFA is $O(\beta(U_{\max}/U_{\min})(U_{\min}/\sigma + \log(D)))$.*

The proof follows easily from the following lemma, Lemma 6 and Corollary 1.

Lemma 7. *Let τ_t be a task obtained by smoothing a β-elementary task, where $\beta < n$. Then, $\mathbf{E}[\Delta_t(s)] \leq \sigma + \beta U_{\max}$ for each node $s \in V$.*

6   Conclusion

In this paper we focused on the asymptotic behaviour of WFA if the request costs of an adversarial task sequence are perturbed by means of a symmetric additive smoothing model. We showed that the smoothed competitive ratio of WFA is much better than its worst case competitive ratio suggests and that it depends on topological parameters of the underlying graph. Moreover, all our bounds, except the one for β-elementary tasks, are tight up to constant factors. We believe that our analysis gives a strong indication that the performance of WFA in practice is much better than $2n - 1$.

An open problem would be to strengthen the universal lower bounds. Moreover, it would be interesting to obtain exact (and not only asymptotic) bounds on the smoothed competitive ratio of WFA.

Acknowledgements. We thank Alberto Marchetti-Spaccamela for his comments on a first draft of this paper. Moreover, we thank Kurt Mehlhorn for helpful suggestions and discussions; due to one of his suggestions we were able to significantly shorten the proof of Theorem 1.

References

1. A. Borodin and R. El-Yaniv. *Online Computation and Competitive Analysis.* Cambridge University Press, 1998.
2. L. Becchetti, S. Leonardi, A. Marchetti-Spaccamela, G. Schäfer, and T. Vredeveld. Average case and smoothed competitive analysis of the multi-level feedback algorithm. In *Proceedings of the Forty-Fourth Annual IEEE Symposium on Foundations of Computer Science (FOCS)*, pages 462–471, 2003.
3. A. Borodin, N. Linial, and M. Saks. An optimal online algorithm for metrical task systems. *Journal of the ACM*, 39:745–763, 1992.
4. M. S. Manasse, L. A. McGeoch, and D. D. Sleator. Competitive algorithms for on-line problems. In *ACM Symposium on Theory of Computing*, pages 322–333, 1988.
5. R. Motwani and P. Raghavan. *Randomized algorithms.* Cambridge University Press, 1 edition, 1995.
6. G. Schäfer and N. Sivadasan. Topology matters: Smoothed competitiveness of metrical task systems. Technical Report MPI-I-2003-1-016, Max-Planck-Institut für Informatik, Saarbrücken, Germany, 2003.
7. D. Spielman and S. H. Teng. Smoothed analysis of algorithms: Why the simplex algorithm usually takes polynomial time. In *ACM Symposium on Theory of Computing*, 2001.

A Randomized Competitive Algorithm for Evaluating Priced AND/OR Trees

Eduardo Sany Laber*

Departamento de Informática da PUC-Rio
laber@inf.puc-rio.br

Abstract. Recently, Charikar et. al. investigated the problem of evaluating AND/OR trees, with non uniform costs on its leaves, under the perspective of the competitive analysis. For an AND-OR tree T they presented a $\mu(T)$-competitive deterministic polynomial time algorithm, where $\mu(T)$ is the number of leaves that must be read, in the worst case, in order to determine the value of T. Furthermore, they prove that $\mu(T)$ is a lower bound on the deterministic competitiveness, which assures the optimality of their algorithm.

The power of randomization in this context has remained as an open question. Here, we give a step towards solving this problem by presenting a $0.792\mu(T)$-competitive randomized polynomial time algorithm. This contrasts with the best known lower bound $\mu(T)/2$.

1 Introduction

A game tree is a rooted tree, where every internal node has either a MIN or MAX label and the parent of every MIN (MAX) node is a MAX (MIN) node. Every leaf is associated to a real number, its value. The value of a MAX (MIN) node is recursively defined as the maximum (minimum) among the values of its children. The value of a tree is the value of its root. Game trees play a central role in Artificial Intelligence, particularly in game-playing programs.

The AND/OR tree is a particular case of a game tree, where every leaf has either value 0 or 1. It is easy to see that a MAX node can be thought as an OR gate while a a MIN node can be thought as an AND gate. The AND/OR trees are interesting in its own right since they have applications in mechanical theorem proving.

Several authors [1,2,3] have considered the problem of determining the value of game trees and AND/OR trees by reading as few as possible leaves. In [4], Charikar et al. investigated this problem under the perspective of the competitive analysis. They consider the more general problem where the cost of reading a leaf x_i is c_{x_i} and the cost of evaluating a tree is the sum of the costs of the leaves that are read in this process. This variant was motivated by possible Internet applications where the costs of the information required to take some

---

* Partially supported by FAPERJ (Proc. E-26/150.715/2003) and by CNPQ, through Edital Universal 01/2002 (Proc. 476817/2003-0)

V. Diekert and M. Habib (Eds.): STACS 2004, LNCS 2996, pp. 501–512, 2004.

decision may vary depending on the acquisition source. What has brought us into this problem, however, are database applications where queries involving no conventional data like images, DNA sequences and tables are handled [5,6]. These queries differ from the traditional ones, since the processing of attributes like images and sequences are much more expensive than that of usual alpha-numeric registers. Since AND/OR trees model an important class of queries, they are particularly important in this scenario.

Now, we explain the competitiveness metric proposed in [4], which will also be adopted here. Let f be a function over a set of variables $V = \{x_1, x_2, \ldots, x_n\}$ (a game tree can be thought as a function f, where the leaves correspond to the variables in V). Each variable x_i has a non-negative cost c_{x_i} and the vector $c = <c_{x_1}, \ldots, c_{x_n}>$ is called the *cost vector*. Given $U \subset V$, we define the cost of U as the sum of the costs of its variables. A *setting* σ of the variables is the choice of a value for each variable. The partial setting restricted to $U \subset V$ is denoted by $\sigma_{|U}$. A set $U \subset V$ is *sufficient* with respect to σ if the value of f is determined by the partial setting $\sigma_{|U}$. Such a U is a *proof* (certificate) of the value of f under σ. The cheapest proof of the value of f under σ is thus the sufficient set with minimum cost. We use $c^f(\sigma)$ to denote the cost of such a proof.

For example, consider the AND/OR tree T presented in Figure 1. For the setting $\sigma_R = (0, 0, 0, 1, 1)$, we have $c^T(\sigma_R) = 3+5+2$. On the other hand, for the setting $\sigma_S = (0, 1, 1, 1, 1)$, we have $c^T(\sigma_S) = 2 + 6 + 4$. An evaluation algorithm

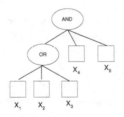

Fig. 1. An AND/OR tree T with vector cost $c = <3, 5, 2, 6, 4>$.

for f sequentially reads the variables in V. The algorithm stops when the set of variables read so far is sufficient with respect to σ. The cost of the algorithm $\mathcal{A}$ for a setting σ is given by $c_\mathcal{A}^f(\sigma)$. As an example, let $\mathcal{A}$ be an algorithm that reads the variables following the sequence $x_1 x_2 x_3 \ldots$ and skipping those variables that cannot affect, at the current point, the value of f anymore. Thus, for the tree T in Figure 1, $c_\mathcal{A}^T(\sigma_R) = 10$, since $\mathcal{A}$ reads the leaves x_1, x_2, x_3. On the other hand, $c_\mathcal{A}^T(\sigma_S) = 18$, since in this case it reads x_1, x_2, x_4, x_5.

The competitiveness of $\mathcal{A}$ is defined by

$$\gamma_c^\mathcal{A}(f) = max_\sigma \left\{ \frac{c_\mathcal{A}^f(\sigma)}{c^f(\sigma)} \right\}.$$

The best possible competitive ratio for any deterministic algorithm, then, is $\gamma_c^f = \min_{\mathcal{A}}\{\gamma_c^{\mathcal{A}}(f)\}$, where the minimum is got over all possible deterministic algorithms $\mathcal{A}$. For the case where f is an AND/OR tree function, Charikar et. al. [4] present a pseudo-polynomial γ_c^f-competitive deterministic algorithm.

Furthermore, they studied the dependence of the competitive ratio on the structure of f, defining the extremal competitiveness $\gamma(f)$ of f as $\gamma(f) = \max_c \gamma_c^f$.

This measure captures somehow the complexity of f, leaving the cost vector at the background. For the case where f is an AND/OR tree T, they show that $\gamma(T) = \max\{k(T), l(T)\}$, where $k(T)$ and $l(T)$ are, respectively, the number of leaves that must be read in the worst case in order to guarantee that the value of $T(\sigma)$ is 1 or 0. A simple method to calculate these values is described in Section 2.

1.1   Our Result

The main open direction according to Charikar et. al [4] is understanding the power of randomization in this context. Here, we give an important step in this direction. Given an algorithm $\mathcal{A}$, its randomized competitiveness is defined by

$$\delta_c^{\mathcal{A}}(f) = \max_{\sigma} E\left[\frac{c_{\mathcal{A}}^f(\sigma)}{c^f(\sigma)}\right] = \max_{\sigma} \frac{E[c_{\mathcal{A}}^f(\sigma)]}{c^f(\sigma)}$$

The optimal randomized competitiveness is defined by $\delta_c^f = \min_{\mathcal{A}} \delta_c^{\mathcal{A}}(f)$. Finally, the extremal randomized complexity of f is defined by $\delta(f) = \max_c \delta_c^f$. In [4], the following is observed.

Theorem 1. *If T is an AND/OR tree, then $\delta(T) \geq (1 + \max\{k(T), l(T)\})/2$*

Clearly, $\delta(T) \leq \gamma(T) = \max\{k(T), l(T)\}$, since any deterministic algorithm can be viewed as a randomized algorithm. Here, we show that $\delta(T) \leq 0.792$ $\max\{(k(T), l(T)\}$

This result is proved through the analysis of a randomized polynomial algorithm that combines three key ideas: an optimal way to evaluate AND/OR trees with depth at most 2; a "binarization" of trees with unrestricted depth and a variation of the WeakBalance algorithm proposed in [4] which specially handles nodes whose children are roots of trees with depth at most 1. The main question that remains open is whether $\delta(T) = (1 + \max\{(k(T), l(T)\})/2$ or not.

1.2   Related Work and Paper Organization

Given an AND/OR trees T, it is known that any deterministic algorithm, in the worst case, must evaluate all leaves of T before determining its value.

Tarsi [1] considered the problem of minimizing the expected number of evaluated leaves for a distribution probability in which every leaf has probability p

of having value 1. He has proved that certain class of deterministic algorithm are optimal for balanced trees (a class that includes uniform trees).

For binary trees, where every internal node has exactly two children and every leaf is at distance $2k$ from the root Snir [2] presents a randomized algorithm which reads at most $n^{0.793}$ leaves in the average, where $n = 2^{2k}$ is the total number of leaves. In [3], Saks and Wigderson show that Snir's Algorithm reads, in fact, $O(n^{0.753})$ leaves in the average. Furthermore, they prove that this algorithm is optimal. For general AND/OR trees, they present techniques for generating upper an lower bounds on the expected number of leaves that need to be read.

The paper is organized as follows. In Section 2, we introduce some additional notation and state some facts that will be useful throughout this text. In Section 3, we prove that $\delta(T) = 1 + \max\{k(T), l(T)\}/2$ for every AND/OR tree T with depth at most 2. Finally, in Section 4, we prove that $\delta(T) \leq 0.792 \max\{k(T), l(T)\}$, the main result of this paper.

2   Notations and Basic Facts

Let T be a rooted tree with costs on its leaves. Define $h(T)$ as the depth of T, that is, the longest path from the root of T to a leaf. If T is a leaf, $h(T) = 0$. Given a node x in T, let T_x be the maximal (w.r.t node inclusion) subtree of T rooted in x. We use c_T to denote the sum of the costs of the leaves of T. Throughout this text we use r to denote the root of T and $T_1, \ldots, T_k$ to denote the subtrees rooted at the children of r.

A general AND/OR tree (G-AND/OR tree) T is a rooted tree where every internal node has either an AND or OR label. Furthermore, to each leaf x of T it is associated a cost c_x and a bit value. The value of an AND internal node is 1 if all of its children have value 1 and it is 0, otherwise. The value of an OR internal node is 0 if all of its children have value 0 and it is 1, otherwise. In some occasions, we use the term variables of T to refer to the leaves of T. The value of T for a setting σ is denoted by $T(\sigma)$. As an example, for the setting $\sigma_R = (0, 0, 0, 1, 1)$ in Figure 1, we have $T(\sigma_R) = 0$. We say that two G-AND/OR trees T and T' are equivalent if $T(\sigma) = T'(\sigma)$ for every σ. Whenever the context is clear we use abuse the notation by using σ to refer to the partial setting restricted to the leaves of T_x.

An AND/OR tree is an G-AND/OR tree where the parent of every AND (OR) node is an OR (AND) node and each internal node has at least two children. A single leaf is a *trivial* AND/OR tree. It is easy to verify the following fact: every G-AND/OR tree T is equivalent to an AND/OR tree T' such that $h(T') \leq h(T)$

The functions $k(T)$ and $l(T)$ can be calculated as follows. If T is a leaf then $k(T) = l(T) = 1$. If r is an AND node, then $k(T) = \sum_{i=1}^{k} k(T_i)$ and $l(T) = \max_{i=1\ldots,k} l(T_i)$. Similarly, if r is an OR node, then $l(T) = \sum_{i=1}^{k} l(T_i)$ and $k(T) = \max_{i=1\ldots,k} k(T_i)$. For example, in the tree of Figure 1, we have $k(T) = l(T) = 3$.

In order to make this reading easier we provide a list of notations: $c^T(\sigma)$, cost of the cheapest proof for the value of T when the setting is σ; c_T, sum of the costs of the leaves of T; $c_{\mathcal{A}}^T(\sigma)$, cost incurred by algorithm $\mathcal{A}$ to determine the value of T when the setting is σ; $T(\sigma)$, value of T when the setting is σ $h(T)$, depth of T.

3   Evaluating Trees of Depth at Most 2

In this section, we prove the following theorem

Theorem 2. *If T is an AND/OR tree and $h(T) \leq 2$, then $\delta(T) = (1 + \max\{(k(T), l(T)\})/2$.*

In [3], Saks and Wigderson defined the class of directional algorithms. An algorithm is directional if it reads the leaves of T following a depth first search in T, in which the next child of the current node to be visited is randomly selected according to some probability distribution.

The proof of Theorem 2 follows from the analysis of EVAL, a directional algorithm presented below. What makes EVAL interesting is the probability distribution employed, in which the next subtree to be visited is selected with a probability that depends on the square of the inverse of the sum of its leaves costs.

EVAL(T: AND/OR tree)
    If T is a leaf then Read T and **Return** the value of T
    $S \leftarrow \{1, \ldots, k\}$ (*)
    For each $i \in S$ make $w_i \leftarrow \frac{1}{(c_{T_i})^2}$
    While $S \neq \emptyset$ do
        $W \leftarrow \sum_{j \in S} w_j$
        Selects an index i from S with probability w_i/W
        If the root of T is an OR gate **then**
            If EVAL(T_i)=1 then **Return** 1
    Else
            If EVAL(T_i)=0 then **Return** 0
        $S \leftarrow S - \{i\}$
    If the root of T is an OR gate then **Return** 0
    Else Return 1

Fig. 2. Eval Algorithm

We have the following lemma whose proof we defer for the extended version of the paper

Lemma 1. *Let $Pr[S, i, j]$ be the probability of EVAL selecting the index i before the index j. Then, $Pr[S, i, j] \leq (w_i)/(w_i + w_j)$*

Lemma 2. *Let T be an AND/OR tree with depth at most 1 and let σ be a setting for T. If $T(\sigma) = 1$, then $E[c_{EVAL}^T(\sigma)]/c^T(\sigma) \leq (1 + l(T))/2$. On the other hand, if $T(\sigma) = 0$, then $E[c_{EVAL}^T(\sigma)]/c^T(\sigma) \leq (1 + k(T))/2$.*

Proof: If $h(T) = 0$, then T is trivial and $k(T) = l(T) = 1$. Therefore, the result holds.

Assume that $h(T) = 1$. We only present the proof for the case where $T(\sigma) = 0$, since the proof for the other case is similar.

Subcase 1) r is an OR node. In this case, $k(T) = 1$ and the minimum proof consists of all leaves, so as $c_{EVAL}^T(\sigma)/c^T(\sigma) = 1 = (k(T) + 1)/2$

Subcase 2) r is an AND node. In this case, $k(T)$ is the number of leaves in T. Let x_j be the leaf with minimum cost among those with value 0 and let X_{ij} be a random variable defined as follows: $X_{ij} = 1$ if x_i is evaluated by EVAL before x_j and $X_{ij} = 0$, otherwise. If $i = j$, define $X_{ij} = 1$. Then,
$E[c_{EVAL}^T(\sigma)]/c^T(\sigma) \leq E[\sum_{i=1}^{k(T)} c_{x_i} X_{ij}]/c_{x_j}$.

It follows from Lemma 1 and from the linearity of the expectation that

$$\frac{E[\sum_{i=1}^{k(T)} c_{x_i} X_{ij}]}{c_{x_j}} = \frac{\sum_{i=1}^{k(T)} c_{x_i} Pr[S, i, j]}{c_{x_j}} \leq 1 + (k(T) - 1) \max_{i \neq j} \left\{ \frac{c_{x_i} c_{x_j}}{c_{x_i}^2 + c_{x_j}^2} \right\} \leq \frac{1 + k(T)}{2},$$

where the last inequality follows from the arithmetic-geometric inequality. $\square$

We can obtain a similar result for trees with depth 2 whose proof we defer for the extended version of the paper.

Lemma 3. *Let T be a AND/OR tree with depth 2 and let σ be a setting for T. If $T(\sigma) = 1$, then $E[c_{EVAL}^T(\sigma)]/c^T(\sigma) \leq (1 + l(T))/2$. On the other hand, if $T(\sigma) = 0$, then $E[c_{EVAL}^T(\sigma)]/c^T(\sigma) \leq (1 + k(T))/2$.*

4   Evaluating AND/OR Trees of Unrestricted Depth

In this section, we describe the RWB algorithm, which combines the ideas presented at the previous section with some of the ideas introduced in the algorithm WeakBalance [4]. For convenience, we explain the algorithm using a G-AND/OR tree T' obtained through a set of transformations on the given AND/OR tree T that we denote by binarization. This new tree has the following properties

(i) T' is equivalent to T, that is, $T(\sigma) = T'(\sigma)$, for all σ ;

(ii) $k(T) = k(T')$ and $l(T) = l(T')$

(iii) If x is an internal node in T' and $h(T'_x) \geq 3$, then x has exactly two children.

It is easy to obtain such a tree T' starting from T. Basically, while the current tree has a node x that does not satisfy the condition (iii), then the following rule is applied

Binarization Rule: Let $LAB \in \{AND, OR\}$ be the label of x and let $N_1, N_2, \ldots, N_k$, with $k > 2$, be the children of x. Replace x by an internal node x' with two children N_1 and N_0. Assign label LAB for both x' and N_0. Make $N_2, \ldots, N_k$ be the children of N_0.

This rule is applied until a tree T' with the desired properties is obtained. It is easy to verify that T' satisfies the desired conditions. Let g be any function of $k(T)$ and $l(T)$. One can prove that $c_{\mathcal{A}}^T(\sigma) \leq g(k(T), l(T))$ by showing that $c_{\mathcal{A}}^{T'}(\sigma) \leq g(k(T'), l(T'))$. We will use this fact in some proofs.

4.1   The Random Weak Balance Algorithm

The algorithm gets as input an AND/OR tree T. If $h(T) \leq 2$, then EVAL(T) is executed. Otherwise, T is converted into a G-AND/OR tree T' through the binarization process.

If $h(T') \geq 3$, RWB executes a loop, where at each iteration exactly one leaf is read. A pseudo-code is presented in Figure 3. Every node x stores a recommendation and a variable Cost$_x$. The recommendation is a pair (L, c_L), where L is a leaf in T'_x of cost c_L. It defines the leaf, among those in T'_x, that will be firstly read by RWB from the current iteration. While the recommendation stored by a leaf L is always (L, c_L), the recommendation of an internal node is updated during the execution of RWB to that stored by one of its unevaluated children. This is detailed in the recommendation scheme presented in the next section. The variable Cost$_x$ keeps track of the cost that RWB has incurred in the subtree T'_x, that is, the sum of the costs of the leaves of T'_x evaluated so far. This information is used in the recommendation updating process. In the pseudo-code, the operation Simplify evaluate as maximum as possible T' after reading the leaf L.

RWB Algorithm

    For every $x \in T'$ **do**   Cost$_x \leftarrow 0$.
    Initialize the recommendation for every node traversing T' bottom-up.
    Let (L, c_L) be the recommendation stored by the root of T'
    Read L; Simplify T'.
    While the value of T' remains unknown **do**
        For every ancestor x of L **do** Cost$_x \leftarrow$ Cost$_x + c_L$
        Let $x_1, \ldots, x_p$ be the unevaluated ancestors of L sorted by
        increasing order of distance to L
        For $i = 1 \ldots p$ **do** update the recommendation of x_i (*)
        Let (L, c_L) be the recommendation stored by the root of T'
        Read L; Simplify T'.

Fig. 3. The RWB Algorithm

The Recommendation Scheme. The recommendation scheme defines how the recommendation of a node is updated (initialized) during RWB execution. In fact, it provides the order in which the leaves are read by RWB. In particular, when the recommendation of an internal x node is updated, it defines the first leaf among those recommended by the x children that will be read.

In order to describe this scheme in detail, we distinguish between three types of nodes. A node x is

- white if $h(T'_x) \leq 2$;
- grey if both $h(T'_x) > 2$ and x has a child y, with $h(T'_y) \leq 1$;
- black if x is neither white nor gray.

The motivation behind this classification is that the evaluation of both white and gray nodes can be optimized using randomization. In fact, we have seen that white nodes can be efficiently evaluated through procedure EVAL.

Now, we present the recommendation scheme for white nodes.

White Nodes. Let x be a white node and let $L_1, L_2, \ldots, L_k$ be the random sequence of leaves that are read when EVAL(T_x) is executed. Then, at the beginning x holds recommendation (L_1, c_{L_1}). When L_i is read, $1 \leq i \leq k - 1$, x recommendation is updated to $(L_{i+1}, c_{L_{i+1}})$. This assures that the order in which the leaves from T'_x are read matches with the order defined by EVAL(T'_x).

Now, we explain the scheme for both black and grey nodes. If x is either a black or grey node in T', then $h(T'_x) \geq 3$ and x has exactly two children that we denote by N_1 and N_2. From now on, we assume w.l.g. that $h(T'_{N_1}) \leq h(T'_{N_2})$. Moreover, we assume that N_1 and N_2 hold recommendations (L_1, c_{L_1}) and (L_2, c_{L_2}), respectively.

Black Nodes. If x has only one unevaluated child, say y, then the recommendation of x is updated to that of y.

Otherwise, the recommendation of x is updated to (L_i, c_{L_i}), with $i \in \{1, 2\}$, such that $(Cost_{N_i} + c_{L_i})/f(T'_{N_i})$ is minimized, where $f(T'_{N_i}) = k(T'_{N_i})$ if x is an AND node and $f(T'_{N_i}) = l(T'_{N_i})$, otherwise.

We remark that the recommendation scheme for the black nodes is exactly the one adopted by the algorithm WeakBalance [4].

Gray Nodes. If x has only one unevaluated child, say y, then the recommendation of x is updated to that of y. Otherwise, RWB takes advantage of the following observation:

Observation 3 *if the cheapest proof for the value of a grey node x consists of only leaves from T'_{N_1}, then the cost of the cheapest proof for T'_{N_1} is $c_{T'_{N_1}}$*

Roughly speaking, the scheme works as follows. First, it defines a threshold parameter p_x whose value is related to $c_{T'_{N_1}}$. Then, while the cost incurred in $T'_{N_2}(Cost_{N_2})$ is smaller than p_x, the recommendation from N_2 is selected. In some sense, by taking this decision, the scheme is implicitly assuming that the cheapest proof consists only of leaves from T'_{N_2}. Even if such assumption is not correct, it is not a big problem, once the cost spent in the "wrong" tree, T'_{N_2}, is not large at all. However, if $Cost_{N_2}$ becomes comparable to p_x, the scheme reviews its policy by tossing an unbiased coin. Depending on the result, it either keeps selecting recommendations from N_2 or it changes to those from N_1. Finally, if $Cost_{N_2}$ becomes larger than $2p_x$, then the scheme only accepts the recommendations from T'_{N_1}. This avoids RWB spending too much in T'_{N_2} when the cheapest proof consists only of leaves from T'_{N_1}.

More formally, the scheme is implemented as follows: let p_x be a threshold parameter whose value will be defined later in the analysis and let $b(x)$ be a random bit obtained at the beginning of RWB execution (the value of $b(x)$ does not change throughout the execution). We have the following cases:

1. $Cost_{N_2} + c_{L_2} \leq p_x$. Then, the recommendation of x is updated to (L_2, c_{L_2}).
2. $p_x < Cost_{N_2} + c_{L_2} \leq 2p_x$. If $b(x) = 0$, then the recommendation of x is updated to (L_1, c_{L_1}). Otherwise, it is updated to (L_2, c_{L_2}).
3. $Cost_{N_2} + c_{L_2} > 2p_x$. Then, the recommendation of x is updated to (L_1, c_{L_1}).

4.2 RWB Analysis

In order to establish our main result, $E[c_{RWB}^T(\sigma)]/c^T(\sigma) \leq 0.792 \max\{k(T), l(T)\}$, we first prove by induction that for every node x of T', the tree obtained from T by binarization, we have $E[c_{RWB}^{T'_x}(\sigma)]/c^{T'_x}(\sigma) \leq \max\{\alpha_1(T'_x) l(T'_x), \alpha_0(T'_x)k(T'_x)\}$, where α_0 and α_1 are functions defined at appendix A that associate a G-AND/OR tree to a real number. Then, our main result is established by proving upper bounds on both α_1 and α_0.

Lemma 4. *Let T' be the G-AND/OR tree obtained from the input AND/OR tree T. Furthermore, let x be a node in T' and let σ be a setting for T'. If $T'_x(\sigma) = 1$, then $E[c_{RWB}^{T'_x}(\sigma)]/c^{T'_x}(\sigma) \leq \alpha_1(T'_x)l(T'_x)$. On the other hand, if $T'_x(\sigma) = 0$, then $E[c_{RWB}^{T'_x}(\sigma)]/c^{T'_x}(\sigma) \leq \alpha_0(T'_x)k(T'_x)$.*

Proof: We only consider the case where $T'_x(\sigma) = 1$, since the proof for the other case is similar. The proof is by induction on the height of T'_x. The basis are the white nodes. If $h(T'_x) \leq 2$, it follows from lemmas 2 and 3 and from the definitions of α for white nodes that the result holds. Now, let x be a node of T' such that $h(T'_x) \geq 3$.

Subcase 1) x is either a gray or black internal node with label AND. In this case, the cost of the minimum proof for T'_x is the sum of the costs of the minimum proofs for its children, that is, $c^{T'_x}(\sigma) = c^{T'_{N_1}}(\sigma) + c^{T'_{N_2}}(\sigma)$. Moreover, the value of T'_x is determined right after the value of the last of its children is determined. Hence, $E[c_{RWB}^{T'_x}(\sigma)] = E[c_{RWB}^{T'_{N_1}}(\sigma) + c_{RWB}^{T'_{N_2}}(\sigma)] = E[c_{RWB}^{T'_{N_1}}(\sigma)] + E[c_{RWB}^{T'_{N_2}}(\sigma)]$.

It follows from the inductive hypothesis that $E[c_{RWB}^{T'_{N_i}}(\sigma)]/c^{T'_{N_i}}(\sigma) \leq \alpha_1(T'_{N_i})l(T'_{N_i})$, for $i = 1, 2$. Thus, we have that

$$\frac{E[c_{RWB}^{T'_x}(\sigma)]}{c^{T'}(\sigma)} = \frac{E[c_{RWB}^{T'_{N_1}}(\sigma)] + E[c_{RWB}^{T'_{N_2}}(\sigma)]}{c^{T'_{N_1}}(\sigma) + c^{T'_{N_2}}(\sigma)} \leq \max_{i=1...2}\{\alpha_1(T'_{N_i})l(T'_{N_i})\} = \alpha_1(T'_x)l(T'),$$

where the second inequality from left to right follows from the fact that $(a + b)/(c + d) \leq \max\{a/c, b/d\}$ if a, b, c, d are positive real numbers. Moreover, the rightmost expression is a consequence of the definition of α^1, equations (5) and (12).

Subcase 2) x is a gray internal node with label OR. Since $T'_x(\sigma) = 1$, we have two possibilities: either the cheapest proof consists of leaves from T'_{N_1} or from

T'_{N_2}. First, we consider the case where the cheapest proof consists of all the leaves in T'_{N_1} (recall Observation 3). Analyzing the cases 1-3 of the recommendation scheme for grey nodes, we can conclude that

$$E[c_{RWB}^{T'_x}(\sigma)] \leq c_{T'_{N_1}} + 1.5p_x \tag{1}$$

Let us consider the case where the cheapest proof consists of some leaves in T'_{N_2}. Then, let $P_1 = Pr\left[c_{RWB}^{T'_{N_2}}(\sigma) \geq 2p_x\right]$ and let $P_2 = Pr\left[c_{RWB}^{T'_{N_2}}(\sigma) \geq p_x\right] - P_1$.

Since, by inductive hypothesis, the expected cost incurred at N_2 when its value is determined is at most $\alpha_1(T'_{N_2})l(T'_{N_2})c^{T_{N_2}}(\sigma)$, we have that

$$P_1 2p_x + P_2 p_x \leq \alpha_1(T'_{N_2})l(T'_{N_2})c^{T_{N_2}}(\sigma) \tag{2}$$

Now, we give an upper bound on $E[c_{RWB}^{T'_x}(\sigma)]$. Assume that RWB spends z to determine the value of T'_{N_2}. If $z > 2p_x$, then the item 3 of the recommendation scheme for OR grey nodes assures that RWB spends $z + c_{T'_{N_1}}$ to determine $T'_x(\sigma)$. Otherwise, RWB pays at most $z + c_{T'_{N_1}}$ with probability $1/2$ and pays z with probability $1/2$. Taking the expectation of z we get that $E[c_{RWB}^{T'_x}(\sigma)] \leq P_1 c_{T'_{N_1}} + 0.5P_2 c_{T'_{N_1}} + \alpha_1(T'_{N_2})l(T'_{N_2})c^{T_{N_2}}(\sigma)$.

It follows from the equation above and from inequality (2) that

$$E[c_{RWB}^{T'_x}(\sigma)] \leq \frac{c^{T_{N_2}}(\sigma)l(T'_{N_2})\alpha_1(T'_{N_2})c_{T'_{N_1}}}{2p_x} + \alpha_1(T'_{N_2})l(T'_{N_2})c^{T_{N_2}}(\sigma) \tag{3}$$

Hence, it follows from inequalities (1) and (3) that

$$\frac{E[c_{RWB}^{T'_x}(\sigma)]}{c^{T'_x}(\sigma)} \leq \max\left\{1 + \frac{3p_x}{2c_{T'_{N_1}}}, \frac{\alpha_1(T'_{N_2})l(T'_{N_2})c_{T'_{N_1}}}{2p_x} + \alpha_1(T'_{N_2})l(T'_{N_2})\right\} \tag{4}$$

At this point, we can finally define a suitable value for p_x by setting it as the value that equalizes the arguments of the max expression above. One can verify, that this value is exactly $(\alpha_1(T'_x)(l(T'_{N_2}) + 1)2c_{T'_{N_1}} - 2c_{T'_{N_1}})/3$, where $\alpha_1(T'_x)$ is given by equation (10). Thus, we have that $E[c_{RWB}^{T'_x}(\sigma)]/c^{T'_x}(\sigma) \leq 1 + 1.5p_x/c_{T'_{N_1}} = \alpha_1(T'_x)(l(T'_{N_2}) + 1) = \alpha_1(T'_x)l(T'_x)$

Subcase 3) x is a black internal node with label OR. In this case, the cost of the minimum proof for T'_x is equal to the cost of the minimum proof for one of its children that outputs 1. We assume w.l.g. that N_1 is such a child. Then, $c^{T'_x}(\sigma) = c^{T'_{N_1}}(\sigma)$.

Let c_1 and c_2 be, respectively, the costs incurred at T'_{N_1} and T'_{N_2} when the value of T'_{N_1} is determined. The recommendation rule assures that $c_2 \leq$

$(l(T'_{N_2})c_1)/l(T'_{N_1})$. Thus, the cost incurred at T'_x when the value of T'_{N_1} is determined is bounded above by $c_1 + l(T'_{N_2}c_1/l(T'_{N_1}) = l(T'_x)c_1/l(T'_{N_1})$. Therefore,

$$\frac{E[c^{T'_x}_{RWB}(\sigma)]}{c^{T'_x}(\sigma)} \leq \left(\frac{l(T'_x)}{l(T'_{N_1})}\right) \frac{E[c^{T'_{N_1}}_{RWB}(\sigma)]}{c^{T'_{N_1}}(\sigma)} \leq \alpha_1(T'_{N_1})l(T'_x) \leq \alpha_1(T'_x)l(T'_x),$$

where the second inequality from left to right follows from the application of the inductive hypothesis on T'_{N_1}. □

Now, we prove our main theorem by describing a method that provides upper bounds on both α_0 and α_1.

Theorem 4. *Let T be a non-trivial AND/OR tree. Then, for every setting σ,*
$E[c^T_{RWB}(\sigma)]/c^T(\sigma) \leq 0.792 \max\{k(T), l(T)\}$.

Proof: If either $h(T) = 1$ or $h(T) = 2$, we have that $\max\{k(T), l(T)\} \geq 2$. By inspection, one can verify that $E[c^T_{RWB}(\sigma)]/c^T(\sigma) = E[c^T_{EVAL}(\sigma)]/c^T(\sigma) = (1 + \max\{k(T), l(T)\})/2 \leq 0.75 \max\{k(T), l(T)\}$

Let us consider the case where $h(T) \geq 3$. Let T' be the tree obtained from T through the binarization process. We only consider the case where $T'(\sigma) = 1$, since the proof for the other case is similar. If we prove that $\alpha_1(T') \leq 0.792$, then the Lemma 4 assures the correctness of the theorem.

Let x be a node in T', with $h(T'_x) \geq 2$. We define a function g such that $g(x) \geq \alpha_1(T'_x)$ as follows

$$g(x) = \begin{cases} 0.75, & \text{if } x \text{ is a white node} \\ \max\{g(N_1), g(N_2)\}, & \text{if } x \text{ is a black node} \\ \max\{0.75, g(N_2)\}, & \text{if } x \text{ is a grey AND node} \\ \dfrac{g(N_2)l(T'_{N_2})+1+\sqrt{(g(N_2)l(T'_{N_2}))^2+g(N_2)l(T'_{N_2})+1}}{2(l(T'_{N_2})+1)}, & \text{if } x \text{ is a grey OR node} \end{cases}$$

We observe that the expression for grey OR nodes decreases with $l(T'_{N_2})$ (the proof for that demands some algebraic manipulation) and increases with $g(N_2)$.

By carefully considering the definitions of g and α_1, one can verify that $\alpha_1(T'_x) \leq g(x)$ for every x such that $h(T'_x) \geq 2$. Furthermore, it is easy to verify that only an OR grey node may have g value larger than the maximum g value of its children. Hence, $g(r)$, where r is the root of T', is either equal to 0.75 or to the g value of the gray OR node with maximum g value in T'. Another careful analysis shows that we can obtain an upper bound on $g(r)$ by computing the maximum of the sequence $(q_1, q_2, \ldots, q_{h(T')})$, where $q_1 = 0.75$ and $q_{i+1} = \left(q_i(i+1) + 1 + \sqrt{(q_i(i+1))^2 + q_i(i+1) + 1}\right)/(2i+4)$.

Through some calculations we obtain that $q_i \leq 0.792$, for all i □

References

1. Tarsi, M.: Optimal search on some game trees. Journal of the ACM **30** (1983) 389–396

2. Snir, M.: Lower bounds on probabilistic linear decision trees. Theoretical Computer Science **38** (1985) 69–82
3. Saks, M., Wigderson, A.: Probabilistic Boolean decision trees and the complexity of evaluating game trees. In: 27th Annual Symposium on Foundations of Computer Science, Toronto, Ontario, Canada, IEEE (1986) 29–38
4. Charikar, Fagin, Guruswami, Kleinberg, Raghavan, Sahai: Query strategies for priced information. JCSS: Journal of Computer and System Sciences **64** (2002)
5. Hellerstein, J.M.: Optimization techniques for queries with expensive methods. ACM Transactions on Database Systems **23** (1998) 113–157
6. Laber, E., Carmo, R., Kohayakawa, Y.: Query priced information on database: The conjunctive case. In Farach-Colton, M., ed.: Proceedings of the LATIN 2004, Buenos-Aires, D.C. (2004)

A   The Function α

Here, we give recursive definitions for $\alpha_0(T')$ and $\alpha_1(T')$. At a first view, these definitions (equations (5)-(12)) seem to be rather non-intuitive. However, they become much more natural when the reader examines the proof of lemma 4. Thus, we strongly suggest the reader to skip the definitions below and come back to them whenever they are refered in the proof of such a lemma.

White Nodes. If x is a white node then define $\alpha_0(T'_x) = (k(T'_x)+1)/2k(T'_x)$ and $\alpha_1(T'_x) = (l(T'_x) + 1)/2l(T'_x)$.

Black Nodes. If x is an AND node, then define

$$\alpha_1(T'_x) = \frac{\max\{\alpha_1(T'_{N_1})l(T'_{N_1}), \alpha_1(T'_{N_2})l(T'_{N_2})\}}{l(T'_x)} \tag{5}$$

$$\alpha_0(T'_x) = \max\{\alpha_0(T'_{N_1}), \alpha_0(T'_{N_2})\}. \tag{6}$$

If x is an OR node, then define

$$\alpha_0(T'_x) = \frac{\max\{\alpha_0(T'_{N_1})k(T'_{N_1}), \alpha_0(T'_{N_2})k(T'_{N_2})\}}{k(T'_x)} \tag{7}$$

$$\alpha_1(T'_x) = \max\{\alpha_1(T'_{N_1}), \alpha_1(T'_{N_2})\} \tag{8}$$

Gray Nodes. If x is an OR node, then define

$$\alpha_0(T'_x) = \frac{\max\{\alpha_0(T'_{N_1})k(T'_{N_1}), \alpha_0(T'_{N_2})k(T'_{N_2})\}}{k(T'_x)} \tag{9}$$

$$\alpha_1(T'_x) = \frac{\alpha_1(T'_{N_2})l(T'_{N_2}) + 1 + \sqrt{(\alpha_1(T'_{N_2})l(T'_{N_2}))^2 + \alpha_1(T'_{N_2})l(T'_{N_2}) + 1}}{2(l(T'_{N_2}) + 1)} \tag{10}$$

If x is an AND node, then define

$$\alpha_0(T'_x) = \frac{\alpha_0(T'_{N_2})k(T'_{N_2}) + 1 + \sqrt{(\alpha_0(T'_{N_2})k(T'_{N_2}))^2 + \alpha_0(T'_{N_2})k(T'_{N_2}) + 1}}{2(k(T'_{N_2}) + 1)}$$

$$\tag{11}$$

$$\alpha_1(T'_x) = \frac{\max\{\alpha_1(T'_{N_1})l(T'_{N_1}), \alpha_1(T'_{N_2})l(T'_{N_2})\}}{l(T'_x)} \tag{12}$$

The Plurality Problem with Three Colors*

Martin Aigner[1], Gianluca De Marco[2], and Manuela Montangero[2]

[1] Freie Universität Berlin, Institut für Mathematik II,
Arnimallee 3, 14195 Berlin, Germany.
aigner@math.fu-berlin.de
[2] Istituto di Informatica e Telematica, Consiglio Nazionale delle Ricerche,
via Moruzzi 1, 56124 Pisa, Italy.
{gianluca.demarco, manuela.montangero}@iit.cnr.it

Abstract. The *plurality problem with three colors* is a game between
two participants: Paul and Carol. Suppose we are given n balls colored
with three colors. At any step of the game, Paul chooses two balls and
asks whether they are of the same color, whereupon Carol answers yes
or no. The game ends when Paul either produces a ball a of the plurality
color (meaning that the number of balls colored like a exceeds those of
the other colors), or when Paul states that there is no plurality. How
many questions $L(n)$ does Paul have to ask in the worst case? We show
that $3\lfloor n/2 \rfloor - 2 \le L(n) \le \lfloor 5n/3 \rfloor - 2$.

1 Introduction

The problem considered in this paper is a generalization of the well known
majority problem in which we are given n balls colored with two colors, for
example white and black, and two players Paul and Carol playing the following
game. At any stage of the game Paul chooses two balls x and y and asks whether
they are of the same color. Carol can answer YES or NO. The game ends when
Paul either produces a ball a of the *majority color* (meaning that the number of
balls with the color of a exceeds those of the other color), or when Paul states
that there is no majority (this happens when, in case n is even, there is the same
number of white and black balls). The *majority problem* asks to determine how
many questions Paul needs in the worst case. This kind of problems finds several
interesting applications in the field of fault diagnosis of systems (*e.g.* see [5]).

The majority problem was first solved by Saks and Werman [8], later Alonso,
Reingold, Schott [3] gave a different proof. The elegant combinatorial result is
that $n - \nu(n)$ questions are necessary and sufficient in the worst case, where $\nu(n)$
denotes the number of 1's in the binary representation of n. Alonso, Reingold,
Schott [4] also gave the solution for the average case. Aigner [2] introduced
several variants and generalizations of this problem. In particular, in the (n, k)-
majority game Paul must exhibit a k-majority ball z (that is, there are at least
k balls colored like z), or declare there is no k-majority. De Marco and Pelc [6]

---

* Work supported in part by the European RTN Project under contract HPRN-CT-
2002-00278, COMBSTRU.

considered randomized solutions for the majority problem in the more general case when the balls correspond to the nodes of an undirected graph and the comparisons can only be made between adjacent nodes (of course, the problem reduces to the original majority problem on the complete graph).

Another natural generalization is to consider more than 2 colors. In this case, two possible problems can arise: we can either seek for a majority ball a (that is, there are at least $\lfloor n/2 \rfloor + 1$ balls colored like a; if no color is used on more than $\lfloor n/2 \rfloor$ balls, Paul has to state that there is no majority) or for a *plurality* ball b. In this case Paul has to produce a ball b of *plurality color* (that is, the number of balls colored like b exceeds those of the other colors), or state that there is no plurality. It is worth to observe that if a *majority* ball exists, then this is also a *plurality* ball; while a plurality ball might exist when there is no majority ball (in case there are only 2 colors there is no difference between majority and plurality).

As for the first problem, Fisher and Salzberg [7] solved the majority problem when the number of colors is any integer up to n, by showing than $\lceil 3n/2 \rceil - 2$ comparisons are sufficient and necessary.

As for the plurality problem, it seems to be surprisingly difficult: while it is mentioned in the 1997 Alonso et al. paper, no results were known, even for the case of 3 colors.

In this paper we consider the plurality problem with 3 colors. We exhibit an algorithm that solves the problem using $\lfloor 5n/3 \rfloor - 2$ comparisons in the worst case. On the other hand, in Section 3 we show that any algorithm that correctly determines the plurality must use at least $3\lfloor n/2 \rfloor - 2$ comparisons. Note that it was not previously known that $n + O(1)$ comparisons would not suffice.

2   The Upper Bound

In this section we show that Paul has a strategy that uses no more than $5n/3 - 2$ comparisons to solve the plurality problem. To indicate a test (comparison) between two balls a and b, we use the notation $a : b$. The outcome of a test (the answer given by Carol) might be YES or NO. We say that Paul wins when the game ends and Paul gives the correct solution. Let $L(n)$ be the number of comparisons that Paul has to ask in the worst case.

Theorem 1. *We have* $L(n) \leq \frac{5}{3}n - 2$, *for* $n \geq 2$.

Proof. The proof is by induction on n. This is clear for $n \leq 3$, so let us assume $n \geq 4$. Paul arranges the balls $b_1, \ldots, b_n$ and compares them one by one according to Phase I. A *color class* is a set of balls having the same color.

Phase I. The phase consists of a sequence of states. Every state S_i (after b_i has been handled) is inductively described by a vector (k_i, ℓ_i, m_i), where $k_i \geq \ell_i \geq m_i$ are the the color classes cardinalities. For $i \geq 1$, let $r_i = n - i$ be the number of the remaining balls (those that have not been involved in any comparison yet) and set $t_i = r_i - (k_i - \ell_i - 1)$. The phase ends at state S_i, for $i \geq 1$, when one of the following conditions arises:

(A) $k_i = \ell_i = m_i$;
(B) $t_i = 0$;
(C) $t_i = 1$.

(Notice that (A) and (B) can not arise together, as well as (B) and (C). Moreover, if (A) and (C) hold, then $i = n$.)

Condition (A) simply says that the three color classes have the same cardinality. The problem can, thus, be reduced to the same problem with smaller size $(n - 3k_i)$ and Paul can use induction.

The special cases when $t_i = 0, 1$ give a precise indication on the plurality and Paul can handle them easily.

Claim. Paul has a strategy such that at every state S_i of Phase I, the following conditions hold:

(i) $k_i \geq \ell_i \geq m_i$;
(ii) a representative ball K_i, L_i of the two largest classes k_i, ℓ_i is known (if not empty);
(iii) the number T_i of comparisons up to (and including) S_i is less than or equal to $2k_i + \ell_i + 2m_i - 2$.

Proof. Proof by induction. After the first ball has been handled, $S_1 = (1, 0, 0)$, $T_1 = 0 \leq 2 \cdot 1 + 0 \cdot 1 + 0 \cdot 1 - 2$, $K_1 = b_1$ and L_1 is unknown as the class is empty. Let $1 \leq i < n$. Suppose K_i and L_i are the representatives of k_i and ℓ_i respectively and that b_{i+1} is handled. Conditions (i),(ii) are clearly preserved if Paul uses the following strategy.

- If $k_i > \ell_i > m_i$:

$$b_{i+1} : L_i \begin{cases} \text{if YES } S_{i+1} = (k_i, \ell_i + 1, m_i) \\ \text{if NO } b_{i+1} : K_i \begin{cases} \text{if YES } S_{i+1} = (k_i + 1, \ell_i, m_i) \\ \text{if NO } S_{i+1} = (k_i, \ell_i, m_i + 1) \end{cases} \end{cases}$$

- If $k_i > \ell_i = m_i$:

$$b_{i+1} : K_i \begin{cases} \text{if YES } S_{i+1} = (k_i + 1, \ell_i, \ell_i) \\ \text{if NO } S_{i+1} = (k_i, \ell_i + 1, \ell_i), L_{i+1} = b_{i+1} \end{cases}$$

- If $k_i = \ell_i$ then $\ell_i > m_i$ (otherwise finished by (A)):

$$b_{i+1} : K_i \begin{cases} \text{if YES } S_{i+1} = (k_i + 1, k_i, m_i) \\ \text{if NO } b_{i+1} : L_i \begin{cases} \text{if YES } S_{i+1} = (k_i + 1, k_i, m_i) \\ \qquad K_{i+1} = b_{i+1}, L_{i+1} = K_i \\ \text{if NO } S_{i+1} = (k_i, k_i, m_i + 1) \end{cases} \end{cases}$$

Unless differently stated $K_{i+1} = K_i$ and $L_{i+1} = L_i$.

As for condition (iii), observe that T_{i+1} is equal to T_i plus one or two, according to the number of comparisons Paul did. The proof follows by induction.

Let, for example, $k_i > \ell_i > m_i$ and assume b_{i+1} has the same color of L_i, so that $S_{i+1} = (k_i, \ell_i + 1, m_i)$. Then $T_{i+1} = T_i + 1 \leq 2k_i + \ell_i + 2m_i - 1 = 2k_i + (\ell_i + 1) + 2m_i - 2 = 2k_{i+1} + \ell_{i+1} + 2m_{i+1} - 2$. All the other cases can be proven analogously.   □

Claim. One of $(A), (B), (C)$ eventually occurs.

Proof. At state S_1, we have $t_1 = n - 1 \geq 3$ as $k_1 = 1$, $\ell_1 = 0$ and $n \geq 4$. Every time a ball is handled t_i changes by $0, -1$ or -2. In fact $t_{i+1} - t_i = -1 - (k_{i+1} - k_i) + (\ell_{i+1} - \ell_i)$ and only the cardinality of exactly one of the three color classes is increased by one. When $i = n$ then $t_n = \ell_n - k_n + 1 \leq 1$ and hence (B) or (C) must occur. $\square$

Let (k, ℓ, m) be the state at the end of Phase I, with K and L representatives of the two largest color classes (if not empty), r remaining balls, $t = r - (k - \ell - 1)$ and

$$T \leq 2k + \ell + 2m - 2 \qquad (1)$$
$$n = k + \ell + m + r \ . \qquad (2)$$

Phase II. Paul acts differently depending on how Phase I ended.

Case 1: (A) occurred first.
This means that $k = \ell = m$ and that the total number of comparisons done in Phase I is $T \leq 5k - 2$, by (1).

If $r = 0$, then there are no remaining balls and Paul learned that the three color classes have the same cardinality. Paul wins the game stating there is no plurality. Hence, as $k = n/3$ concerning the total number of comparisons we have

$$L(n) \leq T \leq 5k - 2 = \frac{5}{3}n - 2 \ .$$

If $r > 0$ the plurality among the n balls is the plurality among the $r = n - 3k$ remaining balls. As $r < n$, by induction, Paul wins the game using $5r/3 - 2$ extra comparisons. Hence

$$L(n) \leq T + \frac{5r}{3} - 2 \leq 5k - 2 + \frac{5(n - 3k)}{3} - 2 = \frac{5n}{3} - 4 \ .$$

Case 2: (B) occurred first.
Paul wins the game claiming that K is of the plurality color. In fact, $t = r - (k - \ell - 1) = 0$ means $k = \ell + r + 1$ and even if all remaining balls have the same color as L, there still is one more ball colored as K. Hence K is the plurality color.

To count the number of comparisons used by Paul observe that

$$\begin{aligned} k &= \ell + r + 1 \\ &= \ell + n - k - \ell - m + 1 \qquad \text{by (2)} \\ &= n - k - m + 1 \ , \end{aligned}$$

and

$$3k = k + (\ell + r + 1) + m + (\ell - m) + r + 1 = n + r + (\ell - m) + 2 \ .$$

Suppose $r = 0$, then $\ell > m$. Because if $\ell = m$, then the terminal state is $(k, k - 1, k - 1)$ and thus the previous state was either $(k - 1, k - 1, k - 1)$ and the game would have finished by (A), or $(k, k - 1, k - 2)$ and the game would have finished by (C). Hence $\max\{r, \ell - m\} \geq 1$, and so $3k \geq n + 3$ implying $k \geq n/3 + 1$.

It follows that

$$
\begin{aligned}
L(n) \leq T &\leq 2k + \ell + 2m - 2 && \text{by (1)} \\
&= 2n - \ell - 2r - 2 && \text{by (2)} \\
&= 2n - (\ell + r + 1) - r - 1 && \\
&= 2n - k - r - 1 && \text{because } t = 0 \\
&\leq 5n/3 - 1 - r - 1 && \text{because } k \geq n/3 + 1 \\
&\leq 5n/3 - 2 \ . &&
\end{aligned}
$$

Case 3: (C) occurred first.

We have that $t = r - (k - \ell - 1) = 1$ if and only if $k = \ell + r$ and, hence, K is of the plurality color unless all the r remaining balls have the color of L (or M if $\ell = m$) or unless there are no remaining balls.

If $r = 0$ then $k = \ell > m$ and the game ends with Paul claiming that there is no plurality. To bound the total number of comparisons, observe that $n = k + \ell + m = 2k + m < 3k$ and hence $k > n/3$. We have

$$
\begin{aligned}
L(n) \leq T &\leq 3k + 2m - 2 && \\
&= 2n - k - 2 && \text{by (2)} \\
&< 5n/3 - 2 \ . &&
\end{aligned}
$$

If $r \geq 1$, Paul takes a ball R from the remaining balls and compares it to the other $r - 1$ balls. As soon as Carol answers NO, Paul wins the game claiming K is of plurality color. If Carol always answers YES then Paul wins using one last comparison.

If $\ell = m$:

$$R : K \begin{cases} \text{if YES } K \text{ is of plurality color} \\ \text{if NO \ \ there is no plurality} \end{cases}$$

If $\ell > m$:

$$R : L \begin{cases} \text{if YES \ there is no plurality} \\ \text{if NO \ \ } K \text{ is of plurality color} \end{cases}$$

Altogether, the total number of comparisons is $L(n) \leq T + r$. As $n = k + \ell + m + r = 2k + m < 3k$ we have $k > n/3$ and so

$$L(n) \leq T + r$$
$$\leq 2k + \ell + 2m - 2 + r \qquad \text{by (1)}$$
$$= 2n - \ell - 2r - 2 + r \qquad \text{by (2)}$$
$$= 2n - k - 2 < 5n/3 - 2 \ .$$

□

3   The Lower Bound

In this section we show a $3\lfloor n/2 \rfloor - 2$ lower bound for the plurality problem with three colors, red, blue and green (r, b and g for short). For sake of presentation, we will first assume that n is even and then explain how to derive the same bound also in the case n is odd.

Any algorithm used by Paul can be seen as a sequence of steps in which Paul selects a pair of balls x, y and receives from Carol the answer YES or NO respectively meaning that x and y are colored with the same color or not.

During the game, Carol builds a graph $H = (V, E)$ (*Carol's graph*), where each node in $V \subseteq [n] = \{1, \dots, n\}$ represents a ball that Paul involved in at least one comparison, and $(x, y) \in E$ if and only if Paul asked to compare x and y, where the edges are labeled with YES or NO according to the answers Carol gave. The edges of H will be called YES-edges or NO-edges if they are labeled with YES or NO, respectively. Moreover, by H_Y and H_N we denote respectively the graph induced by the set E_Y of YES-edges and the set E_N of NO-edges of H. Assume n is even, unless differently specified.

Definition 1. *A graph H is said to be* nice, *if it satisfies the following properties:*

- *$H_N = (S_1 \cup S_2, E_N)$ is a bipartite graph, $V = S_1 \cup S_2$, $S_1 \cap S_2 = \emptyset$;*
- *$|S_1| \leq n/2$ and $|S_2| \leq n/2$;*
- *H_Y has no edge connecting a node $x \in S_1$ with a node $y \in S_2$.*

Let us show by induction that Carol has a strategy such that, at each step of *any* algorithm chosen by Paul, Carol's graph H is nice.

At the beginning of the game, Carol's graph is empty and thus trivially nice. Therefore, assume that Carol has a nice graph $H = (S_1 \cup S_2, E)$.

Let x, y be the pair of balls selected by Paul at the new step. Carol has to deal with one of the following cases.

Case 1: $x \in V$ and $y \in [n] \setminus V$.

Suppose w.l.o.g. that $x \in S_1$. If $|S_2| < n/2$, then Carol adds y to S_2 and answers NO. If $|S_2| = n/2$, then it must be $|S_1| < n/2$. In this case Carol adds y to S_1 and answers YES.

In both cases the new graph $H = (V \cup \{y\}, E \cup \{(x, y)\})$ is nice according to the new partition given by sets $S_1, S_2 \cup \{y\}$ in the former case, and by $S_1 \cup \{y\}, S_2$ in the latter.

Case 2: $x, y \in [n] \setminus V$.

If $|S_1| < n/2$ and $|S_2| < n/2$, Carol adds x to S_1 and y to S_2 and answers NO. Otherwise, suppose w.l.o.g., that $|S_1| = n/2$. Then it must be $|S_2| \leq n/2 - 2$ and Carol adds x and y to S_2 answering YES.

In both cases the new graph $H = (V \cup \{x, y\}, E \cup \{(x, y)\})$ is nice according to the new partition given by sets $S_1 \cup \{x\}, S_2 \cup \{y\}$ in the former case and by $S_1, S_2 \cup \{x, y\}$ in the latter.

Case 3: $x, y \in V$.

If $x \in S_1$ and $y \in S_2$, then Carol answers NO, otherwise she answers YES.

Therefore, in any case the new graph $H = (V, E \cup \{(x, y)\})$ is nice according to the partition sets S_1 and S_2.

Since we have shown that Carol has a strategy that allows her to maintain a graph that is nice, in the following we will always assume that Carol's graph is nice. Observe that Carol is always guaranteed that

$$|E_N| \geq \max\{|S_1|, |S_2|\} \ . \tag{3}$$

In fact, any new node inserted in H is inserted with a new NO-edge incident on it, unless $\max\{|S_1|, |S_2|\}$ is already $n/2$.

In the following we will say that a nice graph admits a coloring if the coloring is consistent with the labelling of YES and NO edges.

Lemma 1. *Let $H = (S_1 \cup S_2, E)$ be Carol's graph at the end of the game. Paul wins the game only if S_1 and S_2 are YES-components of cardinality $n/2$ each.*

Proof. In order to prove the lemma, we will show that if S_1 and S_2 are *not* YES-components of cardinality $n/2$ each, then whenever Paul claims that there is no plurality, Carol is able to show that H admits a coloring c having a plurality color. On the other hand, whenever Paul indicates that u is of plurality color, Carol is able to show that H admits another coloring c in which $c(u)$ is not the plurality color. In the following, given a set $S \subseteq V$ and a color $col \in \{r, b, g\}$, $c(S) = col$ means that all the balls in S are colored with col.

Assume first that $\min\{|S_1|, |S_2|\} = |S_1| < n/2$. Let $V_1, V_2 \subseteq V$ be two disjoint sets of nodes such that $V_1 \cup V_2 = V \setminus (S_1 \cup S_2)$ and $|V_j| + |S_j| = n/2$, for $j \in \{1, 2\}$. Of course, $|V_1| > 0$ and $|V_2| \geq 0$.

If Paul claims that there is no plurality or if he claims that $u \in S_1$ is of the plurality color, Carol shows the coloring c such that $c(S_1) = r$, $c(V_1) = b$ and $c(S_2 \cup V_2) = g$. Graph H admits c but in c there is a plurality color, different from $c(u)$.

If Paul claims that $u \in S_2$ is of the plurality color, Carol shows the coloring c such that $c(S_1 \cup V_1) = r$ and $c(S_2 \cup V_2) = g$. It is easy to see that H admits c, but c has no plurality color.

In any case Paul is wrong.

Therefore, we can assume $|S_1| = |S_2| = n/2$. To prove that S_1 and S_2 have to be YES-components, we can proceed analogously, assuming there is a third YES-component that plays the role of V_1. □

Theorem 2. *To solve the plurality problem with 3 colors, Paul needs at least $3n/2 - 2$ comparisons in the worst case.*

Proof. Let $H = (S_1 \cup S_2, E)$ be Carol's graph at the end of a game Paul won. Then by Lemma 1 S_1 and S_2 are YES-components of cardinality $n/2$ each. Thus, the number of YES-edges in each YES-component is at least $n/2 - 1$. From (3) it follows that the number of NO-edges in H is at least $n/2$.

The number of comparisons used by Paul is the number of edges in H, that is, the number of edges in H_Y plus the number of edges in H_N, i.e., $3n/2 - 2$.

$\square$

Let us now see how to derive the same lower bound in the case n is odd. When n is odd, Carol cannot generalize the strategy she used for the case n even by just building a nice graph in which S_1 has cardinality $\lfloor n/2 \rfloor$ and S_2 has cardinality $\lceil n/2 \rceil$ (or vice-versa). In fact, once Paul has a YES-component of cardinality $\lceil n/2 \rceil$, he wins the game by claiming that the color of the nodes in that YES-component is the plurality color. The point is that Paul can build a YES-component of $\lceil n/2 \rceil$ nodes using only $2\lceil n/2 \rceil = n + 1$ comparisons.

Hence Carol's strategy has to be slightly modified. As in the case n even, she builds a nice graph H where the cardinality of sets S_1 and S_2 is bounded by $\lfloor n/2 \rfloor$. When Paul involves the last node, say l, in a comparison for the first time, Carol puts l in a third set S_3 and answers that the two nodes have different colors. In the sequel, whenever l will be involved in a comparison, Carol will say that the two nodes have different colors and will label all edges incident in l with NN. Such edges are called NN-edges and the set of all NN-edges is denoted by E_{NN}.

Let $H = (S_1 \cup S_2 \cup \{l\}, E)$ be Carol's graph at the end of the game and assume that S_i contains k_i YES-components, for $i = 1, 2$.

It is clear that "no plurality" is always possible by coloring S_1 red, S_2 blue and l green. Hence since Paul wins he must be able to exclude the possibility that there is a plurality. From this we conclude:

(1) l must be connected to S_1 and S_2. Otherwise, if e.g., l is not connected to S_1, $c(S_1 \cup \{l\}) = r$, $c(S_2)$ would be a plurality coloring.

(2) If $k_i \geq 3$ ($i = 1, 2$), then l must be connected to every YES-component of S_i.

Otherwise, if $\mathcal{C} \subseteq S_1$ is a component not connected to l then $c(S_1 \setminus \mathcal{C}) = r$, $c(S_2) = b$ $c(\mathcal{C} \cup \{l\}) = g$ would give a blue plurality.

It follows that l is connected by at least $k_i - 1$ edges to S_i. With $|E_N| \geq \lfloor n/2 \rfloor$ (as in the case when n is even) we have that

$$L(n) \geq |E_N| + |E_Y| + |E_{NN}| \geq \lfloor n/2 \rfloor + 2\lfloor n/2 \rfloor - k_1 - k_2 + (k_1 + k_2 - 2) = 3\lfloor n/2 \rfloor - 2 \ .$$

This concludes the proof of Theorem 2 both for n even and odd.

It is straightforward to see that, using the same argument, the same lower bound for the plurality problem with 3 colors can also be derived for the plurality problem with any number of colors greater than 3. That is, we can state the following more general result.

Theorem 3. *To solve the plurality problem with ≥ 3 colors, Paul needs at least $3n/2 - 2$ comparisons in the worst case.*

$\square$

Acknowledgments. The second and the third author wish to thank Pino Persiano and Janos Simon for many helpful discussions.

References

1. M. Aigner, Combinatorial Search. Wiley 1988.
2. M. Aigner, Two colors and more, preprint.
3. L. Alonso, E. M. Reingold, and R. Schott, Determining the majority, Information Processing Letters 47 (1993), 253-255.
4. L. Alonso, E. M. Reingold, and R. Schott, The average-case complexity of determining the majority, SIAM Journal on Computing 26 (1997), 1-14.
5. L. Alonso, P. Chassaing, E. M. Reingold, and R. Schott, The chip problem, preprint. (Available at http://emr.cs.uiuc.edu/~reingold/chips.ps.)
6. G. De Marco and A. Pelc, Randomized algorithms for determining the majority on graphs, Proc. 28th Int. Symp. MFCS 2003, Bratislava, Slovak Republic, LNCS 2747, 368-377.
7. M. Fisher and S. Salzberg, Finding a majority among n votes, Journal of Algorithms 3 (1982), 375-379.
8. M. E. Saks and M. Werman, On computing majority by comparisons, Combinatorica 11 (1991), 383-387.
9. G. Wiener, Search for a majority element, Journal of Statistical Planning and Inference, to appear.

A Measured Collapse of the Modal μ-Calculus Alternation Hierarchy

Doron Bustan[1], Orna Kupferman[2], and Moshe Y. Vardi[1]

[1] Rice University, Department of Computer Science, Houston, TX 77251-1892, U.S.A.
{doron_b,vardi}@cs.rice.edu[***]
[2] Hebrew University, School of Engineering and Computer Science, Jerusalem 91904, Israel
orna@cs.huji.ac.il[†]

Abstract. The μ-calculus model-checking problem has been of great interest in the context of concurrent programs. Beyond the need to use symbolic methods in order to cope with the state-explosion problem, which is acute in concurrent settings, several concurrency related problems are naturally solved by evaluation of μ-calculus formulas. The complexity of a naive algorithm for model checking a μ-calculus formula ψ is exponential in the alternation depth d of ψ. Recent studies of the μ-calculus and the related area of parity games have led to algorithms exponential only in $\frac{d}{2}$. No symbolic version, however, is known for the improved algorithms, sacrificing the main practical attraction of the μ-calculus.

The μ-calculus can be viewed as a fragment of first-order fixpoint logic. One of the most fundamental theorems in the theory of fixpoint logic is the *Collapse Theorem*, which asserts that, unlike the case for the μ-calculus, the fixpoint alternation hierarchy over finite structures collapses at its first level. In this paper we show that the Collapse Theorem of fixpoint logic holds for a measured variant of the μ-calculus, which we call $\mu^{\#}$-calculus. While μ-calculus formulas represent characteristic functions, i.e., functions from the state space to $\{0, 1\}$, formulas of the $\mu^{\#}$-calculus represent measure functions, which are functions from the state space to some measure domain. We prove a *Measured-Collapse Theorem*: every formula in the μ-calculus is equivalent to a least-fixpoint formula in the $\mu^{\#}$-calculus. We show that the Measured-Collapse Theorem provides a logical recasting of the improved algorithm for μ-calculus model-checking, and describe how it can be implemented symbolically using Algebraic Decision Diagrams. Thus, we describe, for the first time, a symbolic μ-calculus model-checking algorithm whose complexity matches the one of the best known enumerative algorithm.

1 Introduction

The *modal μ-calculus*, often referred to as the "μ-calculus", is a propositional modal logic augmented with least and greatest fixpoint operators. It was introduced in [22], following earlier studies of fixpoint calculi in the theory of program correctness [11, 31,32]. Over the past 20 years, the μ-calculus has been established as essentially the

[***] Supported in part by NSF grants CCR-9988322, CCR-0124077, CCR-0311326, IIS-9908435, and IIS-9978135, by BSF grant 9800096, and by a grant from the Intel Corporation.
[†] Supported in part by BSF grant 9800096, and by a grant from Minerva.

V. Diekert and M. Habib (Eds.): STACS 2004, LNCS 2996, pp. 522–533, 2004.
© Springer-Verlag Berlin Heidelberg 2004

"ultimate" program logic, as it expressively subsumes all propositional program logics, including dynamic logics such as PDL, process logics such as YAPL, and temporal logics such as CTL* [13]. The μ-calculus has gained further prominence with the discovery that its formulas can be evaluated symbolically in a natural way [6], leading to industrial acceptance of computer-aided verification.

A central issue for any logic is the *model-checking* problem: is a given structure a model of a given formula. For modal logics we ask whether a given formula holds in a given state of a given Kripke structure. The μ-calculus model-checking problem has been of great interest in the context of concurrent programs. A significant feature of expressing model checking in terms of the μ-calculus is that it naturally leads to *symbolic* algorithms, which operates on sets of states, and can scale up to handle exceedingly large state spaces [28]. Beyond the need to use symbolic methods in order to cope with the state-explosion problem [6], which is acute in concurrent settings, several concurrency-related problems are naturally solved by evaluation of μ-calculus formulas. This includes checks for fair simulation between two components of a concurrent systems [14,16] and reasoning about the interaction between a component and its environment, which is naturally expressed by means of parity games [8] (solving parity games is known to be equivalent to μ-calculus model checking [12]). Indeed, the model-checking problem for the μ-calculus has been the subject of extensive research (see [10] for an overview and [18,19,20,23,25,27,33] for more recent work). The precise complexity of this problem has been open for a long time; it was known to be in UP$\cap$co-UP [19] and PTIME-hard [25].

From a practical perspective, the interesting algorithms are those that have time bounds of the form $n^{O(d)}$, where n is the product of the size of the structure and the length of the formula, and d is the *alternation depth* of the formula, which measures the depth of alternation between least fixpoint and greatest fixpoint operators. A naive algorithm would have d as the exponent, since alternating fixpoints of depth d yield nested loops of depth d, each of which involves n iterations. This naive algorithm uses space $O(dn)$ [13]. The alternation depth is interesting as a measure of syntactic complexity, since, on one hand, many logics can be expressed in low-alternation-depth fragments of the μ-calculus [13,12], and, on the other hand, the μ-calculus alternation hierarchy is strict [4]. As noted, the naive algorithm can be naturally implemented in a symbolic fashion, operating on sets of states.

The first improvement to the naive approach was presented in [27] (and slightly improved in [33]), who got the exponent down to $d/2$ at the cost of exponential worst-case space complexity. It was then shown By Jurdzinski [20] how to obtained the improved exponent together with the $O(dn)$ space bound. Common to these algorithms is the elimination of alternating fixpoints; they use monotone fixpoint computation that simulates the effects of alternating fixpoints by means of so-called *progress measures*. Progress measures are functions that measure the progress of a computation; see [21,30,24] for other applications. While the improved algorithms have better time complexity, they sacrifice the main practical attraction of μ-calculus – these algorithms are enumerative and no symbolic version of them is known.

It is well known that modal logic can be viewed as a fragment of first-order logic [2]. Thus, the μ-calculus can be viewed as a fragment of *first-order fixpoint logic*, often referred to as "fixpoint logic", which is the extension of first-order logic with least and greatest fixpoint operators. Fixpoint logic has been the subject of extensive research in the context of database theory [1] and finite-model theory [9]. One of the most fundamental theorems in the theory of fixpoint logic is the *Collapse Theorem*, which asserts that, unlike the case for the μ-calculus, the fixpoint alternation hierarchy over finite structures collapses at its first level; that is, every formula in fixpoint logic can be expressed as a least-fixpoint formula [15,17,26]. The key to this collapse is the simulation of the effect of alternating fixpoints by means of so-called *stage functions*, which measure the progress of fixpoint computations.

Our main result in this paper is the unification of these two disparate lines of research. We show that the Collapse Theorem of fixpoint logic can be adapted to the μ-calculus. Both progress measure and stage functions measure the progress of fixpoint computations. The key difference between fixpoint logic and the μ-calculus is that while in fixpoint logic progress measures can be constructed *within* the logic (by means of the Stage-Comparison Theorem [29]), this cannot be done in the μ-calculus [4], since it allows fixpoint operators only on unary predicates. In order to simulate the construction of progress measures *within* the μ-calculus, we define the $\mu^{\#}$-calculus. While in the μ-calculus variables represent characteristic functions, i.e., functions from the state space to $\{0, 1\}$, in the $\mu^{\#}$-calculus variables represent *measure functions*, which are functions from the state space to some measure domain. We then prove a *Measured-Collapse Theorem*: every formula in the μ-calculus is equivalent to a least-fixpoint formula in the $\mu^{\#}$-calculus.

We then show that the Measured-Collapse Theorem provides a logical recasting of the improved algorithm in [20]. By starting with a μ-calculus formula of alternation depth d, collapsing it to a least-fixpoint $\mu^{\#}$-calculus formula with measure domain $\{0, \ldots, n^{d/2}\}$, and then computing the least fixpoint, we get the improved exponent of $d/2$ together with the $O(dn)$ space bound. Furthermore, this logical recasting of the algorithm suggests how it can be implemented symbolically. A symbolic evaluation of μ-calculus formulas uses Binary Decision Diagrams [5] to represent characteristic functions [6]. For the $\mu^{\#}$-calculus, we suggest representing measure functions by Algebraic Decision Diagrams, which extend Binary Decision Diagrams by allowing arbitrary numerical domains [7]. Thus, we describe, for the first time, a symbolic μ-calculus model-check algorithm whose complexity matches the one of the best known enumerative algorithm. In fact as detailed in Section 4, working with $\mu^{\#}$-calculus enables us to decrease the bound of the number of iterations needed for the simultaneous calculations, leading to a slightly better complexity.

2   Preliminaries

The μ-*calculus* is a propositional modal logic augmented with least and greatest fixpoint operators [22]. We consider a μ-calculus where formulas are constructed from Boolean propositions with Boolean connectives, the temporal operators $\Diamond$ ("exists next") and $\Box$ ("for all next"), as well as least (μ) and greatest (ν) fixpoint operators. We assume that μ-calculus formulas are written in positive normal form (negation only applied to atomic propositions).

Formally, let AP be a set of atomic propositions and let X be a set of variables. The set of μ-calculus formulas over AP and X is defined by induction as follows. (1) If $p \in AP$, then p and $\neg p$ are μ-calculus formulas. (2) If $x \in X$, then x is a μ-calculus formula (in which x is free). (3) If φ, ψ, are μ-calculus formulas, then $\varphi \vee \psi, \varphi \wedge \psi, \Diamond \varphi$, and $\Box \varphi$ are μ-calculus formulas, (4) If $x \in X$, then $\mu x.\varphi$ and $\nu x.\varphi$ are μ-calculus formulas (in which x is bound). The semantic of μ-calculus is defined with respect to a Kripke structure $M = \langle S, R, L \rangle$, and an assignment $f : X \to 2^S$ to the variables. Let $\mathcal{F}$ denote the set of all assignments. For an assignment $f \in \mathcal{F}$, a variable $x \in X$, and a set $S' \subseteq S$, we use $f|_{x=S'}$ to denote the assignment in which x is assigned S' and all other variables assigned as in f. A formula ψ is interpreted as a function $\psi^M : \mathcal{F} \to 2^S$. Thus, given an assignment $f \in \mathcal{F}$, the formula ψ defines a subset of states that satisfy ψ with respect to this assignment. For a definition of the function ψ^M see the full version or [22]. When M is clear from the context, we omit it). A formula with no free variables is called a *sentence*. Note that the assignment f is required only for the valuation of the free variables in ψ. In particular, no assignment is required for sentences. For a sentence ψ, we say that $M, s \models \psi$ if $s \in \psi^M(f)$, for (the arbitrarily chosen) f with $f(x) = \emptyset$ for all $x \in X$.

Let λ denote μ or ν. We assume that every variable $x \in X$ is bound at most once. We refer to the fixpoint subformula in which x is bound as $\lambda(x)$. If $\lambda = \mu$, we say that x is a μ-variable, and if $\lambda = \nu$, we say that it is a ν-variable. Consider a μ-calculus formula of the form $\lambda x.\varphi$. Given an assignment $f \in \mathcal{F}$, we define a sequence of functions $\varphi^j(f) : 2^S \to 2^S$ inductively as follows. $\varphi^0(f)(S') = S'$ and $\varphi^{j+1}(f)(S') = \varphi(f|_{x=\varphi^j(f)(S')})$. For a μ-calculus formula ψ and a subformula $\varphi = \lambda x.\lambda(x)$ of ψ, we define the *alternation level* of φ in ψ, denoted $al_\psi(\varphi)$, as follows [3]. If φ is a sentence, then $al_\psi(\varphi) = 1$. Otherwise, let $\xi = \lambda' y.\xi'$ be the innermost μ or ν subformula of ψ that has φ as a subformula, and y is free in φ. Then if $\lambda' \neq \lambda$, we have $al_\psi(\varphi) = al_\psi(\xi)+1$. Otherwise, $al_\psi(\varphi) = al_\psi(\xi)$.

Intuitively, the alternation level of φ in ψ is the number of alternating fixpoint operators we have to "wrap φ with" in order to reach a sub-sentence of ψ. For a variable x, the alternation level of x, denoted $al(x)$ is the alternation level of $\lambda(x)$. Note that it may be that $\lambda(x)$ is a subformula of $\lambda(x')$ and $al(x) = al(x')$. The definition of $al(x)$ partitions X into equivalence classes according to the variable's alternation level. Note that an equivalent class may contain variables that are independent. In order to refine the class further, we define the order $\prec$ to be the minimal relation that satisfies the following. (1) If x' is free in $\lambda(x)$ then $x \prec x'$. (2) If $x \prec y$ and $y \prec x'$ then $x \prec x'$. We define the $\approx$ equivalence relation to be the minimal equivalence relation that contains all pairs (x, x') such that $x \prec x'$ and $al(x) = al(x')$. The relation $\approx$ refines the partition induce by $al(x)$ so that each class contains variables at the same alternation level that do depend on each other and are all are either μ variables or ν variables. We define the width $width(i)$ of an alternation level i as the maximal size of an equivalence class that is contained in the i'th alternation level. Another property of the $\approx$ relation is that for every equivalence class X^e there exists a unique variable $x_m = max(X^e)$ in X^e such that for every other variable $x \in X^e$ we have $x \prec x_m$. We can simultaneously calculate the fixpoint values of all the variables that are in the same equivalence class.

The reason that we use simultaneous fixpoint is that the evaluation of the variables of a μ-calculus formula as defined above is hierarchical, in the sense that in order to update the value of a variable x, we first evaluate all the variables that appear in subformulas of $\lambda(x)$. Since the value of x might be updated up to $|S|$ times, this makes the complexity of the evaluation exponential in the nesting depth of the fixpoint operators. It turns out that this hierarchal computation is needed only when there is alternation of μ and ν variables. Thus, if $\lambda(x)$ is a subformula of $\lambda(y)$ but $x \approx y$, we can compute their value simultaneously. This could reduce the complexity substantially.

Next, we define a simultaneous fixpoint operation over equivalence classes organized in tuples. Let X^e be an equivalence class of variables with respect to $\approx$. Let X' be the set of variables $\{x' | \exists x \in X^e . x \prec x'\}$, and let X'' be the set $\{x'' | \exists x \in X^e . x'' \prec x\}$. Let $x_m = max(X^e)$, then the subformula $\lambda(x_m) = \lambda x_m . \varphi_m$ binds all variables of X^e. Given an assignment $f : X' \to 2^S$ we consider $\varphi_m(f)$ as a function $\varphi_m(f) : (X^e \to 2^s) \to (X^e \to 2^S)$. This function is used to define the simultaneous fixpoint value of X^e. Note, that all the variables in φ_m are either in X'' or in $X' \cup X^e$. Given an assignment $f : X' \to 2^S$, assume that an extension of f to $f|_{X^e = \overline{S'}}$ recursively determines the values of the variables in X'' or more precisely the values of the subformulas $\lambda(x'')$. Thus subformulas that are not determined in φ_m are of the the form $\lambda(x')$ where $x' \in X' \cup X^e$. We determine these values using $f|_{X^e = \overline{S'}}$, then for every variable $x \in X^e$ we can calculate the value of φ_x and determine it's new value. We define the simultaneous fixpoint value of X^e as, $\bigcap \{\overline{S'} : \varphi_m(f)(\overline{S'}) \subseteq \overline{S'}\}$ for μ-class and $\bigcup \{\overline{S'} : \overline{S'} \subseteq \varphi_m(f)(\overline{S'})\}$ for ν-class.

Theorem 1. *For every variable x, the μ-calculus and the simultaneous fixpoint assign the same value to x,*

Theorem 2. (Extended Knaster-Tarski)

- $\bigcap\{\overline{S'} | \varphi_m(f)(\overline{S'}) \subseteq \overline{S'}\} = \bigcap\{\overline{S'} | \overline{S'} = \varphi_m(f)(\overline{S'})\} = \bigcup_{i \geq 0} \varphi_m{}^i(f)(\langle \emptyset, \emptyset, \ldots, \emptyset \rangle) = \varphi_m{}^{|S| \cdot |X^e|}(f)(\langle \emptyset, \emptyset, \ldots, \emptyset \rangle)$.
- $\bigcup\{\overline{S'} | \overline{S'} \subseteq \varphi_m(f)(\overline{S'})\} = \bigcup\{\overline{S'} | \overline{S'} = \varphi_m(f)(\overline{S'})\} = \bigcap_{i \geq 0} \varphi_m{}^i(f)(\langle S, S, \ldots S \rangle) = \varphi_m{}^{|S| \cdot |X^e|}(f)(\langle S, S, \ldots S \rangle)$.

3 The Logic $\mu^{\#}$-Calculus

While a formula of the μ-calculus defines a subset of S, namely a mapping from S to $\{0, 1\}$, a formula of the $\mu^{\#}$-calculus defines a mapping from S to a domain D where D is parameterized by a natural number k and a sequence of natural numbers $n_0, n_1, \ldots n_k$ such that $D = \bigcup_{l=0}^{k}(\{1, 2, \ldots, n_0\} \times \{1, 2, \ldots, n_1\} \times \ldots \times \{1, 2, \ldots, n_l\}) \cup \{\infty, -\infty\}$. We start with the syntax of the $\mu^{\#}$-calculus. As in the μ-calculus, formulas are defined with respect to a set AP of atomic and a set X of variables. In the $\mu^{\#}$-calculus, however, each variable is associated with an arity. We write $x^{(c)}$ to indicate that variable x has arity c. Given AP and X, the set of the μ-calculus formulas (in positive normal form) over AP and X is defined by induction as follows.

- If $p \in AP$, then p and $\neg p$ are $\mu^{\#}$-calculus formulas.
- If $x^{(c)} \in X$, then $x^{(c)}$ is a $\mu^{\#}$-calculus formula (in which x is free).
- If φ and ψ are μ-calculus formulas then

- $\varphi \vee \psi$ and $\varphi \wedge \psi$ are $\mu^{\#}$-calculus formulas,
- $\Diamond\varphi$ and $\Box\,\varphi$ are $\mu^{\#}$-calculus formulas,
- For $x^{(c)} \in X$, we have that $\mathtt{set}x^{(c)}.\varphi$ and $\mathtt{inc}x^{(c)}.\varphi$ are $\mu^{\#}$-calculus formula (in which x is bound).

We define an alternation level, a preorder $\prec$, and an equivalence relation $\approx$ over X in the same way we define it for the μ-calculus. We say that a $\mu^{\#}$-calculus formula is well formed if

- The arity c of a $\mathtt{set}$-variable $x^{(c)}$ is equal to the minimal arity of $\mathtt{inc}$-variables with alternation level smaller than $al(x)$.
- The arity c of a $\mathtt{inc}$-variable $x^{(c)}$ is equal to the minimal arity of $\mathtt{set}$-variables with alternation level smaller than $al(x)$, minus one.

We use $sub(\psi)$ to denote all the subformulas of ψ. Before defining the semantics of the $\mu^{\#}$-calculus, we define a parameterized order over the tuples in D. Intuitively, the order is lexicographic, and the parameter enables us to restrict attention to prefixes of the tuples. Formally, we have the following.

Definition 1. *For $d, d' \in D$ and $l \geq 0$, we say that $d <_l d'$ if either $d' = \infty$ and $d \neq \infty$, or $d' \neq -\infty$ and $d = -\infty$ or $d = (d_0, \ldots, d_i)$ and $d' = (d'_0, \ldots, d'_j)$, and either:*

- *For some $k \leq \min(i, j, l)$ we have $d_k < d'_k$ and for every $0 \leq m < k$, $d_m = d'_m$.*
- *$i < \min(l, j)$ and for every $k \leq i$ we have $d_k = d'_k$.*

Definition 2. *For $d, d' \in D$ and $l \geq 0$, we say that $d =_l d'$ if either $d = d'$ or $d = (d_0, \ldots, d_i)$ and $d' = (d'_0, \ldots, d'_j)$, and $l \leq \min(i, j)$ and for every $k \leq l$ we have $d_k = d'_k$.*

Note that $<_l$ is a total order over the tuples with arity $\leq l$. We sometimes use the order without the parameter, with the usual lexicographic interpretation. Thus, $d < d'$ if $d <_l d'$ for $l = \max\{|d|, |d'|\}$, and the minimum and maximum tuple of a set of tuples are defined similarly.

For $d = (d_0, \ldots, d_i)$ and $l \geq 0$, let $\mathtt{set}_l(d)$ be greatest l-tuple d' such that $d' \leq_l d$. If $d = \infty$ or $d = -\infty$, then $\mathtt{set}_l(d) = d$. Also, let $\mathtt{inc}_l(d)$ to be the smallest l-tuple d' in D such that $d <_l d'$. Since $<_l$ is total, such a unique tuple exists. If $d = (n_0, n_1, \ldots, n_l)$, then $\mathtt{inc}_l(d) = \infty$, if d is ∞ then $\mathtt{inc}_l(d) = d$, and if d is $-\infty$ then $\mathtt{inc}_l(d)$ is the l-tuple $(1, 1, \ldots, 1)$.

Consider a Kripke structure $M = \langle S, R, L \rangle$. A *measure function* for M is a function $g : S \rightarrow D$. For $c \geq 1$, we say that g is a measure function of arity c if for all $s \in S$, we have $g(s)$ is either a c-tuple in D or an element of $\{\infty, -\infty\}$. The semantics of $\mu^{\#}$-calculus is defined with respect to a Kripke structure $M = \langle S, R, L \rangle$ and an assignment $f : X \rightarrow D^S$ to the variables. An assignment f is legal if for all $x^{(c)} \in X$, the measure function $f(x)$ is of arity c. Let $\mathcal{F}^{\#}$ denote the set of all legal assignments. A formula ψ is interpreted as a function $\psi^M : \mathcal{F}^{\#} \rightarrow D^S$. Thus, given a legal assignment $f \in \mathcal{F}^{\#}$, the formula ψ defines a measure function for M with respect to f. The function ψ^M is defined, for all $s \in S$, inductively as follows (when M is clear from the context, we omit it).

- $p(f)(s) = \infty$ if $p \in L(s)$ and $p(f)(s) = -\infty$ if $p \notin L(s)$.
- $\neg p(f)(s) = \infty$ if $p \notin L(s)$ and $p(f)(s) = -\infty$ if $p \in L(s)$.
- For a free variable $x^{(c)}$, we have $x^{(c)}(f)(s) = f(x^{(c)})(s)$.
- $(\varphi \vee \psi)(f)(s) = \max\{\varphi(f)(s), \psi(f)(s)\}$.
- $(\varphi \wedge \psi)(f)(s) = \min\{\varphi(f)(s), \psi(f)(s)\}$.
- $(\Diamond \varphi)(f)(s) = \max\{\varphi(f)(s') \,|\, R(s, s')\}$.
- $(\Box \varphi)(f) = \min\{\varphi(f)(s') \,|\, R(s, s')\}$.
- $\mathtt{set}x^{(c)}.\varphi(f)(s) = \mathtt{set}_c(\varphi(f)(s))$.
- $\mathtt{inc}x^{(c)}.\varphi(f)(s) = \mathtt{inc}_c(\varphi(f)(s))$.

Let λ denote $\mathtt{set}$ or $\mathtt{inc}$. As in the μ-calculus, we assume that every variable $x^{(c)} \in X$ is bound at most once in a $\mu^\#$-calculus formula, and refer to the subformula that bounds $x^{(c)}$ as $\lambda(x)$. We can view a formula as a function $\psi : \mathcal{F}^\# \to \mathcal{F}^\#$. Indeed, given $f \in \mathcal{F}^\#$, all the subformulas of ψ, and in particular $\lambda(x)$, for all $x^{(c)} \in X$, are mapped into measure functions. Formulas of $\mu^\#$-calculus are monotone, in the sense that $\varphi(f) \geq f$. Hence, we can talk about the least fixpoint of a $\mu^\#$-calculus formula.

Let $g_\psi : X \to D^S$ be the result of applying ψ on the assignment g_0 until a fixpoint is reached, where g_0 assigns to every variable $x^{(c)}$, the assignment $S \to -\infty$. Every variable $x^{(c)}$ can be updated at most $|S| \cdot n_0 \cdot n_1 \cdot \ldots \cdot n_k$ times thus the time complexity is $O(|X| \cdot |S| \cdot n_0 \cdot n_1 \cdot \ldots \cdot n_k)$ and the space complexity is $O(|X| \cdot |S| \cdot (log(n_0) + log(n_1) + \ldots + log(n_k)))$.

Given a μ-calculus formula ψ, we associate with ψ a $\mu^\#$-calculus formula $\psi^\#$ that characterizes the same set of states. We define $\psi^\#$ to be ψ where the arity of a variable x is $w(x) = \lceil \frac{al(x)}{2} \rceil$, every μ operator is replaced by a $\mathtt{set}$ operator, and every ν operator is replaced by an $\mathtt{inc}$ operator. In order to check whether a Kripke structure M satisfies $\psi^\#$, we define the domain D where $k = \lceil \frac{max_{x \in X}(al(x))}{2} \rceil$ and for every $0 \leq i \leq k$ we have $n_i = width(2 \cdot i + 1) \cdot |S|$.

Theorem 3. (Measured Collapse) *Let ψ be a μ-calculus formula, and let M be a Kripke structure. Then, $M, s \models \psi$ iff $g_{\psi^\#}(\psi^\#)(s) = \infty$.*

The proof of Theorem 3 is described in the full version. Theorem 3 implies a simple model-checking algorithm for the μ-calculus. Given a μ-calculus formula ψ and a Kripke structure M, translate ψ into $\psi^\#$ and check whether $M \models \psi^\#$. The time complexity of this algorithm is $O(|X| \cdot width(1) \cdot width(3) \cdot \ldots \cdot width(2 \cdot k + 1) \cdot |S|^{k+1})$ where k is the maximum alternation level of ψ. The space complexity is $O(|X| \cdot |S| \cdot (log(width(1)) + log(width(2)) + \ldots + log(width(k))))$. Note that in the model-checking algorithm that uses a reduction to parity games, the time complexity is $O(|X| \cdot |al(1)| \cdot |al(3)| \cdot \ldots \cdot |al(2 \cdot k + 1)| \cdot |S|^{k+1})$.

Recall that for all i, we have that $width(i) \leq al(i)$. Thus, our complexity is better. The improved complexity follows from the fact that the reduction of μ-calculus model checking to parity games does not take into account the fact that some variables with the same alternation level may be independent of each other. On the other hand, the translation to $\mu^\#$-calculus refines the partition induced by the alternating level to the relation $\approx$.

4 Symbolic $\mu^{\#}$-Calculus Model Checking and Parity Games

As discussed in Section 1, the improved algorithms for μ-calculus model checking are not symbolic. In this section we describe a symbolic algorithm for $\mu^{\#}$-calculus model checking. The Measured Collapse Theorem then implies a symbolic algorithm for μ-calculus model checking, and our complexity matches the improved complexity of [20]. In addition, we show how the algorithm in [20], for the equivalent problem of solving parity games, can be viewed as a computation of a least fixed-point over a measured domain, and describe a symbolic implementation for it that follows from this view. A symbolic evaluation of μ-calculus formulas uses Binary Decision Diagrams (BDDs) [5] to represent characteristic functions [6]. For the $\mu^{\#}$-calculus, we use Algebraic Decision Diagrams (ADDs), which extend BDDs by allowing arbitrary numerical domains [7].

Symbolic evaluation of $\mu^{\#}$-calculus formulas. Consider a $\mu^{\#}$-calculus formula ψ and a Kripke structure $M = \langle S, R, L \rangle$. We define the product of ψ and M as the graph $G_{\psi,M} = \langle V, E \rangle$, where

- $V = sub(\psi) \times S$.
- $E((\varphi, s), (\varphi', s'))$ iff one of the following holds.
  - $s = s'$ and there is φ'' such that φ is $\varphi' \vee \varphi''$, $\varphi'' \vee \varphi'$, $\varphi' \wedge \varphi''$, or $\varphi'' \wedge \varphi'$.
  - $R(s, s')$ and φ is $\Diamond\varphi'$ or $\Box\,\varphi'$.
  - $s = s'$ and φ is $\mathtt{set}x^{(c)}.\varphi'$ or $\mathtt{inc}x^{(c)}.\varphi'$.
  - $s = s'$, $\varphi = x^{(c)}$, and $\varphi' = \lambda x^{(c)}.\varphi''$.

We refer to vertices of the form $(\varphi' \vee \varphi'', s)$ or $(\Diamond\varphi', s)$ as *max vertices*, and to vertices of the form $(\varphi' \wedge \varphi'', s)$ or $(\Box\,\varphi', s)$ as *min vertices*.

Let $g_\psi : sub(\psi) \to D^S$ be the least fixpoint of ψ. We describe the calculation of g_ψ by means of a function $f_{\psi,M} : V \to D$ such that $f_{\psi,M}(\varphi, s) = g_\psi(\varphi)(s)$. Note that for all $\varphi \in sub(\psi)$, we have that $s \models \varphi$ iff $f_{\psi,M}(s, \varphi) = \infty$. In order to calculate $f_{\psi,M}$, we describe a sequence of functions $f_0, f_1, \ldots$ such that $f_{\psi,M} = f_i$ where i is the least such that $f_i = f_{i+1}$. The functions $f_i : V \to D$ are defined inductively as follows. We start with f_0.

- If $v = (p, s)$ then $f_0(v) = \infty$ if $s \models p$ and $f_0(v) = -\infty$ if $s \not\models p$.
- If $v = (\neg p, s)$ then $f_0(v) = \infty$ if $s \not\models q$ and $f_0(v) = -\infty$ if $s \models q$.
- For all other vertices $f_0(v) = -\infty$.

Given f_i, we define f_{i+1} as follows.

- If v is of the form (p, s) or $(\neg p, s)$ then $f_{i+1}(v) = f_i(v)$.
- If v is a max vertex, then $f_{i+1}(v) = \max\{f_i(v') \mid (v, v') \in E\}$.
- If v is a min vertex, then $f_{i+1}(v) = \min\{f_i(v') \mid (v, v') \in E\}$.
- If v is of the form $(x^{(c)}, s)$ then v has a single successor v' and $f_{i+1}(v) = f_i(v')$.
- If v is of the form $(\mathtt{set}\ x^{(c)}.\varphi, s)$, then v has a single successor v' and $f_{i+1}(v) = \mathtt{set}_c(f_i(v'))$.
- If v is of the form $(\mathtt{inc}\ x^{(c)}.\varphi, s)$, then v has a single successor v' and $f_{i+1}(v) = \mathtt{inc}_c(f_i(v'))$.

Proposition 1. *Consider a Kripke structure M and $\mu^{\#}$-calculus formula ψ. For all $\varphi \in sub(\psi)$ and $s \in S$, we have $g_\psi(\varphi)(s) = f_{\psi,M}(\varphi, s)$.*

We now describe how to compute $f_{\psi,M}$ symbolically. We use BDDs to represent sets and relations, and use ADDs to represent measure functions. Consider a Kripke structure $M = \langle S, R, L \rangle$ and a formula ψ. Let $G_{\psi,M} = \langle V, E \rangle$ be their product as defined above. We assume that M is given symbolically by one BDD h_R for R, and $|AP|$ BDDs – one BDD h_p for each $p \in AP$, representing the set of states that satisfy p (when the state space is given by truth assignments to AP, there is no need for these BDDs) . Given these BDDs, constructing BDDs that represent V and E is straightforward. In particular, we assume that E is represented by the BDD h_E, and we also have the following BDDs for subsets of V: a BDD h_{AP} for vertices of the form (p, s) or $(\neg p, s)$, BDDs $h_{\max}$ and $h_{\min}$ for the max and min vertices, respectively, a BDD h_X for vertices of the form $(x^{(c)}, s)$ for some c, BDDs $h_{\text{set},j}$ for vertices of the form $(\text{set}x^{(j)}.\varphi, s)$, and BDDs $h_{\text{inc},j}$ for vertices of the form $(\text{inc}x^{(j)}.\varphi, s)$. Finally, the procedure also gets an integer c_{max}, which is the maximal arity of a variable in X.

The algorithm for computing $f_{\psi,M}$ is described in Figure 1. Apart from the Boolean BDD operators OR, AND, and NOT, we use the operator $\to (h, d)$, which gets a BDD $h \subseteq V$ and some $d \in D$, and creates an ADD that maps all the elements of h to d, and the following procedures.

- MAX, which given an ADD $f : V \to D$ and the BDD h_E, returns an ADD that assigns to every vertex $v \in h_{max}$ the value $\max\{f(v')|E(v, v')\}$.
- MIN, which given an ADD $f : V \to D$ and the BDD h_E, returns an ADD that assigns to every vertex $v \in h_{min}$ the value $\min\{f(v')|E(v, v')\}$.
- ASSIGN, which given an ADD $f : V \to D$ and the BDD h_E, returns an ADD that assigns to every vertex $v \in h_X$ the value $f(v')$ for the single v' with $E(v, v')$.
- SET(f,j), which given an ADD $f : V \to D$, the BDD h_E, and $1 \le j \le c_{max}$, returns an ADD that assigns to every vertex $v \in h_{set,j}$ the value $\text{set}_j(f(v'))$ for the single v' with $E(v, v')$.
- INC(f,j), which given an ADD $f : V \to D$, the BDD h_E, and $1 \le j \le c_{max}$, returns an ADD that assigns to every vertex $v \in h_{inc,j}$ the value $\text{inc}_j(f(v'))$ for the single v' with $E(v, v')$.
- OR between ADDs, which gets ADDs that map disjoint subsets of V to D and returns their union (all the ADDs are defined for all the vertices in V, but some vertices are mapped to some special value, which enables us to represent by ADDs also partial functions).

Since all procedures assign values to the vertices according their successors, it is useful to generate, given an ADD f and the BDD h_E, the ADD $f_{suc} : V \times V \to D$ such that $f_{suc}(v, v') = d$ if $E(v, v')$ and $f(v') = d$. If $\neg E(v, v')$, then $f_{suc}(v, v') = \infty$. The ADD f_{suc} is simply the result of an AND operation on h_E and a ADD of f with renamed variables. Using f_{suc}, the implementation of ASSIGN is straightforward as $\exists v'.(f_{suc} \text{ AND } h_x)$. The implementation of INC and SET is similar except that we replace every leaf d in the ADD of $(f_{suc} \text{ AND } h_{\text{inc},j})$ or $(f_{suc} \text{ AND } h_{\text{set},j})$ with $\text{inc}_j(d)$ or $\text{set}_j(d)$ respectively. The procedures MAX and MIN are more complicated and are described in the full version.

```
MODEL_CHECK
    h^T_AP = (OR_{p∈AP}({p} AND h_p))OR (OR_{p∈AP}({¬p} AND NOT (h_p)));
    f^T_q =→ (h^T_q, ∞) ;
    f = f^T_q OR → ((h_V AND NOT h^t_q), -∞);
    repeat
        f_old = f;   f_max = MAX(f_old) ;
        f_min = MIN(f_old) ;   f_x = ASSIGN(f_old) ;
        f_set = false;   f_inc = false;
        for j = 1 to c_max do
            f_set = f_set OR SET(f_old, j);   f_inc = f_inc OR INC(f_old, j)
        f = f_q OR f_max OR f_min OR f_set OR f_inc;
    until f = f_old
```

Fig. 1. The symbolic algorithm for $\mu^{\#}$-calculus model checking.

Let us now analyze the complexity of the procedure. The number of iterations required for the procedure to reach a fixed point is bounded by $|D| \cdot |V|$ which is $|S|^{\lceil \frac{al(\psi)}{2} \rceil} \cdot |S| \cdot |\psi|$. Each iteration involves an applications of the MIN/MAX procedures (that are the most costly). In the full version, we show that these procedures apply at most $|V|^2 \cdot log(|V|) = (|S| \cdot |\psi|)^2 \cdot log((|S| \cdot |\psi|)$ ADD operations. Thus, the overall complexity is $O(|S|^{\lceil \frac{al(\psi)}{2} \rceil + 3} \cdot |\psi|^3) \cdot log((|S| \cdot |\psi|)$ ADD operations.

Parity games. A parity game is played on a graph $\langle V, E \rangle$, where V is partitioned into two sets: V_0 of even vertices and V_1 of odd vertices. Every vertex v has a priority $p(v) \in \{0, 1, \ldots k - 1\}$. A parity game over $\langle V_0, V_1, E, p \rangle$ is played by two players, referred to as the odd and the even player. A play over the game starts by putting a pebble at some initial vertex v and proceeds infinitely many rounds. In each round, one of the players moves the pebble on an edge from the current vertex to one of its successors. If the source vertex is in V_0, the even player moves the pebble; otherwise the odd player moves the pebble. The play generates an infinite sequence of vertices ρ. Let $inf(\rho)$ be the set of vertices that appear infinitely often in ρ. The odd player wins the game if the vertex with minimal priority in $inf(\rho)$ has an odd priority. Otherwise, the even player wins. The problem is to determine, given a game graph $\langle V_0, V_1, E, p \rangle$, the set of vertices from which the odd player has a winning strategy.

In [20], an algorithm for solving parity games is suggested. Below, we describe the algorithm in terms of measure function. Let $D = \bigcup_{j=1}^{\frac{k}{2}} \{0, 1, \ldots, |V|\}^j \cup \{\infty, -\infty\}$, let F be the set of all measure functions $f : V \to D$ and let f_0 be the initial function that assigns $-\infty$ to all vertices. A game graph G induces a function from F to F, where for a measure function $f \in F$, the measure function $G(f)$ is defined, for all $v \in V$, as follows:

$$G(f)(v) = \begin{cases} \max_{(v,v')\in E} f(v') & \text{if } v \in V_1 \text{ and } p(v) \text{ is even.} \\ \max_{(v,v')\in E} \text{inc}_{\lceil \frac{p(v)}{2} \rceil}(f(v')) & \text{if } v \in V_1 \text{ and } p(v) \text{ is odd.} \\ \min_{(v,v')\in E} f(v') & \text{if } v \in V_0 \text{ and } p(v) \text{ is even.} \\ \min_{(v,v')\in E} \text{inc}_{\lceil \frac{p(v)}{2} \rceil}(f(v'))) & \text{if } v \in V_0 \text{ and } p(v) \text{ is odd.} \end{cases}$$

If we denote by f_G to the least fixpoint of G, then the set of winning vertices for the odd player is $\{v|f_G(v) = \infty\}$, and the set of winning vertices for the even player is $\{v|f_G(v) < \infty\}$. The measure function f_G can be used for generating a winning strategy $\pi : V_0 \to V$ for the even player where for every $v \in V_0$ we have $\pi(v) = v'$ such that $f_G(v') = min\{f_G(v'')|(v, v'') \in E\}$. Thus, the even player moves to a successor of v with minimal measure. A symbolic procedure that generate a strategy is given in the full version.

A symbolic implementation of the algorithm similar to the symbolic evaluation of $\mu^{\#}$-calculus formulas is described in Figure 2. The procedure calls the following procedures

- MAXe, which given an ADD $f : V \to D$, the BDD h_E, and an even $1 \le j \le \frac{k}{2}$, returns an ADD that assigns to every vertex $v \in V_1$ with $p(v) = j$, the value $max\{f(v')|E(v, v')\}$.
- MAXo, which given an ADD $f : V \to D$, the BDD h_E, and an odd $1 \le j \le \frac{k}{2}$, returns an ADD that assigns to every vertex $v \in V_1$ with $p(v) = j$, the value $max\{inc_{\lceil \frac{j}{2} \rceil}(f(v')) : E(v, v')\}$.
- MINe and MINo, defined similarly for vertices in V_0.

The symbolic implementation of these procedures is similar to the implementation of the MAX and MIN procedures of the former section, and is described in the next section.

```
PARITY(G)
f =→ (V, −∞);
repeat
    f_old = f;    f = false;
    for j = 1 to k/2 do
        if j is even then f = f OR MAXe(f_old, j) OR MINe(f_old, j);
        if j is odd then f = f OR MAXo(f_old, j) OR MINo(f_old, j);
    end for
until f = f_old;
```

Fig. 2. A symbolic algorithm for solving parity games.

Complexity: Similarly to the previous section, we can bound the number of iterations by $|V|^{\lceil \frac{k}{2} \rceil} \cdot |V|$. Thus, the overall complexity is $O(|V|^{\lceil \frac{k}{2} \rceil + 3} \cdot log(|V|))$ ADD operations.

References

1. S. Abiteboul, R. Hull, and V. Vianu. *Foundations of databases*. Addison-Wesley, 1995.
2. J. F. A. K. van Benthem. *Modal Logic and Classical Logic*. Bibliopolis, Naples, 1985.
3. G. Bhat and R. Cleaveland. Efficient local model-checking for fragments of the modal μ-calculus. In *Proc. TACAS*, LNCS 1055, 1996.
4. J.C. Bradfield. The modal μ-calculus alternation hierarchy is strict. *TCS*, 195(2):133–153, 1998.

5. R.E. Bryant. Graph-based algorithms for boolean-function manipulation. *IEEE Trans. on Computers*, C-35(8), 1986.
6. J.R. Burch, E.M. Clarke, K.L. McMillan, D.L. Dill, and L.J. Hwang. Symbolic model checking: 10^{20} states and beyond. *I&C*, 98(2):142–170, 1992.
7. R. Bahar, E. Frohm, C. Gaona, G. Hachtel, E. Macii, A. Pardo, and F. Somenzi", Algebraic decision diagrams and their applications. *FMSD*, 10 (2/3): 171–206, 1997
8. A. Chakrabarti, L. de Alfaro, T.A. Henzinger, M. Jurdzinski, and F.Y.C. Mang. Interface compatibility checking for software modules. In *14th CAV*, LNCS 2404, pp. 428–441, 2002.
9. H.D. Ebbinghaus and J. Flum. *Finite Model Theory*. Perspectives in Mathematical Logic. Springer-Verlag, 1995.
10. E.A. Emerson. Modal Checking and the μ-Calculus, *Descriptive Complexity and Finite Models*, American Mathematical Society, pp. 185–214, 1997.
11. E.A. Emerson and E.M. Clarke. Characterizing correctness properties of parallel programs using fixpoints. In *Proc. 7th ICALP*, pp. 169–181, 1980.
12. E.A. Emerson, C. Jutla, and A.P. Sistla. On model-checking for fragments of μ-calculus. In *Proc. 5th CAV*, LNCS 697, pp. 385–396, 1993.
13. E.A. Emerson and C.-L. Lei. Efficient model checking in fragments of the propositional μ-calculus. In *Proc. 1st LICS*, pp. 267–278, 1986.
14. K. Etessami, Th. Wilke, and R. A. Schuller. Fair simulation relations, parity games, and state space reduction for Büchi automata. In *Proc. 28th ICALP*, LNCS 2076, pp. 694–707, 2001.
15. Y. Gurevich and S. Shelah. Fixed-point extensions of first-order logic. *Annals of Pure and Applied Logic*, 32:265–280, 1986.
16. T.A. Henzinger, O. Kupferman, and S. Rajamani. Fair simulation. *I&C*, 173(1):64–81, 2002.
17. N. Immerman. Relational queries computable in polynomial time. *I&C*, 68:86–104, 1986.
18. M. Jurdzinski J. Voge. A discrete strategy improvement algorithm for solving parity games. In E. A. Emerson and A. P. Sistla, editors, *Proc 12th CAV*, LNCS 1855, pp. 202–215, 2000.
19. M. Jurdzinski. Deciding the winner in parity games is in UP ∩ co-UP. *IPL*, 68(3):119–124, 1998.
20. M. Jurdzinski. Small progress measures for solving parity games. In *Proc. 17th TACAS*, LNCS 1770, pp. 290–301, 2000.
21. N. Klarlund. Progress measures for complementation of ω-automata with applications to temporal logic. In *Proc. 32nd FOCS*, pp. 358–367, 1991.
22. D. Kozen. Results on the propositional μ-calculus. *TCS*, 27:333–354, 1983.
23. O. Kupferman and M.Y. Vardi. Weak alternating automata and tree automata emptiness. In *Proc. 30th STOC*, pp. 224–233, 1998.
24. O. Kupferman and M.Y. Vardi. Weak alternating automata are not that weak. *ACM ToCL*, 2001(2):408–429, 2001.
25. O. Kupferman, M.Y. Vardi, and P. Wolper. An automata-theoretic approach to branching-time model checking. *J. ACM*, 47(2):312–360, 2000.
26. D. Leivant. Inductive definitions over finite structures. *I&C*, 89:95–108, 1990.
27. D. Long, A. Brown, E. Clarke, S. Jha, and W. Marrero. An improved algorithm for the evaluation of fixpoint expressions. In *Proc. 6th CAV*, LNCS 818, pp. 338–350, 1994.
28. K.L. McMillan. *Symbolic Model Checking*. Kluwer Academic Publishers, 1993.
29. Y. N. Moschovakis. *Elementary Induction on Abstract Structures*. North Holland, 1974.
30. Klarlund N and F.B. Schneider. Proving nondeterministically specified safety properties using progress measures. *I&C*, 107(1):151–170, 1993.
31. D. Park. Finiteness is μ-ineffable. *TCS*, 3:173–181, 1976.
32. V.R. Pratt. A decidable μ-calculus: preliminary report. In *22nd FOCS*, pp. 421–427, 1981.
33. H. Seidl. Fast and simple nested fixpoints. *IPL*, 59(6):303–308, 1996.

An Information Theoretic Lower Bound for Broadcasting in Radio Networks

Carlos Brito, Eli Gafni, and Shailesh Vaya

Department of Computer Science
University of California Los Angeles
Los Angeles - 90049
{fisch,eli,vaya}@cs.ucla.edu

Abstract. We consider the problem of deterministic broadcasting in undirected radio networks with limited topological information. We show that for every deterministic protocol there exists a radius 2 network which requires at least $\Omega(n^{\frac{1}{2}})$ rounds for completing broadcast. The previous best lower bound for constant diameter networks is $\Omega(n^{\frac{1}{4}})$ rounds, due to [23]. For networks of radius D the lower bound can be extended to $\Omega((nD)^{\frac{1}{2}})$ rounds. This resolves the open problem posed by [23].

Of perhaps more interest is our approach for proving the lower bound which is novel. We quantify the amount of connectivity information, about the topology of the network, that the source can learn in arbitrary number of rounds of an a deterministic broadcasting protocol. This approach is much more intuitive and exposes the structure of the broadcasting problem. We believe it is of independent interest and may have other applications.

1 Introduction

Ad-hoc wireless networks have been the subject of extensive research in recent years. These networks find potential applications in scenarios such as battlefields, emergency disaster relief, and situations in which it is very difficult to provide the necessary infrastructure. Techniques and algorithms developed for radio networks also find applications in the ever growing field of wireless computing.

Communication in ad-hoc wireless networks is structured using synchronous time-slots. A global clock, which indicates the current round number, is provided to all the nodes in the network. At every round each node acts either as a transmitter or a receiver. A radio network can be modeled as an *undirected* connected graph as follows. Each node in the graph represents a processor, and two nodes are connected by an edge if the coresponding processors lie within the transmission range of each other. A message transmitted by a node can potentially reach all its neighbors. However, if more than one neighbor sends a message in the same round, then a collision occurs and the node does not receive anything. A node cannot distinguish between a collision and silence, that is, a node cannot decide if none or more than one of its neighbors have transmitted in a given round. We

V. Diekert and M. Habib (Eds.): STACS 2004, LNCS 2996, pp. 534–546, 2004.

will see in the next sections that these restrictions on the communication have a severe impact on the design and performance of algorithms for radio networks.

This paper is about *broadcasting* in radio networks. Broadcasting is one of the most studied problem in radio networks. It consists of a task initiated by a single processor, called source, whose goal is to send a single message to all the processors in the network. The complexity of a broadcasting protocol is measured by the number of rounds it requires to deliver the broadcast message to all the nodes in the network. The following section reviews some to the important results for this problem.

1.1 Related Work

The study of broadcasting in radio networks whose nodes have only limited knowledge of the topology, was initiated by the seminal work of Bar-Yehuda, Goldreich, Itai [3]. In the framework considered by them, nodes know only their own label and the labels of their neighbors. Under this assumption, a simple linear time broadcasting algorithm exists based on distributed depth-first search [2]. Reference [3] also claims a lower-bound of $\Omega(n)$ for constant diameter networks. However, as observed by [23], this result does not hold for the stated model, but seems to hold for a related, more restricted model [26].

For the original model, Kowalski, Pelc [23] established a lower bound of $\Omega(n^{1/4})$ for networks of diameter 4 (and, $(nD^3)^{1/4}$ for diameter D).

A weaker setting, where nodes know their own labels, but do not know the labels of their neighbors, has also been studied. Research in this problem has led to the introduction of an interesting combinatorial concept called *selective family*. The use of selective families in the design of deterministic protocols for unknown networks was introduced by Chelbus et. al. in [9]. Several recent works exploit this combinatorial tool, specifically the use of probabilistic method, for obtaining good lower and upper bounds for the broadcasting problem [12,9,11].

2 Discussion of Results and Techniques

The main result of this work is a lower bound on the number of rounds required by any deterministic protocol to broadcast a message in a radio network, where nodes have limited knowledge about the topology and the underlying graph is undirected. The result is formally stated in the next theorem, and holds for the same model studied in [3], [23].

Theorem 1. *Every deterministic protocol requires at least $\sqrt{n}$ rounds in the worst case to complete broadcast in a radio network.*

Besides the lower bound provided in theorem 1, which considerably improves on previous results, another important contribution of the paper is a set of novel techniques that could be useful in the analysis of related problems. In the following we discuss some subtle aspects of the problem of broadcasting in radio networks, that motivate our ideas.

Consider the simple class of networks illustrated in Figure 1, which can be partitioned into 3 layers: (a) layer L_0 consisting only of the source node; (b) layer L_1 composed by n nodes; and, (c) layer L_2 consisting only of a single node, say v. Communication can only occur between the source and each node in layer L_1, and between an arbitrary set of nodes in L_1 and the node v in L_2. Following [23], we call networks with such topologies *BGI networks*.

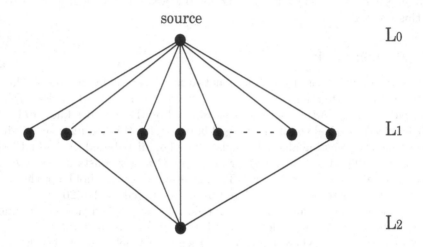

Fig. 1. Example of a BGI newtork

Assuming that the source transmits the broadcast message in round 0 and remains silent thereafter, one can use a hitting set argument [3], to show that any deterministic protocol requires $\Omega(n)$ rounds to complete broadcast in at least one of such networks.

However, as observed in [23], the source can learn some information about the topology during the execution of the protocol. This information can then be transmitted to the other nodes in the network to achieve faster broadcasting. In fact, [23] provides a protocol that completes broadcast in $O(lg_2 n)$ on any *BGI* network.

Our main idea is to estimate the amount of information that can be learned by the source. Then, we show that even if all this information were available to the neighbors of the source at the beginning of the execution, and the source remains silent, still broadcast can not be achieved in less than $\sqrt{n}$ rounds.

For this purpose, we consider a class of networks that can be partitioned into components $C_1, \ldots, C_k$, where each of the components has the structure of a *BGI* network without the source, which is the same for all components (see Figure 2 for an example).

The first important observation is that all the information learned by the source during the execution of a protocol can be summarized by topological information about the components. More specifically, in each round i, if the source receives a message from a node u, then we may assume that the message contains a complete description of the topology of the component of u. In the other case, either no neighbor of the source transmits or a collision occurs during round i, and the source learns nothing in the round, which we denote by ϕ. These ideas are formalized in section 5.

From this observation, it is tempting to conclude that the partial knowledge collected by the source makes broadcasting easy in some components, but is uninformative with respect to the rest of the network. If this were the case, then one could use a hitting set [3] or a selective family [9] argument to obtain lower bounds for completing broadcast.

However, as we show in the next example, depending on the specification of the protocol, the information provided by the source may allow the nodes to obtain additional information about the topology of the network.

Consider a protocol according to which exactly two nodes, say u and v, are scheduled to make a transmission to the source in a specific round, but only if each of them is connected to some other node, say w and z, respectively. Now, if the source receives ϕ in this round it cannot distinguish the case where both u and v transmit from the case in which none of them transmit. On the other hand, with the information that the source receives ϕ in this round, node u can decide if edge (v, z) is present or not based on its own behavior during the round.

To avoid this type of problem we provide an information theoretic argument that is independent of how the information provided by the source is interpreted by the other nodes. Specifically, we first obtain an upper bound on the number of bits required to encode all the information learned by the source in the first $\sqrt{n}$ rounds of an arbitrary protocol. Then, we show that even if all the neighbors of the source receive the same arbitrary string of at most that size, and the source remains quiet in every round, still $\sqrt{n}$ rounds are necessary to complete broadcast.

The rest of the paper proves these facts, and is organized as follows. Section 3 describes the adopted model in more detail and introduces some definitions. Section 4 formally states the facts above in a few lemmas, and gives the proof of our main result. Sections 5, ?? and Appendix ?? provide proofs for all the intermediate results. Finally, we conclude in Section 6

3 Description of the Model and General Definitions

Definition [3],[23]: A broadcast protocol π for a radio network is a multiprocessor protocol which proceeds in rounds as follows:

1. Nodes have distinct labels from the set $\{0, 1, \dots, m\}$, where m is a polynomial in the number of nodes in the network. A distinguished node with label 0 is called the *source*.
2. All nodes execute identical copies of the same protocol π.
3. In each round, every node acts either as a transmitter or as a receiver (or is inactive).

4. A node receives a message in a specific round if and only if it acts as a receiver and exactly one of its neighbors transmits in that round. We assume that the messages are authenticated, that is, when a node receives a message it knows the label of the transmitting node.
5. The action of a node in a specific round is determined by
   a) Initial input, which contains its own label and labels of its neighbors.
   b) Messages received in previous rounds.
6. In round 0 only the source transmits a broadcast message.
7. Only nodes that have received a message are allowed to transmit. That is, the only "spontaneous" transmissions is the one by the source in round 0.
8. Broadcast is completed in r rounds if all nodes receive the source message in one of the rounds $0, 1, \ldots, r - 1$.

3.1 C_2 Networks

The class of networks C_2 is characterized by the fact that nodes can be partitioned into layers satisfying:

1. Layer L_0 consists only of the source node;
2. Layer L_1 contains cn nodes, where c is a constant with respect to n. Each node in layer L_1 is only connect to the source and at most one node from layer L_2.
3. Layer L_2 contains $d\sqrt{n}$ nodes, where d is a constant with respect n and $d < c$. Each node in layer L_2 is connected to exactly $\sqrt{n}$ nodes in L_1, and it is not connected to the source.

For each node u from L_2 in network $\mathcal{N}$, we denote the set composed by all the nodes from L_1 connected to u by $Clan_{\mathcal{N}}(u)$, and say that u is the head of this Clan. A node in L_1 that is not connected to any node in L_2 is said to be *orphan*. Figure 2 shows an example of a C_2 network.

3.2 Advice String $\Upsilon = \Upsilon(\pi, \mathcal{N}, t)$

For a broadcast protocol π, a network $\mathcal{N} \in C_2$, and integer $t \geq 0$, $\Upsilon = \Upsilon(\pi, \mathcal{N}, t)$ is a string that encodes the topological knowledge (potentially) acquired by the source during the first t rounds of execution of protocol π on network $\mathcal{N}$. Viewing Υ as an array with t elements, $\Upsilon[i]$ represents the information obtained by the source during round i, $0 < i \leq t$, and is given by:

1. If the source does not receive any message during round i (either because every node in L_1 was silent, or because a collision occurs), the $\Upsilon = \phi$;
2. In the other case, let w be the node in L_1 that transmits the message received by the source. Then, $\Upsilon[i]$ contains a pair consisting of: (a) a list with the labels of all nodes in the same clan as w; and, (b) the label of the clan of w.

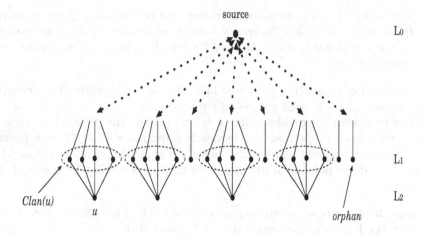

source

Lo

Clan(u)

u

orphan

L1

L2

Fig. 2. Example of a C_2 network

Note that when $\Upsilon[i] \neq \phi$ it encodes all the information about the connectivity among the nodes in the Clan of w.

Let $\mathbb{K}_{\mathcal{A}}(\Upsilon)$ denote the Kolmogorov complexity of string Υ with respect to a decompression algorithm $\mathcal{A}$. Define,

$$\mathbb{K}_{\mathcal{C}_2}(t) = \min_{\mathcal{A}} \ \max_{\pi, \mathcal{N}} \ \mathbb{K}_{\mathcal{A}}(\Upsilon(\pi, \mathcal{N}, t))$$

4   Lower Bound

The lower bound result stated in section 2 is implied by the following theorem:

Theorem 2. *For every deterministic protocol that runs for at most $\sqrt{n}$ rounds, there exists a network $\mathcal{N} \in \mathcal{C}_2$ such that some head node in $\mathcal{N}$ does not receive the source message, and so broadcast is not completed.*

Before proving the theorem, we state two important lemmas developed in this work and a variation of a theorem from [12], that will consist of the main steps of the argument.

The first lemma shows that it is sufficient to analyze protocols that have a simple communication structure, and in which the source only transmits the broadcast message together with an advice string Υ of bounded size, in round 0. This lemma captures the idea that all the help that could be provided by the source to achieve faster broadcast can be encoded in a string containing connectivity information.

Lemma 1. *If there exists a protocol π which completes broadcast in at most r rounds on a network $\mathcal{N} \in \mathcal{C}_2$, then there exists a protocol π' that completes broadcast in at most $3r$ on $\mathcal{N}$, satisfying:*

- *For $i = 0, 1, 2$, nodes in layer L_i transmit in round t only if $t \equiv i \pmod 3$.*
- *In round 0, the source transmits a message containing the broadcast message and a string of length at most $\mathbb{K}_{C_2}(r)$. In every other round the source remains silent.*

The proof of lemma 1 is presented in section 5, and consists of the construction of protocol π' through a series of reductions.

The next lemma provides a lower bound on the size of a set of networks with some special properties. The lemma is proved in section ?? by a counting argument, using estimates on the number of networks that share the same advice string Υ, and the number of distinct clans that appear in at least one of these networks.

Lemma 2. *Let π be an arbitrary protocol and $t > 0$. Then, there exists a subset of networks $\mathcal{X} \subset C_2$ and a head node $v \in L_2$ such that:*

1. *For all $\mathcal{N}_i, \mathcal{N}_j \in \mathcal{X}$, $\Upsilon(\pi, \mathcal{N}_i, \sqrt{n}) = \Upsilon(\pi, \mathcal{N}_j, \sqrt{n})$.*
2. *The clans with which v is associated in each network in $\mathcal{X}$ are distinct;*
3. *$\lg_2 |\mathcal{X}| \geq \frac{13}{14} \sqrt{n} \lg_2(\sqrt{n} + 1)$*

Finally, we will also make use of the next definition and theorem in our proof. They generalize the concept of selective families and the corresponding lower bound given in [12], for the case in which we consider arbitrary sets Δ of subsets of $\{1, \dots, n\}$. The proof of this theorem is given in Appendix A.

Definition 1. *Let n, k be arbitrary positive integers with $k \leq n$, and let Δ be a set of subsets of $\{1, \dots, n\}$. A family $\mathcal{F}$ of subsets of $\{1, \dots, n\}$ is k-selective for Δ if, for every $\delta \in \Delta$ with $|\delta| \leq k$, there is a subset $F \in \mathcal{F}$ such that $|\delta \cap F| = 1$.*

Theorem 3. *Let Δ be a set of $\sqrt{n}$-subsets of $\{1, \dots, n\}$. If Γ is a $\sqrt{n}$-selective family for Δ, then*

$$|\Gamma| \geq \lg_2 |\Delta| - \frac{11}{12} \sqrt{n} \lg_2 \frac{16n}{\sqrt{n}}$$

Proof of Theorem 2: The proof is by way of contradiction. We shall assume that the broadcast protocol runs for $t \leq \sqrt{n}$ rounds. However, we shall show that t should actually be greater then $\frac{1}{85} \sqrt{n} \lg_2 \sqrt{n}$ for broadcast to be complete in all networks.

Suppose that there exists a protocol π that completes broadcast in every network from C_2 in $t \leq \sqrt{n}$ rounds. Then, let π' be a protocol satisfying the conditions of lemma 1 that completes broadcast in every such network in at most $3\sqrt{n}$ rounds.

Now, let $\mathcal{X} \subseteq C_2$ and $u \in L_2$ be a subset of networks and the corresponding head node given by lemma 2 for protocol π.

For a given network $\mathcal{N} \in \mathcal{X}$ and a round i, let subset $\eta_{i,\mathcal{N}}(u)$ be defined as follows:

- If node u does not receive the broadcast message before round i when π
  is executed on $\mathcal{N}$, then $\eta_{i,\mathcal{N}}(u)$ is the subset of nodes from $Clan_{\mathcal{N}}(u)$ that
  would transmit in round i;
- Otherwise, $\eta_{i,\mathcal{N}}(u) = \phi$.

Let $\eta_i(u) = \bigcup_{\mathcal{N} \in \mathcal{X}} \eta_{i,\mathcal{N}}$.

Proposition 1. *Node u receives the broadcast message up to round $3t$ in net-work $\mathcal{N} \in \mathcal{X}$ when protocol π' is run on $\mathcal{N}$ only if*

$$|Clan_{\mathcal{N}}(u) \cap \eta_{3j+1}(u)| = 1, \quad for\ some\ j < t.$$

The proof of this proposition easily follows by induction, by the observation that the behavior of a node $v \in Clan_{\mathcal{N}}(u)$ is independent of the topology of $\mathcal{N}$ up to the first transmission of u.

Since π' completes broadcasting in $3\sqrt{n}$ rounds, it follows that for all $\mathcal{N} \in \mathcal{X}$ there exists a $j \leq \sqrt{n}$ such that $|Clan_{\mathcal{N}}(u) \cap \eta_{3j+1}(u)| = 1$. But this implies that the set $\Gamma = \{\eta_{3j+1}(u) : j = 0, \dots, \sqrt{n}\}$ (where $|\Gamma| = 3\sqrt{n}$) is a $\sqrt{n}$-selective family for the set $\Delta = \{Clan_{\mathcal{N}}(u) : \mathcal{N} \in \mathcal{X}\}$.

Theorem 3, however requires the following relation must hold between Γ and Δ,

$$|\Gamma| \geq \lg_2 |\Delta| - \frac{11}{12}\sqrt{n}\lg_2\frac{16n}{\sqrt{n}} \tag{1}$$

By lemma 2, we have that each network $\mathcal{N} \in \mathcal{X}$ is associated with a distinct clan. So $|\Delta| = |\mathcal{X}|$. And by clause (3) of lemma 2 we have $\lg_2 |\mathcal{X}| \geq \frac{13}{14}\sqrt{n}\lg_2(\sqrt{n}+1)$

Plugging in the values in equation (1) we have,

$$|\Gamma| \geq \lg_2 |\Delta| - \frac{11}{12}\sqrt{n}\lg_2\frac{16n}{\sqrt{n}}$$

$$\geq \frac{13}{14}\sqrt{n}\lg_2(\sqrt{n}+1) - \frac{11}{12}\sqrt{n}\lg_2\frac{16n}{\sqrt{n}}$$

$$\geq \frac{1}{85}\sqrt{n}\lg_2\sqrt{n}$$

for large values of n.

Contradiction, as $|\Gamma| \leq 3\sqrt{n}$. Hence, there exists no deterministic protocol that completes broadcast in at most $\sqrt{n}$ rounds in every $\mathcal{C}_2$ network. $\square$

Note: The combinatorial argument in Lemma 2 can be circumvented by an oracle argument as follows. The advice string provided to nodes in L_1 is composed of $\sqrt{n}$ blocks. Each of these blocks is either ϕ or the connectivity information of a clan. Instead of treating ϕ as one bit of information one can use an oracle argument and substitute ϕ with the connectivity information of two clans, chosen arbitrarily from the set of clans whose member nodes transmitted in the corresponding round. One may now argue that if the advice string has just $o(\sqrt{n})$ blocks then a large number of clans get no help from the source. A Selective family or Hitting set argument can now be used to prove that $\Omega(\sqrt{n})$ rounds are still necessary for completion of broadcasting in the residual network. We note here a weakness of the oracle based argument: For a more general model when ϕ_i (ϕ_2 is received when two nodes transmit) is received by a node when i of its neighbors transmit in the same round, the substitution of ϕ_i by the connectivity information of i clans, whose members transmitted in that round, provides too much information to the network to argue the lower bound.

5   Reductions (Proof of Lemma 1)

Fix a network $\mathcal{N} \in \mathcal{C}_2$. First, we introduce some notation. Let π be a deterministic broadcast protocol, let w be a node in the network, and let $t \geq 0$. Then, we define

- $\mathbb{H}(\pi, \mathbf{w}, \mathbf{t})$ maintains the communication history of node w up to round t, in the form of a list of pairs corresponding to the messages transmitted and received by w in each round.

Note that, from the model description in Section 3, at most one of the elements in each pair of $\mathbb{H}(\pi, \mathbf{w}, \mathbf{t})$ can be different from ϕ. Morever, the behavior of node w during round $t + 1$ is completely determined by its inputs and the contents of $\mathbb{H}(\pi, \mathbf{w}, \mathbf{t})$.

5.1   Reduction 1

This reduction shows that we may consider protocols with a simplified communication structure, at the cost of a constant factor increase in the number of rounds to complete broadcast. In these protocols, the nodes coordinate their transmissions such that collisions involving nodes from different layers do not occur.

Claim. Assume there exists a protocol π that completes broadcast in at most r rounds. Then, there exists a protocol π' that completes broadcast in at most $3r$ rounds, such that, for $i = 0, 1, 2$, nodes in layer L_i transmit in round t only if $t \equiv i (mod 3)$.

Proof. Protocol π' simulates each round t of protocol π with a sequence of 3 rounds: $3t, 3t + 1, 3t + 2$. The idea is that, in round $3t + i$, each node in layer L_i takes the same action that it would take in round t under protocol π.

Assuming that π' has a description of protocol π, it is sufficient to show that each node w can compute the contents of $\mathbb{H}(\pi, \mathbf{w}, \mathbf{t})$ for all $0 \leq t \leq r$. This can be proved by induction as follows.

Suppose that at the beginning of round t node w has the correct history of the communication under protocol π up to this point. This certainly holds for $t = 0$. Now, assuming that this holds for round $t - 1$, it is easy to see that it will hold for round t if the following rule is applied:

- If w transmits message μ in one of the rounds $3t, 3t + 1, 3t + 2$, then append the pair $\langle \mu, \phi \rangle$ to the history list.
- If w does not transmit and exactly one message μ is received in rounds $3t, 3t + 1, 3t + 2$, then append the pair $\langle \phi, \mu \rangle$ to the history list.
- In any other case, append the pair $\langle \phi, \phi \rangle$ to the history list.

Clearly, π' completes broadcast in $3r$ rounds if π completes broadcast in r rounds.

We denote by Π_1 the class of protocols satisfying the conditions of claim 5.1.

5.2   Reduction 2

This reduction shows that instead of transmitting arbitrary messages the source can just send topological information. The idea is that, receiving the labels and connectivity of the nodes in a component, the remaining nodes can recover the original messages by simulation.

Claim. Assume there exists a protocol π from class Π_1 that completes broadcasting in at most $3r$ rounds. Then, there exists protocol π' such that

- the source is provided with Advice String $\Upsilon(\pi, \mathcal{N}, 3r)$ as input;
- for each $0 < t \leq r$, the source transmits $\Upsilon[3t - 2]$ in round $3t$.

that completes broadcasting in at most $3r$ rounds.

Proof. (Sketch) Clearly, it is enough to construct a protocol π' in which the source behaves as described in the claim, and in each round the nodes in layers L_1, L_2 transmit exactly the same messages that they would send under protocol π. In fact, since the nodes in L_2 are not connected to the source, it is sufficient to show that the nodes in L_1 can behave as specified (nodes in L_2 just simulate protocol π).

The argument that follows is based on a simple observation. Let S denote a subset of the nodes in network $\mathcal{N}$. If a node w has the description of protocol π, knows the topology of S (labels and connectivity), and knows all the messages received by a node in S from a node in $\mathcal{N} - S$ up to round t, then w can simulate the behavior of the nodes in S to [recover/compute] all the messages that each of these nodes would send under protocol π up to round $t + 1$.

Assume first that all the messages sent by the source up to round $3(t - 1)$ are ϕ. This means that the source does not receive any message up to round $3(t-1) - 1$ under protocol π. Thus, each node w in L_1 can simulate the behavior of the source under protocol π to recover all the messages that the source would send up to round $3(t - 1)$. Based on this information, node w just simulates its own behavior under protocol π to compute which message to send (if any) in round $3(t - 1) + 1$.

Now, assume that in round $3t$, for the first time, the source transmits a message different from ϕ, consisting of the description of the topology of component C_i. Suppose first that C_i is composed by a single orphan node v. Let w be any other node in L_1. Recall that w knows all the messages sent by the source up to round $3(t - 1)$ under protocol π. So, when w receives the label of v in round $3t$, it can simulate the behavior of node v under protocol to recover the message received by the source in round $3(t-1) + 1$. With this information, w simulates the behavior of the source to recover the message sent by it in round $3t$, and finally simulates its own behavior under protocol π to compute the message it should in round $3t + 1$.

Now, suppose that component C_i consists of head node u and the nodes in $Clan_{\mathcal{N}}(u)$. Then, again, when a node in layer L_1 receives the description of the topology of C_i, it can simulate the behavior of each node in C_i to recover the message received by the source in round $3(t-1) + 1$, then simulate the behavior of the source up to round $3t$, and finally simulate the behavior of w to compute which message to send in round $3t + 1$.

An easy inductive argument completes the proof of the claim.

We denote by Π_2 the class of protocols satifying the properties stated in claim 5.2.

5.3   Reduction 3

The following easy reduction completes the proof of lemma 1.

Claim. Assume there exists a protocol π from class Π_2 that completes broadcasting in at most $3r$ rounds. Then, there exists a protocol π' such that

- In round 0 the source transmits the broadcast message and Advice String $\Upsilon(\pi, \mathcal{N}, 3r)$;
- Source remains silent in every round $t > 0$.

that completes broadcasting at most $3r$ rounds.

6   Conclusions

We proved a lower bound of $\Omega(\sqrt{n})$ rounds for a deterministic protocol to complete broadcasting in radius 2 network. The outstanding open problem resulting from this work is whether this lower bound can be further improved. Kowalski-Pelc [4], conjecture that the lower bound proved here is optimal.

The technique of quantifying the amount of information learned by a node in the first r rounds of an arbitrary protocol, is of independent interest. To the best of our knowledge, this idea has not been explored in the context of radio networks. We believe that it could be useful to prove stronger results to bridge the gap between the lower and upper bounds on the broadcasting problem. It could also be applied on more general networks and other problems in radio networks like gossiping.

Acknowledgements. Dariusz Kowalski and Andrzej Pelc suggested that the lower bound proved by them may be improvable. The class of networks for which we explored the new lower bound was in fact discovered during a discussion with them. Gunes Ercal participated in useful discussions in the earlier stages of the work. Oded Goldreich's, Chen Avin's and annoymous referees comments were helpful in improving the presentation of this work. We thank all of them.

References

1. N. Alon, A. Bar-Noy, N. Linial and D. Peleg. *A lower bound for radio broadcast*, Journal of Computer Science and System Sciences 43(1991),290-298.
2. B. Awerbuch. *A new distributed depth-first-search algorithm*, Information Processing Letters 20 (1985), 147-150.
3. R. Bar-Yehuda, O.Goldreich, and A. Itai. *On the time complexity of broadcast in radio networks: an exponential gap between determinism and randomization*, Journal of Computer and System Sciences 45 (1992), 104-126
4. Andrzej Pelc. Personal communication, November 2002.
5. A. Czumaj, W. Rytter. *Broadcasting Algorithms in Radio Networks with Unknown Topology*, To appear in Proceedings of the 44th Annual IEEE Symposium on Foundations of Computer Science (FOCS'03), Cambridge, MA.
6. B. Bruschi and M. Del Pinto. *Lower bounds for the broadcast problem in mobile radio networks*, Distr. Comp. 10(1997), 129-135
7. I. Chlamtac and A. Farago. *Making transmission schedule immune to topology changes in multi-hop packet radio networks*, IEEE/ACM Trans. on Networking 2(1994), 23-29
8. I. Chlamtac and O. Weinstein. *The wave expansion approach to broadcasting in multihop radio networks*, IEEE Trans. on Communications 39(1991), 426-433.
9. B.S. Chelbus, L. Gasieniec, A. Gibbons, A. Pelc and W. Rytter. *Deterministic broadcasting in unknown radio networks*, 11th ACM-SIAM SODA, 861-870
10. B.S. Chelbus, L. Gasieniec, A. Gibbons, A. Ostlin and J.M. Robson. *Deterministic radio broadcasting*. Proc. 27th Int. Collo. on Automata, Languages and Programming (ICALP'2000),LNCS 1853, 717-728
11. M. Chrobak, L. Gasieniec and W. Rytter. *Fast broadcasting and gossiping in radio networks*, Proc. 41st Symposium an Foundations of Computer Science (FOCS'2000), 575-581
12. A.E.F. Clementi, A. Monti and R. Silvestri. *Selective families, superimposed codes, and broadcasting on unknown radio networks*, Proc. 12th Ann. ACM-SIAM Symposium on Discrete Algorithms (SODA'2001), 709-718
13. Cruz, R., and Hajek, B., *A new upper bound to the throughput of a multi-access broadcast channel.*, IEEE Trans. Inf. Theory IT-28, 3 (May 1982), 402-405.
14. G. De Marco and A. Pelc. *Faster broadcasting in unknown radio networks*, Information Processing Letter 79(2001),53-56.
15. P. Erdös, P. Frankl, and Z. Furedi. *Families of finite sets in which no set is covered by the union of r others*, Israel Journal of Math. 51(1985),79-89.
16. I.Gabour and Y. Mansour, *Broadcast in radio networks*, Proc. 6th Ann. ACM-SIAM Symp. on Discrete Algorithms (SODA'1996),577-585.
17. F.K.Hwang. *The time complexity of deterministic broadcast in radio networks*, Discrete Applied Mathematics 60(1995),219-222.

18. P. Indyk, *Explicit constructions of selector and related combinatorial structures, with applications*, Proc. 13th Ann. ACM-SIAM Symposium on Disceret Algorithms (SODA'2002), 697-704.
19. W.H.Kauz and R.R.C. Singleton, *Nonrandom binary superimposed codes*, IEEE Trans. on Information Theory 10(1964), 363-377.
20. E. Kushilevitz and Y. Mansour, *An $\Omega(D\log(N/D))$ lower bound for broadcast in radio networks*, SIAM J. on Computing 27(1998), 702-712
21. M. MOLLE, *Unifications and extensions of the multiple access communications problem*. Ph.D. Thesis, University of California, Los Angeles, Los Angeles, Calif., July 1981.
22. O. Reingold, S. Vadhan and A. Wigderson, *Entropy waves, the zig-zag product, and new constant degree expanders and extractors*, Proc. 41st Symposium on Foundations of Computer Science (FOCS'2000)3-13
23. Dariusz R. Kowalski and Andrzej Pelc, *Deterministic Broadcasting Time in Radio Networks of Unknown Topology*, Accepted to Proc. 43rd Symposium on Foundations of Computer Science (FOCS'2002)
24. Ming Li, Paul Vitanyi, *Introduction to Kolmogorov Complexity and it's applications*, Springer Verlag, Second Edition
25. Thomas M. Cover, Joy A. Thomas *Elements of Information Theory*, Wiley Series in Telecommunications, 1990
26. *Errata regarding "On the Time-Complexity of Broadcast in Radio Networks: An Exponential Gap Between Determinism and Randomization"*, Dec. 2002, available from $http://www.wisdom.weizmann.ac.il/oded/p_bgi.html$

A New Model for Selfish Routing*

Thomas Lücking[1], Marios Mavronicolas[2][**], Burkhard Monien[1], and
Manuel Rode[1]

[1] Faculty of Computer Science, Electrical Engineering and Mathematics, University
of Paderborn, Fürstenallee 11, 33102 Paderborn, Germany.
{luck,bm,rode}@uni-paderborn.de
[2] Department of Computer Science, University of Cyprus, P. O. Box 20537, Nicosia
CY-1678, Cyprus. mavronic@ucy.ac.cy

Abstract. In this work, we introduce and study a new model for *selfish
routing* over *non-cooperative networks* that combines features from the
two such best studied models, namely the *KP model* and the *Wardrop
model* in an interesting way.

We consider a set of n *users,* each using a *mixed strategy* to ship its
unsplittable traffic over a *network* consisting of m parallel *links.* In a
Nash equilibrium, no *user* can increase its *Individual Cost* by unilaterally
deviating from its strategy. To evaluate the performance of such Nash
equilibria, we introduce *Quadratic Social Cost* as a certain *sum* of Individual Costs – namely, the sum of the expectations of the squares of
the incurred *link latencies.* This definition is unlike the KP model, where
Maximum Social Cost has been defined as the *maximum* of Individual
Costs.

We analyse the impact of our modeling assumptions on the computation
of *Quadratic Social Cost,* on the structure of worst-case Nash equilibria,
and on bounds on the *Quadratic Coordination Ratio.*

1 Introduction

1.1 Motivation and Framework

Nash Equilibria and Outline. *Nash equilibrium* [23,24] is arguably the most
robust equilibrium concept in (non-cooperative) Game Theory.[1] At a Nash equilibrium, no player of a strategic game can unilaterally improve its objective by
switching to a different *strategy.* In a *pure* Nash equilibrium, each player chooses
exactly one strategy (with probability one); in a *mixed* Nash equilibrium, the
choices of each player are modeled by a probability distribution over strategies.
Of special interest to our work is the *fully mixed Nash equilibrium* [22], where

---

* This work has been partially supported by the IST Program of the European Union
under contract numbers IST-1999-14186 (**ALCOM-FT**) and IST-2001-33116 (**FLAGS**),
and by research funds at University of Cyprus.
** Part of the work of this author was performed while visiting Faculty of Computer
Science, Electrical Engineering and Mathematics, University of Paderborn.
[1] See [25] for a concise introduction to contemporary Game Theory.

V. Diekert and M. Habib (Eds.): STACS 2004, LNCS 2996, pp. 547–558, 2004.
© Springer-Verlag Berlin Heidelberg 2004

each user chooses each strategy with non-zero probability. Nash equilibria have some very nice properties; most notably, for finite games, there always exists a mixed Nash equilibrium [24].

In this work, we embark on a systematic study, within a new model for *selfish routing* over *non-cooperative networks* that we introduce, of some interesting algorithmic and mathematical properties of Nash equilibria for some specific *routing game* formulated in this context. Our new model for selfish routing is an interesting hybridization of the two most famous models for selfish routing that were studied in the literature before; these are the so called *KP model* [19] and *Wardrop model* [4,30].

The KP Model and the Wardrop Model. The KP and the Wardrop models differ with respect to the assumptions they are making about: 1. the structure of the *routing network*; 2. the *splittability* or *unsplittability* of the users' *traffics*; 3. the definition of *Individual Cost* for a user they use for defining Nash equilibria; 4. the type of Nash equilibria (pure or mixed) they consider; 5. the specific definitions they employ for *Social Cost*, a performance measure for Nash equilibria, and for *Social Optimum*, an optimality measure for traffic assignments (not necessarily equilibria). The definitions for Social Cost usually relate to Individual Costs. In either model, these two definitions give rise to *Coordination Ratio*, the maximum value of the ratio of Social Cost over Social Optimum; a *worst-case* Nash equilibrium is one that maximizes its particular Social Cost.

In the KP model, a collection of n users is assumed; each user employs a *mixed strategy*, which is a probability distribution over m parallel *links*, to control the shipping of its own assigned *traffic*. In the KP model, traffics are *unsplittable*. For each link, a *capacity* specifies the rate at which the link processes traffic. Allowing link capacities to vary arbitrarily gives rise to the standard model of *related links*. A special case of the model of related links is the model of *identical links*, where all link capacities are identical. Reciprocally, in the model of *identical users*, all user traffics are equal; they may vary arbitrarily in the model of *arbitrary users*. In a Nash equilibrium, each user selfishly routes its traffic on those links that minimize its *Individual Cost*: its *expected latency cost* on that link, given the network congestion caused by the other users. In the KP model, the Social Cost of a Nash Equilibrium, henceforth called *Maximum Social Cost*, is the expectation, over all random choices of the users, of the maximum, over all links, *latency* through a link; the Social Optimum, henceforth called the *Maximum Social Optimum*, is the *least possible* maximum, over all links, latency through a link that could be attained had global regulation been available; correspondingly, the Coordination Ratio in the KP model will henceforth be called the *Maximum Coordination Ratio*. It follows that the Maximum Social Cost in the KP model is the *maximum* of Individual Costs.

In the Wardrop model [11,30], there have been considered *arbitrary* networks with *latency functions* for edges. Moreover, the traffics are *splittable* into arbitrary pieces. Here, unregulated traffic is modeled as a *network flow*. *Equilibrium flows* have been classified as flows with all flow paths used between a given pair of a *source* and a *destination* having the same latency. Equilibrium flows are optimal solutions to a convex program, in case the edge latency functions are convex. An equilibrium in this model can be interpreted as a Nash equilibrium in a game with infinitely many users, each carrying an infinitesimal amount of traffic from a *source* to a *destination*. Thus, the Wardrop model restricts to pure Nash equilibria. The *Individual Cost* of a user is defined as the sum of the edge *latencies* on a path from the user's source to its destination. The *Social Cost* of a Nash equilibrium is the sum of all Individual Costs. The *Social Optimum* is the least possible, over all network flows, sum of Individual Costs.

The New Model for Selfish Routing. Our new model for selfish routing over non-cooperative networks is a hybridization of the KP model [19] and the Wardrop model [11,30]. More specifically, we follow the KP model to consider the simple parallel links network (which, however, is also a special case for the Wardrop model). We also follow the KP model to consider unsplittable traffics and mixed Nash equilibria. The Individual Cost we adopt is also identical to that adopted in the KP model – the expected latency cost on a link. However, we follow the Wardrop model to model Social Cost as a certain *sum* of Individual Costs, which we will later describe. In some sense, our new model is the Wardrop model restricted to the simple parallel links network but modified to allow for unsplittable traffics and for mixed strategies; these two features were borrowed from the KP model. Our work is the *first* step toward accommodating unsplittable traffics within the Wardrop model.

For any link, consider the *square* of the traffic through the link divided by the link capacity; taking the expectation of this and adding up over all links yields the Social Cost for our model. Call it *Quadratic Social Cost*. In correspondence with Quadratic Social Cost, we also define and study in our new model *Quadratic Optimum* and *Quadratic Coordination Ratio*. Naturally, the former is the *least possible* sum of the squares of total traffic through a link divided by the link capacity; the latter is the maximum value of the ratio of Quadratic Social Cost over Quadratic Social Optimum. Since Nash equilibria are defined with respect to Individual Costs (but are independent of Social Cost), the Nash equilibria in our new model coincide with those in the KP-model since the two adopt the same Individual Costs.

Note that the commutativity between expectation and sum in the definition of Quadratic Social Cost has been unavailable (between expectation and maximum) in the definition of Maximum Social Cost for the KP model. So, this commutativity allows hopes for some more tractable analysis of several problems regarding some interesting algorithmic, combinatorial, structural and optimality properties of Nash equilibria in the new model.

1.2 Contribution and Significance

We partition our results into three major groups.

Combinatorial Expressions for Quadratic Social Cost. In the most general model of arbitrary users and arbitrary links, we obtain an elegant, recursive combinatorial formula for Quadratic Social Cost, implying a dynamic programming algorithm to compute Quadratic Social Cost. Furthermore, we derive simple, combinatorial expressions for the Quadratic Social Cost of the fully mixed Nash equilibrium in case of arbitrary users and identical links, and identical users and arbitrary links, respectively.

The Worst-case Nash Equilibrium. A natural problem that arises in the context of Quadratic Social Cost is to identify the *worst-case* Nash equilibrium – the one that maximizes, for each specific choice of user traffics and link capacities, the Quadratic Social Cost. We address this problem in the particular setting of the model of identical users and identical links, where the fully mixed Nash equilibrium always exists. We prove that, in this particular setting, the worst-case Nash equilibrium is the fully mixed Nash equilibrium.

Bounds on Quadratic Coordination Ratio. For the model of arbitrary users and identical links we prove that the Quadratic Coordination Ratio for pure Nash equilibria is precisely $\frac{9}{8}$. In case of identical users and related links, we discover that the Quadratic Coordination Ratio for pure Nash equilibria increases slightly to $\frac{4}{3}$. We next turn to the model of arbitrary users and identical links. Here, we restrict ourselves to the fully mixed Nash equilibrium. For this setting, we prove an upper bound of $2 - \frac{1}{m}$ on Quadratic Coordination Ratio. For identical users the Quadratic Social Cost of the fully mixed Nash equilibrium slightly drops to $1 + \min\{\frac{m-1}{n}, \frac{n-1}{m}\}$ times the optimal Quadratic Social Cost. Since in this setting the fully mixed Nash equilibrium is the worst-case Nash equilibrium, this bound holds for the Quadratic Coordination Ratio.

1.3   Related Work and Comparison

The KP model was first introduced in the work of Koutsoupias and Papadimitriou [19]; it was further studied in [9,10,12,14,16,17,18,21,22]. Fully mixed Nash equilibria were introduced and analyzed in [22]. Bounds on Maximum Coordination Ratio were proved in [9,14,18,22]. The works by Fotakis *et al.* [16], by Gairing *et al.* [17], and by Lücking *et al.* [21] dwelved into the combinatorial structure and the computational complexity of Nash equilibria for the KP model. In particular, the Fully Mixed Nash Equilibrium Conjecture was motivated by some results in [16], explicitly formulated in [17] and further studied in [21]. The Wardrop model was defined in [30] and further studied in [3,4,11]. Recent studies of selfish routing within the Wardrop model include [27,28,29].

Fotakis *et al.* [16, Theorem 8] proved that computing the Maximum Social Cost of an arbitrary Nash equilibrium is a #$\mathcal{P}$-complete problem. This hardness result stands in very sharp contrast to our general, pseudopolynomial algorithm to compute Quadratic Social Cost (Theorem 1).

For the KP model, there are known bounds on Maximum Coordination Ratio of $\Theta\left(\frac{\lg m}{\lg \lg m}\right)$ for the model of arbitrary users and identical links [9,18,19,22], of $\Theta\left(\frac{\lg m}{\lg \lg \lg m}\right)$ for the model of arbitrary users and related links [9], and of $O\left(\sqrt{m}\right)$ for the model of arbitrary users and related links and for pure Nash equilibria [14], which improves the previous bound for small values of m. Some of these super-constant bounds stand in very sharp contrast to some of the constant bounds (independent of m and n) on Quadratic Coordination Ratio we prove in this work. However, for the Wardrop model, there have been shown constant bounds on Coordination Ratio [27,28,29].

Other works that have studied Coordination Ratio include [13] for a network creation game and [2] for a network design game. For a survey of recent work on selfish routing in non-cooperative networks, see [15]. Work in the scheduling literature that has considered quadratic cost functions for *makespan* includes [1, 6,8,20]; work in the networking literature that has considered quadratic cost functions for network delay includes [7].

1.4   Road Map

The rest of this paper is organized as follows. Section 2 presents our definitions and some preliminaries. The Quadratic Social Cost of Nash equilibria is studied in Section 3. Section 4 proves that the fully mixed Nash equilibrium maximizes Quadratic Social Cost in the model of identical users and identical links. Our bounds on Quadratic Coordination Ratio are presented in Section 5. Due to lack of space the proofs are omitted. They can be found in the full version.

2   Framework

2.1   Mathematical Preliminaries and Notation

Throughout, denote for any integer $m \geq 2$, $[m] = \{1, \ldots, m\}$. For a random variable X, denote $\mathcal{E}(X)$ the *expectation* of X. We continue to prove a simple combinatorial inequality.

Lemma 1. *For any* $k, a, b \in \mathbb{N}$ *with* $0 < k \leq a \leq b$, $\frac{1}{a^k}\binom{a}{k} \leq \frac{1}{b^k}\binom{b}{k}$.

Finally, we prove a combinatorial lemma that will be useful in a later proof.

Lemma 2. *Fix any real number* a, *where* $0 < a < 1$, *and positive integer* r, *and set* $A = \frac{r}{a}$. *Then,* $\sum_{1 \leq k \leq r}\binom{r}{k}k^2\left(\frac{1}{a}\right)^k\left(1 - \frac{1}{a}\right)^{r-k} = A + \frac{r-1}{r}A^2$.

2.2   General

We consider a *network* consisting of a set of m parallel *links* $1, 2, \ldots, m$ from a *source* node to a *destination* node. Each of n *network users* $1, 2, \ldots, n$, or *users* for short, wishes to route a particular amount of traffic along a (non-fixed) link from source to destination. (Throughout, we will be using subscripts for users and superscripts for links.)

Denote w_i the *traffic* of user $i \in [n]$. Define the $n \times 1$ *traffic vector* **w** in the natural way. Assume throughout that $m > 1$ and $n > 1$. Assume also, without loss of generality, that $w_1 \geq w_2 \geq \ldots \geq w_n$. Denote $W = \sum_{i \in [n]} w_i$.

A *pure strategy* for user $i \in [n]$ is some specific link. A *mixed strategy* for user $i \in [n]$ is a probability distribution over pure strategies; thus, a mixed strategy is a probability distribution over the set of links. The *support* of the mixed strategy for user $i \in [n]$, denoted sup(i), is the set of those pure strategies (links) to which i assigns positive probability. A *pure strategy profile* is represented by an n-tuple $\langle \ell_1, \ell_2, \ldots, \ell_n \rangle \in [m]^n$; a *mixed strategy profile* is represented by an $n \times m$ *probability matrix* **P** of nm probabilities p_i^j, $i \in [n]$ and $j \in [m]$, where p_i^j is the probability that user i chooses link j.

For a probability matrix $\mathbf{P}$, define *indicator variables* $I_i^j \in \{0,1\}$, where $i \in [n]$ and $j \in [m]$, such that $I_i^j = 1$ if and only if $p_i^j > 0$. Thus, the support of the mixed strategy for user $i \in [n]$ is the set $\{j \in [m] \mid I_i^j = 1\}$. For each link $j \in [m]$, define the *view* of link j, denoted $view(j)$, as the set of users $i \in [n]$ that potentially assign their traffics to link j; so, $view(j) = \{i \in [n] \mid I_i^j = 1\}$. For each link $j \in [m]$, denote $V^j = |view(j)|$.

A mixed strategy profile $\mathbf{P}$ is *fully mixed* [22, Section 2.2] if for all users $i \in [n]$ and links $j \in [m]$, $I_i^j = 1$. Throughout, we will cast a pure strategy profile as a special case of a mixed strategy profile in which all (mixed) strategies are pure.

2.3   System, Models, and Cost Measures

Denote $c^\ell > 0$ the *capacity* of link $\ell \in [m]$, representing the rate at which the link processes traffic. So, the *latency* for traffic w through link ℓ equals w/c^ℓ. In the model of *uniform capacities*, all link capacities are equal to c, for some constant $c > 0$; link capacities may vary arbitrarily in the model of *arbitrary capacities*. Assume throughout, without loss of generality, that $c^1 \geq c^2 \geq \ldots \geq c^m$. Denote $C = \sum_{j \in [m]} c^j$. In the model of *identical traffics*, all user traffics are equal to 1; user traffics may vary arbitrarily in the model of *arbitrary traffics*.

For a pure strategy profile $\langle \ell_1, \ell_2, \ldots, \ell_n \rangle$, the *latency cost for user* $i \in [n]$, denoted λ_i, is $(\sum_{k:\ell_k=\ell_i} w_k)/c^{\ell_i}$; that is, the latency cost for user i is the latency of the link it chooses. For a mixed strategy profile $\mathbf{P}$, denote δ^ℓ the *actual traffic* on link $\ell \in [m]$; so, δ^ℓ is a random variable. For each link $\ell \in [m]$, denote θ^ℓ the *expected traffic* on link $\ell \in [m]$; thus, $\theta^\ell = \mathcal{E}(\delta^\ell) = \sum_{i=1}^n p_i^\ell w_i$. Given $\mathbf{P}$, define the $m \times 1$ *expected traffic vector* Θ induced by $\mathbf{P}$ in the natural way. Given $\mathbf{P}$, denote Λ^ℓ the *expected latency* on link $\ell \in [m]$; clearly, $\Lambda^\ell = \frac{\theta^\ell}{c^\ell}$. Define the $m \times 1$ *expected latency vector* Λ in the natural way. For a mixed strategy profile $\mathbf{P}$, the *expected latency cost* for user $i \in [n]$ on link $\ell \in [m]$, denoted λ_i^ℓ, is the expectation, over all random choices of the remaining users, of the latency cost for user i had its traffic been assigned to link ℓ; thus,

$$\lambda_i^\ell = \frac{w_i + \sum_{k=1, k \neq i} p_k^\ell w_k}{c^\ell} = \frac{(1 - p_i^\ell)w_i + \theta^\ell}{c^\ell}.$$

For each user $i \in [n]$, the *minimum expected latency cost*, denoted λ_i, is the minimum, over all links $\ell \in [m]$, of the expected latency cost for user i on link ℓ; thus, $\lambda_i = \min_{\ell \in [m]} \lambda_i^\ell$. For a probability matrix $\mathbf{P}$, define the $n \times 1$ *minimum expected latency cost vector* λ induced by $\mathbf{P}$ in the natural way.

Associated with a traffic vector $\mathbf{w}$, a capacity vector $\mathbf{c}$ and a mixed strategy profile $\mathbf{P}$ is the *Quadratic Social Cost*, denoted $\mathsf{QSC}(\mathbf{w}, \mathbf{c}, \mathbf{P})$, which is the expectation of the sum of squares of the incurred link latencies; thus,

$$\mathsf{QSC}(\mathbf{w}, \mathbf{c}, \mathbf{P}) = \mathcal{E} \left(\sum_{\ell \in [m]} \frac{\left(\sum_{k:\ell_k=\ell} w_k \right)^2}{c^\ell} \right)$$

$$= \sum_{\langle \ell_1, \ell_2, \ldots, \ell_n \rangle \in [m]^n} \left(\prod_{k=1}^n p_k^{\ell_k} \cdot \sum_{\ell \in [m]} \frac{\left(\sum_{k:\ell_k=\ell} w_k \right)^2}{c^\ell} \right).$$

Since the expectation of a sum is equal to the sum of expectations, we can write

$$QSC(\mathbf{w}, \mathbf{c}, \mathbf{P}) = \sum_{\ell \in [m]} \sum_{A \subset [n]} \left(\prod_{i \in A} p_i^\ell \right) \left(\prod_{i \notin A} (1 - p_i^\ell) \right) \frac{\left(\sum_{k:\ell_k=\ell} w_k \right)^2}{c^\ell}. \quad (1)$$

The *Quadratic Optimum* associated with a traffic vector $\mathbf{w}$ and a capacity vector $\mathbf{c}$, denoted $QOPT(\mathbf{w}, \mathbf{c})$, is the *least possible* sum of squares of the incurred link latencies. Note that while $QSC(\mathbf{w}, \mathbf{c}, \mathbf{P})$ is defined in relation to a mixed strategy profile $\mathbf{P}$, $QOPT(\mathbf{w}, \mathbf{c})$ refers to the *optimum* pure strategy profile.

The *Maximum Social Cost*, denoted $MSC(\mathbf{w}, \mathbf{c}, \mathbf{P})$, which is used in the original KP model, is defined as the expectation of the maximum of the incurred link latencies. Correspondingly, the *Maximum Optimum*, denoted $MOPT(\mathbf{w}, \mathbf{c})$, is the minimum, over all assignments, maximum incurred link latency.

2.4 Nash Equilibria

We are interested in a special class of mixed strategies called Nash equilibria [24] that we describe below. Formally, the probability matrix $\mathbf{P}$ is a *Nash equilibrium* [19, Section 2] if for all users $i \in [n]$ and links $\ell \in [m]$, $\lambda_i^\ell = \lambda_i$ if $I_i^\ell = 1$, and $\lambda_i^\ell > \lambda_i$ if $I_i^\ell = 0$. Thus, each user assigns its traffic with positive probability only on links (possibly more than one of them) for which its expected latency cost is minimized; this implies that there is no incentive for a user to unilaterally deviate from its mixed strategy in order to avoid links on which its expected latency cost is higher than necessary.

Mavronicolas and Spirakis [22, Lemma 15] show that in the model of arbitrary users and identical links, all links are equiprobable in a fully mixed Nash equilibrium.

Lemma 3 (Mavronicolas and Spirakis [22]). *Consider the model of arbitrary users and identical links. Then, there exists a unique fully mixed Nash equilibrium with associated Nash probabilities $p_i^\ell = 1/m$, for any user $i \in [n]$ and link $\ell \in [m]$.*

2.5 Coordination Ratio and Quadratic Coordination Ratio

The *Quadratic Coordination Ratio* is the maximum value, over all traffic vectors $\mathbf{w}$, capacity vectors $\mathbf{c}$, and Nash equilibria $\mathbf{P}$ of the ratio $\frac{QSC(\mathbf{w},\mathbf{c},\mathbf{P})}{QOPT(\mathbf{w},\mathbf{c})}$. In a corresponding way, the *Maximum Coordination Ratio* is defined in [19] as the maximum value, over all traffic vectors $\mathbf{w}$, capacity vectors $\mathbf{c}$ and Nash equilibria $\mathbf{P}$ of the ratio $\frac{MSC(\mathbf{w},\mathbf{c},\mathbf{P})}{MOPT(\mathbf{w},\mathbf{c})}$.

3 The Quadratic Social Cost of Nash Equilibria

In this section, we study the Quadratic Social Cost of arbitrary (mixed) Nash equilibria. We start by proving:

Theorem 1 (Quadratic Social Cost of Arbitrary Nash Equilibrium).
Fix any traffic vector **w**, *any capacity vector* **c**, *and any arbitrary Nash equilibrium* **P**. *Then,* QSC $(\mathbf{w}, \mathbf{c}, \mathbf{P})$ *can be computed in time* $O(nmW)$.

We next establish that the Quadratic Social Cost takes a particularly nice form for the case of the fully mixed Nash equilibrium. We prove:

Theorem 2 (Quadratic Social Cost of Fully Mixed Nash Equilibrium).
Consider the model of arbitrary users and identical links. Then, for any traffic vector **w**,

$$QSC(\mathbf{w}, \mathbf{F}) = W_1 + \frac{2}{m} W_2,$$

where $W_1 = \sum_{i \in [n]} w_i^2$ *and* $W_2 = \sum_{i,k \in [n], i \neq k} w_i w_k$.

The next Lemma is used in the proof of Proposition 1.

Lemma 4. *Let* $a, n \in \mathbb{N}$, a *even, let* $p_i \in [0,1]$ *for all* $1 \leq i \leq n$. *Denote* $P = (p_1, \ldots, p_n)$ *and* $p = \sum_{1 \leq i \leq n} p_i$. *Set*

$$H(P) = \sum_{A \subset [n]} |A|^a \left\{ \prod_{i \in A} p_i \right\} \left\{ \prod_{j \notin A} (1 - p_j) \right\}.$$

Define $\tilde{P}$ *by* $\tilde{p}_i = \frac{1}{n} \cdot p$ *for all* $1 \leq i \leq n$. *Then* $H(P) \leq H(\tilde{P})$.

Proposition 1. *Consider the model of identical users and identical links. Then, for any arbitrary Nash equilibrium* **P**,

$$QSC(\mathbf{P}) \leq \sum_{j \in [m]} \left(\theta^j + \frac{r_j - 1}{r_j} (\theta^j)^2 \right),$$

where $\theta^j = \sum_{i \in [n]} p_i^j$ *and* $r_j = |view(j)|$.

We finally prove:

Theorem 3. *Consider the model of identical users and related links. Then,*

$$QSC(\mathbf{c}, \mathbf{F}) = \frac{n(n + m - 1)}{C}.$$

Corollary 1 (Quadratic Social Cost of Fully Mixed Nash Equilibrium).
Consider the model of identical users and identical links. Then,

$$QSC(\mathbf{w}, \mathbf{c}, \mathbf{F}) = \frac{n(n + m - 1)}{m}.$$

4   The Worst-Case Nash Equilibrium

We now establish that, for the model of identical users and identical links, the worst-case Nash equilibrium is the fully mixed Nash equilibrium. We start our proof with a technical lemma which holds in the more general model of arbitrary users, and then return to the model of identical users and identical links.

Lemma 5. *Consider n arbitrary users on m identical links, and let $j, k \in [m]$.*

1. *If $view(j) = view(k) \neq \emptyset$, then $|view(j)| = 1$ or $\theta^j = \theta^k$ and $p_i^j = p_i^k$ for all $i \in [n]$.*
2. *If $view(j) \subsetneq view(k)$, then $\theta^j > \theta^k$.*

Theorem 4. *Consider the model of identical users and identical links. Then, for any arbitrary Nash equilibrium $\mathbf{P}$, $\mathrm{QSC}\,(\mathbf{w}, \mathbf{c}, \mathbf{P}) \leq \mathrm{QSC}\,(\mathbf{w}, \mathbf{c}, \mathbf{F})$.*

5   Bounds on Quadratic Coordination Ratio

In this section, we present our bounds on Quadratic Coordination Ratio. We start by proving:

Theorem 5 (Quadratic Coordination Ratio for Pure Nash Equilibria).
Consider the model of arbitrary users and identical links, restricted to pure Nash equilibria. Then,

$$\max_{\mathbf{w}, \mathbf{P}} \frac{\mathrm{QSC}\,(\mathbf{w}, \mathbf{P})}{\mathrm{QOPT}\,(\mathbf{w})} = \frac{9}{8}.$$

We give here only a sketch of the proof. Let there be n users and m links. If $n \leq m$, then every pure Nash equilibrium has optimal social cost. Now assume $n > m$. Let $\mathbf{P}$ be any pure Nash equilibrium. Let us first assume that $w_i \leq \frac{W}{m}$ holds for all users $i \in [n]$. Let $B = \min_{j \in [m]} \delta^j$ be the minimum traffic on any of the links. Then $B > 0$, and it has been shown in [17], that on every link the load is bounded by $2B$.

We use some iterative procedure to compute an upper bound for $\mathrm{QSC}(\mathbf{w}, \mathbf{c}, \mathbf{P})$. When the algorithm terminates, then we know that there exists some $k \in [m]$, such that

- $\mathrm{QSC}(\mathbf{w}, \mathbf{c}, \mathbf{P}) \leq \sum_{j \in [m]} x_j^2$,
- $x_j = 2B$ for k links,
- $x_j = B + x$, $0 \leq x \leq B$, for one link, and
- $x_j = B$ for $m - k - 1$ links.

Note, that $\mathrm{QOPT}(\mathbf{w}, \mathbf{c}) \geq \frac{W2}{m}$, and therefore

$$\frac{\mathrm{QSC}(\mathbf{w}, \mathbf{c}, \mathbf{P})}{\mathrm{QOPT}(\mathbf{w}, \mathbf{c})} \leq \frac{((3k + m - 1)B2 + (B + x)2)m}{(mB + kB + x)2} = f(k).$$

Maximizing the function $f(k)$ shows the upper bound for the case that $w_i \leq \frac{W}{m}$ for all $i \in [n]$.

In case that $w_i > \frac{W}{m}$ holds for some user $i \in [n]$, such a user is alone on its link in every Nash equilibrium $\mathbf{P}$, and both the user and the link can be omitted, increasing the coordination ratio. To show tightness, we give an instance.

We continue by a similar result for the reciprocal case of identical users and related links:

Theorem 6 (Quadratic Coordination Ratio for Pure Nash Equilibria). *Consider the model of identical users and related links, restricted to pure Nash equilibria. Then,*

$$\max_{\mathbf{w},\mathbf{c},\mathbf{P}} \frac{\mathsf{QSC}\,(\mathbf{w},\mathbf{c},\mathbf{P})}{\mathsf{QOPT}\,(\mathbf{w},\mathbf{c})} = \frac{4}{3}.$$

We give here only a sketch of the full proof. First, we show that no instance with traffic vector $\mathbf{w} = \{1\}^n$, capacity vector $\mathbf{c}$ and pure Nash equilibrium $\mathbf{P}$ exists with Quadratic Coordination Ratio greater than $\frac{4}{3}$. Therefore, we assume, by way of contradiction, that such an instance exists, and fix the minimal (in the number of links) such counterexample, its worst case Nash equilibrium $\mathbf{P}$ and an optimal assignment $\mathbf{Q}$. We denote the traffic of each link j by $\delta^j(\mathbf{P})$ when referring to $\mathbf{P}$, and by $\delta^j(\mathbf{Q})$ when referring to the optimum assignment. Lemma 6 shows, that $\delta^j(\mathbf{P})$ is at most by one smaller than $\delta^j(\mathbf{Q})$ for any link j. Lemma 7 shows, that for the instance under consideration, only for exactly one link k, $\delta^k(\mathbf{P})$ is greater than $\delta^k(\mathbf{Q})$, and that no link has the same traffic according to $\mathbf{P}$ and $\mathbf{Q}$. This implies $\delta^k(\mathbf{P}) = \delta^k(\mathbf{Q}) + m - 1$, because all remaining links must have $\delta^j(\mathbf{P}) = \delta^j(\mathbf{Q}) - 1$. Lemma 8 shows, that, if not all links except for k have the same capacity c^j and the same traffic, then we can create a new instance with $m - 1$ identical links, having the same traffic, and one additional link, which has at least the same Quadratic Coordination Ratio. Hence, we can consider this new instance in order to bound the Quadratic Coordination Ratio of the original instance from above. To do so, we write down an optimization problem which overestimates the Quadratic Coordination Ratio of the new instance and includes, as constraints, the Nash equilibrium property and optimality criterion from Lemma 9. The optimization problem evaluates to $\frac{4}{3}$, which contradicts the initial assumption.

To proof that the bound is tight, we construct an instance with Quadratic Coordination Ratio $\frac{4}{3}$ for any number of links m.

Lemma 6. *Let $(\mathbf{w},\mathbf{c})$, $\mathbf{Q}$, $\mathbf{P}$, $\delta^j(\mathbf{Q})$ and $\delta^j(\mathbf{P})$ be as in the proof of Theorem 6. Then, $\delta^j(\mathbf{Q}) - \delta^j(\mathbf{P}) \leq 1$ for all $j \in [m]$.*

Lemma 7. *Let $(\mathbf{w},\mathbf{c})$, $\mathbf{Q}$, $\mathbf{P}$, $\delta^j(\mathbf{Q})$ and $\delta^j(\mathbf{P})$ be as in the proof of Theorem 6. Then, $\delta^k(\mathbf{P}) = \delta^k(\mathbf{Q}) + m - 1$ for some $k \in [m]$, and $\delta^j(\mathbf{P}) = \delta^j(\mathbf{Q}) - 1$ for all $j \in [m]\backslash\{k\}$.*

Lemma 8. *Let* $(\mathbf{w}, \mathbf{c})$, $\mathbf{Q}$, $\mathbf{P}$, $\delta^j(\mathbf{Q})$ *and* $\delta^j(\mathbf{P})$ *be as in the proof of Theorem 6. Then, there exists an instance* $(\tilde{\mathbf{w}}, \tilde{\mathbf{c}})$ *that has the same number* m *of links as* $(\mathbf{w}, \mathbf{c})$ *with optimal assignment* $\tilde{\mathbf{Q}}$, *Nash equilibrium assignment* $\tilde{\mathbf{P}}$, *such that* $\delta^k(\tilde{\mathbf{P}}) = \delta^k(\tilde{\mathbf{Q}}) + m - 1$ *for some link* $k \in [m]$, $\delta^i(\tilde{\mathbf{Q}}) = \delta^j(\tilde{\mathbf{Q}})$ *and* $\tilde{c}_i = \tilde{c}_j$ *for all* $i, j \in [m] \backslash \{k\}$ *and* $\frac{\mathsf{QSC}(\tilde{\mathbf{w}}, \tilde{\mathbf{c}}, \tilde{\mathbf{P}})}{\mathsf{QOPT}(\tilde{\mathbf{w}}, \tilde{\mathbf{c}})} \geq \frac{\mathsf{QSC}(\mathbf{w}, \mathbf{c}, \mathbf{P})}{\mathsf{QOPT}(\mathbf{w}, \mathbf{c})}$.

Lemma 9. *Let* $\mathbf{Q}$ *be any pure assignment for an instance* $(\mathbf{w}, \mathbf{c})$ *of the model of identical traffics and related links, let* $\mathbf{w} = (w, \ldots, w)$. *Then,* $\mathbf{Q}$ *is optimal, i.e.,* $\mathsf{QSC}(\mathbf{w}, \mathbf{c}, \mathbf{Q}) = \mathsf{QOPT}(\mathbf{w}, \mathbf{c})$, *if and only if for every pair of links* $i, j \in [m]$

$$\frac{(\delta^i(\mathbf{Q}) + w)^2}{c_i} + \frac{(\delta^j(\mathbf{Q}) - w)^2}{c_j} \geq \frac{(\delta^i(\mathbf{Q}))^2}{c_i} + \frac{(\delta^j(\mathbf{Q}))^2}{c_j}.$$

We next prove:

Theorem 7. *Consider the model of arbitrary users and identical links. Then,*

$$\max_{\mathbf{w}, \mathbf{c}} \frac{\mathsf{QSC}(\mathbf{w}, \mathbf{c}, \mathbf{F})}{\mathsf{QOPT}(\mathbf{w}, \mathbf{c})} \leq 2 - \frac{1}{m}.$$

We next prove:

Theorem 8. *Consider the model of identical users and identical links. Then, for any traffic vector* $\mathbf{w}$, *capacity vector* $\mathbf{c}$ *and mixed Nash equilibrium* $\mathbf{P}$,

$$\frac{\mathsf{QSC}(\mathbf{w}, \mathbf{c}, \mathbf{P})}{\mathsf{QOPT}(\mathbf{w}, \mathbf{c})} \leq 1 + \min \left\{ \frac{m-1}{n}, \frac{n-1}{m} \right\} \leq 2 - \frac{1}{m}.$$

Acknowledgments. We thank Rainer Feldmann and Martin Gairing for several helpful discussions.

References

1. N. Alon, Y. Azar, G. J. Woeginger and T. Yadid, Approximation Schemes for Scheduling, *Proc. of SODA 1997*, pp. 493–500.
2. E. Anshelevich, A. Dasgupta, É. Tardos, and T. Wexler, Near-Optimal Network Design with Selfish Agents, *Proc. of STOC 2003*, pp. 511–520.
3. M. J. Beckmann, On the Theory of Traffic Flow in Networks, *Traffic Quart*, Vol. 21, pp. 109–116, 1967.
4. M. Beckmann, C. B. McGuire and C. B. Winsten, *Studies in the Economics of Transportation*, Yale University Press, 1956.
5. D. Braess, Über ein Paradoxen aus der Verkehrsplanung, *Unternehmensforschung*, Vol. 12, pp. 258–268, 1968.
6. A. K. Chandra and C. K. Wong, Worst-case Analysis of a Placement Algorithm Related to Storage Allocation, *SICOMP 1975*, Vol. 4, pp. 249–263.
7. E. Altman, T. Basar, T. Jimenez and N. Shimkin, Competitive Routing in Networks with Polynomial Costs, *IEEE Transactions on Automatic Control*, Vol. 47, pp. 92–96, 2002.

8. R. A. Cody and E. G. Coffman, Jr., Record Allocation for Minimizing Expected Retrieval Costs on Crum-Like Storage Devices, *JACM,* Vol. 23, pp. 103–115, 1976.
9. A. Czumaj and B. Vöcking, Tight Bounds for Worst-Case Equilibria, *Proc. of SODA 2002,* pp. 413–420.
10. A. Czumaj, P. Krysta and B. Vöcking, Selfish Traffic Allocation for Server Farms, *Proc. of STOC 2002,* pp. 287–296.
11. S. C. Dafermos and F. T. Sparrow, The Traffic Assignment Problem for a General Network. *Journal of Research of the National Bureau of Standards,* Series B, Vol. 73B, pp. 91–118, 1969.
12. E. Even-Dar, A. Kesselman and Y. Mansour, "Convergence Time to Nash Equilibria," *Proc. of ICALP 2003,* J. C. M. Baeten, J. K. Lenstra, J. Parrow and G. J. Woeginger eds., Vol. 2719, pp. 502–513.
13. A. Fabrikant, A. Luthra, E. Maneva, C. H. Papadimitriou, and S. Shenker, On a Network Creation Game, *Proc. of PODC 2003,* pp. 347–351.
14. R. Feldmann, M. Gairing, T. Lücking, B. Monien and M. Rode, Nashification and the Coordination Ratio for a Selfish Routing Game, *Proc. of ICALP 2003,* Vol. 2719, pp. 514–526.
15. R. Feldmann, M. Gairing, T. Lücking, B. Monien and M. Rode, Selfish Routing in Non-Cooperative Networks: A Survey, *Proc. of MFCS 2003,* Vol. 2747, pp. 21–45.
16. D. Fotakis, S. Kontogiannis, E. Koutsoupias, M. Mavronicolas and P. Spirakis, The Structure and Complexity of Nash Equilibria for a Selfish Routing Game, *Proc. of ICALP 2002,* Vol. 2380, pp. 123–134.
17. M. Gairing, T. Lücking, M. Mavronicolas, B. Monien and P. Spirakis, The Structure and Complexity of Extreme Nash Equilibria, submitted for publication, 2003.
18. E. Koutsoupias, M. Mavronicolas and P. Spirakis, Approximate Equilibria and Ball Fusion, *Proc. of SIROCCO 2002,* pp. 223–235.
19. E. Koutsoupias and C. H. Papadimitriou, Worst-case Equilibria, *Proc. of STACS 1999,* G. Meinel and S. Tison eds., Vol. 1563, pp. 404–413.
20. J. Y. T. Leung and W. D. Wei, Tighter Bounds on a Heuristic for a Partition Problem, *Information Processing Letters,* Vol. 56, pp. 51–57, 1995.
21. T. Lücking, M. Mavronicolas, B. Monien, M. Rode, P. Spirakis and I. Vrto, Which is the Worst-case Nash equilibrium?, *Proc. of MFCS 2003,* B. Rovan and P. Vojtas eds., Vol. 2747, pp. 551–561.
22. M. Mavronicolas and P. Spirakis, The Price of Selfish Routing, *Proc. of STOC 2001,* pp. 510–519.
23. J. F. Nash, Equilibrium Points in N-Person Games, *Proceedings of the National Academy of Sciences,* Vol. 36, pp. 48–49, 1950.
24. J. F. Nash, Non-cooperative Games, *Annals of Mathematics,* Vol. 54, No. 2, pp. 286–295, 1951.
25. M. J. Osborne and A. Rubinstein, *A Course in Game Theory,* The MIT Press, 1994.
26. C. H. Papadimitriou, Algorithms, Games and the Internet, *Proc. of STOC 2001,* pp. 749–753.
27. T. Roughgarden, The Price of Anarchy is Independent of the Network Topology, *Proc. of STOC 2002,* pp. 428–437.
28. T. Roughgarden, *Selfish Routing,* Ph. D. Thesis, Department of Computer Science, Cornell University, May 2002.
29. T. Roughgarden and É. Tardos, How Bad is Selfish Routing? *JACM,* Vol. 49, pp. 236–259, 2002.
30. J. G. Wardrop. Some Theoretical Aspects of Road Traffic Research, *Proceedings of the of the Institute of Civil Engineers,* Pt. II, Vol. 1, pp. 325–378, 1952.

Broadcast in the Rendezvous Model

Philippe Duchon, Nicolas Hanusse, Nasser Saheb, and Akka Zemmari

LaBRI - CNRS - Université Bordeaux I, 351 Cours de la Liberation, 33405 Talence, France. {duchon,hanusse,saheb,zemmari}@labri.fr

Abstract. In many large, distributed or mobile networks, broadcast algorithms are used to update information stored at the nodes. In this paper, we propose a new model of communication based on *rendezvous* and analyze a *multi-hop distributed algorithm* to *broadcast* a message in a *synchronous* setting. In the *rendezvous model*, two neighbors u and v can communicate if and only if u calls v and v calls u simultaneously. Thus nodes u and v obtain a rendezvous at a meeting point. If m is the number of meeting points, the network can be modeled by a graph of n vertices and m edges. At each round, every vertex chooses a random neighbor and there is a rendezvous if an edge has been chosen by its two extremities. Rendezvous enable an exchange of information between the two entities. We get sharp lower and upper bounds on the time complexity in terms of number of rounds to broadcast: we show that, for any graph, the expected number of rounds is between $\log n$ and $O(n^2)$. For these two bounds, we prove that there exist some graphs for which the expected number of rounds is either $O(\log n)$ or $\Omega(n^2)$. For specific topologies, additional bounds are given.

Keywords: Algorithms and data structures, distributed algorithms, graph, broadcast, rendezvous model

1 Introduction

Among the numerous algorithms to broadcast in a synchronized setting, we are witnessing a new tendency of distributed and randomized algorithms, also called *gossip-based algorithms*: at each instant, any number of broadcasts can take place simultaneously and we do not give any priority to any particular one. In each round, a node chooses a random neighbor and tries to exchange some information. Due to the simplicity of gossip-based algorithm, such an approach provides reliability and scalability. Contrary to deterministic schemes for which messages tend to route in a particular subgraph (for instance a tree), a gossip-based algorithm can be fault-tolerant (or efficient for a dynamic network) since in a strongly connected network, many paths can be used to transmit a message to almost every node.

The majority of results deal with the *uniform random phone call* for which a node chooses a neighbor uniformly at random. However, such a model does not take into account that a given node could be "called" by many nodes simultaneously implying a potential congestion. A more embarrassing situation is

V. Diekert and M. Habib (Eds.): STACS 2004, LNCS 2996, pp. 559–570, 2004.

the one of the *radio networks* in which a node should be called simultaneously by a unique neighbor otherwise the received messages are in collision. In the *rendezvous model*, every node chooses a neighbor and if two neighbors choose themselves mutually, they can exchange some information. The *rendezvous model* is useful if a physical meeting is needed to communicate as in the case of robots network.

Although the *rendezvous model* can be used in different settings, we describe the problem of broadcasting a message in a network of robots. A robot is an autonomous entity with a bounded amount of memory having the capacity to perform some tasks and to communicate with other entities by radio when they are geographically close. Examples of use of such robots are numerous: exploration [1,7], navigation (see Survey of [16]), capture of an intruder [3], search for information, help to handicapped people or rescue, cleaning of buildings, ... The literature contains many efficient algorithms for one robot and multiple robots are seen as a way to speed up the algorithms. However, in a network of robots [4], the coordination of multiple robots implies complex algorithms. *Rendezvous* between robots can be used in the following setting: consider a set of robots distributed on a geometric environment. Even if two robots sharing a region of navigation (called neighbors) might communicate, they should also be close enough. It may happen that their own tasks do not give them the opportunity to meet (because their routes are deterministic and never cross) or it may take a long time if they navigate at random. A solution consists in deciding on a meeting point for each pair of neighbor robots. If two neighbors are close to a given meeting point at the same time, they have a *rendezvous* and can communicate.

Although there exist many algorithms to broadcast messages, we only deal with algorithms working under a very weak assumption: each node or robot only knows its neighbors or its own meeting points. This implies that the underlying topology is *unknown*. Depending on the context, we might also be interested in *anonymous* networks in which the labeling of the nodes (or history of the visited nodes) is not used. By anonymous, we mean that unique identities are not available to distinguish nodes (processors) or edges (links). In a robot network, the network can have two (or more) meeting points with the same label if the environment contains two pairs of regions that do not overlap. The anonymous setting can be encountered in dynamic, mobile or heterogeneous networks.

1.1 Related Works

How to broadcast efficiently a message with a very poor knowledge on the topology of an *anonymous* network ? Depending on the context, this problem is related to the way a "rumor" or an "epidemic" spreads in a graph. In the literature, a node is *contaminated* if it knows the rumor. The broadcast algorithm highly depends on the communication model. For instance, in the *k-ports model*, a node can send a message to at most k neighbors. Thus our rendezvous model is a 1-port model.

The performance of a broadcast algorithm is measured by the time required to contaminate all the nodes, the amount of memory stored at each node or the total number of messages. In this article, we analyze the time complexity in a synchronous setting of a rendezvous algorithm (although several broadcast algorithms including ours can work in an asynchronous setting, the theoretical time complexity is usually analyzed in a synchronous model).

Many broadcast algorithms exist (see the survey by Hedetniemi *et al.* [10]) but few of them are related to our model. The closest model is the one of Feige *et al.* [8]. The authors prove general lower and upper bounds ($\log_2 n$ and $O(n \log n)$) on the time to broadcast a message *with high probability* in any unknown graph. A contaminated node chooses a neighbor uniformly at random but no rendezvous are needed. In our model, the time complexity increases since a rendezvous has to be obtained to communicate. For a family of small-world graphs and other models (2-ports model but a node can only transmit a given message a bounded number of times), Comellas *et al.* [6] showed that a broadcast can always be done. A recent work of Karp *et al.*[11] deals with the *random phone call model*. In each round, each node u chooses another node v uniformly at random (more or less as in [8]) but the transmission of a rumor is done either from the caller to the called node (*push transmission algorithm*) or from the called node to the caller (*pull transmission algorithm*). The underlying topology is the complete graph and they prove that any rumor broadcasted in $O(\ln n)$ rounds needs to send $\omega(n)$ messages on expectation.

However, the results of random call phone [8,11] do not imply the presented results in the rendezvous model:

- The classes of graphs for which the broadcast runs fast or slowly are different in the rendezvous model and in the random phone call model. For instance, the lower bound is $\Omega(\log n)$ for the two models but for the complete graph, the broadcast time of $O(\log n)$ is close to the lower bound in the random phone call model whereas it becomes $\theta(n \log n)$ in the rendezvous model.
- We deal with the expected broadcast time. Depending on the topology, this time can be either equal or different to the broadcast time with high probability[1].

In the radio network setting (n-ports model), some algorithms and bounds exist whether the topology is known or unknown (see the survey of Chlebus [5]). However, the model of communication is different from ours: simultaneously, a node can send a message to all of its neighbors and a node can receive a message if and only if a unique neighbor send a message. Two kinds of algorithms are proposed in the radio model : with or without collision detection. In our model, there is no problem of collision.

Rendezvous in a broadcast protocol are used in applications like Dynamic Host Configuration Protocol but to the best of our knowledge, the analysis of a *randomized* rendezvous algorithm to broadcast in a network is new. The random rendezvous model was introduced in [13] in which the authors compute the expected number of rendezvous per round in a randomized algorithm. Their algorithm is a solution to implement synchronous message passing in an anonymous network that passes messages asynchronously [17]. Many concurrent programming languages including CSP and Ada use this method to define

---

[1] High probability means with probability $1 - O(n^{-c})$ for some positive constant c.

a communication between pairs of asynchronous processes. Angluin [2] proved that there is no deterministic algorithm for this problem (see the paper of Lynch [12] containing many problems having no deterministic solutions in distributed computing) . In [14], the rendezvous are used to elect randomly a leader in an anonymous graph.

1.2   The Model

Let $G = (V, E)$ be a connected and undirected graph of n vertices and m edges. For convenience and with respect to the problem of spreading an epidemic, a vertex is *contaminated* if it has received the message sent by an *initial vertex* v_0.

The model can be implemented in a fully distributed way. The complexity analysis, however based on the concept of *rounds*, is commonly used in similar studies [8,13,14]. In our article, a *round* is the following sequence:

- for each $v \in V$, choose uniformly at random an incident edge.
- if an edge (v_i, v_j) has been chosen by v_i and v_j, there is a rendezvous.
- if there is a rendezvous and if only v_i is contaminated, then v_j becomes contaminated.

T_G is the *broadcast time* or *contamination time*, that is the number of rounds until all vertices of graph G are contaminated. T_G is an integer-valued random variable; in this paper, we concentrate the study on its expectation $\mathbb{E}(T_G)$.

Some remarks can be made on our model. As explained in the introduction, the rendezvous process (the first two steps of the round) keeps repeating forever and should be seen as a way of maintaining connectivity. Several broadcasts can take place simultaneously and we do not give any priority to any one of them, even if we study a broadcast starting from a given vertex v_0.

We concentrate our effort on $\mathbb{E}(T_G)$ and we do not require that the algorithm finds out when the rumor sent by v_0 has reached all the nodes. However some hints can be given: we can stop the broadcast algorithm (do not run the third step of the round) using a local control mechanism in each node of the network: if identities of the nodes are available (non anonymous networks), each node keeps into its memory a list of contaminated neighbors for each rumor and when this list contains all the neighbors, the process may stop trying to contaminate them (with the same rumor). If the network is anonymous and the number of nodes n is known, then it is possible to prove that in $O(n^2 \log n)$ rounds with high probability, all the neighbors of a contaminated node know the rumor.

In our algorithm, nodes of large degree and a large diameter increase the contamination time. Taking two adjacent nodes v_i and v_j of degrees d_i and d_j respectively, the expected number of rounds to contaminate v_j from v_i is $d_i d_j$. For instance, take two stars of $n/2$ leaves. Join each center by an edge. In the rendezvous model, the expected broadcast time is $\Theta(n^2)$ whereas in [8]'s model, it will be $\Theta(n \log n)$ on expectation and with high probability. Starting from this example, $\mathbb{E}(T_G)$ can easily be upper bounded by $O(n^3)$ but we find a tighter upper bound.

1.3   Our Results

The main result of the paper is to prove in Section 2 that for any graph G, $\log_2 n \leq \mathbb{E}(T_G) \leq O(n^2)$. More precisely, for any graph G of maximal degree Δ, $\mathbb{E}(T_G) = O(\Delta n)$.

In Section 3, we show that there are some graphs for which the expected broadcast time asymptotically matches either the lower bound or the upper bound up to a constant factor. For instance, for the complete balanced binary tree, $\mathbb{E}(T_G) = O(\log_2 n)$ whereas $\mathbb{E}(T_G) = \Omega(n^2)$ for the double star graph (two identical stars joined by one edge). For graphs of bounded degree Δ and diameter D, we also prove in Section 3 that $\mathbb{E}(T_G) = O(D\Delta^2 \ln \Delta)$. This upper bound is tight since for Δ-ary complete trees of diameter D, $\mathbb{E}(T_G) = \Omega(D\Delta^2 \ln \Delta)$. The complete graph was proved [13] to have the least expected number of rendezvous per round; nevertheless, its expected broadcast time is $\Theta(n \ln n)$. Due to space limitations, proofs of lemmas and corollaries are not given.

2   Arbitrary Graphs

The first section presents some terminology and basic lemmas that are useful for the main results.

2.1   Generalities on the Broadcast Process

The rendezvous process induces a *broadcast process*, that is, for each nonnegative integer t, we get a (random) set of vertices, V_t, which is the set of vertices that have been reached by the broadcast after t rounds of rendezvous. The sequence $(V_t)_{t \in \mathbb{N}}$ is a *homogeneous, increasing Markov process* with state space $\{U : \emptyset \subsetneq U \subset V\}$. Any state U contains the initial vertex v_0 and the subgraph induced by U is connected. State V as its sole absorbing state; thus, for each graph G, this process reaches state V (that is, the broadcast is complete) in finite expected time.

The transition probabilities for this Markov chain (V_k) depend on the rendezvous model. Specifically, if U and U' are two nonempty subsets of V, the transition probability $p_{U,U'}$ is 0 if $U \not\subseteq U'$, and, if $U \subseteq U'$, $p_{U,U'}$ is the probability that, on a given round of rendezvous, $U' - U$ is the set of vertices not in U that have a rendezvous with a vertex in U. Thus, the *loop probability* $p_{U,U}$ is the probability that each vertex in U either has no rendezvous, or has one with another vertex in U.

In the sequel, what we call the *broadcast sequence* is the sequence of *distinct* states visited by the broadcast process between the initial state $\{v_0\}$ and the final absorbing state V. A *possible broadcast sequence* is any sequence of states that has a positive probability of being the broadcast sequence; this is any sequence $\mathcal{X} = (X_1, \ldots, X_m)$ such that $X_1 = V_0 = \{v_0\}$, $X_m = V$, and $p_{X_k, X_{k+1}} > 0$ for all k.

By d_u we denote the degree of vertex u. For a bounded degree graph, Δ is the maximal degree of the graph. By D we denote the diameter of the graph.

If $X_k = V_t$ is the set of the k contaminated vertices at time t then Y_k is the set of remaining vertices. We define the cut C_k as the set of edges that have one endpoint in X_k and the other in Y_k.

For any edge $a = (u, v) \in E$, $\mathbb{P}(a) = (d_u d_v)^{-1}$ (resp. $\mathbb{P}(\overline{a})$) is the probability that edge a will obtain (resp. not obtain) a rendezvous at a given round. The product $(d_u d_v)^{-1}$ is also called the *weight* of the edge a.

We also define two values for any set of edges $C \subset E$: $\mathbb{P}(\mathcal{E}_C)$ (resp. $\mathbb{P}(\overline{\mathcal{E}_C})$) where $\mathcal{E}_C$ is the event of obtaining a rendezvous in a round for at least one edge (resp. no edge) in C; and $\pi(C) = \sum_{a \in C} \mathbb{P}(a)$. While $\pi(C)$ has no direct probabilistic interpretation, it is much easier to deal with in computations. Obviously, $\mathbb{P}(\mathcal{E}_C) \leq \pi(C)$ holds for any C. Lemma 2 provides us with a *lower bound* for $\mathbb{P}(\mathcal{E}_C)$ of the form $\Omega(\pi(C))$ provided $\pi(C)$ is not too large.

With these notations, for any set of vertices U, $p_{U,U} = 1 - \mathbb{P}(\mathcal{E}_{C_U})$, where C_U is the set of edges that have exactly one endpoint in U (the *cut* defined by the partition $(U, V - U)$).

Lemma 1. *Let* $a \in E$ *and for any* $C \subset E$, $\mathbb{P}(a \mid \overline{\mathcal{E}_C}) \geq \mathbb{P}(a)$.

Lemma 2. *For any* $C \subset E$, $\mathbb{P}(\mathcal{E}_C) \geq \lambda \min(1, \pi(C))$ *with* $\lambda = 1 - e^{-1}$ *where* $e = exp(1)$.

Corollary 1.

$$\frac{1}{\mathbb{P}(\mathcal{E}_C)} \leq \frac{e}{e-1} \max\left(1, \frac{1}{\pi(C)}\right) \leq \frac{e}{e-1}\left(1 + \frac{1}{\pi(C)}\right). \qquad (1)$$

Lemma 3. *For any graph* G, *any integer* k *and any* $p \in (0, 1)$, *if* $\mathbb{P}(T_G > k) \leq p$ *then* $\mathbb{E}(T_G) \leq k/(1-p)$.

Since the number of contaminated vertices can be at most doubled at each round, we have the following trivial lower bound

Theorem 1. *For any graph* G, $T_G \geq \log_2 n$ *with probability 1.*

2.2   The General Upper Bound

We will prove the following :

Theorem 2. *For any connected graph* G *with* n *vertices and maximum degree* Δ, *the broadcast time* T_G *satisfies*

$$\mathbb{E}(T_G) \leq \frac{e}{e-1}(n-1)(6\Delta + 1). \qquad (2)$$

The proof of this theorem is a bit involved; we will sketch it before stating and proving a few lemmas.

The probability distribution for the full broadcast time T_G is not known, but, when *conditioned* by the sequence of states visited by the broadcast process, it becomes a sum of independent geometric random variables, for which the parameters are known exactly (Lemma 4). Thus, the conditional expectation of the broadcast time becomes the weight of some trajectory, which is defined as a sum of weights for the visited states. Each individual weight is upper bounded by an expression that only depends on individual rendezvous probabilities (Lemma 2 and Corollary 1), and then a uniform upper bound is obtained for the conditional expectations (Lemma 5); this uniform upper bound then straightforwardly translates into an upper bound for the (unconditional) expected broadcast time.

The next lemma is stated in a more general setting than our broadcasting process.

Lemma 4. *Let $(M_t)_{t \in \mathbb{N}}$ be a homogeneous Markov chain with finite state space S and transition probabilities $(p_{x,y})_{x,y \in S}$.*

Let $(T_k)_{k \in \mathbb{N}}$ denote the increasing sequence of stopping times defined by

$$T_0 = 0$$
$$T_{k+1} = \inf\{t > T_k : M_t \neq M_{T_k}\},$$

and let $(M'_k)_{k \in \mathbb{N}}$ be the "trajectory" chain defined by

$$M'_k = \begin{cases} M_{T_k} & \text{if } T_k < \infty, \\ M'_{k-1} & \text{if } T_k = \infty. \end{cases}$$

Then, for any sequence $x_0, \ldots x_N$ such that $x_{k+1} \neq x_k$ and $p_{x_k, x_{k+1}} > 0$ for $0 \leq k \leq N - 1$, conditioned on $M'_k = x_k$ for $0 \leq k \leq N$, $\mathcal{T} = (T_{k+1} - T_k)_{0 \leq k \leq N-1}$ is distributed as a vector of independent geometric random variables with respective parameters $1 - p_{x_k, x_k}$.

Corollary 2. *Let $\mathcal{V}$ denote the trajectory of the loopless broadcast process (written M' in the statement of Lemma 4).*

Let $\mathcal{X} = (X_1, \ldots, X_m)$ be any possible broadcast sequence, and $\mathcal{C} = (C_1, \ldots, C_{m-1})$ the corresponding sequence of cuts. Then

$$\mathbb{E}(T_G | \mathcal{V} = \mathcal{X}) = \sum_{k=1}^{m-1} \frac{1}{\mathbb{P}(\mathcal{E}_{C_k})}.$$

Lemma 5. *Define the weight of any possible broadcast sequence $\mathcal{X}$ as*

$$w(\mathcal{X}) = \sum_{k=1}^{m-1} \frac{1}{\pi(C_k)}. \tag{3}$$

Then

$$w(\mathcal{X}) \leq 6(n - 1)\Delta, \tag{4}$$

where Δ is the maximum degree of G.

Proof. We begin by noting that, since we are looking for a uniform upper bound on the weight, we can assume that $m = n$, which is equivalent to $|X_k| = k$ for all k. If such is not the case in a sequence $\mathcal{X}$, then we can obtain another possible sequence $\mathcal{X}'$ with a higher weight by inserting an additional set X' between any two consecutive sets X_k and X_{k+1} such that $|X_{k+1} - X_k| \geq 2$ (with the condition that $p_{X_k, X'}$ and $p_{X', X_{k+1}}$ are both positive; such an X' always exists, because each edge of every graph has positive probability of being the only rendezvous edge in a given round). This will just add a positive term to the weight of the sequence; thus, the sequence with the maximum weight satisfies $m = n$.

To prove that $\sum_{k=1}^{n-1} 1/\pi(C_k) \leq 6(n-1)\Delta$, we prove that the integer interval $[1, n-1]$ can be partitioned into a sequence of smaller intervals, such that, on each interval, the average value of $1/\pi(C_k)$ is at most 6Δ.

Assume that integers 1 to $k-1$ have been thus partitioned, and let us consider C_k. If $\pi(C_k) \geq 1/(4\Delta)$ (that is, $1/\pi(C_k) \leq 4\Delta < 6\Delta$), we put k into an interval by itself and move on to $k+1$. We now assume that $\pi(C_k) < 1/(4\Delta)$, and set $1/\pi(C_k) = \alpha\Delta$ with $\alpha > 4$.

Let v be the next vertex to be reached by the broadcast after X_k, that is, $\{v\} = X_{k+1} - X_k$. This vertex must have at least one neighbor u in X_k.

Let $d \geq 1$ denote the number of neighbors of v that are in X_k. Each edge incident to v has weight at least $1/(d_v\Delta)$, and d of them are in C_k, so that we have $d/(d_v\Delta) \leq \pi(C_k) = 1/(\alpha\Delta)$, or equivalently,

$$d \leq d_v/\alpha. \tag{5}$$

Thus, $v \in X_{k+1}$ has $d_v - d$ neighbors in $Y_{k+1} = V - X_{k+1}$. Since at most one of them is added to X at each step of the sequence, this means that, for $0 \leq j \leq d_v - d$, Y_{k+1+j} contains at least $d_v - d - j$ neighbors of v. In other words, C_{k+1+j} contains at least $d_v - d - j$ edges that are incident to v, each of which has weight at least $1/(d_v\Delta)$. Consequently,

$$\frac{1}{\pi(C_{k+1+j})} \leq \frac{d_v\Delta}{d_v - d - j} \tag{6}$$

holds for $0 \leq j \leq d_v - d$.

The right-hand side of (6) increases with j, and for $j = \lfloor d_v/4 \rfloor$ (recall eq. (5) and $\alpha > 4$), it is

$$\frac{d_v\Delta}{d_v - d - \lfloor d_v/4 \rfloor} \leq \frac{d_v\Delta}{d_v - 2\lfloor d_v/4 \rfloor}$$
$$\leq \frac{d_v\Delta}{\lceil d_v/2 \rceil}$$
$$\leq 2\Delta.$$

Summing (6) over $0 \leq j \leq \lfloor d_v/4 \rfloor$, we obtain

$$\sum_{j=0}^{\lfloor d_v/4 \rfloor} \frac{1}{\pi(C_k + 1 + j)} \leq 2\Delta \left(1 + \frac{d_v}{4}\right). \tag{7}$$

Since $d_v \geq \alpha$, we also have $1/\pi(C_k) \leq d_v\Delta$. Adding this to 7, we now get

$$\frac{1}{\pi(C_k)} + \sum_{0 \leq j \leq \lfloor d_v/4 \rfloor} \frac{1}{\pi(C_k + 1 + j)} \leq \Delta\left(\alpha + 2 + \frac{d_v}{2}\right)$$

$$\leq \Delta\left(2 + \frac{3d_v}{2}\right).$$

There are $2 + \lfloor d_v/4 \rfloor \geq 1 + \frac{d_v}{4}$ terms in the left-hand side of this inequality, so that the average value of $1/\pi(C_i)$, when i ranges over $[k, k + 1 + \lfloor d_v/4 \rfloor]$, is at most

$$\Delta\frac{2 + \frac{3d_v}{2}}{1 + \frac{d_v}{4}} \leq 6\Delta. \tag{8}$$

This concludes the recursion, and the proof.

Proof (Theorem 2).
    Let $\mathcal{X}$ be any possible broadcast sequence as in Lemma 5. Applying Corollary 1 to $C = C_k$ and summing over k, we get

$$\sum_k \frac{1}{\mathbb{P}(\mathcal{E}_{C_k})} \leq \frac{e}{e-1}\left(n - 1 + \sum_k \frac{1}{\pi(C_k)}\right). \tag{9}$$

By Lemma 5, the right-hand side of (9) is at most

$$\frac{e}{e-1}\left(n - 1 + 6\Delta(n-1)\right) = \frac{e(n-1)(6\Delta+1)}{e-1}. \tag{10}$$

By Lemma 4, the left-hand side of (9) is the conditional expectation of T_G. The upper bound remains valid upon taking a convex linear combination, so that we get, as claimed,

$$\mathbb{E}(T_G) \leq \frac{e(n-1)(6\Delta+1)}{e-1}. \tag{11}$$

Note: It should be clear that the constants are not best possible, even with our method of proof. They are, however, quite sufficient for our purpose, which is to obtain a uniform bound on the expected broadcast time.

3   Specific Graphs

Theorems 1 and 2 provide lower and upper bounds on the expected contamination time for any graph. In this section, we prove that there exists some graphs for which the bounds can be attained.

    The well-known coupon-collector problem (that is the number of trials required to obtain n different coupons if each round one is chosen randomly and independently. See [15] for instance) implies the next lemma:

Lemma 6. *For a star S of n leaves, $\mathbb{E}(T_S) = n \ln n + O(n)$.*

3.1   The l-Star Graphs

An l-star graph S_l is a graph built with a chain of $l + 2$ vertices. Then for each vertex different to the extremities, $\Delta - 2$ leaves are added. Let S_l be a l-star graphs with $n = l(\Delta - 1) + 2$ vertices. According to Theorem 2, $\mathbb{E}(T_{S_l}) = O(\Delta n) = O(\frac{n^2}{l})$. On the other hand, the expected number of rounds to get a rendezvous between centers of two adjacent stars is Δ^2 and, therefore, the expected number of rounds for contaminating all the centers is $\Omega(l\Delta^2) = \Omega(n\Delta)$. As a corollary to this result we have

Proposition 1. *There exists an infinite family of graphs $\mathcal{F}$ of n vertices and maximal degree Δ such that, for any $G \in \mathcal{F}$, $\mathbb{E}(T_G) = \Omega(\Delta n)$.*

It follows that the general upper bound $O(n^2)$ given by Theorem 2 is tight for the any l-star graph with $l \geq 2$ constant.

3.2   Matching the Lower Bound

To prove that the $\Omega(\log n)$ bound is tight, we prove an upper bound that only involves the maximum degree Δ and the diameter D.

Theorem 3. *Let G be any graph with maximum degree $\Delta \geq 3$ and diameter D. Then the expected broadcast time in G, starting from any vertex, is at most $4\Delta^2 (\ln 2 + D + D \ln \Delta)$.*

Our proof of this theorem will make use of the following lemma.

Lemma 7. *Fix a constant $p > 0$, and let S_k denote the sum of k independent geometric random variables with parameter p.*
Then, for any $t \geq k/p$, we have

$$\mathbb{P}(S_k > t) \leq \exp\left(-\frac{tp}{2}\left(1 - \frac{k}{tp}\right)^2\right).$$

Proof (Theorem 3). We prove that the probability for the broadcast time to exceed half of the claimed bound is at most $1/2$ and then use Lemma 3.

Let u be the initial vertex for the broadcast. For each other vertex v, pick a path γ_{uv} from u to v with length at most D. Since all degrees are at most Δ, each edge in γ_{uv} has a rendezvous probability at least $1/\Delta^2$. Hence, the broadcast time from u to v *along the path* γ_{uv} (that is, the time until the first edge has a rendezvous, then the second edge, and so on) is distributed as the sum of independent geometric random variables with parameters equal to the rendezvous probabilities, and is thus stochastically dominated by the sum of D independent geometric random variables with parameter $1/\Delta^2$.

Let T_{uv} denote the time until broadcast reaches v when the initial vertex is u; Lemma 7 and the above discussion imply, for any t,

$$\mathbb{P}(T_{uv} > t) \leq e^{-\frac{t}{2\Delta^2}\left(1 - \frac{D\Delta^2}{t}\right)^2}. \tag{12}$$

Let $1 + n$ denote the number of vertices in G. Moore's bound ensures that $n \leq \Delta^D$.

It is routine to check that, if $t > 2\Delta^2(\ln 2 + D + D \ln \Delta)$, then $t(1 - D\Delta^2/t)^2 > 2\Delta^2(\ln 2 + D \ln \Delta) \geq 2\Delta^2 \ln(2n)$. Thus, for each of the n vertices $v \neq u$, we get

$$\mathbb{P}(T_{uv} > t) \leq e^{-\ln(2n)} = \frac{1}{2n}, \tag{13}$$

so that, summing over v, we get

$$\mathbb{P}(T_u > t) \leq \frac{1}{2}. \tag{14}$$

Corollary 3. *There exists an infinite family of graphs $\mathcal{F}$ such that, for any $G \in \mathcal{F}$, $\mathbb{E}(T_G) = O(\log |G|)$.*

3.3 The Complete Graph

It is seems also interesting to point out that the complete graph K_n has the minimal (see [13]) expected rendezvous number in a round:

$$\mathbb{E}(N_{K_n}) = \frac{\binom{n}{2}}{(n-1)^2},$$

which is asymptotically $\frac{1}{2}$. We prove in this section that its expected broadcast time is however $O(n \ln n)$, which is *significantly shorter* than that of the l-star graph with l constant which is $\Omega(n^2)$.

Lemma 8. $\mathbb{E}(T_{K_n}) \leq 2\lambda^{-1} n \ln n + O(n)$.

Moreover, we have:

Lemma 9. *With probability $1 - n^{-1/2}$, $\mathbb{E}(T_{K_n}) \geq \frac{1}{2} n \ln n$.*

Lemmas 9 and 8 imply:

Proposition 2. $\mathbb{E}(T_{K_n}) = \Theta(n \ln n)$.

3.4 Graphs of Bounded Degree and Bounded Diameter

Lemma 10. *Let G be a Δ-regular balanced complete rooted tree of depth 2. The expected time for the root to contaminate its children is $\Theta(\Delta^2 \ln \Delta)$.*

Theorem 4. *Let G be a Δ-regular balanced complete rooted tree of depth $D/2$ with D even. $\mathbb{E}(T_G) = \Omega(D\Delta^2 \ln \Delta)$.*

Proof. Suppose the broadcast starts from the root v_0. Let us construct a path $v_0, v_1, v_2, \ldots, v_{D/2}$ such that v_i is the last contaminated child of v_{i-1}. T_{v_i} denotes the number of rounds to contaminate v_j by its parent v_{i-1} once v_{i-1} is contaminated. Since $T_G \geq \sum_{i=1}^{D/2} T_{v_i}$ and from Lemma 10, for every $1 \leq i \leq D/2$, $\mathbb{E}(T_{v_i}) = \Theta(\Delta^2 \ln \Delta)$, we have $\mathbb{E}(T_G) \geq \sum_{i=1}^{D/2} \mathbb{E}(T_{v_i}) = \Omega(D\Delta^2 \ln \Delta)$.

Theorem 4 proves that there exists a graph for which the upper bound of Theorem 3 is tight.

P. Duchon et al.

References

1. S. Albers and M. Henzinger. Exploring unknown environments. *SIAM Journal on Computing*, 29(4):1164–1188, 2000.
2. D. Angluin. Local and global properties in networks of processors. In *Proceedings of the 12th Symposium on theory of computing*, pages 82–93, 1980.
3. L. Barriere, P. Flocchini, P. Fraigniaud, and N. Santoro. Capture of an intruder by mobile agents. In *In 14th ACM Symposium on Parallel Algorithms and Architectures (SPAA)*, pages 200–209, 2002.
4. Michael A. Bender and Donna K. Slonim. The power of team exploration: two robots can learn unlabeled directed graphs. In *Proceedings of the 35rd Annual Symposium on Foundations of Computer Science*, pages 75–85. IEEE Computer Society Press, Los Alamitos, CA, 1994.
5. B. Chlebus. *Handbook on Randomized Computing*, chapter Randomized communication in radio networks. Kluwer Academic, to appear. http://citeseer.nj.nec.com/489613.html.
6. Francesc Comellas, Javier Ozón, and Joseph G. Peters. Deterministic small-world communication networks. *Information Processing Letters*, 76(1–2):83–90, 2000.
7. Xiaotie Deng, Tiko Kameda, and Christos H. Papadimitriou. How to learn an unknown environment i: The rectilinear case. *Journal of the ACM*, 45(2):215–245, 1998.
8. Uriel Feige, David Peleg, Prabhakar Raghavan, and Eli Upfal. Randomized broadcast in networks. *Random Structures and Algorithms*, 1, 1990.
9. M. Habib, C. McDiarmid, J. Ramirez-Alfonsin, and B. Reed, editors. *Probabilistic Methods for Algorithmic Discrete Mathematics*. Springer, 1998.
10. S.M. Hedetniemi, S.T. Hedetniemi, and A.L. Liestman. A survey of gossiping and broadcasting in communication networks. *Networks*, 18:319–349, 1988.
11. Richard M. Karp, Christian Schindelhauer, Scott Shenker, and Berthold Vöcking. Randomized rumor spreading. In *IEEE Symposium on Foundations of Computer Science*, pages 565–574, 2000.
12. N. Lynch. A hundred impossibility proofs for distributed computing. In *Proceedings of the 8th ACM Symposium on Principles of Distributed Computing (PODC)*, pages 1–28, New York, NY, 1989. ACM Press.
13. Yves Metivier, Nasser Saheb, and Akka Zemmari. Randomized rendezvous. Trends in mathematics, pages 183–194, 2000.
14. Yves Metivier, Nasser Saheb, and Akka Zemmari. Randomized local elections. *Information processing letters*, 82:313–320, 2002.
15. R. Motwani and P. Raghavan. *Randomized Algorithms*. Cambridge Univ. Press, 1995.
16. N. Rao, S. Kareti, W. Shi, and S. Iyenagar. Robot navigation in unknown terrains: Introductory survey of non-heuristic algorithms, 1993. http://citeseer.nj.nec.com/rao93robot.html.
17. G. Tel. *Introduction to distributed algorithms*. Cambridge University Press, 2000.

Time-Space Tradeoff in Derandomizing Probabilistic Logspace*

Jin-Yi Cai, Venkatesan T. Chakaravarthy, and Dieter van Melkebeek

University of Wisconsin, Madison, USA.
{jyc,venkat,dieter}@cs.wisc.edu

Abstract. Nisan [6] showed that any randomized logarithmic space algorithm (running in polynomial time and with two-sided error) can be simulated by a deterministic algorithm that runs simultaneously in polynomial time and $\Theta(\log^2 n)$ space. Subsequently Saks and Zhou [9] improved the space complexity and showed that a deterministic simulation can be carried out in space $\Theta(\log^{1.5} n)$. However, their simulation runs in time $n^{\Theta(\log^{0.5} n)}$. We prove a time-space tradeoff that interpolates these two simulations. Specifically, we prove that, for any $0 \le \alpha \le 0.5$, any randomized logarithmic space algorithm (running in polynomial time and with two-sided error) can be simulated deterministically in time $n^{O(\log^{0.5-\alpha} n)}$ and space $O(\log^{1.5+\alpha} n)$. That is, we prove that $\mathsf{BPL} \subseteq \mathsf{DTISP}[n^{O(\log^{0.5-\alpha} n)}, O(\log^{1.5+\alpha} n)]$.

1 Introduction

Given an undirected graph and vertices s and t, the undirected st-connectivity problem is to check whether there is a path from s to t. It is one of the most fundamental problems in computer science and has been well-studied for the past three decades. Procedures like depth-first search and breadth-first search solve the problem in polynomial time, but use linear space. On the other hand, Savitch's theorem [10] gives an algorithm (even for directed graphs) that uses only $O(\log^2 n)$ space. However, the algorithm runs in time $n^{O(\log n)}$.

It remains open whether undirected st–connectivity can be solved in logarithmic space. It is known that this can be accomplished if randomness is allowed. Aleliunas et al. [1] showed that the problem can be solved in randomized logarithmic space (with one-sided error). Most subsequent improvements have been via deterministic simulation of the randomized logspace algorithm.

In a major breakthrough, Nisan [5] constructed a pseudorandom generator that stretches a seed of length $O(\log^2 n)$ into a string of polynomial length. He showed that the output of the generator (on a randomly chosen seed) looks almost truly random for any randomized logspace computation (with two-sided

---

* A more detailed version of the paper is available at
http://www.cs.wisc.edu/~dieter. Research supported in part by NSF grants
CCR-9634665, CCR-0208013 and CCR-0133693.

V. Diekert and M. Habib (Eds.): STACS 2004, LNCS 2996, pp. 571–583, 2004.
© Springer-Verlag Berlin Heidelberg 2004

error). Then, if we run through all possible seeds, we get a deterministic simulation. This naive simulation using Nisan's generator needs $O(\log^2 n)$ space and
$n^{O(\log n)}$ time, and hence fails to beat the bounds from Savitch's theorem. However, Nisan [6] showed that, in fact, one can perform the simulation in polynomial time, while using only $O(\log^2 n)$ space. This settled an important problem
of whether randomized logspace algorithms can be simulated in simultaneous
polynomial time and polylog space. Subsequently, Nisan, Szemeredi and Wigderson [7] presented an $O(\log^{1.5} n)$ space algorithm for undirected st–connectivity.
In a sweeping generalization, Saks and Zhou [9] proved that any randomized
logspace algorithm can be simulated deterministically in $O(\log^{1.5} n)$ space. But
the time complexity of this simulation is $n^{O(\log^{0.5} n)}$. In this paper, we generalize
the deterministic simulations of Nisan [6], and of Saks and Zhou [9], and exhibit
a time-space tradeoff interpolating the two.

We denote by BPL the class of all languages that can be recognized by a
randomized algorithm with two-sided error that uses logarithmic space and runs
in polynomial time (for any input and for any random coin tosses). It contains
RL, the one-sided error class. We refer to the excellent survey on probabilistic
space bounded complexity classes by Saks [8] for more background. For a time
bound $t(n)$ and space bound $s(n)$, let DTISP$[t, s]$ denote the class of languages
that can be recognized by a deterministic algorithm that runs in time $t(n)$ and
uses space $s(n)$. With this notation, we can restate the previous results as:

- BPL $\subseteq$ DTISP$[n^{O(1)}, O(\log^2 n)]$ (Nisan [6]).
- BPL $\subseteq$ DTISP$[n^{O(\log^{0.5} n)}, O(\log^{1.5} n)]$ (Saks and Zhou [9]).

In this paper, we establish a time-space tradeoff that generalizes the above two
results:

Theorem 1. BPL $\subseteq$ DTISP$[n^{O(\log^{0.5-\alpha} n)}, O(\log^{1.5+\alpha} n)]$, *for any rational number* $0 \le \alpha \le 0.5$.

2   Preliminaries

As is standard in sublinear space bounded computation, we use an off-line Turing
machine model to measure space complexity. Thus, the input is considered given
on a separate read-only tape and does not count towards the space complexity.
Randomness is provided by a one-way read-only tape containing unbiased and
uncorrelated random bits. The random bit tape does not count towards the space
complexity either.

As is common in prior works, we model the computation of a randomized
logspace polynomial-time Turing machine on an input w as a finite state automaton, and analyze the automaton's behavior using its transition matrix. This way,
the issue of deterministic simulation reduces to approximate matrix powering.
The following definitions and facts will be used for that purpose.

Definition 1. *For positive integers d and m, a (d, m)-automaton Q is a map-
ping $Q : \{0, 1, \ldots, d\} \times \{0, 1\}^m \longrightarrow \{0, 1, \ldots, d\}$, such that, for all $\alpha \in \{0, 1\}^m$,*

$Q(0, \alpha) = 0$. *We say that Q has $d+1$ states numbered $0, 1, 2, \ldots, d$. State 0 is a special state called the* dead state *of Q. We define a mapping $\widehat{Q} : \{0, 1, \ldots, d\} \times (\{0, 1\}^m)^* \longrightarrow \{0, 1, \ldots, d\}$, recursively as follows. For $i \in \{0, 1, \ldots, d\}$, we define $\widehat{Q}(i, \epsilon) = i$, where ϵ denotes the empty string. Let $i \in \{0, 1, \ldots, d\}$ and $\alpha_1 \alpha_2 \ldots \alpha_t \in (\{0, 1\}^m)^+$, where each $\alpha_i \in \{0, 1\}^m$, and t is a positive integer. Then $\widehat{Q}(i, \alpha_1 \alpha_2 \ldots \alpha_t) = Q(\widehat{Q}(i, \alpha_1 \alpha_2 \ldots \alpha_{t-1}), \alpha_t)$.*

Definition 2. *For a $d \times d$ matrix M over the real numbers, define the* norm *of M to be*

$$||M|| = \max_{1 \leq i \leq d} \left(\sum_{j=1}^{d} |M[i, j]| \right),$$

where $M[i, j]$ is the (i, j) entry of M. The matrix M is said to be sub-stochastic *if $||M|| \leq 1$ and $M[i, j] \geq 0$ for any $i, j \in \{1, 2, \ldots, d\}$, i.e., M has non-negative entries with each row sum at most 1. Such a matrix is said to be a (d, m)-matrix if for any $i, j \in \{1, 2, \ldots, d\}$, $2^m M[i, j]$ is an integer.*

Definition 3. *Let Q be a (d, m)-automaton. The* transition matrix *of Q, denoted by $\mathcal{M}(Q)$, is the (d, m)-matrix M with, for $i, j \in \{1, 2, \ldots, d\}$, $M[i, j] = \Pr_{\alpha \in \{0, 1\}^m}[Q(i, \alpha) = j]$.*

We will exploit the following connection between powers of the transition matrix $M = \mathcal{M}(Q)$ and "powers" of Q: For any nonnegative integer k,

$$M^k[i, j] = \Pr_{s \in (\{0, 1\}^m)^k}[\widehat{Q}(i, s) = j], \tag{1}$$

i.e., the (i, j) entry of M^k equals the probability that a random string of length k over the alphabet $\{0, 1\}^m$ "moves" Q from i to j.

Note that different (d, m)-automata Q may have the same transition matrix $\mathcal{M}(Q)$. We will need to invert the operator $\mathcal{M}$ in a canonical way.

Definition 4. *Let M be a (d, m)-matrix. The* canonical automaton *corresponding to M, denoted by $\mathcal{Q}(M)$, is a (d, m)-automaton Q defined as follows. Let $i \in \{1, 2, \ldots, d\}$ and $\alpha \in \{0, 1\}^m$. Let $\underline{\alpha}$ denote the number with binary representation $.\alpha$. If $\underline{\alpha} > \sum_{j=1}^{d} M[i, j]$, then $Q(i, \alpha) = 0$; otherwise, let $k \in \{1, 2, \ldots, d\}$ be the least integer such that $\underline{\alpha} \leq \sum_{j=1}^{k} M[i, j]$, then we let $Q(i, \alpha) = k$. An automaton Q is called* canonical *if it is the canonical automaton corresponding to some M.*

Note that $\mathcal{M}(\mathcal{Q}(M)) = M$ for any (d, m)-matrix M. By applying $\mathcal{Q}$ once more it follows that, for a canonical Q, $\mathcal{Q}(\mathcal{M}(Q)) = Q$.

3   Overall Approach and Main Ingredients

Given a randomized logspace, polynomial-time, two-sided error Turing machine, and an input w of length n, we need to distinguish between the case where the acceptance probability is at least $2/3$, and the case where it is at most $1/3$. We do so by approximating the acceptance probability to within $1/6$ in a deterministic way within the space and time bounds specified in the tradeoff. The problem reduces to matrix powering in the following standard fashion.

Consider the configurations of the machine on input w, where each configuration consists of the state of the machine, position of the tape heads and the contents of work tape. Let the total number of configurations be d. We can label them $1, 2, \ldots, d$. As the machine runs in logspace and polynomial time, $d = n^{\Theta(1)}$. We can assume that the machine reads a fresh random bit b in every step of the computation. The machine then behaves like a $(d, 1)$-automaton. More formally, the function Q that maps (i, b) to the state of the machine after reading random bit b in state i, defines a $(d, 1)$-automaton. Note that Q as well as its transition matrix $M = \mathcal{M}(Q)$ can be computed in logspace given w. Without loss of generality, the initial configuration of the machine is labeled 1, and the machine has a unique accepting configuration labeled d, which is absorbing (i.e., $M[d, d] = 1$). Suppose the machine runs for p steps, where p is polynomial in n. By (1), the acceptance probability of the machine on input w is given by the $(1, d)$ entry of the matrix M^p, which is the same as the $(1, d)$ entry of M^{2^r} for any integer $r \geq \log p$. In Section 4, we sketch a proof of the following approximation result.

Theorem 2. *Given a $(d, 1)$-matrix M, positive integers r, r_1 and r_2, where $r = r_1 r_2 = O(\log d)$, and a positive integer $a = O(\log d)$, there is a deterministic algorithm that computes a matrix M' such that $\|M^{2^r} - M'\| < 2^{-a}$. The algorithm uses space $O(\max\{r_1, r_2\} \log d)$ and runs in time $d^{O(\min\{r_1, r_2\})}$.*

Setting $r_1 = \Theta(\log^{0.5+\alpha} d)$, $r_2 = \Theta(\log^{0.5-\alpha} d)$, and $a = 3$ in Theorem 2 yields Theorem 1.

Hence, given a $(d, 1)$-matrix M and an integer $r = O(\log d)$, our goal is to approximate M^{2^r} within certain time and space bounds. Instead of working with $(d, 1)$-matrices, we consider the problem for (d, m)-matrices. Clearly, any $(d, 1)$-matrix is also a (d, m)-matrix for any $m \geq 1$. A specific value for $m = O(\log d)$ will be fixed later.

3.1   Nisan's Pseudorandom Generator Construction

A standard way of computing M^{2^r} (either exact or approximately) is by repeated squaring. A recursive implementation as in Savitch's Theorem yields a procedure that runs in $\Theta(\log^2 d)$ space and $d^{\Theta(\log d)}$ time: Each of the $\Theta(\log d)$ levels of recursion induces an additive term of $\Theta(\log d)$ to the space complexity, and a multiplicative term of $d^{\Theta(1)}$ to the time complexity for storing and (re)computing intermediate results.

Nisan's breakthrough [5,6] can be viewed as repeated approximate squaring in a way that avoids the need for storing and recomputing intermediate results. The basic ingredient is the following procedure to approximately "square" an underlying automaton using a hash function h.

Definition 5. *Let Q be a (d, m)-automaton, $h : \{0, 1\}^m \to \{0, 1\}^m$, and $\epsilon > 0$. Define Q_h, also denoted by $\mathcal{N}_h(Q)$, to be the following (d, m)-automaton: For any $i \in \{0, 1, \ldots, d\}$ and $\alpha \in \{0, 1\}^m$, $Q_h(i, \alpha) = \widehat{Q}(i, \alpha \circ h(\alpha))$, where $\circ$ denotes concatenation. We denote h as ϵ-pseudorandom for Q if $\|\mathcal{M}(Q_h) - \mathcal{M}(Q)^2\| < \epsilon$.*

By (1), $\mathcal{M}(Q)^2$ corresponds to picking $\alpha, \beta \in \{0, 1\}^m$ independently at random and running Q on $\alpha \circ \beta$. Similarly, $\mathcal{M}(Q_h)$ corresponds to picking only $\alpha \in \{0, 1\}^m$ uniformly at random, and running Q on $\alpha \circ h(\alpha)$. This motivates the use of the term "pseudorandom."

A crucial question is how to find the ϵ-pseudorandom hash functions h we need. Nisan argues that ϵ-pseudorandom hash functions for a (d, m) automaton abound in a universal family of hash functions $\mathcal{H}_m$ from $\{0, 1\}^m$ to $\{0, 1\}^m$ with $m = \Omega(\log d + \log 1/\epsilon)$. We will fix a universal family such that we can uniformly sample from $\mathcal{H}_m$ in $O(m)$ space, as well as evaluate any $h \in \mathcal{H}_m$ on a given input. An example of such a family is the set of all linear functions over a finite field with 2^m elements.

Lemma 1. *Let Q be a (d, m)-automaton, $\mathcal{H}_m$ a universal family of hash functions, and $\epsilon > 0$.*

$$\Pr_{h \in \mathcal{H}_m} [h \text{ is not } \epsilon\text{-pseudorandom for } Q] \leq \frac{d^5}{\epsilon^2 2^m}.$$

Moreover, given Q and ϵ, an exhaustive search for a hash function $h \in \mathcal{H}_m$ that is ϵ-pseudorandom for Q can be performed in space $O(m + \log d)$.

Using Lemma 1, we can approximately square a (d, m)-matrix M as follows: Construct the canonical (d, m)-automaton $Q = \mathcal{Q}(M)$, find a hash function $h \in \mathcal{H}_m$ that is ϵ-pseudorandom for Q, construct Q_h, and transform Q_h into its transition matrix $\mathcal{M}(Q_h)$. The result is a (d, m)-matrix that is no more than ϵ away from M^2 in norm. When we apply this procedure r times successively to approximate M^{2^r}, we can, of course, eliminate the intermediate automaton-to-matrix and matrix-to-automaton transformations. We introduce the following simplified notation for the intermediate automata.

Definition 6. *Let Q be a (d, m)-automaton and $h_1, h_2, \ldots, h_r$ be hash functions over $\{0, 1\}^m$. Then we define $Q_{h_1, h_2, \ldots, h_k}$, also denoted by $\mathcal{N}_{h_1, h_2, \ldots, h_k}(Q)$, as*

$$Q_{h_1, h_2, \ldots, h_k} = (\ldots ((Q_{h_1})_{h_2}) \ldots)_{h_k}.$$

Another important question is how the errors accumulate. The accuracy of the final result is governed by Lemma 2, which uses the following definition [5].

Definition 7. *Let Q be a (d, m)-automaton and $h_1, h_2, \ldots, h_r$ be hash functions over $\{0, 1\}^m$. We say that the sequence $h_1, h_2, \ldots, h_r$ is ϵ-pseudorandom for Q, if $\|\mathcal{M}(Q_{h_1, h_2, \ldots, h_r}) - (\mathcal{M}(Q))^{2^r}\| < \epsilon$.*

Lemma 2. *Let Q be a (d, m)-automaton, and $\epsilon > 0$. Let $h_1, h_2, \ldots, h_r$ be hash functions over $\{0,1\}^m$ such that, for each $1 \leq i \leq r$, h_i is ϵ-pseudorandom for $Q_{h_1, h_2, \ldots, h_{i-1}}$. Then the sequence $h_1, h_2, \ldots, h_r$ is $2^r \epsilon$-pseudorandom for Q.*

It follows from Lemma 1 and 2 that a choice of $m = O(\log d)$ is sufficient to obtain a good enough approximation to M^{2^r} for our purposes.

A straightforward recursive implementation of Nisan's algorithm uses roughly the same amount of resources as the trivial recursive squaring approach, namely $\Theta(\log^2 d)$ space and $d^{\Theta(\log d)}$ time. However, the crucial property in Proposition 1 below allowed Nisan to do better. The following definition plays a central role.

Definition 8. *Let Q be a (d, m) automaton, and $h_1, h_2, \ldots, h_r$ be hash functions over $\{0,1\}^m$. Recursively define $G_{h_1, h_2, \ldots, h_r}$ as a mapping from $\{0,1\}^m$ to $(\{0,1\}^m)^{2^r}$ by $G(\alpha) = \alpha$, and*

$$G_{h_1, h_2, \ldots, h_i}(\alpha) = G_{h_1, h_2, \ldots, h_{i-1}}(\alpha) \circ G_{h_1, h_2, \ldots, h_{i-1}}(h_i(\alpha)).$$

Note that, given hash functions $h_1, h_2, \ldots, h_r \in \mathcal{H}_m$, a bit index, and $\alpha \in \{0,1\}^m$, any bit of $G_{h_1, h_2, \ldots, h_r}(\alpha)$ can be computed in $O(m + \log r)$ space.

Proposition 1. *Let Q be a (d, m)-automaton and $h_1, h_2, \ldots, h_r$ be hash functions over $\{0,1\}^m$. Then for any $i \in \{0, 1, \ldots, d\}$ and $\alpha \in \{0,1\}^m$,*

$$Q_{h_1, h_2, \ldots, h_r}(i, \alpha) = \widehat{Q}(i, G_{h_1, h_2, \ldots, h_r}(\alpha)).$$

Although Proposition 1 looks innocuous, it has far reaching consequences. First, it shows that we obtain our approximations to the probabilities defined by (1) for $k = 2^r$ by subsampling, i.e., by using a pseudorandom generator. The function mapping $(h_1, h_2, \ldots, h_r, \alpha)$ to $G_{h_1, h_2, \ldots, h_r}(\alpha)$ defines a pseudorandom generator stretching $O(rm)$ random bits to $2^r m$ pseudorandom bits that "fool" the automaton Q. We will not explicitly use this fact but it was Nisan's original motivation [5].

Second, and more important for us, Proposition 1 provides a shortcut for storing the intermediate results in the recursive computation of $Q_{h_1, h_2, \ldots, h_r}$. Given $h_1, h_2, \ldots, h_r \in \mathcal{H}_m$, $i \in \{0, 1, \ldots, d\}$, and $\alpha \in \{0,1\}^m$, we can now compute $Q_{h_1, h_2, \ldots, h_r}(i, \alpha)$ in space $O(m + r + \log d)$ instead of $O(r(m + \log d))$. This allows us to deterministically find pseudorandom hash functions h_i for every level of recursion as well as compute $\mathcal{M}(Q_{h_1, h_2, \ldots, h_r})$ from $h_1, h_2, \ldots, h_r$ using only $O(m + r + \log d)$ work space, and therefore in time $2^{O(m+r+\log d)}$. The only additional space needed is $O(rm)$ bits to store the hash functions. This is how Nisan established his result that $\mathsf{BPL} \subseteq \mathsf{DTISP}[n^{O(1)}, O(\log^2 n)]$ [6].

3.2 Saks-Zhou Rounding

The only reason why Nisan's algorithm needs more than logarithmic space is to store the $r = O(\log d)$ hash functions of $O(m) = O(\log d)$ bits each. A natural approach to save space then, is to use the same hash functions at multiple levels of recursion.

Given any *fixed* collection of (d, m)-automata $Q_1, Q_2, \ldots, Q_r$, we can efficiently find a hash function h that is pseudorandom for all of them. This follows from Lemma 1.

Corollary 1. *For any (d, m)-automata $Q_1, Q_2, \ldots, Q_r$,*

$$\Pr_{h \in \mathcal{H}_m} [h \text{ is not } \epsilon\text{-pseudorandom for at least one of } Q_1, Q_2, \ldots, Q_r] \leq \frac{rd^5}{\epsilon^2 2^m}.$$

Moreover, given $Q_1, Q_2, \ldots, Q_r$ and ϵ, an exhaustive search for a hash function $h \in \mathcal{H}_m$ that is ϵ-pseudorandom for all of $Q_1, Q_2, \ldots, Q_r$ can be performed in space $O(m + \log d + \log r)$.

However, the sequence $Q_1, Q_2, \ldots, Q_r$ in Nisan's algorithm is not fixed but depends on the choice of the hash functions: $Q_{i+1} = (Q_i)_{h_i}$. If Lemma 1 guaranteed the existence of a fixed automaton Q^* such that $Q_h = Q^*$ for most choices of h, then we could apply Corollary 1 to the sequence $Q_1, Q_2, \ldots, Q_r$ with $Q_1 = Q$ and $Q_{i+1} = Q_i^*$, and safely use the same hash function h at every level of recursion. Unfortunately, Lemma 1 only tells us that Q_h is "close" to some fixed Q^* for most h and not that it coincides with Q^* for most h. Similarly, Corollary 1 does not guarantee the existence of a hash function h that is pseudorandom for all of Q, Q_h, $(Q_h)_h$, etc.

Saks and Zhou [9] devised a randomized rounding scheme to make the automata at every level of recursion independent of the hash functions at the previous levels (for most choices of these hash functions), namely by randomly perturbing and then truncating the entries of the transition matrices. We will review the details below and see that the rounding requires $O(\log d)$ bits to be stored for a $d \times d$ matrix.

We point out one unfortunate side-effect of the rounding scheme, which wasn't critical for Saks and Zhou but will be for us: the breakdown of the analogue of Proposition 1. We can no longer circumvent the recursion because we need to act on the matrices, and therefore have to transform between automata and matrices at every level of recursion. As a consequence, the processing space increases from $O(m + r + \log d)$ to $O(r(m + \log d))$ again.

The storage space consists of two components: $O(m)$ bits for the hash function h, and $O(r \log d)$ bits for all the perturbations. In order to balance the two components of the space complexity, Saks and Zhou considered a hybrid algorithm that uses r_1 hash functions $\boldsymbol{h} = (h_1, h_2, \ldots, h_{r_1})$ cyclically r_2 times, where $r_1 r_2 = r$, and applies the randomized rounding between cycles. The processing space becomes $O(r_2(m + \log d))$ and the storage space $O(r_1 m + r_2 \log d)$. By setting $r_1 = r_2 = \sqrt{r}$, Saks and Zhou obtained their result that $\mathsf{BPL} \subseteq \mathsf{DTISP}[n^{O(\log^{0.5} n)}, O(\log^{1.5} n)]$ [9].

We now discuss the Saks-Zhou rounding scheme in more detail for the hybrid setting, and adapt it to our needs.

Definition 9. *Let* t, D *be positive integers, and* $\delta \in \{0, 1\}^D$. *We define the rounding operator* $\mathcal{R}_{\delta,t}$ *as the function mapping* $z \in [0, 1]$ *to* $\lfloor \max(z - \underline{\delta}2^{-t}, 0) \rfloor_t$, *where* $\underline{\delta}$ *denotes the number with binary representation* $.\delta$, *and* $\lfloor z \rfloor_t = \lfloor 2^t z \rfloor 2^{-t}$. *The operator extends to real-valued matrices with each entry in* $[0, 1]$ *by entrywise application.*

The effect of $\mathcal{R}_{\delta,t}$ is to perturb the binary expansion of every number after the t-th bit by δ (obtaining a smaller number but never going negative), and then truncate it after the t-th bit. Note that if M is a (d, m)-matrix and $t \leq m$, then $\mathcal{R}_{\delta,t}(M)$ also is a (d, m)-matrix.

Definition 10. *Let* M *be a* $d \times d$-matrix over $[0, 1]$, *and* t, D, r_1, k *be positive integers. Let* $\boldsymbol{\delta} = (\delta_1, \delta_2, \ldots, \delta_k) \in (\{0, 1\}^D)^k$. *We define the* rounded sequence $R(M, \boldsymbol{\delta})$ *with parameters* t, r_1, *and* k *as the following sequence of matrices:*

$$N_0, \widetilde{N}_1, N_1, \widetilde{N}_2, N_2, \ldots, \widetilde{N}_k, N_k$$

where, $N_0 = M$ *and for* $1 \leq i \leq k$,

$$\widetilde{N}_i = N_{i-1}^{2^{r_1}}, \quad N_i = \mathcal{R}_{\delta_i, t}(\widetilde{N}_i).$$

Note that if M is a (d, m)-matrix and $t \leq m$, then every matrix N_i is a (d, m)-matrix. Their canonical automata $\mathcal{Q}(N_i)$ are the "fixed" automata to which Corollary 1 will be applied.

Rounding does not effect the final result by much.

Lemma 3. *Let* M *be a* $d \times d$-matrix over $[0, 1]$, *and* t, D, r_1, k *be positive integers. Let* $\boldsymbol{\delta} = (\delta_1, \delta_2, \ldots, \delta_k) \in (\{0, 1\}^D)^k$. *Then, the matrix* N_k *defined in the rounded sequence* $R(M, \boldsymbol{\delta})$ *with parameters* t, r_1, *and* k *satisfies* $\|N_k - M^{2^{r_1 k}}\| < 2^{-t + r_1 k + \log d + 1}$.

The crucial property of the rounding operator is that for any $z \in [0, 1]$, unless δ is exceptional, $\mathcal{R}_{\delta,t}$ maps any number that is about $2^{-(t+D)}$ close to z to the same value as z. Saks and Zhou formalized this property using the notion of safety. We will distinguish between two levels of safety. We define them right away for matrices.

Definition 11. *Let* M *be a* $d \times d$-matrix over $[0, 1]$, t, D *positive integers, and* $\delta \in \{0, 1\}^D$. *We denote* δ *as* t-safe *for* M *if for any* $d \times d$-matrix Z over $[0, 1]$ satisfying $\|Z - M\| < 2^{-(t+D)}$, $\mathcal{R}_{\delta,t}(Z) = \mathcal{R}_{\delta,t}(M)$. *If the condition holds whenever* Z *satisfies* $\|Z - M\| < 2^{-(t+D+1)}$, *we call* δ t-weakly-safe *for* M.

By definition, t-safeness implies t-weakly-safeness. We will use the following stronger relationship between the two levels of safety.

Lemma 4. *Let* M *and* N *be* $d \times d$-matrices over $[0, 1]$, t, D *positive integers, and* $\delta \in \{0, 1\}^D$. *If* δ *is* t-safe *for* M *and* $\|M - N\| \leq 2^{-(t+D+1)}$, *then* δ *is* t-weakly-safe *for* N.

For any $z \in [0,1]$, there are at most two values of $\delta \in \{0,1\}^D$ that are not t-safe for z (viewed as a 1×1 matrix), and these values are easy to find. We have the following generalization for $d \times d$ matrices.

Lemma 5. *Let M be a $d \times d$-matrix over $[0,1]$, and t, D positive integers. For all but at most $2d^2$ values of $\delta \in \{0,1\}^D$, the operator $\mathcal{R}_{\delta,t}$ is t-safe for M. Moreover, given M, t, and D, an exhaustive search for a $\delta \in \{0,1\}^D$ that is t-safe for M can be performed in space $O(D + \log d + \log t)$.*

Definition 12. *Let M be a (d,m)-matrix, and t, D, r_1, k positive integers with $t \leq m$. Let $\boldsymbol{\delta} = (\delta_1, \delta_2, \ldots \delta_k) \in (\{0,1\}^D)^k$. Let $\boldsymbol{h} = (h_1, h_2, \ldots, h_{r_1})$ be a sequence of hash functions from $\mathcal{H}_m$. We define the* Saks-Zhou sequence $SZ(M, \boldsymbol{h}, \boldsymbol{\delta})$ *with parameters t, r_1, and k as the following sequence of matrices and automata:*

$$M_0, Q_0, \widetilde{Q}_1, \widetilde{M}_1, M_1, Q_1, \widetilde{Q}_2, \widetilde{M}_2, M_2, \ldots, Q_{r_2-1}, \widetilde{Q}_k, \widetilde{M}_k, M_k$$

where, $M_0 = M$, and for $1 \leq i \leq k$,

$$Q_{i-1} = \mathcal{Q}(M_{i-1}), \quad \widetilde{Q}_i = \mathcal{N}_{h_1, h_2, \ldots, h_{r_1}}(Q_{i-1}), \quad \widetilde{M}_i = \mathcal{M}(\widetilde{Q}_i), \quad M_i = \mathcal{R}_{\delta_i, t}(\widetilde{M}_i)$$

See Figure 1 for a schema of the construction of the Saks-Zhou sequence $SZ(M, \boldsymbol{h}, \boldsymbol{\delta})$, the rounded sequence $R(M, \boldsymbol{\delta})$, and their intended relationships (for $k = r_2$). In the figure, the operator $\mathcal{P}$ denotes raising a matrix to the power 2^{r_1}.

Saks and Zhou defined $\boldsymbol{\delta}$ to be t-safe for the sequence $R(M, \boldsymbol{\delta})$ if δ_i is t-safe for $\widetilde{N}_i$, for each i. As can be seen from Lemma 5, for a large enough choice of $D = O(\log d)$, a random $\boldsymbol{\delta}$ will be safe for $R(M, \boldsymbol{\delta})$. When $\boldsymbol{\delta}$ is safe for $R(M, \boldsymbol{\delta})$, one can argue that for most $\boldsymbol{h}$, $M_i = N_i$ for $0 \leq i \leq r_2$, where M_i and N_i are matrices defined in $SZ(M, \boldsymbol{h}, \boldsymbol{\delta})$ and $R(M, \boldsymbol{\delta})$, respectively. In particular, $M_{r_2} = N_{r_2}$ is a good approximation to M^{2^r}.

The fact that M_i and N_i coincide for every $1 \leq i \leq r_2$ can be seen as follows. Let $P_0, P_1, \ldots, P_{r_2}$ be the canonical automata corresponding to the matrices $N_0, N_1, \ldots, N_{r_2}$, respectively. If we choose $\boldsymbol{h}$ at random from $\mathcal{H}_m^{r_1} = \mathcal{H}_m \times \mathcal{H}_m \times \cdots \times \mathcal{H}_m$, then, with high probability, $\boldsymbol{h}$ is ϵ-pseudorandom for all the automata $P_0, P_1, \ldots, P_{r_2}$, for suitably small ϵ. This is guaranteed by Corollary 1 because these automata are defined using only M and $\boldsymbol{\delta}$, and in particular they do not depend on $\boldsymbol{h}$. By definition, $M_0 = N_0 = M$ and thus $Q_0 = P_0$. Therefore $\boldsymbol{h}$ is ϵ-pseudorandom for Q_0. It follows that $\widetilde{M}_1$ is close to $\widetilde{N}_1$. Then $M_1 = N_1$ by δ_1 being safe for $\widetilde{N}_1$. Continuing this way for r_2 steps, we get $M_{r_2} = N_{r_2}$.

Using these properties, the Saks-Zhou [9] algorithm approximates M^{2^r} as the average of the matrices M_{r_2} over all $\boldsymbol{\delta}$ and $\boldsymbol{h}$.

4   The Tradeoff

In this Section, we sketch the proof of Theorem 2. We refer the reader to a longer version of the paper [3] for more details.

Given a (d, m)-matrix M and integers r_1, r_2 with $r = r_1 r_2$, the Saks-Zhou algorithm described in Section 3.2 approximates M^{2^r} in space $O(\max\{r_1, r_2\} \log d)$ but uses time $d^{O(r_1 + r_2)}$. The factor $d^{O(r_1)}$ comes from trying all possible sequences of r_1 hash functions. Our goal is to avoid this exhaustive search and approximate M^{2^r} using space $O(\max\{r_1, r_2\} \log d)$ and time $d^{O(\min\{r_1, r_2\})}$. We will choose $r_1 \geq r_2$, and thus, we want to approximate M^{2^r} in space $O(r_1 \log d)$ and time $d^{O(r_2)}$.

For any sequence $\boldsymbol{\delta} = (\delta_1, \delta_2, \ldots, \delta_{r_2}) \in (\{0, 1\}^D)^{r_2}$, the matrix N_{r_2} defined in the rounded sequence $R(M, \boldsymbol{\delta})$ is a close approximation to M^{2^r}. We want to find a $\boldsymbol{\delta}$ and a sequence of hash functions $\boldsymbol{h} = (h_1, h_2, \ldots, h_{r_1})$ such that we can efficiently compute the matrices $N_0, N_1, \ldots, N_{r_2}$ defined in the sequence $R(M, \boldsymbol{\delta})$ by computing the corresponding matrices $M_0, M_1, \ldots, M_{r_2}$ in the Saks-Zhou sequence $SZ(M, \boldsymbol{h}, \boldsymbol{\delta})$. See Figure 1 for the correspondences.

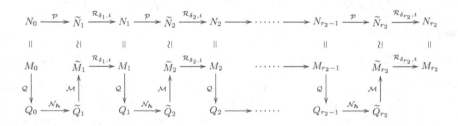

Fig. 1. Rounded and Saks-Zhou sequences

A natural idea is to find the hash functions h_i, one by one, based on Lemma 1. Thus, for the automaton $Q_0 = \mathcal{Q}(M)$, we can find a sequence of hash functions, $\boldsymbol{h} = (h_1, h_2, \ldots, h_{r_1})$, one by one, such that $\widetilde{M_1} = \mathcal{M}(\widetilde{Q_1}) = \mathcal{M}(\mathcal{N}_{\boldsymbol{h}}(Q_0))$ is very close to $\widetilde{N_1} = M^{2^{r_1}}$. This step is essentially Nisan's algorithm for raising M to the power 2^{r_1}. Each step to find the next h_i is carried out by an exhaustive search over $\mathcal{H}_m$, and thus can be done in polynomial time and space $O(r_1 m)$.

Then we can deterministically find a $\delta_1 \in \{0, 1\}^D$ which is safe for $\widetilde{M_1}$. By Lemma 5, we can guarantee the existence of δ_1 by setting $D = O(\log d)$. Since $\widetilde{M_1}$ is very close to $\widetilde{N_1}$, δ_1 will in fact be weakly-safe for $\widetilde{N_1}$, even though we never really compute $\widetilde{N_1}$ exactly. With $\boldsymbol{h}$ already written, the task of finding δ_1 is in logspace (and thus in polynomial time). Since $\widetilde{M_1}$ and $\widetilde{N_1}$ are close, the rounding operator $\mathcal{R}_{\delta_1, t}$ on $\widetilde{M_1}$ and $\widetilde{N_1}$ yields identical matrices $M_1 = N_1$. At this point, we have computed $\boldsymbol{h} = \boldsymbol{h}^{(1)}$ and δ_1, which can be viewed as *a succinct representation* of N_1, which is an approximation to $M^{2^{r_1}}$.

Now we would like to extend this to N_2. Let $Q_1 = \mathcal{Q}(M_1) = \mathcal{Q}(N_1)$. By Corollary 1, it is true that most sequences of r_1 hash functions $\boldsymbol{h}'$ will be simultaneously pseudorandom for Q_0 and Q_1. If we had chosen our $\boldsymbol{h}$ randomly, then with high probability it would be pseudorandom for both Q_0 and Q_1. But we found our h deterministically; there is no guarantee that h will be pseudorandom for Q_1.

Our idea is to find a *new* sequence of hash functions h'. With the *succinct representation* h and δ_1 in hand, we can compute Q_1 and find a new sequence of r_1 hash functions h' which is pseudorandom for both Q_0 and Q_1. Of course, due to the space bound we cannot keep the old h around. So, at this point we want to discard h and replace it by h'.

However, after discarding the old h, we no longer have access to $\widetilde{M}_1 = \mathcal{M}(\mathcal{N}_h(Q_0))$; and it is from $\widetilde{M}_1$ and δ_1 that we defined Q_1, for which the new h' was found to be pseudorandom. If at this point the new $\widetilde{M}_1' = \mathcal{M}(\mathcal{N}_{h'}(Q_0))$ were to lead to an automaton different from Q_1, we would have made no progress.

However, note that δ_1 is weakly-safe for $\widetilde{N}_1$. While $\widetilde{M}_1' = \mathcal{M}(\mathcal{N}_{h'}(Q_0))$ may be different from $\widetilde{M}_1 = \mathcal{M}(\mathcal{N}_h(Q_0))$, both matrices are very close. In fact, the new $\widetilde{M}_1' = \mathcal{M}(\mathcal{N}_{h'}(Q_0))$ will be close to $\widetilde{N}_1$. It follows that when we apply the rounding operator $\mathcal{R}_{\delta_1,t}$, the matrices are the same again, namely $M_1 = N_1$. See the left-hand side of Figure 2. Therefore, we do get back to the same automaton $Q_1 = \mathcal{Q}(M_1) = \mathcal{Q}(N_1)$.

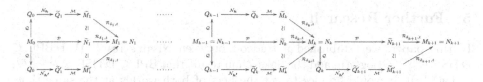

Fig. 2. Finding new sequence of hash functions

We then proceed to find a δ_2 which is weakly-safe for $\widetilde{N}_2 = N_1^{2^{r_1}}$. Note that $\widetilde{N}_2$ is never computed exactly but we choose δ_2 as being safe for the matrix $M_2' - \mathcal{M}(\mathcal{N}_{h'}(Q_1))$, which is very close to the matrix $\widetilde{N}_2$. Then applying $\mathcal{R}_{\delta_2,t}$ to either matrix yields N_2. We have arrived at a *succinct representation* for N_1 and N_2, namely $h' = h^{(2)}$ and (δ_1, δ_2).

Generalizing, we accomplish the computation of our final approximation N_{r_2} to M^{2^r} in r_2 stages as follows (see Figure 2). At the end of stage k, we will have computed a sequence of r_1 hash functions h and a sequence $\delta = (\delta_1, \delta_2, \ldots, \delta_k) \in (\{0,1\}^D)^k$. They constitute a *succinct representation* of the matrices $N_0, N_1, \ldots, N_k$ of the rounded sequence; we can compute these matrices N_i as the corresponding matrices M_i in the Saks-Zhou sequence $\mathrm{SZ}(Q, h, \delta)$. Moreover, each δ_i in δ is weakly-safe for $\widetilde{N}_i$ in $\mathrm{R}(M, \delta)$, $1 \leq i \leq k$.

In the $(k+1)$st stage, we use h and δ to reconstruct the matrices $N_0 = M_0$, $N_1 = M_1$, ..., $N_k = M_k$. We then compute a new sequence of r_1 hash functions h', one by one, which is simultaneously pseudorandom for $Q_0 = \mathcal{Q}(N_0), Q_1 = \mathcal{Q}(N_1), \ldots, Q_k = \mathcal{Q}(N_k)$. Thus, while both h and h' are pseudorandom for $Q_0, Q_1, \ldots, Q_{k-1}$, h' is also pseudorandom for Q_k. Now each

$\widetilde{M}_1' = \mathcal{M}(\mathcal{N}_{h'}(Q_0)), \widetilde{M}_2' = \mathcal{M}(\mathcal{N}_{h'}(Q_1)), \ldots, \widetilde{M}_k' = \mathcal{M}(\mathcal{N}_{h'}(Q_{k-1}))$ are sufficiently close to $\widetilde{N}_1, \widetilde{N}_2, \ldots, \widetilde{N}_k$, respectively, that when we apply the rounding operator $\mathcal{R}$ based on δ and t, we get the matrices $N_1, \ldots, N_k$ of the rounded sequence $\mathrm{R}(M, \delta)$ back. This is because δ_i is weakly safe for $\widetilde{N}_i$, $1 \leq i \leq k$. In addition, we have obtained $\widetilde{M}_{k+1}' = \mathcal{M}(\mathcal{N}_{h'}(Q_k))$, which is close to $\widetilde{N}_{k+1}$. We then find a $\delta_{k+1} \in \{0,1\}^D$ which is guaranteed to be weakly-safe for the matrix $\widetilde{N}_{k+1}$. Again, even though we do not really compute this $\widetilde{N}_{k+1}$ exactly, we find δ_{k+1} as being safe for its close approximation $\widetilde{M}_{k+1}'$. At this point, h' and $\delta' = (\delta_1, \delta_2, \ldots, \delta_k, \delta_{k+1})$ constitute a succinct representation of the matrices $N_0, N_1, \ldots, N_k, N_{k+1}$ in $\mathrm{R}(M, \delta')$, as shown in Figure 2. Now, we discard the old h and replace it with the newly found h', and we append δ_{k+1} to δ.

At the end of r_2 stages, we have found h and $\delta = (\delta_1, \delta_2, \ldots, \delta_{r_2})$ such that the rounded sequence $\mathrm{R}(M, \delta)$ and the Saks-Zhou sequence $\mathrm{SZ}(M, h, \delta)$ agree as in Figure 1.

In terms of time and space complexity, the most time consuming task is to recursively reconstruct the automata and matrices in the Saks-Zhou sequences with a maximum of r_2 levels of recursion, each level involving a polynomial time computation. The most space consuming task is to store the r_1 functions h.

5   Further Research

In this paper, we established a tradeoff between Nisan's result that BPL $\subseteq$ DTISP$[n^{O(1)}, O(\log^2 n)]$, and the Saks-Zhou result that BPL $\subseteq$ DTISP$[n^{O(\log^{0.5} n)}, O(\log^{1.5} n)]$. It would be nice to get the best of both worlds at the same time, i.e., a deterministic simulation of BPL that simultaneously runs in polynomial time and space $O(\log^{1.5} n)$. The breakdown of Proposition 1 seems to be the bottleneck.

Regarding undirected st-connectivity, Armoni et al. [2] managed to reduce the space bound to $O(\log^{4/3} n)$. At a high level, they apply the Saks-Zhou rounding technique to the shrinking strategy of Nisan, Szemeredi, and Wigderson [7]. Does the $O(\log^{4/3} n)$ space algorithm lead to a better time-space tradeoff for undirected st-connectivity than our general result for BPL?

The big open question, of course, is whether BPL can be simulated deterministically in logarithmic space. We know that this is the case if there exists a language in deterministic linear space that requires branching programs of size $2^{\epsilon n}$ for some positive constant ϵ [4].

References

1. R. Aleliunas, R. Karp, R. Lipton, L. Lovasz, and C. Rackoff. Random walks, universal travel sequences and the complexity of maze problems. *FOCS*, 1979.
2. R. Armoni, A. Ta-Shma, A. Wigderson, and S. Zhou. An $O(\log n^{4/3})$ space algorithm for (s,t) connectivity in undirected graphs. *JACM*, 47(2), 2000.
3. J. Cai, V. Chakaravarthy, and D. van Melkebeek. Time-space tradeoff in derandomizing probabilistic logspace. Available at http://www.cs.wisc.edu/~dieter.

4. A. Klivans and D. van Melkebeek. Graph nonisomorphism has subexponential size proofs unless the polynomial hierarchy collapses. *SICOMP*, 31(5), 2002.
5. N. Nisan. Pseudorandom generators for space-bounded computation. *Combinatorica*, 12(4), 1992.
6. N. Nisan. RL⊆ SC. *Computational Complexity*, 4, 1994.
7. N. Nisan, E. Szemeredi, and A. Wigderson. Undirected connectivity in $O(\log^{1.5} n)$ space. *FOCS*, 1992.
8. M. Saks. Randomization and derandomization in space bounded computation. In *IEEE Conference on Computational Complexity*, 1996.
9. M. Saks and S. Zhou. $BP_H SPACE(S) \subseteq DSPACE(S^{3/2})$. *JCSS*, 58, 1999.
10. W. J. Savitch. Relationships between nondeterministic and deterministic space complexities. *JCSS*, 4(2), 1970.

What Can Be Efficiently Reduced to the K-Random Strings?

Eric Allender[1*], Harry Buhrman[2], and Michal Koucký[3**]

[1] Rutgers University, New Brunswick, NJ, USA, alldender@cs.rutgers.edu
[2] CWI and University of Amsterdam, Amsterdam, Netherlands, buhrman@cwi.nl
[3] McGill University, Montréal, PQ, Canada, mkoucky@cs.mcgill.ca

Abstract. We investigate the question of whether one can characterize complexity classes (such as PSPACE or NEXP) in terms of efficient reducibility to the set of Kolmogorov-random strings R_K. We show
that this question cannot be posed without explicitly dealing with issues
raised by the choice of universal machine in the definition of Kolmogorov
complexity. Among other results, we show that although for every universal machine U, there are very complex sets that are $\leq_{dtt}^P$-reducible to
R_{K_U}, it is nonetheless true that $P = REC \cap \bigcap_U \{A : A \leq_{dtt}^P R_{K_U}\}$. We
also show for a broad class of reductions that the sets reducible to R_K
have small circuit complexity.

1 Introduction

The set of *random strings* is one of the most important notions in Kolmogorov
complexity theory. A string is random if $K(x) \geq |x|$. (Given a Turing machine
U, $K_U(x)$ is defined to be the minimum length of a "description" d such that
$U(d) = x$. As usual, we fix one such "universal" machine U and define $K(x)$ to
be equal to $K_U(x)$. In most applications, it does not make much difference which
"universal" machine U is picked; it suffices that U satisfies the property that for
all U' there exists a constant c such that $K_U(x) \leq K_{U'}(x) + c$.) Let R_K denote
the set of random strings, and let R_{K_U} denote the corresponding set when we
need to be specific about the particular choice of machine U.

It has been known since [4] that R_K is co-r.e. and is complete under weak-
truth-table reductions. This was improved significantly by Kummer, who showed
that R_K is complete under truth-table reductions [3] (even under disjunctive
truth-table reductions (dtt-reductions)). Thus there is a computable time bound
t and a function f computable in time t such that, for every x, $f(x)$ is a list of
strings with the property that $f(x)$ contains an element of R_K if and only if x is
not in the halting problem. Kummer's argument in [3] is not very specific about
the time bound t. Can this reduction be performed in exponential time? Or in

---

* Partially supported by NSF grant CCR-0104823.
** Partially supported by NSF grant CCR-0104823. Part of this work was done while
visiting CWI, Amsterdam and while a graduate student at Rutgers University, NJ.

V. Diekert and M. Habib (Eds.): STACS 2004, LNCS 2996, pp. 584–595, 2004.

doubly-exponential time?[1] In this paper, we provide an answer to this question; surprisingly, it is neither "yes" nor "no".

Kummer's theorem is not primarily a theorem about complexity, but about computability. More recently, however, attention was drawn to the question of what can be *efficiently* reduced to R_K. Using derandomization techniques, it was shown in [1] that every r.e. set is reducible to R_K via reductions computable by polynomial-size *circuits*. This leads to the question of what can be reduced to R_K by polynomial-time *machines*. In partial answer to this question, it was also shown in [1] that PSPACE is contained in P^{R_K}.

Question: Is it possible to *characterize* PSPACE in terms of efficient reductions to R_K?

Our goal throughout this paper is to try to answer this question. We present a concrete hypothesis later in the paper. Before presenting the hypothesis, however, it is useful to present some of our work that relates to Kummer's theorem, because it highlights the importance of being very precise about what we mean by "the Kolmogorov random strings".

Our first theorem suggests that Kummer's reduction might be computable in doubly-exponential time.

Theorem 1. *There exists a universal Turing machine U such that $\{0^{2^x} : x$ is not in the Halting problem\} is polynomial-time reducible to R_{K_U} (and in fact this reduction is even a $\leq^{p}_{dtt}$ reduction).*

Note that, except for the dependence on the choice of universal machine U, this is a considerable strengthening of the result of [3], since it yields a polynomial-time reduction (starting with a very sparse encoding of the halting problem). In addition, the proof is much simpler.

However, the preceding theorem is unsatisfying in many respects. The most annoying aspect of this result is that it relies on the construction of a fairly "weird" universal Turing machine U. Is this necessary, or does it hold for *every* universal machine? Note that one of the strengths of Kolmogorov complexity theory has always been that the theory is essentially insensitive to the particular choice of universal machine. We show that for this question (as well as for other questions regarding the set of Kolmogorov-random strings) the choice of universal machine *does* matter.

1.1 Universal Machines Matter

To illustrate how the choice of universal machine matters, let us present a corollary of our Theorem 8.

---

[1] Kummer does show in [3] that completeness under truth-table reductions does *not* hold under some choices of numberings of the r.e. sets; however his results *do* hold for every choice of a universal Turing machine (i.e., "Kolmogorov" numberings, or "optimal Gödelnumberings"). Kummer's result holds even under a larger class of numberings known as "optimal numberings". For background, see [5].

Corollary 1. *Let t be any computable time bound. There exists a universal Turing machine U and a decidable set A such that A is not dtt reducible to R_{K_U} in time t.*

Thus, in particular, the reason why Kummer was not specific about the running time of his truth-table reduction in [3] is that no such time bound can be stated, without being specific about the choice of universal Turing machine. This stands in stark contrast to the result of [1], showing that the halting problem is P/poly-reducible to R_K; the size of that reduction does not depend on the universal Turing machine that is used to define R_K.

Most notions in complexity theory (and even in computability theory) are invariant under polynomial-time isomorphisms. For instance, using the techniques of [2] it is easy to show that for any reasonable universal Turing machines U_1 and U_2, the corresponding halting problems $H_i = \{(x, y) : U_i(x, y)$ halts$\}$ are p-isomorphic. However, it follows immediately from Corollary 1 and Theorem 1 that the corresponding sets of random strings $R_{K_{U_i}}$ are not all p-isomorphic.

Corollary 2. *Let t be any computable time bound. There exist universal Turing machines U_1 and U_2 such that $R_{K_{U_1}}$ is not reducible to $R_{K_{U_2}}$ in time t. In particular, $R_{K_{U_1}}$ and $R_{K_{U_2}}$ are not isomorphic via isomorphisms computable in time t.*

(We believe that the situation is actually even worse than this, in that the quantifiers in the preceding corollary can be switched. Even if we take U_1 to be the "standard" universal machine, and we define $U_2(0d) = U_1(d)$, we do not see how to construct a computable isomorphism between $R_{K_{U_1}}$ and $R_{K_{U_2}}$.)

The lesson we bring away from the preceding discussion is that the choice of universal machine is important, in any investigation of the question of what can be efficiently reduced to the random strings. In contrast, all of the results of [1] (showing hardness of R_K) hold *no matter* which universal Turing machine is used to define Kolmogorov complexity.

Another obstacle that seems to block the way to any straightforward characterization of complexity classes in terms of R_K is the fact that, for *every* universal Turing machine and *every* computable time bound t, there is a recursive set A such that $A \leq^P_{dtt} R_{K_U}$ but such that $A \notin \mathrm{DSPACE}(t)$ (Theorem 10). Thus P^{R_K} may not correspond to any reasonable complexity class. How can we proceed from here?

We offer the following hypothesis, as a way of "factoring out" the effects of pathological machines. In essence, we are asking what can be reduced to the K-random strings, *regardless* of the universal machine that is used.

Hypothesis 2 $\mathrm{PSPACE} = \mathrm{REC} \cap \bigcap_U P^{R_{K_U}}$.

We are unable to establish this hypothesis (and indeed, we stop short from calling it a "conjecture"). However, we do prove an analogous statement for polynomial-time dtt reductions.

Motivation for studying dtt reductions comes from Kummer's paper [3] (presenting a dtt reduction from the complement of the halting problem to R_K), as well as from Theorem 1 and Corollary 1. The following theorem is similar in structure to Hypothesis 2, indicating that it is possible to "factor out" the choice of universal machine in some instances.

Theorem 3. $P = REC \cap \bigcap_U \{A : A \leq_{dtt}^p R_{K_U}\}$.

We take this as weak evidence that something similar to Hypothesis 2 might be true, in the sense that it shows that "factoring out" the effects of universal machines can lead to characterizations of complexity classes in terms of reducibility to the random strings.

1.2 Approaching the Hypothesis

In order to prove Hypothesis 2, one must be able to show that there are decidable sets that cannot be reduced efficiently to R_{K_U} for some U. Currently we are able to do this only for some restricted classes of polynomial-time truth-table reductions: (a) *monotone* truth-table reductions, (b) parity truth-table reductions, and (c) truth-table reductions that ask at most n^α queries, for $\alpha < 1$.

In certain instances, we are able to prove a stronger property. In the case of parity truth-table reductions and disjunctive reductions, if there is a reduction computable in time t from A to R_{K_U} for every U, then A can already be computed nearly in time t. That is, for these classes of reducibilities, a reduction to R_K that does *not* take specific properties of the universal machine into account is nearly useless. We believe that this is likely to be true for any polynomial-time truth-table reduction. Note that this stands in stark contrast to polynomial-time Turing reducibility, since PSPACE-complete problems are expected to require exponential time, but can be solved in polynomial time with R_K as an oracle. An even stronger contrast is provided by NP-Turing reducibilities. The techniques of [1] can be used to show that $NEXP \subseteq NP^{R_K}$; and thus R_K provably provides an exponential speed-up in this setting.

2 Preliminaries and Definitions

In this section we present some necessary definitions. Many of our theorems make reference to "universal" Turing machines. Rather than give a formal definition of what a universal Turing machine is, which might require introducing unnecessary complications in our proofs, we will leave the notion of a "universal" Turing machine as an intuitive notion, and instead use the following properties that are widely known to hold for any natural notion of universal Turing machine, and which are also easily seen to hold for the universal Turing machines that we present here:

- For any two universal Turing machines U_1 and U_2, the halting problems for U_1 and U_2 are p-isomorphic. That is, U_1 halts on input x if and only if U_2 halts on input x' (where x' encodes the information (U_1, x) in a straightforward way). This is a length-increasing and invertible reduction; p-isomorphism now follows by [2].

– For any two universal Turing machines U_1 and U_2, there exists a constant c such that $K_{U_1}(x) < K_{U_2}(x) + c$.

Let U_1 be the "standard" universal Turing machine. If U_2 is any other machine that satisfies the two properties listed above, then we will consider U_2 to be a universal Turing machine. We are confident that our results carry over to other, more stringent definitions of "universal" Turing machine that one might define. This does not seem to us to be an interesting direction to pursue.

We define $R_{K_U} = \{x \in \{0,1\}^* : K_U(x) \geq |x|\}$. When we state a result that is independent of a particular choice of a universal Turing machine U we will drop the U in K_U and refer simply to $K(x)$.

2.1   Reductions

Let $\mathcal{R}$ be a complexity class and A and B be languages. We define the following types of reductions.

– *Many-one reductions.* We say that A $\mathcal{R}$-*many-one reduces* to B ($A \leq_m^{\mathcal{R}} B$) if there is a function $f \in \mathcal{R}$ such that for any $x \in \Sigma^*$, $x \in A$ if and only if $f(x) \in B$.
– *Truth-table reductions.* We say that A $\mathcal{R}$-*truth-table reduces* to B ($A \leq_{tt}^{\mathcal{R}} B$) if there is a pair of functions q and r, both in $\mathcal{R}$, such that on an input $x \in \Sigma^*$, function q produces a list of queries $q_1, q_2, \ldots, q_m$ so that for $a_1, a_2, \ldots, a_m \in \{0,1\}$ where $a_i = B(q_i)$, it holds that $x \in A$ if and only if $r(\langle x, (q_1, a_1), (q_2, a_2), \cdots, (q_m, a_m)\rangle) = 1$.
  If $r = \wedge_i a_i$, then the reduction is called a *conjunctive truth-table reduction* ($\leq_{ctt}^{\mathcal{R}}$). If $r = \vee_i a_i$, then the reduction is called a *disjunctive truth-table reduction* ($\leq_{dtt}^{\mathcal{R}}$). If the function r computes the parity of $a_1, a_2, \ldots, a_m$, then the reduction is called a *parity truth-table reduction* ($\leq_{\oplus tt}^{\mathcal{R}}$). If the function r is monotone with respect to $a_1, a_2, \ldots, a_m$ then the reduction is called a *monotone truth-table reduction* ($\leq_{mtt}^{\mathcal{R}}$). (A function r is monotone with respect to $a_1, \ldots, a_m$, if for any input x, any set of queries $q_1, \ldots, q_m$, and $a_1, \ldots, a_m, a_1', \ldots, a_m' \in \{0,1\}$, where for all i, $a_i \leq a_i'$, if r accepts $\langle x, (q_1, a_1), (q_2, a_2), \cdots, (q_m, a_m)\rangle$ then it is also the case that r accepts the tuple $\langle x, (q_1, a_1'), (q_2, a_2'), \cdots, (q_m, a_m')\rangle$) If the number of queries m is bounded by a constant, then the reduction is called a *bounded truth-table reduction* ($\leq_{btt}^{\mathcal{R}}$). If the number of queries m is bounded by $f(n)$, then the reduction is called a $f(n)$ *truth-table reduction* ($\leq_{f(n)-tt}^{\mathcal{R}}$).
– *Turing reductions.* We say that A $\mathcal{R}$-*Turing reduces* to B ($A \leq_T^{\mathcal{R}} B$) if there is an oracle Turing machine in class $\mathcal{R}$ that accepts A when given B as an oracle.

3   Inside P^{R_K}

We have two kinds of results to present in this section. First we present several theorems that do not depend on the choice of universal machine. Then we present our results that highlight the effect of choosing certain universal machines.

3.1   Inclusions That Hold for All Universal Machines

The following is a strengthened version of claims that were stated without proof in [1].

Theorem 4.

1. $\{A \in \mathrm{REC} : A \leq^{\mathrm{P}}_{\mathrm{ctt}} R_{\mathrm{K}}\} \subseteq P$.
2. $\{A \in \mathrm{REC} : A \leq^{\mathrm{P}}_{\mathrm{btt}} R_{\mathrm{K}}\} \subseteq P$.
3. $\{A \in \mathrm{REC} : A \leq^{\mathrm{P}}_{\mathrm{mtt}} R_{\mathrm{K}}\} \subseteq P/\mathrm{poly}$.

Proof. In all three arguments we will have a recursive set A that is $\leq^{(q,r)}_{tt}$ reducible to R_{K}, where (q,r) is the pair of polynomial-time-computable functions defining the $\leq^{\mathrm{P}}_{\mathrm{ctt}}$, $\leq^{\mathrm{P}}_{\mathrm{btt}}$ and $\leq^{\mathrm{P}}_{\mathrm{mtt}}$ reductions, respectively. For $x \in \{0,1\}^*$, $Q(x)$ will denote the set of queries produced by q on input x.

1. (q,r) computes a $\leq^{\mathrm{P}}_{\mathrm{ctt}}$ reduction. For any $x \in A$, $Q(x) \subseteq R_{\mathrm{K}}$. Hence, $Q = \bigcup_{x \in A} Q(x)$ is an r.e. subset of R_{K}. Since R_{K} is immune (i.e., has no infinite r.e. subset), Q is finite. Hence we can hard-wire Q into a table and conclude that $A \in P$.

2. (q,r) computes a $\leq^{\mathrm{P}}_{\mathrm{btt}}$ reduction. We will prove the claim by induction on the number of queries. If the reduction does not ask any query, the claim is trivial. Assume that the claim is true for reductions asking fewer than k queries. We will prove the claim for reductions asking at most k queries. Take (q,r) that computes a $\leq^{\mathrm{P}}_{\mathrm{btt}}$ reduction and such that $|Q(x)| \leq k$, for all x. For any string x, let $m_x = \min\{|q| : q \in Q(x)\}$. We claim that there exists an integer l such that for any x, if $m_x > l$ and $Q(x) = \{q_1, q_2, \ldots, q_{k'}\}$ then $r(\langle x, (q_1, 0), (q_2, 0), \ldots, (q_{k'}, 0)\rangle) = A(x)$. For contradiction assume that for any integer l, there exists x such that $m_x > l$ and $r(\langle x, (q_1, 0), (q_2, 0), \ldots, (q_{k'}, 0)\rangle) \neq A(x)$. Since A is recursive, for any l, we can find the lexicographically first x_l having such a property. All the queries in $Q(x_l)$ are longer than l and at least one of them should be in R_{K}. However, each of the queries can be described by $O(\log l)$ bits, which is the contradiction. Hence, there exists an integer l such that for any x, if $m_x > l$ then $r(\langle x, (q_1, 0), (q_2, 0), \ldots, (q_{k'}, 0)\rangle) = A(x)$. Thus we can encode the answers for all queries of length at most l into a table and reduce the number of queries in our reduction by one. Then we can apply the induction hypothesis.

3. (q,r) computes a $\leq^{\mathrm{P}}_{\mathrm{mtt}}$ reduction. q is computable in time n^c, for some $c > 1$. We claim that r does not depend on any query of length more than $2c \log n$. Assume that for infinitely many x, r does depend on queries of length more than $2c \log |x|$, i.e., if $Q(x) = \{q_1, q_2, \ldots, q_m\}$ and $a'_1, a'_2, \ldots, a'_m \in \{0,1\}$ are such that $a'_i = 1$ if $q_i \in R_{\mathrm{K}}$ and $|q_i| \leq 2c \log |x|$, and $a'_i = 0$ otherwise, then $r(\langle x, (q_1, a'_1), (q_2, a'_2), \ldots, (q_m, a'_m)\rangle) \neq A(x)$. Since r is monotone, this may happen only for x that belong to A. The set of all such x can be enumerated, by assuming that all queries of length greater than $2c \log |x|$ are not in R_{K} and assuming that all shorter queries are in R_{K}, and then computing successively better approximations to the correct answers for the short queries by enumerating the complement of R_{K}, until an answer vector is obtained on which r evaluates to zero, although x is in A. Note that for better approximations to the true value

of R_K, r will still evaluate to zero because r is a monotone reduction. Hence for given l, we can find the first x of length more than l in this enumeration. One of the queries in $Q(x)$ is of length more than $2c \log l$ and it belongs to R_K. But we can describe every query in $Q(x)$ by $c \log l + 2 \log \log l + \log l + O(1)$ bits, which is less than $2c \log l$. That is a contradiction. Since we have established that r depends only on queries of length at most $2c \log n$, we can encode information about all strings of this size that belong to R_K into a polynomially large table. Thus A is in P/poly.

Theorem 5. *If A is recursive and it reduces to R_K via a polynomial-time $f(n)$-truth-table reduction then A is in $P/(f(n)2^{f(n)3 \log f(n)})$.*

Corollary 3. *If A is recursive and reduces to R_K via a polynomial-time truth-table reduction with $O(\log(n)/\log \log n)$ queries then A is in P/poly.*

Corollary 4. *Let $g(n)$ be such that $g(n)2^{g(n)3 \log g(n)} < 2^n$. Then there exists a recursive A such that A does not reduce to R_K via a polynomial-time $g(n)$-truth-table reduction. In particular for any $\alpha < 1$ there exists a recursive A that does not reduce to R_K via a polynomial-time n^α-truth-table reduction.*

Proof of Theorem 5. W.l.o.g. $f(n)$ is unbounded. Let M be the reduction from A to R_K that uses at most $f(n)$ queries. Let $Q(x)$ be the query set that $M(x)$ generates. We will remove from $Q(x)$ all the strings that have length at least $s_n = 2 \log(f(n)) + 2 \log \log f(n) + c$ for some suitably chosen constant c. Let $Q'(x) = Q(x) \bigcap \{0,1\}^{<s_n}$ be this reduced set.

Note that there are at most 2^{s_n} strings of length less than s_n and that there are at most $\binom{2^{s_n}}{f(n)} < (2^{s_n})^{f(n)} < 2^{f(n)3 \log f(n)}$ possible subsets $Q'(x)$. Partition $\{0,1\}^n$ into equivalence classes, where $[x] = \{y : Q'(y) = Q'(x)\}$. We will show that for each equivalence class $[x]$ there is an answer sequence v_x such that, for all $y \in [x]$, y is in A if and only if M accepts y when the answers to $Q(y)$ are answered according to v_x for all of the queries in $Q'(y)$, and all of the long queries are answered negatively.

Thus the advice string consists of an encoding of v_x, which can be written using $f(n)$ bits, for each possible set $Q'(x)$. This yields the desired advice bound.

It remains only to show that the string v_x exists. Assume otherwise. Thus, given m, there is a recursive procedure that finds the lexicographically first string x of length n such that $\log f(n) > m$ and for all v there is some $y_v \in [x]$ on which the result of running $M(y_v)$ with answer vector v does *not* answer correctly about whether y_v is in A. Let v be the answer sequence for $Q'(x) \cap R_K$, and let r be the number of 1's in v (i.e., r is the size of $Q'(x) \cap R_K$). Thus, given (m, r) we can compute $Q'(x)$ and start the enumeration of the complement of R_K until we have enumerated all but r elements of $Q'(x)$. Thus we can compute v and find y_v. Since $M(y_v)$ is not giving the correct answer about whether y_v is in A, but M *does* give the correct answer when using R_K as an oracle, it follows that $Q(y_v)$ contains an element of R_K of length greater than s_n. However, this string is described by the tuple (m, r, i), along with $O(1)$ additional bits. For the appropriate choice of c, this has length less than s_n, which is a contradiction. □

Note that the preceding proof actually shows that, for every x such that $[x]$ has "small enough" Kolmogorov complexity, we can pick v_x to be the answer sequence for $Q'(x) \cap R_K$. If this were true for *every* x, then it would follow easily that every decidable set A that is reducible to R_K via a polynomial-time truth-table reduction is in P/poly.

3.2 Pathological Universal Machines

Before presenting the results of this section, we digress in order to introduce some techniques that we will need.

The following development is motivated by a question that one can naturally ask: what is the size of $(R_K)^{=n}$? It is a part of folklore that the number of strings in R_K of length n is Kolmogorov random. But is it odd or even? One would be tempted to answer that since $|(R_K)^{=n}|$ is Kolmogorov random, the parity of it must also be random. The following universal Turing machine U_{even} shows that this is not the case.

Let U_{st} be the "standard" universal Turing machine. Consider the universal Turing machine U_{even} defined by: for any $d \in \{0, 1\}^*$, $U_{even}(0d) = U_{st}(d)$ and $U_{even}(1d) =$ the bit-wise complement of $U_{st}(d)$. It is immediate that the size of $(R_{K_{U_{even}}})^{=n}$ is even for all n. To construct a universal Turing machine U_{odd} for which the size of $(R_{K_{U_{odd}}})^{=n}$ is odd for all n (large enough), is a little bit more complicated.

We will need the following definition. For any Turing machine U we can construct an *enumerator* (Turing machine) E that enumerates all pairs (d, x) such that $U(d) = x$, for $d, x \in \{0, 1\}^*$. (The running time of E is possibly infinite.) Conversely, given an enumerator E that enumerates pairs (d, x) so that if (d, x) and (d, x') are enumerated then $x = x'$, we can construct a Turing machine U such that for any $x, d \in \{0, 1\}^*$, $U(d) = x$ if and only if E ever enumerates the pair (d, x). In the following, we will often define a Turing machine in terms of its enumerator.

We define U_{odd} in terms of its enumerator E_{odd} that works as it is described below. E_{odd} will maintain sets of non-random strings $\{N_i\}_{i \in \mathbb{N}}$ during its operation. At any point in time, set N_i will contain non-random strings of length i that were enumerated by E_{odd} so far. E_{odd} will try to maintain the size of sets N_i to be odd (except while they are empty.)

Initialize all $\{N_i\}_{i \in \mathbb{N}}$ to the empty set.[2]

For all $d \in \{0, 1\}^*$, run $U_{st}(d)$ in parallel.

Whenever $U_{st}(d)$ halts for some d and produces a string x do:

    Output $(0d, x)$.

    If $|0d| < |x|$ and $N_{|x|} = \emptyset$ then set $N_{|x|} := \{x\}$.

---

[2] We assume in the usual way that E_{odd} works in steps and at step s it initializes the s-th set of $\{N_i\}_{i \in \mathbb{N}}$ to the empty set. Our statements regarding actions that involve infinite computation should be interpreted in a similar way.

Else if $|0d| < |x|$ and $x \notin N_{|x|}$ then:

    Pick the lexicographically first string y in $\{0,1\}^{|x|} - (N_{|x|} \cup \{x\})$.

    Set $N_{|x|} := N_{|x|} \cup \{x, y\}$ and output $(1d, y)$.

Continue.

End.

It is easy to see that the Turing machine U_{odd} defined by the enumerator E_{odd} is universal. Also it is clear that for all n large enough, $(R_{K_{U_{\text{odd}}}})^{=n}$ is of odd size.

The ability to influence the parity of $(R_{K_U})^{=n}$ allows us to (sparsely) encode any recursively enumerable information into R_{K_U}. We can state the following theorem.

Theorem 6. *For any recursively enumerable set A, there is a universal Turing machine U such that if $C = \{0^{2^x} : x \in A\}$, then $C \leq^{\mathrm{p}}_{\oplus \mathrm{tt}} R_{K_U}$. Consequently, $A \leq^{EE}_{\oplus \mathrm{tt}} R_{K_U}$.*

Proof. Observe, $C \subseteq \{0^{2^i} : i \in \mathbf{N}\}$. We will construct the universal Turing machine U so that for any integer $i > 3$, $0^{2^i} \in C$ if and only if $(R_{K_U})^{=i}$ is of odd size. Then, the polynomial time parity reduction of C to R_{K_U} can be constructed trivially as well as the double-exponential parity reduction of A to R_{K_U}.

Let M be the Turing machine accepting the recursively enumerable set C. We will construct an enumerator E for U. It will work as follows. E will maintain sets $\{N_i\}_{i \in \mathbf{N}}$ during its computations. At any point in time, for every $i > 0$ the set N_i will contain non-random strings of length i that were enumerated by E so far and E will try to maintain the parity of $|N_i|$ unchanged during most of the computation. E will also run M on all strings $z = 0^{2^i}$ in parallel and whenever some new string z will be accepted by M, E will change the parity of $N_{\log|z|}$ by making some new string of length $\log|z|$ non-random. The algorithm for E is the following.

Initialize all $\{N_i\}_{i \in \mathbf{N}}$ to the empty set.

For all $d \in \{0,1\}^*$ and $z \in \{0^{2^i} : i \in \mathbf{N}\}$, run $U_{\text{st}}(d)$ and $M(z)$ in parallel.

Whenever $U_{\text{st}}(d)$ or $M(z)$ halts for some d or $z = 0^{2^i}$ do:

    If $U_{\text{st}}(d)$ halts and produces output x then:

        Output $(00d, x)$.

        If $|00d| < |x|$ and $x \notin N_{|x|}$ then:

            Pick the lex. first string y in $\{0,1\}^{|x|} - (N_{|x|} \cup \{x\})$.

            Set $N_{|x|} := N_{|x|} \cup \{x, y\}$ and output $(01d, y)$.

    Continue.

    If $M(0^{2^i})$ halts and $i > 3$ then:

        Pick the lexicographically first string y in $\{0,1\}^i - N_i$.

        Set $N_i := N_i \cup \{y\}$, and output $(1^{i-1}, y)$.

        Continue.

End.

Clearly, enumerator E defines a universal optimal Turing machine and for any integer $i > 3$, $0^{2^i} \in C$ if and only if $(R_{K_U})^{=i}$ is of odd size.

Parity is not the only way to encode information into R_{K}. The following theorem illustrates that we can encode the information so that one can use $\leq^{\mathrm{P}}_{\mathrm{dtt}}$ reductions to extract it. In particular, this proves our Theorem 1.

Theorem 7. *For any recursively enumerable set A, there is a universal Turing machine U such that if $C = \{0^{2^x} : x \in A\}$, then $\overline{C} \leq^{\mathrm{P}}_{\mathrm{dtt}} R_{\mathrm{K}_U}$. Consequently, $\overline{A} \leq^{EE}_{\mathrm{dtt}} R_{\mathrm{K}_U}$.*

Proof. First, define a universal Turing machine U_{opt} as follows: $U_{\mathrm{opt}}(0d) = U_{\mathrm{st}}(d)$ and $U_{\mathrm{opt}}(1d) = d$. Clearly, for any $x \in \{0,1\}^*$, $\mathrm{K}_{U_{\mathrm{opt}}}(x) \leq |x| + 1$. For any $d \in \{0,1\}^*$ and any $s \in \{0,1\}^5$, U is defined as follows:

On input $0ds$, run $U_{\mathrm{opt}}(d)$ and if $U_{\mathrm{opt}}(d)$ halts then output $U_{\mathrm{opt}}(d)s$.

On input $1d$ do:

    Run $U_{\mathrm{opt}}(d)$, until it halts.

    Let y be the output of $U_{\mathrm{opt}}(d)$.

    Check if $0^{2^{|y|}} \in C$.

    If $0^{2^{|y|}} \in C$ then output $y0^5$.

End.

It is clear that for any $x \in \{0,1\}^*$, $\mathrm{K}_U(x) \leq |x| + 2$. Further, for any $s, s' \in \{0,1\}^5 - \{0^5\}$, $K_U(xs) = K_U(xs')$. Finally, for any $y \in \{0,1\}^*$, $0^{2^{|y|}} \in C$ if and only if $K_U(y0^5) < K_U(y1^5) - 4$. Hence, if $0^{2^{|y|}} \in C$ then $y0^5 \notin R_{\mathrm{K}}$. The $\leq^{\mathrm{P}}_{\mathrm{dtt}}$ reduction of $\overline{C}$ to R_{K} works as follows: on input 0^{2^n}, for all $y \in \{0,1\}^n$ ask queries $y0^5$. Output 0 if none of the queries lies in R_{K} and 1 otherwise.

One could start to suspect that maybe all recursive functions are reducible to R_{K} in, say, doubly exponential time, regardless of which universal Turing machine is used to define R_{K}. We do not know if that is true but the following theorem shows that certainly disjunctive truth-table reductions are not sufficient.

Theorem 8. *For any computable time-bound $t(n) \geq n$, every set A in $\mathrm{REC} \cap \bigcap_U \{A : A \leq^{t(n)}_{\mathrm{dtt}} R_{\mathrm{K}_U}\}$ is computable in time $O(t^3(n))$.*

Theorem 3 is a corollary of Theorem 8.

Proof. It suffices to show that for each decidable set A that is not computable in time $O(t^3(n))$, there is a universal machine U such that A is not $\leq^{t(n)}_{\mathrm{dtt}}$-reducible to R_{K_U}. Fix a set A not computable in time $O(t^3(n))$.

Let U_{st} be a (standard) universal Turing machine, and define U so that for all d, $U(00d) = U_{st}(d)$. Note that, for every length m, fewer than $\frac{1}{4}$ of the strings of length m are made non-random in this way.

Now we present a stage construction, defining how U treats descriptions $d \notin \{00\}\{0,1\}^*$. We present an enumeration of pairs (d, y); this defines $U(d) = y$. In stage i, we guarantee that the i-th Turing machine q_i that runs in time $t(n)$ (in an enumeration of clocked Turing machines computing $\leq^{t(n)}_{\mathrm{dtt}}$ reductions) does not reduce A to R_{K_U}.

At the start of stage i, there is a length l_i with the property that at no later stage will any string y of length less than l_i be enumerated in our list of pairs (d, y). (At stage 1, let $l_1 = 1$.)

Let $\mathcal{T}$ be the set of all subsets of the strings of length less than l_i. For any string x, denote by $Q_i(x)$ the list of queries produced by the $\leq_{\text{dtt}}^{t(n)}$ reduction computed by q_i on input x, and let $Q'(x)$ be the set of strings in $Q_i(x)$ having length less than l_i.

In Stage i, the construction starts searching through all strings of length l_i or greater, until strings x_0 and x_1 are found, having the following properties:

- $x_0 \notin A$,
- $x_1 \in A$,
- $Q'(x_1) = Q'(x_2)$, and
- One of the following holds
  - $Q_i(x_1)$ contains fewer than 2^{m-2} elements from $\{0,1\}^m$ for each length $m \geq l_i$, or
  - $Q_i(x_0)$ contains at least 2^{m-2} elements from $\{0,1\}^m$ for some length $m \geq l_i$

We argue below that strings x_0 and x_1 will be found after a finite number of steps.

If $Q_i(x_1)$ contains fewer than 2^{m-2} elements from $\{0,1\}^m$ for each length $m \geq l_i$, then for each string y of length $m \geq l_i$ in $Q_i(x_1)$, pick a different d of length $m - 2$ and add the pair $(1d, y)$ to the enumeration. This guarantees that $Q_i(x_1)$ contains no element of R_{K_U} of length $\geq l_i$. Thus if q_i is to be a $\leq_{\text{dtt}}^{t(n)}$ reduction of A to R_{K_U}, it must be the case that $Q'(x_1)$ contains an element of R_{K_U}. However, since $Q'(x_1) = Q'(x_0)$ and $x_0 \notin A$, we see that q_i is not a $\leq_{\text{dtt}}^{t(n)}$ reduction of A to R_{K_U}.

If $Q_i(x_0)$ contains at least 2^{m-2} elements from $\{0,1\}^m$ for some length $m \geq l_i$, then note that at least one of these strings is not produced as output by $U(00d)$ for any string $00d$ of length $\leq m - 1$. We will guarantee that U does not produce any of these strings on any description $d \notin \{00\}\{0,1\}^*$, and thus one of these strings must be in R_{K_U}, and hence q_i is not a $\leq_{\text{dtt}}^{t(n)}$ reduction of A to R_{K_U}.

Let l_{i+1} be the maximum of the lengths of x_0, x_1 and the lengths of the strings in $Q_i(x_0)$ and $Q_i(x_1)$.

It remains only to show that strings x_0 and x_1 will be found after a finite number of steps. Assume otherwise. It follows that $\{0,1\}^*$ can be partitioned into a finite number of equivalence classes, where y and z are equivalent if both y and z have length less than l_i, or if they have length $\geq l_i$ and $Q'(y) = Q'(z)$. Furthermore, for the equivalence classes containing long strings, if the class contains both strings in A and in $\overline{A}$, then the strings in A are exactly the strings on which q_i queries at least 2^{m-2} elements of $\{0,1\}^m$ for some length $m \geq l_i$. This yields an $O(t^3(n))$-time algorithm for A, contrary to our assumption that A is not computable in time $O(t^3(n))$.

Theorem 9. *For any computable time-bound $t(n) \geq n$, every set A in REC $\cap$ $\bigcap_U \{A : A \leq_{\oplus tt}^{t(n)} R_{K_U}\}$ is computable in time $O(t^3(n))$.*

Due to space limitations, the proof is omitted.

We conclude with the following observation that is a corollary to Kummer's result [3].

Theorem 10. *For every universal Turing machine U and every time-constructible function $t(n) \geq n$, there is a recursive set $A \notin \mathrm{DSPACE}(t)$ such that $A \leq_{dtt}^{p} R_{K_U}$.*

Proof. Fix any universal Turing machine U and time-bound $t(n) \geq n$. By Kummer's result, there is a time-bound t' such that the Halting problem dtt-reduces to R_{K_U} in time $t'(n)$. W.l.o.g. $t'(n) \geq n$. Let $A \notin \mathrm{DSPACE}(t(t'(2^n)))$ be a recursive set. Consider set $B = \{0^{t'(2^{|x|})-|x|-1}1x : x \in A\}$. Clearly, $B \notin \mathrm{DSPACE}(t(n))$. Since A is recursive, it reduces to R_{K_U} via a dtt-reduction running in time $t'(n^c)$, for some constant c. It follows that $B \leq_{dtt}^{p} R_{K_U}$.

4   Conclusions and Open Problems

Do there exist universal Turing machines U_1 and U_2 so that $R_{K_{U_1}}$ and $R_{K_{U_2}}$ are not recursively isomorphic? Or so that they are not in the same $\leq_m$-degree?

Can one show that not every decidable set is $\leq_{tt}^{p}$-reducible to R_K (at least for some choice of universal machine)?

Is there a proof of Hypothesis 2? It might be more feasible to prove a related hypothesis more in line with Theorems 4 and 5 of Section 3: For any universal machine: $\{A \in \mathrm{REC} : A \leq_T^{p} R_K\} \subseteq \mathrm{PSPACE/poly}$

Acknowledgments. We would like to thank to Kolya Vereshchagin and Troy Lee for helpful discussions.

References

1. E. Allender, H. Buhrman, M. Koucký, D. van Melkebeek, and D. Ronneburger. Power from random strings. In *FOCS: IEEE Symposium on Foundations of Computer Science (FOCS)*, pages 669–678, 2002.
2. L. Berman and J. Hartmanis. On isomorphisms and density of NP and other complete sets. *SIAM Journal on Computing*, 6:305–323, 1977.
3. M. Kummer. On the complexity of random strings. In *Symposium on Theoretical Aspects of Computer Science (STACS)*, volume 1046 of *Lecture Notes in Computer Science*, pages 25–36. Springer, 1996.
4. E. L. Post. Recursively enumerable sets of positive integers and their decision problems. *Bulletin of American Mathematical Society*, 50:284–316, 1944.
5. C. P. Schnorr. Optimal enumerations and optimal Gödel numberings. *Mathematical Systems Theory*, 8:182–191, 1974.

Regular Language Matching and Other Decidable Cases of the Satisfiability Problem for Constraints between Regular Open Terms

Sebastian Bala

Institute of Computer Science
University of Wrocław
Przesmyckiego 20, 51151 Wrocław, Poland
magic@ii.uni.wroc.pl

Abstract. In this work, we investigate computational complexity of the solution existence problem for language equations and language constraints. More accurately, we study constraints between regular terms over alphabet consisting of constants and variables and based on regular operators such as concatenation ($\cdot$), sum ($+$), Kleene-star ($*$). We obtain complexity results concerning three restricted cases of the constraints: for system of language equations in which one side does not contain any occurrences of variables in case arbitrary solutions and with restriction to finite languages; for constraint in form $L \subseteq R$, where R has no occurrences of variables.

1 Introduction

Language equations can be defined over different sets of operators. But, the concatenation must appear among the operators. The properties of language equations have been the field of intensive studies for many variants of sets of operators ([8], [12]) and various restrictions put on the form of equations ([11], [3]), the domain of solutions ([4]), the number of variables, and the size of the alphabet ([11], [9], [5]). Besides, in [11], it was considered not only equations but constraints with inclusion operator. The algebraic properties of language equations such as the existence of the solution, the problem of uniqueness and the existence of the greatest solution, testing whether the system of language equations has finitely many solutions were investigated for linear regular language equations in [10] and [3]. A language equation is linear if each side of the equation has the form of a linear pattern $S_0 \cup S_1 X_1 \cup \ldots \cup S_n X_n$, where $S_1, \ldots, S_n$ are arbitrary formal languages which are called language constants, $X_1 \ldots X_n$ are different variables. In [3], they consider systems of linear language equations in which all language constants are regular. We call them linear regular language equations. In [3], among other things, it was proved that satisfiability problem for linear language equations is $EXPTIME\text{-}complete$ and for linear regular language matching this problem is $PSPACE\text{-}complete$. Moreover, for the above mentioned two cases the satisfiability has that nice property that if the solution exists then the regular one exists too.

Partially supported by Komitet Badan Naukowych grant 8 T11C 043 19.

V. Diekert and M. Habib (Eds.): STACS 2004, LNCS 2996, pp. 596–607, 2004.
© Springer-Verlag Berlin Heidelberg 2004

The results concerning language equations are of independent interest, they frequently appear in other research contexts. Below we mention several interesting applications of the results: in [5] there have been proved undecidability results for the process logic using the result that the satisfiability of equations between regular terms is undecidable; in [3], [4] there was shown computational complexity of certain cases of the unification problem in description logic which was obtained by reduction of the satisfiability of linear regular language equations; in [2] there was considered the satisfiability problem for certain cases of linear regular language equations the motivation of which arise from the coding theory if we make the additional assumption that the operations must be unambiguous.

The regular language equations were investigated almost always in the linear case. In this paper we consider equations between regular terms based on Kleene's operators $\cdot, +, *$ in arbitrary form. In the general case the solution existence problem for equations between regular terms is undecidable even if only one variable is used.

We show computational complexity in three cases of language equations and language constraints: for the system of langauge equations in which one side does not contain any occurrences of variables the satisfiability problem is $EXPSPACE$-complete and if we want to decide does there exist solution over finite languages, not over arbitrary languages, the problem remains $EPSPACE$-complete; the satisfiability problem for constraint of the form $L \subseteq R$, where R has no occurrences of variables, is $PSPACE$-complete. In the first, second and the third cases we show that if the solution exists then the regular one exists too. Besides, we show that if any solution is maximal then it is regular.

2   Notations and Preliminaries

Let $\Sigma, \mathcal{V}$ be two disjoint alphabets. Σ is a finite set of letters (terminal symbols) and $\mathcal{V}$ is a set of variables. We use the lower-case letters a, b, c, d to denote members of Σ and X, Y, U, W to denote variables.

Regular expressions (over some Σ) are usually based on the operator $\cdot$ (concatenations) and the set operators $*$ (Kleene-closure), $+$ (union). But sometimes are considered with additional set operators namely either with intersection or complement. We call them respectively *semi-extended regular expressions* and *extended regular expressions*. Additional operators enable representing regular languages in a more succinct form. $L(R)$ denotes the language generated by a regular expression R.

Let $REGE_{\Sigma \cup \mathcal{V}}$ be a set of regular expressions over $\Sigma \cup \mathcal{V}$. We will call them *open* regular expressions. If $A(X_1, \ldots, X_n) \in REGE_{\Sigma \cup \mathcal{V}}$ and $X_1, \ldots, X_n$ are variables which can occur an arbitrary number of times in term A then one can interpret this term as an operator which takes arbitrary formal languages $L_1, \ldots, L_n \subseteq \Sigma^*$ and provides a new language $L(A(L_1, \ldots, L_n))$. In the further part of this paper we will consider only open and close expressions which are built over $\cdot, *, +$.

Definition 1. *Let $\Diamond$ be a set operator from $\{=, \subseteq, \supseteq\}$. An constraint $A(X_1, \ldots, X_n) \Diamond B(X_1, \ldots, X_n)$ is satisfiable over Σ if there exists nonempty languages $L_1, \ldots, L_n \subseteq \Sigma^*$ such that $L(A(L_1, \ldots, L_n)) \Diamond L(B(L_1, \ldots, L_n))$. In other words, there exists substitution $\theta = \{X_1 \leftarrow L_1, \ldots, X_n \leftarrow L_n\}$ such that $\theta(A(X_1, \ldots, X_n)) \Diamond \theta(B(X_1, \ldots, X_n))$.*

Let's note that the satisfiability problem for the system of regular language equations $A^i(X_1^i, \ldots, X_{n(i)}^i) = B^i(X_1^i, \ldots, X_{n(i)}^i)$, where $1 \le i \le m$, can be reduced to the satisfiability of a single equation by addition of different strings $c_1, \ldots, c_k$ of the same length as a prefix to each side of the equation: $\sum_{i=1}^m c_i A^i(X_1^i, \ldots, X_{n(i)}^i) = \sum_{i=1}^m c_i B^i(X_1^i, \ldots, X_{n(i)}^i)$. A set operator $\Lambda : (\Sigma^*)^n \to \Sigma^*$ is monotonic iff for all languages $L_1 \subseteq M_1, \ldots, L_n \subseteq M_n$ there holds $\Lambda(L_1, \ldots, L_n) \subseteq \Lambda(M_1, \ldots, M_n)$. Let's note the following simple fact:

Fact 2 $\cap, +, *$ *are monotonic operators and every set operator* $\Lambda(X_1, \ldots, X_n)$ *which is equivalent to some open regular expression over* $\{\cap, +, *, \cdot\}$ *is monotonic.*

3   Solving Regular Language Matching

In this section we will show computational complexity of the following two problems:

Problem 3. *(RLM)- Regular Language Matching INSTANCE: An equation between regular terms*

$$A(X_1, \ldots, X_n) = R, \tag{1}$$

where $A(X_1, \ldots, X_n)$ *is an open regular expression and* R *is a regular expression without variables. QUESTION: Is the equation satisfiable ?*

Problem 4. *(CONSTRAINT) INSTANCE: A constraint between regular terms* $A(X_1, \ldots, X_n) \subseteq R$, *where* R *is a regular expression without variables. QUESTION: Is the constraint satisfiable ?*

A regular expression is the synonym of the finite nondeterministic automaton. Throughout this section, we will think about R as a nondeterministic automaton $R = <\Sigma, s, \delta, Q, F>$ where Σ is a finite alphabet, s is a start state, $Q = \{q_1, \ldots, q_k\}$ is a set of states, F is a set of accepting states and δ is a transition function. Without loss of generality, we assume that for each $q \in Q$ and $w \in \Sigma^*$ there exists $p \in Q$ that $\delta(q, w) = p$.

Definition 5 (String R-profile). *A R-profile of a string* w *is a set of pairs* $P^R(w) = \{(q, p) \mid \delta(q, w) = p\}$. $P^R(w)$ *can be also interpreted as vector* $[D_1, \ldots, D_k]$ *of subsets of* Q, *where* $p \in D_i$ *if and only if* $(q_i, p) \in P^R(w)$.

Definition 6 (Language R-profile). *A R-profile of language* L *is the following class* $P^R(L) = \{P^R(w) \mid w \in L\}$.

Definition 7 (R-Projection of a language). *A R-projection of a language* L *on* Σ^* *is a language* $\Pi^R(L) = \{w \mid w \in \Sigma^* \text{ and } P^R(w) \in P^R(L)\}$.

Proposition 8. *For any nondeterministic automaton* R *and any language* $L \subseteq \Sigma^*$, $\Pi^R(L)$ *is regular and it is accepted by automaton which has at most exponentially increased size compared to* R.

Below, we introduce the definition of a new automaton which will characterize the behavior of A with respect to the R automaton after the application of possible substitution on $A(X_1, \ldots, X_n)$.

Definition 9 (R-profile automaton). *A R-profile automaton for a generalized non-deterministic automaton A denoting $L(A(L_1,\ldots,L_n))$ is $A^P = \ <\ \Sigma^P, s^P, \delta^P, Q^P,$ $F^P >$, where $\Sigma^P = P^R(\Sigma) \cup \bigcup_{i=1}^m P^R(L_i)$, $Q^P = Q^A \times 2^Q$, $s^P = [s^A, \{s\}]$, $F^P = \{[f^A, I] \mid I \subseteq Q,\ I \cap F \neq \emptyset,\ and\ f^A \in F^A\}$. $([l_1, R_1], [D_1, \ldots, D_k], [l_2, R_2]) \in \delta^P$ if and only if one of the follows holds: (1) there exists $a \in \Sigma$ such that $P^R(a) = [D_1, \ldots, D_n]$, $(l_1, a, l_2) \in \delta^A$, and $R_2 = \bigcup_{\{i \mid q_i \in R_1\}} D_i$; (2) there exists $X_j \in \Sigma^A$ such that $[D_1, \ldots, D_n] \in P^R(L_j)$, $(l_1, X_j, l_2) \in \delta^A$, and $R_2 = \bigcup_{\{i \mid q_i \in R_1\}} D_i$.*

Lemma 10. *Let R be a nondeterministic finite automaton, A^P be the R-profile automaton for a generalized nondeterministic automaton A associated with a regular term $A(X_1,\ldots,X_n)$ and a certain regular language $L(A(L_1,\ldots,L_n))$. The following conditions are equivalent:*

1. there is no state in $U = \{[f^A, I] \mid I \subseteq Q \setminus F\}$ which is reachable from $[s^A, \{s\}]$,
2. $L(A(L_1,\ldots,L_n)) \subseteq L(R)$,
3. $L(A(\Pi^R(L_1),\ldots,\Pi^R(L_n))) \subseteq L(R)$.

Theorem 11. *The CONSTRAINT problem is PSPACE-complete.*

Proof. First, we show how the $CONSTRAINT$ problem can be decided in $PSPACE$. If the constraint is satisfiable by $L_1,\ldots,L_n$ then one can choose single strings from each of sets $w_1 \in L_1,\ldots,w_n \in L_n$ and from Fact 2 we have $L(A(\{w_1\},\ldots,\{w_n\})) \subseteq L(R)$. Hence, we may try to guess a vector of sets for each w_i such that $P^R(w_i) = [D_1^{w_i},\ldots,D_k^{w_i}]$ and for each $a \in \Sigma$ we can easily obtain $P^R(a)$ out of R automaton. The R-profile automaton for the generalized automaton A denoting $L(A(\{w_1\},\ldots,\{w_n\}))$ has size at most exponentially greater then A and R. Using Savitch's method [13] for the reachability problem we can decide reachability for two states of automaton A^P in $NLOGSPACE$ with respect to size of the automaton A^P. Analyzing definition of A^P it is easy to see that it is possible to guess nondeterministically (in polynomial space) the index of state and the label for transition. Hence, we obtain $NPSPACE (\equiv PSPACE)$ algorithm.

To prove the lower bound it is enough to observe that the left-hand side of the constraint does not contain any occurrences of variables in particular. This means that it can be equivalent to Σ^*. Hence, we obtain the $CONSTRAINT$ problem of the form $\Sigma^* \subseteq L(R) \equiv \Sigma^* = L(R)$. But it was proved in [7] that the universality problem for regular expression is $PSPACE$-hard. $\square$

Theorem 12. *If the RLM problem has solution $\theta = \{X_1 \leftarrow L_1, \ldots, X_n \leftarrow L_n\}$ then it has also the regular solution $\theta^\Pi = \{X_1 \leftarrow \Pi^R(L_1),\ldots, X_n \leftarrow \Pi^R(L_n)\}$.*

Proof. Since θ is a solution of equation (1), the following constraint $L(R) \subseteq L(A(L_1, \ldots, L_n))$ holds. From the fact that $L \subseteq \Pi^R(L)$, for any language L, and from monotonicity (Fact 2) of $A(X_1, \ldots, X_n)$ follows that $L(A(L_1,\ldots,L_n)) \subseteq L(A(\Pi^R(L_1), \ldots, \Pi^R(L_n)))$. However, from Lemma 10 and from the assumption that $L(A(L_1, \ldots, L_n)) \subseteq L(R)$ we obtain $L(A(\Pi^R(L_1), \ldots, \Pi^R(L_n))) = L(R)$. $\square$

In case of the satisfiability problem for linear language equations was proved [3] that if the system of equations is satisfiable then it has a greatest solution and this solution is regular. From above theorem and fact that if we assume $W_L = \{N \subseteq \Sigma^* \mid P^R(N) \subseteq P^R(L)\}$ then $\Pi^R(L) = \bigcup_{M \in W_L} M$, one can conclude that:

Corollary 13. *Every maximal solution of satisfiable system of regular equations of the form (1) is regular.There exists at most double exponentially many maximal solutions in the size of (1).*

Lemma 14. *The RLM problem is in EXPSPACE.*

Proof. The algorithm, using exponential space in the size of the regular expressions R and $A(X_1, \ldots, X_n)$ will be working in the following stages: (1) Convert expression R to nondeterministic automaton R (polynomial in the size of the expression). (2) Guess, nondeterministically, R_{L_i} automata recognizing $\Pi^R(L_i)$ for some potential solution $\theta = \{X_1 \leftarrow L_1, \ldots, X_n \leftarrow L_n\}$. We can do it using exponential space because R_{L_i} has exponential size in the size of the expression R. (3) Convert pattern automaton A for $A(X_1, \ldots, X_n)$ to A' by replacing each of occurrences X_i in A with an automaton R_{L_i}. Hence, A' is a nondeterministic automaton of size exponential in the size of the regular expressions R and $A(X_1, \ldots, X_n)$. (4) The equivalence problem for two nondeterministic automata is in $PSPACE$. Therefore checking whether the automaton A' is equivalent to the automaton R is in $EXPSPACE$ in size of (1).$\Box$

In this section we show that the RLM problem is $EXPSPACE$-hard. In order to obtain this lower bound we exploit the following theorem and a certain detail of its proof:

Theorem 15 [6]. *Let SE be a semi-extended regular expression over finite alphabet Σ. The problem, whether SE is equivalent to Σ^* is $EXPSPACE$-complete*

Now we introduce a particular class of semi-extended regular expressions.

Definition 16. *Let $\Sigma^{\mathcal{A}} = \{A_1, \ldots, A_l\}$ be a finite set of regular expressions over some finite alphabet Σ, where each of A_i has the form $\bigcap_{j=1}^{k(i)} B_j^i$ for some positive integer $k(i)$. Besides each of B_j^i is an ordinary regular expression built over Σ using $\cdot, +, *$. We call such expressions A_i intersection atoms. The semi-extended regular expression SE is intersection one level if SE is regular expression which is built over some set of intersection atoms using the operators $\cdot, +, *$.*

Below, we propose the conclusion from the proof of Theorem 15. The reader, which is interested in verifying this conclusion, should look at the proof of this theorem placed in [1].

Problem 17. *(ONE LEVEL) INSTANCE: An alphabet Σ, a regular expression S which is one level intersection. QUESTION: Is S equivalent to Σ^* ?*

Corollary 18. *The ONE LEVEL problem is $EXPSPACE-hard$.*

Now we show how we can reduce the $ONE\ LEVEL$ problem, in polynomial time, to the RLM problem.

Lemma 19. *The RLM problem is $EXPSPACE$-hard.*

Proof. Let us take any semi-extended regular expression SE which is one level intersection. Besides, let $SE = B(A_1, \ldots, A_l)$ where $B(X_1, \ldots, X_l)$ is an open regular expression without any intersection operator, and A_i are intersection atoms. We should also assume that variables $X_1, \ldots X_l$ are pairwise different and each variable is associated with a single occurrence of intersection atom in the term B. Let us remember that each of A_i atoms has the form $\bigcap_{j=1}^{k(i)} B_j^i$. For each A_i, we will create the system of language equations

$$A_i = \{X_i + B_j^i = B_j^i \mid 1 \leq j \leq k(i)\}. \tag{2}$$

At the end of the reduction, the equation in the following form will be added

$$B = \{B(X_1, \ldots, X_l) = \Sigma^*\}. \tag{3}$$

It remains to justify the correctness of our construction, it means – the system of regular language equations $S = B \cup \bigcup_{i=1}^{l} A_i$ is satisfiable if and only if the expression SE is equivalent to Σ^*.

Obviously, $A_i = \bigcap_{j=1}^{k(i)} B_j^i \subseteq B_k^i$ for $1 \leq k \leq k(i)$ and for each $1 \leq i \leq l$. Therefore $A_i \cup B_j^i = B_j^i$ for any j. Assuming $L(B(A_1, \ldots, A_l)) = \Sigma^*$ we have that substitution $\theta = \{X_1 \leftarrow L(A_1), \ldots, X_l \leftarrow L(A_l)\}$ satisfies simultaneously B equation and A_i equations. In the other direction, (2) and (3) are satisfiable by θ if and only if $\{\theta(X_i) \subseteq B_j^i\}_{j=1}^{k(i)} \equiv \theta(X_i) \subseteq \bigcap_{j=1}^{k(i)} B_j$ and by monotonicity of operator B we have $L(B(A_1, \ldots, A_l)) = \Sigma^*$. $\square$

We will be consider, in a section 4 version of RLM problem where we ask about existence of solution over finite languages domain (further called $FINITE$ $MATCHING$). It is reasonable to mention just here that one level expression which is constructed in the above cited proof [1] has such pleasant property that each intersection atom denotes finite language. Hence, the $FINITE$ $MATCHING$ problem is $EXPSPACE$–hard.

As a corollary from Lemmas 14 and 19 we obtain

Theorem 20. *The RLM problem is EXPSPACE-complete.*

4   Finite Solutions

In this chapter we will show algorithm which decide whether does exists finite solution for equation of type (1). In this place, "finite solution" means language consisting of finite set of strings. Due to theorem 12 we know that if some finite solution L_f of (1) exists then, this solution is a subset of $\Pi^R(L_f)$. Additionally $\Pi^R(L_f)$ is the solution also. Since $K = \{\Pi^R(L) \mid L \subseteq \Sigma^*\}$ contain finite set of languages then we will split our algorithm into two parts. The first part is based on nondeterministic guessing of tuple $(L_1, \ldots, L_n) \in K^n$. In the next step we check whether is $(L_1, \ldots, L_n)$ solution of (1). If the checking returns positive answer (of course, maximal solution need not be unique) it remains for us to solve the following problem:

Problem 21. *(FINITE BASE) INSTANCE: A regular expression $\Lambda(L_1, \ldots, L_n)$. QUESTION: Does tuple of finite languages $(C_1, \ldots, C_n)$ such that $C_1 \subseteq L_1, \ldots, C_n \subseteq L_n$ and $L(\Lambda(L_1, \ldots, L_n)) = L(\Lambda(C_1, \ldots, C_n))$ exist ?*

Before we show algorithm which solve the $FINITE\ BASE$ problem, it is worth to recall that, by proposition 8, every L_i language can be described as nondeterministic automaton of exponential size in the size of input of the matching problem. Hence, a tuple of automata for $(L_1, \ldots, L_n)$ is guessed from double exponential domain and we need only exponential counter to storage of information about which tuple of automata is currently considered.

Let $A = \langle s, Q, E, \delta, \chi, F \rangle$ be a finite automaton with coloring χ. Further, we will think about automaton as directed labelled graph. In turn, Q is a set of vertices (states) E is a set of labelled edges, δ is a function giving the labelling, s is a distinguished vertic which will be called starting, $F \subseteq E$ is a set so called accepting states (vertices), $\chi : E \to \{0, 1\}$. A *path* for finite sequence of labels (word) w is a sequence of vertices joined by sequence of labels w. For some pair of states p and q and word $w \in \Sigma^*$, it can exists more than one path between p and q labelled by letter sequence w. Further, the set of such paths will be denoted by $Path_p^q(w)$. Among all paths for any w we distinguish *accepting paths* i.e. those which start from s and end at some accepting vertic. $Path(w)$ denotes set of all accepting paths for a string w. If we look at particular path we can analyze sequence of colors assigned to sequence of edges associated with the path and find maximal length sequence of 1's not separated by any 0 occurrences. Such length for path p is called *weight* of path p. And it will be denoted by $weight(p)$. For every string w we assign nonnegative integer $Weight(w) = \min\{weight(p) \mid p \in Path(w)\}$. Similarly, $Weight_p^q(w) = \min\{weight(p) \mid p \in Path_p^q(w)\}$. Let define, to further using, function $\beth$ which returns 0 for some path argument p if and only if sequence of edges associated with p are colored solely 0. Let $\beth, \beth_p^q : \Sigma^* \to \{0, 1\}$ be define in the following way: $\beth(w) = 1 \iff \forall_p\ p \in Path(w) \to \beth(p) = 1$ and similarly $\beth_p^q(w) = 1 \iff \forall_p\ p \in Path_p^q(w) \to \beth(p) = 1$. In this section we will consider the problem whether does $\sup\{Weight(w) \mid w \in L(A)\}$ equals ∞. We call it $SUPREMUM$.

The purpose of introducing the definition of automaton with coloring function is reduction the $FINITE\ BASE$ problem to the $SUPREMUM$ problem. We will give here short recipe for obtaining appropriate automaton with coloring. Namely, at the first $\Lambda(X_1, \ldots, X_n)$ should be translated to nondeterministic automaton $A''(X_1, \ldots, X_n)$, without $\epsilon-$ transitions, treating a variable symbols as terminal symbols. Further is assumed that each of L_i does not contain ϵ. Otherwise, one can guess which from L_i languages contain ϵ and start the translation with $\Lambda(\epsilon + X_{i_1}, \ldots, \epsilon + X_{i_k}, X_{i_{k+1}}, \ldots, X_{i_n})$ where $\{X_1, \ldots, X_n\} = \{X_{i_1}, \ldots, X_{i_n}\}$. Next, For every edge $p \xrightarrow{a} q$, where $a \in \Sigma$, let give a color 0. Next, we take, for each $\leq i \leq n$, nondeterministic automaton without $\epsilon-$transitions $M_i = \langle Q_i, \delta_i, s_i, F_i \rangle$ corresponding to L_i. Let paint the all edges of M_i color 1. Next, we starting a process of replacing all edges $p \xrightarrow{X_i} q$ in automaton A with automaton M_i. This is the crucial point of our reduction. Namely, for each $1 \leq i \leq n$, transition $r \xrightarrow{a} f_i \in \delta_i$ where $f_i \in F_i$ and q appropriate to any occurrence of X_i, let add new edge $r \xrightarrow{a} q$ and let set $\chi(r \xrightarrow{a} q)$ on 0. In this way we obtain automaton with coloring $A' = \langle Q', \delta', s', F', \chi \rangle$. Next, for each triple $1 \leq i \leq n$, p appropriate to any occurrence of X_i and transition $r \xrightarrow{a} p \in \delta'$ we add new edge $r \xrightarrow{a} s_i$. We set a color of newly-introduced edge $\chi(r \xrightarrow{a} s_i)$ on 0. Next, we remove all edges labelled by $X_1, \ldots, X_n$. Such created automaton we denote $A = \langle Q, \delta, s, F, \chi \rangle$. After above construction may happen that we obtain automaton with starting state which has no outgoing edges even though $L(\Lambda(L_1,\ldots,L_n)) \neq \emptyset$. In order to prevent such undesirable situation we assume, without loses of generality, that the *FINITE BASE* problem is stated as $\Lambda(L_1,\ldots,L_n) = a\Lambda'(L_1,\ldots,L_n)$. Hence a is the only label which goes out of s in A. After execution of our procedure it may appear two edges between the same pair of vertics which are labelled by the same terminal and colored by differ colors. We allow this situation.

Now we give short justification that $\sup\{Weight(w) \mid w \in L(A)\} = \infty$ if and only if does not exist finite base for $\Lambda(L_1,\ldots,L_n)$. Let assume that finite base $(C_1,\ldots,C_n)$ exist. Let $\Lambda(exp(L_1),\ldots,exp(L_n)))$ be regular expression which arise after substitution of each occurrence of nonterminal symbols X_i in regular expression $\Lambda(X_1,\ldots,X_n)$ for regular expression $exp(L_i)$ denoting language L_i. Let $der(w)$ denotes set of derivations of a word w from expression $\Lambda(exp(L_1),\ldots,exp(L_n)))$ and let $sub(d)$ denotes set of subwords in a derivation d which, inside the derivation, are composed solely from letters which was derived from the same occurrence of subexpression $exp(L_i)$. We write $max(D)$ to denote maximal length word from set of words D. It is obvious that for each $w \in L(\Lambda(L_1,\ldots,L_n))$ there exists derivation $d \in der(w)$ such that maximal subword from $sub(d)$ is at most $max\{|w| \mid w \in C_1 \cup \ldots \cup C_n\}$ long. However if finite base does not exist then it means that we can chose infinite sequence of words $w_0,w_1,\ldots \in L(\Lambda(L_1,\ldots,L_n))$ such that $s_n > d_n$ holds for each positive integer n and $s_n = \min(\{k \mid k = max\{|w| \mid w \in sub(p)\} \text{ and } p \in der(w_n)\})$, $d_n = max(\{s_1,\ldots,s_{n-1}\})$.

Note that: (1) $L(\Lambda(exp(L_1),\ldots,exp(L_n)))) = L(A'')$, (2) for each $w \in L(\Lambda(exp(L_1), \ldots,exp(L_n))))$ and for each $p \in der(w)$ there exist derivation counterpart of word w in automata A'' with properties that every maximal subsequence of letters which in derivation p was derived from one of the occurrences $exp(L_i)$ is colored 1 except last letter (which is colored 0, besides a letters which were not derived from one of the $exp(L_i)$ have color 0) and vice versa.

Now we define finite algebraic structure $\mathcal{B} = \langle \mathbf{B}, \odot \rangle$ for automaton A, and one argument function $[\![\ ]\!]^{\mathcal{B}} : \Sigma^* \longmapsto \mathbf{B}$ which will be used to describe of behavior of coloring on the paths between every ordered pair of states for certain string. B is a set of pairs of true-false (zero-one) square matrixes (L,R) for which formula $[R]_i^j \vee [L]_i^j$ holds for each pair (i,j). Let R^a denotes one step reachability matrix for symbol $a \in \Sigma$. It means that if we assume that rows and columns of R^a are numbered by linear ordered states from Q then at the (p,q) position of R^a ($[R^a]_p^q$) there is 1 iff $(p,a,q) \in \delta$. One can extend definition of reachability matrix to strings. Namely R^w, for $w \in \Sigma^*$, has 1 at the position (p,q) if and only if $(p,w,q) \in \delta$. Matrix L^w has 1 at the position (p,q) if and only if either all paths, for w, from p to q are colored solely by 1 or $(p,w,q) \notin \delta$. What follows that if there is 0 at the position (p,q) in reachability matrix R^w then only 1 can occur at the position (p,q) in L^w matrix. Function $[\![\ ]\!]^{\mathcal{B}}$ is defined in such way that $[\![w]\!]^{\mathcal{B}} = (L^w, R^w)$ for every $w \in \Sigma^*$. More formally

$$[\pi_2([\![w]\!]^{\mathcal{B}})]_p^q = \begin{cases} 1 & : \quad (p,w,q) \in \delta \\ 0 & : \quad \text{otherwise} \end{cases} \tag{4}$$

$$[\pi_1([\![w]\!]^{\mathcal{B}})]_p^q = \begin{cases} 1 & : \quad \text{either } [\pi_2([\![w]\!]^{\mathcal{B}})]_p^q = 0 \text{ or } Weight_p^q(w) = |w| \\ 0 & : \quad \text{otherwise} \end{cases} \tag{5}$$

Let define operation $\odot$ on the above defined structure in such way that will be "keep interpretation" on a result of the operation.

$$(A,R) \odot (B,S) = (A \odot_R^S B, R \cdot S) \tag{6}$$

where $T \cdot S$ is an ordinary multiplication of the boolean matrixes and

$$[A \odot_R^S B]_p^q = \bigwedge_{r \in Q} ([R]_p^r \wedge [S]_r^q) \rightarrow ([A]_p^r \wedge [B]_r^q). \tag{7}$$

The operator $\odot$ "keep interpretation" means $[\![w_1]\!]^B \odot [\![w_2]\!]^B = [\![w_1 w_2]\!]^B$ for every w_1, $w_2 \in \Sigma^*$. Let $[\![\epsilon]\!]^B = (U, I)$, where all elements of U are 1's and I is boolean matrix which only has 1's on diagonal. In other words, $[\![\;]\!]^B$ is homomorphism from monoid $\langle \Sigma^*, concatenation, \epsilon \rangle$ to B. The operation $\odot$ is well-defined because structure $\langle B, \odot, (U, I) \rangle$ is a monoid. Besides $\odot$ "keeps interpretation".

Let define new structure $C = \langle B, \otimes \rangle$ and operation $\otimes$ on B set.

$$(A,R) \otimes (B,S) = (A \otimes_R^S B, R \cdot S)$$

$$[A \otimes_R^S B]_p^q = \bigwedge_{r \in Q} ([R]_p^r \wedge [S]_r^q) \rightarrow ([A]_p^r \vee [B]_r^q).$$

Now we introduce the second function which describe behavior of coloring on the paths for individual strings. Namely, $[\![\;]\!]^C$ is defined formally as follows: $[\pi_2([\![w]\!]^C)]_p^q = [\pi_2([\![w]\!]^B)]_p^q$ and $[\pi_1([\![w]\!]^C)]_p^q = \beth_p^q(w)$. It is left to the reader to prove that $[\![\;]\!]^C$ "keep interpretation" and $\langle B, \otimes, (\overline{I}, I) \rangle$ is monoid, where we write line over matrix $\overline{M}$ to denote matrix which arise from M by replacement each position of value 1 with 0 and each position of value 0 with 1.

Let $A \subseteq M$. A-*closure* of finite monoid $\mathcal{M} = <M, \circ, i>$, denoted by $(A)_\circ^+$, will be the least set containing A and such that if $a, b \in (A)_\circ^+$ then $a \circ b \in (A)_\circ^+$. Let $U, W \subseteq M$ and *composition* of two subsets of monoid $\mathcal{M}$ is defined as $U \circ W = \{a \circ b \mid a \in U$ and $b \in W\}$. A kth power of some subset of M is denoted by U^k.

Below we present algorithm which decide the $SUPREMUM$ problem. After this presentation we give a sketch of proof completeness, soundness and termination of the algorithm.

$INPUT$: automaton A with coloring;
$R = \{R^a \mid a \in \Sigma\} \cup \{I\}$; $S = \{I\}$; $LR = \{(L^a, R^a) \mid a \in \Sigma\}$;
$Factors = \{(U, I)\}$; $Stack = \emptyset$;
repeat
(1) $Factors = Factors \odot LR$;
(2) $Clousure = (Factors)_\otimes^+ \otimes \{(\overline{X}, X) \mid X \in S\}$;
(3)   **if** $\neg(\bigvee_{Y \in Clousure} \bigvee_{q \in F}([\pi_1(Y)]_s^q \wedge [\pi_2(Y)]_s^q))$ **then return false** ;
(4)   **if** $(Factors \times S) \notin Stack$ **then**
(5) $Stack = Stack \cup \{Factors \times S\}$
(6)   **else return true** ;
(7) $S = (S \cdot R) \cup \{I\}$;
until false ;

For each word w accepted by coloring automaton A there is set of accepting paths $Path(w)$. $\sup\{Weight(w) \mid w \in L(A)\} < \infty$ if then only if there exist nonnegative integer η that for each word $w \in L(A)$ there exists path $p \in Path(w)$ such that $weight(p) \leq \eta$. Let call such path a *witness*. Each word $w \in L(A)$ of length greatest than η can be factorized on $\kappa = |w| \; div \; (\eta+1)$ factors of length $\eta+1$ and $tail$ of length $|w| - \kappa(\eta+1) \leq \eta \, (w = w_1 \ldots w_\kappa w_{tail})$. Sometimes we will use term $\eta-factorization$ to emphasize a length of factors. The witness p of w can be factorized according to the factorization of w ($p = p_1 \ldots p_\kappa p_{tail}$). From pigeon hole principle we obtain that each part p_i for $1 \leq i \leq \kappa$ of witness is not colored solely by 1. Let $f(p_i)$ be the first state of ith factor of p and let $l(p_i)$ be the last state of p_i. Hence $\pi_1(\llbracket w_i \rrbracket^{\mathcal{B}})_{f(p_i)}^{l(p_i)} = 0$ and $\pi_2(\llbracket w_i \rrbracket^{\mathcal{B}})_{f(p_i)}^{l(p_i)} = 1$ for all $1 \leq i \leq \kappa$. As far as w_{tail} is concerned we use $\overline{\pi_2(\llbracket w_{tail} \rrbracket^{\mathcal{B}})} \times \pi_2(\llbracket w_{tail} \rrbracket^{\mathcal{B}})$ instead of $\llbracket w_{tail} \rrbracket^{\mathcal{B}}$. In this way we treat every nonempty p_{tail} fragment of path containing at least one edge colored 0 regardless of it is true. Besides, in this way, we want to ensure correct transmission of reachability for any p_{tail}.

It is clear that if $|p_i| = e + 1$ for $1 \leq i \leq \kappa$ and $0 \leq |p_{tail}| \leq e$ and a sequence $S = \pi_1(\llbracket w_1 \rrbracket^{\mathcal{B}})_{f(p_1)}^{l(p_1)}, \ldots, \pi_1(\llbracket w_\kappa \rrbracket^{\mathcal{B}})_{f(p_\kappa)}^{l(p_\kappa)}, \pi_1(\llbracket w_{tail} \rrbracket^{\mathcal{B}})_{f(p_{tail})}^{l(p_{tail})}$ consist solely of 0's than $weight(p) \leq 2e$. However, if S contain at least one occurrence of 1 than $weight(p) > e$. It follows that if for some witness p of string w the length e of factors thanks to which 1's are absorbed is found than this fact show that the $weight(p) \leq 2e$. The most important question is do we can find such length simultaneously for all witnesses corresponding to all $w \in L(A)$?

Thanks to the $\llbracket \; \rrbracket^{\mathcal{B}}$ function and matrix representation we are able to encompass behavior of coloring simultaneously on all paths $p \in Path(w)$ for any $e-$ factorization. $[\pi_2(\llbracket w_i \rrbracket^{\mathcal{B}})_p^q \wedge \neg [\pi_1(\llbracket w_i \rrbracket^{\mathcal{B}})_p^q$ means that for factor w_i a path between p and q exists and from among all paths between p and q we can choose such path that not all edges are colored 1. The operator $\otimes$ detects a path and appropriate sequence $\pi_1(\llbracket w_1 \rrbracket^{\mathcal{B}})_s^{l(p_1)}$, $\ldots, \pi_1(\llbracket w_\kappa \rrbracket^{\mathcal{B}})_{f(p_\kappa)}^{l(p_\kappa)}, \pi_1(\llbracket w_{tail} \rrbracket^{\mathcal{B}})_{f(p_{tail})}^{f \in F}$ which contain only 0's if only such path exist. From above considerations we conclude the following lemma:

Lemma 22.

1. For every $w \in L(A)$ and its $\eta-factorization$ $w = w_1 \ldots w_\kappa w_{tail}$
   $\exists_{f \in F} \neg [\llbracket w_1 \rrbracket^{\mathcal{B}} \otimes \ldots \otimes \llbracket w_\kappa \rrbracket^{\mathcal{B}} \otimes (\overline{\pi_2(\llbracket w_{tail} \rrbracket^{\mathcal{B}})} \times \pi_2(\llbracket w_{tail} \rrbracket^{\mathcal{B}}))]_s^f \Longrightarrow Weight(w) \leq 2\eta$,
2. $\eta - Factors = \{\llbracket w \rrbracket^{\mathcal{B}} \mid w \in \Sigma^\eta \wedge w \in \Sigma^*\}$; $\eta - L(A)Factorizations = \{\llbracket w_1 \rrbracket^{\mathcal{B}} \otimes \ldots \otimes \llbracket w_\kappa \rrbracket^{\mathcal{B}} \mid \exists_{w_{tail}} \exists_{\kappa \in I\!N} w_{tail} \in \bigcup_{j=1}^{\eta-1} \Sigma^j \wedge (\bigwedge_{i=1}^{\kappa} w_i \in \Sigma^\eta) \wedge w_1 \ldots w_\kappa w_{tail} \in L(A) \}$; $(\eta - Factors)_\otimes^+$; $R^{<\eta} = \bigcup_{k=0}^{\eta-1} R^k$ where $R = \{R^a \mid a \in \Sigma\}$ are finite sets and they have size with upper bound which depend solely on the size of automaton A,
3. $\eta - L(A)Factorizations \subseteq (\eta - Factors)_\otimes^+$,
4. Let $C = (\eta - Factors)_\otimes^+ \otimes \widetilde{R^{<\eta}}$ where $\widetilde{R^{<\eta}} = \{(\overline{X}, X) \mid X \in R^{<\eta}\}$,
   $D = \eta - L(A)Factorization \otimes \widetilde{R^{<\eta}}$. A formula $\Phi = \bigvee_{Y \in C} \bigvee_{q \in F}([\pi_1(Y)]_s^q \wedge [\pi_2(Y)]_s^q)$ is equivalent to $\bigvee_{Y \in D} \bigvee_{q \in F}([\pi_1(Y)]_s^q \wedge [\pi_2(Y)]_s^q)$,
5. $\neg \Phi$ if and only if there exists $1 \leq \eta < \infty$ such that for every string $w \in L(A)$ there exists witness $p \in Path(w)$ of weight at most η.

So to find good length $\eta + 1$ of factors for all strings in $L(A)$ we start infinite loop which increase length of factors by one per one execution of the loop – see line (1). Each next value of $R^{<\eta} = S$ is computed in line (7). In the line (2) we compute set of matrixes C and next we compute value of negated formula Φ (line (3)). As for generalized alternative symbols appearing in line (3) it can be simulated by "for" loop. A counter of the "for" loop is proportional to logarithm of power of domain which underline the alternative operation occurrence. If calculated value amounts to *true* then we return *false* what means that $\sup\{Weight(w) \mid w \in L(A)\} < \infty$. It remains to prove that our algorithm terminates. Due to above lemma *Stack* variable is bounded by the size of automaton A. Let note that if we can not add to *Stack* some object in some step of our algorithm then next computed *Factors*'s and *Clouser*'s will repeat itself. Hence, if value of formula from line (3) was *false* until now then it will remain *false* in the next steps. This is time to break our computation with answer *true* what means that $\sup\{Weight(w) \mid w \in L(A)\} = \infty$. We estimate maximal number of different set of *Factors* at $2^{2^{2n^2}}$ where n is number of states of automaton A. A size of S set amounts to at most 2^{n^2} and because during execution, size of S always is increased than we obtain at most 2^{n^2} different occurrences of S. Therefore, the "repeat" loop is executed at most $2^{n^2 + 2^{2n^2}}$ times. Hence, our algorithm works in double exponential time in the size of A. What follows that it solves the $FINITE\ MATCHING$ problem in triple exponential time in the size of equation (1).

Our algorithm can be improved by more reasonable computation of *Factors* and the S set. Namely, we can increase mentioned sets two times in every step. After this improvement the $SUPREMUM$ can be solved in exponential time.

Lemma 23. Let $\lambda = 2^{n^2 + 2^{2n^2}}$, $\kappa = 2^{2n^2}$, $\tau = 2^{n^2}$, $A_\odot^{<\alpha,\beta>} = \bigcup_{i=\alpha}^{\beta} A_\odot^i$, $R = \{R^a \mid a \in \Sigma\}$

1. $(LP)_\odot^\lambda \subseteq (LP)_\odot^{<\lambda,\lambda+\kappa>} = (LP)_\odot^{<\kappa,2\kappa>}$,
2. $((LP)_\odot^\lambda)_\otimes^+ \subseteq ((LP)_\odot^{<\lambda,\lambda+\kappa>})_\otimes^+ = ((LP)_\odot^{<\kappa,2\kappa>})_\otimes^+$,
3. $R^{<\lambda} = R^{<\tau}$.

Lemma 24. Let $\Psi(Y) = \bigvee_{q \in F}([\pi_1(Y)]_s^q \wedge [\pi_2(Y)]_s^q))$, $Cl_1 = ((LP)_\odot^{\lambda+1})_\otimes^+ \otimes \widetilde{R^{<\lambda}}$, $Cl_2 = ((LP)_\odot^{<\kappa,2\kappa>})_\otimes^+ \otimes \widetilde{R^{<\tau}}$. The following condition holds $\bigvee_{Y \in Cl_1} \Psi(Y) \Leftrightarrow \bigvee_{Y \in Cl_2} \Psi(Y)$.

Proof.   Let assume that in the $SUPREMUM$ problem we will apply nonuniform length factors. Namely, each of words $w \in L(A)$ will be factorized on factors of length at least $\lambda + 1$ and at most $\lambda + \kappa$. Let repeat the reasoning which proved soundness and completeness of the algorithm. Firstly, if the $SUPREMUM$ problem has negative solutions then for every accepted string there exists witness p of weight less then $2(\lambda + \kappa) + 1$ – inside each of factors for witness p at least one color 0 will appear. On the other hand if the $SUPREMUM$ has positive answer then there exists string $w \in L(A)$ such that all witnesses for w are at least of λ weight. Therefore, if $Cl_3 = ((LP)_\odot^{<\lambda,\lambda+\kappa>})_\otimes^+ \otimes \widetilde{R^{<\lambda}}$ then $\bigvee_{Y \in Cl_1} \Psi(Y) \Leftrightarrow \bigvee_{Y \in Cl_3} \Psi(Y)$ holds. And from lemma 23 we obtain $\bigvee_{Y \in Cl_3} \Psi(Y) \Leftrightarrow \bigvee_{Y \in Cl_2} \Psi(Y)$. $\square$

Due to lemmas 23 and 24 we can write algorithm solving the $SUPREMUM$ problem which works in polynomial space. Idea of the algorithm is the following: let apply well known Savitch's reachability method everywhere it is possible. Namely, one can recognize (1) does any matrix $M \in \{[\![w]\!]^{\mathcal{B}} \mid w \in \bigcup_{i=\lambda}^{\lambda+\kappa} \Sigma^i\}$ using $O(\log^2(\kappa))$ space, (2) does any $M \in ((LP)_\odot^{\leq\lambda,\lambda+\kappa>})_\otimes^+$ using $O(\log^2(\kappa))$ space assuming that we use oracle from point (1) to recognize of factors, (3) does any $M \in R^{<\tau}$ ("fixed point for reachability set") using $O(\log^2(\tau))$ space. The fact that structures $\mathcal{B}$, $\mathcal{C}$ and $\langle \mathbf{R}, \cdot, I \rangle$, where $\mathbf{R}$ is a set of boolean matrixes are monoid (especially associativity) plays fundamental role for soundness of sketched algorithm.

Theorem 25. *The $FINITE\ MATCHING$ problem is $EXPSPACE-complete$.*

References

1. A. V. Aho, J. E. Hopcroft, J. D. Ullman, *The Design and Analisys of Computer Algorithms*, Addison-Wesley Publishing Company, 1974, chapter 11.3 – A Problem Requiring Exponential Time and Space.
2. M. Anselmo, *A non-ambiguous decomposition of regular languages and facorizing codes*, Discrete Applied Mathematics 126: 129-165, 2003.
3. F. Baader, R. Küsters, *Unification in a Description Logic with Transitive Closure of Roles*, LPAR 2001: 217-232
4. F. Baader, P. Narendran, *Unification of Concept Terms in Description Logics*, J. Symbolic Computation, 31(3): 277-305, 2001.
5. A. K. Chandra, J. Y. Halpern, A. R. Meyer, R. Parikh, *Equations between Regular Terms and an Application to Process Logic*, in Proc. of STOC 1981: 384-390 15, also SIAM J. Comput. 14(4): 935-942 1985.
6. H. B. Hunt III. *The equivalence problem for regular expressions with intersection is not polynomial in tape*, Report TR 73-161. Departament of Computer Science, Cornell University, 1973.
7. H. B. Hunt III, D. J. Rosenkrantz, T. G. Szymanski, *On the, Containment, and Covering Problems for the Regular and Context-Free Languages* J. Computer and System Science 12, 222-268, 1976.
8. L. Kari, *On language equations with invertible operations*, Theoretical Computer Science 132 (1-2): 129-150 1994.
9. E. L. Leiss, *Language Equations Over a One-Letter Alphabet with Union, Concatenation and Star: A Complete Solution*, Theoretical Computer Science, 131(2): 311-330, 1994.
10. E. L. Leiss, *Implicit Language Equations: Existence and Uniqueness of Solutions*, Theoretical Computer Science 145 (1-2): 71-93 1995.
11. E. L. Leiss, *Solving Systems of Explicit Language Relations*, Theoretical Computer Science 186(1-2): 83-105, 1997.
12. A. Okhotin, *Decision problems for language equations with Boolean operations*, Automata, Languages and Programming, 30th International Colloquium, ICALP 2003, Proceedings. Lecture Notes in Computer Science 2719 Springer 2003.
13. W. J. Savitch. *Relationship between nondeterministic and deterministic tape comoplexities*, J. of Computer and System Science, 4:177-192, 1970.

Deterministic Truthful Approximation Mechanisms for Scheduling Related Machines*

Vincenzo Auletta, Roberto De Prisco, Paolo Penna, and Giuseppe Persiano

Dipartimento di Informatica ed Applicazioni "R.M. Capocelli", Università di Salerno,
via S. Allende 2, I-84081 Baronissi (SA), Italy.
{auletta,robdep,penna,giuper}@dia.unisa.it

Abstract. We consider the problem of scheduling jobs on related machines owned by selfish agents and provide the first *deterministic* mechanisms with constant approximation that are *truthful*; that is, truth-telling is a *dominant strategy* for all agents. More precisely, we present deterministic polynomial-time $(2 + \epsilon)$-approximation algorithms and suitable payment functions that yield truthful mechanisms for several NP-hard restrictions of this problem. Our result also yields a family of deterministic polynomial-time truthful $(4 + \epsilon)$-approximation mechanisms for any fixed number of machines. The only previously-known mechanism for this problem (proposed by Archer and Tardos [FOCS 2001]) is 3-approximated, *randomized* and truthful under a *weaker* notion of truthfulness.

Up to our knowledge, our mechanisms are the first non-trivial polynomial-time deterministic truthful mechanisms for this NP-hard problem.

To obtain our results we introduce a technique to transform the PTAS by Graham into a deterministic truthful mechanism.

1 Introduction

The Internet is a complex distributed system where a multitude of heterogeneous entities (e.g., providers, autonomous systems, universities, private companies, etc.) offer, use, and even compete with each other for resources. Resource allocation is a fundamental issue for the efficiency of a complex system. Several efficient distributed protocols have been designed for resource allocation. The underlying assumption is that the entities running the protocol are trustworthy; that is, they behave as prescribed by the protocol. This assumption is unrealistic in some settings as the entities owning the resources might try to manipulate the system in order to get some advantages by reporting false information. For example, a router of an autonomous system can report false link status trying to redirect traffic through another autonomous system.

With false information even the most efficient protocol may lead to unreasonable solutions if it is not designed to cope with the selfish behavior of the

---

* Work supported by the European Project IST-2001-33135, Critical Resource Sharing for Cooperation in Complex Systems (CRESCCO).

V. Diekert and M. Habib (Eds.): STACS 2004, LNCS 2996, pp. 608–619, 2004.

single entities. The field of *mechanism design* provides an elegant theory to deal with this kind of problems. The main idea of this theory is to pay the agents to convince them to perform strategies that help the system to optimize a global objective function. A *mechanism* $M = (A, P)$ is a combination of two elements: an algorithm A computing a solution and a payment rule P specifying the amount of "money" the mechanism should pay to each entity. Informally speaking, each agent i has a *valuation function* that associates to each solution X some value $v_i(X)$ and the mechanism pays i an amount $P_i(X, r_i)$ based on the solution X and on the *reported* information r_i. A *truthful mechanism* is a mechanism such that the payments guarantee that, when $X = X(r_i)$ is the solution computed by the mechanism, $u_i := P_i(X, r_i) + v_i(X)$ is maximized for r_i equal to the true information (see Sect. 1.3 for a formal definition).

Recently, mechanism design has been applied to several optimization problems arising in computer science, networking and algorithmic questions related to the Internet (see [10] for a survey). In the seminal papers by Nisan and Ronen [8, 9] (see also [11]) it is first pointed out that classical results in mechanism design theory, originated from micro economics and game theory, do not completely fit in a context where computational issues play a crucial role [9].

The main purpose of this paper is to provide polynomial-time approximation truthful mechanisms for the problem of scheduling jobs on parallel related machines ($Q||C_{\max}$).

1.1 Previous Work

The theory of mechanism design dates back to the seminal papers by Vickrey [12], Clarke [4] and Groves [7]. Their celebrated *VCG mechanism* is still the prominent technique to derive truthful mechanisms for many problems (e.g., shortest path, minimum spanning tree, etc.). In particular, when applied to combinatorial optimization problems (see e.g., [8,11]), the VCG mechanisms guarantee the truthfulness under the hypothesis that the optimization function is *utilitarian*[1] and the mechanism is able to compute the optimum.

Unfortunately, none of these hypothesis holds for $Q||C_{\max}$ since we aim at minimizing the *maximum* over all machines of their completion times, and the problem is NP-hard [5].

In [2] the authors characterize those algorithms which can be turned into a truthful mechanism for $Q||C_{\max}$. Their beautiful result brings us back to "pure algorithmic problems" as all we need is to find a good algorithm for the original problem which also satisfies the additional *monotonicity* requirement: increasing the speed of exactly one machine does not make the algorithm decrease the work assigned to that machine (see Sect. 1.3 for a formal definition, and Theorem 7 below). The authors then provide (i) an exact truthful mechanism based on the the algorithm computing the (lexicographically minimal) optimal solutio and

---

[1] A maximization problem is *utilitarian* if the optimization can be written as the sum of the agents' valuation functions.

(ii) a *randomized* 3-approximation mechanism that is *truthful in expectation*, a weaker notion of truthfulness.

Nisan and Ronen [8,11] considered the *unrelated* machines case and provide an n-approximation deterministic truthful mechanism for it (n is the number of machines). Rather surprisingly, this mechanism is optimal for the case of $n = 2$. For the case $n > 2$ [8,11] prove that a wide class of "natural" mechanisms cannot achieve a factor better than n, if we require truthfulness. Finally, for $n = 2$ [8, 11] give a *randomized* 7/4-approximation mechanism.

There is a significant difference between the definition of truthfulness used in [8,11] and the one used in [2]. Indeed, the randomized 7/4-approximation algorithm in [8,11] yields a truthful dominant strategy for *any* possible random choice of the algorithm. In [2], instead, the notion of utility is replaced by the *expected utility* one: even though the expected utility is maximized when telling the truth, for some random outcome, there might exist a better (untruthful!) strategy.

This idea is pushed further in [1] where *one parameter agents* are considered for the problem of combinatorial auction. In this work, truthfulness is achieved w.r.t. expected utility and with high probability, that is, the probability that an untruthful declaration improves the agent utility is arbitrarily small.

1.2   Our Contribution

It is natural to ask whether some problems require some relaxation on the definition of truthfulness in order to achieve polynomial-time approximation mechanisms. In this paper we investigate the existence of truthful polynomial-time approximation mechanisms for $Q||C_{\max}$, while maintaining the *strongest* definition of truthfulness: *truth-telling is a dominant strategy over all possible strategies of an agent.*

We first show that, for any fixed number of machines, $Q||C_{\max}$ admits a deterministic truthful $(2+\epsilon)$-approximation mechanism if there exists a monotone allocation algorithm Gc whose cost is within an additive factor of $O(t_{\max}/s_1)$ from the cost of Greedy, where $t_{\max}$ is the largest job weight and s_1 is the smallest machine speed (see Sect. 2). Our result is a modification of the classical PTAS [6]. Notice that this PTAS cannot be used to construct a truthful mechanism because Greedy is not monotone and the allocation produced by the combination of the two algorithms (the optimal and the greedy one) is also not monotone. Our technical contribution here is the analysis of a new algorithm obtained by combining the optimal algorithm and Gc, that preserves the monotonicity *and* whose cost is within a factor of 2 of the cost of the PTAS.

We then show that such a monotone algorithm Gc exists for the following versions of the problem (see Sect. 3):

- speeds are integer and the largest speed is bounded from above by a constant;
- speeds are *divisible*, that is, they belong to a set $C = \{c_1, c_2, \ldots, c_p, \ldots\}$ such that for each i, c_{i+1} is a multiple of c_i.

Thus, for both these cases, we obtain a family of deterministic truthful $(2 + \epsilon)$-approximation mechanisms (see Sect. 4). Observe that all such restrictions remain NP-hard even for two machines [5]. Up to our knowledge, this is the first result in which approximate solutions yield truthful mechanisms, where truthfulness is defined in the strongest sense. Indeed, the mechanism in [2] is only truthful on average. Although our new algorithm is relatively simple, its analysis, in terms of monotonicity and approximability, is far from trivial and goes through several properties of greedy allocations on identical machines.

We emphasize that the importance of an approximating mechanism for the case of divisible speeds is both practical and theoretical. Indeed, on one hand, in many practical applications "speeds" are not arbitrary but they are taken from a pre-determined set of "types", yielding values that are multiple with each other. Moreover, this result implies the existence, for any fixed number of machines, of deterministic truthful $(4 + \epsilon)$-approximate mechanisms for the case of *arbitrary* speeds, for any $\epsilon > 0$.

Observe that, also in the case of divisible speeds, existing and natural approximation algorithms are not monotone, and thus they are not suitable for truthful mechanisms (see [3] for a discussion).

Finally, our mechanisms satisfy *voluntary participation* and are able to compute the payments within polynomial time (see Sect. 4). The latter is a property that cannot be directly derived from the results in [2].

Due to lack of space some proofs are omitted or only sketched. We refer the interesting reader to the full version of this work [3].

1.3 Preliminaries

We consider the problem of scheduling on related parallel machines $(Q||C_{\max})$. We are given the *speed vector* $s = \langle s_1, s_2, \ldots, s_n \rangle$, with $s_1 \leq s_2 \leq \ldots \leq s_n$, of the of n machines and a *job sequence* with weights $\sigma = (t_1, t_2, \ldots, t_m)$. In the sequel we simply denote the i-th job with its weight t_i. The largest job weight in σ is denoted by $t_{\max}$. A schedule is a mapping that associates each job to a machine. The amount of time to complete job j on machine i is t_j/s_i. The *work* of machine i, denoted as w_i, is given by the sum of the weights of the jobs assigned to i. The *load* (or finish time) of machine i is given by w_i/s_i. The cost of a schedule is the maximum load over all machines, that is, its *makespan*. Given an algorithm A for $Q||C_{\max}$, $A(\sigma, s)$ denotes the solution computed by this algorithm on input the job sequence σ and the speed vector s. The cost of the solution computed by algorithm A on input σ and s is denoted by $\text{cost}(A, \sigma, s)$. We will also consider scheduling algorithms that take as third input the parameter h. In this case we denote by $A(\sigma, s, h)$ the schedule output and by $\text{cost}(A, \sigma, s)$ its cost.

We consider $Q||C_{\max}$ in the context of selfish agents in which each machine is owned by an agent and the value of s_i is *privately* known to the agent. A mechanism for this problem is a pair $\mathcal{M} = (A, P)$, where A is an algorithm to construct a solution and P is a *payment function*. In particular, the mechanism asks each agent i to report her speed and, based on the *reported* costs, constructs a solution using A and pays the agents according to $P = (P_1, P_2, \ldots, P_n)$. The profit of agent i is defined as $profit_i = P_i - w_i/s_i$, that is, payment minus the cost incurred by the agent in being assigned work w_i.

A *strategy* for an agent i is to declare a value b_i for her speed. Let b_{-i} denote $b_1, b_2, \ldots, b_{i-1}, b_{i+1}, \ldots, b_n$. A strategy $\overline{b}_i$ is a *dominant strategy* for agent i, if $\overline{b}_i$ maximizes $profit_i$ for *any* possible b_{-i}. A mechanism is *truthful* if, for any agent i, declaring her true speed is a dominant strategy. A mechanism satisfies *voluntary participation* if, for any agent i, declaring her true speed yields a non-negative utility.

An algorithm for the $Q||C_{\max}$ problem is *monotone* if, given in input the machine speeds $b_1, b_2, \ldots, b_n$, for any i and fixed b_{-i}, the work w_i is non decreasing in b_i.

Given a sequence σ of m jobs, we denote by σ_h the subsequence consisting of the first h jobs in σ, for any $h \leq m$; moreover, $\sigma \setminus \sigma_h$ denotes the sequence obtained by removing from σ the h first jobs.

The `Greedy` algorithm (also known as the LISTSCHEDULING algorithm [6]) processes jobs in the order they appear in σ and assigns a job t_j to the machine i minimizing $(w_i + t_j)/s_i$, where w_i denotes the work of machine i before job t_j is assigned; if more than one machine minimizing the above ratio exists then the one of smallest index is chosen.

An *optimal algorithm* computes a solution of minimal cost $opt(\sigma, s)$. Throughout the paper we assume that the optimal algorithm always produces the *lexicographically minimal* optimal assignment. As shown in [2], this algorithm is monotone.

An algorithm A is a c-approximation algorithm if, for every instance (σ, s), $cost(A, \sigma, s) \leq c \cdot opt(\sigma, s)$. A *polynomial-time approximation scheme* (PTAS) for a minimization problem is a family $\mathcal{A}$ of algorithms such that, for every $\epsilon > 0$ there exists a $(1 + \epsilon)$-approximation algorithm $A_\epsilon \in \mathcal{A}$ whose running time is polynomial in the size of the input.

2   Combining Monotone Algorithms with the Optimum

In this section we show how to combine an optimal schedule on a subsequence of the jobs with the one produced by a monotone algorithm on the remaining jobs in order to obtain a good monotone approximation algorithm. Our approach is inspired by the PTAS of R. L. Graham [6] that can be described as follows. First, we optimally assign the h largest jobs. Then, we complete this assignment by running `Greedy` on the remaining jobs according to the work assigned to the machines in the previous phase.

Unfortunately, this PTAS is not monotone. Indeed, even though the first phase is monotone, it is easy to see that `Greedy` is not monotone [2]. Moreover, even if we replace `Greedy` with a monotone algorithm the resulting algorithm is not guaranteed to be monotone. We, instead, propose the following approach.

Let `Gc` be any scheduling algorithm. By `Opt-Gc` we denote the following algorithm.

Algorithm Opt-Gc

Input: a job sequence σ, speed vector s, and parameter h.

Assume that the jobs in σ are ordered in non-increasing order by weight.

A. compute the lexicographically minimal schedule among those that have optimal makespan with respect to job sequence σ_h and speed vector s;

B. run algorithm Gc on job sequence $\sigma \setminus \sigma_h$ and speed vector s assuming that machine i has initial load 0, $i = 1, \cdots, n$;

output the schedule that assigns to machine i the jobs assigned to machine i in Phase A and Phase B.

We have the following lemma.

Lemma 1. *If* Gc *is monotone then* Opt-Gc *is also monotone.*

In the next sections we show that, if Gc has an approximation factor close to the one of the greedy algorithm, then, for each $\epsilon > 0$ and for each number n of machines, it is possible to choose the value of the parameter h so that Opt-Gc outputs a schedule of makespan at most $(2 + \epsilon)$ times the optimal schedule.

We start by defining the notion of a *greedy-close* algorithm.

Definition 1 (greedy-close algorithm). *Let c be a constant. An algorithm* Gc *is c-greedy-close if, for any job sequence σ and any machine speed vector $s = \langle s_1, s_2, \ldots, s_n \rangle$, $\mathrm{cost}(\mathrm{Gc}, \sigma, s) \leq \mathrm{cost}(\mathrm{Greedy}, \sigma, s) + c \cdot t_{max}/s_1$. An algorithm* Gc *is greedy-close if it is c-greedy-close for some constant c.*

2.1   Approximation Analysis of Opt-Gc

In this section, we show that the approximation factor of Opt-Gc is at most twice the approximation factor of PTAS-Gc, where PTAS-Gc computes the optimal schedule on the h largest jobs and then combines it with a greedy-close solution computed using algorithm Gc. Moreover, in order to guarantee a "good" approximability, it makes a *balancing* step in Phase B where jobs are assigned to non-bottleneck machines to reduce the unbalancing, while keeping the solution optimality.

Algorithm PTAS-Gc

Input: a job sequence σ, speed vector s, and parameter h.

Assume that the jobs in σ_h are the h largest jobs of σ.

A. compute the lexicographically minimal schedule among those that have optimal makespan with respect to job sequence σ_h and speed vector s; let $\mathrm{opt}(\sigma_h, s)$ be the makespan of the schedule produced in this phase;

B. reduce unbalancing without increasing cost by running algorithm Greedy as long as it is possible to add jobs without exceeding $\mathrm{opt}(\sigma_h, s)$ and let h' be the last job considered in this phase;

C. run algorithm Gc on job sequence $\sigma \setminus \sigma_{h'}$ and vector speed s assuming that machine i has initial load 0, for $i = 1, \cdots, n$;

output the schedule that assigns to machine i the jobs assigned to machine i in phases A, B and C.

Let PTAS-Greedy be algorithm PTAS-Gc with Gc = Greedy. We define the quantity $\overline{\text{cost}}(\text{PTAS-Greedy}, \sigma, s, h) = \text{opt}(\sigma_h, s) + \text{cost}(\text{Greedy}, \sigma \setminus \sigma_{h'}, s)$, where h' is the value computed in Phase B. It is easy to see that $\overline{\text{cost}}(\text{PTAS-Greedy}, \sigma, s, h) \geq \text{cost}(\text{PTAS-Greedy}, \sigma, s, h)$. Moreover, let Greedy* denote the algorithm that, on input σ and $s = \langle s_1, \ldots s_n \rangle$, returns as output the best schedule among those computed by Greedy on input σ and speed vectors $\langle 0, \ldots, 0, s_k, \ldots, s_n \rangle$ for $k = 1, \ldots, n$. Let us also define $\overline{\text{cost}}(\text{Gc}, \sigma, s, \alpha) := \text{cost}(\text{Greedy}^*, \sigma, s) + (1 + c)t_{\max}/\alpha$.

It is then possible to prove the following results: (i) $\text{cost}(\text{Greedy}, \sigma, s) \leq \text{cost}(\text{Greedy}^*, \sigma, s) + t_{max}/s_1$, (ii) $\text{cost}(\text{Gc}, \sigma, s) \leq \overline{\text{cost}}(\text{Gc}, \sigma, s, s_1)$, and (iii) $\overline{\text{cost}}(\text{Gc}, \sigma, \langle 0, \ldots, 0, s_k, s_{k+1} \ldots, s_n \rangle, s_1) \leq \overline{\text{cost}}(\text{Gc}, \sigma, \langle 0, \ldots, 0, s_{k+1} \ldots, s_n \rangle, s_1)$.

To upper bound the cost of PTAS-Gc, we consider the following quantity:

$$\overline{\text{cost}}(\text{PTAS-Gc}, \sigma, s, h) := \text{opt}(\sigma_h, s) + \overline{\text{cost}}(\text{Gc}, \sigma \setminus \sigma_{h'}, s, s_1),$$

where h' is the index of the last job considered in Phase B of PTAS-Gc. Because of (ii) above, we have that $\overline{\text{cost}}(\text{PTAS-Gc}, \sigma, s, h) \geq \text{cost}(\text{PTAS-Gc}, \sigma, s, h)$.

The next two lemmas provide an upper bound on $\overline{\text{cost}}(\text{PTAS-Gc}, \sigma, s, h)$.

Lemma 2. *For any job sequence σ, any h, and any speed vector s of length n*

$$\overline{\text{cost}}(\text{PTAS-Greedy}, \sigma, s, h) \leq \text{cost}(\text{PTAS}, \sigma, s, h) + \frac{\text{opt}(\sigma, s)}{h \cdot s_1} \left(\sum_{i=1}^{n} s_i \right) (n - 1).$$

Lemma 3. *If Gc is c-greedy-close, then for any job sequence σ, any h, and any speed vector s of length n*

$$\overline{\text{cost}}(\text{PTAS-Gc}, \sigma, s, h) \leq \overline{\text{cost}}(\text{PTAS-Greedy}, \sigma, s, h) + \frac{(1 + c) \cdot \text{opt}(\sigma, s)}{h \cdot s_1} \sum_{i=1}^{n} s_i.$$

We next provide a bound on the cost of PTAS-Gc in terms of $\text{opt}(\sigma, s)$ and s_n/s_1.

Theorem 1. *If Gc is c-greedy-close then, for any job sequence σ, any h, and any speed vector s of length n,*

$$\overline{\text{cost}}(\text{PTAS-Gc}, \sigma, s, h) \leq \text{opt}(\sigma, s) \left(1 + \frac{f(n) + n^2 + c \cdot n}{h} \frac{s_n}{s_1} \right).$$

PROOF. By previous lemmata we have

$$\overline{\text{cost}}(\text{PTAS-Gc}, \sigma, s, h) \leq \text{cost}(\text{PTAS}, \sigma, s, h) + \frac{\text{opt}(\sigma, s)}{h \cdot s_1} \left(\sum_{i=1}^{n} s_i \right) (n - 1)$$

$$+ (1+c) \cdot \frac{\mathsf{opt}(\sigma, s)}{h \cdot s_1} \sum_{i=1}^{n} s_i$$

$$\leq \mathsf{opt}(\sigma, s) \left(1 + \frac{f(n)}{h+1} + \frac{n+c}{h \cdot s_1} \sum_{i=1}^{n} s_i \right)$$

$$< \mathsf{opt}(\sigma, s) \left(1 + \frac{f(n) + n^2 + c \cdot n}{h} \frac{s_n}{s_1} \right),$$

where the last inequality follows from $\mathsf{cost}(\mathsf{PTAS}, \sigma, s, h) \leq \mathsf{opt}(\sigma, s) \left(1 + \frac{f(n)}{h+1}\right)$ (see [6]) and $s_i \leq s_n$. □

The bound given by Theorem 1 is good for small values of s_n/s_1. When instead, s_n is much larger than s_1 it might be convenient to neglect the machine with speed s_1 and run instead PTAS-Gc only on the remaining $n-1$ machines. In the next theorem, we prove that in this way we can obtain $(1+\epsilon)$ approximation for any value of $\epsilon > 0$. The proof of theorem is based on the following technical lemma.

Lemma 4. *If* Gc *is greedy-close, then for all* σ, h *and* $s = \langle s_1, s_2, \ldots, s_n \rangle$

$$\overline{\mathsf{cost}}(\mathsf{PTAS\text{-}Gc}, \sigma, \langle s_1, s_2, \ldots, s_n \rangle, h) \leq \overline{\mathsf{cost}}(\mathsf{PTAS\text{-}Gc}, \sigma, \langle 0, s_2, \ldots, s_n \rangle, h).$$

Theorem 2. *For any positive integer* n *and for any* $\epsilon > 0$, *if* Gc *is a polynomial-time greedy-close algorithm, then there exists an* h *such that, for all* σ *and for all speed vectors* s *of length* n, $\mathsf{cost}(\mathsf{PTAS\text{-}Gc}, \sigma, s, h) \leq (1+\epsilon)\mathsf{opt}(\sigma, s)$. *Moreover, the running time of* PTAS-Gc *is polynomial in* $m = |\sigma|$.

PROOF. We will prove by induction on n that for any $\epsilon > 0$ there exists an h, depending on ϵ and n only, such that $\overline{\mathsf{cost}}(\mathsf{PTAS\text{-}Gc}, \sigma, s, h) \leq (1 + \epsilon)\mathsf{opt}(\sigma, s)$. The base case $n = 1$ is trivial. For the inductive step assume that, for any $\epsilon > 0$, there exists h such that $\overline{\mathsf{cost}}(\mathsf{PTAS\text{-}Gc}(\sigma, \langle 0, s_2, \ldots, s_n \rangle, h) \leq (1 + \epsilon)\mathsf{opt}(\sigma, \langle 0, s_2, \ldots, s_n \rangle)$. If $s_n/s_1 \leq \epsilon$, then by Theorem 1, it is possible to pick $h = h(n, \epsilon)$ so that $\overline{\mathsf{cost}}(\mathsf{PTAS\text{-}Gc}, \sigma, s, h) \leq (1 + \epsilon)\mathsf{opt}(\sigma, s)$. Otherwise, pick ϵ' such that $(1 + \epsilon')(1 + s_1/s_n) \leq (1 + \epsilon)$. Then by Lemma 4 and by inductive hypothesis it is possible to choose $h' = h'(n - 1, \epsilon')$ such that

$$
\begin{aligned}
\overline{\mathsf{cost}}(\mathsf{PTAS\text{-}Gc}, \sigma, \langle s_1, s_2, \ldots, s_n \rangle, h') &\leq \overline{\mathsf{cost}}(\mathsf{PTAS\text{-}Gc}, \sigma, \langle 0, s_2, \ldots, s_n \rangle, h') \\
&\leq (1 + \epsilon')\mathsf{opt}(\sigma, \langle 0, s_2, \ldots, s_n \rangle) \\
&\leq (1 + \epsilon')(1 + s_1/s_n)\mathsf{opt}(\sigma, \langle s_1, s_2, \ldots, s_n \rangle) \\
&\leq (1 + \epsilon)\mathsf{opt}(\sigma, s).
\end{aligned}
$$

Finally, the running time is $O(n^{h+2} + m \log m + \mathsf{poly}(m))$. □

We are now ready to prove the main result of this section.

Theorem 3. *For any positive integer n and for any $\epsilon > 0$, if Gc is greedy-close, then there exists an $h = h(n, \epsilon)$ such that for all sequences of jobs σ and all speed vectors s of length n, $\mathrm{cost}(\mathrm{Opt\text{-}Gc}, \sigma, s) \leq (2 + \epsilon)\mathrm{opt}(\sigma, s)$.*

PROOF SKETCH. Fix $\epsilon > 0$. Let $h = h(n, \epsilon)$ be such that $\mathrm{cost}(\mathrm{PTAS\text{-}Gc}, \sigma, s, h) \leq (1 + \epsilon/2)\mathrm{opt}(\sigma, s)$ (such an h exists by Theorem 2) and let h' be the index of the last job scheduled during phase B by algorithm PTAS-Gc on input σ, s, and h. Construct a new job sequence σ' from σ by adding, just after $t_{h'}$, a copy of the jobs from t_{h+1} to $t_{h'}$. It is possible to prove that the cost of the schedule produced by PTAS-Gc on input σ', s, and h is not less than the cost of the schedule produced by Opt-Gc on σ, s, and h (see [3]).

We observe that the set of new jobs, considered independently from the rest of the sequence, can be scheduled in time $\mathrm{opt}(\sigma, s)$ (using the same schedule computed in phase B of PTAS-Gc) and thus $\mathrm{opt}(\sigma', s) \leq 2\mathrm{opt}(\sigma, s)$. Then, we have

$$\mathrm{cost}(\mathrm{Opt\text{-}Gc}, \sigma, s, h) \leq \mathrm{cost}(\mathrm{PTAS\text{-}Gc}, \sigma', s, h)$$
$$\leq (1 + \epsilon/2)\mathrm{opt}(\sigma', s) \leq (2 + \epsilon)\mathrm{opt}(\sigma, s)$$

and the theorem follows.   □

3   A Monotone Greedy-Close Algorithm

In this section we describe a greedy-close algorithm that is monotone for the case of "divisible" speeds (see Def. 2 below). We present our algorithm for the case of *integer* divisible speeds; this is without loss of generality, as in case the divisible speeds are not integers then they can be scaled to be integers.

Let us consider the following algorithm:

Algorithm `uniform`

Input: a job sequence σ and speed vector $s = \langle s_1, s_2, \cdots, s_n \rangle$, with $s_1 \leq s_2 \leq \cdots \leq s_n$.

A. run algorithm Greedy on job sequence σ and $S = \sum_{i=1}^{n} s_i$ identical machines;

B. order the identical machines by nondecreasing load $l_1, \ldots, l_S$;

C. let $g := GCD(s_1, s_2, \ldots, s_n)$ and split the identical machines into g blocks $B_1, \cdots, B_g$ each consisting of S/g consecutive identical machines. For $1 \leq i \leq g$ and $1 \leq k \leq S/g$, denote by $B_i(k)$ the k-th identical machine of the i-th block. Thus identical machine $B_i(k)$ has load $l_{(i-1) \cdot S/g + k}$.

D. for $1 \leq j \leq n$ let $k_j = \sum_{l=1}^{j-1} s_l/g$; then machine j receives the load of identical machines $B_i(k_j + 1), \cdots, B_i(k_j + s_j/g)$, for each block $1 \leq i \leq g$;

As it is described above, algorithm `uniform` does not run in polynomial time as its running time depends on S which, in general, is not polynomially bounded in n and m. However, `uniform` can be easily modified so to obtain the same allocation in $O(n \cdot m + m \log m)$ time.

3.1   Approximation Analysis of uniform

Let us denote by w_j^i the work of the s_j/g identical machines from block B_i whose loads are assigned to machine j. Then we have that $w_j^i = \sum_{k=1}^{s_j/g} l_{(i-1)\cdot S/g+k}$.

Theorem 4. *For any job sequence σ and any integer speed vector $s = \langle s_1, s_2, \ldots, s_n \rangle$ it holds that* $\mathsf{cost}(\mathsf{uniform}, \sigma, s) \leq \mathsf{opt}(\sigma, s) + t_{\max}/g$, *where $g = GCD(s_1, s_2, \ldots, s_n)$.*

When s_1 divides all s_is, we have that $g = s_1$ and the uniform algorithm is greedy-close. We then define sequences of speeds that enjoy this property, which will be used below to prove the monotonicity of uniform.

Definition 2 (divisible speeds). *Let $C = \{c_1, c_2, \ldots, c_p, \ldots\}$, with the property that c_i divides c_{i+1}. Then a speed vector $s = \langle s_1, s_2, \ldots, s_n \rangle$ is divisible if $s \in C^n$. The restriction to divisible speeds denotes the problem version in which the set C is known to the algorithm and all declared speeds must be in C.*

We thus have following theorem.

Theorem 5. *Algorithm uniform is greedy-close when restricted to divisible speeds.*

3.2   Algorithm uniform Is Monotone

In order to prove the monotonicity of algorithm uniform we first prove some technical results on greedy allocations on identical machines.

Lemma 5. *Let L_i (respectively, l_i) denote the load of the i-th least loaded machine when Greedy uses N (respectively, $N+1$) identical machines. It then holds that $l_{i+1} \leq L_i$, for all $1 \leq i \leq N$.*

Lemma 6. *Let L_i (respectively, l_i) denote the load of the i-th least loaded machine when Greedy uses N (respectively, $N' > N$) identical machines. It holds that $L_i \leq l_i + l_{i+1}$, for $1 \leq i \leq N$.*

PROOF.   We prove the lemma for $N' = N + 1$ since this implies the same result for any $N' > N$. For any $1 \leq i \leq N$, Lemma 5 yields $\sum_{k=1}^{i-1} L_k \geq \sum_{k=1}^{i-1} l_k$ and $\sum_{k=i+1}^{N} L_k \geq \sum_{k=i+1}^{N} l_{k+1}$, thus implying $L_i \leq l_i + l_{i+1}$.   □

Lemma 7. *Let L_i (respectively, l_i) denote the load of the i-th least loaded machine when Greedy uses N (respectively, $N' > N$) identical machines. For any a, b, b' such that $N - b \leq N' - b'$ it holds that*

$$W(a, b) := \sum_{i=a}^{b} L_i \geq W'(a + b' - b, b') := \sum_{i=a+b'-b}^{b'} l_i.$$

PROOF. Let $d = N' - N$. By repeatedly applying Lemma 5 we obtain $L_i \geq l_{i+d}$, for $1 \leq i \leq N$. Since $b' - b \leq N' - N = d$, it holds that $L_i \geq l_{i+d} \geq l_{i+b'-b}$, for $1 \leq i \leq N$. This easily implies the lemma.   □

We can now prove that uniform is monotone. Intuitively, if an agent increases her speed, then the overall work assigned to the other agents cannot decrease.

Theorem 6. *Algorithm* uniform *is monotone when restricted to divisible speeds.*

4   Polynomial-Time Mechanisms

Computing the payments. We make use of the following result:

Theorem 7 ([2]). *A decreasing output function admits a truthful payment scheme satisfying voluntary participation if and only if $\int_0^\infty b_i w_i(b_{-i}, u) du < \infty$ for all i, b_{-i}. In this case, we can take the payments to be*

$$P_i(b_{-i}, b_i) = b_i w_i(b_{-i}, b_i) + \int_0^\infty b_i w_i(b_{-i}, u) du. \tag{1}$$

We next show how to compute the payments in Eq. (1) in polynomial time when the work curve corresponds to the allocation of PTAS-uniform.

Theorem 8. *Let A be a polynomial-time r–approximation algorithm. It is possible to compute the payment functions in Equation (1) in time $poly(n, m)$ when (i) all speeds are integer not greater than some constant M, and (ii) speeds are divisible.*

PROOF.   Observe that since A is an r–approximation algorithm there exists a value $\overline{S} \leq r \cdot S$, where $S = \sum_{i=1}^n s_i$, such that on input $(s_{-i}, \overline{S})$, the algorithm assigns all jobs to machine i. Then, in order to compute the work curve of machine i we have only to consider speed values in the interval $[0, \overline{S}]$. Since A runs in polynomial time, if speeds are integer, it is always possible to compute the work curve within time $O(S \cdot poly(n, m))$. When all speeds are not larger than M, we have that $S \in O(n \cdot M)$ and the first part of the theorem follows.

Suppose now that speeds are divisible. In this case all the speeds belong to the interval $[2^{-l}, 2^l]$, where l is the length in bits of the input. Then, there are $O(\log 2^l)$ distinct speed values that machine i can take. So, the computation of the work curve takes $O(l \cdot poly(n, m)) = O(poly(n, m))$.   □

Truthful approximation mechanisms.

Theorem 9. *There exists a truthful polynomial-time $(2 + \epsilon)$-approximation mechanism for $Q||C_{\max}$ when (i) all speeds are integer bounded above by some constant M, or (ii) speeds are divisible. Moreover, the mechanism satisfies voluntary participation and the payments can be computed in polynomial time.*

Theorem 10. *For every $\epsilon > 0$, there exists a truthful polynomial-time $(4 + \epsilon)$-approximation mechanism for $Q||C_{\max}$. Moreover, the mechanism satisfies voluntary participation and the payments can be computed in polynomial time.*

References

1. A. Archer, C. Papadimitriou, K. Talwar, and E. Tardos. An approximate truthful mechanism for combinatorial auctions with single parameter agents. In *Proc. of the 14th SODA*, 2003.
2. A. Archer and E. Tardos. Truthful mechanisms for one-parameter agents. In *Proc. of FOCS*, pages 482–491, 2001.
3. Vincenzo Auletta, Roberto De Prisco, Paolo Penna, and Pino Persiano. Deterministic truthful approximation mechanisms for scheduling related machines. Technical Report 2, European Project CRESCCO,
   http://www.dia.unisa.it/~penna/papers/related-MDfull.ps.gz, 2003.
4. E.H. Clarke. Multipart Pricing of Public Goods. *Public Choice*, pages 17–33, 1971.
5. M.R. Garey and D.S. Johnson. *Computers and intractability: a guide to the theory of NP-completeness*. Freeman, 1979.
6. R. L. Graham. Bounds for certain multiprocessing anomalies. *Bell System Tech. Journal*, 45:1563–1581, 1966.
7. T. Groves. Incentive in Teams. *Econometrica*, 41:617–631, 1973.
8. N. Nisan and A. Ronen. Algorithmic Mechanism Design. In *Proc. of the 31st STOC*, pages 129–140, 1999.
9. N. Nisan and A. Ronen. Computationally Feasible VCG Mechanisms. In *Proceedings of the 2nd ACM Conference on Electronic Commerce (EC)*, pages 242–252, 2000.
10. C. H. Papadimitriou. Algorithms, Games, and the Internet. In *Proc. of the 33rd STOC*, 2001.
11. A. Ronen. *Solving Optimization Problems Among Selfish Agents*. PhD thesis, Hebrew University in Jerusalem, 2000.
12. W. Vickrey. Counterspeculation, Auctions and Competitive Sealed Tenders. *Journal of Finance*, pages 8–37, 1961.

The Expected Competitive Ratio for Weighted Completion Time Scheduling

Alexander Souza and Angelika Steger

Institute of Theoretical Computer Science, ETH Zürich
Haldeneggsteig 4, CH - 8092 Zürich
{asouza|steger}@inf.ethz.ch

Abstract. A set of n independent jobs is to be scheduled without preemption on m identical parallel machines. For each job j, a so called diffuse adversary chooses the distribution F_j of the random processing time P_j from a certain class of distributions $\mathcal{F}_j$. The scheduler is given the expectation $\mu_j = \mathbb{E}[P_j]$, but the actual duration is not known in advance. A positive weight w_j is associated with each job j and all jobs are ready for execution at time zero. The objective is to minimise the expected competitive ratio $\max_{F \in \mathcal{F}} \mathbb{E}\left[\frac{\sum_j w_j C_j}{\mathrm{OPT}}\right]$, where C_j denotes the completion time of job j and OPT the offline optimum value. The scheduler determines a list of jobs, which is then scheduled in non-preemptive static list policy.

We show a general bound on the expected competitive ratio for list scheduling algorithms, which holds for a class of so called new-better-than-used processing time distributions. This class includes, among others the exponential distribution. Our bound depends on the probability of any pair of jobs being in the wrong order in the list of an arbitrary list scheduling algorithm, compared to an optimum list. As a special case, we show that the so called WSEPT algorithm achieves $\mathbb{E}\left[\frac{\mathrm{WSEPT}}{\mathrm{OPT}}\right] \leq 3 - \frac{1}{m}$ for exponential distributed processing times.

1 Introduction

Scheduling problems were among the first combinatorial optimisation problems to be studied. The usually considered worst-case perspective often does not reflect, that even a scheduling algorithm with bad worst-case behaviour may perform rather well in practical applications. A natural step to overcome this drawback is to consider stochastic scheduling, i.e., to interpret problem data as random variables and to measure algorithm performance by means of expected values. In this paper, we study the so called expected competitive ratio of online list scheduling algorithms for stochastic completion time scheduling problems.

Model, Problem Definition, and Notation. Consider a set $J = \{1, 2, \ldots, n\}$ of n independent jobs that have to be scheduled non-preemptively on a set $M = \{1, 2, \ldots, m\}$ of m identical parallel machines. For each job j, a so called

V. Diekert and M. Habib (Eds.): STACS 2004, LNCS 2996, pp. 620–631, 2004.

diffuse adversary (see [12]) chooses the *distribution* F_j of the random *processing time* $P_j \geq 0$ out of a certain class of distributions $\mathcal{F}_j$. Yet, we assume processing times being independent. The scheduler is given the expectation $\mu_j = \mathbb{E}[P_j]$ of each job j, but the actual realisation p_j is only learned upon job completion. A positive *weight* w_j is associated with each job $j \in J$ and all jobs are ready for execution at time zero. Every machine can process at most one job at a time. Each job can be executed by any of the machines, but preemption and delays are not permitted. The *completion time* C_j of a job $j \in J$ is the latest point in time, such that a machine is busy processing the job.

In *list scheduling*, jobs are processed according to a priority list. For numerous deterministic and stochastic problems, list scheduling strategies are known to be optimal, see e.g., [14]. This is especially true for non-preemptive and non-delay scheduling, since there, any schedule can be described by a list.

Thus, we restrict ourselves to list scheduling and consider the following model. A so called *online list scheduling algorithm* is given weight w_j and mean μ_j for all $j \in J$ and based on that information, at time zero *deterministically* constructs a permutation π of J which is called a *static list*. This list is then *scheduled* in the following *policy*: whenever a machine is idle and the list is not empty, the job at the head of the list is removed and processed non-preemptively and without delay on the idle machine (with least index). Notice that the actual *realisations* of processing times are learned only upon job completion, i.e., the list is constructed *offline*, while the schedule is constructed *online*.

Once a realisation $p = (p_1, p_2, \ldots, p_n)$ of job processing times is fixed, this policy yields a realisation of the random variable $\mathrm{TWC}(\pi) = \sum_{j \in J} w_j C_j$, which denotes the *total weighted completion time* for list π. Thus, for any realisation of job processing times, an *offline optimum list* π^* is defined by

$$\mathrm{OPT}(p) = \mathrm{TWC}(\pi^*) = \min\{\mathrm{TWC}(\pi) : \pi \text{ is a permutation of } J\}. \qquad (1)$$

This yields the random variable OPT of the minimum value of the objective function for the random processing time vector $P = (P_1, P_2, \ldots, P_n)$. Let ALG be an online list scheduling algorithm and let π denote the list produced by it on input $\mu = (\mu_1, \mu_2, \ldots, \mu_n)$ and $w = (w_1, w_2, \ldots, w_n)$. We define the random variable $\mathrm{ALG} = \mathrm{TWC}(\pi)$ as the total weighted completion time achieved by the algorithm ALG. It is important to note that any online list scheduling algorithm deterministically constructs one *fixed* list for all realisations, while the optimum list may be different for each realisation.

For any algorithm ALG, the ratio $\frac{\mathrm{ALG}}{\mathrm{OPT}}$ defines a random variable that measures the relative performance of that algorithm compared to the offline optimum. We may thus define the *expected competitive ratio* of an algorithm ALG by

$$R(\mathrm{ALG}, \mathcal{F}) = \max\left\{\mathbb{E}\left[\frac{\mathrm{ALG}}{\mathrm{OPT}}\right] : F \in \mathcal{F}\right\}$$

where the job processing time distributions $F = (F_1, F_2, \ldots, F_n)$ are chosen by a diffuse adversary from a class of distributions $\mathcal{F} = (\mathcal{F}_1, \mathcal{F}_1, \ldots, \mathcal{F}_n)$. The objective is to minimise the expected competitive ratio, and thus an algorithm is called *competitive optimal* if it yields this minimum over all algorithms.

In the standard classification scheme by Graham, Lawler, Lenstra, and Rinnooy Kan [8], this completion time scheduling problem is denoted

$$P \mid P_j \sim F_j(\mu_j) \in \mathcal{F}_j \mid \max_{F \in \mathcal{F}} \mathbb{E} \left[\frac{\sum_j w_j C_j}{\mathrm{OPT}} \right].$$

Our model can be seen as a hybrid between stochastic scheduling models (see [14]) and competitve analysis (see [1]), since it comprises important aspects of them both.

As done in competitive analysis, our model relates the performance of an algorithm to the offline optimum on each instance. But rather than taking the maximum over all instances, we take the average over all instances weighted with the adversarial distribution. Notice that we are in the *diffuse adversary* model introduced by Koutsoupias and Papadimitriou [12], since our adversary is allowed to choose the distribution of problem relevant data out of a certain class of distributions.

The similarities to stochastic scheduling are that processing times are distributed according to a probability distribution, and that the number n of jobs, their weights w and most importantly their expected durations μ are known. The most important difference is that in stochastic scheduling, the optimum is not defined as the offline optimum, but as the policy that, given w and μ only, minimises the expected total weighted completion time.

Previous Work. Several deterministic completion time scheduling problems can be solved in polynomial time. Smith [22] shows that scheduling jobs in order of non-decreasing processing time and weight ratio (WSPT) is optimal for the single machine problem $1 \mid \mid \sum_j w_j C_j$. For the unweighted problem $P \mid \mid \sum_j C_j$ on identical parallel machines, the optimality of the shortest processing time first (SPT) strategy is shown by Conway, Maxwell, and Miller [5].

In contrast, Bruno and Sethi [3] establish that the problem $Pm \mid \mid \sum_j w_j C_j$ is $\mathcal{NP}$-hard in the ordinary sense for constant $m \geq 2$ machines, while Sahni [19] shows that it admits an FPTAS. For m considered part of the input, the problem $P \mid \mid \sum_j w_j C_j$ is $\mathcal{NP}$-hard in the strong sense [7]. However, Kawaguchi and Kyan [11] establish that WSPT achieves $\frac{1}{2}(1 + \sqrt{2})$ approximation ratio. An exact algorithm is given by Sahni [19], and Skutella and Woeginger [25] establish a PTAS. Several constant factor approximations are known for variants of the problem, see e.g., Phillips, Stein, and Wein [15,16], Schulz [20] Hall, Schulz, Shmoys, and Wein [9], and Skutella [21].

Turning to stochastic scheduling, the expected value of the objective function to a deterministic problem is a natural choice as an objective for the probabilistic counterpart. Thus, in that preformance measure, an algorithm ALG is considered optimal if it minimises the value $\mathbb{E}\left[\mathrm{ALG}\right] = \int_x \mathrm{ALG}(x) f(x) dx$, where $\mathrm{ALG}(x)$ denotes the value of the objective function achieved by ALG on an instance x with density $f(x)$.

Apparently, models that are $\mathcal{NP}$-hard in a deterministic setting sometimes allow a simple priority policy to be optimal for the probabilistic counterpart. For example, scheduling jobs in order of non-decreasing expected processing time (SEPT) is known to be optimal for many problems with the objective $\mathbb{E}\left[\sum_j C_j\right]$, see e.g., Rothkopf [18], Weiss and Pinedo [26], Bruno, Downey, and Frederickson [2], Kämpke [10], and Weber, Varaiya, and Walrand [27]. Moreover, for the problem $1 \mid P_j \sim \text{Stoch}\,(\mu_j) \mid \mathbb{E}\left[\sum_j w_j C_j\right]$, scheduling jobs in non-decreasing order of $\frac{\mu_j}{w_j}$ ratio (WSEPT) is optimal in non-preemptive static and dynamic policies, see e.g., [14]. By using LP relaxations, Möhring, Schulz, and Uetz [13] show $\mathbb{E}\,[\text{WSEPT}] \leq (2 - \frac{1}{m})\mathbb{E}\,[\text{OPT}]$, for several variants of the scheduling problem $P \mid P_j \sim \text{Stoch}\,(\mu_j) \mid \mathbb{E}\left[\sum_j w_j C_j\right]$, where OPT denotes an optimum policy.

One property of the performance measure $\mathbb{E}\,[\text{ALG}]$ is that instances x with small value $\text{ALG}(x)$ tend to be neglected since they contribute few to the overall expected value. Hence, in this measure, algorithms are preferred that perform well on instances x with large optimum value $\text{OPT}(x)$. It depends on the application if such behaviour is desireable, but if one is interested in algorithms that perform well on "many" instances, this measure may seem inappropriate.

Regarding this problem, the measure $\mathbb{E}\left[\frac{\text{ALG}}{\text{OPT}}\right]$ seems to be interesting for the following intuition. The ratio $\frac{\text{ALG}(x)}{\text{OPT}(x)}$ relates the value of the objective function achieved by some algorithm ALG to the optimum OPT on the instance x. Thus, the algorithm performs well on instances that yield small ratio, and fails on instances with large ratio. Hence, if for "most" instances a small ratio is attained, the "few" instances with large ratio will not increase the expectation drastically.

However, it appears that in the context of stochastic scheduling, the measure $\mathbb{E}\left[\frac{\text{ALG}}{\text{OPT}}\right]$ has only been considered by Coffman and Gilbert [4] and in the recent work by Scharbrodt, Schickinger, and Steger [23,24].

The former article [4] is concerned with the makespan scheduling problems $P \mid P_j \sim \text{Exp}\,(\lambda) \mid \mathbb{E}\left[\frac{C_{\max}}{\text{OPT}}\right]$ and $P \mid P_j \sim \text{Uni}\,(0,1) \mid \mathbb{E}\left[\frac{C_{\max}}{\text{OPT}}\right]$ in non-preemptive static list policy.

In the latter papers [23,24], the problem $P \mid P_j \sim \text{Stoch}\,(\mu_j) \mid \mathbb{E}\left[\frac{\sum_j C_j}{\text{OPT}}\right]$ is considered for non-preemptive static list policy. The main result is that the SEPT algorithm yields $\mathbb{E}\left[\frac{\text{SEPT}}{\text{OPT}}\right] = \mathcal{O}(1)$ for identical parallel machines under relatively weak assumptions on job processing time distributions.

Our Results. We introduce the class of distributions that are new-better-than-used in expectation *relative* to a function h (NBUE$_h$), which generalises the new-better-than-used in expectation (NBUE) class. The NBUE$_{\text{OPT}}$ class comprises the exponential, geometric, and uniform distribution.

Allowing the adversary to choose NBUE_{OPT} processing time distributions, we derive bounds to online list scheduling algorithms for the problem

$$P \mid P_j \sim F(\mu_j) \in \text{NBUE}_{\text{OPT}} \mid \max_{F \in \mathcal{F}} \mathbb{E}\left[\frac{\sum_j w_j C_j}{\text{OPT}}\right].$$

Our analysis depends on a quantity α which is an upper bound to the probability for any pair of jobs being in the wrong order in a list of an arbitrary online list algorithm ALG, compared to an optimum list.

Theorem 2 states that $R(\text{ALG}, \text{NBUE}_{\text{OPT}}) \leq \frac{1}{1-\alpha}$ holds for the single machine problem. Corollary 2 claims $R(\text{ALG}, \text{NBUE}_{\text{OPT}}) \leq \frac{1}{1-\alpha} + 1 - \frac{1}{m}$ for m identical parallel machines. These results reflect well the intuition that an algorithm should perform the better, the lower its probability of sequencing jobs in a wrong order.

As a special case, we show that the WSEPT algorithm yields $\mathbb{E}\left[\frac{\text{WSEPT}}{\text{OPT}}\right] \leq 3 - \frac{1}{m}$ for m identical parallel machines and exponential distributed processing times. Simulations empirically demonstrate tightness of this bound.

2   New-Better-Than-Used Distributions

Having to specify a class of distributions open to the diffuse adversary, we generalise the class of distributions that are *new-better-than-used in expectation* (NBUE). The concept of NBUE random variables is well-known in reliability theory [6], where it is considered as a relatively weak assumption. NBUE distributions are typically used to model the aging of system components, but have also proved useful in the context of stochastic scheduling. For the problem $P \mid \sqrt{\text{Var}\,[P_j]} \leq \mathbb{E}\,[P_j] \mid \mathbb{E}\left[\sum_j w_j C_j\right]$ the bound $\mathbb{E}\,[\text{WSEPT}] \leq (2 - \frac{1}{m})\mathbb{E}\,[\text{OPT}]$ of Möhring, Schulz, and Uetz [13] holds for NBUE processing time distributions as an important special case. In addition, Pinedo and Weber [17] give bounds for shop scheduling problems assuming NBUE processing time distributions.

A random variable $X \geq 0$ is NBUE if $\mathbb{E}\,[X - t \mid X \geq t] \leq \mathbb{E}\,[X]$ holds for all $t \geq 0$, see e.g., [6]. Examples of NBUE distributions are uniform, exponential, Erlang, geometric, and the Weibull distribution (with shape parameter at least one).

Let X denote a random variable taking values in a set $V \subset \mathbb{R}_0^+$ and let $h(x) > 0$ be a real-valued function defined on V. The random variable $X \geq 0$ is *new-better-than-used in expectation relative to h* (NBUE$_h$) if

$$\mathbb{E}\left[\frac{X - t}{h(X)} \,\bigg|\, X \geq t\right] \leq \mathbb{E}\left[\frac{X}{h(X)}\right] \tag{2}$$

holds for all $t \in V$, provided these expectations exist.

As NBUE$_1$ variables are NBUE, the NBUE$_h$ concept is indeed a generalisation of NBUE. Now we establish several general properties of NBUE$_h$ distributions.

Lemma 1. *If X is* NBUE$_h$ *and* $\alpha > 0$, *then*

$$\mathbb{E}\left[\frac{\alpha X - t}{h(X)} \,\middle|\, \alpha X \geq t\right] \leq \mathbb{E}\left[\frac{\alpha X}{h(X)}\right]$$

holds for all $t \in V$.

It is natural to extend the concept of NBUE$_h$ distributions to functions h that have more than one variable. Let X denote a random variable taking values in a set $V \subset \mathbb{R}_0^+$, let $y \in W \subset \mathbb{R}^k$ for $k \in \mathbb{N}$ and let $h(x, y) > 0$ be a real-valued function defined on (V, W). The random variable $X \geq 0$ is NBUE$_h$ if

$$\mathbb{E}\left[\frac{X - t}{h(X, y)} \,\middle|\, X \geq t\right] \leq \mathbb{E}\left[\frac{X}{h(X, y)}\right] \tag{3}$$

holds for all $t \in V$ and all $y \in W$, provided these expectations exist.

Lemma 2. *Let X be* NBUE$_h$ *and let Y be a random vector taking values in W independently of X, then*

$$\mathbb{E}\left[\frac{X - t}{h(X, Y)} \,\middle|\, X \geq t\right] \leq \mathbb{E}\left[\frac{X}{h(X, Y)}\right].$$

Let $g(y)$ be a function defined on W taking values in V. Since (3) holds for *all* $t \in V$ it holds especially for $t = g(y)$.

Lemma 3. *Let X be* NBUE$_h$, *let Y be a random vector taking values in W independently of X and let $g(y)$ be a function defined on W taking values in V, then*

$$\mathbb{E}\left[\frac{X - g(Y)}{h(X, Y)} \,\middle|\, X \geq g(Y)\right] \leq \mathbb{E}\left[\frac{X}{h(X, Y)}\right].$$

In fact, exponential, geometric, and uniform distributed random variables are NBUE$_h$ for non-decreasing functions h. We give a proof for the exponential distribution.

Lemma 4. *If $X \sim \mathrm{Exp}\,(\lambda)$ and $h(x, y) > 0$ is non-decreasing in x and y, then X is* NBUE$_h$.

Proof. For all $s \geq 0$ we have $f_{X|X \geq t}(t + s) = f_X(s)$ since X has memoryless density f_X. As h is non-decreasing in x and y it holds that $h(t + s, y) \geq h(s, y)$ for $t \geq 0$. We therefore obtain

$$\mathbb{E}\left[\frac{X - t}{h(X, y)} \,\middle|\, X \geq t\right] = \int_{x=t}^{\infty} \frac{x - t}{h(x, y)} f_{X|X \geq t}(x)dx$$

$$= \int_{s=0}^{\infty} \frac{t + s - t}{h(t + s, y)} f_{X|X \geq t}(t + s)ds$$

$$\leq \int_{s=0}^{\infty} \frac{s}{h(s, y)} f_X(s)ds = \mathbb{E}\left[\frac{X}{h(X, y)}\right]$$

which proves the lemma. $\qquad\square$

3   The Expected Competitve Ratio for Weighted Completion Time Scheduling

From now on, we allow the diffuse adversary to choose NBUE_{OPT} processing time distributions in the following way: all jobs fall into the same class of distribution, e.g., they are all exponential distributed, but the parameter, and thus the mean μ_j of each individual job j is arbitrary. We denote this degree of freedom by $P_j \sim F(\mu_j) \in \text{NBUE}_{\text{OPT}}$ and consider the problem

$$P \mid P_j \sim F(\mu_j) \in \text{NBUE}_{\text{OPT}} \mid \max_{F \in \mathcal{F}} \mathbb{E} \left[\frac{\sum_j w_j C_j}{\text{OPT}} \right],$$

for online list scheduling against a diffuse adversary. In Section 3.1 the single machine case is studied, and the results are generalised to identical parallel machines in Section 3.2.

For all $j, k \in J$ we define the indicator variable $M_{j,k}$ for the event that the jobs j and k being scheduled on the same machine. It is easily observed that for any list π and job j the random completion time satisfies $C_j = \sum_{k \leq^\pi j} P_k M_{j,k}$, where $k \leq^\pi j$ denotes that job k is *not after* job j in the list π.

3.1   Single Machine Scheduling

A list π is called a *weighted shortest processing time first* (WSPT) list (also known as Smith's ratio rule [14]) if the jobs are in non-decreasing order of processing time and weight ratio, i.e.,

$$\frac{p_j}{w_j} \leq \frac{p_k}{w_k} \quad \text{for} \quad j \leq^\pi k. \tag{4}$$

It is a well-known fact in scheduling theory, see e.g., [22,14] that WSPT characterises the offline optimum for single machine scheduling.

Bounding the Expected Competitve Ratio. Recall that $M_{j,k}$ takes the value one if jobs j and k are scheduled on the same machine, which is trivially true in single machine scheduling. Thus, $\text{TWC}(\pi)$ can be rearranged to the more convenient form

$$\text{TWC}(\pi) = \sum_{j \in J} w_j C_j = \sum_{j \in J} w_j \sum_{k \leq^\pi j} P_k M_{j,k} = \sum_{j \in J} P_j \sum_{k \geq^\pi j} w_k.$$

For all $j, k \in J$, we define the random variable $\Delta_{j,k} = w_k P_j - w_j P_k$ and for any fixed list π the indicator variable

$$X_{j,k} = \begin{cases} 1 & \text{if } \Delta_{j,k} > 0 \text{ and } k >^\pi j \\ 0 & \text{otherwise.} \end{cases}$$

The intuition behind $X_{j,k}$ is that the variable takes the value one if the jobs j and k are scheduled in the wrong order in a list produced by an algorithm, compared to an optimum list.

Theorem 1. *For any list π it holds that*

$$\text{TWC}(\pi) = \text{OPT} + \sum_{j \in J} \sum_{k \geq^\pi j} \Delta_{j,k} X_{j,k}.$$

The proof is omitted due to space limitations, but the strategy is as follows: for any processing time vector p, the list π is inductively rearranged into an optimum list π^*, by a sequence of reorderings. In each reordering, the variables $X_{j,k}$ and $\Delta_{j,k}$ are used to record by how much the total weighted completion time decreases.

Theorem 2. *Let ALG be any online list scheduling algorithm for the problem*

$$1 \mid P_j \sim F(\mu_j) \in \text{NBUE}_{\text{OPT}} \mid \max_{F \in \mathcal{F}} \mathbb{E}\left[\frac{\sum_j w_j C_j}{\text{OPT}}\right].$$

If $\Pr[X_{j,k} = 1] \leq \alpha < 1$ holds for all $j \leq^\pi k$ in all ALG lists π, then

$$R(\text{ALG}, \text{NBUE}_{\text{OPT}}) \leq \frac{1}{1 - \alpha}.$$

Proof. Let π denote the fixed ALG list for expected processing times μ and weights w. By Lemma 3 and Lemma 1 we have that

$$\mathbb{E}\left[\frac{\Delta_{j,k}}{\text{OPT}} \,\Big|\, X_{j,k} = 1\right] = \mathbb{E}\left[\frac{w_k P_j - w_j P_k}{\text{OPT}} \,\Big|\, w_k P_j \geq w_j P_k\right] \leq \mathbb{E}\left[\frac{w_k P_j}{\text{OPT}}\right] \quad (5)$$

holds for all NBUE_{OPT} processing time distributions. Theorem 1 and linearity of expectation establish

$$\mathbb{E}\left[\frac{\text{ALG}}{\text{OPT}}\right] = \mathbb{E}\left[\frac{\text{OPT} + \sum_{j \in J} \sum_{k \geq^\pi j} \Delta_{j,k} X_{j,k}}{\text{OPT}}\right]$$

$$= 1 + \sum_{j \in J} \sum_{k \geq^\pi j} \mathbb{E}\left[\frac{\Delta_{j,k} X_{j,k}}{\text{OPT}}\right].$$

By conditioning on $X_{j,k} = 1$, application of (5) and by $\Pr[X_{j,k} = 1] \leq \alpha$ for all $j \leq^\pi k$ we obtain

$$\mathbb{E}\left[\frac{\text{ALG}}{\text{OPT}}\right] = 1 + \sum_{j \in J} \sum_{k \geq^\pi j} \Pr[X_{j,k} = 1] \mathbb{E}\left[\frac{\Delta_{j,k}}{\text{OPT}} \,\Big|\, X_{j,k} = 1\right]$$

$$\leq 1 + \alpha \left(\sum_{j \in J} \sum_{k \geq^\pi j} \mathbb{E}\left[\frac{w_k P_j}{\text{OPT}}\right]\right) = 1 + \alpha \mathbb{E}\left[\frac{\text{ALG}}{\text{OPT}}\right].$$

Finally, rearranging the inequality and $\alpha < 1$ completes the proof. $\qquad\square$

Analysis of the WSEPT Algorithm. Now we consider the popular WSEPT list scheduling algorithm, and calculate the expected competitve ratio for exponential distributed job processing times, i.e., the adversary commits to exponential distribution.

A list π is called a *weighted shortest expected processing time first* (WSEPT) list, if scheduling is done according to non-decreasing expected processing time and weight ratio, i.e.,

$$\frac{\mu_j}{w_j} \leq \frac{\mu_k}{w_k} \quad \text{for} \quad j \leq^\pi k. \tag{6}$$

The random variable WSEPT = TWC(π) defines the total weighted completion time for WSEPT lists π. Notice that WSEPT is an online list scheduling algorithm since WSEPT lists can be determined with the knowledge of the weights and expected processing times, rather than their realisations.

A standard interchange argument, analogous to [24], proves Lemma 5 which states the competitive optimality of WSEPT for single machine scheduling with arbitrary processing time distributions.

Lemma 5. *An online list scheduling algorithm is competitive optimal for the scheduling problem* $1 \mid P_j \sim \text{Stoch}\,(\mu_j) \mid \mathbb{E}\left[\frac{\sum_j w_j C_j}{\text{OPT}}\right]$ *if and only if it is WSEPT.*

In practical applications, processing times are often modelled by exponential distributed random variables. Thus the bound obtained in Theorem 2 is of particular interest in this special case.

Corollary 1. *The WSEPT algorithm for the stochastic scheduling problem*

$$1 \mid P_j \sim \text{Exp}\,(\mu_j^{-1}) \mid \mathbb{E}\left[\frac{\sum_j w_j C_j}{\text{OPT}}\right]$$

yields $\mathbb{E}\left[\frac{\text{WSEPT}}{\text{OPT}}\right] \leq 2$.

Proof. Observe that the function OPT(p) is non-decreasing in p. Hence, by Lemma 4, exponential distributed random variables are NBUE$_{\text{OPT}}$. It is thus sufficient to prove $\Pr\left[X_{j,k} = 1\right] \leq \frac{1}{2}$ for $j \leq^\pi k$ in all WSEPT lists π. As $w_k P_j \sim \text{Exp}\left((w_k \mu_j)^{-1}\right)$ and $w_j P_k \sim \text{Exp}\left((w_j \mu_k)^{-1}\right)$ we have

$$\Pr\left[X_{j,k} = 1\right] = \Pr\left[\Delta_{j,k} > 0\right] = \Pr\left[w_k P_j > w_j P_k\right]$$

$$= \int_{t=0}^\infty \frac{e^{-\frac{t}{w_j \mu_k}}}{w_j \mu_k} \int_{s=t}^\infty \frac{e^{-\frac{s}{w_k \mu_j}}}{w_k \mu_j} ds\, dt = \frac{w_k \mu_j}{w_k \mu_j + w_j \mu_k} \leq \frac{1}{2}$$

because $j \leq^\pi k$ implies $w_k \mu_j \leq w_j \mu_k$ by the WSEPT ordering (6). Application of Theorem 2 completes the proof. □

Simulations of exponential distributed processing times empirically demonstrate tightness of Corollary 1.

3.2   Scheduling Identical Parallel Machines

Now we generalise our results to online list scheduling on m identical parallel machines.

Let $\mathrm{ALG}^{(\ell)}$ and $\mathrm{OPT}^{(\ell)}$ denote the values of the objective function achieved by the algorithm ALG and the offline optimum, respectively, for the processing time vector P on ℓ identical parallel machines. Moreover, the completion time vector for a list π on ℓ identical parallel machines is denoted by $C^{(\ell)}$.

The following lemmata are needed to reduce scheduling on m parallel machines to single machine scheduling. Similar approaches and proofs can be found in [9] and [13,15].

Lemma 6. *Let π be any job list for non-preemptive list scheduling and let P be processing times, then*

$$C_j^{(m)} \leq \frac{1}{m}C_j^{(1)} + \left(1 - \frac{1}{m}\right) P_j.$$

Lemma 7. *For any processing time vector P and the problem $P\,||\,\sum_j w_j C_j$ we have*

$$\mathrm{OPT}^{(m)} \geq \frac{1}{m}\mathrm{OPT}^{(1)}.$$

Theorem 3. *Let ALG be any online list scheduling algorithm for the problem*

$$P\,|\,P_j \sim \mathrm{Stoch}\,(\mu_j)\,|\,\mathbb{E}\left[\frac{\sum_j w_j C_j}{\mathrm{OPT}}\right],$$

then

$$\mathbb{E}\left[\frac{\mathrm{ALG}^{(m)}}{\mathrm{OPT}^{(m)}}\right] \leq \mathbb{E}\left[\frac{\mathrm{ALG}^{(1)}}{\mathrm{OPT}^{(1)}}\right] + 1 - \frac{1}{m}.$$

Proof. Lemma 6 and Lemma 7 establish

$$\frac{C_j^{(m)}}{\mathrm{OPT}^{(m)}} \leq \frac{C_j^{(1)}}{m\mathrm{OPT}^{(m)}} + \left(1 - \frac{1}{m}\right)\frac{P_j}{\mathrm{OPT}^{(m)}} \leq \frac{C_j^{(1)}}{\mathrm{OPT}^{(1)}} + \left(1 - \frac{1}{m}\right)\frac{P_j}{\mathrm{OPT}^{(m)}}.$$

Thus we have

$$\frac{\sum_{j \in J} w_j C_j^{(m)}}{\mathrm{OPT}^{(m)}} \leq \frac{\sum_{j \in J} w_j C_j^{(1)}}{\mathrm{OPT}^{(1)}} + \left(1 - \frac{1}{m}\right)\frac{\sum_{j \in J} w_j P_j}{\mathrm{OPT}^{(m)}} \leq \frac{\sum_{j \in J} w_j C_j^{(1)}}{\mathrm{OPT}^{(1)}} + 1 - \frac{1}{m}$$

by $\mathrm{OPT}^{(m)} \geq \sum_{j \in J} w_j P_j$. Taking expectations completes the proof.   □

Corollary 2. *Let ALG be any online list scheduling algorithm for the problem*

$$P \mid P_j \sim F(\mu_j) \in \text{NBUE}_{\text{OPT}} \mid \max_{F \in \mathcal{F}} \mathbb{E}\left[\frac{\sum_j w_j C_j}{\text{OPT}}\right].$$

If $\Pr[X_{j,k} = 1] \leq \alpha < 1$ *holds for all* $j \leq^\pi k$ *in all ALG lists* π, *then*

$$R(\text{ALG}, \text{NBUE}_{\text{OPT}}) \leq \frac{1}{1-\alpha} + 1 - \frac{1}{m}.$$

Corollary 3. *The WSEPT algorithm for the stochastic scheduling problem*

$$P \mid P_j \sim \text{Exp}\left(\mu_j^{-1}\right) \mid \mathbb{E}\left[\frac{\sum_j w_j C_j}{\text{OPT}}\right]$$

yields $\mathbb{E}\left[\dfrac{\text{WSEPT}}{\text{OPT}}\right] \leq 3 - \frac{1}{m}$.

Acknowledgement. The authors thank the anonymous referees for references and suggestions which helped improving the paper.

References

1. Alan Borodin and Ran El-Yaniv. *Online Computation and Competitive Analysis.* Cambridge University Press, 1998.
2. J. Bruno, P. Downey, and G. N. Frederickson. Sequencing Tasks with Exponential Service Times to Minimize the Expected Flow Time or Makespan. *Journal of the ACM*, 28(1):100 – 113, 1981.
3. E. C. Bruno, Jr. and R. Sethi. Scheduling independent tasks to reduce mean finishing time. *Communications of the ACM*, 17:382 – 387, 1974.
4. Edward G. Coffman, Jr. and E. N. Gilbert. On the Expected Relative Performance of List Scheduling. *Operations Research*, 33(3):548 – 561, 1985.
5. R. W. Conway, W. L. Maxwell, and L. W. Miller. *Theory of Scheduling.* Addison–Wesley Publishing Company, Reading, MA, 1967.
6. I.R. Gertsbakh. *Statistical Reliability Theory.* Marcel Dekker, Inc., New York, NY, 1989.
7. M. R. Garey and D. S. Johnson. *Computers and Intractability – A Guide to the Theory of NP-Completeness.* Freeman, San Francisco, CA, 1979.
8. R. L. Graham, E. L. Lawler, J. K. Lenstra, and A. H. G. Rinnooy Kan. Optimization and approximation in deterministic sequencing and scheduling theory: a survey. *Annals of Discrete Mathematics*, 5:287 – 326, 1979.
9. Leslie A. Hall, Andreas S. Schulz, David B. Shmoys, and Joel Wein. Scheduling to minimize average completion time: Off-line and on-line approximation algorithms. *Mathematics of Operations Research*, 22:513 – 544, 1997.
10. Thomas Kämpke. On the optimality of static priority policies in stochastic scheduling on parallel machines. *Journal of Applied Probability*, 24:430 – 448, 1987.
11. Tsuyoshi Kawaguchi and Seiki Kyan. Worst Case Bound of an LRF Schedule for the Mean Weighted Flow-Time Problem. *SIAM Journal on Computing*, 15(4):1119 – 1129, 1986.

12. Elias Koutsoupias and Christos Papadimitriou. Beyond Competitive Analysis. *Proceedings of the 35th Annual Symposium on Foundations of Computer Science (FOCS '94)*, pages 394 – 400, 1994.

13. Rolf H. Möring, Andreas S. Schulz, and Marc Uetz. Approximation in Stochastic Scheduling: The Power of LP-based Priority Rules. *Journal of the ACM*, 46:924 – 942, 1999.

14. Michael Pinedo. *Scheduling – Theory, Algorithms, and Systems*. Prentice–Hall, Englewood Cliffs, 1995.

15. Cynthia Phillips, Clifford Stein, and Joel Wein. Scheduling Jobs That Arrive Over Time. In *Proceedings of the 4th Workshop on Algorithms and Data Structures (WADS '95)*, volume 955 of *Lecture Notes in Computer Science*, pages 86 – 97. Springer Verlag, 1995.

16. Cynthia A. Phillips, Cliff Stein, and Joel Wein. Minimizing average completion time in the presence of release dates. *Mathematical Programming*, 82:199 – 223, 1998.

17. Michael Pinedo and Richard Weber. Inequalities and bounds in stochastic shop scheduling. *SIAM Journal on Applied Mathematics*, 44(4):867 – 879, 1984.

18. Michael H. Rothkopf. Scheduling with Random Service Times. *Management Science*, 12:707 – 713, 1966.

19. Sartaj K. Sahni. Algorithms for Scheduling Independent Tasks. *Journal of the ACM*, 23:116 – 127, 1976.

20. Andreas S. Schulz. Scheduling to Minimize Total Weighted Completion Time: Performance Guarantees of LP-Based Heuristics and Lower Bounds. In *Proceedings of the International Conference on Integer Programming and Combinatorial Optimization*, volume 1084 of *Lecture Notes in Computer Science*, pages 301 – 315, Berlin, 1996. Springer Verlag.

21. Martin Skutella. Semidefinite relaxations for parallel machine scheduling. *Proceedings of the 39th Annual Symposium on Foundations of Computer Science (FOCS '98)*, pages 472 – 481, 1998.

22. W. E. Smith. Various Optimizers for Single Stage Production. *Naval Research Logistics Quarterly*, 3:59 – 66, 1956.

23. Thomas Schickinger, Marc Scharbrodt, and Angelika Steger. A new average case analysis for completion time scheduling. *Proceedings of the 34th Annual ACM Symposium on Theory of Computing (STOC '02)*, pages 170 – 178, 2002.

24. Thomas Schickinger, Marc Scharbrodt, and Angelika Steger. A new average case analysis for completion time scheduling. *Journal of the ACM*, accepted, 2003.

25. Martin Skutella and Gerhard J. Woeginger. A PTAS for minimizing the total weighted completion time on identical parallel machines. *Mathematics of Operations Research*, 25, 2000.

26. Gideon Weiss and Michael Pinedo. Scheduling tasks with exponential service times on non-identical processors to minimize various cost functions. *Journal of Applied Probability*, 17:187 – 202, 1980.

27. R. R. Weber, P. Varaiya, and J. Walrand. Scheduling jobs with stochastically ordered processing times on parallel machines to minimize expected flowtime. *Journal of Applied Probability*, 23:841 – 847, 1986.

Effective Strong Dimension in Algorithmic Information and Computational Complexity

Krishna B. Athreya[1]*, John M. Hitchcock[2]**, Jack H. Lutz[3]***, and Elvira Mayordomo[4]†

[1] School of Operations Research and Industrial Engineering, Cornell University, Ithaca, NY 14853, USA and Departments of Mathematics and Statistics, Iowa State University, Ames, IA 50011, USA. kba@iastate.edu
[2] Department of Computer Science, University of Wyoming, Laramie, WY 82071, USA. jhitchco@cs.uwyo.edu
[3] Department of Computer Science, Iowa State University, Ames, IA 50011, USA. lutz@cs.iastate.edu
[4] Departamento de Informática e Ingeniería de Sistemas, Universidad de Zaragoza, 50015 Zaragoza, SPAIN. elvira@posta.unizar.es

Abstract. The two most important notions of fractal dimension are *Hausdorff dimension*, developed by Hausdorff (1919), and *packing dimension*, developed independently by Tricot (1982) and Sullivan (1984). Both dimensions have the mathematical advantage of being defined from measures, and both have yielded extensive applications in fractal geometry and dynamical systems.

Lutz (2000) has recently proven a simple characterization of Hausdorff dimension in terms of *gales*, which are betting strategies that generalize martingales. Imposing various computability and complexity constraints on these gales produces a spectrum of effective versions of Hausdorff dimension, including constructive, computable, polynomial-space, polynomial-time, and finite-state dimensions. Work by several investigators has already used these effective dimensions to shed significant new light on a variety of topics in theoretical computer science.

In this paper we show that packing dimension can also be characterized in terms of gales. Moreover, even though the usual definition of packing dimension is considerably more complex than that of Hausdorff dimension, our gale characterization of packing dimension is an exact dual of – and every bit as simple as – the gale characterization of Hausdorff dimension.

Effectivizing our gale characterization of packing dimension produces a variety of *effective strong dimensions*, which are exact duals

---

* This research was supported in part by Air Force Office of Scientific Research Grant ITSI F 49620-01-1-0076.
** This research was supported in part by National Science Foundation Grant 9988483.
*** This research was supported in part by National Science Foundation Grants 9988483 and 0344187.
† This research was supported in part by Spanish Government MCT project TIC2002-04019-C03-03 and by National Science Foundation Grants 9988483 and 0344187. It was done while visiting Iowa State University.

of the effective dimensions mentioned above. In general (and in analogy with the classical fractal dimensions), the effective strong dimension of a set or sequence is at least as great as its effective dimension, with equality for sets or sequences that are sufficiently regular.

We develop the basic properties of effective strong dimensions and prove a number of results relating them to fundamental aspects of randomness, Kolmogorov complexity, prediction, Boolean circuit-size complexity, polynomial-time degrees, and data compression. Aside from the above characterization of packing dimension, our two main theorems are the following.

1. If $\boldsymbol{\beta} = (\beta_0, \beta_1, \dots)$ is a computable sequence of biases that are bounded away from 0 and R is random with respect to $\boldsymbol{\beta}$, then the dimension and strong dimension of R are the lower and upper average entropies, respectively, of $\boldsymbol{\beta}$.

2. For each pair of Δ_2^0-computable real numbers $0 \le \alpha \le \beta \le 1$, there exists $A \in E$ such that the polynomial-time many-one degree of A has dimension α in E and strong dimension β in E.

Our proofs of these theorems use a new large deviation theorem for self-information with respect to a bias sequence $\boldsymbol{\beta}$ that need not be convergent.

1   Introduction

Hausdorff dimension – a powerful tool of fractal geometry developed by Hausdorff [8] in 1919 – was effectivized in 2000 by Lutz [17,18]. This has led to a spectrum of effective versions of Hausdorff dimension, including constructive, computable, polynomial-space, polynomial-time, and finite-state dimensions. Work by several investigators has already used these effective dimensions to illuminate a variety of topics in algorithmic information theory and computational complexity [17,18,1,3,21,10,9,7,11,12,6]. (See [20] for a survey of some of these results.) This work has also underscored and renewed the importance of earlier work by Ryabko [22,23,24,25], Staiger [30,31,32], and Cai and Hartmanis [2] relating Kolmogorov complexity to classical Hausdorff dimension. (See Section 6 of [18] for a discussion of this work.)

The key to all these effective dimensions is a simple characterization of classical Hausdorff dimension in terms of *gales*, which are betting strategies that generalize martingales. (Martingales, introduced by Lévy [13] and Ville [36] have been used extensively by Schnorr [26,27,28] and others in the investigation of randomness and by Lutz [15,16] and others in the development of resource-bounded measure.) Given this characterization, it is a simple matter to impose computability and complexity constraints on the gales to produce the above-mentioned spectrum of effective dimensions.

In the 1980s, a new concept of fractal dimension, called the packing dimension, was introduced independently by Tricot [35] and Sullivan [33]. Packing dimension shares with Hausdorff dimension the mathematical advantage of being based on a measure. Over the past two decades, despite its greater complexity (requiring an extra optimization over all countable decompositions of a set in its definition), packing dimension has become, next to Hausdorff dimension, the most important notion of fractal dimension, yielding extensive applications in fractal geometry and dynamical systems [4,5].

The main result of this paper is a proof that packing dimension can also be characterized in terms of gales. Moreover, notwithstanding the greater complexity of packing dimension's definition (and the greater complexity of its behavior on compact sets, as established by Mattila and Mauldin [19]), our gale characterization of packing dimension is an exact dual of – and every bit as simple as – the gale characterization of Hausdorff dimension. (This duality and simplicity are in the *statement* of our gale characterization; its proof is perforce more involved than its counterpart for Hausdorff dimension.)

Effectivizing our gale characterization of packing dimension produces for each of the effective dimensions above an *effective strong dimension* that is its exact dual. Just as the Hausdorff dimension of a set is bounded above by its packing dimension, the effective dimension of a set is bounded above by its effective strong dimension. Moreover, just as in the classical case, the effective dimension coincides with the strong effective dimension for sets that are sufficiently regular.

After proving our gale characterization and developing the effective strong dimensions and some of their basic properties, we prove a number of results relating them to fundamental aspects of randomness, Kolmogorov complexity, prediction, Boolean circuit-size complexity, polynomial-time degrees, and data compression. Our two main theorems along these lines are the following.

1. If $\delta > 0$ and $\boldsymbol{\beta} = (\beta_0, \beta_1, \dots)$ is a computable sequence of biases with each $\beta_i \in [\delta, \frac{1}{2}]$, then every sequence R that is random with respect to $\boldsymbol{\beta}$ has dimension

$$\dim(R) = \liminf_{n \to \infty} \frac{1}{n} \sum_{i=0}^{n-1} \mathcal{H}(\beta_i)$$

and strong dimension

$$\mathrm{Dim}(R) = \limsup_{n \to \infty} \frac{1}{n} \sum_{i=0}^{n-1} \mathcal{H}(\beta_i),$$

where $\mathcal{H}(\beta_i)$ is the Shannon entropy of β_i.
2. For every pair of Δ_2^0-computable real numbers $0 \leq \alpha \leq \beta \leq 1$ there is a decision problem $A \in \mathrm{E}$ such that the polynomial-time many-one degree of A has dimension α in E and strong dimension β in E.

In order to prove these theorems, we prove a new large deviation theorem for the self-information $\log \frac{1}{\mu^{\beta}(w)}$, where $\boldsymbol{\beta}$ is as in 1 above. Note that $\boldsymbol{\beta}$ need not be convergent here.

A corollary of theorem 1 above is that, if the average entropies $\frac{1}{n} \sum_{i=0}^{n-1} \mathcal{H}(\beta_i)$ converge to a limit $\overline{H}(\boldsymbol{\beta})$ as $n \to \infty$, then $\dim(R) = \mathrm{Dim}(R) = \overline{H}(\boldsymbol{\beta})$. Since the convergence of these average entropies is a much weaker condition than the convergence of the biases β_n as $n \to \infty$, this corollary substantially strengthens Theorem 7.7 of [18].

Our remaining results are much easier to prove, but their breadth makes a strong *prima facie* case for the utility of effective strong dimension. They in some cases explain dual concepts that had been curiously neglected in earlier work, and they are likely to be useful in future applications. It is to be hoped that we are on the verge of seeing the full force of fractal geometry applied fruitfully to difficult problems in the theory of computing.

2   Fractal Dimensions

In this section we briefly review the classical definitions of some fractal dimensions and the relationships among them. Since we are primarily interested in binary sequences and (equivalently) decision problems, we focus on fractal dimension in the Cantor space $\mathbf{C}$.

For each $k \in \mathbb{N}$, we let $\mathcal{A}_k$ be the collection of all prefix sets A such that $A_{<k} = \emptyset$. For each $X \subseteq \mathbf{C}$, we then define the families

$$\mathcal{A}_k(X) = \left\{ A \in \mathcal{A}_k \,\middle|\, X \subseteq \bigcup_{w \in A} \mathbf{C}_w \right\},$$

$$\mathcal{B}_k(X) = \{ A \in \mathcal{A}_k \,|\, (\forall w \in A)\mathbf{C}_w \cap X \neq \emptyset \}.$$

If $A \in \mathcal{A}_k(X)$, then we say that the prefix set A *covers* the set X. If $A \in \mathcal{B}_k(X)$, then we call the prefix set A a *packing* of X. For $X \in \mathbf{C}$, $s \in [0, \infty)$, and $k \in \mathbb{N}$, we then define

$$H_k^s(X) = \inf_{A \in \mathcal{A}_k(X)} \sum_{w \in A} 2^{-s|w|}, \quad P_k^s(X) = \sup_{A \in \mathcal{B}_k(X)} \sum_{w \in A} 2^{-s|w|}.$$

Since $H_k^s(X)$ and $P_k^s(X)$ are monotone in k, the limits

$$H^s(X) = \lim_{k \to \infty} H_k^s(X), \quad P_\infty^s(X) = \lim_{k \to \infty} P_k^s(X)$$

exist, though they may be infinite. We then define

$$P^s(X) = \inf \left\{ \sum_{i=0}^{\infty} P_\infty^s(X_i) \,\middle|\, X \subseteq \bigcup_{i=0}^{\infty} X_i \right\}. \tag{2.1}$$

The set functions H^s and P^s have the technical properties of an outer measure [4], and the (possibly infinite) quantities $H^s(X)$ and $P^s(X)$ are thus known as the *s-dimensional Hausdorff (outer) cylinder measure* of X and the *s-dimensional packing (outer) cylinder measure* of X, respectively. The set function P_∞^s is *not* an outer measure; this is the reason for the extra optimization (2.1) in the definition of the packing measure.

Definition. Let $X \subseteq \mathbf{C}$.

1. The *Hausdorff dimension* of X is $\dim_H(X) = \inf\{s \in [0, \infty)|H^s(X) = 0\}$.
2. The *packing dimension* of X is $\dim_P(X) = \inf\{s \in [0, \infty)|P^s(X) = 0\}$.

The proof of our main result uses a well-known characterization of packing dimension as a modified box dimension. For each $X \subseteq \mathbf{C}$ and $n \in \mathbb{N}$, let $N_n(X)$ be the number of strings of length n that are prefixes of elements of S. Then the *upper box dimension* of X is $\overline{\dim}_B(X) = \limsup_{n \to \infty} \frac{1}{n} \log N_n(X)$.

Box dimensions are over 60 years old, have been re-invented many times, and have been named many things, including Minkowski dimension, Kolmogorov entropy, Kolmogorov dimension, topological entropy, metric dimension, logarithmic density, and information dimension. Box dimensions are often used in practical applications of fractal geometry because they are easy to estimate, but they are not well-behaved mathematically. The *modified upper box dimension*

$$\overline{\dim}_{MB}(X) = \inf \left\{ \sup_i \overline{\dim}_B(X_i) \,\middle|\, X \subseteq \bigcup_{i=0}^{\infty} X_i \right\} \tag{2.2}$$

is much better behaved. (Note that (2.2), like (2.1), is an optimization over all countable decompositions of X.) In fact, the following relations are well-known [4].

Theorem 2.1. *For all* $X \subseteq \mathbf{C}$, $0 \leq \dim_H(X) \leq \overline{\dim}_{MB}(X) = \dim_P(X) \leq \overline{\dim}_B(X) \leq 1$.

The above dimensions are *monotone*, i.e., $X \subseteq Y$ implies $\dim(X) \leq \dim(Y)$, and *stable*, i.e., $\dim(X \cup Y) = \max\{\dim(X), \dim(Y)\}$. The Hausdorff and packing dimensions are also *countably stable*, i.e., $\dim(\cup_{i=0}^{\infty} X_i) = \sup\{\dim(X_i) | i \in \mathbb{N}\}$.

3   Gale Characterizations

In this section we review the gale characterization of Hausdorff dimension and prove our main theorem, which is the dual gale characterization of packing dimension.

Definition. Let $s \in [0, \infty)$.

1. An *s-supergale* is a function $d : \{0,1\}^* \longrightarrow [0, \infty)$ that satisfies the condition

$$d(w) \geq 2^{-s}[d(w0) + d(w1)] \tag{3.1}$$

   for all $w \in \{0,1\}^*$.
2. An *s-gale* is an *s*-supergale that satisfies (3.1) with equality for all w.
3. A *supermartingale* is a 1-supergale.
4. A *martingale* is a 1-gale.

Intuitively, we regard a supergale d as a strategy for betting on the successive bits of a sequence $S \in \mathbf{C}$. More specifically $d(w)$ is the amount of capital that d has after betting on the prefix w of S. If $s = 1$, then the right-hand side of (3.1) is the conditional expectation of $d(wb)$ given that w has occurred (when b is a uniformly distributed binary random variable). Thus a martingale models a gambler's capital when the payoffs are fair. (The expected capital after the bet is the actual capital before the bet.) In the case of an *s*-gale, if $s < 1$, the payoffs are less than fair; if $s > 1$, the payoffs are more than fair.

We now define two criteria for the success of a gale or supergale.

Definition. Let d be an s-supergale, where $s \in [0, \infty)$.

1. We say that d *succeeds* on a sequence $S \in \mathbf{C}$ if

$$\limsup_{n \to \infty} d(S[0..n-1]) = \infty.$$

The *success set* of d is $S^\infty[d] = \{S \in \mathbf{C} | d \text{ succeeds on } S\}$.

2. We say that d *succeeds strongly* on a sequence $S \in \mathbf{C}$ if

$$\liminf_{n \to \infty} d(S[0..n-1]) = \infty.$$

The *strong success set* of d is $S^\infty_{\mathrm{str}}[d] = \{S \in \mathbf{C} | d \text{ succeeds strongly on } S\}$.

We have written conditions (1) and (2) in a fashion that emphasizes their duality. Condition (1) says simply that the set of values $d(S[0..n-1])$ is unbounded, while condition (2) says that $d(S[0..n-1]) \to \infty$ as $n \to \infty$.

Notation. Let $X \subseteq \mathbf{C}$.

1. $\mathcal{G}(X)$ is the set of all $s \in [0, \infty)$ for which there exists an s-gale d such that $X \subseteq S^\infty[d]$.
2. $\mathcal{G}^{\mathrm{str}}(X)$ is the set of all $s \in [0, \infty)$ for which there exists an s-gale d such that $X \subseteq S^\infty_{\mathrm{str}}[d]$.
3. $\widehat{\mathcal{G}}(X)$ is the set of all $s \in [0, \infty)$ for which there exists an s-supergale d such that $X \subseteq S^\infty[d]$.
4. $\widehat{\mathcal{G}}^{\mathrm{str}}(X)$ is the set of all $s \in [0, \infty)$ for which there exists an s-supergale d such that $X \subseteq S^\infty_{\mathrm{str}}[d]$.

Note that $s' \geq s \in \mathcal{G}(X)$ implies that $s' \in \mathcal{G}(X)$, and similarly for the classes $\mathcal{G}^{\mathrm{str}}(X)$, $\widehat{\mathcal{G}}(X)$, and $\widehat{\mathcal{G}}^{\mathrm{str}}(X)$. The following fact is also clear.

Observation 3.1. *For all $X \subseteq \mathbf{C}$, $\mathcal{G}(X) = \widehat{\mathcal{G}}(X)$ and $\mathcal{G}^{\mathrm{str}}(X) = \widehat{\mathcal{G}}^{\mathrm{str}}(X)$.*

For Hausdorff dimension, we have the following known fact.

Theorem 3.2. (Gale Characterization of Hausdorff Dimension – Lutz [17]) *For all $X \subseteq \mathbf{C}$, $\dim_{\mathrm{H}}(X) = \inf \mathcal{G}(X)$.*

Our main result is the following dual of Theorem 3.2.

Theorem 3.3. (Gale Characterization of Packing Dimension) *For all $X \subseteq \mathbf{C}$, $\dim_{\mathrm{P}}(X) = \inf \mathcal{G}^{\mathrm{str}}(X)$.*

By Observation 3.1, we could equivalently use $\widehat{\mathcal{G}}(X)$ and $\widehat{\mathcal{G}}^{\mathrm{str}}(X)$ in Theorems 3.2 and 3.3, respectively.

4   Effective Strong Dimensions

Theorem 3.2 has been used to effectivize Hausdorff dimension at a variety of levels. In this section we review these effective dimensions while using Theorem 3.3 to develop the dual effective strong dimensions.

We define a gale or supergale to be *constructive* if it is lower semicomputable. The definitions of finite-state gamblers and finite-state gales appear in [3]. For the rest of this paper, Δ denotes one of the classes all, comp, p, pspace, p_2, p_2 space, etc. that are defined in [17].

For each $\Gamma \in \{\text{constr}, \Delta, \text{FS}\}$ and $X \subseteq \mathbf{C}$, we define the sets $\mathcal{G}_\Gamma(X)$, $\mathcal{G}_\Gamma^{\text{str}}(X)$, $\widehat{\mathcal{G}}_\Gamma(X)$, and $\widehat{\mathcal{G}}_\Gamma^{\text{str}}(X)$ just as the classes $\mathcal{G}(X)$, $\mathcal{G}^{\text{str}}(X)$, $\widehat{\mathcal{G}}(X)$, and $\widehat{\mathcal{G}}^{\text{str}}(X)$ were defined in Section 3, but with the following modifications.

(i) If $\Gamma = \text{constr}$, then d is required to be constructive.
(ii) If $\Gamma = \Delta$, then d is required to be Δ-computable.
(iii) In $\mathcal{G}_{\text{FS}}(X)$ and $\mathcal{G}_{\text{FS}}^{\text{str}}(X)$, d is required to be finite-state.
(iv) $\widehat{\mathcal{G}}_{\text{FS}}(X)$ and $\widehat{\mathcal{G}}_{\text{FS}}^{\text{str}}(X)$ are not defined.

The following effectivizations of Hausdorff and packing dimension are motivated by Theorems 3.2 and 3.3.

Definition. Let $X \subseteq \mathbf{C}$ and $S \in \mathbf{C}$.

1. [18] The *constructive dimension* of X is $\text{cdim}(X) = \inf \mathcal{G}_{\text{constr}}(X)$.
2. The *constructive strong dimension* of X is $\text{cDim}(X) = \inf \mathcal{G}_{\text{constr}}^{\text{str}}(X)$.
3. [18] The *dimension* of S is $\dim(S) = \text{cdim}(\{S\})$.
4. The *strong dimension* of S is $\text{Dim}(S) = \text{cDim}(\{S\})$.
5. [17] The *Δ-dimension* of X is $\dim_\Delta(X) = \inf \mathcal{G}_\Delta(X)$.
6. The *Δ-strong dimension* of X is $\text{Dim}_\Delta(X) = \inf \mathcal{G}_\Delta^{\text{str}}(X)$.
7. [17] The *dimension* of X in $R(\Delta)$ is $\dim(X|R(\Delta)) = \dim_\Delta(X \cap R(\Delta))$.
8. The *strong dimension* of X in $R(\Delta)$ is $\text{Dim}(X|R(\Delta)) = \text{Dim}_\Delta(X \cap R(\Delta))$.
9. [3] The *finite-state dimension* of X is $\dim_{\text{FS}}(X) = \inf \mathcal{G}_{\text{FS}}(X)$.
10. The *finite-state strong dimension* of X is $\text{Dim}_{\text{FS}}(X) = \inf \mathcal{G}_{\text{FS}}^{\text{str}}(X)$.
11. [3] The *finite-state dimension* of S is $\dim_{\text{FS}}(S) = \dim_{\text{FS}}(\{S\})$.
12. The *finite-state strong dimension* of S is $\text{Dim}_{\text{FS}}(S) = \text{Dim}_{\text{FS}}(\{S\})$.

In parts 1,2,5, and 6 of the above definition, we could equivalently use the "hatted" sets $\widehat{\mathcal{G}}_{\text{constr}}(X)$, $\widehat{\mathcal{G}}_{\text{constr}}^{\text{str}}(X)$, $\widehat{\mathcal{G}}_\Delta(X)$, and $\widehat{\mathcal{G}}_\Delta^{\text{str}}(X)$ in place of their unhatted counterparts. In the case of parts 5 and 6, this follows from Lemma 4.7 of [17]. In the case of parts 1 and 2, it follows from the main theorem in [12] (which answered an open question in [18], where $\widehat{\mathcal{G}}_{\text{constr}}(X)$ was in fact used in defining $\text{cdim}(X)$).

The polynomial-time dimensions $\dim_{\text{p}}(X)$ and $\text{Dim}_{\text{p}}(X)$ are also called the feasible dimension and the feasible strong dimension, respectively. The notation $\dim_{\text{p}}(X)$ for the p-dimension is all too similar to the notation $\dim_P(X)$ for the classical packing dimension, but confusion is unlikely because these dimensions typically arise in quite different contexts.

Observations 4.1. *1. Each of the dimensions that we have defined is monotone (e.g., $X \subseteq Y$ implies $\text{cdim}(X) \leq \text{cdim}(Y)$).*

2. *Each of the effective strong dimensions is bounded below by the corresponding effective dimension (e.g., $\mathrm{cdim}(X) \leq \mathrm{cDim}(X)$).*
3. *Each of the dimensions that we have defined is nonincreasing as the effectivity constraint is relaxed (e.g., $\dim_{\mathrm{H}}(X) \leq \mathrm{cdim}(X) \leq \dim_{\mathrm{pspace}}(X) \leq \dim_{\mathrm{FS}}(X)$).*
4. *Each of the dimensions that we have defined is nonnegative and assigns* $\mathbf{C}$ *the dimension 1.*

5   Algorithmic Information

In this section we present a variety of results and observations in which constructive and computable strong dimensions illuminate or clarify various aspects of algorithmic information theory. Included is our second main theorem, which says that every sequence that is random with respect to a computable sequence of biases $\beta_i \in [\delta, 1/2]$ has the lower and upper average entropies of $(\beta_0, \beta_1, \dots)$ as its dimension and strong dimension, respectively. We also present a result in which finite-state strong dimension clarifies an issue in data compression.

Mayordomo [21] proved that for all $S \in \mathbf{C}$,

$$\dim(S) = \liminf_{n \to \infty} \frac{K(S[0..n-1])}{n}, \tag{5.1}$$

where $K(w)$ is the Kolmogorov complexity of w [14]. Subsequently, Lutz [18] used termgales to define the dimension $\dim(w)$ of each (finite!) string $w \in \{0,1\}^*$ and proved that

$$\dim(S) = \liminf_{n \to \infty} \dim(S[0..n-1]) \tag{5.2}$$

for all $S \in \mathbf{C}$ and

$$K(w) = |w|\dim(w) \pm O(1) \tag{5.3}$$

for all $w \in \{0,1\}^*$, thereby giving a second proof of (5.1). The following theorem is a dual of (5.2) that yields a dual of (5.1) as a corollary.

Theorem 5.1. *For all $S \in \mathbf{C}$, $\mathrm{Dim}(S) = \limsup_{n \to \infty} \dim(S[0..n-1])$.*

Corollary 5.2. *For all $S \in \mathbf{C}$, $\mathrm{Dim}(S) = \limsup_{n \to \infty} \frac{K(S[0..n-1])}{n}$.*

By Corollary 5.2, the "upper algorithmic dimension" defined by Tadaki [34] is precisely the constructive strong dimension.

As the following result shows, the dimensions and strong dimensions of sequences are essentially unrestricted.

Theorem 5.3. *For any two real numbers $0 \leq \alpha \leq \beta \leq 1$, there is a sequence $S \in \mathbf{C}$ such that $\dim(S) = \alpha$ and $\mathrm{Dim}(S) = \beta$.*

We now come to the main theorem of this section. The following notation simplifies its statement and proof.

Notation. Given a bias sequence $\beta = (\beta_0, \beta_1, \dots)$, $n \in \mathbb{N}$, and $S \in \mathbf{C}$, let

$$H_n(\beta) = \frac{1}{n} \sum_{i=0}^{n-1} \mathcal{H}(\beta_i),$$

$$H^-(\beta) = \liminf_{n \to \infty} H_n(\beta),$$

$$H^+(\beta) = \limsup_{n \to \infty} H_n(\beta).$$

We call $H^-(\beta)$ and $H^+(\beta)$ the *lower* and *upper average entropies*, respectively, of β.

Theorem 5.4. *If* $\delta \in (0, \frac{1}{2}]$ *and* β *is a computable bias sequence with each* $\beta_i \in [\delta, \frac{1}{2}]$, *then for every sequence* $R \in \mathrm{RAND}^\beta$, $\dim(R) = H^-(\beta)$ *and* $\mathrm{Dim}(R) = H^+(\beta)$.

Theorem 5.4 says that every sequence that is random with respect to a suitable bias sequence β has the lower and upper average entropies of β as its dimension and strong dimension, respectively. We now describe the most important results that are used in our proof of Theorem 5.4.

Notation. Given a bias sequence $\beta = (\beta_0, \beta_1, \dots)$, $n \in \mathbb{N}$, and $S \in \mathbf{C}$, let

$$L_n(\beta)(S) = \log \frac{1}{\mu^\beta(S[0..n-1])} = \sum_{i=0}^{n-1} \xi_i(S),$$

where

$$\xi_i(S) = (1 - S[i]) \log \frac{1}{1 - \beta_i} + S[i] \log \frac{1}{\beta_i}$$

for $0 \leq i < n$.

Note that $L_n(\beta), \xi_0, \dots, \xi_{n-1}$ are random variables with

$$\mathrm{E}L_n(\beta) = \sum_{i=0}^{n-1} \mathrm{E}\xi_i = \sum_{i=0}^{n-1} \mathcal{H}(\beta_i) = nH_n(\beta).$$

The following large deviation theorem tells us that $L_n(\beta)$ is very unlikely to deviate significantly from this expected value.

Theorem 5.5. *For each* $\delta > 0$ *and* $\epsilon > 0$, *there exists* $\alpha \in (0, 1)$ *such that, for all bias sequences* $\beta = (\beta_0, \beta_1, \dots)$ *with each* $\beta_i \in [\delta, 1 - \delta]$ *and all* $n \in \mathbb{Z}^+$, *if* $L_n(\beta)$ *and* $H_n(\beta)$ *are defined as above, then*

$$\mathrm{P}\big[|L_n(\beta) - nH_n(\beta)| \geq \epsilon n\big] < 2\alpha^n,$$

where the probability is computed according to μ^β.

Lemma 5.6. *If* $\delta > 0$ *and* β *is a computable bias sequence with each* $\beta_i \in [\delta, \frac{1}{2}]$, *then* $\mathrm{cdim}(\mathrm{RAND}^\beta) \leq H^-(\beta)$ *and* $\mathrm{cDim}(\mathrm{RAND}^\beta) \leq H^+(\beta)$.

Corollary 5.7. *If β is a computable sequence of coin-toss biases such that $\overline{H}(\beta) = \lim_{n \to \infty} H_n(\beta) \in (0,1)$, then every sequence $R \in \mathbf{C}$ that is random with respect to β is c-regular, with $\dim(R) = \text{Dim}(R) = \overline{H}(\beta)$.*

Note that Corollary 5.7 strengthens Theorem 7.6 of [18] because the convergence of $H_n(\beta)$ is a weaker hypothesis than the convergence of β.

Dai, Lathrop, Lutz, and Mayordomo [3] investigated the *finite-state compression ration* $\rho_{\text{FS}}(S)$, defined for each sequence $S \in \mathbf{C}$ to be the infimum, taken over all information-lossless finite-state compressors C (a model defined in Shannon's 1948 paper [29]) of the *(lower) compression ratio*

$$\rho_C(S) = \liminf_{n \to \infty} \frac{|C(S[0..n-1])|}{n}.$$

They proved that

$$\rho_{\text{FS}}(S) = \dim_{\text{FS}}(S) \tag{5.4}$$

for all $S \in \mathbf{C}$. However, it has been pointed out that the compression ratio $\rho_{\text{FS}}(S)$ differs from the one investigated by Ziv [37]. Ziv was instead concerned with the ratio $R_{\text{FS}}(S)$ defined by

$$R_{\text{FS}}(S) = \inf_{k \in \mathbb{N}} \limsup_{n \to \infty} \inf_{C \in \mathcal{C}_k} \frac{|C(S[0..n-1])|}{n},$$

where $\mathcal{C}_k$ is the set of all k-state information-lossless finite-state compressors. The following result, together with (5.4), clarifies the relationship between $\rho_{\text{FS}}(S)$ and $R_{\text{FS}}(S)$.

Theorem 5.8. *For all $S \in \mathbf{C}$, $R_{\text{FS}}(S) = \text{Dim}_{\text{FS}}(S)$.*

Thus, mathematically, the compression ratios $\rho_{\text{FS}}(S)$ and $R_{\text{FS}}(S)$ are both natural: they are the finite-state effectivizations of the Hausdorff and packing dimensions, respectively.

6   Computational Complexity

In this section we prove our third main theorem, which says that the dimensions and strong dimensions of polynomial-time many-one degrees in exponential time are essentially unrestricted. Our proof of this result uses Theorem 5.5 and convenient characterizations of p-dimension (due to Hitchcock [11]) and strong p-dimension (in the full version of this paper) in terms of feasible unpredictability. This theorem and its proof are motivated by analogous, but simpler arguments by Ambos-Spies, Merkle, Reimann and Stephan [1].

Theorem 6.1. *For every pair of p-computable real numbers x, y with $0 \le x \le y \le 1$, there exists $A \in \mathbf{E}$ such that*

$$\dim_{\text{p}}(\deg_{\text{m}}^{\text{P}}(A)) = \dim(\deg_{\text{m}}^{\text{P}}(A)|\mathbf{E}) = x$$

and

$$\text{Dim}_{\text{p}}(\deg_{\text{m}}^{\text{P}}(A)) = \text{Dim}(\deg_{\text{m}}^{\text{P}}(A)|\mathbf{E}) = y.$$

In light of Theorem 6.1, the following question concerning the relativized feasible dimension of NP is natural.

Open Question. For which pairs of real numbers $\alpha, \beta \in [0,1]$ does there exist an oracle A such that $\dim_{p^A}(NP^A) = \alpha$ and $\text{Dim}_{p^A}(NP^A) = \beta$?

Acknowledgment. The third author thanks Dan Mauldin for extremely useful discussions.

References

1. K. Ambos-Spies, W. Merkle, J. Reimann, and F. Stephan. Hausdorff dimension in exponential time. In *Proceedings of the 16th IEEE Conference on Computational Complexity*, pages 210–217, 2001.
2. J. Cai and J. Hartmanis. On Hausdorff and topological dimensions of the Kolmogorov complexity of the real line. *Journal of Computer and Systems Sciences*, 49:605–619, 1994.
3. J. J. Dai, J. I. Lathrop, J. H. Lutz, and E. Mayordomo. Finite-state dimension. *Theoretical Computer Science*, 310(1–3):1–33, 2004.
4. K. Falconer. *Fractal Geometry: Mathematical Foundations and Applications*. John Wiley & Sons, 1990.
5. K. Falconer. *Techniques in Fractal Geometry*. John Wiley & Sons, 1997.
6. S. A. Fenner. Gales and supergales are equivalent for defining constructive Hausdorff dimension. Technical Report cs.CC/0208044, Computing Research Repository, 2002.
7. L. Fortnow and J. H. Lutz. Prediction and dimension. *Journal of Computer and System Sciences*. To appear.
8. F. Hausdorff. Dimension und äußeres Maß. *Mathematische Annalen*, 79:157–179, 1919.
9. J. M. Hitchcock. Correspondence principles for effective dimensions. *Theory of Computing Systems*. To appear.
10. J. M. Hitchcock. MAX3SAT is exponentially hard to approximate if NP has positive dimension. *Theoretical Computer Science*, 289(1):861–869, 2002.
11. J. M. Hitchcock. Fractal dimension and logarithmic loss unpredictability. *Theoretical Computer Science*, 304(1–3):431–441, 2003.
12. J. M. Hitchcock. Gales suffice for constructive dimension. *Information Processing Letters*, 86(1):9–12, 2003.
13. P. Lévy. *Théorie de l'Addition des Variables Aleatoires*. Gauthier-Villars, 1937 (second edition 1954).
14. M. Li and P. M. B. Vitányi. *An Introduction to Kolmogorov Complexity and its Applications*. Springer-Verlag, Berlin, 1997. Second Edition.
15. J. H. Lutz. Almost everywhere high nonuniform complexity. *Journal of Computer and System Sciences*, 44(2):220–258, 1992.
16. J. H. Lutz. Resource-bounded measure. In *Proceedings of the 13th IEEE Conference on Computational Complexity*, pages 236–248, 1998.
17. J. H. Lutz. Dimension in complexity classes. *SIAM Journal on Computing*, 32(5):1236–1250, 2003.
18. J. H. Lutz. The dimensions of individual strings and sequences. *Information and Computation*, 187(1):49–79, 2003.

19. P. Mattila and R. Mauldin. Measure and dimension functions: measurability and densities. *Mathematical Proceedings of the Cambridge Philosophical Society*, 121:81–100, 1997.
20. E. Mayordomo. Effective Hausdorff dimension. In *Proceedings of Foundations of the Formal Sciences III*. Kluwer Academic Press. To appear.
21. E. Mayordomo. A Kolmogorov complexity characterization of constructive Hausdorff dimension. *Information Processing Letters*, 84(1):1–3, 2002.
22. B. Ya. Ryabko. Coding of combinatorial sources and Hausdorff dimension. *Soviet Mathematics Doklady*, 30:219–222, 1984.
23. B. Ya. Ryabko. Noiseless coding of combinatorial sources. *Problems of Information Transmission*, 22:170–179, 1986.
24. B. Ya. Ryabko. Algorithmic approach to the prediction problem. *Problems of Information Transmission*, 29:186–193, 1993.
25. B. Ya. Ryabko. The complexity and effectiveness of prediction problems. *Journal of Complexity*, 10:281–295, 1994.
26. C. P. Schnorr. A unified approach to the definition of random sequences. *Mathematical Systems Theory*, 5:246–258, 1971.
27. C. P. Schnorr. Zufälligkeit und Wahrscheinlichkeit. *Lecture Notes in Mathematics*, 218, 1971.
28. C. P. Schnorr. Process complexity and effective random tests. *Journal of Computer and System Sciences*, 7:376–388, 1973.
29. C. E. Shannon. A mathematical theory of communication. *Bell System Technical Journal*, 27:379–423, 623–656, 1948.
30. L. Staiger. Kolmogorov complexity and Hausdorff dimension. *Information and Computation*, 103:159–94, 1993.
31. L. Staiger. A tight upper bound on Kolmogorov complexity and uniformly optimal prediction. *Theory of Computing Systems*, 31:215–29, 1998.
32. L. Staiger. How much can you win when your adversary is handicapped? In *Numbers, Information and Complexity*, pages 403–412. Kluwer, 2000.
33. D. Sullivan. Entropy, Hausdorff measures old and new, and limit sets of geometrically finite Kleinian groups. *Acta Mathematica*, 153:259–277, 1984.
34. K. Tadaki. A generalization of Chaitin's halting probability ω and halting self-similar sets. *Hokkaido Mathematical Journal*, 31:219–253, 2002.
35. C. Tricot. Two definitions of fractional dimension. *Mathematical Proceedings of the Cambridge Philosophical Society*, 91:57–74, 1982.
36. J. Ville. *Étude Critique de la Notion de Collectif*. Gauthier–Villars, Paris, 1939.
37. J. Ziv. Coding theorems for individual sequences. *IEEE Transactions on Information Theory*, 24:405–412, 1978.

A Lower Bound on the Competitive Ratio of Truthful Auctions

Andrew V. Goldberg[1], Jason D. Hartline[1], Anna R. Karlin[2], and Michael Saks[3]

[1] Microsoft Research, SVC/5, 1065 La Avenida, Mountain View, CA 94043.[†]
{goldberg,hartline}@microsoft.com
[2] Computer Science Department, University of Washington.
karlin@cs.washington.edu
[3] Department of Mathematics–Hill Center, Rutgers University. 110 Frelinghuysen
Rd., Piscataway, NJ 08854. [‡] saks@math.rutgers.edu

Abstract. We study a class of single-round, sealed-bid auctions for a set of identical items. We adopt the worst case competitive framework defined by [6,3] that compares the profit of an auction to that of an optimal single price sale to at least two bidders. In this framework, we give a lower bound of 2.42 (an improvement from the bound of 2 given in [3]) on the competitive ratio of any truthful auction, one where each bidders best strategy is to declare the true maximum value an item is worth to them. This result contrasts with the 3.39 competitive ratio of the best known truthful auction [4].

1   Introduction

A combination of recent economic and computational trends, such as the negligible cost of duplicating digital goods and, most importantly, the emergence of the Internet as one of the most important arenas for resource sharing between parties with diverse and selfish interests, has created a number of new and interesting dynamic pricing problems. It has also cast new light on more traditional problems such as the problem of profit maximization for the seller in an auction.

A number of recent papers [6,3,4] have considered the problem of designing auctions, for selling identical units of an item, that perform well in *worst case* under unknown market conditions. In these auctions, there is a seller with ℓ units for sale, and bidders each interested in obtaining one of them. Each bidder has a valuation representing how much the item is worth to them. The auction is performed by soliciting a sealed bid from each of the bidders, and deciding on the allocation of units to bidders and the prices to be paid by the bidders. The bidders are assumed to follow the strategy of bidding so as to maximize their personal utility, the difference between their valuation and the price they pay. To handle the problem of designing and analyzing auctions where bidders may falsely declare their valuations to get a better deal, we will adopt the solution

---

[†] Work was done while second author was at the University of Washingtion.

[‡] Supported by NSF grant CCR-9988526. Part of the work was done while visiting Microsoft Research.

concept of *truthful mechanism design* (see, e.g., [6,11,9]). In a truthful auction, truth-telling, i.e, revealing their true valuation as their bid, is an optimal strategy for each bidder regardless of the bids of the other bidders. In this paper, we will restrict our attention to truthful (a.k.a., incentive compatible or strategyproof) auctions.

In research on such auctions, a form of *competitive analysis* is used to gauge auction revenue. Specifically, a truthful auction's performance on a particular bid vector is evaluated by comparing it against the profit that could be achieved by an "optimal" omniscient auction, one that knows the true valuations of the bidders in advance. An auction is β-*competitive* if it achieves a profit that is within a factor of $\beta \geq 1$ of optimal *on every input*. The goal then becomes to design the auction with the best competitive ratio, i.e., the auction that is β-competitive with the smallest possible value of β.

A particularly interesting special case of the auction problem is the *unlimited supply* case. In this case the number of units for sale is at least the number of bidders in the auction. This is natural for the sale of digital goods where there is negligible cost for duplicating and distributing the good. Pay-per-view television and downloadable audio files are examples of such goods.

For the unlimited supply auction problem, the competitive framework introduced in [6] and further refined in [3] uses the profit of the *optimal omniscient single priced mechanism that sells at least two units* as the benchmark for competitive analysis. The assumption that two or more units are sold is necessary because in the worst case it is impossible to obtain a constant fraction of the profit of the optimal mechanism when it sells only one unit [6]. In this worst case competitive framework, the best known auction for the unlimited supply has a competitive ratio of 3.39 [4].

In this paper we also consider the case where the number of units for sale, ℓ, is limited, i.e., less than the number of bidders. At the opposite extreme from unlimited supply, is the limited supply case with $\ell = 2$.[1] In this case the Vickrey auction [11], which sells to the highest bidder at the second highest bid value, obtains the optimal worst case competitive ratio of 2 [3].

The main result of this paper is a lower bound on the competitive ratio of any randomized auction. For $\ell = 2$, this lower bound is 2 (this was originally proven in [3], though we give a much simpler proof of it here). For $\ell = 3$, the lower bound is $13/6 \approx 2.17$, and as ℓ grows the bound approaches 2.42 in the limit. We conjecture that this lower bound is tight. Yet, even in the case of three units, the problem of constructing the auction matching our lower bound of $13/6$ is open.

The rest of the paper is organized as follows. In Section 2 we give the mathematical formulation of the auction problem that we will be studying, and we describe the competitive framework that is used to analyze such auctions in worst case. In Section 3 we give our main result, a bound on how well any auction can perform in worst case. In Section 4 we describe attempts to obtain a matching upper bound.

---

[1] Notice that the competitive framework is not well defined for the $\ell = 1$ case as the optimal auction that sells at least two units cannot sell just one unit.

2   Preliminaries and Notation

We consider single-round, sealed-bid auctions for a set of ℓ identical units. As mentioned in the introduction, we adopt the game theoretic solution concept of truthful mechanism design. A useful simplification of the problem of designing truthful auctions is obtained through the following algorithmic characterization. Related formulations to the one we give here have appeared in numerous places in recent literature (e.g., [2,10,3,7]). To the best of our knowledge, the earliest dates back to the 1970s [8].

Definition 1. *Given a bid vector of n bids, $\mathbf{b} = (b_1, \ldots, b_n)$, let $\mathbf{b}_{-i}$ denote the vector of with b_i replaced with a '?', i.e.,*

$$\mathbf{b}_{-i} = (b_1, \ldots, b_{i-1}, ?, b_{i+1}, \ldots, b_n).$$

Definition 2 (Bid-independent Auction, BI_f). *Let f be a function from bid vectors (with a '?') to prices (non-negative real numbers). The deterministic bid-independent auction defined by f, BI_f, works as follows. For each bidder i:*

1. *Set $t_i = f(\mathbf{b}_{-i})$.*
2. *If $t_i < b_i$, bidder i wins at price t_i*
3. *If $t_i > b_i$, bidder i loses.*
4. *Otherwise, ($t_i = b_i$) the auction can either accept the bid at price t_i or reject it.*

A randomized bid-independent auction is a distribution over deterministic bid-independent auctions.

The proof of the following theorem can be found, for example, in [3].

Theorem 1. *An auction is truthful if and only if it is equivalent to a bid-independent auction.*

Given this equivalence, we will use the the terminology *bid-independent* and *truthful* interchangeably. We denote the profit of a truthful auction $\mathcal{A}$ on input $\mathbf{b}$ as $\mathcal{A}(\mathbf{b})$. This profit is given by the sum of the prices charged bidders that are not rejected. For a randomized bid-independent auction, $\mathcal{A}(\mathbf{b})$ and $f(\mathbf{b}_{-i})$ are random variables.

It is natural to consider a worst case competitive analysis of truthful auctions. In the competitive framework of [3] and subsequent papers, the performance of a truthful auction is gauged in comparison to the *optimal auction that sells at least two units*. There are a number reasons to choose this metric for comparison, interested readers should see [3] or [5] for a more detailed discussion.

Definition 3. *The optimal single price omniscient auction that sells at least two units (and at most ℓ units), $\mathcal{F}^{(2,\ell)}$, is defined as follows: Let $\mathbf{b}$ be a bid vector of n bids, and let v_i be the i-th largest bid in the vector $\mathbf{b}$. Auction $\mathcal{F}^{(2,\ell)}$ on $\mathbf{b}$ chooses $k \in \{2, \ldots, \ell\}$ to maximize kv_k. The k highest bidders are each* *sold a unit at price v_k (ties broken arbitrarily); all remaining bidders lose. Its profit is:*

$$\mathcal{F}^{(2,\ell)}(\mathbf{b}) = \max_{2 \leq k \leq \ell} k v_k.$$

In the unlimited supply case, i.e., when $\ell = n$, we define $\mathcal{F}^{(2)} = \mathcal{F}^{(2,n)}$.

Definition 4. *We say that auction $\mathcal{A}$ is β-competitive if for all bid vectors $\mathbf{b}$, the expected profit of $\mathcal{A}$ on $\mathbf{b}$ satisfies*

$$\mathbf{E}[\mathcal{A}(\mathbf{b})] \geq \frac{\mathcal{F}^{(2,\ell)}(\mathbf{b})}{\beta}.$$

The competitive ratio of the auction $\mathcal{A}$ is the infimum of β for which the auction is β-competitive.

2.1 Limited Supply versus Unlimited Supply

Throughout the remainder of this paper we will be making the assumption that $n = \ell$, i.e., the number of bidders is equal to the number of items for sale. The justification for this is that any lower bound that applies to the $n = \ell$ case also extends to the case where $n \geq \ell$. To see this, note that an ℓ item auction $\mathcal{A}$ that is β-competitive for any $n > \ell$ bidder input must also be β-competitive on the subset of all n bidder bid vectors that have $n - \ell$ bids at value zero. Thus, we can simply construct an $\mathcal{A}'$ that takes an ℓ bidder input $\mathbf{b}'$, augments it with $n - \ell$ zeros to get $\mathbf{b}$, and simulates the outcome of $\mathcal{A}$ on $\mathbf{b}$. Since $\mathcal{F}^{(2)}(\mathbf{b}') = \mathcal{F}^{(2,\ell)}(\mathbf{b})$, $\mathcal{A}'$ obtains at least the competitive ratio of $\mathcal{A}$.

In the other direction, a reduction from the unlimited supply auction problem to the limited supply auction problem given in [5] shows how to take an unlimited supply auction that is β-competitive with $\mathcal{F}^{(2)}$ and construct a limited supply auction parameterized by ℓ that is β-competitive with $\mathcal{F}^{(2,\ell)}$.

Henceforth, we will assume that we are in the unlimited supply case, and we will examine lower bounds for limited supply problems by placing a restriction on the number of bidders in the auction.

2.2 Symmetric Auctions

In the remainder of this paper, we restrict attention to *symmetric auctions*. An auction is symmetric if its output is not a function of the order of the bids in the input vector, $\mathbf{b}$. We note that there is no loss of generality in this assumption, as the following result shows.

Lemma 1. *For any β-competitive asymmetric truthful auction there is a symmetric randomized truthful auction with competitive ratio at least β.*

Proof. Given a β-competitive asymmetric truthful auction, $\mathcal{A}$, we construct a symmetric truthful auction $\mathcal{A}'$ that first permutes the input bids $\mathbf{b}$ at random to get $\pi(\mathbf{b})$ and then runs $\mathcal{A}$ on $\pi(\mathbf{b})$. Note, $\mathcal{F}^{(2)}(\mathbf{b}) = \mathcal{F}^{(2)}(\pi(\mathbf{b}))$ and since $\mathcal{A}$ is β-competitive on $\pi(\mathbf{b})$ for any choice of π, $\mathcal{A}'$ is β-competitive on $\mathbf{b}$. ∎

2.3 Example: The Vickrey Auction

The classical truthful auction is the 1-item Vickrey auction (a.k.a. the second price auction). This auction sells to the highest bidder at the second highest bid value. To see how this fits into the bid-independent framework, note that the auction $\mathrm{BI}_{\max}$ (the bid-independent auction with $f = \max$) does exactly this (assuming that the largest bid is unique).

As an example we consider the competitive ratio of the Vickrey auction in the case where there are only two bidders. Given two bids, $\mathbf{b} = \{b_1, b_2\}$, the optimal single price sale of two units just sells both units for the smaller of the two bid values, i.e., the optimal profit is $\mathcal{F}^{(2)}(\mathbf{b}) = 2\min(b_1, b_2)$. Of course, the 1-item Vickrey auction sells to the highest bidder at the second highest price and thus has a profit of $\min(b_1, b_2)$. Therefore, we have:

Observation 1 *The Vickrey auction on two bidders is 2-competitive.*

It turns out that this is optimal for two bidders. Along with the general lower bound of 2.42, in the next section we give a simplified proof of the result, originally from [3], that no two bidder truthful auction is better than 2-competitive.

3 A Lower Bound on the Competitive Ratio

In this section we prove a lower bound on the competitive ratio of any truthful auction in comparison to $\mathcal{F}^{(2)}$; we show that for any randomized truthful auction, $\mathcal{A}$, there exists an input bid vector, $\mathbf{b}$, on which

$$\mathbf{E}[\mathcal{A}(\mathbf{b})] \leq \frac{\mathcal{F}^{(2)}(\mathbf{b})}{2.42}.$$

In our lower bound proof we will be considering randomized distributions over bid vectors. To avoid confusion, we will adopt the following notation. A real valued random variable will be given in uppercase, e.g., X and T_i. In accordance with this notation, we will use B_i as the random variable for bidder i's bid value. A vector of real valued random variables will be a bold uppercase letter, e.g., $\mathbf{B}$ is a vector of random bids.

To prove the lower bound, we analyze the behavior of $\mathcal{A}$ on a bid vector chosen from a probability distribution over bid vectors. The outcome of the auction is then a random variable depending on both the randomness in $\mathcal{A}$ and the randomness in $\mathbf{B}$. We will give a distribution on bidder bids and show that it satisfies $\mathbf{E}_{\mathbf{B}}[\mathbf{E}_{\mathcal{A}}[\mathcal{A}(\mathbf{B})]] \leq \frac{\mathbf{E}_{\mathbf{B}}[\mathcal{F}^{(2)}(\mathbf{B})]}{2.42}$. We then use the following fact to claim that there must exist a fixed choice of bids, $\mathbf{b}$ (depending on $\mathcal{A}$), for which $\mathbf{E}[\mathcal{A}(\mathbf{b})] \leq \frac{\mathcal{F}^{(2)}(\mathbf{b})}{2.42}$.

Fact 1 *Given random variable X and two functions f and g, $\mathbf{E}[f(X)] \leq \mathbf{E}[g(X)]$ implies that there exists x such that $f(x) \leq g(x)$.*

As a quick proof of this fact, observe that if for all x, $f(x) > g(x)$ then it would be the case that $\mathbf{E}[f(X)] > \mathbf{E}[g(X)]$ instead of the other way around.

A key step in obtaining the lower bound is in defining a distribution over bid vectors on which any truthful auction obtains the same expected revenue.

Definition 5. *Let the random vector of bids $\mathbf{B}^{(n)}$ be n i.i.d. bids generated from the distribution with each bid B_i satisfying $\mathbf{Pr}[B_i > z] = 1/z$ for all $z \geq 1$.*

Lemma 2. *For $\mathbf{B}^{(n)}$ defined above, any truthful auction, $\mathcal{A}$, has expected revenue satisfying,*

$$\mathbf{E}\Big[\mathcal{A}(\mathbf{B}^{(n)})\Big] \leq n.$$

Proof. Consider a truthful auction $\mathcal{A}$. Let T_i be the price offered to bidder i in the bid-independent implementation of $\mathcal{A}$. T_i is a random variable depending on $\mathcal{A}$ and $\mathbf{B}_{-i}$ and therefore T_i and B_i are independent random variables. Let P_i be the price paid by bidder i, i.e., 0 if $B_i < T_i$ and T_i otherwise. For $t \geq 0$, $\mathbf{E}[P_i \mid T_i = t] = t \cdot \mathbf{Pr}[B_i > t \mid T_i = t] = t \cdot \mathbf{Pr}[B_i > t] \leq 1$, since B_i is independent of T_i. Therefore $\mathbf{E}[P_i] \leq 1$ and $\mathbf{E}\big[\mathcal{A}(\mathbf{B}^{(n)})\big] = \sum_i \mathbf{E}[P_i] \leq n$. ∎

For the input $\mathbf{B}^{(n)}$ an auction attempting to maximize the profit of the seller has no reason to ever offer prices less than one. The proof of the above lemma shows that any auction that always offers prices of at least one has expected revenue exactly n.

3.1   The $n = 2$ Case

To give an outline for how our main proof will proceed, we first present a proof that the competitive ratio for a two bidder auction is at least 2. Of course, the fact that the 1-item Vickrey auction achieves this competitive ratio means that this result is tight. The proof we give below simplifies the proof of the same result given in [3].

Lemma 3. $\mathbf{E}\big[\mathcal{F}^{(2)}(\mathbf{B}^{(2)})\big] = 4$.

Proof. From the definition of $\mathcal{F}^{(2)}$, $\mathcal{F}^{(2)}(\mathbf{B}^{(2)}) = 2 \min \mathbf{B}^{(2)}$. Therefore, for $z \geq 2$, $\mathbf{Pr}\big[\mathcal{F}^{(2)}(\mathbf{B}^{(2)}) > z\big] = \mathbf{Pr}[B_1 > z/2 \wedge B_2 > z/2] = 4/z^2$. Using the definition of expectation for non-negative continuous random variables of $\mathbf{E}[X] = \int_0^\infty \mathbf{Pr}[X > x]\, dx$ we have

$$\mathbf{E}\big[\mathcal{F}^{(2)}(\mathbf{B}^{(2)})\big] = 2 + \int_2^\infty (4/z^2)dz = 4. \quad \blacksquare$$

Lemma 4. *The optimal competitive ratio for a two bidder auction is 2.*

The proof of this lemma follows directly from Lemmas 2 and 3, and Fact 1.

3.2   The General Case

For the general case, as in the two bidder case, we must compute the expectation of $\mathcal{F}^{(2)}(\mathbf{B}^{(n)})$.

Lemma 5. *For n bids from the above distribution, the expected value of $\mathcal{F}^{(2)}$ is*

$$\mathbf{E}\left[\mathcal{F}^{(2)}(\mathbf{B}^{(n)})\right] = n - n\sum_{i=2}^{n} \left(\frac{-1}{n}\right)^{i-1} \frac{i}{i-1}\binom{n-1}{i-1}.$$

Proof. In this proof we will get a closed form expression for $\mathbf{Pr}\left[\mathcal{F}^{(2)}(\mathbf{B}^{(n)}) > z\right]$ and then integrate to obtain the expected value. Note that all bids are at least one and therefore, we will assume that $z \geq n$. Clearly for $z < n$, $\mathbf{Pr}\left[\mathcal{F}^{(2)}(\mathbf{B}^{(n)}) > z\right] = 1$. Let V_i be a random variable for the value of the ith largest bid, e.g., $V_1 = \max_i B_i$. To get a formula for $\mathbf{Pr}\left[\mathcal{F}^{(2)}(\mathbf{B}^{(n)})\right]$, we define a recurrence based on the random variable $F_{n,k}$ defined as

$$F_{n,k} = \max_i (k+i)V_i.$$

Intuitively, $F_{n,k}$ represents the optimal single price revenue from $\mathbf{B}^{(n)}$ and an additional k consumers each of which has a value equal to the highest bid, V_1. To define the recurrence, fix n, k, and z and define the events $\mathcal{H}_i$ for $1 \leq i \leq n$. Intuitively, the event $\mathcal{H}_i$ represents the fact that i bidders in $\mathbf{B}^{(n)}$ and the k additional consumers have bid high enough to equally share z, while no larger set of $j > i$ bidders of $\mathbf{B}^{(n)}$ can do the same.

$$\mathcal{H}_i = V_i \geq z/(k+i) \wedge \bigwedge_{j=i+1}^{n} V_j < z/(k+j)$$

$$\mathbf{Pr}[\mathcal{H}_i] = \binom{n}{i}\left(\frac{k+i}{z}\right)^i \mathbf{Pr}[F_{n-i,k+i} < z].$$

Note that events $\mathcal{H}_i$ are disjoint and that $F_{n,k}$ is at least z if and only if one of the $\mathcal{H}_i$ occurs. Thus,

$$\mathbf{Pr}[F_{n,k} > z] = \mathbf{Pr}\left[\bigwedge_{i=1}^{n}\mathcal{H}_i\right] = \sum_{i=1}^{n}\mathbf{Pr}[\mathcal{H}_i]$$

$$= \sum_{i=1}^{n}\binom{n}{i}\left(\frac{k+i}{z}\right)^i \mathbf{Pr}[F_{n-i,k+i} < z]. \tag{1}$$

Equation (1) defines a two dimensional recurrence. The base case of this recurrence is given by $F_{0,k} = 0$. We are interested in $\mathcal{F}^{(2)}(\mathbf{B}^{(n)})$ which is the same as $F_{n,0}$ except that we ignore the $\mathcal{H}_1$ case. This gives

$$\mathbf{Pr}\left[\mathcal{F}^{(2)}(\mathbf{B}^{(n)}) > z\right] = \mathbf{Pr}[F_{n,0} > z] - \mathbf{Pr}[\mathcal{H}_1]$$

$$= \mathbf{Pr}[F_{n,0} > z] - \tfrac{n}{z}\mathbf{Pr}[F_{n-1,1} < z]. \tag{2}$$

To obtain $\mathbf{Pr}\left[\mathcal{F}^{(2)}(\mathbf{B}^{(n)})\right]$ we can solve the recurrence for $F_{n,k}$ given by Equation (1). We will show that the solution is:

$$\mathbf{Pr}[F_{n,k} > z] = 1 - \left(\frac{z-k}{z}\right)^n \left(\frac{z-k-n}{z-k}\right). \tag{3}$$

Note that (3) is correct for $n = 0$. We show that it is true in general inductively. Substituting in our proposed solution (3) into (1) we obtain:

$$\mathbf{Pr}[F_{n,k} > z] = \sum_{i=1}^{n} \binom{n}{i} \left(\frac{k+i}{z}\right)^i \left(\frac{z-k-i}{z}\right)^{n-i} \left(\frac{z-k-n}{z-k-i}\right)$$

$$= \frac{z-k-n}{z^n} \sum_{i=1}^{n} \binom{n}{i} (k+i)^i (z-k-i)^{n-i-1}. \tag{4}$$

We now apply the following version of Abel's Identity [1]:

$$\frac{(x+y)^n}{x} = \sum_{j=0}^{n} \binom{n}{j} (x+j)^{j-1}(y-j)^{n-j}.$$

Making the change of variables, $j = n - i$, $x = z - k - n$, and $y = k + n$ we get:

$$\frac{z^n}{z-k-n} = \sum_{i=0}^{n} \binom{n}{i} (k+i)^i (z-k-i)^{n-i-1}.$$

We subtract out the $i = 0$ term and plug this identity into (4) to get

$$\mathbf{Pr}[F_{n,k} > z] = \frac{z-k-n}{z^n} \left(\frac{z^n}{z-k-n} - (z-k)^{n-1}\right)$$

$$= 1 - \left(\frac{z-k}{z}\right)^n \left(\frac{z-k-n}{z-k}\right).$$

Thus, our closed form expression for the recurrence is correct.

Recall our goal is to compute $\mathbf{Pr}\left[\mathcal{F}^{(2)}(\mathbf{B}^{(n)}) > z\right]$. Equation (3) shows that $\mathbf{Pr}[F_{n,0} > z] = n/z$. This combined with Equation (2) and Equation (3) gives the following for $z \geq n$:

$$\mathbf{Pr}\left[\mathcal{F}^{(2)}(\mathbf{B}^{(n)}) > z\right] = \tfrac{n}{z} - \tfrac{n}{z}\mathbf{Pr}[F_{n-1,1} < z]$$

$$= \tfrac{n}{z}\mathbf{Pr}[F_{n-1,1} > z]$$

$$= \frac{n}{z}\left(1 - \left(\frac{z-1}{z}\right)^{n-1}\left(\frac{z-n}{z-1}\right)\right).$$

Recall that for $z \leq n$, $\mathbf{Pr}\left[\mathcal{F}^{(2)}(\mathbf{B}^{(n)}) > z\right] = 1$. To complete this proof, we use the formula $\mathbf{E}\left[\mathcal{F}^{(2)}(\mathbf{B}^{(n)})\right] = \int_0^\infty \mathbf{Pr}\left[\mathcal{F}^{(2)}(\mathbf{B}^{(n)}) > z\right] dz = n +$

$\int_n^\infty \mathbf{Pr}\left[\mathcal{F}^{(2)}(\mathbf{B}^{(n)}) > z\right] dz$. In the form above, this is not easily integrable; however, we can transform it back into a binomial sum which we can integrate:

$$\mathbf{Pr}\left[\mathcal{F}^{(2)}(\mathbf{B}^{(n)}) > z\right] = n \sum_{i=2}^n \left(\frac{-1}{z}\right)^i i \binom{n-1}{i-1}.$$

$$\mathbf{E}\left[\mathcal{F}^{(2)}(\mathbf{B}^{(n)})\right] = n + n \int_n^\infty \sum_{i=2}^n \left(\frac{-1}{z}\right)^i i \binom{n-1}{i-1} dz$$

$$= n - n \sum_{i=2}^n \left(\frac{-1}{n}\right)^{i-1} \frac{i}{i-1} \binom{n-1}{i-1}. \quad \blacksquare$$

Theorem 2. *The competitive ratio of any auction on n bidders is*

$$1 - \sum_{i=2}^n \left(\frac{-1}{n}\right)^{i-1} \frac{i}{i-1} \binom{n-1}{i-1}.$$

This theorem comes from combining Lemma 2, Lemma 5, and Fact 1. Of course, for the special case of $n = 2$ this gives the lower bound of 2 that we already gave. For $n = 3$ this gives a lower bound of $13/6$. A lower bound for the competitive ratio of the best auction for general n is obtained by taking the limit. In the proof of the main theorem to follow, we use the following fact.

Fact 2 *For $1 \le k \le K$, $0 < a_k < 1$, then $\prod_{k=1}^K (1 - a_k) \ge 1 - \sum_{k=1}^K a_k$.*

Theorem 3. *The competitive ratio of any auction is at least 2.42.*

Proof. We prove this theorem by showing that,

$$\lim_{n \longrightarrow \infty} \left(1 - \sum_{i=2}^n \left(\frac{-1}{n}\right)^{i-1} \frac{i}{i-1} \binom{n-1}{i-1}\right) = 1 + \sum_{i=2}^\infty (-1)^i \frac{i}{(i-1)(i-1)!} \quad (5)$$

After which, routine calculation shows that the right hand side of the above equation is at least 2.42 which gives the theorem. To prove that (5) holds, it is sufficient to show that

$$\left|\left(1 + \sum_{i=2}^n (-1)^i \frac{i}{(i-1)(i-1)!}\right) - \left(1 - \sum_{i=2}^n \left(\frac{-1}{n}\right)^{i-1} \frac{i}{i-1} \binom{n-1}{i-1}\right)\right| = O\left(\frac{1}{n}\right).$$

We proceed as follows:

$$\left|\left(1+\sum_{i=2}^{n}(-1)^{i}\frac{i}{(i-1)(i-1)!}\right)-\left(1-\sum_{i=2}^{n}\left(\frac{-1}{n}\right)^{i-1}\frac{i}{i-1}\binom{n-1}{i-1}\right)\right|$$

$$\leq\sum_{i=2}^{n}\left|\frac{i}{(i-1)(i-1)!}-\left(\frac{1}{n}\right)^{i-1}\frac{i}{i-1}\binom{n-1}{i-1}\right|$$

$$=\sum_{i=2}^{n}\left|\frac{i}{(i-1)(i-1)!}\left(1-\frac{n(n-1)\cdots(n-i+2)}{n^{i-1}}\right)\right|$$

$$=\sum_{i=2}^{n}\left|\frac{i}{(i-1)(i-1)!}\left(1-\left(1-\frac{1}{n}\right)\left(1-\frac{2}{n}\right)\cdots\left(1-\frac{i-2}{n}\right)\right)\right|$$

$$\leq\sum_{i=2}^{n}\left|\frac{i}{(i-1)(i-1)!}\left(1-\left(1-\sum_{j=1}^{i-2}\frac{j}{n}\right)\right)\right|$$

$$\leq\sum_{i=2}^{n}\left|\frac{i}{(i-1)(i-1)!}\left(\frac{i^{2}}{n}\right)\right|=\frac{1}{n}\sum_{i=2}^{n}\frac{i^{3}}{(i-1)(i-1)!}\leq\frac{1}{n}\sum_{i=2}^{\infty}\frac{i^{3}}{(i-1)(i-1)!}$$

Since $(i-1)!$ grows exponentially, $\sum_{i=2}^{\infty}\frac{i^{3}}{(i-1)(i-1)!}$ is bounded by a constant and we have the desired result. ∎

4   Lower Bounds versus Upper Bounds

As mentioned earlier, the lower bound of 2.42 for large n does not match the competitive ratio of the best known auction (currently 3.39 [4]). In this section, we briefly consider the issue of matching upper bounds for small values of n. For $n = 2$ the 1-item Vickrey auction obtains the optimal competitive ratio of 2 (see Section 2.3). It is interesting to note that for the $n = 2$ case the optimal auction always uses sale prices chosen from the set of input bids (in particular, the second highest bid). This motivates the following definition.

Definition 6. *We say an auction, $\mathcal{A}$, is restricted if on any input the sale prices are drawn from the set of input bid values, unrestricted otherwise.*

While the Vickery auction is a restricted auction, the Vickrey auction with reserve price r, which offers the highest bidder the greater of r and the second highest bid value, is not restricted as r may not necessarily be a bid value.

Designing restricted bid-independent auctions is easier than designing general ones as the set of sale prices is determined by the input bids. However, as we show next, even for the $n = 3$ case the optimal restricted auction's competitive ratio is worse than that of the optimal unrestricted auction.

Lemma 6. *For $n = 3$, no restricted truthful auction, BI_f, can achieve a competitive ratio better than $5/2$.*

Proof. Because BI_f is restricted, $f(a,b) \in \{a,b\}$. For $h > 1$ and $a \geq hb$, let

$$p = \sup_{a,b} \mathbf{Pr}[f(a,b) = b].$$

For ϵ close to zero, let a and b be such that $a > hb$ and $\mathbf{Pr}[f(a,b) = b] \geq p - \epsilon$.

The expected revenue for the auction on $\{a, b + \epsilon', b\}$ is at most $b + \epsilon' + pb$. Here, the $b + \epsilon'$ an upper bound on the payment from the a bid and the pb is an upper bound on the expected from the $b + \epsilon$ bid (as p is an upper bound on the probability that this bid is offered price b). Note that $\mathcal{F}^{(2)} = 3b$ so the competitive ratio obtained by taking the limit as $\epsilon' \to 0$ is at least $3/(1+p)$.

An upper bound for the expected revenue for the auction on $\{a + \epsilon', a, b\}$ is $2pb + (1-p+\epsilon)a$. The $pb + (1-p+\epsilon)a$ is from the $a+\epsilon'$ and the pb is from the a bid. For large h, $\mathcal{F}^{(2)} = 2a$ so the competitive ratio is at least $2h/(2pb + h(1-p+\epsilon))$. The limit as $\epsilon \to 0$ and $h \to \infty$ gives a bound on the competitive ratio of $2/(1-p)$.

Setting these two ratios equal we obtain an optimal value of $p = 1/5$ which obtains a competitive ratio of $5/2$. ∎

This lower bound is tight as the following lemma shows.

Lemma 7. *For $a \geq b$, the bid-independent auction, BI_f with*

$$f(a,b) = \begin{cases} b & \text{with probability } 1/5 \\ a & \text{otherwise.} \end{cases}$$

achieves a competitive ratio of $5/2$ for three bidders.

We omit the proof as it follows via an elementary case analysis. It is interesting to note that the above auction is essentially performing a 1-item Vickrey auction with probability $4/5$ and a 2-item Vickrey auction with probability $1/5$.

Lemma 8. *An unrestricted three bidder auction can achieve a better competitive ratio than $5/2$.*

Proof. For $a \geq b$, the bid independent auction BI_f with

$$f(a,b) = \begin{cases} \begin{cases} b & \text{with probability } 15/23 \\ 3b/2 & \text{with probability } 8/23. \end{cases} & b \leq a \leq 3b/2 \\[2em] \begin{cases} b & \text{with probability } 3/23 \\ a & \text{with probability } 20/23. \end{cases} & a > 3b/2. \end{cases}$$

has competitive ratio 2.3. We omit the elementary case analysis. ∎

Recall that the lower bound on the competitive ratio for three bidders is $13/6 \approx 2.17$. Obtaining the optimal auction for three bidders remains an interesting open problem.

5   Conclusions

We have proven a lower bound of 2.42 on the competitive ratio of any truthful auction. The algorithmic technique used, that of looking at distributions of bidders on which all auctions perform the same and bounding the expected value of the metric (e.g., $\mathcal{F}^{(2)}$), is natural and useful for other auction related problems.

There is a strange artifact of the competitive framework that we employ here (and that which is used in prior work [3,4]). As we showed, the optimal worst case auction for selling two items is the 1-item Vickrey auction. This auction only sells one item, yet we had two items. Our optimal restricted auction for three items never sells more that two items. Yet, under our competitive framework it is not optimal to run this optimal restricted auction for three items when there are only two items for sale. As it turns out, this is not a problem when using a different but related metric, $\mathcal{V}_{opt}$, defined as the k-item Vickrey auction that obtains the highest profit, i.e., $\mathcal{V}_{opt}(\mathbf{b}) = max_i(i - 1)b_i$ (for $b_i \geq b_{i+1}$).

Acknowledgements. We would like to thank Amos Fiat for many helpful discussions.

References

1. N. Abel. Beweis eines Ausdrucks von welchem die Binomial-Formel ein einzelner Fall ist. *Crelles Journal für die Reine und Angewandte Mathematik*, 1:159–160, 1826.
2. A. Archer and É. Tardos. Truthful mechanisms for one-parameter agents. In *Proc. of the 42nd IEEE Symposium on Foundations of Computer Science*, 2001.
3. A. Fiat, A. Goldberg, J. Hartline, and A. Karlin. Competitive Generalized Auctions. In *Proc. 34th ACM Symposium on the Theory of Computing*. ACM Press, New York, 2002.
4. A. Goldberg and J. Hartline. Competitiveness via Concensus. In *Proc. 14th Symp. on Discrete Algorithms*. ACM/SIAM, 2003.
5. A. Goldberg, J. Hartline, A. Karlin, M. Saks, and A. Wright. Competitive auctions and digital goods. *Games and Economic Behavior*, 2002. Submitted for publication. An earlier version available as InterTrust Technical Report STAR-TR-99.09.01.
6. A. Goldberg, J. Hartline, and A. Wright. Competitive Auctions and Digital Goods. In *Proc. 12th Symp. on Discrete Algorithms*, pages 735–744. ACM/SIAM, 2001.
7. D. Lehmann, L. O'Callaghan, and Y. Shoham. Truth Revelation in Approximately Efficient Combinatorial Auctions. In *Proc. of 1st ACM Conf. on E-Commerce*, pages 96–102. ACM Press, New York, 1999.
8. J. Mirrlees. An Exploration into the Theory of Optimal Income Taxation. *Review of Economics Studies*, 38:175–208, April 1971.
9. N. Nisan and A. Ronen. Algorithmic Mechanism Design. In *Proc. of 31st Symposium on Theory of Computing*, pages 129–140. ACM Press, New York, 1999.
10. I. Segal. Optimal Pricing Mechanism with Unknown Demand. *American Economic Review*, 93:509–29, 2003.
11. W. Vickrey. Counterspeculation, Auctions, and Competitive Sealed Tenders. *Journal of Finance*, 16:8–37, 1961.

Errata to Analysis of the Harmonic Algorithm for Three Servers

Marek Chrobak[1] and Jiří Sgall[2]

[1] Department of Computer Science, University of California, Riverside, CA 92521.
marek@cs.ucr.edu
[2] Mathematical Inst., AS CR, Žitná 25, CZ-11567 Praha 1, Czech Republic.
sgall@math.cas.cz, http://www.math.cas.cz/sgall,

In the paper [1] we have presented a tight analysis of so-called HARMONIC algorithm for three servers, the claim being that the algorithm is 6-competitive.

Unfortunately this analysis contains an error which we are not able to correct and thereby we have to withdraw our claim.

The error is in the proof of Theorem 2.1, the analysis of the adversary move. We claim that the potential changes by the change of $H_{11'}$ when the adversary move the server $1'$ and subsequently bound this change. However, also the other components of the potential, namely $H_{22'}$ and $H_{33'}$ for three servers, may change as the metric spaces underlying these random walks do change due to the move of the server $1'$. Thus, overall, the potential can change more than the paper claims and we cannot prove any improved bound on the competitive ratio using this potential.

The framework of random walks (in particular the proofs of the inequalities (A) to (C) for three servers and (D) for any number of servers) remain untouched by this error. We still believe that this type of analysis may be useful for the analysis of HARMONIC. However, the potential function has to be significantly different.

References

1. M. Chrobak and J. Sgall. Analysis of the Harmonic algorithm for three servers. In *Proc. of the 20th Ann. Symp. on Theor. Aspects of Comput. Sci., Lecture Notes in Comput. Sci. 2607*, pages 247–259. Springer, 2003.

V. Diekert and M. Habib (Eds.): STACS 2004, LNCS 2996, p. 656, 2004.
© Springer-Verlag Berlin Heidelberg 2004

Author Index